ISBN 978-1-5285-9690-9
PIBN 11013539

English
Français
Deutsche
Italiano
Español
Português

www.forgottenbooks.com

Mythology Photography **Fiction**
Fishing Christianity **Art** Cooking
Essays Buddhism Freemasonry
Medicine **Biology** Music **Ancient
Egypt** Evolution Carpentry Physics
Dance Geology **Mathematics** Fitness
Shakespeare **Folklore** Yoga Marketing
Confidence Immortality Biographies
Poetry **Psychology** Witchcraft
Electronics Chemistry History **Law**
Accounting **Philosophy** Anthropology
Alchemy Drama Quantum Mechanics
Atheism Sexual Health **Ancient History**
Entrepreneurship Languages Sport
Paleontology Needlework Islam
Metaphysics Investment Archaeology
Parenting Statistics Criminology
Motivational

87 1	87 89	87 203	87 357	87 511	87 642
89 16	89 71	87 659	88 99	88 488	89 357
90 654	91 82	88 438	89 446	90 572	90 475
		91 469	89 502	92 169	
87 12	87 94		91 411		87 644
88 114	87 736	87 206	92 453	87 517	92 368
	90 224	91 350		92 473	
87 14			87 370		87 659
91 13	87 99	87 213	88 458	87 530	92 344
	89 31	87 729	91 243	90 249	
87 17	89 164	90 489			87 685
89 27	91 13	91 270	87 374	87 533	91 156
91 49	91 42	91 587	90 339	89 576	
	91 85			90 305	87 691
87 24		87 220	87 376		89 402
90 589	87 103	92 344	87 492	87 544	
	88 99			88 253	87 705
87 27		87 228	87 381		90 439
87 60	87 105	87 529	91 129	87 545	
90 323	88 175	91 277		92 457	87 708
92 63	88 232	92 514	87 392		90 3
92 77	92 63		89 255	87 558	91 121
		87 233	90 28	92 368	91 123
87 30	87 107	91 358	92 245		91 124
88 99	87 88	91 359		87 563	91 442
89 88			87 395	90 205	91 493
89 102	87 113	87 240	90 251	91 493	92 225
89 103	88 104	89 158			92 286
90 3			87 409	87 569	92 309
90 576	87 121	87 270	88 225	89 635	
91 85	88 3	88 599			87 725
92 30	88 17		87 411	87 575	89 399
	88 51	87 277	91 231	89 32	92 415
87 39	88 120	88 99		89 55	
88 207	88 121	89 402	87 431	92 290	87 733
91 82	89 78	89 446	88 277		89 220
	91 90		88 279	87 577	90 86
87 46	92 69	87 285	88 283	89 549	
87 138	92 72	90 425	91 195	90 543	87 796
87 143			91 196	92 385	88 494
88 131	87 137	87 305	91 339		89 260
88 133	88 175	89 55	91 522	87 584	89 262
88 135	88 232	92 586	92 162	88 441	90 260
88 136			92 184	90 448	92 450
90 594	87 138	87 321			
	87 492	87 497	87 436	87 589	
87 57	90 518		88 396	91 370	
89 71	92 100	87 325	90 144	91 371	
91 82	92 196	92 183	90 379	91 372	
	92 203		90 576	91 375	
87 61		87 328	91 261		
89 71	87 147	88 214		87 605	
91 82	88 208	92 332	87 458	90 85	
			90 253		
87 71	87 154	87 331	91 216	87 610	
87 88	91 175	87 734		89 291	
87 104		89 220	87 493	89 527	
88 99	87 158	90 86	89 362	90 12	
	88 338		89 562	91 415	
87 75	90 155	87 334	91 411	91 416	
88 68		90 488		92 216	
88 100	87 179	90 571	87 500		
	87 497	91 579	88 588	87 618	
87 80			90 236	87 630	
88 37	87 185	87 340	90 311	87 631	
88 238	87 343	89 498		91 252	
	89 497		87 501	91 257	
87 85		87 344	90 57	91 259	
91 47		91 521		91 260	
92 71		92 428			

REPORTS

CASES ARGUED AND DETERMINED

IN THE

SUPREME COURT OF ALABAMA,

DURING THE

DECEMBER TERM, 1888-89.

BY

JNO. W. SHEPHERD,
STATE REPORTER.

VOL. LXXXVII.

MONTGOMERY, ALA.:

BROWN PRINTING CO., STATE PRINTERS.

1889.

OFFICERS OF THE COURT

RULES FOR TAKING THE ORAL EXAMINATION WITNESSES IN CHANCERY CASES.

Every notice required to be given under the following rules, must be given in writing by the party desiring it to the adverse party, or to his solicitor of record, if either resides in the chancery district; but if neither resides therein, the notice may be given by an entry on the order book of the register.

2. Any party to a cause who may require the examination of any witness to be taken orally, shall file such request with the register, and give notice thereof to the adverse party at least three days before the examination is taken.

3. In case interrogatories in writing to a witness are filed, and any party to the cause shall require the examination of such witness to be taken orally, he shall give the other parties to the cause, or their solicitors, notice of such requirement within five days after notice of the filing of such interrogatories, or on failure to give such notice shall be held to have waived the right to any oral examination.

4. Notice shall be given by the solicitor of the party calling the witness to the opposing party or parties of the time and place of the examination, for such reasonable time as the register or examiner or special commissioner may fix by order in each case.

5. The examination of witnesses shall take place in the presence of the parties or their agents by their solicitors, and the witnesses shall be subject to cross-examination and re-examination, which shall be conducted, as near as may be, in the mode in use in the common law courts; but in case either party or his solicitor shall fail to attend at the time and place of such examination after notice, the officer taking such examination may proceed therewith in his or their absence.

6. The depositions taken upon oral examination shall be taken down in writing by the examiner in the form narative, unless some question is r on the legality or pertinency of th terrogatory, or on the legality or ciency of the answer. Questions ing under this exception must be and fully set forth by the examin requested by either party. When pleted, the deposition shall be read to the witness, and shall be signe him in the presence of the partie counsel, or such of them as may at provided that if the witness shall r to sign the same , then the officer such deposition shall state that f his certificate.

7. The officer taking such exa tion may state to the court therei special matters he may think fit any question or questions which m objected to shall be noted upon th position, as stated in rule 6, by the cer taking the examination, but he not have power to decide on the co tency, materiality or relevancy o questions or answers; and the chanc shall have power to deal with the of incompetent, immaterial, or ir vant depositions, or parts of them may place the costs unnecessaril curred on the offending party.

8. The officer taking such exa tion may adjourn the same from ti time, but no adjournment for any l time than two days shall be made e upon the consent of the parties, o pressing necessity, which consent o cessity shall be noted in the depos by the officer taking the same.

9. The deposition when taken be transmitted to the register in same manner as is now provided fo transmission of depositions taken terrogatories.

Adopted to take effect Dec. 10th,

TABLE OF CASES.

ERRATA.

In *Gas-Light Co. v. City Council of Montgomery*, p. 255, 5th line from bottom, for *appointed* read *appraised*.

In *Anderson v. Bellenger & Ralls*, p. 338, 18th line from bottom, before *public officers* insert *contracts made by*.

CASES

IN THE

SUPREME COURT OF ALABAMA.

DECEMBER TERM, 1888.

Herrington v. The State.

Indictment for Embezzlement of County Revenue.

Ex parte Herrington.

Application for Discharge from Custody on Habeas Corpus.

1. *Embezzlement of public revenue; sentence to imprisonment in penitentiary.*—Under the provisions of the statute approved March 6th, 1876, embezzlement of the public revenue was punishable by fine and imprisonment in the penitentiary "not less than one year," one or both, at the discretion of the court (Code, 1876, § 4275); but, by a statute approved on the next day, regulating the punishment of felonies (*Ib.* § 4450), when the sentence to imprisonment "is for twelve months or less," it must be in the county jail, and not in the penitentiary; and this latter statute controls a sentence to imprisonment under the former.

2. *Judgment reversed, as to erroneous punishment only* —The defendant and petitioner in this case having been convicted of felony, and erroneously sentenced to the penitentiary for twelve months, instead of the county jail, this court, reversing the judgment, will not order his discharge, but will reverse the judgment back to the sentence; nor will it correct and render final judgment, though requested by counsel by agreement entered of record.

FROM the Circuit Court of Conecuh.

Tried before the Hon. JOHN P. HUBBARD.

The defendant and petitioner in this case, W. H. Herrington, was indicted for embezzlement; the indictment being found in October, 1886, and charging, in different counts, embezzlement of the county revenues, and embezzlement by an agent or bailee. Being duly arraigned and put on his trial, the defendant pleaded guilty to the first count in the indictment, and a *nolle-pros.* was entered as to the others; and the

1

court thereupon rendered judgment sentencing him to imprisonment in the penitentiary for the term of one year. The defendant afterwards moved to correct and amend this judgment, on the ground that he could not be lawfully sentenced to the penitentiary for a term of twelve months; but the court overruled and refused the motion. On this judgment he then sued out a writ of error to this court, and here assigned the judgment as error; and he also applied by petition for a writ of *habeas corpus*, to procure his discharge from custody. The two cases were argued and submitted together.

N. STALLWORTH, JOHN GAMBLE, and H. A. HERBERT, for the petitioner and plaintiff in error, cited *Gunter v. State*, 83 Ala. 101; *Ex parte McKivett*, 55 Ala. 236; *Ex parte Crews*, 78 Ala. 457; *State v. Metcalf*, 75 Ala. 42; *Smith v. State*, 76 Ala. 69.

W. L. MARTIN, Attorney-General, for the State, cited *De-Bardelaben v. State*, 50 Ala. 179; *Bradley v. State*, 69 Ala. 318; 2 Brick. Digest, 463, §§ 44-5; 3 *Ib*. 749, § 28.

STONE, C. J.—The petitioner for *habeas corpus*—appellant in the case on error—was indicted for embezzlement under section 4275 of the Code of 1876, pleaded guilty, and was convicted. Up to this point, it is not complained that the trial court committed any error. Only the judgment of the court is complained of. The defendant was sentenced to confinement in the penitentiary for one year.

The statute under which the defendant was tried and convicted was a section of the Revenue Law, approved March 6, 1876.—Sess. Acts, pp. 84–5. Its language is: "That if any officer, or person, knowingly converts or applies any of the revenue of the State, or of any county thereof, to his own use, or to the use of any other person, he shall be deemed guilty of a felony, and, upon conviction thereof, must be fined not less than two hundred, nor more than one thousand dollars, and be imprisoned in the penitentiary not less than one year, one or both, at the discretion of the court trying the same; and the prosecution therefor may be commenced at any time within six years from the time of such conversion."

On the next day, March 7, 1876, the act was approved, fixing a new grade of punishment of persons convicted of

[Herrington v. The State.]

felonies.—Sess. Acts, 287.   That statute was carried into
the Code of 1876 as section 4450, and is as follows: "And
in all cases in which the period of imprisonment or hard labor
is more than two years, the sentence must be to imprisonment in the penitentiary; and in all cases of convictions for
felonies, in which the imprisonment or hard labor is for
more than twelve months, and not more than two years, the
judge may sentence the party to imprisonment in the penitentiary, or confinement in the county jail, or for hard labor
for the county, at his discretion; and in all cases in which
the imprisonment or sentence to hard labor is for twelve
months or less, the party must be sentenced to imprisonment
in the county jail, or to hard labor for the county."

Our interpretation of these statutes is, that the one last
approved dominates the other, and that when the punishment
imposed does not exceed one year in duration, there is no
power to imprison in the penitentiary, in a case circumstanced
as this is.—*Gunter v. State*, 83 Ala. 96.   This rule would
probably not apply, if the statute defining the punishment
for the crime had been later in date than the one which fixed
the grades of punishment.   The doctrine of implied repeal,
by later expression of legislative will, would probably prevail in such case.

It is contended that, because the Circuit Court exceeded
its authority in the matter of fixing the punishment, the prisoner should be absolutely discharged.   We can not agree to
this.   He is subject to punishment, and rightly in custody.
The only error is in declaring the kind of punishment he
shall undergo.   The law has declared what kind of punishment may be inflicted on him, and there is not shown to have
been any obstacle in the way of its infliction.—*Ex parte
Simmons*, 62 Ala. 416.

When there is no power to impose either imprisonment or
hard labor, or when the punishment the statute authorizes
can not be carried into effect, by reason of the failure of the
proper authorities to make the necessary orders, or to provide the necessary machinery for its enforcement, then
restraint may, and sometimes does, become unlawful, and
the prisoner will be discharged.—*Ex parte McKivett*, 55 Ala.
236; *State, use, v. Metcalf*, 75 Ala. 42; *Ex parte Crews*,
78 Ala. 451; *Ex parte Buckalew*, 84 Ala. 460.

The judgment in this case, fixing the penalty, must be,
and is reversed, but the prisoner will not be discharged.

Counsel on each side desire, and have so indorsed on the

transcript, that if this case is reversed, and the prisoner not discharged, the cause shall not be remanded for sentence, but that this court proceed to render the proper sentence. We think we have no power to do so. The statute lodges that discretion with the Circuit Court, not with us. We can not know whether that court would elect to impose imprisonment in the county jail, or hard labor for the county, nor whether it would be content with a term of one year in any form of punishment other than imprisonment in the penitentiary. That whole subject the law confides to him. Nor can we know what rate *per diem* the court would allow the prisoner in working out the judgment for costs.—Code of 1876, § 4731; Code of 1886, § 4504.

The judgment of the Circuit Court is reversed, back to the conviction—no farther—and the cause remanded, that the Circuit Court may render the proper sentence.—*Ex parte Simmons*, 62 Ala. 416.

Reversed and remanded.

Ex parte Barker.

Application for Discharge on Habeas Corpus.

1. *Fugitives from justice; extradition proceedings, founded on void or defective process.*—A person who was arrested in Georgia, without legal process, or under a void warrant issued by an Alabama magistrate, and delivered, as a fugitive from justice, into the custody of an agent of the State of Alabama, under extradition proceedings instituted after his arrest, can not claim to be discharged from custody on *habeas corpus*, because his arrest was illegal, nor because of defects in the warrant on which the extradition proceedings were based, when it appears that he is held in custody under a *capias* on an indictment since found, for the same offense, and that the executive authorities of Georgia have not complained of the illegal arrest.

APPLICATION by petition on the part of Wm. M. Barker, for the writs of *habeas corpus, certiorari*, and other necessary remedial process, to procure his discharge from the custody of the sheriff and jailer of Elmore county; a discharge having been refused by Hon. WM. A. AUSTIN, the probate judge of said county, to whom the application for a discharge was first made. The petition alleged, and the accompanying exhibits showed, that on the 8th November,

1888, an affidavit was made before Judge Austin, as judge of the County Court, by one F. L. Barker, charging that the petitioner, W. M. Barker, "took and carried away gold and silver coin," of the value of $3,000, the personal property of Isaiah Barker; that a warrant for his arrest was thereupon issued, returnable before the judge of the County Court, to answer a charge of grand larceny; that the petitioner was arrested under this warrant, on the 18th December, 1888, by the sheriff of DeKalb county, Georgia, where he was teaching school, and was delivered, a day or two afterwards, into the custody of A. M. Powell, the sheriff of Elmore county, Alabama, and Ernest McCain, his deputy, as the agents of the State of Alabama, under extradition proceedings instituted against him as a fugitive from justice; that he was brought back by them into Alabama, and lodged in the jail of Elmore county, to answer the charge of grand larceny. The requisition of Governor Seay, of Alabama, on Governor Gordon, of Georgia, was in regular form, and was dated the 19th December. On the 24th December, after the petitioner had been lodged in the jail of Elmore county, an order of commitment was made by Judge Austin, "sitting as committing magistrate on preliminary hearing," which, after reciting that the defendant, on his arraignment charged with the offense of grand larceny, "came into open court, and waives preliminary examination," commanded the jailer to receive and detain him in custody until legally discharged; and the sheriff was authorized, by indorsement on the order, to admit him to bail in the sum of $2,000, conditioned for his appearance at the next term of the Circuit Court. On the 7th March, 1889, a *capias* for his arrest was issued by the clerk of the Circuit Court, which recited that an indictment for grand larceny had been found against him at the Spring term, 1889; and the sheriff returned it executed, "by arresting said defendant, and retaining him in jail."

The petition for *habeas corpus*, addressed to Judge Austin, was filed on the 7th March, 1889. In it the petitioner alleged that he was a citizen of Georgia at the time of his arrest, and was arrested without any legal warrant or process; that the extradition proceedings against him were void, because founded on an affidavit which charged no offense, and because they were instituted after his arrest in Georgia; and that he was still held in custody "under and by virtue of said process and none other." In his return to the writ, the jailer justified under the original warrant of arrest, with

[Ex parte Barker.]

the affidavit on which it was founded, the extradition proceedings, the subsequent order of commitment made by Judge Austin, and the *capias*, which were made exhibits. The original affidavit, as set out in the return, alleged that the money was taken and carried away *feloniously*. The petitioner traversed the return, alleging that the word *feloniously* was not used in the original affidavit, and that he was held in custody solely under and by virtue of the process set out in his petition. On the hearing, March 14th, the solicitor of the circuit intervened in the name of the State, denied that the petitioner was a citizen of Georgia at the time of his arrest, and alleged that he was a citizen of Alabama at the time of the commission of the offense with which he was charged, and was a fugitive from justice from Alabama at the time of his arrest in Georgia. On the evidence adduced, Judge Austin refused to discharge the petitioner; and on these facts he renewed his application to this court.

PARSONS, DARBY & BURNEY, for the petitioner.—The original affidavit, on which the proceedings against the petitioner were founded, charged no criminal offense.—*Morningstar v. State*, 55 Ala. 148; *McMullen v. State*, 53 Ala. 531; *Williams v. State*, 44 Ala. 396; *Roundtree v. State*, 58 Ala. 381; 1 Hale's P. C. 504; 2 *Ib*. 184. The warrant of arrest, if legal and valid, could have no extra-territorial force or efficacy; and the arrest under it in Georgia, by a sheriff of that State, was a trespass,—a high-handed outrage. But the warrant itself was void, because it was based on an affidavit which charged no offense, and because the officer by whom it was issued had no jurisdiction of felonies.—Code, §§ 4197, 4201, 4204. The extradition proceedings were void, because they were founded on an affidavit which charged no offense, and because it was not made before a proper officer. The extradition of fugitives was once a matter of comity, but now it is a matter of statutory right, and governed entirely by statutory provisions.—U. S. Rev. Statutes, § 5278; *State v. Vanderpool*, 5 Crim. Law Magazine, 50; *Mohr's case*, 73 Ala. 503; Spear on Extradition, 297–8. The extradition proceedings, even if valid and regular on their face, could not justify an illegal arrest, a mere trespass, made or committed before they were instituted; nor can the subsequent judicial proceedings in Alabama be invoked for that purpose. Extradition proceedings are only authorized in specified cases, and intended to secure the

presence of the fugitive to answer the particular charge on
which they were instituted.   He can not be held, after arrest
and surrender, to answer other criminal prosecutions; and
this must include judicial proceedings instituted after his
arrest.—Spear on Extradition, 72, 570–72, 530; 47 Mich.
481; Whart. Crim. Law, 7th ed., vol. 3, p. 34, § 2956 *a*.

WM. L. MARTIN, Attorney-General, *contra*, cited 51 Amer.
Dec. 400; 28 Fed. Rep. 653; 34 *Ib.* 525; *Ker v. People*,
110 Ill. 627; 51 Amer. Rep. 706; 119 U. S. 436; 73 Ala.
503; 9 Wend. 212; 23 Fed. Rep. 32.

SOMERVILLE, J.—The prisoner was arrested in the
State of Georgia, without legal process, and was afterwards
handed over by the officers of the law in that State into the
custody of one McCain, who acted as agent of the State of
Alabama, under a warrant issued by the Governor of the
latter State under the inter-state extradition laws of the
United States.   This was done pursuant to a warrant of the
Governor of Georgia.   These extradition papers are claimed
to have been so defective as to confer no jurisdiction on any
of the officers, in whose custody the prisoner has been
detained.

The return made to the writ of *habeas corpus* by the
deputy-sheriff of Elmore county shows that the petitioner
was detained in his custody, not only under the authority
conferred by these papers, but by virtue of a *capias* issued
on an indictment for the offense of grand larceny—the same
crime for which he was extradited from the State of Georgia
as a fugitive from justice from Alabama.

The proposition contended for by the petitioner's counsel
may be reduced to this: that the petitioner is entitled to be
discharged from custody, and should be allowed reasonable
time to make good his escape again from this State, because
he was illegally arrested in Georgia and brought into Alabama.

This proposition is not sound, and there is an overwhelm-
ing array of authority against it.   We may admit that the
affidavit, charging the offense upon which the extradition
warrant was based, was fatally defective in omitting the
word "feloniously" before the words "took and carried away,"
which purport to charge the crime of grand larceny, and, for
this reason, the affidavit legally charges no crime.   And we
premise also, that when the affidavit in such cases fails on its

face to state facts which constitute a crime, the defect is jurisdictional, and may be ascertained and declared by the investigating tribunal, on an application for the writ of *habeas corpus.*—U. S. Rev. Stat., § 5278; Spear on Extradition, pp. 471–472, 477, 498, 548; 7 Amer. & Eng. Encyc. Law, 632, 637; *People v. Brady,* 56 N. Y. 182.

So, without affecting the merits of this case, it might be admitted for the sake of argument, as contended, that the judge of the County Court of Elmore county had no authority to issue a warrant for the arrest of a person for a felony— although it is obvious that he is invested by the statute with this authority as a lawful magistrate (Code, 1886, §§ 4255, 4279, 4680); and although "an affidavit made before any magistrate of a State or Territory," certified as authentic by the Governor of the demanding State, is obviously sufficient, if otherwise objectionable, under the Federal statute governing the subject of the extradition of fugitives from justice between the States and Territories.—U. S. Rev. Stat. § 5278; Hurd on Habeas Corpus (2d Ed.), 610.

It nevertheless is true, that the courts of a State will not generally investigate, either on *habeas corpus* proceedings, or on final trial, the mode of the prisoner's capture, whether it was legal or illegal—whether it was under lawful process or without any process at all—where he has fled to another State or country, and been brought again into its jurisdiction. The question is the legality of the prisoner's detention, not the legality of his arrest, unless on the complaint of the Governor of the State whose laws were violated by such unlawful arrest. The person making the arrest may be prosecuted criminally for kidnapping, or be held liable to respond in civil damages for false imprisonment; but the prisoner can not himself claim to be released from any legal process for the *same crime,* under authority of which he may be detained in the custody of the law. In other words, the mere fact that the prisoner, being a fugitive from justice, was kidnapped in another State—to put the case strongly—and was brought into this State, is alone no reason why he should be released, unless the demand for release is made by the Governor, or other executive authority of such foreign State. This is the accepted doctrine of the State and Federal courts, and is founded on an ancient and well settled principle of the common law.—Spear on Extradition, pp. 181, 492, 554; 7 Amer. & Eng. Ency. Law, 643, 653, note; *Matter of Fel-*

ter, 57 Amer. Dec. 400, *note*, and cases cited; *Com. v. Shaw*, 6 Crim. Law Mag. (1885), 245.

In *Ex parte Scott*, 9 Barn. & Cress. 446, a case of *habeas corpus*, the prisoner, a female, had been arrested at Brussels, without authority of law, and brought back to England. Lord Tenterden refused to inquire into the circumstances of her arrest, whether legal or illegal, upon its being made to appear that an indictment had been found against her in the proper jurisdiction in England, where the investigation occurred, and the crime was alleged to have been committed. It was not denied, that the foreign country, whose laws may have been violated by the illegal arrest, could vindicate their breach by making demand for the prisoner's return.

In *Dow's case*, 18 Penn. St. 37, the prisoner had escaped from justice in Pennsylvania, and fled to Michigan. He was arrested in the latter State, without legal authority, and brought back to the former State, where a prosecution was pending against him for forgery. He was held not to be entitled to his discharge, his release not being demanded by the executive of Michigan.

In *State v. Brewster*, 7 Vt. 118, where the prisoner had been kidnapped in Canada, and forcibly brought into the State of Vermont, his discharge was refused, and he was held liable to answer an indictment for crime in the latter State.

A like ruling was made in *Ker v. People*, 110 Ill. 627; s. c., 51 Amer. Rep. 706, in the case of one who had been seized by private persons in Peru, without warrant of law, and was brought to California, and from thence to the State of Illinois by process of extradition. The authorities on the subject are ably reviewed in this case by Scott, J.; and the United States Supreme Court, on appeal to that tribunal, declined to disturb the judgment of the Supreme Court of Illinois.—*Ker v. Illinois*, 119 U. S. 436. See, also, Spear on Extradition, 181–186; *Ker's case*, 18 Fed. Rep. 167.

It is not denied that the crime of grand larceny described in the *capias* on the indictment against the prisoner, and under which the sheriff claims to detain him, is the same offense as that intended to be charged in the extradition warrant of the Governor. There can be no serious question, under these circumstances, of the legality of the petitioner's detention under the *capias* on this indictment, irrespective of all other questions discussed in the briefs of counsel.

[Davis v. The State.]

Fetter's case, 23 N. J. Law, 311; s. c., 57 Amer. Dec. 382; 7 Amer. & Eng. Encyc. Law, 627-628.

The application for the writ of *habeas corpus* must be denied.

Davis *v.* The State.

Indictment for Criminal Possession of Burglarious Implements.

1. *Possession of burglarious implements, as criminal offense.*—Under statutory provisions, the possession of "any implement or instrument designed and intended to aid in the commission of burglary or larceny [in this State or elsewhere]," is declared to be a misdemeanor (Code, § 3788); but, while the offense consists of the possession, with the criminal intent to use the implements, the bracketed words are no part of it, and the statute is to be read as if they were omitted.

FROM the City Court of Montgomery.

Tried before the Hon. THOS. M. ARRINGTON.

The indictment in this case charged, that the defendant "had in his possession an implement or instrument designed and intended by him to aid in the commission of burglary or larceny, in this State or elsewhere, against the peace," &c. There was no demurrer, or other objection to the indictment; and issue being joined on the plea of not guilty, the trial resulted in a verdict of guilty, and the imposition of a fine of $300; to which the court added twelve months hard labor for the county, and an additional term of 209 days on non-payment of the costs. The refusal of a charge asked by the defendant, which is set out in the opinion of the court, is the only matter to which an exception was reserved.

E. P. MORRISSETT, for appellant.—The possession of burglarious tools is not a statutory offense (Code, § 3788), unless the party has the criminal intent to use them. The use of such implements burglariously elsewhere would not be an offense against the laws of Alabama; nor can the intent to so use them elsewhere, while in possession here, be an offense against our laws, without giving them an extra-territorial operation. To constitute a crime, a criminal act must concur with a criminal intent, both being aimed against the laws of the jurisdiction which seeks to punish it.

W. L. MARTIN, Attorney-General, *contra*, cited *Ivey v. State*, 12 Ala. 276.

CLOPTON, J.—The statute, under which appellant was indicted and convicted, declares "any person, who has in his possession any implement or instrument designed and intended to aid in the commission of burglary or larceny in this State or elsewhere," to be guilty of a misdemeanor. Code, 1886, § 3788. On the trial, the defendant requested the court to instruct the jury, that before they can convict, they must be satisfied beyond a reasonable doubt that the implements or instruments found in his possession were designed and intended to aid in the commission of burglary or larceny in this State. By the limited terms of the charge, no effect or operation is allowed to the words, *or elsewhere*, as used in the statute. It is predicated upon the interpretation of the statute, that the offense which it proposes to punish is the *intent* to commit burglary or larceny. The argument, based on this hypothesis, is, that it is not competent for the legislature to enact a law to punish the intent to commit a crime beyond the territorial limits of the State; and that, as the operation of the words referred to is to give the statute an extra-territorial force, it should be read as if those words were expunged.

It is true, that the mere possession of burglarious implements or instruments does not constitute the offense created by the statute; neither is the mere *intent* to commit either of the crimes designated. The denunciation of the statute is directed against the *possession* of such implements or instruments, with the design or intent to use them in the attempt to commit either burglary or larceny, as, where, and when opportunity may offer. The unlawful act, and the vicious intent, must concur to complete the statutory offense. The purpose of the statute is the security of property, and the prevention of crime, by declaring the possession of implements or instruments which are capable of aiding the commission of burglary or larceny, with the design and intent to use them, a criminal offense. The terms, *in this State or elsewhere*, constitute no part of the definition of the statutory offense. They are used for the purpose of excluding a conclusion, that the place where it may be intended to use the implements or instruments is a constituent of the offense denounced by the statute.—*Ivey v. State*, 12 Ala. 276. The charge was properly refused.

Affirmed.

Emmonds *v.* The State.

Indictment for Burglary.

1. *Sufficiency of indictment in averring ownership of house.*—An indictment for burglary, in breaking and entering the store-house "of the Perry Mason Shoe Company," must either allege that said company is a corporation, or, if it be a partnership, must allege that fact, and state the names of the individual partners, showing that the defendant is not one of them.

FROM the Criminal Court of Jefferson.

Tried before the Hon. S. E. GREENE.

The defendants in this case, John Emmonds and Henry Williams, were jointly indicted for burglary, in breaking and entering "the store of the Perry Mason Shoe Company;" were jointly tried and convicted, and sentenced to the penitentiary for the term of two years. There was no demurrer to the indictment, and no motion in arrest of judgment. On the trial, as the bill of exceptions states, "it was proved that the Perry Mason Shoe Company was a corporation, duly organized under the laws of Alabama, and composed of divers persons;" and thereupon the defendants asked the court to charge the jury, "that if they find from the evidence that the Perry Mason Shoe Company is a corporation, there is a fatal variance between the allegations and the proof, and they can not find the defendants guilty." The court refused this charge, and the defendants excepted.

No counsel appeared in this court for the appellants.

W. L. MARTIN, Attorney-General, for the State, cited 1 Bish. Crim. Pro., § 576; *Seymour v. Thomas Harrow Co.*, 81 Ala. 250; An. & Ames on Corp., § 632; 1 Archb. P. & Ev. 245; 2 *Ib.* 1167; *Lockett v. State*, 63 Ala. 5; 4 Amer. & En. Encyc. Law, 285, note.

[Emmonds v. The State.]

McCLELLAN, J.—The indictment charges the breaking and entering "of the store of the Perry Mason Shoe Company," with the intent to steal, &c. The sole question presented by the record for our consideration is, whether the allegation as to the ownership of the house entered is sufficient. One of the essentials of a charge, in offenses against property, is the negation of the defendant's ownership, by such averments as show affimatively, that the property, general or special, against which the crime is laid, is in another. It is on this principle that indictments charging offenses against the property of partnerships are bad, unless the names of the individuals composing the firm are set out; for otherwise it is not shown that the crime could have been committed of the property, as *non constat*, but that the defendant is one of the partners, and as such is entitled to do, with respect to the partnership property, the precise thing charged against him as a crime.—*Davis v. State*, 54 Ala. 88; *Beall v. State*, 53 Ala. 460; *Graves v. State*, 63 Ala. 134.

If the property is laid in a corporation, it is not necessary to state the names of its shareholders, as they, in their individual capacities, have no more control or possession of it than strangers, and whether the defendant be a shareholder or not is immaterial. But the indictment should aver facts which show that the company is a corporation. The use of a name which may import a corporation, or which, on the other hand, may be that of a voluntary association or a simple partnership, will not suffice. It is enough in civil causes, depending on corporate character, at least on appeal, to allege a name appropriate to a corporation (*Seymour v. Thomas Harrow Co.*, 81 Ala. 252); but the rule which requires indictments to aver every fact necessary to an affirmation of guilt, is not satisfied, as long as any one of these facts is left to implication or inference. The Perry Mason Shoe Company bears a name appropriate to corporate existence; yet it may be that of a voluntary association of two or more individuals, each having the right to break into and enter the store-house of the company, and, for aught that appears in the indictment, the detendant may be one of these associates; so that, if every fact set forth be admitted, the court could not say that the defendants were guilty of the crime of burglary. These considerations lead us to the conclusion, which is supported by the weight of authority, that when property, against or in reference to which an offense is charged, belongs to a private corporation, the fact that the company is a corporation must be alleged —*People v. Swartz*, 32 Cal. 160; *Wallace v. People*, 63 Ill. 452; *State v. Mead*, 27 Vt. 722; *Cohen v. People*, 5 Park. C. R. 330; 2 Russ. on Crimes, 100; Whart. Cr. Pl. & Pr., § 110 (n. 1); *Johnson v. State*, 73 Ala. 483.

If the Perry Mason Shoe Company is a corporation, that fact is not alleged; if it be a partnership, the names of the partners are not given; and in either view, the indictment was bad.

The judgment must be reversed, and the cause remanded.

Coleman *v.* The State.

Indictment for Grand Larceny.

1. *To what witness may testify.*—A sheriff, or constable, testifying to a conversation had by them with the defendant, prior to his arrest, in which they asked him whether he had any of the money stolen from the prosecutor, not making any accusation against him, may testify "that he did not stand still, but kept turning around and kicking the ground, and would not look at them;" but not "that he was restless, nervous, and excited."

2. *General objection to evidence, partly admissible.*—A general objection to evidence, a part of which is admissible, may be overruled entirely.

3. *Testimony as to defendant's arrest, or surrender.*—The sheriff, by whom the defendant was arrested, or to whom he surrendered, having testified that, not being able to find the defendant, "he told his friends that he had a warrant for the arrest of the defendant, and sent him word to come in and give himself up—that the case against him amounted to nothing, and he would have no trouble to get out of it; that the defendant did come in and surrender a day or two afterwards, but he did not know the defendant got his message;" *held*, that this evidence was improperly admitted, against the objection of the defendant.

4. *Argument of counsel to jury.*—Counsel should not be allowed, in argument to the jury, to state as fact that which is damaging to the defendant, and of which there is no legal evidence.

5. *Charge as to circumstantial evidence.*—A charge asserting that, "to justify conviction, circumstantial evidence ought to exclude a rational probability of innocence, and a conviction ought not to be had on circumstantial evidence, when direct and positive evidence is attainable," is properly refused, as tending to mislead and confuse the jury, when there is some direct and positive evidence, and the record does not show that any other was attainable.

FROM the Circuit Court of Lauderdale.

Tried before the Hon. H. C. SPEAKE.

The defendant in this case was indicted for the larceny of

one hundred dollars in gold coin, the personal property of
Thos. P. Earnest, consisting of four $20 pieces, one $10
piece, and two $5 pieces.　On the trial, the prosecutor testi-
fied to the loss of his money, stated circumstances tending
to show that it had been stolen, and identified a $20 gold
coin, which had a peculiar mark on it, as one of the lost
pieces.　The coin, as one Price testified, who was a constable,
was delivered up to him by Peter McDaniel, the father of
Hilliard McDaniel, who said that he got it from Hilliard,
and that Hilliard said he had won it.　This occurred at the
house of said Peter, when the sheriff and constable had gone
there to arrest Hilliard, who was charged with the larceny.
Hilliard was arrested, and was under indictment for the
offense, when he was introduced as a witness for the prosecution in this case; and he testified, in substance, that he
went with the defendant to Earnest's house the night the
money was stolen, and held his mule while the defendant
went into the house, and that the defendant gave him the
gold coin on their return.　The constable further testified
that, after the arrest of Hilliard, he went with the sheriff
to see the defendant, "and asked him if he had any of Hilliard's money, not mentioning any particular kind of money;
that they made no charge against him, and said nothing about
arresting him, but only asked if he had any of Hilliard's
money; that defendant replied, that he had not, nor anybody elses money except his own, and that was greenbacks.
Witness was then asked, if he observed anything unusual
in the defendant's manner during this conversation; to which
question the defendant objected, and excepted to its allowance.　The witness answered, that the defendant, during
said conversation, was restless, nervous, and excited; that
he did not stand still, but was continually changing his position, and kicking the ground, and would not look at them.
The defendant objected to this answer, and moved to exclude
it from the jury; which motion the court overruled, and
the defendant excepted."　The testimony of the sheriff, as
to what occurred at this interview, was the same in substance,
and almost in words; and a similar exception was reserved
to its admission.

　　The sheriff testified, also, that a warrant for the defendant's
arrest was placed in his hands a few days after the arrest of
Hilliard; that he went to defendant's house, but could not
find him, and could learn nothing about him by inquiry
among his neighbors.　"Witness was then asked, if he

arrested defendant, and, if so, how; and answered, that he adopted a ruse and entrapped him, and was satisfied this brought about his arrest. To this the defendant objected, and the court sustained the objection, but told the witness he could state what he did, and not give his opinion. Witness then stated, that some of defendant's friends came to town, and he told them that he had a warrant for defendant's arrest, and sent him word by his friends to come in and give himself up—that the case against him amounted to nothing, and he would have no trouble to get out of it; and that a day or two thereafter the defendant did come in and surrender. Witness stated, also, that he did not know that defendant got the message. Defendant objected to this evidence, and moved to exclude it from the jury; which motion the court overruled, and the defendant excepted."

"The counsel for the prosecution, in his argument to the jury, stated that defendant fled to the woods after the arrest of Hilliard McDaniel, and was arrested by a ruse on the part of the sheriff. The defendant asked the following charges in writing: (1.) 'There is no proof in this case that the defendant took to the woods, and the fact that he was not at the place where the officer sought to find him, if it be a fact, is not alone evidence that he was avoiding arrest.' (2.) 'To justify conviction, circumstantial evidence ought to exclude a rational probability of innocence; and a conviction ought not to be had on circumstantial evidence, when direct and positive evidence is attainable.' The court refused each of these charges, and the defendant duly excepted to the refusal of each."

EMMET O'NEAL, for appellant.

WM. L. MARTIN, Attorney-General, for the State.

STONE, C. J.—The statement of the sheriff, and of the constable, when on the witness stand, that on a certain occasion, before his arrest, the defendant was "restless, nervous and excited," if properly objected to, would have been inadmissible.—*Gassenheimer v. State*, 52 Ala. 313; *McAdory v. State*, 59 Ala. 92. But, if part of the testimony offered be legal, and the objection is to the whole in a lump, the court is not bound to separate the legal from the illegal, but may overrule the entire objection.—3 Brick. Digest, 443, § 570. The other portions of the evidence, to which, as a whole, a single objection was interposed, were legal, and properly allowed; and there is nothing in these objections. 3 Brick. Dig. 437, §§ 455, 458; *Pollock v. Gantt*, 69 Ala. 373, 378.

The sheriff was allowed to testify as a witness, "that some of the defendant's friends came to town, and he told them that he had a warrant for the arrest of defendant; that he sent defendant word by his friends to come in and give himself up—that the case against defendant amounted to nothing, and that he would have no trouble to get out of it; and that a day or two thereafter defendant did come in and surrender. Witness also stated, that he did not know that defendant got the message." Defendant excepted to the admission of this evidence. The Circuit Court erred in this ruling.

There was no legal evidence that defendant had "fled to the woods," if indeed there was *any evidence* that such was the case. Counsel should not be permitted to state as fact that which is damaging to defendant, and of which there is no legal proof.

Charge 2 asked by the defendant, though possibly true in some states of proof, was rightly refused in this case. It was not adapted to the testimony. There was some positive proof—that of Hilliard McDaniel—that defendant did steal the money, and the record does not tend to show that any additional, positive testimony could be obtained, or was in existence. The tendency of the charge, if given, would have been to mislead and confuse the jury.—3 Brick. Digest, 111, §§ 73, 79.

Reversed and remanded.

Carl *v.* The State.

Indictment for Selling Intoxicating Liquors contrary to Law.

1. *Violation of prohibitory liquor law; what decoctions or mixtures are within statute.*—Prohibitory liquor laws are designed to prevent the sale of intoxicating liquors as a beverage, and do not apply to medicinal preparations, articles for toilet use, or for culinary purposes, of which alcohol may be a necessary ingredient; the question being one of fact for the determination of the jury, whether it was made and sold in good faith for the purpose indicated, or was intended for use as a

2

beverage, and was so used; but, if made and sold in good faith as a tonic or beverage, its misuse by the purchaser, though producing partial intoxication, does not render the seller criminally liable.

2. *Evidence as to intoxicating properties of article sold.*—In a criminal prosecution for the sale of intoxicating liquors in violation of a local prohibitory liquor law, the article sold being compounded by a druggist, and the bottles labeled *"Elixir Cinchona,"* or *"Cinchona Bitters;"* it is permissible for the prosecution to prove that it was bought and used by many persons as a beverage, the use to which it was applied being illustrative of its nature and properties; and a person who had swallowed it may state its exhilarating effect on himself, and, though not technically an expert, may testify that, "in his opinion, it would produce intoxication."

FROM the Circuit Court of Escambia.

Tried before the Hon. JOHN P. HUBBARD.

The indictment in this case was found in October, 1887, and contained two counts; the first charging that the defendant, H. C. Carl, "sold vinous or spirituous liquors, without a license, and contrary to law;" and the second, "that he did unlawfully sell, keep for sale, or otherwise dispose of vinous, spirituous, or malt liquors, or other intoxicating beverages or bitters, within the limits of said county." On the trial, as appears from the bill of exceptions, the evidence showed that the defendant kept for sale, and had sold several bottles of "Elixir Cinchona," or "Cinchona Bitters," a tonic or mixture prepared and sold by Dr. J. W. Hale, a druggist in Montgomery, who testified, as a witness for the defendant, that the mixture "contained gentian-root, bitter orange-peel, cardeman seed, red peruvian bark, snake-root, syrup and water, and enough spirits to prevent fermentation; that there were six pints of water in a gallon of the mixture, and one pint of proof spirits; that there was not more than twenty per-cent. of spirits in the article sold, and there was not less than that in any liquid medicine manufactured or sold in any drug-store; that he lost the preparation the first time he experimented with it, and found that twenty per-cent. of proof spirits was necessary to prevent fermentation; that it was a tonic and stimulant, but not an intoxicant; that he had seen parties take it, and had seen it taken repeatedly for about three years, but had never seen the least effect of intoxication produced by it; that it was not an intoxicant, and a man could not, in his opinion, drink enough of it to make him intoxicated." W. H. O'Bannon, a witness for the prosecution, testified "that he bought from the defendant, about ten or twelve months ago, a bottle of said elixir as a medicine for his wife; that she could not take it, and he took a drink of it

[Carl v. The State.]

himself; that it made him sick, and about half drunk; that a dose was about a table-spoonful; that it was sold as a medicine all the time; that the defendant, when he went into business a short time before, proposed that witness should go into the business with him, said there was money in it, and that they could have it put up in different ways to suit customers, but said nothing about the quantity of spirits in it; that he (witness) had been in the whiskey business for several years, had drank whiskey, and knew the effect of it; that said elixir had the same effect as whiskey, and would, in his opinion, produce intoxication. To the opinion of the witness, as thus testified to, the defendant objected, and excepted to its admission as evidence." The witness testified, also, "that said elixir was sold generally in Brewton as a beverage;" and the court admitted this evidence, against the objection and exception of the defendant.. Other witnesses for the prosecution, who had bought and drank the elixir, testified to its exhilarating effects, while several practicing physicians in Brewton, who had used and prescribed it, testified to its tonic and medicinal properties.

The court charged the jury as follows: "Although Dr. Hale, in the manufacture of said elixir, did not use enough spirituous liquor to render it intoxicating in its ordinary use, yet, if the defendant bought that article, and put into the bottle sold to O'Bannon sufficient spirituous, vinous or malt liquors to render it intoxicating in its ordinary use, it is such an article as is prohibited by the statute; and if the jury find that he sold it to O'Bannon, he would be guilty, if in other respects his guilt was made out; and whether he put any of such liquors in it, is for the jury to decide from the evidence. . . If the article sold by defendant to O'Bannon contained a sufficient quantity of liquor to produce intoxication in its ordinary use, although Dr. Hale put no more liquor in it than was actually necessary to prevent it from fermenting, and this was done by him honestly; yet it is such an article as comes within the prohibition of the statute. . . If a man goes and gets this article, and it is an intoxicant in its ordinary use, and the intoxicating element is spirituous liquor; and he uses it as a beverage, and gets drunk in its ordinary use; it is an article prohibited by the statute, and he (?) would be guilty, though it was the best of medicines, if he sold it, and if the other elements of the offense are made out. . . Was there in this compound, whether bought as a medicine or not, a sufficient quantity of spirituous liquor to produce intoxication in its ordinary use? If there was, then it is an article prohibited by the statute, whether it is the best of medicines or not."

JOHN GAMBLE, for the appellant, cited *Wall v. State*, 78 Ala. 417; *Carson v. State*, 69 Ala. 235; *Ryall v. State*, 78 Ala. 410; *Knowles v. State*, 80 Ala. 9.

WM. L. MARTIN, Attorney-General, for the State.

SOMERVILLE, J.—The defendant, being indicted, was convicted of selling spirituous liquors without a license, and contrary to law. The article sold was labelled "Elixir Cinchona," or "Cinchona Bitters." The evidence on the part of the State tended to prove that it contained spirituous liquor sufficient to make it intoxicating in its ordinary use as a beverage, and that it was frequently sold and used as a beverage in the community, especially since the enactment of a local law prohibiting the sale of spirituous liquors in Escambia county, and that it was sold by the defendant more as a beverage than as a medicine. The testimony offered by the defendant, on the contrary, tended to prove that the decoction contained twenty per cent. of proof spirits, or only enough to prevent it from fermentation, and no more; that it was manufactured in good faith as a medicine, and that it was a valuable tonic and stimulant, and not as an intoxicant in its ordinary use; that it contained barks and herbs of known medicinal qualities, and was sold in good faith as a medicine, and not as a beverage.

The purpose of prohibitory liquor laws is to promote the cause of temperance, and prevent drunkenness. The mode adopted to accomplish this end is the prevention of the sale, the giving away, or other disposition of intoxicating liquors. The evil to be remedied is the use of intoxicating liquors as a beverage, rather than as an ingredient of medicines and articles for the toilet, or for culinary purposes; and the object of the law in this particular must not be lost sight of in its interpretation. It is true, and we have so held in *Carson's case*, that if the article sold was spirituous, or other intoxicating liquor, the fact that it was sold for medicine would be no defense, unless there was an express exception in the statute. But we observed in that case as follows: "We are not to be supposed as intimating that physicians or druggists would be prohibited, under such a statute as the one

in question, from the *bona fide* use of spirituous liquors in
the necessary compounding of medicines manufactured,
mixed or sold by them. This would not be within the evils
intended to be remedied by such a prohibitory enactment,
nor even within the strict letter of the statute."—*Carson v.
State*, 69 Ala. 235, 241; *Woods v. State*, 36 Ark. 36; s. c.,
38 Amer. Rep. 22. We again said in discussing this same
subject, in *Wall v. State*, 78 Ala. 417: "There may be
cases, perhaps, where the *bona fide* use of a moderate quantity of spirituous liquor, in a medicinal tonic, would not alone
bring a beverage [or decoction] within the statute."

This question is exhaustively discussed in the *Intoxicating
Liquor Cases*, 25 Kans. 751; 37 Amer. Rep. 384, decided in
the year 1881. The Kansas statute prohibited the sale of
"all liquors, and mixtures, by whatever name called, that
will produce intoxication." It was held not to embrace
standard medicines, and toilet articles, not ordinarily used as
beverages, such as tincture of gentian, bay-rum, and essence
of lemon, although containing alcohol. Whether it embraced certain cordials, or bitters, was held to be a question
of fact, dependent on the evidence as to their intoxicating
qualities and ordinary use. It was said that "bay-rum, co-
logne, paregoric, and tinctures generally, all contain alcohol,
but in no fair or reasonable sense are they intoxicating
liquors, or mixtures thereof." And as to the cordials and
bitters, the question was said to be one of fact, which should
be referred to the jury. "If the compound or preparation,"
said the court, "be such that the distinctive character and
effect of intoxicating liquor are gone—that its use as an
intoxicating beverage is practically impossible by reason of
the other ingredients—it is not within the statute. The
mere presence of the alcohol does not bring the article within
the prohibition. The influence of the alcohol may be coun-
teracted by the other ingredients, and the compound be
strictly and fairly only a medicine. On the other hand, if
the intoxicating liquor remains as a distinctive force in the
compound, and such compound is reasonably liable to be
used as an intoxicating beverage, it is within the statute, and
this though it contain many other ingredients, and ingredients of an independent and beneficial force in counteracting
disease, or strengthening the system. 'Intoxicating liquors,
or mixtures thereof;' this, reasonably construed, means
liquors which will intoxicate, and which are commonly used
as beverages for such purposes, and also any mixture of such

liquors as, retaining their intoxicating qualities, it may be fairly presumed may be used as a beverage, and become a substitute for the ordinary intoxicating drinks."

In *King v. State*, 58 Miss. 737; 38 Amer. Rep. 344 (1881), the defendants were indicted for selling intoxicating liquor without a license, and contrary to law. The article sold was "Home Bitters," a decoction composed of thirty per cent. of alcohol, and the rest of water, barks, seeds, herbs, and other like ingredients. It was alleged by the defendant to have been sold as a medicine. It was held that, if the compound was intoxicating, and was sold as a beverage, the jury should convict; but, if it was sold in good faith, only as a medicine, they should acquit. It was said: "One authorized to sell medicines ought not to be held guilty of violating the laws relative to retailing, because the purchaser of a medicine containing alcohol misuses it, and becomes intoxicated; but, on the other hand, these laws can not be evaded by selling as a beverage intoxicating liquors containing drugs, barks, or seeds which have medicinal qualities. The uses to which the compound is ordinarily put, the purposes for which it is usually bought, and its effect upon the system, are material facts, from which may be inferred the intention of the seller. If the other ingredients are medicinal, and the alcohol is used as a necessary preservative or vehicle for them—if, from all the facts and circumstances, it appears that the sale is of the other ingredients as a medicine, and not of the liquor as a beverage—the seller is protected; but, if the drugs and roots are mere pretenses of medicines, shadows and devices under which an illegal traffic is to be conducted, they will be but shadows when interposed for protection against criminal prosecution." See, also, *Wall's Case*, 78 Ala. 417; *Ryall's Case, Ib.* 410. To the same effect, substantially, is the case of *Com. v. Ramsdell*, 130 Mass. 68 (1881).

We have quoted at length from the foregoing authorities, because they seem to be carefully considered, and furnish suitable tests for the determination of what may be considered intoxicating liquors within the meaning of our prohibition liquor laws, as accurate and just as seems to be practicable. We accordingly adopt the doctrine of these cases, as the correct rule for the government of this case on another trial.

The rulings of the Circuit Court are not in accord with this view, and for this reason the judgment must be reversed.

It was competent to prove the intoxicating qualities of the

elixir, or bitters in question, by the experimental effect of its use.—*Knowles v. State*, 80 Ala. 9. Or the same fact could be proved by any witness who is shown to have had an opportunity of personal observation, or of experience, such as to enable him to form a correct opinion. He need not be a technical expert, and it is no objection that his statement of the fact is made in the form of an opinion. *Carson v. State*, 69 Ala. 236; *Merkle v. State*, 37 Ala. 139. So, it was proper to prove that this article was bought and used for a beverage, and drank as such by many persons in the community, or elsewhere. Its nature was illustrated by the uses to which it was put. The court did not err in its rulings on the evidence.

The judgment is reversed, and the cause remanded for a new trial.

Andy *v.* The State.

Indictment for Robbery.

1. *Severance of trial.*—Under the statute now of force (Code, § 4451), when two or more persons are jointly indicted, either one of them is entitled to a severance as matter of right, if he claims it in proper time.

FROM the Criminal Court of Jefferson.
Tried before the Hon. S. E. GREENE.

CLOPTON, J.—On the day set for the trial, but before a jury was organized, appellant, who was jointly indicted with others, moved for a severance as to himself. Section 4451 of Code of 1886 declares: "When two or more defendants are jointly indicted, they may be tried either jointly or separately, as either may elect." Under the statute, as it stood prior to this enactment, and also in the absence of statutory regulations, it was held, that the allowance of a separate trial was discretionary with the court.—Code, 1876, § 4892; *Hawkins v. State*, 9 Ala. 137; *Wade v. State*, 40 Ala. 74. The purpose and operation of section 4451 are to abrogate the former rule, and to entitle either defendant to a separate trial as matter of right. Under the present statute, when two or more persons are jointly indicted, and either so elects in proper time, the allowance of a separate trial is imperative.

Reversed and remanded.

NOTE.—See Rule of Practice, since adopted, regulating severances.—86 Ala. VIII.

White v. The State.

Indictment for Burglary and Grand Larceny.

1. *Contradicting or impeaching party's own witness.*—While a party can not, as a general rule, contradict or impeach his own witness, he may, when put at disadvantage by an unexpected answer, or for the purpose of refreshing the memory of the witness, ask him whether, at a certain time and place, he has not made other statements inconsistent with his testimony as just given.

2. *Same.*—The general rule, which denies to a party the right to impeach his own witness, applies to a witness who is summoned and examined by and for each party; that is, the party who first introduces him, can not impeach him when introduced and examined by the other.

FROM the City Court of Mobile.

Tried before the Hon. O. J. SEMMES.

The indictment in this case contained two counts, one charging the defendant with burglary, and the other with larceny from a dwelling-house; the house broken and entered, and the goods stolen therefrom, being alleged to be the property of Emma Harris. On the trial, as the bill of exceptions shows, the State introduced said Emma Harris as a witness, and she testified to the burglary and larceny from her house; stating, also, that she found some of the stolen articles, a few days afterwards, in the defendant's house, and the others in the possession of one Gertrude Loyd. "Said witness was asked, on cross-examination, if she did not go to the house of Gertrude Loyd, a few days before the meeting of the grand jury, and try to induce her to false-witness against the defendant; which question she answered in the negative." The defendant afterwards introduced said Gertrude Loyd as a witness, and asked her, "whether Emma Harris had not gone to her house, a few days before the meeting of the grand jury, and said something about getting

her to false-witness against the defendant; and the witness
answered in the negative." The defendant's attorney then
asked the witness: "Did you not tell me, here in this court-
room, a few minutes before the trial, that Emma did come
to your house, a few days before the meeting of the grand
jury, and say something about getting you to false-witness
against the defendant?" The solicitor objected to this
question, "on the ground that a party can not impeach his
own witness." The defendant's attorney then stated, "that
he expected the witness to answer in the affirmative." The
court sustained the objection to the question, and the
defendant excepted.

The State introduced as a witness Catherine White, who
was the mother of the defendant, and who testified that the
defendant brought home the articles the morning after the
burglary. The witness was then turned over to the defendant,
and her attorney asked the court, "whether he had the right
to examine the witness then as his own, or must wait until
the State had rested its case. The court said, 'You may do
either;' and the defendant's attorney answered, 'Then I shall
do so now.'" The testimony of the witness, on examination
by the defendant's counsel, is then stated; among other
things, "that Emma Harris is a woman of bad reputation,
and witness would not believe her on oath." The defendant's
counsel, in his argument before the jury, "comparing the
relative weight to be attributed to the testimony of Emma
Harris and Catherine White, said that the defendant had
impeached Emma Harris, but the State had not even sought
to impeach Catherine White. The solicitor replied, in his
argument to the jury, that, as matter of law, he could not
impeach her, as she was his own witness. The defendant's
attorney objected, under the circumstances, to this proposition being stated as a rule of law, on the ground that said
Catherine White, being a witness for the defendant as well
as for the State, could be impeached. The court overruled
the objection, and allowed the proposition to be stated; and
the defendant thereupon excepted."

JNO. E. MITCHELL, for appellant, cited *Campbell v. State*,
23 Ala. 77; *Hemingway v. Garth*, 51 Ala. 530; 1 Greenl.
Ev., §§ 444–47; 2 Phil. Ev. 450; *Wright v. Beckett*, 1 M.
& W. 414; *Barker v. Bell*, 46 Ala. 217.

W. L. MARTIN, Attorney-General, for the State.

McCLELLAN, J.—A party may ask his witness, for the purpose of refreshing his memory, or of showing that he has been put at a disadvantage by unexpected evidence, whether at a certain time and place he has not made certain statements inconsistent with his testimony on the stand, even though the admission of such inconsistent statements will injuriously affect the witness' credibility with the jury. *Campbell v. State*, 23 Ala. 77; *Hemingway v. Garth*, 51 Ala. 530; Roscoe's Cr. Ev. 103; 1 Greenl. Ev. § 444. While this can not be done, when the purpose and only effect of such evidence is to impeach the witness (*Gandy v. State*, 81 Ala. 68); yet, the mere fact that the party expects the witness to admit the contradictory statements is not sufficient to show that the purpose and sole effect of the examination is to impeach the witness, or to justify the exclusion of the testimony.   Therefore, the defendant's witness, Lloyd, having, in reply to defendant's counsel, sworn that the State's witness, Harris, had not attempted to get her to "false-witness" the defendant, proper predicate having been laid for the impeachment of Harris, the court should have allowed counsel to ask Lloyd, if she had not, at a given time and place, stated to him that such attempt was made.   The refusal of the court to allow this question to be put and answered was error, for which the case must be reversed.

"When a party offers a witness in proof of his cause, he thereby, in general, represents him as worthy of belief;" and he will not be permitted to impeach the witness' general reputation for truth, or otherwise show that he is unworthy of credit.   The ground upon which the right to impeach his own witness is denied to a party—the reason of the rule—would apply equally to the witness after he had been examined and discharged by the one, and introduced by the other party; and would extend throughout the particular case. For such party to attack the credibility of the witness, in that case, even after he had become the witness of his adversary, would be inconsistent with his implied assurance of his worthiness of belief.   And while a party may show that the fact is not as it was testified to by his witness, either during the time he continued to be so, strictly speaking, or after he had been offered as to new matters by the other party; it can not be said that, at any time, or under any circumstances, in that trial, he has a right to impeach him.   As we have shown above, for certain purposes, other than impeachment, a art may show, by the witness himself, inconsistent statements; but, even with respect to these, he is not permitted to assume an attitude repugnant to his representation of general credibility. In the usual sense of the term, therefore, the statement of the solicitor, that the law did not allow him to impeach the witness, Catherine White, was a correct exposition of the rule, and a proper argument in reply to the position taken by defendant's counsel.—1 Gr. Ev. § 442.

Reversed and remanded.

Tolbert *v.* The State.

Indictment for Gaming in Public Place.

1. *Sufficiency of indictment* —-An indictment which charges that the defendant "bet at a game played with cards, dice, or some device or substitute for either cards or dice, in a public house, highway, or other public place, or at an outhouse where people resort" (Code, §§ 4052, 4057), is fatally defective, unless it also alleges that a game *was played*.

2. *Objections to question and answer.*—When an objection is made and sustained to a question propounded to a witness, but the record does not show what answer was expected, nor that the witness had any knowledge or information on the subject, this court can not consider the correctness of the ruling.

3. *Conversations between third persons; admissibility as evidence.*—Conversations between third persons, tending to implicate the defendant, but not had in his presence, are not admissible as evidence against him; and if they did not relate to the particular offense with which he is charged, they would be inadmissible because irrelevant.

4. *Evidence as to character of house, or room.*—On a prosecution for playing cards in a public house, or for betting at a game played in a public house, evidence as to the character of the house, whether public or private, is relevant and admissible; the presumption being that the house is an entirety.

5. *Sentence to hard labor for county, on non-payment of costs.*—On conviction of a misdemeanor, a fine being assessed as the punishment, followed by a sentence to hard labor for the county for a specified number of days for the fine, "and an additional term for the costs, not exceeding eight months, at thirty cents per day;" this court will not say that the judgment is erroneous, because it does not specify the amount of costs for which additional hard labor is imposed, but suggests that this should always be done, or it should be otherwise made definite and certain.

FROM the Circuit Court of Conecuh.

Tried before the Hon. JOHN P. HUBBARD.

The indictment in this case charged that the defendant, Sanford Tolbert, "bet at a game played with cards, dice, or

some device or substitute for either cards or dice, in a public
house, highway, or other public place, or at an outhouse
where people resort." The defendant demurred to the indictment, because it did not allege that a game "was played"
at any one of the places specified; and his demurrer being
overruled, he pleaded not guilty. By the verdict of the jury
he was found guilty, and a fine of $100 imposed; and the fine
and costs not being presently paid or secured, the court rendered judgment sentencing him to "hard labor for the county
for thirty days for the fine, and to an additional term of
hard labor for the costs, not exceeding eight months, at
thirty cents per day."

On the trial, as the bill of exceptions shows, it appeared
that the defendant and several other persons were arrested
one night, in a small room over a "livery and feed stable,"
where a game of "craps" was being played on a blanket on
the floor, cloths being hung over the openings of the room.
The defendant reserved several exceptions to the rulings of
the court on evidence, among which were the following:
"Capt. M. A. Gantt, the first witness examined on the part
of the State, testified in substance, in connection with other
things, as follows: 'The night on which the defendant, with
others, was arrested, John Stamps, the night watchman, came
to my house, awoke me, and asked me to go with him.' Defendant objected to the witness testifying as to what passed
between himself and the watchman, unless the defendant
was present; which objection the court overruled, and the
defendant excepted. The solicitor then asked said witness,
for what purpose the room was used in which the playing
took place; to which he answered, that he did not know.
The solicitor then asked him, for what purpose it was used
when he occupied the building, which was about six months
before the alleged offense; to which question, and to the
answer of the witness, the defendant objected, because a room
might, under certain circumstances, be a public place at one
time, and not at another time; which objections the court
overruled, and the defendant excepted." Further testifying,
the witness said, that when he, in company with Stamps and
another person, went to the room in which the playing was.
going on, and demanded admittance, "they (meaning the
persons in the room) blew out the light as quick as snapping
his finger, and escaped through the windows;" and to this
testimony, also, the defendant objected and excepted, as
irrelevant and illegal.

[Tolbert v. The State.]

STALLWORTH & BURNETT, for appellant, cited *Dreyfus v. State*, 83 Ala. 54; *Johnson v. State*, 75 Ala. 7; *Collins v. State*, 70 Ala. 19; and they also contended that the judgment was erroneous.

WM. L. MARTIN, Attorney-General, for the State.

STONE, C. J.—The indictment in this case is defective, and will not support the conviction.   To constitute a good indictment for the offense attempted to be charged in this case, it must be averred that a game *was played* "with cards or dice," or a substitute therefor, at one of the places mentioned in the statute, and that the defendant did bet at such game.—Code of 1886, §§ 4052, 4057; *Jacobson v. State*, 55 Ala. 151; *Mitchell v. State*, *Ib.* 160; *Collins v. State*, 70 Ala. 19.   The indictment in the present case is not specific enough.   While it avers that the game on which the bet was made was one played with cards or dice, or some device or substitute for either cards or dice, it fails to aver that the game on which the bet was made was in fact played.   This precise question was so ruled in *Dreyfus v. State*, 83 Ala. 54, and in *Johnson v. State*, 75 Ala. 7; also, *Smith v. State*, 63 Ala. 55.

Several objections were made and sustained, to questions propounded to witnesses; but it is not shown what answers the witnesses were expected to give, nor, indeed, that they could have given any information on the subjects inquired about, affecting the defendant.   We can not consider these objections.—3 Brick. Dig. 444, §§ 577 to 579.   Conversations tending to implicate the defendant, had when he was not present, should not have been received; and if they did not relate to the case on trial, they were irrelevant, and inadmissible on that account.   The character of the house, whether public or private, was an issue in the cause, and legitimate evidence—not a general opinion or conclusion of the witness—was competent to prove whether the house fell within one of the classes in which gaming is prohibited. This question, however, must be treated on the *prima facie* intendment that a house is an entirety, or unit.—*Huffman. r. State*, 29 Ala. 46; *Moore v. State*, 30 Ala. 550; *Russell v. State*, 72 Ala. 222.

We do not feel at liberty to declare that a trial court, in sentencing to hard labor for non-payment of costs, commits a reversible error, by failing to ascertain and insert in the judgment the sum of the costs for which additional labor is imposed. The sentence can not extend to all costs that may have been incurred. The classes of costs for which the convicted offender may be sentenced to perform hard labor, are defined in *Bradley v. State*, 69 Ala. 318. In passing sentence, the trial court would avert uncertainty and possible expense, by either expressing the amount of costs the defendant is sentenced to pay with his labor, or by giving such directions as to the classes of costs he is liable to so pay, or, what is the same thing, by expressing the classes of costs that are not to be computed in fixing the amount, for the payment of which he is sentenced to perform additional hard labor.

Reversed and remanded.

Perry *v.* The State.

Indictment for Murder.

1. *Former testimony of absent witness.*—The testimony of a witness on a former trial of the defendant, or on his preliminary examination by a committing magistrate, is admissible as evidence against him on the trial, on proof that the witness is beyond the jurisdiction of the court, being either permanently or indefinitely absent.

2. *To what witness may testify.*—A witness who, as a member of the coroner's jury, had seen the dead body of the child alleged to have been murdered, may testify that its neck, which was broken, "looked like it had been struck with a hot iron, and looked scarred."

3. *Charge as to reasonable doubt.*—A charge asked in a criminal case, asserting that "the probability of reasonably accounting for the death of the deceased by accident, or by any other cause than the unlawful act of the defendant, must be excluded by the circumstances proved; and it is only when no other hypothesis will explain all the conditions of the case, and account for all the facts, that it can be safely and justly concluded that it was caused by him,"—is properly refused.

4. *Same; charge tending to mislead* —A charge requested, asserting that "it is the safer and better practice for the jury to acquit a guilty person, rather than run the risk of convicting an innocent one," is properly refused, as tending to mislead.

5. *Charge as to argument of counsel.*—A charge instructing the jury that "the suggestions of counsel in their argument, founded on the evidence, may give rise to such a reasonable doubt as will justify the jury in acquitting the defendant," being merely argumentative, and tending to mislead, is properly refused.

6. *Insanity as defense; charges as to, when abstract.*—Charges as to the defense of insanity in criminal cases are properly refused, without regard to their correctness as abstract legal propositions, when there is no evidence in the case showing any form of mania, or mental incapacity, to a degree which confers irresponsibility for crime.

Vol. LXXXVII.

7. *Same; how pleaded; ex post facto laws.*—By statutory provision, insanity as a defense in criminal cases must be specially pleaded, and is not available under the plea of not guilty generally (Sess. Acts 1888-9, pp. 742-6); and this statute, relating only to the mode of procedure, applies to all cases tried since its passage, although the offense was committed before that date.

FROM the City Court of Mobile.

Tried before Hon. O. J. SEMMES.

The defendant in this case, Caroline Perry, a negro woman, was indicted for the murder of her daughter Mary, a child between ten and twelve years of age; was convicted of murder in the second degree, and sentenced to the penitentiary for the term of ten years. The defendant was blind, and was usually led about by the child. The child was killed one morning in June, 1888; and an examination of its body before the coroner's jury showed that its neck was broken, and it was badly bruised and beaten. The defendant, testifying as a witness on the trial, denied that she killed the child, or that she beat or injured it in any way; and the evidence against her was entirely circumstantial. No one was in the house at the time except the defendant and the child. Her statement to the jury was, that while she was sitting in the door and talking to the child, "she heard it hiccough, and fall to the floor, called it, but it did not answer; got up and felt around, and found the child lying on the floor; picked it up, and found it cold, but its heart was still beating; called Charlotte Patterson [her sister, who lived on the same lot] to come and see what was the matter;" and that she afterwards washed and dressed the child for burial, "because nobody else came." Two women in the neighborhood, who came in on hearing of the death of child, found it dressed for burial; and they testified that the defendant objected to having it undressed.

Charlotte Patterson was examined as a witness on the preliminary examination of the defendant before a justice of the peace, but she was not present at the trial; and it was shown that she "was out of the State, and beyond the jurisdiction of the court;" the magistrate further testifying, "that she told him she was going to leave, for fear the defendant would charge her with having killed the child." Her testimony, as detailed by the magistrate, was: "I was going out of the yard gate to pick blackberries, and met the child. She was, to all appearances, well and hearty. When I returned, about one hour afterwards, I found the defendant in the house with the child. It was dead, and she said it had

[Perry v. The State.]

fallen in a fit, she believed, and she thought it was dead."
The defendant objected and excepted to the admission of this
evidence. W. Forbes, a witness for the prosecution, who
was a member of the coroner's jury, thus testified: "The
child was badly bruised all over, as if beaten, and its neck
was broken. The child's neck looked like it had been struck
with a hot iron, and looked scarred." The bill of exceptions
then proceeds: "The defendant objected to this portion of
said witness' testimony. because it was the expression of an
opinion, and was not competent evidence;" and an exeception
was reserved to the overruling of the objection.

It was proved on the part of the defendant, that she was
subject to epileptic fits; that she "talked and acted foolish"
after these fits, and sometimes just before a fit came on; that
she had a fit on the evening of the day of the child's death,
and two on the next day; but there was no evidence that she
had a fit on the morning the child was killed, and she herself testified that she had none. Two physicians testified as
to the different kinds of epilepsy, and the effects of each.

· The defendant requested seven charges to the jury, and
duly excepted to the refusal of each. The first charge was
in these words: "The probability of reasonably accounting
for the death of the deceased by accident, or by any other
cause than that of the unlawful act of the defendant, must
be excluded by the circumstances proved; and it is only when
no other hypothesis will explain all the conditions of the
case, and account for all the facts, that it can be safely and
justly concluded it was caused by the defendant." The
second, third, fourth and fifth charges, each related to the
defense of insanity, and, under the decision of this court,
require no notice. The other charges were: (6.) "The
suggestions of counsel in their argument to the jury, founded
on the evidence in the case, may give rise to such a reasonable doubt as will justify the jury in acquitting the defendant." (7.) "It is the safer and better course for the jury to
acquit a guilty person, rather than run the risk of convicting
an innocent one."

SAM. B. BROWNE, and A. ANDERSON, for appellant.

W. L. MARTIN, Attorney-General, for the State.

SOMERVILLE, J.—1. The witness Charlotte Patterson was shown to have been out of the State, and beyond

the jurisdiction of the court at the time of the trial, being either permanently or indefinitely absent. This was sufficient reason to authorize the introduction of secondary evidence of what this witness had previously deposed to, on the preliminary investigation of the same case before a committing magistrate. In *Lowe v. State*, 86 Ala. 47, we held this principle to be applicable as well to criminal as to civil cases; and this rule has been since re-affirmed in *South v. The State*, decided at the present term; 6 So. Rep. 52.

2. The statement of the witness Forbes, who was one of the coroner's jury, and had investigated the cause of the death of the deceased child, was to the effect that "it was badly bruised all over, as if beaten, and its neck was broken." "The child's neck," the witness said, *"looked like it had been struck with a hot iron, and looked scarred."* Construing the exception taken to apply only to the latter part of this witness' testimony, we think it free from the objection that it was the expression of a mere opinion, and not the statement of a fact. The resemblance of things—or their likeness, similitude, or similarity—is ordinarily rather a conclusion of fact than of opinion; and it is common for witnesses to be permitted to depose to it as an element of description, if not impracticable for the man of average intelligence to express himself. The similarity testified to in this instance is one of common knowledge, and involved nothing requiring skillful comparison by an expert physioligist. There was no error in admitting this testimony.

3. It is not *any doubt*, arising out of the evidence, which authorizes a jury to acquit on trial for crime, but only a *reasonable* doubt of such guilt, generated by the evidence in the cause—not a possible, speculative, or imaginary doubt. *Kidd v. State*, 83 Ala. 58. So, an acquittal should follow, if the killing, or other act charged as a crime, be satisfactorily accounted for on any other *reasonable* hypothesis than the guilt of the accused. If the hypothesis suggested, which in the present case was accidental injury, be unreasonable, or otherwise not authorized by the evidence, it would afford no ground upon which the accused could claim an inference of innocence justifying her acquittal. The first charge requested by the defendant was, under this principle, properly refused.

4. The seventh charge, asserting that "it is the safer and better course for a jury to acquit a guilty person, rather than run the risk of convicting an innocent one," announced no

proposition of law, but was a mere comparison of abstract justice, which tended to mislead the jury.—*Garlick v. The State*, 79 Ala. 265; *Ward v. The State*, 78 Ala. 442; *Farrish v. The State*, 63 Ala. 164.

5. The sixth charge is susceptible of the construction, that the jury would be authorized to consider the suggestions of counsel made in the progress of the argument, either as in the nature of evidence, or as correct expositions of law, that might legitimately affect their verdict. While all proper weight should be given to such suggestions, when founded on the evidence, in enabling the jury to properly understand the facts of the case, and to throw light on the issues in dispute, the guilt or innocence of the party charged is to be determined, not by the strength or logic of the arguments, but on the force and weight of the facts. The charge in question is not only misleading, but it is merely argumentative, and for these reasons was properly refused.

6. All the other charges relate to the alleged insanity of the defendant, and are based upon that portion of the evidence which tends to prove that the defendant was subject to periodic attacks of epileptic fits. Probably the refusal of these charges could be justified upon the ground, that there is no evidence tending to prove that the defendant was afflicted with any epileptic manifestations on the day of the killing, or that the killing was the product or outgrowth of the alleged disease, or in fact of any form of mania, or mental incapacity, to a degree which confers irresponsibility for crime.—*Gunter v. State*, 83 Ala. 101; *Parsons v. The State*, 81 Ala. 597; 60 Amer. Rep. 193. The only testimony bearing on this point is that of the defendant herself, and she testifies to a state of facts entirely rebutting such a conclusion.

7. But we prefer to rest our ruling as to these charges on another ground. This case was tried on March 25th, 1889, and the evidence in reference to the defendant's state of mind was in support of the defense of insanity, which seems to have been introduced under the plea of not guilty. At that time, the act of February 27th, 1889, was in force, entitled "An act in relation to criminal insane persons, who are charged by indictment with murder and other high crimes."—Acts 1888–89, pp. 742-746. It is provided in section four of that act, that in prosecutions for murder, rape, robbery, or burglary, or any grade of these crimes, "where the defense of insanity is set up, *it shall be inter-*

posed *by special plea* at the *time of his* [the defendant's]
arraignment, which in substance shall be 'not guilty by
reason of insanity;' which plea shall be entered of record
upon the docket of the trial court. Such plea shall not
preclude the usual plea of the *general issue, which shall not,
however, put in issue the question of irresponsibility of the
accused by reason of his alleged insanity, this question being
triable only under the special plea."* The act further requires that the jury shall return a *special verdict* on the
question of the defendant's sanity *vel non.*—Acts 1888–89,
p. 744, §§ 5 and 6.

The purpose of the act is plainly to require the defense
of insanity to be tried only under a special plea, to require
this plea to be interposed at the time of arraignment, and
to require a special verdict on this issue. This defense can
not now be introduced under the plea of "not guilty," as it
formerly could be.

It being made to appear from the record that no special
plea of insanity was interposed in the court below, the question of insanity *vel non* was not an issue properly before the
court or jury. The court could, without error, have ruled
out all the evidence bearing on the subject of the defendant's
alleged insanity. There was consequently no error in refusing any or all of the charges seeking to raise this question.

8. The law under consideration is one governing only the
mode of procedure in criminal cases, and the custody of the
prisoner *ad interim* during the pendency of the prosecution.
It works no injustice to the defendant, and deprives him of
no substantial right which he would otherwise have. It is
not, therefore, objectionable as an *ex post facto,* when applied,
as in the present case, to a crime already committed at the
time of its enactment, any more than a statute authorizing indictments to be amended, or conferring additional challenges
on the government, or authorizing a change of venue, or
other like statutes regulating the mode of judicial or forensic
proceeding in a cause.—Cooley on Const. Lim. (5th Ed.)
329–330.

We find the record free from error of any kind, and the
judgment is affirmed.

Fomby *v.* The State

Indictment for Forgery.

1. *What writing is subject of forgery; averment of extrinsic facts in indictment.*—A written instrument which is on its face unintelligible, not purporting to create or discharge any pecuniary liability, nor otherwise showing that another person might be injured by it, will not support an indictment for forgery (Code, § 3852), unless extrinsic facts are averred supplying its deficiencies.

FROM the Criminal Court of Jefferson.

Tried before the Hon. S. E. GREENE.

The indictment in this case charged that the defendant, Henry Fomby, with intent to injure or defraud, "did forge an order or instrument in writing, purporting to be the act of one Greene Milligan, which order is in the words and figures following," setting it out. The writing set out in the indictment, as copied into the transcript, is unintelligible, but it seems to have been signed "*Grenn Milisic,*" addressed to "Mr. Odom," and in these words, or letters: Please *ete* this man have *surthanges, an illitz riai jor then untill* Payday;" and after the signature the words were added, "*He is all right.*" The original writing was attached to the transcript as an exhibit, by order of the court below; but it seems to have been returned to that court, and has not come to the hands of the Reporter. The bill of exceptions states that the defendant demurred to the indictment, assigning as grounds of demurrer the unintelligibility of the writing set out, and its incapacity to deceive or defraud, or to create or discharge a pecuniary liability; but this does not appear in the judgment-entry. The bill of exceptions contains this additional statement: "In his argument to the jury, after the evidence on both sides had been closed, the solicitor attempted to interpret, construe and translate the said alleged forged writing, by spelling out certain words, and explaining their meaning; to which attempted translation and construction the defendant duly objected and excepted."

LEA & GREENE, for appellant, cited *Holt v. State*, 75 Ala. 1; *Rembert v. State*, 53 Ala. 467; *Given v. State*, 5 Ala. 747;

[Fomby v. The State.]

2 Bish. Crim. Law, §§ 506-512; Wharton's Crim. Law,
§§ 740, 696-7.

W. L. MARTIN, Attorney-General, for the State, contended
that the ruling on demurrer to the indictment, not being
shown by the judgment-entry, was not presented for revision; citing *Steele v. Savage*, 85 Ala. 230; *Perry v. Danner,*
74 Ala. 485; *Tyree v. Parham*, 66 Ala. 424; *Smith v. State*,
68 Ala. 424; *Buckley v. Wilson*, 56 Ala. 393; *Petty v. Dill*,
52 Ala. 641.

CLOPTON, J.—It is well established that an indictment
which merely sets out a writing, on which the forgery
charged is predicated, wanting in the legal requisites to its
validity, or so imperfect or incomplete that it can not be the
foundation of a legal liability, and its real meaning and terms
are not intelligible from the words and characters used, does
not charge an offense. If the legal force of the writing, not
being apparent on its face, arises from extrinsic facts, or,
being incomplete or unintelligible, its meaning and capacity
to effect a fraud are derived from extrinsic facts, such facts
must be averred with certainty to make judicially apparent
that the instrument is the subject of forgery.—*Rembert v.
State*, 53 Ala. 467; *Hobbs v. State*, 75 Ala. 1.

The instrument, for forging which the defendant was convicted, is set forth in the indictment *in hœc verba*. On its
face, so far as it can be deciphered, it does not purport to
create a pecuniary liability on another, nor does it show that
another might be injured by it. It is not apparent, that, if
genuine, it would operate as the basis of another person's
liability. It is uncertain, and some of the words and characters used are so obscure and unintelligible, that its meaning and vicious capacity can not be ascertained from the
writing as set forth in the indictment, nor what effect, if
any, it should have. In such case, the extrinsic facts connected with a forged instrument, should be averred, so that
the court may see its capacity to create a liability, or to effect
a fraud. No extrinsic facts are averred, which show or tend
to show its vicious capacity, nor is its apparent obscurity
explained or removed by inuendo or otherwise. The demurrer to the indictment should have been sustained.

Reversed and remanded.

Cagle *v.* The State.

Indictment for Selling Liquor to Minor.

1. *Illegal sale of liquor by infant, or agent.*—An unmarried girl, seventeen years old, living with her mother, may be convicted of selling liquor to a minor, on proof that she poured out and delivered the liquor under the order or instructions of her mother, to whom it belonged, and to whom the money was paid by the purchaser.

FROM the Circuit Court of Etowah.

Tried before the Hon. JOHN B. TALLY.

The indictment in this case was found in April, 1889, and charged that Rachel Cagle and Sis Cagle, who was her daughter, "did sell or give spirituous liquors to Jep Elkins, a minor." Sis Cagle being on trial alone, as the bill of exception states, "Jep Elkins testified, on the part of the State, that he was a minor, fifteen years old; that he got ten cents worth of whiskey from a woman named Rachel; that Sis Cagle measured it out to him, and put it in a bottle for him; that she put the whiskey in the bottle, and set it on the table, and witness took it and left the house; that he paid the money to Rachel, and said nothing to Sis Cagle about either the purchase or the price; that Rachel was in the bed at the time; that he got the liquor, and went away, but Sis Cagle never sold nor gave it to him. The defendant then testified in her own behalf, that she was about seventeen years old at the time mentioned by said Elkins, lived with her mother, said Rachel, and was under her control; that she simply poured out the whiskey according to her mother's instructions, and had no interest in it, nor in the sale thereof; and that she never at any time sold or gave away whiskey to said Elkins. This being substantially all the evidence, the court charged the jury, on the written request of the solicitor, that they must find the defendant guilty, if they believed the evidence;" and refused to instruct them, as requested in writing by the defendant, that they should find him not guilty, if they believed all the evidence. To the charge given, and to the refusal of the charge asked, the defendant duly excepted.

[Johnson v. The State.]

W. L. MARTIN, Attorney-General, for the State.

McCLELLAN, J.—The bill of exceptions shows that the defendant was present, and aided and abetted in the sale of spirituous liquor to a minor. The fact that she did not own the whiskey, and received nothing for it, constituted no defense.—*State v. Hill*, 62 Ala. 168. Nor is she any the less guilty, because what she did in measuring and delivering the liquor to the minor was done at the request or command of her mother, to whom it belonged, and who received the price of it.—1 Bish. Cr. Law, §§ 355, 367; *People v. Richmond*, 29 Cal. 414. There was no error in giving the general charge at the instance of the State, nor in refusing the charge asked by the defendant.

Affirmed.

Johnson *v.* The State.

Indictment for Murder.

1. *Declarations of defendant as evidence.*—Declarations made by the defendant himself, before or after the commission of the homicide with which he is charged, tending to connect him with it, are admissible as evidence against him, although a conspiracy between him and the other persons implicated may not be established.

2. *Declarations and conduct of conspirators, as evidence against each other.*—Under the rule laid down in the case of *McAnally v. State*, (74 Ala. 9), when the evidence establishes, *prima facie*, the existence of a conspiracy between the defendant and others, to commit the crime with which he is charged, the acts, declarations and conduct of the others, in promotion of the purpose or object of the conspiracy, or in relation to it, are competent and admissible as evidence against him; and such evidence was properly admitted in this case.

3. *New trial; refusal not revisable.*—By the settled practice of this court since its organization, a motion for a new trial is addressed to the discretion of the lower court, and its refusal is not revisable by this court on error or appeal.

FROM the City Court of Selma.

Tried before the Hon. JONA. HARALSON.

The defendant in this case, Willie Johnson, was indicted, jointly with Saunders Collier, for the murder of Frances Rodgers, by shooting her with a pistol; and being tried separately, a severance having been granted, was convicted of murder in the first degree, and sentenced to death by hanging. The deceased was shot and killed on Saturday night, November 19th, 1887, between the hours of eight and nine, by a man who came to her house and called her to the door. Harriet Gladden, who lived in the house with her, thus testified on the part of the prosecution: "I went to the door. A man stood in the porch. He asked me if Frances Rodgers lived there. I said yes. He said he wanted to see her. I asked him if I would not answer. He said no, he wished to see her—that he had a message for her. I told Frances what the man said, and she went to the door. The pistol fired, and she fell." The assailant was not recognized by any one, and he escaped. Other evidence adduced by the prosecution showed that two men made inquiries that night for the house of Frances Rodgers, and went there together, one stopping at the gate, while the other went in and called her out; and the prosecution proceeded on the theory, that these men were the defendant and said Saunders Collier, and that they were instigated to the murder by one Wiley Lewis, who had married a daughter of Frances Rodgers. The defendant adduced evidence tending to show . that he was, until late in the evening on the day the murder was committed, in Birmingham, where he, Collier and Lewis lived, or resided most of the time.

The principal witness on the part of the prosecution was one Willie Clark, who testified to several conversations he had heard between the defendant, Collier and Lewis, and conversations he had had with one or more of them, tending to prove the alleged conspiracy between them. Numerous exceptions were reserved by the defendant to the testimony, but they can not be set out at length. The nature of the testimony, and the grounds of objection, are shown by the following extracts: "The solicitor asked the witness" [after he had testified to his acquaintance with the several parties in Birmingham], "if he had ever heard the defendant say anything about the killing of Frances Rodgers, before the killing occurred, to tell what it was; to which question the defendant objected, on the ground that no conspiracy had been proved, and duly excepted to the overruling of his objection. The witness answered: 'I recollect once, about a week and a half before Frances Rodgers was killed, defendant told me that Wiley Lewis had asked him to come to Selma and kill Frances Rodgers. He said that he went to collect a debt from Lewis, and Lewis would not pay him, and that he told Lewis, if he did not pay him, he would tell what he

(Lewis) had tried to get him to do—to kill Frances Rodgers.' The defendant moved to exclude these declarations, on the ground that no conspiracy had been proved; and his motion being overruled, he excepted." The witness continued: "At first, defendant said he would tell me, if I promised not to tell. I said I would not tell, and asked what it was. He said Wiley Lewis had been trying to get him to come to Selma, to kill a woman. I asked him who it was, and he said Frances Rodgers, and that Lewis had been trying to buy a pistol to do it with. He told me, if Lewis tried to buy the pistol I had, not to let him have it; and said he gussed he would have been gone, if he could have got a pistol. I told him not to go—to have nothing to do with it, and I tried to persuade him to do nothing of the kind." The bill of exceptions then states, that the defendant "objected to each and every declaration as next above set out, on the ground that no conspiracy has been shown," and an exception was reserved. The witness further testified, that the defendant came to him "about the middle of the week before November 19th," and asked if he had let Lewis have the pistol, and he answered that he had not; that Saunders Collier then came up, and, in the defendant's presence, proposed to buy it, saying that he wanted it for a particular purpose;" that he refused to sell the pistol, but it was stolen Friday night; and that he heard of the murder on Sunday morning. The witness then continued: "I saw the defendant Sunday, about dark. Saunders Collier was with him. I had a talk with them, and said to Saunders, 'Hello, you all got back?' He said 'Yes.' I asked him where my pistol was. He said he had it, and pulled it out, but would not let me have it. He said that nobody knew what had been done but me, and if I told it, he would keep the pistol to blow me up with. I told him he ought to give me the pistol, as he had done what he wanted to do with it; but he said no, that he might give it to me after awhile. The defendant was present all this time, and I asked him who did the shooting. He said Saunders did it. I asked him how many times he shot, and he said once. I then asked Saunders to let me see how many balls were out of the pistol; he showed it to me, and one ball was out. Neither of them mentioned the name of anybody who was shot, and the name of Frances Rodgers was not mentioned." The defendant objected and excepted to the admission of each part of this evidence, and other similar exceptions were reserved. The character of Clark was impeached on cross-examination, and by other evidence adduced by the defendant.

G. A. ROBBINS, and CHAS. D. CLARKE, for the appellant, cited Whart. Crim. Ev. 698; 2 Whart. Crim. Law, § 1406; 2 Russ. Crimes, 696–8, note z; 1 Greenl. Ev. §§ 111, 214–19; 3 *Ib.* § 92; Archb. Crim. Pl. by Waterman, vol. 3, pp. 618–9; 2 Stark. Ev. 326; *Reg. v. Murphy*, 8 C. & P. 297; *Reg. v. Shellard*, 9 C. & P. 277; *Stewart v. State*, 26 Ala. 44; *Martin & Flinn v. State*, 28 Ala. 71; *Steele v. State*, 43 Ala. 1; *McAnally v. State*, 74 Ala. 9; *Insurance Co. v. Moog*, 78 Ala. 284, and authorities there cited; Wells on Cir. Ev. 88; 1 Leach, C. C. 299; *Rice v. State*, 47 Ala. 38; *Kelso v. State*, 47 Ala. 573; *Burns v. State*, 49 Ala. 370; *McAdory v. State*, 62 Ala. 154.

W. L. MARTIN, Attorney-General, for the State, cited *Amos v. State*, 83 Ala. 1; 1 Brick. Digest, 451, §§ 51–54; 3 *Ib.* 288, § 596; *Bedwell v. Bedwell*, 77 Ala. 587.

STONE, C. J.—Dallas county has a jury system, secured to it by statute, which is peculiar to itself.—Sess. Acts 1882-83, p. 273; *Ib.* 1884–5, p. 192; *Ib.* 1886–7, p. 209. We are not informed that any objection was made to the formation of the grand or petit jury, and we find in the record no ground for objection to this part of the proceedings. Since the decision in *Evans v. State*, 80 Ala. 4, the jury law of Dallas county has been so changed, as that "whenever the judge of the Circuit, or the judge of the City Court of Selma, shall deem it proper to set two or more criminal cases for trial on the same day, said judge may draw and have summoned one jury, or one *venire*, for the trial of all such cases so set for one day."

The chief objections to testimony have for their predicate that there was not sufficient evidence of a conspiracy between the accused and others not on trial, to authorize the admission of the evidence. Much of the testimony to which this objection was interposed, consists of alleged declarations and statements made by the accused himself. These, being in their nature pertinent to the offense charged, and to the defendant's participation therein, were competent evidence against him, whether there was a conspiracy or not.—3 Brick. Dig. 425–6, §§ 286 *et seq.; Ib.* 283, §§ 504 *et seq.*

There was, however, testimony received and excepted to,

[Johnson v. The State.]

the legality of which depended on the establishment of a conspiracy to murder Frances' Rodgers. The alleged conspiracy was between the defendant, one Collier, and one Lewis; the last two not on trial. In *McAnally v. State*, 74 Ala. 9, 16, we said: "In charges of crime which, in their nature, may be perpetrated by more than one guilty participant, if there be a previously formed purpose or conspiracy to commit the offense, then the acts, declarations and conduct of each conspirator, done or expressed in promotion of, or in relation to the object or purpose of such conspiracy, become the acts, declaration, or conduct of each co-conspirator, and may be' given in evidence against him. But, to allow such testimony to go to the jury, a foundation must be laid by proof sufficient, in the opinion of the judge presiding, to establish *prima facie* the existence of such conspiracy."

The case of *Williams v. State*, 81 Ala. 1, contains a full collection and discussion of many authorities; and while it does not conflict in the least with the principles declared in *McAnally's case*, it lays down certain other principles that are not raised in this case. See, also, *Amos v. State*, 83 Ala. 1.

Under the principles declared in *McAnally's case*, we hold that the testimony of the witness Clark, considered in its entirety, establishes, if believed, at least a *prima facie* case of conspiracy to murder Frances Rodgers, and that the acts, declarations and conduct of each conspirator, done or expressed in apparent promotion of the common object, were competent evidence against each of the others. We speak of Clark's testimony in its entirety, because it is immaterial at what stage of his examination he proved the conspiracy, if he proved it all.—*Bedwell v. Bedwell*, 77 Ala. 587.

What we have said relates to the competency of the testimony, and its sufficiency to make a *prima facie* case, so as to let in testimony of the acts, declarations and conduct of one, as evidence against the other. Its ultimate credibility and sufficiency to justify conviction, was a question for the jury.—*McAnally's case, supra*. We find no errors in the admission of testimony.

It has been the settled rule of this court from its very organization, and never departed from, that we will not review the action of the primary court, in granting or refusing to grant a new trial.—2 Brick. Dig. 276; 3 *Ib.* 676; *Bedwell v. Bedwell*, 77 Ala. 587.

The judgment of the City Court is affirmed. And inasmuch as the day fixed for the execution of the prisoner is now passed, it is the judgment and order of this court, that on Friday, August 9, 1889, the said Willie Johnson be hanged by the neck until he is dead; and the sheriff of Dallas county is charged with the execution of this sentence, in strict conformity to the requirements of the statute.—Code of 1886, §§ 4665 to 4669, inclusive.

Affirmed.

Bailey *v.* The State.

Indictment for Larceny, and for Receiving Stolen Goods.

1. *Sentence to hard labor for county, on non-payment of costs; local law in Jefferson.*—In a criminal case, the costs not being presently paid or secured (Code, §§ 4502-04), a sentence to hard labor for the county for their satisfaction is not violative of the constitutional provision which prohibits imprisonment for debt; and the local law prevailing in Jefferson county, authorizing convicts sentenced to hard labor to be employed in working on the public roads, and giving the officers and witnesses recourse only against the fine and forfeiture fund of the county for the recovery of their fees (Sess. Acts 1887-8, p. 818), does not in any manner change this principle.

FROM the Criminal Court of Jefferson.

Tried before the Hon. S. E. GREENE.

The indictment in this case contained two counts, the first charging the defendants, W. W. Bailey and others, with the larceny of a trunk and its contents, alleged to be worth $250; and the second, that they received, concealed, or aided in the concealment of the trunk and its contents, knowing that the same had been stolen, and not having the intent to restore the property to its owner. On the trial, Bailey was found guilty under the second count, the value of the stolen property being assessed at $20; and he was thereupon sentenced by the court to hard labor for the county for six months, and to an additional term of 143 days on non-payment of the costs. He afterwards made a motion to have the costs re-taxed, and excepted to the overruling of his motion.

B. M. ALLEN, for the appellant.

W. L. MARTIN, Attorney-General, for the State.

SOMERVILLE, J.—The defendant, being convicted of larceny, was sentenced to perform hard labor for the county of Jefferson, for a period of time not exceeding eight months, to satisfy certain costs incurred in the prosecution of the case, and taxed as fees in favor of the solicitor, clerk of the court, sheriff, and certain State witnesses. The sentence seems to have been made in accordance with the rules prescribed by section 4504 of the present Code, which provides for the sentence of convicts to additional hard labor imposed for costs, if not presently paid, or if judgment is not confessed therefor, as provided by law.

We have repeatedly held that imprisonment of one convicted of crime, for the satisfaction of costs incurred by the State in his prosecution, or to which the State, if it were liable for costs, should be subjected, is not an infringement of that provision of the Constitution, which provides that "no person shall be imprisoned for debt."—*Bradley v. State*, 69 Ala. 318; 3 Brick. Dig. p. 141, §§ 197 *et seq.*, and cases cited. The authority of these decisions is not denied. But it is contended that, inasmuch as the defendant in this case is sentenced to hard labor under the provisions of the act approved February 18th, 1887, entitled "An act relating to the working of male convicts sentenced to hard labor for the county of Jefferson, upon the public roads of said county" (Acts 1886–87, pp. 818–21), the fees are no longer due the officers and witnesses, and there is no authority for the enforcement of their collection by hard labor.

The only sections of this act which bear particularly on the case are sections 11 and 16. There is nothing any where found in its provisions that can be construed as intended to repeal sections 4502 to 4504 of the present Code (1886), which authorize the defendant to pay the fine and costs, or confess judgment therefor, with good and sufficient sureties, as in other cases. It is only where the fine and costs are not presently paid, or secured by confession of judgment, with proper sureties, that any sentence to hard labor can be enforced for their satisfaction. The general law on this subject, as contained in the above cited sections of the Code, is perfectly consistent with the provisions of the special act in question, relating to the county of Jefferson.

Section 11 of the latter act, in effect, transfers to the

county of Jefferson the right to the labor of all convicts sentenced in that county to hard labor for such county to pay the fine and costs assessed against them on conviction in prosecutions for crime, and this without liability to pay either the fine or costs incident to such conviction. Section 16 gives the officers of court and witnesses recourse only against the fine and forfeiture fund of the county for the recovery of their fees. We can not perceive that this transfer of rights, as to the benefits accruing from the enforcement of a satisfaction of the costs, in any manner changes the nature of the defendant's imprisonment. It is precisely for the same length of time, and is exacted to satisfy the same demand—viz., the costs incurred at the instance of the State in the prosecution of the defendant.—*Smith v. State*, 82 Ala. 40; *Wynn v. State, 1 b.* 55. The only persons affected by the change are the officers of court and the witnesses, and it is not shown that they either do, or can, legally complain, that the benefit of their services has to some extent been taken away from them, and given to the county of Jefferson. Costs and fees of this character are *ex gratia*, and not *ex debito*. They are conferred by the statute, and may be taken away in the same mode.

It is our opinion that the act of February 18th, 1887, under consideration, authorizes the imposition of additional hard labor to pay the fine and costs in conformity to the provisions of the general law, as contained in sections 4503 and 4504 of the present Code; and that the objections taken to its constitutionality are without merit.

The judgment is accordingly affirmed.

Ex parte State, *in re* Long.

Application for Prohibition to Probate Judge, in matter of Discharge on Habeas Corpus.

1. *Hard labor for county, on non-payment of fine and costs.*—On conviction of a misdemeanor punishable by fine only, or so punished in the particular case, followed by a sentence to hard labor for the county to enforce its payment, an additional term of hard labor may be imposed for the payment of costs (Code, §§ 4502-04), as if hard labor or imprisonment had been part of the punishment originally imposed. (CLOPTON, J., *dissenting.*)

2. *Same; discharge on habeas corpus.*—On a conviction of vagrancy before a justice of the peace, a fine of $20 being imposed, followed by a sentence, in default of payment of the fine and costs, that the defendant be detained in custody "until he performs twenty days hard labor for the county for said fine, and sixty days for said costs," is a nullity, and not void only for the excess of hard labor which might have been imposed; and the prisoner is entitled to be discharged from custody on *habeas corpus.*

APPLICATION in the name of the State, on the relation of the Attorney-General, for a writ of prohibition to Hon. F. C. RANDOLPH, judge of the Probate Court of Montgomery, for the purpose of reviewing and quashing certain proceedings had before him on the petition of Joe Long, who was discharged from custody on a hearing on *habeas corpus.* Said Long was convicted of vagrancy before B. H. Screws, a justice of the peace, and fined $20; and the justice's *mittimus* to the jailor directed him to take said Long into custody, "in default of payment of said fine, and costs amounting to $18.25, and detain him until he performs twenty days hard labor for the county for said fine, and sixty days for payment of said costs, subject to the order of the Board of Revenue." Judge Randolph discharged the prisoner, on the ground that the sentence to hard labor for twenty days, on non-payment of the fine, was void.

WM. L. MARTIN, Attorney-General, and T. LOMAX, for the State.

GEO. F. MOORE, *contra.*

CLOPTON, J.—It appears from the return of the sheriff to the writ of *habeas corpus,* that the petitioner is retained under a *mittimus,* following a judgment of conviction on a prosecution for vagrancy, rendered by a justice of the peace. The justice assessed a fine of twenty dollars; and the *mittimus* commands the officer to take the petitioner, in default of the payment of the fine and costs, "into custody, and detain him until he performs twenty days hard labor for the county for said fine, and sixty days for payment of said costs, subject to the order of the Board of Revenue." On the hearing of the application, the judge of probate ordered the petitioner to be discharged, on the ground that the justice had exceeded his jurisdiction in the sentence and judgment. This proceeding is an application for a writ of prohibition, or other proper remedial writ, to vacate and annul the order of discharge, and to prevent its enforcement.

The authority of the justice to impose additional hard labor for the payment of costs is claimed under section 4504 of the Code of 1886. The corresponding section (4731) of the Code of 1876 read as follows: "If, on conviction before the County, Circuit or City Court, judgment is rendered against the accused, that he perform hard labor for the county, and if the costs are not presently paid, then the court may impose additional hard labor for the county, for a term sufficient to cover all costs and officers' fees, allowing not exceeding forty cents *per diem*, for the additional labor imposed." In *Ex parte McKivett*, 55 Ala. 236, it was held, that this statute conferred no authority on a justice of the peace to sentence to hard labor for the county for the payment of costs, the authority being confined by the words of the statute to the County, Circuit and City Courts. The section was amended by the act of February 26, 1881, by prescribing a limit to the term for which additional hard labor may be imposed, reducing the rate to thirty cents *per diem*, and adding other provisions not material in this case. The section as amended is incorporated in the Code of 1886 as section 4504, except that the words, *before the County, Circuit or City Court*, are omitted. The argument is, that by the omission of these words, in view of the judicial construction previously placed upon the statute, the legislature intended a change, and that the effect is to confer on all courts, having jurisdiction to try and convict of criminal offenses, authority to impose additional hard labor for the county for costs. The general rule is, that a material change in the phraseology of a subsequent statute, revising a pre-existing statute, indicates a changed legislative intent. The force of the argument must be admitted; and it may be that it was the intent to extend such authority to all courts having criminal jurisdiction in cases to which the section is applicable. Conceding this, there yet lies behind it the question, whether the case of the petitioner falls within the operation of section 4504.

There are other sections of the Code relating to the same subject. Section 4502 provides: "When a fine is assessed, the court may allow the defendant to confess judgment, with good and sufficient sureties, for the fines and costs." And section 4503 declares: "If the fine and costs are not paid, or a judgment confessed according to the provisions of the preceding section, the defendant must either be imprisoned in the county jail, or, at the discretion of the court, sentenced to hard labor for the county, as follows;" and the section then proceeds to specify the terms of days, for which the defendant may be imprisoned or sentenced to hard labor, regulated by, and increased in proportion to the amount of the fine. The statutes composing sections 4503 and 4504, except as amended, have co-existed since 1866, and are embodied in the same article of the same chapter of the present Code. They should, therefore, be read as continuous sections of the same act, and so construed as to harmonize each with the other. A separate and distinct field should be assigned to each, in which its provisions may operate, without colliding with any of the provisions of the other, or covering the same space.

Legal punishments are defined by the statute as follows: "Fines, hard labor for the county, imprisonment in the county jail, imprisonment in the penitentiary, which includes hard labor for the State, and death by hanging."—Code, 1886, § 4492. Different crimes are differently punished. Some misdemeanors are punishable by fine only; others by fine, to which imprisonment in the county jail, or hard labor for the county, may be added; and in all cases in which the imprisonment or sentence to hard labor is for twelve months or less, the defendant must be sentenced to imprisonment in the county jail, or to hard labor for the county. Chapter ten of the Code, which contains all the sections herein above referred to, relates to the subject of punishment, and forms a complete system, constructed in view of, and in relation to the different kinds and degrees of punishment affixed by the statutes to different crimes. Sections 4502 and 4503 relate specially and particularly to fines, and apply and govern when, on conviction, the accused is fined only—when hard labor for the county can not be by law, or is not, when discretionary with the court, superadded. Section 4503 does not provide punishment which must or may be imposed in the first instance, but a substituted punishment, which must be imposed only when there is a failure to pay the fine and costs, or confess judgment therefor, as allowed by section 4502. In the imposition of such substituted punishment, the court has no authority to exceed the term of imprisonment or hard labor, for the fine and costs, or either of them, expressly fixed by the statute.

Section 4504 has another and different field of operation. By its terms, authority to impose additional hard labor for the costs is confined to cases where, on conviction, judgment

4

is rendered that the accused perform hard labor for the
county, and the costs are not presently paid; that is, where
the accused is convicted of a crime, to which the special
statute, in regard to the particular offense, affixes the punishment of hard labor for the county as one of the authorized
modes of punishment; and the court may render judgment
that the defendant perform hard labor for the county, as the
primary, not the alternative punishment authorized by section 4503. To illustrate : We have said that several
statutes affix, as punishment on conviction of certain misdemeanors, that the defendant must be fined, and may be imprisoned in the county jail, or sentenced to hard labor for
the county not exceeding a specified term; in such case, if
the court should render judgment that the accused be fined
only, or, in addition, be imprisoned in the county jail, section 4504 confers no authority to impose hard labor for the
costs. Under section 4503, though the defendant may pay
the fine, should he fail or refuse to pay or confess judgment
for the costs, he may, nevertheless, be imprisoned or sentenced to hard labor for the term of days specified in the
section.—*Morgan v. State*, 47 Ala. 34. But the term of
days for which he may be sentenced must, under the statute,
be determined by the amount of the fine, and not the costs.
To hold that, in such case, additional hard labor for the
county may be imposed for the cost under section 4504,
would be tantamount to an imposition of double punishment.

The present case affords a fair illustration of our views.
The punishment for vagrancy, the offense of which petitioner
was convicted, is, that the defendant, "on conviction for the
first offense, be fined, not less than ten, nor more than fifty
dollars; and on a second conviction, within six months after
the first, must be fined not less than fifty, nor more than one
hundred dollars, and may be imprisoned in the county jail,
or sentenced to hard labor for the county, for not more than
six months."—Code, 1886, § 4047. The petitioner was convicted for the first offense, and fined twenty dollars. Under
section 4503, failing to pay or confess judgment for the fine
and costs, the petitioner could and should have been sentenced to imprisonment in the county jail, or to hard labor
for the county, for ten days; but beyond this, the justice
could not sentence him, either for the fine or costs. Should
he be convicted a second time, within six months after the
first, and fined, and also sentenced to hard labor for the
county, then, under section 4504, the court could impose

[Ex parte State, in re Long.]

additional hard labor for costs. A sentence to hard labor, according to the provisions of section 4503, does not constitute a basis for the imposition of additional hard labor for the costs under section 4504. The latter was not designed to be supplemental to the former section. By this construction, each has a distinct and independent sphere of operation, and distinct purposes. Our conclusion is, that the justice, having assessed a fine only, had no authority to impose the additional hard labor for the county for the costs.

But the justice also exceeded his authority by imposing hard labor for twenty days for the fine. The amount of the fine assessed being twenty dollars, the petitioner could not, under the statute, be sentenced to hard labor for the county for a longer term than ten days. It is contended, however, that this is an error or irregularity for which he should not be discharged on *habeas corpus;* and we are referred, as sustaining this position, to *Ex parte Simmons*, 62 Ala. 416; *Ex parte Hubbard*, 65 Ala. 473, and *Ex parte Herrington*, at the present term; 5 So. Rep. 831. When the defendant is retained by virtue of process from a court having jurisdiction of the subject-matter, *habeas corpus* is not an appropriate mode to correct mere errors or irregularities in the sentence and judgment. To justify a discharge, the process must not be authorized by any provision of the law. Illegality, usurpation, or excess of jurisdiction is essential. This is also the statutory rule.—Code, 1886, § 4785. In each of the cases cited by counsel, the error or irregularity intervened in a matter which the court had jurisdiction to hear and determine. In respect to the term of hard labor to which the petitioner could be sentenced, nothing rested in the discretion or judgment of the justice. He had but to declare the term positively and absolutely fixed by the statute. The informality of the *mittimus*, in commanding the jailor to detain petitioner until he performed the hard labor to which he was sentenced, may be considered an irregularity, which of itself would not authorize his discharge. That this sentence to twenty days hard labor for the county for the fine, and sixty days for the costs, is in excess of the jurisdiction of the justice, was expressly decided in the analogous case of *Ex parte McKivett, supra*, where it is said: "When the justice passed beyond the term of ten days as a term of hard labor for the county, he exceeded his jurisdiction. The sentence is consequently void, and the *mittimus* expressing it as a cause of detention is also void." The same principle was asserted and sustained in the subsequent cases of *Ex parte City Council of Montgomery*, 79 Ala. 275; and *Ex parte Mayor of Anniston*, 84 Ala. 21. Had the justice sentenced the petitioner to ten days' hard labor for the fine, and sixty days for the costs, we should have regarded the latter part of the sentence only as void, and the petitioner would have been required to work out the ten days before entitled to a discharge. But, the sentence being for twenty days hard labor for the fine, and an additional term for the costs, the *mittimus* is unauthorized by any provision of the law, and is a nullity.

Prohibition denied.

[On application for rehearing].

McCLELLAN, J.—The Penal Code prepared by Stone and Shepherd was adopted by an act of February 23, 1866. Acts 1865–6, pp. 121–124.

Section 213 of that Code was carried without amendment, in any particular, into all subsequent Codes, and is found at section 3760 Revised Code of 1867; at 4455, Code of 1876; and at section 4503, Code of 1886.

Section 511 of the Penal Code of 1866 read as follows: "If, on conviction before the County, Circuit or City Court, judgment is rendered against the accused, that he perform hard labor for the county, and if the costs are not presently paid, then the court may impose additional hard labor for the county, for a term sufficient to cover the costs to the county, for State witnesses and judges' fees, allowing not exceeding forty cents *per diem* for the additional hard labor imposed."

This section was amended by the act of February 10, 1867, by striking out the words, "the costs to the county for State witnesses and judges' fees," and inserting in lieu thereof the words "all costs and officers' fees."—Acts 1866-7, pp. 513-514.

As thus amended, this law became section 4061 of the Revised Code of 1867, and section 4731 of the Code of 1876.

This section was amended by the act of February 26, 1881, so as to read as follows: "If, on conviction before the Circuit, City or County Court, judgment is rendered against the accused, that he perform hard labor for the county, and if the costs are not presently paid, or judgment confessed therefor, as provided for in section 4454 of the Code, then the court may impose additional hard labor for the county, for such period, not to exceed eight months in cases of misdemeanors, and fifteen months in cases of felony, as may be sufficient to pay the costs, at a rate not less than thirty cents *per diem* for each day. Any person sentenced to hard labor to pay costs, must be discharged from such sentence on the payment of such costs, or any balance thereof, by the hire of such convict or otherwise; and the certificate of the judge or clerk of the court in which such conviction was had, that the costs, or the residue thereof, after deducting the amount realized from the hire of the convict, have been paid, or that the hire or labor of the convict, as the case may be, amounts to a sum sufficient to pay the costs, shall be sufficient evidence to authorize such discharge."—Acts 1880–81, pp. 37–38.

As thus amended, with the additional change in phraseology effected by the substitution of the words, "*as provided by law,*" for the words "as provided for in section 4454 of the Code," this law became section 4504 of the Code of 1886.

The law thus referred to as section 4454, Code of 1876, was section 3759 of the Revised Code of 1867, and section 212 of the Penal Code of 1866; and has been, at least since the year last named, and is now, as embodied, without modification, in the Code of 1886 at section 4502, the law, and the only law, which provides for the confession of judgment by convicts. By its terms, which are, "When a fine is assessed, the court may allow the defendant to confess judgment, with good and sufficient sureties, for the fine and costs," and from the nature of things, since only a money judgment could be confessed and secured, it applies only to cases in which fines are assessed, and, it would seem, necessarily to all cases in which a fine is assessed, whether that be the sole punishment or not.

An analysis of the amendment of February 26, 1881, and of the codification of the statute as amended, will demonstrate that, so far as the cases in which hard labor for costs may be imposed are concerned, section 4504 of the Code of 1886 is in identically the same language as section 511 of the Penal Code of 1866, except that the words, "or judgment confessed therefor as provided by law,'" are inserted in the section as embodied in the present Code. To my mind, this shows not only a legislative construction, evidenced both by the act of 1881 and the adoption of the Code of 1886, that section 4504, as to hard labor for costs, applied to cases provided for, as to the imposition of hard labor for the fine, by section 4503, but also an affirmative expression of the legislative will that such should thereafter be the effect of section 4504, whether it had been so theretofore or not.

But, aside from this consideration, enough has been said to show that there has been no change in the statute now constituting section 4504 of the Code, which tends, in any degree, to the exclusion from its operation of any case originally embraced in its terms. In 1876, in a case in which upon conviction the only penalty provided by law, and the only penalty in fact imposed, was the assessment of a fine, this court held that it was competent for the court below, the fine and costs not being presently paid, to sentence the defendant to hard labor for the payment of the fine under section 3760 of the Revised Code (§ 4455, Code of 1876; and § 4503, Code of 1886), and to hard labor for the payment of costs under section 4061 of the Revised Code (§ 4731, Code of 1876; and § 4504, Code of 1886).—*Williams v. State*, 55 Ala. 166.

These statutes have each been re-enacted several times since this judicial construction was engrafted upon them, and it must now be considered to have been adopted by the legislature as a part of the laws themselves.—*O'Byrnes v. State*, 51 Ala. 25; *Ex parte Matthews*, 52 Ala. 51; *E. T., V. & G. R. R. Co. v. Bayliss*, 74 Ala. 150.

This construction receives support from section 4501 of the present Code, which has come down, with the other sections under consideration, from the Penal Code of 1866. It is there provided that a prosecutor, who has been taxed with costs, may be sentenced to hard labor if he fail to pay it. It would be anomalous to authorize this to be done, and at the same time to withhold a like power with respect to a convicted defendant.

Upon these several considerations, we feel constrained, in response to the application for a rehearing, to recede from the position heretofore taken, as to the power of courts to impose hard labor for costs on conviction for offenses punishable, or punished, by fine only; and to so modify our former opinion as to hold, that in all cases in which the defendant is sentenced to hard labor as a punishment for the offense of which he has been convicted, either in default of the payment of, or confession of judgment for the fine assessed, or in execution of the original judgment, the court may impose additional hard labor, as provided by section 4504 of the Code, for the payment of costs.

SOMERVILLE, J.—I concur in the foregoing opinion of Judge McCLELLAN, as a proper construction of sections 4502 to 4504 of the present Code. The case of *Williams v. State*, 55 Ala. 166, decided in 1876, is conclusive of the main question raised, the statutes then in force being substantially the same as those embodied in these sections. It is immaterial that the reasons there given for the correctness of the decision are subject to criticism, if the decision itself be correct. Since that deliverance was promulgated, it has been followed by many others in which the principle settled was tacitly assumed by this court as free from all doubt. The original statutes have been one or more times re-adopted by the General Assembly since that decision was made, without material change of phraseology; and this presumptively carries with it the judicial construction previously given. The uniform practice of the *nisi prius* courts all over the State, for the past twenty years, moreover, has been to sentence convicts to additional hard labor to satisfy costs, as well where a fine only has been imposed, followed by a sentence to hard labor to enforce its payment, as where the accused has been sentenced by the court, in the first instance, to perform hard labor for the county. The overruling of *Williams'* case would greatly disturb the administration of justice in criminal trials; and I should be disposed to adhere to it, even if I doubted its correctness, which I do not.

CLOPTON, J., dissenting.—My convictions constrain me to dissent from the conclusion to recede from the construction of the statutes announced in the opinion delivered in the first instance. The reasons for the construction then given are fully stated therein, and I do not propose to repeat or elaborate them. In *Williams v. State*, 55 Ala. 166, the rule, that the different sections of a Code, relating to the same subject, should be construed in reference to each other, and as the several sections of a single statute, was held inapplicable, on the ground stated in the opinion then rendered as follows: "It is well known that many acts were passed after the adoption of the original Code of 1852, that were

supplementary to, as well as many that were amendatory of
its provisions.   Of the former sort was the act of the 16th
of February, 1867, which is incorporated as section 4061 in
the Revised Code."   On this ground section 4061, which
corresponds to section 4504 of the Code, 1886, was construed
to be supplementary to section 3760 of the Revised Code,
which corresponds to section 4503 of the Code of 1886.
Now, the fact is, the originals of sections 4503 and 4504
were first and contemporaneously introduced into the Penal
Code of 1866, and the act of February 16, 1867, was not an
original act, but merely amendatory in respect to the *particular costs* for which additional hard labor might be imposed.
The mistake in the legislative history of the sections, on
which the construction in *Williams v. State* was based,
greatly impairs, if it does not destroy its weight as authority.

As to the presumption that the legislature had adopted
that judicial construction of the sections, arising from their
re-enactment, it may be said, that, except the amending act
of February 26, 1881, there has been but one re-enactment
since that decision was made—the adoption of the Code of
1886.   In the previous Codes, the sections were arranged in
different chapters, under different titles, and in relation to
different subjects; whereas, in the Code of 1886, they are
collocated in the same chapter, under the same title, and in
reference to the same subject.   This collocation brings them
within the operation of the rule, that they should be construed as several sections of a single act.—Endlich on
Interp. Stat. § 40.   The mode and manner of the re-enactment overcomes the presumption, which ought not to be
rigidly indulged as to penal statutes.

I am unable to appreciate the force of the argument based
on the amending act of February 26, 1881.   The purpose
of that amendment was to give the accused the right to confess judgment for the costs, and escape the additional hard
labor.   This is sought to be accomplished by mere reference
to section 4454 of Code of 1876, not as giving the right to
confess judgment, but as requiring good and sufficient sureties.   The amendment does not provide that judgment may
be confessed for *fines*, but only for *costs*, in cases where judgment is rendered that the accused perform hard labor for
the county.   A confession of judgment when a fine is assessed as the punishment, was already provided for, and the
amendatory act was not intended to have any reference to
such cases, but to a distinct class of cases.

[Goley v. The State.]

If the legislature originally intended, when a fine only is the assessed punishment, that hard labor could be imposed for the costs under section 4504, why was it, that the term of days, for which the accused could be sentenced to hard labor, in the event he failed to pay or confess judgment for both the *fine* and *costs*, was specified in section 4503? This excludes any inference of an intention, that the accused could be sentenced to hard labor, for either fine or costs, for a longer time than the *specified* number of days, as a part of the alternative punishment provided by section 4503. The construction placed upon the statutes by a majority of the court leads to this result. The accused is convicted, and a fine only is assessed. He pays the fine, but fails to pay or confess judgment for the costs. It is admitted that additional hard labor for the costs can not be imposed, unless judgment be rendered that he perform hard labor for the county. Now, though the fine has been paid, the court may sentence him to hard labor for the term specified in section 4503, as preliminary and in order to impose additional hard labor for the costs under section 4504—two distinct sentences to hard labor, one under each section, because of the failure to pay or confess judgment for the *costs*. A construction, that could lead to such result, should not be placed on the statutes.

I can not perceive how the future administration of justice in criminal trials can be possibly disturbed by overruling *Williams v. State.* And if it has been the practice of the *nisi prius* courts to impose punishment unauthorized by law, such practice can not be stopped too soon.

Goley *v.* The State.

Indictment for Murder.

1. *When case is properly triable.*—The statutory provision requiring the criminal docket to be taken up on the second Monday of the term, when the term continues two weeks (Code, § 751), was intended to expedite speedy trials of criminal cases, and does not deny to the court the right to proceed with the trial of a criminal case before that time; and the further provision requiring the clerk of the court to set the trial of criminal cases for particular days, "except capital cases," and declaring that "no case so set shall be called for trial before such day" (*Ib.* § 4447), does not apply to a capital case improperly set for trial by the clerk.

[Goley v. The State.]

2. *Admissibility of declarations, as part of res gestæ.*—This court can not revise the ruling of the trial court in refusing to admit the defendant's declarations as evidence, as a part of the *res gestæ*, when the declarations are not set out, and it is not shown that they related to the act charged, or threw light on it, or tended to elucidate it, or would have been beneficial to the defendant, or were in any way material.

3. *Same.*—The offer of the defendant to lift up the deceased, made two or three minutes after the shooting, is not admissible evidence as a part of the *res gestæ*, not being shown to have been made so immediately after the act as to authorize the presumption that it was part of the main fact, and not an afterthought intended to give a false coloring to it.

4. *General exception to refusal of several charges.*—An exception expressed in these words, "The defendant asked the court to give the following charges, each of which the court refused to give, whereupon the defendant duly and legally excepted," is a general exception, and can not avail if any one of the charges was properly refused.

5. *Charge as to adequate motive.*—A charge asked, assuming that the prosecution has failed to prove an "adequate motive" for the crime, is properly refused, when there is any evidence of motive, however weak and inconclusive; and if the bill of exceptions does not purport to set out all the evidence, this court would presume, if necessary, that there was other evidence of motive.

FROM the Circuit Court of Conecuh.

Tried before the Hon. JOHN P. HUBBARD.

The defendant in this case, Ed. Goley, was indicted for the murder of William Luckey, by shooting him with a gun, and on the first trial was convicted of murder in the second degree, and sentenced to the penitentiary for ten years; but the judgment was reversed by this court, on a former day of the present term, and the cause remanded.—85 Ala. 333. On a second trial, as shown by the present record, he was again convicted of murder in the second degree, and sentenced to the penitentiary for fifteen years. The bill of exceptions does not purport to set out all the evidence that was introduced, but, after stating that each of several named witnesses "testified substantially as follows," adds, "Here the testimony ended." It appeared that, on the evening of the killing, the defendant, the deceased, and one Chester, all freedmen, went into the woods to hunt squirrels, and came out of the woods, into the road, after sunset, when it was getting dusk; that they met two girls in the road, with whom they walked some distance, and when the girls turned off the defendant was walking some distance in front of the deceased; that the deceased asked him to wait for him, and as he came up the defendant rose from the ground, on which he was sitting or lying, and discharged his gun, shooting the deceased in the breast, and inflicting wounds from which he died. The defendant testified, in his own behalf, that the killing

[Goley v. The State.]

was accidental—that his finger touched the trigger of his gun accidentally as he rose from the ground; and he proved the dying declarations of the deceased, "I don't know why he shot me." Chester testified, on the part of the prosecution, that when he turned around, on hearing the report of the gun, the defendant seemed to have the gun at his shoulder. Several witnesses testified that friendly relations existed between the parties; but one Oliver testified, that about two months before the killing, while they were working with him on a building, "they got to fussing and cursing one another," and he heard defendant say, "I've got your company, nigger, and I'll get you yet." The defendant requested the following (with other) charges in writing, and excepted to their refusal: (3.) "In determining whether or not the defendant intended to take the life of the deceased, the jury may take into consideration the fact that the State has failed to prove any adequate motive or intent on the part of the defendant." (4.) "While the jury are authorized to presume malice from the use of a deadly weapon, still such presumption can not be indulged when the State fails to prove any adequate motive." Other exceptions were reserved by the defendant during the trial, which, under the decision of this court, require no special notice; and an exception was also reserved to the action of the court in proceeding with the trial of the case before the day for which it had been set by the clerk.

JAS. F. JONES, for appellant.—The court erred in proceeding with the trial of the case, against the objection of the defendant, in advance of the day for which it was regularly set for trial.—Code, §§ 751, 4447. The court erred, also, in excluding as evidence the declarations of the defendant, which were a part of the res gestæ.—Allen v. State, 60 Ala. 19; Blount v. State, 49 Ala. 381; Wesley v. State, 52 Ala. 182; Smith v. State, 52 Ala. 407; Gandy v. Humphreys, 35 Ala. 617.

W. L. MARTIN, Attorney-General, for the State.

McCLELLAN, J.—Section 751 of the Code must be construed with reference to the constitutional and legislative policy of the State to secure to defendants a speedy trial, and to mean that the criminal dockets shall be taken up on the second Monday of the term to the exclusion of civil

business, but not to deny the court the right to proceed with
the trial of criminal cases before that time. To hold otherwise would be, in many instances, to enforce idleness on the
Circuit Courts during a part of their terms, and to impede
and delay the administration of justice,—a result diametri-
cally opposed to the spirit and purpose of the statute. Defendant's objection to being put on trial during the first week
of the term is untenable.

Section 4447 of the Code makes it "the duty of the clerk
of the Circuit or City Court to set for trial all criminal cases
in his court, except capital cases and cases of parties in custody, for particular days;" and provides that "no case so set
shall be called for trial before such day." This case was set
for a particular day of the second week of the term. On
Wednesday of the first week, the defendant being in court
and not objecting, the case was called, and the plea of former
acquittal of murder in the first degree, by reason of a conviction of murder in the second degree, which had been reversed by this court, was interposed, confessed by the solicitor,
proved by the records of the court, and adjudged good.
Until this action was taken, the case of the defendant was a
capital one, and expressly excepted from the operation of
the statute quoted above. The action of the clerk, therefore, in setting the case was a nullity, and there was no
error in the order of the court setting another and an earlier
day for the trial, or in proceeding with the trial on the day
so set.

Several exceptions are reserved to the refusal of the court
below to allow declarations of the defendant, made just after
the fatal shot, to be given in evidence, as a part of the *res
gestœ*. It is not shown in this record what these declarations were—whether they related to the act charged, or threw
light on it, or tended to elucidate it, or would have been
beneficial to the defendant, or were in any way material to
the inquiry. Under these circumstances, it is impossible
for this court to affirm that the action of the Circuit Court
in this regard was erroneous.—*Roberts v. State*, 68 Ala. 524;
Stewart v. State, 63 Ala. 199; *Burns v. State*, 47 Ala. 370;
Tolbert v. State, at present term.

Only one declaration or statement of the defendant is at
all indicated in the bill of exceptions. This consisted of an
offer on his part, made two or three minutes after the shooting, "to lift deceased up." Even conceding the relevancy
of this remark, it is not shown to have been made so imme-

diately after the act as to authorize the presumption that it arose from, and was part of the main fact, but, on the contrary, might be a part of a course of conduct determined on after the act, and intended to give a false coloring to it. *Garrett v. State*, 76 Ala. 21.

The bill of exceptions states, that "the defendant asked the court to give the following charges, which were in writing, and numbered one, three and four, each of which charges the court refused to give; whereupon the defendant then and there duly and legally excepted." This is a general exception, and the ruling of the court will be upheld, if any one of the charges was erroneous.—*McGehee v. State*, 52 Ala. 224; *Black v. Pratt Coal & Coke Co.*, 85 Ala. 511, and cases there cited.

Without deciding that either of these charges was a correct statement of law, it is patent that the third and fourth were bad, in that they assumed that the State had failed to prove an "adequate motive" for the crime; and if given, they would have withdrawn from the jury the evidence on that subject, which, though weak and inconclusive it may have been, they had a right to consider.—*Commander v. State*, 60 Ala. 1; *McAdory v. State*, 62 Ala. 154; *Marler v. State*, 67 Ala. 55. The bill of exceptions not purporting to set out all the evidence, the presumption will be indulged here, if necessary to sustain the refusal of these charges, that there was other testimony than that shown in the record going to prove motive for the crime.

The judgment of the Circuit Court is affirmed.

Dick *v.* The State.

Indictment for Rape.

1. *General exception to charge.*—A single exception to an entire charge can not be sustained, unless each principle asserted by it is faulty.

2. *Charge as to sufficiency of evidence.*—A charge which instructs the jury, in a criminal case, that "the State is not required to prove the guilt of the defendant to a mathematical certainty," asserts a correct proposition.

3. *Charge as to testimony of defendant.*—A charge asked, instructing the jury that, "in considering the testimony of the defendant, while they may look to the fact that he is a party to the suit, yet that does

[Dick v. The State.]

not render him less creditable [credible?] than he would be if he were
not a party," is properly refused.

4. *Special venire in capital case.* —In a capital case, when the arraignment and the trial occur in the same week, the special *venire* should
include, not "those summoned on the regular juries for the week"
(Code, § 4320), but only those who have appeared, and who constitute
the regular juries in fact; though the rule is different, when the trial is
set for a subsequent week.

FROM the Circuit Court of Dale.

Tried before the Hon. JESSE M. CARMICHAEL.

The defendant in this case was indicted for rape, was convicted, and sentenced to the penitentiary for life. The
order for the special *venire* is set out in the opinion of the
court. The bill of exceptions, after setting out the testimony
of the prosecutrix, contains the following statement as to the
charge (or charges) given by the court: "The court, at the
instance of the State, gave the following charge in writing:
It is the duty of the jury, in considering what [weight?]
they will give to the evidence of the defendant, to remember
the fact that he is the defendant, and interested in the result
of the verdict; and they may, for this reason, if the jury
think it sufficient, entirely discard and disbelieve his statement as a witness. They will consider the written evidence
of Chever in connection with all the other evidence; and if
it is contradicted by other witnesses, they may disbelieve it.
The State is not required to prove the guilt of the defendant to a positive, absolute, mathematical certainty; and the
jury can not acquit, although they may believe that may be,
perhaps, or possibly the defendant is not guilty. To the
giving of each of which the defendant then and there severally excepted." Opposite each of the sentences composing
this charge, respectively, on the margin of the transcript,
are written the words, "Charge No. 1," "Charge No. 2,"
"Charge No. 3." The defendant also excepted to the refusal
of the following charge, which was asked in writing: "While
the jury, in considering the evidence of the defendant, may
look to the fact that he is a party to the suit; yet being
defendant, or party to the suit, does not render him any less
creditable than he would be if he were not a party to the
suit."

WM. L. MARTIN, Attorney-General, for the State, cited
Code, § 4320; *Jackson v. State*, 77 Ala. 18; *Floyd v. State*,
55 Ala. 61; *Shelton v. State*, 73 Ala. 5; *Lang v. State*,
84 Ala. 1; *McKleroy v. State*, 77 Ala. 95,

VOL. LXXXVII.

[Dick v. The State.]

STONE, C. J.—The charge of the court, as shown in
the bill of exceptions, is not divided into sections, paragraphs,
or separate divisions. The exception is, "to the giving of
each of which the defendant then and there severally excepted." We have many times ruled that an exception thus
reserved is equivalent to a general exception to the whole
charge, and will not be considered by us, unless the charge
is faulty in each principle it asserts.—3 Brick. Digest, 80,
§§ 34, 37. Some of the principles announced in the charge,
if stated separately, we might consider misleading, if not
erroneous; but the assertion that "the State is not required
to prove the guilt of the defendant to a mathematical certainty," is unquestionably the law.

Any artificial rules for determining the credibility of testimony, should generally be avoided. Jurors, who observe
the witness while he is testifying, his manner, his intelligence, his appearance, his bias, or the absence of it, and
many other nameless *indicia*, are, as a rule, the best deter-
miners of the truth or falsity of parol testimony. It is their
highest duty to arrive at the truth if they can, and in doing
so, they must accord to the entire evidence that weight, and
only that weight, with which it impresses them. In criminal
prosecutions, the testimony must establish the guilt of the
accused beyond a reasonable doubt; or, which is the same
thing, to a moral certainty. If, weighing the whole testimony, it comes up to this standard—that is, convinces the
jury to a moral certainty that the accused is guilty—then
the verdict should be "guilty," notwithstanding there may
remain a *possibility*, a *perhaps*, or a *may be* that he is not
guilty. The doubt which demands acquittal against such
criminating evidence, must be a reasonable doubt, and not
a mere possibility of innocence.

The charge asked by defendant was properly refused.

The prisoner was arraigned on Thursday, January 17th,
1889, and the ensuing Saturday, 19th, was set for his trial.
The court ordered, "that the sheriff be, and is hereby,
directed and commanded to summon sixty jurors, including
those summoned on the regular juries for the week," from
which to organize a jury for the trial of the accused. It will
be observed that the day set for the trial was during the same
week in which the order was made; and the trial was had on
the day appointed. This order was made under section 4320,
Code of 1886,—section 4874, Code of 1876. Of the petit
jurors summoned for the week, one failed to appear, and con-

sequently was not in attendance, nor one of the number composing the juries organized for the week. In *Floyd v. State*, 55 Ala. 61, interpreting the section of the Code referred to, it was decided that the true construction was, that only such of the jurors summoned as were in attendance on the court, should constitute a part of the *venire* for the trial of a capital felony. See § 4324, Code of 1886. That case was followed in *Lee v. State*, 55 Ala. 259; *Posey v. State*, 73 Ala. 490, and *Jackson v. State*, 77 Ala. 18. The court erred in putting on the defendant a juror, who, though summoned, was not a member of either of the juries organized for the week, and was not in attendance on the court. The effect was to deny to the accused one of the sixty persons, which the order of the court had directed should constitute the special *venire*.

The rule is different, when the trial and the order setting a day for it occur in different weeks. It not being ascertainable what number of the summoned jurors will be in attendance, the statute is conformed to when the jurors summoned for the particular week are made a part of the *venire.—Morrison v. State*, 84 Ala. 405.

We are aware that, in the order for a special *venire* in this case, the presiding judge pursued the exact language of section 4320 of the Code of 1886—section 4874, Code of 1876; section 4175, Code of 1867. In *Floyd's case*, 55 Ala. 61, which arose under the Code of 1867, we interpreted that section in connection with section 4324, and decided that, in cases like the present, where the order setting a day for the trial, and the trial itself, occur in the same week, only those jurors summoned for the week who are in attendance, are to be placed on the special *venire*. We held that this was the legitimate interpretation of the two sections, when construed together. We pursued and emphasized that ruling in *Shelton's case*, 73 Ala. 5; and the ruling in *Posey's case, Ib.* 690, rests on the same principle. The interpretation we then gave, and which we adhere to, casts on the presiding judge the duty of being specific in his directions, and leaves to the sheriff no room for mistakes. This is the safer practice. Since *Floyd's case* was decided, those sections have passed through two Code revisions, without change; and this is, at least, some evidence that the codifiers and the legislature have approved the interpretation.

Reversed and remanded.

Poe *v.* The State.

Indictment for Murder.

1. *To what witness may testify.*—On a prosecution for murder, a witness for the defense can not be allowed to testify that the defendant "was afraid" to work in the field alone, or to go out about his premises after dark, on account of threats made against him by the deceased; such testimony being merely the opinion of the witness, based on the conduct or declarations of the defendant himself, or unsupported by any fact at all.

2. *Self-defense; charge as to duty to retreat; explanatory charge.*—In a case of homicide, a charge instructing the jury that, "if the deceased was the assailant, the party assailed must retreat, unless retreat will endanger his safety, and must refrain from taking life, if there *is* any other reasonable mode of escape," states the rule in the ordinary language of the decisions; and if it be objectionable, as requiring the party assailed to act on the actual (and not an apparent) necessity, this qualifying principle should be invoked by an explanatory charge. (The 7th head-note to the case of *Tesney v. The State*, 77 Ala. 33, in stating that the charge therein set ont "is erroneous," instead of "too narrow and restricted," is "not justified by the opinion of the court" in that case.)

3. *Same; charge ignoring duty to retreat.*—A charge requested, instructing the jury that, "if they believed the deceased was trying to draw a deadly weapon, or that he acted in such a manner as to convey to the defendant the impression that he was trying to draw a deadly weapon, for the purpose of attacking the defendant," who was armed with a shot-gun, "and thereby put defendant in fear of great bodily harm, he was justified in doing whatever was necessary to preserve his own life;" and a charge asserting that, if the deceased came towards the defendant, using angry and insulting language, "and placed his hand in his pocket in such a manner as to indicate to a reasonable mind that his purpose was to draw and fire, then the defendant was authorized to draw and fire first," each is erroneous, in excluding from the jury all consideration of the inquiry as to any duty to retreat.

4. *Charge as to threats, with overt act, excusing retreat.*—No threats, or overt acts, which do not, actually or apparently, justify a reasonable apprehension of danger to life, or of great bodily harm, will justify the party assailed in killing his adversary, without resorting to retreat; and a charge requested which ignores the duty to retreat, without regard to the character of the threats, is properly refused.

5. *Misleading charge assuming facts to be true.*—A charge requested, which assumes as true certain facts which are controverted, instead of referring to the jury the sufficiency of the evidence relating to them, is properly refused.

FROM the Circuit Court of Tuskaloosa.

Tried before the Hon. S. H. SPROTT.

The defendant in this case, Jasper Poe, was indicted for the murder of Wallace Cooper, by shooting him with a gun;

5

was convicted of murder in the first degree, and sentenced
to the penitentiary for life. The parties were both freedmen, and it seems that they had married sisters, the
daughters of Tom and Mary Hailey. The homicide was committed one morning in July, 1888, when the defendant, passing through Hailey's yard, and having his shot-gun on his
shoulder, encountered the deceased, and shot him. The
wound made by the shot was "about the size of a dollar,"
and the deceased died within fifteen minutes. Mary Hailey,
who seems to have been the only eye-witness of the killing,
testified on the part of the State, that the defendant, having
his gun thrown across his shoulders, with one hand on each
end of it, came up near her as she was sitting in the door of
her house, "and asked where they all were;" that she told
him they were all gone, and he turned off to leave; "that he
had gone about seven steps when he met Cooper, and asked
him 'if he was going down yonder to-day'; that Cooper said,
'he did not know'; that defendant then walked on about seven
steps, turned and fired, striking Cooper in the back, and
killing him." The wife of the deceased also testified, on behalf of the State, that she saw the fatal shot fired, and that
the defendant then presented his gun, and threatened to shoot
her; but, on cross-examination, she said that she did not see
the gun fired, and that the house was between her and the
parties at the time, though she saw her husband fall. The
defendant, testifying in his own behalf, said that he had
been out turkey-hunting that morning, passed Hailey's house
on his road home, had some few words with Mary Hailey as
he passed her, and then started to go home; and he then
proceeded: "I had taken four or five steps, when Cooper
came around the corner of the house, meeting me. I tried
to pass him, when he pressed towards me, with the remark,
*'There is the damned son of a bitch now, and I am going on
him.'* I had my gun on my shoulder, and was eight or ten
feet from him. He put his hand in his pocket, and attempted
to draw his pistol. I presented my gun while he was still
attempting to get out his pistol, and he had succeeded in getting it out far enough for me to see the but-end, though the
barrel was still in his pocket. When I saw what he was
going to do, I fired, and he fell. I am certain his side was
towards me when I fired, and he flirted around just as I
fired."

The prosecution adduced evidence, also, that the defendant
and the deceased had had a personal difficulty, in January,

[Poe v. The State.]

or February, 1888, in which the deceased was shot in the arm; and that the defendant declared, as one witness testified, "in cotton-planting time," that he would kill Cooper. On the other hand, evidence was adduced by the defense, of repeated declarations by the deceased, to different persons, and at different times, that he would kill the defendant if it took him ten years to do it; that these threats had been communicated to the defendant before the killing; that the deceased, at the time of the difficulty between them, in January or February, 1888, had waylaid the defendant, and attempted to shoot him from ambush; and that the deceased was a quarrelsome, turbulent, and dangerous man. Andrew Clines, in whose employment the parties were at the time, thus testified in behalf of the defendant: "Defendant and Cooper were not on good terms, and Tom Hailey and defendant were at outs. I saw Cooper after he was shot. He was shot over the right hip. The load seemed to range straight through, and the wound could have been covered with a dollar. Cooper was a dangerous man. When I got to him he was dead, and I saw no pistol on or near him." During the examination of said Clines as a witness, "defendant offered to prove by him that, previous to the killing, and after defendant had heard of the threats made by Cooper, defendant was afraid to work in his field by himself, and was afraid to go after dark to the spring, or to the horse-lot"; and he excepted to the exclusion of this evidence, on objection by the State.

The court charged the jury, on request of the solicitor in writing, as follows: "If the deceased was the assailant, the party assailed must retreat, unless retreat will endanger his safety, and must refrain from taking life, if there is any other reasonable mode of escape." To this charge the defendant excepted, and he also excepted to the refusal of each of the following charges, which were asked by him in writing: (2.) "If the jury believe from the evidence that the deceased was trying to draw a deadly weapon, or that he acted in such a manner as to convey to the defendant the impression that he was trying to draw a deadly weapon, for the purpose of attacking the defendant, and thereby put him in fear of great bodily harm, the defendant was justified in doing whatever was necessary to preserve his own life." (5.) "If the jury believe the evidence given by the defendant, they will find him not guilty." (6.) "If the jury believe that the defendant did not provoke, or bring on the difficulty, but met the deceased in a peaceable and orderly manner; that the deceased used angry and insulting language to him, and came towards him, and placed his hand in his pocket in such a manner as to indicate to a reasonable mind that his purpose was to draw and fire; then the defendant was authorized to draw and fire first; and the rule would not be varied, if it should afterwards turn out that the deceased was in fact unarmed." (7.) "If the jury believe that the deceased had previously waylaid the defendant to kill him, and had afterwards repeatedly threatened to kill him; and that these threats were communicated to the defendant; and that the deceased was a dangerous man, and the defendant knew the fact; and that they casually met; and that the deceased made threats, and used abusive language, and made any overt act to carry these threats into effect; under these circumstances, the defendant is not required to retreat, or flee, but may kill the deceased, if he honestly believes it is necessary to preserve his life." (8.) "The party once assailed by an enemy who has threatened to kill him, is not bound to run, and thereby escape that assault, leaving the danger still impending, and perhaps increased by the act of running." (9.) "When a man has been threatened with death, by a vindictive, reckless, and determined man, and has once escaped assassination at his hands; and his enemy has lain in wait to kill him; and they meet accidentally; and his enemy reiterates his purpose to kill him, at the same time putting his hand in his pocket, as if to draw a pistol; and he thereupon shoots and kills his enemy, and it afterwards turns out that he had no pistol at the time, that fact does not render him culpable."

J. J. MAYFIELD, and THOS. L. BEATTY, for appellant. (1.) The testimony of Clines was admissible, (1) as tending to prove the character of the defendant, which is always permissible; (2) as tending to show that he apprehended danger at the hands of the deceased, at the time of the killing; and (3) to rebut the idea of malice, arising from the use of a deadly weapon.—*Armor v. State,* 63 Ala. 173; *Kilgore v. State,* 74 Ala. 1; *Fields v. State,* 47 Ala. 603; Burr. Cir. Ev. 509-10, 520-24 ; 5 Geo. Rep. 85; 2 Halst. 226; 6 Blackf. 299. (2.) The charge given by the court, at the instance of the State, was erroneous, (1) because it ignored the murderous intent and character of the assault; (2) because it required the party

[Poe v. The State.]

to act on the real (instead of the apparent) necessity; and
(3) because it was not warranted by the evidence.—Hor. &
Th. Cases of Self-defense, 30, 31, 34, 137; 1 Bish. Crim.
Law, § 850; 26 Amer. Rep. 52; 71 Ala. 351, 329; 92 Amer.
Dec. 417; 80 *Ib*. 481; 61 *Ib*. 49; 95 Mo. 322; 5 Amer. St.
Rep. 882; 17 Ala. 587; 83 Ala. 33; 66 Ala. 548; 67 Ala.
87.   (3.) The charges asked and refused correctly stated
the law of self-defense.   Neither law nor reason requires a
man to flee, or even offer to retreat, when he is without fault
in bringing on the difficulty, and the assault is felonious in
its purpose, fierce in its character, and deadly in its agency.
1 Bish. Crim. Law, §§ 850, 865; 2 Whart. Crim Law, § 1019;
Foster's Crown Law, 273; 2 Stark. Ev. 721; Hor. & Th.
Cases, 30, 31, 92, 109; 8 Amer. Rep. 474; 77 Ala. 18;
75 Amer. Dec. 52; 80 *Ib*. 398; 2 Crim. L. Magazine, 119;
51 Ala. 1.

W. L. MARTIN, Attorney-General, for the State.

SOMERVILLE, J.—The statement of the witness Clines,
that the defendant "was afraid" to work in the field alone,
or to go out about his premises after dark, on account of
threats made against him by the deceased, for whose homicide he stands indicted, was, at most, but the opinion of the
witness, based either on the conduct or declarations of the
defendant himself, or else unsupported by fact at all; and it
was properly excluded by the court.   Such evidence would
open the way for easy manufacture of testimony by defendants.   The fears of a man, moreover, may be no proper evidence of the danger even apparently confronting him.

"The right of self-defense," as the rule is sometimes
stated, "can not be carried to the last resort of taking human
life, until the defendant has availed himself of all proper
means in his power to decline combat by retreat, provided
there is open to him a safe mode of escape—that is, when he
can safely and conveniently retreat, without putting himself
at a disadvantage by increasing his own peril in the combat."—*Carter v. State*, 82 Ala. 13, and cases there cited;
Brown v. State, 74 Ala. 478; *Rogers v. State*, 62 Ala. 170.

The charge given by the court, at the request of the solicitor, asserted that "if the deceased was the assailant, the
party assailed must retreat, unless retreat will endanger his
safety, and must refrain from taking life, if there is any
other reasonable mode of escape."   This instruction states

the rule in the ordinary language of our decisions, and of the books. The main objection taken to it is, that it requires the party assailed to act only on the *actual,* and not the *apparent* necessity. Such is not the construction generally imputed to charges in this form, which purport only to assert a rule of law in general terms. The defendant, in estimating the peril which surrounds him—in its bearing both on the necessity of taking life, as well as of retreat—may certainly act on reasonable appearances, where this phase of fact enters into the evidence. This qualifying principle should be invoked by an explanatory charge. An instruction given by the court, which ignores it, may be misleading, as too narrow and limited, but it is not erroneous, the giving of a misleading charge not always being ground of reversible error. The case of *Tesney v. State,* 77 Ala. 33, does not go further than this, the seventh head-note not being justified by the opinion of the court.

The second and sixth charges requested by the defendant were erroneous, in excluding from the consideration of the jury all inquiry as to any duty of retreat. The mere fact that the alleged attack by the deceased on the defendant was with a pistol, the defendant himself being armed with a shot-gun, did not warrant the withdrawal of this inquiry from the jury, and its decision as matter of law by the court.—*Storey's case,* 71 Ala. 329, 337.

The seventh charge is predicated upon the idea, that the making of threats and using of abusive language, without regard to the character of such threats, if accompanied by an overt act to carry them into effect, would justify the party assailed in killing his adversary, without resorting to retreat. This is not the law. No threats or overt acts, which do not, actually or apparently, justify a reasonable apprehension of danger to life, or great bodily harm, will avail as an excuse of taking human life. There was no error in refusing this charge.—*Eiland v. State,* 52 Ala. 322; *Storey's case, supra; State v. Benham,* 92 Amer. Dec. 417.

The eighth and ninth charges are misleading, in assuming as true certain facts, without referring the sufficiency of the evidence bearing on them to the jury. The former assumes that in this case a retreat by the defendant, on the uncontroverted facts, would have left the danger confronting him still impending, and perhaps increased. The latter charge assumes as true the testimony of the defendant rendered on the trial, to the effect that the deceased had "put his hand in his pocket as if to draw a pistol," which was controverted; to say nothing of its failure to refer to the jury the credibility of other testimony tending to support other facts hypothesized in the charge.

This disposes of all the exceptions taken to the rulings of the court. We discover no error in the record, and the judgment must be affirmed.

Clarke *v.* The State.

Indictment for Murder.

1. *Special venire in capital case.*—In drawing a special *venire* for the trial of a capital case, under the provisions of the general jury law approved February 28th, 1887 (Sess. Acts 1886-7, pp. 151-8, § 10; Code, p. 134, note), the court has a discretionary power as to the number to be drawn, within the limits specified, and can not be required, on demand of the defendant, to draw fifty, the maximum number specified, which was the minimum under the former law (Code, § 4320).

2. *Peremptory challenges; when and how demanded.*—An exception reserved during the drawing of the special *venire*, in these words, "The defendant then made a motion that, as matter of law he was entitled to twenty challenges, which motion the court overrule, and the defendant excepted," does not show a reversible error (Code, § 4330), when it does not appear that he in fact challenged or offered to challenge any juror who was drawn.

3. *Testimony of defendant in his own behalf.*—In a criminal case, if the defendant fails or declines to testify in his own behalf, this does not create any presumption against him, and is not the subject of comment by counsel (Code, § 4473); but, if he elects to testify, and fails or refuses to explain or rebut any criminating fact, when he can reasonably do so, this is a circumstance in the nature of an implied admission, on which counsel may properly comment.

FROM the Criminal Court of Jefferson.

Tried before the Hon S. E. GREENE.

The defendant in this case, Ralph Clarke, was indicted for the murder of James Leatherwood, by shooting him with a gun or pistol; was convicted of murder in the first degree, and sentenced to the penitentiary for life. The material facts attending the killing are stated in the former report of the case (78 Ala. 474-81), and a statement of them here is unnecessary. "On Monday, June 4th," as the bill of exception recites, a special *venire* was drawn, the defendant demanding that said *venire* should be composed of fifty jurors, but the court permitted only thirty to be drawn; to

which the defendant excepted. On June 7th, the case came
to trial, and, both sides announcing themselves ready, the
court proceeded to impannel a jury. Several jurors were
called, five in all, who were returned not found; to which
the defendant excepted, and exception overruled. The defendant then made a motion to the following effect, that he
was entitled, as matter of law, to twenty challenges; which
motion the court overruled, and the defendant excepted. The
jury being impannelled, the State produced the following
witnesses," &c. "The defendant testified, that he knew
John Allen, but never had any row with him before Leatherwood's death; that after Leatherwood's death, acting as constable, he served process on Allen, and had some words with
him, but thought nothing further about it afterwards; that
he heard of Leatherwood's death, but did not know him, and
had never seen him; denied the killing of Leatherwood, and
said that about that time he was a constable in Allen's court in
Birmingham." In his argument to the jury, the assistant
solicitor "commented at length on defendant's taking the
stand as a witness, thus having an opportunity of explaining
his whereabouts on the night of Leatherwood's death, and
his failure to do so. The defendant's counsel here objected
to this manner of presenting the case, and contended that
while the accused was a witness, he was also the defendant,
and any failure on his part to testify could not be adverted
to by the State as a condemning circumstance; which
objection was overruled, and exception noted. The solicitor
continued on this line of argument at length, and with great
force."

W. L. MARTIN, Attorney-General, for the State.

CLOPTON, J.—When the names of persons to be summoned as special jurors for the trial were being drawn, defendant demanded that fifty names should be drawn, but the
court permitted only thirty. The jury law, which was in
force in Jefferson county at that time, provides, that when
any capital case stands for trial, the court shall cause the
jury-box to be brought into the court-room, and the presiding
judge shall draw therefrom not less than twenty-five, nor
more than fifty names, to constitute a part of the *venire*,
from which the jury to try the case shall be selected.—Acts
1886–7, p. 151. The statute gives the accused a right to
have the *minimum* number drawn, but not the *maximum*, at

his election, or on his demand. How many names between the prescribed numbers shall be drawn is intrusted to the discretion of the court, having reference to the circumstances, and the exercise of the discretion is not revisable.

A motion relating to the number of challenges without cause to which the accused is of right entitled, preliminary to the drawing of the names on the *venire* for the purpose of selecting a jury, is not the proper mode to raise the question. Such declaration, at such time, would not be the adjudication of a practical question, which arose during the trial, but the expression of the then opinion of the presiding judge, notwithstanding which the court may have accorded defendant his full right in respect to challenges, when and so far as he sought to exercise it during the selection of the jury. In such case, he would have no cause to complain. The record does not show that the court decided, at any stage of the trial, the number of peremptory challenges to which defendant was entitled, or that he was denied the right to exercise any challenge allowed by law. Moreover, the number specified in the motion is not strictly correct, under the statutes in force at the time of the trial, and we can not indulge a presumption, in order to put the court in error, that defendant was refused his legal right of challenge to its full extent.—*Todd v. State*, 85 Ala. 339.

Defendant, at his request, became a witness, and testified in his own behalf. The bill of exceptions recites that, during the argument, the prosecuting attorney commented at length on defendant having taken the stand as a witness, thus having an opportunity to explain where he was on the night of the killing, and his failure to do so. To this course of argument, counsel for defendant objected. Section 4473 of Code of 1886 provides: "On the trial of all indictments, complaints, or other criminal proceedings, the person on trial shall, at his own request, but not otherwise, be a competent witness; and his failure to make such request shall not create any presumption against him, nor be the subject of comment by counsel." The statutory protection against unfavorable presumptions or comments extends only to an entire failure or omission to testify. The accused can not be made a witness, except at his option; but, when he exercises the option to be a witness, he waives his constitutional right to protection against compulsory self-crimination, as to any fact or matter pertinent to the issue, or connected with the transaction; subjects himself to the test of cross-examination, within proper limitations; assumes the obligation to tell the whole truth, and can not elect to disclose only such facts as may suit his interest, or be to his advantage, nor decline to disclose inculpatory facts. We so declared the rule, and the limitation upon the privilege of cross-examination, when this case was previously before the court. When the defendant became a witness at his own request, and testified, thus placing himself in the category of a witness, we see no sufficient reason why the same presumptions, indulged in the case of other witnesses, should not arise against him, from his failure or omission to deny, explain or rebut any circumstances and testimony tending to show his connection with the offense, when the facts are within his knowledge, and the denial, explanation or rebuttal is in his power. Common experience teaches that, when a person, charged with the commission of a crime, undertakes to exculpate himself, he uses the opportunity, if innocent, to contradict or explain the criminating facts and accusatory evidence, if in his power. The unfavorable presumption, created by his failure, rests on this common experience. The manner of the accused while testifying, and his testimony, may be subject of comment by counsel, the same as the manner and testimony of other witnesses. The evidence was circumstantial. Witnesses had testified to having seen defendant on the night of the killing, in the vicinity of the place where it occurred. It was in his power to contradict or explain, for he certainly knew where he was on that night. His failure to do so, under such circumstances, was properly the subject of comment. The record does not set forth the remarks of counsel, nor show their character; and in the absence of an affirmative showing to the contrary, we must presume they were legitimate.—*Stover v. People*, 56 N. Y. 315; *Huber v. State*, 57 Ind. 341; Whart. Crim. Ev. § 435a.

The exceptions, going to the rulings of the court on the admissibility of evidence, were decided adversely to appellant on the former appeal—*Clarke v. State*, 78 Ala. 474; 56 Amer. Rep. 45.

Affirmed.

Cotton *v.* The State.

Indictment for Rape.

1. *Evidence identifying defendants as perpetrators of offense.*—Where the defendants deny their guilt, though identified by the prosecutrix, and show that, before their arrest, she had given a description of the guilty parties which did not suit their appearance, it is competent for the prosecution to prove that, after their arrest, she identified and pointed them out among a large number of prisoners.

2. *Objection to party's own evidence.*—A party can not object or except to the admission of evidence which he has himself elicited.

3. *Privileged communications between attorney and client.*—An officer, having the legal custody of a prisoner, should allow him every reasonable opportunity, consistent with his safe keeping, for private consultation with his attorney; yet he may testify to communications made in his presence, although they might be privileged as between the attorney and his client.

4. *Evidence of prior contradictory statements of defendant.*—The defendant testifying in his own behalf to an *alibi*, it is competent for the prosecution to prove his prior contradictory statements, by affidavit or otherwise, as to his whereabouts on the day named; but evidence of prior statements made, not inconsistent with his testimony on the trial, is not admissible.

5. *Charge on part of evidence.*—Where the evidence adduced by the prosecution is both direct and circumstantial, a charge requested, as to the sufficiency of circumstantial evidence to authorize a conviction, ignoring the direct evidence, is properly refused.

6. *Special venire in capital case.*—When the arraignment and the trial, in a capital case, occur in the same week, the special *venire* should include, not "those summoned on the regular juries for the week" (Code, § 4320), but only those who have appeared, and who constitute the regular juries in fact.

FROM the Circuit Court of Dale.

Tried before the Hon. JESSE M. CARMICHAEL.

The defendants in this case, Greene Cotton and William Hendrix, freedmen, were jointly indicted, tried and convicted of committing a rape on Martha Fralish, and were sentenced to the penitentiary for life. "On the trial," as the bill of exceptions states, "evidence was produced by the State tending to show the defendants' guilt. The prosecutrix swore positively to the commission of the offense, and that the defendants committed it; also, that it was the first time she ever saw them. The defendants produced evidence tending to prove an *alibi*, and that they were not guilty; averring positively that they did not commit the offense, and that they never were in the vicinity where it was committed. The pros-

ecutrix, while on the stand as a witness, was asked by the
defendant, if she did not, in the evening after she said the
offense was committed, and at the place where she said it
was committed, in describing the parties who she said committed it, tell Mr. Baker and Mr. Cherry, witnesses for the
defense, a description of the men that would not conform to
defendants; and she answered, that she did not. The defendants then introduced said Cherry and Baker, who testified that the description she gave them, at the time and place
named, did not correspond to the defendants. The State
then asked the prosecutrix, if nine other negroes were brought
to her for identification soon after the offense was committed,
and before the defendants were arrested, and if she identified either of the nine as the guilty parties; and she answered,
that they were brought before her, and that she did not
identify any of them." The defendants objected to each of
these questions and answers, and excepted to their allowance.
"The State then asked the prosecutrix, if she went to Milton, Florida, and there saw the defendants; and she said, yes.
The State then asked her, if she saw them in jail in Ozark
in January, 1888, and there identified them; and she answered, yes."

"The defendants introduced one Hatton as a witness, and
asked him, if he was at the place where the offense was said
to have been committed; and he replied, that he was at a
place where said Baker and Cherry told him the offense was
committed, and that said Baker fell down and rolled over, to
see if he would leave any signs of scuffling. The defendants
then asked him, if the prosecutrix told him that was the
place; and he answered, no. The defendants then moved to
exclude the said testimony of Hatton, 'that he was at a place
where said Baker and Cherry told him the offense was committed'; and they excepted to the overruling of their motion."

The defendants also objected and excepted to the testimony
of one Mosely, the county jailor, as to declarations he had
heard Greene Cotton, while in his custody, make to one J. C.
Cotton, his attorney; the facts being thus stated in the bill
of exceptions: "After the proper predicate had been laid as
to time and place, the State proposed to ask the defendant
Cotton, if he did not tell said Mosely that he was at Westville on the 25th October, 1887, on Maj. Landrum's front (?)
for nearly a half-day, and that he met at DeFuniack, Florida,
on the 26th October, a lawyer from Milton, Florida, named

Perrinote, and talked with him, and tried to borrow money from him, saying that he was strapped, and that he could prove these facts, if he had that lawyer here. The evidence showed that said Mosely was the jailor at the time, and had the charge and custody of the defendants; and that said Mosely heard said defendant make said statements to one J. C. Cotton, a practicing lawyer, who was defendants' attorney at the time. The defendants objected to the question put to said Greene Cotton, and excepted to its allowance. The court having permitted said Mosely to testify to the declarations of said Greene Cotton to his attorney, J. C. Cotton, defendants offered said J. C. Cotton as a witness, and asked him if said Greene Cotton, at the time mentioned by Mosely, told him that he was in DeFuniack on Wednesday, October 26th; and he replied, that Greene Cotton told him he was in DeFuniack on Thursday, and in Milton on Wednesday, October 26th. The State then asked J. C. Cotton, if said Greene Cotton did not tell him that, on the 25th October, he was a half day on Maj. Landrum's front (?) in Westville, Florida; which the witness declined to answer, because it called for a privileged communication. The State then moved to exclude that part of said J. C. Cotton's testimony, wherein he said that Greene Cotton told him he was in De-Funiack on Tuesday, and in Milton on Wednesday, October 25th, this being the conversation testified to by Mosely. The witness, being informed by the court that he need not testify to confidential communications between himself and his client, asked to withdraw said statements; which was done, and no objection or exception taken."

"The defendants requested each of the following charges in writing: (1.) 'To justify conviction, circumstantial evidence ought to exclude a rational probability of innocence; and a conviction ought not to be had on circumstantial evidence, where direct and positive evidence is attainable.' (2.) 'The true test of the sufficiency of circumstantial evidence is, whether the circumstances as proved produce moral conviction, to the exclusion of every reasonable doubt.' (3.) 'The humane provision of the law is, that upon circumstantial evidence there should not be a conviction, unless to a moral certainty it excludes every other reasonable hypothesis than that of the guilt of the accused.' The court refused to give either of said charges, and to such refusal defendants excepted."

H. L. MARTIN, for the appellants.

WM. L. MARTIN, Attorney-General, for the State.

McCLELLAN, J.—The defendants in the court below were identified by the prosecutrix, as the perpetrators of the crime. It was attempted to be shown that, before their arrest, she had given descriptions of them, which were not accurate. The purpose, and only legitimate effect of this testimony was, to engender in the minds of the jury a doubt as to the certainty of her subsequent identification of the parties. To meet this tendency, it was entirely competent to show that she fixed upon these men as the criminals, out of a number who had been brought before her. To be able to select one or more out of a multitude, or out of any greater number, is one of the ordinary tests of the correctness of the identification; and the fact that the prosecutrix did this, goes to show that, although she may have expressed an inaccurate description, she evidenced no hesitation or uncertainty in pointing out the defendants, when they and others were brought before her.

A defendant can claim no advantage, on appeal, for an error which he superinduced; nor can he predicate an assignment of error on the refusal of the trial court to exclude testimony, which he has adduced before the jury. The action of the Circuit Court in overruling the defendants' motion to exclude the evidence of the witness Hatton, whether erroneous or not, abstractly considered, can not avail the appellants.—*Ex parte Winston*, 52 Ala. 421; *Shelton v. State*, 73 Ala. 5.

The rule as to the inviolability of professional confidences applies, as between attorney and client, only to communications made and received for the purposes of professional action and aid, and the secrecy imposed extends to no other persons than those sustaining to each other the confidential relationship, except the necessary organs of communication between them, such as interpreters, and their own agents and clerks. If the parties choose to hold their conferences in the presence and hearing of third persons, whether they be officers of the law, and, as such, charged with the custody of the client, and hence necessarily present, or indifferent bystanders, there is no rule of law which forbids such third persons to depose to facts thus coming to their knowledge. The evidence of the witness Mosely, who was the jailor, as

[Cotton v. The State.]

to what one of the defendants told his attorney in his presence, was properly admitted. We, of course, are not to be understood as intimating that it is not the duty of officers, having the custody of alleged criminals, to afford them every opportunity, consistent with the safe-keeping of their prisoner, for private consultation with their attorneys.

The defendant Greene Cotton having testified that he was in Milton, Florida, on the 26th day of October—the day on which the offense was committed—it was entirely competent for the State to impeach and discredit his evidence in this connection, a proper predicate therefor having been laid, by showing that, either in court or elsewhere, he had made statements, by affidavits or otherwise, as to his whereabouts on that day, which were inconsistent with his statements on the trial.

We are unable to see that the testimony adduced by the State, to the effect that the defendant Hendrix had sworn, on his application for a continuance made at a former term, that there was a large number of witnesses, at different points in Florida, whose names were unknown to him, and could not be ascertained in time to be stated in the application, &c., was pertinent to any issue in the case. As the matter is presented in the bill of exceptions, this statement is not inconsistent with any fact deposed to by this defendant on the trial; and it was therefore irrelevant for the purpose of impeachment, for which it appears to have been introduced. It should have been excluded.

The evidence which tended to establish the guilt of the defendants, was both direct and circumstantial. The charges requested by the defendants ignored entirely all the positive testimony in the case, and required the court to direct the attention of the jury alone to the circumstances which, in greater or less degree, bore upon the question of guilt. Their tendency was to obscure the most potent facts adduced before the jury, and to authorize a determination of the question of guilt *vel non* upon a consideration of a part, and that probably the least important part of the evidence. They were clearly misleading, if not in a certain sense abstract, and were properly refused.—*A. G. S. R. R. Co. v. Jones*, 71 Ala. 487.

In the case of Vandy Dick, at this term, *ante*, p. 61, it was held that an order for the organization of a special jury under the law applicable to Dale county, which directed the sheriff to summon "sixty persons, including those summoned on the

[Burney v. The State.]

regular juries for the week," was irregular and erroneous, when, as in that case, and in this, the order for the jury, and setting a day for the trial, was made, and the trial had in the same week. Such was the order in this case; and on the authority of the case referred to, the judgment of conviction will be reversed, and the cause remanded.

Reversed and remanded.

Burney *v.* The State.

Indictment for Receiving Stolen Money.

1. *Accomplice; corroborating evidence; charge invading province of jury.*—On a prosecution for receiving stolen money, a witness who, according to her own testimony, stole the money at the instigation of the defendant, and gave it to him, having further testified that, when he came back again, and gave her a message which purported to come from her mother, as had been agreed upon between them, she replied, *"There aint no more to get;"* held, that the testimony of another witness, who overheard this remark, but heard nothing else, would be corroborative evidence tending to connect the defendant with the commission of the offense (Code, § 4476), if the jury believed that it referred to the money; but that this was an inference of fact which only the jury could draw, and which the court could not assume as matter of law in instructions to them.

2. *Sufficiency of indictment.*—An indictment for receiving stolen money (Code, § 3794), must aver the number and denomination of the coins, or some of them, or must allege that the same was unknown to the grand jury; and an averment that it was "two hundred dollars in gold coin," without other descriptive words, is not sufficient.

From the Circuit Court of Pike.

Tried before the Hon. John P. Hubbard.

The indictment in this case contained two counts, the first of which alleged that the defendant, Wes. Burney, "did receive, conceal, or aid in concealing two hundred dollars in gold coin of the United States, the personal property of James D. Sikes, knowing that it was stolen, and not having the intent to restore it to the owner;" and the second, that he "feloniously took and carried away two hundred dollars, the personal property of James D. Sikes." The defendant pleaded not guilty, without objection to the indictment. The jury returned a verdict in these words: "We, the jury, find the defendant guilty, and assess the value of the property stolen at $75." On the trial, as the bill of exceptions shows,

[Burney v. The State.]

said Sikes testified to the loss of his money, stating that it was wrapped in a cloth, and placed in a box, which was kept in a trunk, of which his wife had the key; that he first missed fifty dollars, but lost altogether about two hundred dollars; that it was all in gold coins of different denominations, $20, $10, $5, &c.; that some of it was lost about a week before Christmas, 1887; that the key was on a ring, on which a shoe-buttoner was also fastened; that the ring was sometimes in the possession of Maria Sharp, who was a servant in his family in attendance on his children, and who was also the defendant's step-daughter; and that he had seen the defendant at his house several times talking with the girl, "and one time shortly before Christmas, 1887." The prosecution then introduced Maria Sharp as a witness, who testified, in substance, that she stole the money at the instigation of the defendant, who was her mother's husband; that he promised to send her to school, if she "would get him some money from Mr. Sikes' trunk, who, he said, was making barrels of it, and would not miss it;" that she only took money once, and gave it to her mother; "that when the defendant came for her to get money for him," by agreement between them, he brought a pretended message from her mother; that he came two or three times; that he came to the back gate on the second occasion, and delivered the message agreed on, but she told him "*There aint any more to get*," and went off to the house. Frank Coskrey, another witness, "referring to the time last above named by Maria Sharp," testified that he was standing about fifty yards distant when the defendant came and called her to the back gate, and heard her make the remark above quoted, but did not hear anything else that was said between them. On this evidence, the court gave the charge which is copied in the opinion of this court, and to which the defendant excepted. There was other evidence in the case, but it requires no notice.

W. L. PARKS, for appellant, cited *Griffin v. State*, 76 Ala. 29; *Murphy v. State*, 6 Ala. 845; *Grant v. State*, 55 Ala. 201.

W. L. MARTIN, Attorney-General, for the State, cited *May v. State*, 85 Ala. 14: *Grattan v. State*, 71 Ala. 344; *Chisholm v. State*, 45 Ala. 66; 11 Ind. 195; 16 Gray, 240; 11 Cush. 142; 59 Ala. 104; 63 Ala. 5; 76 Ala. 35.

STONE, C. J.—Defendant was indicted under section 3784, Code of 1886, for receiving and concealing stolen money, knowing it to be stolen, and "not having the intent to restore it to the owner." The money was alleged to have been stolen from Sikes. about Christmas, 1887. An accomplice was the witness by whom the most important criminating facts were proved. Another witness, Coskrey, was examined, with a view of corroborating the testimony of this accomplice. He testified that, about the time of the larceny, he, the witness, was at Mr. Sikes' mother's, about fifty yards from Mr. Sikes' back gate, and heard Maria, the accomplice, say to defendant, in reply to something said by defendant, which witness did not understand, "There aint no more to get." Maria then walked off from defendant, and witness heard no more. It was then about dusk.

Under our statute, "a conviction of felony can not be had on the testimony of an accomplice, unless corroborated by other evidence, tending to connect the defendant with the commission of the offense."—Code, 1886, § 4476, and note. The court charged the jury: "If you believe from the evidence that Frank Coskrey heard a conversation at or near the gate between Wes. Burney and Maria Sharp, the accomplice, and heard Maria, to what he said, reply, 'There aint no more to get;' this is corroborative evidence, tending to connect defendant with the commission of the offense, if committed."

It will be seen that this remark—all that the witness Coskrey is claimed to have heard—does not mention money, nor expressly refer to it. That may have been her meaning, and if so, it is not only not improbable, but very likely, that his remark, not heard by the witness, referred to the same subject, and that his request was that she should bring him money. If so, this would "tend to connect defendant with the commission of the offense." But, to have this effect, there was an inference to be drawn, and only the jury could draw that inference. The charge under discussion was a charge on the effect of the evidence; and such charge should never be given, when a material inquiry of fact rests in inference.—3 Brick. Dig. 110, §§ 48, 53, 55, 56. The court erred in giving this charge.

The indictment in this case is bad. It should have averred the number and denomination of the coins, or of some of them, or that the same were to the grand jury unknown. Such have been the rulings of this court; and as this requirement is both reasonable and easily conformed to, we are unwilling to depart from it.—*State v. Murphy*, 6 Ala. 845; *Du-Bois v. State*, 50 Ala. 139; *Grant v. State*, 55 Ala. 291; Whar. Cr. Pl. § 218.

Reversed and remanded.

Whaley *v.* The State.

Indictment for Retailing Spirituous Liquors without License.

1. *Selling liquor "drunk on or about premises."*—Under the former decisions of this court, which have received legislative sanction by the re-adoption of the statute without change of phraseology in successive Codes, a conviction may be had for selling liquor "which was drunk on or about the premises" (Code, § 4036), on proof that it was drunk by the purchaser and his friends in the public road, within five or six steps of the defendant's store, and in full view of his premises; and the fact that the defendant did not see it is no excuse.

FROM the Circuit Court of Covington.

Tried before the Hon. JOHN P. HUBBARD.

The indictment in this case, which was found in March, 1886, charged that the defendant, "not having first procured a license as a retailer from the proper legal authority, did sell vinous or spirituous liquors, which *was* drunk on or about the premises." On the trial, as the bill of exceptions states, one R. C. Teele testified on the part of the prosecution, that he had several times bought liquor from the defendant, in quantities less than a quart, and drank some of the liquor on the premises; that on Christmas eve, 1885, he bought a quart of whiskey from the defendant, and went, with others, out into the public road which run by the defendant's store, and there drank some of the liquor out of the bottle; that this was in full and open view of the defendant's front door, and about four or five steps from his front piazza; also, that the defendant had told him not to drink the liquor on his premises, as it was against his orders; and that he was not on friendly terms with the defendant. The prosecution having elected to proceed for this particular sale, the defendant proved that he had taken out a license as a wholesale liquor dealer in April, 1885, and he testified in his own behalf, that he never sold any liquor in less quantity than a quart; that he always informed persons that it was against his orders for any one to drink whiskey on or about his premises; that on Christmas eve, 1885, Teele and others had some whiskey in bottles, which they had bought at his store, "and they drank some of it in the public road above and below his store, about four or five steps from the front door; that he had no control over them in the public road, and made no effort to prevent said drinking." On this evidence, the court charged the jury, "that if the liquor was drunk in the public road, five or six steps from the defendant's store, and in front thereof, and in full view thereof, the place was about the defendant's premises within the meaning of the statute;" also, "that if the defendant did not see Teele drink the liquor on his premises, or in his house, this, of itself, was no excuse." To each of these charges the defendant excepted, and also to the refusal of the following charges, which were asked by him in writing: (1.) "If the defendant did not know that Teele drank the liquor on or about the premises, and if they further believe that he exerted reasonable effort and caution and means to prevent the drinking by Teele or others on or about the premises; then he is not guilty, although they may believe that Teele did drink it on or about the premises." (2.) "After carefully considering all the testimony, unless the jury believe beyond a reasonable doubt, and to a moral certainty, that the defendant sold whiskey which was drunk by Teele on or about the premises over which the defendant had control, or the legal right to exercise authority, or at a place over which he may not have such control, yet is so near thereto, and so situated, that it is within the mischief intended to be remedied,—then they should find the defendant not guilty."

WM. L. MARTIN, Attorney-General, for the State.

SOMERVILE, J.—The rulings of the Circuit Court in this case must be pronounced correct, on the authority of the following cases: *Christian v. State*, 40 Ala. 376; *Pearce v. State, Ib.* 720; *Brown v. State*, 31 Ala. 353; *Patterson v. State*, 36 Ala. 297; *Powell v. State*, 63 Ala. 177; *Easterling v. State*, 30 Ala. 46; Clark's Man. Cr. Law, §§ 1609-1610. Under the authority of these decisions, if the liquor sold by the defendant was drunk within five or six steps of his store, and in full view of the premises, it was drunk "about his premises" within the meaning of the statute. Code, 1886, § 4036. It would avail nothing, that the liquor was drunk by the purchaser in the public road, over which the defendant had no legal control, or that the defendant failed to notice the fact and time of its being drunk.

This rule is a severe one in its consequences, and its reasonableness, in my judgment, may well be questioned; but the statute was long ago repeatedly so construed, and has been several times since re-adopted by the General Assembly, without change of phraseology; and on this ground, I adhere to this construction.

Affirmed.

Norris v. The State.

Indictment for Assault with Intent to Ravish.

1. *Constituents of offense.*—Force is an essential ingredient of the crime of rape, and an intent to use force, if necessary, is essential to an assault with intent to ravish (Code, § 3751); yet, where it is shown that the defendant put his arms around the prosecutrix, forcibly held and pressed her, making indecent proposals, and only released her on her threats to call assistance, this is sufficient to support a conviction, although he may have had no intention to commit a battery on her.

. 2. *Charge as to weight or effect of evidence.*—It is the exclusive province of the jury to reconcile the testimony of the different witnesses, if possible, or, if irreconcilable, to determine whom they will believe, or what credit they will give to a witness who is contradicted or impeached; and a charge which institutes a comparison between the weight and force of the testimony of different witnesses, equally credible and having equal opportunities for knowing the facts, is properly refused, as tending to confuse and mislead the jury, and invading their peculiar province.

3. *Charge as to testimony of defendant.*—When the defendant in a criminal case has testified in his own behalf, a charge instructing the jury that "the interest he has in the case may be considered by them in weighing his own evidence" is not erroneous.

FROM the Circuit Court of Madison.

Tried before the Hon. H. C. SPEAKE.

The indictment in this case was found in February, 1882, and charged that the defendant, J. Taylor Norris, forcibly assaulted Mrs. Sallie Rodgers, a married woman, with the intent to ravish her. The trial was had in March, 1889, on issue joined on the plea of not guilty; the defendant being found guilty of an assault, and fined $225. The prosecutrix testified positively that, on a specified day in January, 1882, the defendant came to her house during her husband's absence, "put his arms around her, forcibly held and pressed her, and only released her on her threats to call assistance," and that she made complaint to her husband, on his return in the evening; and her husband corroborated her as to the complaint made. The defendant, testifying for himself, denied that he made any assault on the prosecutrix, and said that he only went to the house for the purpose of getting a bridle, which she brought out to him; and his testimony was corroborated, in some particulars, by one George Miller, who was with him a part of the time. The bill of exceptions purports to set out "all the testimony," but a full statement of it is not necessary to an understanding of the points here decided.

The court charged the jury, on request of the solicitor, "that the interest the defendant has in the case may be considered by them in weighing his own evidence." The defendant excepted to this charge as given, and he also excepted to the refusal of each of the following charges, which were asked by him in writing: (1.) "If the jury believe from the evidence that the defendant had no intention to commit a battery on Mrs. Rodgers, then there was no assault, and the defendant must be acquitted." (2.) "The burden is on the State to establish the guilt of the defendant beyond a reasonable doubt; and if the prosecutrix is the only witness on behalf of the State, testifying to the charge; and if the defendant and George Miller testified, on behalf of the defendant, that the offense was not committed; and if the jury find from the evidence that each witness is equally credible, and their opportunities of knowing the facts are equal, then the State has not made out its case, and the defendant should be acquitted." (3.) "If the prosecutrix testifies to the assault, the fact that the defendant was in proximity to the place where, as she alleges, the offense was committed, does not make him guilty of anything—the law does not recognize any such absurdity." (3.) "If the jury believe from the evidence that the defendant did put his arm around the neck of the prosecutrix, but the proof does not show more, there is an absence of that intent which must be shown to justify a conviction." (4.) "In considering the testimony of the prosecutrix, and of her husband as corroborative testimony, to whom she testified that she complained, the jury may consider whether the offense testified to by her is the same of which she complained to him, and whether it is the same with which he is now charged; and it is the duty of the jury to reconcile the statements of these two witnesses, if they can; and if they can not upon a consideration of the whole testimony, and have a reasonable doubt as to the defendant's guilt, they must acquit him."

LAWRENCE COOPER, JNO. D. BRANDON, and L. W. DAY, for the appellant, cited *Lawson v. State*, 30 Ala. 54; *Johnson v. State*, 35 Ala. 363; *Gray v. State*, 63 Ala. 66; *Lane v. State*, 85 Ala. 11; *Wharton v. State*, 73 Ala. 366.

W. L. MARTIN, Attorney-General, and D. D. SHELBY, for the State.

CLOPTON, J.— When the charges requested by the defendant are referred to the evidence, we discover no error in the refusal of the court to give them.

The indictment charges the offense of assault with intent to ravish. Defendant asked the court to instruct the jury, if they believed from the evidence there was no intention to commit a battery, then there was no assault, and he must be acquitted. Generally, to constitute an assault, a battery must be attempted, intended, or threatened—the commencement of an act, which, if not prevented, would produce a battery. As force is an essential constituent of the crime of rape, the intent to use force, if necessary to consummate the carnal connection, is essential to a conviction of assault with intent to ravish. But in this offense the force may be actual or constructive.—*McQuirk v. State*, 84 Ala. 435. Though there may be no intention in fact to apply actual force to the person, the offense of rape is complete, when unlawful intercourse is accomplished by overcoming resistance, and procuring submission on the part of the woman, by means of threats, or otherwise exciting fears of bodily harm; and in such case, should the accomplishment of the purpose be prevented by extraneous causes, there is an assault with intent to ravish.

Defendant was convicted of an assault merely. The verdict of the jury is explainable only on the theory, that they believed the testimony of the prosecutrix as to the conduct and acts of the defendant at the time of the alleged offense, but found that his intent was to induce consent by taking indecent liberties with her person, and not to compel acquiescence by force. If her testimony be true, defendant, without any indication of willingness or inclination on her part, put his arms around her, held and forcibly pressed her, and only released her on threats to call assistance. Imposition of his arms on her person, and holding and pressing her against her will, is, in legal contemplation, force, though there may have been no intention to hurt—unquestionably an assault and battery.—*Goodman v. State*, 60 Ga. 509. In the absence of proof of justification or excuse, the law implies the criminal intent, when the act is unlawful in itself. The charge requested by the defendant would have imported to the jury, when referred to the evidence, that it was incumbent on the State to make proof of intention to commit a battery, other than the presumption arising from its actual and intentional commission.

The other charges asked by defendant required the court to instruct the jury as to the sufficiency of the evidence. The reconcilability of the testimony of different witnesses, or, if irreconcilable, what witness they will believe, or what credit shall be given to a witness who is impeached by proof of contradictory or inconsistent statements, are questions exclusively in the province of the jury. And we have uniformly disapproved charges, which institute a comparison between the weight and force of the testimony of different witnesses, who may be regarded as equally credible, and as having equal opportunities of knowing the facts.—*Ala. Fert. Co. v. Reynolds*, 85 Ala. 19.

The defendant having placed himself in the position of a witness at his own request, he subjected himself, as to determining what credit was due to his evidence, to all the considerations applicable in cases of other witnesses, who sustain a close relation to the party calling them, or who have an interest in the result of the suit.—*Clarke v. State, ante,* 71. It was competent for the court to instruct the jury, that in weighing the evidence of defendant, they could consider his interest in the case. In *Allen v. State,* at this term, in reference to a charge on this subject, it is said: "The court should not have gone further in this connection, than to instruct the jury that, in determining the weight they would give to the defendant's testimony, they should consider, along with all other circumstances having any bearing on the matter, the fact that he was the defendant." The charge in that case was declared erroneous, because it went further, and authorized the jury to disregard the defendant's testimony, for the reasons only that he was the defendant, and was contradicted by other witnesses. The credence to be given to his testimony should be left to the jury, unembarrassed by direct or indirect instructions from the court bearing on its sufficiency. The charge in this case does not violate this rule.

Affirmed.

Adams v. The State.

Indictment for Assault with Intent to Murder.

1. *Tenancy in common in crops, between owner of land and agricultural laborer.*—Under a contract between the owner of land and an agricultural laborer, by which the former agrees to furnish the lands and necessary teams, and the latter the labor, the crops to be divided equally between them, the parties are tenants in common of the crop until divided; though the statute (Code, § 3065) gives the laborer a lien, and process of attachment to enforce it.

2. *General exception to several charges given or refused.*—A general exception to several charges given can not avail anything, unless all of them are erroneous; nor to the refusal of several charges asked, unless each of them stated a correct principle of law applicable to the case.

From the City Court of Montgomery.

Tried before the Hon. Thos. M. Arrington.

Indictment for assault with intent to murder. Conviction of assault and battery. Exceptions to charges given, and to the refusal of charges asked. Material facts stated in opinion.

W. L. Martin, Attorney-General, and Tennent Lomax, for the State.—Under the undisputed facts of this case, by express statutory provision, the contract of hire existed between the parties, and the defendant had a lien on the crops, enforceable by process of attachment.—Code, § 3065. At common law, without this statute, the parties may have been tenants in common of the crops, with equal right of possession; but this relation can not exist where one has an express lien, which necessarily implies that the title and right of possession are in the other. The exception to charges given and refused is too general.—3 Brick. Digest, 80, § 41.

McCLELLAN, J.—The appellant was convicted of an assault and battery, under an indictment which charged an assault with intent to murder. In determining whether he was in fault in bringing on the difficulty, in which the assault was alleged to have been made, the ownership of certain corn became a material inquiry. The proof was, that this corn was a part of a crop raised by the defendant under a contract between him and one Turnipseed, by the terms of which the latter "furnished the land and teams, the defendant furnished the labor, and the crop was to be equally divided between them." A part of the corn had been gathered by the defendant, under the direction of Turnipseed, who ordered defendant to store it in his, Turnipseed's, crib. Two wagon-loads were thus gathered and stored; but the third load was stored in a crib belonging to, or under the control of the defendant. The assault charged in the indictment was consequent upon an effort of Turnipseed to get possession of this corn, and defendant's resistance thereto. On this state of the facts, the court charged the jury as follows: "The legal title to the corn was in Mr. Turnipseed, and the defendant had no right to it other than a lien, which could be enforced by attachment." This charge is not in harmony with the decisions of this court. These adjudications have fully settled the doctrine, that crops grown under a contract, such as the one proved in this case, belong to the contracting parties as tenants in common, and that this relation is changed by section 3065, only for the purpose, and to the extent of furnishing the agricultural laborer a remedy against the unfair dealings of his co-tenant, by the process of attachment; and until this remedy, which may be regarded in a sense as cumulative, is resorted to, the relations and rights of the parties are those of tenants in common, each having the same title, and the same right of possession as the other.—*Collier v. Falk*, 69 Ala. 58; *Holcombe v. State*, 69 Ala. 218; *McCall v. State*, 69 Ala. 227; *Smith v. State*, 84 Ala. 438.

Two or more charges were given at the request of the State, and eight charges asked by the defendant the court refused to give. To the action of the court in each particular, there was one general exception. These exceptions could not avail the defendant, unless, in the one instance, all the charges given at the request of the solicitor were bad; and in the other, all those of the defendant which were refused, correctly stated principles of law bearing on the case. We are satisfied that some, at least, of the former were good, and some, at least, of the latter were bad. It follows, that the action of the court on the special charges given and refused is not presented so as to authorize revision by this court.—*Black v. Pratt C. & C. Co.*, 85 Ala. 511; *Bedwell v. Bedwell*, 77 Ala. 587; *Stevenson v. Moody*, 83 Ala. 418; *Mc-Gehee v. State*, 52 Ala. 225.

For the error in the general charge pointed out above, the judgment must be reversed, and the cause remanded.

Bobbitt v. The State.

Indictment for Obtaining Money by False Pretenses.

1. *False pretenses.*—A conviction may be had for obtaining money by false pretenses (Code, § 3811), on proof that the defendant, representing himself to be a lawyer from Chicago, and an agent of a company there organized to loan out money in the South on lands to be purchased by freedmen, and as having a large amount of money with him for the purpose, thereby obtained from the prosecutor $35 as a fee for examining the title to a tract of land, which he represented must be done before any money would be loaned.

2. *Trial on Good Friday.*—Although Good Friday has been declared a legal holiday (Sess. Acts 1888-9. p. 56), a trial may be lawfully had and judgment and sentence rendered on that day.

FROM the Circuit Court of Tuskaloosa.

Tried before the Hon. S. H. SPROTT.

The indictment in this case charged that the defendant, "J. O. Bobbitt, whose christian name is to the grand jury unknown, did falsely pretend to Columbus Dunlap, with intent to defraud, that representing some company, which is to the grand jury unknown, that desired to purchase land in this country, he had one hundred thousand dollars in Tuskaloosa, with which to purchase lands; and, by means of such false pretenses, did obtain from the said Columbus Dunlap thirty-five dollars in money, as a fee to investigate the titles to certain lands, which he then and there proposed to buy for the said Columbus Dunlap, a description of which said lands is to the grand jury unknown." The defendant, conducting his own defense, moved to quash the indictment, "on the ground that the averment, 'he had one hundred thousand dollars in Tuskaloosa,' is too vague and indefinite; and on the further ground, that the averment, 'J. O. Bobbitt, whose christian name is to the grand jury unknown,' is inconsistent and contradictory." The court overruled the motion, and also overruled a demurrer to the indictment, on the same grounds.

The trial took place on April 19th, 1889, which was Good Friday; and the defendant reserved a bill of exceptions, in which the facts are thus stated: "The State introduced evidence tending to show that the defendant, who is a colored man, came to Tuskaloosa some time in January, or February, 1889, and went out into the country, and saw different colored men, representing that he was a lawyer from Chicago, and that he represented a company who wished to loan out money in the South on lands to be purchased by the colored people; that he had $100,000 in the city of Tuskaloosa for that purpose; and that he would have to examine the titles to the land, before they could get the money. Upon this representation, he obtained from Columbus Dunlap the sum of $35. This was on Thursday, and he instructed said Dunlap to meet him in Tuskaloosa on Saturday, and that he would then let him have the money, or would refund the $35; but, on that night, the defendant took the south-bound train, and was arrested, some time afterwards, in New Orleans, where he had assumed another name. The defendant, testifying in his own behalf, swore that he did represent a company, and was prepared to make advances upon land; that he left Tuskaloosa suddenly, because he had heard of some threats of violence made against him that evening, and took the first train in order to escape. He admitted, on cross-examination, that he had changed his name after going to New Orleans; that he had obtained money in the same manner, in Autauga and Wilcox counties, Alabama, and also in Mississippi and Louisiana; that he went by a different name at each of these places, but could not recollect the names he assumed; and that he had made no loans, because he was run off each time before he had time to fix up the papers. He admitted, also, on cross-examination, that he did not investigate the titles to any of the lands which the party from whom he obtained the $35 wished to purchase; nor did he see the owners of the land to ascertain if they could be purchased; nor did he inform said Dunlap that he was going to leave, or make any effort to refund said $35. The court charged the jury, among other things, as follows: 'A false pretense, to be indictable, must be calculated to deceive and defraud; it must be of a material fact, on which the party to whom it is made has a right to rely,—not the mere expression of an opinion, and not of facts open to his present observation, and in reference to which, if he observed, he could obtain correct knowledge. As a general rule, if the pretense

[Cagle v. The State.]

is not, of itself, absurd or irrational, or if he had not, at the very time it was made and acted on, the means at hand of detecting its falsehood, if he was really imposed on, his want of prudence is not a defense.' To this part of the charge of the court the defendant duly excepted."

W. C. FITTS, for appellant.

W. L. MARTIN, Attorney-General, for the State.

STONE, C. J.—We have examined the record in this case with care, and are not able to perceive any error in the rulings of the court. The pretenses alleged to have been falsely made were of fact, and not mere opinion, or promise broken. They were calculated to deceive; and if they were intentionally made, were acted on, and a thing of value parted with in the confidence of their truth, while in fact they were false and intended to defraud, every requirement of the statute was met, and the defendant was and is guilty.—Code of 1886, § 3811.

The indictment is sufficient.—Form 47, Code of 1886, Vol. 2, p. 272.

The charge of the court is free from error.—3 Brick. Dig. 207.

There is nothing in the objection that the trial was had on Good Friday—a legal holiday.—*Belmont C. & R. R. Co. v. Smith*, 74 Ala. 206; *Pfister v. State*, 84 Ala. 432.

Affirmed.

Cagle *v.* The State

Indictment for Selling Spirituous Liquors without License.

1. *Illegal sale of liquor by infant, or agent.*—A girl seventeen years old, living with her mother, may be convicted of selling liquor without a license and contrary to law (Code, §§ 4036-38), on proof that she measured out and delivered the liquor under the order or instructions of her mother, to whom it belonged, and to whom the money was paid by the purchaser.

FROM the Circuit Court of Etowah.
Tried before the Hon. JOHN B. TALLY.

W. L. MARTIN, Attorney-General, for the State.

SOMERVILLE, J.—The defendant was convicted of sell-ing spirituous liquors without a license, and contrary to law. The evidence showed that she was a minor, about seventeen years of age, and sold the liquor by instruction of her mother, and as her mother's agent or servant. This was no excuse for the act. There is no pretense that she was so far under the age of discretion by reason of infancy as to affect her legal capacity to commit crime. Nor does it avail that she had no interest in the article sold, and was only acting, with-out compensation, as the servant of the owner. No one can legally authorize another to do an act prohibited by law; and the agent can not, therefore, protect himself by showing the authority of his principal, where the same act, if done by the principal, would be indictable as a crime. The instruc-tion from her mother, moreover, afforded the defendant no protection, in the absence of any evidence showing that she was acting under compulsion so as to deprive her of her free agency.—*Reese v. The State*, 73 Ala. 18; *Martin v. State*, 59 Ala. 34; 1 Whart. Cr. Law (9th Ed.), § 94*a*; 1 Bish. Cr. Law (7th Ed.), § 658; Bish. Stat. Crimes, § 1024.

The rulings of the court are free from error, and the judg-ment is affirmed.

Munkers *v.* The State.

Indictment for Seduction.

1. *Misnomer; pleadings as to* —The difference between the names *Munkers* and *Moncus* is sufficient to support a plea of misnomer, when a demurrer is interposed to it; if, by local usage, the names have the same pronunciation, issue should be taken on the plea, or a replication should be filed.

2. *Evidence corroborating prosecutrix.*—By statutory provision, a con-viction of seduction can not be had on the uncorroborated testimony of the woman herself (Code, § 4015); the corroboration must be as to a material matter, must connect the defendant with that matter, and must be sufficient to satisfy the jury, beyond a reasonable doubt, of the truth of the woman's testimony; and the defendant's own admission to third persons of an engagement between him and the woman, and of his intention to marry her, are admissible as evidence against him, and sufficient to meet the statutory requirement, though they may not be sufficient to satisfy the jury beyond a reasonable doubt.

3. *Chastity of prosecutrix; charge on different aspects of evidence.*—The

[Munkers v. The State.]

chastity of the prosecutrix, at the time of the alleged seduction, is an essential ingredient of the offense, and is to be presumed in the absence of evidence to the contrary; but a reasonable doubt of its existence entitles the defendant to an acquittal, and if the testimony of the parties is in irreconcilable conflict, as to the fact of prior illicit intercourse between them, he is entitled to have charges given based on the supposed truth of his own testimony.

4. *Reasonable doubt; and "reason to believe."*—A charge asked, assert·ing the right to an acquittal if the jury "have reason to believe" certain facts hypothetically stated, is properly refused, since ·the expression is not the equivalent of *belief*, and does not correctly state the doctrine of reasonable doubt.

FROM the Circuit Court of Clay.

Tried before the Hon. LEROY F. BOX.

The defendant in this case was indicted, by the name of Richard *Munkers*, for the seduction of Dora Wright, an unmarried woman; and pleaded in abatement that his true name was Richard *Moncus*, and that he had always been known and called by that name. A demurrer was interposed to this plea, on the ground that each name was *idem sonans*, and it was sustained; and the cause was tried on issue joined on the plea of not guilty. On the trial, the prosecutrix swore positively to her seduction by the defendant, under promise of marriage, in December, 1887; that she allowed him to have sexual intercourse with her on two occasions during that month, and had never had intercourse with him or any other man at any other time. The defendant, testifying for himself, denied that he had ever made any promise of marriage, and said that he had had sexual intercourse with the prosecutrix once or twice each week, with intervals, from November, 1886, until her miscarriage in July, 1888. The State adduced evidence of the defendant's declarations or admissions, made to several different persons in December, 1887, or about that time, of his intention to marry the prosecutrix; and the court admitted this evidence, against the objection and exception of the defendant.

The court charged the jury, at the instance of the solicitor, "that if the evidence corroborates the prosecutrix in material facts, and satisfies the jury that she is worthy of credit, then the corroboration is sufficient." The defendant excepted to this charge as given, and also to the refusal of each of the following charges, which were asked by him in writing: (1.) "If the jury believe from the evidence that the defendant had sexual intercourse with Dora Wright in November, 1886, and continued in such acts of sexual intercourse until December, 1887, they must find him not guilty." (2.) "Although Dora Wright's general character may have been good in December, 1887, yet, if the jury have reason to believe from the evidence that the defendant had been having sexual intercourse with her once or twice a week, from November, 1886, to December, 1887; they must find him not guilty." (3.) "If the jury have a reason to believe from the evidence that the defendant had sexual intercourse with Dora Wright in November, 1886, and continued to have sexual intercourse with her once or twice a week until within a few weeks of July, 1888, then they must find him not guilty."

KELLY & SMITH, for appellant, cited *Nutt v. State*, 63 Ala. 184; *Lynes v. State*, 5 Porter, 236; 11 Atlantic Rep. 602; *Wilson v. State*, 73 Ala. 528.

W. L. MARTIN, Attorney-General, for the State.

CLOPTON, J.—The demurrer to the plea of misnomer, interposed by appellant to the indictment, presented for decision by the court the question, whether Richard *Munkers*, by which name the defendant is indicted, is *idem sonans* with Richard *Moncus*, which the plea avers to be his true name, by which he has always been called and known. Though this is strictly a question of pronunciation, when raised by demurrer, it may be treated as a question of law; but, in such case, the judgment of the court should express the conclusion of law from facts or rules of which judicial notice may be taken. When there is no generally received English pronunciation of the names as one and the same, and the difference in sound is not so slight as to be scarcely perceptible, the doctrine of *idem sonans* can not be applied without the aid of extrinsic evidence, unless, when sound and power are given to the letters, as required by the principles of pronunciation, the names may have the same enunciation, or sound. There is a material difference in orthography, and a perceptible difference between *Moncus* and *Munkers*, when ordinary sound and power are given to the variant letters. They are as different names as some which this court has held not to be *idem sonans.*—*Lynes v. State*, 5 Port. 236; *Humphrey v. Whitten*, 17 Ala. 30; *Nutt v. State*, 63 Ala. 180; *Adams v. State*, 67 Ala. 89. If by local usage the names have the same pronunciation, it becomes a question of fact, which must be referred to the jury. The court erred in

[Munkers v. The State.]

sustaining the demurrer to the plea. The State should have taken issue, or replied.

The defendant was convicted of seduction, under section 4015 of Code, 1886, which declares: "No indictment or conviction shall be had under this section, on the uncorroborated testimony of the woman upon whom the seduction is charged." This clause of the statute was fully considered in *Cunningham v. State*, 73 Ala. 51. It was then construed as not requiring that other witnesses shall testify to every fact testified to by the woman; but that its requirements are met, when the corroboration is of some matter which is an element of the offense, and its effect is to satisfy the jury that the corroborated witness has testified truly. The true rule is stated as follows: "That the corroboration shall be such as to convince the jury, beyond reasonable doubt, that the witness swore truly; but, to produce this conviction, it must be in a matter material to the issue, and must tend to connect the defendant with that material matter, and the matter itself must not be in its nature formal, indifferent, or harmless." This construction was re-affirmed in *Wilson v. State*, 73 Ala. 527, at a subsequent term of the court. The corroborating evidence consisted of the defendant's frequent visits to the female for whose seduction he was indicted, his escorting her to church, parties, and other social gatherings, and his admissions of an engagement and intention to marry her, made about the time of the alleged seduction. A promise of marriage is one of the alternative elements of the offense denounced by the statute. The corroboration was as to this act, with which the evidence connected defendant. His admissions were properly received in evidence. The phraseology of the charge of the court on this subject may be objectionable, as importing to the jury that the *corroborating testimony* was sufficient. Evidence may be sufficient to meet the statutory requirement as to corroboration, and yet not sufficient to satisfy the jury beyond a reasonable doubt that the woman swore truly.

The chastity of the woman, at the time of the criminal connection, is an essential ingredient of the offense. The statute provides, "No conviction shall be had, if on the trial it is proved that such woman was, at the time of the alleged offense, unchaste." The female, upon whom the seduction is charged, testified that, though the defendant had solicited her three or four months previously, she did not yield to his persuasions until December, 1887, during which month she

7

had sexual intercourse with him on two occasions, and had never had sexual intercourse with him or any other man prior to or since that time. This was the time elected by the State, and no evidence tending to show a seduction at any other time was offered. The defendant offered himself as a witness, and testified, that he first had sexual intercourse with her in November, 1886, under circumstances, which, if true, tended to show that it was through her inclination as well as his; and that he continued to do so once or twice a week, until a short time before her miscarriage in July, 1888. He further testified, that he did not promise to marry her. There is an irreconcilable conflict between his testimony and that of the female. It was for the jury to determine whom they would believe. If his testimony be true, as to which we intimate no opinion, the sexual intercourse, in its inception, was not induced by "temptation, deception, arts, flattery or a promise of marriage," and was continuous in practice. If such be the facts, the woman was unchaste at the time of the alleged seduction, in December, 1887. It was the right of defendant to have given to the jury instructions based on the hypothesis which his evidence tended to establish, thus submitting its credibility to them; especially as a reasonable doubt of the chastity of the woman is fatal to a conviction.—*Wilson v. State, supra.* Her chastity will be presumed, in the absence of evidence of a want of chastity; but, when there is contrary evidence, though it may be regarded insufficient, the court should not withdraw its consideration from the jury.

On the case as presented by the record, and in view of the fact that the woman and defendant are the only witnesses as to the act of seduction, the first charge asked by the defendant should have been given. The others are objectionable, in that acquittal is based on the ground that the jury have *reason* to believe from the evidence that the parties had previous sexual intercourse. Verdicts should be founded on belief, not a mere reason to believe. There may be a reason, yet insufficient as a predicate of belief. In this case, the belief of prior sexual intercourse should be strong enough to create a reasonable doubt of the pre-existing chastity of the woman.

Reversed and remanded.

Marks *v.* The State.

Indictment for Mnrder.

1. *General objection to evidence partly admissible.*.—A general objection to the admission of evidence, a part of which is admissible, may be overruled entirely.

2. *Error without injury in exclusion of evidence.*—As a general rule, the doctrine of error without injury does not obtain in criminal cases; yet, where evidence is erroneously excluded, but the record affirmatively shows that its admission could only have prejudiced the defense, the error will not work a reversal.

FROM the Circuit Court of Tuskaloosa.

Tried before the Hon. S. H. SPROTT. ·

The defendant in this case, Dinah Marks, was indicted for the murder of Julia Cannon; was convicted of manslaughter in the first degree, and sentenced to the penitentiary for ten years. The only exceptions reserved during the trial relate to the exclusion of evidence, as shown in the opinion of the court.

COCHRANE & FITTS, for appellant.

W. L. MARTIN, Attorney-General, for the State.

McCLELLAN, J.—E. R. King, a witness for the State, testified on his examination in chief to several distinct matters, each having a tendency to inculpate the defendant, and each bearing the same relation to defendant's motion to exclude, to the overruling of which an exception was reserved. This witness' testimony was, in effect, that at the time of the crime he was marshal of the city of Tuskaloosa, but had nothing to do with the arrest of the defendant; that after her commitment he found some bloody clothing of the defendant; that about Tuesday of the week after she was put in jail, he carried the clothing to her in jail; that she claimed it, and attempted to explain the appearance of blood on the garments; that he then left her; that a few days afterwards she sent for him, and he went to her again on Friday of that week; that she then made certain statements to him about the homicide with which she was charged;

that he made no threats, nor held out any inducements, nor
made any promises to get her to confess, but that she commenced the conversation herself, without any suggestion of
any kind on his part; that her statements to him were purely
voluntary on her part; and that she then proceeded to tell
him the facts and circumstances of the homicide, which the
witness then repeated to the jury. At the conclusion of the
examination in chief of this witness, during which he had
testified to all the foregoing facts, the bill of exceptions sets
forth, "The defendant then moved the court to exclude this
testimony from the jury; the court overruled the motion,
and the defendant then and there in open court duly
excepted." Beyond all question, under the repeated decisions of this court, this motion to exclude went to all of the
testimony of the witness King on his examination in chief;
the exception to the overruling of the motion was, of necessity, likewise general, having reference to all of this evidence; and if any fact testified to by this witness was competent, the appellant can take nothing by the exception, though
other parts of the evidence against which it is directed
should be palpably inadmissible.—3 Brick. Dig. p. 80,
§§ 41, 42; *Reynolds v. State*, 68 Ala. 502; *Boswell v. State*,
63 Ala. 307; *Black v. Pratt C. & C. Co.*, 85 Ala. 511.

Even should it be admitted, that the confessions deposed
to by this witness were inadmissible, because of the supposed continuing influence of antecedent inducements, as insisted by counsel, there can be no question of the competency
of the evidence relating to the clothing of the defendant;
and hence there was no error in the overruling of the motion
to exclude evidence of which this constituted a part.

The theory of the prosecution obviously was, that Isom
Cannon was implicated with the defendant in the homicide.
The confessions, which constituted the chief criminating
evidence, clearly connect Isom with the defendant on trial,
in the commission of the offense. The only legitimate
tendency of the evidence sought to be drawn out by the defendant, as to the relations between Isom and the deceased,
the pendency of an indictment against Isom and his flight,
was to corroborate the confessions, and support the State's
theory of the case. It is utterly inconceivable how this testimony could have benefitted the defendant. On the contrary, we can see that its influence on the jury could not
have been other than prejudicial to the defense. We are of
one mind that the exclusion of this evidence will not work a

reversal of the judgment. Without intending to impinge upon the former expressions of this court, to the effect that the doctrine of error without injury does not obtain in criminal proceedings, as that rule was applied in the several cases in which these expressions were employed, this case enforces the recognition of a limitation on, or an exception to the rule, which may be thus formulated: When this court can affirmatively determine from the record that evidence, to the exclusion of which the defendant excepts, could only have prejudiced the defense, the action of the trial court, though it may be technically erroneous, will not furnish ground for reversal.—*Vaughn v. State*, 83 Ala. 55; *Williams v. State, Ib.* 16; *Diggs v. State*, 49 Ala. 314; *Roberts v. State*, 68 Ala. 524; *Burns v. State*, 49 Ala. 373; *State v. Kinney*, 26 W. Va. 143; s. c., L. A. R. (Book 2), 668.

All of the testimony offered by the defendant, tending to connect Isom Cannon with the homicide, except perhaps that having reference to his habit of quarreling and threatening his wife, was properly excluded on other grounds. *Levison v. State*, 54 Ala. 520; *West v. State*, 76 Ala. 98.

The judgment of the Circuit Court must be affirmed.

DuBois v. The State.

87
105

Indictment for Selling Liquor in Prohibition District.

1. *Sale of liquor; purchase for another.*—A conviction can not be had for an illegal sale of liquor within a district in which a general prohibitory law is of force, on proof that the defendant bought a quart of liquor outside of the district, at the request of a third person, and delivered it to him within the district, on repayment of the money which he had advanced for it.

87
143

FROM the Circuit Court of Tallapoosa.

Tried before the Hon. JAMES R. DOWDELL.

The indictment in this case charged that the defendant, Barney DuBois, "sold vinous or spirituous liquor, without a license, and contrary to law."   On the trial, as appears from the bill of exceptions, the prosecution proved by one Mace "that he saw the defendant sell to one J. B. Thayer three pints of whiskey, for which said Thayer paid him $1.50; and that this occurred in said county, within a half-mile of Tallassee Factory, within twelve months before the finding of the indictment." The prosecution offered in evidence, also, the act of the General Assembly incorporating the Tallassee Factory, which prohibits the sale of spirituous liquors within four miles of the company's factories.—Sess. Acts 1851-2, p. 262. The defendant then testified in his own behalf, "and stated that, on the day before the alleged sale to Thayer, he was hired by Buckner & Son to go to Sentell's bar-room, which was more than four miles from Tallassee Factory, and purchase for them two quarts of whiskey; that he met said Thayer on his way, who asked him to get three pints of whiskey for him, and said that he would pay when he came for it next morning; that he (defendant) then went to said bar-room, and bought one gallon of whiskey, which was put in a jug, and for which he paid $4.00 out of his own money; that he let Buckner & Son have two quarts of whiskey out of this jug, and let said Thayer have three pints, for which Thayer paid him $1.50, the same price which he had paid." This being all the evidence, the court charged the jury, on request of the solicitor, "that they must find the defendant guilty, if they believed the evidence;" to which charge the defendant excepted.

JNO. A. TERRELL, for appellant, cited *Morgan v. State*, 81 Ala. 72; *Campbell v. State*, 79 Ala. 271; *Young v. State*, 58 Ala. 358.

W. L. MARTIN, Attorney-General, for the State.

STONE, C. J.—If the testimony of the defendant be true, he neither sold, nor aided in selling the liquor to Thayer. He purchased it for Thayer, at a point which is shown to have been without the prohibited district. He was not interested in the sale, and in no sense was he the agent of the seller. He was agent of Thayer, the buyer, and did not assume to represent the seller. He advanced the money, not buying for his own use, but as an accommodation loan to Thayer, the purchaser. He made no profit, but received back only the money he had paid out for the liquor. If this testimony be true, the defendant is not guilty.—*Young v. State*, 58 Ala. 358; *Campbell v. State*, 79 Ala. 271; *Morgan v. State*, 81 Ala. 72.

Reversed and remanded.

Cotton *v.* The State.

Indictment for Larceny of Ox.

1. *Testimony of defendant in his own behalf.*—In a criminal case, if the defendant fails or declines to testify in his own behalf, his failure does not create any presumption against him, and is not the subject of comment by counsel (Code, § 4473); but, if he elects to testify, and fails or refuses to explain or rebut any criminating fact, when he can reasonably do so, this is a circumstance in the nature of an implied admission, on which counsel may comment, and which the jury may consider in determining his guilt or innocence.

FROM the Circuit Court of Pike.

Tried before the Hon. JOHN P. HUBBARD.

The defendant in this case was indicted for the larceny of an ox, the personal property of *Henry* Flowers; and was indicted by the name of "William Holland, *alias* John Cotton." On the trial, he reserved a bill of exceptions, as follows: "The State introduced evidence tending to show that one *Hussey* (?) Flowers owned a steer, which was missing; and that he and Rollin Ballard came to the beef-market in Troy, soon after the ox was missed, and there found the hide and horns, which they described as those of the missing steer. The market-man testified, that he bought the steer from the defendant a short time before that, and butchered it, and that the hide and horns found were those of the steer about which said Flowers and Ballard testified. The defendant introduced the affidavit sued out in a preliminary trial, under which he was bound over, made by the market-man; and the charge in the affidavit was against one John Holland, *alias* John Cotton. The defendant then testified that, after he was arrested, he asked Beasley, the market-man, why he had him arrested; and that Beasley told him, that a Mr. Davis told him that he (defendant) was the man who sold him the steer; which Beasley denied. The defendant was sworn and examined on his own request, and refused to deny that he took the steer, or that he sold it to Beasley. The time and venue were properly proved, and this was all the evidence in the case. In his argument to the jury, the solicitor commented on the fact, that the defendant had failed to make the above denial; and thereupon, after the court had

given an oral charge to the jury, the defendant requested the
following charge in writing: 'Unless the jury are satisfied
beyond a reasonable doubt of the guilt of the defendant, by
the other evidence in the case except the evidence of his
refusal to deny the charge, then the defendent is not guilty.'
The court refused to give this charge, and the defendant excepted to its refusal."

W. L. MARTIN, Attorney-General, for the State.

SOMERVILLE, J.—Where a defendant in a criminal
prosecution elects to become a witness in his own behalf, as
he may do under the statute, he waives the constitutional
guaranty which protects him from answering questions
touching the merits of the case which may tend to criminate
him.   He may be examined by the State as to all material
facts pertinent to his guilt, and his failure to explain or rebut
any criminating fact, where he reasonbly can do so, is a circumstance which may be considered by the jury as prejudicial to his innocence.   This being so, it is clearly in reason,
that his silence or refusal to testify as to such fact may become the subject of legitimate criticism on the part of the
State's counsel, just as the testimony of any other witness
may be under like circumstances.   And the guilt or innocence of the defendant is to be determined on the entire
evidence, including the testimony of the defendant himself.
The authorities fully sustain this view.—*Clarke v. State*,
ante, p. 71, at present term; *Stover v. People*, 56 N. Y. 315;
State v. White, 27 Amer. Rep. 137, *note* 144; Whart. C. Ev.
(9th Ed.), §§ 432-3; *Clarke v. State*, 78 Ala. 474; 56 Am.
Rep. 45.

It is only where the defendant fails to become a witness
at all, or to request to become one, that section 4473 of the
Code affords him any protection against the criticism of counsel.   In such event, his failure to become a witness is not
allowed to create any unfavorable presumption against him,
nor to be the subject of any comment by counsel.—Crim.
Code, 1886, § 4473.

The charge requested by the defendant was based on the
false idea, that nothing the defendant said, or failed to say,
of a criminative character, should be allowed to have any
weight whatever with the jury in securing his conviction;
and erroneously affirmed, that they should acquit him, unless
they are satisfied beyond a reasonable doubt of his guilt by

other evidence in the case, irrespective of his own testimony on the stand, including any implied admission of guilt. The charge was palpably erroneous, and was properly refused.

Affirmed.

Skinner v. The State.

Indictment for Gaming in Public House.

1. *Trial by court, without jury; how considered on error or appeal.* When a criminal case is submitted to the decision of the court without a jury, as authorized by a special statute, the decision of the court on a question of fact, as to which the evidence is conflicting, or where inferences are to be drawn dependent on its sufficiency, will not be reversed, unless a verdict would be set aside on the same evidence; but, when the facts are undisputed, and only a legal conclusion is to be drawn from them, the decision is regarded as if given in charge to the jury, and its correctness is a question of law.

2 *Gaming; what is public house.*—A room in the second story of a building, rented and occupied as a private bed-room, and accessible by a pair of steps running up on the outside, through a front hall with which it was connected by a door, is not a public house within the statute against gaming (Code, § 4052), because the front hall is public, and is used once or twice a week as a dancing hall.

FROM the Criminal Court of Pike.

Tried before the Hon. H. C. WILEY, as special judge.

W. L. PARKS, for the appellant, cited *Dale v. State*, 27 Ala. 31; *Wilson v. State*, 31 Ala. 371.

WM. L. MARTIN, Attorney-General, for the State, cited *Cochran v. State*, 30 Ala. 542; *Smith v. State*, 52 Ala. 384; *Bentley v. State*, 32 Ala. 596; *Cawthorn v. State*, 63 Ala. 157; *Summers v. State*, 70 Ala. 16; *Gilliam v. State*, 71 Ala. 10; *Wren v. State*, 70 Ala. 1.

CLOPTON, J.—Appellant was convicted, in the Criminal Court of Pike county, of the offense of betting at a game played with dice in a public house, under section 4057 of Code of 1886. A jury not having been demanded, as provided by the act establishing the Criminal Court, the facts were properly triable by the presiding judge. In such case, his finding of fact will not be reversed on appeal, unless so clearly erroneous that the verdict of a jury would be set aside by the trial court, if rendered on the same testimony. *Jacques v. Horton*, 76 Ala. 238; *Gilliam v. State*, 71 Ala. 10; *Nooe v. Garner*, 70 Ala. 443. This rule applies, when there is a conflict in the evidence, or inferences are to be drawn therefrom dependent upon its sufficiency; but it has no application where the judgment of the court is a conclusion of law from undisputed facts.—*Hardy v. Ingram*, 84 Ala. 544.

The constituents of the offense, with which defendant was charged, consist in betting at a game played with cards or dice, or any device or substitute therefor, at one of the interdicted places. The finding as to the first constituent—that defendant bet at a game played with dice—depends on the sufficiency of the evidence to establish the fact beyond a reasonable doubt. To this finding the rule applies. But the finding as to the second constituent—that the game was played in a public house, within the meaning of the statute —must be regarded a conclusion of law from undisputed facts, there being no contradiction in the evidence, and no such inference of fact to be drawn therefrom; and it should be considered the same as if, on trial by jury, the court had so instructed them. Otherwise, when the accused does not demand a jury, he would be deprived on appeal of the benefit of exception to an erroneous ruling on a question of law.

The undisputed facts are: The game was played in a building, the first story of which was used and occupied as a storehouse; in the second story there was a public hall, used, once and sometimes twice a week, as a dancing hall; and at one end of the hall there were two rooms, which were approached by going up a stairway on the outside of the building, into the hall, and entering the room through a door opening into the hall. The game was played in one of these rooms, which was rented by Pres Thomas, and occupied by him as a private bed-room. The hall was under the control and management of the owner of the building. The room was controlled by Thomas, who held and occupied it as a tenant of the owner. The room and the hall were under the control of different persons. Whether a room, situated and occupied as this was, is a public house within the meaning of the statute, was decided more than thirty years ago. It was held, that separate parts of the same building, disconnected and appropriated to distinct and separate uses, were the same in law as if they were two buildings, so far as this offense

[Allen v. The State.]

is concerned; and that a room, rented and occupied by one person as a bed-room, does not partake of the character of another part of the same building used by another person in a public manner, and for public purposes, so as to warrant a conviction of the statutory offense.—*Dale v. State*, 27 Ala. 31; *Wilson v. State*, 31 Ala. 371.

Since this construction was placed upon it, the statute has been re-enacted several times, without change in phraseology. The room being rented and occupied by Thomas as his sleeping apartment, and under his exclusive control, we are forced to hold, under the influence of the previous decisions, that it is not a public house within the meaning of the statute.

Reversed and remanded.

Allen *v.* The State.

Indictment for Rape.

1. *Complaint of prosecutrix; impeaching witness by proof of contradictory statements.*—On a prosecution for rape, the mother of the prosecutrix having testified that her daughter complained to her immediately after the commission of the offense, the defendant has a right to elicit the particulars of the complaint; and he may impeach the witness, a proper predicate having been laid, by proof of prior contradictory statements out of court.

2. *Charge as to testimony of defendant.*—Where the defendant has testified in his own behalf, a charge instructing the jury that, in considering what weight they will give to his statements, ' it is their duty to remember that he is the defendant, and interested in the result of the verdict: and they may, for this reason, if they think it sufficient, entirely disregard his statement, if it is in conflict with the other evidence,'' is erroneous, and ground of reversal.

3. *Consent implied from conduct.*—Although the prosecutrix may not have consented in fact, yet, if her conduct towards the defendant, at the time of the alleged rape, was such as to create in his mind an honest and reasonable belief that she had consented, or was willing for him to have connection with her, a conviction should not be had; and the court should so instruct the jury, on request.

FROM the Circuit Court of Russell.

Tried before the Hon. JESSE M. CARMICHAEL.

The defendant is this case, Isham Allen, a freedman, was indicted for committing a rape on Annie Capers, a negro girl about sixteen years old; was convicted under the charge of the court, and sentenced to the penitentiary for life. On the trial, as appears from the bill of exceptions, the prosecutrix testified to the commission of the offense by the defendant, stating time, place, and circumstances; while the defendant, testifying in his own behalf, admitted that he had connection with her at the time and place named, but said that it was with her consent, and that he had had connection with her before. Aggie Capers, the mother of the prosecutrix, was examined as a witness for the State, and testified that the prosecutrix, immediately on her return home, had complained to her that the defendant "had ravished her;" and that she, witness, then went to the house of Capt. Glenn, on the same evening, and talked with him about it. The defendant then asked her, "if she did not then tell Capt. Glenn that Annie said, 'Isham tried to rape her, but did not do it, because she called some one and stopped him'; to which she replied, that she did not tell Capt. Glenn this." Capt. Glenn was afterwards introduced as a witness by the defendant, and was asked if, on the evening of the alleged rape, when the mother of the prosecutrix came to see him, "she did not tell him that Annie said, 'Isham tried to rape her, but did not do it, because she called some one and stopped him';" to which question the court sustained an objection, and the defendant excepted.

The court gave the following charge to the jury, on request of the solicitor: "In considering the statement made on oath by the defendant, and what weight they may give to it, it is the duty of the jury to remember that he is the defendant, and interested in the result of the verdict; and they may, for this reason, if they think it sufficient, entirely disregard his said statement, if it is in conflict with the other evidence in the case.". The defendant excepted to this charge, and also to the refusal of the following charge, which was asked by him in writing: "(3.) If the jury believe from the evidence that the conduct of the prosecutrix towards the defendant, at the time of the alleged rape, was such as to create in the mind of the defendant an honest and reasonable belief that she consented, or was willing for him to have connection with her, they must acquit the defendant."

JOHN V. SMITH, for appellant, cited *Griffin v. State*, 76 Ala. 29; *Barnett v. State*, 83 Ala. 40; *Williams v. State*, 74 Ala. 18; *McQuirk v. State*, 84 Ala. 435.

W. L. MARTIN, Attorney-General, for the State, cited 2 Brick. Digest, 548, § 117.

[Allen v. The State.]

McCLELLAN, J.—1. The defendant had the right to elicit from the witness Aggie Capers the particulars of the complaint made to her by the prosecutrix.—*Griffin v. State*, 76 Ala. 29; *Scott v. State*, 48 Ala. 420; *Barnett v. State*, 83 Ala. 40. This evidence was material, therefore; and it was competent to impeach the witness, by showing that she had stated these particulars out of court to be other than those to which she testified on the trial. This was proposed to be done by asking the witness Glenn, whether Aggie had not told him that the prosecutrix complained to her that the defendant had tried to rape her, but had not succeeded, a sufficient predicate having been laid for impeachment in this case; and the refusal of the court to allow this question to be put and answered was erroneous.

2. It is unquestionably the duty of the jury to bear in mind, in reaching their conclusions on the evidence, every circumstance properly brought to their attention, affecting the credibility of witnesses who have deposed before them. The fact that a witness is a party to the suit, and interested in the result to be worked out by the verdict, is, both in civil and criminal cases, such a circumstance, and should, therefore, be remembered by them in their deliberations. It is also clearly within the power and right of the jury, to wholly disbelieve and discard the testimony of any witness, whether a party in interest or to the record or not; but this they are not authorized to do arbitrarily and capriciously, in any case, or with respect to any witness. Certainly the one isolated fact of interest, however great, on the part of the witness, can not be affirmed, as a matter of law, to authorize the jury to disregard his testimony. Nor, even when to interest is added a conflict between the evidence of such witness and other evidence in the case, does it follow that he is not entitled to credence. It would be entirely competent for the jury to accord credibility to such testimony, and reach the conclusion to which it pointed, notwithstanding its infirmities, both of interest and contradiction, as there might be overbalancing infirmity in the conflicting testimony. The charge given at the request of the State was violative of these well-settled principles. It authorized the utter disregard of the defendant's testimony, for the two reasons alone, that he was the defendant, and that he was contradicted by other witnesses, although, notwithstanding both these facts, the jury might still have believed him. The court should not have gone further in this connection, than

[Ex parte Pierce]

to instruct the jury that, in determining the weight they
would give to the defendant's testimony, they should
consider—along with all other circumstances having any
bearing on the matter—the fact that he was the defendant, and the fact, if they so found, that his testimony was in
conflict with other evidence in the case.—*Williams v. State*,
74 Ala. 26; *Chappell v. State*, 71 Ala. 322; *Beasley v. State*,
Ib. 328; *State v. White*, 27 Amer. Rep. 144, note.

3. The third charge requested by defendant should have
been given. It asserts a correct legal proposition, and there
was evidence tending to show conduct, from which a belief
that the woman had consented might have resulted, though
there had been no expression of consent, and though there
may, in fact, have been no consent at all.—*McQuirk v. State*,
84 Ala. 435.

The judgment of the Circuit Court is reversed, and the
cause remanded.

Ex parte **Pierce.**

*Application for Mandamus to Probate Judge, on Refusal
to grant License for Retailing Spirituous Liquors.*

1. *Prohibitory liquor laws in Butler county; amending and revising
statutes.*—Beat No. 12 in Butler county was exempted from the operation
of the general law regulating the granting of licenses to retail liquors,
under the provisions of a special statute approved November 27th,
1886, which authorized a local election to determine whether or not the
sale of liquors in that beat should be prohibited; another statute was
approved February 19th, 1887, which prohibited the sale of liquors
"within five miles of Goodwater Academy, Coosa county, and in the
county of Butler except in Beat No. 12," while a general prohibitory
law, applicable to the whole of Butler county, was approved on the
26th February, 1887, a subsequent day of the same session of the General Assembly; and each of these two acts went into effect on the 1st
January, 1888. On the 20th February, 1889, during the next session of
the General Assembly, the act of February 19th, 1887, was amended by
excepting the town of Goodwater from its operation; but the amendatory law set out the title and the 1st section of the former act in full,
including the exemption in favor of said Beat No. 12, and re-enacted it
with the addition of a proviso excepting the town of Goodwater. *Held,*
that the effect of this last statute was to revive the exemption in favor
of said Beat No. 12, although it had been repealed by the general prohibitory law of February 26th, 1887.

[Ex parte Pierce.]

APPLICATION by petition on the part of William Pierce,
for a writ of *mandamus* directed to Hon. L. M. LANE, probate judge of Butler county, requiring him to issue to the
petitioner a license to retail spirituous liquors in the town
of Greenville. The petitioner had complied with all the
statutory pre-requisites, and a license was refused solely on
the ground that Greenville was governed by the general
prohibitory law of February 26th, 1887, which went into
effect on the 1st January, 1888, and by its terms applied to
the whole of Butler county. An application for a *mandamus*
was first made to Hon. JOHN P. HUBBARD, the presiding circuit judge, and was by him refused.

The case involves a consideration of the effect of the following statutes: (1.) By an act approved December 12th, 1882,
the general law (Code, 1876, § 1544) was amended "so far
as it relates to the counties of Pike, Butler and Coffee," by
requiring the applicant for a license to retail spirituous liq-
ors to produce the recommendation of a majority of the
qualified electors residing in the precinct.—Sess. Acts
1882-3, p. 272. (2.) On the 27th November, 1886, this
act was amended so far as it applied to Precinct No. 12,
which includes the town of Greenville, by providing for an
election in the precinct, to ascertain the sense of the people
on the question of prohibition.—Sess. Acts 1886-87, p. 706.
An election was held under the provisions of this act, and
resulted in favor of "No Prohibition." (3.) On the 19th
February, 1887, a later day of the same session of the General Assembly, an act was passed prohibiting the sale of
liquor "within five miles of Goodwater Academy, Coosa
county, and in the county of Butler except Beat No. 12 of
said county;" but this act, by its terms, did not go into
effect until January 1st, 1888.—Sess. Acts 1886-7, p. 695.
(4.) On the 26th February, 1887, a still later day of the
same session, another act was passed prohibiting the sale of
liquor in Butler county generally, not making any exceptions; and this act went into effect on the 1st January, 1888.
Sess. Acts 1886-7, p. 700. (5.) On the 20th February,
1889, an act was passed by the General Assembly amending
the 1st section of said act of February 19th, 1887, by excepting the town of Goodwater from its provisions; the
enacting part being as follows: "SEC. 1. *Be it enacted*," &c.,
"that section 1 of 'An act to prohibit the sale, giving away,
delivery, transfer, parting with, procuring, or other disposition of spirituous, vinous or malt liquors, or any intoxicating

bitters or mixtures, within five miles of Goodwater Academy, Coosa county, and in the county of Butler except Beat 12 of said county,' approved February 19th, 1887, be amended so as to read as follows: SEC. 1. *Be it further enacted*," &c., "that it shall be unlawful for any person to sell, give away, deliver, transfer, part with, procure, or otherwise dispose of spirituous, vinous or malt liquors, or other intoxicating bitters or mixtures, within five miles of Goodwater Academy, Coosa county, and in the county of Butler except Beat No. 12 of said county; *provided*, the provisions of this act shall not apply to social drinking in family circles; *and provided further*, that the provisions of this act shall not apply to the corporate limits of the town of Goodwater."—Sess. Acts 1888-9, p. 512. The second proviso to this act, and a third proviso, which has no connection with this case, show the only changes made in the amended act of February 19th, 1887.

CHAS. WILKINSON, for the petitioner, cited *Riggs v. Brewer*, 64 Ala. 285; *George v. Skeates & Co.*, 19 Ala. 738; *Wilkinson v. Ketler*, 59 Ala. 308; *Washington v. State*, 72 Ala. 276; Endlich on Statutes, § 187, p. 259.

PER CURIAM.—The present application presents a single question, namely: Whether the act approved February 20th, 1889—Sess. Acts, 512—repealed the prohibition statute for Butler county, approved February 26, 1887—Sess. Acts, 700-1. It is manifest that the two statutes are incompatible, and both can not stand. In such case, the rule is that the latest expression of the legislative will must dominate the older.

It is true, that the act of February 19, 1887—Sess. Acts, 195—had been superseded and repealed, so far as it affected Butler county, by the prohibitory enactment of February 26, 1887. After that time, the provision in the older statute, which exempted Beat No. 12 in Butler county from its operation, ceased to be the law. The act of •February 20, 1889, however, relieved the exemption of Beat No. 12 of the prohibitory provision, and restored it to its former *status*. Under our rulings, we feel constrained to hold that the act of February 20, 1889, revived and re-enacted section 1 of the act approved February 19, 1887, and thenceforth the prohibitory liquor law for Butler county was and is not of force in Beat No. 12 of that county.—*Wilkinson v. Ketler*,

59 Ala. 306; *Tally v. Grider*, 66 Ala. 119; *State v. Warford*, 84 Ala. 15.

A rule is ordered to be issued from this court, directed to the Hon. L. M. LANE, judge of probate of Butler county, commanding him to show cause to the next term of the Circuit Court of Butler county, why a peremptory writ of *mandamus* shall not issue, commanding him to issue the license prayed for by the petitioner.

Let the costs of this proceeding be paid by the petitioner.

Carter *v.* The State.

Indictment for Assault.

1. *Mistake as to identity of person assaulted, and drunkenness, as defenses.*—Neither a mistake in the identity of the person assaulted, nor the drunkenness of the defendant at the time, is a defense to a prosecution for an assault.

FROM the County Court of Jackson.

Tried before the Hon. R. SCOTT PARKS, as special judge.

The defendant in this case was indicted for an assault on a young lady, pleaded not guilty to the charge, but was convicted, and fined one cent. The evidence adduced on the trial, all of which is set out in the bill of exceptions, showed that the defendant, on the day of the assault, had been drinking all the morning, and was very drunk; that as the young lady passed him on the street, where he was sitting down, he got up and staggered after her, extending his hands, and declaring, with an oath, his intention to have intercourse with her; that she screamed, and jumped aside, and he fell on his face, and was picked up by the town marshal, who was standing some distance off. The evidence for the defense tended to show that the defendant mistook the young lady for a common prostitute of the town, to whom he had paid some money in the morning, and who had invited him to follow her; but the defendant, testifying in his own behalf, said that he was too drunk to remember anything about the assault. The court charged the jury, among other things, as follows: "To constitute an assault, there must be an attempt, though interrupted, to inflict personal violence; and

8

the jury may look to the evidence, to determine whether or not the defendant intended to commit an assault. The law looks to the intention, to determine the guilt of persons; and it always maintains, that a person can not be guilty who has an innocent mind. If the jury believe that the defendant intended to inflict personal violence on another person, but was mistaken in the person, that will not excuse him. If the jury believe that he had a reckless disregard, and did not care whom he dealt with, that will not excuse him. If he intended to violate forcibly the person of a prostitute, that will not excuse him; but the jury may look to the evidence whether or not he intended an assault. The fact that the defendant was in a state of intoxication can not excuse him." To each of these parts of the general charge of the court the defendant duly excepted.

WM. L. MARTIN, Attorney-General, for the State.

SOMERVILLE, J.—It is unquestionably the law, that if the defendant intended to inflict personal violence on another person than the one assaulted, a mere mistake in the identity of the person would not excuse him. It was no justification of the assault charged in this case that the defendant was drunk, or that he erroneously believed the person assaulted to be a common prostitute. The charges of the court correctly stated the law on this, and other questions involved. The exceptions taken were all properly overruled.
Affirmed.

Squire v. The State.

Indictment for Murder.

1. *Charge as to self-defense; when properly refused.*—In a prosecution for murder, a charge requested, instructing the jury that the defendant is entitled to an acquittal, if the assault was unprovoked by him, and he appeared at the time to be so menaced as to create a reasonable apprehension of danger to his life, or of grievous bodily harm, and could not have retreated without danger to his life or person, is properly refused, when the evidence as to the assault is conflicting, and the defendant's own testimony shows that, when he fired the fatal shot, he was beyond the reach of the axe in the hands of the deceased.

FROM the Circuit Court of Clarke.

Tried before the Hon. WM. E. CLARKE.

The defendant in this case, Ben Squire, was indicted, jointly with one Dick Hawthorn, for the murder of William Johnson, by shooting him with a pistol; was found guilty of murder in the second degree, and sentenced to the penitentiary for the term of twenty years. The homicide occurred one Sunday morning in July, or August, 1887, at the house of one Levi Corsey, or in his front yard, under the following circumstances, as detailed by the eye-witnesses, said Corsey and his two daughters: The deceased and one Eden boarded at Corsey's house, and were sitting out on the front porch, in company with Corsey and his daughters, when the defendant and said Hawthorn came to the front gate, and called them out. Some angry words passed between the parties, when, as Corsey and his daughters each testified, the defendant and Hawthorn each drew a pistol; but Eden picked up a long stick, or pole, and knocked the defendant's pistol out of his hand, and then ran into the house and got a gun. The defendant picked up his pistol, and, on Hawthorn saying "Shoot the damned rascal," shot the defendant in the side; and on the appearance of Eden, with the gun in his hands, they both ran off. The deceased died, from the effect of the wound, on the next day. The defendant thus testified in his own behalf: "I went to Levi Corsey's gate with Dick Hawthorn. Dick hailed, and Levi asked us to come in. I told him we didn't have time, and that we wanted to see Eden and Johnson. Eden and Johnson started out to the gate. Eden pulled off his coat, and said, '*If you want a fuss, you can get it.*' I told Dick to tell him that we did not want any fuss, but just a quiet talk. Eden picked up a stick, and knocked Dick down; and he then struck me on the head, and broke the stick, and then knocked the pistol out of my hand. I picked up my pistol, and Eden went into the house. Levi and Adeline Corsey came out, and told us all to stop. Johnson got an axe, and made a lick at me with it. I backed off some fifteen steps, and shot him. When I fired, Johnson walked off towards the house, carrying the axe with him, and dropped it between the gate and the house. Eden then came out with his gun, and snapped at me, and Dick and I ran off." An axe was afterwards picked up at the spot. On these facts, the defendant requested the following charges to the jury, and duly excepted to their refusal: (1.) "If the jury believe from the evidence that the assault was unpro-

voked by the defendant, and that he appeared to be so menaced at the time as to create a reasonable apprehension of
danger to his life, or of grievous bodily harm; the defendant
is entitled to an acquittal, provided he could not have
retreated without danger to his life or person." (2.) "If
the defendant did nothing to bring on the difficulty, but
only fought in necessary self-defense, then he should be
acquitted."

W. L. MARTIN, Attorney-General, for the State.

CLOPTON, J.—There was no error in the refusal to
charge the jury, at the request of defendant, if they believed
from the evidence that the assault was unprovoked by him,
and he appeared to be so much menaced at the time as to
create a reasonable apprehension of danger to his life, or of
grievous bodily harm, he is entitled to an acquittal, provided
he could not have retreated without danger to his life or
person. If it be conceded that the hypothesis of the charge
sufficiently supposes the facts essential to the plea of self-
defense, it was properly refused on two grounds: First, it
assumes as a fact, that an assault was made upon defendant
by deceased; which, being disputed, and dependent on conflicting oral testimony, was a question exclusively for the
jury. A charge which assumes as proved a controverted
fact, is an invasion of the province of the jury, and properly
refused. Second, the hypothesis is not sustained by the
proof. The bill of exceptions purports to set out the entire
evidence; and it fails to disclose any tending to show, or
from which an inference can be drawn, that defendant appeared to be so menaced as to create in the mind of a reasonable man an honest belief of present, impending peril, or
that he could not have retreated without danger. Defendant
himself is the only witness, who testifies to an assault by deceased. Assuming the truth of his testimony, and using his
own language, when he was struck at with the axe, he "backed
off some fifteen steps and shot him." Evidently he was at
that time beyond the reach of the axe. There is no pretense
that deceased was pursuing, or attempting to pursue him;
and no reasons are shown, why he could not have retreated
with safety, so as to have avoided any necessity to take life,
as easily as he escaped a blow with the axe by backing the
distance of fifteen steps.—*Williams v. State*, 81 Ala. 1.

Affirmed.

Wilson *v.* The State.

Prosecution for Trespass after Warning.

1. *"Legal cause, or good excuse" for trespass.*—In a prosecution for trespass after warning (Code, § 3874), by driving a loaded wagon along a neighborhood road, which had been opened through the lands of the prosecutor, by his permission, to give convenient access to a cane-mill, and which was afterwards closed by him; it being shown that the defendant might have had access to the mill "by cutting out a new road, a short distance through open piney woods, perhaps 100 yards, and cause-waying a small boggy branch;" *held*, that a "legal cause or good excuse" for the trespass was not shown.

FROM the Circuit Court of Coffee.

Tried before the Hon. JESSE M. CARMICHAEL.

This was a prosecution for trespass after warning, instituted by H. A. Goodman against W. J. Wilson, and was commenced before a justice of the peace, on the 8th November, 1888. On the trial in the Circuit Court, as the bill of exceptions shows, the prosecutor testified, "that he warned the defendant on the 6th November, 1888, not to go on his lands or premises, and that the defendant went on the land the next day with his oxen and wagon;" and he further testified, on cross-examination, "that the part of the land that the defendant went on was a settlement road, leading from the public road to William Haney's cane-mill." It was admitted that the land belonged to said Goodman, and that he had obstructed the road by placing a pole across it, which rested on the fence on one side, and on a stump on the other. Said Haney testified, on the part of the defense, that he had a cane-mill at his place, about one mile from the public road, where he had lived about five years; that when he first moved to the place, he cut out a road from his house to the public road; that Goodman told him he might cut out a straight road from his house to the public road, putting it by the side of his fence, and he should have no trouble about it, as it would protect the fence from fire; that he then cut out a straight road by the side of Goodman's fence, a part of it being cut out by one Carroll, who lived between him and the public road; "that said road had been used by all the neighbors in the settlement ever since, about two years,

and is still open and in general use by all persons who desire
to travel it, except that Goodman had put a pole across it,
and had posted up notice not to travel it;" also, that the defendant had hauled a load of cane to his mill on the 5th
November, and was hauling another on the 7th, when he
committed the alleged trespass, having been warned on the
6th; and that he could not have got to the mill in any other
way, only by cutting out a new road, a short distance through
open piney woods, perhaps 100 yards, and cause-waying a
small boggy branch." Said Carroll testified, also, that the
road was cut out by himself and Haney, by permission of
Goodman; "that it runs through wild and uninclosed land
belonging to Goodman, near his fence, and is still opened
and used by all the neighbors, and the public who desire to
pass along it, over the protest of Goodman." This being all
the evidence, the defendant requested the court to charge the
jury, "that if they believed from the evidence that the defendant had carried a part of his cane to Haney's mill before
he was warned not to travel said road, they may consider
whether or not it was a good excuse for him to carry the
balance of his cane along the road under the proof in the
case." The court refused this charge, and the defendant
excepted.

W. L. MARTIN, Attorney-General, for the State.

McCLELLAN, J.—The charge requested by the defendant was properly refused. It was in evidence, that "by cut-
ing out a new road, a short distance through open piney
woods, perhaps 100 yards, and cause-waying a small boggy
branch," any necessity the defendant would otherwise have
been under to use the road across the land of the prosecutor,
which he had been warned not to do, would have been obvi-
ated. Without undertaking to define those terms as employed in the statute creating the offense of trespass after
warning (Code, § 3874), we are satisfied that there was no
such conduct on the part of the prosecutor, with respect to
the opening of the road originally, and no such necessity for
the defendant to use it after warning, as would furnish "legal
cause or good excuse" for the act charged.

This being the only point reserved for consideration, the
judgment of the Circuit Court is affirmed.

[The State v. Sloss.]

The State *v.* Sloss.

*Action against Agent, for Taxes assessed against Foreign
Corporation.*

1. *When action lies.*—To sustain an action against the agent of a foreign corporation engaged in the business of lending money on mortgage, for taxes assessed on the gross receipts of its business, a valid assessment must be shown, as claimed, against that particular corporation.

2. *Name of corporation; variance.*—The *American Mortgage Company of Scotland,* and the *American Mortgage Company,* are, *prima facie,* different corporations; and an assessment of taxes against the latter, if regular on its face, will not support an action against an agent of the former.

3. *Assessment of taxes against foreign corporation.*—An assessment of taxes against a foreign corporation, in these words: "Value of personal property, less exemptions, $15,200; State tax, $91.20; county tax, $76.00; total tax, $167.20," does not show an assessment of two per cent. on the gross receipts of the corporation from its business in this State, and will not support an action against its agent to recover such assessment on receipts.

FROM the Circuit Court of Madison.
Tried before the Hon. H. C. SPEAKE.

This action was brought in the name of the State of Alabama, against Joseph H. Sloss, "agent of American Mortgage Company of Scotland," a foreign corporation alleged to be engaged in the business of lending money on mortgages of land in this State, to recover the sum of $200, said to have been assessed against said agent as taxes due from said corporation to the State of Alabama and Madison county, on the gross receipts of its business during the year 1885; and was commenced on the 2d June, 1887. On the trial, as appears from the bill of exceptions, the plaintiff proved by Alonzo Ware, deputy-assessor of Madison county in 1886, that after April 1st of that year, finding that the defendant, "as agent of the American Mortgage Company of Scotland, Limited," had not made any returns to the tax-assessor, as to the gross receipts of the company's business during the preceding year, he "proceeded to make a supplemental assessment from the best information he could get," and made an assessment as follows: "*American Mortgage Company:* Value of personal property, less exemptions, $15,200; State tax, $91.20; county tax, $76.00; total tax,

$167.20." Witness stated, that the assessment "should have been against the *American Mortgage Company of Scotland, Limited,*" and that the additional words were omitted "by a clerical error" on his part; but the court excluded this testimony, on objection by the defendant, and the plaintiff excepted. The defendant then moved to exclude all the testimony of the witness, "on account of the variance between it and the allegations of the complaint," and the court sustained the motion; to which the plaintiff excepted, and thereupon took a nonsuit.

Wm. RICHARDSON, for appellant, cited *Preston v. Dunham,* 52 Ala. 217; *Farris & McCurdy v. Dudley,* 78 Ala. 124; *Offutt v. Scott,* 47 Ala. 104; Burr. Taxation, 251.

L. W. DAY, and D. D. SHELBY, *contra,* cited *People v. Whipple,* 47 Cal. 618; Law of Assessments by D. W. Welty, 1886, §§ 60-62, notes.

STONE, C. J.—This suit is instituted against Sloss, "agent of American Mortgage Company of Scotland." The averments of the complaint show the suit is brought for the recovery of taxes due from, and assessed against the "American Mortgage Company of Scotland," a corporation of which Sloss was agent. The taxes claimed as due, and as having been assessed, accrued, if at all, and were assessed under section 6, subd. 8 of the Revenue Law, approved December 12, 1884.—Sess. Acts, pp. 10 and 11. We say they accrued, if at all, and were assessed under that provision of the Revenue Law, for that is the provision which allows suit and recovery against the agent of the "person, company, association or corporation, · · · who, by themselves or agent, is engaged in the business of loaning money, or thing of value, upon mortgage or lien upon any property in this State;" and the averments in the complaint prove that a recovery was claimed under that provision of the statute. This was necessary; for, without such averments, the complaint would have shown no right of recovery against Sloss, the mere agent of the tax-payer.

The attempted assessment of taxes in this case must be pronounced ineffectual and void, for more reasons than one. First: Taxes, such as those claimed in this case, must be assessed against the person, company, association, or corporation, which is liable for their payment. "American Mort-

[Hussey v. The State.]

gage Company," and "American Mortgage Company of Scotland," are not, *prima facie*, one and the same.—Burroughs Taxation, 203-4. The assessment was not against the corporation, of which Sloss, according to the averments of the complaint, was agent. Hence, the assessment did not tend to show assessed taxes, for which the statute made Sloss liable. Second: The entire assessment neither tends to show gross receipts, nor to show an assessment of two per-cent. on gross receipts. It shows the contrary. It sets down personal property of the tax-payer, valued at $15,200, and then fixes the State tax rate, not at two per-cent., the rate the statute prescribes, but at six mills, which was then our tax rate on property proper. In other words, the assessment was on "personal property," owned by the American Mortgage Company, and the suit seeks to recover from Sloss, agent of the American Mortgage Company of Scotland, taxes on the gross receipts derived from business done by that company. The assessment can, in no sense, maintain the claim asserted in the complaint, even if there had been no error in the name of the corporation.

Affirmed.

Hussey v. The State.

Indictment for Murder.

1. *Change of venue.*—In a criminal case, a change of venue is a matter of right, if the application is made in due time, and is supported by sufficient evidence (Code, § 4485); but it is properly refused, when, on all the evidence adduced for and against the application, the court is not reasonably satisfied that an impartial trial and an unbiased verdict could not reasonably be expected in the county in which the indictment was found.

2. *Same; counter affidavits.*—By the established practice in this and other States, on application for a change of venue, counter affidavits may be received against those offered in support of it; and this practice is not violative of the constitutional principle which gives to the accused the right to be "confronted by the witnesses against him."

3. *Dying declarations*—The declarations of the deceased in this case, made to different persons, at intervals, during the three days he lived after receiving the fatal wound, always expressing the belief that he would die from the effects of the wound, were properly admitted as evidence, although some of his friends declared to him their belief that he was not seriously wounded, and one of his attending physicians had expressed to him the hope that he might recover.

4. *Proof of character.*—A witness, testifying to the character of the

[Hussey v. The State.]

defendant as a peaceable and quiet man, may be asked whether he "ever heard of his having any other difficulty than the one in question," and may testify that he had not.

Objection to question and answer.—When a question is in proper form, and calls for evidence which is *prima facie* relevant and legal, the refusal to allow it is a reversible error, although the proposed or expected answer of the witness is not stated.

5. *Proof of character.*—Evidence of character, at least on direct examination, goes to general reputation only, and can not be extended to particular acts, or specified conduct; nor can a witness give his own opinion as to the person inquired about;—as, that he was a "model man," or "was a timid man, and would rather avoid than provoke a difficulty."

6. *Same; cross-examination of witness; impeaching.*—Witnesses for the prosecution having testified to the good reputation of the deceased as a peaceable and quiet man, and having denied, on cross-examination, that they had ever heard of certain specified personal difficulties in which he was said to have been involved; the defendant can not prove the existence and general notoriety of these difficulties, for the purpose of discrediting their testimony.

7. *Character of deceased; evidence as to.*—On a trial for murder, the prosecution may adduce evidence of the character of the deceased as a peaceable and quiet man, although the defense has only proved particular traits of his character, as a quick-tempered, violent man, easily provoked, and likely to provoke a difficulty.

8. *Charge as to effect of evidence of good character.*—The court may properly instruct the jury in a criminal case, that proof of good character is not permitted to go to them for the purpose of shielding the defendant from the consequences of his conduct, but simply as a circumstance to be considered by them with the other evidence in the case; that if, from all the evidence, they believe the defendant guilty beyond a reasonable doubt, they should say so as firmly against a man of good character as bad; that good character does not shield from the consequences of a criminal act, proved to the satisfaction of the jury beyond a reasonable doubt, though it may raise a reasonable doubt that the act was done with the criminal intent.

9. *Testimony of physician as expert; hearsay.*—A practicing physician, who examined the deceased after he was wounded, and has given his own diagnosis of the case, can not be allowed to testify that other physicians concurred with him in opinion.

10. *Wife as witness for husband.*—In a criminal case, the wife is not a competent witness for her husband.

FROM the Circuit Court of Madison.

Tried before the Hon. H. C. SPEAKE.

The bill of exceptions in this case purports to set out "all the material evidence," and the opinion of this court states the facts bearing on each point decided. The defendant reserved an exception "to so much of the general charge of the court as follows," the charge being given in writing: "All men, whether of good or bad character, are liable to punishment, and should receive punishment when they violate the laws of the land. Proof of good character, then, is not permitted to go to the jury for the purpose of shielding the defendant from the consequences of his conduct, but simply as a circumstance to be considered by the jury with the other evidence in the case; and if, from all the evidence in the case, the jury believe the defendant to be guilty beyond a reasonable doubt, they should say so by their verdict, as firmly against a man of good character as of bad. Good character does not shield from the consequences of a criminal act, proved to the satisfaction of a jury beyond a reasonable doubt, though it may raise a reasonable doubt of the act having been done with the criminal intent."

R. A. McClellan, Milton Humes, and R. C. Brickell, for appellant.—(1.) The orders for a special *venire*, including the jurors *drawn*, instead of those *in attendance*, were erroneous.—*Goley v. State*, 85 Ala. 333; *Jackson v. State*, 77 Ala. 18; *Posey v. State*, 73 Ala. 490; 55 Ala. 61. The order for the special *venire* at the February term, 1889, when the trial was had, was also erroneous.—Code, § 4449; cases *supra*. (2.) The challenge to the array ought to have been allowed.—61 Ala. 169; 47 Ala. 726; 5 So. Car. 429; Th. & M. on Juries, 132, 144. That the challenge to the array was part of the record, see Proffatt, 153; 1 Denio, 281, 308; 4 Wend. 229, 239; 21 Wend. 509, 445; 6 Cowen, 555. (3.) One of the special jurors being also one of the regular jurors for the week, the list served was one less than the number ordered; and this was an error.—68 Ala. 515. If one name may be duplicated, why not twelve or more? (4.) The application for a change of venue ought to have been granted.—*Seams v. State*, 84 Ala. 410; 47 Ala. 68; 45 Ala. 32. That counter affidavits ought not to have been received, see 1 Bish. Crim. Pro., 72; 28 Ala. 28, 38. (5.) The dying declarations ought not to have been received. 78 Ala. 441, 471; 74 Ala. 1; 68 Ala. 502; 55 Ala. 39; 52 Ala. 192. (6.) The court erred in excluding the proposed evidence of character.—Whart. Cr. Ev. 57; 11 Ohio St. 114; 22 Minn. 407; 67 Ala. 67; 71 Ala. 351; 77 Ala. 18; 55 Ala. 28; 13 Ala. 718; 22 Ala. 23; 28 Ala. 53; 58 Iowa, 208; 68 Ind. 238; 51 Texas, 65; 33 Gratt. 413; 10 Cox, C. C. 25; 69 Eng. C. L. 877.

Wm. L. Martin, Attorney-General, and D. D. Shelby, *contra.*—(1.) The application for a change of venue came too late.—*Fallin v. State*, 86 Ala. 13; *Shackelford v. State*, 79 Ala. 26; 3 Amer. & Eng. Ency. 102–05; 72 Ill. 95; 75 Ill. 198; 71 Ill. 250. It was properly denied on its

merits.—*Kelly v. State*, 52 Ala. 367; *Seams v. State*, 84 Ala.
410.   Counter affidavits were properly received.—*Edwards
v. State*, 49 Ala. 334; *Chase v. State*, 43 Ala. 303; *Birdsong
v. State*, 47 Ala. 68; 84 Ala. 410.   (2.) As to *venire*, motion
to vacate service, and construction of jury law, see Code,
§ 4449; *Goley v. State*, 85 Ala. 333.   The failure of the
clerk to sign the *venire* was immaterial.—Th. & M. on
Juries, §§ 70, 77; 14 Ga. 43; *People v. Williams*, 24 Mich.
156; *Brown v. State*, 74 Ala. 483; *Spicer v. State*, 69 Ala.
161; *Paris v. State*, 36 Ala. 232; *Rash v. State*, 61 Ala.
90.   Besides, the question can not be first raised after verdict.
Th. & M. on Juries, § 76; Proff. Juries, 143; *Brister v.
State*, 26 Ala. 107; 2 Brick. Digest, 166, § 62.   (3.) The
dying declarations were properly received.—6 Amer. & Eng.
Encyc. Law, 127, 122; *Ward v. State*, 78 Ala. 441; *Kilgore
v. State*, 74 Ala. 7; Whart. Cr. Ev., 9th ed., §§ 282-4; Whart.
Hom., § 756.   It is immaterial at what time the predicate is
proved.—*Edwards v. State*, 49 Ala. 334.   As to test of
credibility, see Whart. Hom., § 756.   (4.) Evidence of character confined to proof of general reputation.—*Jones r. State*,
76 Ala. 6; *Davenport v. State*, 85 Ala. 338; Whart. Cr. Ev.,
9th ed., 58; *Reg. v. Rawton*, L. & C. Cr.   Cases, 520; *DeAr-
man v. State*, 71 Ala. 351.   The refusal to allow a question,
when the record shows character was fully proved, will not
work a reversal.—11 Ohio St. 114; 37 Penn. 108.   (5.) As
to competency of jurors, see *Bales v. State*, 63 Ala. 30;
Carson v. State, 50 Ala. 134; *Pearson v. State*, 72 Ala. 191.
(6.) As to charge on character, see *Armor v. State*, 63 Ala.
173; 5 Cush. 334; 74 Ala. 1.

SOMERVILLE, J.—The prisoner in this case was tried
for the murder of Matt. Strong, and, being convicted of
murder in the second degree, was sentenced to confinement
in the penitentiary for a period of twenty-five years.   The
questions presented have been ably and exhaustively argued,
both at the bar and in the written briefs of counsel.
   1.   A careful examination, by each of the judges, of the
application made by the prisoner for a change of venue in
this case, including the affidavits both in support of the motion, and those offered in opposition to it, has led us unani-
mously to the conclusion that it was properly overruled.   The
evidence fails to show to our reasonable satisfaction that an
impartial trial and an unbiased verdict could not reasonably
be expected, according to the ordinary course of justice, in

[Hussey v. The State.]

the county of Madison where the indictment was found. Regarding the application as having been made in due time, which we need not decide, it will be overruled on the authority of the rule declared in *Seams v. The State*, 84 Ala. 410.

2. In determining the merits of this application, we have considered the counter affidavits offered by the State, to the introduction of which the record shows objection was duly taken in the court below. It is our opinion that the exception based on the admission of these affidavits was properly overruled. The reasons urged in argument against this evidence are two-fold: *First*, it is said to be in violation of section 7 of Article I of our State constitution, which provides that, "in all criminal prosecutions," the accused shall have the right "to be confronted by the witnesses against him"; and, *secondly*, that such evidence is *ex parte*, and of an unreliable nature, the deponents not being subject to cross-examination, and there being no compulsory method of forcing them to swear to affidavits.

The objection urged against the value, or weight of such evidence, is unquestionably well taken, and is suggestive of admitted elements of weakness in this kind of testimony. It goes, however, to the question of its sufficiency, rather than that of its competency; and it applies to every class of cases where *ex-parte* affidavits are held to be admissible, whether civil or criminal, or in courts of law or equity, which are numerous. It has always been said that this species of evidence is of a very low order, and that it ought to be received with caution and closely scrutinized; and the propriety of its reception in many instances is, for this reason, addressed to the sound discretion of the lower court. On principles of necessity and convenience, it has long been received by courts of equity, upon applications for the appointment or discharge of receivers, and various other interlocutory motions; by courts of law, to grant new trials, enter satisfaction of judgments, obtain attachments, and the like; and in criminal proceedings, for leave to file an information, to mitigate or aggravate punishment after convictions of misdemeanor, to discharge from wrongful arrests; and in applications for discharge in *habeas corpus* cases. The same practice is authorized, and has long prevailed in this and other States, in motions made for changes of venue in both criminal and civil cases. From the earliest period of our State's history, *ex-parte* affidavits have been received on the part of both the defendant and the State, in applications of this character. The com-

petency of such testimony, whatever may be its value, is well
established by uniform practice, as well as by authority.
1 Bishop Cr. Proc. (3d Ed.), § 73; *Seams' case, supra; Ex
parte Chase,* 43 Ala. 303; *Birdsong's case,* 47 Ala. 68; *Edwards' case,* 49 Ala. 334.

The supposed constitutional objection can not be sustained
to such counter affidavits when offered by the State. It is
only in "criminal prosecutions" that the right of the accused
to be confronted by his witnesses is secured. This has reference only to the trial proper—or those proceedings which
follow between the commencement of the trial and the verdict of acquittal or conviction. It manifestly has never been
supposed to extend to the preliminary proceedings in the grand
jury room, upon which the indictment is founded, or other
collateral proceedings. It is akin to the right to be heard
by counsel, to demand the nature and cause of the accusation, to have compulsory process for witnesses, to be exempt
from giving evidence against oneself, and to have a speedy
trial by an impartial jury; which are guaranties enumerated
in the same clause of the constitution, and must be interpreted by the principle of *noscitur a sociis.*—Const. 1875,
Art. I, § 7. All these are rights secured during the trial of
the defendant—not on the investigation of issues collateral,
or preliminary to his prosecution.

This construction was long ago placed by the United States
Supreme Court on the analogous clause of the Federal constitution, which declares that, "in all criminal prosecutions,
the accused shall enjoy the right . . . to be confronted
with the witnesses against him." In *Ex parte Bollman,*
4 Cranch (U. S.), 75, which was an application for *habeas
corpus,* the question arose, whether an *ex-parte* affidavit,
made before a magistrate to obtain a warrant of arrest, could
be used as evidence on a motion to commit, and whether the
accused was not entitled to demand *viva voce* evidence rendered in his presence. The affidavit was held admissible, on
the ground that the preliminary investigation, instituted to
determine whether the accused should be discharged or held
to trial, was not, strictly speaking, "a prosecution," within
the meaning of this clause of the constitution. The same
question was raised shortly afterwards in the case of Aaron
Burr, before the Circuit Court of the United States at Richmond, which was an application for discharge on *habeas corpus.* Chief-Justice MARSHALL held, that an *ex-parte* affidavit was admissible on the same ground stated in the other

case, such evidence not being, in a case of that nature, objectionable on constitutional grounds.—Burr's Tr. 97. This view of the constitution has not been seriously questioned since that time in this country—the word prosecution being generally conceded to embrace only the trial proper of a criminal cause, and not collateral motions merely incidental to the cause.—Hurd on *Habeas Corpus*, §§ 207–220; 5 Cr. Law Mag. (1884), p. 798, and cases cited in note 2; 1 Bish. Cr. Proc. (3d Ed.), § 75. The right to change the venue, it may be added, is a statutory, not a constitutional right of the citizen. It may therefore be given or taken away *ad libitum* by legislative enactment. This being true, the privilege may be burdened, when given, by such reasonable conditions as the law-making power may elect to attach to it. Had the General Assembly declared that one of the conditions of exercising the right to make such an application should be the admission of affidavits on the part of the State, the condition would be valid, because that to which it is attached is of grace, and not of right. The principle can not vary because the condition is attached by judicial construction, and not by the express words of the statute.

We adhere to the established practice on this subject, which has uniformly authorized the admission in evidence of counter affidavits introduced by the State, in answer to the defendant's evidence of like kind in support of his motion for a change of venue.

3. One of the points most earnestly pressed on our attention in this case is the admission of the dying declarations of the deceased, which were made at different times, to various witnesses, between the time he received the fatal wound, on Wednesday in the forenoon, and the hour of his death, on the afternoon of the following Saturday. The contention is, that no sufficient predicate was laid for the admission of this evidence.

The rules of law on this subject have been too often discussed by this court to justify any additional attempt on our part to restate them at any great length. The difficulty does not lie in the rules themselves, but in the just and proper application of them to the particular facts in each case. The purpose of the court should be to arrive at the state of the declarant's mind when the declarations were made, taking into consideration all that was said by him, and the surrounding circumstances of the case, including the nature of the injury which produced decedent's death, and his probable

appreciation of its fatal character. The inquiry is, were
such declarations uttered under the sense of impending dissolution—under the solemnity of the conviction that death
was near at hand, and that there was no hope of the declarant's recovery? Was he fully conscious of the fact that he
could not rally from the effects of his injury—so that he
entertained no expectation of ultimate recovery? If this be
true, then what he said under this conviction—this despair
of recovery—touching the homicide and its attendant circumstances—which carried with it all the solemnity of a
sworn declaration, is admissible, although in point of fact
there was no rapid succession of death, and no apprehension
of such event immediately following.

The wound in question was inflicted by a pistol shot—the
ball being described as conical, and "38 calibre." It passed
into the left side of the deceased, and lodged in his back
near the surface of the skin, from which it was extracted by
the attending physician on the day after the shooting. The
physician, Dr. Dement, expressed the opinion that it passed
through the lung of deceased, and fractured the rib, producing much suffering from nervous shock. The deceased
fell to the ground at the time he was shot, and was never
able afterwards to stand, remaining in bed to the hour of his
death, which occurred three days afterwards.

All his utterances made on the first day show unmistakably his belief that death was imminent, and that he entertained no hope whatever of recovery. He declared immediately after the occurrence to the witness Patton, whom he
requested to help him up from the place he had fallen in the
open field, that "he would never get over it." On the same
morning, and at the same place, he said to his brother,
James Strong, that "he could not get well, and that he would
be dead in a few minutes"; and, after requesting not to be
put in a vehicle to be carried home, he repeated, that "he
knew he could not live." About eleven o'clock on the same
day, while in bed at home, he said to the witness Newman
Jones, when asked how he felt, that "he was a dead man;"
and to the suggestion that he was "more scared than hurt,"
he replied that he was "worse hurt than the witness thought
he was." To his wife, Mrs. Strong, who was with him
during his entire confinement, he said "he was bound to die,"
and that "he was going to die, *every time.*" To Dr. Dement
he said "he did not think he could get well"; and this in
reply to words of encouragement given him, and, it seems,

[Hussey v. The State.]

in face of the fact that Dr. Mastin, also one of his attending physicians, expressed the hope, in his presence, that he would recover. Every utterance made on the day of the shooting makes it clear to our minds that the deceased did not then entertain the faintest hope of recovery. And while the expressions afterwards used are not so strong, still they show with sufficient clearness that there was no revivor of hope, but a settled conviction in despair of life. On Thursday— the day the ball was extracted—when told by Robert Strong that he hoped he would get well, he persisted in asserting that he did not think he would," and again that "he did not think he could live." The testimony of his brother James Strong, who was with him every day, was "he *always* said he would die."

A careful examination of all the evidence bearing on this subject leads us to the conclusion that, under the principles so often declared by us in adjudged cases heretofore decided, the Circuit Court properly admitted all the dying declarations testified to by the several witnesses, as set out in the bill of exceptions. The predicate laid satisfactorily convinces us that they were made under a sense of impending dissolution, and without the least hope of recovery on the part of the declarant. We could arrive at no other conclusion without in effect overruling many of our reported cases. *Jordan v. State*, 82 Ala. 1; s. c., 81 Ala. 20; *Johnson v. State*, 17 Ala. 618; *Kilgore v. State*, 74 Ala. 7; *Ingram v. State*, 67 Ala. 67; *Ward v. State*, 78 Ala. 441; *Sylvester v. State*, 71 Ala. 17; *Reynolds v. State*, 68 Ala. 502; *Wills v. State*, 74 Ala. 21; Whart. Cr. Ev. (8th Ed.), §§ 282–284; *State v. Johnson*, 9 Cr. Law Mag. (1887) 451, and 453, *note.*

4. The rulings of the court below raise in this case a question of evidence which is of great importance, as it occurs to us, in the practical administration of justice. It involves the right of a defendant to introduce *negative testimony* in support of his good character—a right which does not seem to be recognized by the old text-writers and authorities, but may be said to be accorded from necessity, almost universally, by the *nisi prius* courts in the trial of causes. The defendant was allowed to prove his good character generally for peace and quiet—an issue having reference to the nature of the charge against him, which was murder. Two witnesses were asked the question, whether they had "ever heard of the defendant having any other difficulty except the one in question?" This question was objected to by the

9

State, and on such objection was excluded. There is good authority in support of this ruling of the Circuit Court, but we are all of one opinion that the question should have been allowed. Bare evidence by a witness that he knows the general character of a given person, and it is good, or very good, or excellent, is, after all, closely analogous to a mere opinion in the nature of a fact, and, standing alone, carries with it an impression that it is lacking in some element to give force to the statement. The party testifying can render it more satisfactory and convincing by showing the foundation on which it rests. It is well to prove a person to be reputed honest, or truthful, or a woman chaste, or a man loyal to his country, or peaceably disposed towards all his neighbors. But great emphasis is added by the declaration that the witness, who has had every opportunity to know, has never heard any human being challenge the honesty or veracity of the one, or breathe the slightest breath of suspicion on the virtue of the other, or assert any fact which goes to deny the loyalty, or question the humanity and orderly conduct of the third. It is only to put the matter in a slightly different form, to inquire of the deposing witness whether he had ever heard of any act or conduct in refutation of the good repute which he has affirmed of the person in question. To say his character is good, is a positive expression of the fact. To say that the witness has never heard any thing *against* his character, as to the particular phase in which it is put in issue, is negative in form, but often more satisfactory than evidence of a positive character.

The propriety of this rule, permitting negative evidence of good character, is gradually forcing itself upon the recognition of the courts, and there is a current of modern authority rapidly forming in support of it.

Mr. Taylor, in his work on Evidence, after observing that the term "character" is not synonymous with "disposition," but simply means reputation, or the general credit which a man has obtained in public opinion, observes as follows of the practice of the English judges on this point: "Aware that 'the best character is generally that which is the least talked about,' they have found it necessary to permit witnesses to give negative evidence on the subject, and to state that 'they have never heard any thing *against* the character of the person on whose behalf they have been called.' Nay, some of the judges," he continues, "have gone so far as to assert that evidence in this negative form is the most cogent proof of a man's good reputation."—1 Taylor's Ev. § 350. In support of this view he cites the late case of *Reg. v. Cary*, 10 Cox Cr. Cases, 25, where Cockburn, C. J., observes: "I am ready to admit that negative evidence to which I have referred, of a man saying 'I never heard any thing against the character of the person of whose character I come to speak,' should not be excluded. I think, though it is given in a negative form, it is the most cogent evidence of a man's good character and reputation, because a man's character does not get talked about until there is some fault to be found with him. It is the best evidence of his character, that he is not talked about at all. I think the evidence is admissible in that sense."

Mr. Wharton recognizes the same principle, and says : "In view of the fact that the best character is generally that which is least talked about,' the courts have found it necessary to permit witnesses to give negative evidence on the subject, and to state that 'they never heard any thing *against* the character of the person on whose behalf they have been called."—Whart. Cr. Ev. (8th Ed.), § 58; 1 Whart. Law Ev., § 49; and to the same purport is the view of Mr. Bishop. 1 Bish. Cr. Proc. (3d Ed.), § 1117.

A well considered case in direct support of this doctrine is that of *State v. Lee*, 22 Minn. 407; 21 Amer. Rep. 796, where Berry, J., observes: "A very sensible and commendable instance of the relaxation of the old and strict rule is the reception of negative evidence of good character—as, for example, the testimony of a witness who swears that he has been acquainted with the accused for a considerable time, under such circumstances that he would be more or less likely to hear what was said about him, and has never heard any remark about his character—the fact that a person's character is not talked about at all being, on grounds of common experience, excellent evidence that he gives no occasion for censure, or, in other words, that his character is good." It was held accordingly that a witness might, when a proper predicate of knowledge had been laid, be permitted to testify negatively to one's good character by affirming that he had never heard his character discussed, or spoken of by any one.

To the same effect is *Gandolfo v. The State*, 11 Ohio St. Rep. 114, where negative evidence of a defendant's good character was allowed to be given. "Such evidence," it was said, "is often of the strongest description; as, where a character for truth is in issue, that among those acquainted with the party, it had never been questioned; and so, as to character for peace and quietness, that among those with whom the party associates, no instance has been known or heard of, in which he has been engaged in a quarrel."

In *State v. Nelson*, 68 Iowa, 208, the same rule was recognized, and a witness was allowed to testify that he had never heard anything against the defendant's character or reputation; the court observing that, in the absence of such a rule, "a person, who had so far lived a blameless life as to provoke but little discussion respecting his character would oftentimes be utterly unable to support his character when assailed."

So in *Davis v. Foster*, 68 Ind. 258, an instruction to the jury was held good, which asserted that, "if a man's neighbors say nothing whatever about him, as to his truthfulness, that fact of itself is evidence that his general reputation for truth is good." And in *Davis v. Franke*, 33 Grat. (Va.) 413, a witness who had an opportunity to know another's character was allowed to testify that he never heard it called in question; Staples, J., observing: "Possibly, in many cases, the highest tribute that can be paid to the witness is that his reputation as a man of veracity is never called in question, or even made the subject of conversation in the community where he resides."

In *Childs v. State*, 55 Ala. 28, a witness, who claimed to know the character of another witness, "but never heard his character discussed," was held competent to speak to the question of character. A like principle was declared in *Hadjo v. Gooden*, 13 Ala. 718.

Under the principle established by these authorities, we hold that the Circuit Court erred in excluding the question propounded, as to whether the two witnesses named in the record had ever heard of the defendant's having any other difficulty except the one in question. It was equivalent to the inquiry, whether the witnesses had ever heard anything *against* the character of the defendant for quiet, peace, or good order; and should have been allowed by the court.

The question propounded, calling for evidence *prima facie* relevant and legal, the refusal to allow it was error, although no answer, or proposed answer of the witnesses was stated. *Phœnix Ins. Co. v. Moog*, 78 Ala. 284.

5. The court did not err, however, in its rulings on the evidence otherwise bearing on the subject of the defendant's character. Particular acts, whether good or bad, or the repu-

tation of having done them, can not be shown in proof or rebuttal of good character, on the direct examination, although the rule is often otherwise on cross-examination. Evidence of character goes to general repute, not particular acts, or specified conduct, the parties litigant being presumed to be prepared to meet the one and not the other, which might often do injustice by taking by surprise. "This point," says Mr. Greenleaf, "has been much discussed, but may now be considered at rest."—1 Greenl. Ev. (14th Ed.), § 461; *Steele v. State*, 83 Ala. 20; *Jones v. State*, 76 Ala. 8; Whart. Crim. Ev. §§ 259–60. Such evidence, moreover, must be in the nature of reputation, and not the individual opinion of the witnesses as to the disposition or tendency of the prisoner's mind.—*Reg. v. Rowton*, 10 Cox Cr. Cases, 25. It was not competent to prove that the defendant was a member of the church; or that he was "a model man" in respect to the use of profane language, which he had been charged with using. So, the mere "opinion" of the witness Anderson that the defendant "was a timid man, and would rather avoid than provoke a difficulty."

6. The State introduced several witnesses who testified to the good reputation of the deceased, in the community in which he lived, for peace and quiet. The defendant, on cross-examination, was permitted to inquire of these witnesses, by way of testing the ground of their statement, whether they knew or had ever heard of various specified and notorious difficulties in which deceased had been involved, and in which he had used or threatened to use a deadly weapon. These witnesses having denied that they had ever heard of these difficulties, the defendant proposed to prove, as an independent fact, that these several difficulties had actually occurred, and also to prove their notoriety. The declared object of this evidence was to impeach these witnesses. This evidence was properly excluded. Under the rule above declared, it was incompetent to prove these specified difficulties in proof or rebuttal of good character. They were collateral and irrelevant to the issues in the case. And the rule is too well settled for discussion, both in practice and by authority, that "a witness can not be cross-examined as to any fact, which is collateral and irrelevant to the issues, merely for the purpose of contradicting him by other evidence, if he should deny them, and thereby discredit his testimony. And, if a question is put to the witness, which is collateral, or irrelevant to the issue, his answer can not be contradicted by

the party who asked the question; but it is conclusive against him."—1 Greenl. Ev. § 449. Of course, the rule is different where the fact inquired about is material, as affecting the credit of the witness, as showing bias or hostility against the opposite party; or where the witness has on a former occasion given a contradictory account of the same matter; or where one of the parties to the cause had offered to suborn his testimony, and other like cases.—*Bullard v. Lambert,* 40 Ala. 210; *McHugh v. State,* 31 Ala. 317; *Melhurst v. Collier,* 69 Eng. C. L. 377; *Harralson v. The State,* 82 Ala. 47. The proposal to prove the notoriety of the difficulties, in refutation of the denial of the witnesses that they had ever heard of them, was necessarily irrelevant, if the facts themselves were so, as independent transactions.

7.   There was no error in allowing the State to prove the good character of the deceased for peace and quiet. The ground of objection to this evidence seems to be, that the general reputation of the deceased had not been put in issue, but only the particular traits of his character as a quick-tempered, violent man, easily provoked, and likely to provoke a difficulty. If these traits of disposition are provable at all—which we do not decide—they are not separable from the question of character. It is plain that the State could rebut this evidence by proof of defendant's reputation for peace and quiet, the whole question of character often going to the intent with which an alleged crime was committed, "the prevailing character of the party's mind, as evinced by the previous habits of his life, being a material element in discovering that intent in the instance in question."--1 Greenl. Ev. § 54, n. 3.

8.   The portion of the court's charge which seems to have been copied from the opinion of this court in *Armor v. The State,* 63 Ala. 173, was a correct statement of the law bearing on this subject.—*State v. McMurphy,* 52 Mo. 251; *Coleman v. State,* 59 Miss. 490; *Kilgore v. State,* 74 Ala. 1; *Webster's case,* 5 Cush. (Mass.) 324; Ram on Facts, 96–7.

9.   The testimony of Dr. Dement, to the effect that other physicians concurred with him in his opinion as to the nature of the wound of the deceased, was clearly hearsay, and not admissible. There is no more reason for permitting the unsworn assertions of experts to be detailed second-handed in court, than the like testimony of other persons. Each is equally hearsay, within the strictest meaning of the term.

A. G. S. R. R. Co. v. Arnold, 80 Ala. 600; *Vicksburg & Mer. R. R. Co. v. O'Brien*, 119 U. S. 99.

10. The defendant's wife was not a competent witness for him, as heretofore uniformly held by us, and she was properly excluded from testifying.—*Woods v. State*, 76 Ala. 35; *Johnson v. State*, 47 Ala. 7; 3 Brick. Dig. 824, §§ 35-42.

We need not consider in detail the other rulings on the evidence. We need only observe that we discover no error in them.

The other points raised, as to the alleged irregularities in the organization of the jury, the competency of the juror Williams, and other like contentions, need not be considered, as they will not probably arise on another trial. .

The judgment will be reversed for the error above pointed out, and the cause will be remanded for a new trial. In the meanwhile, the defendant will be retained in custody until discharged by due course of law.

Cooper *v.* The State.

Indictment for Burglary.

1. *Recent possession of stolen goods; flight* —The possession of a part of the stolen goods, recently after a larceny or burglary, imposes on the party the *onus* of explaining how he acquired them; and being unexplained, in connection with proof of attempted flight when arrested for the offense, would authorize a conviction for the offense.

FROM the Circuit Court of Shelby.

Tried before the Hon. LEROY F. BOX.

The indictment in this case was found in October, 1885, and charged that the defendant, John Cooper, "with intent to steal, broke into and entered the store of W. W. Brame, in which goods or merchandise was kept for use, sale, or deposit." "On the trial," as the bill of exceptions states, "the evidence on the part of the State tended to show that the store of W. W. Brame, in which goods were kept for sale, was broken into and entered one Saturday night in the summer of 1885, and goods stolen from it; that one J. H. Duran, on Tuesday following, being in search of the persons suspected of the burglary, saw the defendant at a distance of two or three hundred yards, heard some one say *Run*, and

[Cooper v. The State.]

saw the defendant running off; that one Hill pursued and
overtook him, attempted to arrest him, and told him it was
for breaking into Mr. Brame's store; that the defendant then
ran off again, but was pursued and arrested by Hill; that
Hill found upon his person, at the time of his arrest, a new
pocket-knife, and a pair of socks in his pocket; and said
Brame identified said articles as his property, and a part of
the goods stolen from his store on the night of the burglary.
The evidence for the State tended to show, also, that about
a sack-ful of goods, consisting of various articles, were stolen
from the store on the night of the burglary, the greater part
of which was found in the possession of other persons than
the defendant. This being substantially all the evidence,
the court charged the jury, among other things, that if they
believed from the evidence the burglary was committed in
Shelby county, within three years before the finding of the
indictment, and that goods were also stolen from the house
at the time of the burglary, and that the defendant was found
in the possession of a part of the goods recently after the
commission of the burglary; this would cast on him the
burden of explaining his possession of them. To this charge
the defendant excepted, and requested the following charges
in writing: (1.) 'If the jury believe the evidence, they will
find the defendant not guilty.' (2.) 'The defendant is not
required to account to the satisfaction of the jury for his
possession of the goods, although the jury may believe that
they were stolen.' The court refused each of these charges,
and the defendant excepted to the refusal of each."

W. L. CARY, and A. P. LONGSHORE, for appellant.

W. L. MARTIN, Attorney-General, for the State.

CLOPTON, J.—There is no error in the charge given by
the court, nor in the refusals to charge as requested by the
defendant. The burglary was committed on Saturday night,
and the defendant was arrested on the following Tuesday, at
which time some of the articles stolen were found in his
possession. His attempted flight, upon being informed of
the offense of which he was accused by the person who was
endeavoring to arrest him, and his recent possession of some
of the stolen articles, were facts sufficient to authorize the
inference that he was guilty of the burglary with which he
was charged. Though the court might have declared, as

[Wynn v. The State.]

matter of law, that the possession was recent, its recency was submitted to the jury. Without charging upon the effect of the evidence, the court instructed the jury, if the defendant, recently after the commission of the burglary, was found in the possession of a part of the goods stolen, this would cast on him the burden of explaining his possession. The settled rule in this State is, that the possession of goods, recently after a larceny or burglary, which were stolen in the commission of the offense, imposes on the possessor the *onus* of explaining his possession, if he would repel the inference of complicity in the crime. Defendant offered no explanation whatever. The sufficiency of the evidence to satisfy the jury of defendant's guilt beyond a reasonable doubt was submitted to them. The charge did not invade their province.—*Neal v. State*, 53 Ala. 465; *Ross v. State*, 82 Ala. 65; *Dodson v. State*, 86 Ala. 60.

Affirmed.

Wynn *v*. The State.

Indictment for Slander.

1. *Trial by court without jury; revision of finding on facts.*—A trial by jury not being demanded, in a criminal prosecution before the Criminal Court of Pike (Sess. Acts 1888-9, p. 631, § 7), this court can not review the conclusions of the judge on the evidence adduced.

2. *Hard labor for county, on non-payment of fine and costs.*—On conviction of a misdemeanor, punished by fine only, followed by a sentence to hard labor for the county to enforce its payment, an additional term of hard labor may be imposed for the costs (Code, §§ 4502-04).

FROM the Criminal Court of Pike.

Tried before the Hon. WM. H. PARKE.

The defendant in this case was indicted for verbal slander in charging that Jack Parker had committed perjury in testifying as a witness on the trial of a criminal prosecution against said defendant and his son. On the trial, the defendant pleaded not guilty, but did not demand a trial by jury. On the evidence adduced, all of which is set out in the bill of exceptions, the court adjudged the defendant guilty, and further, "that the following punishment be awarded—a fine of $20, and ten days hard labor for the county, and the costs of this proceeding; and the fine and costs not being pres-

[Ex parte Reynolds.]

ently paid, nor judgment confessed therefor, the defendant must also perform hard labor for the county for ten days, and an additional term, not exceeding eight months, as is sufficient to pay the costs, at 30 cents per day."

WM. L. MARTIN, Attorney-General, for the State, cited *Knowles v. State*, 80 Ala. 9; *Bell v. State*, 75 Ala. 25; *Gilliam v. State*, 71 Ala. 10; *Cawthorn v. State*, 68 Ala. 157; *Summers v. State*, 70 Ala. 16.

McCLELLAN, J.—The appellant, having waived a jury, was tried and convicted before the judge of the Criminal Court of Pike county. The exception reserved goes only to the correctness of the court's finding on the facts. The statute establishing that court does not authorize us to review the conclusions of the judge on the evidence adduced before him.—Acts 1888-89, p. 631. Without statutory authority in that behalf, this court has no jurisdiction in such cases. *Knowles v. State*, 80 Ala. 9; *Bell v. State*, 75 Ala. 25. Were this otherwise in the present instance, appellant would take nothing by this appeal. The judgment below is abundantly supported by the evidence.

It may be that this record was intended to bring under review the action of the Criminal Court in sentencing defendant to hard labor for the payment of costs, and that reliance in that regard is had upon the opinion of this court in *Ex parte Long*, at this term. That case, in respect to the imposition of hard labor for costs, has been reconsidered, and the opinion modified, so as to leave no doubt of the power to impose such sentence.—*Ex parte Long, ante,* p. 47.

The judgment of the Criminal Court is affirmed.

Ex parte Reynolds.

Application for Habeas Corpus and Certiorari.

1. *Title and subject-matter of laws, under constitutional provisions; act amending charter of Anniston.*—The act approved February 14th, 1887, entitled "An act to amend section 3 of an act entitled 'An act to incorporate the town of Anniston, Calhoun county,' approved February 4, 1879" (Sess. Acts 1886-87, pp. 307-32), is violative of the constitutional provision which declares, "Each law shall contain but one subject,

[Ex parte Reynolds.]

which shall be clearly expressed in the title" (Art. IV, § 2), because it contains more than one subject, and because no one of its subjects is clearly expressed in its title.

2. *Prohibiting sale of spirituous liquors in Anniston; local option; judicial notice of election.*—The provision contained in the charter of Anniston, giving the authority to "license, tax and regulate grocers, merchants, retailers," &c. (Sess. Acts 1888-9, p. 612, § 7, subd. 10), does not confer the power to prohibit the sale of spirituous liquors within the corporate limits; and if the power be conferred by the further provision empowering the municipal government to provide for the punishment of "any offense punishable by the laws of the State of Alabama" (subd. 22, § 7), it must be shown that the sale of liquor there is prohibited by law, since Calhoun county is governed by a "local option" law, and the court can not take judicial notice of the result of an election held under that law.

3. *Sentence to hard labor, under municipal ordinance.*—A sentence to hard labor, imposed by a municipal court, which has power to punish only by fine or imprisonment, is illegal and void, and the defendant is entitled to be discharged on *habeas corpus.*

APPLICATION by petition on behalf of Jeff. Reynolds, for the writs of *habeas corpus* and *certiorari*, to procure his discharge from the town marshal of Anniston, after a discharge had been refused by the City Court of Anniston, Hon. W. F. JOHNSTON presiding. The exhibits to the petition show that the petitioner was, on the 8th May, 1889, convicted of "violating prohibition ordinance," and sentenced to "thirty days on the streets." On the hearing before Judge JOHNSTON, two municipal ordinances were read in evidence, prohibiting the sale of spirituous liquors within the corporate limits of Anniston, and punishing such sale by fine, imprisonment, or hard labor. One of these ordinances was dated May 27, 1887; and the other, March 8th, 1889. The several statutes relating to the charter of Anniston, or the material parts thereof, are cited and stated in the opinion of the court. They may be found in the Sessions Acts as cited, and are too long for insertion in this report.

MACDONALD & WILLIAMS, for the petitioner.—(1.) The act approved February 14, 1887, purporting to amend the charter of Anniston, is a nullity, being in palpable violation of the constitutional provision as to the title and subject-matter of statutes.—*Ballentyne v. Wickersham,* 75 Ala. 533; *Medical College v. Muldon,* 46 Ala. 603. (2.) If this act ever had any force or validity at all, it was repealed by the later amendatory act of February 23d, 1889, which only confers the power to "license, tax, and regulate;" and this does not include the power to prohibit.—*Miller v. Jones,* 80 Ala. 89. (3.) If the municipal authorities of Anniston have any

[Ex parte Reynolds.]

power to punish for an offense against the State laws relating
to the sale of liquors, it can avail nothing in this case, because it is not shown that Calhoun is a "prohibition" county;
and if an election has ever been held, and resulted in favor of
prohibition, this court can not take judicial notice of the fact.
(4.) The power to punish by fine, or imprisonment, does
not give the power to punish by hard labor. (5.) The violation of a municipal ordinance is not a "crime," as the word
is used in constitutional provisions.—*Posey's case*, 36 Ala.
252; 5 Vroom, N. J. Law, 367.

AGEE & MICOU, *contra.*—The amendatory charter of February 14th, 1887, confers express authority to "license, tax,
regulate or prohibit traffic in vinous, malt, or spirituous
liquors."—Sess. Acts 1886-7, par. 13, subd. 11. If other
parts of that statute be unconstitutional, because not included
in the title, they may be rejected.—*Pollard v. Wood*, 40 Ala.
77. This provision is not repealed by the later charter of
February 23, 1889, because not inconsistent with it; and
repeals by implication are never favored. Aside from these
provisions, the sale of liquor in Calhoun county is prohibited
by law, and this court must take notice of the result of the
election, as of any other historical fact.—*Ashley v. Martin*,
50 Ala. 537; *Lewis v. Burton*, 74 Ala. 317.

STONE, C. J.—The City Council of Anniston, by an
ordinance adopted March 8, 1889, prohibited the sale of intoxicants within the police jurisdiction of that city. The
penalty prescribed for its violation is a fine of not less than
one, nor exceeding one hundred dollars, or imprisonment or
hard labor on the streets, for a term not exceeding six months.
Petitioner was convicted under this ordinance, and sentenced
to thirty days hard labor on the streets. Contending that
the sentence was illegal, petitioner sued out a writ of *habeas
corpus*, returnable to the City Court of Anniston. That
court adjudged the sentence to be lawful, and remanded the
petitioner to the custody of the city authorities. Thereupon
petitioner applied to this court for appellate *habeas corpus*,
and for a review of the City Court's ruling.

The city of Anniston appeared by counsel, and contests
the discharge. It is admitted that the petition truly sets
forth the facts, and it is both consented and desired that we
consider and determine the merits of the application, without the issue of the preliminary writ.

[Ex parte Reynolds.]

The act "to incorporate the town of Anniston, Calhoun county, Alabama," was approved February 4, 1879.—Sess. Acts, 353. It consists of eight sections, and conforms in the main to the usual routine observed in the incorporation of towns by special enactment. Section 1 gives the dimensions of the town. Section 2 provides for holding elections. Section 3 prescribes the oath of office, constitutes the intendant and councilmen a body corporate, with authority to sue and be sued—the intendant to preside and preserve order and decorum at all meetings of the council; and empowers the corporation "in general to do and perform all acts which are incident to bodies corporate, and to purchase, hold and dispose of, for the benefit of said town, real, personal and mixed property, to the value of twenty thousand dollars." We have now summarized all the powers conferred by the third section. All other powers usually granted to municipal corporations are granted in the other sections of the statute. Among these are the power to open, improve and light the streets; to levy taxes; to prevent nuisances; to establish a police, jail, or guard-house; to impose and provide for inflicting punishment; to grant occupation licenses; to regulate places of amusement, and to preserve the good order and quiet of the town by appropriate ordinances and their enforcement. We have only glanced at the powers conferred by sections 4 to 8, inclusive. To be fully understood, they must be read.

The act with the title "To amend section 3 of an act entitled 'An act to incorporate the town of Anniston, Calhoun county, Alabama,' approved February 4, 1879," was approved February 14, 1887.—Sess. Acts, pp. 307 to 332. Under this caption, or title, will be found a most elaborate statute, changing the name of the corporation to that of "The Mayor and City Council of Anniston." It then proceeds to enumerate and confer all the powers deemed necessary to a full-rigged city government, with great fullness and particularity of detail. It not only specifies and confers all the powers which the entire act of February 4, 1879, had conferred, but it enumerates and grants many other powers necessary to a well appointed city government. It then expressly repeals sections 4, 5, 6, 7, and 8, of the act approved February 4, 1879. This act also must be read to be understood.

Our constitution, Article IV, section 2, declares that "Each law shall contain but one subject, which shall be clearly expressed in the title." The title of the present enactment is to amend section 3 of the act approved February 4, 1879. No one reading that section would have the slightest intimation of one tenth of the provisions contained in the act approved February 14, 1887. And, in addition to this, the later enactment repeals the last five sections of the older statute. It thus violates each of the provisions of the constitutional clause copied above. It contains more subjects than one, and neither of the subjects of which it treats is sufficiently expressed in the title, if indeed it is expressed at all. In *Ballentyne v. Wickersham*, 75 Ala. 533, we considered this subject so fully, that we consider it unnecessary to reproduce the argument.—*Chiles v. Monroe*, 4 Metc. 72; *State v. Harrison*, 11 La. An. 122; *Dorsey's Appeal*, 72 Pa. St. 192; *People v. Allen*, 42 N. Y. 404.

The attempted enactment of February 14, 1887, being unconstitutional, can exert no influence whatever in the decision of this case. It not only failed to confer the power it assumed to confer, but it failed to repeal any part of the act of February 4, 1879. We must, then, decide this case as if the act of February 14, 1887, had never been attempted to be enacted.

The authority of the city government of the city of Anniston to prohibit the sale of intoxicants must, then, be determined by the act approved February 23, 1889.—Sess. Acts, 601 to 624. It is not contended that act is unconstitutional; and if such contention were made, we discover nothing in the statute to authorize us to question its constitutionality. Subdivision 10 of section 7 of that act—p. 612—is the only provision which bears directly on this question. It confers the power to "license, tax and regulate grocers, merchants, retailers," &c., but it confers no power to prohibit the sale of liquors.—*Miller v. Jones*, 80 Ala. 89.

It is contended, in opposition to relief, that subdivision 22 of section 7 supplies the requisite authority. That subsection does empower the city government to provide for the punishment "of any offense punishable by the laws of the State of Alabama." But it empowers the municipal authorities to punish such case by *fine or imprisonment.* It confers no authority to impose labor on the streets as a punishment. So, if it be true, as contended, that Calhoun is a prohibition county, and that the sale of intoxicants in that county is, in consequence, an "offense punishable under the laws of Alabama," that is no answer to the present application. The punishment inflicted in the present case is labor on the

[Smoke v. The State.]

streets, when, even according to the contention, the statute only authorizes fine and imprisonment. Conceding the entire scope of the argument, the petitioner is illegally restrained of his liberty, for the mayor had no power to impose the kind of punishment he did inflict.—*State, ex rel. Long*, which cites the authorities; *ante*, p. 47.

We must not be understood, however, as deciding that, if the punishment had been either fine or imprisonment, the provision of the statute we are considering would have upheld the conviction. Calhoun is not absolutely a prohibition county. The statute authorizes a popular election, to determine whether intoxicating liquors shall be sold in the county, or their sale prohibited.—Act approved December 7, 1886 —Sess. Acts, 671—and act approved February 26, 1887. Sess. Acts, 700. We have decided that we will not take judicial cognizance that the county had voted for prohibition. *Grider v. Tally*, 77 Ala. 422. We need not decide, if the county did so vote, that this would constitute a violation of the prohibition an "offense punishable by the laws of the State of Alabama," so that the city government, by an ordinance, could make it a punishable offense against the municipality. We decide nothing on this question.

The petitioner is illegally restrained of his liberty, and is entitled to his discharge.

The writs of *habeas corpus* and *certiorari* will be granted, unless the petitioner, on being certified of this opinion, is content to renew his application before a court of original jurisdiction.

Smoke *v.* The State.

Indictment for Arson.

1. *Sufficiency of indictment; averment of ownership of building.*—An indictment which charges the burning of a "cotton-house containing cotton of M. B." (Code, § 3781), is fatally defective, in not alleging with sufficient clearness the ownership of the house.

FROM the City Court of Selma.

Tried before the Hon. JONA. HARALSON.

The indictment in this case contained four counts, the first charging that the defendant "willfully set fire to or burned the cotton-house containing cotton of Montgomery Beasley;" the second, "the cotton-pen containing cotton of Montgomery Beasley;" the third, "the cotton-house containing cotton of Bettie Beasley;" and the fourth, "the cotton-pen containing cotton of Bettie Beasley." There was a demurrer to the indictment, and also a motion in arrest of judgment, because the indictment did not allege the ownership of the building alleged to be burned; each of which was overruled.

W. L. MARTIN, Attorney-General, for the State.

SOMERVILLE, J.—The indictment, in our opinion, was bad, in failing to aver with sufficient clearness the ownership of the "cotton-house," or "cotton-pen," alleged to have been set fire to, or burned.—Crim. Code, 1888, § 3781. Each of the four counts must be construed to aver only the ownership of the cotton contained in the house or pen, and not of the structure itself which contained the cotton.

The demurrer should have been sustained, and it was error to overrule it.

The judgment will be reversed, and the usual order made for holding the defendant in custody until legally discharged.

Reversed and remanded.

Ballou *v.* The State.

Indictment for Peddling without License.

1. *Peddling; selling stoves by samp'e.*—Under an indictment which charges that the defendants engaged in the business of peddling in a two-horse wagon, without a license as required by law (Code, § 629, subd. 31, 40), a conviction can not be had on proof that they were the agents of a foreign company engaged in the manufacture of stoves; that one of them travelled about in a wagon, carrying a single stove with him, selling stoves by the sample, and taking the purchaser's note payable on delivery within sixty days; and that the other afterwards carried the stoves around in a wagon, delivered them, and received payment of the notes, if the purchasers elected to pay cash at a reduced price.

FROM the Circuit Court of Geneva.

Tried before the Hon. JESSE M. CARMICHAEL.

W. D. ROBERTS, for appellants.

WM. L. MARTIN, Attorney-General, for the State.

CLOPTON, J.—The indictment charges the defendants with a violation of the revenue law, by engaging in, or carrying on the business of peddling, in a wagon drawn by two horses, without a license. The evidence shows the facts to be as follows: The only article sold or delivered by the defendants was a stove, called the "Wrought Iron Range Stove," which was manufactured in St. Louis, Missouri, by a company having their principal place of business in that city. The stoves were shipped from St. Louis, by the carload, to Caryville, Florida, and kept in a warehouse for delivery as sales were made. The defendants were agents of the company, one being the managing agent, having his place of business in Geneva in this State; and the others, salesmen and delivery-men. The following was the mode of doing business: The managing agent sent salesmen, who would go through the country, carrying a sample stove in a two-horse wagon, from house to house, and procure orders for stoves. When an order was obtained, the purchaser gave a note for sixty-five dollars, conditioned to be void if the stove was not delivered in thirty days. The orders and notes were delivered to the managing agent, who, within twenty or thirty days thereafter, would send other men with stoves, in two-horse wagons, to deliver on the orders, and put them up for the purchasers. These men took the notes with them, to give the purchaser an opportunity to pay the cash price of sixty dollars, if he preferred, which he had the option to do. The sample stove was not sold by the salesman, but was usually left on his return from a trip to Geneva, for the delivery-man, at the last house at which he procured an order, who sometimes, by agreement with the purchaser, would put it up, instead of the stove carried for that purpose.

On these facts, the question is, were the defendants required to take out a license as peddlers, under sub-division 31 of section 629 of Code, 1886. There being nothing in the context indicating a different intention, the term *peddler* must be construed in its ordinary popular sense. In *Randolph v. Yellowstone Kit*, 83 Ala. 474, its popular signification is said to be, "a small retail dealer, who, carrying his merchandise with him, travels from house to house, or from place to place, either on foot or on horse-back, or in a vehicle

10

drawn by one or more animals, exposing his goods for sale, and selling them." The distinctive feature does not consist in the *mode* of transportation, though one of the statutory modes is essential to constitute a peddler, but in the fact that a peddler goes from house to house, or place to place, carrying his articles of merchandise with him, and concurrently sells and delivers. The defendants, who were salesmen, carried no stoves with them, but sold by sample, and took orders for subsequent delivery; and the defendants who delivered made no sales. They were not *peddlers*, in the sense in which the term is ordinarily understood.

The conclusion, that the business in which they were engaged is not within the provision relating to peddlers, does not rest solely on unaided construction. If not rendered conclusive, it is strongly supported by the different and specific provisions of the revenue law, classifying other itinerant dealers in goods, wares and merchandise, and companies or persons engaged in selling stoves or ranges. As one of the occupations for which a license is required, subdivision 34 of section 629 provides: "For transient or itinerant auctioneers, or dealers in goods, wares and merchandise, other than licensed peddlers, and other than travelling agents of whole-sale dealers in said articles, making sale thereof by sample, fifty dollars." And sub-division 40 of the same section specially provides: "Each sewing-machine, stove, range or clock company, selling sewing-machines, stoves, ranges, or clocks, either in person, or through agents, or consignees, and all persons who engage in the business of selling sewing-machines, stoves, ranges or clocks, shall pay to the State twenty-five dollars for each county in which they may so sell." There is an exception in favor of merchants engaged in a general business, which is only material as showing that the legislature exacted a license only for those who, it was contemplated, would be itinerant, going from county to county. Thus it appears, that the legislature has arranged, as to requirement of licenses, different kinds of itinerant dealers into separate and distinct classes, making variant provision for each. The defendants, being engaged in the sole business of selling stoves as agents of the manufacturing company, come within the letter of sub-division 40; and being included in this provision of the revenue law, are, by clear implication, excluded from the operation of subdivision 31. A double license fee will not be intended.

It is said, however, that subdivision 40 is unconstitutional

[Prestwood v. The State.]

as to foreign companies or persons, on the authority of *State v. Agee*, 83 Ala. 110. This question it is unnecessary to decide; for its unconstitutionality, if conceded, would not destroy or impair its effect as evidence of the legislative intent, nor operate to bring the defendants within a class not intended.

Reversed and remanded.

Prestwood v. The State.

Indictment for Enticing away Laborer.

1. *Constituents of offense; consent of employer.*—The consent of the employer, expressed in writing, or given in the presence of a credible person, is a defense to a prosecution for enticing away a laborer in service under a written contract (Code, § 3757); if the consent is conditional, as on payment of the amount due the employer, performance of the condition must be shown; and the person in whose presence the consent is given being presumed to be credible, in the absence of evidence to the contrary, the defendant is entitled to have the jury pass on the sufficiency of the evidence.

2. *Local jurisdiction.*—If the employer and the defendant resided near each other, but in adjacent counties, and the acts requisite to the consummation of the offense occurred in both counties, the jurisdiction is in either. (Code, § 3719.)

FROM the Circuit Court of Dale.
Tried before the Hon. JESSE M. CARMICHAEL.

W. L. MARTIN, Attorney-General, for the State.

. CLOPTON, J.—The defendant was indicted under section 3757 of Code of 1886, which makes penal knowingly interfering with, hiring, employing, enticing away, or inducing to leave the service of another, any laborer or servant, who has contracted in writing to serve such other person for a specified time, not to exceed one year, before the expiration of the time so contracted for, without his consent given in writing, or in the presence of some credible person. The purpose of the statute is the protection of the employer against unlawful interference with his laborers, who have contracted in the prescribed manner. His consent given in writing, or in the presence of some credible person, is requisite to justification or excuse; but the consent may be conditional, and, on the performance of the condition, constitutes a full defense. There was evidence on the part of defendant, tending to show that the party with whom the laborer had contracted in writing, consented, in the presence of John Prestwood, who, in the absence of proof to the contrary, is presumed to be credible, that defendant might hire him, if he would pay the employer the amount due him by the laborer, and that the amount claimed to be due was paid. If these be the facts, the defendant did not commit the offense denounced by the statute. Defendant had the right to ask that the sufficiency of the evidence to establish these facts should be submitted to the jury. The third charge requested by defendant hypothetically states these facts, and should have been given.

The local jurisdiction is not necessarily in the county in which the defendant made the contract of hire with the laborer. If the acts requisite to the consummation of the offense occurred in both the counties of Dale and Coffee, the jurisdiction is in either county.—Code, 1886, § 3719.

Reversed and remanded.

Ex parte Printup; *Ex parte* Elliott.

Applications for Mandamus to Chancellor, on refusal to allow Petitioners to come in as Parties.

1. *Intervention of third persons as parties by petition*—By the general rule of practice in courts of equity, third persons can not be allowed to come in as parties to a pending suit on their own motion, or by petition, against the objection of the complainant; but are required to propound their interests by original bill in the nature of a cross-bill, or in the nature of a supplemental bill.

2. *Same.*—The only recognized exceptions to this general rule are—1st, that the beneficiaries of a trust are sometimes allowed to intervene by petition in a suit to which the trustee is a party; and, 2d, where a person has an interest in a fund which is in the custody, or under the control of the court, and he desires to secure its proper administration and distribution.

APPLICATIONS by petition, by John S. Printup and James M. Elliott, respectively, for the writ of *mandamus* to Hon. S. K. McSPADDEN, presiding in the Chancery Court of Etowah, requiring and commanding him to allow them to

[Ex parte Printup; Ex parte Elliott.]

intervene as parties in a suit pending in said court between other persons, on the facts stated in the opinion of the court.

JOHN T. MORGAN, for the petitioners, cited Cook on Stockholders, § 659; 2 Black, 715; *Bayliss v. Railroad Co.*, 2 Biss. 193; *Stout v. Lye*, 103 U. S. 66; *Bronson v. Railroad Co.*, 2 Wall. 285, 304; 34 Texas, 125; *Scott v. Ware*, 64 Ala. 182; *Lyons v. Hamner*, 84 Ala. 197; *Bingham v. Jones*, 84 Ala. 202; *Ex parte Branch*, 53 Ala. 140; *Carlin v. Jones*, 55 Ala. 624; *Dodge v. Woolsey*, 18 How. 331; 105 U. S. 13; 111 U. S. 518; 52 Me. 115.

JNO. H. DISQUE, WM. H. DENSON, and R. F. FOUCHE, *contra*, cited *Ex parte Branch*, 53 Ala. 140; *Renfro Bros. v. Goetter, Weil & Co.*, 78 Ala. 311; *Hill v. Miller*, 9 Gill & J. 73; *Bank v. Man. Co.*, 10 Paige, 481; 6 Blatch. 151; Story's Eq. Pl. § 72; Dan. Ch. Pr., vol. 1, p. 190.

McCLELLAN, J.—On April 29, 1889, John S. Printup filed his petition in the Chancery Court of Etowah, setting forth a state of facts, which it is unnecessary to recapitulate here, tending to show that he had an interest in the subject-matter involved in a cause pending in that court, in which Daniel S. Callahan was complainant, and the Rome & Decatur Railroad Company and others were defendants; and prayed therein "that he may be admitted as a party defendant in said cause in this honorable court, to defend against the bill of the American Trust Company" (a defendant which had filed a cross-bill), "in the same manner and with the same effect as he would have been if originally made a party defendant therein, and that he may make his defense by motion, demurrer, plea, or answer."

On 22d of May, 1889, James M. Elliott filed his petition in said court, propounded therein the interest of the estate of Daniel S. Printup in the subject-matter of said suit, and prayed to be appointed administrator *ad litem* of Printup's estate, and in that capacity to be admitted into the cause as a party, "to defend and protect the interests of said estate as he may be advised, by answer, cross-bill, plea or demurrer to the bill and cross-bill, or any other pleading in said cause; and also in any original suit that should be instituted by petitioner in said court of chancery to secure full justice and equity to said estate."

On May 24, 1889, a decree was entered, denying the petition of James M. Elliott; and on motion of the complainant in the cross-bill, striking the petition of John C. Printup from the files. Motions are now made in this court for writs of *mandamus*, to compel the chancellor to reinstate, and grant the prayers of said petitions, respectively.

It is manifest from the foregoing statement, that the purpose of the petitioners is to intervene generally in a pending cause, and to exercise therein all the rights of original parties. It is also clear, from the record exhibited in this case, that the privilege to thus intervene is not claimed by the petitioners upon any idea of a trust relation existing between them and the parties in the court, or upon any theory that a fund is being administered in this proceeding, in which the petitioners are entitled to share, and that they should be allowed to come in merely for the purposes of distribution. On the contrary, it is patent that this case involves—pretermitting consideration of the power of the court in any case to appoint an administrator *ad litem* of an estate not before, in any manner, represented in the litigation—the naked question of the right of a stranger, on his own petition, and against the objection of the parties litigant, to be made a party to the record. To a satisfactory determination of this question, a brief review of the authorities will be advantageous, if not essential.

The result of the adjudged cases is stated by text-writers to be, that a motion to be admitted as a defendant in a suit is irregular, and that in equity jurisprudence there is no such practice as making a person a defendant in a pending cause upon his own application, and over the objection of the complainant.—1 Daniel's Ch. Pl. & Pr. 287.

Upon this general rule but two exceptions have been engrafted. One of these, growing out of trust relations between a party and third persons—relations which do not exist, as we have seen, in this case—is thus formulated by Judge Story: "If the *cestuis que trust* should not be made parties to the suit, and their interests are apparent, a court of equity will sometimes, as a matter of indulgence, and to prevent further delay and expense, allow them to bring forward their claims by petition, in order to have their interests ascertained, and their rights protected."—Story Eq. Pl. § 208; *Drew v. Harman*, 5 Price, 319.

The other exception is illustrated in those cases where the petitioner desires to intervene only for the purpose of the proper administration and distribution of a fund, which is in the custody or control of the court, and in which he, though not a party, is entitled to share.—*Carlin v. Jones*, 55 Ala. 630.

In *Shields v. Barrow*, 17 Howard, 417, it is said: "If the plaintiff desires to make new parties, he amends his bill, and makes them. If the interest of the defendant requires their presence, he takes the objection of non-joinder, and the plaintiff is forced to amend, or his bill is dismissed. If, at the hearing, the court finds that an indispensable party is not on the record, it refuses to proceed. These remedies cover the whole subject" of the introduction of new parties into a pending cause.

In *Drake v. Goodrich*, 6 Blatch. 151, it is said, that no such practice is known in equity, as making a person a defendant to a suit on his own application, or as compelling a plaintiff to join as co-plaintiff a person not a party, on the application of such person.

To the same effect is the case of *Coleman v. Martin*, 6 Blatch. 119.

And these cases are referred to in the case of *Stretch v. Stretch*, 2 Tenn. Ch. 140, and the principle announced in them fully indorsed. In the latter case, as in the case at bar, the subject-matter of the litigation was in the hands of a receiver, who had been appointed in the suit to which the petitioners sought to be made parties. Chancellor Cooper, in delivering the opinion in that case, uses this language: "Where there is no privity, a stranger interested in the subject-matter or objects of a suit must bring forward his claim by an original bill in the nature of a supplemental bill, or in the nature of a cross-bill, as the case may be, so that those interested adversely may have process, with a copy of the bill, served on them, and may have an opportunity to avail themselves of the regular modes of defense against such bill; and even where a third person claims under or in privity with one of the parties litigant, his interest can only be brought before the court by bill. It can not be done by petition.—*Foster v. Deacon*, 6 Md. 59; *Carow v. Mowatt*, 1 Edw. Ch. 9."

The case of *Searles v. J.; P. & M. R. R. Co.*, 2 Woods, 621, involved a relationship between the petitioning and litigant parties, very like that existing in the facts in this case. That was a bill filed by the owners of the first-mortgage bonds of a railroad, to foreclose the mortgage, and sell the road in payment of the bonds. The petitioner claimed to be the owner of second-mortgage bonds of the defendant company, and as such desired to set up certain equities he had against the right of complainant to foreclose and apply the proceeds of foreclosure to the payment of the first-mortgage bonds. The motion to be made a party was denied by Mr. Justice BRADLEY; and it was held, that "a complainant can not be compelled to add parties to his bill, if he chooses to take the responsibility of their not being made parties."

The doctrine of these cases, and the general principle in this behalf announced in the texts referred to, have received the unqualified indorsement of this court. The case of *Ex parte Branch* was strikingly like the present one in its facts, except it had progressed further towards a final determination. In each, the effort was to foreclose a mortgage on a railroad. In each, unsecured creditors sought to intervene to defeat foreclosure. While it is true in that case prominence was given to the fact that a decree of foreclosure had passed, and had been partially executed; yet one ground of the opinion, which denied the right of intervention, clearly was, that the petitioners "required a larger field for the development and opportunity for more vigorous action than is afforded generally to one who comes into a cause to attend to the details of the distribution of a fund in court, and a claim to his share;" thus evidencing the understanding of the court that intervention by petition could only be allowed for the limited purposes indicated.—*Ex parte Branch*, 53 Ala. 149.

The point really involved and decided in the case of *Carlin v. Jones* goes no further than this, though the language employed may be susceptible of a broader significance; and both these cases are in harmony with the general principle announced in the outset, that intervention by petition may be allowed when the purpose of the petitioner is to assert his interest and right to share in a fund which is in the custody of, and being administered by the court. Manifestly, this is not the purpose of the petitioners in the case at bar. They do not seek to share in the fund which will be brought into court as result of the proceeding to which they ask to be made parties, but, on the contrary, their avowed purpose is to defeat the only action of the court which could produce a fund to be administered and distributed.—*Carlin v. Jones*, 55 Ala. 630.

As a deduction from all the authorities, the rule was stated in the later case of *Renfro Bros. v. Goetter Weil & Co.*,—a case in which, like that of *Stretch v. Stretch, supra*, and the case at bar, the subject-matter of the litigation was in the hands of a receiver, so that no independent suit could be instituted in regard to it, except by leave of the court first had—to be, that "when a person, not a party to a pending suit, between whom and the complainant there is no privity, but who has a claim or lien on the property, or is interested in the subject-matter of the suit, desires for his own protection to present his new claim, to assert his independent right, and raise new issues, he must do so by a formal bill, containing appropriate allegations—an original bill in the nature of a cross-bill, or of a supplemental bill, as the case may be."—*Renfro v. Goetter*, 78 Ala. 314; *Cowles v. Ledyard*, 39 Ala. 130.

Two cases are relied on by the petitioners, as supporting their right to intervene in the cause presented by the record before us. One of these is *Carlin v. Jones, supra*. If that case goes further than we have construed it to go above, as counsel insists it does, we feel constrained by our own adjudications, and the great weight of authority in other jurisdictions, not to follow it. The other case, upon which reliance is had, is that of *Bronson v. La Crosse Railroad Co.*, 2 Wall. 283, in which the position of petitioners unquestionably finds support, in so far as it is sought to intervene here in the capacity of stockholders in the Rome & Decatur Railroad Company. Even in that case, the right was admitted with hesitation, and the remedy was said to be an extreme one, growing out of the necessities of the case. The conclusion reached is not supported by any citation of authority, either in the opinion of the court, or in the brief of counsel; it is opposed to all other adjudications on the point, and we can not concur in it.

Upon a careful examination and review of all the cases, we have no hesitancy in re-affirming the rule announced in *Renfro v. Goetter, supra*, and holding the petitioners were not entitled to the relief prayed for.

This conclusion renders it unnecessary to consider questions arising on the application of Elliott to be appointed administrator *ad litem* of the estate of Daniel Printup.

The applications for writs of *mandamus* are denied.

Ala. Sipsey River Navigation Co. *v.* Geo. Pacific Railway Co.

Action for Damages on account of Bridge obstructing Navigation of River.

1. *Alabama Sipsey River Navigation Company; power to remove obstructions, and exclusvie right to navigate river.*--Under the charter of the Alabama Sipsey River Navigation Company (Sess. Acts 1875-6, pp. 318-22), "the exclusive right and privilege to navigate said stream, from its mouth to the county line of Marion," is granted to said corporation for thirty years, but only "from and after the completion of said work" --that is, when the navigation of the river is opened up as far as the county line of Marion; and power is given to it to remove obstructions, but not until they are reached in the progress of its work.

2. *When action lies for obstruction to navigable river.*--The obstruction of a navigable river is a public nuisance; but an individual can not maintain an action on account of it, unless he shows some special injury to himself, independent of the general injury to the public.

3. *Sipsey River as navigable stream.*--The Sipsey river being above tide-water, and having been included as land in the public surveys, it is *prima facie* not navigable; and the *onus* of proving that it is navigable in fact is on the party who asserts it.

4. *Error without injury.*--When the plaintiff below recovered nominal damages only, but adduced no evidence which could serve as a basis for the computation or assessment of his damages, rulings adverse to him, even if erroneous, are no ground of reversal, and the court will not consider their correctness.

APPEAL from the Circuit Court of Fayette.

Tried before the Hon. SAM. H. SPROTT.

This action was brought by the Alabama Sipsey River Navigation Company, a corporation chartered by a special act of the General Assembly, approved March 2, 1876, against the Georgia Pacific Railway Company, to recover damages on account of an alleged obstruction of said river by the defendant; and was commenced on the 13th February, 1888. The obstruction of the river was caused by a railroad bridge, which the defendant had built across the river in 1883, in Fayette county, about twenty miles from the boundary line between Fayette and Marion counties. The original complaint contained but a single count, to which a demurrer was interposed, but overruled; and a second count was afterwards added by amendment. The cause was tried, as the judgment-entry shows, on issue joined "on the pleas of *nul tiel* corporation, the statute of limitations of one year, and not guilty."

The jury returned a verdict for the plaintiff, for one cent damages; and the court thereupon rendered judgment for the costs against the plaintiff. Each party reserved a bill of exceptions during the trial, and each assigns as error, on cross appeals, the several rulings to which exceptions were thus reserved. The decision of this court renders it unnecessary to state these rulings.

MARTIN & McEACHIN, and McGUIRE & COLLIER, for the appellant.

NESMITH & SANFORD, and JAS. WEATHERLY, *contra*.

STONE, C. J.—The appellant in this action, plaintiff below, was incorporated by special act of the legislature, approved March 2, 1876.—Sess. Acts, 318. Its object was to have the navigation of Sipsey river improved. To accomplish this purpose, it created certain persons corporators, and prescribed rules for organizing the corporation. The powers of the corporation necessary to be considered in this action are sections 11 and 12.

SEC. 11. "That said company shall have fifteen years in which to complete their work upon said river, in opening up the same to navigation, and shall have the exclusive right and privilege to navigate said stream from its mouth to the county line of Marion county, for thirty years, from and after completion of said work; *Provided*, that said company may authorize other persons or companies to navigate said stream upon payment to the company of a resonable toll therefor."

SEC. 12. "That any obstruction hereafter created or placed upon said stream, by the erection of bridges, mills, dams, or otherwise, shall, whenever the company have, in the progress of its work, reached the point of any such obstructions, be liable to be removed by said company."

Our construction of these sections is, that whenever the incorporated company, "in the progress of its work," shall reach the point of any obstruction to the navigation of said river, it may remove it; but till it reaches it, the charter confers no power to remove the obstruction.—*Olive v. The State*, 86 Ala. 88; s. c., 5 So. Rep. 653. A second proposition follows, namely, that till the work of improvement is completed, and the river opened up to navigation to the line of Marion county, the corporation, by virtue of its charter, can claim no "exclusive right and privilege to navigate said stream." That exclusive privilege was conferred only on the completion of the work, which was required to be done in fifteen years. The result of these clear principles is, that neither the pleadings nor the testimony in this case shows that defendant has violated any charter-right or privilege of the plaintiff.

It is manifest that this action was brought for no alleged violation of the charter-rights of the Alabama Sipsey River Navigation Company. We have shown that it has presented no right of recovery on that ground. It has failed to aver or prove that the entire work has been completed, and it has equally failed to aver or prove that in the progress of its work the company has reached the point of the alleged obstruction. So, if the case presented no other question, we would hold that the general charge ought to have been given in favor of the defendant, and we would consider no other ruling.—3 Brick. Dig. 109, §§ 41 to 44.

The amended complaint presents another claim of damages, which is entirely independent of its chartered rights. It avers that "the Sipsey River is a navigable river; . . . that for many years, to-wit, for forty years before the commencement of this action, the said river has been used by the public for the floatage of saw-logs, and for transporting cotton, coal, staves, and other products of the fields, forests and mines, from points extending to the line of Marion county, Alabama, to points below on the river, as far down as the city of Mobile; that the said river has been used for said purpose for many years before this action was brought, and said river has been capable of said use for the most part of the winter and spring months, to-wit, six months in the year; that there are fertile fields all along said river to the Marion county line, and large forests of valuable pine and other timber, and coal and iron lands of large extent; and said lands, timber and minerals, to a very great extent, have no other means of convenient transportation; that the said bridge, which is now standing over said river, completely prevents all of said navigation and floatage above; and plaintiff avers that nearly all of said timber and minerals are above said bridge."

We are satisfied these averments were not intended as a substantive, independent ground of complaint. Their purpose was to set forth damages plaintiff had suffered from having its alleged right of exclusive navigation obstructed and cut off, as to all that section above the bridge. We have shown the navigation company had and have no such exclusive right, and it follows that the part of the complaint we have copied above must stand or fall alone. Considered by itself, it is fatally defective. It avers enough to show the bridge was a public nuisance, if the Sipsey was a navigable river; but that is not enough to enable an individual to maintain an action. It must show a special injury to itself, independent of the general injury to the public, before a suit for individual damages can be maintained.—Cooley on Torts, 614–5, and note; *Mayor v. Rogers*, 10 Ala. 37; *Crommelin v. Coxe*, 30 Ala. 318. The plaintiff does not set forth any special interest it has in the navigation of the Sipsey river above the bridge, and hence neither of the counts contains a good cause of action. But there was no demurrer to the amended count.

We know that the Sipsey river is not subject to the ebb and flow of the tides, and that it was included in the Government surveys as land, and not thrown into fractions by running meandering lines on the borders of the stream. It was and is, then, *prima facie* non-navigable, and the burden of proving it navigable was on the plaintiff, who asserted it. This is a question for the jury, and the rules for determining when such stream is, and when it is not navigable, have been so often declared by this court that they need not be repeated.—*Ellis v. Carey*, 30 Ala. 578; *Rhodes v. Otis*, 33 Ala. 596; *Peters v. N. O., M. & C. R. R. Co.*, 56 Ala. 528; *Walker v. Allen*, 72 Ala. 456; *Lewis v. Coffee County*, 77 Ala. 190; *Sullivan v. Spotswood*, 82 Ala. 163.

There is no proof in the record tending to show that the bridge caused the plaintiff any special damage, nor is there proof that plaintiff had any interest or enterprise above the bridge to be the subject of special damage. So, while under the issue, the plaintiff may have been entitled to recover (3 Brick. Dig. 711, §§ 6, 7), it furnished the jury no data for fixing the amount of the damages. It did recover nominal damages, and, under the proof, it is entitled to no more. No matter what the rulings were, they could amount to nothing more than error without injury.—3 Brick. Dig. 405, § 20. We will not further consider charges asked by plaintiff.

Some of the charges asked by defendant may assert correct propositions of law, if they were properly presented in the pleadings. They are not so presented. The others, construed in reference to the issues, are misleading, and were properly refused on that account.

The first count of the complaint is defective, but the demurrers did not reach or point out the defects.

There is no error in the record, of which either appellant can complain.

Affirmed.

Sheffield Land, Iron & Coal Co. *v.* Neill.

Bill in Equity by Vendor, for Rescission of Contract.

1. *Registration as constructive delivery of deed.*—The intentional delivery of a deed by the grantor to the probate judge, for registration, may be a sufficient delivery to the grantee, though he never had actual possession, and was even ignorant of the existence of the deed; and a delivery for registration, by mistake of the grantor's clerk, may, by long acquiescence, operate as a valid and effectual delivery, on the presumption that the mistake has been waived.

2. *Rescission of contract at suit of vendor.*—On a sale of town lots by a private corporation at auction, part of the purchase-money to be paid in cash, when a deed would be delivered, and notes and mortgages executed for the deferred payments; the general manager of the corporation having accepted from a purchaser his draft at thirty days instead of a payment in cash, and, by mistake, delivered the deed to the probate judge for registration, afterwards paying the fee, and retaining possession of the deed, the draft not having been paid; the right to a rescission in equity is barred by *laches* after the lapse of more than two years and a half, when it appears that the vendor still retained the notes and mortgage, and that the market value of the land had but recently increased.

APPEAL from the Chancery Court of Colbert.

Heard before the Hon. THOMAS COBBS.

The bill in this case was filed on the 22d December, 1886, by the appellant corporation, against William M. Neill; and prayed the rescission of a contract for the sale of several town lots in Sheffield, and the cancellation of the appellant's conveyance to the defendant, as a cloud on the title, it having been recorded by mistake as alleged. The chancellor sustained a demurrer to the bill, and his decree is here assigned as error. The opinion states the material facts.

EMMET O'NEAL, for appellant, cited *Alexander v. Alexander*, 71 Ala. 298; *Smith v. Cockrell*, 66 Ala. 79; 13 Vesey, 224; 2 Story's Equity, § 780; *Kirby v. Harrison*, 59 Amer. Dec. 680; *Remington v. Kelly*, 7 Ohio, 97; *Higley v. Whitaker*, 8 Ohio, 201; *Johnson v. Evans*, 50 Amer. Dec. 678;

5 Rich. Eq. 370; 1 Hoff. Ch. 123; 6 Wheat. 528; 15 Mich. 499; 4 Mich. 573; 4 John. Ch. 559; 8 Paige, 426; 2 Beav. 183; 6 *Ib.* 126; 3 Leigh, 161; 2 Clark, Iowa, 126.

J. B. MOORE, *contra*, cited *Long v. Brown*, 4 Ala. 622; 31 Ala. 123; 94 U. S. 214; 5 John. Ch. 29; Waterman on Spec. Performance, §§ 457-8, 462; 1 Sm. & Mar. Ch. 376; 3 Pomeroy's Equity, § 1408; Whart. Contracts, vol. 1, § 258; 2 *Ib.* § 888; *Elsberry v. Boykin*, 65 Ala. 341; *Williams v. Higgins*, 69 Ala. 522.

SOMERVILLE, J.—The present case is argued by appellant's counsel mainly upon the theory, that the case made by the bill is one for a mere cancellation of a deed to appellee Neill, delivered to the probate judge by mistake, and duly recorded by him on the book of records for deeds; said deed purporting to convey to the grantee certain urban lots in the town of Sheffield, and being alleged to be a cloud on the title of the complainant. A close analysis of the allegations of the bill, however, taken in connection with its prayer, shows that its true scope and purpose are to rescind a sale of land which may be regarded as executory, or executed, according to the inferences which we may be authorized to draw from the conduct of the contracting parties.

These lots were sold at public auction by the appellant corporation, on May the 9th and 10th, 1884; terms, one-fourth cash, the remainder of the purchase-money payable by notes of the purchaser in one, two and three years, secured by mortgage on the property. The managing agent of the company, A. H. Moses, without authority, accepted a draft of the purchaser on certain Montgomery bankers, for the first cash installment, and had the deed, notes and mortgage all prepared in due form, with the understanding that, when the draft was paid, the deed was to be delivered. The deed was delivered on May 12th, 1884, by mistake of a clerk of the general manager, to the probate judge, and was by him recorded. After discovery of this fact, the fees for registration were paid by A. H. Moses, and the deeds were taken from the office of the probate judge. The appellee's draft was not paid, for want of funds in the hands of the drawees. The appellee was requested to pay the amount due, and neglecting to do so, was asked to make a quit-claim deed back to the company, which he failed to do. When this request was made does not appear, except that it is alleged to have been before the considerable rise in value of the land, which seems to have occurred since the sale. The present bill was filed on December 22d, 1886, or more than two and a half years from the recording of the deed.

The intentional delivery of a deed to the probate judge for registration, although the grantee may never be in actual possession of the instrument, has been held to be a sufficient delivery to the grantee, although he was at the time ignorant of its existence.—*Elsberry v. Boykin*, 65 Ala. 336. In *Alexander v. Alexander*, 71 Ala. 295, it was left an open question, whether the presumption of delivery arising from this state of facts would be overturned by the retention of the deed in the possession of the grantor after it had been thus recorded. However this may be, it is apparent that the registration of a deed, although it was done by mistake, and the paper was retained by the grantor after being recorded, may be ratified by the grantor, by subsequent acts satisfactorily importing an intention to affirm the transaction as a valid delivery. By long acquiescence he may be presumed to have waived the mistake, and by failure to correct he may be inferred to have accepted the registration with its attendant consequences. The grantor, in other words occupies a position where he may by his conduct either affirm or disaffirm the act of registration as an act of delivery, especially when, as in this case, delivery itself is by agreement made to depend on the payment in cash of a single installment of a sum of money, and an executory sale by auction has already been made.

We deem it important, that a valid executory contract of sale between the parties had already been made by auction, the requisite memorandum being made to take it out of the operation of the statute of frauds. The papers, as above said, were all prepared—deed, notes and mortgage—to take effect when a cash payment should be made of one-fourth of the purchase-money. An unauthorized draft had been taken by the general manager for this payment, which itself, though 'not originally taken as cash, was capable of being so treated by the company as to operate as a waiver of such cash payment. The delay in seeking to rescind, we repeat, has been over two years and a half.

The rule is, that the right to rescind, when it does exist, must be exercised within a reasonable time. Undue *laches*, or want of diligence in asserting the right, will operate as a

[Sheffield Land, Iron & Coal Co. v. Neill.]

waiver of it.—*Bryant v. Isburgh*, 74 Amer. Dec. 662, *note*, and cases cited. Time is not generally regarded in a court of equity as of the essence of a contract, where delay has worked no harm to the opposite party, although it may be made essential by the·clearly expressed intention of the contracting parties.—3 Pom. Eq. Jur. § 1408. Especially is time not considered essential in ordinary contracts for the sale of land, where specific perfórmance is sought to be enforced, the execution of such contracts often being compelled after years of delay. This general rule "is usually applied where the purchaser fails to pay the purchase-money at the appointed time. There, the compensation for delay can be easily adjusted, by allowing interest on the amount up to the date of payment."—*Bullock v. Adams*, 20 N. J. Eq. 371.

In such cases, where the purpose of the seller is to rescind, he should give an explicit notice to that effect, or do some positive act of equivalent import, which will put the opposite party on his guard, or else manifest his intention to rescind by filing his bill. It has been held in many cases, that a vendor of land can not put an end to a contract of sale, without a formal and *reasonable* notice that, unless the purchaser shall fulfill it, the vendor will not hold himself further bound.—*Falls ∨v. Carpenter*, 1 Dev. & Bat. Eq. 237; s. c., 28 Amer. Dec. 592. It has accordingly been decided, that "a notice that non-performance by a certain day would be regarded as equivalent to a refusal to fulfill the contract, is not tantamount to a notice that the contract would then be considered as rescinded."—*Johnson v. Evans*, 50 Amer. Dec. 678, *note*. We may safely say, in the absence of suit brought, or of a formal notice, that no word or act will operate as notice of such intention, which is not positive in its character, and unambiguous in meaning, as showing a clear purpose to put an end to the contract, unless the opposite party shall comply with his part of the agreement in a reasonable time.—*Bryant v. Isburgh*, 74 Amer. Dec. 659, *note*.

Prompt action, moreover, is required in all such cases, where a party is invested with an option to rescind, where there has been, or is likely to be, a rapid fluctuation in the market-price value of the property.—*Gilmer v. Morris*, 80 Ala. 78; s. c., 60 Amer. Rep. 85. "He will not be permitted", it has been said, "to lie by, and wait for the rise or fall in the value of the property, and then act according to his interest in the matter."—*Johnson v. Evans*, 50 Amer.

11

Dec. 678, *note.* The just reason, given by Chief Justice Ruffin, in *Falls v. Carpenter*, 28 Amer. Dec. 607, *supra*, is, "because a favorable change ought not to profit him who would not run the risk of an unfavorable one." This principle, it is true, might, under other circumstances, affect the appellee, who was defendant in the court below, but it most equitably and chiefly affects that party upon whom the law casts the duty of affirmative action. That party, in the present case, is the complainant.

We think the delay in filing the bill in this case is fatal to the right of relief. The bill, as amended, alleges no fraud. Its object is to rescind on the ground of a default, which time may condone, and a mistake allowed to remain uncorrected for between two and three years. The complainant has not exercised due diligence in seeking to rescind the sale. No explicit notice of a purpose to rescind is shown, until the present suit was brought—a delay of two years and seven months. In the meanwhile, the deed to the purchaser has all along stood registered on the public record for conveyances, the fees for recording being paid by the general manager of the complainant. The draft has never been returned to the purchaser, but his notes and mortgage have been retained by the vendor, so as to hold the option to waive the cash payment at any time, recognize the registered deed as a delivery, and enforce the payment of the mortgage debt. The complainant must be charged with knowledge of these transactions on the part of its vice-president and general manager, who was invested with power to sell the lands of the company. The exercise of proper diligence on the part of the directors would have informed them as to these acts of its agent. Long acquiescence is ratification.

The decree of the chancellor, sustaining the demurrer to both the original and amended bills, is free from error, and must be affirmed.

CLOPTON, J., not sitting.

Bank of Eutaw (Barnes) *v.* Alabama State Bank.

Statutory Detinue for One Hundred Bales of Cotton.

1. *Mortgage of property to be afterwards acquired; executory contract of pledge.*—A verbal agreement between private bankers and one of their customers who was engaged in the business of buying cotton, to the effect that they would advance money to be used by him in the purchase of cotton; that all cotton bought by him, and paid for by checks on them, should be their property, and they should have the right to take, hold and sell the same, until the money advanced for it had been repaid; and that on their failure to sell, the customer might ship and sell the cotton, but should give them a draft for the proceeds, with bill of lading attached,—does not create a legal mortgage, nor operate as a pledge of any particular cotton, until it has been delivered, or otherwise specifically appropriated.

2. *Same.*—A subsequent agreement between the parties, after other transactions between them, to the effect that the bankers, on paying a note held by another bank, should take up and cancel a bill of lading for one hundred bales of cotton, held by that bank as security for the debt, and should hold all the customer's cotton then on hand, which he had bought with money advanced by them, until a specified future day, and, if not sold or shipped by the customer before that day, should have the right to take possession, ship and sell it, applying the proceeds of sale to the payment of the customer's indebtedness to them,—like the previous agreement, creates only an equitable lien, which, coupled with possession wrongfully taken, can not defeat an action by the owner of a superior equitable lien, who procured the legal title by an indorsement of the warehouse receipts after such wrongful possession taken.

3. *Equitable lien with possession, as against prior lien with subsequent legal title.*—While possession of personal property wrongfully taken by a person who has an equitable lien on it, can not prevail against a prior or superior equitable lien, coupled with a legal title acquired after the wrongful taking; yet the title of the latter does not attach, as against the former, to property which was substituted by the owner, under whom each party claims, for a part of the property covered by the lien which he had disposed of.

FROM the Circuit Court of Greene.

Tried before the Hon. SAM. H. SPROTT.

This action was brought by the Alabama State Bank, a corporation doing business at Birmingham, against the Bank of Eutaw, a partnership composed of B. B. Barnes and others, who conducted business as bankers at Eutaw, to recover one hundred bales of cotton; and was commenced on the 13th August, 1884. The cotton had belonged to Cleage Brothers, a partnership engaged in the business of buying cotton,

during the years 1883–4, in Eutaw and other places; and
each of the parties claimed title under them. The plaintiff
claimed it under a contract which originated in an application by Cleage Brothers for a loan of money, and which, as
reduced to writing and signed by them, was dated at Birmingham, April 30th, 1884, and in these words: "The Alabama State bank having this day loaned us $11,385.91, on
230 bales of cotton, now stored in warehouses at Tuskaloosa
and Eutaw," specifying weight and quality; "we agree to
keep said cotton covered by insurance in good, solvent companies, the loss (if any) payable to said bank, and also, on
the demand of the said bank, and within forty-eight hours
after notice sent to us by mail or telegraph, to pay them such
additional sum as they may deem necessary to cover any decline in the price of cotton. Should we fail to keep and perform promptly any agreement herein at maturity, or fail to
pay said loan at maturity, said bank, or its agents, may sell
said cotton in such manner as they deem best, and without
notice, and apply the proceeds, after paying all expenses,
costs and charges incurred by them, or lawfully claimed
against said cotton, to the payment of said note."

Of said 230 bales of cotton, 130 were stored in a warehouse in Tuskaloosa, and 100 in the "McGee Warehouse" at
Eutaw, of which Cleage Brothers were the lessees; and a
warehouse receipt for these 100 bales was then held by the
National Bank of Birmingham, as security for a loan or advance of $3,000. By the terms of the agreement between
plaintiff and Cleage Brothers, though not expressed in the
writings, plaintiff paid or advanced to the National Bank at
Birmingham the amount due from Cleage Brothers, and
received from said bank, without indorsement, the warehouse
receipt for the cotton. The receipt, which was dated February 2d, 1884, was signed by J. W. Deadrick, who was in
fact the clerk or agent of Cleage Brothers, the lessees of the
warehouse; but the receipt did not disclose or indicate the
fact, and the plaintiff had no knowledge of it until a short
time before the commencement of this suit. At the time this
receipt was given, Cleage Brothers had a large quantity of
cotton in said warehouse; and "at or about said date," as
plaintiff's evidence tended to show, "they caused 100 bales
of said cotton to be marked with tags, numbered from 1368
to 1468 inclusive, and set apart to itself in the warehouse, for
the purpose of including them in said receipt." These bales
remained in the warehouse, kept apart from the other cotton,

until about the first June, 1884, when one Payne became the lessee and proprietor of the warehouse; and they were then removed from the warehouse by Cleage Brothers, "without the knowledge or consent of plaintiff," and placed on the platform at the railroad depot, but still kept separate and apart from the rest of their cotton. On or about June 15th, Cleage Brothers, having contracted to sell 50 bales of cotton, of a particular grade or quality, to a purchaser, and not being able to make up the number from the rest of their cotton on hand, took 24 of the 100 bales for the purpose of filling their contract, removing the tags from the bales sold, and placing them on 24 other bales then substituted in their stead. This was done without the knowledge or consent of plaintiff, who was not informed of it until a few days before the commencement of this suit, after the defendants had taken possession of the cotton (including the substituted bales); "and when so informed, plaintiff ratified and assented to such exchange and substitution." In the early part of July, 1884, while the cotton was still on the platform, in charge of an agent of Cleage Brothers, defendants sent their agents and servants, with instructions to remove the tags, and to mark and number the bales in their names; and they succeeded in doing so, against the protest and efforts of the agent of Cleage Brothers, who attempted to prevent it by removing the new tags as fast as they were affixed, but no breach of the peace was committed. On the morning after the completion of this work, the defendants removed the cotton to another warehouse. The plaintiff was informed of these transactions a day or two afterwards, and instituted an inquiry into defendants' claim to the cotton; and afterwards, but before the commencement of this suit, obtained from Cleage Brothers an indorsement of said warehouse receipt.

The defendants adduced evidence showing that the cotton in controversy, with a large quantity of other cotton, was bought by Cleage Brothers with money furnished by them, or paid for by checks drawn on them; and that these transactions were had under and pursuant to agreements between them, which are thus stated in the bill of exceptions: "Defendants' evidence tended to show that, in August, 1883, before Cleage Brothers began the purchase of cotton that season, defendants entered into a contract with them, whereby they agreed to advance to said Cleage Brothers money with which to pay for cotton which Cleage Brothers should buy, at Eutaw and any other points in Greene county, during said season, by paying their checks on defendants for the price, as the cotton should be purchased by them, on the express condition and understanding, that all cotton so bought by Cleage Brothers, with money so advanced, or paid on their checks, should be the property of defendants, until they were repaid all moneys so advanced, and they should have the right to take, hold, ship and sell the same, whenever deemed necessary for their protection; that otherwise Cleage Brothers should ship and sell the cotton to such persons as they desired, but, whenever they made a shipment, they should give defendants a draft for the proceeds, with bill of lading attached;" and defendants' evidence tended to show that the cotton here in controversy was bought and paid for under this agreement. The bill of exceptions adds in this connection: "On cross-examination of defendants' witnesses on this point, it was shown that this agreement was intended by the parties merely as security for the money so advanced; that in fact Cleage Brothers never actually turned over to defendants the cotton purchased by them with money furnished by defendants, but bought said cotton in their own name, retained possession of it, sold and shipped it in their own name, and otherwise dealt with it as their own property; but that generally, when they sold such cotton, they drew on the purchaser for the purchase-money, in favor of the defendants, attaching the bill of lading to the draft, and left them with the defendants, to be collected and placed to their credit."

The plaintiff had adduced evidence showing that, about October 1st, 1883, Cleage Brothers had entered into a written contract with defendants, relative to the purchase of cotton, and the division of the profits between them; "that said agreement lasted only a few days, when, in lieu of the division of net profits under said written agreement, Cleage Brothers agreed to pay said B. B. Barnes, and did pay him, $500." This written agreement, which was produced, was dated October 1st, 1883, signed by the Cleage brothers individually and B. B. Barnes, and in these words: "For and in consideration of a mutual agreement between" the said parties, naming them, "it is hereby agreed, that B. B. Barnes, as cashier of the Bank of Eutaw, is to furnish no other cotton-buyers with funds with which to purchase cotton; and it is agreed by said Cleage Brothers, that they will use every effort to throw cotton business into the hands of said bank; and it is further agreed by them, that all purchases of cotton made by them

at Eutaw, Stewart Station, Akron, and Boligee, Alabama, are
to be paid for by said bank; that they are to keep a regular
buyer in the market, and are to make an equal division of
any profits arising from the purchase of cotton at the above
places, with said B. B. Barnes. It is understood that said
Barnes is to be held in no way responsible for any losses,
should any occur, on the above transactions, after a final
settlement of the season's business. It is further understood,
that $500 be paid to J. H. Armstrong, for classing said cot-
ton, and that all necessary expenses arising from the purchase and sale of said cotton must be paid before any division
is made. It is understood, also, that said bank is to charge
the usual exchange for cashing drafts. This agreement is
to be considered as a secret contract until the 29th February,
1884, commencing on the 17th October, 1883."

The defendants adduced evidence showing that, a few days
before May 23d, 1884, they learned that Cleage Brothers
had obtained from the railroad agent at Eutaw a bill of lading
for 100 bales of cotton, "to some point of destination not
remembered," and had procured a loan of $5,000 from a
bank in Chattanooga, Tennessee, on the faith of said bill of
lading, which was attached to their note for the money loaned;
that on the 23d May, 1884, the active partner of Cleage
Brothers and said Barnes, acting for the defendants, had an
interview, at which Cleage requested defendants to pay off
this debt, and to have the bill of lading returned and cancelled; "that thereupon they made a computation of the
value of all the cotton on hand held by Cleage Brothers in
Greene county, and purchased as aforesaid, which consisted
of 158 bales at Eutaw and 50 bales at Boligee, in which estimate they included the cotton now in controversy, and also
an estimate of the indebtedness of Cleage Brothers to defendants, which was about $6,000, to which was added the
$5,000 due to the Chattanooga bank, from which deducting
the estimated value of said cotton, there remained a balance
of some $2,000 due to defendants; that thereupon it was
orally agreed between them, that defendants would pay the
$5,000 to the Chattanooga bank, would charge the amount
so advanced to Cleage Brothers, take up said bill of lading,
and have it cancelled; that Cleage Brothers should secure
them with collaterals, which they did; that defendants should
hold all the cotton then on hand in Greene county, including
the cotton now in controversy, until June 15th, 1884, and if
said cotton had not been shipped and sold by Cleage Broth-

ers by that time, and draft for the proceeds given to defendants, then defendants should ship and sell the same, and
apply the proceeds to the payment of said indebtedness of
Cleage Brothers;" and their evidence showed that they had
complied with the terms of this contract on their part, and
that they had no knowledge, notice or information of plaintiff's claim to this cotton, until after they had taken possession of it as above stated, nor any notice of the warehouse
receipt signed by Deadrick. The bill of exceptions here
adds: "But, on cross-examination of defendants' witnesses
on this point, it was developed that defendants never in fact
had actual possession of any of the cotton of Cleage Brothers
under this agreement, nor did they attempt to take actual
possession of any of said cotton until, as above stated, in
July, and that said agreement was only intended as security
for the indebtedness of said Cleage Brothers; and the evidence was conflicting as to the making of said agreement,
the plaintiff's evidence tending to show that no such agreement was ever made." There was a conflict in the evidence,
also, as to the cotton included in the bill of lading held by
the Chattanooga bank; the defendants claiming that it was
the cotton here in controversy, while the plaintiff's evidence
tended to show that no particular cotton was described in the
bill of lading, and that no cotton was in fact delivered to
the railroad agent when he signed and issued the bill of
lading.

On the facts above stated, the court charged the jury, on
request of the plaintiff, "that, if they believe the evidence,
the plaintiff is entitled to recover in this action all of the
cotton seized under the writ which was a part of the 100
bales selected, set apart and included in the warehouse receipt
of February 2d, 1884; and the jury may assess its alternate
value at the market value at Eutaw when defendants took
possession, with interest to the time of trial." To this
charge the defendants excepted, and they here assign it as
error.

The court charged the jury, also, on request of the defendants, "that, if they believed the evidence, they must find for
the defendants for all the cotton in controversy not included
in the 100 bales for which said warehouse receipt was
issued by Deadrick, but which was afterwards substituted by
Cleage Brothers for cotton included in said receipt." The
plaintiff excepted to this charge, and here assigned it as error
on a cross-appeal.

J. B. HEAD, with whom was E. W. DE GRAFFENBEID, for appellants, defendants below.—(1.) As between defendants and Cleage Brothers, leaving plaintiff's title out of view, the original contract between them gave defendants a legal title to the cotton, as it was purchased and paid for. This contract was not in the nature of a mortgage upon property not then in existence, or to be afterwards acquired, as security for an existing debt; for there was no debt then existing, and none was then contracted. It was simply an executory contract, made in contemplation of future transactions between the parties, and intended to govern their rights and duties as and when those transactions occurred; and it is to be construed as if a separate and independent contract had been made in reference to each particular purchase of cotton, or as if cotton had been purchased and paid for while a statute was of force containing similar provisions; in either of which cases, it can not be doubted, defendants would have acquired a legal title to the cotton as purchased, on which they might have maintained detinue against Cleage Brothers. *Greenway v. Fuller*, 47 Mich. 557; *Rees v. Coats*, 65 Ala. 256; *Jackson v. Rutherford*, 73 Ala. 155; *Evington v. Smith*, 66 Ala. 398; Jones on Chattel Mortgages, ch. IV; *Pennock v. Coe*, 23 How. 117; *Seymour v. Railroad Co.*, 25 Barb. 284; *Railroad Co. v. Cowdrey*, 11 Wall. 459. (2.) The subsequent contract of May 23, 1884, had no reference to future purchases, but related only to cotton then on hand; and it certainly gave defendants the right, as against Cleage Brothers, to take peaceable possession of the cotton, as they did. (3.) Against defendants' title under these contracts, even though it be equitable merely, coupled with possession peaceably taken in ignorance of plaintiff's claim, plaintiff can not claim protection, because of the admitted usury in the loan to Cleage Brothers.—*Wailes v. Couch*, 75 Ala. 134; *McCall v. Rogers*, 77 Ala. 349; *Meyer v. Cook*, 85 Ala. 417. (4.) As to the substituted cotton, the charge of the court was correct.—*Ala. State Bank v. Barnes*, 82 Ala. 607.

WEBB & TILLMAN, for plaintiff below, relied on the former decision in this case, 82 Ala. 607-15, and cited the following additional authorities.—*Jackson v. Bull*, 1 John. Cases, 81; *Vaughn v. Marable*, 64 Ala. 66; *Thompson v. Marshall*, 36 Ala. 512; *Burns v. Campbell*, 71 Ala. 288; *Huddleston v. Huie*, 73 Ala. 216; *Morrow v. Turney*, 35 Ala. 133.

CLOPTON, J.—The present record, and the record which was before us on the former appeal, do not materially vary as to the facts. By the cross-appeals, substantially the same questions which we then decided are again presented, and we are asked to reconsider the conclusions then announced. *Ala. State Bank v. Barnes*, 82 Ala. 607. On the former appeal we held that the agreement of August, 1883, created neither a mortgage nor a pledge of specific cotton. Not controverting that a mortgage upon property, to be acquired in the future, does not operate to convey the legal title, if it be to secure any antecedent debt, but is only an agreement to convey when the property is acquired; counsel now insist, that, as there was no existing debt at the time the agreement was made, it was simply a contract prescribing rules for the government and construction of future transactions when had,˙ and that the cotton, under the agreement, became the property of defendants, and the legal title vested in them, as and when the cotton was purchased and paid for. The terms of the agreement were, that defendants would advance money to pay for cotton purchased by Cleage Brothers in Greene county during the ensuing cotton season, by paying checks drawn by them on defendant as the cotton was purchased, on the condition and understanding that all cotton so bought and paid for should be the property of defendants until they were repaid all money advanced, and that they should have the right to take, hold, ship and sell the same, whenever deemed necessary for their protection; otherwise, Cleage Brothers could ship and sell the cotton to such persons as they desired; but whenever a shipment was made they should give defendants a draft for the proceeds, with bill of lading attached. The advances were to be made, and the property acquired in the future.

It is manifest from the terms of the agreement it was not intended that the cotton should become the absolute property of defendants, or that the title thereto should vest in them, but merely a security for money advanced—not for a present, subsisting debt, but for future advances. Had Cleage Brothers, at the time the agreement was made, owned the cotton, it may be that the words, *should be the property of defendants*, would have been sufficient to have constituted a legal mortgage. At law, a mortgage can operate only on property actually or potentially belonging to the mortgagor. If he does not own the property, there is nothing upon which the conveyance can operate. The rule is otherwise in equity ;

but, even in equity, a contract to transfer property to be subsequently acquired, does not operate as a present alienation, but merely to transfer the beneficial interest immediately on the acquisition of the property. On the principle that a future acquisition, merely expected or contemplated, is not the subject of a mortgage at law, rest all our decisions, holding that a mortgage on an unplanted crop does not pass the legal title, even when the crop comes into existence, unless the mortgagor does some new act for the purpose of carrying it into effect; though it creates an equitable interest, which attaches when the crop comes into existence, and which a court of equity will protect and enforce. The same principle controls the effect and operation of the agreement under consideration.

It is further contended, that the agreement of May, 1884, was made with reference to the agreement of August, 1883, and for the purpose of carrying the latter agreement into effect. The terms of the agreement are stated in the opinion delivered on the former appeal, and need not be repeated. We then ruled, that it created only an equitable lien, such as may exist without the delivery of possession, and did not authorize defendants to take possession of the cotton against the objection of Cleage Brothers, so as to defeat the legal title which plaintiff acquired by the indorsement of the warehouse receipt. The contract of May, 1884, is a separate, distinct and independent contract, designed to meet new and different conditions, without reference to the contract of August, 1883, except to originate an additional equitable lien for the balance due on account of the money previously advanced. This becomes manifest when the contract of October 1, 1883, an intervening contract, is considered. By this last agreement, B. B. Barnes, one of the defendants, and who was cashier of the Bank of Eutaw, stipulated that the bank should pay for all cotton purchased by Cleage Brothers at designated places in Greene county, and would not furnish other cotton buyers with funds with which to purchase cotton. Cleage Brothers were to keep a regular buyer in the market, and use efforts to throw the cotton business into the hands of the bank. The bank was to charge the usual exchange, and the profits to be divided between Cleage Brothers and B. B. Barnes. This agreement continued only a few days, when it was changed; the change being, that in lieu of one-half of the profits, Cleage Brothers agreed to pay Barnes five hundred dollars. It is said that this was a pri-

vate agreement with Barnes, with which the other defendants
had no connection.   It is apparent, however, that it was
made also for the benefit of the bank, which was bound by
the stipulations of the cashier and managing partner.   The
agreement was intended to supersede, and did supersede, the
agreement of August, 1883; or, at least, operated to break
any possible connection which might otherwise have existed
between the latter agreement and the agreement of May,
1884.

On the cross-appeal, plaintiff contends that the indorsement of the warehouse receipt related back to the time of
the substitution of other cotton for a portion of the one hundred bales originally included in the receipt, which had been
sold by Cleage Brothers, and vested in plaintiffs a title to
the substituted cotton sufficient to maintain detinue.   The
argument is, that by the substitution plaintiff acquired an
equitable claim to the substituted cotton, and having such
interest, and Cleage Brothers having an interest in upholding
its validity, they could, without committing maintenance,
put the plaintiff in a position to maintain its lien on the cotton.   This may be conceded, but the equitable interest of
the plaintiff was inchoate, and not itself acquired until ratification.   Defendants had previously acquired an equitable
interest, without notice of plaintiff's claim; and a subsequent
ratification, by which only an equitable interest is acquired,
does not operate to cut off the intervening equity of defendants.   Whatever may have been the operation of the
indorsement of the warehouse receipt, as between plaintiff
and Cleage Brothers, it does not pass, as against the equity
of defendants, the legal title to cotton not originally included
in the receipt.

After careful consideration of the questions raised and
argued, we adhere to, and affirm the rulings on the former
appeal.

Affirmed.

Abraham *v.* Nicrosi.

Attachment for Rent by Landlord.

1. *Landlord's lien for rent, on goods in store-house.*—Under statutory provisions giving to landlords of store-houses, dwelling-houses and other buildings "a lien on the goods of their tenants for rent" (Code, §§ 3069-74), construed in the light of the rules of the common law governing the remedy by distress, the lien attaches, where the tenancy is continued, by express contract, or by implication, to goods brought on the premises after the expiration of the original term, and remaining there when the attachment is sued out to enforce it; and this lien must prevail against the claim of a third person in possession by purchase from the tenant.

2. *Practice in attachment suits, on interposition of claim by third person, and motion to dissolve attachment and dismiss levy.*—In an attachment suit, the defendant only appearing for the purpose of moving to dissolve the attachment and dismiss the levy, the attached property having been claimed by a third person as purchaser; although the court may correctly adjudge that the property is, on the facts proved, subject to the attachment, it should only render judgment overruling the defendant's motions, and delay final judgment, until the determination of the adverse claim to the property; and the defendant himself may assign as error the rendition of final judgment against him.

APPEAL from the City Court of Montgomery.

Tried before the Hon. THOS. M. ARRINGTON.

This action was brought by P. M. Nicrosi against Jacob Abraham, and was commenced by attachment sued out on the 10th January, 1887. The cause of action was the defendant's promissory note for $225, which was dated July 30th, 1885, payable on the 1st July, 1886, and given for one month's rent of a store-house in the city of Montgomery; and the attachment was levied on the stock of goods in the store-house on the day the attachment was sued out, to which a statutory claim was thereupon interposed by David Abraham, who was a son of Jacob Abraham. At the ensuing March term of the court, the defendant appeared by attorney, but only for the special purpose of making three motions, which were, in substance, to dissolve and dismiss the attachment, and to discharge the levy, on the ground that the goods levied on were not subject to the attachment; which motions being heard together by consent, and issue joined as to whether the goods were subject to the levy of the attachment, "the said issue was, by order of the court, submitted for trial to a jury;" and this issue being found in favor of

the plaintiff, the court rendered judgment declaring the
property subject to the levy, and then rendered final judgment by *nil dicit* against the defendant.

On the trial of the issue before the jury, as appears from
the bill of exceptions, the plaintiff having read in evidence
the note on which his action was founded, it was proved on
the part of the defendant, by said David Abraham, his son,
that on the 30th July, 1885, the day on which the note was
given, defendant leased from plaintiff the store-house in the
city of Montgomery in which the goods were when the
attachment was levied on them; that the lease was for the
term of one year, commencing on the 1st October, 1885;
that said note was given for rent accruing under said lease;
that the defendant, at the expiration of the lease, again
leased the store-house for another year, and continued to
occupy it as before; that the goods levied on were bought
by the defendant, and brought into the store-house, after the
expiration of the first lease, and during the term of the second lease, and that on the 7th January, 1887, three days
before the levy of the attachment, he (witness) bought from
his father the entire stock of goods in the store-house. On
cross-examination of said witness, he further testified that
his father, during the year 1885-6, "was constantly buying
and selling goods, and kept his stock up to about the same
amount;" and the court admitted this evidence, against the
objection and exception of the defendant. On the part of
the plaintiff, John Nicrosi, his agent, testified that, when the
note fell due, and was presented for payment, defendant
asked indulgence on it, promising to pay the notes given on
the new lease promptly as they fell due; that he assented to
this, and all of the notes subsequently maturing were paid.

On these facts, the court charged the jury, on request of
the plaintiff, "that if the goods were on the rented premises
at the time of the levy, it makes no difference whether they
were bought before or after the 1st October, 1886." The
defendant excepted to this charge, and requested the court,
in writing, to instruct the jury, "that they should find a
verdict for the defendant, if they believed the evidence;"
which charge the court refused, and the defendant excepted.

The admission of the evidence objected to, the charge
given, the refusal of the charge asked, and the final judgment, are now assigned as error.

ARRINGTON & GRAHAM, for appellant.—(1.) The statute

[Abraham v. Nicrosi.]

giving landlords a lien, such as is sought to be enforced in
this case, is in derogation of the common law, and must be
strictly construed. — *Nation v. Roberts*, 20 Ala. 544;
Zackowski v. Jones, 20 Ala. 189; *Kirksey v. Dubose*, 19 Ala.
43; *Scaife v. Stovall*, 67 Ala. 237; *Beale v. Posey*, 72 Ala.
323; *Cook v. Meyer*, 73 Ala. 580. (2.) The statute gives a lien
on the goods of the tenant in the store-house, or other building; and each contract of lease is to be construed as if the
statute were incorporated in it. If so incorporated, the lien
would extend only to goods brought into the house during
the term; and there can be no presumption that the parties
contemplated, or provided for, a continuation of the lease.
(3.) The judgment of condemnation, and the judgment by
nil dicit, is each erroneous.—*Moore v. Dickerson*, 44 Ala.
485; *Nabors v. Nabors*, 2 Porter, 162; *Lampley v. Beavers*,
25 Ala. 534. (4.) The evidence objected to was irrelevant,
and should have been excluded.—65 Ala. 88; 56 Ala. 235;
17 Ala. 566; 8 Porter, 511. (5.) The motions were the
proper remedy for reaching the irregularity complained of.
Rich v. Thornton, 69 Ala. 473; *Brown v. Coats*, 56 Ala. 439;
Drakeford v. Turk, 75 Ala. 339.

WATTS & SON, *contra*, cited *Hadley v. Bryers*, 58 Ala.
139; *Stewart v. Goode & Ulrick*, 29 Ala. 476; *Eaton v.
Harris*, 42 Ala. 491; *Sevier v. Throckmorton*, 33 Ala. 512;
Roberts v. Burgess, 85 Ala. 192; *Harmon v. Jenks*, 84 Ala.
74; *Lucas v. Goodwin*, 6 Ala. 831; *Thornton v. Winter*,
9 Ala. 613; *Betancourt v. Eberlein*, 71 Ala. 461.

McCLELLAN, J.—The act of February 23, 1883, as
amended by the act of February 17, 1885 (now constituting
sections 3069–3074 of the Code), giving to "landlords of
store-houses, dwelling-houses and other buildings, a lien on
the goods of their tenants for rents," must be construed in
the light of the common law, and be accorded such operation and effect, not inconsistent with its terms, as was given
to the landlord's remedy under the old law of distress. The
main points of difference between the statutory and common-
law systems are, that the former substitutes the process of
courts for the personal distraint of the landlord allowed by
the latter, and confines the distress to the property of the
tenant; whereas, under the latter, the right to distrain extended to the goods of a stranger found on the demised
premises. These changes were necessary, to conform the

law to the genius of our institutions, which is inimical alike to the taking of property without due process of law, and to the subjection of the goods of one man to the satisfaction of the debt of another, on the mere fortuitous circumstance of their being on the premises of the debtor. Aside from the cardinal points of difference, and such changes in detail as were necessary to limit and effectuate the new remedy, it is apprehended that the principles of the common law, as to rent and the remedies for its collection, apply also to the statutory right and remedy we are considering. At common law, there would be no distress, unless the relation of landlord and tenant existed. Under our statute, the existence of this relation is essential to the right of attachment. At common law, the right to distrain pertained only to property which was, or had been within a certain period, on the premises. There is no express, or necessarily implied limitation of this kind, in our statute, but, following the common law, we have adjudged that the right to attach extended only to goods which enjoyed the protection of the premises for which rent is claimed.—*Ex parte Barnes,* 84 Ala. 540. Distress could only be made, at common law, during the term of the lessee; and doubtless, under the statute, an attachment could not be maintained after the termination of the demise, except it may be in the enforcement of a lien which had attached before. What was a termination of a lease, in the sense which operated to put an end to the right of distress, became the point of many decisions at common law; and no reason occurs to us for not according to the principles settled in these cases a controlling influence in the construction of our statute, or, rather, in determining whether, in a given case, the term has ceased in that sense which defeats the right to attach. It is thoroughly established by these adjudications, that where the tenant holds over, after the term originally stipulated, the relation of landlord and tenant continues; the original term is held to be enlarged, and the right to distrain for the rent of any part of the tenure still exists.—Taylor Land. & Ten., p. 448, § 564.

This rule is based on the implication, which the law raises, that the parties have agreed to a continuation of the lease, and looking back from any point during the holding over, to the inception of the relation, the whole time is in law considered but one term. The courts, seizing on the reason for this result—the implication of an agreement to continue the

[Abraham v. Nicrosi.]

term—gave the rule a wider operation, and extended it to
cases in which the contract for a continuation of the tenancy
was expressed, as it before applied to contracts which were
implied from the situation of the parties. It thus became
the settled law, that where there are successive leases from
year to year, for the purpose of distress, all of such successive years are regarded as constituting but one term. In a
leading case on this subject, there was a rental for the year
1839, another for the year 1840, evidenced by a different
instrument, and yet another for the year 1841, evidenced by
an indorsement on the contract for 1840; and a distress in
1840 for the rent in arrear for 1839. Holding the distress
well made, the court uses this language: "What is there in
the nature of the case to prevent us taking a stand at the
time of the distress, and computing backwards, according to
the acts of the parties? Had the renewal for the several
years been by implication, it would, according to the language of the writers, have been construed to spring out of,
and continue to enlarge the first lease. Shall an express
renewal have a less important effect? There is just as much
room for implication and constructive continuation in the one
case as the other."—*Webber v. Shearman*, 6 Hill, 20. This
case was followed by subsequent ones; and it may now be
considered as settled law, that where there are leases from year
to year, and the rent of a former is in arrear during a subsequent year, the goods of the tenant then on the premises may
be distrained for such rent.—*Bell v. Potter*, 6 Hill, 497; *Parker's Appeal*, 5 Penn. St. 390; Taylor Land. & Ten., p. 504,
§ 572.

Substituting the lien of our statute, and the remedy by
which the lien is effectuated, for the old lien and remedy by
distress, and applying the principles above stated to the operation of the statute in this case, the result is, that the plaintiff below had a lien on the goods in the store-house at the
time of the attachment, for the rent in arrear for the previous year, whether those goods were in the store before the
end of that year or not; and the charges given by the court
asserting this proposition are free from error. The lien
attached to the goods the moment they were brought into
the house, if, when brought in, they belonged to the tenant;
and the alleged sale of January 7th, 1887, to the tenant's
son, conveyed no right to the property, which could prevail
over the lien, so long as the goods remained on the demised
premises. If these positions be well taken, it follows that

12

the evidence offered on the trial of the motion to dissolve
raised a wholly immaterial inquiry; and if error was committed in the admission of testimony, in rebuttal of irrelevant evidence introduced by the defendant, it was error
without injury; and if error, and injurious, the error is not
one of which the defendant can complain.—*Harmon v. Jenks*,
84 Ala. 74.

The judgment invoked by the motions should have been
confined to the motions. If the court had found that the
property was not subject to the attachment, for the reason
that the debt sued on was not for rent for the payment of
which a lien existed on the property, the attachment should
have been dissolved. Having, as we have seen, correctly
found that the note was for rent for which a lien on the property of defendant in the store during the second year of the
lease existed, the judgment should have been simply that the
motions be denied. The case would then have been precisely in the same condition as if the motions had not been
made. So considered, it presents the features of an ordinary
attachment suit, in which there has been a limited appearance
by the defendant, and a claim interposed by a third person,
under the statute, which was still pending. The jurisdiction
of the court to proceed to final judgment, depended on
whether the levy had been made on property which belonged
to the defendant. That question could not be determined
on the motions. The interposition of the claim by D. Abraham had the effect of rebutting the presumption of that fact
which arose from the sheriff's return, and postponed its ascertainment until the trial of the issue between the plaintiff and
the claimant. Until the trial was had, and the property
found in it to be subject to the attachment, there was no such
service of process on the defendant, by levy on his property,
as would support a judgment by default. That the court, in
passing on defendant's motion, had adjudged the property to
be his, can make no difference. It could not cut off the
claim in that trial. And if, on the trial of the claim suit,
the issue should be found in favor of D. Abraham, and the
property be adjudged to belong to him, the court would be
put in the attitude of having rendered a personal judgment
against J. Abraham, without personal service, without an
appearance on his part, and without constructive service by
levy on his property. These considerations lead us to the
conclusion, that the court erred in entering up judgment
against the defendant; a conclusion that is also strongly sup-

ported by the statute, which clearly contemplates that the suit against the defendant shall stand in abeyance, or at least not proceed to a judgment of condemnation, until the claim suit has been determined.—Code, §§ 3012–3013; *Moore v. Dickerson*, 44 Ala. 485; · *Lampley v. Beavers*, 25 Ala. 533.

It follows, that the judgment of condemnation was also erroneous; and for these reasons, the judgment will be reversed, and the cause remanded.

Reversed and remanded.

Campbell *v.* Hopkins.

Action on Attachment Bond.

1. *Composition with creditors; fraudulent proposal.*—A proposal by an insolvent or embarrassed debtor to his creditors, offering to surrender all of his property to them on condition of receiving an absolute release from further liability, is fraudulent, and, if accepted, would avoid the discharge, when it appears that some of the assets included in his schedule had been previously transferred to one of his creditors as collateral security, and were in his hands only for the purpose of collection; that the names of several small creditors were omitted, because he had "laid aside the money to pay them, and regarded them as paid," although the payment was in fact not made for two or three days afterwards; and that he also omitted a power-press, on which he had paid one half of the purchase-money, the vendor retaining a lien until full payment was made.

2. *Attachment, on ground of fraudulent disposition of property.*—A proposal for a composition with his creditors by an embarrassed debtor, offering to surrender all of his property on condition of receiving a release in full, is good ground for suing out an attachment (Code, § 2930), when it appears that his schedule of assets includes claims which he had already transferred to one of his creditors as collateral security, and omitted property in which he had a valuable interest, and that the names of several small creditors were omitted, money being retained and laid aside to pay them.

APPEAL from the Circuit Court of Madison.

Tried before the Hon. HENRY C. SPEAKE.

This action was brought by Frank W. Hopkins, against Allen R. Campbell and Archibald Campbell, to recover damages for the wrongful and vexatious suing out of an attachment, as alleged; and was commenced on the 24th December, 1884. The defendants pleaded "the general issue, in short by consent, with leave to give any special matter in evidence," and issue was joined on this plea. Under the rulings of the court, in the matter of charges given and refused, the plaintiff had a verdict and judgment for $2,572. The attachment was sued out on the 4th December, 1884, at the suit of Mallory, Crawford & Co., wholesale merchants in Memphis, Tennessee, on the ground, as stated in the affidavit, that said F. W. Hopkins "has fraudulently disposed of his property." The defendants here sued were sureties on the attachment bond. At the time the attachment was sued out, Hopkins was doing business as a merchant at Greenbier, Limestone county, and had become embarrassed, if not insolvent; and he addressed a circular letter to his creditors, which was dated December 1st, 1884, and in these words:

"In consequence of the almost total failure of the cotton crop in my section, I think it to your interest that I make the following statement, as it appears on my books. The same I herewith inclose. This statement excludes about $1,500 in doubtful and bad debts due me, on which something might possibly be realized. I made my purchases with intention of paying $ for $, and would have done so but for the disastrous crops. My proposition is, to make a fair and equitable distribution of my assets (counting at cost) among my creditors, expecting a release in full from each. I can claim under the law, as exempt, property to the amount of 1 m. dollars. I do not propose, however, to avail myself of this feature of the law, if it can be avoided; and in consideration of my not doing so, and making a clear surrender, I shall expect to be released of all further liability. I make to each of my creditors a *fac simile* statement."

On receipt of this circular letter, one of the partners of Mallory, Crawford & Co. came out to Greenbrier, and had an interview with Hopkins; and the attachment was at once sued out, and levied on plaintiff's stock of goods, garnishments being served on several of his debtors. The testimony of the plaintiff himself in reference to this circular, his condition at the time, and other attendant circumstances, or the material portions thereof, are stated in the opinion of the court. Many charges were asked by the defendants, and refused by the court, based on the facts stated as authorizing an attachment, and among them this: "(22.) If the jury believe the evidence, they must find for the defendants." The refusal of the several charges asked, and the charges given, to which exceptions were duly reserved, are now assigned as error.

[Campbell v. Hopkins.]

LAWRENCE COOPER, and MILTON HUMES, for appellants, contended that the general charge ought to have been given, citing *City Nat. Bank v. Jeffries*, 73 Ala. 183; Waples on Attachment, 52; 1 Smith's L. C. 29–30, 9th ed.; *Lukens v. Aird*, 6 Wall. 78; Bump on Fraud. Conv., 24, 190; *Wiswall v. Ticknor*, 6 Ala. 185; *Wiley, Banks & Co. v. Knight*, 27 Ala. 347; *Montgomery v. Kirksey*, 26 Ala. 172; *Reynolds v. Welch*, 47 Ala. 203; *Levy v. Williams*, 79 Ala. 171; *Sims v. Gaines*, 64 Ala. 392; *Stevens v. Helpman*, 29 La. Ann. 635; *Powell v. Matthews*, 10 Mo. 49; *Farmer's Bank v. Fonda*, 32 N. W. Rep. 664; 51 Maine, 418; 11 Metc. 231; 16 Fed. Rep. 206.

R. W. WALKER, *contra*, argued each of the assignments of error, and cited the following cases: *Durr v. Jackson*, 59 Ala. 206; *Pollak v. Searcy*, 84 Ala. 262; *Adams v. Thornton*, 78 Ala. 489; *Hodges v. Coleman*, 76 Ala. 103.

STONE, C. J.—The present suit was by Hopkins against Campbell *et al.*, for wrongfully and vexatiously suing out an attachment, under which the former's merchandise and other chattels were levied on and sold.

The following facts are clearly proved, and are undisputed: Mallory, Crawford & Co. were wholesale merchants, doing business in Memphis, Tennessee. Hopkins was their customer, and was a retail merchant, doing business at Greenbrier, Limestone county, Alabama. He was financially embarrassed, or cramped, at the opening of the year 1884, and made an agreement with Mallory, Crawford and Co., hereafter called M., C. & Co., that with certain assistance from them, he could tide his affairs over, and at the close of the season could and would pay them in full. Under this agreement, M., C. & Co. advanced to Hopkins in money and merchandise, until in November he owed them over twenty-two hundred dollars, nearly one half of his entire indebtedness.

Hopkins' principal business was advancing to planters, and his custom was to secure the repayment of such advances by mortgages and liens on the crops and stock of the planters to whom the advances were made. Of such debts from his customers, together with the securities taken for their payment, he had turned over to M., C. & Co., as collateral security for the debt due and to become due to them, different claims amounting to some eighteen hundred dollars. When harvest time arrived, M., C. & Co. returned these claims

and liens to Hopkins, that he might, as their agent, collect
them, and remit to them the proceeds. He proceeded to
collect several hundred dollars on them, and made some
remittances; but, at the time of the attachment, hereafter
described, he still held of these claims, uncollected, as much
as one half or more. He also had in his hands some of the
money collected, which he had not paid over; and he had
some horses which he had recovered from mortgagors—part
of the claims he had turned over to M., C. & Co. as collateral security.

Hopkins was a member of the partnership known as Hopkins, Seat & Son. Their business was ginning and packing
cotton, for hire, or toll. Hopkins had himself purchased a
power-press, used in that business; had paid $150, half of
the purchase-money, and his note was out for the other half,
with a year's interest, due December 1, 1884, with a lien on
the press for its payment. It is not shown, or pretended,
that the firm of Hopkins, Seat & Son had any part in this
purchase, was bound for the unpaid purchase-money, or that
it claimed any ownership in the press. So far as the record
discloses, the press was the individual property of Hopkins,
subject to the lien for $162. Hopkins also owed two other
small debts, evidenced by notes containing a waiver of exemptions. The aggregate of these three debts was something over two hundred and twenty dollars, due to Findley,
to Matthews & Co., and to Rison.

On December 1, 1884, Hopkins addressed a circular letter
to his creditors. The reporter will insert a copy of that circular, omitting the schedule, as furnished in the testimony
of Crawford. This circular stated on its face, that it set
forth all his creditors and the amount due to each, and that
it scheduled all his assets of every description. The gross
amount of liabilities, as set forth, was $4,762, and the aggre-
gate value of the assets he tendered was estimated at $4,200.
His offer was to turn over his entire assets, not excepting or
reserving his exemptions, on the condition, and only on the
condition, that all his creditors would accept them in full
payment of their claims, and give him a full discharge.
He said he proposed to make a "clear surrender," and, in
return, expected to be "released of all further liability."

Among the assets he proposed to surrender are the following items: "6 head of horses and mules, $400.00; collect-
ible debts, $781.30." Large part of the claims he charac-
terized as collectible, and proposed to turn over as part of

[Campbell v. Hopkins.]

his assets, was composed of the claims he had hypothecated, or placed as collaterals with M., C. & Co., and which were then in his hands as agent for collection. So, of the six head of horses and mules, three had been received by him in payment, or part payment, of the claims and mortgages so held by M., C. & Co. as collateral security. Neither the circular letter, nor the schedule, gave any notice of these facts.

In his schedule of creditors he did not place the name of Findley, Matthews & Co., or Rison. Nor did he mention the money then in his possession, something over two hundred and forty dollars. In regard to these, he testified before the jury as follows: "On November 29, 1884, I had on hand $228.04. · · · That was on Saturday. I laid this money aside to pay my note to C. D. Findley, $162.05, and the account of Matthews & Co., $21.60, and of J. L. Rison, for $36.97. · · · I made the entry on my book on Saturday, November 29, showing the payment of the Findley note. But in some way I did not send the money and check to W. R. Rison & Co. that day." [W. R. Rison & Co. were bankers.] "The next day was Sunday. On Monday, I was engaged all day in writing letters and statements to my creditors. And it was not until Tuesday, December 2, that I sent the money to W. R. Rison & Co., and requested them to pay the Findley note. But, on the Saturday before, I had laid aside this money to pay the Findley, Matthews, and Rison debts, and in making the statements to my creditors, neither the debts themselves, nor the money with which they were paid, were included. I regarded them as paid." He further testified as follows: "Several weeks prior to December 1, 1884, I realized my embarrassed condition, and contemplated making a statement and proposition to my creditors, which I did make on that day."

The plaintiff's own testimony shows that, in presenting his list of creditors, he omitted three of his debts, which were then unpaid; for setting apart money to pay them, was not paying them. He still owed the debts, and the money remained his. It would remain his, and subject to his control, until it was actually applied in their liquidation. And this "laying aside" on his part was part and parcel of his scheme to compound his debts, and obtain a discharge from them; for he had contemplated submitting his statement and proposition for "several weeks." This, then, was a naked proposition, ostensibly to make a full surrender of all his property, for the general benefit of all his creditors, while he secretly withheld what money he had for the payment of certain preferred creditors in full, whose names, and the fact and amounts of their several claims, he also withheld. This, if successful, would have been such a fraud on his other creditors, as that they could have set aside Hopkins' discharge from his debts, because they would have been obtained by fraud.—*City Nat. Bank v. Jeffries,* 73 Ala. 183; 3 Amer. & Eng. Encyc. of Law, 396-398.

Other features of this transaction deserve comment. Of the assets proposed to be turned over to the creditors, a material part had been previously pledged to Mallory, Crawford & Co., as collateral security; and yet the offer contained nothing that could give the slightest notice of such lien or incumbrance. Not even M., C. & Co. would have detected that such was the case. If the offer had been accepted, the result must needs have been to take from M., C. & Co. what had been specially pledged to them, or to obtain from the other creditors a discharge, upon the surrender of assets greatly less valuable than they were represented to be. This would have been a fraud, which would have set aside Hopkins' discharge; for the law requires good faith on the part of a debtor in compounding with his creditors.—3 Amer. & Eng. Encyc. Law, 391.

There is yet another damaging feature of this transaction. The largest part— $162—of the money "set apart" by Hopkins was to be paid to Findley, final payment of the power-press. When that payment was made, the press became the unincumbered property of Hopkins. In his report of his assets to his creditors, no reference whatever is made to this power-press. This secured a benefit to Hopkins, of relatively.considerable value—secured it secretly, and as the result of the composition he proposed to make. This, of itself, would have been a fraud, which would have invalidated the composition and discharge. And the fraudulent disposition, or attempt fraudulently to dispose of a part, of a failing debtor's effects, is sufficient ground for attachment.—*Smith v. Baker,* 80 Ala. 318; *Sims v. Gaines,* 64 Ala. 392-8; *Lehman v. Kelly,* 68 Ala. 192; *Seaman v. Nolen, Ib.* 463; *Levy v. Williams,,* 79 Ala. 171; *Prichett v. Pollack,* 82 Ala. 169; *Lukins v. Aird,* 6 Wall. 78.

There are many rulings of the Circuit Court which can not be reconciled with our views. According to the testi-

[Harrison v. Yerby.]

mony of the plaintiff, he was not entitled to recover. Charge
No. 22 asked by defendant ought to have been given.

Reversed and remanded.

Harrison *v.* Yerby.

*Bill in Equity by Purchaser, for Injunction against Sale
under Unrecorded Mortgage.*

1. *Dissolution of injunction on answer.*—On motion to dissolve an injunction, even when the answer contains a full and complete denial of
the material allegations of the bill, the court is invested with a wide
latitude of discretion, in the exercise of which it will consider and balance the probable resulting damages to the respective parties; and if
it appears that irreparable mischief may result from a dissolution, or
that greater injury may thereby result to the complainant than to the
defendant from continuing the writ in force, a special injunction will be
retained until final hearing.

2. *Same; case at bar.*—When the bill prays an injunction against a
sale under a mortgage, the complainant having purchased from the
mortgagee, as agent of the mortgagor (to whom he had previously sold
and conveyed), and alleging that the defendant fraudulently concealed
from him the existence of the mortgage, which was then unrecorded;
the injunction may properly be retained, notwithstanding the denials
of fraud in the answer, when it appears that the mortgagor and vendor
is a non-resident, and that he has transferred one of the complainant's
notes for the purchase-money, to an assignee, who is asserting a prior
lien on the land.

APPEAL from the Chancery Court of Tuskaloosa.

Heard before the Hon. THOMAS COBBS.

The bill in this case was filed on the 9th November, 1888,
by J. Stephen Yerby, against J. C. Harrison, Geo. F. Lupton, and J. O. Prude; and sought (1) to enjoin a threatened
sale, under a power in a mortgage, of certain lots of land,
which the complainant had bought from said Harrison, who
was the agent of said Lupton; (2) to have the mortgage
cancelled, as to the lots, as a deed on the complainant's title;
and (3) to enjoin said Prude from enforcing the collection
of a note given for a part of the purchase-money, which he
claimed was a prior lien on the lots. The said lots were
part of a tract or parcel of land adjoining the city of Tuskaloosa, which was sold and conveyed by said Harrison and
wife to Lupton, on the 16th April, 1887, at the price of
$4,000; and at the same time Lupton executed to Harrison
a mortgage on the property, to secure the payment of two

notes, each for $1,333.33, given for the deferred payments;
one of said notes falling due April 16th, 1888, and the other
October 16th.   This mortgage was filed for record in the
office of the probate judge, as shown by his certificate, on
the 7th July, 1887; but it was not proved by the attesting
witness, and was not acknowledged by the grantor until the
11th July, 1887.   Immediately after the purchase of the
land, Lupton had it divided into lots, and left the property
in the hands of said Harrison, or J. C. Harrison & Co., real
estate agents in Tuskaloosa, for sale.   On April 21st, 1887,
complainant (Yerby) bought two of said lots from Harrison,
as agent for Lupton, for the aggregate price of $1,950, pay-
ing $650 cash, and giving his two notes for $650 each, payable twelve and eighteen months after date; and on August
6th afterwards he bought a third lot, at the price of $700,
of which $500 was paid in cash, and a note for $200 given
for the residue.   On each of these sales, a bond for titles
was executed by said Lupton, conditioned in the usual form.
The first note for $650, which fell due on the 21st April,
1888, was discounted before maturity, and paid by complainant on the 7th May, 1887; and the note for $200 was paid
at maturity, April 10th, 1888.   The second note for $650,
which fell due on the 16th October, 1888, was transferred
by Lupton to J. O. Prude, as collateral security for an existing debt; and said Prude asserted it as a prior lien on the
two lots first sold to complainant, when, as the bill alleged,
said Harrison advertised them for sale under his mortgage
from Lupton.

The bill alleged that all these transactions occurred between the complainant and said J. C. Harrison, acting as the
agent of Lupton, and sought equitable relief against the
mortgage and threatened sale on these grounds: (*Par.* 11.)
"During all these transactions, said Harrison kept your
orator in ignorance of the fact that he held said mortgage on
said property, or any adverse claim thereto, but, on the contrary, represented the title as good, and repeatedly told
your orator that a good and perfect title could and would be
delivered as soon as all the purchase-money was paid; and
said Harrison never in any way so much as intimated that
he held a mortgage on said property, but fraudulently misled
your orator, and procured him to purchase said property, and
to receive said bond for title therefor, and also fraudulently
and designedly procured your orator to take up and satisfy
said note before maturity; the said Harrison having never

filed his said mortgage, nor so much as procured an acknowledgment thereof before an officer." And the complainant
declared his readiness, willingness and ability to pay the
unpaid note for $650, with interest, so soon as he could ob-
tain from Lupton a good and sufficient conveyance, as
required by the terms of his bond for title.

In response to these allegations of the bill, the answer of
Harrison contained the following averments: "In answer to
the 11th part of the 1st paragraph of said bill of complaint,
extending from line 21, page 9, to line 3, of page 11,
respondent denies the same wholly and entirely, as being
untrue in each and every statement thereof. He denies that,
during the said transactions, he kept complainant in ignorance of the fact that he held the said Lupton mortgage upon
said premises. He denies that he told complainant a good
and perfect deed could and would be delivered to him so
soon as all of the purchase-money should be paid to said
Lupton; and asserts that he did say to complainant that a
good and sufficient deed could be made by said Lupton to
complainant, so soon as all of the purchase-money due on
respondent's mortgage should be paid to him by said Lupton.
He denies that he fraudulently misled and procured complainant to purchase said property, and to receive therefor
said bond for title; and denies that he fraudulently procured
complainant to take up and satisfy said note before it became due; and he denies that his said mortgage was not filed
within the time prescribed by law." And a subsequent
paragraph of his answer contained these averments: "Respondent believes and asserts that, during the entire time of
the negotiation for the purchase of said property, complainant
was fully aware that said Lupton had bought said property
from him, and that a part of the purchase price was not paid,
and that respondent held a mortgage on said property to
secure the payment of the same. But, if there could be any
possible doubt about complainant being informed of the existence of said mortgage during the negotiations, it was
ended and set at rest when the parties met in the office of
said J. C. Harrison & Co. for the purpose of completing said
sale; at which time the question came up, as to what kind of
instrument said Lupton should execute to complainant; and
it was stated that he would give him a bond for title, conditioned to make title upon payment of the amount due. Complainant then inquired if he could not have a deed for the
property, and respondent stated to him that, on account of

[Harrison v. Yerby.]

Lupton having paid only a part of the purchase-money for the property, and having given this respondent a mortgage on the property for the unpaid price, which mortgage was then unsatisfied, said Lupton could not then make a deed, but could do so when he had satisfied said mortgage, so far as respondent was concerned. And respondent avers, that this entire matter, as to the kind of transfer and said unsatisfied mortgage, was fully discussed, talked of, and understood by all present; and that there was no concealment or misrepresentation used by this respondent, or any other person, towards complainant, but that said sale was open, fair and square, and everything connected with the title of said property was open to complainant's examination, and that he fully knew of the existence of said mortgage to respondent."

An answer was also filed by Lupton, and an answer and cross-bill by Prude; but these require no notice. After answers filed, a motion was submitted by Harrison, to dissolve the injunction on the denials of his answer; which motion being overruled and refused by the chancellor, his decree is here assigned as error by said Harrison.

WOOD & WOOD, for appellant.—The bill seeks to set up an equitable estoppel against the legal title to land, but its allegations are scarcely sufficient.—Bigelow on Estoppel, 4th ed., 679; 2 Herman on Estoppel, § 966; *Turnipseed v. Hudson*, 50 Miss. 249; 7 Amer. & Eng. Encycl. Law, 12; 2 Pom. Equity, § 806; 3 Washb. Real Property, 88; 80 Ala. 354. Admitting the sufficiency of the bill, its material allegations are denied fully, explicitly, and with particularity; and the injunction ought to have been dissolved on the denials of the answer.—*Weems v. Weems*, 73 Ala. 464; *Bishop v. Wood*, 59 Ala. 253; *Jackson v. Jackson*, 84 Ala. 344; *Satterfield v. John*, 33 Ala. 132; High on Injunctions, 2d vol., §§ 1472, 1505; *Collier v. Falk*, 61 Ala. 105; *Garrett v. Lynch*, 44 Ala. 683; *Dunlap v. Clements*, 7 Ala. 539; 67 N. C. 422. The insolvency of the defendants is not averred in the bill, nor any other facts stated from which an inference of irreparable damage may be drawn.

COCHRANE & FITTS, *contra*.—There is no inflexible rule, which requires the dissolution of an injunction on the denials of the answer. On the contrary, it is a matter of sound judicial discretion, to be exercised on a consideration of all the facts and circumstances of the particular case; and this

[Harrison v. Yerby.]

discretion has a wider range where fraud is charged, and where irreparable injury may result from a dissolution. Another principle requires the court to weigh the relative benefit or injury which may result to the respective parties; and the appellate court will not disturb the ruling of the chancellor, unless the record shows an abuse of his discretion. An application of these principles to the facts of this case justifies the decision of the chancellor.—High on Injunctions, §§ 508–14, 900, 905, 1467, 1543; *Collier v. Falk*, 61 Ala. 105; *Chambers v. Ala. Iron Co.*, 67 Ala. 353; *Bibb v. Shackelford*, 38 Ala. 611; *E. & W. Ala. R. R. v. E. T., Va. & Ga. R. R.*, 75 Ala. 275; *Miller v. Bates*, 35 Ala. 580; *Rembert v. Brown*, 17 Ala. 667; *Walker v. Tyson*, 52 Ala. 593.

SOMERVILLE, J.—The motion made before the chancellor was to dissolve the injunction, on the denial of the facts constituting the equity of the bill, as contained in the answer of the respondent. This motion was overruled, and from this ruling the present appeal was taken.

The denials contained in the answer are not so full and complete as we might desire. But, considering that they are sufficiently so, the rule is not imperative, that the injunction shall in all such cases be dissolved, The court is invested with a wide latitude of discretion in acting on such cases. It will especially weigh the relative degree of injury or benefit to the parties which may ensue from the maintenance of the injunction on the one hand, or its dissolution on the other; and if the continuance of the writ will probably cause less injustice and inconvenience to the defendant, than its dissolution will to the complainant, the court, upon balancing the question of relative damage, always feels at liberty to exercise its discretion in furtherance of justice, by maintaining the injunction; especially where the discretion of the lower court, which is entitled to great respect, has been apparently exercised without abuse. Where irreparable mischief to the complainant will be likely to follow from a dissolution, the appellate court always feels authorized to allow a special injunction to remain in force, until a final hearing can be had on the merits.—*Bibb v. Shackelford*, 38 Ala. 611; *East & West R. R. Co. v. East Tenn., &c. R. R. Co.*, 75 Ala. 275; *Chambers v. Ala. Iron Co.*, 67 Ala. 353; *Collier v. Falk*, 61 Ala. 105; *Columbus & West. R. R. Co. v. Witherow*, 82 Ala. 190; 2 High on Inj., § 150 *et seq*;

Doughty v. S. & E. R. R. Co., 51 Amer. Dec. 267; *Mc-Brayer v Hardin*, 53 Amer. Dec. 389.

There is no question as to the equity of the bill. If the facts alleged in it are satisfactorily proved, the complainant is unquestionably entitled to a perpetual injunction of the mortgage sale of the land. The defendant, Lupton, the vendor of the land, is a non-resident of the State. He has transferred the last note due for the purchase-money to the defendant Prude, who himself claims priority of lien on the premises. It is important to the complainant to have settled the relative priority of this lien and that of the mortgage executed by Lupton to the defendant Harrison. Without such adjustment, much embarrassment and consequent loss will probably ensue to complainant, which may prove irreparable. The defendants, on the contrary, can suffer no very great inconvenience by keeping the injunction in force, being fully protected against loss by the injunction bond.

The decree of the chancellor keeping the injunction in force is free from error, and is affirmed.

Aycock *v.* Adler.

Bill in Equity for Redemption, by Judgment Debtor.

1. *Redemption by judgment debtor; surrender of possession on demand.* On bill to redeem by the judgment debtor (Code, §§ 1879-81), if it appears that he had rented out the land to a tenant, who quit the possession before the sale, and that the purchaser entered, within ten days, without demand, and without objection, this shows a substantial surrender of possession within ten days after the sale.

2. *Same; outstanding title acquired by purchaser, or sub-purchaser.* On bill to redeem by a judgment debtor, showing a substantial compliance with statutory requisitions, neither the purchaser, nor a sub-purchaser under him, can attack the validity of the debtor's original title, or set up, by cross-bill, a title subsequently acquired from a third person.

APPEAL from the Chancery Court of Etowah.

Heard before the Hon. S. K. McSPADDEN.

The bill in this case was filed on the 7th February, 1888, by Ike Adler, against W. L. Aycock and W. L. Echols; and sought to redeem a house and lot in Gadsden, containing about one acre, which had been sold under execution against the complainant, in January, 1887, and of which the defendants were in possession, as sub-purchasers under Amos E.

Goodhue, the purchaser at the sheriff's sale.   The complainant had bought the land at a sale under a mortgage executed by Mrs. Anne E. Wharton to Dean, Whaley & Co., which was dated August 11th, 1883, the mortgagees' conveyance to him being dated July 23d, 1885.   The defendants denied the complainant's right to redeem, and attacked the validity of the sale under the mortgage; and having obtained a conveyance to themselves from the trustees in the mortgage, they sought by cross-bill to set aside the complainant's purchase at the mortgage sale, and to be let in to redeem as purchasers from the mortgagor.   On final hearing, on pleadings and proof, the chancellor rendered a decree for the complainant; and his decree is here assigned as error.

JAMES AIKEN, DORTCH & MARTIN, and GEO. D. MOTLEY, fro appellants.

A. E. GOODHUE, *contra.*

CLOPTON, J.—Appellee seeks by the bill to enforce the statutory right of redemption.   The land, which is sought to be redeemed, was sold under an execution against the appellee, and was purchased by Amos E. Goodhue.   The bill alleges, and the proof shows, a tender of the purchase-money, with ten per cent. *per annum* thereon, and an offer to pay all lawful charges.   Goodhue conveyed the land by quit-claim deed to appellant, Aycock, who conveyed an undivided half interest to his co-appellant.   Complainant was in possession of the land at the time of the execution sale, and claimed title by purchase at a sale previously made under a power contained in a mortgage, executed by Mrs. Wharton to Dean, Whaley & Co.   After the execution of the mortgage, Mrs. Wharton sold and conveyed the land to Jesse Looney and others, trustees, from whom defendants deduce title, other than the title acquired from the purchaser at the sheriff's sale.   Defendants refused to accept the tender of complainant, and denied the right to redeem, on the alleged ground, that the mortgage sale, under which complainant derived title, was void by reasons of irregularities and non-compliance with the conditions of the mortgage.

The statute confers on complainant the right to redeem the land, within two years after the execution sale, if possession was delivered within ten days thereafter, on demand of the purchaser, by paying or tendering the purchase-money, with ten per cent. *per annum* thereon, and all other lawful charges.—Code, 1886, §§ 1879-1881.   The agreed statement of facts shows, that complainant had rented the land to a tenant, who left it about a month prior to the sheriff's sale, and that within ten days after the sale the purchaser went into possession, without having made demand, and without objection, and remained in possession until he conveyed to Aycock, who has been in possession ever since.   The tender and surrender of possession by complainant were sufficient.

A compliance, or tender of compliance with the statutory requirements, has the effect to re-invest the debtor with the title which he possessed at the time of the sale; and the purchaser, if a conveyance has been made to him, is required to re-convey to the debtor such title as he acquired by the purchase.   Any other right or title which the purchaser, or those claiming under him, may have acquired after the sale, is not affected by the redemption, and he can not set up such title in bar of a bill to redeem.   After the purpose of the statute has been effectuated, by restoring the debtor to the right and possession he had at the time of the sale, the person from whom the debtor redeems may assert any superior title which he may have subsequently obtained, by any appropriate remedy.   The object of the cross-bill, filed by defendant, is to call upon the court to determine the validity of the title of the execution debtor.   This, the court will not do, on a bill to redeem; such inquiry being foreign to the issues.   The essential facts existing—a sale under execution, an entry into possession by the purchaser, and an offer to redeem in compliance with the statute—entitle the complainant to the relief he seeks, without regard to any other title the defendants may have subsequently acquired from any other source.—*Posey v. Pressley*, 60 Ala. 243; *Hanna v. Steele*, 84 Ala. 305.

In the bill, complainant tenders and offers to pay the purchase-money, with ten per cent. *per annum* thereon, and all lawful charges, and avers that he is ready, able and willing to pay, and submits himself to the jurisdiction of the court. Under such offer and submission, the court may compel him to pay as the condition of granting the relief.   The bill sufficiently offers to do equity.—*Rogers v. Torbut*, 58 Ala. 523.

Affirmed.

Hewlett, Schwarz & Co. *v.* Alexander.

*Action on Common Count for Work and Labor, with Special
Count on Contractor's Lien.*

1. *Breach of contract, and waiver thereof; rescission.*—Under a contract by which plaintiff undertook to furnish materials and build a house for defendant at a specified price, to be paid as the work progressed on the certified estimate of the supervising architect, the defendant's failure to make partial payments on the certified estimates is a breach of the contract, but is waived by plaintiff's consent to wait for the money, and continuing to perform the work; and if the plaintiff himself violates the stipulations of the contract by furnishing materials and work of an inferior quality, and fails to correct the resulting defects, after repeated requests and promises to do so, the defendant may discharge him, and treat the contract as annulled and rescinded, notwithstanding the breaches on his part which had been thus waived.

2. *Contract for construction of building; completion by owner, on default of contractor.*—On a contract for furnishing the materials and building a house, containing a stipulation that, on default by the contractor, and after notice to him, the owner might himself complete the building, deducting the expenses from the stipulated price, or the unpaid residue thereof, and accounting to the contractor only for the excess; if the expenses incurred in completing the house exceed the balance due to the contractor, no action lies in his favor.

APPEAL from the City Court of Birmingham.

Tried before the Hon. H. A. SHARPE.

This action was brought by John G. Alexander, against the appellants as partners, to recover an alleged balance due for materials furnished and work done by plaintiff in erecting a large brick building for defendants in the city of Birmingham; and was commenced on the 21st October, 1887. The complaint contained the common count for materials furnished and work and labor done, and a special count which sought to enforce a contractor's lien on the property. The defendants pleaded the general issue, payment, set-off, and recoupment of damages; and issue was joined on these several pleas. The cause being submitted to the court without a jury, judgment was rendered for the plaintiff, for $958.20, and a statutory lien on the building declared in his favor. The defendants excepted to the decision and judgment of the court, and they here assign it as error. The material facts, as found by this court, are stated in the opinion.

13

FEAGIN & WILKERSON, for appellants, cited Bish. Contracts, § 829; *Brigham v. Carlisle*, 78 Ala. 243; 30 N. W. Rep. 446; *Smith v. Brady*, 17 N. Y. 179, or 72 Amer. Dec. 442; *English v. Wilson*, 34 Ala. 201; *Allen v. McKibben*, 5 Mich. 455; 26 Mich. 473; 7 Pick. 181, or 19 Amer. Dec. 268, and notes; *Bragg v. Bradford*, 33 Vt. 35; *Dyer v. Jones*, 8 Vt. 205.

MOUNTJOY & TOMLINSON, *contra*, cited *Canal Co. v. Gordon*, 6 Wall. 561; *Railroad Co. v. Howard*, 13 How. 343; *U. S. v. Peck*, 102 U. S. (12 Otto), 64.

McCLELLAN, J.—This case was tried by the judge below, without jury, under section 12 of the act of December 9, 1884, establishing the City Court of Birmingham, which makes it our duty on appeal to review "the conclusions and judgment of the (city) court on the evidence." Upon a consideration of the whole evidence, we are led by a preponderance of testimony to the following conclusions: 1. That appellants committed breaches of their contract on the 1st and 8th days of October, 1887, in failing to pay the estimates of work done and materials furnished by appellee, as certified to them by the supervising architect. 2. That the breach of October 1st was waived by appellee's consent to wait for the money until Hewlett's return, and his continuing to perform the contract. 3. That the breach of October 8th was waived by appellee's tacit assent to further delay in the payment of the estimates, and continued performance of the contract. 4. That there were breaches of the contract on the part of appellee, prior to October 1st, with respect to the kind and quantity of material supplied by him, the manner of its use, and the character of work done in the construction of the house. 5. That these breaches of the contract were not waived by appellants, but that they at all times insisted on appellee's remedying the defects resulting from them, and upon his final refusal to do so—after having all the while previously promised to correct them—they discharged him, and annulled the contract, as by stipulations in the contract itself they were authorized to do, upon his failure and refusal to comply with its terms.

The contract being thus rightfully terminated before the completion of the building, the rights and interests of the parties are to be determined in accordance with the stipulations entered into by them with respect to this contingency.

These stipulations are as follows: Upon the termination of the contract "all claim of the contractor, his executors, administrators; or assigns shall cease; and the proprietor may provide materials and workmen sufficient to complete the said works, after giving forty-eight hours notice, in writing, directed and delivered to the contractor, or at his residence, or place of business; and the expense of the notice and the completing of the various works will be deducted from the amount of contract, or any part of it, due or to become due to the contractor. . . . . . But, if any balance on the amount of this contract remains after completing in respect to the work done during the time of the defaulting contractor, the same shall belong to the persons legally representing him; but the proprietor shall not be liable or accountable to them in any way for the manner in which he may have gotten the work completed."

The appellants completed the building, under the right to do so given by these provisions of the contract, at an aggregate outlay, including payments made to appellee and others before the termination of the contract, of $21,178.50. It was satisfactorily shown that the expenditure of this sum, even with some modifications of the original plans which lessened the cost of the work, was reasonable and necessary. The contract price fixed in the original agreement was $19,514. It was claimed by appellee that the cost of rebuilding a part of the wall, which gave way without fault of his, should be added to this sum. This item was $242, and allowing his claim in that particular the total contract price was $19,756. It is apparent, therefore, that there was no balance of the amount which was due, or could under any circumstances have become due to appellee, remaining after the completion of the work by appellants. On the contrary, the payments by the proprietors exceeded to the extent of $1,422.50 the greatest sum that appellee would have been entitled to under the contract had he fully performed it. On this state of proof, if we are to give any effect to the language of the contract—if the court is to be governed at all by the agreement which the parties themselves made, and as to the true intent and meaning of which there can be no doubt—the plaintiff below was not entitled to recover in this action.

The judgment below must be reversed, and the cause remanded.

Gunter *v.* Stuart.

Action on Account, for Goods Sold and Delivered.

1. *Admission by agent, after termination of agency.*—The clerk of a steamboat, having authority to make purchases and to state accounts for the boat, can not bind the owners by his written admission of the correctness of an account after the termination of his agency, but must be examined as a witness to prove its correctness, if known by him.

APPEAL from the Circuit Court of Jackson.

Tried before the Hon. JOHN B. TALLY.

This action was brought by John B. Stuart, against R. C. Gunter and others, late partners doing business under the name of the Decatur & Chattanooga Packet Company; and was commenced on the 17th August, 1886. The complaint contained a count on an account stated, claiming $108.43 for goods sold and delivered by plaintiff to defendants, "through their agents, from July 7th, 1883, to February 9th, 1886;" and a count on an open account was added by amendment. The defendants pleaded *non assumpsit*, payment and set-off, in short by consent; and issue was joined on these several pleas. On the trial, as the bill of exceptions snows, it appeared that the plaintiff was a general merchant, doing business at Decatur; that the defendants had been engaged in business as partners, owning and running several steamboats on the Tennessee River, between Decatur and Chattanooga; and that the goods, the price of which was the cause of action, were sold to or for the use of their several boats. The plaintiff did not produce an itemized account, but had his books in court, and testified that he had sent an itemized account, by mail, to S. C. Capehart, one of the defendants; and he produced a statement of account against each boat, showing the balance due on account. At the foot of each of these statements, or accounts, were written the words, "This statement is correct," or words the same in substance, to which was signed the name of "J. B. McKee, clerk;" one of which was dated May 22d, 1886, and the others, October 31st, 1885. The defendants introduced evidence showing that their partnership in the steamboat business was dissolved on October 5th, 1885; that said McKee, who had

[Gunter v. Stuart.]

been their clerk, quit their employment in June, 1885, and that he was in the service of another boat when he signed said stated accounts. On this evidence, the defendants asked the following charges in writing: (2.) "If the jury believe from the evidence that McKee was not in the employment of the defendants at the time he stated said accounts with plaintiff, then the defendants are not bound thereby." (3.) "If the jury believe from the evidence that the defendants' partnership was dissolved and ceased to exist before McKee indorsed said accounts, then his acts do not and can not bind the defendants." The court refused each of these charges, and the defendants duly excepted; and these rulings are here assigned as error.

HUNT & CLOPTON, for appellants.

J. E. BROWN, *contra.*

STONE, C. J.—Part of Stuart's evidence, on which he relied for recovery against the steamboat company, the appellants, consisted in certain stated accounts, certified to be correct by one McKee, styling himself clerk. These certificates, several of them bear date in October, 1885, and some of the items appear to be later than this. There was testimony tending to show that McKee ceased to be clerk or agent of appellants about June 1, 1885, and that he was not afterwards in their employment. It is too clear to admit of argument, that after McKee ceased to be clerk and agent of appellants, he could neither do any act, state an account, or make an admission that would bind them. While the relation of principal and agent exists, the agent can bind his principal by any act done within the scope of his authority, and by any admission made contemporaneous with, and explanatory of the act of agency so done.—3 Brick. Dig. 25, §§ 107-8. And it may be that, acting as clerk of the boat, it was within the purview of his duties to make purchases for the boat, and to state accounts. All these powers, however, would necessarily terminate when his connection with the boat was severed. To obtain, after that time, any information he might possess, he must needs have been made a witness. Charges 2 and 3 asked by appellants ought to have been given

Reversed and remanded.

Clark *v.* Allen.

*Bill in Equity to establish Equitable Title to Homestead,
and for Injunction against Judgment at Law.*

1. *Homestead tract containing more than eighty acres; equitable rights
of purchaser from debtor, as against purchaser at execution sale.*—Where
the owner of a homestead tract of land containing more than eighty
acres, having made and filed a declaration and claim of exemption,
which was valid though irregular, sold and conveyed the entire tract on
the 6th March, 1880, putting the purchaser in possession; and the land
was afterwards sold under an execution lien, which was existing at the
time of this sale and conveyance, and the continuity of which was never
broken; the plaintiff in execution becoming the purchaser with notice
of the sale and conveyance by the debtor, and afterwards recovering a
judgment at law for the land, against the grantee and his tenants, with
damages for the rents; *held*, that the debtor's grantee acquired an
equitable title to the homestead, not exceeding eighty acres of the entire tract, and was entitled to have it set apart in equity, and was also
entitled to an injunction against the judgment for damages (or rents),
so far as the rents accrued or arose from the land allotted to him.
2. *Same; setting aside sale under execution.*—In ordinary cases, a court
of equity will not take jurisdiction to set aside a sale of lands under execution by the sheriff, even at the instance of a person who claims an
equitable interest by purchase from the defendant, because he has an
adequate remedy by motion to set aside the sale; but, when any distinct ground of equity intervenes, or when a motion to set aside the sale
is not a complete and adequate remedy, he may invoke the jurisdiction
of a court of equity.

APPEAL from the Chancery Court of Greene.

Heard before the Hon. THOS. B. WETMORE, as special
chancellor.

The bill in this case was filed on the 4th November, 1884,
by Mrs. Martha J. Allen, against Thomas C. Clark and John
P. Spencer; and sought to establish the complainant's equitable title and interest in a tract of land, which had been
sold and conveyed to her by said Spencer, by deed dated
March 6th, 1880, and which was afterwards sold under execution against him by the sheriff, said Clark becoming the
purchaser; and Clark having afterwards recovered a judgment in ejectment for the land, against the complainant and
her tenants, with $150 damages on account of rents, the
bill also prayed a partial injunction of this money judgment, to the extent of her equitable interest in the land as
ascertained by the decree of the court. Spencer died pending the suit, and it was abated as to him.

[Clark v. Allen.]

The tract of land contained eighty-eight acres, and was owned and occupied by said Spencer, as he claimed, as a homestead, prior to his sale and conveyance, March 6th, 1880, to the complainant; and on the 22d October, 1878, he had made and filed for record, in the office of the probate judge, a declaration and claim of exemption for the whole tract, not selecting any particular part. The execution under which the land was sold by the sheriff, on the first Monday in August, 1881, was issued on a decree in chancery which Clark had obtained against Spencer in July, 1879. The chancery suit was founded on a debt contracted in 1871, and it was pending when said declaration and claim of exemption was filed. The first execution on this decree was issued on October 22, 1879, returnable on the first Monday in January, 1880; and it was "returned for *an alias*," January 2d, 1880. A second execution was issued on the 5th January, 1880, returnable on the first Monday in June; and having been levied on said tract of land, it was returned, June 2d, "Levy discharged on claim of exemption filed." A third execution was issued December 2d, 1880, returnable on the fourth Monday in January, 1881, and returned January 25th, "No property found." A fourth execution, issued March 17th, with the return day in blank, was levied on the land on the 14th April, 1881; and it was returned June 6th, 1881, indorsed "Returned for *alias pluries*, by order of plaintiff." The fifth and last execution was issued June 6th, 1881, and returnable on the first Monday in September; and the land was sold under it, as above stated. Notice was given, at the sale, of Spencer's sale and conveyance to Mrs. Allen, and of her claim to the homestead interest of eighty acres. Mrs. Allen had taken possession of the land soon after her purchase, and claimed to be in possession, by her tenants, at the time of the sheriff's sale. In March, 1882, Clark brought an action of ejectment, or statutory action in the nature thereof, against Spencer and the tenants in possession; and Mrs. Allen defended the suit as landlord. In that suit, judgment was rendered in favor of the plaintiff, on October 25th, 1883, for the possession of the land, and for $150 damages on account of rents; and that judgment was affirmed by this court on appeal, as shown by the reported case of *Clark v. Spencer* (75 Ala. 49–58), which should be entitled *Spencer v. Clark*. This is the judgment, against which the complainant sought an injunction, to the extent of her interest in the land; and she also asked the appointment of commissioners, to set aside and allot to her eighty acres of the land, as the homestead interest acquired by her purchase from said Spencer.

A demurrer to the bill, for want of equity, was interposed, but overruled; and on final hearing, on pleadings and proof, a decree was rendered for the complainant, appointing commissioners to set aside and allot to her eighty acres of the land, and granting a partial injunction of the judgment for damages, or rents, as prayed. The defendant appeals from this decree, and assigns each part of it as error.

Thos. R. Roulhac, for appellant.—By her purchase and conveyance from Spencer, Mrs. Allen acquired only his estate and interest in the land, which was subject to Clark's execution lien; and that, if anything, was a legal, as distinguished from an equitable estate or interest, and has been lost by *laches*, or the failure to presént it in proper form. All the facts on which she now relies were presented in the action at law, and were adjudged unavailing as a defense against Clark's title acquired by his purchase at the sheriff's sale.—*Clark v. Spencer*, 75 Ala. 49. It was expressly decided in that case, that though the claim of exemption was informal, it ought to have been contested; that the sale, without a contest, was irregular, and would have been set aside on timely application; but that "it can not be declared void on collateral attack." A motion to set aside the sale was the direct mode of impeaching it, and that was an adequate remedy.—Freeman on Executions, § 310; Freeman on Judgments, § 485; *Watts v. Gayle & Bower*, 20 Ala. 817; *Hair v. Lowe*, 19 Ala. 224; *Coffin v. McCullough*, 30 Ala. 107; *Henderson v. Sublett*, 21 Ala. 626; *Stockton v. Briggs*, 5 Jones' Eq. 309. As matter of fact, such an application was made, as the answer averred, and was overruled because not made within a reasonable time; but the special chancellor held that the fact was not properly presented to him, and could not be noticed for that reason. If the motion was made and overruled, the judgment is conclusive; if it was not made, the right to make it is now lost by *laches;* and in either case, equitable relief can not now be had against the judgment at law, except on the ground of fraud, accident, or mistake, as in the case of any other judgment at law.—Freeman on Executions, § 307; *McCaskell v. Lee*, 39 Ala. 132; *Henderson v. Henderson*, 66 Ala. 558; *Beadle v. Graham*,

66 Ala. 102; *Collier v. Falk*, 66 Ala. 223; *Broda v. Green-wald*, 66 Ala. 541.

J. B. HEAD, *contra*. (No brief on file.)

SOMERVILLE, J.—The bill is filed by the appellee, Mrs. Allen, for the purpose of asserting an equitable interest in certain described lands, of which the legal title is in the appellant, Clark, who was defendant in the court below. The incidental relief sought is an injunction against a judgment for rent, obtained by Clark against the complainant and one Spencer, in an ejectment suit for the lands, in which Clark proved successful, which judgment was affirmed on appeal to this court.—*Clark v. Spencer*, 75 Ala. 49.

Two or three settled principles of law, in our opinion, require an affirmance of the chancellor's decree granting to the complainant the relief prayed.

The land in controversy belonged to one Spencer, and contained eighty-eight acres, or eight more than he was entitled to have set apart to him as a homestead, as against the execution under which it was sold, and purchased by Clark. Mrs. Allen bought the land from Spencer, for a valuable consideration, he at the time residing on it as a homestead. This sale, by deed duly executed, passed to her as purchaser an equitable title to Spencer's right of homestead—consisting of eighty acres, to be set apart or selected out of the whole tract—the remaining eight acres only being liable to Clark's execution. Clark, nevertheless, was vested with the legal title to the whole, until the exempted portion was set aside. When so designated and identified, the homestead would be rescued from the execution sale, because, as to the homestead, this sale was void.—*Clark v. Spencer, supra; DeGraffenreid v. Clark, Ib.* 425; *Hardy v. Sulzbacker*, 62 Ala. 44. Under this state of facts, the title of the complainant was purely equitable, and not legal; and she could invoke the aid of a court of chancery in asserting it, and having it confirmed. That court would have power to appoint commissioners, and authorize them to set aside the homestead by metes and bounds, so as to embrace an area of eighty acres, including the dwelling of the vendor, and not exceeding in value the sum of two thousand dollars. *McGuire v. Van Pelt*, 55 Ala. 344, 364. This is precisely the relief granted by the special chancellor in his decree.

It is contended, however, that the complainant had a

[Clark v. Allen.]

right to go into the Circuit Court, and have the sheriff's execution sale set aside for manifest irregularities; and for this reason, it is said, the bill is without equity. It is true, that under the practice in this State, it has been held that a third person, who has an equitable interest in lands, equally with one holding a legal title, connected by purchase with the defendant in execution, may, in a proper case, make a motion to set aside an execution sale, if his interests are thereby prejudiced.—*Henderson v. Sublett*, 21 Ala. 626; *Lee v. Davis*, 16 Ala. 516. But it by no means follows, that he is bound to pursue this remedy. If there is any distinct ground of equity jurisdiction, entitling him to invoke the aid of chancery, or if setting aside the execution sale is an incomplete and inadequate remedy, as in this case, he may make his choice of the forum in which he will enter for relief. He is not bound to select the inadequate remedy. *Ray v. Womble*, 56 Ala. 32. It may be admitted that a court of equity will not take jurisdiction to set aside a sheriff's sale in ordinary cases, independently of some specific ground of equitable jurisdiction. Nor is that the primary purpose of the present bill. Clark, as we have said, holds the legal title of the entire tract of land. He bought it with full knowledge of the complainant's rights, as claimed in the bill. He holds the legal title, therefore, charged with her equity, as a trustee for her benefit. The bill seeks to carve this equity out of his legal title, and to set aside a judgment for rents to which, in equity, the trustee was not entitled, because the land belonged not to him, but to the complainant as his beneficiary. All this can be accomplished without the formality of setting aside the execution sale, by a mole devestiture of the legal title, and perpetually enjoining the judgment in the ejectment suit, as done in the chancellor's decree. The complainant's remedy at law obviously was not adequate. The judgment for rents was properly apportioned, in view of the fact that the complainant is entitled to only eighty out of the eighty-eight acres embraced in the land, the remainder going to the defendant, Clark, under his purchase at the sheriff's sale.

The decree is affirmed.

Case v. Edgeworth.

Statutory Action in nature of Ejectment.

1. *What title will support action; receiver's receipt on homestead entry.* As against a mere trespasser, a receipt given by the receiver of a land office of the United States, for money paid on a homestead entry (U. S. Rev. Statutes, §§ 2290-97), confers a title on which ejectment, or the statutory action in the nature thereof, may be maintained before the expiration of five years (Code, § 2782); and the defendant can not be heard to allege a breach of the conditions on which the entry may be perfected.

APPEAL from the Circuit Court of DeKalb.
Tried before the Hon. JOHN B. TALLY.

This action was brought by D. C. Case against E. L. Edgeworth and T. A. Lumsden, to recover the possession of a tract of land containing 160 acres, which was a part of section 28, township 7, range 7 east; and was commenced on the 7th February, 1887. The defendants pleaded not guilty, and issue was joined on that plea. On the trial, as the bill of exception shows, the plaintiff offered in evidence, after proving its execution, a receipt given to him by the receiver of the land office at Huntsville, which was dated November 29th, 1886, and acknowledged the payment of $14 in full of fees on homestead entry of the land; and this was all the evidence adduced. The court thereupon charged the jury, on request, that they must find for the defendants, if they believed the evidence. The plaintiff excepted to this charge, and he here assigns it as error.

WATTS & SON, and W. J. HARALSON, for appellant, cited *White v. St. Guirons*, Minor, 331; *Bullock v. Wilson*, 2 Porter, 436; s. c. 5, Porter, 338; *Cruise v. Riddle*, 21 Ala. 791; *Bates v. Herron*, 35 Ala. 117; *Watson v. Prestwood*, 79 Ala. 416; Code, § 2782.

DOBBS & HOWARD, *contra.*—The plaintiff was never in possession of the land, and showed no legal title in himself, the title being in the United States until the issue of a patent.—*Goodman v. Winter*, 64 Ala. 410; *Wilkerson v. McDougall*, 48 Ala. 383; *Baucum v. George*, 65 Ala. 259;

Wilson v. Glenn, 68 Ala. 383; *Slaughter v. McBride*, 69 Ala. 510; *Scranton v. Ballard*, 64 Ala. 402; *Bruce v. Bradshaw*, 69 Ala. 360; *Pollard v. Hanrick*, 74 Ala. 334.

CLOPTON, J.—The general rule, that a plaintiff in eject-ment must recover on the strength of his own title, and must show a legal title to the premises, is elementary and familiar; an equitable estate or claim will not support the action. The evidence which the plaintiff introduced in sup-port of his title, was a receipt in the usual form given by the receiver of the public moneys to him, for the sum of fourteen dollars, being the amount of fee and compensation of register and receiver, for the entry of the land sued for, under section 2290 of the Revised Statutes of the United States. The decisions of the Supreme Court of the United States, holding that until the patent issues the fee is in the government, and that a certificate of entry vests only an equitable claim, which will not support ejectment, are founded on the general rule.

Conceding that, independent of statute, a certificate of entry is not a title complete or legal in its character, there is in this State a statute which declares: "All certificates issued pursuant to any act of Congress, by any board of commissioners, register of a land office, or by any one authorized by law to issue such certificate, upon any warrant or order of survey, or for any donation or pre-emption claim, vests the legal title in the holder or his assignee, and must be received as evidence of such title."—Code, 1886, § 2782. This statute has been in force, with immaterial changes in phraseology, since 1812; and under it, certificates given by the receiver of public moneys, on the entry of public lands, have been held sufficient evidence of title to enable the holder to maintain the action of ejectment. The first case was *Bullock v. Wilson*, 2 Port. 436, in which the only evi-dence of title offered by the plaintiff was a receipt, which expressed to be in full for the land described in the declara-tion. It was held that the receipt was within the equity of the statute, and, until the patent issues, was the best evi-dence of the plaintiff's right which the case admits of, and was sufficient evidence of title to authorize the holder to maintain an action of trespass to try titles. This ruling was re-affirmed in the subsequent cases of *Cruise v. Rid-dle*, 21 Ala. 791; and *Bates v. Herron*, 35 Ala. 117.

Section 2290 of the Revised Statutes provides, that any

[Case v. Edgeworth]

person applying to enter land, for the benefit of the homestead, shall, upon making the prescribed affidavit, and paying the requisite sum, be permitted to enter the land specified. The succeeding section declares, that he shall be entitled to a patent, if, after the expiration of five years, he proves by two credible witnesses, that he resided on, or cultivated the same, for the term of five years immediately succeeding the time of filing the affidavit; and makes affidavit that no part of the land has been alienated, except as authorized by law, and that he will bear true allegiance to the government of the United States. It is true, the same section declares, that no certificate or patent shall issue until the expiration of five years from the date of the entry; but this evidently refers to the certificate to be issued after proof that the conditions of the entry have been complied with. Compliance with the provisions of section 2290, and an entry made in accordance therewith, vest an estate or right in the settler—a right to enter the land and occupy. This is manifest from the provisions of section 2297, which provides: "If at any time, after the filing of the affidavit and before the expiration of the five years, it is proved, after due notice to the settler, that the person having filed such affidavit has actually changed his residence, or abandoned the land for more than six months at any time, the land so entered shall revert to the government." There can properly be no reversion, unless some right or estate has passed out of the grantor.

The defendants showed no title or right whatever. So far as the evidence discloses, they are mere trespassers. The estate of the plaintiff acquired by the entry, whatever may be its extent or the character of the title, is an estate on condition. Whether the condition has been complied with, or whether there has been a forfeiture, can only be ascertained in a direct proceeding instituted for that purpose. A mere trespasser can not inquire whether there has been a breach of the condition, and can not set up as a defense a failure to perform the condition. Though the title of the plaintiff does not become complete until the conditions have been performed, the receipt given by the receiver of the public money in full, for lands entered under section 2290, vests in the plaintiff, under the statute in this State, a legal title sufficient to maintain an action of ejectment, or the corresponding statutory real action, and must be received as evidence of such title in such action.

It follows that the court erred in giving the affirmative charge in favor of the defendant.

Reversed and remanded.

Moore & Handley Hardware Co. *v.* Towers Hardware Co.

Bill in Equity for Injunction, in nature of Bill for Specific Performance of Contract.

1. *Contract in restraint of trade.*—A contract by which a partnership, engaged in the business of selling hardware, and selling out their stock of plow-blades and plow-stocks to a rival company, agree "not to handle any more plow-blades or plow-stocks," construed in connection with the attendant circumstances showing the extent of country over which the rivalry in business extended, is not an unreasonable restriction or restraint of trade.

2. *Corporation; how far bound by acts or contracts of stockholders individually, before incorporation.*—A corporation is a legal entity, and is not affected by the personal rights, obligations or transactions of its individual stockholders with third persons, whether before or after incorporation; although it may be charged with the engagements of its promoters in anticipation of incorporation, which it has ratified, or the benefits of which it has received, and although a court of equity will not allow partners or associates, by combining as a "paper corporation," thereby to evade responsibility for their individual obligations, but will hold the nominal corporation to a discharge thereof; yet this principle will not be applied, where an injunction is sought against a private corporation, to restrain its violation of a contract entered into, before incorporation, by its principal corporators and stockholders individually, when it is not averred or shown that the corporation was organized fraudulently, as a device to evade the personal obligation of the contractors.

APPEAL from the Chancery Court of Jefferson.

Heard before the Hon. THOMAS COBBS.

The bill in this case was filed on the 3d December, 1888, by the Towers Hardware Company, a private corporation, against the Moore & Handley Hardware Company, another private corporation; and sought an injunction to restrain the defendant from selling "plow-stocks and plow-blades," in violation of a contract made between the complainant and a partnership doing business under the name of Moore, Moore & Handley, which was composed of James D. Moore, Benj. F. Moore, and William A. Handley, who, as the bill alleged, afterwards formed the defendant corporation. The com-

[Moore & Handley Hardware Co. v. Towers Hardware Co.]

plainant was incorporated, under the general statutes, on the 1st February, 1887, and the defendant on the 12th March, 1888; each having its principal place of business in Birmingham, and selling hardware throughout the northern counties of the State mostly on orders effected through their travelling salesmen. The partnership of Moore, Moore & Handley had been engaged in the same business, and on the 27th May, 1887, they sold out their entire stock of plow-stocks and plow-blades, at the price of $728 paid in cash, to the complainant; signing an agreement, which was written at the foot of the memorandum, or bill of sale, in these words: "In consideration of above sale, we agree not to handle any more plow-stocks or plow-blades, except railroad plows." The bill alleged that the price paid was about $100 more than the market value of the articles, and that complainant was induced to make said purchase "solely by said written promise and undertaking of said Moore, Moore & Handley." By the terms of defendant's articles of incorporation, its capital stock was $100,000, of which said partners each subscribed $25,000, and one Thos. P. Wimberly $25,000; but the bill alleged that, "if said Wimberly ever really had any interest in said corporation. or the capital stock thereof, by virtue of having paid anything on his subscription, he no longer has any interest therein, nor has had since before (to-wit) August 8th, 1888;" also, on information and belief, that said Moores and Handley "are the sole owners of the capital stock of said corporation, and have been since August 10th, 1888," J. D. Moore being president, Handley vice-president, and B. F. Moore secretary, ever since its organization; that the defendant corporation was organized for the purpose of carrying on the same business which the partnership had carried on; that its capital stock "was paid for wholly and entirely in the stock of goods and assets of said partnership;" that it "succeeded to all the property rights and assets of said partnership, as well as all the liabilities thereof;" that said defendant corporation "is none other than said J. D. Moore, B. F. Moore and Wm. A. Handley, who constituted said partnership, and row constitute said corporation. Your orator can not say whether or not said Moores and Handley organized said corporation for the purpose of evading the force and effect of their said agreement with your orator, but does say and charge that the effect of their doing so would be to perpetrate a fraud on your orator, if they should be allowed to handle plow-blades and plow-stocks; that the defendant's business, as now conducted, is identically the same as that conducted by said Moores and Handley, is conducted by the same persons, and in substantially the same manner as before, and that the only change in fact has been in the name of the concern. And your orator alleges that said Moores and Handley, in making said agreement with your orator, thereby meant and intended, and such was your orator's intention, that they would not again engage in selling or handling plow-blades or plow-stocks in connection with their said business in the city of Birmingham, so long as your orator was engaged in the like business."

The defendant answered the bill, admitting its allegations as to the contract between the complainant and Moore, Moore & Handley, and the nature of the business carried on by the several parties; denying that it assumed, or in any manner became liable for, the obligations of said partnership, or of its individual partners. or that it acquired any interest in the outstanding notes and accounts due to said partnership, or the real estate owned by the partners, which was more than sufficient to pay all their outstanding debts and liabilities; alleging that Wimberly owned a one-fourth interest in the corporation at its organization, and for some time acted as its treasurer, but admitting that the Moores and Handley had since bought out his interest; insisting that said contract was illegal and void, because in restraint of trade, and, if valid, was not binding on the defendant; and demurring to the bill for want of equity.

After answer filed, the defendant submitted a motion to dissolve the temporary injunction, and to dismiss the bill; and this appeal is taken from the decree of the chancellor overruling and refusing these motions.

SMITH & LOWE, for appellant.—(1.) The bill in this case asks an injunction against an alleged violation of a contract, in the nature of a decree for specific performance; and it presents the anomaly of seeking this relief against a third person, who was not a party to that contract, and is not bound by it. For it is well settled, that a corporation is a legal entity separate and distinct from the individuals who, from time to time, may be its stockholders; deriving all its powers from its charter, or articles of incorporation, in connection with statutory provisions, and liable only for its own contracts, engagements and defaults. Whatever may be the

complainant's rights or remedies against the Moores and
Handley individually, the bill shows no cause of action
against the defendant corporation.—*State Bank v. Gibson*,
6 Ala. 814; *U. S. v. Planters' Bank*, 9 Wheat. 907; *Kentucky v. Wister*, 2 Pet. 318; *Bank v. Gibbs*, 3 McCord, 377;
Mor. Corp., §§ 547–8; *Milk Asso. v. Wall*, 17 Hun, N. Y.,
494. (2.) The alleged contract is void, because in restraint
of trade.—*Caswell v. Gibbs*, 33 Mich. 331.

CABANISS & WEAKLEY, *contra.*—(1.) The contract, construed in connection with the attendant circumstances, was
not an unreasonable restraint of trade, nor otherwise illegal.
Robbins v. Webb, 68 Ala. 399; *Hubbard v. Miller*, 27 Mich.
15; *Beall v. Chase*, 31 Mich. 490; *Smalley v. Greene*, 35 Am.
Rep. 267; Bish. Contracts, §§ 513–20; 2 High Inj., § 1170;
2 Benj. Sales, 696, n. 15. (2.) A court of equity regards
the substance, rather than the form of things, and will not
permit parties to screen themselves behind the legal fiction
of a corporation's separate entity, in order to carry on a business which they can not conduct in their own names—will
not allow them to do by indirection what they can not do
directly; but will look beyond technical rules, when necessary to do justice, or to prevent fraud.—Mor. Corp., 1, 227,
1012, 1031; *Gas Co. v. West*, 52 Iowa, 16; *Beall v. Chase*,
31 Mich. 490; 20 Fed. Rep. 699, 700; 28 N. J. Eq. 151;
3 Amer. Rep. 164.

McCLELLAN, J.—The equity of the bill, so far as the
injunction is concerned, and the sufficiency of those of its
allegations which are not denied by the answer to sustain the
injunction, depend primarily on two questions: *first*, whether
the contract relied on is void, as being in unreasonable restraint of trade; and, *second*, whether a negative undertaking
entered into by persons who subsequently organize, and for
the time constitute, a corporation for the prosecution of the
business with respect to which the contract was made, can be
inforced by injunction against the corporation.

1. It is insisted that the agreement of Moore, Moore &
Handley, "not to handle any more plow-blades or plow-stocks," is an unreasonable restriction on trade, in that it
contains no limitation as to the place or locality at or in which
they are to refrain from carrying on the specified business.
It is true that such contracts must be limited as to the space
they are intended to cover, or they can not be supported.

14

The meaning of a contract of this character, however, is not to be found solely from a consideration of its expressed terms. Courts look to all the circumstances surrounding the parties, and attendant upon the transaction, and from a consideration of these circumstances, in connection with the expressions of the undertaking, they will first construe the contract, and then proceed to pass upon its reasonableness as thus construed. In the case at bar, the facts were, that both parties were engaged in a certain business, in and covering that part of the State of Alabama which embraces and lies north of the city of Birmingham. It was a character of business, as conducted by them, which could reasonably and naturally be carried on throughout the territory. Over this space they were dealing in competition with each other, and presumptively the operations of each were detrimental to the trade of the other, and the agreement of either to desist from these operations redounded to the advantage of the other. The bill alleges, and the answer does not deny, that the written agreement, copied above, was made with respect to the trade thus carried on in the territory including, and north of Birmingham, in Alabama. The contract will, therefore, be construed with reference to these facts, and held to mean that Moore, Moore & Handley would not handle plow-stocks and blades in competition with, or opposition to the Towers Hardware Company, within the territory covered by their previous competition, and described as that part of Alabama which includes and lies north of Birmingham. Thus construed, it becomes specific as to time, space, and character of the dealing intended to be restrained, and is reasonable and valid.—*Hubbard v. Miller,* 27 Mich. 15; *Curtis v. Gokey,* 68 N. Y. 300; *Warfield v. Booth,* 33 Md. 63; *Dethlifs v. Tomsen,* 7 Daly, 354; *Beal v. Chase,* 31 Mich. 490; *Havner v. Graves,* 7 Bing. 735; *Whittaker v. Howe,* 3 Beav. 383; *Tallis v. Tallis,* 1 El. & Bl. 391; *Morse Machine Co. v. Morse,* 103 Mass. 73; *O. S. Nav. Co. v. Winsor,* 20 Wallace, 64.

2. The general doctrine is well established, and obtains both at law and in equity, that a corporation is a distinct entity, to be considered separate and apart from the individuals who compose it, and is not to be affected by the personal rights, obligations and transactions of its stockholders; and this, whether said rights accrued, or obligations were incurred, before or subsequent to incorporation.—Morawetz on Priv. Corp. 227–234, 547–549; *Morrison v. Gold Mt. G.*

M. Co., 52 Cal. 309; *Hawkins v. Mansfield G. M. Co., Ib.*
515; *Gent v. M. & Mut. Ins. Co.*, 107 Ill. 658; *Caledo-
nian R. Co. v. Helensburgh*, 2 Macg. 391; *Penn. Mat.
Co. v. Hapgood*, 141 Mass. 147.

There is a class of contracts, however, which are entered
into between the promoters or prospectors of a contemplated
corporation and third persons, on the faith of the corporation,
intended to enure to its benefit, and which in point of fact do
enure to its benefit, on which the corporation will be charged,
even in the absence of an express promise to perform, or ratification on the part of the company after it is *in esse;* on
"the familiar principle, that one who accepts the benefit of a
contract, which another volunteers to perform in his name,
and on his behalf, is bound to take the burden with the benefit."—Redfield on Railways (5th Ed.), 18; *Edwards v.
Grand Junc. R.*, 1 M. & Cr. 650; *Stanley v. Birkenhead R.*,
9 Sim. 264; *L. R. & Fel. S. R. Co. v. Perry*, 37 Ark. 164;
Perry v. L. R. & Fet. S. R. Co., 44 Ark. 383; *Bommer v.
Am. Spiral Co.*, 81 N. Y. 468.

And in those cases where "associates combine together to
create a paper corporation, to cover a partnership or joint
venture, and where the stockholders are partners in intention," and have resorted to the fiction of separate corporate
entity to free themselves from individual obligations which
had attached to them, with respect to the business they propose to carry on, prior to the organization of the company,
courts of equity, when the ends of justice require it, will
disregard and look beyond the fiction of corporate entity, and
hold the corporation to a discharge of the liabilities resting
on its members; and this may be done, although some of the
shareholders had not originally incurred the obligation
sought to be enforced, provided they had notice of it before
entering the corporation, and participated in the effort to
avoid it.—*Davis Imp. Wrought Iron W. W. Co. v. Davis
Wrought Iron W. Co.*, 20 Fed. Rep. 700; *Beal v. Chase*,
31 Mich. 490, 495, 532.

The contract of Moore, Moore & Handley, sought to be
enforced against the Moore & Handley Hardware Company,
was not an undertaking between promotors of the company
and third parties, nor made on the faith of the corporation,
nor intended to enure to its benefit, nor did it enure, in point
of fact, to the benefit of the corporation. It is not of that
class of contracts which courts enforce against corporations,
on the ground that they were made in the corporate name by

anticipation, and that the corporation received and accepted the benefits resulting from them.

There is no allegation of fraud made against the corporation, or its shareholders, and the implication of the fraudulent effect of the corporate action complained of is denied. It is not shown that this is a mere "paper corporation," to cover a joint venture, in which the corporators are partners in intention, and have resorted to this form for the purpose of evading and avoiding obligations which they had taken upon themselves as individuals, or for the purpose of evading the promise relied on here. If these things had appeared in the case, we should not hesitate to hold the corporation answerable for the individual obligation. But, in the absence of fraud, "no authorities have gone the length of holding that any contract made with individuals, exclusively upon individual credit, will become the contract of any future corporation that may be formed for the more convenient management and use of the benefits of it."—*L. R. & Ft. S. R. Co. Cases, supra.*

If the case of *Beal v. Chase, supra,* goes beyond this doctrine, we can not indorse it. We do not think it does. In that case, the corporation had been formed *for the purpose* of violating a contract not to engage in a certain business. All the corporators were held to have participated in this purpose. The business was to be conducted by the corporation, in connection with the promisor in his individual capacity. He had an interest in it, both individually and as the principal shareholder of the company; and the court enjoined the corporation, not generally, but from carrying on the business with or for the individual contracting party. To put the case at bar in line with that case, it would have to appear, not only that the corporators organized for the purpose, and with the intention of evading their contract, through the separate entity of corporate existence, but also that they reserved an interest in the business distinct from their interests as stockholders. None of these facts are shown. The effect of allowing the injunction in this case to continue, would necessarily be to hold all future shareholders in the corporation to the performance of a contract which neither they nor the corporation had ever entered into, and of which they may not even have had notice. Such a result could only be justified on the ground of bad faith in the creation of the company. To thus hamper a *bona fide* corporation, would be inequitable, and have the effect of

[Beck v. West & Co.]

establishing a doctrine fraught with much danger to corporate rights, powers and property.

The allegations going to show a ratification, by the corporation, of this contract of Moore, Moore & Handley, are denied by the answer, and hence can not be considered in passing on the decree overruling the motion to dissolve the injunction. Those allegations of the bill which are not denied, were not sufficient to authorize a continuance of the injunction, and the decree on that point was erroneous, and is reversed.

The contract relied on here is such a one as the respondent corporation could have made under its charter. It is, therefore, one which, being already in existence between complainant and the individuals composing the defendant company, the corporation had the power to ratify and adopt. The bill, in our judgment, sufficiently avers such ratification or adoption. These allegations give equity to the bill, and the decree overruling the demurrer is affirmed.

The cause will be remanded, with instructions to the chancellor to dissolve the injunction, unless the complainant amends its bill so as to entitle it to a continuance of the writ, under the principles we have announced.

Reversed and remanded.

Beck *v.* West & Co.

Action for Breach of Special Contract of Employment.

1. *Demurrer; when ruling on is revisable.*—Rulings on demurrer, shown only by the bill of exceptions, are not revisable on error or appeal.

2. *Construction of writings, by court, or by jury.*—When the contract sued on is evidenced only by the written correspondence of the parties, it is the duty of the court to construe the writings, and to instruct the jury as to their meaning and legal effect.

3. *Contract of employment as travelling salesman; damages for breach.* Under a contract by which defendants, tobacco merchants, employed plaintiff as a travelling salesman, agreeing to supply him with samples, to allow him as compensation one-half of the profits on sales effected by him, and to advance to him, by paying his drafts at the commencement of his work, $50 at the end of every two weeks, to be repaid out of his share of the profits, while he was to furnish his own outfit; on a breach by defendants, refusing to pay plaintiff's drafts, and instructing him to quit work before the expiration of the stipulated term, plaintiff is entitled to recover as damages, not only his share of the profits on sales perfected and consummated, but also on sales negotiated

so far that it can be ascertained with certainty that they would be completed, and the extent or amount thereof; but mere expectations, doubtful offers, or other vague or indefinite assurances of intention to purchase, without expression of quantity or value, are speculative merely, and not recoverable; opinions as to what sales he could, or probably would have made, are also speculative and contingent; nor can he prove or recover for the cost of his horse and buggy, the value of his services per month, or the damages to his credit by being thus thrown out of employment.

APPEAL from the Circuit Court of Escambia.

Tried before the Hon. JOHN P. HUBBARD.

This action was brought by Wilson Beck against J. P. West & Co., and was commenced by attachment, sued out on the 2d January, 1888, on the ground of the defendants' non-residence. The defendants were tobacco manufacturers and dealers, doing business in Lynchburg, Virginia, and had employed the defendant, who lived in or near Brewton, Alabama, to serve them as travelling salesman. The contract between the parties was negotiated by letters, several of which were read in evidence on the trial, as follows: On the 30th August, 1887, defendants wrote to plaintiff, acknowledging the receipt of a letter which was not produced, and saying in reply: "We think, if you will work regularly, you will no doubt be worth $50 and more per month; but we would prefer to pay you according to your work. We will give you half you can make, you paying your own expenses. Will furnish you samples, &c., and will give you a letter of credit, so you may draw $50 every two weeks, or $100 per month. If you will go to work, and travel two weeks, then draw for $50, and so on, every two weeks, will send you check to balance your half of profits at end of each month. You only furnish your expenses for first two weeks, then your letter of credit entitles you to draw $100 per month thereafter, in two drafts of $50 each every two weeks. Now, if you will work regularly, we will make above terms until end of year, and will continue same terms next year, or will estimate your work and pay you salary next year. If you accept, get ready for work at once, and write us by return mail, and we will furnish samples and letter of credit at once, and will comply strictly with this letter. . . The trade will no doubt be good now. Awaiting reply at once," &c. This letter seems to have miscarried in the mails, as shown by plaintiff's answer to it, which is dated September 13th, and in which, after alluding to the delay in its transmission, he said: "I will now say in reply, that I will try

[Beck v. West & Co.]

the tobacco business again, though I have said I would never again sell tobacco on commission; but, as I feel satisfied I can do well in the business, I will try it again. So now I will make myself ready to go to work, and will be ready by the time you can get your samples here. Please send a nice lot of samples," &c. To this letter defendants replied, under date of September 16th, saying: "All right. We are going to stand up to you, and will expect steady, square work on your part. We send you, by to-day's express, a full line of samples, with list of cost and selling prices; but we do not mean to confine you to selling prices, allowing you to make prices according to lots and competition. Spread yourself." The rest of the letter relates to the counties in which the plaintiff should begin business, and other details of the trade. The plaintiff's letter of credit from defendants, dated September 21st, 1887, was in these words: "This is to certify, that you are instructed to draw on us, for one hundred dollars per month, as follows: After you have worked for us regularly two weeks, draw for $50, and after two weeks more regular work for us draw for $50 more. Good until January 1st, 1888."

Under the contract shown by these letters, plaintiff bought a horse and buggy, as he testified, and entered on the discharge of his duties, travelling through Butler, Covington, Conecuh and other counties, exhibiting his samples, soliciting orders from merchants, &c.; on October 24th he drew on defendants for $50, on November 9th for $25, and on November 14th for $25; and a few days afterwards, while at Hayneville, Lowndes county, he received from defendants the following letter: "Yours of 9th inst. just at hand, and we write at once, and will say to go home at once and wait until trade opens. You are not doing anything, and why in the name of common sense do you keep travelling. We wrote you before you left Brewton not to go yet, as you had made a trip and found the trade was not buying. You did not start when you could have made sales. Now go home, and when trade opens we will send you money to start, but can not promise you any money to throw away now." To this letter plaintiff replied at once, denying defendants' right to make him discontinue his work, and notifying them that he should return home and hold himself subject to their orders according to the terms of the contract; and he testified that he did so.

The complaint set out the contract substantially as shown

by these letters, alleged performance on plaintiff's part, and breaches thereof by defendants, as follows: (1) in failing and refusing to pay his said drafts; (2) in failing to pay him his commissions on the goods sold by him; (3) in discharging him and ordering him to quit work without legal cause or excuse. For these breaches the complaint claimed damages as follows: $500 "for loss of credit and reputation by reason of defendants' failure to cash plaintiff's said drafts;" $150, "for money laid out and expended by plaintiff for horse and buggy in preparing and fitting out for said business;" $500, "for loss of commissions on sales which plaintiff would have made if said defendants had complied with their said contract;" and $500 for the breaches generally. The judgment-entry recites that issue was joined on the plea of *"not guilty;"* but the bill of exceptions further states, that a demurrer was interposed and sustained to so much of the complaint as claimed $500 damages "for loss of commissions on sales which plaintiff would have made if defendants had complied with their contract;" and that plaintiff was permitted to amend his complaint "by claiming $150 damages for board of self and horse, and for his expenses while travelling in defendants' service; also, $150 for use of horse and buggy, and his commissions earned while in the service of defendants."

"Plaintiff offered to prove, during the progress of the trial, what he paid for his horse and buggy to equip himself for service under said contract;" also, "what amount of goods he would have sold for defendants by the 1st January, 1888, if they had cashed his drafts, and permitted him to continue to travel, and what his commissions on the same would have amounted to;" also, "how the orders of a travelling salesman of tobacco, on his second trip through the same territory, would compare in amount with his orders on his first trip;" also, "that he was out of employment, from November 16th, 1887, to January 1st, 1888, and also up to the time of the trial;" also, "what his time was worth, per month, from October 6th, 1887, to January 1st, 1888, and from that day to the trial;" also, "that on his trip through the counties named, in addition to the orders secured, he had made arrangements with certain merchants to place their orders for tobacco, cigars and snuff, through plaintiff, on defendants' house, on his second trip, in November and December, and offered to prove the names of such merchants, with the amounts of goods each one proposed to take, and what

[Beck v. West & Co.]

his commissions on such proposed sales would have been;" also, "that the hire and use of his horse and buggy was worth $2.00 per day, the cost of board of himself and horse was over $1.50 per day, and that he paid out these amounts from the 6th October to about 20th November, when he reached home in Brewton." The court excluded each part of this evidence, on objection by defendants, and plaintiff duly excepted.

Under the rulings of the court, the plaintiff had a judgment on verdict for $45.44, from which he now appeals, assigning as error the several rulings above stated, with others.

JAMES M. DAVISON, and WATTS & SON, for appellant.

M. A. RABB, contra.

STONE, C. J.—This action was brought by Beck against West & Co., and claims damages, first, for unpaid commissions on sales made by Beck; and, second, for failing to supply him with expense money agreed to be supplied, and thereby preventing his performance of the contract, and throwing him out of employment. Other grievances are complained of, but we will show further on that they furnished no ground of recovery.

It is said in the bill of exceptions that there was a demurrer, and a ruling on it; but, inasmuch as this appears only in the bill of exceptions, we can not consider it.—3 Brick. Dig. 78, § 7; Ib. 705, § 82.

The contract, for an alleged breach of which this action was brought, appears to have been made entirely by correspondence. There is no testimony tending to show that the contracting parties ever had a personal interview. Terms were offered by West & Co., which were accepted without modification by Beck. It was the duty of the court to interpret those writings, and hence it became its duty, and not that of the jury, to determine what obligations the writings imposed on each of the contracting parties. We concur with the trial court, in holding that no contract was made which bound either party to its observance for a longer term than January 1, 1888. We hold further, that, up to that time, there was a binding contract, requiring West & Co. to give employment to Beck as their travelling salesman, and, in consideration thereof, binding Beck to serve them as a

travelling salesman for the same term. Beck's compensation
was to be half the profits made on sales effected through
his agency; but he was to pay his own expenses, and, with
the exception of samples, he was to provide his own outfit.
West & Co. were to furnish samples; and, to enable Beck to
meet expenses until profits should be realized, they bound
themselves to honor and cash his orders to be drawn on
them, for fifty dollars for every two weeks he should have
continuously worked for them in said business. These were
not payments to Beck, but loans or advances to be made to
him, to be repaid out of his share of the profits on the sales
of merchandise he was expected to make. It is manifest
that both parties contracted in the honest belief and expectation that Beck's share of the profits on the sales he would
make, would at least equal fifty dollars for every two weeks;
and they made no provision for the contingency that they
might not reach that sum. Yet, West & Co. gave no guaranty as to the amount of the profits Beck should realize.
This was left dependent on his success as a salesman. We
hold that West & Co. bound themselves to give Beck employment as a travelling salesman until January 1, 1888, to
furnish him samples, and to lend to, or advance for him fifty
dollars for every two weeks he was actually engaged in such
service. The contract confers no discretion in the performance of these stipulations. And the contract equally
bound Beck to serve them as travelling salesman with energy
and fidelity, to allow them to retain of his share of the
profits until they reimbursed themselves for the loans or
advances made to him; and if such share of the profits fell
short of reimbursing them, then Beck would owe them the
balance.

The interpretation we have given the contract places the
parties in an embarrassing predicament, but it is chargeable,
perhaps, to a want of foresight in framing it. It is not in
our power to modify the terms they agreed on.

On the testimony found in this record, we are not able to
affirm that plaintiff violated any term of his contract, while
the testimony, if believed, shows that West & Co. broke
their contract, by refusing to honor and pay Beck's drafts.
What, then, are proper elements of damages, entitling him
to a recovery?

He was clearly entitled to recover his share of the profits
on sales made by him. So, if he had agreements for later
sales, which he could have perfected during his term, he is

equally entitled to his share of the profits. But, to fall within this class, the negotiations must have proceeded so far, as that it can be ascertained with certainty that the sale would be made, and the extent of it. Mere expectations, doubtful offers, or other vague or indefinite assurances of intention to purchase, without expression of quantity or value, must be classed as speculative, and hence not recoverable. Being thrown out of employment was also an element of damages, if it were not that no standard can be fixed for ascertaining its extent. Opinion as to what sales he could, or probably would have made, all fall within the category of the speculative, are contingent, and do not tend to show a right of recovery.—*Pollock v. Gantt*, 69 Ala. 373; *Brigham v. Carlisle*, 78 Ala. 243; *Higgins v. Mansfield*, 62 Ala. 267; *Culver v. Hill*, 68 Ala. 66; *Union Refining Co. v. Barton*, 77 Ala. 148; *Bell v. Reynolds*, 78 Ala. 511.

The cost of plaintiff's horse and buggy, the value of his services per month, and damage to his credit, were each and all irrelevant testimony, and properly ruled out.

Plaintiff, as a witness for himself, offered to testify, that "he had made arrangements with certain merchants to place their orders for tobacco, cigars and snuff, through plaintiff, on defendants' house, on his second round in November and December, and offered to prove the names of such merchants, with the amount of goods each one proposed to take, and what plaintiff's commission on such proposed sales would have been." This testimony he was not allowed to give. This was error. To constitute this a right of recovery, however, his proof must come up to the rule as to certainty, which we have declared above.

The charge, "that in no event can the plaintiff recover more than the amount of his commissions" on sales actually made and completed, was probably correct on the testimony that was before the jury. No data had been placed before them, on which they could have rendered a verdict for greater damages. If the testimony, which we have decided the court should have received, had been put in, and had shown a case for recovery under the rules we have declared, then the charge would have been erroneous.

Reversed and remanded.

Moore v. Johnston.

Action for Breach of Covenants in Conveyance.

1. *Dedication of streets.*—There can be no complete dedication of land to public uses, without an acceptance by the public, by use or otherwise; and where the owner of a tract of land adjoining the limits of an incorporated town or city, having had it mapped and subdivided into lots and blocks, separated by s'reets, afterwards sells a part of the tract extending to the middle of a street as laid down on the map, this narrows the street at that point to one half of its original width on the map.

2. *Conveyance of lot bounded by street.*—A conveyance of a lot bounded by a street, in an incorporated city or town, passes to the grantee the fee to the centre of the street, subject to the public easement; and the same rule applies to a conveyance of lots outside of the corporate limits, which have been laid off with a view to future extension of the corporate limits.

3. *Covenant of seizin; breach of.*—A covenant of seizin is broken, if there is an outstanding estate in a third person, or a material deficiency in the quantity of land conveyed, or where the grantor has not substantially the same estate, both in quantity and quality, which he professes by his deed to convey; but the existence of a public easement, as a street or right of way, is not a breach of such covenant.

APPEAL from the City Court of Birmingham.
Tried before the Hon. H. A. SHARPE.

E. W. PETTUS, and W. M. BROOKS, for the appellants, cited *Sibley v. Holden,* 10 Pick. 250; *Tyler v. Hammond,* 11 Pick. 211.

WARD & HEAD, *contra,* cited *Steele v. Sullivan,* 70 Ala. 589; 90 Amer. Dec. 224, note; 58 Amer. Rep. 143, note; Washb. Easements, 235; Tied. Real Prop., § 851; 15 John. 483; 19 Amer. Dec. 140; *Railway Co. v. Witherow,* 82 Ala. 190; *Perry v. Railroad Co.,* 55 Ala. 413; Angell on Highways, §§ 302, 326; 44 Amer. Dec. 138.

SOMERVILLE, J.—The action is one brought by the appellant, Moore, against the appellee, Johnston, for alleged breach of a covenant of *seizin* contained in a deed of land. The land sold the plaintiff by the defendant is "the north-easterly portion of the block of land lying between Twenty-first Street and Twenty-second Street, bounded on the east by said Twenty-second Street, and on the north by Avenue G, fronting north on said avenue, three hundred and forty (340) feet, and extending back perpendicularly to Avenue H, of the uniform width one hundred and ninety feet, to an alley." According to the plaintiff's contention, the defendant has sold him forty feet of land on the *west* side of the purchased lot, to which he had no title, and which was owned by one Mrs. Bustin, and in her adverse possession at the time of the sale. The defendant contends, that the forty feet lay on the *east* side, and extended to the centre of Twenty-second Street, as originally marked on the map of the Elyton Land Company. This so called street was outside of the corporate limits of Birmingham, was not opened or used, being mere woodland, and was the property of the Elyton Land Company. The deed from this company to Bustin, and from Bustin to Johnston, conveyed to the centre of the street. A fence had been built inclosing this half of the so called street, so as to make it only forty instead of eighty feet wide at this point, on paper, where it alone existed. The only issue is, whether the fee in this forty feet was conveyed by the deed, or whether the intention of the parties was to sell on the one hand, and buy on the other, the forty feet on the west side belonging to Mrs. Bustin.

The evidence, in our opinion, supports the view, that the Elyton Land Company, by selling to the centre of Twenty-second Street, had narrowed the street at this point, so as to reduce it to forty feet. There can be no valid and complete dedication, without an acceptance by the public; and it is not pretended that there was any acceptance in this case, by use or otherwise. It is true, that the owner may often be estopped to deny a dedication, where he maps out his lands, and sells them with reference to a plat describing them by streets, alleys and blocks. But the plaintiff here visited the premises, and saw the land as inclosed by a fence. The contracting parties thus treated this fence as constituting the western boundary line of the street, and the eastern boundary line of the lot. The plaintiff went into possession of this piece of land, which contained 340 feet—or all in quantity he claimed to have purchased.

There may possibly be purchasers of lots who could successfully challenge the right of the Elyton Land Company to lessen the dimensions of this street; but the plaintiff is in no condition to do so, being himself the purchaser and occupant of this portion of the narrowed street. The plain-

[Moore v. Johnston.]

tiff, moreover, in any event, is the owner of the fee to the centre of Twenty-second Street, which he acquired by virtue of his deed from Johnston. Conceding that there was a dedication of the street on the principle of estoppel, the conveyance nevertheless, in any aspect of the case, carried a *fee* to the centre of the highway, subject only to a future easement in the public. This is the accepted doctrine in Alabama, and in the majority of our States —*Columbus & West. Railway Co. v. Witherow*, 82 Ala. 190, and cases cited. The cases of *Tyler v. Hammond*, 11 Pick. 193, and *Sibley v. Holden*, 10 Pick. 251, holding the contrary view, and cited by appellant's counsel, have been entirely repudiated by the Massachusetts court in its more recent decisions.—*Paine v. Woods*, 108 Mass. 171; *Boston v. Richardson*, 13 Allen, 152.

A covenant of *seizin* is broken as soon as made, if the covenantor has no title to the estate granted.—*Anderson v. Knox*, 20 Ala. 156. So, it will constitute a breach, if there is an outstanding estate in a life tenant, or a tenant in common; or if there is a material deficiency in the amount of land conveyed; or, in general, where the grantor has not substantially the very estate, both in quantity and quality, which he professes by his deed to convey.—Boone on Real Property, §§ 310–311; *Mecklem v. Blake*, 22 Wis. 495; s. c., 99 Amer. Dec. 68; *note*, pp. 73–81. But it is well settled by the authorities, that the existence of a public easement over land, or other equitable incumbrance, which does not in any way affect the technical seizin of the purchaser, is no breach of the covenant of seizin. The reason is, that there is no inconsistency between the public having the right of way over land, and at the same time the vesting of a freehold in the owner of the soil.—Boone on Real Property, § 311; 4 Amer. & Eng. Encyc. Law, p. 479; Tiedeman on Real Prop. § 851; *Fitzhugh v. Croghan*, 19 Amer. Dec. 140, 148; *Lewis v. Jones*, 44 Amer. Dec. 138; *Kellogg v. Malin*, 11 Amer. Rep. 426; *Cortelyou v. Van Brundt*, 2 Johu. 357; s. c., 3 Amer. Dec. 439; *Lamb v. Danforth*, 8 Amer. Rep. 426.

The plaintiff owned the fee in the forty feet on the east side of the lot running to the centre of the street, and has not been disturbed in his possession of it. His occupancy of it may never be challenged by any one in the future. If evicted, he has his remedy on his covenants of warranty and against incumbrances. There is no breach of the covenant of *seizin*.

The judgment of the City Court, so holding, is affirmed.

Garland v. Board of Revenue of Montgomery County.

$\begin{smallmatrix}87\\127\\\hline 87\\135\end{smallmatrix}$

Bill in Equity for Injunction against County Board of Revenue, in matter of Erecting Public Bridge.

$\begin{smallmatrix}87\\127\end{smallmatrix}$

1. *Constitutionality of statutes; rule of judicial construction.*—In adjudicating the constitutionality of a statute, it is the duty of the courts, in deference to the legislative department of the government, to so construe both the constitutional and the statutory provisions, if possible, that the statute may be upheld; but a constitutional provision, protective of the rights of persons and property, and remedial in its nature, is not to be construed so literally or strictly as to defeat the purposes for which it was intended; and a new provision, incorporated in a revised constitution, is to be construed in connection with the facts of public history, showing the causes in which it originated, and the mischief it was intended to remedy and prevent.

2. *Bridge across Alabama river between Montgomery and Autauga counties, for railroad purposes, wagons, and persons on foot; constitutionality of law authorizing.*—The act of the General Assembly, approved February 27th, 1889, authorizing the Boards of Revenue of Montgomery and Autauga counties to erect a bridge across the Alabama river near the city of Montgomery, making it a "free foot and wagon bridge, or a railroad bridge, or both combined," to issue county bonds to pay for it, and to levy a special tax to pay the annual interest on the bonds (Sess. Acts 1889, p. 756), so far as it authorizes the counties to build a bridge for railroad purposes, or a foot and wagon and railroad bridge combined, is violative of the constitutional provision which declares that no county, city or municipality shall "lend its credit, or grant public money or thing of value, in aid of or to any individual, association, or corporation" (Art. iv, § 55); and is also violative of the constitutional limitation (Art. xi, § 5) imposed on the taxing power of the counties.

APPEAL from the City Court of Montgomery, in equity.

Heard before the Hon. THOS. M. ARRINGTON.

The bill in this case was filed on the 19th June, 1889, by Alex. B. Garland, as a citizen and tax-payer of Montgomery county, against the Board of Revenue of said county, and the members thereof individually; and sought to enjoin and restrain the defendants from issuing county bonds, or doing any other acts in furtherance of the erection of a bridge across the Alabama river, as they had resolved to do under authority supposed to have been conferred on them by an act of the General Assembly, approved February 27th, 1889, which is quoted in the opinion of the court. There was a motion to dissolve the injunction, and to dismiss the bill for want of equity, which motion the court sustained; and this judgment and decree is here assigned as error.

GEO. F. MOORE, and JNO. GINDRAT WINTER, for appellant.

H. C. TOMPKINS, and A. A. WILEY, *contra.*

CLOPTON, J.—An act of the General Assembly, approved February 27, 1889, provides, "That the Boards of Revenue of the counties of Montgomery and Autauga be, and they are hereby, authorized and empowered to erect a bridge across the Alabama river, at or near the city of Montgomery; and are also authorized, within their discretion, to make said bridge either a free foot and wagon bridge for the travelling public, or a railroad bridge, or both combined;" and the Boards of Revenue are further severally authorized to issue bonds, not exceeding the sum of one hundred thousand dollars, for the purpose of paying for the bridge. Acts 1888–9, p. 756. Under the authority of this act, the Board of Revenue of Montgomery county, by resolution, authorized the issuance of bonds to the amount of sixty thousand dollars, to be sold at not less than their face value, and the proceeds to be solely used in the construction of a toll-bridge across the Alabama river, at or near the city of Montgomery, such bridge to be constructed as a foot and wagon bridge and railroad bridge combined. Appellant files the bill in the capacity of property-holder and tax-payer, and seeks to enjoin the issue of the bonds. The bill alleges, that the resolution providing for their issuance conforms in all respects to the requirements of the act. The right to maintain the injunction is based on the ground, that the act is in conflict with section 55 of Article IV of the Constitution, which declares: "The General Assembly shall have no power to authorize any county, city, town, or other subdivision of this State, to lend its credit, or to grant public money or thing of value, in aid of, or to any individual, association, or corporation whatever, or to become a stockholder in any such corporation or company, by issuing bonds or otherwise."

We are not unobservant of the rule, that in adjudicating the constitutionality of a statute, it should be so construed, if possible, as to bring it within the scope of the constitutional powers of the General Assembly. The presumption is, that the legislative department has not transgressed the limitations and inhibitions upon its powers. In deference

to a co-ordinate department of the government, it is our
judicial duty not to impute a violation of the organic law
binding equally on every department; and in declaring upon
the validity of a legislative enactment, to seek such a construction, if reasonable, as that the constitution and the
statute can co·exist. But constitutional provisions, protective of the rights of persons and property, and remedial in
their nature, are not to be construed so literally as to defeat
the protection intended and provided. New provisions,
incorporated in a revised constitution, are to be interpreted
and given such operation as will accomplish the purposes for
which they were introduced; and if, when so interpreted, a
legislative enactment is not fairly susceptible of a construction consistent with such provisions, it becomes the plain,
though delicate, duty of the court, to declare its invalidity.

With a view to comprehend the scope of the inhibitory
provision of the Constitution under consideration, and to
ascertain the purpose of its introduction, the causes in which
it originated, and the mischiefs designed to be remedied,
may be properly and helpfully considered. Under the constitutions preceding the present, the legislature had unlimited power over the subject. Several of the counties had,
by legislative authority, subscribed for stock in railroad corporations, and issued bonds to pay for the same, in anticipation of their future public benefit. The disastrous consequences which ensued are common knowledge. . Either from
mismanagement or fraud, insolvency of the companies, and
failure to complete the roads, supervened, the stock became
worthless, and the indebtedness exceeded the ability of the
counties to pay. Expensive and protracted litigation was
inaugurated; taxation became oppressive; legal proceedings
to compel the levy of taxes were prosecuted by the bondholders; confiscation of the property of the citizens was impending, and the counties reduced to such condition as to be
designated "the Strangulated Counties." To prevent a re-
currence of such ruinous consequences to the governmental
agencies, which had either transpired, or were clearly apparent at the time of the formation of the present constitution, the inhibitory provision was introduced. Its terms are
comprehensive enough to include any aid, by issuing bonds
or otherwise, by which a pecuniary liability is incurred,
furnished by the municipalities named to private enterprises.
In reference to a similar clause in the Constitution of Ohio,
it was said in *Walker v. City of Cincinnati*, 21 Ohio St. 15:

15

"In no project originated by individuals, whether associated or otherwise, with a view to gain, are the municipalities named permitted to participate in such manner as to incur pecuniary liability. They can neither become stockholders, nor furnish money or credit for the benefit of the parties interested therein." Operation should be given to the provision in the constitution co-extensive with the evils to be prevented. A loan of credit, or grant of money or thing of value, *in aid* of an individual or corporation, in any mode, directly or indirectly, falls within its operation. A direct loan or grant to the individual or corporation is not essential. *Jarrett v. City of Moberly*, 5 Dillon, 253; s. c., 103 U. S. 580; *Wyscaver v. Atkinson*, 37 Ohio St. 80.

The act authorizes the Board of Revenue to issue bonds, and use the proceeds in the construction, within their discretion, of a free foot and wagon bridge for the travelling public, or a railroad bridge, or both combined. It is manifest that authority is conferred to erect a bridge, which may be exclusively a railroad bridge. It would seem from the terms of the act, that the primary and principal object was the erection of a railroad bridge, in whole or in part, and that the construction of a foot and wagon bridge is incidental. A railroad bridge, as such, is useless, unless it forms a part of a railroad. The counties having no power to construct a railroad, it was evidently contemplated that the bridge would be used and operated by some railroad company. The act being silent as to what use or disposition shall be made of the bridge, if erected as a railroad bridge, after it is completed, there is implied authority to permit its free use by individuals or a corporation operating a railroad. Power to lease it may be regarded, under the statute, a question of grave doubt; but, if conceded, the right to allow free use, and the right to lease, are of equal authority in the statute. There can be no question that the erection of a bridge by the issue of county bonds, and giving a railway company the right to control and use it free of charge, would be, in the meaning of the Constitution, a loan of credit in aid of such company. There is as little room for doubt, that constructing a railroad by the use of bonds of the county, and leasing it for a term of years to a railroad corporation, would be the grant of a thing of value in aid of such corporation. The legislature has equal power to authorize the municipalities named in the Constitution to erect manufactories, and issue bonds to pay for the same, for the purpose of leasing them to individuals or corporations, or repair shops for the purpose of leasing them to a railway company. All such methods are in aid of private enterprises, and constitute authority to indirectly accomplish that which, if done directly, would be a manifest infraction of the Constitution—a conversion of the municipalities into trading corporations.

The act further authorizes the levy of a special tax on the taxable property in the counties, to pay the semi-annual interest and the principal on the bonds. Independent of the constitutional provisions, there are limitations upon the taxing power, inherent in our system of government and political institutions. An essential limitation is, that no tax shall be levied for other than a public purpose.—*Loan Asso. v. Topeka*, 20 Wall. 655. There are express limitations in the Constitution upon the taxing power of the counties. Section 5 of Article XI declares: "No county shall be authorized to levy a larger rate of taxation, in any one year, on the value of the taxable property therein, than one-half of one per centum." The provisos in the section authorize an additional rate, to pay debts existing at the ratification of the Constitution, and special taxes for the erection of necessary buildings and bridges. A county can not levy a *special* tax for any purpose other than those expressed. The bridges referred to are bridges erected for use by the community, and under the control of the municipal authorities—constituting parts of the county highways. Though corporations, organized to build railroads, possess some characteristics of a public nature, such as the right of eminent domain, they are mainly private enterprises for purposes of gain. What we do affirm is, that a railroad bridge, to be used and operated by a corporation distinct from the county, does not come within the classes of bridges, for the erection of which the imposition of a special tax may be authorized under the Constitution.

We therefore hold, that those parts of the act which authorize the erection of a railroad bridge, or a foot and wagon and railroad bridge combined, are unconstitutional. We do not mean to intimate, that the legislature has no power to authorize the counties named in the act to erect a foot and wagon bridge across the Alabama river. Neither do we decide that the counties and a railroad company may not be authorized to erect jointly a foot and wagon and a railroad bridge combined, each paying their proportion of the cost, and owning separately and severally their respective interests

in the property. This question is not presented by the
record, and we leave it open. Other questions are presented
in the argument, relating to the extent the act is invalid;
but, as they are not raised by the record, it would be unbe-
coming to decide them.

Reversed, and judgment will be here rendered making the
injunction permanent.

Reversed and rendered.

Stevenson *v.* Anderson.

Bill in Equity for Partition and Account.

1. *Parties to bill; heirs and administrator.*—To a bill filed by the heirs
at law of a deceased non-resident, against the surviving tenant in common, seeking a partition of lands and an account, and alleging that the
decedent left no debts, and that no administration has been granted on
his estate, a personal representative of his estate is not a necessary
party.

2. *Absence, or non-residence, as exception to statute of limitations.*—In
computing the bar of the statute of limitations, the period of the defendant's absence from the State, and not of his non-residence, is to be
deducted (Code, § 2622); yet, where the bill alleges that the defendant
was a non-resident of Alabama, and resided in Tennessee, when the
cause of action accrued, and ever since, this is sufficient, on demurrer,
to avoid the bar.

3. *Statute of limitations in favor of purchaser, as against tenant in
common of vendor.*—The statute of limitations is not a bar, as against one
tenant in common, in favor of a purchaser from the other, unless ten
years have elapsed since his purchase, or unless he can claim the benefit of adverse possession by his vendor.

4. *Adverse possession, between tenants in common.*—Actual possession,
such as the land reasonably admits of, is an essential element of adverse
possession; an entry by two tenants in common, surveying and laying
the land out in lots, without more, does not constitute such actual possession; and a sale and conveyance of one or more of the lots by one of
them, after the lapse of ten years, does not, as against the other, establish an adverse possession of the other portions of the land.

5. *Stale demands*—As between tenants in common, a bill for partition is not a stale demand so long as a right of entry is not barred.

APPEAL from the Chancery Court of Jackson.

Heard before the Hon. THOMAS COBBS

The bill in this case was filed on the 19th September,
1887, by V. K. Stevenson and others, as heirs at law of V.
K. Stevenson, deceased, against John F. Anderson, Isaac
Hames, and others; and sought a partition of certain lands

[Stevenson v. Anderson.]

between complainants and said Anderson, and an account of
the purchase-money received by Anderson on the sale of lots,
or parcels of the land, more than ten years before the bill
was filed. The tract of land, now the site of the town of
Stevenson in said county, was sold and conveyed to said
Stevenson and Anderson, in 1852, or 1853, by one John A.
Price; and they had it surveyed and laid out in lots, some
of which they sold at public auction, and others at private
sale. Afterwards, as the bill alleged, Anderson sold and conveyed several of the lots; a sale to J. F. Martin being made
in December, 1867, and another to Isaac Hames on the 16th
November, 1885; and it was alleged that each of the purchasers was put in possession. A demurrer to the bill was
filed by Anderson, on the ground that the personal representative of V. K. Stevenson, deceased, was a necessary party;
and on the further grounds, that the demand was stale, and
was, on the averments of the bill, barred by the statute of
limitations; and his demurrer was adopted by Hames. The
chancellor sustained the demurrer on these grounds, and his
decree is here assigned as error.

WM. L. MARTIN, for appellants.—(1.) The personal representative of V. K. Stevenson was not a necessary party
to the bill.—*Wright v. Lang,* 66 Ala. 389; *Alexander v.
Caldwell,* 70 Ala. 212; *Sullivan v. Lawler,* 72 Ala. 68;
Glover v. Hill, 85 Ala. 41; *Marshall v. Marshall,* 86 Ala.
383. (2.) Under the allegations of the bill, there was no
adverse possession by Anderson, and no relief was sought
against purchasers who had been in possession for ten years.
Neither the statute of limitations, nor staleness of demand,
was a bar to the relief sought.—Freeman on Co-tenancy &
Partition, §§ 221-228, 197; *Lipscomb v. McClellan,* 72 Ala.
151; *Walker v. Crawford,* 70 Ala. 567; *Carpentier v. Webster,* 27 Cal. 549; *State Bank v. Seawell,* 18 Ala. 616;
Wright v. Strauss, 73 Ala. 227.

J. E. BROWN, and R. C. HUNT, *contra,* cited *Warfield v.
Lindell,* 38 Mo. 561; s. c., 30 Mo. 273; *Marcus Unger v.
Mooney,* 63 Cal. 586; *Scruggs v. Decatur M. & L. Co.,*
86 Ala. 173; *State Bank v. Seawell,* 18 Ala. 616.

McCLELLAN, J.—The bill in this cause was filed by the
heirs at law of Vernon K. Stevenson, Sr., for partition of
certain lands between them and J. F. Anderson and certain

other persons, who had within ten years purchased parts of
the common property from said Anderson, and for an account
with said Anderson for the purchase-money of certain other
parts of the land sold by him, more than ten years before
the bill was filed. The bill alleged that Stevenson and Anderson, about the year 1852, purchased the tract of land in
question from one Price, each paying an equal part of the
purchase-money, and went into possession thereof as tenants
in common; that soon afterwards they laid the land, or a
portion of it, out in town lots, and sold a number of the lots
jointly; that beginning in December, 1867, less than twenty
years before this suit was instituted, and continuing down
to the year 1885, Anderson sold a number of the remaining
lots and parts of said tract, received the purchase-money
therefor, without accounting to his co-tenant, and executed
to the several purchasers conveyances purporting to convey
the entire interest and title therein, and that said purchasers
went into possession, claiming under these conveyances, and
are now so claiming and holding. It is shown that V. K.
Stevenson died in 1884, leaving no debts in Alabama or
elsewhere, and that there has been no administration on his
estate in this State. It is further alleged, that said Anderson was, at the time of the original purchase from Price,
has even since been, and is now a non-resident of the State
of Alabama. It does not appear from the bill that there
has ever been any actual possession of the land (unless the
surveying and plotting it in 1852 or 1853 by Anderson and
Stevenson was such possession), except by the vendees of
Anderson and Stevenson, under the sales made by them
jointly in 1852 or 1853, and by the vendees of Anderson
under the sales made by him in 1867 and subsequently.

To the case made by the bill, and under its allegations
that V. K. Stevenson owed no debts at his death in 1884,
and there had been no administration in Alabama on his
estate, the heirs alone of the deceased co-tenant were necessary parties complainant, and the demurrer of respondent
Anderson, on the ground that the administrator of the estate
of their ancestor should have been made a party, was improperly sustained.—*Glover v. Hill*, 85 Ala. 41; *Marshall
v. Marshall*, 86 Ala. 383.

It is quite true, that to bring a case within the exception
to the statute of limitations provided for by section 2622 of
the Code, absence from the State, and not mere non-residence,
must be shown.—*Huss v. Centr. R. R. & Bank. Co.*, 66 Ala.

[Stevenson v. Anderson.]

476. But, in this case, the position taken by the demurrant, in seeking to have the action adjudged to be barred by the statute of limitations, is necessarily, that it appears by the averments of the bill that the cause of action has passed under the bar of the statute. The averments on this point are, that the defendant Anderson was, at the time the cause of action accrued, and ever since has been, a non-resident of this State, and then resided, and ever since has resided, and now resides in the State of Tennessee. On these averments, the *prima facie* presumption of law is, that he has been all the time present at his place of domicil, and, of consequence, absent from the State of Alabama. On the face of the bill, therefore, it is not shown that the bar of the statute of limitations of either six or ten years has been perfected, or, indeed, that the statute has begun to run at all in favor of Anderson; and his demurrers which affirm that these facts do appear of the bill, were not well taken.—*State Bank v. Seawell*, 18 Ala. 616; *Wright v. Strauss*, 73 Ala. 227.

The right of action against Anderson not being cut off by the lapse of time, it follows that purchasers from him can not claim immunity from suit under the statute, unless it appears that, disconnected with him, a sufficient time has run since the cause of action accrued against them to perfect the bar. The respondent Hames purchased in 1885. Complainant had no right to sue him until that purchase and entry by him under it. Manifestly, therefore, the action of the chancellor in sustaining his demurrer, predicated on the ground that the statute of limitations of ten years had run in his favor, was erroneous.

It remains to be considered whether the bill discloses that the defendant Anderson had had adverse possession of the land sought to be partitioned, for ten years before the institution of the suit. One essential element of the possession, which the lapse of the statutory period will ripen into title, is that it must be *actual*. "Actual possession is the same as *pedis possessio*, or *pedis positio;* and these mean a foothold on the land, an actual entry, a possession in fact, a standing upon it, as a real demonstrative act done. It is the contrary of a possession in law, which follows in the wake of title, and is called constructive possession."—*Churchhill v. Onderdonk*, 59 N. Y. 134. The possession which a lapse of the statutory period will ripen into title, must consist of such corporal presence and physical control as the land reasonably admits of, as well as a present power and right of dominion over it; and is usually evidenced by occupation and such use as is appropriate to the locality and quality of the property.—*Minturn v. Burr*, 16 Cal. 107; *Coryell v. Cain, Ib.* 567; *Staininger v. Andrews*, 4 Nev. 59; *Fleming v. Maddox*, 30 Iowa, 240.

Does the bill disclose actual possession of the land sought to be partitioned, in Anderson, within the meaning of these definitions? We think not. It is shown, indeed, that he and Stevenson went upon the land, and laid it out into town lots in 1852 or 1853, but this possession in Anderson manifestly was not adverse to Stevenson. It may be, that Anderson subsequently had a like possession in the absence of Stevenson; but this, without more, would not be in hostility to his co-tenant; and if this were otherwise, such holding would not be of a character which, by continuance for ten years, would vest title in him. The possession of land merely for the purpose of surveying and laying it out into lots, even when accompanied by the payment of taxes and the execution of a conveyance of it, is not actual possession, in the sense necessary when adverse holding is relied on to defeat an action.—*Simpson v. Creswell*, 18 Fla. 29. And it does not appear by the bill that Anderson was in the possession involved in mapping the land, so to speak, except in conjunction with Stevenson. It is true, that the bill alleges that Anderson, assuming to be the sole owner, sold and conveyed sundry lots, or distinct part of the lands, and that his vendees went into actual possession under such sales. But it is not sought to partition this part of the land, except where the sales have been made within ten years. That there may be an ouster as to, and an adverse holding of a part of the common premises, without affecting the *status*, as between the co-tenants, of the remainder, is well settled.—Freeman Cot. & Part., § 228; *Carpentier v. Webster*, 27 Cal. 449. That the several vendees of Anderson took and held possession, certainly to no greater extent than the descriptions in their respective deeds, is equally free from doubt.—*Prescott v. Nevers*, 4 Mason, C. C. 330.

It may be admitted, for all the purposes of this case, that the actual possession of a part of a tract of land will be construed to be the actual possession of the whole of it, where the same right of possession, or color of such right, pertains alike to the entire tract. That is not the case here. The vendees of Anderson and Stevenson, and of Anderson assuming to convey without Stevenson, severally hold certain distinct lots. Their possession, aside from being limited to the respective lots, is wholly disconnected from Anderson, and from his relations to the remainder of the land. It does not appear from the bill that Anderson ever had actual possession of the land. or any part of it. The bill, therefore, does not disclose that he had had ten years adverse possession, and his demurrer on that ground should have been overruled.—*Lipscomb v. McClellan*, 72 Ala. 151; *Black v. Pratt C. & C. Co.*, 85 Ala. 504.

The bill showing no adverse possession in Anderson, no actual holding by him in hostility to Stevenson, his constructive possession is also the possession of his co-tenant, and it is not conceivable that the latter's demand asserted in this cause, to have a partition of the common property, could ever become stale so long as the joint possession continued. As we understand the averments of the bill, it is not sought to partition any of the lands held by the vendees of Anderson, where their possession has continued for ten years. We do not think that a demand for partition becomes stale within the time necessary to bar the right of entry.

The decree of the chancellor must be reversed, and a decree here rendered overruling the demurrers of Anderson and Hames, which were sustained by the court below.

Troy *v.* Walter Bros.

Bill in Equity by Purchaser, for Removal of Cloud on Title, Injunction of Action at Law, and other Relief.

1. *Unrecorded deed; statutory protection to purchasers without notice.* As against subsequent purchasers and judgment creditors without notice, an unrecorded deed is inoperative and void (Code, §§ 1810-11); and possession, acquired or held under it, charges a purchaser or creditor with constructive notice *only* when there is an actual change of possession.

APPEAL from the Chancery Court of Montgomery.
Heard before the Hon. JOHN A. FOSTER.

The bill in this case was filed on the 2d July, 1887, by Walter Brothers, suing as partners, against D. S. Troy, J. T. May, and C. B. Ferrell; and was called an "original bill in the nature of a cross-bill to a suit instituted by said May

[Troy v. Walter Bros.]

against said Walter Brothers, Troy and Ferrell," which sought to enforce a vendor's lien on land. The tract of land was sold by Ferrell to Walter Brothers, on the 12th May, 1885, at the agreed price of $1,800, and a bond for title given; but a conveyance was not executed until August 13th, and it was proved and filed for record on that day. Ferrell held the land under the will of his deceased wife, which contained a clause in these words: "I give and bequeath unto my husband, C. B. Ferrell, all of my land and real estate, during his natural life only; which said lands and real estate he shall have the right and power of selling, either in whole or in part, if he chooses, and investing the proceeds in such manner as he may think best for the interest of himself and my children; and after his death, the said lands and real estate, or the proceeds arising from the sale of the same, shall be equally divided among all my children, share and share alike." Walter Brothers gave their three notes for the purchase-money, each for $600, dated May 12th, 1885, and payable on the 1st September, 1886, 1887, and 1888, respectively. The two notes first falling due were transferred and assigned by Ferrell to J. T. May, and the third was also assigned to some person alleged to be unknown. May brought an action at law on the notes assigned to him, and also filed a bill in equity to enforce them as a lien on the land; and the bill in this case was filed in the nature of a cross-bill to that suit.

At the time of the sale by Ferrell to Walter Brothers, a suit was pending against him, in the United States Circuit Court at Montgomery, in favor of one Sweatman; and a judgment was rendered for the plaintiff in that suit, on the 12th June, 1885, for $941.62, besides costs. An execution was issued on this judgment, and placed in the hands of the United States marshal, on the 20th June; and the execution being levied on said land, the same was sold by the marshal on the 14th September, 1885, D. S. Troy becoming the purchaser. The bill alleged that the land, "at the time of said purchase by complainants, and of the execution of said deed to them, was rented out, and in the possession of a number of tenants; that said Ferrell was not, after said 12th May, 1885, in the actual possession of said land, but the same was, from that time until the execution and delivery of said deed to complainants, in the actual possession of a number of tenants, who were fully informed of complainants' purchase; but said Ferrell, by the terms of said contract of sale, reserved the rents for the year 1885; and after and upon the execution of said deed to them, complainants went into, and have ever since been in possession of said land." It was alleged, also, that complainants, at the time of their purchase, had no knowledge or information of the pending suit against Ferrell, nor of the judgment or execution until after they had received their deed; that Ferrell was insolvent; that Troy threatened to sue for the land, and they were unable to defend at law; that said deed, if invalid in equity, is a cloud on complainants' title; that they are willing and able to pay said notes, when assured that said deed to Troy is ineffectual; but, if said deed is effectual against them, they claim that they are entitled to a deduction from said notes held by May, equal to the value of the life-estate of said Ferrell in said lands, and they can not safely pay said notes, or any of them, until the effect of said deed to Troy is determined."

On these allegations the bill prayed an injunction against May; "that the validity of said deed to Troy, as against the life-estate of said Ferrell in said lands conveyed to complainants, may be determined, and, if found ineffectual, may be cancelled as a cloud upon their title; that if it be found effectual to convey the life-estate of said Ferrell as against complainants' title, the value of said life-estate, and the other damages complainants may have sustained by reason of the breach of warranty of title by said Ferrell, be computed, and allowed to complainants as a deduction against said notes held by May; that, if this can not be done, the said sale to complainants may be set aside; that the court will, on final hearing, settle, define, and decree to said Troy, and also to said May, all of their rights in the premises;" and the general prayer was added, the complainants offering to perform whatever might be required of them by the decree of the court.

The bill was afterwards amended by adding the following allegations: "That at the time of said sale, to-wit, on May 12th, 1885, said Ferrell put your orators in possession of all of said lands, subject only to the rights of said tenants for the year 1885; and your orators have, from that day to the present, been in possession of, and exercising acts of ownership over all of said lands, subject only to the rights of said tenants as above stated; and on the said day of said sale, said Ferrell and your orators informed and notified the said tenants of the sale of said lands by him to your orators; and said tenants thereafter recognized your orators as the owners of said lands, subject only to their rights as tenants for the year 1885.

Troy filed an answer to the original bill, in which he alleged that neither he, nor any other member of his law firm, nor their client, had any knowledge, notice or information, as to the alleged sale by Ferrell to complainants, until after the issue and levy of the execution under which he bought; insisted that by his purchase he acquired the life estate of Ferrell in the lands; and, "as to the averment that the tenants in possession of said land were fully informed of complainants' purchase," said that he had "no knowledge or information except that contained in said bill of complaint." In his answer to the amended bill he said, "This defendant denies that said Walter Brothers were in possession of said land at the time of the recovery of said judgment, or at the time of the issue of the execution thereon."

On final hearing on pleadings and proof, this cause and the original suit by May being heard together, the chancellor rendered a decree in favor of May, for the full amount due on the two notes held by him, and ordered a sale of the land unless the money was paid into court by Walter Brothers within ten days after the adjournment of the court; and in his opinion accompanying the decree he placed it on this ground: "It appears to the court that Walter Brothers went into possession of the land, under a valid contract of purchase, on May 12th, 1885, and that Sweatman obtained his judgment on the 12th June afterwards. The fact that Walter Brothers were in possession, under their bond for title, was sufficient to put Sweatman, and those acquiring rights under him, on inquiry as to their title or equity. The tenants on the place had been informed that Walter Brothers were the owners of the land, and had consented to recognize and regard them as such, although the rent notes were still to be paid to Ferrell, their former landlord. The court is of the opinion, that May's vendor's lien is a superior equity to the title acquired by Troy, the purchaser at execution sale."

Troy alone assigns this decree as error.

TOMPKINS, LONDON & TROY, for appellants, cited *King v. Paulk*, 85 Ala. 186; s. c., 86 Ala. 332.

GRAVES & BLAKEY, *contra.*—Troy, as a purchaser without notice, can claim nothing under his deed from the marshal, because the deed of Walter Brothers was on record before that time, and he had actual notice of it; nor can his legal title avail against their prior equity, if he is chargeable with notice of it.—*LeNeve v. LeNeve*, 3 Atk. 654; 13 Vesey, 114; Wade on Notice, § 55; *Sawyer r. Baker*, 66 Ala. 292; *Brunson v. Brooks*, 68 Ala. 248; *Burt v. Cassety*, 12 Ala. 734. A purchaser at execution sale succeeds to all the rights of the judgment creditor, as they existed when the judgment was rendered, and is entitled to all the protection given by statute to the creditor, but no more. Possession is the visible evidence of title, and is, to some extent, title. Whoever buys land in the actual possession of any other person than his vendor, is bound to inquire into the possessor's title, is chargeable with notice of every fact which inquiry would have disclosed, and can claim no protection against an equity which would have been brought to his knowledge, if he had made inquiry. The chancellor found, and we think correctly, that the tenants in possession of the land had been notified of the sale to Walter Brothers, and recognized their title and ownership, though the rent for the year was reserved by Ferrell. If inquiry of the tenants would have disclosed these facts, the creditor and purchaser are chargeable with notice of them, and are not entitled to protection.—*Montgomery v. Tutwiler*, 73 Ala. 263; *Chadwick r. Carson*, 78 Ala. 116; *Herbert v. Hanrick*, 16 Ala. 581; *Yarbrough v. Avant*, 66 Ala. 526; Tied. R. P., § 701; *Scroggins v. McDougald*, 8 Ala. 384; Wade on Notice, §§ 279, 286; 16 Vesey, 252; *Powell v. Allred*, 11 Ala. 318; *Harris v. Carter*, 3 Stew. 233; *Brewer v. Brewer*, 19 Ala. 489; 2 Sugden on Vendors, 9th ed., 291-2, mar. *King v. Paulk*, 85 Ala. 186, it is submitted, is not in harmony with these authorities, and a reconsideration of it is asked.

STONE, C. J.—We are asked in this case to review our ruling in *King v. Paulk*, 85 Ala. 186; s. c., 86 Ala. 332. That case was followed and re-affirmed in *Fitzgerald v. Williams*, 85 Ala. 585. And each of these cases followed, substantially, our older rulings in *McCarthy v. Nicrosi*, 72 Ala. 332, and *Watt v. Parsons*, 73 Ala. 202. They rest on the solid ground, that a change of title, or ownership, without visible change of possession, is neither actual nor constructive notice. We consider that ruling as resting on justice and solid reasoning, and are not inclined to depart from it.

It is contended for appellees, that when Ferrell agreed to sell to Walter Brothers, the tenants attorned to the latter;

and that this operated as constructive notice to all persons
who claim to have acquired liens or rights affecting the
property after that time. *Tutwiler v. Montgomery*, 73 Ala.
263; *Brunson v. Brooks*, 68 Ala. 248, and *Brewer v. Brewer*,
19 Ala. 481, are relied on in support of this view. But the
appellees do not bring themselves within the principle of
Tutwiler v. Montgomery. There is not only no proof that
the tenants in possession of the lands when Ferrell sold to
Walter Bros. attorned to the latter, but the proof is express
that they did not. They remained Ferrell's tenants, and paid
the accruing rent to him; and there was no testimony that
Walter Bros. had taken any kind of possession under their
alleged purchase.

Troy, by his purchase at marshal's sale, acquired a title
to the lands, to continue during Ferrell's life, that is superior
to all other rights presented by this record.—*Preston v.
McMillan*, 58 Ala. 84; 2 Pom. Eq. § 724; *Dickerson v. Carroll*, 76 Ala. 377.

In scaling the amount of purchase-money for which the
Walter Bros. are liable, should they be held to their purchase, the rule of the inverse ratio of the alienation of the
purchase-money notes will furnish the proper guide.

Reversed and remanded.

Clements *v.* Beatty.

Action for Breach of Contract for Sale of Trees.

1. *Measure of damages.*—In an action for the breach of a contract,
by which defendants sold to plaintiff all the standing trees on a tract
of land suitable for saw-logs of specified size, at a named price per
thousand feet, and afterwards sold all the timber on the land to a third
person, who entered and cut some of the trees to which plaintiff was
entitled; the measure of damages is the market value of the trees so
cut and carried away, *less* the price which plaintiff was to have paid
for them, but which he had not paid.

APPEAL from the Circuit Court of Tuskaloosa.
Tried before the Hon. SAM. H. SPROTT.
This action was brought by C. C. Beatty, against Alsey
Clements and Morgan Clements, to recover damages for the
alleged breach by the defendants of a written contract, by
which they sold to plaintiff all the pine timber then standing

[Clements v. Beatty.]

on a tract of land particularly described, "which will make
saw-logs twelve feet long, and will square ten inches;" and
was commenced on the 20th March, 1888. The only plea
was the general issue. On the trial, as the bill of exceptions
shows, the plaintiff read in evidence the written contract between himself and the defendants, which was dated 21st October, 1886, and which stipulated that the plaintiff should
pay for the timber, or lumber, "one dollar per thousand feet
board measure;" and he then offered in evidence another
written contract, dated June 29th, 1887, by which defendants
leased said tract, with other lands, for the term of five years,
to one W. A. Goold, giving him the right to cut and use "all
timber that may be necessary for coal mining and coke oven
purposes." "The plaintiff then introduced evidence tending
to show that, in July, or August, 1887, said Goold entered
upon said lands embraced in plaintiff's contract with defendants, and cut down pine trees of the dimensions described
in said contract, which was also necessary for mining purposes; and plaintiff proved the market value of said trees,
as they stood upon the stump. Upon this evidence, the court
charged the jury, that if they found for the plaintiff, the
measure of damages would be the market value of the trees
cut by Goold, as they stood upon the stump." The defendants excepted to this charge, and they here assign it as error.

F. S. Moody, and J. M. Foster, for the appellants, cited
Johnson & Thornton v. Allen & Jemison, 78 Ala. 387;
2 Benj. Sales, 973, 977–8.

A. B. McEachin, Foster & Jones, and Thos. L. Beatty,
contra, cited *Murrell v. Whiting*, 32 Ala. 54; *George v.
C. & M. Railroad Co.*, 8 Ala. 234; *Lecroy v. Wiggins*,
31 Ala 13; *Culver v. Hill*, 68 Ala. 66; *Trustees v. Turner*,
71 Ala. 429.

SOMERVILLE, J.—The proper measure of the plaintiff's
damages could not be more than a just recompense for the
actual injury he had sustained, by reason of the alleged
breach of the contract by the defendants. The recovery
could not, therefore, exceed the market value of the trees cut
by Goold, which the defendants had given the plaintiff a
license to cut, *less* the amount the plaintiff had agreed to
pay for them, with lawful interest on this balance. This is
the established rule for a breach of contract to deliver goods,

where no money has been paid by the vendee. If the price had been paid in advance by the vendee, which is not the case here, a different rule would prevail.—2 Greenl. Ev. (14th Ed.), § 261; 2 Addison on Contr., § 589; *Bell v. Reynolds*, 78 Ala. 511; s. c., 56 Amer. Rep. 52; *Trustees of Howard College v. Turner*, 71 Ala. 429; s. c., 46 Amer. Rep. 326; *Johnson v. Allen*, 78 Ala. 387.

Neither the evidence, nor the rulings of the court, present any question as to the plaintiff's right to recover profits as damages.—*Reynolds v. Bell*, 84 Ala. 496; *Griffin v. Colver*, 69 Amer. Dec. 718; *note*, 724.

The charge given by the court was in conflict with this view of the law, and was erroneous.

Reversed and remanded.

Judson *v.* City of Bessemer.

Bill in Equity for Injunction against Issue of Bonds by Municipal Corporation.

1. *Charter of Bessemer, under constitutional provision as to title and subject-matter of laws; power to issue municipal bonds* —The act approved December 12th, 1888, entitled "An act to amend the charter of the town of Bessemer, and to re-incorporate the same as the city of Bessemer, and to establish a charter therefor," is not violative of the constitutional provision which declares, "Each law shall contain but one subject, which shall be clearly expressed in its title" (Art. iv, § 2); the title and the body of the act, construed together, show a single purpose, and relate to a single subject; and the grant of power, in the 38th section, to issue negotiable bonds for specified municipal purposes, is germane to that subject as expressed in the title.

2. *Same; amendatory laws, and unconstitutional repealing laws.*—The subsequent statute amending the 38th section of said charter, "by striking out the word *fifty*, and inserting *thirty* in lieu thereof," is violative of the further constitutional provision, contained in the same article and section, that, in amendatory laws, so much of the former law as is amended "shall be re-enacted and published at length;" and said amendatory law being unconstitutional and void, the power of the corporation to issue bonds payable in fifty years, as at first provided, is unimpaired.

3. *Municipal bonds payable in gold coin.*—A grant of power to a municipal corporation to issue bonds, without limitation as to the kind of currency in which they shall be payable, confers the authority to make them payable "in gold coin of the United States of America, of the present standard weight and fineness."

[Judson v. City of Bessemer.]

APPEAL from the City Court of Birmingham, in equity. Heard before the Hon. H. A. SHARPE.

The bill in this case was filed on the 25th April, 1889, by W. H. H. Judson and A. J. Robinson, citizens, tax-payers, and owners of property in Bessemer, against the corporate authorities of said city; and sought to enjoin the issue of certain corporate bonds for municipal purposes. The City Court dismissed the bill, on motion, for want of equity; and this decree is here assigned as error.

FEAGIN & WILKERSON, for appellants.

WEBB & TILLMAN, contra.

CLOPTON, J.—Appellants seek by the bill to enjoin the issuance and sale of municipal bonds, which appellees claim authority to issue under power conferred by an act of the General Assembly, incorporating the city of Bessemer. The right to the injunction is founded on the alleged grounds, that the act is unconstitutional; and if constitutional, as amended, it does not authorize the issue of bonds of the character and terms provided by the ordinance adopted by the municipal authorities.

The first point of contention is, that the act violates the mandate of the Constitution, which declares, "Each law shall contain but one subject, which shall be clearly expressed in its title." It is entitled "An act to amend the charter of the town of Bessemer, and to re-incorporate the same as the city of Bessemer, and to establish a charter therefor." This caption is followed by an enactment consisting of forty-four sections, which is new and independent legislation, complete in itself.—Acts 1888-9, p. 185. The bill does not inform us when, or in what manner, the town of Bessemer was incorporated; and as we know of no legislative act of incorporation, and our attention has been called to none, we assume, for the purposes of this case, that it was incorporated under the general laws. On this assumption, the act does not purport or profess to amend, revise or enlarge any former legislative act. True, the first section, after declaring that the inhabitants of the town of Bessemer are re-incorporated as the city of Bessemer, provides, "that the charter of the present town of Bessemer be altered, amended and enlarged in conformity herewith." The effect of the act, if these words had been omitted, would have been to amend,

16

abrogate, or supersede by implication, the charter of Bessemer as a town. The use of the words quoted impart no other or greater force or effect. They may be regarded as superfluous. The act, therefore, is not amendatory or revisory in its character and operation, otherwise than by implication.

In pronouncing upon the constitutionality of statutes, as tested by the clause of the Constitution referred to, we have uniformily observed two leading and controlling rules of interpretation: (1.) The mandate should not be so narrowly construed, or exactly enforced, as to embarrass or obstruct legislation. (2.) Sentence of nullity will not be declared because of the mere generality of the title. The subject may be expressed in general terms. It is sufficient, if the terms in which the subject is expressed are so comprehensive, that all the minor provisions of the enactment are embraced in, or referable, or cognate to that subject.—*Ballentyne v. Wickersham*, 75 Ala. 533; *Stein v. Leeper*, 78 Ala. 517; *Hare v. Kennerly*, 83 Ala. 608.

It is insisted that the statute contains two subjects, both of which are expressed in the title—one to amend the charter of the town, and the other to incorporate the city of Bessemer. It is well settled, that a statute which contains two subjects, both of which are expressed in the title, falls within the constitutional inhibition; and when a statute contains two subjects, only one of which is expressed in the title, the portions not pertinent and germane to the subject so expressed will be declared unconstitutional. If, as appellants contend, two subjects are expressed in the title, but the enactment contains only one of them, it is not violative of the Constitution. The constitutional mandate is not, that two subjects shall not be expressed in the title; but that "each law shall contain but one subject, which shall be clearly expressed in its title." A statute does not come within the letter or spirit of the constitutional inhibition, merely because two subjects may be expressed in the title. In such case, the subject so expressed, but not contained in the law, may be rejected as surplusage. If the enactment assailed contains only one of the subjects which is expressed in the title, and only minor provisions connected with, and proper or necessary to the full accomplishment of its object, the constitutional mandate is satisfied, though there may be two subjects expressed in the title. But are ¡two subjects expressed? If the words, *to amend the charter of the town of*

[Judson v. City of Bessemer.]

Bessemer, were omitted from the title, there would be no doubt that only one subject would be expressed. On the authority of *Gandy v. State*, 86 Ala. 20, these words may be rejected from the title as surplusage. When the title and the act are compared and construed jointly, and its sole purpose considered, it is obvious that but one subject is expressed—the incorporation of the town of Bessemer as a city, and to establish a charter therefor.

The only provision, which, it is insisted, is not cognate to the subject of incorporating the town as a city, is the authority to issue the bonds in question. Section 38 of the act confers authority on the Mayor and Aldermen to issue bonds of the city to an amount not exceeding thirty thousand dollars, payable in fifty years from their issuance, with coupons attached, bearing interest at a rate not exceeding eight per cent. *per annum*, and payable annually to bearer, at some place designated by the board. By section 41, the Mayor and Aldermen are authorized to negotiate and sell the bonds, the proceeds "to be used and applied in building and constructing sewers in said city, and in erecting city buildings in said city, and in grading and making improvements of any and all kinds upon the streets of said city." It is not infrequent that municipal authorities are necessitated to borrow money, to carry into full effect the objects of the incorporation. Negotiable bonds can not be issued without authority, express or implied. The bonds are authorized to be issued only for municipal purposes, and authority to issue them is germane to the primary objects of the incorporation, and are referable and cognate to the subject expressed in the title.

The ordinance provides for the issuance of bonds payable fifty years after date of issuance. It is insisted that the municipal authorities are not authorized to issue bonds payable at such time. This contention is based on an act of the General Assembly, passed at a subsequent day of the same session, which, it is claimed, amends section 38. The amending act reads as follows: "That section 38 of the charter of the city of Bessemer, Alabama, be, and the same is hereby, amended by striking out the word '*fifty*,' in the sixth line of said section, and inserting the word '*thirty*' in lieu thereof." The section is not re-enacted and published at length as amended.—Acts 1888–9, p. 901. It is too plain for argument, that the amendatory act is in contravention of the clause of the Constitution, which provides: "That no law shall be revised, amended, or the provisions thereof extended or conferred, by reference to its title only; but so much thereof as is revised, amended, extended or conferred, shall be re-enacted and published at length."—*Stewart v. County Commissioners*, 82 Ala. 209. The amending act, being unconstitutional and void, has no force or effect whatever. Section 38 remains unaffected, and as originally passed.—*Tims v. State*, 26 Ala. 165.

The remaining contention is, that the bonds are invalid, because of a want of authority to make them payable "in gold coin of the United States of America, of the present standard weight and fineness," as provided by the ordinance. The general rule is, that corporations, upon whom is conferred power to give securities, may exercise such power in the same mode and manner as natural persons may under similar circumstances, there being no legislative restriction nor specification of a particular mode.—*Trustees v. Moody*, 62 Ala. 389. The charter, while specifying the amount and denominations of the bonds to be issued, the time in which they may be made payable, and the rate of interest, is silent as to the kind of currency in which they shall be payable. The purpose is to authorize the issue of bonds, which, by usage and judicial adjudications, are negotiable securities. The limitation is, that they shall possess the elements of negotiability. There being different kinds of currency, the legislative intent is to leave this matter to the discretion and judgment of the municipal authorities—a matter of contract. The evident purpose of making the bonds payable in gold coin, of the present standard weight and fineness, is to give them a fixed and stable value on their face, not subject to be affected by fluctuations in the value of the various kinds of circulating medium, or to future appreciation or depreciation. of the present value of gold coin. Express and general power to issue negotiable bonds, in the absence of legislative restriction, carries the implied or incidental power to make them payable generally; that is, in currency which is constitutionally a legal tender, or payable in the particular coin which constitutes the legal and commercial standard by which the value of other kinds of currency is measured. Under such express power, the city of Bessemer has an authority to agree that the bonds shall be payable as provided by the ordinance.

Affirmed.

Montgomery Gas-Light Co. v. City Council of Montgomery.

Bill in Equity for Injunction against Municipal Corporation, in matter of Contract with Gas Company.

1. *Remedy for breach of contract with municipal corporation, granting exclusive privilege.*—On the breach of a contract between a municipal corporation and private persons, or a private corporation, granting the exclusive privilege of lighting the streets with gas for a term of years, the city may treat the contract as abrogated, and grant the privilege to other persons, although it might also maintain an action at law for damages; but a bill for specific performance would not lie, where the breach consists in the failure to appoint appraisers of the property, on the election of the city to purchase, as authorized by the terms of the contract.

2. *Contract between city of Montgomery and Montgomery Gas-Light Company; election by city to purchase at appraised value, on expiration of twenty-five years.*—Under the contract by which the city of Montgomery granted to Jeffrey & Co., their successors and assigns, now the Montgomery Gas-Light Company, the exclusive privilege of lighting the streets of the city with gas, for the term of fifty years from November 1st, 1852; the provision contained in the 8th section, giving the city "the right or privilege," at the expiration of twenty-five years, "of purchasing from said Jeffrey & Co., their associates, successors and assigns, all the pipes, buildings and apparatus constituting the gas works, at such price as may be determined by five disinterested men," to be selected as therein provided, confers only a right of election to purchase, at a price to be afterwards ascertained, and not a right to have appraisers appointed, with a view to a subsequent election to purchase based on their appraisement; and the company is not in default, because of a refusal to appoint appraisers in advance of an election to purchase.

3. *Same; when election may be exercised.*—This right of election on the part of the city, conceding that it might be exercised within a reasonable time after the expiration of the twenty-five years, is certainly lost after the lapse of eight years more; and a bill then filed by the gas company, seeking to enforce its rights under the contract, or to enjoin any violation by the city, need not aver an open and continuing offer to the city to purchase.

4. *Injunction against municipal corporation in matter of exclusive franchise.*—If an individual, or a private corporation, having granted an exclusive franchise or privilege, afterwards attempts to repudiate it by an inconsistent grant to another person, which would cast a cloud on the title held under the first grant, a court of equity will interfere by injunction; and if a municipal corporation should grant an exclusive franchise or privilege, and afterwards, in violation thereof, grant a similar franchise or privilege to other persons, who threaten to exercise it to the injury of the original grantees, a court of equity would enjoin the threatened action; but it would not interfere by injunction to prevent the passage of an ordinance by the municipal corporation, or the making of a contract by it, on the ground that such action would be violative of the franchise already granted.

APPEAL from the City Court of Montgomery in equity. Heard before the Hon. THOS. M. ARRINGTON.

The bill in this case was filed on the 28th December, 1885, by the Montgomery Gas-Light Company, a private corporation, against the corporate authorities of the city of Montgomery; and prayed an injunction, restraining the defendants "from entering into any contract, or passing any ordinance, granting to any person or corporation the right to lay pipes for conducting gas under any street, alley or thoroughfare within the corporate limits of said city, before the 1st day of November, A. D. 1902," in violation of an exclusive franchise claimed by the complainant under a former contract and ordinance. On final hearing, on pleadings and proof, the bill was dismissed; and the decree dismissing it is now assigned as error. The opinion of the court states all the material facts.

TOMPKINS, LONDON & TROY, and JNO. GINDRAT WINTER, for the appellant.—(1.) The bill makes a clear case for an injunction, if the appellant's construction of the contract be correct.—*Casey v. Holmes*, 10 Ala. 776. (2.) The contract gave the city a right of election to purchase the property, on the expiration of twenty-five years, at a valuation to be fixed by appraisers; but not a right to require the appointment of appraisers in advance, "with a view to purchase;" and until the city declared its election to purchase, the company was not bound to appoint appraisers. It was nothing more or less than an offer by the company to sell its property to the city on a future day, at a price to be fixed by appraisers, if the city elected to purchase.—1 Chitty on Contracts, 15, note; 1 Benj. Sales, p. 54; *Newton v. Newton*, 23 Amer. Rep. 476. But this offer was not continuing; the option was to be exercised at the expiration of twenty-five years, and the company was not bound to extend it for a further period of eight years.—*Richardson v. Hardwick*, 106 U. S. 252; *Longworth v. Taylor*, 1 McL. 395. (3.) Even if the city's construction of the contract be correct, the failure of the company to appoint appraisers gave it no right to declare the contract abrogated, or to treat the franchise as forfeited. Its remedy was by an action at law for damages, or a bill in equity for specific performance, under which the court would have appointed appraisers.—*Chapin v. School District*, 35 N. H. 445; *Emerson v. Simpson*, 80 Amer. Dec. 184; 10 Amer.

& Eng. R. R. Cases, 234; *Smith v. Peters,* 15 Eng. Rep. 463; 1 Sm. & G. 184; *Durham v. Bradford,* L. R. 5 Ch. 519.

WM. S. THORINGTON, with whom was SAM. F. RICE, *contra.* (1.) By the terms of the contract between these parties, the city of Montgomery, acting for the public, granted to the complainant a valuable franchise, for a long period of time, but reserved to itself the privilege of purchasing the property, at the expiration of twenty-five years, at an appraised valuation. Whether this stipulation was intended to act *in terrorem,* securing better service on the part of the company, or was inserted from economic considerations, it was in the interest of the public as represented by the city, and was intended for the benefit of the city. To make an election— to exercise the privilege of purchasing understandingly—an appraisement of the property was an indispensable prerequisite. An election, made without knowledge of the facts, is not binding in any case. To require the city to elect to purchase, without an appraisement of the property on which to base its election, would destroy the benefit intended to be secured, and might work great injury. The contract is in the nature of a legislative grant, and is to be construed most strongly in favor of the public.—*Wright v. Nagle,* 101 U. S. 794; *Railroad Co. v. Litchfield,* 23 How. 66, 88; *Slidell v. Grandjean,* 111 U. S. 437; Endlich Stat., §§ 349, 354; *Willard v. Taylor,* 8 Wall. 557; *Home v. Rouse,* 8 Wall. 437. That a contract may be obligatory on one party, and optional as to the other, see 2 John. Cases, 254; Doug. Rep. 23; 1 T. R. 132; Cowp. 818; 2 Chitty on Contracts, 1061, 11th Amer. ed. (2.) The appointment of appraisers was requested "with a view to purchase;" and if the contract bound the city to purchase, the company could not legally refuse to appoint appraisers. (3.) The city had a right to treat the contract as rescinded, on the breach by the company.—Bish. Contracts, § 837; Anson on Contracts, 253–4. (4.) The bill does not make a case for injunction. 44 Iowa, 505; 25 Conn. 19; 2 Story's Equity, § 959a, note 6; 1 Beasley, N. J. 499.

McCLELLAN, J.—This bill was filed by the Montgomery Gas-Light Company, against the City Council of Montgomery, to enjoin the city authorities from "entering into any contract, or passing any ordinance granting to any person or corporation the right to lay pipes for conducting gas under any street, alley or thoroughfare within the corporate limits of said city, before the first day of November in the year 1902." The facts upon which this relief is sought may be epitomized as follows:

On the 30th day of August, 1852, the City Council of Montgomery passed an ordinance "to provide for the lighting of the city of Montgomery with gas," in and by the first section of which it was provided, "that the exclusive privilege shall be, and the same is hereby, granted for the term of fifty years from the first day of November, A. D. 1852, to John Jeffrey & Co., of Cincinnati, Ohio, their associates, successors and assigns, of laying pipes for conducting gas under any street, alley or thoroughfare within the corporate limits of the city." This grant is made to depend upon certain conditions, specified in section 2 of the ordinance, which is in the following language: "That the privilege herein granted is upon the condition, that the said John Jeffrey & Co. shall, on or before the first day of May, A. D. 1854, have completed the requisite apparatus for manufacturing gas, and shall have laid in connection therewith three miles of main pipe in the streets of Montgomery, and shall further lay, from time to time, such additional main pipes in any street, alley or thoroughfare, as shall be required by the city council; *Provided,* that the demand for gas to be supplied by such extensions, shall afford a reasonable prospect for a fair remuneration." Subsequent sections required Jeffrey & Co., their successors and assigns, to furnish from time to time, and at all times, for the public use and benefit, such quantities of gas, of the most approved quality, as might be needed for lighting the streets of the city, at one-half the price per cubic foot, at which gas is furnished to individuals; and that gas in like quantity, and of the same quality, should be furnished the inhabitants of said city, at as low a price as gas, under similar conditions, is furnished to the inhabitants of any other Southern city of equal or greater population.

By section 8, with the terms of which we are chiefly concerned, it is provided: "That at the expiration of twenty-five years from the first day of November, A. D. 1852, the City Council of Montgomery shall have the right or privilege of purchasing from the said John Jeffrey & Co., their associates, successors and assigns, all the pipes, buildings and apparatus constituting the gas-works, at such price as may be ascertained and determined by five disinterested men, two of whom shall be chosen by the City Council of Montgomery, two by said John Jeffrey & Co., their associates, successors and assigns, and the fifth by the four thus chosen."

Section 9 evidences the purpose and contemplation of the parties, that Jeffrey & Co. should secure a legislative charter, in order to afford citizens and the City Council the opportunity to take shares in the capital stock of a corporation, to be organized thereunder as the successor of the original grantees. The ordinance was assented to by Jeffrey & Co., and went into effect on October 14th, 1852.

The contract thus made, by the adoption of the ordinance on the part of the city and the assent of Jeffrey & Co. to its terms, was soon afterwards assigned by Jeffrey & Co. to certain associates, who were constituted a body corporate by an act of the General Assembly, approved February 15, 1854, which act expressly ratified and confirmed the original contract, as a compact between said company, the complainant in this cause, and the City Council. Under this contract, the gas company established a plant for the manufacture of gas, and laid pipes under the streets for its distribution to and throughout the city, and carried on the business in accordance with the ordinance, for the first twenty-five years of the grant. At the end of this time, the City Council sought to avail itself of the right and privilege guaranteed to it by section 8 of the ordinance, as that section was construed on the part of the city; and "with a view to purchasing" the property of the gas-company, appointed two men, who were citizens of Montgomery and gas-consumers, to act, with two others to be appointed by the company, and a fifth to be selected by the four thus appointed, in the valuation of such property. The company was notified of this action, and requested to name the two appraisers on its part. This the company declined to do, on two grounds: *first*, that the right reserved to the city, by section 8, was the right to purchase the property, and not the right to have it appraised with a view to purchasing, and that the city had not made its election, upon which alone depended both the necessity and right to have the price fixed; and, *second*, that the city had failed to comply with the terms of section 8 as to the character of the appraisers it had appointed, in that those named by it were not "disinterested men," as therein required. The City Council, considering that this refusal and failure on the part of the company was a breach of the contract, in such sort that the city was authorized to repudiate it *in toto*, notified the gas company of its determination so to do, and has ever since treated it as ended. Acting upon the assumption that the contract was no longer binding upon it, and no longer secured to the company the exclusive use of the streets in the distribution of gas, the city, in 1885, was about to grant this privilege to other parties, and to enter into contracts with them for furnishing gas to the city and its inhabitants. The appellant's right to enjoin this threatened action by the municipal authorities is now presented for our consideration.

It may be taken as conceded by the arguments at the bar, that the grant of the exclusive privilege to lay pipes in the streets of the city, for the considerations stipulated, was a valid exercise of corporate power, confirmed, as it was, by legislative action. Whether a like grant would be upheld under the provisions of the constitution now in force, we need not decide. It will also be treated as admitted, that the Montgomery Gas-Light Company succeeded to all the rights of John Jeffrey & Co., and for the first twenty-five years of the grant complied with all its terms and conditions; and hence was, for that time, entitled to the exclusive privilege conferred by the ordinance.

Much has been said in argument concerning the rights of the city in the premises, assuming a breach of the contract, in the particular referred to, to have been committed, on the part of the gas company. The appellant insists, that the city's remedy for such violation lay in an action for damages; or, if this mode of redress should be held inadequate, full relief could be had on a bill for specific performance. On the other hand, the appellee contends, that commensurate relief could only be had by treating this contract as abrogated, and securing the benefits, which the default of the company had denied to it, through another contract with other parties, on whom it proposed to confer the privilege of using the streets for the purpose of distributing gas. This right is denied by the appellant, because, it is said, to allow it would be to give section 8 the effect and operation of a condition subsequent, which its terms do not import or require; and we are referred to the authorities which support the doctrine, that such conditions are not favored in the law, and the language of contracts should be construed, in cases of doubt, against the divestiture of an estate by acts or omissions occurring after its creation. Without, for the present at least, entering upon an elaborate consideration of these questions, it will suffice to say generally, that it would seem that the city is without adequate remedy for the alleged breach, unless it is permitted to avail itself of the right to annul the contract ; at least to the extent of avoiding the consequence of the exclusive grant of the privilege of laying pipes in the streets. It is readily conceivable that actions for damages would fall short of conferring exact justice between the parties; and, were this otherwise, the existence of this remedy would not be inconsistent or incompatible with the exercise of the right of abrogation.

The other mode of redress suggested by the appellant does not exist. There is no principle better settled in reason and by authority, than that an executory contract for the sale of property, by the terms of which the price to be paid for the whole subject-matter is to be determined by appraisers, to be selected directly or indirectly by the parties, can not be specifically enforced in equity, so long as there is a failure from any cause to appoint referees, or a failure of such referees, after appointment, to assess the value.—*Vickers v. Vickers*, 3 Eq. Cases (L. R.) 532; *Milnes v. Gery*, 14 Vesey, 400; *Cooth v. Jackson*, 6 Ves. 84; *Thurnell v. Balburnie*, 8 M. & W. 786; 1 Benj. on Sales, p. 54; 2 Benj. Sales, p. 755. A different rule prevails, where the thing which is to be appraised by such valuers constitutes only a minor part of the subject-matter of the contract; as, for instance, where land is purchased at a fixed price, but the contract of sale also includes fixtures, or timber, or furniture, the valuation of which is to be determined by third persons; or, as in the case of a contract of partnership, containing a stipulation for a sale by one co-partner to the other, on dissolution, at a price to be ascertained by arbitrators. But the case at bar is not of this class.—*Smith v. Peters*, 20 Eq. Cas. (L. R.) 511; *Dinham v. Bradford*, 5 Ch. App. Cas. 521.

The attitude of the city could be justified, by treating its contract as a grant of the right to lay pipes in its streets, coupled with a covenant not to grant a like privilege to others for fifty years; and so regarded, it would be competent for the city, upon the failure of one of the considerations on which it so covenanted, through the default of the company with respect to the right of purchase given by section 8 of the ordinance, to hold itself no longer bound thereby. This view, we think, might be taken, and this construction resorted to, if necessary to the ends of justice. Whether it is necessary depends, of course, upon the question, whether

there was a default on the part of the company with respect
to the duties imposed on it by section 8; and this, in turn,
depends solely on the construction that should be given to
that section, for the facts are undisputed. And this brings
us to the consideration of what must be regarded as the
main question in the case : *Was the action or non-action of
the company, in the matter of the appraisement of the gas
works, a breach of its contract ?* Undoubtedly, the only
valuable, substantive right secured to the city by section 8,
was the right to purchase. If it had an opportunity to make
its election, under and as contemplated by that section, the
company has not been in default. What was essential to the
exercise of the right, within the purview of the terms which
granted it? Was it necessary to have a valuation made
before the duty of election devolved on the city? Or does
the contract mean that the election should be made by the
city, unaided and unadvised in the premises by the appraisement provided for in the instrument? Was the fixing of the
price by five disinterested men to serve in the first instance
as a basis for the exercise of the option, and then as a basis
of settlement between the parties only in the event the city,
as admonished thereby, should elect to buy? Or were these
men to act only after the election to purchase had been
made, and then to ascertain and determine what sum should
be paid and received by the parties respectively? It is to
be borne in mind that the right to purchase was secured
many years before it was to be exercised. Neither the value
of the property, nor the ability of the city to pay for it, at
any price, great or small, could be foreseen. Nor could it
be determined so long in advance whether, granting that a
reasonable and fair valuation, and one within the financial
competency of the city, should be fixed, it would be to the
interest of the city to purchase. To enable the city to deal
with a present condition into which all these future contingencies should have resolved themselves, and to effectuate
whatever it might in 1877 conceive to be its interest, it was
given the right and privilege, without any corresponding
obligation, to purchase when a certain time elapsed, at such
price as might be ascertained by disinterested third persons.
It is not to be assumed that either party expected to gain
any advantage over the other by this stipulation. They
contracted *in limine*, upon terms of equality. Is there
anything in the contract to warrant the inference that it was
contemplated that, at any time, or with respect to any matter

under the contract, the situation of the parties should be so changed as to put either in a better position with reference to the subject-matter than the other? To admit the construction of section 8 insisted on by the city, would have this effect. Under that construction, the company would have been compelled to sell its property at the assessment of the referees, but there was no compulsion on the city to make its election on that basis. On the contrary, it would have had the further right to pass its own judgment on the fairness and reasonableness of the price thus fixed. This would be to bind the company absolutely by the appraisement, but to impose no correlative obligation on the city. The company had no option to decline the price so ascertained, however inadequate in point of fact, while the city was bound to pay that price only on the condition and in the event its judgment coincided with that of the valuers.

The presumption would be, that a construction which produces such an unequal *status* of parties, who, in the outset, at the time of executing the stipulation in question, and with reference to that stipulation, dealt on terms of the utmost equality, is not in accordance with their intention; and it should not be allowed to obtain, unless the language employed by them requires it. Does the language of section 8 lead to this result? It is possible to impute two purposes to the parties in the use of the words, "at such price as may be ascertained and determined by five disinterested men," &c. One of these purposes could have been subserved by holding the meaning to be that, after the city had elected to purchase, there should be an ascertainment and a determination by five men of the amount it should pay. The only other possible meaning is, that the appraisement should be first made, and the city's election predicated on it. Considering, on the one hand, that many things might have transpired between the date of the contract and the time at which the option of the city was to be exercised, to make the sale objectionable to the company, and to induce it to throw obstacles in the way of the city's acquisition of its property; and on the other hand, that the property of the company was of such public character, so open to inspection, especially on the part of the municipal authorities, is it not more reasonable that the provision quoted was intended to further and secure the consummation of the sale after election made, than to afford the city data upon which to make the election. It would, we apprehend, have been an easy matter for the city officers, with their necessarily intimate knowledge of the pipes, apparatus and buildings constituting the gas-works, to have sufficiently approximated their value as to determine intelligently whether it would be to the interest and within the ability of the city to buy the plant; but it would have been simply impossible for a sale to have been consummated, or the gas company put in default in respect to it, if the company was unwilling to dispose of its property, without the arbitration of third persons. Nor is it conceivable that this interpretation of the contract works any detriment to the city. As we have said, it can not be taken for granted to have been in the contemplation of the parties that any undue benefit was to accrue to either of them. On the contrary, care was taken to secure an impartial, fair, and reasonable valuation. The presumption is, that the *consensus* of five disinterested men would have attained the purpose, and ascertained and determined that the city should pay, and the company should receive, the fair and just equivalent of the property, no more and no less. So long as the right of the city to acquire the gas-works at a fair price is not denied, or abridged, can it be said that the real and only substantive right which section 8 secured to the city—the right to purchase at a fair price— has been defeated? If not, it would seem that the construction which the appellant insists on would meet all the exigencies of the case. The idea of equality and mutuality between the parties would be maintained, so that neither, with respect to the right provided for in section 8, would be put at a disadvantage; the intention of the parties, which surely could not have been other than that the city might purchase the gas-works at the value the referees should fix, would be fully effectuated; and the rights of the parties would be protected.

The same conclusion would be reached by considering the question from another point of view. The legal effect of section 8 of the ordinance was to impose on the gas company the duty of offering its property to the city, at a price to be ascertained and determined in a certain way. The rights of the parties on November 1, 1877, were precisely the same as if the contract had been silent as to the city's right to purchase, and the company, of its own volition, not induced thereto by an antedecent obligation, had then offered to sell its property to the city "at such price as may be ascertained and determined by five disinterested men," to be selected in a prescribed manner.—*Hunt v. Wyman*, 100 Mass. 198; *Newton v. Newton*, 23 Amer. Rep. 478; *McCall v. Powell*, 64 Ala. 254. The right secured to the city was to say whether it would accept or reject this offer, in the identical terms in which it was made. The offer was not open to qualification by the acceptance. Any attempt to accept, which imported new terms, would have been a rejection. Any suggestion of a different contract than was proposed by the offer, was a rejection of it. The offer put it on the city to say, not that it would have the valuation made, and then determine whether it would accept the proposition, but to say whether it would buy at such valuation as might be ascertained and determined in the prescribed manner. The offer implied that the seller took the chances of a fair valuation by appraisers. The acceptance, to be responsive, must assume the same uncertainty on the part of the purchaser. To accept upon the condition that the appraisers shall first determine upon a price the acceptor is willing to pay, is manifestly not only no acceptance at all, but is an affirmative rejection of the offer.—*Hutcheson v. Blakeman*, 3 Met. (Ky.) 80, and authorities therein cited; *Fox v. Turner*, 1 Ill. App. 153; 1 Benj. on Sales, pp. 53-54; *Falls v Gaither*, 9 Port. 605. The gas company having made the offer in accordance with its contract so to do,—for it is abundantly shown by the record that nothing was done by the company to hinder in any degree the city's exercise of its election,— thus discharged the only duty then resting upon it. Its further duty depended upon the city's acceptance of the offer in the terms in which it was made. The city not having accepted the offer, it was not incumbent on the company to appoint appraisers, and its failure in that regard was not a breach of its contract.

It is thus seen that, from whatever point of view section 8 of the ordinance is regarded, the same result as to its interpretation is reached. Every consideration of fact presented by the transaction, and every principle of law applicable to it, concur in the enforcement of the conclusion, that the right of the city was to make its election with reference to the purchase of the property at a price to be thereafter appointed; until the city exercised this option in such way as to bind it to purchase, there was no obligation on the company to proceed with the appraisement; that the city did not elect to purchase, and the company was not in default by reason of its failure to appoint appraisers.

The view thus taken of this case renders it unnecessary to consider the other objection on the part of the gas company to proceeding with the appraisement. The mere appointment of appraisers by the city, however unexceptionable the appointees may have been, did not, in the absence of an election to purchase, impose any duty on the company to proceed with the appraisement; and whether appraisers selected by the city were disinterested men, within the meaning of the contract, is an immaterial inquiry.

Considering the effect of section 8 to be, as we have said, to require an offer to be made by the gas company on November 1, 1877, to sell its property to the city, and the rights of the parties on that day to have been the same as if the offer had not been induced by the contract, it follows that the subsequent rights of the parties are to be determined by the principles of law applicable to ordinary offers to sell, in which there is no limitation or specification of the time in which the proposition is to be passed on and accepted or rejected by the other party. Under such circumstances, the rule is well settled, that the acceptance must be made within a reasonable time. What would have been a reasonable time in this case, we need not undertake to determine with any approach to precision—a week, it may be, or a month, or perhaps longer—as the question here is, whether the proposition was open to acceptance up to December 28, 1885, when the bill was filed; and we have no hesitancy in saying that was far in excess of our conception of what would have been a reasonable time during which the gas company should have held itself ready to consummate the sale to the city council. 1 Benj. on Sales, p. 61, n; *Judd v. Day*, 50 Iowa, 247; *Martin v. Black*, 21 Ala. 721.

This construction comports with the language employed by the parties, which gives the right of purchase "at," and not after a particular time, or for an indefinite period; and is the more reasonable in view of the fact that the property is of that character in which investments are usually made with regard to their permanency, and that an outstanding indefinite right of purchase would naturally depreciate its value. The company, at the time of instituting this suit, was, therefore, under no obligation to sell to the city, and was not required to embody an offer to do so in its bill.

It remains to be considered whether the case presented by the bill of complaint is such a one as calls for, or admits of the interposition of a court of equity by injunction. If an

[Montgomery Gas-Light Co. v. City Council of Montgomery.]

individual or private corporation had granted a franchise like that involved here, and was about to repudiate the grant, and make other contracts with respect to its subject-matter, which would cast a cloud on the title held under the first grant; or, if in this case, the city had already passed an ordinance granting the privilege to private parties, who were threatening to exercise it to the injury of the original grantee; in either of these cases, unquestionably a court of equity would enjoin the threatened action.—*B. & P. M. St. Railway Co. v. B. St. Railway Co.*, 79 Ala. 465; High on Inj., §§ 902 *et seq.* But the prayer of this bill is to enjoin—not the use of the streets, or any infringement, in point of fact, or any other actual encroachment upon the exercise of that privilege by the company—but the passage of an ordinance, granting this privilege to others, or providing for the execution of a contract with others under which they will be authorized, so far as the threatened action can have that effect, to lay pipes in the streets, the grant to the appellant to the contrary notwithstanding. In the well considered case of the *Des Moines Gas Co. v. City of Des Moines*, which was precisely identical with this case in the particular under consideration, it was held, in an able and exhaustive opinion, that the bill to enjoin the city authorities from the adoption of an ordinance repealing a former grant of the exclusive privilege to lay gas pipes in the streets of the city, and granting that privilege to others, would not lie. The decision was put on the ground, mainly, that the threatened action was legislative in its character, and as such, at least within charter limitations, was as fully exempted from judicial control as the action of the General Assembly of the State in the passage of laws. A further reason for denying the relief sought is thus stated by the learned judge: "If the ordinance sought to be enjoined is void by reason of its unconstitutionality, the plaintiff can be in nowise injured by its passage. A void law is no law, and this without doubt is true as to an ordinance. No injury, much less one of an irreparable character, can be inflicted by such an ordinance."—*Des Moines Gas Co. v. City of Des Moines*, 44 Iowa, 505.

The principle announced in this case has received the indorsement of such text-writers as Dillon and High, and is supported by the weight of adjudications.—High on Injunc. § 1246; 1 Dillon Mun. Corp. § 308; *Chicago v. Evans*, 24 Ill. 52; *Smith v. McCarthy*, 56 Penn. St. 359.

We consider this the better view of the question, though

17

there are one or two cases which seem to hold the contrary, with respect to an ordinance, the purpose of which was to make a contract—a distinction which is expressly repudiated in the leading case *supra*—but, at the same time concede the general doctrine, that legislative action of municipal corporations can not be enjoined; and upon this ground the decree of the City Court will be affirmed.

CLOPTON, J., not sitting.

Leinkauff & Strauss *v.* Forcheimer & Co.

Garnishment on Judgment; Contest with Claimant of Fund.

1. *Promise to one person, for benefit of another.*—On a sale of personal property, where the purchaser promises, as evidenced by the bill of sale, to pay the agreed price to several named creditors of the seller, ratably according to their respective debts, the assent of each creditor will be presumed, since the promise is apparently for his benefit; he may recover the money by action of debt, or *indebitatus assumpsit*, against the purchaser; and until he manifests his election, the money can not be reached by other creditors of the vendor. But, if he refuses to accept the money, the right to it revests in the vendor, and it is subject to garnishment at the suit of other creditors.

2. *Estoppel by election between inconsistent rights*—An embarrassed or insolvent debtor having sold certain bales of cotton, stating in the bill of sale that the purchaser promised and agreed to pay the purchase-money to several creditors, a specified sum to each; a creditor can not, while attacking the sale for fraud, claim his share of the money in the hands of the purchaser; and if he is unsuccessful in his suit attacking the sale, he can not afterwards assert a claim to the money, as against another creditor, who, having accepted his share of the money, recovered a judgment for the balance of his debt, and sued out a garnishment against the purchaser; nor is the latter creditor estopped, by his acceptance of the money in the first instance, from afterwards maintaining such garnishment.

APPEAL from the Circuit Court of Mobile.

Tried before the Hon. WM. E. CLARKE.

This was a statutory contest, between Forcheimer & Co., judgment creditors of A. J. Harris, who had sued out a garnishment against Lehman, Durr & Co., as the debtors of said Harris; and Leinkauff & Strauss and C. A. Stern & Co., each claiming a part of the fund which the garnishees admitted to be in their hands, and which they paid into court.

VOL. LXXXVII.

The case was submitted to the court on an agreed statement
of facts, with leave to either party to except and appeal. It
appears from the agreed statement of facts that the money
in controversy, $1150.14, was part of the agreed price of 64
bales of cotton, sold by said Harris to Lehman, Durr & Co.,
on the 30th October, 1886, when he executed to them a bill
of sale, as follows: "Know all men," &c., "that for and in
consideration of the sum of $2,300, which Lehman, Durr &
Co. agree and bind themselves to pay to the creditors of my
Geneva business, as follows: to Keith & Son, $334.71; to C.
A. Stern & Co., $422.05; to Leinkauff & Strauss, $728.09;
to M. Forcheimer & Co., $548.05; to J. Pollock & Co.,
$217.05; and to Cavanaugh, Barney & Co., $50.05; I hereby
sell, transfer and convey to the said Lehman, Durr & Co. 64
bales of cotton now in the warehouse, and around and about
the warehouse in the town of Geneva, Alabama, a list of the
marks and weights of which cotton is hereto attached. Witness my hand," &c. It was agreed, also, that $2,300 was
the fair market value of the cotton at that time, and the
cotton was delivered to the purchasers. At the time of
this sale, Harris, who had been carrying on business as a
merchant at Geneva, had become embarrassed, if not insolvent; and a few days before, on October 25th, he had transferred his stock of goods, notes and accounts, to Lehman,
Durr & Co., and other creditors in Montgomery. On the
28th October, Leinkauff & Strauss and C. A. Stern & Co.
each sued out attachments against said Harris, on the ground
that he had fraudulently disposed of his property; and garnishments were issued and served under these attachments,
which have no relevancy to the issues involved in this suit.
When informed by Lehman, Durr & Co. of the money in
their hands to be paid out to the creditors named in the bill
of sale, Forcheimer & Co. accepted the amount to be paid to
them, but Leinkauff & Strauss and C. A. Stern & Co. each
refused to accept; and on the 18th November, 1886, they
each sued out *alias* attachments, which were levied on the
cotton sold by Harris to Lehman, Durr & Co. The latter
interposed a claim to the cotton, made affidavit, and gave
bond for a trial of the right of property; and on the trial a
judgment was rendered in their favor, which judgment was
affirmed by this court, on appeal, July 1st, 1887. "Within
the first ten days of November," Forcheimer & Co. and several other creditors named in the bill of sale also sued out
attachments against Harris, on the ground that he had fraud-

ulently disposed of his property; "but, admitting the validity of said sale of cotton to Lehman, Durr & Co., they gave
credit on their respective debts for the amounts to be paid
them by Lehman, Durr & Co., and levied their attachments
only on the stock of goods; and these attachment suits were
pending when the attachments of Leinkauff & Strauss and
C. A. Stern & Co. were levied on said cotton." The Montgomery creditors, the transferrees of the stock of goods, interposed a claim to the property thus attached, and gave
bond to try the right of property; but the suits were settled
by compromise, the goods sold, and the proceeds of sale
divided among the several claimants, Forcheimer & Co. receiving $134.74 on their debt. The attachment suits were
prosecuted to judgment on the 25th March, 1887, the judgment in favor of Forcheimer & Co. being for $895; and on
this judgment they sued out a garnishment on March 31st,
which was served on Lehman, Durr & Co. as the debtors of
Harris. Forcheimer & Co. claimed the money in the hands
of Lehman, Durr & Co., or their proportionate part of it,
under this garnishment.

On the facts above stated, the court rendered judgment in
favor of Forcheimer & Co. for $431.58, as their share of the
money paid into court by the garnishees; to which judgment
Leinkauff & Strauss and C. A. Stern & Co. excepted, and
they here assign it as error.

GAYLORD B. CLARK & F. B. CLARK, for appellants.—These
claimants attacked the sale of the cotton for fraud, honestly
believing there was fraud, and having facts sufficient to
make out a *prima facie* case of fraud, though they were judicially explained in the course of the litigation. But they
gained nothing by their attack on the sale, and did not put
their opponents in any worse position; on the contrary, the
litigation resulted in a benefit to the appellees, whose title to
the money they received from Lehman, Durr & Co. was
thereby confirmed. On the admitted facts, there is no estoppel against the appellants.—Bigelow on Estoppel, 98–100,
503; *Hunley v. Hunley*, 15 Ala. 92; *Gwynn v. Hamilton*,
29 Ala. 233; 7 Amer. & Eng. Encyc. Law, 22–3, notes;
Bump's Fraud. Conv. 466–8; 9 Penn. St. 203; 104 Penn. St.
615; Bispham's Equity, § 294; *Williams, Deacon & Co. v.
Jones*, 77 Ala. 294. On the contrary, Forcheimer & Co.,
having accepted their part of the purchase-money of the cot-

ton, can not now heard to claim the part which was assigned to these appellants.—*Hatchett v. Blanton*, 72 Ala. 424.

J. L. SMITH, with PILLANS, TORREY & HANAW, *contra.* Appellants could not, while attacking the sale of the cotton for fraud, claim the money thereby appropriated for their benefit, for one can not claim both under and against an assignment. The money left in the hands of Lehman, Durr & Co., when appellants refused to accept it, belonged to Harris, and was subject, of course, to legal process at the suit of his creditors. Lehman, Durr & Co. assert no claim to the money, but have paid it into court; and their title to the cotton was admitted by Forcheimer & Co. before it was confirmed by judicial decision. Forcheimer & Co. have never attacked the sale of the cotton, and they do not now assail it, but only seek to reach the money left in the hands of the purchasers, which other creditors have refused to accept. They invoke the doctrine of estoppel, on the authority of *Henry v. Murphy*, 54 Ala. 252; *Price v. Masterson*, 35 Ala. 489; *Coleman v. Hatcher*, 77 Ala. 222; *Hatchett v. Blanton*, 72 Ala. 433; *Caldwell v. King*, 76 Ala. 155; Burr. Assignments, §§ 479, 491; *Espy v. Comer*, 80 Ala. 338; *Watts v. Eufaula Bank*, 76 Ala. 480; *Lehman v. Meyer*, 67 Ala. 403; 33 Penn. St. 40; Herm. Estoppel, 1176; *Iron Works v. Renfro*, 71 Ala. 577; *Abrams v. Carter*, 53 Ala. 8; *Treadway v. Treadway*, 56 Ala. 390; *Lehman v. Warren*, 53 Ala. 535; 65 Ala. 211.

STONE, C. J.—When Harris and Lehman, Durr & Co. concluded their contract of sale and purchase of the sixty-four bales of cotton, the result was that, *prima facie*, Lehman, Durr & Co. became debtors to Leinkauff & Strauss in the sum they had promised to pay them, $728. This was part of the purchase-price of the cotton; and the promise, made as part of the contract of purchase, being to pay to Leinkauff & Strauss, the law, in the absence of all other facts, presumes their acquiescence in, and acceptance of it, because it appears to be for their benefit. It clothed them with such right to the money, as that they could have maintained *indebitatus assumpsit* for its recovery. Any attempt, made at that time, to subject this indebtedness of Lehman, Durr & Co. to the payment of other debts of Harris, would have failed.—*Coleman v. Hatcher*, 77 Ala. 217.

The presumption, however, that Leinkauff & Strauss would

and did accept this provision for their benefit, and would agree to accept Lehman, Durr & Co. as their debtors, was not conclusive. It was made without their concurrence, and was open to their ratification or rejection. If, on being informed of it, they repudiated the arrangement, and sought other remedies inconsistent with it, this would be equivalent to a rejection of the benefit, and, at least so long as they prosecuted the inconsistent claim, would annul or suspend the promise to pay them, made by Lehman, Durr & Co. They could not, at one and the same time, attack the sale of cotton made to Lehman, Durr & Co. as fraudulent, and claim the provision that sale had procured for their benefit. 3 Brickell's Digest, 341, §§ 160, 161; *Butler v. O'Brien,* 5 Ala. 316.

We are within safe bounds when we hold, that when Leinkauff & Strauss rejected the offer made in the contract, for Lehman, Durr & Co. to pay them the specified sum of money, and attacked for fraud the trade of which that promise was a part, that money became due and payable to Harris, if to any one. If Lehman, Durr & Co. did not lose the cotton, which was the consideration of the promise, they owed the money; and Leinkauff & Strauss refusing to receive it, they owed it to Harris, from whom the consideration had moved. It then, like any other money debt due to Harris, became subject to garnishment at the suit of his judgment creditors.

Pending the suit of Lienkauff & Strauss, to subject to their claim the cotton which Harris had sold to Lehman, Durr & Co., for alleged fraud in the sale, Forcheimer & Co., having obtained a judgment against Harris, had a writ of garnishment served on Lehman, Durr & Co., as supposed debtors of Harris. Lehman, Durr & Co. answered the garnishment, setting forth the facts, and deposited the money in court. Leinkauff & Strauss, having failed to subject the cotton to their demand, then set up a claim to the money paid into the court by Lehman, Durr & Co. The conflicting claims of Forcheimer & Co., as attaching creditors, on the one side, and Leinkauff & Strauss on the other, constituted the issue in this cause. The Circuit Court adjudged the money to Forcheimer & Co.

Like Leinkauff & Strauss, Forcheimer & Co. had been provided for in the cotton sale to Lehman, Durr & Co. It was one of the provisions of that contract, that Lehman, Durr & Co. should pay them $548. In this respect, they stood precisely in line with Leinkauff & Strauss. They accepted the

provision made for them, and thereby estopped themselves
from assailing the cotton sale made to Lehman, Durr & Co.
And so long as the transaction remained as originally agreed
on, they would not be heard to gainsay the validity of the
provision therein made for Leinkauff & Strauss.—*Sloan v.
Frothingham*, 72 Ala. 589; *Hatchett v. Blanton, Ib.* 423.

When, however, Leinkauff & Strauss refused to accept the
provision made for them, and took steps to set the sale aside
as fraudulent, this released the promise as made by Lehman,
Durr & Co. to pay them, and left the fund subject to attachment at the suit of any of Harris' creditors, if the other facts
authorizing attachment existed. We are not able to perceive
any reason why Forcheimer & Co., because they were also
provided for in the sale, should be debarred this right. It
was not an attempt to claim against the deed, after accepting
a benefit conferred by it. It was, at most, an effort to condemn what had not been allowed to pass by the provisions of
the deed.

Affirmed.

Tompkins *v.* Levy & Brother.

*Bill in Equity by Creditors of Husband, to subject Proceeds
of Policy of Insurance in favor of Wife and her Heirs.*

1. *Insurance on life of husband, for benefit of wife and children, or
heirs; validity as against creditors.*—Under statutory provisions (Code,
1876, §§ 2733-4), since changed in phraseology (Code, 1886, §§ 2356),
the husband might insure his wife, paying an-
nual premiums not more than $500, and might make the policy payable
to her children, in the event of her death before his; and these statutory provisions operating in the nature of an exemption law, the proceeds of the policy could not be subjected by creditors to the payment
of the husband's debts. But the interest of the wife terminated, on her
death before her husband; and the policy being made payable to
"her heirs, executors or assigns," her children acquired no interest
which could prevail against the husband's creditors, on his subsequent
death.

2. *Same.*—Where the husband takes out a policy of insurance on his
own life, in favor of his wife, "her heirs, executors, or assigns," paying
the premiums with his own funds, a provision to the effect that, after
the expiration of fifteen years, on surrender of the policy, none of its
provisions having been violated, the company would pay to him, his
heirs, executors or assigns, the equitable value of the policy, "as an endowment in cash," is the reservation of a benefit to himself, and renders the policy fraudulent as against his creditors.

3. *Parties to bill.*—The personal representative of the deceased husband, though he might be a proper party, is not a necessary party to
a bill filed by creditors, seeking to subject the proceeds of a policy of
insurance on his life, as against the claims of his children, to the payment of their debts.

4. *Action by partnership.*—A suit may be maintained in the name of
a late partnership, stating the names of the late partners, notwithstanding its dissolution.

APPEAL from the Chancery Court of Mobile.

Heard before the Hon. THOS. W. COLEMAN.

The bill in this case was filed on the 22d September, 1888,
by M. Levy & Brother, "a late mercantile partnership, which
was composed of Maurice Levy and Samuel Levy," as creditors of Milton J. Brasfield, deceased, against Margaret J.
Tompkins, as the administratrix of his deceased wife, Mrs.
Sallie A. Brasfield, and their two infant children, Kate and
Sallie Brasfield; and sought to reach and subject, in the
hands of said administratrix, the proceeds of a policy of insurance which said Milton J. Brasfield had effected on his
own life, to the payment of complainants' debts against him
or his estate. The policy, which was for $5,000, was issued
in July, 1878, by the Mobile Life Insurance Company, and
was made payable to Mrs. Sallie A. Brasfield, "her heirs,
executors, or assigns," the annual premium being $113.50;
and it contained the following (with other) provisions:
"The said company do further promise and agree within
ninety days after the expiration of fifteen years from the
date of this policy, or within ninety days after the expiration of any subsequent period of five years, and on surrender
of same properly receipted, provided all the stipulations,
conditions and agreements herein contained shall have been
duly observed, to pay to said Milton J. Brasfield, his heirs,
executors or assigns, at their office in the city of Mobile,
the full equity, or interest of said policy in the assets of the
company, as an endowment in cash. . . The surplus
arising from the payments of all members of the life endowment class of 1878, in which this policy is included, shall
be kept intact and accumulated by the said company for fifteen years; at the expiration of which time, or in 1893, said
accumulated surplus shall be wholly and exclusively divided,
in equitable proportions, among the surviving members of
said class; that is to say, among those members who have
survived the said period of fifteen years, in each case from
date of the issue of the policy, and who have complied with

all the conditions and agreements herein contained, and who have paid each year the stipulated premiums."

Milton J. Brasfield died about February 10th, 1887, and the bill alleged that his wife had died about eight years before. At the time of his death, said Brasfield was indebted to complainants in the sum of $978.48, balance due on account. He had commenced dealing with them in 1877, and the balance due at the end of each year was carried forward into the account of the next year. In addition to this balance, the complainants had bought from Arrington & Steinhart an account against him for $61.24. After the death of said Milton J. Brasfield, letters of administration on the estate of his deceased wife were granted to said Margaret J. Tompkins, and the proceeds of the policy of insurance were paid to her. It was alleged that the estate of said Brasfield was insolvent, and that he was insolvent for several years before his death. It was alleged, also, that said Brasfield kept up said policy after the death of his wife, "paying the annual premiums out of his own funds, or with funds advanced to him by your orators for that purpose, as hereinafter stated, up to the time of his death;" and in a subsequent paragraph it was alleged, with particularity, that the balance of the account due to complainants at the end of each year included the annual premium advanced to or for him by them; but the averments of this latter paragraph were struck out by amendment, after demurrer was filed. It was alleged, also, that letters of administration on the estate of said M. J. Brasfield had been granted to one of the complainants, and the bill asked the appointment of an administrator *ad litem* to represent his estate.

A demurrer to the bill was filed by the administratrix of Mrs. Brasfield, assigning these specific grounds: 1st; "because the bill is filed in the name of a mercantile partnership which did not then exist;" 2d, "because the premiums paid by said Brasfield to keep up said policy, were paid with the knowledge, consent and assistance of complainants, and, therefore, was no fraud upon them;" 3d, "because the administrator of said M. J. Brasfield has not been made a party;" 4th, "because said policy was taken out by said Brasfield for the benefit of his wife, and the annual premiums paid by him were less than $500, and hence the proceeds of said policy are not liable to the claims set up in the bill."

The chancellor overruled the demurrers, and his decree is now assigned as error.

[Tompkins v. Levy & Brother.]

AUSTILL & ERVIN, for appellant.—(1.) The policy was
clearly intended for the benefit of the wife, or of the wife
and children, and it must be construed liberally, to advance
the known policy of the statute.—*Felrath v. Schonfield*,
76 Ala 202. The word *heirs* is without meaning, unless it
is construed to mean *children*, as it is frequently construed
in wills.—*Braden v. Cannon*, 1 Grant's Cases, 60; *King v.
Beck*, 15 Ohio, 559; 5 Ind. 283; *Collier v. Collier*, 3 Ohio,
N. S. 369; 1 Sneed, 1; 2 Redf. Wills, 390, note; *Gould v.
Emerson*, 99 Mass. 154; Stewart on H. & W., § 133.
(2.) The policy could not operate a fraud on the complainants, when, as they allege, they furnished the money to pay
the annual premiums.

GREG. L. & H. T. SMITH, *contra.*—(1.) The bill was
properly filed in the name of the late partnership.—1 Lindley
on Partnership, 266, ed. 1888; *Sims v. Jacobson*, 51 Ala.
186; *Davidson v. Weems*, 58 Ala. 189. (2.) In the absence
of any statute on the subject, the policy would be subject to
the debts of the husband, as a voluntary conveyance; and if
it does not conform substantially to the provisions of the
statute, it is equally subject to his debts.—*Insurance Co. v.
Webb*, 54 Ala. 702; *Fearn v. Ward*, 80 Ala. 558. But the
policy is not protected by the statute. It is not made payable to the wife, "in case she survives him," nor is it made
"payable after death to her children;" but it is payable to
her, "her heirs, executors or assigns." The word *heirs*,
when applied to personalty, means *distributees;* and the policy must be read as if payable to the wife, "her executors
or assigns."—*Scudder v. Van Arsdale*, 13 N. J. Eq. 110;
88 Ill. 251; 13 Bush, Ky. 489; 13 Daly, N. Y. 522; 1 Hun,
N. Y. 601. If the children take any interest in the policy,
it is not under this special exemption statute, but as distributees of their mother's personal estate.

SOMERVILLE, J.—The purpose of the bill is to subject
the proceeds of a policy of insurance on the life of Milton
J. Brasfield, deceased, to the payment of certain debts of the
decedent. The policy was made payable to his wife, "Sallie
A. Brasfield, her *heirs*, executors, or assigns." The premiums were paid by the assured out of his own funds. He died
in the year 1887, having survived his wife about eight years,
she having deceased in the year 1879, leaving two minor
children. It is claimed that these children are entitled to

the fund, under the provisions of sections 2733 and 2734 of the Code of 1876, authorizing married women to insure the lives of their husbands free from the claims of creditors, or the claims of the husband's personal representatives. The word "heirs," it is contended, must be construed to mean "children;" and such a construction is asserted, to entitle the two children to the fund under the statute.

It is manifest that the fund is liable to the claims of the husband's creditors, unless it is rescued from such liability by the terms of the statute, which we have held to be in the nature of an exemption law, and, for this reason, to be liberally construed to effect the purpose of its enactment —*Fearn v. Ward*, 65 Ala. 33: s. c., 80 Ala. 555; *Felrath v. Schonfield*, 76 Ala. 199; s. c., 52 Amer. Rep. 319; *Continental Life Ins. Co. v. Webb*, 54 Ala. 688; *Appeal of Elliott's Ex'rs*, 88 Amer. Dec. 525, 531, *note*.

The statute provides, that a policy of insurance taken out under its provisions, on the husband's life, for the benefit of the wife, shall be payable to her, "in case of her *surviving her husband*."—Code, 1876, § 2733. It is further declared, in the following section, that "in case of the death of the wife, before the decease of the husband, the amount of the insurance *may* be made payable after death to her children, for their use, and to their guardian, if under age."—Code, 1876, § 2734.

The wife here has not survived her husband, and there is no clause in the policy making the amount of the insurance payable to the children in case of her death before his decease. It is too plain to admit of argument, that the statute does not, *proprio vigore*, make such policies payable to the children, on the death of the wife before the husband, irrespective of the contract, but it only authorizes such a provision to be incorporated in the contract of insurance, so as to rescue such contract from the taint of fraud, and exempt the proceeds of the policy from liability to creditors or administration.

It is equally obvious, that by the terms of the statute the wife's interest is contingent on her surviving her husband, and in event of her death before his it is gone. The New York statute of 1840, from which our own is substantially copied, has been construed by the Court of Appeals of that State to be enabling, and not declaratory of the common law. In *Eadie v. Slimmon*, 26 N. Y. 9; s. c., 82 Amer. Rep. 395, after holding that a policy upon the life of the husband, for the benefit of the wife, could not be assigned so as to destroy the right of the wife—a point as to which we intimate no opinion—the following language was used by Denio, C. J.: "By the general rules of law, a policy on the life of one sustaining only a domestic relationship to the insured would become inoperative by the death of such insured in the life-time of the *cestui que vie;* or, if it could be considered as existing for any purpose after that event, it would be for the benefit of the personal representatives of the insured; but, by this act, the contract may be continued in favor of the children of the insured wife, after her death."

The Connecticut statute is substantially like that of New York and Alabama. In *Connecticut Mut. Life Ins. Co. v. Burroughs,* 34 Conn. 305; s. c., 91 Amer. Dec. 725, it was said, that while the doctrine of *Eadie v. Slimmon,* 26 N. Y. 9, *supra,* as to the non-assignability of such policies, seemed reasonable and just, where the husband paid the premiums; yet, where the wife paid them from her own separate estate, it was difficult to suggest a reason why she should not have the same power to assign her interest in the policy that she has to assign any other *chose* in action belonging to her. Nevertheless, it was decided, where she attempted to make such assignment, her interest being contingent on her surviving her husband, and she having died before he did, her interest terminated, and her assignee acquired nothing under the assignment. To the same purport is the reasoning upon which the decision of this court rests in *Continental Life Ins. Co. v. Webb,* 54 Ala., *supra.* See, also, May on Insurance (2d Ed.), § 391; and *Appeal of Elliott's Ex'rs,* 88 Amer. Dec. 532, *note.*

We hold that, upon the death of Mrs. Brasfield, her interest in the policy of insurance on her husband's life ceased.

Was it continued by the terms of the statute, for the benefit of her children? Under the most liberal construction of the statute which we feel authorized to give it, we can not hold that it was. It could lawfully have been made payable to the children upon the death of the wife, but it is sufficient to say that it was not so made. The word "heirs," as used in the policy, must, under all the authorities, be construed with reference to the species of property which is the subject of disposition, whether real or personal; and when used with reference to personal property, it must be held to mean distributees, or next of kin. This is especially so, when associated with the words "executors," and "assigns."

Scudder v. Van Arsdale, 13 N. J. Eq. 109; *Hodges' Appeal*,
Pa. 9 Ins. L. J. 709; *Kaiser v. Kaiser*, 13 Daly, 522;
Cushman v. Horton, 1 Hun, N. Y. 601; *Gauch v. St. Louis
Mut. Life Ins. Co.*, 88 Ill. 251. And while it is true that
the children might be distributees of their mother's estate,
they could only be so in the event that her interest in the
fund did not terminate on her death. But, having terminated,
it could not pass to her estate, or distributees, in the order of
usual succession. The interest of the distributees, being
derived through her, was also contingent on the wife's surviving the husband, which, as we have seen, never happened.
Fuller v. Linzee, 135 Mass. 468.

We might or might not construe the statute in like manner, if the premiums on the policy had been paid with funds
belonging to the wife's separate estate. But, in this case,
they were paid with the husband's funds, and we confine the
construction to the case before us. The phraseology of the
new Code, it will be noticed, has been materially changed in
several particulars touching this matter.—Code, 1886,
§ 2356.

There is another feature about this policy, which stamps
it as fraudulent against creditors, and takes it out of the
protection of the statute. It is the interest which Milton
Brasfield reserved to himself, in the event of his surviving
for fifteen years after its issue. It is expressly provided,
that after the expiration of this number of years, on surrender of the policy, none of its conditions having been violated, the company would pay to Brasfield himself, "his
heirs, executors, or assigns," the equitable value of the policy, "as an endowment in cash." It is obvious that the interest of Mrs. Brasfield in this policy was contingent upon
her husband's dying before the expiration of fifteen years
from date, and, had he survived for this length of time, the
cash value of the policy could have been claimed by him,
free from any trust in favor of the wife.—*Levy v. Van Hagen*,
69 Ala. 17. That a reservation of this kind would be such
a locking up of the debtor's property from creditors, for his
own beneficial use, as to evince an intent to hinder, delay, or
defraud creditors, has never been doubted since the doctrine settled in *Twyne's Case*, decided near three centuries
ago.—*Benedict v. Renfro*, 75 Ala. 121; s c , 51 Amer. Rep.
429; *Murray v. McNealy*, 86 Ala. 234; s. c., 5 So. Rep.
565; *Woodall v. Kelly*, 85 Ala. 368.

The personal representative was not a necessary, although

he may have been a proper party defendant to the bill. *Coffey v. Norwood*, 81 Ala. 512.

There is nothing in the suggestion, that the bill was improperly filed in the name of the partnership which had been dissolved. It is described as a late partnership, and the names of the individual members of the firm are set out. This was clearly sufficient.

The second ground of demurrer suggests the point, that the premiums paid by Milton Brasfield to keep the policy in force were paid with the knowledge and assent of complainants, and such payment was not, therefore, a fraud on them. The allegations of the seventh paragraph of the bill, bearing on this point, refer for explanation to those set out in the tenth paragraph; and the latter having been stricken out by amendment, the remaining averments are not sufficiently clear and specific to raise the question. We do not, therefore, consider it. It can be raised by plea or answer to the bill.

The extent to which the proceeds of the policy in question are liable to the demand of the complainants, is not raised by the demurrer. If any portion of the fund is liable, as we have held it is, the demurrer raising this question was properly overruled.

The decree of the chancellor so ruling is affirmed.

Jackson *v.* Stanley.

Bill in Equity to enforce Vendor's Lien on Land.

1. *Waiver of vendor's lien* —A vendor's lien on land for the unpaid purchase-money is presumptively waived by the acceptance of any distinct and independent security, such as the note or bond of a third person, or of the purchaser himself with personal security, or a mortgage on other lands, or a pledge of stock as collateral security; but it is in each case a question of intention, in determining which all the facts and attendant circumstances should be considered.

2. *Same; acceptance of husband's notes for purchase-money. on sale to wife.*—When the contract is negotiated by the husband as the agent of the wife, and the conveyance is executed to her, the acceptance of his notes for the purchase-money is not, under our decisions, a presumptive waiver of the vendor's lien; but it is a circumstance, of more or less weight, to be considered in connection with the other facts and circumstances of the particular case.

3. *Same; pledge of stock as collateral security.*—A pledge of stock in a private corporation, as collateral security for the purchase-money, is

presumptively a waiver of the vendor's lien; and though the transfer afterwards proves to be invalid, no fraud being practiced, this does not affect the question of intended waiver; as where the stock belongs to the wife, who is the purchaser, and the transfer is not effectual to convey her interest.

4. *Retention of lien by agreement; case at bar.*—Though a vendor's lien is presumptively waived by the acceptance of independent or collateral security, this presumption may be rebutted and overcome by proof of an oral agreement or understanding that it was retained; but the *onus* of establishing such agreement is on the vendor, who asserts it; and it is not established by the evidence in this case, against the uncontroverted facts and the face of the writings.

5. *Husband's admissions, as evidence against wife.*—When the contract of sale is negotiated by the husband for the benefit of the wife, and the conveyance is executed to her, though his notes are given for the purchase-money, his subsequent admissions or declarations, when pressed for payment, that the vendor had retained a lien on the land, are not competent or admissible as against the wife.

APPEAL from the Chancery Court of Chilton.

Heard before the Hon. S. K. MCSPADDEN.

The bill in this case was filed on the 11th February, 1887, by J. F. B. Jackson, against C. W. Stanley and his wife, Mrs. Mary E. Stanley; and sought to establish and enforce a vendor's lien on land for the unpaid purchase-money. The contract for the sale of the land was made between complainant and said C. W. Stanley, who executed his several notes for the purchase-money, which were past due and unpaid when the bill was filed. A conveyance for the land was at the same time executed to Mrs. Stanley, but the bill alleged that this was done at the instance and request of her husband; while the answer of the defendants alleged that she was the real purchaser, and that the contract was made by her husband, as her agent, in her name, and for her benefit. At the time the contract was made, and as part of it, Stanley and wife deposited with the complainant a certificate of several shares of stock in the "Prattville Manufacturing Company No. 1," which belonged to Mrs. Stanley; and the complainant gave a receipt for it, which stated that he had received the certificate from Mrs. Stanley "as collateral security for the notes of her husband," and that it was to be surrendered on prompt payment of the notes; and further, "should said notes not be paid, this stock to be lawfully sold by me [him], and any balance after payment of said notes to be paid to her." This receipt, as copied in the transcript, appears to be signed by the complainant and Mrs. Stanley, after which the words are added, "This is agreed to by us;" to which is signed the name of "C. W. Stanley, husband of Mary E. Stanley" The receipt appears, also, to be attested by John N. Webb and S. J. Brock as subscribing witnesses; but Stanley testified, on the part of the defendants, that Webb signed as attesting witness to complainant's signature, and Brock afterwards as witness to the signatures of himself and his wife. The certificate was retained by the complainant, and was in his possession when the bill was filed; but he offered to return it, alleging that the pledge of it was illegal and void, because the stock belonged to Mrs. Stanley, and could not be pledged or transferred as security for her husband's debt.

The conveyance to Mrs. Stanley, the complainant's receipt for the certificate of stock, and Stanley's notes for the purchase-money, were all dated April 7th, 1884, the day on which the contract was consummated. In November, 1882, the complainant had sold and conveyed the same lands to David H. Mullens, taking his notes for the purchase-money, and a mortgage on the lands to secure their payment; and these notes being past due and unpaid at the time of the sale to Stanley and wife, complainant transferred them to Mrs. Stanley, by writing dated April 7th, 1884; and two days afterwards, April 9th, he executed a formal quit-claim to Mrs. Stanley, of all his interest in the mortgaged lands, on the recited consideration of $750 in hand paid. On the 22d April, 1884, Mullens and wife executed to Mrs. Stanley a quit-claim deed to the land, the consideration being the surrender of his unpaid notes for the purchase-money. The complainant alleged in his bill, and testified as a witness for himself, that a vendor's lien on the land was retained, by express agreement between him and said Stanley; and he took the deposition of Geo. L. Morris, who was jointly interested in the land with him, and who testified to the same effect. Complainant also took the deposition of J. M. Bivings, to whom he had sent two of Stanley's notes for collection; and said Bivings testified, that when he pressed Stanley for payment of the notes, or for permission to sell the stock, Stanley said that he ought to be willing to wait, as he had a lien on the land. To this testimony objection was made by Mrs. Stanley. The defendants, in their answer, denied that any lien on the land was retained by the complainant, and alleged that Mrs. Stanley refused to buy unless she could get an absolute title unincumbered by any lien. In proof of their contention, they adduced as exhibits the several transfers and other writings above mentioned, and also a letter written by complainant to Stanley, which is without date, but said to

have been written two or three days before the consummation of the contract, after a personal interview between Stanley and Morris. The letter is in these words: "I wrote you
several days since, accepting your proposition, taking your
notes in place of Mullens, by you putting up one thousand
dollars of Pratt stock, as you proposed, to secure payment.
Answer, and oblige," &c. On receipt of this letter, Stanley
alleged and testified, he at once went to Blount Springs,
where complainant was, and there consummated the contract
with him. The defendants also took the deposition of
Charles Maxwell, who testified to a conversation between
complainant and C. W. Stanley, "in Birmingham, in April,
1884," in which Jackson "told Stanley he would waive a lien
on the land, if Stanley would give him power of attorney to
sell certain factory stock, if the notes for the land were not
paid; to which Stanley assented." The complainant objected to this testimony.

On final hearing, on pleadings and proof, the chancellor
dismissed the bill; and his decree is here assigned as error.

W. A. COLLIER, for appellant.

WATTS & SON, *contra.*

CLOPTON, J.—The lien which equity, on principles of
natural justice, creates as security for the purchase price of
land sold and conveyed. is the subject of waiver, express, or
implied from the acts of the parties. Generally, the lien
will be regarded as waived, if the grantor accepts any distinct and independent security. The authorities vary in the
application of the rule to particular facts; and it would be
difficult to formulate a general definition, specific, and yet
comprehensive enough to include all acts which will operate
to displace the lien. Ordinarily, this result is produced by
the acceptance of the note or bond of a stranger, or of the
grantee with personal security, or with a mortgage on other
land, or a pledge of stock, or other personal property. There
are cases, in which no one of several acts is, of itself, sufficient. In such cases, all the facts and circumstances should
be considered, and if it appears that the vendor did not intend to look to the land, but to rely on a substituted, independent security, or on the personal responsibility of the
vendee, the presumption is rebutted, and the retention of the
lien repelled.—*Walker v. Struve,* 70 Ala. 167; *Carroll v.*

18

Shapard, 78 Ala. 358; *Stringfellow v. Ivie*, 73 Ala. 214; *Tedder v. Steele*, 70 Ala. 349.

The undisputed facts are: Appellant, who seeks by the bill to assert and enforce the equitable lien, sold and conveyed the lands in controversy, in 1882, to D. H. Mullens, for the sum of nine hundred dollars. Mullens gave his five notes for the purchase-money, the last maturing November 15, 1886, and executed a mortgage on the lands to secure the same. On April 7, 1884, complainant conveyed the lands to Mrs. Stanley, a married woman, on the expressed consideration of seven hundred and fifty dollars. For this sum, her husband gave his four notes, payable at long intervals of time, and Mrs. Stanley and her husband deposited with complainant two shares of the capital stock of the Prattville Manufacturing Company No. 1, of the par value of one thousand dollars each, as collateral security for the notes given by her husband, with power to sell the same on default in payment of the notes. Contemporaneously, and as part of the same transaction, complainant transferred to Mrs. Stanley, by instrument in writing, the notes and mortgage of Mullens.

The first inquiry is the sufficiency of the uncontroverted facts to show, *prima facie*, an intention to look to other independent security, instead of to the land, for the purchase-money. It satisfactorily appears, that the negotiations were conducted by Mrs. Stanley through her husband as agent, who bought the lands in her name, and for her benefit. It is unnecessary, for the purpose of this case, that we should go so far as to decide, as some respectable authorities hold, that where a married woman purchases land, taking a conveyance in her own name, and the husband gives his notes for the purchase-money, in whole or in part, he is regarded, in legal contemplation, a third person, and that the acceptance of his notes is, presumptively, a waiver of the equitable lien. The contrary is the logical tendency of our own decisions; which rather regard taking the husband's notes, in such case, as a mode of effecting a sale not voidable by the husband during coverture, and not as authorizing the wife to hold the lands without paying the purchase-money. *Carter v. Eads*, 65 Ala. 190; *Marks v. Cowles*, 53 Ala. 499. Though the acceptance of the husband's notes does not, of itself, rebut the presumption of a reservation of the vendor's lien, it is a fact or circumstance of more or less import and significance, dependent on its connection with, and the nature of the other facts and circumstances of the transaction.

Accepting the husband's notes, secured by a mortgage or pledge of other property, has the same operation and effect as if the notes of the grantee were taken, secured in like manner. The shares of the capital stock of the manufacturing company, which were deposited as collateral security for the notes of the husband, were the statutory separate estate of Mrs. Stanley. The evidence shows that there was in fact only one subscribing witness to the signatures of herself and her husband to the instrument in writing by which the stock was pledged, though, on its face, there purports to be two. On this ground, and because of her incapacity to pledge the stock for her husband's debts, it is contended that it should not be allowed the effect of a waiver of the lien. Whether or not the lien has been waived, is wholly a question of intention, and does not involve, in the absence of fraud, the sufficiency or invalidity of the independent security taken and accepted. At the time of its acceptance, the complainant considered the stock as ample security.; it was the security for which he stipulated, and both parties believed the pledge to be valid and binding. The case does not come within that class of cases, in which an invalid mortgage on the land sold and conveyed is taken. Such mortgage evinces an intention to look to the land as security. There is no pretense that any fraud was practiced. It is simply a case of taking an invalid security, supposed to be good, under a mistake of law. Under such circumstances, taking the stock as collateral security for the notes of the husband has the same effect as evidence of intention, as if the pledge were unexceptionable. Its invalidity does not necessarily operate to prevent a waiver. To whatever other rights and remedies complainant, under the circumstances, may have been entitled, equity can not relieve from the consequences of an election and waiver once made, by restoring and re-establishing the vendor's lien, the transaction being free from fraud.—*Partridge v. Logan*, 3 Mo. App. 509; 2 Wash. Real Prop. 96.

The lands had been previously sold and conveyed by complainant to Mullens, and a mortgage taken back to secure the purchase-money notes. At the time of the sale and conveyance to Mrs. Stanley, these notes were outstanding and unpaid, and the mortgage in full force. Complainant, by virtue of the mortgage, had, at law, only a defeasible legal title, and in equity a security for the mortgage debt. The notes and mortgage were transferred to Mrs. Stanley, which armed her with powers, by foreclosure of the mortgage, to destroy the vendor's lien, if any had been retained. The equitable lien would have been insecure. In this condition of facts, it was natural and reasonable that the vendor should require other independent security. Considering the whole transaction, all the undisputed facts, which consist of the writings, conspire to show an intention not to look to the lands as security for the purchase-money.

It is, however, further insisted, that a vendor's lien was retained by express agreement, which presents the next inquiry. It is well settled in this State, that the presumption of a waiver of the lien, arising from the acts of the parties, may be rebutted and overcome by proof of an oral understanding or agreement that it should be retained.—*Woodall v. Kelly*, 85 Ala. 368. The burden of proof is, in the first instance, on the party asserting a waiver of the lien; but, when it is shown that a distinct or independent security, sufficient to operate as a waiver, has been taken and accepted, the *onus* is shifted on the vendor, to prove an understanding or agreement for its reservation. On this question of fact, we can not consider the evidence of Bivings. Had the proper predicate been laid, the admissions or declarations of Stanley, as proved by him, would have been receivable for the purpose of impeachment; but, having been made long after the consummation of the purchase, are not receivable to affect otherwise the rights of Mrs. Stanley.—*Carver v. Eads, supra*. The other parol evidence consists of the testimony of the complainant and Morris, who was interested in the land, on the one side, and of Stanley and Maxwell on the other. True, Stanley's character for veracity was impeached by several witnesses; sustained, however, by a much larger number. A partial impeachment may possibly impair his credibility more or less; but he is corroborated by Maxwell, who is a disinterested and unimpeached witness, and also by all the written instruments, and by the letter of Stanley, written by complainant pending the negotiations, in which he accepted the former's proposition to give his notes, their payment secured by a deposit of factory stock, without any allusion to the retention of the equitable lien. The complainant retained the shares of stock without an offer to return them, until the filing of the bill, which were regarded as ample security until the destruction of the factory by flood. On this state of the proof, the burden being on complainant,

[Calhoun v Hannan & Michael.]

we can not say that the evidence is sufficient to overcome a presumption of the waiver of the lien.

Affirmed.

Calhoun *v.* Hannan & Michael.

Action on Attachment Bond.

1. *When action lies* —Although an attachment may have been sued out vexatiously and maliciously, an action can not be maintained on the bond, unless it was also wrongfully sued out—that is, unless it was sued out without the existence of any one of the facts which authorize a resort to the process.

2. *Damages; error without injury.*—In an action on an attachment bond, a judgment on verdict for the defendants conclusively determines that the writ was not wrongfully sued out; and the rulings of the court on the pleadings and evidence, or in the matter of charges given or refused, relating only to the question of exemplary damages, if erroneous, could not have injured the plaintiff.

3. *Pleading over, after demurrer sustained; error without injury.* Where the record shows that, after demurrer sustained to a plea or replication, the party had the full benefit of the same matter under an amended pleading, the ruling on demurrer, if erroneous, could have worked no injury, and is not a reversible error.

4. *Abstract charge.*—A charge requested, which is not supported in all of its hypotheses by the evidence, is abstract, and is properly refused on that account.

5. *Struck jury; competency of juror.*—In an action on an attachment bond, a struck jury being demanded (Code, § 2752), a clerk in the employment of another attaching creditor of the plaintiff, on whose bond another suit is pending in the same court, and set for trial on the same day, is not subject to challenge for cause on the ground of bias or prejudice, although it is shown that the two attachments were sued out at the same time, and under the same circumstances; these facts not being sufficient to raise a presumption of disqualifying bias, though sufficient to support a challenge for favor, which would require an investigation by the court into the question of bias as matter of fact.

6. *General objection to evidence.*—A general objection to the admission of a promissory note as evidence, not specifying any particular ground of objection, does not raise the objection that its execution has not been proved.

7. *Burden of proof as to consideration and good faith of conveyance.* The fact that property has been conveyed by a debtor, on the recited consideration of an antecedent debt, raises a presumption of unfairness and bad faith, as between the debtor and his other creditors, and casts on him the *onus* of showing that the sale was fair, and made in good faith; and the proof must be fuller and clearer when the conveyance is made to a relative.

8. *Burden of proof, as to ground for attachment.*—In an action on an attachment bond, the *onus* is on the plaintiff to prove the falsity of the affidavit on which the attachment was sued out.

9. *Charge as to sufficiency of proof.*—When the burden of proof as to the truth or falsehood of an alleged fact is on the plaintiff, he must

reasonably satisfy the jury in that regard; and the court may instruct the jury, on request, "that if the evidence leaves them confused and uncertain as to its truth or falsity, they must find for the defendant."

APPEAL from the City Court of Mobile.

Tried before the Hon. O. J. SEMMES.

This action was brought by Joseph C. Calhoun, against Hannan & Michael as partners, with others their sureties; was founded on an attachment bond, and was commenced on the 19th September, 1887. The bond was dated December 20th, 1886, and was conditioned, in the words of the statute, for the payment to the defendant of "all such damages as he may sustain by the wrongful or vexatious suing out of said attachment." The attachment was sued out, on said 20th December, by John E. Michael, a partner of said firm, on the ground that said Calhoun "has fraudulently disposed of his property;" and it was levied on certain real estate in Mobile, including property which said Calhoun had conveyed by deed to his wife some time before, though the deed was not put on record until the day on which the attachment was sued out. The debt claimed by the attaching creditors was $1,671.58, and they obtained judgment in the attachment suit, May 25th, 1887, for $1,731.90. Other attachments were sued out against plaintiff on the same day, by Leinkauf & Son, Cavanagh, Barney & Co., and others, and were levied on the same lands; and the lands were sold, on September 5th, 1887, under writs of *vend. exponas* on these several judgments. John E. Michael became the purchaser at the sheriff's sale, at the aggregate price of $5,345, which paid the several judgments in full, with costs.

The complaint alleged, that the plaintiff had not fraudulently conveyed or disposed of his property, nor committed nor contemplated any fraudulent act whatever, nor done any other act which subjected him or his property to the process of attachment; that the attachment was sued out wrongfully, vexatiously, and maliciously; and he claimed damages on account of the injury to his credit and reputation in business as a commission-merchant, and on account of the sacrifice of his property under the sheriff's sale, and for his attorney's fees and costs in defense of the attachment suit. The defendant pleaded, (1) not guilty, on which plea issue was joined; (2) that sufficient cause existed for suing out the attachment, to which plea a demurrer was sustained; and (3) that John E. Michael, at the time he sued out the attachment, "had probable cause to believe, and in good faith

did believe, that said plaintiff had then fraudulently disposed
of his property, and acted without malice in suing out said
attachment." To this 3d plea the plaintiff replied specially,
(1) "that before said attachment was sued out, one of the
members of the firm of Hannan & Michael, for whose benefit
said attachment was sued out, knew that plaintiff had made
but one recent conveyance of any part of his property, and
had been informed that said conveyance was not fraudulent,
and had an opportunity of ascertaining whether the same
was fraudulent or not, and knew that John E. Michael was
going to sue out said attachment;" (3) "that at the time said
attachment was sued out, one of the members of said firm,
for whose benefit said attachment was sued out, knew that
plaintiff had not then made any fraudulent disposition of his
property." To each of these replications the court sustained
a demurrer, because the name of the partner who had the
alleged knowledge was not stated; and an additional replication was then filed, alleging that Patrick C. Hannan, a member of said partnership, had knowledge of said alleged facts.

On the trial, the defendants having demanded a struck
jury, a list of twenty-four persons was furnished to the parties, from which to select the jury. "Before the striking of
the jury commenced, the plaintiff challenged one of the
twenty-four for cause, and proved to the court, in support of
said challenge, that he was a clerk in the employment of
Cavanagh, Barney & Co., who had sued out an attachment
against plaintiff on the same day, on the same ground,
through the same attorney, and under the same circumstances as the attachment sued out by said Hannan &
Michael; that said attachments were both levied on the same
property; and that he had brought suit on the attachment
bond of said Cavanagh, Barney & Co., in said City Court,
which suit was now pending, and was set for trial on the
same day with the present suit. The court refused to allow
the challenge, and put said juror on the *venire;* to which
the plaintiff excepted."

The chief point of contention on the trial was as to the
bona fides and consideration of the conveyance executed by
the plaintiff to his wife, under which the defendants justified
the suing out of the attachment. This conveyance is not set
out in the bill of exceptions, nor is it said to have been produced on the trial; but it is said that it was "written in the
summer of 1886, acknowledged several months afterwards,
and not put upon the record until the day the attachments

were sued out." The plaintiff, testifying in reference to it, stated, that the consideration was a debt which he owed his son in 1880, and which the son gave to his mother; that on a settlement between him and his son in 1883, the amount of this indebtedness being ascertained, he executed his note to his wife for the amount, and afterwards, on her request, executed said conveyance in full discharge of the note; that the property conveyed was worth about $10,000; that the conveyance was executed in good faith, without the reservation of any benefit to himself; that he had other property more than sufficient to pay all his debts; that when the debts of Hannan & Michael and Leinkauf & Son were about to fall due, finding that he could not meet them, he submitted to his creditors a proposition for a settlement, giving them a list of his debts and a schedule of his property, which he proposed to convey in discharge of his debts; and that the attachments were sued out before he had received a definite answer to this proposal. The evidence on the part of the defendants tended to show, on the other hand, that the creditors would not accept the proposal because the value of the property he proposed to convey was over-estimated, because he owned other property which he did not include in his proposal, and because his list of creditors included his sons, whose debts the other creditors were not willing to recognize. John E. Michael, one of the defendants, through whom the proposal to the creditors was made by plaintiff, testified that plaintiff, in conversation with him, being asked what was the consideration of the conveyance to his wife, replied, "that it was for a legacy which had been left to her, and which he had spent;" also, that plaintiff, in another conversation with him, "putting his hand on his pocket, said, that he had given his creditors a chance to select their man, but they had failed to do so, and now he had selected his own man, and had the papers in his pocket already drawn up." During the examination of said Michael as a witness he was asked several questions, as to his consultation with an attorney before suing out the attachment, his statements to the attorney, and the attorney's advice, or reply; but the rulings of the court on these questions and answers, which were excepted to, are immaterial in the view taken of the case by this court.

W. H. Leinkauf, one of the defendants, who was a surety on the attachment bond, was introduced as a witness for the defendants, "was shown two notes, which he identified, and

was asked by defendants, if he held said notes at the time
defendants' attachment was sued out. Plaintiff objected to
this question, but the court overruled the objection, and
allowed the witness to testify that he did have said notes at
the time said attachment was sued out. The defendants
offered said notes in evidence, and the plaintiff objected to
their admission; which objection the court overruled, and
plaintiff excepted." The notes were for $750 each, payable
to W. H. Leinkauf & Son, and fell due on the 17th December, 1886.

The plaintiff asked the following charge in writing, and
duly excepted to its refusal: "If the jury believe from the
evidence that John E. Michael, one of the defendants, stated
fully and fairly [to an attorney?] all the facts within his
knowledge relative to the transaction of the plaintiff, and that
such attorney thereupon advised him to sue out an attachment, but did not mean thereby to say that there was probable cause for suing it out, but only that he, if he were acting instead of Michael, would sue out the attachment, and
take the chance of being made liable for it; and if the jury
further believe from the evidence that said Michael so understood said advice, and that he had no reasonable ground to
believe that plaintiff had fraudulently disposed of his property, or was about fraudulently to dispose of it, and that
plaintiff did not have money, property or effects, liable to
satisfy his debts, which he fraudulently withheld, and that
none of said grounds in fact existed,—then the attachment
was sued out both wrongfully and vexatiously."

The plaintiff excepted, also, to several charges given by
the court at the instance of the defendants, among which
were these: (1.) "If the jury believe from the evidence
that the plaintiff, while indebted to Hannan & Michael in a
part of the amount to collect which they sued out the writ
of attachment against his estate, conveyed a large and valuable property to his wife; the presumption is that such conveyance, unexplained, was fraudulent; the burden of showing that it was fair and *bona fide* devolves on the plaintiff,
and unless he has reasonably satisfied the jury that it was
fair and *bona fide*, they must find for the defendants."
(2.) "The burden of proof is on the plaintiff to show the
falsity of the affirmation of fraud, upon which the attachment was sued out, and he must reasonably satisfy their
minds of such falsity; and if the evidence leaves them confused or uncertain as to the truth or falsity of such charge, they

must find for the defendants." The other charges given at
the instance of the defendants, relating to the right of the
plaintiff to recover attorney's fees or exemplary damages,
require no notice, as they are not considered by this court.

The refusal of the court to allow the challenge of one of
the jurors, the several rulings on the pleadings and evidence
adverse to the plaintiff, the refusal of the charge asked by
the plaintiff, and the giving of the several charges asked by
the defendants, are now assigned as error.

GREG. L. & H. T. SMITH, for appellant.—(1.) Knowledge
by one partner, or notice to him, charges the partnership
with notice or knowledge, and the name of the particular
partner is immaterial.—Bates on Partnership, § 390; *Renfro
v. Adams*, 62 Ala. 302; 8 Wheat. 668; *Thames v. Jones*,
N. C., 1 S. E. Rep. 692. (2.) The clerk of Cavenagh,
Barney & Co. was not a competent juror, and the challenge
to his competency ought to have been sustained.—*Davis v.
Allen*, 11 Pick. 466; *Jeffries v. Randall*, 14 Mass. 405;
8 Cush. Mass. 73; 17 Johns. 403; 10 Excheq. 131; Thompson & M. on Juries, §§ 180, 195-7; *Hubbard v. Rutledge*,
57 Miss. 7. (3.) The court erred in its rulings as to the
consultation with an attorney, the statements made to him,
and his advice.—*Murphy v. Lawson*, 77 Ill. 172; *Stanton v.
Hurt*, 27 Mich. 539; *Ash v. Marlowe*, 20 Ohio, 119; *Hill
v. Palm*, 38 Mo. 13; *Sharp v. Johnston*, 59 Mo. 557; 50 How.
Pr. 105; 50 Mo. 83; 57 Md. 282. (4.) The charge asked
by plaintiff ought to have been given.—*Chandler v. McPherson*, 11 Ala. 918; *McLeod v. McLeod*, 73 Ala. 45, and authorities last above cited. (5.) The notes held by Leinkauf
were not relevant to any issue in this case, and, if relevant,
were not admissible as evidence without proof of their execution. (6.) The first and second charges given at the instance of defendants were erroneous.—17 Cal. 508; 29 Mo.
259; *Durr v. Jackson*, 59 Ala. 204; *Adams v. Thornton*,
78 Ala. 489; 41 Ala. 40; 38 Ala. 636; 27 N. W. Rep. 333;
57 Ala. 517; 76 Ala. 182; 34 Ala. 90.

WATTS & SON, *contra.*—(1.) As the plaintiff recovered
no actual damages, the attachment was not sued out wrong-.
fully; and the several rulings of the court as to the advice of
counsel, probable cause, &c., relating only to the question of
exemplary damages, are immaterial, being, at most, only
error without injury.—73 Ala. 183; 75 Ala. 97. (2.) The

[Calhoun v. Hannan & Michael.]

challenge for cause was not well taken.—9 Car. & P. 480;
Brown v. Wheeler, 18 Conn. 199. (3.) The proof of indebtedness was relevant, the question of fraud being involved.
Allen v. Hubbard, 59 Ala. 283. The general objection to
the admission of the notes did not raise the question as to
the proof of their execution.—*Wallis v. Rhea*, 10 Ala. 451;
57 Ala. 551. (4.) The charge asked by plaintiff was partly
abstract, and was properly refused on that account.—*Williams v. Barksdale*, 58 Ala. 288; *Thrash v. Bennett*, 57 Ala.
156; *Brewer v. Watson*, 71 Ala. 299. (5.) The first charge
given at the instance of defendants was correct.—62 Ala.
34; 64 Ala. 263; 2 Brick. Digest, 21, § 100; 3 *Ib.* 520, § 173.
(6.) As to the correctness of the second charge, see *Durr
v. Jackson*, 59 Ala. 203; *Flournoy v. Lyon*, 70 Ala. 308;
61 Ala. 270; 73 Ala. 183.

McCLELLAN, J.—Many of the assignments of error are
predicated upon the rulings of the primary court on the sufficiency of pleadings and the admissibility of evidence, having reference solely to the defendant's liability for punitive
or exemplary damages. The matters presented by the
pleadings in this behalf, and the evidence in support or denial of them, were material only upon the assumption, that
none of the statutory grounds for the issuance of the attachment existed, and that the writ was, therefore, wrongful.
However malicious and vexatious the suing out of the writ
may have been, the plaintiff was not entitled to recover in
this action, unless it had been shown its issuance was also
wrongful, in the sense of not being based upon some one of
the facts which authorize a resort to this extraordinary
process.

In determining this primary question of the rightfulness
of a resort to the writ, neither the allegations nor proof, in
respect to facts which go only in aggravation or mitigation
of the act complained of, can exert any legitimate influence
in shaping the issue, or on the minds of the jury. There
must be an unlawful act, before the good or bad faith with
which the act was done can become a material inquiry.—*City
Nat. Bank v. Jeffries*, 73 Ala. 183; *Jackson v. Smith*,
75 Ala. 97.

The verdict was in favor of the defendants. This was a
determination that the attachment was rightfully sued out.
A different finding could not have been reached or justified
by a consideration of any conceivable state of pleadings or

proof in regard to malice or vexation. The action of the
court on these matters could have had no effect on the verdict; and whatever might have been the conclusion of the
jury as to the existence *vel non* of bad faith or recklessness
on the part of the plaintiff in attachment, no recovery could
have been had. The rulings of the City Court, therefore, on
the demurrers to plaintiff's replications, on the admissibility
of evidence as to the attachment having been sued out by
advice of counsel, on the charge requested by the plaintiff,
and on the third, fourth and fifth charges requested by the
defendants, which replications, evidence and charges related
exclusively to exemplary damages, if erroneous, were without
injury to the appellant, and furnish no ground for a reversal
of the judgment.—*Foster v. Johnson*, 70 Ala. 249; *Thomason v. Gray*, 82 Ala. 291.

The error, if error there was, in sustaining demurrers to
plaintiff's first and third replications to the third plea, is
shown to have worked no detriment to the appellant, by the
further fact that these replications were redrawn, so as to
obviate the infirmity pointed out by the demurrer, again
filed, and the benefit of the matters set up by them fully
secured to the plaintiff.—*Phœnix Ins. Co. v. Moog*, 78 Ala.
284; *Owings v. Binford*, 80 Ala. 421.

The charge requested by the plaintiff was not supported in
all of its hypotheses by the evidence, and the court's refusal
to give it may also be justified on this ground. The charge
was abstract.—*Williams v. Barksdale*, 58 Ala. 288; 3 Brick.
Dig. p. 133, §§ 106 *et seq.*

There was no error in disallowing plaintiff's challenge of
the juror, who was an employee of the defendants in another
suit brought by the plaintiff in this action, involving the same
issues, pending in the same court, and set down for trial on
the same day as this case. The facts shown were sufficient
to support a challenge for favor, the effect of which is to require an investigation by the court into the question, whether
the juror is biased in point of fact; but, of themselves, they
are not sufficient to show this, or to raise a disqualifying
presumption of bias.—Thompson & Mer. on Juries, 170, 171;
Brown v. Wheeler, 18 Conn. 199; *Strawn v. Cogswell*, 28 Ill.;
Com. v. Boston R. R. Co., 3 Cush. 25.

The objection to the testimony of Leinkauff, as to certain
notes purporting to be signed by the plaintiff and another,
and to the introduction of the notes themselves in evidence,
was too general. If these notes were, what they appeared to

be on their face, the obligations of the plaintiff, and if they were held by the witness, as he testifies, at the time of the attachment, they were admissible, as showing indebtedness of Calhoun at the date of the writ, which is also shown to have been the time at which the execution of the conveyance by plaintiff to his wife was perfected. The real objection to this testimony lay in the fact that the execution of the notes was not proved. This infirmity was not suggested in the objection actually made, and there was no error in overruling the very general and indefinite objection which was made. *Dyer v. Lewis*, 57 Ala. 551; *Steele v. Tutwiler*, 57 Ala. 113; *Tus. Cot. Oil Co. v. Perry*, 85 Ala. 158.

The fact that property has been conveyed on the recited consideration of an antecedent debt, by one otherwise indebted, raises a presumption of unfairness and *mala fides*, and casts upon the debtor, as between him and creditors who attack the conveyance for fraud, the *onus* of showing that the sale was fair, and made in good faith; and this he must do more fully and clearly, when it is shown, as here, that the conveyance was made to a relative. The first charge given at the request of the defendants was a correct exposition of this principle.—*Pollak v. Searcy*, 84 Ala. 259; *Tutwiler v. Munford*, 68 Ala. 124; *Dudley v. McKiernan*, 62 Ala. 34; *Garrett v. Garrett*, 64 Ala. 263.

The burden of proof being on the plaintiff to show the falsity of the affidavit in respect to the ground alleged for the issuance of the attachment, he must reasonably satisfy the minds of the jury in this regard. Manifestly, if their minds are left in a state of confusion and uncertainty on this point, the plaintiff has failed to make out this very essential part of his case, and can not recover. The second charge given at the request of defendants was, therefore, when referred to the evidence, free from error.—*Durr v. Jackson*, 59 Ala. 203.

Affirmed.

Hall *v.* Caperton.

Statutory Action in Nature of Ejectment.

1. *Specific performance of executory agreement to convey.*—A written instrument in the form of a deed, though defective as a conveyance for

[Hall v. Caperton]

the want of attestation or acknowledgment, is a valid executory agreement to convey, the specific performance of which a court of equity will
enforce, when it is shown that the consideration was paid, and that
possession was given and taken under it.

2. *Statute of limitations; possession under executory agreement to convey.*—When two persons execute to each other written instruments in
the form of deeds, which are defective as conveyances for the want of
attestation or acknowledgment, each instrument being the consideration
of the other, and possession is given and taken by each, the statute of
limitations at once commences to run, and, after the lapse of ten years,
perfects a title which will maintain or defeat an action of ejectment.

3. *Sale of lands for partition.*—To justify proceedings in the Probate
Court for a partition of lands, or a sale for partition (Code, §§ 3237, 3253),
each part owner must be interested in the entire lands sought to be sold
or partitioned.

4. *Conclusiveness of judgment or decree as bar.*—A decree rendered in
an interpleader suit, in favor of one of the adverse claimants of rents
in the hands of the complainant, is conclusive in a subsequent action
between them for the land from which the rents accrued, each asserting the same title under which he claimed the rents.

APPEAL from the Circuit Court of Jackson.

Tried before the Hon. HENRY C. SPEAKE.

This action was brought by A. D. Hall, Minerva George,
and George A. Love, minors, suing by their next friend,
against Samuel Caperton, to recover the possession of a
tract of land containing about 105 acres, which was particularly described in the complaint; and was commenced on
the 1st October, 1886. One of the plaintiffs was the daughter of Mrs. Delaney Caperton, who died on the 7th September, 1885, and who was the surviving widow of George W.
Caperton, who died on the 8th July, 1868; and Samuel
Caperton, the defendant, who was a son of said George W.
Caperton by a former marriage. The land sued for was part
of a tract of 848 acres, which had once belonged to said
George W. Caperton, and which was conveyed by him, by
deed dated November 2d, 1867, on the recited consideration
of $2,324.87, to four of his sons by his first marriage—
namely, Samuel, Adam H., Hugh E., and John F. Caperton.
Mrs. Delaney Caperton, then the wife of said George W.,
did not join in the conveyance, nor otherwise relinquish her
dower in the land. On the 31st May, 1870, two of the
grantees in said deed (Hugh E. and John F.) having died
without children or their descendants, Adam H. and Samuel
Caperton, the surviving grantees, procured from Mrs. Caperton a release of her dower interest in the tract of land, in
consideration of their conveyance to her of the 105 acres
here sued for; and instruments to that effect were recipro-
cally executed and delivered, neither of which was attested

or acknowledged. The conveyance to Mrs. Caperton was to her for life, with remainder to her four children by said George W. Caperton. The possession of the land was delivered to Mrs. Caperton under this instrument, and she continued in uninterrupted possession until her death. The plaintiffs in this suit claimed as her heirs at law, and as remainder-men under the deed.

The defendant denied that the plaintiffs ever had any legal title to the land, and asserted title in himself, (1) under the original deed from George W. Caperton; (2) under a purchase at a sale made under a probate decree, on the 17th December, 1881, under a petition filed by himself asking a sale for partition among the several tenants in common; and (3) as sub-purchaser at a sale made under an execution for costs issued from the Chancery Court. Mrs. Delaney Caperton, who was then living, was not made a party to the proceedings in the Probate Court, but the plaintiffs in this action were joined with the other defendants as tenants in common; and the entire tract of land, including said 105 acres, was sold under the decree. The chancery suit, under which the land was sold, was instituted on the 24th September, 1879, by Mrs. Ruth A. Caperton, the widow and administratrix of said Adam H. Caperton, with their children as his heirs at law, and Samuel Caperton, the defendant in this suit, against the other heirs at law of said George W. Caperton; and sought (1) a reformation of said deed from him to his four sons, by correcting an alleged mistake in the description of a part of the tract of land; (2) an account of the rents and profits of the land received by the several grantees, and also of the purchase-money paid by them respectively; and (3) that a lien be declared on the land in favor of the complainants, for an alleged excess of purchase-money paid by said Adam H. and Samuel Caperton over and above their share. On final hearing, on pleadings and proof, the chancellor reformed the deed, but refused to grant any other relief to them; and he divided the costs equally between the parties. The land was sold under executions for costs issued on this decree, and bought by one Samuel E. Norwood, from whom the defendant afterwards redeemed and purchased. Mrs. Delaney Caperton was not made a party to the chancery suit.

On the trial, the plaintiffs offered in evidence the original deed from George W. Caperton to his sons, and the two written instruments executed between Mrs. Delaney Caperton and Samuel and Adam H. Caperton, above described; and they also offered in evidence a transcript of the record of a chancery suit under a bill of interpleader filed by one Marcus Rudder, involving the right to the rent of the land for the year 1885, which was awarded to these plaintiffs by the decree of the chancellor, and his decree was affirmed by this court on appeal.—*Caperton v. Hall*, 83 Ala. 171. The defendant offered in evidence transcripts of the proceedings in the Probate Court and in the Chancery Court, and the several conveyances to himself. The court charged the jury, on request, that they must find for the defendant, if they believed the evidence. The plaintiffs excepted to this charge, and they here assign it as error.

BROWN & KIRK, for appellants.—The written instrument executed by Samuel and Adam H. Caperton to Mrs. Delaney Caperton, though defective as a conveyance of the legal title, was good as color of title; and Mrs. Caperton's possession under it, for more than ten years, gave her a good title against all the world. On her death, intestate, this title descended to her heirs, the present plaintiffs; and it is unaffected by the sales under the probate and chancery decrees, because Mrs. Caperton was not made a party to these proceedings, and her interest was in no way involved in either suit.—Freeman on Judgments, § 259. Moreover, the decree in the interpleader suit is conclusive of the rights of the parties.—*Caperton v. Hall*, 83 Ala. 171; *Liddell v. Chidester*, 84 Ala. 508.

W. L. MARTIN, *contra.*—The decree in the interpleader suit has none of the elements of an estoppel, and is not conclusive of anything in this suit.—*Gilbreath v. Jones*, 66 Ala. 129; *McCall v. Jones*, 72 Ala. 368; *Hamner v. Pounds*, 57 Ala. 348; *Watts v. Rice*, 75 Ala. 289; Freeman on Judgments, § 249. The decision of this court in that case was put on the express ground, that the plaintiffs had a superior equitable right to the rents. In this action, only the legal title is involved, or can be considered; and the plaintiffs' equitable rights can not prevail against the defendant's legal title.

STONE, C. J.—On the 2d day of November, 1867, George W. Caperton executed a deed of conveyance to his four sons, Adam H., Hugh E., Samuel, and John F. Caperton, by which

he conveyed to them, with warranty, a tract of more than
eight hundred acres of land, on a recited valuable consideration of over two thousand dollars. The grantees were
four of eleven children of the said George W., the fruit of
his first marriage. He had married a second time, and the
second wife, Delaney Caperton, filled that relation when the
deed was made, and did not join in the conveyance, or otherwise relinquish her dower. The said George W. died July
8, 1868, leaving Delaney, his widow, surviving him. By
her he had and left four children, one of them of posthumous
birth. Hugh Caperton, one of the grantees in the deed,
died October 23, 1867, before the death of his father, George
W.; and John F., another of the grantees, died August 10,
1868. Neither of these left lineal descendents, and their
brothers and sisters became their heirs at law.

On the 31st day of May, 1870, Adam H. Caperton and
Sam. Caperton had an agreement with Mrs. Delaney Caperton, the widow, by which they agreed to convey to her one
hundred and five acres, the land in controversy in this
suit—part of the tract conveyed by Geo. W. Caperton to his
four sons—in consideration of which she agreed to relinquish
her dower claim to the residue of the tract. They attempted to carry this agreement into execution. Adam and Sam,
describing themselves as "surviving partners with Hugh E.
Caperton and John F. Caperton, deceased," executed a paper, by which they attempted to convey to Delaney Caperton
the lands herein sued for; and she, at the same time, by
written instrument, attempted to relinquish to them her
dower interest in the residue of the lands. Each of these
instruments is correct in form to accomplish the purpose
attempted, but each was and is inoperative, as a conveyance
of title, because each is without subscribing witnesses, and
without certificate of acknowledgment.—3 Brick. Dig. 297,
§ 11. By the terms of this agreement, each of these instruments was the consideration of the other, but neither
conveyed a legal title. No purchase-money remained unpaid
from Mrs. Caperton, for by the agreement she was to pay
none. The imperfectly executed deed to her was a sufficient
executory agreement to convey, took it without the influence
of the statute of frauds, and chancery would compel its
specific performance.—*Jenkins v. Harrison*, 66 Ala. 345;
Roney v. Moss, 74 Ala. 390. There are other provisions of
this agreement which we will notice further on.

The proof is clear and undisputed, that on the making of
19

this agreement—May 31, 1870—Mrs. Delaney Caperton
went into immediate possession of the one hundred and five
acres of land attempted to be conveyed to her, and that she
held the same in her own individual, independent right until
her death in 1885. Sam. Caperton proves this himself, and
proves further that he owned lands adjoining, and her possession and right of possession were never questioned during
her life. Other testimony proves that, during that time, she
received and enjoyed the income and profits, aud held exclusive and notorious possession and control of the premises as
of right, and exercised the customary acts of ownership.
She became an adverse holder from the time she took possession, and asserted rightful ownership, and from that time
the ten years statute of limitations commenced to run in her
favor.—*Potts v. Coleman*, 67 Ala. 221; *Tillman v. Spann*,
68 Ala. 102; *Morgan v. Casey*, 73 Ala. 222.

Nor can it be said that she entered and held as dowress.
There was no allotment of dower, and no proceedings were
instituted looking to that result. She entered pursuant to
the agreement with Adam and Sam. Caperton; and there is
no pretense that there was ever any change of the terms
under which she held, by any consent or act of hers. This,
after ten years of such holding, gave her not only a right to
defend against any adversary claim, no matter how well
fortified it might be by a documentary title, but it went
further, and clothed her with a title on which she could
maintain a suit, even against the holder of a perfect paper
title.—*Coker v. Ferguson*, 70 Ala. 284; 3 Brick. Dig. 621,
§§ 63, 68, 69; *Black v. Coal & Coke Co.*, 85 Ala. 504.

The title which Mrs. Caperton had acquired by adverse
holding, was the only legal title she held—the only title we
can consider in this action at law. She died the holder of a
legal title acquired by adverse holding; and at her death
that title devolved immediately on her heirs at law, and
armed them with the same right to sue and defend, which
she could assert if living.—3 Brick. Dig. 325, §§ 33, 34.

There are other features of this case which must not be
overlooked. When Adam and Sam Caperton contracted with
Mrs. Delaney Caperton in reference to her dower, they subscribed themselves as "surviving partners." This language
favors the conclusion, that their interpretation of their father's deed was, that it conveyed the title to the four brothers
as joint tenants, and that they as survivors had succeeded to
the entire estate. If this was their construction of the deed,

[Hall v. Caperton.]

they fell into an error. They took, under our statute, as
tenants in common, between whom the right of survivorship
does not obtain.—3 Brick. Dig. 692, §§ 98 et seq. It follows, that the attempted conveyance by Adam and Sam.
Caperton only bound their two one-fourth interests, equal to
one undivided half, and left the remaining undivided half to
descend equally and alike to all the heirs at law of Hugh E.
and John F. Caperton, deceased, with no discrimination
between the whole and the half blood. Some of them were
possibly minors, and possibly some had died, leaving minor
descendants. The record does not inform us sufficiently.
This inquiry may affect the running of the statute of limitations as to some of the interests which it seems had centered
in Sam. Caperton—the result of the two sales under the
chancery and probate decrees.

In *Black v. Pratt Coal & Coke Co.*, *supra*, and authorities
therein cited, the rule for determining when the statute is,
and when it is not suspended as to persons not *sui juris*, is
laid down. Mrs. Caperton had acquired a perfect title by
the statute of limitations, against the original half belonging to Adam and Sam. Caperton, and against all the heirs at
law of Hugh E. and John F. Caperton who can not bring
themselves within some exception to the statute of limitations. So, to this extent, the plaintiffs have a clear right to
recover in this action at law against Sam. Caperton. The
precise undivided proportion of the land they are entitled to
recover in this action, the record does not enable us to determine.

Neither the suit in equity, instituted by Ruth A. Caperton,
administratrix, and others, nor the proceedings in the Probate Court and sale under it, can affect the legal title vested
by independent, adverse holding in Delaney Caperton, nor
of her heirs, on whom that title devolved at her death. She
was not made a party to either of the suits, and neither she,
nor those who are her successors in legal interest, are, as to
that legal interest, concluded thereby. The tract of one
hundred and five acres involved in this suit, was improperly
included in the probate court proceedings, and the sale for
division or distribution. As we have shown, the claims of
Adam and Sam. Caperton to the land, as well as that of all
the other heirs, whose rights had become barred under the
principles declared above, had vested in Mrs. Delaney Caperton by adverse holding, and, hence, could not be joined with
the other lands in one and the same proceeding, having for

[Hall v. Caperton.]

its object the partition of the land, or its sale for division
or distribution.   To justify proceedings in the Probate Court
for partition of lands, or for a sale for division, each part
owner must be interested in the lands sought to be partitioned.

The deed from George W. Caperton to his four sons devested out of him all title to the lands conveyed, and vested
it in the grantees.   There could, therefore, be no one claiming an interest in the lands as heirs of George W. Caperton.
He had parted with the title, and thereby left in himself no
estate to transfer.   When Hugh E. and John F. Caperton
died, each the holder of an undivided fourth interest in the
lands, their living brothers and sisters, and the descendants,
if any, of such as had died, became inheritors from them,
and not from George W. Caperton, their father.   So, it was
the tenancy in common, created by the devolution of the title
of Hugh E. and John F. Caperton on their deaths, which
gave rise to the partition proceedings in the Probate Court.
No part of their interest or title devolving on Mrs. Delaney
Caperton, she was not, and could not be classed as an in-
heritor from either of them; and hence her possession could
not be as heir, or as one of the tenants in common.   If it
had been, possibly it would require twenty years of hostile,
adversary holding by her, to bar the partition proceedings.
Bozeman v. Bozeman, 82 Ala. 389.   But we need not decide
this, as she filled no such relation.   She held in independent
claim of right, and hostile to the whole world, except her
own children, as we shall hereafter show.

The only legal title in the lands in controversy, which Sam.
Caperton can maintain, are those possible interests in the
descent from Hugh E. and John F. Caperton, which, by
reason of exceptions from the statute of limitations, were not
barred by Mrs. Delaney Caperton's long adverse holding.
The legal title to these possible interests, it would seem,
vested in Sam. Caperton by virtue of his purchases, and these
can not be recovered in this action at law.

The lands in controversy were let to rent for the year 1885,
by Rudder, acting as agent of Mrs. Delaney Caperton.
During the year, and before the rent matured, Mrs. Caperton died, leaving four surviving heirs at law; one daughter,
Mrs. Love, and three grandchildren, offspring of her other
daughters, who had previously died.   When the rent matured, Rudder, the agent, collected it of the tenant, and had
it in hand.   The said fours heirs at law of Mrs. Caperton

claimed the money, on two grounds: first, as express remainder-men under the deed of Mrs. Caperton; and second, as her heirs at law. Sam. Caperton also asserted claim to the rent money, claiming that the land was his, and that the rent should follow the title. He rested his claim on the several alleged chains of title referred to above—namely, the titles acquired under the chancery sales, and under the probate sale for division. He had acquired these several titles before the death of Mrs. Caperton in 1885. So, as we have said, each party claimed the rent money, as an incident to the claim and title each asserted.

Rudder, having the money, and being only a stake-holder, in March, 1886, filed his bill of interpleader, making the said Sam. Caperton and the said heirs at law of Delaney Caperton, the plaintiffs in this suit, parties defendant, and prayed that they be decreed to interplead, and determine which party was entitled to the rent money. No defect in the bill of interpleader is pointed out, and none is perceived. The chancellor entertained the bill, and the parties did interplead. In March, 1887, he rendered his final decree in the cause. In his decree, the chancellor said: "Samuel Caperton has not been successful in sustaining his right to the money due for the rent of said land for 1885. These rents would follow the title." He decreed that the rent money should be paid the said heirs at law of Delaney Caperton, and that Sam. Caperton should pay the costs. The case had been submitted "on register's report, pleadings and proof, as noted by the register, for final decree."

Sam. Caperton appealed to this court, and the decree of the chancellor was affirmed.—*Caperton v. Hall*, 83 Ala. 171. This court, without passing on the legal title of Delaney Caperton's heirs, speaking of the unattested instrument which Adam and Sam. Caperton had given to Delaney in 1870, said: "The instrument operates to confer on appellees an equitable title, and a consequent claim to the rent, which equity will regard and uphold." We then proceeded to declare, that the claim of Delaney Caperton's heirs was, in equity, paramount to all claim and right of Sam. Caperton in the very lands in controversy in this suit, and upon the very title here relied on, and that, as a consequence, they were entitled to the rents. The case was decided in this court on the equity feature of the very title in issue in this case, and between identically the same parties; and it was held that the equitable title of the plaintiffs in this action is superior to

[Sparks v. Woodstock Iron and Steel Company.]

Sam. Caperton's title. This is *res judicata*, and is conclusive on him in any and all proceedings between them involving the same title.—*Liddell v. Chidester*, 84 Ala. 500.

The imperfectly executed instrument from Adam and Sam. Caperton to Mrs. Delaney Caperton assumes to convey the land to her for life, remainder to her children. That is the instrument which was construed in *Caperton v. Hall*, 83 Ala. 171. Should Sam. Caperton, in the future trial of this case, be able to show that he has an unbarred legal title to any undivided part of the land sued for, and thus partially defeat a recovery in this suit, he will be but a trustee of the legal title so vested in him, and on a proper bill by the heirs it will be devested out of him, and vested in them. This, on the principle that this question is *res judicata*, and is not open to further controversy.

The Circuit Court erred in giving the general charge in favor of the defendant.

Reversed and remanded.

Sparks *v.* Woodstock Iron and Steel Company.

Bill in Equity for Specific Execution of Defective Conveyance.

1. *Specific execution of defective instrument, as agreement to convey.* When a written instrument, purporting to convey land, is signed by the grantor, and has all the elements of a valid deed, except in the necessary attestation of subscribing witnesses, a court of equity will specifically enforce it, against the heirs of the deceased grantor, as an agreement to convey, unless some sufficient reason is shown why specific performance should not be decreed.

2. *Same; case at bar.*—On the evidence shown by the record in this case, the court holds that the written instrument sought to be enforced against the heirs of the deceased grantor was signed by her voluntarily, with full knowledge of its contents, was founded on an adequate consideration, and was fair, just and reasonable in all of its parts; and that the charges of fraud, duress, and unfair advantage, set up in the answer, are not sustained.

3. *Organization of corporation.*—Under statutory provisions relating to the formation of private corporations for business purposes (Code, 1876, § 1807), the judge of probate is required, "upon the completion of the organization of the company," as shown by the certified statement to him, to issue a certificate of the fact that the company is fully organized, and is authorized to commence business under its charter; but this

certificate is not a condition precedent to the complete organization of the company, and the want of it does not establish the plea of *nul tiel* corporation, in an action brought by the company.

APPEAL from the Chancery Court of Calhoun.
Heard before the Hon. S. K. MCSPADDEN.

The bill in this case was filed on the 26th February, 1888, by the Woodstock Iron and Steel Company, and the Anniston City Land Company, two private corporations organized under the general statutes, against Mrs. Eliza A. Sparks and others, heirs at law of Mrs. Sallie J. W. McAdams, deceased; and sought the specific execution of a defective conveyance of a tract of land, executed by Mrs. McAdams in her lifetime to George W. Brannon, under whom the complainants derived title; also, a divestiture of the legal title out of the defendants, and an injunction of an action at law which they had brought to recover the land. The written instrument of which a specific execution was sought, and which was dated October, 1884, conveyed to said Brannon, with covenants of warranty, a tract of land containing forty acres, on the recited consideration of $300 in hand paid, "and the further consideration that the said party of the second part has agreed and by these presents does agree and bind himself, to take care of her [the grantor]. and to provide for her support and maintenance during her life;" and it was signed by the grantor, and attested by two subscribing witnesses, each signing by mark only; but there was no attesting witness to their signatures, or marks. The complainants alleged that Brannon paid the $300 as recited, and took care of Mrs. McAdams until her death in May, 1885; and that he continued in the possession of the land until August 26th, 1886, when he sold and conveyed to the Woodstock Iron & Steel Company, who afterwards sold and conveyed a part of the land to the Anniston City Land Company.

The defendants answered the bill, and denied both the execution and the validity of the said written instrument; alleging that, if Mrs. McAdams ever signed it, she did so in ignorance of its contents, and when she was mentally incapable of making any contract; that the instrument was procured from her by fraud, duress, and undue influence, and was not supported by an adequate consideration; and they also filed a special plea of *nul tiel* corporation, denying that the Woodstock Iron & Steel Company was ever legally incorporated.

The complainants produced a transcript from the records

of the Probate Court containing the proceedings relating to the
organization of the Woodstock Iron & Steel Company, setting out—1st, the articles of incorporation, which stated the
names of the corporators, the name and business of the proposed corporation, &c.; 2d, the written order of the probate
judge, appointing two of the corporators as commissioners
to open books of subscription, and to make report of their
proceedings; 3d, the report of the commissioners showing
their proceedings, and stating the names of the subscribers,
with the amount subscribed and paid in, and the names of
officers elected; 4th, an order by the probate judge, reciting
. the filing of the report, "that a certificate of authority issue
to said company authorizing them to proceed to business as
set out in its declaration, and according to law." A great
deal of evidence was taken by each of the parties, showing
the circumstances attending the execution of the written instrument by Mrs. McAdams, the relations then existing
between her and Brannon, her pecuniary condition, and her
mental and physical capacity. A summary of this evidence,
if possible within the limits of a report, is not necessary to
an understanding of the opinion of the court, and therefore
is not attempted; and the arguments of counsel, addressed
chiefly to a discussion of the evidence, are omitted for the
same reason.

On final hearing, on pleadings and proof, the chancellor
rendered a decree for the complainants, as prayed; and his
decree is here assigned as error.

BROTHERS, WILLETT & WILLETT, for appellants.—(1.) The
Woodstock Iron & Steel Company, claiming incorporation
under the general statutes, must show a substantial compliance with all statutory requisitions. The proceedings shown
by the transcript from the Probate Court are fatally defective, because—1st, the report of the commissioners, or board
of corporators, does not show that, at the meeting held for
the purpose of organizing and electing officers, a majority
in value of the subscribers were present, either in person or
by proxy; and, 2d, no certificate appears to have been issued
by the probate judge, and his order is not the equivalent of
a certificate.—1 Mor. Corp., §§ 27, 15; *People v. Selfridge*,
52 Cal. 331; *Factory Asso. v. Clarke*, 61 Maine, 351; *Stowe
v. Flagg*, 72 Ill. 397; *Field v. Cook*, 16 La. Ann. 153;
Bridge Co. v. Wood, 14 Geo. 84; 17 Cal. 136. (2.) Specific performance is not a matter of right, but is a matter of

sound judicial discretion, as determined by the circumstances of each particular case; and it will not be granted, where there is a suspicion of fraud, undue influence, or improper advantage; nor where there is inadequacy of consideration, and the contract is not fair, just and reasonable in all its parts.—*Irwin v. Bailey*, 72 Ala. 467; *Moon v. Crowder*, 72 Ala. 79; *Derrick v. Monette*, 73 Ala. 75; *Gould v. Womack*, 2 Ala. 83; *Radcliffe v. Warrington*, 12 Vesey, 332; *Willard v. Tayloe*, 8 Wall. 565; *Manning v. Wadsworth*, 4 Md. 59; 21 Gratt. 23; 38 N. H. 400; 5 Harr. Del. 74; 73 Ill. 63; 43 Iowa, 43; *Blackwilder v. Loveless*, 21 Ala. 371; 8 Vesey, 337; 14 Vesey, 273; 3 M. & K. 339; 2 Sch. & L. 31; 1 H. L. Cases, 724; 2 Strob. Eq. 72; 1 N. J. Eq. 320; 21 Barb. 381; 20 N. Y. 184; 12 Wisc. 382; 9 N. J. Eq. 332; 40 Miss. 507; 20 Md. 482; 2 Jones Eq. (N. C.) 224; 9 N. J. Eq. 332; *Lester v. Mahan*, 25 Ala. 445; *Shipman v. Furniss*, 69 Ala. 555; *Thompson v. Lee*, 31 Ala. 292; *Meyer v. Mitchell*, 75 Ala. 475. (3.) An application of these principles to the facts of this case, as disclosed by the evidence, is fatal to the plaintiffs' case.

CALDWELL & JOHNSTON, CASSADY & BLACKWELL, and KNOX & BOWIE, *contra*, cited *Goodlett v. Hansell*, 66 Ala. 159; *Chambers v. Ala. Iron Co.*, 67 Ala. 353; *Thames v. Rembert*, 63 Ala. 561; 67 Ala. 353; 76 Ala. 222.

SOMERVILLE, J.—1. The instrument bearing date October 20th, 1884, purporting to convey the land in controversy to Brannon by Mrs. McAdams, as grantor, has every element of a good and valid deed of conveyance, except as to its attestation by the requisite witnesses. It is defective in the latter particular, on the ground that neither of the attesting witnesses wrote their names, but the name of each was written by some one else, and was authenticated only by the making of the witnesses' "marks" respectively. If actually signed by the grantor, it was good nevertheless, as an agreement to convey, and a court of equity will enforce its specific execution by compelling the heirs of the deceased grantor to convey, unless some sufficient reason is shown why this divestiture of title should not be decreed.—Code, 1886, § 1789; *Roney v. Moss*, 74 Ala. 390; 3 Brick. Dig. p. 362, § 435.

2. We have examined and weighed the testimony in the case, and are of opinion that it shows satisfactorily that the

instrument was voluntarily signed by the grantor, Mrs. Mc-Adams, with a full knowledge of its contents, and that she was of sound mind at the time of its execution. The pre-ponderance of the testimony, moreover, favors the conclusion reached by the chancellor, that the consideration shown to have been satisfied in money and services by the grantee, Brannon, under whom the appellees claim title, was of a character to render the contract not only fair, just and rea-sonable in all its parts, but one that was, under the peculiar circumstances, quite advantageous to the grantor. The charge of fraud, duress, or unfair advantage, is not, in our judgment, supported by the evidence.

3. The contention that the Woodstock Iron and Steel Company, one of the complainants in the bill, is not a legally organized corporation, is not well taken. It is not denied that all proper steps were taken to organize the company under the statute relating to business corporations, except the issue of the requisite *certificate* of organization required by section 1807 of the Code of 1876. It is shown that the proceedings as to organization, regular in form, were certi-fied by the directors to the probate judge, which was required to be done by this section of the Code, "upon the comple-tion of the organization of the company," and after the payment of twenty per cent. of the capital subscribed. The judge was requested to issue the certificate, and made an order that it should issue. The provision of the statute is, that, after these steps are taken, the probate judge "shall issue to the company a certificate that they have fully organized ac-cording to the laws of Alabama, under the name and for the purposes indicated in their written declaration, and that they are fully authorized to commence business under their char-ter."—Code, 1876, § 1807. The duty of the probate judge, in this particular, was ministerial, and *mandamus* would clearly lie to compel its performance.—1 Morawetz on Corp. (2d Ed.) § 15. This certificate was not a condition prece-dent to the company's incorporation becoming complete un-der the statute, but it is the mere evidence of the fact that it had already become so. The very language of the statute, on the contrary, shows the legislative intention to be, that such a certificate could only issue "upon the *completion of the organization* of the company." Whether necessary to a license, or pre-requisite of the right to carry on business after organization, is another question, which can not affect the rightful existence of the corporation—the only inquiry

here raised by the defendants' plea of *nul tiel corporation.*
1 Morawetz on Corp. §§ 29, 27, 30.

We discover no error in the decree of the chancellor,
granting relief prayed by the complainants, and it is affirmed.

Peddy *v.* Street.

Motion to Substitute Record of Destroyed Judgment.

1. *Amendment by striking out part of papers.*—On motion to substitute a judgment, the record of which has been lost or destroyed, an
amendment may be allowed striking out the summons and complaint
as a part of the papers to be substituted.

2. *Defenses against substitution.*—On motion to substitute the record
of a judgment which has been lost or destroyed, the copy proposed to
be substituted reciting the service of process on the defendant, he may
controvert the correctness of the copy in this particular, but not the
recitals of the original judgment as to the service of process on him.

APPEAL from the Circuit Court of Clay.
Tried before the Hon. LEROY F. BOX.

WATTS & SON, for appellant.

CLOPTON, J.—This is an appeal from an order of the
Circuit Court, substituting the record of a destroyed judgment rendered at the Fall term, 1869, of the same court.
The proceedings, as originally instituted, also sought to substitute the summons and complaint in the cause in which the
judgment was rendered. The motion for substitution was
amended by striking out so much as referred to the summons
and complaint. The movant certainly had the right to aban-
don the whole, or any part of his application; and the
amendment was merely an abandonment of the part stricken
out. We discover no valid objection to the amendment.

The appellant appeared, and filed pleas, setting up that a
copy of the summons and complaint in the original suit was
not served on him; that he had no notice of such suit; and
that the court, in rendering judgment, did not have jurisdiction of his person. The judgment proposed to be substituted
recites, that a copy of the summons and complaint was served
on appellant. On a motion to substitute, appellant can not
contest the truth of the recitals of the record, though he may

(Chandler v. Chandler.]

show that the lost or destroyed record did not contain such recitals. On such motion, the court does not render, or revive the judgment; but merely supplies the record evidence of one already in existence. The whole purpose is to re-establish evidence of its existence, in itself conclusive, and to dispense with the necessity of resorting to secondary evidence.—*May v. Parham*, 68 Ala. 253. If the court is fully satisfied by the proof as to the correctness of the proposed substitute, it will order the judgment enrolled as it stood originally; and when enrolled, it possesses neither more nor less validity than the original judgment.—*Atkinson v. Keel*, 25 Ala. 551; *Lilly v. Larkin*, 66 Ala. 110; *Ward v. State*, 78 Ala. 455. On a proceeding to substitute a lost record, the court can not consider a collateral issue.

Affirmed.

Chandler *v.* Chandler.

Final Settlement of Executor's Accounts.

1. *What is revisable; matters of record, shown only by bill of exceptions.*—On appeal from a probate decree rendered on final settlement of an executor's accounts, this court can not consider an assignment of error based on an order setting aside a prior decree allowing a claim of exemptions filed by the widow, when such order, and the decree setting it aside, are shown only by the bill of exceptions; though the court may consider the transcript as showing the fact that the claim was filed, its date, and the property embraced in it.

2. *Exemptions of personalty in favor of widow and children.*—A liberal construction has always been given to the statutory provisions allowing exemptions to the widow and minor children of deceased debtors; the right is not made to depend on a dissent from the will, making a testamentary provision for their support; the claim is allowed to attach to any kind of personal property, or to the proceeds of any personal property which has been sold or exchanged by the personal representative; and if the whole of the personal property does not exceed $1,000 in value, and is in the possession of the widow, her right of exemption does not require a selection, or formal claim, to perfect it. But, when no claim of exemptions has been interposed, a sale by the personal representative, if made by authority, cuts off the right of exemption; though, if made without authority, the property may be recovered by a succeeding administrator, and again become subject to a claim of exemption.

3. *Executor's power to sell property under will.*—A testamentrry provision d recting that all of the testator's property, real, personal and mixed, shall be collected together by the executor, and used in the settlement of debts, and that any residue, after the settlement of debts, shall be equally distributed among his children, does not confer any other or greater power of sale than is given by statutory provisions.

[Chandler v. Chandler.]   •

4. *Executor's authority to sell personalty.*—Independent of testamentary provisions, an executor has the full legal title to all *choses* in action, and may dispose of them absolutely without an order of court; but he has not such power to dispose of the tangible personal property, and his sale without an order of court does not affect the right of exemption of the widow and children.

5. *Payment of taxes by executor.*—An executor is entitled, on final settlement of his accounts, to a credit for taxes paid by him which were assessed during the year of the testator's death.

6. *Allowance to executor, for costs paid.*—It being the duty of an executor to collect, by suit or otherwise, debts due the estate, he is entitled to a credit on final settlement, as against the widow and children, for costs paid in prosecuting a suit against a debtor.

APPEAL from the Probate Court of Marshall.

Heard before the Hon. THOS. A. STREET.

In the matter of the estate of Elisha R. Chandler, deceased, on final settlement of the accounts and vouchers of John D. Chandler as executor, which were contested by the widow and minor children of said decedent. The record proper shows that the executor filed his accounts and vouchers for a settlement in January, 1888, and the 12th March was then appointed as the day for a final settlement; that the settlement was continued from one day to another, until June 11th, when a final settlement was made, and a decree rendered, ascertaining a balance of $72.70 in favor of the executor. On the settlement, as the bill of exceptions states, the executor moved the court to set aside a decree which had been rendered on the 21st November, 1887, allowing a claim of exemptions filed by the widow, October 18th, 1887, in favor of herself and the minor children; and the court granted the motion, and set aside that decree, against the objection and exception of the widow, who here assigned that ruling as error. Entering on the settlement of the executor's accounts as stated, the widow objected to each item on each side of the account, and reserved exceptions to the allowance of each item; and these several rulings are also assigned as error. The appellee submitted a motion to strike out the first assignment of error, on the ground that the appeal was not sued out from the decree setting aside the allowance of exemptions, and that decree was shown only by the bill of exceptions; and to strike out the other assignments of error, because the record does not show that the appeal is taken from the decree rendered on final settlement of the executor's accounts.

LUSK & BELL, for appellant.

WATTS & SON, and JNO. G. WINSTON, *contra.*

McCLELLAN, J.—Considering the certificate of appeal in connection with the bond in this case, we think it is sufficiently shown that this appeal is taken from the decree of the court below on the final settlement of the appellee as executor of E. R. Chandler, deceased. That decree appears here as from the record of the primary court, and the motion to dismiss this appeal, on the ground that it is prosecuted from the action of the Probate Court in reference to the claim of exemption, and that the decree in that matter is shown here only by the bill of exceptions, must be overruled. There is, however, an assignment of error, directed against this latter decree, which is not appealed from; and for this reason that assignment will not be considered. The application of the widow to have the personal property set apart as exempt to her and the minor children, the decree of the court thereon, the petition of the executor asking that that decree be vacated, and the order granting that petition, are all matters of record in the Probate Court, and can not be considered by this court, for the purpose of reviewing the action of the court below in that behalf, when presented, as is the fact in this case, only by the bill of exceptions.—*Ex parte Knight,* 61 Ala. 482; *Slernan v. Marx,* 58 Ala. 608.

The transcript of these matters of record may, however, be looked to, on this appeal, as showing the *facts* that such claim was filed, its date, and the property embraced in it.

On the final settlement of the executor, the widow appeared for herself and the minor children, and objected to each item on both sides of the account, on the ground that the debits consisted of personal property exempted from administration, and the credits consisted of payments made out of the proceeds of such exempt property. It was admitted that the personalty of the estate did not exceed one thousand dollars in value; that that part of it charged in the account against the executor, had been disposed of by him, and the proceeds applied to the payment of the debts of the estate, before the widow's claim of exemption was filed; and that all of this had been done within eighteen months after grant of letters testamentary. The court overruled the widow's objection, and passed and allowed the account as stated, bringing down a small balance in favor of the executor. This action is here assigned as error.

This court has uniformily given a liberal construction to

the statutes allowing exemptions to the widow and minor children of decedents, in furtherance of the manifest legislative policy to secure, as far as possible, the comfort and well-being of those who, without the protection thus afforded, might be left in want. It is settled, that the exemption secured to them by statute is not defeated by testamentary provision being made for their support; and, therefore, that the widow is not required, as a condition to securing the statutory right, to dissent from the will in such cases. *Hubbard v. Russell*, 73 Ala. 578; *Bell v. Bell*, 84 Ala. 64. The claim may attach to any kind of personalty belonging to the estate—chattels, *choses* in action, or money—and to the proceeds of any personal property which has been sold or exchanged by the personal representative.—*Little v. McPherson*, 76 Ala. 556; *Darden v. Reese*, 62 Ala. 311.

But, while the beneficent purpose of the statute has been recognized, and the utmost liberality of construction has obtained in furtherance of its objects, it is well settled, that the right given by it, like all other statutory exemptions, must be claimed, and, if not claimed in some of the modes provided by or within the contemplation of the act, it will be held to have been waived.—*Henderson v. Tucker*, 70 Ala. 384; *Little v. McPherson*, 76 Ala. 555. The exemption will be held to have been abandoned, in all cases in which there has been a failure on the part of the widow, the guardian of the minors, and the probate judge, through commissioners, to make the selection, until, in consequence of such neglect, the personal representative subjects the property to administration for the payment of debts, or for distribution.—*Tucker v. Henderson*, 63 Ala. 280; *Henderson v. Tucker*, 70 Ala. 384; *Mitcham v. Moore*, 73 Ala. 546.

In the case last cited, there is an intimation, that the necessity for an assertion of the claim is not the same in those cases where the whole of the personal property of the estate does not exceed one thousand dollars in value. This suggestion proceeds more on the situation of the property, so to speak, than upon any consideration of its value. If the whole property is of less value than one thousand dollars, the widow would be entitled to all of it; and if she had it in possession, there could be no necessity for a selection by her, the guardian of the minors, or commissioners; but, whether the value be greater or less than the sum named, if the property be not in the possession of those to whom it is exempted, a claim would have to be interposed, to defeat the executor's qualified right to sell or distribute it in the course of administration.

In no case has the right to the exemptions been admitted, after the property, to which it would otherwise have attached, has been sold; and with respect to exemption in lieu of homestead, the tendency is to hold the claim waived, unless made before a decree of sale.—*Seals v. Pheiffer*, 84 Ala. 361; *Toenes v. Moog*, 78 Ala. 558. To have the effect of cutting off the claim of exemption, however, the sale must be such as the personal representative is authorized to make; otherwise, the title to the property remains in the estate, and the property itself may be recovered by a succeeding administrator, and when recovered, be delivered to the widow and minor children under their claim of exemptions.—*Riddle v. Hill*, 57 Ala. 324; 1 Brick. Dig. 935, § 303.

As to the tangible personal property, the executor in this case had no power of sale. It is admitted that no order of the court to that end had been made, but, on the contrary, he had disposed of the property at private sale, on the assumption that the will gave him power so to do. The provision of the will, upon which reliance was had, is as follows: "All the rest and residue of my estate, real and personal and mixed, I desire to be collected together by my executor, and be used in the settlement of my just debts, and if there is any left, after the settlement of my debts, to be equally divided among my eight children." This is no more than a dedication of the property to the uses to which the law itself would have devoted it, and leaves the executor with precisely the same rights in respect to it, which he would have had in the absence of the provision quoted—the right to take possession of the property and sell it for the payment of debts, under and as directed by the orders of the Probate Court.

A considerable part of the personalty consisted of *choses* in action. As to this class of property, an entirely different rule prevails. The personal representative takes the full legal title to the *choses* in action of the estate, and may, without an order of court, or testamentary authorization, transfer, release, compound or discharge them, as fully as if he were the absolute owner, subject only to a liability for improvidence in the exercise of the power.—3 Brick. Dig. 464, § 139; *Curry v. Peebles*, 83 Ala. 225.

It results from these considerations, that the claim of the widow and minor children, to have the tangible personal property set apart to them as exempt, was not cut off by the disposition of that property by the executor. That property was not assets of the estate, for the purpose of administration ; the representative should not have been charged with it in the first instance, nor credited with the proceeds arising from its sale, and paid out on the debts of the estate.

The sale of the *choses* in action having, as we have shown, been made with authority, as to them the claim of exemption must be held to have been waived, and the executor was properly charged with their value, and credited with the amount of the proceeds arising from their disposition and devoted to the debts of the estate.

The rulings of the Probate Court were not in accord with the foregoing principles, and its judgment must be reversed.

The executor was properly allowed a credit for the taxes paid by him. It appears from a receipt offered in evidence, that the taxes paid were those for the year 1886, in which the testator died. The assessment was not only a charge on all of his property, but also a personal charge against him, and as such was properly paid by his representative.

It was not only the right, but the duty of the executor, to collect debts due the estate, by suit or otherwise; and he was properly allowed credits for costs which he had incurred and paid in his efforts to perform this duty.

For the errors indicated above, the judgment is reversed, and the cause remanded.

Tabler, Crudup & Co. *v.* Sheffield Land, Iron & Coal Co.

Action on Common Counts, for Money Paid.

1. *When action lies for money paid.*—To maintain an action for money paid by plaintiffs to the holders of certain non-transferable "labor-tickets" issued by the defendant corporation to workmen in its employment, it must be shown that plaintiffs took the tickets at the instance or request of the corporation, acting through some agent lawfully authorized to bind it; or, if the agreement was made by an agent not duly authorized, that it was afterwards ratified by the corporation.

2. *General charge on evidence.*—A general charge should never be given in favor of either party, unless the evidence is so clear and convincing that a demurrer might properly be sustained to it; never when

[Tabler, Crudup & Co. v. Sheffield Land, Iron & Coal Co.]

there is a conflict in the evidence, or when it is circumstantial, or when a material fact rests in inference.

3. *Testimony of party as to transactions with decedent.*—In an action by a partnership against a private corporation, one of the plaintiffs can not testify as a witness in their behalf to a transaction or conversation between himself and the president or general manager, since deceased, of the corporation (Code, § 2765).

4. *Ratification of agent's unauthorized act or agreement.*—A payment by the defendant corporation, on presentation, of labor-tickets which the plaintiffs had taken from the holders to whom they were issued, on the faith of a promise by an agent of the corporation that they would be paid on presentation, is a ratification of the agent's promise, and authorizes plaintffis to continue to purchase the tickets until notified that they would not be paid.

APPEAL from the Circuit Court of Colbert.

Tried before the Hon. HENRY C. SPEAKE.

This action was brought by the appellants, suing as partners, against the appellee, a private corporation; and was commenced on the 25th August, 1884. The cause of action was numerous printed certificates, called "labor-tickets," which the defendant had issued to the workmen in its employment, for their wages, and each of which was marked "not transferable;" and the plaintiffs claimed to have taken or purchased them from the workmen to whom they were issued, at the special instance and request of the defendant, through its agents, who promised that the corporation would pay or redeem them on presentation. On the second trial, as shown by the present record, the special counts on the tickets were struck out by amendment, leaving only the common counts; to which the defendant pleaded the general issue, with leave to give any special matter in evidence. The tickets were in the form shown by the former report of the case (79 Ala. 377), and the letters *E. P. M.* were written across the end of each, being the initials of one E. P. Miller, who was, as he testified on the trial, at that time in the employment of the defendant corporation "as general superintendent of the hands employed by defendant to clear off and grade the streets and avenues of Sheffield." Said Miller testified, also, that prior to the issue of these tickets the workmen were paid only once a month, and became dissatisfied because they could not procure provisions and medicines when they needed them; that he stated these facts to Walter Gordon, who was then the president and general manager of the defendant corporation, "and from whom he received all his instructions and orders about the work," and the tickets were prepared by arrangement between them to meet this necessity; that the tickets were left in his possession, to be given out to the workmen as earned, his initials being written on each when it was issued; "that although the tickets were marked 'not transferable,' it was understood and agreed between him and said Gordon, at the time, that the workmen were to be informed they could use said tickets at the defendant's commissary store in Sheffield, at two boarding houses there, and at plaintiffs' commissary store in Tuscumbia, to obtain supplies and medicines, or money to buy them with; that he so informed the workmen under him, and also informed plaintiffs of the arrangement, under the directions of said Gordon, and requested them to let the hands have commissary supplies, medicines and money, and to take said tickets in payment, and that defendant would take up the tickets, and pay them on presentation;" also, that plaintiffs did furnish supplies and medicines to the workmen under this arrangement, taking said tickets in payment. W. M. Wiley, who was a clerk in plaintiffs' store at the time, testified in substance that plaintiffs furnished goods, medicines, &c., to defendant's workmen, taking said tickets in payment, to the amount of nearly $1,000. D. L. Duncan, one of the plaintiffs, was also examined as a witness on their behalf, and testified that they took the tickets from defendant's workmen on the faith of the statements made by Miller as to their payment by the defendant, and of similar statements afterwards made to them by said Gordon as president; but the conversation with Gordon was excluded as evidence, on objection by the defendant, and the plaintiffs excepted. Duncan testified, also, that on May 20th, 1884, he carried a large number of tickets which they had taken, amounting to $1,302.05, to the defendant's office in Sheffield, and presented them for payment; that "the amount was paid to him by defendant, acting through A. H. Moses, the vice-president and general manager, or by some one acting for defendant in his presence;" and that the tickets on which this action was founded were taken by plaintiffs afterwards, before they heard that Moses objected to their taking them. J. Nathan was then introduced as a witness by plaintiffs, and testified that he was acting as paymaster for the defendant at the time of said payment on May 20th, 1884, "and that on the day he made said payment he told one J. T. Cooper, a clerk and bookkeeper of plaintiff, that no more of said tickets would be paid by defendant except to the laborers themselves." Said Duncan was then recalled by plaintiffs, "and testified that he was present when the payment alluded to by Nathan was

made, and that he heard no such conversation as that made
by said Nathan."

This was all the evidence introduced by plaintiffs, and defendants introduced none.   The court thereupon charged the
jury, on request, that they must find for the defendant, if
they believed the evidence.   The plaintiffs excepted to this
charge, and they here assign it as error.

J. B. MOORE, and JAMES JACKSON, for appellants.—Gordon was the president and general manager of the defendant corporation, and the plaintiffs were justified in presum-
ing that he had the right to bind it by his contracts and
engagements in his name—Mor. Corp. §§ 538,616; *Gold
Life Ins. Co. v. A. & M. Asso.*, 54 Ala. 73; *Oxford Ins. Co.
v. Spradley*, 46 Ala. 98; Angell & Ames on Corporations,
198; *Railway Co. v. McCarthy*, 96 U. S. 258.   Even if
Gordon had no authority to make such contract, yet his
promise or contract might be ratified by the corporation; and
the payment made on May 20th, 1884, was a ratification of
it.—*McKenzie v. Stevens*, 19 Ala. 691; *Taylor v. A. & M.
Asso.*, 68 Ala. 238; 2 Waterman on Corporations, 370; 96 U. S.
258.   The general charge of the court was erroneous.
67 Ala. 13; 70 Ala. 499; 73 Ala. 295.

EMMET O'NEAL, and WATTS and SON, *contra*, cited *Stanley v. Sheffield Land, Iron & Coal Co.*, 83 Ala. 262; and
Tabler, Crudup & Co. v. Sheffield Land, Iron and Coal Co.,
79 Ala. 377.

STONE, C. J.—This is the second time the present case
has been before this court on appeal.   When here before,
the appeal was prosecuted from the rulings of the lower
court upon the pleadings; and this court held, that the plaintiffs, who are appellants in both appeals, could not maintain
their action as transferrees of the "labor-tickets."—*Tabler,
Crudup & Co. v. Sheffield Land, Iron & Coal Co.*, 79 Ala.
377.   Upon remandment of the cause, the special counts of
the complaint, in which plaintiffs claimed a recovery as
transferrees of the "labor-tickets," were abandoned, and issue was joined on the common counts.

The right of the plaintiffs to recover in this action can be
maintained only upon the theory, that they took up the
"labor-tickets"—the basis of the suit—at the instance or request of the defendant corporation, acting through some

lawfully authorized agent or agents; or, if upon agreement with some officer or agent not duly authorized to bind the company thereby, that the defendant corporation subsequently ratified the agreement.—*Stanley v. S. L., I. & C. Co.*, 83 Ala. 260.

There was much testimony introduced by the plaintiffs, tending to show that they became the purchasers of the said "labor-tickets," giving in exchange therefor "supplies, and medicines, or money," under a special arrangement and agreement with the president, who was also general manager, and with a special agent of the defendant, that the corporation would take up the said "labor-tickets," for their full value, upon presentation by the plaintiffs. There was also evidence on the part of the plaintiffs, tending to show that upon presentation of a number of such tickets, the defendant paid the plaintiffs the full amount represented by them. There was no conflict in this evidence. One witness for plaintiff, however, testified that "on the day he made such payment to plaintiffs, he told one J. T. Cooper, a book-keeper and clerk of plaintiffs, that no more of said tickets would be paid by defendant, except to the laborers themselves;" while Duncan, one of the plaintiffs, testified that on the day of the payment he was present, and "heard no such conversation" as that testified to by the witness. This constitutes a conflict in the testimony, which will not authorize the general charge. To support the general charge, the evidence must be so clear and convincing as that the court could rightly sustain a demurrer to the evidence of the opposite party. If the evidence be in conflict, or if it be circumstantial, or if a material fact in the case rests in inference, the general charge should not be given. The Circuit Court erred in giving the charge requested by the defendant.—*Ala. Gold Life Ins. Co. v. Mobile Mut. Ins. Co.*, 81 Ala. 329; *Seals v. Edmondson*, 73 Ala. 295; *S. & N. Ala. R. R. Co. v. Small*, 70 Ala. 499; *Smoot v. M. & M. Railway Co.*, 67 Ala. 13.

There was no error in the court excluding that part of the testimony of the witness Duncan relating to an alleged conversation had between him and one Walter Gordon, who was at the time president and general manager of the defendant corporation, but was shown to be deceased when the trial was had. It was evidence of one interested in the result of the suit, and related to an agreement or conversation alleged to have been engaged in by one who, at the time, occupied a

[Tabler, Crudup & Co. v. Sheffield Land, Iron & Coal Co.]

fiduciary relation to the defendant. The statute is very plain in this respect; and the adjudications thereon render further comment unnecessary, to give a clearer understanding of its meaning.—Code, 1886, § 2765, and citations; *Miller v. Cannon*, 84 Ala. 59; *Stanley v. S. L., I. & Co.*, 83 Ala. 260; *Warten v. Stranc*, 82 Ala. 311.

The payment, testified to have been made by the defendant to the plaintiffs on the 20th of May, 1884, was after the alleged agreement entered into with plaintiffs. If, after said agreement, the defendant made such payment, with a full knowledge of all the facts and circumstances, it thereby ratified said agreement, and bound itself to meet all obligations arising therefrom. If the "labor-tickets" had once been paid without objection or disapproval by the corporation, the plaintiffs were justified in indulging the presumption, that all other tickets purchased by them would be also paid. Such ratification would bind the defendant corporation to pay the tickets bought by plaintiffs, until they were notified that no more of the tickets would be paid "except to the employees themselves."

By such payment, the defendant recognized and ratified the authority of its agent to bind it by the agreement with plaintiffs; and until notice was brought home to the plaintiffs that no more of the tickets would be paid by them, the obligation to pay would still rest with the defendant, and is sufficient to maintain an action against the corporation. The principle is the same as when a father, without objection, pays an account contracted by his minor son; the payment is equivalent to a recognition by the father of the son's authority to bind him, and will render him liable on a similar account subsequently contracted.—2 Greenl. Ev. (14th Ed), §§ 65–66; Story on Agency, § 56; 1 Pars. on Contr., §§ 50–51; Ewell's Evans on Agency, p. 66; 2 Waterman on Law of Corp., 370; 2 Morawetz on Corp., §§ 604, 630–632; *Taylor v. A. & M. Asso.*, 68 Ala. 229; *Talladega Ins. Co. v. Landers*, 43 Ala. 136; *Stone v. Britton*, 22 Ala. 542; *McKenzie v. Stevens*, 19 Ala. 691; *Whitney Arms Co. v. Barlow*, 63 N. Y. 62; *Railway Co. v. McCarthy*, 96 U. S. 258; *Hurd v. Green*, 17 Hun, 327; *Howe v. Keeler*, 57 Conn. 538.

The judgment is reversed, and the cause remanded.

CLOPTON, J., not sitting.

[Insurance Companies v. Raden.]

Insurance Companies (Niagara Fire, and Hamburg-Bremen) *v.* Raden.

Bill in Equity to reinstate Cancelled Policies of Insurance.

1. *Cancellation of policy; authority of agent.*—An agency to procure insurance is ended when the policy is procured and delivered to the principal; and the agent has no power afterwards to consent to a cancellation, or to accept notice of an intended cancellation by the insurer.

2. *Same; dual agency*—An express stipulation in the policy authorizing the company to terminate it at any time on giving notice to that effect to the assured, "or to the person who may have procured the insurance to be taken," can not be applied to a case where the same person acted as agent for both parties in procuring and issuing the policy, and notice of the intended cancellation was not given to the assured in person.

3. *Ratification of cancellation.*—A ratification of the cancellation of a policy, which was procured for the insured by an agent of the insurance company, will not be presumed from his acceptance, after a loss, of a policy in another company, which was procured by the same agent, when it is not shown that the assured was fully informed of all the facts connected with the supposed cancellation and substitution, and of his legal rights as determined by those facts; nor will it be presumed from the institution of a suit on the substituted policy, which was induced by the misrepresentation of the agent to the attorneys of the assured.

APPEAL from the City Court of Birmingham, in equity. Heard before the Hon. H. A. SHARPE.

HEWITT, WALKER & PORTER, for appellants.—The policies here sought to be reinstated were procured for complainant by Smith, on his cancellation of her original policy in the London, Liverpool & Globe Insurance, which was procured through the agency of Flanagan & Langley, and which was cancelled by Smith in obedience to orders from said company; and these policies were afterwards (but before a loss) cancelled by him, as per instructions from the companies, and other policies substituted in their stead. There is no question that all this was done in good faith. On the day after the fire, the substituted policies was delivered by Smith to the complainant, and were accepted by her after consultation with one or two friends; and suits on these substituted policies are now pending. These facts show a ratification by complainant of the acts of Smith as her agent, and estop her from now denying his authority.—*Clealand v. Walker*, 11 Ala. 1058; *Stark v. Sikes*, 69 Amer. Dec. 270; *Persons v. McKibben*, 5 Ind. 261; *Blevins v. Pope*, 7 Ala. 371; *Wood v. McCain*, 7 Ala. 800; *Reynolds v. Dothard*, 11 Ala. 531; Story on Agency, § 244; *Dearing v. Lightfoot*, 16 Ala. 28; *Jones v. Atkinson*, 72 Ala. 248; 2 M. & S. 485; *Routh v. Thompson*, 13 East, 279; 1 Phil. Insurance, 519; 2 *Ib.* 337, 369; 4 Moore, 8; 5 Metc. 192; 72 N. Y. 385; 36 Mich. 502.

WEBB & TILLMAN, and MCINTOSH & ALTMAN, *contra.* (1.) The policies sought to be reinstated were never legally cancelled.—*Insurance Co. v. Forcheimer & Co.*, at present term, 86 Ala. 541; *Herman v. Insurance Co.*, 100 N. Y. 411; 109 U. S. 278; 23 Fed. Rep. 709; 17 Fed. Rep. 630; 115 Mass. 241; May on Insurance, § 574. (2.) The attempted cancellation was never ratified, because the complainant was never informed of the facts, nor of her legal rights as governed by the facts.

SOMERVILLE, J.—The bill is filed by the appellee, Mrs. Raden, to restore or reinstate two policies of fire insurance alleged to have been cancelled by fraud, or mistake of fact, and to re-establish these instruments as evidences of the liability of the defendant companies by which they were issued, and to incidentally enforce them by the rendition of moneyed decrees for the amount of the loss by fire, not exceeding the amount of the policies, which were each for the sum of $1,250. The court below granted the full relief prayed in the bill, holding both of the policies to be of binding force.

A demurrer was filed to the bill, but no assignment of error is based on the action of the court in overruling it. Objection to this ruling is expressly waived, and the only question presented by the record is, whether the insurers—the Niagara Fire Insurance Company, and the Hamburg-Bremen Insurance Company—one or both, are liable on these policies, under the facts disclosed by the evidence.

The complainant's property in Bessemer is shown to have been destroyed by fire on the night of July 19th, 1887; and no controversy is raised as to its value, or the amount of the loss. The property was originally insured in the Liverpool, London & Globe Insurance Company, on July 2d, 1887, for $2,500; but this policy was cancelled, and the two policies

here in controversy were substituted in its place, by consent
of the insured, a week or ten days after this cancellation.

The defense to the present suit is, that each of the policies in controversy was cancelled on July 18th, 1887—the
day before the occurrence of the loss. This is alleged to
have been effected by giving notice of such cancellation to
one Langley, who is claimed to have been the agent of Mrs.
Raden, the insured, and to him was paid the return premium.
It is not denied that cancellation was effected, if Langley
was the agent of the insured for the purpose of receiving
the notice and the return premium. The whole question of
cancellation hinges on this one fact.

One John G. Smith was the agent of the defendant companies at Birmingham, Alabama. He was also agent for the
Liverpool, London & Globe Insurance Company, in which the
first policy was obtained. Flanagan & Langley were insurance agents at Bessemer, Alabama, their exact relations
towards Smith not being made very clear by the testimony.
The testimony is very conflicting on the point as to whether
they acted as agents of Smith, or of Mrs. Raden, or merely
as insurance brokers in procuring the first policy, as to the
cancellation of which no controversy exists. Flanagan says
they acted for Smith, and Smith asserts they acted for Mrs.
Raden. This Mrs. Raden denies. Langley says they acted
as insurance brokers, dividing commissions with Smith. It
is quite clear to us, that Langley, as he himself testifies,
solicited the insurance of Mrs. Raden; that she was induced
to make a written application for the first policy, and that it
was countersigned by Flanagan & Langley, as agents of the
Liverpool, London & Globe Company, and was transmitted
by them to Smith, at Birmingham. This document appears
in the record as an exhibit to Langley's deposition, and is
more trustworthy than the less certain memory of witnesses.

All of this testimony relates, as we have said, to the first
policy, admitted to be cancelled. We do not deem it necessary to discuss this part of the evidence at length, as it does
not seem to be of controlling importance. The question is,
who procured the issue of the policies here in controversy?
Did Langley, or his firm, do so as the agents of Mrs. Raden?
If not, the notice to Langley, and the payment of the return
premium to him, did not operate to cancel these policies, or
rescind the contract of insurance evidenced by them.

We are satisfied from the testimony that Smith, and not
Langley, procured these policies to be issued. There is

scarcely enough conflict in the evidence to raise any serious controversy on this point. Smith was himself the authorized agent of these defendant companies at Birmingham. Flanagan & Langley had no connection with them. When ordered to cancel the Liverpool, London & Globe policy, he at once volunteered to substitute for the cancelled policy the two policies in controversy, which he transmitted to Mrs. Raden through Flanagan & Langley for delivery; and this seems to be all the latter firm had to do with the matter. Smith, it is true, insists on the fact of this firm's agency for the insured, and testifies that they were her agents; but the facts stated by him refute the existence of the alleged agency. He says: "After the cancellation [of the Liverpool, London & Globe policy], Mrs. Raden's property was insured in other companies *by me*, and the policy in the Liverpool, London & Globe was surrendered by me to Flanagan & Langley. In order to secure her from loss, *I* insured her property in other companies." And again, on cross-examination: "When the Liverpool, London & Globe Insurance Company policy was cancelled, I issued the policies in the defendant companies, without the knowledge of Mrs. Raden, or her agents, Flanagan & Langley."

As to the policy of one of the defendants—the Hamburg-Bremen Insurance Company—we need say but little. Even if it were admitted that Langley had procured this policy to be issued, or if it be assumed that Smith did so, the agency ceased when the policy was delivered to the insured. We have decided at the present term, that "an agency to procure insurance is ended when the policy is procured, and the policy delivered to the principal; and the agent employed to procure the insurance has no power, after the policy is so delivered, to consent to cancellation."—*Ins. Co. of North America v. Forcheimer & Co.*, 86 Ala. 541. This doctrine is fully supported by the adjudged cases. *Herman v. The Niagara Fire Ins. Co.*, 100 N. Y. 411; 1 Wood on Fire Ins. (2d Ed.), 337, § 142. Notice of cancellation to Langley, therefore, with his consent to rescission, was no notice to, or consent by Mrs. Raden.—*Grace v. American Cent. Ins. Co.*, 109 U. S. 278; May on Insurance, (2d Ed.), § 138.

As to the policy of the other defendent—the Niagara Fire Insurance Company—a slightly different view must be taken, because of the following provision relating to the cancellation of policies: "This insurance may be terminated at any time, by request of the assured, or by the company on giving notice to that effect to the assured, or to the *person who may have procured this insurance* to be taken.ˑ On surrender of the policy, the company shall refund any premium that may have been paid, reserving the usual short rates in the first case, and *pro rata* rates in the other case."

This policy, as we have shown, was obtained for Mrs. Raden by Smith, not by Langley. Smith was the person who procured it to be taken, within the meaning of the policy. Now, Smith was the agent of the company to issue the policy. He therefore occupied an ambiguous attitude, or a double agency, involving conflicting rights and duties. The provision above cited was not intended to cover a case of this character. It could not have been contemplated that the agent of the company should give notice to himself, as agent also of the insured, of the cancellation, or rescission of the contract of insurance, nor that he should pay to himself the return premium required to be paid under the terms of the contract, without which payment there could be no cancellation. If susceptible of this construction, the provision would be invalid as in violation of all sound principles of public policy, and we would so declare it. The law will not permit an agent thus to serve two masters with conflicting interests.—*Commercial Fire Ins. Co. v. Allen*, 80 Ala. 571, and cases cited on p. 576; *Piedmont & A. Ins. Co. v. Young*, 58 Ala. 476; 2 Wood on Fire Ins. (2d Ed.), 833 *et seq.*, §409; *Kausal v. Minnesota &c. Association*, 47 Amer. Rep. 776.

Under these principles, Mrs. Raden had no notice of the cancellation until the loss by fire had occurred, and the liability for such loss had been fastened on the insurers. Nor was the return premium paid back to her before such loss, the payment to Langley being no payment to her.

We come next to the question of ratification. It is contended that Mrs. Raden ratified the alleged cancellation, in two ways: *first*, by accepting two other policies of insurance —one in the Mobile Fire Insurance Company, and the other in the St. Paul Fire and Marine Insurance Company—which were substituted by Smith for the policies in controversy, covering the same property, and for like amounts; and, *secondly*, by having brought suit on these substituted policies, before filing the present bill. And it is said that all this was done by Mrs. Raden with a full knowledge of the facts of the case on her part.

These policies were not delivered to Mrs. Raden until after her property was destroyed by fire, and her right to indemnity for the loss had accrued, although they had been taken out by Smith, without her knowledge, before the fire. Smith, again, in this matter acted as agent for Mrs. Raden. He was an insurance agent, shown to be intelligent, and presumably an expert in matters pertaining to this subject. She was a foreigner by birth, and evidently ignorant as to her legal rights, unless fully instructed as to them. Under this state of facts, Smith owed her peculiar duties before she can be declared by a court of equity to have voluntarily abandoned her claim under these policies against the defendants. He should not only have disclosed to her all the facts bearing on the case, known to him, but it should be shown to the court that she knew the transaction to be *impeachable* —that is, that she knew she had a legal right to refuse to accept the new policies, and to claim indemnity under those in controversy.— *Voltz v. Voltz*, 75 Ala. 567. The inference is fair, that Smith was aware of the fact that Mrs. Raden had a valid claim against the defendant companies, and it is clear that she was ignorant of this legal right. This misapprehension he should have rectified, and his failure to do so is a sufficient ground for equitable relief.—2 Pom. Eq. Jur. §847.

It is not shown, moreover, that Mrs. Raden knew, at the time of her alleged ratification, that Smith had procured the new policies upon the representation that no other insurance existed on the property—based, no doubt, on the idea that the policies in the defendant companies had been cancelled, which, as we have seen, was not true. Whether this would, or would not vitiate the new policies in the Mobile and St. Paul companies, we do not decide. We say only that the fact in question was one material in its bearings, and that a ratification made in ignorance of it, can not be held to be binding.

The suits at law brought on these policies by Mrs. Raden's attorneys are clearly shown to have been instituted under a mistake of fact. Smith led these attorneys to believe that Langley was the agent of their client, and that the notice of cancellation given, and the return premium paid to him, effected a rescission of the policies in the defendant companies—the Niagara Fire and the Hamburg-Bremen Insurance Companies. These suits can not, for this reason, operate as a ratification by Mrs. Raden of the acceptance of the new policies, and as an intentional abandonment of her vested rights under the policies in existence when the loss occurred.

Our judgment is, that the chancellor did not err in holding the policies here in controversy to be binding on the insurers, and that his decree granting the relief prayed is free from error, and must be affirmed.

Pritchett *v.* Jones.

Bill in Equity for Settlement of Assignment; Contest between Creditors.

1. *Fraudulent sale of goods by insolvent debtor; right of purchaser, on payment of judgment, to claim as creditor under deed of assignment.*—A sale of goods by an insolvent debtor having been held fraudulent at the instance of attaching creditors, on the trial of a statutory claim suit instituted by the purchaser, the payment of their judgments by him, which were less than the assessed value of the property, does not subrogate him to their rights as creditors under a deed of assignment executed by the debtor after the sale of the goods, nor give him any other rights as a creditor to participate in the assets in the hands of the assignee, although a part of said assets consists of money paid by him in cash on the purchase of the goods.

APPEAL from the Chancery Court of Wilcox.

Heard before the Hon. THOS. W. COLEMAN.

In the matter of the assignment by John W. McCaskey to Edward N. Jones, as trustee, for the benefit of the creditors of the late firm of McCaskey & Ratcliff, a petition was filed in the said court, on the 22d April, 1886, by the trustee, asking an order requiring creditors to file their claims, and for a partial distribution of the assets among them. Under the order requiring creditors to file their claims, a claim was filed by D. S. Pritchett, which was contested by the assignee and the other creditors, and was disallowed by the chancellor; and the order rejecting it is now assigned as error. The opinion states the facts connected with the claim.

J. N. MILLER, for the appellant, cited *Humes v. Scruggs*, 64 Ala. 40; *McLeod v. Powe*, 76 Ala. 418; Benjamin on Sales, § 490, note *r*.

JNO. Y. KILPATRICK, for the creditors, and JONES & JONES, for the assignee, cited *Shealy & Finn v. Edwards*, 75 Ala.

412; *Williams v. Higgins*, 69 Ala. 518; *Pickett v. Pipkin*, 64 Ala. 522; *Watts v. Nat. Bank*, 76 Ala. 475; Wait's A. & D., vol. 1, p. 80, §13; Ib. vol. 5, p. 216, §21.

CLOPTON, J.—On April 13, 1886, John M. McCaskey, a member of the mercantile firm of McCaskey & Ratcliff, made an assignment to E. N. Jones, for the benefit of the partnership creditors, a list of whose names was appended. On a petition filed by the assignee for a partial distribution, under the order of the Chancery Court, the chancellor directed the register to ascertain and report the creditors who were entitled to share in the distribution, and the amount and character of their respective claims. On the reference, appellant presented and filed claims, which originated under the following circumstances: Prior to the execution of the assignment, appellant purchased from the firm their stock of goods, and some notes and accounts, and paid for them in part with partnership indebtedness, in part with individual notes of the partners, and in part with cash. J. Pollock & Co. and M. P. Levy & Co., who were creditors of the partnership, and whose names were included in the list appended to the assignment, caused attachments to be sued out against McCaskey & Ratcliff, and levied on the goods; to which appellant interposed a claim under the statute. On trial of the right of property, the goods were found subject to the attachments, their value assessed by the jury, and judgment rendered condemning them to the satisfaction of the plaintiffs' demands. On appeal, the judgment in favor of Pollock & Co. was affirmed by this court, on the ground that the conveyance to appellant by McCaskey & Ratcliff was fraudulent as to the partnership creditors.—*Pritchett v. Pollock & Co.*, 82 Ala. 169. After the affirmance, the appellant paid the judgments rendered in the attachment suits, and also the costs of the trial of the right of property. The amounts thus paid constituted the claims presented by him to the register. A portion of the money paid by appellant to McCaskey, on the purchase of the goods, was included in the assignment. The question is, whether, on these facts, appellant is entitled to share with the other creditors in the distribution of the trust fund.

It will be observed that appellant did not file his original demands against the partnership. These seem to have been regarded as extinguished. His claims being founded on the payment of the judgments of the attaching creditors, their allowance depends on his equity to be subrogated to their right to participate in the distribution of the assigned fund. Subrogation is a mode adopted, in the administration of equity, to reimburse a party who has been compelled to pay a debt, or discharge a liability, which another was, either in law or in equity, primarily bound to pay or discharge, out of any fund to which the creditor could resort in the first instance. The object of the doctrine is, to enforce natural justice in favor of a person who occupies the situation of a surety or guarantor, whether he is nominally or actually such, or merely stands in a position which compels him to pay to protect his own interests. The payment of a debt without a previous request, or an obligation, or under circumstances from which a request may be implied, is insufficient; and if the debt, in contemplation of equity, is extinguished, there remains nothing on which to found the right of subrogation.

The doctrine, though most usually applied in cases of sureties or guarantors strictly, is of liberal and extensive application, and may be generally said to reach all cases in which, the essential conditions existing, its application is necessary to obtain the ends of justice. It is not without qualifications. Being purely of equitable creation, it is controlled by equitable principles and considerations. A material qualification is, that it will not be enforced if the effect is to defeat or prejudice the rights of third persons. The party seeking such relief, must show a superior equity; for the equities being equal, the law will be allowed to take its course.—*Knighton v. Curry*, 62 Ala. 404; *Sawyers v. Baker*, 72 Ala. 49; 2 Lead. Cas. Eq. 285-290; Brandt on Suretyship, § 265.

It is not contended that appellant was a surety, or in any manner bound for the debts of the attaching creditors, before the rendition of the judgments condemning the goods. On his failure to deliver the goods to the sheriff, within thirty days after the rendition of the judgments, and the return of his claim bond forfeited, executions could have been issued against him and his sureties for the amounts of the plaintiffs' judgments, they being less than the assessed value of the property.—Code, 1886, § 3008. Though the conveyance of the goods by McCaskey to appellant was valid as between the parties, being fraudulent, it was void as to the assailing creditors. The judgment of condemnation is conclusive on appellant, that the goods were, as to the creditors, the property of the attached debtors. It results, so far as the creditors are concerned, that the payment of the judgments in favor of the attaching creditors was payment under compulsion by the judgment of condemnation, and was, to all legal intents and purposes, the payment of a judgment against the appellant himself, with the funds of McCaskey & Ratcliff. At least, the payment of the judgments by appellant was without a previous request, or an obligation, or under circumstances from which a request could be implied, and the judgments were extinguished in law and in equity.

There are cases in which a fraudulent conveyance will be allowed to stand as security for the consideration actually paid. Of this class are conveyances constructively fraudulent, because of inadequacy of consideration, there being no actual fraud, nor participation on the part of the grantee in any fraudulent intent of the grantor.—*Caldwell v. King*, 76 Ala. 149. When a conveyance is founded in actual fraud, it will not be permitted to stand for the purpose of reimbursing or indemnifying the grantee. In such case, he is regarded as *particeps criminis*, and will not be allowed to assert, as against creditors, any right founded on such conveyance.—*Gordon v. Tweedy*, 71 Ala. 202. It has been held that a fraudulent purchaser of property can not be reimbursed for prior incumbrances discharged by him. *Wiley, Banks & Co. v. Knight*, 27 Ala. 336. In *Williamson v. Goodwyn*, 9 Gratt. 503, a fraudulent grantee of slaves, who had applied the proceeds of the sale of some of them to the payment of just debts of the grantor, claimed that she should be protected against the other creditors, to the extent of the price of the slaves so applied. It is said: "After the fraud is detected and brought to the light, the fraudulent vendee should not be allowed to compound the fraud by giving up a portion of the property, or its avails, and be exempt from liability for another portion, although that portion may have gone to pay *bona fide* debts." We are at a loss to conceive any sound or just principle on which a grantee can deduce any equity from a conveyance fraudulent in fact, which will be enforced to the prejudice of the creditors of the grantor. "He that hath committed iniquity, shall not have equity." The complicity of appellant in the fraud deprives him of any right or equity of subrogation.

Affirmed.

Tillman *v.* Thomas.

Bill in Equity by Heirs, to set aside Sale of Lands under Probate Decree on application of Administrator.

1. *Filing bill in double aspect.*—A bill filed in a double aspect, seeking to set aside a sale of lands under a probate decree, on the ground (1) that the proceedings are void on their face, or (2) that they are void for fraud in their procurement, is demurrable; but the objection must be taken by demurrer specially assigned.

2. *Demurrer; adequate legal remedy.*—A demurrer to a bill, on the ground that there is an adequate legal remedy, is properly overruled, when the legal remedy is adequate to only one of the two aspects in which the bill is filed.

3. *Sale of lands under probate decree; setting aside in equity on ground of fraud.*—A sale of lands under a probate decree, on the petition of the administratrix of the deceased owner, will be set aside in equity at the instance of the heirs, on averment and proof that it was procured by fraudulent collusion between the purchaser and the administratrix, in payment of her individual debt to him.

4. *Same; sub-purchaser with notice.*—A sub-purchaser from the original fraudulent purchaser, having knowledge of facts sufficient to put him on inquiry, is chargeable with notice of the fraud, and can not claim protection against the equity of the heirs.

APPEAL from the Chancery Court of Russell.

Heard before the Hon. JOHN A. FOSTER.

The bill in this case was filed on the 2d July, 1883, by Edward Thomas and John Thomas, children and heirs at law of John R. Thomas, deceased, against W. L. Tillman, B. R. Burts, Mrs. Rebecca P. Kennedy, and others; and sought to vacate and set aside a sale of certain lands, which had belonged to the decedent in his life-time, and were sold under a probate decree on the petition of the widow as administratrix. As the bill is copied in the transcript, L. D. Odom, who had married a daughter of the decedent, was joined as a complainant; but he was also made a defendant, and a decree *pro confesso* was entered against him; and it was alleged that his wife and only child were dead. John R. Thomas died in December, 1862, or January, 1863. Letters of administration on his estate were granted to his widow, Mrs. Rebecca P., who afterwards married W. L. Kennedy. She filed a petition in the Probate Court, in February, 1872, asking an order to sell the lands for the payment of debts. An order of sale was granted on 20th March, and the lands

21

were sold under it on April 15th, 1872. W. L. Tillman became the purchaser at the sale, and was so reported to the court, by which the sale was confirmed; and he afterwards sold and conveyed a part of the land to Burts. The complainants sought to set aside the sale, to cancel the several conveyances, and to recover the possession of the land, on the ground that the sale was procured by fraudulent collusion between Mrs. Kennedy and her husband and said Tillman, to whom they were indebted; and on the further ground that the proceedings were void on their face as against the complainants.

Separate answers were filed by Tillman and Burts, each insisting on the validity and conclusiveness of the probate decree; and each demurred to the bill, on the ground that the bill was barred by the statute of limitations, and that the complainants had an adequate remedy at law. Burts also claimed protection as a purchaser for valuable consideration without notice. The chancellor overruled the demurrer, and, on final hearing on pleadings and proof, rendered a decree for the complainants as prayed. Tillman and Burts appeal from this decree, and here assign it as error.

WATTS & SON, and J. B. MITCHELL, for appellants, cited *Watts v. Frazier*, 80 Ala. 186; *Lanford v. Dunklin*, 71 Ala. 594; *Farley v. Dunklin*, 76 Ala. 530; *Gordon v. Ross*, 63 Ala. 366; *Pettus v. McClanahan*, 52 Ala. 60; *Dugger v. Tayloe*, 60 Ala. 519; *Kellam v. Richards*, 56 Ala. 240; *Riggs v. Fuller*, 54 Ala. 148; *Strang v. Moog*, 72 Ala. 465; *Chardavoyne v. Lynch*, 82 Ala. 376.

HOOPER & WADDELL, *contra*.

McCLELLAN, J.—This is a bill by heirs, seeking to set aside and vacate the proceedings of the Probate Court, under which lands belonging to the estate of their ancestor were sold by his personal representative. As amended, the bill is presented in two aspects. In one, it is sought to vacate the order of sale and confirmation, on the ground of fraud in their rendition. In the other, the same result is attempted to be reached, on the ground that the probate proceedings are void on their face. A cause, if proper objection be interposed, can not thus be presented to a court of equity in a double aspect, unless the complainant is entitled to the same relief on each phase of his allegations.

[Tillman v. Thomas.]

That is not true in the case at bar. On the contrary, in that aspect in which the ground of relief is fraud, he would, if the averments are supported by the evidence, be entitled to a decree vacating the order of sale, and annulling all proceedings thereunder; while in that aspect in which the decree is alleged to be void on its face, he would be entitled to no relief in equity, but would be remitted to the law courts. *Florence v. Paschal*, 50 Ala. 28; *Tyson v. Brown*, 64 Ala. 244. If the latter allegation be not treated as merely redundant, it would seem that the bill presented two claims for relief, which ought not to have been joined. But the objection on that ground could only be taken by demurrer, and no demurrer going to this point was interposed.—*Seals v. Robinson*, 75 Ala. 363.

There was a general demurrer to the bill, as amended, on the ground that it disclosed that complainants had an adequate remedy at law. This objection was well taken to only one of the two aspects in which relief was prayed. Under the allegations that the proceedings sought to be vacated were void on their face, it was disclosed that an adequate remedy at law existed. But the complainants had no such remedy under their claim for relief on the ground of fraud. The rule is of general application, that where the bill sets forth two or more claims for relief in equity, and a general demurrer is filed by respondents, it should be overruled, and the relief granted, if any of the grounds upon which relief is sought are of equitable cognizance.—1 Dan. Ch. Pr. & Pl. 550; *Dimmock v. Bixby*, 20 Pick. 374; *Morton v. Grenada Acad.*, 8 Sm. & M. 773. In Alabama, this principle has been applied to a case very like the present one. A bill was filed to have a deed cancelled as a cloud on title. The allegations disclosed one state of facts on which the remedy was in chancery, and another on which the remedy was at law. There was a demurrer to the whole bill, on the ground that the complainant had an adequate legal remedy. The opinion of this court was, that "the bill contains two distinct independent grounds on which the claim for relief is based; and that, if either ground is sufficient, its force is not impaired by the fact that it is joined cumulatively with another alleged ground, which, of itself, will not maintain the equity of the bill;" and it was accordingly held, that the demurrer was properly overruled.—*Shipman v. Furniss*, 69 Ala. 563.

We concur with the chancellor's finding on the evidence,

that the order of the Probate Court for the sale of the lands, described in the bill, and all the proceedings in that behalf were procured to be made, had and done, by and through the fraudulent collusion of the defendants (appellants here), Tillman, W. L. Kennedy and Rebecca P. Kennedy, the latter being the administratrix of the estate. We are satisfied, also, that the purchase-money of the land was never intended to be paid, and was not in fact paid; and that neither the estate, nor the complainants, ever received any benefit from the sale of said lands. On these facts, there can be no doubt of the power of the Chancery Court to declare the orders of sale and confirmation void, and make all other decrees necessary to a complete rehabilitation of the title of the heirs, and to a full redress of the injuries they have suffered through the wrongful disseizin of their lands. It is one of the honorable boasts of our system of equity juprisprudence, that "the infection of fraud will be made to vitiate even the most solemn transactions, and adjudications of courts form no exception to the salutary rule.—Freeman on Judgments, § 449; *Eslava v. Eslava*, 50 Ala. 32; *Lee v. Lee*, 55 Ala. 590; *Humphreys v. Burleson*, 72 Ala. 1; *Dunklin v. Wilson*, 64 Ala. 162.

We also concur with the chancellor, that the evidence sufficiently shows the *mala fides* of the respondent Burt in his purchase of the lands from Tillman. It is in proof that he knew the lands belonged to the estate of Thomas, and so were being sold in a fiduciary capacity by Mrs. Kennedy. He admits that the uncle of the minor heirs, who was also a surety on the administration bond, had told him that whoever bought this land would buy a law-suit. He swears that he had reason to believe that Tillman bought the land in satisfaction of a mortgage he held on Kennedy and wife, and that he knew Tillman had furnished them supplies, and that Kennedy told him that the land was to be sold to reimburse him, Kennedy, moneys he had paid out for the estate. While it may be that no one of these facts would have been sufficient to put him on inquiry, yet all of them combined are adequate to that end. Holding him, as all men must be held, to know the law, he had notice that a trust estate was being sold to pay the individual indebtedness of the agent of the trustee to his vendor, and that objection was being made to this transaction by a near relative of the infant *cestuis que trust*, and in their behalf. This should have put him on inquiry.—*Pendleton v. Fay*, 2 Paige, 202; *Slanghill v. Ausley*, 1 DeG., M. & G. 635.

Had the inquiry been prosecuted, the legal presumption is, that the real facts would have been ascertained. Had he gone, for instance, to Mrs. Kennedy, who was the trustee thus converting the trust estate, the law presumes that she would have told him the whole truth, as she seems to have done in this case, and he would have been fully apprised of the infirmity of his vendor's title; and had he gone to the records of the Probate Court, which contained the evidence of one link in the title he was about to buy, he would have found, indeed, that the proceedings were not void on their face; but at the same time, and as a part of the same record, he would have found the most solemn asseverations, on the part of the heirs and the sureties of the administratrix, of fraud and crime in the administration of the trust property. Equity will hold him to a knowledge of all the facts that these inquiries would have disclosed to him; to a knowledge in this case of no more or no less than that the title of his vendor was the issue of fraud and collusion, and was void.

The decree of the chancellor is, therefore, affirmed.

Harmon *v.* Goetter, Weil & Co.

Statutory Detinue by Seller against Sub-Purchaser of Goods.

1. *Sale of goods; when title passes.*—A sale of goods, on the condition that the price is to be paid on receipt of an invoice, is a sale for cash; and no title passes to the purchaser until the price is paid.

2. *Evidence as to delivery and reception of invoice.*—Where the seller seeks to recover the goods from a sub-purchaser, the price being payable on delivery of an invoice, it is competent for the plaintiff to prove the sending and the reception of the invoice, as showing performance on his part, and that the purchase-money was due.

3. *Evidence as to value of goods.*—The goods sued for by the seller, the price never having been paid (as stipulated) on delivery of an invoice, being part of a stock of goods afterwards sold by the purchaser to the defendant, the validity of that sale is not involved in the issue; and evidence as to the value of the stock of goods, or offers to sell them, which might be admissible if the sale were attacked for fraud, is not relevant or competent.

4. *Evidence tending to prove possession; admission implied from silence.* Where the defendant in detinue denies his possession of the goods sued for, alleging that they were in the possession of the sheriff at the commencement of the suit, the plaintiff may prove, by a witness who was present, that the sheriff said, in the presence of the defendant, that he had not then made a levy under the other writs, and that the defendant said nothing.

APPEAL from the Circuit Court of Pike.

Tried before the Hon. JOHN P. HUBBARD.

This action was brought by Goetter, Weil & Co., suing as partners, againt John F. Harmon, to recover certain goods which plaintiffs had sold to Harmon Brothers, with damages for their detention; and was commenced on the 7th January, 1887. The transcript contains what purports to be a bill of exceptions, but it is not signed by the presiding judge, and the record shows no agreement or admission supplying the defect. It is shown by this bill that one of the plaintiffs testified, on the trial, that the goods sued for were sold by plaintiffs to Harmon Brothers on the 28th December, 1886; that they "refused to sell on time, and said they must have cash; that it was then agreed that they would ship the goods, and that Harmon Brothers would remit the price on receipt of the invoice, which was to be sent by mail; and that said goods were shipped the same day." The witness testified, also, that the invoice was forwarded by mail on the same day, and that he afterwards saw it in the possession of said Harmon Brothers; and this evidence was admitted by the court, against the objection and exception of the defendant.

Goldman, a witness for plaintiffs, "testified, that he was present when the sheriff took possession of the goods sued for; that he went to the sheriff, who told him that he had not levied on these goods, the defendant being present at the time, and making no reply, and the sheriff having the attachment writ. The defendant moved to exclude said declarations of the sheriff, and excepted to the overruling of his motion." Said Goldman testified, also, "that he went with the sheriff to the store where the goods were; that two persons were inside of the store, with the defendant, one of whom unlocked the door; that he demanded the goods of the defendant, who replied, that they were in the possession of the sheriff," and, after consultation with his attorney, declined to point them out. The testimony of the defendant tended to show that, at the time the suit was commenced, certain creditors of Harmon Brothers had sued out attachments against them, the sheriff had taken possession of said goods, and had the keys of the store in which they were, and was proceeding to take an inventory of said goods for the purpose of levying on such portions thereof as might be necessary to satisfy said attachments; that he replied to Goldman's demand for the goods, that they were in the possession of the

[Harmon v. Goetter, Weil & Co.]

sheriff, and to his request to point out the goods, that he had been advised by his attorney not to do so."

The defendant claimed the goods under a purchase from Harmon Brothers, on the 2d or 3d January, 1887, of their entire stock of goods, in payment of an antecedent indebtedness of about $5,000; and he adduced testimony tending to show that the goods sued for, with the rest of the stock, was delivered to him immediately after his purchase; "that he knew nothing of the time and manner of the purchase of said goods;" and that the value of the entire stock of goods, at first cost, was about $4,500. "Defendant proposed to testify, in his own behalf, that when he bought said stock of goods, he offered them for sale to the merchants of Union Springs, before any attachments were sued out against Harmon Brothers, or there had been any interference with them in any way, and that he could not get an offer of more than 65 cents on the dollar of first cost." The court excluded this evidence, on objection by the plaintiffs, and the defendant excepted.

These rulings on the evidence, with other matters, are now assigned as error.

GARDNER & WILEY, for appellant.

FLEMING LAW, *contra.*

STONE, C. J.—This action counts in detinue; being brought by the appellees against the appellant, for the recovery in specie of certain described articles of merchandise.

1. The goods were sold to the vendors of the defendant by the plaintiffs, upon the condition that the price therefor was to be paid upon the receipt of an invoice of the goods. This rendered the transaction between the plaintiffs in this action and the sellers of the defendant, a sale for cash. Until the fulfillment of the condition—the payment of the price of the goods—the sale was not completed, and the title to the goods remained in the plaintiffs. The payment of the purchase-money was a condition precedent to a consummation of the trade; and until such payment, the title to the goods never passed out of the seller, and no right of possession accrued to the buyer. Harmon Brothers, the vendees of the plaintiffs and the vendors of the defendant, totally failed to comply with the condition of the sale.

Hence the title to the goods, and the right of possession, never passed out of the plaintiffs, which gave them a right of action for the recovery of the goods.—*Sumner v. Woods,* 67 Ala. 139; *Holman v. Lock,* 51 Ala. 281; *McCall v. Powell,* 64 Ala. 254; *Jones v. Pullen,* 66 Ala. 306; *Fairbanks v. Eureka Co.,* 67 Ala. 109; *Shines v. Steiner,* 76 Ala. 258; 1 Benj. on Sales, § 425.

2. There was no error in the admission of evidence relating to the sending and receiving of the invoice. As the receipt of the invoice was the time when the purchase-price fell due, it was competent to prove the sending and the reception of the invoice, in order to show that the sellers had performed their part of the contract, and that the purchase-money was due.

3. The evidence of the defendant, tending to show his attempt to sell the goods to other merchants in Union Springs, and that he was only offered a certain price for them, was irrelevant to the issues involved, and therefore incompetent. The sale of the goods from Harmon Brothers to J. F. Harmon, the defendant, was not attacked for fraud. The *bona fides* of the transfer to the defendant not being assailed, this evidence was wholly irrelevant.—1 Greenl. Ev. (14th Ed.), § 49, note.

4. The testimony of the witness Goldman, as to the declaration of the sheriff, was competent evidence, as tending to prove an admission, implied from silence, on the part of the defendant, that the goods were still in his possession. The defendant's motion to exclude this evidence from the jury was properly overruled.

There was no error in the court giving and refusing the charges set out in the record.

The judgment is affirmed.

Woodward Iron Co. *v.* Cabaniss.

Application for Prohibition, or Mandamus, to Probate Judge, in matter of Statutory Proceedings for Condemnation of Right of Way by Railroad Corporation.

1. *Trial by jury, under constitutional provisions.*—A lawful jury, as the term is used in constitutional provisions, means a jury of twelve

men, according to the principles of the common law; and a jury consisting of a less number, under statutory provisions, is not a lawful jury, unless an appeal is given to a higher court, where a jury of twelve men may be impanelled on demand.

2. *Statutory proceedings for condemnation of right of way; appeal, and trial by jury.*—Under statutory provisions authorizing the condemnation of a right of way by railroad corporations (Code, § 3210; Sess. Acts 1888-9, p. 112), the jury of appraisers may consist of only six men, and no appeal is given to a court of which a trial by jury is a constituent part; yet, under the general statute regulating appeals from the Probate Court (Code, § 3640), construed in connection with the constitutional provision which secures an appeal from "any preliminary assessment of damages," and gives a right of trial by jury, "as to the amount of damages, in all cases of appeal," an appeal lies from the Probate to the Circuit Court, and a jury of twelve men may be there impanelled to assess the damages.

3. *Same; when prohibition or mandamus lies.*—Since an appeal lies from the Probate Court to the Circuit Court, in the matter of proceedings for the condemnation of a right of way at the suit of a railroad company, a writ of prohibition or *mandamus* from the Circuit Court will not be awarded to prevent further proceedings.

APPEAL from the Circuit Court of Jefferson.

Heard before the Hon. JAMES B. HEAD.

In the matter of the petition of the Woodward Iron Company, a private corporation, addressed to the presiding judge of said circuit, for a writ of prohibition, *mandamus*, or other appropriate process, directed to Hon. E. H. CABANISS, presiding as special judge of probate in and for said county of Jefferson, "restraining and prohibiting him from further proceedings" in the matter of a petition filed by the Birmingham, Powderly & Bessemer Street Railroad Company, another corporation organized under the general statutes, by which the latter corporation attempted to condemn and acquire a right of way over and through the lands of the petitioner. The circuit judge sustained a demurrer to the petition, and dismissed it; and his judgment is here assigned as error.

WEBB & TILLMAN, for appellant.

CHAS. B. POWELL, *contra.*

SOMERVILLE, J.—The application is for a writ of prohibition, *mandamus*, or other appropriate writ, directed to the appellee, sitting as special judge for the trial of an *ad quod damnum* proceeding pending in the Probate Court of Jefferson county, and seeking to restrain him from further proceeding in the cause.

The ground upon which the petition rests is the alleged

unconstitutionality of the present statute providing for the condemnation of lands for public uses.—Code of 1886, §§ 3207-3220. The particular objection urged is, that the statute fails to provide for the right of trial by jury, on appeal from the preliminary assessment of damages made by the award of viewers, or commissioners; and that for this reason it offends section 7 of Article XIV of the Constitution. This section, after providing that all corporations and individuals, invested with the right of eminent domain, shall first make just compensation for the property taken, injured or destroyed by the construction or enlargement of their works, highways, or improvements, declares: "The General Assembly is hereby prohibited from depriving any person of an appeal from any preliminary assessment of damages against any such corporations or individuals, made by viewers or otherwise; and *the amount of such damages, in all cases of appeal, shall, on demand of either party, be determined by a jury according to law.*"—Const., 1875, Art. XIV, sec. 7.

We concede, for the sake of argument, that the remedy here invoked would be appropriate, if this contention is correct. We are inclined, also, to the view of appellants' counsel, that section 3210 of the present Code, as amended by the act approved February 28th, 1889 (Acts 1888-89, p. 112), contemplates nothing more than a preliminary assessment, and not a final trial by a lawful jury. That section, as amended, authorizes a jury of as few as six jurors. A lawful jury, within the meaning of the Constitution, means a jury of twelve men, according to the usages of the common law. We shall also consider this contention well taken.

In this aspect of the case, we hold that the right of appeal to the Circuit Court was secured to the appellant, by section 3640 of the present Code. And on the authority of *Montgomery So. Railway Co. v. Sayre*, 72 Ala. 443, the constitutional provision invoked was so far self-executing as to entitle the appellant to demand a trial by jury in that court, to determine the amount of damages assessed. The statutes construed in that case, giving the right of appeal, do not essentially differ from those embodied in the present Code; and while the correctness of the decision is not entirely free from doubt, the court is unanimous in the opinion that it should be followed, and it is conclusive of the present case.

The petition was properly dismissed, and the judgment is affirmed.

Moritz & Weil *v.* Miller, Schram & Co.

Creditor's Bill in Equity, to set aside Fraudulent Conveyance.

1. *Receiver; appointment without notice.*—A receiver should not be appointed without notice, on the filing of a bill by a simple-contract creditor to set aside, on the ground of fraud, a transfer by an insolvent debtor of all his outstanding notes and accounts, when the bill merely alleges, on information and belief, that the transferrees are rapidly collecting the notes and accounts, and placing them beyond the reach of creditors, but does not allege that they are insolvent, or unable to respond to any decree which might be rendered against them; and the accompanying affidavit only states that, in the belief of the affiant, based on information, to give notice of the application would cause delay, which would probably defeat the receiver, and prevent him from taking possession and recovering the notes and accounts; it further appearing that all the defendants reside in the city in which the bill was filed.

APPEAL from the City Court of Montgomery, in equity.
Heard before the Hon. THOS. M. ARRINGTON.

The appeal in this case is sued out from an order for the appointment of a receiver, under a bill filed by Miller, Schram & Co., as simple-contract creditors of Moritz & Weil, against their said debtors and others, seeking to set aside as fraudulent a transfer of their outstanding notes and accounts by said Moritz & Weil.

TOMPKINS & TROY, for appellants, cited High on Receivers, §§ 111-13; *Briarfield Iron Works v. Foster*, 54 Ala. 622.

RICE & WILEY, *contra.*

CLOPTON, J.—As receivers are ordinarily appointed without requiring of the applicant bond indemnifying the other party against damages which may be caused by a wrongful appointment, the utmost care and circumspection should be observed in administering this extraordinary remedy. The court should ever be reluctant to summarily take property from the possession of a defendant claiming right or title thereto, and putting it into the control and management of an appointee of the court, without affording the claimant and possessor opportunity to be heard in

opposition.   When the most provident care is used, it not
infrequently happens that great injustice, and sometimes
irreparable injury, is occasioned.   In view of these probable
evils, and for the purpose of avoiding, as far as practicable,
an improper and injudicious exercise of this jurisdiction, the
statute provides: "Receivers may be appointed by the
chancellor in term time or vacation, and by the register in
vacation, upon application in writing; and when the application is made in vacation, reasonable notice of the time of
such application, and the person to whom it will be submitted, must be given, or a good reason shown to the chancellor or register for the failure to give the same."—Code,
1886, § 3534.

   The complainants, who are simple-contract creditors of the
firm of Moritz & Weil, seek by the bill to set aside a transfer
of their books, notes, accounts and other *choses* in action,
to the other defendants, on the alleged ground, that the
transfer was made upon a simulated and fictitious consideration, with intent to hinder, delay or defraud complainants
and the other creditors of the firm.   The equity of the bill
may be conceded.   The question on this appeal is not,
solely, whether the bill makes a *prima facie* case for the
appointment of a receiver—a case in which it does not seem
reasonable that the assets should be left in the possession of
the defendants pending the litigation.   A decision as to the
propriety and necessity of appointing a receiver would be
premature, in advance of a showing by defendants against
it, or an opportunity to make such a showing.   The receiver
being appointed without notice, and before service of process, the material question is, whether a good reason is
shown for the failure to give notice.

   By the established practice, independent of statute, courts
of equity, being averse to interference *ex parte*, will
entertain, in ordinary cases, an application for the appointment of a receiver, only after notice, or rule to show cause.
The exceptional cases are, when the defendant is beyond
the jurisdiction of the court, or can not be found, or when
some urgent emergency is shown rendering interference,
before there is time to give notice, necessary to prevent
waste, destruction or loss; or when notice itself will jeopard-
ize the delivery of the property, over which the receivership
is extended, in obedience to the order of the court.   The
statute being silent as to what will constitute a good reason,
precedents and adjudged cases under the general practice, in

the absence of statutory regulations, will afford a sufficient
guide. The bill alleges that the defendants, to whom the
books, notes and accounts were transferred, are rapidly collecting the indebtedness, and placing the money beyond the
reach of the creditors. If, in connection with this averment,
the insolvency of these defendants, or their inability to
respond to any decree which may be rendered against them
if the transfer be declared fraudulent, had been alleged, it
may be that a good reason would have appeared for the failure to give notice.—*Sims v. Adams*, 78 Ala. 395; *Ashurst
v. Lehman*, 86 Ala. 370; 5 So. Rep. 731; *Micou v. Moses*,
72 Ala. 439. But the bill contains no such allegation; and
the averment made is verified on information and belief,
without stating the source of the information, its character,
or when obtained. The reason for failure to give notice,
deducible from the mere allegations of the bill, is a mere
suspicion, opinion or belief, that defendants may spirit away
the effects, and place them beyond the power of the court to
compel their delivery.

The only other reason is found in the affidavit of one of
the complainants, made for the appointment of the receiver,
which states, upon information and belief, that to give notice
of the application for a receiver would cause delay, which
would probably defeat the receiver, and prevent him from
taking possession of, and preserving the books, accounts and
choses in action. In *Verplanck v. Mercantile Ins. Co.*,
2 Paige, 438, Chancellor Walworth says: "In every case,
when the court is asked to deprive the defendant of the
possession of his property without a hearing, or an opportunity to oppose the application, the particular facts and circumstances, which render such a summary proceeding
proper, should be set forth in the bill or petition on which
such application is founded. Oglevie's affidavit in this case,
that he was satisfied of the necessity of such a proceeding,
was not sufficient. He should have stated the facts on which
his opinion was founded, to enable the court to judge of its
correctness." This ruling was approved and followed in
French v. Gifford, 30 Iowa, 148. The affidavit in the
present case is not as strong as those in the cases cited. It
merely states, that in the belief of the witness, based on
information, notice of application would *probably* defeat the
receiver. He should have stated the facts, of which he had
been informed, on which he founded his belief. The receiver
was appointed on the same day on which the bill was filed,

and process was not served until next day. It appears from
the bill that all the defendants reside in the city of Montgomery, where the order was made. They could have been
speedily served with notice, without causing any unusual or
probable injurious delay.

On the foregoing principles, we are forced to the conclusion, that the allegations of the bill, and the affidavit for the
appointment of a receiver, do not justify such appointment
without notice. To hold otherwise, would render the statute
nugatory.—*Frichert v. Burgess*, 11 Md. 452; High on
Receivers, §§ 111–112.

The order appointing the receiver must be reversed, and
the cause remanded. Complainants can make another application, if so advised.

Reversed and remanded.

Anderson *v.* Bellenger & Ralls.

Action on Statutory Claim Bond.

1. *Discharge of surety, by alteration of contract.*—A surety has the
right to stand upon the very terms of his contract, and he is discharged
by any alteration made without his consent, whether he is thereby
injured or not, and even though it appears to be to his advantage, as by
the addition of another as co-obligor; but alterations in the writing by
a third person, who was not a party to it, can not change its legal operation and effect, and do not discharge the surety.

2. *Same; alteration of statutory claim bond, by adding name of another
surety as co-obligor.*—After a statutory claim bond, having been signed
by the principal obligor and two sureties, has been accepted and
approved by the sheriff, it is his duty to return it at once to the court
from which the process issued, and he has no authority, though retaining possession of the bond, to induce or accept the subsequent signature
of a third person as surety; and such signature and acceptance being
unauthorized, the liability of the original sureties is not thereby discharged or affected.

3. *Contracts made on Sunday.*—A statutory claim bond, accepted by
the sheriff on Sunday, is within the statute declaring void "all contracts made on Sunday" (Code, § 1749); and when the plaintiffs in the
action bring suit on the bond, it is not necessary that a plea, alleging its
invalidity because it was accepted on that day, should also allege the
plaintiffs' complicity in such acceptance.

4. *Signature to bond procured by fraud and mistake.*—In an action on
a statutory claim bond, it is a good plea by one of the sureties, that he
was fraudulently induced by the sheriff to sign it after it had been
accepted and approved with the signatures of the other two sureties
only, and that he signed it under a mistake of fact induced by the misrepresentations of the sheriff.

Vol. lxxxvii.

APPEAL from the Circuit Court of Etowah. Tried before the Hon. JOHN B. TALLY.

This action was brought by Bellenger & Ralls, suing as partners, against James Lancaster, T. M. Anderson, F. M. Reeves, and W. L. Aycock; was founded on a statutory claim bond, which was signed by said Lancaster as principal, and by the other defendants as his sureties; and was commenced on the 16th August, 1888. The plaintiffs had commenced a suit in detinue against one G. W. Lancaster, for 3,000 lbs. of seed-cotton; and after the cotton was seized by the sheriff, a statutory claim to it was interposed by said James Lancaster, and the bond here sued on was given conditioned as required by the statute. The claim suit was decided against the claimant, and the plaintiffs afterward recovered judgment in the detinue suit; and the cotton not being produced in accordance with the condition of the claim bond, this action on the bond was instituted. The action was discontinued as to James Lancaster, who was not served with process, and prosecuted to judgment against the other defendants.

The defendants jointly pleaded "the general issue," and issue was joined on that plea. Anderson and Reeves further filed a special plea of *non est factum*, called plea No. 2, alleging that after they had signed said bond with said Lancaster, and said bond was approved and accepted by the sheriff, "he, the said sheriff, without the consent, request or procurement of these defendants, or of said James Lancaster, their principal, procured and obtained the signature of said W. L. Aycock to said bond." They also filed another plea, No. 3, alleging that said bond "was delivered to the said sheriff, and by him approved, on Sunday, contrary to the statute in such case made and provided." A special plea was also filed by said Aycock, No. 4, alleging "fraud and misrepresentation, in that the said sheriff, after he had approved and accepted the said bond upon which 'plaintiffs' action is founded, falsely and knowingly represented to this defendant that said T. M. Anderson, who was at the time a co-surety on said bond, had requested him, said Aycock, to go upon said bond; that by virtue of said representations, so made by said sheriff, this defendant was induced to sign said bond as a surety, when in truth and in fact said Anderson made no such request, nor authorized any one to do so for him, nor was said sheriff authorized to make said representations for either James Lancaster or F. M. Reeves; and that said sheriff made said representations well knowing that they were untrue." To each of these special pleas the court sustained a demurrer, and its judgment is now assigned as error.

W. L. WHITLOCK, J. H. DISQUE, and GEO. D. MOTLEY, for appellant, cited *Giles v. Williams*, 3 Ala. 316; *Clay v. Dennis*, 3 Ala. 375; *Tamplin v. Still's Adm'r*, 77 Ala. 374.

DORTCH & MARTIN, *contra*, cited *Railroad Co. v. Hurst*, 9 Ala. 513; *Hammons v. State*, 59 Ala. 164; *Cranson v. Goss*, 107 Mass. 439, or 9 Amer. Rep. 45; *Johns v. Bailey*, 45 Iowa, 241; *Knox v. Clifford*, 38 Wisc. 651, or 20 Amer. Rep. 28.

McCLELLAN, J.—The contract of suretyship must be strictly construed in favor of the surety. His obligation is voluntary, without any consideration moving to him, without benefit to him, entered into for the accommodation of his principal, and generally, also, for that of the obligee; and courts see to it that his liabilities thus incurred are not enlarged beyond the strict letter of his undertaking. To the extent, and in the manner, and under the circumstances pointed out in his obligation, he is bound, and no further. His contract can not be changed in any respect. Whether an alteration is or is not to his benefit, is not open to inquiry. "He has a right to stand upon the very terms of his contract," and if a variation is made which extends its liability "to another person, or to any other subject, or for any other period of time than such as may be included in its words," and he does not assent to it, such variation is fatal to his obligation, whether he is injured thereby or not.—*Miller v. Stewart*, 9 Wheaton, 681; *Taylor v. Johnson*, 17 Ga. 521; *Gardner v. Walsh*, 5 El. & Bl. 89; *Bowers v. Briggs*, 20 Ind. 139; *Henry v. Coats*, 17 Ind. 161; *Wallace v. Jewell*, 21 Ohio St. 163; *Dickerman v. Miner*, 43 Iowa, 508; *City of Montgomery v. Hughes*, 65 Ala. 204.

Variations of the contract of suretyship which operate the discharge of the surety must, however, be such as are material, and change the legal import of the instrument, assuming the genuineness of the paper thus modified. Interlineations and changes may be made in the paper which evidences the liability, or in the words which express it, without destroying the validity of the contract, provided such modifications do not go beyond the mere form of the undertaking, or beyond the expression of the obligation which the law ascribes to it, in the absence of such expression, by implication. But, if the alterations exceed these limits, and change the real meaning of the undertaking which the parties have entered into, whether presumptively to the detriment or advantage of the surety, and whether the effect is to add to or take from the liability, by the introduction of additional parties or otherwise, the surety is discharged.—*United States v. Tillotson*, 1 Paine, 305; *Taylor v. Johnson*, 17 Ga. 521; *O'Neal v. Long*, 4 Cranch, 60; *People v. Brown*, 2 Doug. (Mich.) 9; *Portago Br. Bank v. Lane*, 8 Ohio St. 360.

There is another important limitation on the general doctrine which we have been considering, applicable to contracts generally, and exerting its influence on contracts of suretyship as well as all others. It is now well settled in this country, though the contrary rule formerly prevailed, and does yet to a large extent in England, that erasures, interlineations, spoliations and changes, made in and of contracts by strangers to them, however material abstractly considered, are, in legal contemplation, wholly immaterial, and ineffective to give to the instrument any other or different meaning or operation than that which attached to it before such intermeddling.—*Brown v. Jones*, 3 Porter, 422; *Davis v. Carlisle*, 6 Ala. 709; 1 Green. Ev., §§ 565–568; Byles on Bills, 323, and notes; 2 Parsons on Contr. 716 *et seq.*

In this case, it is averred by the defendants Anderson and Reeves, that after the bond had been signed by them and their principal, it was delivered to, and accepted and approved by the sheriff. It was the latter's duty to pass on the sufficiency of the bond as to amount and solvency. When he accepted and approved it, with these names on it, the contract was complete, and his duties, so far as the execution of the instrument was concerned, were then at an end. His further duty with respect to the bond was to file it in the office of the clerk of the court.—Code, 1876, §§ 2942, 2946. The sheriff was merely the agent of the law to take the bond of the defendant, payable to the plaintiff, and return it into court. After taking it, he had only the naked custody for a particular purpose, and not to extend beyond a given time. In all other respects, and for all other purposes, he was an utter stranger. Of course, the defendant Aycock was also a stranger to the contract. The addition of Aycock's name as an obligor, after the undertaking had thus been perfected, was the act of these two strangers to it,

22

[Anderson v. Bellenger & Ralls.]

the one inducing and accepting the signature, and the other
signing.   Under this state of facts, the alteration was no
alteration in point of law.   No change in the *status* of the
parties was effected by it; nothing was added to, or taken
from their rights or liabilities; and the contract is to be
treated by the parties as if the matter thus injected into it
was not a part of the paper, as it is not a part of the undertaking which the paper evidences.   The second plea of
Anderson and Reeves discloses that the contract had thus
been altered by strangers to it,—a fact which could exert no
influence on their liability; and the plea presented therefore
an immaterial issue.   The demurrer to it was properly sustained.—*United States v. Spalding*, 2 Mason, 478.

Contracts made on Sunday are absolutely void.—Code,
§ 1749.   A contract delivered on Sunday, is a contract made
on that day, within the meaning of this statute.—*Flanagan
v. Meyer*, 41 Ala. 132; *Burns v. Moore*, 76 Ala. 342.   The
contract of the defendants, while running to the plaintiffs,
and enuring to their benefit, was required by law to
be made, and could only be made with the sheriff.   If
delivered to him on Sunday, it was absolutely void,
and imported no liability whatever.   The plaintiffs had,
and could have had, no connection with the making of
the contract, and no control over the sheriff's action
in relation to it.   To hold that it was not void as
between the plaintiffs and defendants, would be to add
another term to the statute, and make it inapplicable to public officers, and enuring to third persons.   The case of *Salt-
marsh v. Tuthill*, 13 Ala. 390, is not in point.   That adjudication related to a negotiable instrument, and depended for
the result reached on the general principle which frees commercial paper from infirmities of which subsequent holders
have no notice.   Besides, the present statute "is more
sweeping and vitiating in its effect than the act of 1803,"
under which that case was decided; and "all contracts," of
whatever nature, are rendered void by it, if made on Sunday, unless they fall in one of the classes of cases specially
excepted.—*Burns v. Moore, supra*.   It was not necessary,
therefore, for the third plea of Anderson and Reeves to aver
the complicity of the plaintiffs in the execution of the contract, and the demurrer to that plea should have been overruled.

Fairly construed, the plea interposed by Aycock is an
averment that he was fraudulently induced to sign the bond,

after it had been accepted and approved. This goes to the consideration. The purpose of the bond was to secure to the principal the possession of the property. When the sheriff had accepted and approved the bond, as this plea alleges he did, the right to possession was perfect, and the duty on the part of the sheriff to deliver possession was absolute. It was immaterial whether possession had actually passed. The bond could have no other effect than to create this right and corresponding duty as to the possession. If these existed by reason of the acceptance and approval of the bond before it was signed by Aycock, it was without consideration as to him; and he should have been allowed to prove these facts, if he could.—*Jackson v. Jackson*, 7 Ala. 791; *Rutledge v. Townsend*, 38 Ala. 706; Brandt on Suretyship, 9.

This plea of Aycock also disclosed that his signature constituted an alteration of the contract made by him through a mistake of fact, being mislead by the sheriff so to do; and on this ground, also, we hold that it was well pleaded, and the demurrer to it was properly overruled.

Reversed and remanded.

Pendry *v.* Shows.

Petition for Habeas Corpus, in matter of Custody of Child.

1. *Bill of exceptions; matters of record.*—When matters which constitute a part of the record proper in the court below, are shown only by the bill of exceptions, the appellate court can not consider them for any purpose, but will disregard them *ex mero motu.*

APPEAL from the Probate Court of Crenshaw.

Heard before the Hon. B. A. WALKER.

In the matter of the petition of Thos. W. Shows, for a writ of *habeas corpus* directed to James P. Pendry, alleging his illegal detention of Frances W. Davis, an infant, to whose custody the petitioner claimed to be entitled. Several rulings of the court on pleadings, shown only by the bill of exceptions, with other matters, are here assigned as error.

GAMBLE, BRICKEN & GAMBLE, PARKS & PARKS, and WATTS & SON, for appellant.

M. W. RUSHTON, *contra.*

STONE, C. J.—What is claimed as a record in this case, is made up almost entirely of a bill of exceptions. All the pleadings, process, execution of the same, and the rulings on the pleadings, are shown only in the bill of exceptions. Outside of it, the record shows only the following: Note of petition filed, writ of *habeas corpus* awarded to J. P. Pendry, and trial set for October 6, 1888; writ issued October 2; and note of filing of petition made September 25, 1888; continued to October 24, 1888, by order made October 6; trial had October 24, 25 and 26, testimony heard, argument had, and judgment, "that T. W. Shows, to whom said child had been regularly apprenticed, is the proper custodian of said child." This is the substance of all that is shown, except what appears in the bill of exceptions. We repeat, neither the petition for *habeas corpus*, the writ, the sheriff's return, the pleadings nor the rulings on them, is shown any where else than in the bill of exceptions. Without these record facts before us, there is nothing we can review. Our uniform ruling has been, that when matters which are properly the record of the suit, and which constitute the record in the court below, are brought before us only in the bill of exceptions, we will disregard them *ex mero motu.*—3 Brick. Dig. 78, § 7. The present record shows no available error in the trial court's rulings.

There is no error in the record, of which appellant can complain.

Affirmed.

Kinney *v.* Ensminger.

Bill in Equity for Reformation of Conveyance and Notes for Purchase-Money.

1. *Parties to bill.*—When a bill is filed by the vendor of lands, seeking to correct his conveyance, and also the notes given for the purchase-money, by inserting an express provision for the retention of the vendor's lien, both of the makers of the notes are proper parties defendant, whether they were joint purchasers, or one was merely a surety for the other.

2. *Reformation of conveyance and notes for purchase-money, on ground of mistake or fraud.*—A vendor of lands, having executed a conveyance to the purchaser, and taken his notes for the purchase-money, may maintain a bill in equity to reform and correct them, by inserting an

[Kinney v. Ensminger.]

express provision for the retention of a vendor's lien, on averment and proof that such provision was omitted by mistake or fraud, without fault on his part.

3. *Same; signing or accepting writings without reading them.*—If the bill alleges that the complainant was not able to speak or understand the English language well, and that the contract was negotiated on his part by an agent, or an attorney in fact, who fraudulently colluded with the purchasers to omit from the writings the agreement for a retention of the vendor's lien, he relieves himself from the imputation of negligence, which generally attaches to a person who signs a writing without reading it, without inquiry, and without excuse for his neglect.

4. *Dissolution of injunction on answer.*—An injunction should not be dissolved on the denials of the answer, unless they are full and positive, especially where irreparable injury might result to the complainant from such dissolution.

APPEAL from the Chancery Court of Morgan.
Heard before the Hon. THOMAS COBBS.

W. T. L. COFER, for appellants.—(1.) In cases like this, where a party seeks to change the terms of a written instrument by oral evidence, the court proceeds with great caution, and requires the mistake to be established clearly and satisfactorily.—*Campbell v. Hatchett*, 55 Ala. 548; *Turner v. Kelly*, 70 Ala. 85; *Hinton v. Insurance Co.*, 63 Ala. 488; *Alexander v. Caldwell*, 55 Ala. 517; *Berry v. Sowell*, 72 Ala. 14. (2.) The complainant does not acquit himself of negligence.—*Watts v. Burnett*, 56 Ala. 340; *Dawson v. Burrus*, 73 Ala. 111; Benj. Sales, 436, § 452. (3.) The demurrers to the bill ought to have been sustained.—*McDonald v. Insurance Co.*, 56 Ala. 468; *Lake v. Loan Asso.*, 72 Ala. 207; *Flewellen v. Crane*, 58 Ala. 627; *Pickett v. Pipkin*, 64 Ala. 520; *Chamberlain v. Dorrance*, 69 Ala. 40. (4.) The injunction ought to have been dissolved on the denials of the answer.—*Collier v. Falk*, 61 Ala. 105; *Chambers v. Ala. Iron Co.*, 67 Ala. 353; 3 Brick. Digest, 352, § 303.

SOMERVILLE, J.—The bill is filed by the appellee, Ensminger, to reform a land deed recently executed to the appellants, and also the notes given for the purchase-money, so as to make the papers show on their face that a vendor's lien was retained, in accordance with what is alleged to have been the mutual agreement between the contracting parties. An injunction was prayed and granted, staying the threatened sale of the land in the meanwhile, it appearing that the purchase-money notes were not yet due, and that the defendants were insolvent. The appeal is taken from an interlocutory decree of the chancellor overruling a demurrer to the bill, and refusing to dissolve the injunction.

The several grounds of demurrer were, in our judgment, properly overruled.

According to the allegations of the bill, the defendant, P. H. Kinney, was one of the purchasers of the land, and not a mere surety on the purchase-money notes, as averred in the answer. In either event, whether interested as a co-vendee or a mere surety, he was a proper party defendant to the bill.—*Tedder v. Steele*, 70 Ala. 347; *Ramage v. Towles*, 85 Ala. 588.

If the facts alleged in the bill are true, the case is clearly brought within the jurisdiction of chancery, under the equity head of reformation of written instruments on the ground of mistake or fraud, unless the failure of the complainant to inform himself as to the contents of the deed and notes be such culpable negligence as to bar him of his remedy in a court of conscience. The bill avers a distinct agreement between the parties, that the deed and notes should show on their face a retention of a vendor's lien, and that the omission of this stipulation from these papers was through the fraudulent collusion of the defendants and one Harrison, who, as real estate agent, negotiated the sale as attorney in fact of the complainant.—*Berry v. Sowell*, 72 Ala. 14; 2 Pom. Eq. Jur. §§ 870, 1375; 3 Brick. Dig. 358, §§ 379 *et seq.*

The bill, in our opinion, shows no such culpable negligence on the part of the complainant as to bar his right to seek correction of the mistake sought to be rectified. It is not every negligence that will operate to bar in such cases, as is sometimes inaccurately asserted. "It would be more accurate to say," observes Mr. Pomeroy, in discussing this subject, "that where the mistake is wholly caused by the want of that care and diligence in the transaction which should be used by every person of reasonable prudence, and the absence of which would be a violation of a legal duty, a court of equity will not interpose its relief."—2 Pom. Eq. Jur. § 856. After adding that each instance of negligence must depend largely upon its own circumstances, he further says: "The conclusion from the best authorities seems to be, that the neglect must amount to the violation of a positive legal duty. The highest possible care is not demanded. Even a clearly established negligence may not, of itself, be sufficient ground for refusing relief, if it appears that the other party has not been prejudiced thereby."—*Ib.* § 856.

While courts will act on this principle in granting relief,

[Kinney v. Ensminger]

they will do so with great caution, so as to not unduly
encourage the want of ordinary prudence, on the part of
persons signing important papers, in making examination or
inquiry as to their contents.—*Watts v. Burnett*, 56 Ala. 340.
And generally an unexplained signing, without excuse for
neglecting to read, or to make inquiry, and without any
fraud, deceit or misrepresentation being practiced on the
maker or grantor, by which he was induced to execute the
paper, is not ground for relief, or defense to an action on
this paper.—*Cannon v. Lindsey*, 85 Ala. 198; *Dawson
v. Burrus*, 73 Ala. 111; *Pacific Guano Co. v. Anglin*, 82 Ala.
492; *Burroughs v. Pacific Guano Co.*, 81 Ala. 255; *Ken-
nerty v. Etiwan Phosphate Co.*, 53 Amer. Rep. 669; *Murrel
v. Murrel*, 49 Amer. Dec. 664. Especially is this true,
where the rights of an innocent third person are involved,
or the subject of the transaction is commercial paper, which
is not this case.—*Montgomery v. Scott*, 30 Amer. Rep. 1.

The complainant's illiteracy and inability to understand
the English language, coupled with his probable confidence
in his trusted agent, Harrison, who acted for him in negotiating the sale, are *prima facie* sufficient, under the facts of
this case, to acquit him of such culpable negligence, in failing
to be informed as to the contents of the deed and notes, as
would prevent him from obtaining relief in a court of equity.

The bill is not wanting in equity, and there was no error
in refusing to dissolve the injunction on this ground. The
demurrer to it was also correctly overruled.

As to the denials of the answer, they are not so full and
positive as to justify a dissolution of the injunction, based
alone on such denials, especially in view of the irreparable
injury which might ensue to complainant in the event the
land is sold to a *bona fide* purchaser, without notice of his
alleged vendor's lien.—*C. & W. Railway Co. v. Witherow*,
82 Ala. 190; *Burnley v. Cook*, 65 Amer. Dec. 79; *Harrison
v. Yerby, ante*, p. 185.

Affirmed.

McCLELLAN, J., not sitting, having been of counsel.

Chewacla Lime Works *v.* Dismukes, Frierson & Co.

Action for Price of Goods Sold and Delivered.

1. *Variance in name of corporation; appeals from justice's court.*—In an action commenced in a justice's court, which, on appeal, is required to be tried *de novo*, according to equity and justice, without regard to any defect in the process or proceedings before the justice (Code, § 3405); the defendant corporation being sued by the name given by its amended charter, which also made it liable for all debts created by the corporation under its original name and charter; the cause of action, as indorsed on the justice's warrant, being an account for goods sold and delivered to it by its amended name, while the proof shows that the goods were sold and delivered to the corporation before its change of name,—there is no material variance.

2. *Private corporation; power to carry on mercantile business.*—A private corporation, authorized by its charter "to have, purchase, receive, possess and enjoy lands, rights, tenements, hereditaments, goods, chattels and effects, in any amount the body corporate may deem necessary to carry all the objects of said corporation into full force and effect; which objects are to mine lime rock and manufacture the same, to keep up and run such machinery as may be necessary to saw lumber and make barrels for the packing of said lime, and the same to sell, devise, grant, alien, and dispose of"—has no implied or incidental power to carry on a general mercantile business.

3. *Estoppel against corporation; contract ultra vires.*—Under the decisions of this court, a corporation which has received the benefits of a contract *ultra vires*, is not thereby estopped from setting up the invalidity of the contract, in defense of a suit to enforce it.

APPEAL from the Circuit Court of Lee.

Tried before the Hon. JESSE M. CARMICHAEL.

This action was brought by the appellees, suing as partners, against the appellant, a private corporation; and was commenced before a justice of the peace on the 5th of January, 1884. The cause of action, as indorsed on the justice's warrant, was, "$80, due June 22, 1882, for goods, wares and merchandise sold by plaintiffs to defendant on the 22d of February, 1882, with the interest thereon." On appeal to the Circuit Court, the defendant filed two pleas: the first alleging that the defendant never bought the goods, nor promised or assumed in any manner to pay for them; and the second, that the goods were bought by the Chewacla Lime Company, without authority of law; that the contract was *ultra vires*, and not binding on the defendant as the successor of said Chewacla Lime Company. Issue was

[Chewacla Lime Works v. Dismukes, Frierson & Co.]

joined on both of these pleas. On the trial, as the bill of exceptions shows, the plaintiffs proved the sale of the goods to the Chewacla Lime Company, and their value; and the defendant, after introducing the original act incorporating the Chewacla Lime Company, and the amendatory act changing its name, proved that said corporation, at the time of the sale of the goods, "was keeping a store and carrying on a mercantile business, and bought said goods for the purpose of selling the same at a profit, as other merchants do." The original act of incorporation was approved on the 9th December, 1862, and the amendatory act on the 15th February, 1883. The material parts of each are copied in the opinion of this court. This being all the evidence, the court charged the jury, on request, that they must find for the plaintiff, if they believed the evidence. The defendant excepted to this charge, and it is here assigned as error.

HARRISON & LIGON, for appellant, cited *Savings Bank v. Dunklin*, 45 Ala. 471; *Chambers v. Falkner*, 65 Ala. 448; *City Council v. Plank-road Co.*, 31 Ala. 76; *Grand Lodge v. Waddell*, 36 Ala. 313; *Smith v. Life Ins. and Trust Co.*, 4 Ala. 558; *Central R. R. and B. Co. v. Smith*, 76 Ala. 572.

JOHN M. CHILTON, *contra*, cited *Spence v. Shapard*, 57 Ala. 598; Green's Brice's *Ultra Vires*, 65, notes.

CLOPTON, J.—By an act of the General Assembly, amending the act "to incorporate the Chewacla Lime Company," the name of the corporation was changed to the "Chewacla Lime Works." The fifth section of the amendatory act provides: "That the said Chewacla Lime Works shall succeed, and does hereby succeed, to all the rights, privileges and immunities, and franchises and property, that was of and belonging to the said Chewacla Lime Company, and shall be subject to all liabilities and charges legitimately due from the said Chewacla Lime Company."—Acts 1882-3, p. 369.

This action was commenced in a justice's court, and was brought by appellees to recover the price of goods, which the indorsement on the summons avers were sold to the Chewacla Lime Works, by which name the corporation is sued; while the evidence shows that the goods were sold to the Chewacla Lime Company, before the amendment of the charter. On appeals from judgments of justices of the peace, the cause "must be tried *de novo*, and according to equity and justice, without regard to any defect in the summons or other process, or proceedings before the justice." Code, 1886, § 3405. The corporation, notwithstanding the change of name, is one and the same entity. The averments of the statement of the cause of action might have been more formal, but there is no substantial variance between them and the proof.

It clearly appears that, at the time of the sale and delivery of the goods, the corporation was engaged in carrying on a general mercantile business, for which purpose they were bought. The material ground on which the defendant resists a recovery is, that the Chewacla Lime Company had no authority to engage in such business, and that the contract of purchase is *ultra vires*. The question raised involves the application of only a few principles of law, which may be regarded elementary. As corporations derive their existence and capacity from a special statute, or a general law empowering them to organize, they can not exercise any power, or act in any capacity, not authorized by the act of incorporation, or the general law. A corporation has no implied authority to engage in any business other than the particular enterprise for which it is chartered, or to do any act, or make any contract, not in pursuance of the purposes for which it was created. Authority to carry on a particular business, includes authority to conduct it in the usual and customary modes. Within the scope and purview of the chartered powers, the business, for which the corporation was chartered may be conducted in the same manner as individuals would conduct the same enterprise under similar circumstances. But any transaction or contract beyond this, not necessary or proper to enable the corporation to answer the purposes of its creation, is void.

The grant of powers conferred on the Chewacla Lime Company by the original act of incorporation, on which plaintiffs base the authority, is in the following language: "Shall be, and are hereby, made able and capable in law to have, purchase, receive, possess and enjoy, and realize to them and their successors, lands, rights, tenements, hereditaments, goods, chattels and effects, in any amount the body corporate may deem necessary to carry all the objects of said corporation into full force and effect, which objects are, to mine lime-rock, and manufacture the same; and to keep up and run such machinery as may be necessary to saw lumber

[Chewacla Lime Works v. Dismukes, Frierson & Co.] ·

and make barrels for the packing of said lime, and the same
to sell, devise, grant, alien and dispose of."—Acts, 1862,
p. 127.   It is manifest that the act of incorporation grants no
express authority to engage in a general mercantile business.
Is there implied authority?   The declared objects of the
corporation are the mining and manufacture of lime-rock,
and putting the product in a marketable condition.   These
purposes constitute limitations upon the exercise of the express and implied powers.   There may be circumstances
under which a manufacturing company would have implied
authority to connect a *supply store*, with the business of the
corporation, as being ancillary thereto.   In such case, the
real and primary object must be auxiliary to the main enterprise of the corporation, for the purpose of providing supplies for the employees and laborers, founded on necessity
arising from situation and condition.   No circumstances are
shown which bring the present case within this exception.
A general mercantile business does not pertain to the purposes of mining and manufacturing lime-rock.   They are
separate and distinct in their nature and objects.   A coal
mining company has no implied authority to buy coals in
the market, for the purpose of re-sale as a speculation.
Alexander v. Caldwell, 83 N. Y. 480.   A corporation authorized and organized to manufacture lime, can not buy lime
manufactured elsewhere for the purpose of trade, in order
to raise funds to carry on the corporate business.   As well
might such corporation engage in any other distinct business
as that of merchandizing, because it may be deemed profit-
able, and will thus contribute, indirectly, to promote the objects of the corporation.   A general mercantile business,
being a distinct branch of business, the Chewacla Lime
Company had no authority, express or implied, to engage in
carrying on the same.

The established rule in this State is, that a corporation is
not estopped, by reason of having received the benefits of a
contract which is *ultra vires*, from setting up its invalidity in
defense of a suit brought to enforce it.—*Sherwood v. Alvis,*
83 Ala. 115; s. c., 3 Amer. St. Rep. 695.

The Circuit Court erred in giving the affirmative charge .
in favor of the plaintiffs.

Reversed and remanded.

Skinner *v.* Dawson.

Application for Mandamus to President of Board of Convict Inspectors.

1. *Assessed value of stolen property, as part of costs on conviction of larceny.*—On a conviction of larceny and sentence to hard labor for the county, the assessed value of the stolen property, or the part thereof which has not been restored to the owner, is an item of the costs, and payable as other items are (Code, § 3792); but the statute does not extend to convictions followed by a sentence to the penitentiary.

APPEAL from a judgment rendered by Hon. JOHN MOORE, the presiding judge of the Fourth Judicial Circuit, refusing to grant a *mandamus* to Hon. R. H. DAWSON, as President of the Board of Inspectors of Convicts, requiring him to restore and allow an item of $80.75 as a part of the costs in a criminal prosecution against one Frank Smith, who had been convicted of grand larceny, and sentenced to the penitentiary for the term of four years. The application for the writ was made by John L. Skinner, the owner of the stolen property. The value of the property, or the part thereof which had not been restored to the owner, was assessed by the jury at $80.75; and it was included in the statement of the items of costs, certified by the clerk, with a copy of the judgment and sentence, to said Dawson; but it was struck out and disallowed by him, in his certified statement to the contractors to whom the convict was assigned, leaving the balance of costs as allowed $61.15. Judge Moore refused to grant a *mandamus*, and this appeal seeks to review his decision.

J. N. MILLER, for the petitioner.

W. L. MARTIN, Attorney-General, *contra*.

Per Curiam.—The real question involved in this proceeding is, whether the legislature has subjected the State to the liability of paying the assessed value of stolen property, on a conviction of the thief and his sentence to the penitentiary. Prior to the enactment of the present statute (Code

of 1886, § 3792), there was no law which authorized the
court, on conviction of a person charged with larceny, to
make the assessed value of the property stolen or embezzled
an item of cost. The statute provides, that when the costs
are paid or worked out, including the value of the property
stolen, the court of County Commissioners must order a warrant upon the county treasurer, in favor of the owner, for
the value thereof, to be paid out of the fund arising from the
proceeds of such labor.—Code of 1886, § 3792. This clearly
has reference to county convicts, whose labor is under the
control of the Commissioners Court. It can not, and does
not, apply to penitentiary convicts. It is a summary remedy, gratuitously given by the legislature, and it rested
entirely with the legislature to provide the extent and method
of payment. Indeed, the legislature might repeal the statute after the commission of a larceny and before the trial,
and the owner of the stolen property could not complain.
It is a mere matter of grace.

Prior to the passage of the act of February 17, 1885, "To
further define and regulate the convict system."–Acts, 1884-5,
pp. 187-196—the State paid no costs, although the defendant was sentenced to the penitentiary. The statute, in section 34, provides for the payment of the costs generally, out
of the convict fund, on the warrant of the Auditor.

The Code, section 4609, *specifies the items of cost* which
are to be paid by the State, and makes it the duty of the contractor to pay them. The act of February 28, 1887, p. 86,
requires a certified copy of the bill of costs to be sent to the
president of the Board of Inspectors of convicts, it must be
inferred, for his approval. The general term "costs," as employed in section 4609, applies to the special words, "the
particular items," mentioned in the preceding part of the
section.—3 Brick. Dig. p. 749, § 21. And the act of February 28, 1887, must be read and construed in connection
with section 4609 of the Code. The word "costs" has the
same meaning in the statute—the items enumerated.

The costs specified are to be paid by the contractor, for
the State. He advances that amount on the hire of the convicts, and it is credited with the amount so paid on his next
settlement with the convict bureau.—Acts 1886-7, p. 86.
This is the State paying the costs. The law must be strictly
construed in favor of the State.—*Pollard v. Brewer*, 59 Ala.
130; Code, 1886, § 4892.

The purpose of the statute was to compensate witnesses

and officers. If the stolen property in this case is a part of the costs to be paid by the State, the same rule would apply in a case where very large sums are stolen or embezzled; and on a *pro rata* distribution of the $150, the maximum amount allowed, the witnesses and officers would get comparatively nothing.

With slight verbal alterations, we have adopted the argument of the Attorney-General as our opinion.

Writ denied.

Tillison *v.* Ewing.

Bill in Equity for Cancellation of Conveyance.

1. *Fraudulent concealment, as avoiding statute of limitations, at law and in equity.*—The fraudulent concealment of facts on which a right of action depends, such as avoids the bar of the statute of limitations (Code, § 2630), is available at law, and will not uphold a suit in equity, in the absence of facts showing a necessity for special equitable relief.

APPEAL from the Chancery Court of Etowah.

Heard before the Hon. S. K. McSPADDEN.

The bill in this case was filed on the 16th February, 1888, by William S. Tillison and the heirs at law of Francis M. Tillison, deceased, against W. T. Ewing; and sought the cancellation of a conveyance for a tract of land, executed to the defendant, in 1863, by Thomas Hollingsworth, since deceased. The chancellor dismissed the bill, on motion, for want of equity; and his decree is here assigned as error. The opinion states the material facts.

WALDEN & SON, for appellant.

WM. H. DENSON, *contra.* (No briefs on file.)

STONE, C. J.—According to the averments of the bill, Francis M. Tillison and W. S. Tillison became the owners of the land in controversy by purchase from Hollingsworth, in April, 1843, and being transferrees of the receiver's certificate of entry, a patent was issued to them from the Government of the United States, in June, 1845. Francis M. Tillison and Hollingsworth lived together on the land until the close

[Tillison v. Ewing]

of the year 1845, when the said Francis M. died. Hollingsworth remained in possession until 1863, when he conveyed
to Ewing, who continued in possession until this suit was
brought, in February, 1888. W. S. Tillison, living at a distance, was never informed that he or his brother had any
interest in, or claim to the lands, until 1887—less than a
year before this bill was filed. (They were associated in
land speculations.) The other complainants are the heirs at
law of Francis M. Tillison, and they had no knowledge of
said claim, until, by an accidental discovery of the patent in
1887, W. S. Tillison and the heirs ascertained its existence,
and their right to the land.

The bill anticipates the defense of staleness and the statute of limitations, and attempts to avoid it by the following
averred facts: That soon after the death of F. M. Tillison,
W. S., the surviving brother, visited F. M.'s late residence,
and called on Hollingsworth for his papers; that the latter
gave him one insignificant paper, and said nothing about the
patent, or the land transaction had with F. M.; that said
patent was accidentally discovered, as shown above, and the
present suit was brought in less than twelve months afterwards. The attempted answer to the statute of limitations
is, that Hollingsworth perpetrated a fraud in concealing the
fact of the issue of the patent, and that the fraud was never
discovered by complainants, until the time mentioned above.
Code of 1886, § 2630.

According to our former rulings, and to the weight of
American authority, this answer to the statute of limitations
is available at common law; and as fraud is not a sufficient
ground to uphold a suit in equity, in the absence of averments showing a necessity for special equitable relief, the
bill was properly dismissed for want of equity.—*Proskauer
v. Peop. Sav. Bank*, 77 Ala. 257; *Curry v. Peebles*, 83 Ala.
225; *Peebles v. Burns*, 77 Ala. 290; *Smith v. Cockrell,* ·
66 Ala. 64; *Porter v. Smith*, 65 Ala. 169; *Wear v. Skinner*,
24 Amer. Rep. 517.

When the present bill was filed, F. M. Tillison had been
dead forty-two years. During the first seventeen of those
years, we infer that Hollingsworth claimed the land, and exercised acts of ownership over it. We draw this inference,
because the bill is silent as to its use or occupation during
this period, and because in 1863 he conveyed the lands to
Ewing, the defendant in this cause. We also infer from the
averments that from the date of said conveyance in 1863,

until this bill was filed—over twenty-four years—Ewing and others in his right are charged to have been in control and possession of the lands.

The bill, as amended, contains this clause: "That said F. M. Tillison died in possession of said land-patent at the house of said Hollingsworth, the 29th of December, 1845; that said Hollingsworth, in fraud of orators' right to said patent, took said patent, and concealed it from orators; and that defendant, at and before he purchased the land of Hollingsworth, had knowledge from said Hollingsworth of complainants' right to the land under said patent, and was partaker in the fraud perpetrated by said Hollingsworth, by concealing from orators the knowlege of their cause of action, until it was discovered as stated by orators in this bill, as complainants are informed and believe, from the discovery of the patent, as stated in the bill." *Sec. 7.* "Complainants charge and aver that, at the time, and previous to accepting said deed, the defendant, W. T. Ewing, had notice that said Hollingsworth deraigned no title to said lands from the patentees thereof, their heirs or legal representatives."

If this averment, in each of its aspects, be proved, we are not prepared to say the case is not brought within the exceptional section 2630 of the Code of 1886. If, however, there is a failure to prove that Ewing had the notice that he is charged to have had, it would seem he could not have aided in concealing the fraud, charged to have been perpetrated and concealed by Hollingsworth; and that, therefore, the twenty years presumption is a complete protection to him.—*Phillippi v. Phillippi*, 61 Ala. 41, and authorities; *Solomon v. Solomon*, 81 Ala. 505; s. c., 83 Ala. 394; *Holt v. Wilson*, 75 Ala. 58; *McCarthy v. McCarthy*, 74 Ala. 546; *Wear v. Skinner*, 24 Amer. Rep. 517. But this question is not decided, not being necessary to the result of the present suit.

Affirmed.

Brown *v.* Williams.

Application to correct Mistake in Description of Lands sold under Probate Deree.

1. *Correcting mistake in description of lands sold under probate decree.* Under statutory provisions (Code, 1886, §§ 2129-30; 1876, § 2472; 1867, § 2128), when a mistake has been made in the description of a decedent's lands sold under a probate decree, whether in the petition, order, or other proceedings, the court ordering the sale has authority to correct it, on the application of the purchaser, or any one claiming under him; and the provisions regulating the practice in such cases, as now of force, being remedial in their character, are applicable to sales made while the former statutes were in force.

2. *Same; effect of decree correcting mistake; defenses against.*—A decree correcting a mistake, under these statutory provisions, only has the effect of placing the parties in the same position they would have occupied if no mistake had occurred, but it gives no additional validity to the original order of sale; other defects in the order, or in the proceedings connected with it, assailing its validity, are no defense against the application; and the lapse of seventeen years since the sale, no adverse possession being shown, is no bar to a correction of the mistake.

3. *Costs, as against guardian ad litem.*—The rule of this court has always been, not to tax a guardian *ad litem* with costs, though he be the unsuccessful appellant.

APPEAL from the Probate Court of Pike.

Heard before the Hon. W. J. HILLIARD.

In the matter of the application of Jonathan Williams, for the correction of a mistake in the description of lands sold under a probate decree in 1871, as contained in the petition and order of sale. The lands had belonged to W. A. Carpenter, deceased, and were sold on the petition of his administrator, alleging (1) a deficiency of personal assets to pay debts, and (2) that the lands could not be equally divided without a sale. The petition for the correction of the mistake in the description of the lands was filed in March, 1888, the petitioner claiming under the sale as a sub-purchaser; and it was contested by Mrs. Ida Lee, a minor, who was the only child of said W. A. Carpenter, by M. P. Brown as her guardian *ad litem*. The defenses set up by the guardian *ad litem* were: 1st, that the application was barred by the statute of limitations; 2d, that the land was in fact not sold under said order, but under a subsequent order amending it (*Lee v. Williams*, 85 Ala. 189); 3d, that

23

the statute in force when the order was made did not authorize the court to correct it, and the statute now of force had no retroactive operation; 4th, that the order of sale, and the petition on which it was founded, were void on their face. The court overruled each of these defenses, and rendered a decree correcting the mistake in the petition and order of sale. The guardian *ad litem* excepted to the several rulings, and also to the decree of the court, and he here assigns them as error.

WATTS & SON, and J. E. P. FLOURNOY, for appellant, cited *Lee v. Williams*, 85 Ala. 189; *Gillespie v. Nabors*, 59 Ala. 441; *Kidd v. Montague*, 19 Ala. 619; *Insurance Co. v. Boykin*, 38 Ala. 510.

SOMERVILLE, J.—The present application is made to the Probate Court, under the provisions of section 2129 of the Code of 1886, for the purpose of correcting a mistake in the description of certain lands sold under order of the court, in the year 1871, at an administrator's sale. The lands were erroneously described as lying in section *36*, township *9*, range 23. The correct description sought to be made places them in section *6*, township *8*, range 23. The application is made by one holding under the purchaser at the sale, is verified by affidavit, and alleges substantially all the facts required by the statute. The jurisdiction here conferred is analogous to that possessed by courts of chancery to reform written instruments under the equity of reformation and re-execution. This jurisdiction of equity has, in this State, been enlarged by statute, so as to authorize the reformation of administrators' deeds, made under authority of the Probate Court, so as to correct misdescriptions of the lands conveyed.—*Ganey v. Sykes*, 84 Ala 348; s. c., 76 Ala. 421.

To economize expense, it was provided as far back as 1852, that a like jurisdiction might be exercised by the Probate Court, where the lands of a decedent had been sold *bona fide* under its order, and possession accompanied the sale. On application of the purchaser, or any person holding under him, and after notice to the personal representative of the decedent, the Probate Court was authorized, on proper proof, to order title to be made to the applicant by such representative, by proper description of the lands by the corrected numbers.—Code, 1867, § 2128; Code, 1876, § 2472. This section was amended by the act approved December 3, 1884, by authorizing a correction of a mistake in the description of *boundaries* as well as of numbers, and authorizing the appointment of a special administrator to represent the estate, where there was no administrator.—Acts, 1884-85, p. 76. The present Code (§ 2129) confers no new or additional jurisdiction, but is only more elaborate in explaining the details of such application, and the requisite proceedings under it. It authorizes the Probate Court to correct any such mistake in the description of lands sold under its order, "either in the petition, order or other proceedings," under like circumstances provided for by section 2128 of the Code of 1867. It also states the requisite contents of the application, and provides for notice to the heirs or devisees of the decedent, as well as to his personal representative, and for the appointment, in a proper emergency, of an administrator *ad litem* to represent the estate, as well as a guardian *ad litem* to represent the minor heirs.—Code, 1886, § 2129.

The whole purpose of such proceeding is to correct, by reformation, a mistake in *the description* of the lands sold, and to authorize such rectification of error by the execution of a new deed, conveying to the purchaser, or applicant, "the lands according to the description as corrected." Code, 1886, § 2130. It creates no new contract between the parties, and imposes no additional burdens or obligations. It merely reforms the record evidence, so as to make it speak the truth as to the real contract. The conveyance is only made effective by applying it to the property sold by one party and bought by the other, in accordance with the original and mutual intention of the contracting parties. The court thus, through the equity of specific performance, and sometimes by an application of the just doctrine of equitable estoppel, compels the seller, by re-execution of the conveyance, to convey to the purchaser a legal title, where before he only had an equitable one.—*Gardner v. Gates*, 75 Ala. 394; s. c., 51 Amer. Rep. 454; *Styers v. Robbins*, 76 Ind. 547; *Robertson v. Bradford*, 73 Ala. 116. But, as said by Mr. Pomeroy, "the reformation of a deed does not directly restore the grantee to the dominion and possession of the land which has been omitted; but it places him in a position which enables him, if necessary, to assert his dominion, and recover the possession."—3 Pom. Eq. Jur. § 1375.

There can be no doubt that the provisions of the statute

under consideration, with its several amendments as appearing in the present Code of 1886 (§ 2129), being remedial in their character, are all applicable to the case in hand, notwithstanding the sale of the lands in controversy was made in 1871—prior to the enactment of the amendatory features of the statute to which we have above alluded at some length. The jurisdiction conferred has been rather regulated by these amendments, than newly created, or materially enlarged. Code, 1867, § 2128; Code, 1876, § 2472; Acts 1884-85, p. 76; Code, 1886, § 2129.

The legal effect of such a proceeding, however, we repeat, is only to accomplish a single purpose. It only corrects the misdescription in the lands sold and conveyed, and places the purchaser, or applicant holding under him, in the same situation he would have been had the correct description been originally inserted in the petition, the order of sale, and the administrator's deed; or, in other words, in precisely the position he would have occupied had there been no misdescription in the lands sold. In other respects, the validity of the proceedings is unaffected. If the sale is void for want of proper jurisdictional averments in the petition, or because the lands sold belonged to minors, or persons of unsound mind, and the order of sale was made without taking proof, as in chancery cases, showing the necessity of the sale, as required by statute, or on any other ground than inaccuracy in the description of the lands, it is void still, notwithstanding the action of the court in making a correction of this particular error or mistake. The Probate Court, in exercising this limited jurisdiction to correct misdescriptions, must be confined to its statutory power, and has no authority to enter upon an investigation as to the validity of the order based on other grounds. All such inquiries are left open for consideration by the proper court, when the purchaser, or applicant, may undertake to assert his dominion over the lands by suit in ejectment, or otherwise. The validity of the sale may be then attacked on any other ground than error in the description of the lands, this inquiry alone being *res adjudicata* in any application made to the Probate Court under section 2129 of the Code (1886), and acted on favorably by that tribunal, as in the present case.

The applicant having been in possession of the premises—or, at least, there having been no adverse possession in hostility to the title—the lapse of seventeen years since the alleged mistake was committed constitutes no bar to its

[Knowles v. Street.]

correction.—*Harold v. Scott*, 72 Ala. 373; *Nabors v. Meredith*, 67 Ala. 333.

An application of these principles leaves no doubt of the fact that the Probate Court committed no error either in the rulings on the evidence, or in the decree rendered.

The judgment is accordingly affirmed.

NOTE.—On a subsequent day of the term the following opinion was delivered.

SOMERVILLE, J.—The judgment in this case will be corrected, so as to relieve the appellant of all liability for costs. The rule of this court has always been, not to tax a guardian *ad litem* with costs. On the authority of *Perryman v. Burgster*, 6 Por. 99, the judgment will be reversed and rendered, so as to make the correction indicated.

Knowles *v.* Street.

Trover for Conversion of Stock of Goods.

1. *Sale of stock of goods by insolvent debtor to creditor; validity as against other creditors.*—A sale of his entire stock of goods by an embarrassed or insolvent debtor, in absolute payment of a *bona fide* existing debt, will be sustained as against other creditors, without regard to the question of fraudulent intent, when there is no material difference between the value of the property and the amount of the debt, and no use or benefit is reserved to the debtor himself.

2. *Charge not applicable to evidence.*—A charge asked which asserts a legal proposition not applicable to the facts of the case, though correct as a general abstract proposition, is properly refused.

3. *Estoppel by words or conduct.*—In an action against a purchaser of goods at execution sale, by one claiming under a prior purchase from the defendant in execution, a charge asserting that, "if plaintiff used such words to and in the presence of defendant, at or near the time of the sale of the goods, as would cause a reasonably prudent man to act, and to alter his condition to his prejudice, on the faith of such statements, and defendant did alter his condition to his prejudice on the faith of such statements, then plaintiff was guilty of a fraud, and can not recover," is properly refused, because it submits to the jury the sufficiency of the statements to constitute an estoppel.

4. *Authority of agent to collect; purchase in payment of debt.*—Although authority to a clerk to sell goods and collect the debts may not empower him to purchase a stock of goods in payment of a debt; yet, where a general agent is left in charge of his principal's business, and is specially instructed to look after a particular debt, to collect something on it, or arrange it in some way, it can not be assumed that his authority was limited to the collection of debts in the usual mode on the sale of goods.

APPEAL from the Circuit Court of Clay.

Tried before the Hon. JAMES W. LAPSLEY.

This action was brought by Merit Street against John W. Knowles, to recover damages for an alleged conversion of a stock of goods, and was commenced on the 24th March, 1885. The stock of goods had belonged to one H. A. Manning, who was engaged in business as a merchant at Ashland in said county, and under whom each party claimed; the plaintiff under a purchase at private sale, in payment of an antecedent debt, and the defendant under a purchase, a few days afterwards, at a sale under execution by the United States marshal. The bill of sale to the plaintiff, which was dated December 1st, 1884, recited an indebtedness by Manning to him of $5,599.88, as evidenced by two promissory notes, and a sale of the goods "in order to reduce and pay as much of said indebtedness as possible;" the groceries being taken at invoice price, and the other goods at twenty per cent. less. The purchase was effected for plaintiff, while he was absent in Montgomery, by his son and agent, J. C. Street, who testified on the trial, that his father, when starting to Montgomery, "gave him instructions in regard to the collection of the debt on Manning—instructed him to look after the claim, and told him to collect something on it, or to arrange it in some way." The plaintiff's clerks and agents at once took possession of the goods, and commenced to make an invoice of them, selling by retail each day, until December 6th, when the execution was levied by the marshal. The execution was issued on December 4th, on a judgment rendered that day by the United States Circuit Court at Montgomery, in favor of Slade & Etheridge, against said Manning; and the defendant became the purchaser at the marshal's sale under the levy, at the price of $1,400. The plaintiff's attorney gave public notice at the sale of his claim to the goods, but the defendant testified that he did not hear the notice, and that he quit bidding when he learned that such notice had been given; and he further testified in this connection: "There was then an interval of a half-hour when no bidding was going on. During this interval Street came up to witness, and asked if that was his bid; to which witness replied that it was not—that he had understood notice had been given that whoever bought the goods would buy a lawsuit. Street then said, that the goods were going very low, and that witness would not be in any danger if he bought them. Street then asked, if witness did not need the goods;

[Knowles v. Street.]

and witness answered, 'Yes, and if you say buy them, I'll do it.' Street then said, 'I don't think you will be in any danger, if you buy them.' Witness then made one or two more bids, and the goods were knocked down to him.'' The defendant introduced two witnesses who corroborated his testimony as to the conversation between himself and the plaintiff, while the plaintiff, testifying for himself, denied that he made any such statements in the conversation between himself and the defendant.

The defendant requested nineteen charges in writing, and duly excepted to the refusal of each Among these charges were the following: (1.) "If the jury believe from the evidence that the plaintiff, at or near the time of the sale of said goods, used such words to and in the presence of defendant as would cause a reasonably prudent man to act, and to alter his condition to his prejudice, on the faith of such statement, and that the defendant did alter his condition, to his prejudice, on the faith of such statements so made to or in his presence by plaintiff, plaintiff would thereby be guilty of a fraud, and can not recover in this case, and the jury must find for the defendant." (2.) "Authority to sell goods, and to collect debts for the principal, does not constitute such an agency, nor authorize an agent to purchase a stock of goods in payment of such debts." The other charges related to the question of fraud in the sale by Manning to plaintiff, and it is unnecessary to state them. The errors assigned are founded on the refusal of the several charges asked.

C. A. STEED, and BRICKELL, SEMPLE & GUNTER, for appellant, cited the following cases: "(1.) On the question of estoppel—*Harrison v. Pool*, 16 Ala. 167; *Stone v. Britton*, 22 Ala. 543; *Powers v. Harris*, 68 Ala. 409; *McCravey v. Remson*, 19 Ala. 430; *Auerbach v. Pritchett*, 58 Ala. 451; *Hendricks v. Kelly*, 64 Ala. 388; *Leinkauf v. Munter*, 76 Ala. 194; *Dickerson v. Colgrove*, 100 U. S. 578; 6 Wait's A. & D. 682, § 2; 689, § 2; *Abrams v. Seal*, 44 Ala. 299; *Watson v. Knight*, 44 Ala. 352. (2.) As to the validity of the plaintiff's purchase of the stock of goods, under the facts stated hypothetically in the several charges asked—*Bryant v. Young*, 21 Ala. 272; *Wiley, Banks & Co. v. Knight*, 27 Ala. 347; *Hodges v. Coleman & Carroll*, 76 Ala. 103; Code, § 1735. (3.) As to the authority of J. C. Street to make the *purchase*—*Robinson v. Murphy*,

69 Ala. 543.; *Cameron v. Clarke*, 11 Ala. 259. (4.) That
a subsequent ratification of the purchase by plaintiff could
not affect the intervening rights of defendant—*Jackson
v. Ramsay*, 15 Amer. Dec. 246.

CLOPTON, J.—Appellant purchased the goods, the subject of suit, at a sale by the marshal under an execution in
favor of Slade & Ethridge against H. A. Manning, which
was issued on a judgment rendered December 4, 1884, by
the United States Circuit Court. Appellee, who brings the
action for a conversion of the goods, deduces title by a purchase from Manning on December 1, 1884.

The evidence establishes that Manning had been for some-
time prior, and was at the time of the purchase, largely
indebted to plaintiff, and that the latter purchased the goods
in payment, *pro tanto*, of the indebtedness. The *bona fides*
of the debt is not seriously controverted; the notes which
evidenced it were produced in evidence, and their considerations proved; and there is no pretense that plaintiff paid
Manning other or additional consideration. The case, therefore, comes within that class of cases, in which a creditor
purchases, or takes property from an embarrassed or insolvent debtor, in payment of his debt. The defendant requested
the court to charge the jury, that if Manning yielded a
preference to plaintiff, in his diligence to collect his debt,
which was participated in by him, for the purpose of defeating the rights of the plaintiffs in execution, the jury must
find for the defendant.

Since the decision in *Hodges v. Coleman*, 76 Ala. 103,
which has been uniformly followed, it should be regarded as
settled law in this State, that a sale of the whole, or a part
of his property, by an embarrassed or ·insolvent debtor to
his creditor, in payment of an antecedent debt, will be upheld,
if the debt be *bona fide*, its amount not materially less than
the fair and reasonable value of the property, and payment
of the debt is the solè consideration, and no use or benefit
is· secured or reserved to the debtor. In such case, the
inquiry should be directed to the *bona fides* of the debt, the
sufficiency of the consideration, and the reservation of a
benefit to the debtor. If the transaction is not assailable
on some one of these grounds, fraud otherwise has no room
for operation. Whether there exist the ordinary badges of
fraud, whether the debtor intended to hinder or defraud his
other creditors, whether the purchasing creditor was swift

in the race of diligence for the purpose of defeating other creditors who were pressing their demands, or whether such is the necessary consequence, are not material inquiries. By devoting his property to the payment of an honest debt, the debtor merely performs a lawful act, which causes no legal injury to any one; and without injury there can be no actionable fraud.—*Meyer v. Sulzbacher*, 76 Ala. 120; *Levy v. Williams*, 79 Ala. 121; *Carter v. Coleman*, 84 Ala. 256; *Morrison v. Morris*, 85 Ala. 196. The rule settled by these cases is a qualification of the general rule as to fraudulent conveyances.

On the question of fraud, the defendant asked several other charges, which were refused. Whether properly refused does not depend solely upon the correctness of the abstract legal propositions of the charges, but also upon their applicability to the case as presented by the evidence. Though correct, if inapplicable, they were properly refused. All these charges ignore the qualification to the general rule above stated, and their tendency would have been to divert the minds of the jury from the proper inquiries. *Jeff. Co. Sav. Bank v. Eborn*, 84 Ala. 529.

The defendant further requested the court to charge the jury, that if the plaintiff used such words, to and in the presence of defendant, as would cause a reasonably prudent man to act, and alter his condition, to his prejudice, on the faith of such statements, and the defendant did alter his condition to his prejudice on the faith of such words, the plaintiff was guilty of a fraud, and the jury must find for the defendant. The principle intended to be invoked by the instruction is, that when a party by his declaration induces another to buy property, which otherwise he would not have bought, he will not be permitted to set up against such purchaser a title in himself. The essential elements of an estoppel *en pais*, in such case, are, a statement inconsistent with the title proposed to be set up, an act done by the other party on the faith of such statement, and injury as the result of allowing the statement to be shown to be untrue. Ordinarily, the declarations must be made with the intention to induce action; but intention to willfully mislead is not essential. It is sufficient if a statement is made in such manner that a sensible man would receive it as true, and believe that it was intended that he should act on it. This qualification, however, applies to the *manner* in which the statement is made, there being no positive intention that it should be believed and acted upon. It has no reference to the *charac-ter* of the statement itself. A declaration may be made in such manner as would induce a sensible man to believe it to be true, and intended to be acted on, and yet insufficient of itself to constitute an estoppel. Whether a statement is of such character as would cause a reasonable man to act, is not the test of the sufficiency. The character and sufficiency of the statement are for the determination of the court.

There being evidence that the goods were purchased by the agent of plaintiff during his absence, the defendant further asked the court to charge the jury, that authority to sell goods and collect debts does not authorize an agent to purchase a stock of goods in payment of such debts. The evidence tended to show that the son of plaintiff was his general agent, and was specially directed to look after the Manning claim, and collect something on it, or to arrange it in some way—had authority to settle the claim. The charge is obnoxious to the objection, that it would have authorized the jury to infer that the authority was limited to selling goods and collecting debts in the usual and customary mode, an inference which could not be reasonably drawn from the evidence. Such being the authority of the agent, no question arises as to the effect of a subsequent ratification upon the intervening rights of the plaintiffs in execution.

Affirmed.

Comer *v.* Lehman, Durr & Co.

Bill in Equity, for Reformation and Foreclosure of Mortgage.

1. *Mortgage of personalty; indefinite description; reformation in equity.*—A mortgage conveying "twenty head of mules and horses now in use upon my said plantation," without other descriptive or identifying words, is void for uncertainty and indefiniteness, when it is shown that the mortgagor in fact had nearly twice that number on the plantation at that time; and a court of equity will not reform it, on averment and proof that he proposed to mortgage all of his horses and mules, and represented that they were twenty in number.

2. *Mortgage of crops, "to extent of one hundred bales of cotton."*—A mortgage conveying "the entire crop of corn, cotton, fodder, cotton seed, and all other crops of every kind or description, which may be made and grown during the present year on said lands, to *the extent of one hundred bales of cotton, which is to be the first cotton picked*," and de-

[Comer v. Lehman, Durr & Co.]

claring the mortgagor *"may mortgage to other parties any balance after such one hundred bales;"* the italicized words being written, and the others part of a printed form, conveys not only one hundred bales of cotton, but the other crops also as security for the delivery of the one hundred bales, or their value. (McClellan, J. *dissenting,* held that it conveyed only the one hundred bales of cotton.)

3. *Foreclos re of mortgage; extent of relief as to matters cognizable at law; interest.*—Under a bill to foreclose a mortgage on crops, a purchaser with notice being joined as a defendant, he may be held responsible, not only for the cotton then in his possession, but also for cotton received and sold by him before the bill was filed, although the mortgagee might maintain an action at law for its conversion; and he is chargeable with interest on the value of the cotton so sold, although, by agreement of the parties to the cause, he has been allowed to sell the cotton in possession, giving a bond to account for its value.

APLEAL from the Chancery Court of Bullock.

Heard before the Hon. JOHN A. FOSTER.

The original bill in this case was filed by Lehman, Durr & Co., commission-merchants in Montgomery, against J. F. Comer and H. M. Comer & Co., a partnership doing business in Savannah, Georgia; and sought principally to enforce and foreclose a mortgage on crops, horses, mules, &c., executed to plaintiffs by said J. F. Comer; also, the appointment of a receiver to take possession of the mortgaged property, and to hold H. M. Comer & Co. accountable for some of the mortgaged property which was in their possession, and for the value of some of the cotton which they had received and sold, having knowledge, as alleged, of the mortgage to the . complainants. The mortgage was dated May 12th, 1886, and recited an indebtedness of $7,000 for money loaned and advanced. It was a printed form, with blanks filled up and additions made in writing. The material parts are quoted in the opinion of the court. A copy of this mortgage, partly printed and partly written, like the original, was made an exhibit to the bill, and was sent to this court for inspection. The mortgage was duly recorded in Bullock and Barbour counties, in which the plantations of the mortgagor were situated.

An answer to the bill was filed by J. F. Comer, in which, admitting the execution of the mortgage, he insisted that it only conveyed to complainants one hundred bales of cotton, the first to be picked and ginned, and that the mortgage was void as to the mules and horses for uncertainty, because he then had on his plantations about thirty-six mules and horses; and he alleged that, on November 30th, 1886, being indebted to H. M. Comer & Co. in the sum of about $15,000, he had conveyed to them, in absolute payment of said indebtedness, his plantations, all of his horses and mules, and about fourteen bales of cotton, the last of his crop, after more than one hundred bales had been picked and ginned. An answer was also filed by H. M. Comer & Co., substantially the same as the answer of J. F. Comer, denying that they had any knowledge, information or notice, until after November 30th, 1886, that complainants had or claimed any mortgage or lien whatever upon the crops of J. F. Comer, except upon the first one hundred bales of cotton. The complainants then filed an amended bill, alleging that J. F. Comer, when he made application for a loan of money, and pending the negotiations for the same, proposed to mortgage all of the horses and mules he had which were unincumbered, representing that he had about twenty, and that he could not give any particular description of them; that the complainants, trusting to these representations, so expressed the number in the mortgage; and praying that the mortgage be reformed, so as to express and include the true number. The amended bill alleged, also, that prior to November 30th, 1886, H. M. Comer & Co. had received from J. F. Comer, of the crops covered by the complainants' mortgage, about seventy-five bales of cotton, some of which they had sold, and still had possession of the remainder; and prayed that they might be held accountable for this cotton, or its proceeds. In their answer to the amended bill, H. M. Comer & Co. admitted that they had received the cotton as alleged, but said that they had sold it, and had accounted to J. F. Comer for the proceeds of sale, before the bill was filed, and before they had any notice or information that complainants asserted any claim to it; and they demurred to the amended bill, so far as it sought relief as to this cotton, on the ground that complainants had an adequate remedy at law.

On the filing of the bill, an application being made to the register for the appointment of a receiver, it was thereupon agreed between the parties, "in order to save costs and expenses, that H. M. Comer & Co. should retain the possession of all of said property, upon their entering into bond conditioned that, if, on the final decision of said cause, it is ascertained and decided that Lehman, Durr & Co. are entitled to any part of the said property, under and by virtue of the mortgage which they claim to hold on the same; and if thereupon H. M. Comer & Co. shall pay, or cause to be paid to the said Lehman, Durr & Co., any decree which may be rendered against them, for the value of any of said property

[Comer v. Lehman, Durr & Co.]

embraced or covered by said mortgage, then said obligation to be void;" and a bond was executed by H. M. Comer & Co., conditioned as stipulated. It was agreed, also, that the chancellor should consider the question of allowing interest, as against H. M. Comer & Co., on the cotton received and sold by them before the bill was filed, the interest amounting to $462.

The chancellor held the mortgage void as to the horses and mules, and refused to reform it; but he further held that it conveyed, not only one hundred bales of cotton, but also all the other crops, corn, cotton-seed, fodder, &c., and that the complainants were entitled to hold H. M. Comer & Co. liable in this suit for the proceeds of all the cotton which they had received and sold before the bill was filed; and he ordered a reference to the register, to ascertain the indebtedness of J. F. Comer to the complainants, and the amount for which H. M. Comer & Co. were responsible. The register reported the indebtedness of J. F. Comer, principal and interest, to be $6,120.80, and that of H. M. Comer & Co. to be $4,991. The report was confirmed, and a personal decree was then rendered against the defendants separately, with a direction that all sums paid by H. M. Comer & Co., or collected from them, should be credited on the decree against said J. F. Comer ; but the chancellor refused to allow interest against H. M. Comer & Co. on the proceeds of the cotton which they had received and sold before the bill was filed.

The defendants appeal from this decree, and here assign it as error, particularly in the construction given to the mortgage on the crops. By consent, the complainants below file cross-assignments of error: 1st, the refusal to reform the mortgage as to the horses and mules; 2d, the refusal to allow interest against H. M. Comer & Co., as claimed.

G. L. COMER, for appellants.—(1.) The mortgage being a printed form, with written changes and additions, the written words must control in the construction of the instrument; and they limit the conveyance to one hundred bales of cotton, the first to be picked and ginned.—*Bolman v Lohman*, 79 Ala. 67. (2.) As to the mules and horses, the mortgage was void for uncertainty, and the chancellor properly refused to reform it.—Jones on Chattel Mortgages, § 55, and authorities cited; *Stewart v. Jaques*, 77 Geo. 365; *Richardson v. Lumber Co.*, 40 Mich. 203; *Blakely v. Patrick*, 67 N. C.

40; 1 Kans. 259; *Mobile Savings Bank v. Fry*, 69 Ala. 348; *Hurt v. Redd*, 64 Ala. 85. (3.) As to the cotton received and sold by H. M. Comer & Co. before the bill was filed, if it was a part of the one hundred bales first picked and ginned, complainants had an adequate remedy at law, by action of trover, or special action on the case. (4.) Complainants received the highest market price for the cotton which went into the hands of H. M. Comer & Co., and they were not entitled to interest on it also.

TROY, TOMPKINS & LONDON, *contra.*—(1) As to the mortgage on the mules and horses, the complainants were entitled to have it reformed and foreclosed on all the animals, or, at least, to be allowed to select twenty of the number. The proof is undisputed, that Comer proposed to mortgage all of his horses and mules, and that complainants accepted his proposal as made, trusting to his representations as to the number. To refuse relief as to the horses and mules under these circumstances, would be to allow a party to take advantage of his own fraud or wrongful act.—*Love v. Graham*, 25 Ala. 187; *Smith v. Jordan*, 97 Amer. Dec. 232; 55 *Ib.* 137; 1 Story's Equity, §§ 147, 154; 2 Pom. Equity, §§ 870, 872; 3 *Ib.* § 1376; *Call v. Gray*, 75 Amer. Dec. 141. (2.) As to the cotton and other crops, the chancellor adopted the proper and most reasonable construction. When a written instrument is fairly susceptible of two or more constructions, it will be construed most strongly against the grantor; and though it be partly printed, and partly written, effect must be given to every word, if possible, since it is not to be presumed that the parties intended to insert inconsistent provisions.—1 Brick. Digest, 386, § 162; *Wilson v. Manning*, 53 Ala. 549; *Robinson v. Bullock*, 58 Ala. 618; *Ins. Co. v. Crane*, 77 Amer. Dec. 289; *Hutchinson v. Lord*, *Ib.* 381, 388; 1 Chitty on Contracts, 120; *Bolman v. Lohman*, 79 Ala. 67. (3.) H. M. Comer & Co. are chargeable as purchasers with notice, actual and constructive.—Jones on Chattel Mortgages, § 312; *Price v. McDonald*, 54 Amer. Dec. 657; *Morrison v. Kelly*, 74 Amer. Dec. 178; 15 Wall. 165-75; *Wade on Notice*, §§ 17, 90, 183; *Westmoreland v. Foster*, 60 Ala. 455; 2 Story's Equity, §§ 1255-6. As to the right to hold them responsible in this suit for the proceeds of cotton sold before the bill was filed, see *Stow v. Bozeman*, 29 Ala. 397; *Scruggs v. Driver*, 31 Ala. 274; *Alexander v. Rea*, 50 Ala. 450. (4.) But the chancellor erred in not allowing the complainants interest on the proceeds of this cotton, which was not included in the terms of the bond given by H. M. Comer & Co.—*Flinn v. Barber,* 64 Ala. 193; *State v. Lott,* 69 Ala. 147; *Bradley v. Harden,* 73 Ala. 70; *Chambers v. Wright,* 52 Ala. 444; *Broughton v. Mitchell,* 64 Ala. 210..

McCLELLAN, J.—The negotiations of the parties, which led up to and resulted in the execution of the mortgage, may, on the case as presented by the complainants, be epitomized thus: Comer desired to borrow seven thousand dollars from Lehman, Durr & Co. The latter required that the loan be secured by mortgage. Comer proposed to secure them by assigning certain *choses* in action, and by mortgage on certain crops, and on all his mules and horses then in use on his plantations in Barbour and Bullock counties, and represented that there were twenty head of such mules and horses, though he in fact had thirty-six horses and mules on said plantations at the time, as afterwards transpired This proposition was accepted, the mortgage drawn accordingly, and the money advanced. The contract thus reduced to writing was the contract upon which the minds of the parties had met. The agreement was for twenty head of mules and horses—the contract was so written. The intention of the parties was to cover that number, and that intention was embodied in the paper. Had complainants known the real facts, they might have declined to advance the money, unless Comer would put thirty-six instead of twenty mules and horses in the mortgage; and Comer might or might not have done so. The intentions of the parties might have been other than they were, had all the facts been known to the complainants; on the facts as represented, the intention was clear, and is clearly expressed in the instrument. Equity will reform written contracts, so as to make them evidence what they were intended to evidence—the pact between the parties; but it will not amend a contract entered into under a misapprehension of facts by one party or both, so as to make of it an agreement which the parties, or either of them, did not contemplate, and which the parties, or one of them, might have declined to execute, had both been cognizant of all the facts. This would be, not to make the writing speak the true terms of the agreement—the real intent of the parties—but to make a new contract embodying terms on which the minds of the parties not only had not met, but with respect to which, in this case, according to the aspect of the evidence most favorable to the complainants, one of the parties had resorted to misrepresentation to avoid. This may have been fraud; it may have afforded ground for equitable relief against the contract made; but it is not ground for making a new contract between the parties. We discover no error in the decree of the chancellor on this part of the case.

The granting part of the mortgage, or so much of it as is material for us to consider, is in the following words: "*I*, the said *J. F. Comer*, do by these presents grant, bargain, sell and convey, to the said Lehman, Durr & Co., the following real and personal property, to-wit, the entire crops of corn, cotton, fodder, cotton-seed, and all other crops of every kind or description, which may be made and grown during the present year on the lands in *Bullock and Barbour* county, which *I am* cultivating and causing to be cultivated during the present year, *to the extent of one hundred bales of cotton, which said cotton is to be the first cotton picked and raised on any of my plantations; said cotton is to weigh five hundred pounds average to the bale; any balance after such 100 bales cotton he may mortgage to other parties.*" In making this mortgage, a printed form was used, and the instrument as executed was partly printed and partly written. Of the clause quoted above, that part which is italicized is written, and the other is printed. The instrument also undertook to convey twenty mules and horses, and to transfer and assign certain *choses* in action, amounting to ten thousand dollars, to secure a loan of seven thousand dollars. The chancellor construed that part of the granting clause of the mortgage which is quoted above to embrace and convey one hundred bales of cotton, and all of the other crops grown on the plantations referred to. My own opinion is, that it covers only the one hundred bales of cotton. I base this conclusion on the following considerations: (1.) The words, "entire crops of corn, cotton, cotton-seed," &c., appear in the printed form. They are inconsistent with the written limitations, which, to my mind, refer to the substantive term, "entire crops," and confine the operation of the instrument to one hundred bales of cotton out of the crop. The use of the words, "of corn, cotton-seed," &c., is due to the fact that they were a part of the printed paper intended for general application, and is not referable to the intention of the parties to this particular transaction. In such cases, the rule is to discard the irreconcilable printed words, and look alone to those that are written, as being the best exponents of intention.—*Amer. Ex. Co. v. Binckney*, 29 Ill. 410; *Robertson v. French*, 4 East, 130. (2.) The property which this interpretation leaves nominally subject to the mortgage, was amply sufficient to secure the money advanced; and it is not to be assumed, as showing intention, that the mortgagees would have demanded, or the mortgagor would have consented to give, more security than was necessary, especially when the paper itself evidences that it was contemplated by both parties that Comer would have to execute other mortgages to secure additional advances. (3.) The correspondence of the parties between the execution and the law-day of the mortgage tends strongly to show that each and all of them treated and construed it as covering no part of the crops except the one hundred bales of cotton.

But a majority of the court have reached a different conclusion. They take a middle ground between my position and that of the chancellor, and hold that the instrument is an absolute mortgage, so to speak, on one hundred bales of cotton, and that it covers also the other crops, but only for the purpose of securing the delivery of one hundred bales of cotton, or the payment of the value thereof, and only to the extent necessary to an effectuation of that purpose. This conclusion has been reached mainly on the consideration, that no other construction will admit of some meaning being given to each of the words employed. Under this construction, the chancellor will so shape his further action in the premises as to subject the other crops, or the proceeds arising from a sale of them, to the end that the complainants shall receive the full value of the one hundred bales of cotton, of the quality indicated in the mortgage.

The Chancery Court having taken jurisdiction to foreclose the mortgage on the crops which were in the possession of H. M. Comer & Co. in Alabama, at the time the bill was filed, properly took cognizance of complainants' claim against said H. M. Comer & Co., on account of cotton covered by the mortgage, which had been received and disposed of by them before the suit was instituted.

This cotton, it appears, was not embraced in the forthcoming bond which Comer & Co. executed, and the consideration which rendered it inequitable to decree interest on the value of the property covered by that bond did not apply to the proceeds of the cotton. The decree should have allowed complainants interest on the value of the cotton which had

24

been disposed of by Comer & Co. before bill filed, from the time of its sale by them.

For the errors above indicated, the decree is reversed, and the cause is remanded.

Brown *v.* Alabama Great Southern Railroad Co.

Action for Damages against Railroad Company, for Injuries to Stock.

1. *Jurisdiction of justice of the peace, under constitutional and statutory provisions.*—Under constitutional and general statutory provisions (Const. Ala., Art. vi, § 26; Code, § 839), the jurisdiction of a justice of the peace, in cases of tort, is limited to $50; and the special statute which gives him jurisdiction "of all actions for injury to, or destruction of stock, by the locomotive or cars of a railroad, if the sum in controversy does not exceed $100" (Code, § 1149), being a discrimination against corporations, is unconstitutional and void as to the excess of jurisdiction attempted to be conferred.

APPEAL from the Circuit Court of Tuskaloosa.

Tried before the Hon. SAM. H. SPROTT.

This action was brought by R. R. Brown, against the appellee, a domestic corporation, to recover $65 as damages for the loss of two cows and ten turkeys, alleged to have been negligently killed by the defendant's locomotive and cars; and was commenced in a justice's court, on the 6th September, 1887. The defendant pleaded in abatement to the jurisdiction of the justice, and moved to dismiss the suit because the amount claimed was beyond his jurisdiction; but the justice overruled the plea and the motion, and rendered judgment for the plaintiff, for $65 besides costs. On appeal to the Circuit Court, the plaintiff filed a complaint claiming $65 as damages; and the defendant again pleaded in abatement to the jurisdiction of the justice, and moved to dismiss the suit; which motion the court sustained. The judgment dismissing the suit is here assigned as error.

HARGROVE & VANDEGRAAFF, for appellant.—This action was commenced before the present Code went into effect, and is governed by section 1711 of the Code of 1876, the phraseology of which differs materially from section 1149 of the Code of 1886. The former gives an action, for injuries to stock, against "all corporations, person or persons, owning or controlling any railroad;" while the latter gives an action "for injury to, or destruction of stock, by the locomotive or cars of a railroad." It is submitted that the statute, in either form, is not a discrimination against corporations, but only relates to the remedy and procedure in a particular class of cases—injuries to live stock by railroads. Railroads, like manufacturing establishments, steamboats, mills, &c., "may be owned and operated without incorporation. and by a single proprietor."—*Smith v. L. & N. Railroad Co.*, 75 Ala. 450; *Wilks v. Ga. Pac. Railway Co.*, 79 Ala. 180. The statute is not directed against corporations, but against the owners of railroads, or persons operating them, whether as owners or lessees. Under constitutional provisions, one hundred dollars is the limit of a justice's jurisdiction, in civil cases, whether founded on contract, or sounding in damages; and certain kinds of action are expressly excepted.—Art. VI, § 26. Under the general statute, he has jurisdiction of "all actions founded on any wrong or injury, when the damages claimed do not exceed $50," except of the particular actions specified in the constitution; and also "in such other cases as jurisdiction is or may be given by law, not contrary to the constitution." What effect is to be given to this last clause, except to allow his jurisdiction to be increased in cases of tort, as the General Assembly may deem proper? Of the kind or class of cases to be committed to his jurisdiction, the General Assembly is the proper judge. This statute has been of force for more than ten years, and it has passed through two Code compilations. Its constitutionality will be upheld, unless the mind of the court is clearly convinced to the contrary.

WOOD & WOOD, *contra*, cited *L. & N. Railroad Co. v. Morris*, 65 Ala. 193; *Home Protection Insurance Co. v. Richards*, 74 Ala. 467; *Smith v. L. & N. Railroad Co.*, 75 Ala. 449; Cooley's Const. Lim., 3d ed., § 393.

STONE, C. J.—Our decisons are uniform, that under our constitution and statutes, the jurisdiction of the justices of the peace, in cases of tort, is limited to fifty dollars. This is the language of the general statute.—Code of 1886, § 839; *Taylor v. Woods*, 52 Ala. 474; *Burns v. Henry*, 67 Ala. 209; *Carter v. Alford*, 64 Ala. 236; *Rodgers v. Gaines*, 73 Ala.

218; *Alabama Great Southern Railroad Co. v. Christian*, 82 Ala. 307.

In the Code of 1886, § 1149, is the following provision: "A justice of the peace has jurisdiction of all actions for injury to, or destruction of stock, by the locomotive or cars of a railroad, if the sum in controversy does not exceed one hundred dollars." We have thus the naked inquiry, whether the constitutions, Federal and State, permit the legislature to discriminate between railroad corporations and other persons, natural or artificial, in the matter of the jurisdiction of an inferior tribunal; or, in other words, whether it is competent for the legislature to limit a justice's jurisdiction to fifty dollars, in suits against tort-feasors generally, and to enlarge it to one hundred dollars, when a railroad corporation is the offender. Our former rulings compel us to declare section 1149 of the Code of 1886 to be unconstitutional. *S. & N. R. R. Co. v. Morris*, 65 Ala. 193; *Zeigler v. S. & N. R. R. Co.*, 58 Ala. 594; *Smith v. L. & N. R. R. Co.*, 75 Ala. 449; *Mayor v. Stonewall Ins. Co.*, 53 Ala. 570; *Green v. State*, 73 Ala. 26.

The judgment of the Circuit Court is affirmed.

Bullock *v.* Vann.

Action on Promissory Note, by Assignee against Maker.

1. *Transfer of promissory note by husband and wife* —Under the statute regulating the separate estates of married women. which has been in force since February 28th, 1887 (Sess. Acts 1886-7, p. 81; Code, §§ 2346, 2348), a promissory note which is the separate property of the wife, having been made payable to her while sole and unmarried, may be transferred by her written assignment, to which the husband's consent is affixed in writing, as well as by a joint assignment.

APPEAL from the Circuit Court of Russell.

Tried before the Hon. JAMES M. CARMICHAEL.

This action was brought by Osborn C. Bullock, against John C. Vann; was founded on the defendant's promissory note under seal, for $281.74, which was dated April 9th, 1887, and payable on the 1st December, 1887, "to the order of Fannie L. Paschal, or bearer;" and was commenced on the 9th March, 1888. The plaintiff sued as the assignee of the note, alleging that it was his property, The defendant filed a special plea, verified by affidavit, denying the plaintiff's ownership of the note, and alleging that it still belonged to the payee, then the wife of A. R. Calhoun. Issue was joined on this plea. On the trial, the plaintiff offered the note in evidence, with the indorsements thereon, which consisted of an assignment by Mrs. Calhoun, in these words, "For value received, I hereby assign the within note to O. C. Bullock," to which her name was signed; and underneath the words were added, "I hereby consent to the above assignment," to which the name of Calhoun was signed. On objection by the defendant, the court excluded the indorsements as evidence; to which ruling the plaintiff excepted, and took a non-suit.

WATTS & SON, for appellant.

L. W. MARTIN, *contra.*

SOMERVILLE, J.—The defendant's sworn plea denies the plaintiff's ownership of the promissory note, which is the subject of the suit.

The evidence shows that the note was the separate property of Mrs. Calhoun, who is a married woman, and that she assigned the instrument in writing to the plaintiff after February 28th, 1887, when the new married woman's law of that date went into effect. To this assignment, the husband, A. R. Calhoun, appended his consent in writing, which he duly subscribed. The act above cited, now comprised in the present Code, provides that "the wife has full legal capacity to contract in writing as if she were sole, with the assent or concurrence of the husband expressed in writing."—Code, 1886, § 2346; Acts 1886-87, sec. 6, p. 81.

The note was personal property of the wife, within the meaning of this term as used in the statute, and the title unquestionably passed to the plaintiff by the assignment. Code, 1885, § 2348; § 2, sub-div. 3. A strictly joint contract of transfer or assignment was unnecessary.

Reversed and remanded.

Maund *v.* Loeb & Brother.

Trover for Conversion of Goods.

1. *Continuance on payment of costs; itemized bill of costs.*—When a continuance is granted to the defendant, "on the payment of all costs within ninety days, as a condition precedent, or judgment to go against him at next term," his consent to the terms is implied in his acceptance of the continuance; and the costs not being paid within the ninety days, the court may enter judgment by *nil dicit* against him on the first day of the next term, although he then offers to pay them; nor is it necessary that an itemized bill of costs should have been furnished to him by the clerk or sheriff.

2. *Judgment by nil dicit; presumption in favor of.*—On judgment by *nil dicit* in regular form, the appellate court will presume, if necessary to sustain it, that it was so rendered because the defendant failed or declined to plead, and not because he failed to pay the costs as required by a former order granting him a continuance.

3. *Same; evidence as to damages.*—After judgment by *nil dicit* in an action of trover, the only question to be referred to the jury, as to which evidence can be adduced, relates to the amount of damages.

APPEAL from the Circuit Court of Henry.

Tried before the Hon. JESSE M. CARMICHAEL.

This action was brought by J. Loeb & Brother, suing as partners, against Wm. T. Maund, to recover damages for the conversion of certain goods particularly described; and was commenced on the 30th March, 1887. At the September term, 1888, an order was entered in the cause, in these words: "Continued by defendant, upon payment of all costs to date, as a condition precedent, to be paid in ninety days, or judgment to go against defendant at next term;" and the bill of exceptions states, that this order "was made in open court, in the presence and hearing of the defendant's counsel." At the next term, as the bill of exceptions further states, "when the case was called for trial, the court inquired of the clerk if the costs had been paid as required by said order, and was informed that they had not been paid in accordance with said order. The defendant then offered to prove that he had not been furnished with an itemized bill of said costs, by the clerk, sheriff, or other officer;" also, "that he had no knowledge or information of the terms imposed by said order of continuance, until said cause was called at this term;" also, "that he had paid all the costs of the case on the first

day of this term, since the cause was called for trial." On
objection by the plaintiff, the court excluded each part of this
evidence as offered, and the defendant excepted.   The bill of
exceptions then proceeds: "The plaintiffs introduced two
witnesses, who testified as to the value of such goods as
were mentioned in the complaint, at the time of the alleged
conversion by the defendant; and each of them stated that
he knew nothing about the identical goods sued for.   This
was all the evidence in the case.   Thereupon, the defendant
requested the following charges in writing: (1.) Before the
plaintiffs can recover in this action, they must prove a legal
title to the property sued for. (2.) If the plaintiffs parted with
the property sued for to Lumley for a consideration, and
Lumley sold the same to defendant for a consideration, and
the transaction between plaintiffs and Lumley was honest;
then the jury may find a verdict for the defendant.   (3.) If
the jury believe the evidence, they will find for the defendant."
The court refused each of these charges, and the defendant
excepted.

The judgment is by *nil dicit* in regular form, with damages assessed by the jury at $169.31.   The defendant appeals,
and assigns as error the rulings of the court excluding the
evidence offered by him, and the refusal of the charges
asked.

J. F. ROPER, for appellant.

R. H. WALKER, and WATTS & SON, *contra.*

CLOPTON, J.—The continuance of a case is in the discretion of the court, and such terms may be imposed, under
the rule of practice, as to the court may seem proper.   At
the Fall term, 1888, of the Circuit Court, defendant obtained
a continuance, upon payment of all the costs as a condition
precedent, to be paid in ninety days, or judgment to go
against him at the next term.   The costs were not paid
until the first day of the next term, and after the case was
called for trial, which was more than ninety days from the
time of the order.   Defendant having applied for, obtained,
and accepted the continuance, we must infer that he consented to the terms upon which it was granted.   It was no
excuse, that an itemized bill of costs had not been furnished,
when it is not shown that defendant offered to pay the costs,
or applied for such bill; and the court was not bound to

accept payment after the expiration of the prescribed time, as a compliance with the condition upon which the continuance was obtained. The court was authorized to render judgment *nil dicit* against defendant.—*Waller v. Sultzbacher*, 38 Ala. 318.

But the record does not show that the judgment was rendered because of defendant's failure to pay the costs. The judgment-entry recites, that defendant said nothing in bar or preclusion of the plaintiff's demand. The defendant was in court, in person, and by attorney. No pleas appear by the record to have been filed, and none were offered to be filed. If necessary to sustain the action of the court, we would presume, from the recitals of the minute-entry, that judgment was rendered because defendant failed or declined to plead. After a judgment *nil dicit* in an action of trover, the only question to be referred to the jury, of which plaintiff is required to make proof, relates to the amount of damages. All the charges asked by defendant go to plaintiff's right to recover at all, and were inapplicable, and properly refused.

Affirmed.

Bay Shell-Road Co. *v.* O'Donnell.

Trespass for Wrongfully Impounding Cattle.

1. *Constitutional provisions as to amending or extending laws by reference to title; estraying cattle on Bay Shell-Road in Mobile.*—The second section of the act "for the protection of life and property upon the Bay Shell-Road" in Mobile, approved February 17th, 1885 (Sess. Acts 1884-5, pp. 392-3), so far as it authorizes any officer or employee of the road company to take up any animal found running at large on its road, and to estray the same in the manner provided by the general law governing estrays, referring to said law only by the numbers of the article, chapter and title in the Code of Alabama, in which it is found, is violative of the constitutional provision (Art. IV, § 2), which provides, that no law "shall be revived, amended. or the provisions thereof *extended or conferred*, by reference to its title only, but so much thereof as is revived, amended, *extended or conferred*, shall be re-enacted and published at length."

APPEAL from the City Court of Mobile.

Tried before the Hon. O. J. SEMMES.

This action was brought by John O'Donnell, against the Bay Shell-Road Company, a private corporation, to recover

[Bay Shell-Road Co. v. O'Donnell.]

damages for an alleged trespass committed by defendant's servants and agents, in seizing plaintiff's cattle while trespassing on said shell-road, and detaining them until plaintiff paid the required fees and expenses in order to procure their release; and it was commenced on the 12th April, 1887. The defendant pleaded not guilty, and filed a special plea justifying the seizure under an act of the General Assembly, the material provisions of which are quoted in the opinion of the court. The court below sustained a demurrer to the special plea, and the ruling thereon is here assigned as error, with other matters which require no special notice.

OVERALL & BESTOR, for appellant.

R. INGE SMITH, contra.

McCLELLAN, J.—By section 2 of an act "for the protection of life and property upon the Bay Shell Road," approved February 17, 1885, it is provided, "that it shall be unlawful for any person to allow any loose animal belonging to them to run at large upon said Bay Shell Road, and any animal found running at large on said road may be, by any officer or employee of said Bay Shell Road Company, taken up and estrayed in the manner as is provided by Article I, Chapter 7, Title 13, Part 1 of the Code of Alabama."—Acts 1884-5, pp. 392-3.

To an action of trespass brought against the Bay Shell Road Company by John O'Donnell, for impounding cattle belonging to him and found running at large on the road, the company, in addition to the general issue, pleaded this statute. The special plea was demurred to, on the ground of the alleged unconstitutionality of the act; the demurrers were sustained, and a trial was had on the general issue, resulting in a judgment for the plaintiff, from which this appeal is prosecuted.

It may admit of doubt, whether the statute is unconstitutional for either of the reasons assigned in the demurrers; but, if the act is bad on any ground, or as being violative of any provision of the constitution, the action of the court, in sustaining the demurrers interposed on the grounds stated, would bear a striking analogy to the ascription of a wrong reason for a correct decision, in which case the decision would be upheld; and in any aspect, if error at all, would be without injury to the defendant company, as it could never justify under the void law.

That the provision of this statute, under which justification was attempted, is void, we entertain no doubt. Section 2 of Article IV, Constitution of 1875, provides that "No law shall be revived, amended, or the provisions thereof extended or conferred, by reference to its title only; but so much thereof as is revived, amended, extended or conferred, shall be re-enacted and published at length." By the act we are considering, the estray law of this State is amended so as to embrace the Bay Shell Road, in addition to residences and plantations; its provisions are extended to said road, and the rights and powers which it gives to owners of residences and plantations are conferred upon the Bay Shell Road Company; and all this is attempted to be done by even less than a reference to its title, and without any pretense of re-enacting the law, all of the provisions of which are thus amended, extended and conferred, or of publishing it at length. The purpose of this constitutional requirement was, to have each bill considered by the General Assembly in and of itself present the full scope, operation and effect of the proposed law, so that members might know and intelligently consider the details of every measure, and vote neither *aye* or *nay* "in blind ignorance of its provisions, or even in trusting confidence to the representations of others."

It would be difficult to conceive a more effective method of defeating this important and salutary purpose, than that adopted in this statute, by which the legislature attempted to amend, extend and confer all the provisions of an intricate and important statute, by a general reference to the subject-matter of that law, and to the book and page where it is published at length. So much of the act, therefore, as attempts to give the right to "estray" animals found running at large on the Bay Shell Road, is unconstitutional and void.—*Stewart v. Commissioners of Hale County*, 82 Ala. 209.

It is not necessary for us to decide, in this case, whether the whole of section 2 of the act is violative of the organic law; and we express no opinion on that subject.

The bill of exceptions does not purport to set out all the evidence; and in support of the ruling of the court in allowing the plaintiff to testify about loss of time in making a trip to the city, it will be presumed that this trip to the city was necessitated by the wrongful act of the defendant, in such sort that the loss of time in making it was an element of the damages which he was entitled to recover.

The facts about the taking of the cattle were undisputed. This taking, we have seen, was wrongful. The charge directing the jury to return a verdict for plaintiff's actual damages was free from error.

The judgment is affirmed.

Walden *v.* Speigner.

Statutory Action of Unlawful Detainer, by Widow of Deceased Mortgagor, against Purchaser at Mortgage Sale.

1. *Who may redeem; widow of deceased mortgagor.*—Under statutory provisions giving and regulating the right to redeem lands sold under execution, or power of sale in a mortgage (Code, §§ 1879, 1888, 1891), the right is not conferred upon the widow of a deceased mortgagor, who joined with her husband in a mortgage of the homestead, under which the land was sold after his death; although his estate was insolvent at the time of his death, and was so declared after the foreclosure of the mortgage by sale under the power, and the premises were afterwards set apart to her as her homestead, subject to the mortgage incumbrance.

APPEAL from the Circuit Court of Talladega.

Tried before the Hon. LEROY F. BOX.

This action was brought by Mrs. Emily P. Walden, the widow of George S. Walden, deceased, against J. H. Speigner, to recover the possession of a house and lot in Talladega; and was commenced on the 23d of April, 1887. The house and lot was the family residence of said George S. Walden at the time of his death, and was mortgaged by him in September, 1879, to L. E. Parsons, his wife joining with him in the conveyance. The mortgage was assigned by Parsons to M. W. Cruikshanks, and the property was sold, under a power of sale contained therein, in April or May, 1885, after the death of said Walden. The defendant became the purchaser at the sale, and possession was delivered to him by the widow, who had continued in possession after her husband's death. Walden left no surviving minor child or children, and was insolvent at the time of his death; and his estate was declared insolvent soon after the sale under the mortgage. The property was afterwards set apart to the widow as her homestead, subject to the mortgage incumbrance; and she made a tender and offer to redeem

[Walden v. Speigner.]

within two years after the sale, which was refused by the
defendant, on the ground that she had no right to redeem.
These facts were alleged, in substance, in the amended complaint filed in the Circuit Court. The court sustained a
demurrer to the complaint, on the ground that the plaintiff
showed no right to redeem; and this ruling is here assigned
as error.

KNOX & BOWIE, for appellant.—The redemption statute
was intended to prevent the sacrifice of real estate, and is
highly remedial. It should receive a liberal construction,
and its benefits be extended to all persons who come within
the mischief intended to be remedied. The plaintiff here,
though not a debtor, was a party to the mortgage, and had
an interest in the property sold—not only a right of dower,
but a right of homestead. Without her signature and
acknowledgment, the mortgage would have been a nullity.
Her right of homestead has now become perfected, subject
only to the incumbrance of the mortgage; and the property
is sacrificed, if she is not allowed to redeem, since it is not
subject to administration, and the administrator can not
redeem in the interest of creditors. It would be a strange
construction of a remedial statute, to extend its provisions to
solvent estates, but withhold them from estates which are
insolvent, and which most need its protection. A person
may be entitled to redeem, although he is not *the debtor*,
strictly speaking; as where one man mortgages his property
for the debt of another; and where two tenants in common
mortgage the property for the debt of one; in either of which
cases, it is believed, the right of redemption could not be
denied.

BROWNE & NEWMAN, *contra*, cited *Powers v. Andrews*,
84 Ala. 289; *Holden v. Rison*, 77 Ala. 515; *Searcy v. Oates*,
68 Ala. 111; 74 Ala. 331; 75 Ala. 297; 73 Ala. 387.

STONE, C. J.—I was dissatisfied with the ruling in
Powers v. Andrews, 84 Ala. 289. I preferred then, and
would still prefer, to follow the decisions made by this court
in *Paulling v. Meade*, 23 Ala. 505, and *Bailey v. Timberlake*,
74 Ala. 221. I think the statute should be liberally interpreted, and that whoever, at the time of the sale, is the
owner of the equity of redemption, or *residuum* of the estate,
whether by purchase, succession, or by devolution, should be

[Cobb v. Thompson.]

let in to redeem; in other words, that the statutory right to redeem, within two years after sale, should be the necessary resultant of the equitable right to redeem or disincumber by paying off the incumbrance before sale.

The rule was differently announced in *Powers v. Andrews, supra*, at the last term. We then held, that only persons who fall within one of the enumerated classes can claim this right. In addition to judgment creditors, whose right is not presented in the present record, we enumerated all the classes upon whom the statute confers this right. Mrs. Walden was and is neither the debtor, his personal representative, his heir or devisee, nor a child who was the grantee of Walden, who owned the land sold. She was and is only his widow, claiming the right to redeem, because the property was the family homestead at the date of the mortgage, at the time of his death, and at the time of the sale under the mortgage. She supplements her claim by showing that Walden, her husband, was insolvent when he died, and that in less than two years after the sale the estate was declared insolvent, and the property set apart to her, as her homestead.

Under the principles declared in *Powers v. Andrews*, we feel bound to deny her the right to redeem.

Affirmed.

Cobb *v.* Thompson.

Certiorari and Supersedeas on Justice's Judgment.

1. *Replevy (or forthcoming) bond in attachment case, before justice of the peace.*—In an attachment case before a justice of the peace, a replevy bond conditioned to have the property forthcoming within *twenty* days after the rendition of judgment, is substantially defective as a statutory bond (Code. §§ 3334–41), and does not authorize a summary execution on a return of forfeiture; and the defect being one of substance, it is not cured by the statutory provision as to defects of form (*Ib.* § 3357).

2. *Certiorari and supersedeas to justice of the peace; when proper remedy.*—When a forthcoming bond in an attachment case, before a justice of the peace, is illegally returned by the constable as forfeited, and a summary execution is thereupon wrongfully issued against the obligors, a petition for a *certiorari* and *supersedeas* from the Circuit Court is the proper remedy, since the defects would not be available on appeal from the justice's judgment.

[Cobb v. Thompson.]

APPEAL from the City Court of Anniston.
Tried before the Hon. W. F. JOHNSTON.

The record in this case shows these facts: On the 28th October, 1887, an attachment for rent was sued out before a justice of the peace, in favor of Mrs. C. A. Thompson against Percy Olmstead, and was levied on certain articles of household furniture, on which several executions had already been levied, one in favor of R. W. Miller, and the others in favor of E. J. Cobb; and said Cobb and Miller thereupon signed, as sureties for said Olmstead, a replevy bond conditioned for the forthcoming of the property within twenty days after the rendition of judgment in the attachment case, which bond was approved by the justice who issued the attachment. In the attachment suit, judgment was rendered for the plaintiff on the 15th November, 1887, and the attached property was ordered to be sold for the satisfaction of the judgment. On the 12th December, 1887, the constable returned the replevy bond forfeited; and on the next day the justice issued a summary execution on the bond, against all the obligors. On the 29th December, 1887, Cobb and Miller, the sureties on the bond, filed their petition, addressed to Hon. JOHN P. HUBBARD, presiding judge of the Circuit Court at Montgomery, asking a *supersedeas* of the execution, and a *certiorari* to the justice of the peace, to remove the proceedings into the Circuit Court. Judge Hubbard granted a *fiat* for a *certiorari* generally, and under it the proceedings were certified to the Circuit Court; but, by agreement, the case was afterwards transferred to the City Court of Anniston. On the trial in that court, as the judgment-entry recites, "the plaintiff demurred to the petition for the writ of *certiorari*, and moved to dismiss the *certiorari*," which motion and demurrer were overruled by the court; "and issue being then joined, and the case submitted to the court without a jury, it is considered that the plaintiff is entitled to recover; and that the said C. A. Thompson have and recover of the said defendants, E. J. Cobb and R. W. Miller, the sum of $106.89, with the costs in this behalf expended." This judgment is now assigned as error by Cobb and Miller. There is no bill of exceptions in the record.

MACDONALD & WILLIAMS, for appellants.

CASSADY & BLACKWELL, *contra*.

[Cobb v. Thompson.]

SOMERVILLE, J.—The purpose of the petition is to supersede an execution summarily issued on a replevy or forthcoming bond executed by a defendant and his sureties, in an attachment proceeding before a justice of the peace, and returned by a constable as forfeited.—Code, 1886, §§ 3334–3341. The bond bore date October 28th, 1887, and was declared forfeited December 12th, 1887, on the ground that the replevied property had not been returned to the constable according to the condition of the bond.

If the undertaking is not a statutory bond—that is, if it does not substantially conform to the requirements of the statute—and its defects are not cured under the provisions of section 3357 of the present Code, the summary remedies given by the statute for the enforcement of its obligations will not lie. The instrument will be good only as a common-law bond, and must be sued on as such.

A fatal defect in the undertaking, so far as concerns its conformity to the statute, is the *time* when the replevied property is to be returned to the constable, which is not only material, but of substance, and not mere form. The Code provides, where personal property, levied on under a writ of *attachment* issuing from a justice's court, is replevied, it "must be delivered to the constable within *ten days* after judgment against the defendant, unless an appeal is prosecuted from the judgment; and on failure thereof, the constable must indorse the bond forfeited, upon which execution must issue against the obligors therein."—Code, 1886, § 3341. Where the levy is under *execution*, the condition of the bond is, "to have the property forthcoming at twelve o'clock of the day, and at the place appointed for *the sale*." Code, § 3354. The present case involves a levy under attachment, not execution. The condition of the delivery bond should, therefore, have been to deliver the attached property to the constable, within *ten days* after judgment against the defendant in attachment, unless an appeal should be prosecuted from the justice's judgment.

The bond in the present case binds the obligors to return the attached property to the constable within *twenty* days after judgment in the attachment suit. This is a material variance from the time fixed by the statute, which, as we have seen, is ten days. It is settled by the authorities, that a forthcoming bond, which provides for the delivery of property on a day different from the day prescribed by law, is not good as a statutory bond, but only as a common-law

[Cobb v. Thompson.]

bond, and it can not be declared forfeited summarily by sheriffs or constables, as only statutory bonds can be.—Murfree on Official Bonds, § 384; *Adler v. Green*, 18 West Va. 201; *Irvin v. Eldridge*, 1 Wash. (Va.) 203; 1 Wade on Attach. §§ 195–197. The power to render such summary judgments, which involves a waiver of the right of trial by jury on the part of the obligors, is based on the contract of the parties that they will submit to such a remedy, provided the undertaking conforms to the statutory requirements. If it does not, they have the right to assume that the implied agreement is that it will be enforced only by the ordinary common-law remedies, and not by those summarily conferred by statute, and affixed only to statutory undertakings.

This defect is not, in our opinion, cured by section 3357 of the Code. While that section would seem to authorize a forthcoming bond to be approved by either a justice or constable, and might, therefore, operate to cure any defective approval of the undertaking, which more regularly should have been taken and approved by the officer making the levy, it goes no further than to cure defects of form, and not of substance. The defect of time here is clearly one of substance.

That a proceeding by *certiorari* or *supersedeas* is the appropriate remedy to quash a summary execution, issued on a forthcoming bond, illegally returned by a sheriff or constable as forfeited, is well settled.—*Rhodes v. Smith*, 66 Ala. 174; 3 Brick. Dig. 755, §§ 1-13; *Gravett v. Malone*, 54 Ala. 19; *Dunlap v. Clements*, 18 Ala. 778; 2 Brick. Dig. 465, §§ 1-33; *Crenshaw v. Hardy*, 3 Ala. 653. An appeal from the justice's judgment, on his refusal to quash the execution, would clearly furnish no adequate remedy. The trial in the Circuit Court would be *de novo*, on the merits of the whole case, and would not reach any alleged defect in the forthcoming bond, or determine its character as a statutory or common-law undertaking.

The City Court erred in refusing to quash the execution against the appellants. The judgment is reversed, and the cause remanded, that the execution issuing on the bond may be quashed and vacated according to the prayer of the petition.

Reversed and remanded.

Weaver *v.* Bell.

Statutory Detinue for Bale of Cotton.

1. *Verbal mortgage.*—By statutory provisions now of force (Code, § 1731), a mortgage of personal property is required to be in writing, and subscribed by the mortgagor, and a verbal mortgage has no validity.

2. *Estoppel by words or conduct.*—The breach of a mere executory agreement or promise does not constitute an estoppel *en pais;* as where plaintiff, in a conversation with defendant, relative to furnishing supplies to a third person to make a crop, said that he would not claim the crops in the fall if defendant would furnish the supplies, and defendant thereupon furnished supplies on the faith of a verbal mortgage only, these facts do not estop plaintiff from afterwards taking a mortgage on the crops for supplies subsequently furnished by him.

APPEAL from the Circuit Court of Cherokee.

Tried before the Hon. JOHN B. TALLY.

This action was brought by M. C. Bell against J. A. Weaver, to recover a bale of cotton; and was commenced in a justice's court, on the 3d of November, 1885. The cotton was raised during the year 1885 by one J. W. Foster, under whom each party claimed; the plaintiff under a mortgage for advances dated September 11th, 1885, and the defendant under a verbal mortgage given in March or April, 1885, for supplies furnished to said Foster during the year 1885; and the defendant also sought to establish an estoppel against the plaintiff, as created by a conversation which is stated in the opinion of the court. The plaintiff's mortgage was duly recorded, and the defendant had actual notice of it at the time the cotton was delivered to him by Foster. The rulings of the court, in the charges given and refused, were in favor of the plaintiff; and these rulings, to which the defendant excepted, are now assigned as error.

WALDEN & SON, for appellant.

BURNETT & SMYER, *contra.*

CLOPTON, J.—The mortgage, from which the plaintiff derives title to the cotton sued for, was executed by J. W. Foster September 11, 1885. In April preceding, defendant

25

and Foster, made an agreement, by which the latter gave the former a verbal lien on the crops covered by the mortgage, to secure supplies furnished by defendant, with the understanding that the crop of cotton should be his until the supplies were paid for. Defendant bases his right on a delivery of the cotton to him by Foster in pursuance of this agreement. It is not disputed that the cotton in controversy is embraced in the mortgage under which plaintiff claims, and that defendant had notice of it at the time he received the cotton. The only ground of defense is, that plaintiff is estopped from asserting title against the claim of defendant. It is claimed that the estoppel arises on a conversation about furnishing Foster with supplies, which defendant testifies occurred between him and plaintiff about the last of March, or first of April, 1885. We state the conversation in his own language: "I asked Bell to furnish Foster that year. He said he would not; that Foster already owed him. Bell said, 'You furnish him.' I replied, 'If I do, you'll come up in the fall, and want the crops.' Bell then said he would not." Thereafter defendant made the agreement with Foster above stated, and furnished him supplies.

By the agreement defendant obtained only a parol mortgage of the crops. This was invalid under section 1731 of Code of 1886, which was in force at that time. The section declares: "A mortgage of personal property is not valid, unless made in writing and subscribed by the mortgagor." Defendant was a creditor without a lien, without right in or to the cotton, until its delivery to him.

A false representation by word or conduct, or a concealment of material facts, upon which another has been induced to act to his prejudice, is essential to constitute an estoppel *en pais*. In ordinary cases, the representation or concealment must have reference to past or present facts. A representation, relating to future action or conduct, operates as an estoppel only when it has reference to the future relinquishment or subordination of an existing right, which is made to induce, and by which the party to whom it was addressed has been induced to act. If the mortgage of plaintiff had been an existing lien at the time of the conversation, and his declaration had reference to its waiver or abandonment should defendant furnish Foster with supplies, this might form the basis of an estoppel, the other essential elements being established. But such is not the case. Plaintiff's mortgage was not executed until several months afterwards.

VOL. LXXXVII.

[Smith v. Alexander.]

It will be observed that the only representation of fact, made by plaintiff, was that Foster already owed him. There is no attempt to prove any facts different from the state of things as represented in the conversation. The declaration of plaintiff to defendant can be regarded only as a declaration of intention, which may be modified, or, at the utmost, as a promise or agreement. Hence the claim of defendant is, that plaintiff, by his declaration of intention or promise, as it may be construed, estopped himself from the future acquisition of a lien on the crops, which he can set up against the right of defendant, as a creditor without a lien. If any injury has resulted to defendant, it was occasioned by the failure of the plaintiff to perform his contract, for which, if it be a binding contract, he is liable in damages. The breach of an executory agreement does not constitute an estoppel *en pais*. It possesses none of the essential elements.—*Starry v. Korah*, 65 Iowa, 267; *Jackson v. Allen*, 120 Mass. 64; *Ins. Co. v. Mowby*, 96 U. S. 544.

The court did not err in refusing the charges requested by defendant.

Affirmed.

Smith *v.* Alexander.

Bill of Interpleader, filed by Sheriff.

87
133

1. *Intervention of third person as party by petition; waiver of objection.* Although it is irregular, after an interpleader suit is regularly at issue, to allow a third person to intervene as a claimant of the fund, on his own petition; yet, if no objection to his intervention is made until after the lapse of more than seven years, when he has lost all other remedies by lapse of time, the objection comes too late.

2. *Same; error without injury.*—If the party objecting was not, and could not have been injured, by allowing the petitioner to remain in the cause as a party, he can not complain of the ruling, even if it was erroneous; as when he disclaims all interest in that portion of the fund allotted to the petitioner.

3. *Interest against attorney, on money received from fund in court.* When a fund in court, in an interpleader suit, is paid to the attorney of one of the parties pending the litigation, on his own motion, he is properly charged with interest on it at the final hearing.

APPEAL from the Chancery Court of Randolph.

Heard before the Hon. S. K. McSpadden.

SMITH & LOWE, for appellant.

W. H. FORNEY, W. D. BULGER, and AIKEN & BURTON, *contra.*

McCLELLAN, J.—In the year 1859, Jeremiah Smith obtained a decree in the Chancery Court of Randolph county divorcing him from M. E. Smith. This decree allowed M. E. Smith one hundred dollars *per annum* as alimony. Soon afterwards, M. E. Smith removed to Texas, where she died in 1867, only one installment of alimony—that for the year 1860—having been paid. In 1872, the death of M. E. Smith not being known to her attorney in Alabama, executions were issued, and the amount due on the decree for alimony was collected by the sale of Jeremiah Smith's property. While the money was in the hands of the sheriff, W. J. Borden claimed the fund as M. E. Smith's administrator, and W. H. Smith, insisting that she was still in life, claimed that the fund should be paid to him as her attorney. The sheriff, W. J. Alexander, being unable to determine for himself to which of these claimants he should pay the fund, filed his bill in the Chancery Court of Randolph, offered to bring the money into court, and prayed that Borden, as such administrator, and W. H. Smith be required to interplead in respect to it, and that he be discharged. A decretal order was made, directing the fund to be paid into court, and, on motion of W. H. Smith, it was paid to him pending the litigation.

In 1875, a decree was entered, requiring Borden and W. H. Smith to interplead. During the further progress of the cause, Jeremiah Smith was made a party on his own petition, without objection at the time; and upon the final hearing, it was decreed, that the complainant, Alexander, was entitled to a part of the gross sum, for his counsel fees and expenses in and about the litigation; that Borden, as administrator of M. E. Smith, deceased, was entitled to that part of the money which was collected as alimony for the years prior to her death; that out of this fund W. H. Smith should be allowed to retain a certain sum, as counsel fees for services rendered by him to M. E. Smith in her life-time; that Jeremiah Smith should be paid the remainder of the fund; and it was also decreed that W. H. Smith should pay interest on the money while it was in his hands. From this decree he prosecutes an appeal to this court; and assigns as error (1) that the court below overruled his motion to strike the petitions, motions, statements, answers, and all other papers presented by Jeremiah Smith, from the files; and (2) that the chancellor decreed interest against him on the fund which he held under an order of the court.

1. The motion directed against the pleadings, &c. of Jeremiah Smith proceeded on the ground, that he had never been properly admitted as a party to the cause. The chancellor overruled this motion, expressly on the ground, that it was not seasonably made, the said Smith having been admitted to the cause on his own petition, and "without objection at the time." Precisely when he was so let in, the record does not with certainty inform us. It is shown, however, that the respondent, W. H. Smith, in a demurrer which he filed to the original bill on July 14, 1875, "craves *oyer* of the petition of Jere. Smith, filed in this court, alleging that Margaret E. Smith is dead, and the proceedings had thereof;" and while neither that petition nor the action of the court upon it is set out in the transcript, the presumption, in support of the decree, will be here indulged, that in that petition Jeremiah Smith prayed to be made a party, and that the "proceedings had thereof" were those which resulted in the order allowing him to interplead in the cause. No objection appears to have been filed until September, 1882,—more than seven years after Jeremiah Smith became a party; and the motion then made appears not to have been brought to the attention of the court, or insisted on in any way, until October, 1887,—more than twelve years after the order of the court granting his petition to be made a party to the cause.

An objection to his admission, or a motion, seasonably made afterwards, to dismiss him, should have prevailed; but, to so dismiss him after he had come in without objection, and been recognized as a proper party until all other remedies he might have had, for the assertion of his unquestioned rights in the premises, had been barred by the lapse of time, would be in the highest degree inequitable. The chancellor was clearly right in refusing to do so.

2. But, had this action of the court been erroneous, it involved no injury to W. H. Smith. His only interest in the litigation consisted in his claim against the estate of M. E. Smith, for counsel fees and expenses. Whether Jeremiah Smith continued in the case or not, W. H. Smith could have asserted no claim whatever to that part of the fund which was adjudged to belong to him. On the con-

trary, W. H. Smith expressly disclaimed all interest in the money, except as against M. E. Smith's administrator, for certain fees which the decree allowed him. He could not have been prejudiced, therefore, by the fact that either Jeremiah Smith or Alexander was allowed to remain in the cause; and if to allow them to do so was error, it was without injury to him, and will not authorize a reversal of the decree.—*Norwood v. M. & C. R. R. Co.*, 72 Ala. 563, and cases cited.

3. It only remains to consider whether W. H. Smith should have been charged interest. The record shows that the fund was paid to him at his own instance; he has had it for many years, and it is not shown that he has not used it. The presumption. is, that he procured the money to be paid to him for the purpose of using it, and that he did use it. Had the fund not been paid to him, it could have been put at interest by an order of court. Having thus by his action, in inducing the court to have the fund paid to him, prevented other disposition of it pending litigation, for the benefit of the parties who were finally decreed to be entitled to it, and having himself had the advantage and profit resulting from its use, it was right and proper that he should pay interest, and the decree of the chancellor in this regard is free from error.

Affirmed.

Walden *v.* Speigner.

Statutory Action of Unlawful Detainer, by Judgment Creditor, against Purchaser at Sale under Mortgage.

1. *Filing claim against insolvent estate; who may redeem as judgment creditor.*—A judgment rendered against a debtor while living, which is not presented as a claim against his insolvent estate within the time allowed by law (Code, § 2238), is forever barred as a debt against the estate; and the plaintiff therein, or his assignee, can not claim, as a judgment creditor (*Ib.* § 1883), the right to redeem lands sold under a mortgage executed by the debtor while living.

APPEAL from the Circuit Court of Talladega.

Tried before the Hon. LEROY F. BOX.

This action was brought by Mrs. Emily P. Walden, the widow of George S. Walden, deceased, against J. H. Speig-

[Walden v. Speigner.]

ner, to recover the possession of a house and lot in Talladega;
and was commenced in a justice's court, on the 22d of April,
1887. The house and lot was the family residence of said
George S. Walden at the time of his death, in 1885, and
was mortgaged by him, in September, 1879, to L. E. Parsons,
his wife joining with him in the conveyance. The mortgage
was assigned by Parsons to M. W. Cruikshanks, and the
property was sold, under a power of sale contained therein,
in April, or May, 1885, after the death of said Walden.
The defendant in this action became the purchaser at the
sale, and possession was delivered to him by the widow. A
judgment had been rendered against said Walden, in March,
1884, in favor of Isbell, McMillan & Co.; and this judgment
having been assigned to his widow, she made a tender and
offer to redeem the property as a judgment creditor. The
tender was made within two years after the sale, and fully
complied with all the statutory requisitions; but it was refused by the defendant, on the ground that Walden's estate
had been declared insolvent, and the judgment had not been
filed as a claim against it within the time prescribed by law.
The court sustained this defense, and rendered judgment for
the defendant; and this judgment is here assigned as error
by the plaintiff.

KNOX & BOWIE, for appellant.—The failure to file the
judgment as a claim against the insolvent estate of the
deceased debtor, although it forever barred the debt as a
claim against the estate, in favor of all persons interested
therein, did not satisfy or extinguish it, nor take away
any collateral or independent remedies which the creditor
might have, suc has a vendor's lien, or a mortgage.—*Du-
val's Heirs v. McLoskey*, 1 Ala. 744; *Puryear v. Puryear*, 34 Ala. 556; *Mahone v. Haddock*, 44 Ala. 99;
Molton v. Henderson, 62 Ala. 433; *Inge v. Boardman*,
2 Ala. 331; *George v. George*, 67 Ala. 192; *Locke v. Palmer*,
26 Ala. 312; *Prince v. Prince*, 47 Ala. 283; *Hooks v. Br.
Bank*, 8 Ala. 580; *Minter v. Br. Bank*, 23 Ala. 762; *Evans
v. Evans*, 16 Ala. 465; *McBroom v. Governor*, 1 Porter, 41;
Mardis v. Smith, 2 Ala. 382. The statute was intended for
the benefit of the estate, or parties interested therein; and
only parties, or their privies, can plead the statute. For
analogous cases, see *Mooney v. Parker*, 18 Ala. 708; *Boren
v. McGehee*, 6 Porter, 432; *Fournier v. Curry*, 4 Ala. 321;
Trimble v. Williamson, 49 Ala. 525; *Jones & Blair v. Burden*, 20 Ala. 382.

CECIL BROWNE, *contra*, cited *Murdock v. Rousseau*, 32 Ala. 611; *Puryear v. Puryear*, 34 Ala. 556; *Watson v. Rose*, 51 Ala. 292.

STONE, C. J.—It has long been settled in this State, that a claim against an estate which has been decreed insolvent, that is not filed within nine months after the decree of insolvency, is forever barred as a debt against the estate. *Murdock v. Rousseau*, 32 Ala. 611; *Puryear v. Puryear*. 34 Ala. 555; *Watson v. Rose*, 51 Ala. 292. A claim in suit pending against an estate, if revived and prosecuted to judgment, is excepted from the rule stated above. In such case, the fact of making the personal representative a party to the suit, is regarded as the equivalent of filing:—3 Brick. Dig. 477, § 341.

The offer to redeem in this case, as a creditor of the deceased mortgagor, comes within the principle stated above. Walden, the mortgagor, had died, and his estate had been declared insolvent. The judgment, under which the redemption was attempted, had been rendered before Walden's death. More than nine months had elapsed after the decree of insolvency, and the claim was never filed against the insolvent estate. It had ceased to be a valid claim against the estate, and the owner of it had ceased to be a creditor. The Circuit Court rightly ruled that, as a creditor, Mrs. Walden showed no right to redeem.

Affirmed.

Louisville & Nashville Railroad Co. v. Perry.

Action by Brakeman against Railroad Company, for Damages on account of Personal Injuries.

1. *Negligence, as question of fact or law.*—The question of negligence, or contributory negligence, in any case, is properly left to the determination of the jury as a question of fact, unless the evidence is free from conflict, and the inferences to be drawn from it are clear and certain.

APPEAL from the Circuit Court of Montgomery.
Tried before the Hon. JOHN P. HUBBARD.

[Louisville & Nashville R. R. Co v. Perry.]

This action was brought by S. G. Perry, against the appellant corporation, to recover damages for personal injuries sustained by the plaintiff while in the defendant's employment as a brakeman; and was commenced on the 5th April, 1888. The accident occurred on the 29th May, 1887, at a wayside station on the defendant's road, where the plaintiff, a brakeman on the road, was standing on the track, for the purpose of making a coupling with the rear section of the freight train, which was coming on a down grade towards him; and his back was turned towards the moving cars when he was struck and injured, necessitating the amputation of one of his legs. The principal defense was contributory negligence on the part of the plaintiff himself, (1) in going in between the cars to make the coupling, instead of using a "coupling stick," as required by the rules of the railroad company; and (2) in not using due care and diligence to watch the approaching cars, which he knew were coming down from above. The bill of exceptions purports to set out "substantially all the evidence," and shows that the following rule, with others, was read in evidence on the part of the defendant: *"Rule No. 222.* Coupling cars by hand is strictly prohibited. Any violation of this rule will be severely dealt with. Yard-masters and conductors must see that it is strictly observed, and must report any infringement of it to the proper officer."

The defendant requested the following charges in writing, and duly excepted to their refusal: (1.) "If the jury believe the evidence, they must find for the defendant." (4.) "The regulation forbidding brakemen to make a coupling without the use of a coupling-stick is a reasonable and proper regulation; and if the jury believe that, at and before the happening of the injury complained of in this case, there was in force, and duly promulgated, a regulation of said railroad company forbidding brakemen to make a coupling without the use of a coupling-stick, and that plaintiff was injured while attempting to make a coupling without the use of a coupling-stick, then the jury might find for the defendant, unless they also find that said injuries were caused by the wanton or intentional act of the defendant or its servants, or by such recklessness as amounts to an indifference to plaintiff's safety." (5.) "If the jury believe from the evidence that, by the rules of the defendant, coupling cars by hand was prohibited, then plaintiff had no right to go upon the railroad for the purpose of coupling cars by hand; and if

the jury believe from the evidence that plaintiff, at the time
he was injured, was violating this rule, then he can not recover." (7.) "If the jury believe that, at and before the time
of the injury to plaintiff, there was in force a rule of the
defendant requiring brakemen to use a coupling-stick in
coupling cars; and that plaintiff, when he received the injuries, did not use a coupling-stick, and did not heed the signal whistled by the fireman just before the injury (if they
find that such signal was so given); and that plaintiff had
time after said signal was given, if in fact it was given, by
the exercise of ordinary care and prudence, to have gotten
safely from between the engine and the car to which it was
to be coupled; then, if the jury find these facts to exist, the
plaintiff can not recover."

The refusal of each of these charges is assigned as error.

JONES & FALKNER, for appellant.

WATTS & SON, *contra*.

SOMERVILLE, J.—The plaintiff, who was a brakeman,
was seriously injured while engaged in the act of coupling
cars on the defendant's road, near a switch on a wayside
station. The accident was produced by a rear section of
loaded cars being allowed to run down grade and strike the
next section, which plaintiff was attempting to couple to the
engine. The defense is contributory negligence, the evidence showing that the plaintiff was standing on the railroad
track at the time he was hurt, attempting to couple the cars
with his hands, without the use of a coupling stick, which
was in violation of the company's rules.

The evidence was conflicting as to the rate of speed at
which the rear section of cars was moving at the time of the
collision, and whether this speed was faster than usual or
not; whether the section came·to a complete stop, or moved
continuously down grade; whether the conductor gave a
signal to come fast or slow; and on other points bearing on
the question of negligence. And the inference, moreover,
was uncertain whether the plaintiff, who had been in the
service of the company only six or eight weeks, had any
knowledge of the rule in question, or was negligent in not
knowing it.

The degree of negligence on the defendant's part, in some
of these aspects, thus affects the inquiry as to the plaintiff's

[Winston v. Mitchell]

alleged contributory negligence, which is the main defense to the action.

It is insisted, however, that upon the uncontroverted facts of the case, the general affirmative charge should have been given for the defendant.

We have attentively examined this evidence, with an earnest desire to do exact justice to the parties. It would accomplish no good to discuss it in detail, each member of the court having thoroughly considered it in all its bearings.

Our conclusion is, that under the principles so frequently declared by us, the evidence is not sufficiently free from conflict, nor the inference of negligence so clear and certain, as to make the question of its existence a question of law. It was, we think, under the circumstances, properly left for the determination of the jury, as one of fact.—*City Council of Montgomery v. Wright*, 72 Ala. 411; *Mayor &c. Birmingham v. McCrary*, 84 Ala. 470; *Eureka Co. v. Bass*, 81 Ala. 200; s. c., 60 Amer. Rep. 152; *Ala. Gr. So. R. R. Co. v. Arnold*, 84 Ala. 160.

The court properly refused to give the general affirmative charge to find for the defendant.

The other three charges requested by the defendant withdrew from the consideration of the jury all inquiry as to the plaintiff's knowledge or notice of the existence of the rule forbidding the coupling of cars without the use of a stick. In the absence of this element of fact, the question of negligence *vel non* was properly left to the jury.—*Ga. Pac. Ry. Co. v. Propst*, 83 Ala. 518, 521.

The judgment must be affirmed.

Winston *v.* Mitchell.

Bill in Equity to establish Resulting Trust in Lands.

1. *Correspondence of pleadings and proof.*—When the bill seeks to establish a resulting trust in lands, a closer correspondence between the pleadings and the proof is required than in other cases, except bills for the reformation or specific performance of contracts, which are strictly analogous.

2. *Resulting trust in lands; variance.*—Where the father procures a transfer to himself of a judgment against his daughter's husband, for which he was also bound as surety on a *supersedeas* bond, and sells the husband's lands under execution issued on it, becoming himself the

purchaser, and taking the title in his own name with the word *agent* added; a resulting trust will be declared in favor of the wife and daughter, on averment and proof that the transfer of the judgment was procured at her instance, under an agreement between her father and herself, and paid for with the proceeds of the sale of certain bank stock belonging to her statutory estate, in order that the lands might be bought and held for her benefit; but, if the evidence shows that the bank stock was in fact not sold for a year after the transfer of the judgment, and that the agreement between the parties did not contemplate a sale and purchase of the lands under execution on the judgment, there is a fatal variance between the allegations and the proof.

3. *Same.*—If the bill had alleged that the judgment was purchased with money raised by a pledge of complainant's bank stock, and claimed a resulting trust in all of the lands, while the evidence showed that only a part of the money was procured by a pledge of the bank stock, the variance would have been fatal to relief, though the complainant might have had relief under another bill.

4. *Constructive trust arising from use of wife's funds.*—If the judgment was purchased by the father, by agreement with his married daughter, with money borrowed on a pledge of her bank stock, she having no legal capacity to bind herself or her statutory estate by a contract for the loan of money, the agreement could not be enforced against him, unless he is estopped from setting up the want of mutuality; but a trust arises by implication of law from such illegal use of her statutory funds, which she may follow into the lands purchased with them, unless she elects to hold the parties personally liable for the conversion; and seeking to enforce a trust in the lands, she may claim interest accruing since February 28th, 1887, when the statute now of force became operative.

APPEAL from the Chancery Court of Sumter.

Heard before the Hon. THOS. W. COLEMAN.

The bill in this case was filed on the 1st of February, 1887, by Mrs. Martha A. Mitchell, who was the wife of Daniel Mitchell and the daughter of Augustus A. Winston, against her said father and husband; and sought to establish and enforce a resulting trust in her favor, in certain lands which had belonged to her husband, and which had been sold under execution against him, her father becoming the purchaser, and taking the title in his own name. The lands consisted of three separate tracts, or places: 1st, the "Patton tract," containing about fifteen hundred acres, of which said Mitchell owned an undivided one-half interest; 2d, the "Harrison tract," containing about 390 acres; and, 3d, the "Long place," the area of which is not shown. These lands were sold by the United States marshal on the 6th of June, 1881, under an *alias* execution, issued on a judgment of the Circuit Court of the United States at Mobile, in favor of Catherine Moore against said Daniel Mitchell, for $6,350.44, as affirmed by the U. S. Supreme Court on appeal; Winston being surety for Mitchell on a *supersedeas* bond in the case. Three separate deeds were executed by the marshal to said Winston, the word *agent* being added after his name in each case, at the following prices: 1st, the Patton tract, $3,025; the Harrison tract, $505; and the Long place, $505, all aggregating $4,035; and copies of these deeds were made exhibits to the bill. The allegations of the bill as amended, on which complainant sought to establish a trust in her favor in these lands, were in these words: " Your oratrix was then the owner of $10,000 of bank stock in the Gainesville National Bank, which she owned as her statutory separate estate. . . Prior to April, 1878, one Catherine Moore obtained a judgment in the United States Circuit Court at Mobile, against said Daniel Mitchell, for several thousand dollars, besides costs of suit. . . On or about April 17, 1878, said judgment was transferred to said A. A. Winston, for the sum of $6,811.12, including costs of suit, which sum was derived by him from the proceeds from her said statutory separate estate; and your oratrix alleges that said transfer to said Winston was made to him as her agent, for the purpose of saving the land of her husband, and buying the same in for herself, in case the same was sold under execution on said judgment; which said Winston well knew, agreeing to assist your oratrix in effecting that end, advising her therein, and using her statutory separate estate therefor. . . Afterwards an *alias fi. fa.* was issued on said judgment, and levied on said lands, together with some personal property; and the same was bought in by said A. A. Winston, as her agent, at the price of $4,572.50. The three deeds made to said Winston by the U. S. marshal, copies of which are hereunto annexed as exhibits, show that he bid for it as agent, paid for it as agent, and took the title to himself as agent. Your oratrix alleges that said judgment was her own; that she furnished the money to pay for it; that the land was sold under said *fi. fa.* for the purpose of putting the title in her, and that said Winston bid for, bought, paid for, and got the title thereto as her agent and trustee, and by her said means." The defendant Winston denied the material allegations of the bill, out of which a resulting trust was claimed to arise; alleging that he bought the judgment with his own funds, and that the proceeds of the complainant's bank stock, afterwards transferred, were used with her knowledge and consent in paying other debts of her husband, on which he was bound as surety.

On final hearing, on pleadings and proof, the chancellor rendered a decree for the complainant; and his decree is here assigned as error by defendant Winston.

PILLANS, TORREY & HANAW, D. C. ANDERSON & SONS, and R. CHAPMAN, for appellant, cited *Lehman v. Lewis*, 62 Ala. 134; *Shelby v. Tardy*, 84 Ala. 329; *White v. Farley*, 81 Ala. 563; *Bibb v. Hunter*, 79 Ala. 351; *Rose v. Gibson*, 71 Ala. 35; *Edwards v. Rogers*, 81 Ala. 571; Perry on Trusts, §§ 133-7; 2 Pom. Equity, § 1038; 51 Amer. Dec. 756, *note; Botsford v. Burr*, 2 John. Ch. 408; *Patton v. Beecher*, 62 Ala. 579; *Baker v. Vining*, 50 Amer. Dec. 617.

A. G. SMITH, and T. B. & R. P. WETMORE, *contra*.

CLOPTON, J.—Mrs. Mitchell, appellee, seeks by the bill to have declared and established in her favor a resulting trust of the legal estate in the lands therein mentioned. A judgment had been obtained by Catherine Moore against Daniel Mitchell, the husband of complainant, in the United States Circuit Court at Mobile, for several thousand dollars, besides the costs of suit. The special averments, on which complainant claims that a trust results, are: "That on or about the 17th day of April, 1878, the said judgment against the said Daniel Mitchell was transferred to the said Augustus A. Winston, for the sum of $6,811.12, including costs of suit, which sum was derived by him from the proceeds of her statutory separate estate; and your oratrix alleges, that said transfer to said Winston was made to him as her agent, for the purpose of saving the lands of her husband, and buying the same in for herself, in case the same were sold under execution on said judgment, which said Winston well knew, agreeing to assist your oratrix in effecting that end, and advising her therein, and using her statutory separate estate therefor." The separate estate alluded to consisted of one hundred shares of the capital stock of the Gainesville National Bank, of the par value of one hundred dollars per share, which were given to her by her father in 1871. The bill further alleges, that the lands, which consisted of three several tracts, known as the "Patton tract," the "Harrison land," and the "Long, or Frost place," were sold by the marshal under an *alias* execution issued on the judgment, and were bought in by defendant, at the price of $4,572.50, who took the title to himself, as agent; that she furnished the money to pay for the judgment; that the lands were sold for the purpose of putting the title in her; and that defendant "bought, paid for, and got the title thereto as her agent and trustee, and by her said means."

[Winston v. Mitchell.]

It is manifest from its allegations, that the bill proceeds upon the theory, that defendant acted as the agent of complainant in purchasing the judgment, using the proceeds of her statutory separate estate to pay for the same, upon an agreement that he would advise and assist her in obtaining the lands for herself, in the event they were sold; and that, in pursuance of such agreement, he subsequently purchased them at the execution sale, used the judgment in paying for the same, and took the title in his own name as agent. It does not seek to establish a trust which results from the facts independent and exclusive of an agreement—a trust resulting by mere implication or construction of law. The trust claimed by complainant, if it exists, has its origin and foundation in the purchase of the judgment. It is therefore essential to sustain the case made by the bill, that complainant establish, by satisfactory proof, that defendant acted as her agent in the transaction, and purchased the judgment with the proceeds of her bank stock, under an agreement to bid off the lands for her benefit, if sold under an execution. In cases of this character, "a closer correspondence between the pleadings and proof is required than in any other, except the analogous cases of bills for the reformation, or for the specific performance of contracts."—*Patton v. Beecher,* 62 Ala. 579.

The first question, then, is, does the evidence sufficiently establish the special averments of the bill, on which complainant rests her title to relief? In the consideration of this question, we shall discard the oral evidence of the parties in respect to their intention, meaning, and understanding. Both concur that the agreement and understanding between them was all had by correspondence. All the letters which passed are professedly attached to their respective depositions, except some which were destroyed, the contents of which are not proved. The presumption is, that they were unimportant, otherwise they would have been preserved with those regarded valuable. From the correspondence, though not clear and explicit in some respects, considered in the light of the attendant and subsequent circumstances, we must ascertain, as satisfactorily as we may, the real facts and nature of the transaction.

A statement of a few indisputable facts is essential to a full understanding of some allusions in the letters, and of the relative positions occupied by the parties. Complainant and defendant bear to each other the relation of father and daughter. He had become liable, either as indorser or acceptor, for the accommodation of her husband, on paper for large sums of money held by the Gainesville Bank, and by W. O. Winston; and her husband was also largely indebted to Jones & Co., and others. Their financial difficulties culminated on the affirmance of the judgment against Mitchell by the Supreme Court of the United States, defendant being surety on his *supersedeas* bond. As the collection of the judgment could be speedily enforced by levy and sale, prompt measures were requisite to prevent a sacrifice of property, and probable financial ruin. In this state of affairs, the correspondence commenced. As to the plan which should be adopted, and the arrangements made to meet the emergencies, the parties differed totally in their views. Complainant's proposals are expressed in her letter of March 13, 1878, evidently in reply to one written by defendant, not produced. Impressed with the fact that her husband could never pay his indebtedness, nor even the interest, she urged her father to sell her bank stock, pay the debt due to the bank and W. O. Winston, for which he was liable, and secure himself, as to the judgment, by the Patton tract and other lands; and this being done, she hoped that, by economy, they would be able to pay Jones & Co., and eventually work out of debt. Defendant's suggestions are contained in his letter of March 24th, 1878, in response to complainant's. They were, to borrow money by a pledge of her bank stock, pay the judgment and the Winston debt, and secure herself, for the use of her stock, by a mortgage on her husband's land; sell the lands at private sale, and save his indorsement and the stock. If this was agreed to, and they would send the notes and the numbers of the lands, he proposed to get an attorney to prepare the mortgage. Five days thereafter, he wrote another letter, in which he expressed apprehensions that Jones & Co. were endeavoring to get complainant to secure their debt, or let her stock go to pay the judgment. He reiterated his wish, that her stock, if used, should be secured by mortgage on the Patton tract, and urged, if she thought he would protect her, to let him have it fixed his way.

From the letter of defendant of April 1, 1878, addressed to Mitchell, it appears that two notes had been sent to him. For what purpose, must be collected from the following extracts: "I received the two notes, and no letter. I return the inclosed, for W. A. Gage to witness Martha A. Mitchell's

[Winston v. Mitchell.]

signature. Send the stock with this, as the bank stock is held with the notes, when used, and returned *paid.* Send land numbers, so I can secure Martha and children." After suggesting to Mitchell to obtain, at once, the amount of each dividend received on the stock, and give complainant a note for it, he adds: "All I wish is to secure Martha and children, and give you a chance to work out, without being sold out, or annoyed by J. W. Jones & Co. If attended to as I request, you will get time, and either sell or work out." It is evident from the letter of April 11, 1878, written by defendant to complainant, that the paper referred to as indorsed, was returned with complainant's indorsement, but without an accompanying letter. In this last letter, defendant writes: "I wrote Mr. Mitchell and yourself at length, and no reply to-day. I received again, in a blank envelope, your indorsement, without one word. My child, I do not wish anything that you both do not approve of; it looks as though it was not agreeable, by the second letter, without a word of approval or dissent." The record contains another letter written by complainant, which defendant testifies was received two days after the date of the letter last mentioned, and which carries internal evidence that it was written about that time. She re-urges her proposals as to the settlement of the debts, and says that she is more than willing to give up her bank stock to relieve her father, and if he is not willing to her plan, he could do as he said, and she would have nothing more to say. With this, the correspondence is suspended for several months. The judgment was transferred to defendant, April 17, 1878.

We have fully considered this portion of the correspondence, and made the foregoing extracts, because the positions and views of the parties, immediately preceding the purchase of the judgment, would be thereby more manifest. We search in vain for any proposition, or any understanding, express or implied, upon which the minds of the parties met, looking to the purchase of the judgment by defendant, as agent of complainant, for the purpose of buying the land for her, if it was sold under execution. A sale under execution was not suggested by either; on the contrary, in his letter of March 15th, 1878, defendant expressed his decided objection to a sale by the marshal, on the ground that a sacrifice of the property and ruin of Mitchell's credit would be the consequence. The prominent wish of complainant was to relieve her father from liability, to accomplish which she was

26

[Winston v. Mitchell.]

willing to give up her bank stock; and defendant not only sought this, but also desired that she should be secured, if she pledged her stock. Neither proposed or suggested a purchase of the judgment for any ulterior purpose of benefit to complainant, but its payment, and her security by a mortgage on the land. Her stock was not then or subsequently sold, as will be hereafter shown; hence its proceeds could not have been used in purchasing the judgment, at the time it was purchased.

It is insisted, however, that the defendant's plan for arranging the debts was substantially carried out, by borrowing money by pledge of complainant's stock, and the judgment held open as complainant's security, instead of a mortgage on the lands. This inference is founded on the fact, that the original certificate, which was in the name of Mitchell, as trustee, was surrendered April 8, 1878, and new certificates issued in the name of Mrs. Mitchell; and on the admissions of defendant in subsequent letters, written by him to complainant, on February 11 and 20, 1879; such as: "The debt to the Savings Bank with you and your stock pledged, I promised Smith L. & Co. to see their debt paid;" and, "Your bank stock was put in your name, and by you pledged to raise money to pay U. S. court debt." It must be admitted that the change of the certificates at that particular time, and the admissions referred to, strongly sustain the reasonableness of the inference; and in the absence of evidence showing that the stock was *not* in fact pledged at that time, we should regard the inference as irresistible. It may be, that in the letters the defendant referred to the paper which he returned in his letter of April 1, 1878, which it is probable had some connection with, or relation to a pledge of the stock, and which he regarded as a pledge. Be this as it may, it is manifest from the negative and positive evidence, that the certificates of stock had not been sent, and were not in the possession of defendant at the time he took a transfer of the judgment. His letter of April 11, 1878, in which he acknowledged the receipt of complainant's indorsement—that is, the paper which he had inclosed in his previous letter—is silent as to the stock, and evidently expresses disappointment at not receiving an approval or dissent from his plan. He testifies that the certificates were not sent; and complainant and her husband, not only omit to testify that they were sent at that time, but directly and positively testify that they were, in fact, sent subsequently. The evidence of complainant is, that the note for $6,400, which was signed by her and her husband, dated April 15, 1879, and payable to the order of defendant twelve months after date, was given to pay off the judgment, and when the judgment was paid, she was to have the lands, and that the certificates of stock were sent to the defendant at the time she signed this note. The evidence of her husband is substantially to the same effect. If this evidence be true, and complainant and her husband certainly know when the certificate was sent, it was not placed in the defendant's possession until about one year after the judgment was purchased; so that the money used in purchasing the judgment could not have been raised by a pledge of the stock, in law or in fact.

But, were it conceded that her stock was pledged to borrow money for the purpose, complainant, being under the disabilities of coverture, was incapable, under the statute in force at that time, to contract a debt for the loan of money, binding her personally, or her separate estate; and if the defendant agreed or promised to take a transfer of the judgment, and use it in purchasing the lands for her benefit, such agreement or promise could not be enforced, for the want of mutuality.—*Lehman v. Lewis*, 62 Ala. 129. If, however, the money was thus raised, or was advanced by defendant for complainant, and he was subsequently re-imbursed from the proceeds of her separate estate, he would be estopped to set up the want of mutuality. Without a review in detail, the evidence convinces us, that the money, with which the judgment was purchased, was borrowed by request of complainant, or advanced by defendant, having in view both his own protection and the benefit of his daughter and her children. His declaration is: "The U. S. debt was paid from money borrowed at your request, and the bank stock was sold to pay that money back to the Savings Bank."

The note for $6,400 was evidently given for the purpose of re-imbursing defendant, not to pay off the judgment, and was paid with proceeds of complainant's bank stock. It is true that Woodruff testifies, and the receipts of defendant show, that on closing the affairs of the bank, the amount distributed to complainant on account of her stock, was applied to the payment of the paper of Mitchell indorsed by defendant, and held by the bank, in January, 1880, and charged to defendant's accounts on the books of the bank.

On March 1, 1880, defendant receipted the National Commercial Bank for $6,400, on account of eighty shares of complainant's stock in the Gainesville Bank. The note for $6,400 matured about two weeks thereafter, and across the face of it is written, in defendant's handwriting, "Paid by 80 shares, $6,400 of it Martha A. Mitchell, Gainesville Bk. stock." This memorandum defendant neither denies, nor satisfactorily explains.

The National Commercial Bank was the disbursing agent of the Gainesville Bank in winding up its affairs, and the defendant was the president of the former bank. The memorandum on the note was made at a time when the facts were known, and fresh in recollection. From these facts, the inference is irresistible, that there was some unexplained connection between the settlement of Mitchell's notes with the Gainesville Bank and the payment of the note for $6,400. On this theory alone can the evidence be reconciled; otherwise, either the entry on the note and the declaration of the defendant, or the testimony of Woodruff and the recitals of the receipt, are false. The proceeds of the stock could not have been used to pay two separate and distinct debts, each equal or larger in amount. This transaction occurred before the sale of the lands, which was in June, 1881. Under these circumstances, complainant had an election, to make defendant and the bank personally liable for such unauthorized and illegal disposition of the proceeds of her stock, or to follow them into the lands, in purchasing which the judgment was used. Had the proceeds of her separate estate, thus used, been sufficient to repay or re-imburse defendant to the full amount borrowed or advanced by him, in the purchase of the judgment, a trust of the legal estate would result by implication of law. But complainant does not claim or pretend that she ever paid more than $6,400. This amount was less than the sum paid by defendant for the judgment, and was considerably less, if interest be calculated thereon until the maturity and payment of the note. A trust of the legal estate in the *entire* lands will not result, unless it is both averred and proved, that complainant paid the entire purchase-money of the judgment.—*Bibb v. Hunter*, 79 Ala. 351; *Preston v. McMillan*, 58 Ala. 84; *McGowan v. McGowan*, 74 Amer. Dec. 668. On the pleadings and proof, a trust of the entire legal estate does not result to complainant.

But it does not follow that complainant is without equity.

[Winston v. Mitchell.]

A constructive trust arises, when a trustee or an agent, either by agreement or by a breach of confidence, which chancery impresses with a trust *in invitum*, uses the funds of another in part purchase of, or part payment for property, and takes the title in his own name. In such case, the beneficiary is entitled to charge the property with the amount thus invested.—*Tilford v. Torrey*, 53 Ala. 120. Neither complainant, nor her husband, nor defendant, nor all together, were capable to appropriate the *corpus* of her separate estate to the payment of her husband's debts; and on account of such use of her funds chancery holds the defendant to be a trustee *in invitum*. Under the statute in force at the time of the transaction, her husband was the trustee of complainant's statutory separate estate, and entitled to receive and dispose of the income. It has been held, that when the wife seeks, by bill in equity, to charge lands with her funds used by her husband in their purchase, she was not entitled to recover interest.—*Sawyer v. Baker*, 77 Ala. 461. The reason of this rule ceased with the passage of the act "to define the rights and liabilities of husband and wife," approved February 28, 1887. By this statute, the trusteeship of the husband was abrogated, and the wife became entitled to sue for and recover the rents, income and profits of her separate estate. In such case, the equity of complainant is, to charge the lands with the sum of $6,400, with interest from February 28, 1887. It appears that defendant has executed a deed to complainant to the "Long place." If the parties agree that she may retain this land, its valuation should be deducted from the amount, and interest calculated on the balance. If they do not agree, the deed should be cancelled.

We have thus considered the equity of complainant in every aspect of the case as presented by the evidence, in the hope that there will be an amicable adjustment between the parties on the basis stated, or on some other equitable basis, and a litigation terminated, the continuance of which can only result in widening the estrangement between father and daughter, and fomenting domestic discord; evils, against which mere pecuniary considerations should not be allowed a feather's weight in the balance.

The cause will be remanded, that complainant may amend her bill, as she may be advised, to meet the state of the evidence; and defendant allowed to set up any defense which may be regarded available.

Reversed and remanded.

Bentley *v.* Dailey.

Final Settlement of Guardian's Accounts.

1. *Annual settlements as evidence.*—On final settlement of a guardian's accounts, former annual or partial settlements made by him are a part of the record, and it is the right and duty of the court to look to them as evidence in the cause.

2. *Conclusiveness of annual settlements.*—On final settlement of a guardian's accounts, credits allowed him on an annual or partial settlement are presumptively correct (Code, § 2458), and the *onus* of disproving their correctness is on the ward.

3. *Confederate money received by guardian.*—A guardian having been allowed a credit, on a partial settlement in 1870-71, for Confederate money received from a debtor during the late war, and left on his hands at the close of the war, the credit ought not to be disallowed on final settlement, on evidence showing merely that the money was collected on notes given for the purchase-money of land, which the guardian had received, in 1859-60, as his ward's distributive share on settlement of an estate; this evidence, without more, not being sufficient to overcome the presumption in favor of the allowance on annual settlement.

4. *Allowance to guardian, for board of ward.*—An allowance to the guardian on an annual or partial settlement, for board paid to the ward's step-father on his account, is properly disallowed on final settlement, on the uncontradicted testimony of the ward that he owed nothing for board; the step-father, though living in the county, not being produced as a witness.

APPEAL from the Probate Court of Calhoun.

Heard before the Hon. EMMETT F. CROOK.

In the matter of the final settlement of the accounts and vouchers of Jacob F. Dailey, as guardian of William C. Bentley. The guardianship commenced before the war, but at what time the record does not show; and several annual or partial settlements had been made—one in 1870, and another in 1871. On these settlements, the guardian was allowed a credit for $548, Confederate money received by him during the war, and left on his hands at the close of the war. On the final settlement, the ward objected to this credit, and excepted to its allowance; and this ruling is here assigned as error. On said former settlement in 1871, the guardian was allowed a credit for two vouchers, which purported to be receipts given to him in August and December, 1870, by Nat. Cobb, for board of the ward for nine months, together amounting to $93.50. In reference to these items the ward thus testified for himself: "I never owed said Cobb anything for board, nor for anything else. He was married to my mother, and I lived with him prior to 1869, and worked for him, and boarded with him. My board was worth about $8 per month, and my work about $10. I never lived with him, or boarded with him, after I boarded at my mother's and went to school in Oxford. I boarded at my mother's in Oxford in 1869, or 1870, and went to school. While boarding there, Cobb would come down on Sundays. He supported my mother at Oxford for about three months, but no longer; and I worked out on evenings and Saturdays, and my sister took in sewing, and we supported ourselves and our mother. Cobb now lives in this county." The guardian himself thus testified in reference to these items: "I do not know that said Bentley ever owed Cobb anything for board, or for anything else. He boarded with his mother in Oxford, and she was then Cobb's wife." This being all the evidence relating to these items, the court allowed the credits as claimed; to which ruling the ward excepted, and he now assigns it as error.

· KELLY & SMITH, for appellant.

ELLIS & STEVENSON, and BROTHERS, WILLETT & WILLETT, contra.

McCLELLAN, J.—This is an appeal from a decree on the final settlement of a guardianship. Two exceptions reserved by the ward in the court below are insisted on here, and these only will be considered, though the assignment of errors embraces others.—1 Brick. Dig. p. 102, § 285.

These exceptions go to the allowance on this settlement of a credit of $548, collected in Confederate currency, which became valueless by reason of the result of the war, and the amount paid by the guardian to one Cobb, for board of the ward in 1870 and 1871, both of which credits had been allowed on previous annual settlements; and the action of the court now complained of seems to have been influenced by the fact of such former allowance. The court had a right, and it was its duty, to look to the records of all the annual settlements which had been made according to law. The records of former annual settlements were a part of the cause on the final settlement.—Foust v. Chamblee, 51 Ala. 75. The annual settlements of 1870 and succeeding years appear to have been regularly made. The allowance of the credits excepted to, in the settlements of 1870 and 1871, raises a

[Bentley v. Dailey.]

presumption of their correctness, which shifted the burden of proof in regard to them from the guardian to the ward. The former may stand upon the settlement, and the latter must impeach it by affirmatively showing the incorrectness of the allowance.—Code, § 2458; *Ashley's Adm'r v. Martin,* 50 Ala. 537; *Radford's Adm'r v. Morris,* 66 Ala. 283.

The fact that the Confederate money was collected on land notes taken by the guardian in 1859 and 1860, in payment of a decree for his ward's distributive share in the estate, is not sufficient to overturn the presumption of correctness. For aught that appears in the record, this action on the part of the guardian may have been to the best interest of the ward, and the only means of collecting the decree; and if, in receiving the notes, he acted with care and diligence, and was also diligent in their collection in funds current at their maturity, he should not be charged for taking them in the place of money in the first instance; nor for receiving Confederate money in payment of them; nor for the loss of this money in his hands, if he exercised the diligence and care which would have characterized the conduct of a prudent man under like circumstances, in dealing with it after he received it.—*Mason v. Buchanan,* 62 Ala. 110; *Stewart v. McMurray,* 82 Ala. 269.

The evidence offered by the ward to charge the guardian with this item, shows only the receipt of the notes in partial satisfaction on the distributive decree, that they were collected in Confederate currency, and that this money was in the guardian's hands, and, of course, valueless after the war. This is wholly insufficient to rebut the presumption of good faith and diligence raised by the decree on the annual settlement of 1870, and the guardian was properly allowed credit for this item.

As to the credits for board paid to Cobb, we are satisfied that the court erred. The uncontroverted evidence of the ward shows, that he never owed Cobb for board or anything else; and if this testimony was untrue, it could have been contradicted by the evidence of Cobb himself, who is shown to have been a resident of the county at the time of the trial. The presumption of correctness, arising from the former allowance of these credits, was overturned; they were shown to be incorrect, and their allowance by the court was error, for which the decree must be reversed, and the cause remanded.

Reversed and remanded.

Huckaba *v.* Abbott.

Statutory Action in nature of Ejectment.

1. *Mortgage for future advances; parol evidence affecting consideration.* A mortgage given to secure payment for future advances by the mortgagee, is a valid security as between the parties; and when the recited consideration is an indebtedness by promissory note, oral evidence may be received to show that part of the actual consideration was supplied or advances to be afterwards furnished, and which were furnished.

2. *Nominal partner testifying as to transactions with decedent.*—In an action by a mortgagee against the widow of the deceased mortgagor, payment of the mortgage debt being suggested and pleaded (Code, §§ 1870, 2707), the plaintiff's son, who was in his employment as clerk when the mortgage was given, and held himself out to the public as a partner, though he had no interest in the business, may testify to transactions with the deceased mortgagor in reference to the mortgage debt, not being within the statutory disqualification (*Ib.* § 2765), either as a party, or as interested.

APPEAL from the Circuit Court of Randolph.

Tried before the Hon. JAMES W. LAPSLEY.

This action was brought by Henry H. Huckaba against Mrs. Elizabeth Abbott, the widow of James W. Abbott, deceased, to recover the possession of a tract of land particularly described in the complaint; and was commenced on the 3d May, 1887. The plaintiff claimed the land under a mortgage executed to him by the defendant and her deceased husband, which was dated December 26th, 1882, and purported to be given to secure the payment of a promissory note for $500, of even date with the mortgage, and payable on the 1st October, 1883; and the defendant suggested and pleaded payment and satisfaction of the mortgage debt. On the trial, as the bill of exceptions shows, the plaintiff read the note and mortgage in evidence, and then introduced his son, W. T. Huckaba, as a witness, who testified that a balance of $285 was still due on the mortgage and secured note. He testified, also, on cross-examination, that he had no interest in his father's mercantile business in December, 1882, when the mortgage was given, but was employed as a clerk on a salary; that he afterwards put up over the door of the store, without consultation with his father, a sign reading 'H. H. Huckaba & Son,' and it had remained there ever since. The witness further stated, on cross-examination, that said J. W.

[Huckaba v. Abbott.]

Abbott was only indebted to H. H. Huckaba, at the time said note and mortgage were given, in the sum of about $100; and that, acting as agent for his father, he had accepted a horse in payment, at the agreed price of $100. Plaintiff then asked said witness, what was the further consideration for said note and mortgage; and he answered, that it was future advances or supplies which H. H. Huckaba agreed to furnish from his store during the year 1883." The defendant objected to this answer, and moved to exclude it from the jury, "on the ground that it was a transaction with a party since deceased, whose estate was interested in the result of the suit, and said witness was incompetent to testify in reference to it; and on the ground, that oral evidence was inadmissible to show that said mortgage was given to secure future advances." The court sustained the objections, and excluded the evidence; and this ruling, to which the plaintiff excepted, is now assigned as error.

N. D. DENSON, for appellant, cited *Tison v. Peoples' Asso.*, 57 Ala. 323; *Forsyth v. Preer*, 62 Ala. 443; *Collier v. Faulk*, 69 Ala. 58.

SMITH & SMITH, *contra.*

STONE, C. J.—It is settled in this State, that a mortgage for future advances is a valid security, and that when it recites an existing debt as its consideration, it is no violation of the law of evidence to receive proof that the actual consideration was advances to be afterwards made.—*Tison v. People's Sav. & L. Asso.*, 57 Ala. 323; *Forsyth v. Preer*, 62 Ala. 443; *Collier v. Faulk*, 69 Ala. 58. Such mortgage, if not assailed on other grounds, is valid between the parties; but this rule has some limitations, when assailed by outside creditors or purchasers.—*Faulk v. Martin*, 69 Ala. 59; *Marks v. Robinson*, 82 Ala. 69.

The witness W. T. Huckaba testified, that he had no interest in the suit, and was not a partner of H. H. Huckaba, his father, in the mercantile business. He had held himself out as partner, and had permitted the business to be conducted in the name of Huckaba & Son, he being the son. This, it is contended, rendered him liable for the mercantile debts, and made him interested in maintaining the suit. It is not shown that there were any debts, nor that the father was not amply able to meet the liabilities, if any existed.

This interest is too remote and contingent, to fall within the statutory rule of exclusion.—Code of 1886, § 2765; *Miller r. Cannon*, 84 Ala. 59. The Circuit Court erred in excluding the testimony of W. T. Huckaba, as to transactions with the deceased mortgagor.

Reversed and remanded.

Schloss & Kahn *v.* Montgomery Trade Company.

Action by Corporation, on Subscription for Stock.

1. *Action by corporation; proof of corporate character* —In an action by a corporation, the plea of *nul tiel* corporation being interposed, the plaintiff is required to prove its corporate character, either by producing its charter, or by some admission on the part of the defendant, or to show facts constituting an estoppel. (But, by statute, a sworn plea is now required.—Sess. Acts. 1888-9, p. 57.)

2. *Estoppel as between corporation and subscriber for stock.*—In an action by a corporation suing as such, against a subscriber to its capital stock before incorporation, the payment by the defendant of former installments as called for, and an averment that the installment sued for was "duly and regularly called in by plaintiff, and demand therefor made upon defendant," do not, without more, show an estoppel against him to deny that there ever was any corporation.

3. *Organization of business corporation; when authorized.*—By statutory provision (Code, 1886, § 1663; Code, 1876, § 1806,) changing the rule of the common law, a business corporation may be organized before all of the capital stock has been subscribed for.

APPEAL from the City Court of Montgomery.

Tried before the Hon. THOS. M. ARRINGTON.

This action was brought against Schloss & Kahn as partners, by the "Montgomery Trade Company, a corporation," as described in the complaint, or, as described in the summons, "a corporation organized under the laws of Alabama;" and was commenced on the 15th September, 1888. The complaint contained the common count on an account stated, and a special count which claimed $300, "due on account of the subscription by defendants, in writing, to the capital stock of plaintiff, with interest thereon from January 9th, 1888;" and the special count averred, "that said defendants subscribed, by instrument in writing, to fifteen shares of the capital stock of said company, of the par value of $100 per share; that said defendants paid all of said subscription, except twenty per cent. thereof; that on the 9th January, 1888, the said twenty per cent. was duly and regularly called in by the plaintiff, and demand therefor made upon said defendants, but they neglected and refused to pay the same, and still neglect," &c. The defendants demurred to the special count, assigning several special grounds of demurrer, which were, in substance, that it did not allege or show that the plaintiff was ever legally incorporated, nor that plaintiff had ever tendered to defendants a certificate for their stock, or was ready to issue such certificate. The court overruled the demurrer, and the defendants then filed several pleas, the first and sixth of which denied the plaintiff's corporate existence; the second alleged that the plaintiff "issued its stock without actually receiving money or property therefor, or getting any consideration in labor done for it;" the third alleged a special agreement and understanding between the subscribers for stock in the Montgomery Trade Company, that not more than twenty per cent. of their subscriptions should be paid in before the organization of the corporation; the fourth alleged that the defendants were induced to make their subscription for stock by the promise of the corporators who were getting up the subscriptions, to the effect that not more than eighty per cent. should ever be called for; the fifth was the general issue, and the seventh claimed a set-off. The court sustained a demurrer to all of these pleas except the fifth and the seventh, on which issue was joined. The defendants also filed three additional pleas, namely: 1st, that plaintiff never issued, nor offered to issue to defendants, any shares of stock, or certificates for shares; 2d, that the plaintiff does not aver its readiness or ability to issue any certificates for stock; 3d, that the capital stock of the proposed corporation was $50,000, and not more than $45,000 was subscribed for. The court sustained a demurrer to each of these additional pleas.

The rulings on the pleadings are now assigned as error.

ARRINGTON & GRAHAM, for appellants.—(1.) The demurrer to the complaint ought to have been sustained. In an action against a subscriber for stock in a proposed corporation not then organized, the fact of incorporation must be proved, if the plaintiff sues as a corporation; and if denied, it must be proved.—*Threshing Machine Co. v. Davis*, 41 N. W. Reporter, 1026; 28 Cent. L. J. 448; *Knox v. Childersburg Land Co.*, 86 Ala. 180; Cook on Stock and

Stockholders, §§ 67, 168.   (2.)   No estoppel is shown by the pleadings against the defendants.—Cook, Stock, § 186; 68 Ind. 388; *Grangers' Insurance Co. v. Kamper*, 73 Ala. 325; *Railroad Co. v. Cushing*, 45 Maine, 524; 5 Nebr. 50.

TOMPKINS & TROY, *contra*, cited *Lehman, Durr & Co. v. Warner*, 61 Ala. 466; *Central A. & M. Asso. v. Insurance Co.*, 70 Ala. 120; Code, § 1663; Mor. Corp., § 269; *Smith v. Plank-road Co.*, 30 Ala. 650; Cook on Stock, §§ 137-8; 91 U. S. 45.

SOMERVILLE, J.—It is true, that where one contracts with an alleged corporation as such, and in such manner as to recognize its corporate existence *de jure* or *de facto*, he will often be estopped to deny the fact thus admitted, whether the denial go to the question of an originally legally organized body, or to that of a cessation of corporate existence. These are cases where the action is brought against one who contracts with the plaintiff in its real or asserted corporate capacity.

But this principle has no reference to cases where a subscription for stock is made by one in anticipation of organizing a corporation, which is at the time only in process of formation.   "The rule that a person contracting with a corporation recognizes thereby its capacity to contract, and can not afterwards deny it in that transaction, does not apply to one who subscribes before incorporation.   He may insist upon the organization of a regular and legal corporation." Cook on Stock and Stockholders, §§ 185-186, and cases cited in *note* 2, p. 173.

It is perfectly well settled, that before a suit can be maintained by an alleged corporation, although it may not be necessary to prove the *legality* of the existence of such corporation, its actual or *de facto* existence must be proved, or else a state of facts shown which will operate to estop the defendant from denying such *de facto* existence.   When the plea of *nul tiel* corporation in proper form is interposed, in the absence of any regulating statute on the subject, the burden is on the plaintiff corporation, if private, to prove its existence, either by production of its charter or articles of corporation, or by some express or implied admission on the part of the defendant, or else to show an estoppel which precludes a denial of the fact.—2 Morawetz on Corp. (2d Ed.), §§ 770, 772, 774, 776; *Lehman v. Warner*, 61 Ala. 455.   The act

approved February 26, 1889 (Acts 1888-89, p. 57), provides,
that when a suit is brought by a corporation, the plaintiff
must not be required to prove the existence of such corporation, unless the same is denied by sworn plea, filed within
the time allowed for filing pleas in abatement. But that act
was not in force when the present case was tried, and hence
did not govern it.

A subscriber to stock may, like any other person, be
estopped from disputing the *de facto* existence of a corporation, especially as against creditors, where he attends the
meetings of stockholders, or otherwise participates in the
business of the company, thereby inducing others to act
upon the faith of his admissions to their prejudice, or for his
benefit. "But, "to warrant holding a person estopped from
disputing the existence of a corporation, on the ground that
he has co-operated in its organization and action, the acts
shown must be unmistakably *corporate* acts."—2 Herman
on Estoppel, § 1247. If the act done, or admission made,
is just as consistent with the existence of an unincorporated
association, as of one incorporated, its ambiguous character
will be so equivocal as not to raise an estoppel.—*Fredenburg
v. M. E. Church*, 37 Mich. 476.

Conceding that the mere description of the plaintiff in the
title of the cause as "a corporation" is sufficient, without any
positive averment in the complaint of its corporate character,
or without alleging whether it is a foreign or domestic corporation, defendants, in their first and sixth pleas, deny that
there was at the commencement of this suit any such corporation as the Montgomery Trade Company—the name in
which the suit is brought. This cast on the plaintiffs, under
the principles above stated, the burden either to prove their
corporate existence *de jure* or *de facto*, by admission of the
defendant, or by production of their charter, with some evidence of user or acceptance, or by other competent evidence,
or else to show an estoppel which would operate to preclude
the defendant from denying the plaintiff's corporate existence. The only fact relied on to raise such estoppel, suggested in the demurrer to these pleas, is the conduct of the
defendants in having paid all of their subscription for the
fifteen shares of stock except the twenty per cent. here sued
for, which latter sum is alleged to have been "duly and regularly called in by the plaintiff, and demand therefor made
upon said defendants," which they refused to pay. We perceive no element of estoppel in this fact, standing alone. The

[Aderholt v. Henry.]

circumstances under which this subscription was paid, are no where stated. It does not appear that it was called for by assessments made even under color of corporate organization or capacity. The payment made does not imply a recognition of corporate existence, or of an unequivocal corporate act performed by the plaintiff, or any participation by the defendants in the corporate meetings or proceedings. There is nothing inconsistent between the facts alleged in the complaint, and the fact of defendants' payment of eighty per cent. of their subscription preliminary to any corporate organization then contemplated, or in anticipation of such event.—*Somerset & K. R. R. Co. v. Cushing*, 45 Me. 524; *Cabot v. Chapin*, 6 Cush. 51; *Kansas City Hotel v. Harris*, 51 Mo. 464; *Knox v. Childersburg Land Co.*, 86 Ala., 180.

The fact that all the capital stock was not subscribed for, might have been a good defense to this suit against the defendants, under the general rule of law, apart from the statute.—Cook on Stock and Stockholders, § 176. But the statute has changed this rule, so as to authorize the organization of corporations of the class to which plaintiffs *prima jacie* belong, upon the payment of fifty per cent. of the proposed capital stock, which may have been subscribed.—Code, 1886, § 1663; Code, 1876, § 1806; Acts, 1882-83, p. 5.

The other contentions of appellant are without merit.

It follows from what we have said, that the City Court erred in sustaining the demurrer of the plaintiff to the first and sixth pleas of the appellants, but not in sustaining the demurrers to the other pleas.

Reversed and remanded.

CLOPTON, J., not sitting.

Aderholt *v.* Henry.

Bill in Equity to enforce Vendor's Lien on Land; Petitions between Purchasers of Different Parcels.

1. *Vendor's lien; priority as between sub-purchasers.*—As a general rule, in enforcing a lien or incumbrance on land, which has been sold and conveyed in parcels to different persons, a court of equity pursues the inverse order of alienation, first subjecting the unsold portions remaining in the hands of the incumbrancer; but the principle extends

[Aderholt v. Henry.]

only to sub-purchasers with covenants of warranty, and is never allowed
to work injustice, being subject to modification by particular facts and
circumstances affecting the rights and equities of the several purchasers
as between themselves.

2. *Same; case at bar.*—In this case, a bill was filed to enforce a vendor's lien on land, after the death of the purchaser, who had sold and
conveyed some portions of it, with covenants of warranty, to different
persons, charged some parcels with the payment of debts, and devised
the residue to his children; and the executor having sold the parcels
charged with the payment of debts, a purchaser of two lots or parcels
paid the purchase-money for one, but failed to pay for the other, which
was afterwards resold under a decree enforcing the vendor's lien of the
executor, for less than the amount of the decree; and the purchaser at
the resale having afterwards bought the decree in the original suit, and
attempted to subject the other portions of the land to its satisfaction,
it was held—1st, that the lot bought and paid for at the sale by the executor must be first subjected, because its owner was primarily liable
for the unpaid purchase-money of the other lot; 2d, that the purchaser
at the resale was not entitled to claim exemption from liability, but
stood on an equality with the several devisees, and must each contribute
suitably to the discharge of the common burden; and, 3d, that each
portion should be estimated at its present value, including improvements erected by the owner.

APLEAL from the Chancery Court of Etowah.

Heard before the Hon. S. K. McSpadden.

This is a branch of a case which has been before the court
on three former appeals.—*Prickett & Maddox v. Sibert*,
71 Ala. 194; s. c., 75 Ala. 315; *Aderholt v. Henry*, 82 Ala.
541. The original bill was filed on the 2d of September,
1879, by O. W. Ward, against Mrs. Rebecca J. Maddox
(now Aderholt), widow and executrix of J. W. Maddox, deceased, with their several children, his heirs and devisees,
and other persons; and sought to enforce a vendor's lien on
a tract of land, for the balance of purchase-money remaining
unpaid. The land was sold and conveyed to said Maddox,
in October, 1872, by J. P. Ralls, partly for cash, and partly
on credit; and the complainant in the bill had become the
owner of one of the notes, by indorsement from Ralls, and
had obtained a judgment on it before filing the bill. Maddox in his life-time had sold and conveyed some portions of
the tract of land, with covenants of warranty, to different
persons, who were made defendants to the bill; and he died
in May, 1876, having executed his last will and testament,
by which he charged particular parcels with the payment of
his debts, giving his executrix power to sell them for that
purpose, and devised the residue to his children. In December, 1876, the executrix sold the parcels which the testator had charged with the payment of debts, C. B. Maddox
becoming the purchaser of a lot, for which he paid $250;

[Aderholt v. Henry.]

and he and W. P. Prickett bid off the "Mill tract," as it is called, containing about forty acres, at the price of $1,950, but failed to pay the purchase-money. On the 22d of September, 1879, the executrix filed a bill against them in said court, seeking to subject said tract of forty acres to sale in satisfaction of her vendor's lien; and she obtained a decree on the 24th of April, 1880, for $2,307.59. At a sale by the register under this decree, Sam. Henry became the purchaser of the "Mill tract" at the price of $400; and having paid the amount of his bid, he received a deed from the register, dated 12th February, 1881. In the meantime, Ward, the complainant in the original bill, had died, and the suit had been revived in favor of his widow and W. J. Sibert as administrators; and a decree was rendered in their favor, on the 14th of November, 1883, for $1,167.59, principal and interest. On the 1st of August, 1884, Henry procured from the administrators a transfer of said decree to himself, paying the full amount due on it, with costs; and he signed a written agreement, that he would indemnify them against any costs incurred in the further prosecution of his rights, as assignee of the decree, in their names; and that he would file a petition in the Chancery Court, or institute other proper proceedings, to have the court determine the order in which the different parcels of land should be sold, in satisfaction of the outstanding incumbrance for unpaid purchase-money. Henry afterwards sued out an execution on this decree, and had all of the lands sold except the "Mill tract," becoming himself the purchaser. The other defendants and claimants objected to the confirmation of this sale, and moved to set it aside; and this court sustained their contention on the last appeal, and set aside the sale.—*Aderholt v. Henry,* 82 Ala. 541.

After the remandment of the cause, Henry filed a petition, claiming exemption of the "Mill tract," and asking a sale of the other portions of the land; and counter petitions were filed by the other defendants. On the hearing of the petitions, the chancellor rendered a decree as follows: "It is adjudged, ordered and decreed, that in proceeding to sell said Maddox lands purchased from Ralls, under the Sibert-Ward decree, the register will first sell the land, if any, not alienated or bequeathed by said J. W. Maddox in his lifetime, except the 'Mill tract'; then the lands alienated by him on the 25th of May, 1876, to John H. Burton, C. B. Maddox, and J. F. W. L. Maddox, respectively, and the

27

lands bequeathed by will to Rebecca J. Maddox; and should
said lands fail to pay said Sibert-Ward decree, then the
register will sell the land known as the 'Mill tract,' with the
appurtenances thereunto belonging." Mrs. Aderholt and the
other defendants, except Henry, appeal, and assign this decree as error.

A. E. GOODHUE, for appellants, cited *Aderholt v. Henry*,
82 Ala. 541; *M. D. Insurance Co. v Huder*, 35 Ala. 713;
Cullum v. Erwin, 4 Ala. 452; *Prickett v. Sibert*, 75 Ala. 319.

WM. H. DENSON, and WATTS & SON, *contra*, cited *Hill v.
McCarter*, 27 N. J. Eq. 41; *Shannon v. Marselis*, Saxt. N.
J. Eq. 413; *Guion v. Knapp*, 6 Paige, 35: *Patty v. Paige*,
8 Paige, 277; *Caldwell v. Smith*, 77 Ala. 158; *Ewing v.
Peck*, 17 Ala. 339; *Dothard v. Sheid*, 69 Ala. 135; *McCall
v. Jones*, 72 Ala. 368; *Smith v. Perry*, 56 Ala. 266; *Wallace v. Nichols*, 56 Ala. 321; *Johnson v. Toulmin*, 18 Ala.
50; *Wells v. Morrow*, 38 Ala. 125; *Craft v. Russell*,
67 Ala. 9; *May v. Wilkerson*, 76 Ala. 543.

CLOPTON, J.—A court of equity, in charging land subject
to an incumbrance, which has been successively sold and conveyed in parcels, with covenant of warranty, to different persons, pursues the inverse order of alienation. This general
rule has been so repeatedly and uniformly affirmed, that, as
has been said, it should be regarded *res adjudicata.—Mobile M. D. & Mut. Ins. Co. v. Huder*, 35 Ala. 713; *Prickett
v. Sibert*, 75 Ala. 315. The application of the rule rests on
the equitable principle, that an incumbrancer, having a paramount lien on the entire land, shall first exhaust that parcel,
the sale of which will not prejudice a *bona fide* purchaser of
another parcel. In order to successfully invoke the protection of the rule, the alienees first in time must be *bona fide*
purchasers, and the successive alienees have notice, actual or
constructive, of the antecedent sale and conveyance. Want
of notice of the common incumbrance is not requisite. If
any are *bona fide* purchasers without notice, their right to
hold the property discharged of the incumbrance is governed
by different principles. Generally, the rule may be invoked
whenever the alienee has a right, as against the common vendor, to have the parcel bought and paid for by him free from
the incumbrance. Facts and circumstances affecting and
qualifying the rights and equities of the different purchas-

ers, as between themselves, may materially modify the application of the rule; it will not be applied, if its application works injustice. With this general statement of the rule and its qualifications, we pass to a consideration of the equities of the parties.

A bill was filed by the transferrees of a note given by J. W. Maddox for a part of the purchase-money of the land, which had been bought by him in October, 1872, to enforce a vendor's lien. A final decree of sale was made in November, 1883. Maddox having died before the filing of the bill, his heirs and devisees were made defendants. He sold and conveyed, in his life-time, parcels of the land to different persons, and by his will devised a part of it to be sold for the payment of his debts, and other portions to some of his children. The alienations, first in the order of time, bear date May 25, 1876; on which day he conveyed, with covenant of warranty, by three separate conveyances, different parcels to John H. Burton, C. B. Maddox, and F. W. L. Maddox. It is satisfactorily shown by the evidence, that the first two conveyances were made on a valuable consideration; the last is a voluntary conveyance. As to Burton, the evidence discloses no fact or circumstance which impairs or displaces his right to a preference over the others. Being a *bona fide* purchaser, with a stipulation for a good and unincumbered title, he is unquestionably entitled to have the other portions of the land sold before his is resorted to. C. B. Maddox, though a purchaser for a valuable consideration, occupies an entirely different position, as will be hereafter shown.

The next point of consideration relates to the equities between appellee, Henry, and the devisees; to a clear understanding of which a statement of other facts is requisite. On the same day on which the conveyances above mentioned were made, J. W. Maddox made his will, and died a few days thereafter. By the will, power was conferred on the executrix to sell, for the payment of his debts, those parts of the land designated in the record as the "Mill tract," and a half interest in three acres previously conveyed to C. B. Maddox, and also one acre on which the store-house stood. The executrix executed the power of sale December 22, 1876. At the sale, C. B. Maddox purchased the one acre, and the half interest in the three acres, the purchase-money for which he paid. C. B. Maddox and Prickett purchased the "Mill tract." In consequence of their failure to pay the purchase-money, the executrix filed a bill in September, 1879, to subject it to the payment thereof. On October 23, 1880, a decree was rendered ascertaining that Maddox and Prickett were indebted about the sum of $2,300, and ordering the land to be sold for its payment. It was sold by the register under the decree, January 3, 1881, and bought by Henry for $400.

The bill, on which the present decree of sale was made, was filed *before* the bill on which the decree was rendered under which Henry bought, and was pending at the time of his purchase. He necessarily had notice of the vendor's lien, and purchased subject to it. There is evidence showing that the existence and amount of the vendor's lien were considered and estimated by him in determining the price which he was willing to pay for the land. The rule, to pursue the inverse order of alienation, does not extend to a case, where a part of the land is sold subject to the paramount incumbrance. When a vendor sells a part of a tract, subject to a mortgage, which covers the entire tract, the vendor and purchaser stand on the same level, and must contribute in proportion to their respective interests. Successive purchasers of an equity of redemption, sold by the sheriff in parcels at different times, are not liable in the inverse order of alienation. Black, C. J., says: "Two purchasers at a sheriff's sale, subject to a mortgage, which is a common incumbrance on the land of both, stand on a level. Neither of them has done or suffered any thing, which entitles him to a preference over the other. Equality is equity. They must pay the mortgage in proportion to the value of their respective lots."

The contention of counsel, that the devisees are estopped by the decree under which Henry bought, on the ground that they were parties, can not be sustained. By the purchase, Henry acquired all the title and interest in and to the "Mill tract," which they had as heirs and devisees, and they are estopped from asserting any right or title to that particular land. But, the question here is not a question of right or title to the land, but of the equities between successive purchasers and devisees of parcels of land covered by a common vendor's lien, subject to which all of them took their respective interests. The devisees are affected by all the equities to which the devised parcels were subject in the hands of the testator, and Henry's equity is the same as if he had purchased from the testator, subject to the vendor's lien. If a mortgagor sells a part of the mortgaged lands, subject to the mortgage, the part which he retains, and the part sold, are ratably liable to the mortgage debt. Henry, having purchased subject to the vendor's lien, has no claim to a preference over the devisees. The equities between them are equal, and equality of burden becomes equity. Their several parcels are liable to contribute in proportion to their respective values. In such case, the principle of contribution applies. The same observations apply to F. W. Maddox's part, he being a mere volunteer.—2 Lead. Cas. Eq. 304. "When the deeds to the successive grantees are not warranty, or equivalent thereto, but simply purport to convey the mortgagor's title, right and interest in the parcels, the intention is clear, that the grantees respectively assume their portions of the burden."—3 Pom. Eq. Jur. § 1225.

The remaining question relates to the equities between C. B. Maddox and the other parties. The interest of the testator in the "Mill tract" was specially charged with the payment of his debts, and sold for that purpose. C. B. Maddox became the purchaser. The payment of the purchase-money of the "Mill tract," and its application to the debts, would have relieved the land of the vendor's lien, and the devisees and Henry would have received their parts or parcels free of incumbrance. C. B. Maddox owes now, on account of the purchase-money, more than enough to pay the amount of the decree of sale. Being aware that the "Mill tract" was specially charged and sold to pay the debts of the testator, his purchase imposed an obligation to furnish the money for that purpose, and thus relieve the balance of the land. It is still his legal and equitable duty to pay what he owes in exoneration of the other parcels. Says Mr. Pomeroy: "Although the deeds are warranties, so that the doctrine will otherwise apply, any particular grantee may, by his subsequent omissions, or by his subsequent dealings with other parties, disturb the order of the equities in his own favor, and create equities in behalf of other owners, and even render his own primarily liable as between all the grantees."—3 Pom. Eq. Jur. § 1225. It would be inequitable to allow him, by his failure to pay the purchase-money for the "Mill tract," to throw the burden of the vendor's lien on the other owners, and be himself relieved. The other parties have a superior equity, and in adjusting the equities between them, the court should direct his land to be first sold.

In determining the proportions which should be contributed by the parcels owned by Henry, F. W. Maddox and the devisees, the court will be governed by the rule settled in *Mo. & Mar. Dock & Mut. Ins. Co. v. Huder*, 35 Ala. 713.

Reversed and remanded.

Calera Land Co. *v.* Brinkerhoff.

Action for Trespass to Realty.

1. *Competency of party to testify to handwriting of subscribing witness to deed.*—A party to the suit, who is the grantee in a deed which he offers in evidence, may testify to the handwriting of the subscribing witness (Code, § 2765), on making satisfactory proof as to his failure to produce the witness himself.

APPEAL from the Circuit Court of Shelby.

Tried before the Hon. LEROY F. BOX.

This action was brought by W. E. Brinkerhoff, against the Calera Land Company, a private corporation, and Arthur Adams, its agent as alleged; was commenced on the 5th March, 1887, and sought to recover damages for an alleged trespass on land. The defendants pleaded the general issue, and several special pleas, on which issue was joined. "On the trial," as the bill of exceptions states, "the plaintiff offered in evidence a quit-claim deed for the premises, from David Adams to himself; which deed not having been registered, the court held that it must be proved by the subscribing witness thereto, O. W. Buck. The plaintiff was then called as a witness in his own behalf, and the absence of said subscribing witness was accounted for by him; and the plaintiff himself was then offered as a witness to prove the handwriting of the subscribing witness to said deed. The defendants objected to the plaintiff's thus testifying, on the ground that he was a party to the suit." The court overruled the objection, and allowed plaintiff to testify as proposed; to which ruling the defendants excepted, and they now assign it as error.

W. R. OLIVER, for appellants.

TROY, TOMPKINS & LONDON, *contra.*

[Kyle v. Perdue.]

McCLELLAN, J.—The only question presented by this record goes to the competency of a party to prove the handwriting of an attesting witness to a deed, the failure to introduce the latter being properly accounted for. We entertain no doubt of the correctness of the action of the court below in allowing the plaintiff to testify to the handwriting of the absent attesting witness. Section 2765 of the Code removes all objection to the competency of witnesses predicated on interest, or the fact of their being parties to the record, with certain exceptions, within which the testimony involved here clearly does not fall; and a party may testify to any material, relevant fact not falling within these exceptions.—*Davis v. Tarver*, 68 Ala. 98; *Gold Life Ins. Co. v. Sledge*, 62 Ala. 566; *O'Neal v. Reynolds*, 42 Ala. 197.

This is not the question of the competency of an attesting witness to a deed in his favor, and is not within the decision in *Coleman v. State*, where it was essential to produce or account for the absence of the subscribing witnesses, before other evidence of execution could be received, and it appeared that the donee and two others had attested the execution of the instrument. The absence of the other attesting witnesses was not accounted for, but it was proposed to satisfy the rule requiring at least one of such witnesses to be introduced, or sufficient reason shown for a failure to do so, by offering the grantee; and the exclusion of this witness was held proper, not because he was incompetent to testify to any fact at issue in the cause, but on the ground that he was incapacitated to be an attesting witness, and his introduction as such did not fulfill the requirements of the rule.—*Coleman v. State,* 79 Ala. 50.

Affirmed.

Kyle *v.* Perdue.

Bill in Equity for Foreclosure of Mortgage, or Deed of Trust.

1. *Written instrument operating partly as deed, and partly as will.* A written instrument in the form of a deed, signed by the grantor, attested by two witnesses, and probated as a deed; by which the grantor, reciting her physical incapacity to look after and care for her property, her desire to have it cared for during her life, to make pro-

[Kyle v. Perdue.]

vision for her comfort and welfare during life, and the further purpose of disposing of her property, and having the utmost confidence in the grantees, and for the further consideration of one dollar in hand paid by them, bargains, sells and conveys to them, by present words, all her property of every kind and description, to them and their assigns forever. "in trust nevertheless, and upon the uses and purposes hereinafter mentioned"—namely, to take charge of said property, collect and receive the rents and profits, keep the property in good repair, pay all taxes and other charges or assessments against it, and pay the residue to the grantor during life,—vests in the grantees a present right, interest, and legal title to all the property, but charged with a trust for the uses and purposes specified; although a subsequent provision is added, which is testamentary in its character, and can only take effect after the death of the grantor—namely, that after her death the property "shall revert" to the grantees in fee simple, in equal shares; and further, that in consideration of services rendered by them to her, and also one dollar in hand paid, she sells and conveys to them all the property of which she may die seized and possessed, "hereby revoking all other arrangements, either verbal or written, as to the disposition of my [her] property."

2. *Foreclosure of mortgage by trustee of tenant for life.*—As a general rule, when a person holds the legal title to property, charged with the duty of accounting for the rents and profits to a tenant for life, he is a trustee to that extent, and has no power to change the *status* of the property, except possibly in extreme cases, subject to the direction and approval of a court of equity; yet, where the widow and sole devisee of a deceased mortgagor, and grantor in a deed of trust in the nature of a mortgage, has conveyed all of her property to trustees, with a life interest in herself in the rents and profits after payment of taxes, repairs, &c., and a testamentary provision in their favor after her death, the trustees may maintain a bill to foreclose the mortgage, and the court may, if necessary to prevent danger from conversion of the trust fund, require proper security for the income during her life.

3. *Parties to bill.*—The trustee in a mortgage, or deed of trust in the nature of a mortgage, where the mortgage debt has been bequeathed and devised by the defendant mortgagee to his widow, and she has conveyed all of her property to trustees, charged with the payment of taxes, repairs, &c., and the residue of the rents and profits payable to herself for life, with a testamentary provision in favor of the trustees after her death, may join with the said trustees in a bill to foreclose the mortgage, against the widow and the mortgagor.

APPEAL from the Chancery Court of Etowah.

Heard before the Hon. S. K. MCSPADDEN.

The bill in this case was filed on the 8th February, 1887, by W. H. Denson as trustee, and R. B. Kyle and Sam. Henry, against Daniel Liddell and wife, and Mrs. Augusta E. Perdue, deceased; and sought to foreclose a mortgage, or deed of trust in the nature of a mortgage, which said Liddell and wife had executed to said W. J. Perdue in his life-time, conveying a quarter-section of land as security for a note of $153.25, dated April 11th, 1884, and payable April 9th, 1886. W. J. Perdue died at a time not stated in the record, and his last will and testament was duly admitted to probate on the 19th January, 1885, by which he bequeathed and devised all of his property, by very general words of description, to his widow, Mrs. Augusta E. Perdue, whom he appointed executrix, and relieved her of giving bond. Mrs. Perdue qualified as executrix, and on the 9th August, 1886, she executed an instrument of writing, a copy of which was made an exhibit to the bill, and which was in these words:

"State of Alabama, Etowah County: This indenture, made this 9th day of August, 1886, between Augusta E. Perdue, of the State and county aforesaid, of the first part, and R. B. Kyle and Sam. Henry, of said county and State, of the second part, *witnesseth*, that whereas the said Augusta E. Perdue, being in feeble health, but of sound mind, and unable to look after and care for her property, and being desirous of having her property cared for during her natural life, and to make provision for her comfort and welfare during her natural life, and for the further purpose of disposing of my property, real, personal and mixed, and having the utmost confidence in my friends, R. B. Kyle and Sam. Henry; now, therefore, in consideration of the sum of one dollar in hand paid by the said R. B. Kyle and Sam. Henry, the receipt of which is hereby acknowledged, hath this day bargained, sold, released, conveyed and confirmed, and by these presents doth bargain, sell, release, convey and confirm, unto the the said R. B. Kyle and Sam. Henry, all my property, real, personal, and mixed, together with the tenements, hereditaments, and appurtenances thereunto belonging, and the reversions, remainder, rents, issues and profits thereof; also, all the estate, right, title, interest, claim and demand whatsoever of the said party of the first part, in the above described property; to have and to hold, unto the said R. B. Kyle and Sam. Henry, and their assigns forever; in trust nevertheless, and upon the uses and purposes hereinafter mentioned, namely, first, to take charge of said property, take, collect and receive the rents, issues and profits thereof, and out of the proceeds to keep the said premises in good order and repair, and to pay all charges, taxes and assessments that may be imposed thereon, and pay the residue to Augusta E. Perdue during her life. And the said Augusta E. Perdue *do* by these presents hereby stipulate, and it is hereby understood, that at and after the death of the said Augusta E. Perdue, the property above mentioned shall revert to the said R. B. Kyle and Sam. Henry, in fee simple, and in equal shares; and for and in consideration of valuable services rendered to me by the said R. B. Kyle and Sam. Henry, and the further sum of one dollar to me in hand paid, the receipt of which is hereby acknowledged, I do hereby grant, bargain, sell and convey to the said R. B. Kyle and Sam. Henry all my property, real, personal or mixed, that I may die seized or possessed, together with all the tenements, hereditaments, and appurtenances thereto belonging; to have and to hold to the said R. B. Kyle and Sam. Henry, in equal shares, and to their assigns forever, less one-eighth of an acre each to be given to Ellen Anderson and Bookie Whorton. And the said R. B. Kyle and Sam. Henry are charged with the duty of, and are hereby fully authorized to lay off to Ella Anderson one-eighth of an acre of land, including the building now occupied by her, and one-eighth of an acre of land to Bookie Whorton, including the building now occupied by her, and to execute deeds in fee simple to each of them for said land; and I hereby revoke all other arrangements, either verbal or written, as to the disposition of my property. In witness thereof, I have hereunto set my hand and seal, the day and date above written. Erasures on the 19th and 20th lines of second page made before signing." (Signed by Mrs. Perdue, under seal, attested by two subscribing witnesses, and admitted to record as a deed, December 7th, 1886, on proof by one of the subscribing witnesses.)

The bill alleged that the complainants had never had possession of the note secured by the mortgage, and had not been able to find it after diligent search; and that Kyle and Henry had requested Denson, in writing, to foreclose the mortgage. Mrs. Perdue was made a defendant both individually and as executrix, and she filed a demurrer to the bill, assigning numerous grounds. The chancellor sustained the demurrer, on these grounds: 1st, that the written instrument was testamentary in its character, and gave the complainants, Kyle and Henry, no present or vested interest in the property; 2d, that, even if the instrument operated as a deed, the interest or estate conveyed to Kyle and Henry was charged with certain trust duties, and the bill did not show that they had ever accepted the trust; 3d, that, even if they had accepted the trust, they had no right to foreclose the mortgage, thereby changing the *status* of the property, against the consent of the grantor. The complainants appeal from this decree, and here assign it as error.

Liddell and wife made no defense to the suit, and by

written agreement, entered of record in this court, consented that the case might proceed as if a decree *pro confesso* had been entered against them.

W. H. DENSON, and WATTS & SON, for appellants.—(1.) The writing executed by Mrs. Perdue to Kyle and Henry, though some of its provisions may be regarded as testamentary, is in form and purpose a deed, and conveys to the grantees, for valuable consideration, a present estate and interest; vesting in them the legal title to the property, but charged with certain trusts.—*Golding v. Golding,* 24 Ala. 122; *Strong v. Gregory,* 19 Ala. 146; *Pollard v. Maddox,* 28 Ala. 321; *Comer v. Bankhead,* 70 Ala. 136; *Bryant v. Bryant,* 35 Ala. 315; *McPherson v. Harris,* 59 Ala. 620; *Evington v. Smith,* 66 Ala. 398; *Mason v. Ala. Iron Co,* 73 Ala. 270; *Campbell v. Gilbert,* 57 Ala. 569; *Jenkins v. Cooper,* 50 Ala. 419; *Kyle v. Bellenger,* 79 Ala. 516; *Bryant v. Stephens,* 58 Ala. 636; *Rice v. Rice,* 68 Ala. 216; *Daniel v. Hill,* 52 Ala. 430; *Trawick v, Davis,* 85 Ala. 342; *Hall v. Burkham,* 59 Ala. 349; *Jordan v. Jordan,* 65 Ala. 301; *Elmore v. Mustin,* 28 Ala. 309; *Bolman v. Overall,* 80 Ala. 451; *Nelson v. Manning,* 53 Ala. 549. (2.) If the latter provisions of the instrument are inconsistent with the former, the former must prevail.—*Petty v. Boothe,* 19 Ala. 634; *Gould v. Womack,* 2 Ala. 83; 12 N. W. Rep. 382; 4 Greenl. Cruise, pp. 300-07. (3.) The filing of this bill shows a sufficient acceptance of the trust.—80 Ala. 165. (4.) The proper parties are joined.—*Hitchcock v. U. S. Bank,* 7 Ala. 425; *Owen v. Bankhead,* 76 Ala. 143.

DORTCH & MARTIN, *contra,* contended (1) that the instrument was testamentary; (2) that, if it could operate at all as a deed, it showed only a voluntary executory trust, which a court of equity would not enforce; (3) that it gave Kyle and Henry, as trustees, no power to foreclose the mortgage; (4) that it was void for uncertainty. They cited 2 Ala. 152; 6 Ala. 631; 35 Ala. 628; 42 Ala. 365; 65 Ala. 305; 28 Ala. 313; 5 Amer. Rep. 530; Perry on Trusts, 436.

STONE, C. J.—The points at issue in this cause arise mainly out of a written instrument, bearing date August 9, 1886, and signed by Augusta E. Perdue. One of the controverted questions is, whether that instrument is a deed or a will. It was drawn manifestly by an inexperienced draughtsman. The reporter will set it out *in extenso.*

The conveyance has many of the characteristics of a deed of bargain and sale. It twice recites a consideration. In one place, the language is, "in consideration of the sum of one dollar in hand paid by the said R. B. Kyle and Sam. Henry, the receipt of which is hereby acknowleged." In the other place, the recital is, "for and in consideration of valuable services rendered to me by the said R. B. Kyle and Sam. Henry, and the further sum of one dollar to me in hand paid, the receipt of which I do hereby acknowledge." Now, each of these recitals is of a consideration deemed valuable in the law, as distinguished from one merely good. Each would authorize proof of other valuable consideration in aid of it; and each is sufficient to uphold a conveyance, when not assailed by creditors.—*Houston v. Blackman*, 66 Ala. 559; *Tutwiler v. Munford*, 68 Ala. 124. The instrument has many other properties of a deed. The following are some of them: "Hath this day bargained and sold, released, conveyed and confirmed, and by these presents doth bargain, sell, release, convey and confirm" &c. "To have and to hold unto the said R. B. Kyle and Sam Henry, and their assigns forever; in trust nevertheless, and upon the uses and purposes hereinafter mentioned, namely: First, to take charge of said property, to take, collect and receive the rents, issues and profits thereof, and out of the proceeds to keep the said premises in good order and repair, and to pay all charges, taxes and assessments that may be imposed thereon, and pay the residue to Augusta E. Perdue during her life." There are many other expressions and clauses which properly pertain to deeds, and do not to wills.

Under the instrument, Kyle and Henry are to take charge of the property, collect the rents, and look after the taxes and repairs—all in the life-time of Mrs. Perdue. This gives to the instrument a large operation during the life-time of the maker, and stamps it a deed, not a will. We have so often and so recently considered the differences which distinguish the one instrument from the other, that we consider it unnecessary to repeat them.—*Trawick v. Davis*, 85 Ala. 342; *Sharp v. Hall*, 86 Ala. 110; *Griffith v. Marsh*, 86 Ala. 302; s. c., 5 So. Rep. 569; *Elmore v. Mustin*, 28 Ala. 309; *Jordan v. Jordan*, 65 Ala. 301.

We hold, then, that Mrs. Perdue's conveyance vested in Kyle and Henry, at the time of its execution, the title to the property she then owned; but the title was received by them clothed with a trust, and that trust was so stamped upon it in the face of the title-papers, that it would follow the property into whose hands soever it might go. The trust was, that they should have power to collect the rents, issues and profits, pay the taxes, and keep up the repairs; and any excess of rents, issues and profits beyond this, they were bound to account for and pay to Mrs. Perdue. That was absolutely hers. And if any of the profits accruing to her under this provision, or any property in which it may be invested, should remain undisposed of, or unconsumed at the time of her death, this will have become property of her estate, and, possibly, will not vest in Kyle and Henry, by virtue of the conveyance as a *deed*. The clause of the instrument in reference to such remaining income and profits can, probably, take effect only as a testament.—*Kinnebrew v. Kinnebrew*, 35 Ala. 628.

We have shown above that the title to all the property which Mrs. Perdue owned at the time she executed the instrument, vested at once in Kyle and Henry, incumbered with a trust during the life of the grantor. Of what that property consists, save the single item involved in this suit, we are not informed. The general rule is, that one who holds property charged with the duty of accounting to another for the income and profits, is to that extent a trustee, and subject to the disabilities, of a trustee. He has no power to change the *status* of the property, except, possibly, in extreme cases, subject to the approval and direction of the Chancery Court.—2 Pom. Eq. §§ 1062, 1065, 1067.

When Mrs. Perdue executed the deed, she, under the provisions of her husband's will, had become the owner of a debt due from Liddell, secured by a trust deed on land, in which Denson was named the trustee. The debt was due and payable April 9, 1886, and the trust deed provides, that should any part of said debt remain due and unpaid at maturity, then, upon the written request of Perdue, the payee of the note, his agent or attorney, Denson, the trustee, was required to take possession of the land, and, after advertising, sell the same and pay the debt. The present bill was filed in February, 1887, and avers that Kyle and Henry, claiming to be owners of the debt and its security, had notified Denson, in writing, to foreclose the deed and collect the money. The bill is filed in the name of Kyle, Henry and Denson as complainants, and makes Liddell and wife and Mrs. Perdue, defendants. Liddell and wife offered no defense to the suit.

[Kyle v. Perdue.]

Mrs. Perdue demurred to the bill, and the chancellor sustained the demurrer, holding that Kyle and Henry have no power to foreclose the trust deed, or mortgage.

A mortgage of land to secure the payment of a debt, creates a peculiar estate. While it vests a legal title in the mortgagee, upon which he can maintain an action at law against the mortgagor, it does not make him a freeholder. On his death, it does not descend to his heir, as land held by him in absolute right descends. The naked legal title may descend to the heir; but the latter receives and holds it, not as his own property, but as security for the debt, which is payable to, and demandable by the personal representative. When the debt is paid, the purposes of the mortgage are accomplished, and the right to the land (but not always the title) revests in the mortgagor, who has all the while been, as to the whole world, except the mortgagee, the freeholder, entitled to all the rights and privileges which freehold confers.—3 Brick. Dig. 645, § 177. Mrs. Perdue's property, then, was not the land conveyed by Liddell's mortgage. It was Liddell's debt, secured by the mortgage or trust deed.

The loan of money on mortgage security, the debt having a long time to run, as simply an interest-bearing investment, has not been common with us. We find nothing in the Liddell mortgage which induces us to think such was the intention in this case. We regard it as an ordinary debt from Liddell to Perdue, secured by a deed of trust on land. It gives to Perdue, the beneficiary, neither title to the land, nor the right to take possession of it. It gives to Denson, the trustee, the right to take possession after default, but only on written request, and for the purpose of sale under the power in the trust deed. Nothing is said about default in payment of interest. That the debt, if uncollected, would increase, goes without saying; and we have nothing from which to infer the security would increase in value. On the face of the proceedings, the debt appears, *prima facie*, to be of a class which it is safest to collect, rather than indulge; and we fail to find anything tending to show that Kyle and Henry are abusing the trust or powers the deed confers upon them. If there be danger or risk in allowing them to convert a *chose* in action into money, the chancellor can provide against that, by requiring security, or so securing the fund as that Mrs. Perdue shall enjoy its income for her life. *Dunham v. Milhous*, 70 Ala. 596.

There is no misjoinder of parties complainant.—*Hitchcock v. U. S. Bank*, 7 Ala. 386.

The chancellor erred in sustaining the demurrer to the bill as amended.

Reversed and remanded.

Dudley *v.* Collier & Pinckard.

Action for Compensation under Special Contract.

1. *Foreign corporations; constitutional and statutory restrictions on right to do business here; action by agent on contract violative of.*—An agent of a foreign corporation engaged in the business of lending money on mortgages, not having complied with the conditions imposed by constitutional and statutory provisions on the right to do business in this State (Const. Ala , Art. XIV, § 4; Sess. Acts 1886-7, pp. 102-04), can not maintain an action to recover compensation agreed to be paid him for procuring a loan from the corporation.

APPEAL from the Circuit Court of Lowndes.
Tried before the Hon. JOHN MOORE.

WATTS & SON, and WILLIAMSON & WILLIAMS, for appellant, cited *Amer. U. Tel. Co. v. Western U. Tel. Co.*, 67 Ala. 26; *Smith v. Insurance Co.*, 4 Ala. 558; *Lindsey v. McGehee*, 6 Ala. 16: *Morrell v. Quarles*, 35 Ala. 544; *Walker v. Gregory*, 36 Ala. 180; *Oxford Iron Co. v. Spradley*, 46 Ala. 98, and 51 Ala. 171; *Speed v. Cocke*, 57 Ala. 209; *Ware v. Jones*, 61 Ala. 288; *Pac. Guano Co. v. Dawkins*, 57 Ala. 115; *Mullen v. Pac. Guano Co.*, 66 Ala. 582; *Robertson v. Hayes*, 83 Ala. 290; *Woods v. Armstrong*, 54 Ala. 150; *Lee v. Cassen*, 61 Ala. 312; Chitty on Contracts, 982, note: 2 Parsons on Contracts, 673-4; *Robertson v. Robinson*, 65 Ala. 610; *Ware v. Curry*, 67 Ala. 274; *Toler v. Armstrong*, 11 Wheat.; 13 Amer. Rep. 737; 44 Penn. St. 9.

ROQUEMORE, WHITE & LONG, and W. R. HOUGHTON, *contra.*

SOMERVILLE, J.—The suit is brought by the appellees, for a stipulated compensation agreed to be paid them by the appellant, Dudley, for services rendered in procuring a loan of money for his use.

The court sustained a demurrer to the sixth, seventh and

ninth pleas jointly. and this ruling is assigned as error.   If
either of these pleas constituted a good defense, the ruling is
erroneous.

The sixth plea avers that "the loan and contract of borrowing were to be made with a foreign corporation, company
or association, having no authority to do any business within
the State of Alabama, and that an agreement to pay the borrowed money and interest thereon, and to make a mortgage
upon lands in this [Lowndes] county [Alabama], was to be
made with a foreign corporation, located in Great Britain,
known as the   of London, England;
and the said corporation had no known place of business, nor
authorized agent within the State of Alabama, and had never
been authorized, under the laws of Alabama, to do business
within the State of Alabama, and that the plaintiffs were in
fact the agents of such corporation."

It is declared in Art. XIV, section 4 of our present Constitution, that "no foreign corporation shall do any business
in this State, without having at least one known place of
business, and an authorized agent or agents therein."—
Const. 1875, Art. XIV, § 4.   We have construed this to be
a police regulation, "just as much," we said, "a police regulation for the protection of the property interests of the citizens of the State, as a law forbidding vagrancy among its
inhabitants."—*Amer. Un. Tel. Co. v. West. Un. Tel. Co.*,
67 Ala. 26; s. c., 42 Amer. Rep. 90.   The General Assembly passed an act approved February 28, 1887, to give force
and effect to this section of the Constitution, in which it required that every foreign corporation or company, before engaging in business in this State, shall file in the office of the
Secretary of State an instrument in writing, under seal of
such company, and signed officially by the president and secretary, "designating at least one known place of business in
the State, and an authorized agent or agents residing there-
at."   It is declared that "it shall not be lawful" for any person to act as agent, or transact any business, directly or indirectly, for or on behalf of any such company or corporation, until this requirement is complied with.   Any one who
shall act as such agent, or transact any business for such foreign company, without having first complied with such requirement, is subjected a penalty of five hundred dollars,
payable to the State.   The company itself that transacts or
engages in any business in this State, before filing such in-

[Dudley v. Collier & Pinckard.]

strument, is liable to a penalty of one thousand dollars.—
Acts 1886-87, pp. 102-104.

The contract for services here sued on bears date March
8th, 1887, and is therefore subsequent to the foregoing prohibitory enactment. The case, then, is reduced simply to
this, assuming the facts stated in the plea to be true, as admitted by the demurrer. The plaintiffs are the agents of a
foreign corporation, which has failed to comply with the requirements of this statute. Neither the corporation nor the
agents, therefore, are authorized to transact any business in
Alabama. A loan or borrowing of money, by or from such
company, in this State, is an unlawful act, subjecting both
the agents and the company to a heavy penalty. The services here sued for are for the doing of this prohibited act.
The consideration of the defendant's promise is an act in
express violation of the Constitution and laws of Alabama.
The contract to pay for such illegal services is itself necessarily illegal, as a promise made in consideration of an act
forbidden by law; and being executory, the courts will not
lend their aid to its enforcement.

It is an established rule of law, supported by uniform
authority, that when a statute goes no further even than to
impose a penalty for the doing of an act, a contract founded on
such act as a consideration is void, although the statute does
not pronounce it void, nor expressly prohibit it.—*Woods v.
Armstrong*, 54 Ala. 150; 25 Amer. Rep. 671, and *note*, 675-
678. In the present case, there is both a penalty and an
express prohibition.

In *Woods v. Armstrong, supra*, it was accordingly held,
where a statute of this State imposed a penalty for selling
any fertilizer which had not been inspected, analyzed and
stamped in the mode prescribed by law, a note given for the
purchase-money of such fertilizer sold in violation of this
requirement was void. This ruling has been followed by us
in many other cases.

In *Milton v. Haden*, 32 Ala. 30, a note given for the lease
of a ferry was held void, on the ground that the lessor had
no license, and the running of an unlicensed ferry was prohibited under penalty.

In *Harrison v. Jones*, 80 Ala. 412, we held that no recovery could be had for medical services rendered by an unlicensed physician, the practice of medicine in this State
without such license being impliedly prohibited by a penalty.
This ruling rests upon the general principle, that when a

28

statute forbids under a penalty, or otherwise, the carrying on of any particular business without a license, a contract made for services rendered, or goods sold, in violation of the requirements of such statute, is void; especially if it appears that the object of the legislature was for police purposes, and not solely for the purpose of raising revenue; or, in other words, where the legislative intent, in imposing the condition, was "the maintenance of public order or safety, or the protection of the persons dealing with those on whom the condition is imposed." Such, at least, seems to be the better and later view, sustained by the more recent authorities.—3 Amer. & Eng. Ency. Law, 872; Bishop on Contr. § 547; Greenhood on Public Policy, 580-583. Mr. Wharton states the rule as follows: "When a statute imposes a penalty, not as a tax, but as a punishment, then a contract to do the thing on which the penalty is imposed is ordinarily unlawful; and so when an act is absolutely prohibited. And when conditions on the exercise of a business are imposed in a statute for the maintenance of public order, or the protection of parties, or on grounds of public policy, the contracts by such persons, in violation of the statute, are void."—1 Whart. Contr. § 365; *Melchoir v. McCarty,* 11 Amer. Rep. 605; *Robertson v. Hays,* 83 Ala. 290; *Prescott v. Battersby,* 119 Mass. 285; *Burton v. Hamblen,* 32 Me. 448.

In the present case, it is perfectly manifest that the act of February 28, 1887, above cited, does not contemplate the assessment of the penalties imposed for revenue, but only for punishment. It is even provided that, in case of non-payment of such penalties, the offending party shall be imprisoned, or sentenced to hard labor, for a period not exceeding six months.—Acts 1886-7, p. 10.

The case of *Thorne v. Traveller's Ins. Co.,* 80 Penn. St. 15; Amer. Rep. 89, is one not unlike this in principle. The statutes of Pennsylvania provided, that any foreign insurance company, desiring to transact business in that State, should first appoint a resident agent in that State, on whom process could be served, and file in the office of the Auditor-General a certified appointment of such agent, and a copy of the company's charter. A written application for a license to transact business in the State, signed by such agent, was also required to be filed in some public office, with a bond of the agent with a specified sum, with resident securities, approved in the mode and on the conditions prescribed. An agent who transacted any insurance business in the State for such foreign company, without previous compliance with the provisions of the statute, including the procuring of the license, was made guilty of a misdemeanor, and subjected to a fine of five hundred dollars. The conditions of the statute not having been complied with by the plaintiff insurance company, it was held that a suit against the agents and the sureties on his bond would not lie, for moneys collected by the agent in the course of his agency. The principle on which this conclusion was based is, that the doing of the business by the agent was expressly prohibited by the statute, and was authoiized by the company, and that no recovery could be had on the bond without proving that the company and the agent had both violated the law; or, in other words, without the aid of the illegal transaction the company had no case.

Under the principles settled by the foregoing authorities, to which many others might be added, we are of opinion that the facts stated in the sixth plea constituted a good defense to the action, showing that the contract of loan was one in violation of the statute, and void, therefore, for illegality. The promise of the defendant as a consideration for procuring such a loan was equally illegal and void, as an agreement to pay for the doing of an act prohibited by law, and punishable by a penalty.

Analogous statutes in other States regulating the doing of business by foreign corporations have been frequently construed by the highest courts of those States in accordance with the views which we have above expressed.—*Cincinnati Assur. Co. v. Rosenthal,* 55 Ill. 85; *Ætna Ins. Co. v. Harvey,* 11 Wisc. 394; *Hoffman v. Banks,* 41 Ind. 1; *Union Cent. Life Ins. Co. v. Thomas,* 46 Ind. 44; *Bank v. Page,* 6 Oreg. 431; *In re Comstock,* 3 Sawy. (C. C.) 218; *Semple v. Bank,* 5 Ind. 88; *Williams v. Cheney,* 3 Gray, 215; *Jones v. Smith, Ib.* 500; 2 Morawetz on Corp. (2d Ed.) §§ 661-665.

Whether a foreign corporation, when sued, could take advantage of its own failure to comply with the requirements of the statute by setting up the invalidity of its contract, presents another question, which does not arise in this case. *Brooklyn Life Ins. Co. v. Bledsoe,* 52 Ala. 538.

The case of *Sherwood v. Alvis,* 83 Ala. 115; 3 Amer. St. Rep. 695, was based on a transaction occurring prior to the enactment of the above statute enforcing the constitutional provision; and what was said in that case, in reference to the

[Woodstock Iron Co. v. Roberts.]

effect of this statute, was not necessary for the decision of
the case. The mortgage securing the loan, moreover, had
been foreclosed under the power of sale, so as to cut off the
equity of redemption, and the transaction was, in a measure,
an executed contract. We held that, in such a case, an action of ejectment for the land purchased at the mortgage
sale would lie by the purchaser. That case is, on these and
other grounds, distinguished from this.—*Elston v. Piggott*,
94 Ind. 14,

The court erred in sustaining the demurrer to the pleas;
and for this error, the judgment must be reversed, and the
cause remanded.

Reversed and remanded.

Woodstock Iron Co. *v.* Roberts.

Statutory Action in nature of Ejectment.

1. *Certified copy of patent from land office.*---Under statutory provisions, a copy of a patent for lands issued by the United States may be
certified by the "acting commissioner" of the General Land Office
(Code, § 2787); and such certified copy is admissible as evidence without producing or accounting for the absence of the patent itself. (Overruling *Jones v. Walker*, 47 Ala. 175, as to the last point.)

2. *Infancy as exception to statute of limitations.*—By statute (Code,
§ 2624), an infant is allowed three years after attaining his majority,
within which to bring suit, or make entry; but his disability is not allowed, in any case, to extend the period of limitations beyond the lapse
of twenty years from the accrual of his right of action or entry; this being a statutory affirmation, as applicable to infants, of the doctrine of
proscription.

3. *Adverse possession, under permissive possessor.*—A permissive
possession does not become adverse, without an open and distinct disavowal of the title of the true owner, and the assertion of a hostile
title brought to his notice; but, if the permissive possessor dies in possession, and the land is afterwards sold by his administrator for the
payment of debts, a deed executed to the purchaser purporting to convey the entire estate in the land, the purchase-money paid, and possession delivered, such possession is adverse to the true owner, and will
ripen into a title if continued for the statutory period.

4. *Continuity of possession, as affected by trespass.*—The intrusion of
a mere trespasser on land, who enters without claim or title, does not
interrupt the continuity of possession, unless continued so long that
knowledge by him is presumed, and he fails to resort to legal remedies
before adverse rights are acquired.

5. *Actual and constructive possession.*—Possession under title, or col-
or of title, is not limited to that part of the land which is actually occupied, but extends to the entire tract covered by the written instru-

[Woodstock Iron Co. v. Roberts.]

ment; while the possession of a trespasser, without color of title, extends only to the land actually occupied.

6. *To what witness may testify.*---A witness may testify that a person went into the possession of lands "and thereafter *controlled* them;" this being merely the statement of a collective fact.

APPEAL from the Circuit Court of Calhoun.

Tried before the Hon. JOHN B. TALLY.

This action was brought by Marshall Alexander (now Roberts) against the Woodstock Iron Company, and the Anniston City Land Company, private corporations, to recover the possession of a large tract of land containing more than eight hundred acres; and was commenced on the 13th of May, 1887. The plaintiff was the only child and heir of Marshall J. Alexander, who died on the 12th of September, 1862, and she claimed the land in that capacity; while the defendants claimed as sub-purchasers under persons who had bought the several parcels of the tract, at a sale made by the administrator of the estate of Samuel P. Hudson, deceased, during the year 1866. The defendants pleaded the general issue, and the statutes of limitation of ten and twenty years; and the trial was had on issue joined on these pleas. On the trial, the defendants reserved numerous exceptions to the rulings of the court on the admissibility of evidence, and in the matter of charges given and refused; and these rulings, twenty in number, are now separately assigned as error. The opinion of this court renders unnecessary a statement of these rulings in detail.

KNOX & BOWIE, and CALDWELL & JOHNSTON, for appellant.

BROTHERS, WILLETT & WILLETT, *contra.*

CLOPTON, J.—Transcripts of patents to portions of the land sued for, authenticated by the certificate of the "Acting Commissioner of the General Land Office," were received in evidence, against the objection of defendant. The grounds of objection are, that an acting commissioner is not authorized by law to make such certificate, and that the absence of the original patents was not accounted for. The certificate itself does not appear in the record, and we must assume, in favor of the ruling of the court, that it was in due and proper form. Under the statute which declares that "the certificate of the head of any bureau or department of the general government is a sufficient authentication of any paper or document appertaining to his office," which now constitutes section 2787 of Code, 1886, it was held in *Stephens v. Westwood*, 25 Ala. 716, that a transcript from the books or papers on file in the General Land Office, if properly certified under the seal of the department by the acting commissioner, is admissible in evidence. That case is decisive of the first ground of objection. In *Hines v. Greenlee*, 3 Ala. 73, it was held, that a certified copy of a patent by the commissioner of the General Land Office was receivable in evidence, without attempting in any manner to account for the absence of the original. The decision is based on the principle, that the record of the patent, being required by law, is a public act, and therefore a public document; a duly certified transcript of which is of as high authority, and has the same effect, as the original. Inconsistent with this principle is the ruling in *Jones v. Walker*, 47 Ala. 175, where it was said, that a certified transcript of a deed by the commissioner of the General Land Office is only admissible as secondary evidence, after notice to produce the original. Notice in such case would be useless. The party has not, and is not entitled to possession of the original, and can not be reasonably required to produce an original paper, which is required by law to be kept on file in a department of the government. We reaffirm the ruling in *Hines v. Greenlee*, and *Jones v. Walker* is overruled in this respect.

The plaintiff derives title to the lands as the only child and heir of Marshall J. Alexander, to whom they were sold and conveyed by James A. McCampbell, by deed dated January 18, 1855. The defendant may assail the genuineness of the deed, the *factum*, and date of its execution; but, its execution being proved, it is valid as between the parties, and vests a title in the grantee, valid as to all persons except purchasers from McCampbell and his creditors. The execution of the deed does not appear to be seriously controverted, though the circumstances may be somewhat suspicious. The jury found in favor of its execution, and we shall therefore assume its genuineness. The patents issued to McCampbell, the deed to Alexander, and the proof of the heirship of plaintiff, establish the legal title to be in her, which entitles her, *prima facie*, to maintain the action. The defendant does not pretend to claim title from McCampbell or Alexander. The real defense is adverse possession under color of title, for a sufficient time to defeat the plaintiff's right of action. Whether or not Alexander had actual possession of the lands, is unimportant; he had the legal title, which gave the right, and drew the possession. On the presentation of the case, as made by the record, all issues, except the issue joined on the plea of the statute of limitations, become immaterial. The case will be simplified, and the confusion of immaterial issues avoided, if the inquiry is solely directed to this issue. In our view of the case, we shall limit the consideration to the principles underlying the material and decisive issue, upon which the rights of the parties must ultimately depend.

The plaintiff's father died September 12, 1862; she was born May 31, 1863, and the suit was commenced May 13, 1887. Immediately on the death of an ancestor, his lands descend to his heirs, who are entitled to possession, unless intercepted by the exercise of the statutory authority of the personal representative. The heirs can successfully maintain ejectment against any person in possession, claiming to hold adversely, except the widow or the personal representative of the deceased, though the widow's dower has not been allotted or assigned. Until allotted, she has no legal estate or interest in any specific part of the land, and her right to an assignment of dower does not suspend the heirs' right of action.—*Rives v. Brooks*, 80 Ala. 26; *Turnipseed v. Fitzpatrick*, 75 Ala. 297.

The plaintiff's cause of action accrued as soon as there was any person in the adverse possession of the lands, claiming by independent right. Section 2624 of Code, 1886, provides, if any one entitled to bring suit, or make entry, is, at the time the cause of action or right of entry accrues, a minor, or under other legal disability, he shall have three years after the termination of such disability, in which to bring suit or make entry. This general provision is, however, qualified by the further express provision: "But no disability shall extend the period of limitation, so as to allow such action to be commenced, or entry or defense made, after the lapse of twenty years from the time the cause of action or right accrued." This is a statutory affirmation of the doctrine of prescription, which is so extensive in its scope and operation, that proof of no disability whatever arrests or rebuts the presumption.—*McCartney v. Bone*, 40 Ala. 536; *Garrett v. Garrett*, 69 Ala; 429; *Harrison v. Heflin*, 54 Ala. 552; *Matthews v. McDade*, 72 Ala. 377. Governed by the same policy of security and repose to society, and the necessity of quieting litigation, on which the doctrine of prescription is founded, the statute of limitations prohibits any legal disability to extend the period of limitation beyond twenty years.

It is contended, that the possession of Samuel P. Hudson, under whom the defendant claims, and who, it appears, had been some time prior, and was at the time of his death, in possession, was permissive in its inception; and that it could not become adverse, without a distinct and open disavowal of the title of the true owner, and the assertion of a hostile title brought to her notice. Such is the settled rule. Had Hudson lived, his possession, if permissive, could not have become adverse without such disavowal and assertion. But a possession, however rightfully it may originate, may be converted into a possession hostile and adverse. It appears that, after his death, his administrator sold the lands as the property of his estate, in March, 1866, at which sale different parcels were purchased by different parties. The sales were reported and confirmed by the Probate Court, and, on payment of the purchase-money, conveyances were made to the purchasers, respectively, under order of the court. It is admitted that the proceedings in the Probate Court, and the conveyances of the administrator, were sufficient to invest the purchasers with all the right, title and interest which Hudson had at the time of his death. There is evidence tending to show that the purchasers went into possession immediately after the sale, and that they and those to whom they sold and conveyed, and their sub-vendees, have been in possession ever since. On this question, however, there is a conflict of evidence. The defendant derives title by *mesne* conveyances from the purchasers at the administrator's sale.

If a purchaser of land, under an executory contract, sells and conveys to a third person for a valuable consideration, which is paid, and places him in possession, under a conveyance which is claimed and asserted to pass the entire estate, and under which such third person claims to hold, his possession is adverse to the original vendor, though the first purchaser had not paid the purchase-money, nor received a conveyance.—*Walker v. Crawford*, 70 Ala. 567; *Beard v. Ryan*, 78 Ala. 37. If, after the death of Hudson, his administrator sold the entire estate in the lands, and on payment of the purchase-money executed conveyances to the purchasers, asserting that they passed the entire estate, such conveyances constituted color of title, and were inconsistent

[Woodstock Iron Co. v. Roberts.]

with, and antagonistic to the title of plaintiff; and if the purchasers were placed in possession under such color of title, their possession became hostile and adverse.

It is well settled that possession, in order to ripen into a title, and bar an entry by the true owner, must not only be open, notorious, and adverse, but also continuous for the statutory period. There being some evidence tending to show that the possession was interrupted. defendant, in order to meet this aspect of the evidence, requested the court to instruct the jury, that the entry of a mere intruder, or trespasser, who enters upon land without claim or title, would not interrupt the continuity of defendant's possession. The charge states the rule too broadly. Some courts hold, that a fraudulent or wrongful entry operates to break the continuity of possession, so as to defeat the operation of the statute of limitations. This doctrine is qualified by our decisions. The rule, as settled in this State, is, that the unknown intrusion of mere trespassers will not interrupt the continuity, unless continued for such length of time that knowledge of the intrusion is presumed, or so as to become assertions of adverse rights. If they are known, they become adverse assertions of right, and operate to break the continuity, unless legal remedies are resorted to in a reasonable time to regain possession, and prosecuted to a successful termination.—*Beard v. Ryan, supra; Bell v. Denson*, 56 Ala. 444; *Farmer v. Eslava*, 11 Ala. 1028.

The defendant's possession, being under color of title, is not limited to the lands actually occupied, but extends to the contiguous lands, embraced in the color of title. The possession of a trespasser, without color of title, is confined to his actual occupancy. There being several parcels of land, the intrusion of a mere trespasser would not break the continuity of defendant's possession, except as to that portion of the land actually occupied by such trespasser.

We should remark that the charge requested by defendant, on the effect of the proceedings in the Probate Court, and the sales by the administrator of Hudson, is defective, for the reason, that it omits from its hypothesis the continuity of the possession for the statutory period.

It was competent for the witness Skelton to testify that the defendant went into the possession of the lands "and thereafter *controlled* them." Control is a statement of collective facts. involving management and acts of ownership. If the plaintiff desired to know on what the witness founded his conclusion of facts, he should have drawn it out on cross-examination.   When the character of the possession is in issue, it can not be proved by general reputation, nor by the opinion of individuals as to the actual condition of the property, as was held in *Benje v. Creagh*, 21 Ala. 151.   But control of property is not the opinion of the witness; it is his conclusion of facts—a collective statement.—*Turnley v. Hanna*, 82 Ala. 139; *Elliott v. Stocks*, 67 Ala. 290.

For the error in excluding the testimony of the witness, the judgment must be reversed, as we can not assume that it was without injury.

Reversed and remanded.

Stevenson *v.* Murray.

Petition to set aside Order for Sale of Decedent's Lands.

1. *Sale of decedent's lands for payment of debts; competency of administrator as witness; identity of name as showing identity of person.*—On application by an administrator for an order to sell lands for the payment of debts, when minors are interested in the estate (Code, §§ 2111, 2114), he is not a competent witness to prove the necessity for a sale; yet, if the order is granted, and application is made to set it aside at a subsequent term, the proceedings being regular on their face, it will not be presumed that one of the witnesses was the administrator merely because his name was the same.

APPEAL from the Probate Court of Calhoun.

Heard before the Hon. EMMETT F. CROOK.

In the matter of the estate of Edward C. Murray, deceased, on the petition of the infant heirs to set aside an order for the sale of the lands of the estate, which had been granted on the petition of Hugh Stevenson, the administrator, alleging that a sale was necessary to pay debts.   The order of sale was made on the 19th May, 1887, and the petition to set it aside was filed on the 25th March, 1889.   The court overruled a demurrer to the petition, and set aside the order of sale as prayed; and this judgment is here assigned as error by the administrator.

KNOX & BOWIE, and CALDWELL & JOHNSTON, for appellant.
(1.) The administrator was a competent witness to prove the necessity for a sale, and he knew the condition of the estate

[Steverson v. Murray.]

better than any one else.—*Davis v. Tarver*, 65 Ala. 98;
Quarles v. Campbell, 72 Ala. 64; *Garrett v. Bruner*, 59 Ala.
513. (2.) Even if he was incompetent, the objection was
waived because not taken at the hearing; nor can it be raised
in this collateral proceeding, when the record recites that
the witnesses were disinterested. (3.) The proceedings
connected with the order of sale are regular on their face,
and show that the jurisdiction of the court had attached;
and mere irregularities can not avail on collateral attack.
Pettus v. McClannahan, 52 Ala. 55; *Robertson v. Bradford*,
70 Ala. 387; *Lyons v. Hamner*, 84 Ala. 197; *Ford v. Ford*,
68 Ala. 141; *Carter v. Waugh*, 42 Ala. 452.

BROTHERS, WILLETT & WILLETT, *contra.*—On application
to sell lands for the payment of debts, the administrator and
the heirs are adversary parties.—*Curry v. Peebles*, 83 Ala.
225. Being a party in interest, and a party to the record,
the administrator certainly is not a competent witness to
prove his own side of the issue. His interest and incompetency appear on the face of the record, and render void
the order of sale founded on his testimony.—Code, §§ 2111,
2114; *Davis v. Tarver*, 65 Ala. 98; *Quarles v. Campbell*,
72 Ala. 64; *Robertson v. Bradford*, 70 Ala. 385; *Pettus v.
McClannahan*, 52 Ala. 55.

McCLELLAN, J.—On the 8th day of April, 1887, Hugh
Stevenson, as the administrator of the estate of Edward C.
Murray, deceased, filed a petition in the Probate Court of
Calhoun county, alleging that said estate owed debts to the
amount of five thousand dollars, and that the personal property belonging to the estate was insufficient to pay them, and
praying for an order to sell certain real estate for that purpose. On May 19, 1887, an order of sale was made in
response to this petition. The order recites, among other
things, "the application of said Hugh Stevenson, administrator," &c., notice of the same, appointment, appearance, and denials of a guardian *ad litem* for the
minor heirs of the decedent; and that "it further appearing
to the satisfaction of the court, by the oaths of Hugh Stevenson and August Lorenzen, disinterested witnesses, whose
testimony has been taken by depositions as in chancery proceedings," &c. On March 25th, 1889, the minor heirs of
said intestate filed, by their next friend, a petition in said
Probate Court praying that the order of sale be vacated, on

the ground that the necessity therefor had not been proved by two disinterested witnesses, and alleging that one of the two witnesses, whose deposition had been taken as recited in the order, was the administrator of the estate. The administrator demurred to the petition. The demurrer was overruled, and, no further defense being made, the prayer of the petition was granted, the order of sale vacated and annulled; and this appeal is prosecuted from the decree of the court in that behalf.

It is admitted, and the record shows, that all the proceedings, including and resulting in the decree of sale, were regular, unless the rendition of the decree on the evidence of Hugh Stevenson and another was an irregularity. There is, of course, no question made as to the requirement that the necessity for a sale of the decedent's lands must be shown by two disinterested witnesses.—Code, §§ 2111, 2114. It is equally clear, that an order of sale made in the absence of such proof, taken as in chancery proceedings, where the land has descended to minors, is void.—Code, § 2114; *Robertson v. Bradford*, 70 Ala. 386; *Pettus v. McClannahan*, 52 Ala. 58. The administrator is the movant—the party plaintiff—in proceedings for the sale of lands to pay the debts of the estate, and the heirs of the estate are the parties defendant thereto. The personal representative on the one hand, and the heirs on the other, are adversary parties, with all the incidents implied in that relation.—*Garrett v. Bruner*, 59 Ala. 515; *Davis v. Tarver*, 65 Ala. 98; *Curry v. Peebles*, 83 Ala. 225. Nor is the administrator a mere nominal party to the record. He has a direct interest to subserve in the subjection of the lands of the estate to the payment of its debts. To do so may, in certain contingencies, relieve him from personal accountability, and, in any event, would rédound to his advantage, to the extent of the commissions allowed him on assets which pass through his hands. We entertain no doubt, therefore, that he is not a disinterested witness, within the meaning of sections 2111 and 2114 of the Code. It follows, that if it can be legally determined in this proceeding, that one of the two witnesses, upon whose testimony the order of sale was based, was the administrator of the estate, the order was void, and the decree of the Probate Court so declaring must be affirmed.

The application for the order of sale, as we have seen, stated all the facts necessary to give the court jurisdiction. By the unbroken current of our decisions, a decree based on such a petition will be upheld against collateral attack, even though it should appear that many and gross irregularities had characterized the supervening proceedings.—*Robertson v. Bradford*, 70 Ala. 385. The one exception to the rule is that established by section 2114 of the Code, which renders an order of sale void, notwithstanding the jurisdictional sufficiency of the petition, if the Probate Court has failed to take evidence showing the necessity of sale by depositions as in chancery.—*Pettus v. McClannahan*, 52 Ala. 55. But, even where this is the case, and there has in fact been such irregularity in this respect as by the terms of the statute would avoid the decree upon a direct assault: yet, when the attack is collateral, either by the validity of the order being drawn in question incidentally in other suits or proceedings, or by a petition to vacate the decree made, in and at a subsequent term of the court which rendered it, the rule is well settled with respect to this, as well as all other judgments and decrees in cases in which jurisdiction has attached, that the matter relied on as avoiding the adjudication must appear affirmatively on the face of the record.—Freeman on Judg. § 98; *Johnson v. Glasscock*, 2 Ala. 522; *Pettus v. McClannahan*, 52 Ala. 57–9.

The petition in this case, on which the order of sale was vacated, was filed after the term at which the order was made. The decree vacating the order was made at a subsequent term. The action of the court in vacating the order of sale must, therefore, find its justification on the face of the record, of which the vacated order constituted a part. That record shows that Hugh Stevenson was the administrator; that as such administrator he filed the petition for an order to sell the lands, and that upon the hearing of that petition it appeared "to the satisfaction of the court, by the oaths of Hugh Stevenson and August Lorenzen, disinterested witnesses," that the statutory necessity for a sale of the lands existed, &c. Does it affirmatively appear by this recital, that the Hugh Stevenson who was the administrator, and the Hugh Stevenson whose testimony was taken in support of the application, were one and the same person? Conceding that, ordinarily, the same name will be presumed to indicate and designate the same person (*Wilson v. Holt*, 83 Ala. 541), yet, can it be said—is there any warrant for the indulgence of the presumption—that the Hugh Stevenson who was administrator, and as such so connected with the proceeding as that he could not be a disinterested witness in

[Graham v. Gray.]

the cause, is the same Hugh Stevenson who is affirmed by
the records of the court to be a disinterested witness in that
proceeding? Is not any *prima facie* presumption of the
identity of person, which might have arisen from the identity of name, rebutted and overturned by the solemn assertion of the judgment-entry, that Hugh Stevenson, witness,
was without interest in the pending proceeding—an affirmation, which was not and could not, under any circumstances,
have been true with respect to Hugh Stevenson, administrator? We are of the opinion, that the record of this judgment does not show that the administrator was one of the
two witnesses by whom the necessity for a sale was established. This alleged infirmity could not be shown *aliunde*.
The petition, with its exhibits, presented the whole case on
the part of the movants. The case so presented did not
authorize the setting aside of the order of sale, and the demurrer of the administrator should have been sustained.

The decree of the court overruling the demurrer, and vacating the order of sale, is reversed, and a decree will be
here rendered, dismissing the petition of appellees, at the
cost of their next friend in this court and in the court
below.

Reversed and rendered.

Graham *v.* Gray.

*Bill in Equity for Injunction of Judgment, and Settle-
ment of Partnership Accounts.*

1. *Accounts between partners, at law and in equity.*—When one partner buys out his co-partner's interest in the partnership, giving his note
for the balance of purchase-money not paid in cash, with the understanding that it was subject to abatement on settlement of the partnership accounts, for any balance found in his favor; possibly this defense
could not be made at law, against an action on the note, as it involved
a settlement of the partnership accounts, and, therefore, the failure to
make it does not bar equitable relief against the judgment.
2. *Answer as evidence.*—When an answer is made on oath, as required by the foot-note to the bill, its denials can only be overcome by
the testimony of two witnesses, or of one with proper corroboration.

APPEAL from the Chancery Court of Calhoun.
Heard before the Hon. S. K. McSPADDEN,

[Graham v Gray.]

The bill in this case was filed on the 24th of November, 1885, by J. R. Graham, his wife and daughter, against E. M. Gray and M. T. W. Christian; and sought an injunction against a judgment at law for $284, which the defendants had obtained against J. R. Graham, and a settlement of the accounts of a partnership which had formerly existed between all the parties to the suit. On final hearing, on pleadings and proof, the chancellor dissolved the injunction, and dismissed the bill. The errors assigned are, the refusal of the chancellor to strike the answer from the file on motion, and the dissolution of the injunction.

BROTHERS, WILLETT & WILLETT, for appellants.

E. H. HANNA, *contra.*

STONE, C. J.—The partnership adventure out of which the present litigation grew, was formed in Calhoun county, Alabama, by persons, all of whom were, at that time, residents of that county. The partners, four in number, and equal in interest, were Gray, Christian, Mrs. Graham, wife of J. R. Graham, and Maggie Wilson, Graham's daughter. In forming the partnership, J. R. Graham represented his wife and daughter, and contributed their share of the capital, less one hundred dollars belonging to Mrs. Graham. With the exception of the said one hundred dollars, Graham appears to have made the investment of his funds as a provision for his wife and daughter, vesting the said interest in their respective names.

The purpose of the adventure was to purchase land in Florida, plant and cultivate an orange grove upon it, and engage in the growth of other products; but of what kind, or with what intent, the record does not inform us. The partnership agreement was entered into in 1882. If it was in writing, that fact is not shown.

In pursuance of the agreed adventure, lands were purchased in Florida, labor, stock and other appliances supplied, and Gray was placed in the management and control of it, at an agreed compensation of sixty dollars per month. He continued in the management and control of it until some time in the year 1883, when Gray and Christian sold out their interests to J. R. Graham, at an estimated value of thirty-six hundred dollars, subject to some rebates. Gray had had charge of the entire enterprise—of its expendi-

[Graham v. Gray.]

tures, and the disbursements of its funds—and knew the state
of its accounts.   He had handled all its money.   In the sale
he represented himself and Christian.   The trade was made
with Graham on the faith of his representation of the expenditures he had made, and of the outstanding liabilities
of the partnership.   It is not pretended that either of the
other partners had any personal knowledge on this subject.

The record facts show, without conflict, that in the purchase from Gray and Christian, Graham paid one thousand
dollars cash, gave his note for a second thousand dollars,
which he afterwards paid, and gave a second note for five
hundred dollars.   On this last note he paid two hundred and
fifty dollars; and refusing to pay the balance, suit was instituted by Gray and Christian, and judgment recovered
upon it.   The record does not inform us that the remaining
eleven hundred dollars was ever closed by note, or any part
of it paid.

The present bill was filed to enjoin the collection of the
judgment for the balance of the five hundred dollar note,
and a preliminary injunction was obtained.   The *gravamen*
of the bill, as averred, is, that he, Graham, in his purchase,
had to rely, and did rely, on the representations of Gray, as
to the amount of capital paid in by Gray and Christian, as
to the amount of expenditures in and for the enterprise, and
as to the amount of outstanding liabilities against the firm.
These last Graham assumed to pay, and it is charged and
proved that he had paid them.   He charges that Gray mis-
represented the facts, and deceived him in two respects: in
overstating the amounts he and Christian had paid in, and
in reporting as paid certain claims which were unpaid, and
which Graham had to pay.   He also charged that, among
the expenditures Gray claimed to have made for the firm,
there were several items incurred for his private use.   The
bill further charges that, when the note for five hundred
dollars was given, it was agreed that it was not to be used or
enforced until a settlement of the partnership was had, but
that it was to be held subject to such rebates as Graham
might be entitled to on settlement of partnership accounts.
The bill then charges that Graham has so far overpaid his
share of the expenses and debts, as that nothing is due to
Gray and Christian on the note on which they recovered
judgment.   It charges that Christian is insolvent, and that
Gray has no property in Alabama.   The prayer is, that
these alleged over-payments be set off against the judgment,

[Graham v. Gray.]

and for a perpetual injunction. It prays for a settlement of the partnership accounts, as a means, and the only means, of ascertaining whether he had over-paid, and the extent of it.

The bill charges that Gray, while in the paid employment of the firm, had lost considerable time in attending to his own private business, and that he converted one of the mules of the partnership to his own private use, and thereby caused his death. It seeks to bring these items into the partnership settlement, against Gray. It is fully shown, and not denied, that Graham, when he purchased from Gray and Christian, had full knowledge of these derelictions on the part of Gray; and inasmuch as the partnership settlement is material in the present suit only to the extent it affects Graham's liability on the judgment, he can not raise this question. We will not consider it.

The bill was demurred to, assigning several grounds; among them, the failure to make defense at law. Possibly this defense could not be made at law, as it involved a settlement of the partnership accounts.—*Vincent v. Martin,* 79 Ala. 540; *Chandler v. Wynne,* 85 Ala. 301; *Tate v. Evans,* 54 Ala. 16; *Kelly v. Allen,* 34 Ala. 663; *Martin v. Mohr,* 56 Ala. 221; *Bank of Mobile v. Poelnitz,* 61 Ala. 147; *Wood v. Steele,* 65 Ala. 436; *Goldthwaite v. Nat. Bank,* 67 Ala. 549; *Watts v. Sayre,* 76 Ala. 397; *Campbell v. Conner,* 78 Ala. 211; *Glover v. Hembree,* 82 Ala 324.

The pivotal point of this case probably rests on the averment, that when the note for five hundred dollars was given (the note on which the judgment was rendered), it was agreed that it should not be collected or used, but should be kept by the payees, subject to abatement, as the settlement might show the true state of the partnership account. The bill, in its foot-note, calls for sworn answers from the defendants; and they answered under oath, denying that there was any such condition in the giving of the note. This cast on the complainant the burden of overcoming the denials in the answer, by the testimony of two witnesses, or one with proper corroboration. Only one witness, Graham himself, gives testimony in support of this averment of the bill, and it is not corroborated.—*Beene v. Randall,* 23 Ala. 514; *Garrett v. Garrett,* 29 Ala. 439; *Camp v. Simon,* 34 Ala. 126; *Bryan v. Bryan, Ib.* 516; *Easterwood v. Linton,* 36 Ala. 175; *Marshall v. Croom,* 52 Ala. 554; *Turner v. Flinn,* 67 Ala. 529.

So far from there being corroboration of this testimony,

29

two facts tend to weaken it: *First*, Graham paid half of the note, without requiring a settlement; and, second, there were eleven hundred dollars of the purchase-price, above the twenty-five hundred for which cash and notes were given, of which the record gives no satisfactory account. There being a failure to connect the alleged agreement and the note for five hundred dollars, it is not shown that one should discount the other. Nor is it satisfactorily shown that the complainant can not be indemnified in the eleven hundred dollars, which he does not aver he has paid.

Several questions were raised on the equity of the bill, and for misjoinder of parties, which we need not consider.

The decree of the chancellor is affirmed.

Graves *v.* Smith.

Bill in Equity for Injunction against Windows in Party-Wall.

1. *Party-walls; right to open windows.*—When a party-wall is erected by the owners of two adjoining lots, they do not own it as tenants in common, but each owns one half in severalty, with an easement in the other half; and each may increase the height, at least, of his half, if not of the entire wall, when it can be done without damage to the other proprietor; but, in the absence of statutory provisions, or express agreement between the parties, neither has the right to make windows or other openings in the wall; nor is such right conferred by an agreement giving either one the right "to use said party-wall free of expense in the erection of any building which he may wish to erect on said lot."

2. *Injunction against windows in party-wall.*—A court of equity will interfere by injunction, at the suit of one of the part owners of a party-wall, to prevent the other from making windows, or other openings in it.

APPEAL from the Chancery Court of Jefferson.
Heard before the Hon. THOMAS COBBS.

MARTIN & MCEACHIN, GRAVES & BLAKEY, and WATTS & SON, for appellant, cited Wood on Nuisances, §§ 226–32; *Rouse & Smith v. Martin & Flowers*, 75 Ala. 510; *Antomarchi v. Russell*, 63 Ala. 356; *Partridge v. Gilbert*, 15 N. Y. 601; *Brooks v. Curtis*, 50 N. Y. 639; *Ray v. Lynes*, 10 Ala. 63; *St. James Church v. Arrington*, 36 Ala. 546; *Moody v. McClelland*, 39 Ala. 45; *Rosser v. Randolph*,

7 Porter, 238; *Ferguson v. Selma*, 43 Ala. 398; Washb.
Easements, 621–25; *Platt v. Eggleston*, 20 Ohio St. 414;
State v. Mayor of Mobile, 5 Porter, 279; 1 High on Inj.
§§ 739, 788; 2 Story's Equity, § 925; 38 Md. 128; 28 Ind.
79; 45 Amer Dec. 347, 351, note; 4 Sandf. N. Y. 480;
70 N. Y. 440; 11 Humph. 412; *Davidson v. Isham*,
1 Stockt. 186; 12 Mass. 223; 19 Eng. L. & Eq. 639; 3 My.
& K. 169.

WEBB & TILLMAN, *contra*, cited Lloyd on Buildings, § 184;
Vollmer's Appeal, 61 Penn. St. 128; *Danenhauer v. Devine*,
32 Amer. Rep. 627; 35 Iowa, 531; 4 Allen, Mass. 149;
Nininger v. Norwood, 72 Ala. 281; Wood on Nuisances,
777; High on Injunctions, § 792; *White v. Flanagan*,
54 Amer. Dec. 668; 10 Amer. Rep. 545.; Washb. Easements,
453.

SOMERVILLE, J.—The bill was filed by the appellee,
Smith, to enjoin the appellants from raising the height of a
party-wall, with windows and openings constructed in it, so
as to impair it as a dead or solid wall. The wall was two
stories high, and eighteen inches thick, being so constructed
as to occupy nine inches of each of the adjoining lots of the
complainant and the defendant Graves, respectively, the
former holding under one Wright by purchase. It was
agreed in writing between Graves and Wright—and it is not
denied that this covenant so runs with the land as to bind
Smith—"that the said wall is, and always shall remain, a
party-wall between the said owners of said lots, their heirs
and assigns; and the said Wm. H. Graves, his heirs and
assigns, shall have the right to use the said party-wall free
of expense, in the erection of any building which he or they
may wish to build upon said lot."

The agreement in terms creates a party-wall out of this
division wall; and by a party-wall we must understand a wall
between the estates of adjoining owners, which is used for the
common benefit of both, chiefly in supporting the timbers
used in the construction of contiguous houses on such estates.—1 Wash. Real Prop. (5th Ed.), 385. Where such a
wall is erected, one-half on the land of each adjoining proprietor, it does not render them tenants in common, but each
is the owner in severalty of his part, both of the wall and
the land on which it stands; but the title of each is qualified
by a cross-easement in favor of the other, which entitles him

to support his building by means of the half of the wall belonging to his neighbor.   In other words, each proprietor
owns his own half in severalty, with an easement of support
from the other half of his neighbor's.—*Bloch v. Isham*,
28 Ind. 37; s. c., 92 Amer. Dec. 287; *note*, pp. 291–2;
2 Wash. Real Prop. (5th Ed.), 386; Tiedeman on Real
Prop., § 620.   It is commonly held, that each part-owner
may certainly increase the height of *his half* of the wall, or
so much as stands on his own land, if he does not thereby
endanger or injure the wall, he being responsible for the
resulting damage occasioned by any change in the structure
not required for repairs.—*Andrew v. Haseltine*, 58 Wis.,
395; s. c., 46 Amer. Rep. 635. And, according to the better
view, as supported by the weight of authority, each proprietor has the lawful right to increase the height of the
entire party-wall, when it can be done without injury to the
adjoining building, and without impairing the value of the
cross-easement, to which the neighboring proprietor is entitled.—*Brooks v. Curtis*, 50 N. Y. 639; 10 Amer. Rep. 545;
Bloch v. Isham, 92 Amer Dec., *note*, 295.

This right to raise the height of the wall, however, seems
to be implied in the privilege conferred on Graves by the
agreement, which gives him "the right to use said party-
wall free of expense, in the erection of any building which
he may wish to build upon said [adjoining] lot."   This
right, moreover, is conceded to the defendants, and no effort
is made by the complainant to prevent the mere raising, or
increasing the height of the wall.   The prayer for injunction goes only to restraining the insertion of the windows or
openings.

There is no statute in this State regulating the subject of
party-walls, as in England and some of the American States.
The question is, therefore, to be determined by the principles of the common law bearing on easements of this nature.
It is our opinion, that a party-wall must ordinarily be construed to mean a solid wall, without windows or openings.
Such openings tend to weaken the strength of the structure,
and impair its value for lateral support of the adjoining
building.   They prevent, or render inconvenient, the utilization of the wall for the erection of an additional story for the
building.   They also increase the hazards of fire, and injuriously affect the adjoining proprietor by unduly exposing
his premises in various other objectionable ways, which
readily suggest themselves without any elaborate enumera-

tion. If allowed to continue, moreover, for a period of twenty years, the privilege of the adjoining owner would mature into a perfect legal right, under the doctrine of prescription.—*Ulbricht v. Eufaula Water Co.*, 86 Ala. 587; s. c., 6 So. Rep. 78. The cross-easement which the appellee had in the wall was, in our opinion, violated by the attempt of the defendants to create the openings for the windows, sought to be restrained by injunction.

It is too obvious for argument, that the doctrine of ancient lights has no sort of bearing on this case, in any aspect in which it can be viewed. The difference is between the maintenance of windows in one's own walls and those of another.

The authorities fully support this view, and leave no doubt of the jurisdiction of equity to interfere in such cases by injunctive relief.—*Danenhauer v. Devine*, 51 Tex. 480; 32 Amer. Rep. 627; *Vansyckle v. Tryson*, 6 Phila. Rep. 401; *Sullivan v. Graffort*, 35 Iowa, 531; *Bloch v. Isham*, 92 Amer. Dec., note, 297; *St. John v. Sweeney*, 59 How. Prac. (N. Y.) 175; *Vollmer's Appeal*, 61 Penn. St. 118.

The case of *Weston v. Arnold*, 8 Law Rep. (Ch. Ap. Cas.) 1090, (1872) seems to support the view, that a wall may be a party-wall to such height as it belongs in common to two adjoining buildings, and cease by implication to be such for the rest of its height; but this decision is opposed to the weight of authority, and we decline to approve it.

The chancellor did not err in granting the relief prayed in the bill, and in perpetuating the injunction on the proof made in the case.

Affirmed.

Brown *v.* Scott.

Bill in Equity for Foreclosure of Mortgage.

1. *Set-off against note.*—A demand against an intermediate holder of a promissory note is not available as a set-off to the maker, either at law or in equity, unless founded on an agreement supported by a new consideration, in pursuance of which the intermediate holder procured it, or which was entered into by the parties while it was in his hands; and this rule applies to a non-commercial note transferred after maturity.

2. *Proof of payment.*—The *onus* of proving payment is on the party who asserts it; and if the evidence leaves the fact in doubt and uncertainty, he must fail.

3. *Transfer of note as collateral security; set-off in equity.*—When a note secured by mortgage is purchased by one of the heirs of the deceased mortgagor, and transferred as collateral security for his own debt, and the transferree files a bill to foreclose, he is only entitled to recover the amount of his debt, with attorney's fees and costs; and the transferror being indebted to the estate of the mortgagor, the other heirs may by cross-bill set off that indebtedness against the balance due on the mortgage debt.

APPEAL from the Chancery Court of Calhoun.

Heard before the Hon. S. K. McSPADDEN.

The bill in this case was filed on the 10th March, 1886, by Amelia C. and Lula D. Brown, the partners composing the firm of Rowan, Dean & Co., and Isaac L. Swan as trustee, against W. S. Scott, Winfield Scott and others, heirs at law of William Scott, deceased; and sought the foreclosure of two mortgages, or deeds of trust in the nature of mortgages, executed by said William Scott to Swan as trustee, to secure two notes due to Rowan, Dean & Co. The mortgages and secured notes were transferred by Rowan, Dean & Co., for valuable consideration, to said Winfield Scott; and were afterwards transferred by him, as collateral security, to said Amelia C. and Lula D. Brown. The defendants, except Winfield Scott, insisted in their answer that his purchase of the notes and mortgages was made for the benefit of the mortgagor's estate, and operated a payment and extinguishment of the debts; and they filed a cross-bill, alleging that he was indebted to the estate, and seeking to set off that indebtedness against the mortgage debt. The chancellor overruled a demurrer to the cross-bill, but seems to have granted no relief under it; and on final hearing, on pleadings and proof, he dismissed the original bill. The complainants appeal, and assign these decrees as error.

BROTHERS, WILLETT & WILLETT, for the appellants, cited *Alston v. Alston*, 34 Ala. 16; *Goodwin v. McGehee*, 15 Ala. 232; *Davis v. Cook*, 65 Ala. 622; 7 John. Ch. 252; 54 Ala. 688; 23 Ala. 219; 1 Ala. 43; 50 Ala. 10; 67 Ala. 549.

JOHN H CALDWELL, and CALDWELL & JOHNSTON, *contra*, cited *Harrison v. Hicks*, 1 Porter, 423; *Ross v. Pearson*, 21 Ala. 473; *Prater v. Stinson*, 26 Ala. 456; 3 Rand. Com. Paper, § 1435; *Mount v. Vaughan*, 45 Ala. 134; *Goldthwaite v. Nat. Bank*, 67 Ala. 549; *Sims v. Sampey*, 64 Ala. 230; *Atkins v. Knight*, 46 Ala. 539; 7 Porter, 543.

CLOPTON, J.—Appellants, as transferrees, seek by the bill to foreclose two deeds of trust in the nature of mortgages, which were executed by William Scott,—one on January 18, 1875, and the other April 7, 1877, to secure the payment of two notes made by him to Rowan, Dean & Co. The grantor died in 1878. On May 9, 1879, Rowan, Dean & Co. transferred the deeds of trust, and delivered the notes, to Winfield Scott, who transferred them, June 23, 1882, to complainants, as collateral security for borrowed money. The execution of the conveyances, the justness of the debts, and the transfers, are not controverted; and if they were, are clearly proved.

Winfield Scott, who is a son and one of the heirs of the grantor, was indebted to his father at the time of his death, for money paid as his surety. The other heirs of William Scott seek by cross-bill to set off the indebtedness of Winfield Scott against the notes secured by the deeds of trusts—a demand against an intermediate holder. Courts of equity, there being no special and intervening equities, adopt and follow the rules at law in relation to set-off. The well-settled and uniform construction of the statute is, that the maker of a note will not be allowed to set off a demand against an intermediate holder, unless founded on an agreement supported by a new consideration, in pursuance of which the intermediate holder procured the note, or which was entered into by the parties while it was in his hands.—*Goldthwaite v. Nat. Bank*, 67 Ala. 549. Though the transferree of a note not commercial takes it subject to all the equities existing between the original parties, he does not take it subject to any equities which may arise between the maker and an intermediate holder. This settled and uniform construction of the statutes is essential to the transfer of such paper unobstructed by risks other than the original equities between the original parties. The cross-bill alleges no agreement founded on a new consideration, nor any special or intervening equity, which withdraws their demand from the operation of the general rule.

The defendants set up the further defense, that the transactions by which Winfield Scott obtained the transfer of the notes and deeds of trusts, operated a payment and extinguishment. It satisfactorily appears that Winfield Scott used his own funds to pay Rowan, Dean & Co., and took a written transfer of the deeds of trust with the delivery of the notes. These facts, unexplained, indicate a purchase. W. J. Scott, who was the administrator and also an heir of William Scott, was present when the transfer was made. His testimony, as to what was said in respect to the character of the indorsements which should be put on the deeds, is denied by Winfield Scott, who testified that he said he wanted the papers transferred to him; and is unsupported by Dean, who did not remember the words, but did remember that Winfield Scott said, in substance, he wanted the indorsements to show that the indebtedness was paid by him. It seems that, if payment and satisfaction were intended, the notes and the deeds of trust, instead of being transferred to Winfield Scott as a subsisting demand, would have been surrendered to the administrator, who went with him, and was present at the time of the transaction, but made no claim to have the papers cancelled and surrendered to him. If they were discharged, he was entitled to their possession.

The theory of payment, in satisfaction of the notes and extinguishment of the deeds of trust, is inconsistent with the subsequent acts of the parties. The notes and deeds of trust were left uncancelled in the possession of Winfield Scott, and in that condition remained in his possession until he transferred them to complainants. The administration of the estate of William Scott was finally settled in January, 1886, and no demand for the papers was made, prior to, at the time of, or subsequently to that settlement. His possession of the papers under such circumstances, and for so long a period, is strongly pursuasive of an intention and understanding that they should be regarded as continuing unsatisfied, and, unless explained, should preponderate, when the evidence of payment is so conflicting as to leave it in uncertainty.—*Doty v. Jones*, 28 Wisc. 219.

There are other material and significant acts. The administrator held a note on Winfield Scott for six hundred dollars, dated August 8, 1872, payable to his father. Instead of settling the mutual demands, and exchanging papers, on the next day after the deeds of trust were transferred, a small payment was made, and a credit entered on the note, for the express purpose of preventing the bar of the statute of limitations, and the administrator retained possession of it. In explanation of permitting him to keep possession of the papers, the administrator testifies, that he said to Winfield Scott, as he had only discharged his own debt, the papers should be delivered to him, as he was administrator, and ought to have possession of them. Winfield Scott declined

[Brown v. Scott.]

to deliver them, saying that it was better that he should keep them for the present, on account of a suit then pending against his father's estate, and if judgment was obtained, the homestead might be involved and sold. On hearing this, the administrator acquiesced in his having possession of the notes and deeds of trust. This conversation Winfield Scott wholly denies; and the assertion, that in paying the notes he only discharged his own debt, is not sustained by proof. The evidence clearly establishes that the note for twelve hundred and sixty-nine dollars was the personal debt of William Scott, with which Winfield Scott had no connection in any wise. Without alluding to the avowed fraudulent purpose, for which the papers were left in his possession uncancelled, the explanation is unsatisfactory in view of the fact, that on May 10, 1885, just six years thereafter, a similar payment was made, and credit was entered on the same note, for the same purpose. The reason assigned by Winfield Scott, why he had better keep possession of the papers, had certainly ceased before then.

The statement of Winfield Scott, that when he paid the notes to Rowan, Dean & Co., he regarded his debt to his father as paid and settled, and more than settled, would tend to support the contention of defendant, were it not that his meaning is explained by the further statement, that he kept them, not only to show that his debt was paid, but also the excess paid by him for his father, and to collect the same if it became necessary.

The burden rests on defendants to prove payment. On which party the law casts the burden of proof, should be regarded and taken into consideration in weighing the sufficiency of the evidence as to any question of. fact. The rule is not technical, nor a fiction. Its observance will serve to promote the ascertainment of truth. Keeping in mind that the *onus* is on the defendants to establish the defense of payment, and considering the whole evidence, we can not say that payment, or satisfaction and extinguishment, is satisfactorily proved. At least, the mind is left in doubt and uncertainty, in which case the defendants must fail for want of proof. Both the indebtedness of Winfield Scott to his father, and the indebtedness of his father to Rowan, Dean & Co., were discharged and extinguished, or neither was. The inquiry is pertinent; if paid, why the resort to a mode to prevent the presumption of payment arising from the operation of the statute of limitations? We conclude, that it was not intended to discharge the notes and deeds of trust, but that the mutual demands should be kept uncancelled for future set-off and settlement, which, from neglect or other cause, was never consummated.

The complainants are in equity entitled to receive only the amount of their claim against Winfield Scott, and attorney's fees. If they recovered the full amount of the notes, they would hold the excess for him. The defendants have a clear equity to set off his indebtedness against this excess. The decree should be moulded so as to effectuate a complete adjustment of the rights and equities of all the parties. If the land is divisible, it should be sold in parcels, and only so much sold as will be sufficient to pay the amount ascertained to be due complainants by Winfield Scott, and reasonable attorneys' fees and costs of suit. His indebtedness should be set off against the balance of the notes. To authorize such decree, the cross-bill will have to be amended, so as to strike out all the averments in relation to payment, which is not the subject of a cross-bill.

Reversed and remanded.

Globe Iron Roofing and Corrugating Co. *v.* Thacher.

Bill in Equity by Material-man, to enforce Statutory Lien; or, as Creditor without Lien, to set aside Fraudulent Conveyances.

1. *Filing bill in double aspect.*—A creditor can not file a bill in a double aspect, seeking as contractor, or material-man, to enforce a statutory lien (Code, § 3018-48), to set aside subsequent conveyances of the property (with other property) as void, and to subject it to the satisfaction of his debt; or, in the alternative, as a simple-contract creditor without a lien, to set aside the conveyances as fraudulent.

2. *Statutory lien of contractor or material-man; verification of.* --- Under the statute requiring the claim of an original contractor or material-man to be verified "by the oath of the claimant, or some other person having knowledge of the facts" (Code, § 3022), if the claimant is a private corporation, the affidavit of one of its officers, to the effect that the statement of the claim "is true as to the best of his knowledge and belief," without more, is not a sufficient verification.

3. *Validity of mortgage, as against creditors; allegations of fraud.*— When a creditor files a bill to set aside, on the ground of fraud, a mortgage or deed of trust executed by an insolvent corporation, which purports to convey all of its property to secure the payment of certain in-

[Globe Iron Roofing and Corrugating Co. v. Thacher.]

terest-bearing bonds payable ten years after date, and which reserves to the corporation the right to use the property until foreclosure; alleging that it was really given to secure an antecedent debt to two banks, which had taken some of the bonds as collateral security, and was intended to hinder, delay and defraud other creditors; that these debts were partly simulated, and that they included usurious interest; these allegations, in connection with the provisions of the mortgage, are sufficient to impeach it, showing the reservation of a benefit to the debtor, a fraudulent intent, and participation by the beneficiaries.

4. *Same.*—A mortgage executed by an insolvent debtor, though with a fraudulent intent on his part, for the benefit of certain *bona fide* creditors, who are not charged with knowledge or notice of such fraudulent intent, or any participation therein, will not be declared fraudulent as against other creditors; and this principle is not affected by the facts, that the debtor is an insolvent corporation, and that the preferred creditors, or some of them, are stockholders or officers.

5. *General assignment for benefit of creditors; validity of.*—A general assignment for the benefit of creditors, which fixes no time for foreclosure, and reserves to the grantor the use of the property until foreclosure, is not on that account fraudulent as against creditors, since the assignee may at any time foreclose, and any creditor may compel him to do so.

APPEAL from the Chancery Court of Morgan.

Heard before the Hon. THOMAS COBBS.

[ ]The appeal in this case is sued out from a decree, or interlocutory order, sustaining a demurrer to a bill, which was filed on the 30th of June, 1888, by the Globe Iron Roofing and Corrugating Company, a corporation chartered under the laws of Ohio, against Edwin Thacher, Daniel Mooar, the Decatur Iron Bridge and Construction Company, a private corporation under the statutes of Alabama, the First National Bank of Decatur, and the Exchange Bank of Decatur. The complainant claimed to be a creditor of the Decatur Iron Bridge and Construction Company to the amount of $659.25, balance due for materials furnished under contract, and used in the construction of certain buildings and improvements on lots particularly described; and sought to enforce a statutory lien on this property, to cancel certain conveyances, hereinafter described, as void, and to have the property sold, or so much thereof as might be necessary to satisfy the debt, with interest and costs; and also, in the alternative, as a creditor by simple contract without a lien, to set aside the conveyances as fraudulent and void, and subject the property to the satisfaction of the complainant's debt, as more particularly shown by the prayer hereinafter set out.

The conveyances sought to be set aside were: (1.) A mortgage, or deed of trust, dated November 1, 1887, executed by the Decatur Iron Bridge and Construction Company, and signed in its name, "*per* Geo. S. Mooar, president;" by which was conveyed to Daniel Mooar, as trustee, all the property then owned by said corporation, or which it might afterwards acquire "while this instrument remains in force," with its franchises, reserving to the corporation the right to use the same until foreclosure; "to be held in trust by said Mooar, his successor or successors, to secure the payment of the principal and interest of the following described bonds, issued and to be issued as the necessities of said company may require; which said bonds are dated November 1st, 1887, payable to bearer, amounting in all to $30,000, payable ten years after date, bearing annual interest at eight per cent., payable semi-annually, on the 1st of May and November each year, at the First National Bank of Decatur, Alabama; there being sixty of said bonds, for $500 each, having interest coupons attached: Now, the true intent and object of this instrument is to secure the payment of the aforesaid bonds and coupons, as they may fall due, to whomsoever may be the holders thereof; a failure on the part of said company to pay any of said coupons, for three months after the same shall have become due, and shall have been presented at the office of the company and refused, shall cause the principal of said bonds at once to become due and payable, and a right of action for the foreclosure of this instrument shall at once accrue. But, if the said company shall well and truly pay off and discharge said bonds, and interest thereon, according to the true intent and meaning hereof, then these presents are to be void," &c.

(2.) A mortgage said to have been executed by said company on the 30th of April, 1888, to said Daniel Mooar, conveying all of its property "to secure him for the alleged sum of $5,500, and to save him harmless against all loss and damage he might sustain by reason of his indorsement and suretyship for said company on debts due to the First National Bank of Decatur, and three years salary to said defendant Edwin Thacher, as chief engineer of said company." A copy of this mortgage was not made an exhibit to the bill, but it was alleged in this connection, that the principal stockholders of the company were said George S. Mooar, president; Daniel Mooar, his son, who was its attorney and counsellor; Edwin Thacher, chief engineer; and Robert Curtis, vice-president and general manager.

(3.) A general assignment executed by said company to said Thacher as trustee, in trust for the benefit of all its creditors, specifying their names and the amount of their respective debts. This instrument was alleged to have been executed on the 9th of May, 1888, and that date is signed at the bottom of the copy which is made an exhibit to the bill, with the name of E. L. Olmstead as secretary; but there is no signature to the instrument, and there are no attesting witnesses.

In reference to these instruments the bill contained the following allegations: "Complainant further alleges, that the execution of said mortgage on the 1st of November, 1887, was for the purpose of securing an antecedent debt, but complainant does not admit that the whole amount claimed by said banks was or is justly due from said company; on the contrary, it alleges that the debt due them from said company is much less than the amount claimed, and that the execution of said mortgage, or deed of trust, of November 1st, 1887, and of said mortgage of April 30th, 1888, was an effort on the part of said company to make the said Daniel Mooar and said two banks preferred creditors, and the same is fraudulent as against complainant and its other creditors; that the said deed of trust to said Daniel Mooar was executed after said company became indebted to said banks, and said deed was executed, and the bonds therein mentioned were issued and hypothecated by said company, as collateral security for said indebtedness; and that a portion of said indebtedness is usurious interest charged by them, at different times, to said company, and that said company was insolvent" when each of said instruments was executed.

In the original bill, the complainant sued "in behalf of itself and such other creditors as may desire to join in this suit;" but these words were struck out by amendment, and the prayer of the bill as amended was in these words: "That your Honor take jurisdiction of this cause, and, on final hearing thereof, decree and enforce complainant's lien on said property for materials furnished; that the said property described in this bill, and set out in Exhibit C [the claim filed asserting a lien], be subjected to the payment of said debt, with interest thereon, and that complainant's lien be declared superior to said deed of trust and mortgage executed to said Daniel Mooar; and that said deed of trust, said mortgage and said assignment be, as to complainant, declared void; and that said property be sold, under an order of this court, to satisfy complainant's lien, to the amount of their said debt, with interest and costs. Or, if your Honor finds that

[Globe Iron Roofing and Corrugating Co. v. Thacher.]

complainant has not the lien herein claimed under section 3018 of the Code of Alabama, then complainant prays that said deed of trust and said mortgage to Daniel Mooar, and said assignment to Edwin Thacher, be set aside and declared void; that all of the property thereby conveyed, or so much thereof as may be necessary, be sold under a decree of this court to pay said debt and costs;" and the general prayer was added.

The defendants filed separate demurrers to the bill, specifying the following (with other) grounds of demurrer: 1st, to the whole bill, because (1) it asked inconsistent and repugnant relief in the alternative, and (2) because it joined distinct causes of action; 2d, to so much thereof as claimed a statutory lien for materials furnished, because the verification of the claim was insufficient, and because a compliance with statutory provisions in other respects was not shown; 3d, to so much of the bill as assailed the several conveyances on the ground of fraud, because (1) the allegations of fraud were too general and indefinite, and because (2), on the facts alleged, the conveyances were not shown to be fraudulent. The chancellor sustained these several grounds of demurrer, and his decree is here assigned as error

KIRK & ALMON, for the appellants.—(1.) The statute gives a contractor, or material-man, a right to come into equity to enforce his lien; and provides that, even in actions at law, all persons interested in the property may be made parties to the suit.—Code, §§ 3048, 3030. (2.) The complainant was an original contractor within the terms of the statute, and the verification of the claim was sufficient. *Lane & Bodley Co. v. Jones*, 79 Ala. 156; *Chandler v. Hanna*, 73 Ala. 394; *Townsend v. Steel*, 85 Ala. 580; *Ruhl v. Rogers*, W. Va., 2 S. E. Rep. 798. (3.) The bill is not multifarious, nor is there a misjoinder of defendants.—*Tindal v. Drake*, 51 Ala. 574; *Merritt v. Phœnix*, 48 Ala. 87; *Forrest v. Luddington*, 84 Ala. 1; 84 Ala. 600. (4.) The alternative prayers for relief are neither repugnant nor inconsistent. In each aspect of the bill, the complainant seeks only to subject the property to the satisfaction of its debts, and to set aside conveyances which are a cloud on the title. The bill, as originally framed, was in favor of the complainant and such other creditors as might choose to come in and make themselves parties; but this was struck out by amendment, and the complainant was left suing alone as a creditor

1888.] OF ALABAMA. 463

[Globe Iron Roofing and Corrugating Co. v. Thacher.]

by simple contract. Two or more creditors by simple contract only can not unite in a bill to set aside a fraudulent conveyance.—*Railway Co. v. McKenzie*, 85 Ala. 546. But a mortgagee may join as complainant in a creditor's bill, although he asserts a prior lien on the property.—Story's Eq. Pl., §§ 101, 286. (5.) On the averments of the bill, when assailed by demurrer, each of the conveyances is fraudulent and void as against creditors.—*Sims v. Gaines*, 64 Ala. 392; *Seaman v. Nolen*, 68 Ala. 463; *Clews v. Woods*, 9 Amer. Dec. 346; *Com. Bank v. Brewer*, 71 Ala. 574; *Benedict v. Renfro*, 75 Ala. 121; *LeGrand v. Nat. Bank*, 81 Ala. 123; *Meyer v. Cook*, 85 Ala. 417.

BRICKELL & HARRIS, *contra.*—(1.) The bill presents the complainant's case in a double aspect, asking relief, in the alternative, which is inconsistent and repugnant. In one aspect, the complainant asserts a statutory lien as contractor or material-man; in the other, asks relief as a creditor by simple contract without a lien; and the averments and prayer, in each aspect, are equally repugnant. Such a bill can not be maintained.—*Micou v. Ashurst*, 55 Ala. 607: *Eufaula v. McNab*, 67 Ala. 588; *Mooy v. Talcott*, 72 Ala. 210; *Heyer v. Bromberg*, 74 Ala. 524; *Lehman v. Meyer*, 67 Ala. 404; *Rives v. Walthall*, 38 Ala. 333. (2.) The claim of a contractor's lien must fail, because it was never verified as the statute requires.—Code, § 3018; *Young v. Stoutz*, 74 Ala. 574: *Welch v. Porter*, 63 Ala. 225; 2 Jones on Liens, § 1454; Phill. Mech. Liens, § 357. (3.) The allegations of the bill, as to fraud in the several conveyances assailed, are too vague and indefinite.—*Flewellen v. Crane*, 58 Ala. 627; *Pickett v. Pipkin*, 64 Ala. 520; *Morgan v. Morgan*, 68 Ala. 80; *Chamberlain v. Dorrance*, 69 Ala. 40. (4.) The allegations of the bill do not show fraud in any of the conveyances.—Burr. Assignments, 166, § 118; *Baskins v. Calhoun*, 45 Ala. 582; *Fielder v. Varner*, 45 Ala. 429; *Pope v. Brandon*, 2 Stew. 401; *Turner v. McFee*, 61 Ala. 468; *Steiner v. McCall*, 61 Ala. 406; *Turnilick v. Marbury*, 91 U. S. 589; *Graham v. Lockhart*, 8 Ala. 9; *Abercrombie v. Bradford*, 16 Ala. 560; *Shackelford v. P. & M. Bank*, 22 Ala. 238.

McCLELLAN, J.—The bill in this case is filed in a double aspect. In one view, the claim sought to be enforced is that of a lienor under sections 3018 *et seq.* of the Code;

in the other, the right relied on is that of a simple-contract creditor.   In one aspect, it is sought only to enforce the demand of the complainant; in the other, it is sought to subject the property of the Decatur Bridge Company to the satisfaction of the claims of other creditors, as well as the complainant.   In the phase of the case first presented, the effort is to subject only certain town lots belonging to the bridge company, to the satisfaction of a particular debt; in the phase last presented in the bill, the effort is to subject not only these lots, but all the property of the defendant company, to the satisfaction not only of the complainant's debt, but also of the debts of all other *bona fide* creditors. By one set of averments, it is attempted to make a case, in which complainant's claim will be held superior to certain conveyances made by the bridge company, to, or which enured to the benefit of, the other defendants; by other allegations, the attempt is made to have these conveyances— which in this part of the bill are treated as nominally superior to complainant's claim—declared void as to the debt of complainant, and other *bona fide* creditors.   It thus appears that, whether regard be had either to the character or amounts of the claims involved in the respective aspects of the bill, or to the quantity of property to be affected by the decree, or to the character or extent of the relief sought in the two presentments of the cause of action, there is a manifest dissimilarity, repugnance and inconsistency in and between the two parts of the bill of complaint.

The cardinal requirement with respect to bills framed in the alternative is, that each alternative must entitle the complainant to precisely the same relief, in kind if not in degree; so that, if the bill be confessed, the court, in decreeing the relief prayed on one state of facts, would also respond and grant the relief appropriate to the alternative state of facts. That the relief which would be appropriate to either of the alternatives of this bill would be entirely inappropriate to the other, we entertain no doubt.—*Lehman v. Myer*, 67 Ala. 403; *Micou v. Ashurst*, 55 Ala. 607; *Heyer Bros. v. Bromberg*, 74 Ala. 528; *Gordon v. Ross*, 63 Ala. 363; *Moog v. Talcott*, 72 Ala. 210.

The complainant was an original contractor, within the meaning of the statute giving to mechanics and materialmen liens on buildings or improvements, to the making or erection of which they have contributed labor or material; and had six months from the accrual of the debt involved in

[Globe Iron Roofing and Corrugating Co. v. Thacher.]

this suit, in which to file a verified statement of the claim in the office of the probate judge of Morgan county. We do not understand that it is seriously denied that the statement required by section 3022 of the Code was filed within six months after the debt accrued. It is, however, strenuously insisted, that the statute was not complied with in respect to the verification of the statement so filed. The section last referred to requires that the statement must "be verified by the oath of the claimant, or some other person having knowledge of the facts."

It is thoroughly well settled in principle, and by the adjudged cases, that liens of this class are dependent for their vitality upon a strict compliance, in all matters of substance, with the provisions of the statutes under which alone they have any existence. There is deemed no inequity, says Mr. Phillips, in this strict adherence to the requirements of the law, in view of the fact that the lienor claims, by the terms of the enactment, to fasten an extraordinary right on the lands of another, with priority over all other creditors. The claimant must seek his lien under the statute, and in accordance with its terms, or not at all.—Phillips on Mechanic's Liens, §§ 10, 297; *Chandler v. Hanna*, 73 Ala. 394.

The verification of the statement filed in this case was made by an officer of the claimant corporation. It may be conceded, that under the circumstances, an officer of the incorporated company is to be considered "the claimant," within the meaning of the clause quoted above, and does not come within the terms, "other person having knowledge of the facts." It may be further conceded, that when the statutory affidavit is made by the claimant himself, it need not affirmatively show that the affiant knew the facts; and hence, that the verification made by an officer of a corporation need not affirm that he was cognizant of the facts to which he deposed. The existence of such knowledge, in the absence of anything to the contrary, will be presumed. But the statute, we have no doubt, from its very terms, contemplates and requires that this extraordinary charge should not be placed on the property of another, unless the facts out of which the lien springs are vouched for on oath by some person, whether the claimant himself or another, who knows them to exist. The affidavit relied on here is, that "the foregoing statement is true as to the best of the affiant's knowledge and belief." This affirmatively shows that the affiant, whether he be considered the claimant or another

30

person, did not have a *knowledge* of the facts embraced in the statement. He does not swear, that he knows them to be true, or that they are true, without more; but, on the contrary, the construction of the verification most favorable to the lien would be, that some of the facts were known to be true, and others, though not within the knowledge of the affiant, were believed to be true. This verification is insufficient, and fails to fix the lien on the property of the bridge company.—*Dorman v. Crozier*, 14 Kan. 224; *Childs v. Bostwick*, 12 Daly, N. Y. 15; *Dennis v. Coker*, 34 Ala, 61; Jones on Liens, § 1454.

In its second alternative, the bill seeks to have certain conveyances executed by the bridge company declared fraudulent and void, and the property covered by them subjected to complainant's debt, With respect to one of these conveyances—the deed of trust of November, 1887—it is alleged that the bridge company was, at the time of its execution, insolvent; that it covered all of the grantor's property; that it was made to hinder, delay and defraud other creditors of the grantor; that it reserves a benefit to the company, in that the bonds for which it is security do not mature for ten years, during which time the property conveyed is to continue in the possession and use of the company; that said deed of trust was executed to secure the payment of $30,000 in negotiable bonds; that these bonds were issued and delivered to the First National and Exchange Banks of Decatur, as collateral security for an antecedent debt due to them; that this debt was alleged to be $30,000, and bonds to that amount were issued and deposited to secure the same, but that in truth and fact the debt was less than that sum, and, moreover, was made up in part of usurious interest charges. As we read the averments of the bill relied on to show fraud in this deed of trust, it charges, to recapitulate, insolvency on the part of the bridge company; conveyance of all its property to secure these two creditors; reservation of benefit; intent to hinder, delay and defraud; notice of this intent on the part of the real beneficiaries under the deed, the banks, and their constructive participation in the covinous purpose resulting from their acceptance of the issues of the deed of trust to secure an usurious debt, and simulation of the debt itself, without regard to usury; and when to the case thus made is added the suspension of the banks' right of action on their debt, resulting from their acceptance of the collateral security, having ten years in which to mature,

[Globe Iron Roofing and Corrugating Co. v. Thacher.]

and the delay of other creditors necessarily growing out of this fact, we are clearly of the opinion, that these averments are sufficient to impeach the deed of trust of November 1, 1887, as fraudulent and void as to the complainant.

Whatever may have been the intent of the bridge company in the execution of the mortgage of April, 1888, there is no allegation of bad faith on the part of any of the beneficiaries thereunder; no imputation of simulation of the debts sought to be secured; no averment of notice on the part of the creditors preferred by the mortgage, of the *mala fides* of the grantor, nor of their participation in such intent, if it existed. Clearly, these allegations do not make out a case of fraud. A debtor may prefer a *bona fide* creditor, whatever intent on the part of the debtor may characterize the act, provided the creditor does not participate therein.—*Crawford v. Kirksey*, 55 Ala. 282; *Hodges v. Coleman*, 76 Ala. 103. And the fact that the *bona fide* creditors who are thus secured by the mortgage of April, 1888, or some of them, are stockholders and officers of the bridge company—which fact constitutes the only special infirmity laid against this instrument—does not render it fraudulent. *Turinlick v. Marbury*, 91 U. S. 589.

The only other matter urged upon our attention relates to the general assignment of May, 1888, which is alleged to be rendered fraudulent by reason of the reservation of a benefit to the assignor. It is true, no time is fixed for the foreclosure of this assignment, and the use of the property, until foreclosure is had, is reserved to the bridge company. Any creditor had the right, at any time, to compel, and the assignee, at all times, had the power to proceed with, foreclosure; and the reservation of the possession and use of the property contingent upon the exercise of the right to foreclose, thus residing in both the assignee and beneficiaries, will not avoid the conveyance for fraud.—*Graham v. Lockhardt*, 8 Ala. 9; *Abercrombie v. Bradford*, 16 Ala. 560; *Shackelford v. P. M. Bank*, 22 Ala. 238.

The decree of the chancellor, in so far as it sustained demurrers to those averments of the bill which sought to impeach the deed of trust of November, 1887, is erroneous, and must be reversed. We discover no error in the rulings of the court below on the other grounds of demurrer.

Reversed and remanded.

Clifton Iron Co. *v.* Dye.

Bill in Equity by Riparian Proprietor, for Injunction against Pollution of Steam.

1. *Judicial notice of public facts.*—The courts will take judicial notice of the facts, that large sums of money have been invested in the recent development of the mineral resources of the State; that the utilization of these ores, which must be washed before using, necessarily requires the placing of sediment where it may flow into the streams which constitute the natural drainage of the surrounding country, and that this must cause a deposit of sediment on the lands below.

2. *Injunction against pollution of running stream.*—A riparian proprietor on a small running stream may maintain an action at law for damages, on account of injuries caused by the pollution of the stream and the deposit of sediment from a smelting furnace and washers for iron ore, by an upper proprietor; but a court of equity, balancing the probable injury to the respective parties, and considering the public interests involved in such industrial enterprises, will refuse to interfere by injunction, where it appears that the complainant has on his land another stream, amply sufficient for all the purposes to which he had ever applied the water of the polluted stream; that the upper proprietor owned a large tract of land chiefly valuable for its iron ore and other minerals, and had expended a large sum of money in the erection of a smelting furnace and other works necessary to convert the ore into pig metal; and further, that the stream was necessarily polluted by the sewerage of a neighboring town containing about fifteen hundred inhabitants.

3. *Same; laches.*—In this case, an injunction should be refused on the additional ground of *laches*, it appearing that the defendant's first "washer" for the ore was erected more than three years before the bill was filed, the second about one year afterwards, and that plaintiff did not object or complain until after the erection of the third.

APPEAL from the Chancery Court of Talledaga.

Heard before the Hon. S. K. McSPADDEN.

The bill in this case was filed on the 7th September, 1886, by James T. Dye, against the Clifton Iron Company, a private corporation; and sought to enjoin and restrain the defendant from so using the "washers" and other appliances connected with its smelting furnace at Ironaton, as to pollute the water of a small running stream, called the "Dry Fork of Cheha Creek," which flows through complainant's lands below, and otherwise injuring it by the deposit of dirt and refuse materials. The chancellor overruled a demurrer to the bill, for want of equity; and on final hearing, on pleadings and proof, he rendered a decree for the complainant, grant-

[Clifton Iron Co. v. Dye.]

ing a perpetual injunction. This decree is here assigned as error.

KNOX & BOWIE, for appellant, contended—1st, that the defendant's use of the stream was lawful, and could not give complainant a right of action; 2d, that the evidence showed he had suffered no material injury, as matter of fact; 3d, that though he might have a legal cause of action, the court would not interfere by injunction; and, 4th, that the right to relief was lost by *laches*. They cited *Penn. Coal Co. v. Sanderson*, 113 Penn. St. 126; *Esmond v. Chew*, 15 Cal. 137; *Williams v. Gibson*, 85 Ala. 228; *Hughes v. Anderson*, 68 Ala. 284; *R. R. Mills v. Wright*, 30 Minn. 249; *Lewis v. Stein*, 16 Ala. 214; *Wood v. Sutcliffe*, 2 Sim. N. S. 163; *Van Winkle v. Curtis*, 3 N. J. Eq. 426; 18 N. J. Eq. 293; High, Inj. § 598; *Smith v. Clay*, Amb. 645; 27 N. J. Eq. 1; *Union Tel. Co. v. Judkins*, 75 Ala. 428; Pierce on Railroads, 167–8; 47 N. H. 439; 18 Ohio St. 169; 2 Bland's Ch. 99.

BISHOP & WHITSON, *contra.*—The equity of the bill rests on the settled principles, that a riparian proprietor has a right to the use of the water of a running stream, for all proper and usual purposes, undiminished in quantity, and unpolluted in quality; that any invasion of this right is a continuing nuisance, for which an action will lie, without proof of special damage, and which a court of equity will enjoin, because of the inadequacy of the remedy at law, and to prevent a multiplicity of suits.—*Gardner v. Newburgh*, 2 John Ch. 161, or 7 Amer. Dec. 526; *Burden v. Stein*, 27 Ala. 113; s. c,, 29 Ala. 130; *Merrifield v. Lombard*, 13 Allen, Mass. 16; *Lockwood Co. v. Lawrence*, 52 Amer. Rep. 763; 40 Amer. Rep. 419; 14 Amer. Rep. 658; *Nininger v. Norwood*, 72 Ala. 277; *Ogletree v. McQuaggs*, 67 Ala. 581; 2 Story's Equity, §§ 925–27; Wood's Law of Nuisances, 441–2, 777–81; Washb. Easements, 316–17; 39 Barb. 89; 41 Amer. Rep. 829. Neither the usefulness of the defendant's works, nor their absolute necessity, nor the care and skill employed in their construction and use, nor the fact that they can not be carried on without producing the injury complained of, is an excuse or defense.—Wood, Nuisances, §§ 436–8, 450; 14 Amer. Rep. 658; 14 N. J. Eq. 335; 11 H. L. Cases, 642. The fact that others contributed to the pollution of the stream, is no defense.—Wood, Nuisances, §§ 438–40, notes; 56 Amer. Rep. 81.

[Clifton Iron Co. v. Dye.]

STONE, C. J.—We do not deem it necessary to decide whether the flowing of the dirt and other material from the washers of the appellant, upon the land of the appellee, entitles the latter to recover therefor. If it be conceded that it does, the question presented is, whether the injuries complained of, and damages inflicted and to accrue hereafter, are such as should call forth the extraordinary, restraining powers of a court of equity. It is shown that the Clifton Iron Company owns a valuable body of iron ore land at Ironaton, and for the purpose of converting this iron ore into pig iron the company has erected a smelting furnace and other improvements, at a very large cost. It is further shown that the washing of these ores, substantially in the manner detailed, is necessary for their use; and, as an incident of such washing, the particles of earth and other materials are carried down into the creek or stream which crosses appellee's land, thereby polluting the stream, and causing a deposit of the sediment on appellee's land.

It is neither averred nor proved that there is any other available outlet for the impurities complained of. There is some conflict in the testimony, as to the nature and extent of the alleged injury. It is affirmatively shown that this stream or creek is not the only source of water supply which appellee has; for the undisputed evidence shows that he has a spring and branch on his land quite as conveniently located as the creek is, and which affords an ample and certain supply of water for his uses.

The only asserted use made of the water of the creek by appellee, prior to the erection of the washers, was for fishing, bathing, and watering a few horses, cattle and hogs. The first washer was erected in 1882, or 1883, the second in 1884, and the third or last in 1885-86. It is not shown that, since these washers were erected, appellee has suffered any material injury, or been deprived of the means of giving water to his horses, cattle and hogs. Under these circumstances, should a court of equity enjoin the operations of the company, or leave complainant to his remedy of law for such injury as he has sustained, or is likely to sustain in the future?

Counsel have pressed the proposition, that mere convenience in the use of its property by the company does not entitle it to pour down upon the appellee's land, and into the stream on his land, the debris from the washers erected by it, and we think the contention is reasonable. But it is not every case of nuisance, or continuing trespass, which a court of equity will restrain by injunction. In determining this question, the court should weigh the injury that may accrue to the one or the other party, and also to the public, by granting or refusing the injunction.— *Wood v. Sutcliffe*, 2 Sim. N. S. 162; *E. & W. R. R. Co v. E. T., V. & G. R. R. Co.*, 75 Ala. 295; *C. & W. R. R. Co. v. Witherow*, 82 Ala. 190; 1 High, on Injunc. § 598; *Davis v. Sowell*, 77 Ala. 262; *Torrey v. Camden R. R. Co.*, 18 N. J. Eq. 293; *McBryde v. Sayre*, 86 Ala. 458.

The court will take notice of the fact, that in the development of the mineral interests of this State, recently made, very large sums of money have been invested. The utilization of these ores, which must be washed before using, necessitates, in some measure, the placing of sediment where it may flow into streams which constitute the natural drainage of the section where the ore banks are situated. This must cause a deposit of sediment on the lands below; and while this invasion of the rights of the lower riparian owner may produce injury, entitling him to redress, the great public interests and benefits to flow from the conversion of these ores into pig metal should not be lost sight of. As said by the Vice-Chancellor in *Wood v. Sutcliffe, supra*, "Whenever a court of equity is asked for an injunction in cases of such nature as this [a bill to enjoin the pollution of a stream], it must have regard, not only to the dry, strict rights of the plaintiff and defendant, but also to the surrounding circumstances."

Tested by these rules, we think the chancellor should have declined to make the injunction perpetual, and have remitted the plaintiff to a court of law for the recovery of such damages as he may be able to show he has sustained. The evidence shows that the drainage from the town of Ironaton goes into the stream above appellee's land, and to this extent the stream is polluted; and if the injunction as to the appellant is sustained, it can not remove or restrain the pollution from the drainage of the town of Ironaton. The pollution incident to an increase of population must be borne by appellee, and the court for this can afford no remedy. The pollution of the stream on this account, and to some extent, was and will be inevitable.

But there is another ground which is fatal to complainant's right in a court of equity. The bill in this case was filed September 7th, 1886, more than three years after the

first washer was erected. Complainant saw the effect of it
on the stream, and made no objection thereto. The company
then erected the second washer in 1884, and nearly two
years elapsed before relief was sought. Clearly it was the
duty of complainant to give the company some intimation
of his objection, and not to stand by with full knowledge,
and permit it to make large outlays on these washers, and
then seek the aid of a court of equity to arrest their operations. Reasonable diligence in the assertion of his rights
was the measure of complainant's duty in this case; and
failing in this, he must now seek relief in a court of law, for
any damage he may have suffered.—1 High on Injunc.
§ 797; *Wood v. Sutcliffe, supra.*

Reversed, and bill dismissed.

Sterrett *v.* Miles *&* Co.

Garnishment on Judgment.

1. *Order by client on attorney, not constituting assignment; what may
be reached by attachment or garnishment.*—A written order from a client
to his attorney, instructing him to pay to certain named creditors, when
collected, money arising from claims placed in his hands for collection,
does not operate an assignment of the claims, or the money collected
on them; and the ownership of the claims being thereby unchanged,
the debtors are subject to attachment or garnishment at the suit of the
client's creditors.

2. *Parol evidence varying writing.*—A witness, testifying as to a written order drawn on an attorney by his client, directing him to pay certain
creditors out of moneys, when collected, on claims placed in his hands
for collection, which does not constitute an assignment in law, can not
speak of it as an assignment.

APPEAL from the City Court of Birmingham.

Tried before the Hon. H. A. SHARPE.

The appellees in this case, Robert J. Miles & Co., obtained a judgment in said City Court, on the 23d August,
1887, against Gabert & Ratliff as partners, and, on the 28th
November, 1887, sued out a garnishment on it, which was
served on Mrs. N. A. Bustin, as the debtor of said Gabert
& Ratliff. The garnishee appeared, and answered, that she
was indebted to said Gabert & Ratliff, by judgment rendered
in said court against her, in their favor, on the 26th November, 1887; and that she had been notified by R. H. Sterrett

that he claimed said debt, as trustee, by assignment from Gabert & Ratliff. Sterrett also appeared, and asserted his claim to the debt under a written order addressed to him by said Gabert & Ratliff, which was dated March 19th, 1887, and in these words: "Out of the collections made by you out of the claims placed in your hands against J.B.F. Jackson, Mrs. Bustin and others, on which you have filed liens against their respective properties, and have either brought or been instructed to bring suits, you will please pay the Ala. National Bank of Birmingham the sum of $750, R. J. Miles $200, Smith, Marbury & Co. $115, Thompson, Francis & Chenoworth $115, and Ullman Hardware Co. of Birmingham $700;" and at the foot of the writing these words were added: "The remainder of any sum of money so realized by you, you will pay over to the First Nat. Bank of Birmingham, on a note of $900 given by us to them on this date, March 21st, 1887." The claimant introduced Jos. F. Johnston as a witness, who was the president of said Ala. National Bank at Birmingham, "and asked him to state what arrangements, if any, had been made by Gabert & Ratliff to secure the claim of the bank and other creditors; to which he replied, that Gabert told him they had assigned, or that they would assign, certain claims in their favor which were in the hands of R. H. Sterrett for collection, against J. B. F. Jackson and Mrs. N. A. Bustin, for the purpose of securing or paying said debts. The plaintiffs asked if said assignment or transfer was in writing; and the witness having answered in the affirmative—that it was reduced to writing immediately after the conversation—the plaintiffs moved to exclude the answer of the witness, to the effect that Gabert agreed to assign claims for the purpose of paying or securing said debts. The claimant then stated to the court, that he did not offer said statement to contradict, vary or alter the written instrument, but only for the purpose of explaining the same. The court sustained the objection, and excluded the evidence; to which the claimant excepted." The court charged the jury, on request, that they must find for the plaintiffs, if they believed the evidence. The claimant excepted to this charge, and here assigns it as error, with the exclusion of the evidence offered.

STERRETT & CAMPBELL, for appellant.

CUMMING & HIBBARD, *contra*.

SOMERVILLE, J.—The written order given by Gabert
& Ratliff, bearing date March 19th, 1887, directing the appellant, Sterrett, to pay certain preferred creditors out of the
claims placed in his hands for collection, including the judgment against Mrs. Bustin in favor of the drawers of the said
order, did not operate to transfer or assign the judgment, or
the fund, to either Sterrett, or the creditors. No words of
transfer or assignment are used in the instrument, and no
present valuable consideration is shown to have moved from
the drawee, or said creditors, to the makers of the order.
Nor does it appear that the drawee either accepted the order,
or entered into any promise or arrangement with the creditors, by which he would be prejudiced by the revocation of
the order. The ownership of the judgment, or fund, was
therefore unchanged, and it could be reached by an attaching or garnishing creditor. The cases of *Clark r. Cilley*,
36 Ala. 652; *Coleman v. Hatcher*, 77 Ala. 217, and *Thweat
v. McCullough*, 84 Ala. 517; s. c., 5 Amer. St. Rep. 391, are
conclusive of the question raised, and require an affirmance
of the judgment.

The testimony of the witness Johnston tended to change
the legal effect of the order, so as to make it operate as an
assignment of the judgment to Sterrett, in trust for the creditors named; and being in parol, was properly excluded.

The judgment must be affirmed.

Clark *v.* Jones & Brother.

Action on Common Counts, for Goods Sold and Delivered.

1. *Statute of frauds; promise to answer for debt, default. or miscarriage
of another.*—When goods are sold to one person, or at his instance, for
the use and benefit of another, and the sole credit is given to him, his
promise to pay for them is an original and absolute undertaking, and
not a promise to answer for the debt, default, or miscarriage of another
(Code, § 1732) ; otherwise, if any credit whatever was given to the person for whom the goods were bought.
2. *Same; words of doubtful meaning* —Where the plaintiffs testify that
the defendant applied for the goods in the name of a company of which
he was a member, but they refused to sell on the credit of the company,
and proposed to let the company have the goods on his credit, to which
he agreed; but further, on cross-examination, that they agreed to take,
at the expiration of thirty days, the company's acceptance with the defendant's indorsement for the balance not paid for by the acceptance of

[Clark v. Jones & Brother.]

a third person, which was received as cash; while the defendant denies that he ever offered, directly or indirectly, to become responsible for the goods: *Held*, that the words used might import (1) a collateral undertaking by defendant to indorse the company's acceptance, which would be within the statute of frauds, or (2) an original and independent promise to pay for the goods, with an understanding that plaintiffs would take, in lieu thereof, at the expiration of thirty days, the company's acceptance with the defendant's indorsement, whic.. would be a novation of the original contract, and not within the statute of frauds; and the words being susceptible of these two meanings, it was a question for the jury to determine which was intended by the parties.

3. *Same; charging goods on books to third person, and extending time of payment.*—The fact that the goods were charged on the plaintiffs' books to the company for which they were bought, with the words added, "*Vouched for by*" defendant, does not conclusively show that any credit was given to the company, especially when they were so charged at the instance and request of the defendant; and the fact that plaintiffs afterwards took the company's acceptance for the balance, and then their note with a further extension of time, though proper for the consideration of the jury in determining whether any credit was given to the company, does not conclusively establish, as matter of law, that credit was so given, when it also appears that plaintiffs notified defendant, at the time, that they did not intend thereby to release him.

4. *Company, as corporation, or partnership.*—The name *Wetumpka Lumber Company* does not, *ex vi terminorum*, import that the company is a corporation, rather than an unincorporated association, or a partnership; nor does any presumption of incorporation arise from the fact that its business is transacted by and through a president and secretary; and where the plaintiffs declare against the defendant individually, but seek to charge him with the debt of the company as a partner, and adduce evidence *prima facie* establishing a partnership, the *onus* of proving incorporation is on the defendant.

5. *Action against partner, for debt of partnership.*—In an action against a partner individually, the complaint containing the common counts only, a recovery may be had on proof of a debt against the partnership.

APPEAL from the Circuit Court of Montgomery.

Tried before the Hon. JOHN P. HUBBARD.

This action was brought by W. B. Jones & Brother, suing as partners, against Henry W. Clark, and was commenced on the 17th September, 1886. The complaint contained only the common counts, claiming $500 "due from defendant by account on 1st January, 1886, for money loaned by plaintiffs to him, and the like sum, due on said 1st January, 1886, for merchandise, goods and chattels sold by plaintiffs to him during the year 1885." The defendant pleaded the general issue, the statute of frauds, and payment; and issue was joined on these pleas. W. B. Jones testified on behalf of the plaintiffs, as appears from the bill of exceptions, that defendant came into plaintiffs' store one day in October, 1885, and said that he wanted to get some goods "for his company," the Wetumpka Lumber Company, which he said, in reply to an inquiry by Jones, was composed of himself, his son, and W. R. Weston, and "was good." Jones said: "I don't know anything about the company, but I know you, Mr. Clark, and I will let your company have goods on your credit;" and repeated: "I will sell you the goods, or to the company on your credit." He further testified, that the defendant "agreed to this, but requested witness to have the account made out against the company, for the purpose of enabling him to settle with his company; and witness agreed to this." It was agreed, also, that plaintiffs would take the acceptance of one P. H. McEachin, for something less than one hundred dollars, as part payment in cash; and the acceptance was delivered a few days afterwards, and was paid at maturity. This action involves only the unpaid balance, $273.91, or, possibly, includes a small bill of goods sold and delivered several days after the first; the verdict for plaintiffs being for $328.69.

Said Jones further testified, on cross-examination, "that when defendant first applied to get the goods for his company, he (witness) agreed that for all goods over and above those paid for by the McEachin acceptance defendant was to settle, at the expiration of thirty days, by giving the acceptance of the company, indorsed by himself." Two of the plaintiffs' clerks, who heard the conversation between Jones and Clark, testified substantially as Jones had. Jones testified, also, "that at the time he had the conversations and transactions with defendant, he understood that the Wetumpka Lumber Company was a corporation—thought it was from its name, but knew nothing about it." The defendant testified in his own behalf, "that he told plaintiffs he wanted the goods for his company, but never offered, either directly or indirectly, to become responsible for them, and was never asked to become so until about November 14th, when the time came to give the acceptance, but he did not, specifically, deny the conversation as detailed by Jones and his two clerks."

It appears from the plaintiffs' books, which were in evidence, that the goods were there charged to the Wetumpka Lumber Company, with the words added, "Vouched for by H. W. Clark;" but their clerk testified, that he added these words some time subsequently, by the direction of W. B. Jones, who said his original entry was wrong. At the expiration of about twenty days, the defendant called at the plaintiffs' store, when, as Jones testified, "they demanded that he either pay the balance of the bill, after deducting the

[Clark v. Jones & Brother.]

McEachin acceptance, or give the paper of his company, indorsed by himself; that he refused to do so, but assured plaintiffs that, if they would draw on the company for the balance of the account, payable on 21st December, the company would certainly pay it;" and thereupon Jones wrote a draft for $277.65, dated November 14th, and payable December 21st, on which defendant wrote the acceptance of the company, by himself as its president. The acceptance not being paid at maturity, a note for $280.83 "was taken in lieu of it," as Jones testified, "on the assurance of Clark that it would be paid at maturity;" the note being dated December 28th, payable on January 21st, and the name of the company being signed to it, "by H. W. Clark, Jr., secretary." The plaintiffs' testimony showed that they took said acceptance and note, not as payment, but under protest, and only on the assurance of the defendant above stated; and that they informed him, at the time, they would not release him from his liability to them for the account."

The court charged the jury, *ex mero motu*, as follows: "If the jury believe from the evidence that the goods were sold to a firm of which the defendant was a member, then he would be liable therefor in this action." To this charge the defendant excepted, and also to several charges which were given on request of the plaintiffs, among them the following: (1.) "If the goods were sold by plaintiffs at the request of H. W. Clark, and on his credit; then he would be liable, and the statute of frauds would be no obstacle to a recovery." (3.) "If the evidence shows that the Wetumpka Lumber Company was composed of H. W. Clark, Weston, and H. W. Clark, Jr.; then, if the goods were sold at the request of H. W. Clark, then he would be liable as a partner, unless it is shown that said company is a corporation, and it is not necessary to declare against him as a partner." (4.) "Even if the goods were charged directly to the Wetumpka Lumber Company, and Clark's name nowhere appeared on the account, still the plaintiffs may explain why that was done." (5.) "If the entry was innocently made by the shipping-clerk, plaintiffs would have the right to correct it, in order to make it conform to the terms of the original sale." (6.) "If the jury believe from the evidence that the credit was given to Clark on the sale of the goods, then it matters not how they were charged, and plaintiffs would be entitled to recover." (7.) "The fact that plaintiffs took a draft accepted by the Wetumpka Lumber Company, and afterwards a note of the company in renewal of the draft, is subject to explanation by them; and if the jury are satisfied from the evidence that neither was taken by them with the intent of accepting said company as paymaster instead of Clark, but that it was merely done at his request; then he is not released, if he was originally bound for the payment of the account." The defendant also requested several charges in writing, duly excepting to their refusal, and among them the following: (1.) "If the jury believe all the evidence, they will find for the defendant." (2.) "It is not the duty of the defendant, in this case, to prove that the Wetumpka Lumber Company was a corporation."

The charges given, and the refusal of the charges asked, are now assigned as error.

TOMPKINS, LONDON & TROY, for appellant.—(1.) On the plaintiffs' own testimony, the defendant's promise was a collateral undertaking, and void under the statute of frauds. Browne on Stat. Frauds, §§ 174, 183; *Carville v. Crane,* 40 Amer. Dec. 364; *Taylor v. Drake,* 53 Amer. Dec. 680; *Foster v. Napier,* 74 Ala. 393; *Clark v. Jones,* 85 Ala. 127; Throop on Verb. Agreements, §§ 209–12. (2.) There was no evidence that the Wetumpka Lumber Company was a partnership; its name rather indicated that it was a corporation, and its business was conducted through a president and secretary. The *onus* was certainly not on the defendant to prove incorporation, or to negative partnership. The charges of the court, then, based on the existence of a supposed partnership, of which there was no evidence, were erroneous. *Wise v. Falkner,* 51 Ala. 359; *Boddie v. State,* 52 Ala. 395; *Lehman v. Warren,* 53 Ala. 535; *Henderson v. State,* 49 Ala. 20. (3.) Even if there was any evidence of a partnership, the defendant could not be charged as a partner in this action, which was against him individually. There would have been a fatal variance between the pleadings and the proof.

WATTS & SON, *contra.*—(1.) By statutory provision, partnership debts are made joint and several, and an action may be maintained by the creditor against the partnership as an entity, or against one or more parties individually and separately.—Code, § 2605; *Duramus v. Harrison,* 26 Ala. 326; *Hall v. Cook,* 69 Ala. 87; *Tarleton v. Herbert,* 4 Ala. 359; *McCulloch v. Judd, Sons & Co.,* 20 Ala. 703; *Emanuel v.*

[Clark v. Jones & Brother.]

Bird, 19 Ala. 596; *Waldron v. Simmons*, 28 Ala. 629; *Van Wagner v. Chapman*, 29 Ala. 172; *Haralson v. Campbell*, 63 Ala. 278. (2.) The name of the defendant's company, in this case, does not necessarily import a corporation, nor is a corporation to be presumed because its business was conducted by and through a president and secretary.—*Thomas Hurrow Co. v. Seymour*, 81 Ala. 250; 27 La. Ann. 607; 45 N. Y. 410; 55 Mo. 310; 7 Wend. 542. There was some evidence, also, that the company was not a corporation, namely, the defendant's own declaration as to its members, and the note afterwards given by the company, which contains a waiver of exemptions. (3.) The questions arising under the statute of frauds were properly submitted to the jury.—*Rhodes v. Leeds*, 3 Stew. & P. 212; *Boykin & McRae v. Dohlande & Co.*, 37 Ala. 577; *Bates v. Starr*, 6 Ala. 697; *Scott v. Myatts & Moore*, 24 Ala. 482; *Sanford v. Howard*, 29 Ala. 684; *Ledlow v. Becton*, 36 Ala. 596.

CLOPTON, J.—The instructions of the court based the liability of defendant for the price of the goods, to recover which appellees bring this action, on two hypotheses: *first*, as the real and sole purchaser; *second*, as a member of a partnership for whom the goods were bought. As to the first ground of liability, the contestation is, whether the promise of the defendant to pay for the goods comes within the provision of the statute of frauds relating to "every special promise to answer for the debt, default, or miscarriage of another." In solving this question, the main and decisive inquiry is, Was the promise original and absolute, or collateral and conditional? As the plaintiffs seek by the action to charge the defendant with the price of the goods delivered to the Wetumpka Lumber Company, the rule applicable, and which must govern, may be thus stated: If the goods were sold on the sole credit of the defendant, his promise is original, and without the statute; but, if any credit was given to the company, who received the goods, the promise is collateral, and within the statute. In the latter case, it is immaterial to which party the credit was principally given. *Boykin v. Dohlande*, 37 Ala. 577. To bring such promise within the operation of the statute, there must be concurrent liabilities, each of which is capable of being enforced.

The evidence on the part of the plaintiffs tends to show, that, on application being made by defendant to obtain goods for the company, they refused to sell on the company's credit, but proposed to let the company have the goods on the defendant's credit, to which he agreed.   On cross-examination of one of the plaintiffs, it was brought out that, at the time defendant applied to get the goods, they agreed, for all goods not paid for by the acceptance of McEachin, which defendant proposed to turn over to them, to take, at the expiration of thirty days, the company's acceptance, with defendant's indorsement.   In his testimony, the defendant denies that he offered, directly or indirectly, to become responsible for the goods; but did not otherwise contradict the evidence on behalf of plaintiffs, as to what occurred at the time.   There is an absence of evidence that the company made, at the time or previously, application to procure the goods, or assumed any liability therefor, other than the application and promise of defendant.   Taking and considering all the words used, it is apparent that they are susceptible of two meanings: one importing a collateral undertaking to indorse the company's acceptance, to which the statute applies; the other an original and independent promise to pay for the goods, with an understanding or agreement that plaintiffs would take, at the expiration of thirty days, in lieu thereof, the company's acceptance with defendant's indorsement—a novation of the primary promise, which takes the statute out of the case.   When the words employed are susceptible of two meanings, the question must necessarily be submitted to the jury to determine in which sense they were used and understood.—Throop Verb. Ag., § 180.

The mere fact that the goods were charged to the company on the books of plaintiffs, in the manner shown, is not conclusive that any credit was given to the company.   The manner in which the account was entered on the books is consistent with the intention of the defendant to bind himself as the real purchaser, especially when it appears from the uncontradicted evidence that they were so charged by his request, and for his accommodation.   The same observations apply to the subsequent taking of the unindorsed acceptance of the company, and its renewal by note.   There is evidence tending to show that the acceptance and note were not taken as payment, and that defendant was informed at the time that plaintiffs would not release him from liability.   Giving credit subsequently to the company did not, under the circumstances, operate to change the character of the original promise.   These were facts and circumstances to be referred to the jury, to determine whether credit was given exclu-

[Clark v. Jones & Brother.]

sively to defendant.—*Sanford v. Howard*, 29 Ala. 684; *Led-low v. Becton*, 36 Ala. 596. On the entire evidence, it can not be said, as matter of law, that any credit was given to the company, or that the company incurred any enforceable liability, at the time the goods were obtained and the promise of defendant was made.

The charges of the court, to the effect that, if the goods were sold at the request of the defendant, and on his credit, he is liable, and the statute of frauds would be no obstacle to a recovery, is in accord with the foregoing principles. If the hypothesis of the charge be true, the goods were sold on the sole credit of the defendant; that is, were really sold to him.—*Boykin v. Dohlande, supra.* The charges properly submit to the jury the determination of the facts supposed, on consideration of the entire evidence. If the defendant apprehended that the jury might be misled by the generality of the terms of the instruction, he should have asked qualifying charges, based on the hypothesis in his favor which the evidence tends to establish.

In relation to the second ground of liability. the court instructed the jury, if the goods were sold to a firm of which the defendant was a member, he was liable in this action. The first objection urged to this charge is, that there is no evidence on which to predicate an inference that the Wetumpka Lumber Company is a partnership. It may be conceded, that, as the name may fairly import either a corporation, an unincorporated association, or a partnership, no presumption arises from the *mere name* that the company is either the one or the other. It may be further conceded, that, as plaintiffs declare against defendant individually, and yet seek to charge him as a partner, it is incumbent on them, in the first instance, to show a partnership; but, when they have introduced evidence which *prima facie* establishes a partnership, or from which it may be reasonably inferred, the burden is cast on the defendant to show incorporation, when he seeks to avoid individual liability on the ground that the company is a corporation. At the time the defendant proposed to purchase the goods, he represented that the company was composed of himself, his son and another, and that it was solvent, without any assertion or intimation that it was a corporation. This representation *prima facie* imports a voluntary association of three persons, combining their capital, labor and skill in the business, which was carried on for their common benefit. The fact that the company

31

had a president and secretary is not conclusive of corporate character. The material respects, in which unincorporated associations differ from a partnership, are, that the former are generally composed of a larger number of persons than the latter, and the business is usually conducted by officers acting for all the members. No presumption of incorporation arises from the fact that the business of the company was transacted by a president and secretary. There was sufficient evidence, whether weak or strong is immaterial, in the absence of any other evidence of incorporation, on which to predicate the charge.

It is further objected, that proof of a demand against a partnership, of which defendant is a member, does not authorize a recovery on a complaint which counts on an account stated between plaintiffs and defendant individually, and for goods sold to him alone. This question should be regarded as *res adjudicata* in this State. Under the statute, which declares, "any one of the associates, or his legal representative, may also be sued for the obligation of all," it has been uniformly held, that a partnership creditor may sue one of the members of the firm, for a debt contracted in the partnership name, whether by account or otherwise, and declare upon the demand as his individual liability.—Code, 1886, § 2605; *Duramus v. Harrison*, 26 Ala. 326; *Hall v. Cook*, 69 Ala. 87; *McCulloch v. Judd*, 20 Ala. 703.

Affirmed.

Bolling & Son *v* LeGrand.

Action on Bill of Exchange of Corporation, against Corporator as Partner.

1. *Private industrial corporation; declaration and certificate of incorporation; constitutional provisions as to title and subject-matter of laws, and as to amendatory laws.*—Under the statutory provisions which were of force in May, 1886, relating to the incorporation of private industrial enterprises (Sess. Acts 1882-3, pp. 5, 40; Code, 1876, §§ 1803-07), the board of corporators, on the completion of the organization of the company, the payment "in cash of at least twenty per cent. of the capital subscribed payable in money, and the payment of the remainder of the capital so subscribed, payable in money, being secured to be paid in such installments and at such times as may be provided in the written declaration required by section 1803 of the Code," and also the delivery of twenty per cent. of the property subscribed, "with security for the

delivery of the remainder so subscribed, as may be promised [provided] by said written declaration required by section 1803,'' were authorized to certify these facts to the probate judge of the proper county, who thereupon issued to them a certificate of incorporation; but these provisions did not require that the board of corporators should, in the written declaration required by said section 1803, specify when or how the unpaid portion of the subscribed capital was secured to be paid, nor make the failure to do so a defect fatal to the incorporation; and to give them that construction would be to make them amendatory of said section 1803, in violation of constitutional provisions (Art. IV, § 2).

APPEAL from the Circuit Court of Montgomery.
Tried before the Hon. JOHN P. HUBBARD.

This action was brought by R. E. Bolling & Son, suing as partners, against M. P. LeGrand; was commenced on the 18th December, 1888, and was founded on a bill of exchange for $2,664.05, which, as described in the complaint, was drawn on the 1st June, 1887, by the Southern Railway Construction and Land Company, upon C. W. Scofield, as president of said company, and also as president of the Montgomery & Florida Railway Company, and by him accepted as president, payable to R. B. McKenzie, sixty days after date; which bill, before maturity, was indorsed to the plaintiffs. The first count alleged that, "at the time of said acceptance, said Southern Railway Construction and Land Company was a partnership, or voluntary association; that said Scofield and this defendant, with others, were members thereof, and that defendant is liable on said bill as such partner, or member of said association." The second count alleged that the Southern Railway Construction and Land Company "was never organized as a corporation under the laws of Alabama, but was, at the time of said acceptance, a partnership; that said Scofield and said defendant, with others, were at that time members thereof; that said acceptance was within the scope and authority of said partnership, and that defendant is liable on said bill as such partner."

The defendant filed two pleas, the first of which was a special plea of *non est factum*, setting out all the proceedings had in the matter of the incorporation of the Southern Railway Construction and Land Company, of which defendant was a director and stockholder; alleging that the bill of exchange was made by said corporation after its organization, and while it was doing business as such, and that he "never made, nor authorized any one else to make for him the said bill of exchange, and, save as stockholder and director as aforesaid, had no connection with, or interest in said company." The second plea, after repeating the facts connected with the incorporation of the company, alleged that said Mc-Kenzie made a written contract with said corporation for the performance of certain work in building a railroad, for the construction of which the corporation had contracted; that the corporation became thereby indebted to him, and executed said bill of exchange in part payment of said indebtedness; and that said McKenzie, in making said contract, and in receiving said bill of exchange, "dealt with said company as a corporation, and not otherwise."

All the proceedings in connection with the incorporation of the company, copies of which were made exhibits to the pleas, were had in May, 1886. The declaration was filed on the 24th May, and contained these statements: "We do hereby declare in writing: (1.) That the names and residences of your corporators and declarants are, C. W. Scofield, of the city of New York; M. P. Le Grand and Jas. A. Farley, of Montgomery, Alabama; and John D. Roquemore, of Eufaula, Alabama. (2.) That the name of said corporation shall be, the *Southern Railway Construction and Land Company;* that its principal place of business shall be at Montgomery, Alabama; that the general purpose of said corporation shall be the construction of railroads, and the purchasing, owning, selling, improving, and dealing in lands. (3.) That the capital stock of said corporation shall be $10,000, to be divided into one hundred shares, of the par value of $100 each. (4.) That said corporation shall have the power to purchase, own, sell, and deal generally in real estate; to improve the same, and to sublet any contract it may have for the construction of railroads." On the filing of this declaration, a commission was issued by the probate judge of Montgomery to said Le Grand and Roquemore, authorizing them to open books of subscription, on one day's notice through the newspapers. The books were opened on the 26th May, and fifty shares subscribed for by the corporators, $5,000, of which twenty per cent. ($1,000) was paid in cash; and these facts being certified to the probate judge, with the election of officers, he issued a certificate of incorporation on the same day.

The plaintiffs' demurred to each of the defendant's pleas, and the judgment overruling their demurrers is now assigned as error.

E. P. MORRISSETT, for appellants.—(1.) If the Southern Railway Construction and Land Company was never legally

incorporated, never had a legal existence, its individual stockholders or members are liable as partners on its contracts
and engagements.—Wordsworth on Joint Stock Companies,
3; Cooke on Stock and Stockholders, § 233; Angell & Ames
on Corporations, §§ 591-2; Waite on Insolv. Corp., § 477;
Story on Partnership, 109; 7 Wendell, 542; 73 Ill. 197;
16 La. Ann. 153; *Hill v. Beach*, 12 N. J. Eq. 31; 36 N. J.
Law, 250. *Fay v. Noble*, 7 Cush. (Mass.), asserts a contrary doctrine, and it is adopted by Morawetz; but that decision is founded on the false reason, as assigned, that to
hold them liable as partners would be holding them "to a
liability neither contemplated nor assented to by them." The
liability of a party is determined by his acts, and the resulting implications, not by his intentions. A contract which
the parties intended to make, but did not make, can not be
set up in place of one which they did make.—*Sanford v.
Howard*, 29 Ala. 684. An agent, or trustee, may bind himself personally, although that was not his intention.—*Mc-
Calley v. Wilburn & Co.*, 77 Ala. 552; and many other authorities. (2.) Said company was never legally organized
as a corporation. The proceedings relied on as an incorporation show that the capital stock was to be $10,000, of which
$5,000 was subscribed by the corporators, but only twenty
per cent. ($1,000) was paid in; and that no security was
given for the payment of the residue. Under the statutory
provisions then of force, it was not only required that twenty
per cent. of the capital subscribed for, payable in money,
should be paid in cash, but that security should be given for
the payment of the balance; and the declaration of incorporation was required to state how this unpaid balance was
secured to be paid—in what installments, when, and how
payable; and this was a condition precedent to a valid incorporation.—Sess. Acts 1882-3, p. 40. Any other construction
of the amendatory law would render it useless and nugatory,
since the persons proposing to form a private corporation,
limiting their liability to their unpaid subscriptions, already
had the option of specifying, in their declaration of incorporation, how their unpaid subscriptions, whether of money
or property, should be paid or discharged; and they needed
no additional legislation in this regard. They already had
the power to specify in their written declaration, under subdivision 4, "any other matters which it may be desirable to
set forth in the organic law"; and it is not to be supposed
that it would be desirable to them to incur any other or

further liability than was compulsory. The General Assembly, it is to be presumed, did not enact a special statute which no one needed, and which accomplished nothing after its enactment. On the contrary, the amendatory law was enacted in the interest of third persons—to protect the unwary public against possible imposition and fraud, on the part of those who would induce confidence and secure credit by a pretense of specious capital, seeking corporate privileges while limiting their personal liability; to check the abuse of the loose system of incorporation then existing, by requiring not only payment in cash of one-tenth of the proposed capital stock, but security for the payment of the balance. This construction only can give any effect to the new law.—Dwar. Statutes, 702-7; Sedgw. St. & Const. Law, 245-6; 41 Ala. 479; 59 Ala. 219; 68 Ala. 317. That the word *may*, in a statute, is to be construed as mandatory when the rights and interests of the public are concerned, see *Ex parte Banks*, 28 Ala. 35; 17 Ala. 527; 9 Porter, 390; 3 Atk. 166; 2 Bouv. Dic. 150. (3.) This construction of the statute can not be assailed on constitutional grounds. Sections 1803 and 1807, as well as the intermediate sections, relate to the same subject, and are closely connected, and they are to be construed as *in pari materia*. The constitutional inhibition is against the insertion of matters foreign to the main object of the bill—matters not easily discerned by reading the law, or which might operate a surprise or fraud on legislators. Its requirements are not to be exactingly enforced, nor in such manner as to cripple legislation, or obstruct the machinery of government.—*Ballentyne v. Wickersham*, 75 Ala. 533; *Moses v. Mayor*, 52 Ala. 198; *Falconer v. Robinson*, 46 Ala. 340; 82 Ala. 211; 44 Ala. 639. (4.) The plaintiffs are not estopped from asserting that the company never had a corporate existence, and holding the defendant liable as a partner.—*Chambers · v. Falkner*, 65 Ala. 448; 36 Ala. 313; 31 Ala. 76; 46 Md. 373; 73 Ill. 201; 56 Iowa, 109; Waite's Insolv. Corp. 34, § 23.

SAYRE, STRINGFELLOW & LE GRAND, TOMPKINS & TROY, and ROQUEMORE, WHITE & LONG, *contra.*—(1.) The appellants' construction of the statute amending section 1807 of the Code of 1876, not only does violence to the words used, but perverts the meaning and purpose of the statute, and would make it accomplish by implication what could not have been done expressly and directly without a violation of

[Bolling & Son v. LeGrand.]

mandatory constitutional provisions. Sections 1803 and 1807
relate to the same general subject, and both of them, possibly, might have been modified, or even repealed, by a general affirmative statute which did not mention either of them.
But an act which, by its title, purports "to amend section
1807," could not include also an amendment of section 1803;
and yet the argument is that it does this by implication, and
by reference only to the number of that section.—Const.,
Art. IV, § 2; *Dane v. McArthur*, 57 Ala. 448; *Ballentyne v.
Wickersham*, 75 Ala. 533; *Rogers v. Torbut*, 58 Ala. 523;
Todd v. State, 85 Ala. 339; 82 Ala. 209, 339; 41 Ala. 9;
43 Ala. 224; 46 Ala. 348; 49 Ala. 349. The provision in
the statute was not intended for the benefit of the public;
for the nature of the security is not specified, but is left discretionary with the corporators themselves, for whose benefit
it was intended; and when they deem it desirable to specify
the security, the installments, &c., in their declaration of
incorporation, then it must be certified by them to the probate judge.   (2.) The declaration in this case, it is admitted,
complied strictly with the requirements of section 1803 of
the Code, as then amended; and that, it is insisted, in connection with the certificate of the probate judge, gave it a
corporate existence.   But, even if there was a defect in the
organization or incorporation of said company, the plaintiffs
can not take advantage of it in this action.—*Lehman, Durr
& Co. v. Warner*, 61 Ala. 455; *Agr. & Mech. Asso. v. Insurance Co.*, 70 Ala. 120; *Sherwood v. Alvis*, 83 Ala. 115;
Savings Bank v. Dunklin, 54 Ala. 471; *Sprowl v. Lawrence*,
38 Ala. 690; *Duke v. Cahaba Nav. Co.*, 16 Ala. 372; *Railroad Co. v. Tipton*, 5 Ala. 808; 32 Md. 671; 19 N. Y. 482;
25 N. Y. 208; 26 N. Y. 75; 57 N. Y. 331; 12 Heisk. (Tenn.)
494; 38 Mich. 776; 69 Geo. 159; 35 Ohio St. 158; 58 Penn.
St. 399; 62 Mo. 247; 95 U. S. 665; Mor. Corp., § 748;
12 Wall. 358; 51 Ind. 60; 89 Ind. 389; 32 Wisc. 162;
113 Ill. 618; 12 Amer. & Eng. Corp. Cases, 40.

McCLELLAN, J.—The theory upon which this suit was
instituted, and this appeal prosecuted, is, that the efforts of
the defendant below—appellee here—and others acting with
him, to organize a corporation, were so far abortive that the
would-be corporators, instead of forming a body corporate,
in law and fact constituted a partnership, or voluntary association of individuals, and as individuals became bound on
the contracts purporting to be made by the corporation and

in its name. Two defenses were relied on in the court below: First, that the corporation, whose existence as such is thus attempted to be impeached, was duly and regularly organized, and is alone liable on the contract sued on; and, second, that this contract was made with it as a corporation, and the plaintiff is now estopped to deny its corporate existence and capacity. Manifestly, the consideration of this second defense will be important only in the event that it shall be determined that there was a failure on the part of the declarants to attain corporate existence, and that question will be first considered.

The infirmity in the proceedings had and taken by and at the instance of the defendant and his associates, which is relied on as defeating their purpose to organize a corporation, is alleged to result from non-compliance with two acts of the General Assembly passed at the session of 1882-3, amending respectively sections 1803 and 1804 and section 1807 of the Code of 1876.

By an act of December 6, 1882, sections 1803 and 1804 of the Code of 1876 were amended so as to read as follows, respectively:

"§ 1803. *Declaration filed with Probate Court; contents.*—Two or more persons desiring to form themselves into a private corporation, for the purpose of carrying on any manufacturing, mining, immigrating, industrial or other lawful business, not otherwise specifically provided for by law, may file with the Probate Court of the county, in which it is proposed that such company shall have its only or principal place of business, a written declaration, signed by themselves, setting forth:—

"1. The names and residences of the petitioners.

"2. The name of the proposed corporation, the place at which it proposes to have its principal or only place of business, the general purpose of the corporation, and the nature of the business which it proposes to do.

"3. The amount of the capital stock, and the number of shares into which it is to be divided, showing the par value of each share.

"4. Any other matter which it may be desirable to set forth in the organic law.

"§ 1804. *Commission issued to board of corporators; books of subscription; when and where opened.* Upon the filing of the declaration as above, the probate judge of the county shall issue to the parties, or to any two or more of them, a commission constituting them a board of corporators, giving them authority to open books of subscription to the capital stock of the proposed company, at such time and place as they deem fit."

By an act "to amend section 1807 of the Code," approved February 5, 1883, that section was made to read as follows:

"§ 1807. *Certificate of organization.*—Upon the completion of the organization of the company, and the payment to the treasurer of the company, or some officer designated for that purpose, in cash, of at least twenty per cent. of the capital subscribed, *payable in money, and the payment of the remainder of the capital so subscribed for, payable in money, being secured to be paid in such installments and at such times as may be provided in the written declaration required by section 1803 of the Code; and also the delivery to such officer of at least twenty per cent. of the property so subscribed to the capital of such corporation, with security for the delivery of the remainder of said property, so subscribed to the capital as may be promised by said written declaration required by section 1803*; the board of corporators shall, in writing, over their signatures, certify the same to the probate judge of the county, who shall issue to the company a certificate that they have been fully organized according to the law of Alabama, under the name and for the purpose indicated in their written declaration, and that they are fully authorized to commence business under their charter."

By the first of the acts copied above, section 1803 of the Code of 1876 was amended by inserting the words, "*or other lawful business, not otherwise specifically provided for by law*"; and section 1804 was amended so as to take away from the probate judge the power and duty of requiring the board of corporators to give such notice of the time and place of opening the books of subscription, as he might deem fit, and, in lieu thereof, require that officer to authorize the corporators to open books for subscription "at such time and place as they deem fit." The amendment of section 1807 of the Code attempted to be made by the second statute set out, is indicated by the italization in the body of the act as quoted.

While the statutes were in force, and with the unamended sections of Article 1, Chapter 1, Title 1, Part Second of the Code of 1876, constituted the law under which certain classes of corporations were required to be organized,

the defendant in this action, with others, undertook
to organize a corporation to be called "The Southern Railway Construction and Land Company," and
to that end filed in the office of the judge of probate of
Montgomery county, where it was proposed the said company should have its principal or only place of business, a
declaration in strict compliance with the statute quoted first
above, amendatory of section 1803, and setting forth, under
clause 4 of that section, "that said corporation shall have
the power to purchase, own, sell and deal generally in real
estate, to improve the same, and to sublet any contract it may
have for the construction of railroads." This declaration nowhere attempts to provide for, or specify the installments,
in which that part of the capital stock of the proposed corporation which is not paid in cash, shall be paid, nor the
times at which deferred installments shall be paid, nor does
it provide for or require any kind of security for the payment of deferred installments; and in point of fact, no other
security than the individual obligation of each subscriber to
the stock of the company, evidenced by their respective subscriptions, was ever required or given, for the payment of
that part of the money subscribed which was not paid on organization. It is clear, that neither the original section
1803, nor as it was amended by the act of December 6, 1882,
above set out, required that the declaration of persons desiring to form themselves into a private corporation should
state the installments into which subscriptions should be
divided, nor the time at which subscriptions should be paid,
nor prescribe that any security should be given for the payment of subscriptions in whole, or in any part or parts,
presently, or at any time or times in the future. The
original section 1804 required that twenty per cent. of
the capital subscribed should be paid in, and the fact certified to the judge of probate, before it became the duty of
that officer to issue a certificate of organization; and it appears that this provision was complied with in the present
case.

This section, as amended by the act of February 5, 1883,
refers also to the eighty per cent. of the subscribed capital
stock which is not required to be paid in before certification
of organization, and makes the fact of that part of the capital
"being secured to be paid in such installments and at such
times as may be provided in the written declaration required
by section 1803," one of the conditions upon which arises

[Bolling & Son v. LeGrand.]

the duty of the probate judge to certify the organization of
the company, and that it is fully authorized to commence
business under its charter. This provision of the amendatory act is susceptible of two constructions. The legislature
may have intended thereby to require that the declaration
for the formation of the corporation should set forth the installments into which the unpaid capital should be divided,
and the times at which such installments should be paid, and
that the fact that the deferred capital had been secured to
be paid in the installments, and at the times therein indicated, should be certified to the probate judge in all cases,
before he should authorize the corporation to commence business. On the other hand, recognizing that section 1803
already contained a clause under which corporators, if they
desired so to do, might provide in their declaration that the
deferred subscriptions should be paid in certain amounts, and
at stated times, it may have been the legislative purpose to
provide a method by which the declared intent of the corporators could be effectuated, by requiring security to be
given for the payment in all cases in which the corporators
had availed themselves of the right to prescribe the time
and amounts of such payments. It is patent that the former
interpretation involves the interpolation of a new provision
into section 1803—injects into it a requirement that the
declaration should set forth, in addition to what the section
itself provides, the further statement, that that part of the
capital stock not paid up on organization, should be paid in
certain installments, and at certain times. To thus amend
section 1803 would, in our judgment, violate at least two
provisions of the organic law. Section. 2, Art. IV of the
Constitution, among other things, provides, that "Each law
shall contain but one subject-matter, which shall be clearly
expressed in its title." If the act of February 5, 1883, with
its title to amend section 1807 of the Code, be construed to
inject the new provision into section 1803, which we have
been considering, it clearly contains two subjects-matter, one
of which—the amendment of section 1807—is expressed in
the title, and the other—the amendment of 1803—is in no
manner expressed, or even indicated in the title. The reading of this act by its title, as the Constitution requires it to
be read, in each house of the General Assembly, would have
given to the members of that body no information of its real
contents, or intimation that its purpose was to amend section
1803, as well as 1807 of the Code. To construe it to have

that effect, brings it within both the letter and spirit of the constitutional inhibition.—*Ballentyne v. Wickersham*, 75 Ala. 533, and cases cited; *Ex parte Reynolds, ante,* p. 138, and cases cited; *Chiles v. Monroe,* 4 Met. (Ky.) 72.

Another clause of the section quoted from above provides, that "No law shall be revised, amended, or the provisions thereof extended or conferred, by reference to its title only; but so much thereof as is revised, amended, extended or conferred, shall be re-enacted and published . at length." Giving to the act of February 5, 1883, the effect of amending section 1803 in the particular indicated, the result would be to amend or extend that section, in a matter the importance of which this case fully attests, by a bare reference to an arbitrary number, which has been attached to it for the purpose of physical identification, and which fails absolutely to give any information or hint of its contents, and with no pretense of re-enacting the section and publishing it at length as amended. Such an amendment is clearly within the inhibition of the constitution last quoted, as expounded in the former adjudications of this court.—*Rodgers v. Torbut,* 58 Ala. 523; *Stewart v. County Commissioners,* 82 Ala. 209; *Bay Shell Road Co. v. O'Donnell, ante,* p. 376 ; *Ex parte Reynolds, ante,* p. 138.

Having thus reached the conclusion, that to adopt the construction of the act of February 5, 1883, contended for by appellants, would render it unconstitutional, it becomes the duty of courts to give to that statute, if it can be done consistently with its terms, an interpretation which will leave it a field of operation within constitutional limitations. *Wilburn v. McCalley,* 63 Ala. 436. This result may be attained by adopting the construction indicated above, and holding it to have been the purpose of the General Assembly. as gathered from the language employed, and hence to be the effect of this act, to require unpaid subscriptions to be secured to be paid in certain installments and at certain times, in those cases only in which the corporators have de-. clared, under clause 4 of section 1803, that that part of the subscribed capital which is not paid on organization shall be paid in stated amounts and at particular times. Indeed, the particular expression used in the act of 1883, aside from any other consideration, tends strongly to support this conclusion. It is there provided, that certification of organization shall be made upon the payment of at least twenty per cent. of the capital subscribed, and upon the remainder being secured to be paid in such manner &c. as *may be* provided in the declaration. There is nothing to indicate a legislative purpose to require that such provision should be made, or that security should be given in the absence of any provision for amounts and times of payments; but, in recognition of the discretion left in the corporators to set out a provision of this character, or not to do so, the operation of this amendment of section 1807 is upon a provision in this behalf resulting from the voluntary election of the corporators to include and set it forth in their declaration. As we have seen, there is no such declaration filed for the incorporation of the Southern Railway Construction and Land Company, but, on the contrary, the declarants conceived it "to be desirable to set forth," under the fourth clause of section 1803, other matters, having reference to the general powers of the company.

Our conclusion is, that the corporation was regularly organized, and is alone liable on the contract sued on in this case. This renders it unnecessary to consider the question of estoppel.

Affirmed.

McDowell *v.* Steele.

Bill in Equity by Judgment Creditor, to set aside Mortgages as Fraudulent.

1. *Conveyance by failing or insolvent debtor to creditor; validity as against other creditors.*—A failing or insolvent debtor may select one or more of his creditors, and pay them in full, even though he thereby disables himself to pay anything to the others; but, if the conveyance or arrangement, going beyond the limits of full payment or security, stipulates or provides, openly or secretly, for a benefit to the debtor himself beyond what the law allows or secures to him, it is fraudulent on his part; and if the grantee, or secured creditor, knows of the existence of other debts left unprovided for, or has knowledge of facts calculated to put him on inquiry as to them, he is charged with participation in the fraud.

2. *Mortgage by embarrassed debtor to creditor, stipulating for long time; validity as against other creditors.*—A mortgage executed by an embarrassed (if not insolvent) debtor, conveying lands as security for a debt less than their value, which was to be paid in nine annual installments, the whole interest payable annually, and with power of sale on default in the payment of the third installment; followed on the next day by a second mortgage on the property, to the mortgagor's wife,

who was the mother of the first mortgagee.—*held* fraudulent in law, both as securing a valuable benefit to the mortgagor, and as hindering and delaying another creditor, whose debt was reduced to judgment on the next day, of which debt the mortgagee had notice, actual or constructive, having knowledge of facts sufficient to put him on inquiry.

APPEAL from the Chancery Court of Wilcox.

Heard before the Hon. THOS. W. COLEMAN.

The bill in this case was filed on the 3d March, 1885, by David A. Steele, as a judgment creditor of John R. Mc-Dowell, with an execution returned "No property found," against said McDowell, his wife, Daniel S. Pritchett, and others; and sought to set aside, as fraudulent, two mortgages executed by said McDowell, one to his wife, and the other to said Pritchett, and to subject the property to the satisfaction of the complainant's judgment. The complainant died pending the suit, and it was revived in the name of O. D. Steele as his administrator. The complainant's debt originated in the liability of his guardian, R. H. Dawson, on whose bond said John R. McDowell and one P. D. Burford were sureties. A final settlement of the guardian's accounts was had in the Probate Court on the 13th March, 1884, when a decree was rendered against him, in favor of the ward, for \$2,830.75, besides costs. An execution on this decree was issued on the 10th April, 1884, which was returned "No property found;" and another execution was then issued against the guardian and his sureties, on which the same return was made, on the 7th February, 1885. The mortgage to Pritchett was dated March 14th, 1884, and was given to secure a recited indebtedness of \$7,000, evidenced by McDowell's nine notes, of even date with the mortgage, each for the sum of \$777.78, payable on the 1st December, each year, from 1885 to 1893 respectively, with interest payable annually; and it contained a power of sale, on default in the payment of the third note. The mortgage to Mrs. McDowell, the wife of said John R. McDowell, was dated March 15th, 1884, and purported to secure an indebtedness of \$6,674.28; conveying the same lands, and containing a power of sale if the debt was not paid by the 15th December, 1885. The bill alleged, on information and belief, that these mortgages conveyed all the lands belonging to said McDowell; that he was in fact not indebted to either of the mortgagees; that all of the parties had knowledge of the decree in favor of the complainant, and that the mortgages were intended to hinder and delay him in the collection of

[McDowell v. Steele.]

his debt, and to prevent the property of McDowell from being subjected to liability on the guardian's bond. Burford, the other surety on the bond, had died before the probate decree was rendered, and his administratrix was made a defendant to the bill; but the points raised by her in defense have no bearing on the present appeal.

A demurrer to the bill was overruled by Chancellor Mc-SPADDEN, and his decree was affirmed by this court on appeal.—*Burford v. Steele*, 80 Ala. 147. Separate answers were filed by the defendants. McDowell denied all the charges of fraud; denied that he had knowledge of the decree in favor of the complainant when he executed the mortgages, and denied that they conveyed all of his lands; and he alleged that the indebtedness recited in each mortgage was a valid and subsisting debt. The indebtedness to his wife, he said, was for moneys belonging to her statutory estate, which he had received at different times during coverture, and for which he had never accounted to her; and the debt to Pritchett, he said, accrued in this way: Respondent was the administrator of the estate of David Kennedy, deceased, and on the final settlement of his accounts, in June, 1882, two decrees were rendered against him, in favor of Pritchett as guardian of one of the minors, which together amounted to $5,157.86; and at his instance and request, at the time the mortgage was executed, Pritchett assumed the payment of these decrees, the ward having attained majority, and advanced to him in cash the balance of the recited $7,000, taking the mortgage as security for the entire amount. Pritchett and Mrs. McDowell, in their respective answers, asserted the validity of their respective mortgages, and stated the consideration substantially as McDowell had stated it; and each denied knowledge or notice of the indebtedness to the complainant at the time their mortgages were taken.

On final hearing, on pleadings and proof, the chancellor rendered a decree for the complainant, declaring each of the mortgages to be fraudulent and void; and this decree is here assigned as error by each of the defendants separately.

WATTS & SON, and J. N. MILLER, for appellants.—The mortgages assailed in this case are not fraudulent, either in law or in fact. The indebtedness secured by each, as recited on its face, is proved strictly as alleged; and each is a valid debt which might be thus secured. That the indebt-

edness of the husband to his wife, for moneys belonging to
her statutory estate, which he has received and appropriated,
may be thus paid or secured, see cases cited in Brick. Digest, vol. 3, p. 543, § 19. The indebtedness to Pritchett was
created at the time his mortgage was executed, the greater
part of it being his assumption of a decree in his own favor,
on which he might have had execution issued; and it is
shown that this settlement of the matter had been a subject
of negotiation between the parties for several months. If a
fraud on other creditors was intended, they would not have
waited until after the complainant's demand was reduced to
judgment, before consummating their arrangements by
proper writings. The value of the mortgaged property is
proved to have been between $9,000 and $10,000; more than
$2,000 above the debt to Pritchett, but $3,000 less than the
aggregate of the two debts. If the mortgage to Pritchett
had been an absolute conveyance, this excess of value might
have been fatal to it; but the principle has no application to
a mortgage. There is no proof that McDowell owed any
other debt than the complainant's decree, of which the mortgagees had no notice, and the amount of which did not equal
the value of McDowell's other property. McDowell's liability to complainant was contingent until reduced to judgment.
His testimony shows that he had no actual knowledge of the
decree, and he might well have rested secure, knowing that
the funds of Dawson's ward had been loaned to Burford, the
other surety on the bond, whose estate was primarily liable
for the debt; and if the sureties were equally bound to pay
the decree, less than $3,000, his share was less than $1,500.
The mortgagees had no notice of this contingent liability,
and the mortgagor himself, having personal property of
value more than $2,000, and other lands worth $4,000,
might lawfully give them security. The grant of long time
in a mortgage, while the mortgagor retains possession of the
property, is a badge of fraud; but the long time granted in
the mortgage to Pritchett is more specious than real, since
a power to foreclose is given on default in the payment of the
third note, and the interest on all of the notes is payable annually. It must be remembered, too, that fraud is never to
be presumed, but must be affirmatively proved.—*Thames v.
Rembert*, 63 Ala. 561; 51 Ala. 235; 50 Ala. 590; Jones on
Mortgages, vol. 1, § 627; Bump on Fraud. Conv. 46; 64 Ala.
520; *Crawford v. Kirksey*, 55 Ala. 282; 68 Ala. 149;
26 Ala. 184.

[McDowell v. Steele.]

JNO. Y. KILPATRICK, *contra*, relied on the chancellor's opinion, and cited the following authorities: *Thames v. Rembert*, 63 Ala. 561; *Williams v. Avery*, 38 Ala. 115; *McLeod v. Powe*, 76 Ala. 418; *Lehman, Durr & Co. v. Kelly*, 68 Ala. 192; *Levy v. Williams*, 79 Ala. 171.

STONE, C. J.—The testimony is very satisfactory in support of the proposition, that in March, 1884, McDowell was indebted to Pritchett, and to Mrs. McDowell, in the sums severally claimed by them. We think, also, that the property mortgaged to them was not excessive in value, taking into account the amount of the indebtedness. It is also well settled, under our system, that a failing debtor, who is unable to pay all his debts, may elect whom he will pay, and pay them in full, although he thereby disables himself to pay any thing to his other creditors. But this last principle has its limit, which is as well defined and universal as the principle itself. It is this: The arrangement or adjustment by which the creditor secures, or attempts to secure his own claim, must not stipulate for, or openly or secretly secure or provide, any benefit to the debtor beyond what the law, without such agreement, would secure to him. If the security transcend this boundary, it is fraudulent as to the failing debtor; and if the secured creditor knows of other debts unprovided for, or, what is the same thing, has information calculated to put him on inquiry, which, if followed up, would lead to the discovery of other debts, then it is fraudulent as to him. 3 Brick. Dig. 517, § 137; *Hodges v. Coleman*, 76 Ala. 103; *Pope v. Wilson*, 7 Ala. 690; *Wiley v. Knight*, 27 Ala. 336; *Reynolds v. Welch*, 47 Ala. 200; *McWilliams v. Rogers*, 56 Ala. 87; *Lehman v. Kelly*, 68 Ala. 192; *Seaman v. Nolen*, *Ib.* 463; *Pritchett v. Pollock*, 82 Ala. 169; *Hopkins v. Campbell*, *ante*, p. 179; *Lukins v. Aird*, 6 Wall. 78; 3 Brick. Dig. 679, § 10; *Tillman v. Thomas*, *ante*, p. 321.

It is contended that McDowell, after making these mortgages, retained sufficient unincumbered property to pay the debt which the bill seeks to enforce. We have examined all the testimony bearing on this question, and, without commenting on it, we hold it wholly insufficient to make this contention good. We hold that, at and before making the mortgages, Mr. McDowell was practically insolvent. Else why want twelve years within which to work out and pay his debts?

Is there sufficient evidence that Pritchett had actual knowl-

32

edge, when he obtained his mortgage, that McDowell was otherwise indebted than to him, Pritchett, and to Mrs. McDowell?

Pritchett testifies that, at that time, he did not know that McDowell owed any other than the two debts; the one to himself, and the other to Mrs. McDowell, his mother. The questions may naturally arise, why should he demand a mortgage security of McDowell, if the latter owed no other debts? and, on what principle could he account for McDowell's wish to obtain twelve years indulgence, and his own consent to grant him more than nine? McDowell, Pritchett's witness, sheds light on this. He testified as follows: "The last of November, or first of December, 1883, I had been trying to sell the Fail plantation, to meet that debt [the chief consideration of the mortgage made to Pritchett, March 14, 1884], but could not effect a sale of it. So I proposed to him [Pritchett], as he had money, that he would pay up said decrees, and give me time to pay him, and to pay up my other debts. He asked what time I wanted. I told him, if he gave me twelve years, I thought I could pay him some along every year, and pay up my other debts. He said, 'No; but I tell you what I will do: if you will give me a mortgage on more lands than the Fail place, I will give nine years.' . . . I told him I would do it, and that was agreed to by both of us."

Pritchett's testimony of this transaction is as follows: "I wanted to help him [McDowell], if possible, by giving him time, and, at the same time, wanted to secure the money for my ward; and not knowing of any other debts, I thought he could eventually pay me out." In another place he says: "McDowell asked for twelve years time, on additional security that he was to make me. I told him I would give him nine years time; so we agreed on this."

Mrs. McDowell testified that, when her husband asked her to unite in the mortgage to Pritchett (the night before its execution), he stated "that Pritchett would give him nine years to pay it in, and he thought it would enable him to pay up all his other debts. This is the only way he spoke to me of other debts." It is not shown that Pritchett was informed of this.

The present suit grew out of Dawson's guardianship of D. A. Steele. McDowell was one of Dawson's sureties on his bond as guardian. The settlement of the guardianship was had in Wilcox Probate Court March 13, 1884, and a decree

[McDowell v. Steele.]

was rendered against the guardian for something over twenty eight hundred dollars. Judge Purifoy, then judge of probate of Wilcox, testified, that in the evening of the day on which the settlement was made, Pritchett inquired of him if Dawson had attended the settlement; and on being informed that he had not, he became irritated, and used some harsh expressions. He testified further that he then informed Pritchett of the result of the settlement. Pritchett testified this conversation occurred March 15, 1884.

The mortgage from McDowell and wife to Pritchett was executed and filed for record March 14, 1884. The debt of six thousand dollars was divided into nine equal installments, due December 1, severally and annually, commencing with 1885, and ending with 1893, with a provision that the entire accruing interest was to be paid annually; and if the mortgagor made default in paying the third note at its maturity, December, 1887, then the mortgagee was empowered to foreclose the mortgage by sale.

The testimony is very strong, that Pritchett, at and before he took his mortgage, had knowledge that McDowell owed a debt or debts, other than those he owed to him, Pritchett, and to his mother, Mrs. McDowell. Be this as it may, the testimony and the surroundings clearly convince us that he had sufficient notice to put him on inquiry, which would have led him to a discovery of such debt or debts. Finding this to be the fact, the conclusion is irresistible, that the long delay granted to McDowell, during which the possession and use of the property were proposed to be secured to him, and other creditors denied the right to enforce the collection of their demands, rendered the mortgage doubly fraudulent : First, in securing a valuable benefit to McDowell, and, second, in delaying and hindering all other creditors in the assertion of their claims.

Forbearance and generosity to an embarrassed and struggling debtor, are highly praiseworthy; but the law's stern morality can not permit their exercise, when the palpable effect of thus favoring the debtor is to hinder and obstruct other creditors in the enforcement of their equally meritorious claims. When there is a conflict between the mandate of justice and the instinct of charity, the latter must yield, in all human tribunals.

The chancellor's reasoning and conclusions in this case are striking and convincing. His decree is in every respect affirmed.

Teague *v.* Martin.

Bill in Equity for Cancellation of Fraudulent Conveyance, as Cloud on Title.

1. *Fraudulent conveyance, as cloud on title.*—A purchaser at sheriff's sale under execution, of lands which have been fraudulently conveyed by the judgment debtor, has a plain and adequate remedy at law, and can not, while out of possession, maintain a bill in equity to cancel the conveyance as a cloud on his title.

APPEAL from the Chancery Court of Cleburne.

Heard before the Hon. S. K. MCSPADDEN.

The bill in this case was filed on the 29th February, 1888, by L. G. Teague, against C. A. Martin; and sought to cancel, as a cloud on complainant's title to a tract of land, which he had bought at sheriff's sale under execution against one Joseph E. Burns, a conveyance executed by said Burns to the defendant, and which was alleged to be without consideration, and to have been executed with the fraudulent intent of hindering and delaying the creditors of the grantor. The conveyance to the defendant was dated the 3d June, 1886, and the sheriff's deed to the complainant was dated November 11th, 1887. On final hearing, on pleadings and proof, the chancellor dismissed the bill; and his decree is here assigned as error.

KELLY & SMITH, for appellant.

SOMERVILLE, J.—In *Smith v. Cockrell*, 66 Ala. 64, it was held that a purchaser of land at a sheriff's sale, under execution against a debtor who has made a fraudulent conveyance of the legal title to his vendee, had a plain and adequate remedy at law by action of ejectment, and, for this reason, he can not, before recovery of possession, file a bill against the purchaser to cancel the fraudulent deed as a cloud on his title. I dissented from the conclusion reached by the majority of the court in that case, and have had no reason to change my opinion as then expressed, in support of which I might add other authorities if I were disposed to re-open the discussion.—*Sands v. Hildreth*, 14 John. Ch. 493; *Hildreth*

[Mobile & Girard R. R. Co. v. Ala. Midland R'y Co.]

r. Sands, 2 John. Ch. 36; *Leigh v. Everhart's Ex'r*, 4 T. B. Mon. 379; s. c., 16 Amer. Dec. 160. But *Smith v. Cockrell* has been uniformly and many times followed since it was decided, and the practice is now settled in accordance with that ruling; and for this reason I am now disposed to follow it. *Grigg v. Swindlall*, 67 Ala. 187; *Pettus v. Glover*, 68 Ala. 417; *Betts v. Nichols*, 84 Ala. 278.

On the authority of these cases, the bill in this case was properly dismissed, as being without equity.

Affirmed.

Mobile & Girard Railroad Co. *v.* Ala. Midland Railway Co.

Statutory Proceedings by Railroad Company, for Condemnation of Right of Way.

1. *Condemnation of right of way by railroad corporation; interference with franchise of older corporation; jurisdiction of Probate Court.* Under statutory provisions authorizing and regulating proceedings for the condemnation of a right of way by railroad corporations (Code, §§ 1580-82, 3207-18), construed in connection with the constitutional provision pertaining to the exercise of the right of eminent domain (Art. I, § 24), a railroad corporation organized under the general statutes, without a special legislative charter, may institute such proceedings for the purpose of condemning a part of the right of way of an older corporation, and the Probate Court has jurisdiction to make an order of condemnation; but the right of condemnation in such case, and the jurisdiction of the court, are subject to the limitations hereinafter stated.

2. *Same; limitations on right of condemnation.*—Under such statutory proceedings, the right of condemnation does not authorize an unnecessary interference with the free exercise of the franchise of the older corporation, nor extend to that part of its right of way which is in actual use, and the use of which is reasonably necessary to the safe and proper management of its business—not merely used to prevent another corporation from condemning it; and a reasonable necessity must be shown for the condemnation of any other part.

3. *Same; reasonable necessity, as determined by practicability of another route, cost, etc.*—A necessity, such as authorizes one railroad corporation to condemn a part of the right of way of another, does not mean an absolute and unconditional necessity as determined by physical causes, but a reasonable necessity under the circumstances of the particular case, dependent upon the practicability of another route, considered in connection with the relative cost to one and probable injury to the other; and the right of condemnation is not made out, unless the petitioning company shows that the cost of acquiring and constructing its road on any other route clearly outweighs the consequent damage which may result to the older company, not including the question of competition for the business of a manufacturing (or other large) establishment on the line of the proposed route.

APPEAL from the Probate Court of Pike.

Heard before the Hon. W. J. HILLIARD.

In the matter of the petition of the Alabama Midland Railroad Company, a corporation organized under the general statutes of the State, seeking to condemn a right of way for its road along and across the track of the Mobile & Girard Railroad Company, near and through the city of Troy in Pike county. The petition was contested by the Mobile & Girard Railroad Company, which was incorporated under a legislative charter granted on the 21st January, 1846; but it appeared that the road and franchises of said defendant corporation had been leased, for the term of ninety-nine years, to the Central Railroad & Banking Company of Georgia. The defendant corporation demurred to the petition, assigning as grounds of demurrer (with others), that the petitioner did not show any legal right to disturb or interefere with the franchises of the defendant corporation, and did not show that no other route than that proposed was practicable; and a motion was also submitted to dismiss the petition on these grounds. The court overruled the motion and the demurrers, and held that the petitioner was entitled to condemn a right of way as prayed. A jury was then impannelled to assess the defendant's damages, and exceptions were reserved by the defendant to several rulings of the court on questions of evidence; but these rulings require no notice. The appeal is sued out from the judgment of condemnation, and from the rulings of the court on the pleadings and evidence, which are here assigned as error.

NORMAN & SON, ROQUEMORE, WHITE & MCKENZIE, and JOHN PEABODY, for appellants.—(1.) While railroad corporations, like all others, under constitutional provisions, hold their property and franchises subject to the right of eminent domain, that right can only be exercised, to their detriment, by the General Assembly, which is the sole judge of the public interests involved which justify or require its exercise. Railroads incorporated under the general statutes are organized for purposes of private gain, having no element of public interest, except indirectly. They select their own *termini* and route, having knowledge of the routes of other existing corporations; and to allow them to seriously obstruct or interfere with the vested rights of other corporations, as their own private interests may dictate, would lodge a dangerous power in their hands. No such power has been given to them, and no jurisdiction has been conferred on the Probate Court.—1 Wood's Railway Law, § 229, note; Pierce on Railroads, 152; *A. & C. Railroad Co. v. J., G. & A. Railroad Co.*, 82 Ala. 297, 300; *Pilgreen v. L. & N. Railroad Co.*, 62 Ala. 305; *T. & C. Railroad Co. v. East Ala. Railway Co.*, 75 Ala. 517; 40 Amer. Rep. 743; 118 Mass. 391; 124 Mass. 368; 3 Eng. & Amer. R. R. Cases, 516, 522, and notes. (2.) If such power can be conferred on these corporations, or has been conferred by the general statutes, it can not extend to that part of the right of way of the older corporation which is in actual use, or which is reasonably necessary to the free exercise of its franchises; and a necessity must be clearly shown for the condemnation or invasion of any other part. Here, it is submitted, no necessity whatever was shown, unless a question of costs and expenses involves a legal necessity; and the order of condemnation includes a part of the appellant's right of way which is in actual use, and absolutely necessary for the free and full exercise of the franchises granted by a legislative charter.

A. A. WILEY, *contra.*—Under constitutional provisions, the property and franchises of corporations may be taken for public uses, "the same as individuals." The General Assembly may exercise the reserved right of eminent domain, by acting upon each particular case presented for its consideration, or may, as by general statutes it has done, delegate it to a court and jury, regulating the proceedings by law.—*E. & W. Railway Co. v. E. T., Va. & Ga. Railroad Co.*, 75 Ala. 284; *A. & F. Railroad Co. v. Kenney*, 39 Ala. 307; *Railroad Co. v. Ker*, 72 N. Y. 330; *R. & P. Railroad Co. v. Louisa Railroad Co.*, 13 How. 71; 24 Amer. Rep. 550; *A. & C. Railroad Co. v. J., G. & A. Railroad Co.*, 82 Ala. 301; *Cooper v. A. & A. Rallroad Co.*, 85 Ala. 108. The proceeding in this case followed the statute, and, it is believed, no error intervened.

CLOPTON, J.—This appeal is taken from a decree of the Probate Court of Pike county, condemning a part of the right of way of the Mobile & Girard Railroad Company, on proceedings instituted by appellee. The contest is between corporations, and involves the authority of a railroad company, incorporated under the general laws, to take, by condemnation proceedings, the property, or any part of another corporation, already devoted, by legislative authority, to a public use. The Mobile & Girard Railroad Company was incorporated in 1846, by an act of the General Assembly, and acquired the right of way condemned under authority conferred by the act of incorporation. The Alabama Midland Railway Company was organized under, and possesses the powers granted by the general laws provided for the incorporation of railroad companies. Importance attaches to the questions presented by the proceedings and order of condemnation brought for review, in view of the advancement of public improvements, and the development of the industrial and mineral resources of the State, so largely dependent on the railroads constructed and projected, which, passing at a period not remote through its entire territory, will, of necessity, intersect, run parallel to a greater or less extent, and concentrate at places, present and prospective railroad centers, where the ways of entrance may be restricted. But, however important in material aspects, their importance should not be permitted to obscure the necessity for the preservation of the rights of private property, of keeping persons or corporations, invested with the extraordinary power of dispossessing others of their property by an enforced sale, within the strict limits of the delegated authority. A relaxation of the rule against corporations would form a basis of subsequent departures in cases of individuals. Public and private interests require, that the line of authority shall be clearly and distinctly marked; and if deemed insufficient to meet the probable exigencies of the future, the remedy rests with the law-making power. What authority, and to what extent, shall be delegated, is a question for the legislature; what has been delegated, a question for the court.

Section 24 of the Declaration of Rights declares: "That the exercise of the right of eminent domain shall never be abridged, nor so construed as to prevent the General Assembly from taking the property and franchises of incorporated companies, and subjecting them to public use, the same as individuals. But private property shall not be taken or applied to public use, unless just compensation be first made therefor; nor shall private property be taken for private use, or for the use of corporations other than municipal, without the consent of the owner; *Provided, however*, that the General Assembly may, by law, secure to persons or corporations the right of way over the lands of other persons or corporations, and by general laws provide for and regulate the exercise by persons and corporations of the rights herein reserved; but just compensation shall, in all cases, be first made to the owner." The section does not profess to grant, but simply recognizes a right which existed prior to the constitution, as an incident of sovereignty; and is declaratory of the doctrine, that the property and franchises of corporations are held subject to the eminent domain, the same as the property of individuals. Its purpose is to reserve in the General Assembly, as the conservator of the public welfare, unabridged and unimpaired, the exercise of an existing right, and to prevent a construction discriminating in favor of corporations. The office of the proviso is to authorize the legislature, by delegating the power of condemnation or otherwise, to secure to persons or corporations the right of way over the lands of others, and to provide for and regulate, by general laws, the exercise of the right.

The government can not be coerced to grant the privilege of exercising this prerogative power to any citizen, company or corporation. It is only granted when the public welfare will be promoted or conserved by the grant. It can not be exercised or granted in aid of any interest that is not public; and when part of this sovereign power is granted to a railroad corporation, it is not solely, nor chiefly, that the corporation may be aided thereby. It is alone for the actual or supposed benefit to the public, that this grant is, or can be made. True, the railroad corporation may, and probably will be, benefitted by the grant. If it were not for this prospective profit, such stupendous enterprises would not by undertaken. It is on these reciprocal benefits and burdens that the whole theory of the inviolability of corporate franchises rests. The use to the public is increased facility of travel and transportation. This is the public use, which arms the sovereignty with the power to grant. The labor and expense incident to the construction of the railroad, are the consideration on which, independent of constitutional or statutory provisions, the franchise has been adjudged to be irrevocable.

But the power of eminent domain is not exhausted by any grant it may make, though accepted and acted on. Being granted for the public welfare, it may be revoked or modified, whenever the public good requires it. The public good being the pole-star, whenever that object or *desideratum* will be best accomplished by retaking or withdrawing the whole, or a part of the franchise granted, the sovereignty will not stay its hand, but will again assert itself, if the public welfare demand it. To that grand aim of all good government, all mere private enterprises, or exclusive channels of commerce, must yield.

The power of the General Assembly to take the property and franchises of incorporated companies, and to apply them to another public use deemed more important, upon just compensation being first made, is conceded. Appellant's contention is, that the authority has not been delegated to railroad companies organized under the general laws, and that jurisdiction to condemn such property and franchises has not been conferred upon the Probate Court. The contention brings for construction the general laws, which should be construed in the light of well settled rules. A delegated power to take private property for public use can be exercised only so far as the authority extends, either in express terms, or by clear implication. Statutes delegating the paramount right of eminent domain must be strictly construed, and the authority strictly pursued in the manner prescribed. They are not to be extended by implication further than is necessary to accomplish their general purpose; but not so literally construed as to defeat the manifest objects of the legislature. *Matter of City of Buffalo*, 68 N. Y. 167; Mills' Em. Domain, § 46; 1 Wood's Railway Law, § 224.

The authority of the appellee to take the portions of the right of way of appellants condemned, is claimed under section 1580 of Code 1886, which confers on railroad companies incorporated under the general laws power to acquire and hold, by gift or purchase, or in payment of subscriptions for stock, or by condemnation in the mode prescribed by law, such lands as may be necessary for a way and right of way, not exceeding one hundred feet in width throughout the entire length of the road. Sections 3207 to 3218, inclusive, prescribe the mode of condemnation. The jurisdiction of the Probate Court is claimed under section 3207, which provides: "Any corporation organized under the laws of the State, or any person or association of persons, proposing to take lands, or to acquire an interest or easement therein, for any uses for which private property may be taken, may, if there be no other mode of proceeding prescribed by law, apply to the court of probate of the county in which such lands, or a material portion thereof, may be situate, for an order of condemnation thereof for such uses." By express terms, the statutes give authority to acquire by condemnation proceedings only those kinds of property, which are included in the comprehensive and generic term, *land*. The term is used in the constitution and the statutes in its broad signification, and comprehends the right of way of a railroad corporation. As a general proposition, it may be said, that railroad companies, organized under the general laws, are authorized by the statutes to acquire by condemnation the right of way of another corporation, when essential to the accomplishment of their principal purposes, or when there is space for the tracks of parallel roads without obstructing the use of the same. The statutes have been so construed, and to that construction we adhere.—*Annis. & Cin. R. R. Co. v, Jacksonville, G. & A. R. R. Co.*, 82 Ala. 297; *East & West R. R. Co. v. E. T., Va. & Ga. R. R. Co.*, 75 Ala. 275.

The general terms, on which the authority is granted, are qualified and limited by the operation and intervention of other controlling principles. There must be no material interference, or obstruction of the free and reasonably necessary use by the company, whose right of way is taken, of the franchise to which it is subject. In *Matter of City of Buffalo, supra*, Folger, J., says: "In determining whether a power generally given is meant to have operation upon lands already devoted by legislative authority to a public purpose, it is proper to consider the nature of the prior public work, the public use to which it is applied, the extent to which that use would be impaired or diminished by the taking of such part of the land as may be demanded for the subsequent public use. If both uses may not stand together, with some tolerable interference, which may be compensated by damages paid; if the latter use, when exercised, must supersede the former, it is not to be implied from a general power given, without having in view a then existing and particular need therefor, that the legislature meant to subject lands devoted to a public use already in exercise, to one which might thereafter arise. A legislative intent, that there should be such an effect, will not be inferred from a gift of power in general terms."

The settled rule is, that the legislative intent to grant authority to one railroad to take and condemn a franchise of another must appear in express terms, or must arise from necessary implication, founded on an existing and particular need. No room for doubt or uncertainty must be left. Should the General Assembly empower a company to construct a railroad between designated and fixed terminal

points, and, to accomplish this object, it becomes necessary
to take the franchises, or any part, of another corporation,
power to do so arises from necessary implication; the presumption being that the legislature deemed the later use the
more important, and of greater public benefit. The implication rests on the general rule, that the grant of power to
do a particular thing of a public nature carries with it implied authority to do all that is necessary to accomplish the
principal and general purpose. Whether such implication
arises in favor of railroad companies incorporated under the
general laws, the corporators themselves, and not the legislature, fixing the terminal points, it is unnecessary to decide.
If the purposes for which the Alabama Midland Railway
Company was incorporated, can be reasonably accomplished,
and every power granted in the general terms of the statutes
can be exercised, without materially impairing the usefulness
of the right of way condemned as a franchise, implication of
authority does not necessarily result. The statutes above
referred to confer all the authority to take private property,
whether of persons or corporations, that exists in railroad
companies organized under the general laws. Authority to
take the franchise, or any part, of another corporation, is not
given in express terms, except so far as necessary to cross
or intersect another railroad, and, if not necessarily implied,
it does not exist.—*Matter of Bos. & Al. R. R. Co.*, 53 N. Y.
574; *M. & St. P. Railway Co. v. Faribault*, 23 Minn. 167.

A franchise to acquire, hold and use land for a right of
way, is in its very nature exclusive, that the privileges and
powers granted in respect to its use may be fully exercised.
Dispossession of property, subject to the use of a franchise
and in actual use, is, to all intents, deprivation of the right
to exercise the franchise as to such property—tatamount, in
its legal effect, to the taking of the franchise *pro tanto.* We
adopt the rule as stated 1 Wood's Railway Law, § 229:
"One public corporation can not take the lands or franchises of another public corporation *in actual use by it*,
unless expressly authorized to do so by the legislature; but
the lands of such a corporation, not in actual use, may be
taken by another corporation authorized to take lands for its
use *in invitum*, whenever the lands of an individual may be
taken, subject to the qualification, that there is a necessity
therefor"; with the modificatiou, in order to avoid misunder-
standing, that the authority may be implied in a proper case,
and the use must be reasonably requisite to the free exercise

of the franchise—not for the mere purpose to prevent the exercise of the right of eminent domain. This rule furnishes the boundary of the delegated authority to take; which is *actual* use of the property by the adversary corporation, and the reasonable necessity of its use to the safe, proper and convenient management of the corporate business, and the accomplishment of the purposes of its creation. Taking the property must not materially diminish or impair the usefulness of a franchise in exercise. As a general rule, a corporation to whom the right of eminent domain is delegated, having the right to locate the line of its road between the terminal points, has also the correlative right, to some extent, to select the lands to be taken. But the discretion must be reasonably exercised, so as to cause as little damage as is practicable; and if abuse in the selection is made apparent, the court, before whom the proceeding is pending, should interfere to control the discretion, and prevent the abuse by refusing an order of condemnation.—*N. Y. Cent. & H. R. R. R. Co. v. M. G. L. Co.*, 63 N. Y. 326; 6 Amer. & Eng. Encyc. Law, 541.

According to the rule stated above, the liability of any portion of the right of way of the Mobile & Girard Railroad Company, though not in actual use, to condemnation for the use of the Alabama Midland Railway Company, is subject to the qualification of a necessity therefor. It would be difficult to lay down any specific rule as to the measure of the necessity, of sufficient scope to include all cases. It may be observed generally, that *necessary*, in this connection, does not mean an absolute or indispensable necessity, but reasonably requisite and proper for the accomplishment of the end in view under the particular circumstances of the case. On the evidence, there is little room for doubt, that the route selected by the Alabama Midland Railway Company to get into the city of Troy, and out to the west, is the most practicable, if not in its proper sense the only practicable route. The contention arises at the point where the line selected enters the right of way of the Mobile & Girard Railroad Company near the corporate limits of the city. To go out of Troy by the proposed route, it is necessary to cross the road-bed of the latter company from the west to the east side, either at the point now proposed, or at a point designated on the map as section 27, or near thereto. The real controversy is, whether the Alabama Midland Railway Company shall locate its road on the west or on the east side of

the Mobile & Girard Railroad. The controversy arises on
the facts, that no part of the right of way on the west side is
in actual use; while on the east side, there is a side track
running from the main track to the Troy Fertilizer Works,
situated on the east line of the right of way.   The road of
the Alabama Midland Railway Company, if located on the
east side, would cross this track diagonally, which is in daily
use.   By an amendment of the petition, and by the order of
the court, this side track is excepted from condemnation, but
the condemnation extends up to the track on each side. Under
these circumstances, it is incumbent on the applicant to show
a necessity for the location of its road over the right of way
on the east side; that is, that the route on the west side is
not practicable under the rules we proceed to state.

When the cost of right of way, the labor and expense of
constructing a road-bed so as to be convenient and safe, and
the completion of the road on a particular line of survey, are
not disproportioned to the benefit likely to accrue; then the
route is practicable. In electing between two or more routes,
regarded practicable, expensiveness of acquisition and construction, and interference with, or obstruction to other rights
of property or franchises, must be taken into consideration.
If the advantages to the petitioner for the condemnation of
one route over another practicable route (the public welfare
being in equipoise), do not clearly outweigh the antagonistic
rights and interests it proposes to invade; then the right of
condemnation is not made out, and condemnation should be
withheld.   So far as the element of expensiveness may enter
into the consideration as to the practicability of the route on
the west side of the Mobile & Girard Railroad, the rule for
this case may be stated as follows: If the cost of construction on the west side, with the attendant circumstances, is so
much greater than on the east side as to clearly outweigh
and sensibly exceed the injury. which would proximately result to the Mobile & Girard Railroad Company from crossing the side track alluded to (the question of competition
for the business of the Fertilizer Works being eliminated
from the consideration), then it would be proper to condemn
the right of way on the east side. in the manner sought by
the petition as last amended; if otherwise, condemnation
should be withheld, unless the route on the west side is
shown to be impracticable on account of other considerations.   This rule of election applies specially to cases in
which one corporation seeks to acquire and occupy a part of

the right of way, or other franchise, of another corporation of older organization.

The evidence set forth in the record does not show the impracticability of the route on the west side, under the rules we have stated. Under the circumstances of this case, the inquiry should be specially directed to the question of expensiveness, and the safety and practicability of the necessary crossings to pass from the west to the east side. Under these rules, the order of condemnation is reversed, and case remanded, that the controverted question may be retried on the petition as it now stands, and further proof adduced as to the impracticability of the route on the west side, in respect to the elements of consideration herein suggested: or the applicant may amend the petition, if deemed advisable.

Reversed and remanded.

Knox *v.* Armistead.

Bill in Equity by Mortgagor, for Redemption.

1. *Purchase by mortgagee, at sale under power.*—When a mortgage contains an express provision authorizing the mortgagee to purchase at a sale under the power, and he does become the purchaser, the mortgagor can not disaffirm the sale, and be allowed to redeem, except upon the allegation and proof of facts which would invalidate it if a third person had become the purchaser.

APPEAL from the Chancery Court of Montgomery.

Heard before the Hon. JOHN A. FOSTER.

The bill in this case was filed on the 10th October, 1887, by Edward N. Knox, against William B. Armistead and Elliott S. Armistead; and sought to set aside a sale of land under a power in a mortgage, which the complainant and his wife had executed to the defendants as partners doing business under the name of W. B. Armistead & Son, and to redeem. The sale under the mortgage was made on the 28th December, 1885, said E. S. Armistead becoming the purchaser; and the complainant claimed that his equity of redemption was not thereby cut off. The chancellor dismissed the bill, on demurrer and motion, for want of equity; and his decree is now assigned as error.

R. M. WILLIAMSON, for appellant.

SAYRE, STRINGFELLOW & LEGRAND, *contra*, cited Jones on
Mortgages, §§ 1883, 1876; Jones on Chat. Mortgages, § 806;
Boone on Mortgages, § 220; 3 Pom. Equity, p. 171, § 1193;
Tied. Real Property. § 365; Story's Equity, 12th ed., § 1027,
note 3; 2 Perry on Trusts, § 602; *Elliott v. Wood*, 45 N. Y.
71; s. c., 53 Barb. 285; *Hall v. Bliss*, 118 Mass. 554; *Dexter v. Shepherd*, 117 Mass. 480; *Montague v. Dawes*, 14 Allen, 369; *Robinson v. Amateur Asso.*, 14 S. C. 148; *Ramsay
v. Merriam*, 6 Minn. 168; 52 Ill. 130; 6 Texas, 174;
50 Texas, 203.

McCLELLAN, J.—On March 20, 1885, the appellant—
being joined therein by his wife, Daisy Knox—executed to
the appellees a mortgage on certain lands to secure them
against a contingent liability, which they had assumed as
accommodation acceptors for him.

The mortgage contained a power of sale and an authorization to the mortgagees to purchase at any sale that should
be had thereunder, in the following words: "In the event
of said sale, the said W. B. Armistead & Son, or either of
them, their heirs, assigns, agents or attorneys are authorized
and empowered to purchase said property the same in all
respects as if they were strangers to this conveyance. And
should they so purchase said property, the auctioneer making
said sale is hereby directed and empowered to make and execute a deed to them for the same. And we do covenant
with the said W. B. Armistead & Son, that we will forever
warrant and defend the title so made against the lawful
claims and demands of all persons." The mortgagees,
having had to pay their acceptance, sold the land under and
in conformity with the mortgage, and, as alleged in the bill,
Elliott Armistead, one of the firm of W. B. Armistead & Son,
became the purchaser, and with the said W. B. took, and
has since held, possession of said land. The bill filed by
E. N. Knox, relying on the naked facts above stated, and
without in any manner, or with respect to any matter connected directly or indirectly with the transaction, imputing
fraud or unfairness, or bad faith, or oppression, or inadequacy
of price, or a failure to comply with the terms of the instrument, "disavows said sale as an execution of the mortgage,"
and seeks to redeem the land from the mortgagee upon such
terms as to the court may seem just. There was a demurrer

[Knox v. Armistead.]

to, and a motion to dismiss the bill for want of equity. The demurrer was sustained, the bill dismissed, and the decree of the Chancery Court to that end is here assigned as error.

It is well settled in this State, in consonance with the general doctrine elsewhere, that where a mortgagee purchases at a sale made under a power to that end contained in the mortgage, the instrument not authorizing the mortgagee to become the purchaser, he thereby "arms the mortgagor with the option, if expressed in a reasonable time, of affirming or disaffirming the sale, and this without reference to the fairness of the sale, or the fullness of the price." *Garland v. Watson*, 74 Ala. 324; *Harris v. Miller*, 71 Ala. 26; *Ezzell v. Watson*, 83 Ala. 120.

Such sales, it is manifest, are not absolutely void, but voidable only at the election of the mortgagor. Doubtless he might effectually ratify the sale immediately after its consummation, so at least as to put on him the *onus* of affirmative impeachment of its fairness in any subsequent attack he might make upon it. It is axiomatic, that an act which may be ratified is *in limine* capable of authorization. The point appears never to have been passed on in this court, but all the text-writers and adjudications of other courts, while maintaining in its severest integrity the doctrine of the cases cited above, are equally pronounced in the assertion of the correlative principle, that the mortgage may expressly confer the power and authority to purchase upon the mortgagee, and his exercise of that power in good faith will not vitiate the sale.—Perry on Trusts, § 625; Tiedeman Real Prop. p. 290, § 365; 2 Story Eq. Jur. § 1027, n. 3; 2 Jones on Mortg. § 1883; *Elliott v. Wood*, 45 N. Y. 71; *Hall v. Bliss*, 118 Mass. 554; *Robinson v. Amateur Asso.*, 14 S.C. 148.

Mortgagors are allowed to redeem from a mortgagee who has purchased under a power which did not authorize him to do so, on the theory, that there has been no sale made— no valid execution of the power. It would be to the last degree anomalous to allow that theory to obtain with respect to a sale and purchase made in strict harmony with the terms of the instrument, and in strict compliance with an authorization which all the cases concur in holding the mortgagor was fully competent to make and bind himself by. To so hold would be to render nugatory an important stipulation of the contract, entirely within the competency of the parties to enter into, and not offensive to any principle of law.—Perry on Trusts, p. 166, § 602y; *Doolittle v. Lewis*, 7 Johns. Ch. 45.

33

The true rule, we apprehend, is stated in Jones on Mortgages to be, that the court will not interfere with a purchase by a mortgagee under such a provision, unless there be some other objection, which would generally invalidate a purchase by any one else under the same circumstances.—2 Jones on Mortg. p. 730, § 1883.

The effect of such authorization is, at least, to waive the mortgagor's right to treat the trust as continuing, and to redeem from the purchasing mortgagee, without reference to the fairness of the sale, and to put upon him the *onus* of impeaching the transaction by appropriate allegation sustained by that measure of proof which is ordinarily essential to support affirmative averments. The bill in this case is devoid of such allegations, as we have seen; and the demurrer to it for want of equity was properly sustained.

Affirmed.

Cobb *v.* Malone & Collins.

Action for Damages for Conversion of Crop, by Mortgagee against Purchaser with Notice.

1. *Accord and satisfaction; novation.*—If the mortgagor of personal property, having sold to a third person a part of the mortgaged property, afterwards executes another mortgage on other property, which is accepted by the mortgagee "in settlement of said matter for" the property so sold, or is so accepted by his agent, whose act is afterwards ratified by him, this constitutes a valid substitutionary contract, healing the breach of the first, and is available to the purchaser as a defense to a subsequent action for the alleged conversion of the property sold to him.

APPEAL from the Circuit Court of Geneva.

Tried before the Hon. JESSE M. CARMICHAEL.

This action was brought by A. A. Cobb, against Malone & Collins as partners, to recover special damages for an alleged conversion by defendants of a bale of cotton, on which plaintiff claimed a lien under a mortgage for advances, of which lien he alleged that the defendants had notice when they received and sold the bale of cotton; and was commenced on the 6th October, 1887. The case was tried on issue joined on the plea of not guilty, and resulted in a verdict for the defendants. On the trial, as the bill of excep-

tions shows, the plaintiff read in evidence, without objection,
the mortgage under which he claimed the bale of cotton;
which was executed by one C. D. Crutchfield, was dated
February, 1887, and given to secure a debt of $50 for ad-
vances to make a crop, with such additional advances as
might be made during the year; and it conveyed the mortgagor's entire crop for the year, with one horse, plantation
implements, &c., the law-day being October 1st. The mortgage was duly filed for record on March 4th, 1887. "The
testimony of the plaintiff, in his own behalf, tended to show
that, at the time of the trial, said Crutchfield was indebted
to him, for advances made under said mortgage, in the sum
of $125, having paid him on the same one bale of cotton
and 1,200 lbs. of seed-cotton, of the value of $75; that the
defendants admitted, prior to the bringing of this suit, that
they had received from said Crutchfield the bale of cotton
sued for; and that the highest market value of the cotton
since September 13th, 1887, the date of the alleged conversion, was 9½ cents per pound. Said plaintiff was asked by
defendants, on cross-examination, if Crutchfield did not, in
May, 1887, execute to him another mortgage, to secure an
amount over and above the $50 mentioned in said former
mortgage; and answered, that said Crutchfield did, in May,
1887, execute to him another mortgage for a larger amount."
The plaintiff objected to this question and answer each, and
duly excepted to the overruling of his objections.

"The plaintiff next introduced said Crutchfield as a witness, who testified, in substance, that he sold to defendants
the bale of cotton in controversy some time in the Fall of
1887, and that it was covered by plaintiff's mortgage. The
cross-examination of said witness tended to show, that an
agreement was had between him and one Douglas Cobb,
plaintiff's clerk, to the effect that, if he (Crutchfield) would
execute to plaintiff another mortgage, covering a yoke of
oxen, a wagon, and his entire crop for the year 1887, with
all rents coming to him, and all other stock owned by
him at that time, plaintiff would dismiss his suit; that this
was in settlement of said matter of the bale of cotton involved in this suit, and that plaintiff agreed to dismiss his
suit; and that a mortgage was made in September, 1887,
pursuant to this agreement. The plaintiff objected to the
introduction of this evidence, and excepted to its admission.
The evidence tended to show, also, that plaintiff was absent
at the time said agreement was made, and that said clerk had

no authority to make it; and further, that plaintiff, on his
return, took said mortgage, and had it recorded in the office
of the judge of probate, and still holds and claims it.   The
evidence for plaintiff further tended to show, that said agreement between his clerk and Crutchfield was, that if Crutchfield would execute a new mortgage to plaintiff, and pay the
same in two weeks, plaintiff would dismiss his suit against
the defendants in this case, and that plaintiff sent letter in
relation to the matter.   Crutchfield denied that he was to
pay said new mortgage in two weeks; and defendants then,
in connection with the evidence of said Crutchfield, read in
evidence a record copy of said mortgage of September, 1887;"
which mortgage was dated September 23d, 1887, purported
to secure an indebtedness of $75 for advances to make a crop,
and the law-day of it was October 1st.   The plaintiff objected and excepted to the admission of said mortgage as
evidence.

The rulings of the court on the evidence, as above stated,
are the only matters assigned as error.

M. E. MILLIGAN, and J. F. MILLIGAN, for appellant.

STONE, C. J.—The record before us contains a meagre
presentation of the facts, and fails to affirm it contains all
the evidence.   In such case, it is our duty to indulge every
reasonable intendment in favor of the correct ruling of the
trial court, which is compatible with the averments and recitals found in the record.   Error can not be presumed, but
must be affirmatively shown.—3 Brick. Dig. 406, § 40.

One of the grounds, if not the main ground of defense in
this case, was, that after Crutchfield had sold to Malone &
Collins the bale of cotton on which Cobb had a mortgage
lien, Crutchfield executed a second mortgage to Cobb, conveying additional property, on an agreement that the giving
of this additional security "was in settlement of said matter
of the bale of cotton involved in this suit."   This was the
testimony of Crutchfield; and that pursuant to it he gave
the second mortgage, which was put in evidence.   True,
there was conflict in the testimony, and plaintiff's proof negatived the extent of the agreement; and there was also a
denial of the authority of the agent to make the alleged
agreement.   There was, however, some testimony tending to
show Cobb's ratification of the agreement.—3 Brick. Dig.

20, §§ 17, 19, 20.   Each of these matters of controversy was a question for the jury.—*Carew v. Lillienthall*, 50 Ala. 44.

All the testimony objected to, tended to prove the defense alluded to above.   It was not so entirely insufficient in any of its bearings, as to call for its rejection as matter of law.   Whether it authorized the finding of all the facts necessary to the verdict rendered, could have been raised on proper charges requested.   It is not shown that charges were given or requested, and we must presume that the trial court gave proper instructions.—3 Brick. Dig. 406, § 43.

If the jury believed the testimony of Crutchfield, and further found that Cobb either authorized, or with knowledge ratified the act of his agent, then the second security was a sufficient consideration for the surrender of his lien on the bale of cotton, and constituted the second a valid, substitutionary contract, healing the breach of the first.   The second mortgage bears date in September, 1887, and the present suit was brought afterwards.

Affirmed.

Miller *v.* Lehman, Durr & CO.

Creditor's Bill in Equity to set aside Fraudulent Conveyance.

1.   *When creditor without lien may come into equity.*—Under statutory provisions (Code, § 3544), a bill filed by a creditor without a lien, seeking to set aside a fraudulent conveyance by his debtor, alleging the existence, amount and consideration of his debt, the insolvency of his debtor, a conveyance by the debtor to his brothers, without valuable consideration, or on a simulated consideration, in secret trust for the debtor himself, and with the intent to hinder, delay and defraud his creditors, of which fraudulent intent it is alleged the grantees had knowledge, is not wanting in equity.

2.   *Receiver; appointment by register in vacation; how reviewed.*—Under statutory provisions regulating the appointment of receivers (Code, §§ 3515, 3614), an appeal lies to the chancellor, from an order of the register appointing a receiver in vacation, and an appeal to this court, from the chancellor's order confirming the appointment; but, if the defendant, not having taken an appeal from the appointment by the register, afterwards submits to the chancellor a motion to vacate the order, which motion is heard and overruled at the same time with a motion to dismiss the bill for want of equity, that ruling can not be revised on appeal from the refusal to dismiss the bill.

[Miller v. Lehman, Durr & Co.]

APPEAL from the Chancery Court of Lowndes.

Heard before the Hon. JOHN A. FOSTER.

The bill in this case was filed on the 12th November, 1888, by Lehman, Durr & Co. and Aaron Richards, as creditors of Charles L. Miller, against him and his two brothers, J. E. Miller and F. B. Miller; and sought to set aside, on the ground of fraud, a conveyance of a stock of goods and other property, executed by said C. L. Miller to his brothers on the 8th November, 1888, and to subject the property to the satisfaction of the complainants' debts. Attached to the bill was a petition, addressed to the register, asking the appointment of a receiver to take charge of the goods and property conveyed; and a receiver was at once appointed. After answer filed, the defendants submitted a motion "to vacate the order appointing the receiver," and also to dismiss the bill for want of equity; and these two motions, being argued and submitted to the chancellor at the same time, were both overruled; but he further held that there was a misjoinder of complainants (*McKenzie v. M. & F. Railway Co.*, 85 Ala. 546), and gave the complainant's leave to amend. The appeal is taken from the order overruling the motion to dismiss the bill for want of equity, and errors are also assigned on the refusal to vacate the order for the appointment of a receiver; which latter assignments of error the appellees moved to strike out.

RICE & WILEY, and R. M. WILLIAMSON, for appellants.

WATTS & SON, and TOMPKINS & TROY, *contra*.

SOMERVILLE, J.—The motion to dismiss the bill for want of equity clearly had no merit, and was properly overruled. The bill distinctly alleges the existence of a debt due by the defendant, C. L. Miller, to the complainants, and its amount, with the consideration upon which it is based. It further avers the insolvency of said Miller, and the transfer by him of a stock of goods, and other property, to his co-defendants, who are his brothers, and that this transfer was made without any valuable consideration, or on a mere simulated consideration, in secret trust for the benefit of the grantor, and with intent to hinder, delay and defraud the complainants, and other creditors of the grantor; and that the grantees in this conveyance knew of the fraudulent motives of the grantor in making the transfer. This was man-

[Miller v. Lehman, Durr & Co.]

ifestly sufficient in every particular, and fully justified the
prayer of the bill.

The other assignments of error are based on the refusal
of the chancellor to sustain the motion of the defendants to
vacate the order appointing a receiver in the cause. A motion is made in this court to strike these assignments from
the record, as unauthorized in the present *status* of the
cause. This motion must, in our judgment, be sustained.
The receiver was appointed by the register in chancery,
under the authority conferred on him by the statute. If the
defendants were dissatisfied with the appointment, they had
the right to appeal from the action of the register, to the
chancellor, and have it reviewed before him; and, in the
meanwhile, to have the order suspended, upon giving bond
with sufficient sureties.—Code, 1886, § 3535. And if the
chancellor confirmed the appointment, an appeal would lie to
this court, within thirty days from the filing of the order
with the register, to be tried as a preferred case, and as an
appeal specially authorized by statute from an interlocutory
order.—Code, § 3614. By neglecting to pursue this course,
the defendants waived their right to review, in the mode
now attempted, the regularity and propriety of the appointment, under color of a motion to vacate the order. The
rule is well settled, that the appointment and removal of
receivers are matters which rest in the discretion of the
Chancery Court; and the appellate court will not, on appeal,
undertake to review or control the exercise of this discretionary power, except so far as it may be authorized to do so
by statute. And the statutes of this State give no right of
appeal from the refusal of a court of chancery to *vacate* an
order appointing a receiver, which, as we have said, is purely
interlocutory in its nature.—Beach on Receivers, § 781;
Connolly v. Kretz, 78 N. Y. 620; *Seney v. New York Stage
Co.*, 28 How. Prac. 481; *Mansony v. U. S. Bank*, 4 Ala. 735;
Kerr on Receivers, 139-140, note 1; Code, 1886, §§ 3611,
et seq.

The motion to strike is sustained, and the judgment
affirmed.

Mobile & Girard Railroad Co. *v.* Ala. Midland Railway Co.

Bill in Equity between Railroad Corporations, for Injunction against Statutory Proceedings for Condemnation of Right of Way.

1. *Statutory proceedings for condemnation of right of way between railroad companies; injunction against.*—A court of equity will not interfere by injunction, at the suit of one railroad company, to prevent or restrain statutory proceedings by another for the condemnation of a part of its right of way, pending an appeal from the judgment of condemnation; since the appeal is an adequate remedy for the correction of errors and irregularities in the proceedings, if only irregular and erroneous, and the defendant is a trespasser if they are void; and the prosecution of the work by the defendant pending the appeal, having paid the assessed damages into court, does not add equity to the bill.

2. *Same; payment of assessed damages into court.*—Under former statutory provisions, the petitioning railroad company, on paying into court the assessed damages, or condemnation money, was authorized to proceed with its work pending an appeal from the judgment of condemnation (Code, 1876, § 3593); but this statutory provision is not now of force, and the payment of the money into court, pending the appeal, is not authorized, and has no effect on the rights of the parties.

3. *Same; how far one railroad company may condemn part of another's right of way.*—Under statutory proceedings for the condemnation of a right of way by a railroad company (Code, §§ 3207–18), a part of the road-bed of another railroad can not be condemned, including a sufficient space on each side for the safe passage of trains; but the road-bed does not include all the space covered by necessary embankments and excavations.

APPEAL from the Chancery Court of Pike.

Heard before the Hon. JOHN A. FOSTER.

The bill in this case was filed on the 19th April, 1889, by the Mobile & Girard Railroad Company, and its lessee, the Central Railroad & Banking Company of Georgia, against the Alabama Midland Railroad Company, a corporation organized under the general statutes of Alabama; and sought to enjoin and restrain the defendant from further obstruction or interference with the right of way and franchises of said Mobile & Girard Railroad Company, and from the further prosecution of its work under the judgment of condemnation rendered by the Probate Court of Pike county, under statutory proceedings instituted for that purpose. The proceedings referred to are those shown by the report of the

[Mobile & Girard R. R. Co v. Ala. Midland R'y Co.]

case between the same parties, *ante*, p. 501. The bill set out all the proceedings had inthat case, stating the grounds of demurrer filed to the petition, the rulings of the court thereon, and judgment of condemnation; and further alleged that the complainant had taken an appeal to this court from that judgment, and that the defendant, notwithstanding the appeal, had entered on complainant's right of way under said judgment, having paid the assessed damages to the probate judge, and had a large force employed in grading the same for its own purposes. The chancellor held that the bill contained equity, but dissolved the injunction on the denials of the answer; and the complainant appeals, assigning as error the decree dissolving the injunction.

ROQUEMORE, WHITE & McKENZIE, NORMAN & SON, and JOHN PEABODY, for appellant.—The bill is filed on the theory, that a court of equity will interfere by injunction to restrain corporations, invested with the right of taking private property by compulsory measures, from possessing themselves of property by such measures except in strict conformity to law—to keep them within the limits of their authority, and to enforce obedience to the constitution. *E. & W. Ala. Railroad Co. v. E. T., Va. & Ga. Railroad Co.*, 75 Ala. 275; Kerr on Inj., § 622; 15 Md. 199; 1 Bald. 205; 24 Penn. St. 159; 4 N. J. Eq. 57. There is now no statute of force authorizing the prosecution of the work pending an appeal, on paying the condemnation money into court; yet the defendant in this case is doing so, and the complainant is without remedy to prevent it except by injunction.—13 Kan. 514; 18 Kan. 331; 47 Ala. 609.

A. A. WILEY, *contra.*—The bill does not show a case of irreparable injury, and is utterly wanting in equity. If its allegations are true, the defendant is simply a trespasser, and an action at law is an adequate remedy. A void judgment can not cast a cloud on the title, and does not give a court of equity jurisdiction.—*Ewing v. St. Louis*, 5 Wall. 418; *Secombe v. Railroad Co.*, 23 Wall. 108; 82 Ala. 301; *Cooper v. Railroad Co.*, 85 Ala. 109; *Murphree v. Bishop*, 79 Ala. 404; *W. U. Tel. Co. v. Judkins*, 75 Ala. 428; High on Inj., § 629; *Boulo v. Railroad Co.*, 55 Ala. 480; *Glass v. Glass*, 76 Ala. 368. If the proceedings are only irregular, or erroneous, an appeal is the proper and only remedy to correct them.

CLOPTON, J.—Every question raised by the present bill is purely a legal question, and, according to the averments of the bill, an appeal to this court was pending, which was intended to bring, and did bring, each of these questions before us for review. The case of *Cooper v. Anniston & Atlantic R. R. Co.*, 85 Ala. 106, was very like the present one, except that in that case it was charged that the defendant railroad company was insolvent. That charge is not made in this case. We pronounced that bill wanting in equity, and for a stronger reason, if possible, the present bill is without merit. The injunction was rightly dissolved, for want of equity in the bill.—*A. & C. R. R. Co. v. G. & A. R. R. Co.*, 82 Ala. 297.

The case of *Cooper v. A. & A. R. R. Co.*, *supra*, arose under our former statute, Code of 1876, § 3593. That section provided, that "No appeal shall, during the pendency of it, prevent or hinder the petitioner from occupying the lands involved therein, and proceeding to work thereon"; with a proviso, or condition, which was complied with in this case. The Code provision, copied above, is not found in the Code of 1886. In the absence of that statutory provision, paying or depositing the condemnation money does not authorize the petitioner, while the appeal is pending, to occupy the land, or work upon it. The acts, then, charged against the Midland Railway Company, and complained of, are a naked trespass on the possession and right of the Mobile & Girard Railroad Company, with no facts averred tending to show that the injury inflicted, or threatened, would work an irreparable injury. Of such trespass equity has no juridiction.—*Boulo v. Railroad*, 55 Ala. 480.

The complainants, in their bill, show sufficient title and possession to maintain an action at law.—*T. & C. R. R. Co. v. E. A. Railway Co.*, 75 Ala. 516.

In the case of *Anniston & Cin. R. R. Co. v. Jacksonville & A. R. R. Co.*, 82 Ala. 297, we said: "The Probate Court has no jurisdiction to condemn the road-bed of one incorporated railroad company, for the use of another." What is meant by the term "road-bed", is fully shown in the opinion. Speaking of Davis' Gap, the subject of contention in that case, our language was: "It is no where shown that the respondent railroad company can not obtain room for its track over complainant's right of way, without obstructing complainant's free and ample use of the same. If such is the case, the Probate Court has jurisdiction to condemn so much thereof as is necessary for defendant's road-bed." Road-bed is here used as the synonym of the road's track—the track in use, or intended to be used, on which to operate its trains—and must include a sufficient space on either side, to allow trains to pass each other in safety. It was used in the same sense in *E. & W. R. R. Co. v. E. T., Va. & Ga. R. R. Co.*, 75 Ala. 275, 282. It was not intended to include, necessarily, the whole embankment which supports the track; for that, in cases of high embankments, would be required to be very broad at the base, to furnish the requisite lateral support. The real intention was, that the track or tracks of one railroad that were in use, together with sufficient space for their safe use, could not be condemned by another railroad company for its use; or, what is the same thing, that that part of a railroad company's right of way which was in actual use, and necessary for such actual use, could not be taken from it, and given to another railroad company, thus destroying. or greatly obstructing, all that was useful in one corporate franchise, and vesting it in another corporation. The legislature had not conferred this power and jurisdiction, we said.   On the other hand, if a second condemnation can be so carved out of a right of way previously granted to another railroad company, as to leave the latter's track without such hindrance or obstruction as to render its use unsafe, or materially obstructed, then the Probate Court has jurisdiction to order the condemnation, and the Chancery Court is without jurisdiction to interfere with it.   And in condemning a part of the right of way of an older corporation, previous excavations or embankments do not, as such, enter into the question of jurisdiction.   That is not the road-bed or track (we use them convertibly) which the legislature has given no power to take.   The inquiry is, whether the new condemnation can be made, without destroying the use and usefulness of that part of the first acquired right of way which is in actual use, or so obstructing, hindering or embarrassing it as to render it unsafe.   So long as there is no attempt to appropriate or destroy that part of another corporation's right of way which is in actual use. or to so obstruct or impair it as to render it unsafe, or to materially embarrass its use, the jurisdiction of the Probate Court is ample, and, in the first instance, exclusive.

We have not given the authorities which support our views.   They are cited in our own decisions referred to in this opinion.

[Cary v. Simmons.]

Provision is made in Art. XIV, § 21, of our constitution, securing to a railroad corporation the right to "intersect, connect with, or cross any other railroad." And the statute (Code of 1886, § 1582) has provided the mode of enforcing this right.

Affirmed.

Cary *v.* Simmons.

Bill in Equity by Administrator, for Removal of Settlement.

1. *Decedent's estate; removal of settlement into equity by administrator.*—When an administrator seeks to remove the settlement of the estate into equity, it is immaterial whether or not proceedings for a settlement have been commenced in the Probate Court: in either case, he must aver and show some special ground for equitable intervention.

2. *Same; advancements made by administrator for distributees.*—By statutory provision (Code, §§ 2150–60), an administrator may, on final settlement of his accounts in the Probate Court, be allowed a credit, as against the distributive shares of the several distributees, for moneys paid out and expended by him for their support and education during infancy; and this statute operating on the remedy only, it will be held to apply to and include such expenditures made before its passage, which would then have been allowed in equity; consequently, such prior payments are now no ground for equitable interposition.

3. *Same; removal of incumbrances on land.*—As to lands which never belonged to the intestate, but which accrued to the distributees, as tenants in common with the administrator, from some other source, the administrator may, by paying taxes, or removing incumbrances, acquire as against the distributees a claim for reimbursement; but such claim can not be enforced or allowed on settlement of his accounts, either at law or in equity—neither in the Probate Court, nor in the Chancery Court.

4. *Same; partnership accounts; statute of limitations, as bar to suit for settlement.*—Where it appears that the administrator and his intestate had been partners in business, and the partnership was dissolved by consent, but no settlement of accounts was had; and the intestate then removed to Georgia, and there died after the lapse of several years; the administrator might have a settlement of the partnership accounts in equity, and a decree for any balance in his favor, which would bind any personal assets in his hands, notwithstanding the bar of the statute of limitations; but, when his bill shows that he had no personal assets, and that he seeks to change the lands in the hands of the heirs, or the rents thereof, the statute of limitations is a bar to the suit.

APPEAL from the Chancery Court of Bullock.

Heard before the Hon. JOHN A. FOSTER.

The bill in this case was filed on the 1st December, 1888, by Murrell R. Simmons, as the administrator of the estate of Mrs. Helen G. Cary, deceased, who was his sister, against Charles Cary and others, children and heirs at law of said decedent, and distributees of her estate; and sought to remove the settlement of the administrator's accounts into the Chancery Court. According to the allegations of the bill, the complainant and Mrs. Cary, then a widow, formed a partnership on the 1st January, 1869, for the purpose of conducting a boarding-house at Union Springs, and carried on that business until December 30th, 1870, when the partnership was dissolved by mutual consent, because they found that they were losing money. By the terms of the partnership, as alleged, the family of each of the partners was to board at the house; but, on account of the difference in the numbers composing their families, Mrs. Cary was to pay or allow complainant $8.00 per month. On the dissolution of the partnership, Mrs. Cary removed to Georgia; and she there died on June 3d, 1873, intestate, leaving her three children, then infants, her only heirs at law and distributees of her estate. No settlement of the partnership accounts was ever had, and the complainant claimed that Mrs. Cary was indebted to him, on partnership account, in the sum of over $3,600. Letters of administration on Mrs. Cary's estate were granted to the complainant, July 30th, 1873, by the Probate Court of Bullock county, and he gave bond, and entered on the discharge of his duties. At the time of Mrs. Cary's death, she owned personal property in Bullock county of the value of $216, and a plantation in said county containing about 320 acres; but the estate was largely indebted, and she owed, among other debts, one to Ware, Murphy & Co. for $1,028.30, which was secured by mortgage on said lands. Her children, then minors, as the bill alleged, "had no source or means of support, nor any property other than their interest in their mother's estate, excepting an undivided interest in a plantation in Georgia known as the 'Ossabaw plantation,' which had been sold for taxes, and was held adversely, and was not productive of any income for the benefit for said children, neither of whom ever had a legally appointed guardian. . . . Said lands or plantation being in bad repair, and in consequence of the expenditures necessary for repairs to keep said place in a tenantable condition, the large indebtedness of said estate, the maintenance and education of her children, and in order that he might save said lands from sale under said mortgage, or for the payment of debts, complainant during said administration

[Cary v. Simmons.]

incurred personal liabilities, and made advances for and on account of the support, maintenance and education of said children, and especially for said Mary H. Cary, who, after the death of her mother, lived with him; and for the reasons above set forth, and for the further purpose of saving to said children the costs and expenses which would have been incident to the appointment of a guardian for them, complainant's administration of said estate has been thus long continued. . . Some time during the year 1870, complainant and others, who were joint owners with said children of said Ossabaw tract of land, undertook to and did redeem the same from tax sale, and recover the possession thereof; and in said redemption, and the litigation that was necessary for such recovery, complainant expended for and in behalf of said children, and for the protection of their interests in said Ossabaw lands, the sum of $200; and he avers that said sum, together with other advancements made by him for and in their behalf as aforesaid, should be allowed him as charges against their respective distributive shares of said estate, on final settlement and distribution thereof."

On these allegations, the bill prayed that the settlement of his administration might be removed into the Chancery Court; that an account of the partnership transactions might be stated, and any balance found in his favor "be decreed to be allowed him as a proper charge against said estate;" and that an account might also be stated of his expenditures for the children, and the balance in his favor be declared a charge against their respective distributive shares.

The defendants demurred to the bill, specially assigning as grounds of demurrer, (1) that no facts were alleged which justified a removal of the settlement from the Probate Court; (2) that the claim for an account of the partnership transactions was a stale demand, and was barred by the statute of limitations; (3) that the debts of the estate were presumptively paid, and (4) that the complainant had an adequate remedy at law for the enforcement of any legal demands he might have. The chancellor overruled the demurrer, holding that the bill contained equity; and his decree is now assigned as error.

TOMPKINS & TROY, for the appellants, cited *Chambers v. Wright*, 52 Ala. 444; *Teague v. Corbitt*, 57 Ala. 529; *Weakley v. Gurley*, 60 Ala. 399: *Glenn v. Billingslea*, 64 Ala. 345; *Newsom v. Thornton*, 66 Ala. 311; *Whorton v.*

[Cary v. Simmons.]

Moragne, 59 Ala. 641; *Wells v. Brown*, 83 Ala. 162; *Chandler v. Wynne*, 85 Ala. 301; *Trimble v. Fariss*, 78 Ala. 260; *Grimball v. Mastin*, 77 Ala. 553; *Scott v. Ware*, 64 Ala. 174; Code, § 2159; *Alexander v. Fisher*, 18 Ala. 374.

F. Law, and Norman & Son, *contra*, cited *Knight v. Godbolt*, 7 Ala. 304; *Milam v. Ragland*, 19 Ala. 85; *Bailey v. Munden*, 58 Ala. 104.

McCLELLAN, J.—1. It did not appear by any matter embraced in the submission, from the decree on which this appeal is prosecuted, that the jurisdiction of the Probate Court had been put in exercise for the settlement of the estate of complainant's intestate before the filing of the bill. The chancellor, assuming, as of course he was authorized to do under the circumstances, that the active jurisdiction of the Probate Court had not attached, seems to have been influenced, to some extent, by a consideration of this fact in the conclusions he reached as to the sufficiency of the bill to invoke the interposition of a court of equity. Had the bill been filed by the distributees of the estate, it would have been proper to look to this fact; but not so on a bill exhibited, as this one is, by the personal representative. Whether proceedings for final settlement are pending in the Probate Court or not, the administrator can not come into chancery, without averring some specific fact or circumstance which renders a resort to that court necessary. There must be an allegation of some ground of equitable jurisdiction.—*McNeill v. McNeill*, 36 Ala. 109; *Teague v. Corbitt*, 57 Ala. 537; *Weakley v. Gurley*, 60 Ala. 409.

2. Two grounds are set up and relied on in this bill as predicates for equitable action. One of these is, that the administrator had made advances to the minor heirs of his intestate, for their support and education, and also to disincumber certain lands which belonged to them; for which, on final settlement, it is insisted, the Probate Court was without power to allow him credit. As to the advances made for the support and education of the infant distributees, we have no doubt that the statute of 1877, now constituting sections 2159 and 2160 of the Code, confers ample authority on the Probate Court to allow the administrator credit on his final settlement. The right to such credit was recognized in equity before that act. The operation of the act was on the remedy, rather than on the right itself; and for this reason, the

statute would have been accorded a retrospective operation, without the express provision to that effect embodied in its section. It is, therefore, immaterial, that the third section has been repealed by omission from the Code of 1886; and the fact that the advances claimed were made prior to the passage of the act, does not defeat the jurisdiction of the Probate Court.—*Ex parte Buckley*, 53 Ala. 42; *Eskridge v. Ditmars*, 51 Ala. 245.

3. As we understand the averments of the bill in relation thereto, the Ossabaw land had not been the property of complainant's intestate, and did not belong to the estate at all, but had come to the distributees of the estate from some other source. We are unable to to see what right the complainant had, *as the administrator* of the Cary estate, to make advances to disincumber lands with which neither the estate nor its distributees, as such, had any connection. It may be, the complainant, who is alleged to be a tenant in common with the defendants in that land, would have, in that capacity, a claim against them for money advanced for the common benefit; but he would not be entitled, either in law or equity—either in the Probate or the Chancery Court—on final settlement of his administration, to a credit for such advances. They were not made either for the support or education of the minors, or in the prosecution of the business of the estate.

4. The other facts relied as giving equity to the bill are, that in and for the years 1869 and 1870, the complainant and the intestate constituted a partnership; that the partnership was dissolved December 30, 1870, leaving his co-partner largely indebted to complainant: that she died in 1873, without a settlement of the partnership accounts, and that the partnership is still unsettled; and the bill prays to have an account taken of said partnership accounts and transactions, and that the amount found thereon to be due the complainant may be allowed him on final settlement of her estate. It further appears by the bill, that on January 3, 1871, the partnership having been dissolved, and its business abandoned, by mutual consent, on December 30th next before, the intestate removed to the State of Georgia, and continued to reside there until her death. The statute of limitations of six years is set up by the heirs in their demurrer to the bill. The statute began to run immediately on the dissolution of the partnership, and the subsequent death of Helen Cary did not, of itself, suspend its operation,

[Cary v. Simmons.]

as against her heirs.—*Daniel v. Day*, 51 Ala. 431. But her removal and continued absence from the State did have that effect.—*Minniece v. Jeter*, 65 Ala. 222. And while the statutory exception, in this connection, results only from personal absence, as distinguished from domicil elsewhere ; yet the averment of residence in another State will, on demurrer, be construed to mean, that the person against whom the exception is invoked has been absent during the period of such residence.—*State Bank v. Seawell*, 18 Ala. 616; *Stevenson v. Anderson, ante*, 208. The appellants rely, therefore, on the lapse of time since the complainant became—in 1873—the administrator of the estate of their ancestor, as perfecting the bar of the statute against his claim to have an account taken of the partnership, and a decree in his favor on final settlement for what ever may be found due him in that behalf.

It is conceded, that such an account might be had, and a decree passed thereon, if there were any personal assets of the estate in his hands to be applied in satisfaction of it; and this, notwithstanding the lapse of sufficient time to perfect the bar.—*Knight v. Godbolt*, 7 Ala. 304; *Milam v. Ragland*, 19 Ala. 85. But the bill shows, construing its averments most strongly against the complainant, that the administrator has no personal assets of the estate in his hands. Not only so, but it appears that the personalty of the estate was of the gross value of $216.10, which, the presumption is, has long since been administered; and even should that sum be considered as still in the hands of the personal representative, it is manifestly inadequate to the satisfaction of the decree for which he prays. It thus becomes evident, that the relief on account of the partnership sought by the complainant must be worked out by the subjection of the lands of the estate, or of the rents of those lands, to the payment of the amount found to be due the complainant on the settlement of the partnership. These lands descended to the heirs upon the death of Mrs. Cary. The rents subsequently accruing from them belonged to the heirs. Neither the lands, nor the issues therefrom, became the assets of the estate for the purposes of administration. True, the personal representative had, under statutory provisions, the right to intercept the descent, and apply both the rents and the land itself, if need be, to the payment of the debts of the estate. But, when this is sought to be done, the heirs have a right to interpose any objection to such a disposition

34

of their property which could have been made by their
ancestor. To any suit or proceeding for this purpose,
instituted by the administrator, whether to secure a debt due
himself or to any other creditor of the estate, they may set
up and rely on the statute of limitations, as against the debt
sought to be thus collected. The administrator was under
no disability, certainly after the lapse of eighteen months
from the grant of letters, with respect to proceeding in
equity for a settlement of this partnership, and of his
administration of the estate. He had at that time the same
right to file a bill for those purposes, so far as disability or
incapacity of parties to sue and be sued is involved, as he
had to do so in 1889—fifteen years afterwards—when this
bill was filed. The bill, under the circumstances of the case,
should have been filed within six years after the lapse of
eighteen months from the grant of letters of administration.
As against the heirs, and for the purpose of subjecting
either their lands or the rents thereof to the payment of the
claim of the personal representative, growing out of the
partnership transactions, the case made by the bill was
barred by the statute of limitations of six years.— *Wells v.
Brown,* 83 Ala. 162; *Chandler v. Harris,* 85 Ala. 312;
Harwood v. Harper, 54 Ala. 659; *Teague v. Corbitt,* 57 Ala.
529; *Mundin v. Bailey,* 70 Ala. 69; *Scott v. Ware,* 64 Ala.
174; *Trimble v. Farris,* 78 Ala. 260.

The decree of the chancellor on the demurrers is not in
harmony with the foregoing views, and is reversed and the
cause remanded.

Reversed and remanded.

Baker *v.* Swift & Son.

Statutory Detinue for Horses, Mules, &c.

1. *Entries on docket, as part of record.*—Extracts from the docket of
the court below, copied into the transcript by the clerk, but not made a
part of the record by bill of exceptions or otherwise, are the mere unauthorized memoranda of the clerk, and can not be considered by this
court for any purpose.

2. *Summons not signed by the clerk; waiver of defect.*—In a statutory
action for the recovery of personal property *in specie,* the summons not
being signed by the clerk, though the indorsement requiring the sheriff
to take possession of the property was properly signed; the sheriff

[Baker v. Swift & Son.]

having taken the property from the possession of the defendant, and no objection to the defective summons being raised for four or five terms during which the suit was pending, before a judgment by default was taken; *held*, that the defect in the summons was waived.

APPEAL from the Circuit Court of Lee.

Tried before the Hon. JESSE M. CARMICHAEL.

This action was brought by George P. Swift & Son, suing as partners, against R. P. & R. H. Baker, to recover several mules, horses, and other personal property; and was commenced on the 19th December, 1885. The summons, as copied into the transcript, was not signed by the clerk; but indorsed on it was an order of seizure to the sheriff, in regular form, which was dated December 19th, and was signed by the clerk. The sheriff returned the writ, December 21st, 1885, executed by service on R. P. Baker, and not found as to R. H. Baker, and that he had taken the property into possession; and further, December 30th, that the defendants had failed to give bond within the time prescribed by law, and he had delivered the property to the plaintiffs, who had executed the statutory bond. At the May term, 1888, a judgment by default was rendered, in regular form, followed by the verdict of a jury in favor of the plaintiffs, assessing the separate value of the several articles sued for, and a judgment for the plaintiffs for the property or its alternate value as assessed. The clerk has copied into the transcript, also, without explanation, several entries, or memoranda, which seem to have been copied from the docket of the court below; each being the statement of the case at each term, with the names of the attorneys, and each showing the entry of an attorney's name for the defendants except at the May term, 1888, when the entry is "*Appearance* withdrawn;" and the clerk appends a certificate, stating that those words were written by the presiding judge at that term, and that no appearance was ever entered for defendants on the *Appearance Docket*. The judgment is now assigned as error, because the record shows that the summons was not signed by the clerk.

HARRISON & LIGON, and J. J. ABERCROMBIE, for appellant, cited *Costley v. Driver*, 45 Ala. 230; *Wilson v. Owen*, 45 Ala. 451; *Shapard v. Powers & Bros.*, 50 Ala. 377; *Harrison v. Holley*, 46 Ala. 484; *Gregg v. Gilmer*, 54 Ala. 425.

A. & R. B. BARNES, *contra*, cited *Cooley v. Lawrence*, 12 How. Pr. 176; 5 Duer, 605; 1 Tidd's Practice, 86.

STONE, C. J.—This was a statutory action for the recovery of personal chattels in specie, a substitute, with additional powers, for the common-law action of detinue. The summons, which accompanied the complaint, was not signed by the clerk; but the indorsement upon it, stating that plaintiffs had made the necessary affidavit and given bond, and commanding the sheriff to seize the chattels, was signed by the clerk officially, and bears the same date as the summons.   Under this order of seizure, the sheriff did take possession of the chattels; and the defendants failing to give a replevin bond within five days, the plaintiffs gave the requisite bond, and took the property into possession.—Code of 1886, §§ 2717 *et seq.*

We agree with counsel that what purports to be extracts from the docket in the Circuit Court below is no part of the record, and can not be looked to by us.   The docket is not a record, and what the transcript purports to set forth, as part of it, is but the unauthorized, unofficial statement of the clerk.   We will treat this case as if that were stricken out.

This case remained on the docket of the Circuit Court for over two years, when a judgment by default was taken against the defendants, with a writ of inquiry, executed.   No objection was taken in the court below, for the failure of the clerk to sign the summons, nor are we informed whether the copy-summons was signed or not.   As we have said, the writ of seizure, which the law requires to be indorsed on the summons, was signed by the clerk officially, and bears the same date as the order of filing indorsed by the clerk. Code of 1886, § 2717.   We think this record, in the absence of any objection raised in the court below, furnishes sufficient evidence that the summons was issued by the clerk. Code of 1886, § 2652.

In support of the conclusion we have reached, we feel justified in referring to the fact that, under the process and order of seizure, the sheriff took from the possession of defendants the property sued for, including, among other things, one mule and one mare; and these were never restored to defendants.   The defendants certainly had notice of the suit, and we hold, if they had ground of objection, they have waived it.—*Lenoir v. Broadhead*, 50 Ala. 58 ; *Young v. Broxson*, 23 Ala. 684.   This case is distinguishable from *Harrison v. Holley*, 46 Ala. 84, in several particulars.

We have now noticed the only question assigned as error.
Affirmed.

Weaver *v.* Brown.

Bill in Equity to enforce Vendor's Lien on Land.

1. *Vendor's lien; transfer of note for purchase-money, by delivery merely.*—The transfer of a note given for the purchase-money of land, by delivery merely, prior to the enactment of the statute now of force (Code, § 1764), did not carry with it the vendor's lien; and if the transferree obtains judgment on the note against the maker, sells the land under it, becoming himself the purchaser, and having notice of another unpaid note in the hands of the vendor, he does not acquire, and can not convey to another person, a title which can prevail against the vendor's lien attached to that note.

2. *Set-off against vendor's lien.*—In a suit to enforce a vendor's lien on land, the defendant may set off any legal demands existing in his favor, against the complainant, at the institution of the suit, on which he might maintain an action of debt or *indebitatus assumpsit* in his own name.

3. *Same; conclusiveness of judgment.*—The complainant having obtained a judgment on the note for the unpaid purchase-money, before filing a bill to enforce his lien on the land, the defendant is not precluded from setting off a cross demand which would have been available as a set-off in the action at law, but which was not introduced in that suit.

4. *Cross-bill.*—The benefit of a set-off, in equity, can only be claimed by cross-bill.

5. *Judgment as evidence.*—A judgment by default, rendered by a court of general jurisdiction, is admissible as evidence in a suit which seeks to enforce the demand as a lien on land, in the purchase of which the debt was created, although the record does not show the service of process, the presumption being indulged that the court had acquired jurisdiction of the person.

APPEAL from the Chancery Court of Randolph.

Heard before the Hon. S. K. McSPADDEN.

The original bill in this case was filed on the 5th May, 1880, by Jesse M. Weaver, against Thomas N. Brown, his wife and son; and sought to establish and enforce a vendor's lien on land, for unpaid purchase-money. Garrett Wilder was also made a defendant to the bill, but he died before answer, and the suit was abated as to him. The contract for the sale of the land was made on the 4th April, 1866, and consummated by the execution of a deed by the complainant to said Thomas N. Brown, which recited the payment of $3,000 as its consideration, the payment of which was acknowledged, but afterwards stated that "$1,000 of the consideration [was] unpaid;" while Brown conveyed to him a tract of land in Georgia, at an agreed price, and executed his two notes for the balance of the purchase-money, each for $500. These notes were dated April 4th, 1866, payable to "J. M. Weaver or bearer, by the 25th December, 1867," and 1868, respectively; and each recited that it was "given for the payment of" the land, describing it, "provided it is not cancelled by the Federal Government." On the 22d February, 1870, the complainant recovered a judgment against Brown, on the note first falling due, for $864.66; a copy of which was made an exhibit to the bill, and it was alleged that the same was unpaid, and constituted a lien on the land. The other note was delivered to said Garrett Wilder, or he procured possession of it; and he obtained a judgment on it against Brown, on the 22d August, 1872, for $405.60, the balance then due. The land was sold, under an execution issued on this judgment, in February, 1873, and bought by said Wilder, at the price of $502.26, the amount due on said judgment; and the sheriff executed a conveyance to him as the purchaser, which was dated February 3d, 1873. Wilder afterwards sold and conveyed parts of the land to Brown's wife and son; and they were in possession when the bill was filed, claiming under the conveyances from him, and also under a conveyance from said Brown himself.

The bill alleged that the several defendants, at the time they acquired their respective interests in the land, had notice, both actual and constructive, of the lien for the unpaid purchase-money. The defendants filed a joint and several answer, in which they denied that they had any notice of an outstanding lien for unpaid purchase-money; denied that complainant had any lien, or that any of the purchase-money was unpaid; denied that he had recovered a judgment against Brown, and required proof thereof. As to the note held by Wilder, they alleged that, at and before the consummation of the contract for the sale of the land, complainant was indebted to Wilder in the sum of about $650, and delivered said note to him, soon after it was executed, in part payment of said indebtedness; "that it was agreed said note was and should be a lien on said lands, and said Wilder received it with this express agreement;" that complainant, "at and before the delivery of said note to said Wilder, assured him that it was a lien on said land, and that the description of the land being in said note the land was bound therefor; and said Wilder, relying on these representations as true, accepted said note in part payment of said debt." They also asked to set off against the complainant's judgment, if anything should be found due him, certain cross demands, particularly described, due from him to said Brown at and before the commencement of this suit, and at the date of said judgment; and they prayed that their answer be taken and allowed as a cross-bill for this purpose.

The complainant answered the cross-bill, denying its allegations as to the transactions between him and Wilder, and alleged that Wilder obtained possession of the note by fraud; denied the validity of the cross demands, and pleaded that they were barred by staleness and the statute of limitations: and he demurred to the cross-bill, and moved to dismiss it for want of equity. The grounds of demurrer assigned were—1st, that it was not alleged that the note was transferred to Wilder by written indorsement; 2d, that "a set-off can not be relied on to defeat a suit for the enforcement of a vendor's lien;" 3d, "that the judgment, upon which the original bill was founded, precludes an investigation into joint [cross] claims anterior to said judgment."

The complainant's deposition was taken in his own behalf, in which he stated the facts as alleged in his pleadings—denying the transaction with Wilder, alleging that he obtained possession of the note by fraud, and that public notice of the facts was given at the sheriff's sale at which Wilder became the purchaser; and he was corroborated by the testimony of Richard Moore, as to the manner in which Wilder procured the note from the complainant's wife. Thomas N. Brown, whose deposition was taken on the part of the defendants, testified to the facts as stated in the answer and cross-bill. The complainant offered in evidence a certified copy of his judgment against Brown, which set out the summons and complaint, and the judgment by default; but it did not show any service of process, or acknowledgment of service, and the defendants objected to its admission on this account. On the hearing, the defendants also submitted a motion to dismiss the bill for want of equity, and on account of the staleness of the demand sought to be enforced.

The chancellor overruled the motion to dismiss the bill, and also overruled the demurrer to the cross-bill, except as as to the first ground assigned; but, "on consideration of all the pleadings and proof," he dismissed the complainant's bill, without prejudice. The complainant appeals from this decree, and assigns as error the dismissal of his own bill, and the refusal to dismiss the cross-bill.

SMITH & SMITH, for appellant.

SOMERVILLE, J.—1. The transfer of the note to the defendant Wilder, by the complainant Weaver, having been effected by delivery merely, without indorsement—and prior to the statute authorizing a transfer of a vendor's lien by mere delivery of purchase-money notes given for land (Code, 1886, § 1764)—the transferree did not acquire the vendor's lien, nor any right to enforce it on the land in controversy. *Prickett v. Sibert*, 71 Ala. 194; *Bankhead v. Owen*, 60 Ala. 457; *Hightower v. Rigsby*, 56 Ala. 126. The title, therefore, which Wilder acquired at the sheriff's sale, must be sustained, if at all, without regard to any lien which he was supposed to have on the land for his judgment debt against appellee Brown, based on the note for the purchase-money, transferred by delivery as above stated. Wilder's title was that of an execution creditor buying at his own sale—his co–defendants claiming under him with notice of complainant's equity. The bill alleges, and the testimony satisfactorily proves, that Wilder himself had full knowledge of the existence of the lien for unpaid purchase-money on the land claimed by the complainant. This lien was, therefore, superior to that of Wilder's execution, and the chancellor erred . in not giving it precedence. His decree dismissing complainant's bill was erroneous, and will be reversed.

2. The defendants will be entitled to set off against complainant's claim for unpaid purchase-money any legal demands against complainant which were owned by the judgment debtor, Thomas N. Brown, at the time the suit was brought, and upon which Brown could have instituted an action of debt, or *indebitatus assumpsit*, in his own name. It is no objection to such set-off, that the complainant's demand is an equitable lien on the land, and enforceable as such. *Hooper v. Armstrong*, 69 Ala. 343; *Gafford v. Proskauer*, 59 Ala. 264. The second ground of demurrer to the defendant's cross-bill, based on this suggestion, was properly overruled.

3. We construe the third ground of demurrer to mean, that no set-off can be introduced, which could have been made available at the time the judgment was rendered in favor of the complainant. This view of the law is incorrect, a set-off being a defense which may be made or not, at the option of the defendant. It is not compulsory on him to

make it, and the judgment does not preclude its future introduction.—*Wharton v. King*, 69 Ala. 365.

4. Such a set-off being maintainable in equity only by cross-bill, the refusal of the court to dismiss the cross-bill of defendants is free from error.—*Beall v. McGehee*, 57 Ala. 438; *Chambers v. Wright*, 52 Ala. 444.

5. The judgment in favor of the complainant against the defendant Brown, upon which this suit is based, is a judgment by default; and although it affirmatively shows no appearance on the part of the defendant, or his attorneys, it will be presumed, on collateral objection, that the Circuit Court, which rendered it, had proper jurisdiction of the defendant's person, it being a court of general and not limited jurisdiction.—*Pettus v. McClannahan*, 52 Ala. 55; *Hunt v. Ellison*, 32 Ala. 173; 3 Brick. Dig. p. 587, §§ 5-6; Freeman on Judg. (3d Ed.), §§ 124-131. This judgment is clearly admissible in evidence in the present suit.

Reversed and remanded.

Sykes *v.* Betts.

87
104

Bill in Equity to enforce Vendor's Lien on Land.

1. *Vendor's lien, when legal title is not retained; sale of real and personal property in gross.*—A vendor's lien, after he has conveyed the legal title, is a mere creation of equity. while it is a lien by contract so long as he retains the legal title; but, while the presumption is that he retains the legal title as security for the purchase-money, that presumption may be repelled by the terms and character of the contract, or by the circumstances; and when there is a sale of real and personal property for a sum in gross, no *data* being furnished by which the separate value of the land can be ascertained, it is immaterial whether a conveyance was or was not executed—a vendor's lien is not retained, and it does not arise by operation of law.

2. *Same; contract for division of decedent's estate.*—Under a written agreement between two married sisters, their husbands uniting with them, for a "distribution and final settlement of the estate" of their deceased father, by which it is stipulated that one is to take certain lands, and pay the other $500, while the second is to take certain other lands, with all the personal property, pay all the debts, and save the first harmless against them; no words of conveyance being used, but provisions to the effect that "all proper instruments and conveyances necessary to carry out this agreement are to be executed between the parties," and that "this instrument is to be recorded as a final settlement and distribution of said estate;" a vendor's lien to enforce the payment of the $500 does not arise by operation of law, and the facts repel the presumption that it was retained by contract; and though it

is alleged that there were in fact no outstanding debts, and that the personal assets were valueless, these allegations do not show that the $500 was one half of the estimated difference in value of the lands only.

APPEAL from the Chancery Court of Madison.

Heard before the Hon. THOMAS COBBS.

The bill in this case was filed on the 5th May, 1886, by Andrew J. Sykes and wife, against Edward C. Betts and wife; and sought to enforce an alleged vendor's lien on a tract of land, on account of the non-payment of $500, part of the agreed price, under the terms of a written contract between the parties for the division and distribution of the estate of John M. Swoope, deceased, who was the father of Mrs. Sykes and Mrs. Betts. The agreement, a copy of which was made an exhibit to the bill, was under seal, dated October 1st, 1869, signed by all the parties, and attested by four witnesses; and in the following words, omitting immaterial portions: "This agreement, entered into this   .   .   , witnesses, that the undersigned," naming them, "have by this agreement effected a distribution and final settlement of the estate of John M. Swoope, deceased, between themselves, on the following grounds, viz.: The said Betts and wife are to have the plantation on the Courtland and Brown's Ferry road, in which Mrs. Swoope is allotted dower, subject to said dower, and are to have possession of the same at the end of the present year; and the said Betts and wife are to pay Sykes and wife the sum of $500, on the 1st January, 1871. The said Sykes and wife are to have the plantation near Courtland, between the Brown's Ferry and Lamb's Ferry roads, the house and lot in which Mrs. John M. Swoope now resides (being lots Nos. 293 and 294), subject to her right of dower, and all the other property, real, personal, mixed, and *choses* in action belonging to said estate; and the said A. J. and Emma Sykes also agree to pay all the debts of said estate, and hereby bind themselves to said E. C. and Virginia Betts that they will save them harmless against any and all liability for any and all debts owing by the estate of said John M.. Swoope, and that they will themselves pay the same. And all proper instruments and conveyances are to be executed between the parties; and this instrument is to be recorded in the Probate Court of Lawrence county, Alabama, as a final settlement and distribution of said estate. Witness our hands," &c.

A demurrer was interposed to the original bill, which was overruled by the chancellor then presiding (Hon. S. K. Mc-

[Sykes v. Betts.]

SPADDEN); but, on appeal to this court, his decree was reversed—82 Ala. 378. Afterwards, the death of A. J. Sykes having been suggested, an amendment of the bill was filed in the name of Mrs. Sykes, as follows: "Your oratrix states, on information and belief, that the defendants deny that the lands allotted to said Virginia A. on said division are subject to a lien for the payment of said $500, with interest thereon, and assert and claim that the consideration of the aforesaid promise and obligation to pay said $500 was not solely the purchase-money of the lands, nor the excess in value of the lands allotted to the said Virginia A., over and above the value of the lands allotted to your oratrix on said division. Your oratrix avers that, on said division, and by the said agreement, she parted with, and transferred to the said Virginia A., only her undivided one-half interest in and to said lands, and that, in equity, your oratrix has a lien on such undivided one-half interest, for the payment of said sum of $500, with interest thereon. And your oratrix avers, that at the time of said agreement and division, there were no unpaid debts against the estate of said John M. Swoope, and no charge against his estate, nor was there any personal property of said estate, of any kind, subject to distribution, except some *choses* in action of no value, from which nothing has ever been realized; that the lands allotted to the said Virginia A., on the division aforesaid, exceeded in value, by more than $1,000, the lands allotted and assigned to your oratrix; and that the consideration of said promise and obligation to pay said sum of $500 was equalizing such division of the lands of their ancestor between said Virginia A. and your oratrix."

The chancellor sustained a demurrer to the bill as amended, and his decree here assigned as error.

R. C. BRICKELL, for appellant.—The amendment of the bill fully meets the objections raised on the former appeal, and shows that the $500 was only on account of the estimated difference in value between the two tracts of land, the personal property and the debts being of no value whatever. But it is submitted that, on the facts shown by the record, the former decision is wrong, in not recognizing the distinction between a vendor's lien, or grantor's lien, more properly called, and the security which the vendor carves out for himself, or retains, when he has not parted with the legal title. The vendor's lien, strictly speaking, is the mere creation of equity; it arises by operation of law, when he has parted with the legal title, and is founded on the equitable principle, that it is unconscientious for one man to get and keep the estate of another without paying for it. But, when the vendor retains the legal title in himself—executing only a bond for the title, or taking a mortgage if he has executed a conveyance—the rights of the parties are matter of contract; if binding on one, it is equally binding on the other, and either may compel a specific performance—that is, the purchaser may compel the execution of a conveyance, on payment of the purchase-money; and the vendor may subject the land to the payment of the purchase-money, and obtain a personal decree for any unpaid balance. This distinction is recognized by text-writers, and runs through many adjudicated cases.—3 Pomeroy's Equity, § 1260; 1 Jones on Mortgages, § 225; *Haley v. Burnett,* 5 Porter, 452; *Chapman v. Chunn,* 5 Ala. 397; *Relfe v. Relfe,* 34 Ala. 500; *Bankhead v. Owen,* 60 Ala. 460; *Gilman v. Brown,* 1 Mason, 221; *Teague v. Wade,* 59 Ala. 369; *Kelly v. Payne,* 18 Ala. 371; Pomeroy on Contracts, § 6; Waterman on Specific Performance, § 15; 66 N. C. 501; 80 N. C. 258; 16 N. J. Eq. 147; 6 Gray, 25. Here, the legal title was retained, and express provision was made for the execution of conveyances in the future; and it is not to be presumed that it was intended or contemplated that one should get the property of the other without paying the agreed price.

D. D. SHELBY, *contra,* cited and relied on the former decision in this case.—82 Ala. 378.

CLOPTON, J.—When this case was before the court at a former term, on appeal taken from a decree overruling a demurrer to the bill, we held that its averments were insufficient to bring the claim of complainant within the principle, on which rests the equitable doctrine of enforcing a vendor's lien for the unpaid purchase-money of land. The agreement between the parties was regarded in form a single contract, intended to make, without resort to administration, a full settlement and distribution of the estate of their intestate ancestor. The decision was rested on the ground, that the contract and the allegations of the bill left in doubt and uncertainty whether Mrs. Betts' promise to pay five hundred dollars was based solely on an agreed difference in the value of the lands, or whether some other consideration entered into it. It was said: "To come within the principle, the debt must be contracted in the purchase of real estate, and no other consideration must, in the slightest degree, enter into it. If it be uncertain whether the debt sought to be collected rests alone for its consideration on the lands on which the bill seeks to fasten the lien, or whether it rests on something else, or on the lands and something else, then the doctrine can not be applied for most obvious reasons." 82 Ala. 378.

After the remandment of the case, the bill was amended, a demurrer again interposed, and sustained. The present appeal is taken from the decree sustaining that demurrer. The amendment substantially alleges, that Mrs. Sykes parted with, and transferred to Mrs. Betts, an undivided interest in lands only; that the decedent owed no debts, and there were no charges against his estate at the time of his death, nor was there any personal property subject to distribution, except some *choses* in action, which were valueless; that the lands allotted and assigned to Mrs. Betts exceeded in value, by more than one thousand dollars, the lands allotted and assigned to Mrs. Sykes; and that the consideration of the promise to pay the five hundred dollars was the equalization of the division of the lands.

Appellant insists that the principles announced in the opinion delivered on the former appeal, are only applicable to the lien of the vendor which equity creates after a conveyance is made, and not to the lien reserved by the contract, when the legal title is retained. The argument is, that there is a broad and plain distinction between the rights and interests of a vendor and vendee before and after conveyance. After conveyance, the lien of the vendor is a mere equitable charge, without any estate in the lands; and when no conveyance is made, the vendor retains the legal title, a more efficient security, of which he can not be divested, except by payment of the purchase-money, which the retention of the legal title was intended to secure. In other words, in the former case, the lien is a mere creation of equity; in the latter, a lien by contract. Our own decisions have recognized a marked distinction between the lien of a vendor after a conveyance, and the security carved out by the retention of the legal title, though each may be denominated a lien in the extended signification of the term. It has been repeatedly declared, that the essential incidents of a mortgage attached to a contract for the sale of lands, when by its

[Sykes v. Betts]

terms the vendor retains the legal title as security for the price—such as a bond conditioned to make titles on payment of the purchase-money—and that such security is not impaired by taking personal security.—*Chapman v. Chunn*, 5 Ala. 397; *Kelly v. Paine*, 18 Ala. 371. In such case, the remedy may be regarded reciprocal. Generally, the vendor may maintain a bill to enforce his security, whenever the vendee, if he had paid the purchase-money, could maintain a bill for specific performance.—*Hopper v. Hopper*, 6 N. J. Eq. 147.

It may be conceded, that whenever the vendor retains the legal title, the presumption is, that he retains it as security, unless such presumption is repelled by the terms and character of the contract, or by the circumstances. It is not conclusive. When, by the contract, no lien or security is carved out or reserved, either expressly or by implication, when it becomes a matter of presumption, whether or not the presumption arises before conveyance is made, depends on the same principles applicable after a conveyance is made. When there is a blending and commingling in the same note or contract of the aggregate price of real and personal property sold at the same time, and the agreed price of the real property can not be separated and definitely ascertained, by reference to either the writing, or extrinsic evidence, or both, the presumption of the retention of the equitable lien is rebutted. In *Stringfellow v. Ivie*, 73 Ala. 209, it is said: "When the considerations are blended and combined, and it is impossible, without resort to conjectural inquiries, to separate them, the presumption must be, that the vendor did not look to the lands for payment, but relied exclusively on the personal responsibility of the vendee." The same rule applies, when, from the contract, it appears that there has been a sale of real and personal property for a sum in gross, though no conveyance is made.

By the agreement between the parties, specified lands were allotted to Mrs. Betts, and she agreed to pay five hundred dollars,·while Mrs. Sykes was alloted other specified lands, and all other property of the estate, " real, personal, mixed, and *choses* in action," and obligated herself to pay the debts. True, Mrs. Sykes transferred no personal property to Mrs. Betts, and there is not a blending of the aggregate price of real and personal property; but the principle is the same, whenever any consideration other than the purchase of lands enters into the debt, and no *data* exist from which the particular price agreed to be paid for the land can be distinguished and ascertained. It is evident that the parties intended to make, and did make, a full settlement and division of the entire estate of their deceased father between themselves, the only heirs and distributees. The agreement purports to be a full settlement, division and distribution of the entire estate *in præsenti*. As appears from its face, the consideration of Mrs. Betts' promise to pay five hundred dollars is based on the estimated difference between the value of the portion of the estate allotted to her, and of the portion allotted to Mrs. Sykes, the latter reduced by the amount of the debts assumed to be paid; that is, it was estimated that five hundred dollars would equalize the benefits received and the burdens imposed upon the parties respectively. There is manifestly a blending of considerations, and the agreed value of the lands can not be separated and ascertained by reference to the contract. The presumption that the legal title was retained as security for the purchase-money of the lands, is repelled by the stipulations and character of the contract.

Neither do the extrinsic facts alleged in the amendment of the bill remove the objections to which the claim asserted by complainant is otherwise obnoxious. To effectuate this, it is essential that the price agreed to be paid for the lands should have been fixed and agreed on in the making of the contract, and the relation of vendor and vendee established as matter of separate negotiation.—*Alexander v. Hooks*, 84 Ala. 605; *Stringfellow v. Ivie, supra*. The amendment fails to aver that, at the time of making and consummating the agreement, it was understood and agreed that there were no debts or charges against the estate, or that the personal property was valueless, or that one thousand dollars was the difference in the value of the lands. It is consistent with the allegations of the amendment, that the parties at the time regarded the personal property as of some value, and it subsequently proved to be worthless; and they may have believed that there were debts, and it was afterwards discovered there were none. The question is not, what were the facts as subsequently disclosed, but how did the parties consider and estimate the matters in making the settlement and division of the estate. Considering the frame of the bill, we regard the averment that the consideration of Mrs. Betts' promise was the equalizing the division of the lands, as the mere conclusion of the pleader from the facts alleged.

Affirmed.

Paul *v*. Malone *&* Collins.

Motion to set aside Return showing Service of Process.

1. *Service of process, as shown by sheriff's return; evidence impeaching.*
The return of a sheriff, showing service of process, imports verity,
and casts on the party assailing it the burden of adducing evidence
sufficient to overcome the presumption that the officer did his duty;
and on motion to set aside the return, the bill of exceptions reciting that
"the defendant introduced himself as a witness, and his testimony
tended to show that the summons and complaint were never served on
him," &c., and that "this was all the evidence in the cause," these
recitals are not sufficient to enable this court to say that the lower court
error in refusing to set aside the return.

APPEAL from the Circuit Court of Geneva.
Tried before the Hon. J. M. CARMICHAEL.

M. E. MILLIGAN, for appellant.

McCLELLAN, J.—The defendant below, appellant here,
moved the court to set aside the return of the sheriff showing the service of a copy of the complaint on him. An
issue of fact was made up on this motion, and submitted to
the court; and the refusal of the court to vacate the return
on the evidence introduced, constitutes the only matter now
assigned as error.

The return of the sheriff imports verity, and the burden of
proving it to be false rests on the party assailing it, and must
be discharged by evidence sufficient to overcome the presumption arising from the fact that it was made in the line of
his duty by a sworn officer.—*Dunklin v. Wilson*, 64 Ala. 162.

The bill of exceptions in this case recites: "In support of
said motion, defendant introduced himself as a witness, and
his testimony *tended* to show that the summons and complaint were never served on him," &c.; and that this was
"all the evidence in the cause." Construing these statements
of the evidence most strongly against the appellant, as the
rule requires—3 Brick. Dig. p. 81, § 51—it appears that
there was only a *tendency* of the evidence to establish certain
facts. In cases like this, where this court is required to pass
on the sufficiency of the evidence to support the conclusion
of fact reached by the court below, it will not suffice to state

the mere tendency of the evidence. It can not be assumed
that this mere tendency was sufficiently strong to overturn
the presumption of the verity of the officer's return, and to
reasonably satisfy the mind of the court that there had been
no service of process. And, upon this ground, though it
might be justified also on others, the judgment of the Circuit
Court will be

Affirmed.

Moorer *v.* Moorer.

Bill in Equity by Creditors, to set aside Fraudulent Conveyance.

1. *Assignment of judgment or decree; suits by assignee.*—The statutory
provisions relating to mesne or final process issued upon an assigned
judgment or decree (Code, §§ 2927–28), have no application to suits on
such judgment or decree, whether at law or in equity. An action at
law can not be prosecuted by the assignee in his own name, but he may
maintain a bill in equity in his own name.
2. *Sufficiency of consideration of deed.*—When a bill seeks to set aside
a conveyance of land as fraudulent against creditors, alleging that the
land was worth $1,000 or more, and the recited consideration only $30;
while the conveyance itself, made an exhibit to the bill, shows that the
grantor conveyed only whatever interest and title he had by reason of
his survivorship of his wife, to whom the land belonged, no data being
furnished from which the value of his interest can be ascertained,—the
deed can not be declared fraudulent.

APPEAL from the Chancery Court of Butler.

Heard before the Hon. JOHN A. FOSTER.

The record in this case does not show when the bill was
filed, nor does it show the date of any of the preceedings in
the cause, except that the chancellor's decree is dated January 22d, 1889. The bill was filed by Mrs. Tommie C.
Moorer, the wife of W. J. Moorer, and J. A. Alston, who
was the surviving husband of her deceased sister, against
Nelson J. Moorer and his children; and, as originally framed,
sought a discovery of assets which might be subjected to the
satisfaction of complainant's decree against said Nelson J.
Moorer, and also to set aside a conveyance of land to his
children as fraudulent; but, by amendment, the allegations
and prayer as to a discovery were stricken out, and relief
was sought only against the conveyance, a copy of which

35

was made an exhibit. Mrs. T. C. Moorer, the complainant, and her deceased sister, Mrs. Alston, were the only children and heirs at law of J. C. Johnson, who died in Lowndes county, Alabama, in 1862, and on whose estate letters of administration were granted to said Nelson J. Moorer on December 23d, 1862. On final settlement of the accounts of said administrator, a decree was rendered against him by the Probate Court, in favor of John A. Tyson, as administrator *de bonis non*, for $8,901.24; but, on bill in equity to review and to correct errors in this decree, the amount was reduced to $3,677.20, by decree rendered April 9th, 1874. On this decree, the bill alleged, executions were issued, and returned "No property found;" and the decree itself was "transferred in writing" by said Tyson to the two children and heirs at law of the decedent. A demurrer was filed to the bill, assigning numerous specific grounds of demurrer; one of which was, that the bill showed no assignment of the decree which authorized the complainants to file the bill in their own names; and another, that the averments of the bill did not show that the deed was fraudulent. The chancellor overruled the demurrer, and his decree is here assigned as error,

Richardson & Steiner, for appellants.

J. M. Whitehead, *contra.*

STONE, C. J.—Sections 2927-8 of the Code of 1886 provide a remedy for assignees of judgments or decrees, who seek to enforce them by mesne or final process, issued upon the judgment assigned. These sections have no application to separate or independent suits, brought for the collection of debts evidenced by judgments or decrees. When the effort is made, as it generally may be, to collect by suit a debt due by judgment or decree, different rules prevail. Code, § 2170. If an action at law be resorted to, then the judgment is not such a contract for the payment of money, as that the beneficial owner can sue on it in his own name. *Smith v. Harrison*, 33 Ala. 706; *Lovins v. Humphries*, 67 Ala. 437. The rule is different in chancery. Whoever has the rightful ownership, whether legal or equitable, is the proper complainant.

We think the present bill must be held insufficient. We suppose its purpose was to uncover, and subject to the payment of N. J. Moorer's debt, certain lands, which it charges were conveyed by the latter to his children, after incurring the liability the bill seeks to enforce.   The bill avers that the land so conveyed was worth one thousand dollars, and that the consideration of the conveyance was thirty dollars. It makes the deed of conveyance a part of the bill as an ex- hibit.   The *habendum* clause of the deed is, "To have and to hold whatever interest and title I may and do have by reason of my survivorship of my late wife, Mrs. M. S. Moorer, to whom said lands belonged."   We have now stated every thing the bill contains, tending in the slightest manner to assail the *bona fides* of the transaction.

If the conveyance had been of the title in fee of a tract of land worth a thousand dollars, on the paltry consideration of thirty dollars, it would probably be our duty to pronounce the consideration so grossly inadequate, as to stamp the transaction as fraudulent.   But that is not this case.   Moorer sold and conveyed only the interest and title he had, and we have not been furnished with the data for finding them out. The bill does not dispute the payment of the consideration, does not allege the conveyance was voluntary, does not aver what interest Moorer had, nor what it was worth, and gives no predicate for ascertaining its value.   It does not even aver that the consideration was inadequate, but leaves that to be worked out from the meagre statements set forth above. Pleadings must be more definite than this.—*Matthews v. Mo. Mut. Ins. Co.*, 75 Ala. 85; *Burford v. Steele*, 80 Ala. 147; *Flewellen v. Crane*, 58 Ala. 627; *Pickett v. Pipkin*, 64 Ala. 520; *Gordon v. Tweedy*, 71 Ala. 202; *Caldwell v. King*, 76 Ala. 149.

We will not make any order of dismissal, but will leave that for the chancellor's action, after considering a motion for leave to amend, should it be made.

Reversed and remanded.

Ex parte Williams.

Application for Mandamus, on Order Abating Suit.

1. *Inebriates' estates; powers and duties of trustee; death of inebri- ate pending suit by trustee.*—The estate, powers and duties of the trustee

of an inebriate's estate, under statutory provisions (Code, §§ 2502-06), like the committee of a lunatic in England, terminate with the death of the inebriate, though he still remains liable to account; and having filed a bill in equity to set aside a conveyance of land executed by the inebriate after his appointment, the suit abates by the death, and can not be continued or revived in the name of the heirs of the inebriate jointly with the trustee.

APPLICATION by petition in the name of Robert S. Williams, for a writ of *mandamus*, or other appropriate writ, directed to Hon. THOS. M. ARRINGTON, judge of the City Court of Montgomery, sitting in equity, requiring him to set aside an order for the abatement of a suit lately pending in said court, wherein the petitioner was plaintiff, as trustee of his son, Thomas W. Williams, since deceased, and J. R. Pinkston was defendant; and to allow the suit to be revived and prosecuted in the names of the decedent's sisters, as his heirs at law, jointly with the petitioner. The material facts are stated in the opinion of the court.

BRICKELL, SEMPLE & GUNTER, for the petitioner.

SOMERVILLE, J.—The application is for *mandamus*, or other remedial writ, to compel the judge of the City Court of Montgomery, sitting in equity, to vacate an order abating a suit brought in that court by the petitioner, R. S. Williams, against one J. R. Pinkston, and refusing to allow its prosecution to be continued in his name jointly with others, who were proposed by the amendment to the bill to be made co-plaintiffs in the cause.

The petitioner had been appointed trustee of his son, one William Thomas Williams, under the provisions of sections 2502-2506 of the Code of 1886 (Code, 1876, §§ 2815-2819), which provide that, "when an unmarried man, over twenty-one years of age, is, by reason of intemperance, unfit to manage his estate, or is wasting or squandering it, and is thereby in danger of being reduced to poverty and want, his brothers, or sisters, or next of kin, or any or either of them, may . . . file their bill in chancery to preserve the estate of such intemperate person from further waste, and for general relief."—§ 2502.

The trustee appointed under this section is charged with authority and duty to "manage and superintend the affairs of the estate, and from the avails thereof provide for the support of such intemperate person, or of his wife and children, in the event he has married after the institution of the suit;

which support must be suitable to the means and estate of such intemperate person."—§ 2504.

The chancellor is invested with authority to secure the estate against further waste, by injunction or otherwise, pending the proceeding, and may order the estate to be restored to the *cestui que trust*, on satisfactory proof of his restoration.

The suit of Robert S. Williams against Pinkston, pending in the City Court, was instituted for the purpose of setting aside a conveyance of land made by the *cestui que trust*, or ward, to the defendant, after the complainant's appointment as trustee under the foregoing statute. The ground upon which the suit was declared to be abated was the death of the ward, William Thomas Williams, *pendente lite*. The co-complainants proposed to be introduced as parties were heirs of the deceased.

The statutes in question are analogous to those regulating the estates of lunatics in England, which are said to have been declaratory of the common law, and which authorized the King to act as "*parens patriæ*—as the person to take care of those who are incompetent to take care of themselves." This function he exercised through the agency of the Chancery Court, by the appointment of a "committee," or trustee, who, as said by Lord Redesdale in *Ex parte Fitzgerald*, 2 Sch. & Lef. 431, "is considered as a mere bailiff, appointed by the Crown, and under its control, to take care of the property [of the lunatic], acting according to the duty imposed on the Crown, and liable to account, to censure, to punishment, and to be removed, if he shall misconduct himself." It was said, moreover, to be the duty of the court "to see that the committee [or trustee] does not use his office to the prejudice of the lunatic in his life-time, or of those entitled to his property after his death." The death of the lunatic was said to determine the trustee's authority, although he was still subject to the control of the court; and "the court," it was observed, "ought not to permit the committee [or trustee] to interefere with the title [of the heirs] to the possession. It must consider him in the situation of a bailiff, manager, or receiver; as one who is to act merely officially, and not to interfere in any manner with the rights of third persons, on determination of his authority as committee." "He continues liable to account, and liable to all the consequences of any misconduct on his part, and to act in delivering possession as the court shall direct."

[Ex parte Williams.]

In *Matter of Colvin*, 3 Md. Ch. 278, the inquiry arose, as to what effect the death of the lunatic would have on the trust; and the question is discussed at length. It was held to determine the office of the committee, "that officer, by the death of the lunatic, becoming *functus officio*," and the only power retained over him, as such, by the Chancery Court was held to be, to compel him to account, and deliver possession of the property, if any he has, as the court shall direct. In other words, upon the death of the lunatic, the jurisdiction of chancery remains only to the extent, and for the purpose of having the necessary accounts taken, and directing the fund or estate in possession of the trustee to be paid over, or delivered to the party or parties entitled. It was further held, that chancery could not, after the death of the lunatic, administer the estate for the benefit of creditors, or adjudicate questions of conflicting rights between opposing claimants. This is evidently upon the ground, that the trust relationship has been extinguished, except for the purpose of accounting, and the preservation of the estate by the court *pendente lite*.

The same view is taken in *Guarard v. Gaillard*, 15 S. C. (L. R.) 22; the court holding that the committee, invested with the full power of management, had no legal title to the property of the lunatic, and that "the office of committee expired at the death of the lunatic." If in possession, the trustee was held, however, to the duty of taking care of the estate of the lunatic, for the benefit of those who may have succeeded to the inheritance, until ordered by the court to account and give it up, although, it was said, he might act at his peril without such order.

Mr. Adams, in his work on Equity, summarizes the principle thus: "On the death of the lunatic, the power of administration is at an end, except as to orders which have been already made, or which are consequential on reports or petitions already made or presented. But the committee continues under the control of the court, and will be ordered, on the application of the lunatic's heirs, to deliver up the possession of the estate." In a note to the Seventh American Edition, p. 297 (*298), the doctrine of the Maryland and South Carolina cases above cited is concisely stated, and approved by the editor. See, also, *Dean's Appeal*, 90 Penn. St. Rep. 106; Schouler's Dom. Relations, 424-425; 1 Lewin on Trusts, 346.

Under the principles settled by these authorities, it is clear

[Pollak v. Davidson.]

that the death of William Thomas Williams, the ward of the trustee, terminated the trust relationship existing between him and the petitioner, as his trustee under the statute, who was clothed only with the power of management and control, not with the legal title of the ward's estate. The extinguishment of the trust terminated his further power of control, except to take proper care of any trust fund or property in his possession, and to account to the Chancery Court. He had no further power to collect rents, or to sue for possession of the property of the decedent. The suit in question was, therefore, properly ordered by the court to abate.

The court had no authority, after such abatement, to allow the suit to be prosecuted in the name of the heirs. The proposed introduction of entirely new parties complainant was the introduction of a new and distinct cause of action, which is not authorized by the statute of amendments.

The above view of this case renders it unnecessary that we should consider the suggestion as to the invalidity of the chancellor's decree appointing the petitioner trustee of the ward's estate. For the purpose of this decision, we have considered that decree to be valid—a point in regard to which there is some doubt.

The application is denied.

Pollak *v.* Davidson.

Trover between Mortgagees, for Conversion of Mules.

1. *Charge to jury unsupported by evidence.*—A charge to the jury which, though it asserts a correct legal proposition, is not supported by any evidence in the case, should not be given, because it tends to mislead the jury; but the giving of such a charge is not a reversible error, unless it is apparent that the jury were thereby misled, to the prejudice of the appellant, since he could protect himself by asking explanatory or qualifying charges.

2. *Registration of mortgage as constructive notice; removal of property to another county.*—A mortgage of personal property is required to be recorded, not only in the county in which the mortgagor resides, but also in the county in which the property then is; and on its removal to another county, the mortgage must be there recorded within six months afterwards (Code, §§ 1806, 1814); and the fact that the mortgaged animals (mules) are carried over and worked in the former county by day, but carried back each night into the new county, does not dispense with the necessity for such new registration.

3. *Constructive notice of mortgage, as implied from knowledge of indebtedness, character of business, &c.*—Knowledge of the existence of a debt, is not constructive notice of an unrecorded mortgage given to secure it; nor can notice of such unrecorded mortgage be implied from the additional facts, that the mortgagee was a merchant making advances to planters, and that his house of business was not more than one hundred and fifty yards distant from that of the second mortgagee; nor are these facts sufficient to put the second mortgagee on inquiry.

4. *Charge referring question of law to jury.*—A charge should not be given which refers to the jury the decision of a question at law; as, what diligence in making inquiry the law requires of a purchaser.

5. *Damages for conversion by mortgagee, on return of property to mortgagor.*—In trover by the first, against a second mortgagee of personal property, the material question being whether the defendant was chargeable with notice, actual or constructive, of plaintiff's prior mortgage, the fact that the defendant, at the termination of a lawsuit with the mortgagor, sold and returned to him a part of the mortgaged property, does not relieve him of damages for its conversion, if otherwise he was guilty of a conversion.

6. *Failure of party to testify, as evidence against him.*—In an action by the first, against the second mortgagee, for a conversion of the mortgaged property, the failure of the defendant to testify in his own behalf, that he had no notice of the plaintiff's prior unrecorded mortgage, is not a circumstance from which an unfavorable presumption against him is to be indulged, when the record shows that he was absent from the State at the time of the trial, and that the plaintiff's evidence did not make out against him a *prima facie* showing of notice.

APPEAL from the Circuit Court of Montgomery.

Tried before the Hon. JOHN P. HUBBARD.

This action was brought by J. & T. Davidson suing as partners, and revived in the name of T. Davidson as surviving partner, against I. Pollak, doing business under the name of Pollak & Co., to recover damages for the alleged conversion of seventeen mules; and was commenced on the 21st November, 1887. The plaintiffs claimed the mules under a mortgage executed to them by A. J. Simmons and others, which was dated in January, 1885, to secure a debt for advances to make a crop; and in which the mules were described as being "on Taylor place in Bullock county, and the Charles & Hood place, Montgomery county." The mortgage was duly recorded in Montgomery county, but not in Bullock county. The defendant also claimed the mules under a mortgage executed to him by said Simmons, which was dated December 15th, 1886; and he had obtained possession by legal proceedings instituted against Simmons after the law-day of the mortgage. The only matters here assigned as error are, two charges given by the court below at the instance of the plaintiff, and the refusal of fifteen charges asked by the defendant. The substance of these charges,

[Pollak v. Davidson.]

and the material facts bearing on them, are stated in the opinion.

TOMPKINS, LONDON & TROY, and RICE & WILEY, for appellant.

E. P. MORRISSETT, and WATTS & SON, *contra.*

CLOPTON, J.—Both parties deduce title to the mules, for the conversion of which appellee sues, from successive mortgages executed by a common mortgagor; the first about January 13, 1885, to J. & T. Davidson, of which firm appellee is the surviving partner; and the other December 15, 1886, to Pollak & Co., of which appellant is the sole member. No question arises as to the claim of defendant to protection as a *bona fide* purchaser for a valuable consideration, if he took his mortgage without notice of the prior mortgage. The contestation between the parties is, which mortgage has the superior lien; and notice is the pivotal question.

So far as shown by the record, plaintiff asked only two charges, both in relation to implied notice. The first is, substantially, that whatever is sufficient to put a party upon inquiry, is sufficient to charge him with notice, and whenever a person making a purchase, or taking a mortgage, has such information as would put a prudent man on inquiry, and inquiry would lead to knowledge of an adverse prior claim, it is his own folly if he does not act on the information, and make inquiry; and he can claim no protection against a prior mortgage, or other incumbrance, of which he would have been informed if diligent inquiry had been made. The correctness of the legal proposition of the charge is not controverted; but it is specially objected, that there is no evidence on which to predicate it. If the objection be well founded, the charge should have been refused. The court should carefully avoid giving instructions unsupported by any evidence, their tendency being to mislead the jury, and withdraw their consideration from the material and real issues. But, having been given, it does not authorize a reversal, unless it is apparent that the jury were mislead to the prejudice of appellant. We have substantially stated the charge at length, for the purpose of considering, in connection with it, qualifying instructions asked by defendant, based on the want of evidence tending to prove the fundamental hypothetical fact stated therein—information such as would put a prudent man on inquiry.

[Pollak v. Davidson.]

The qualifying charges are: *First*, that the only evidence of any notice to the defendant, of plaintiffs' mortgage, is the evidence of the mortgagor; and unless the jury are satisfied from all the evidence that the mortgagor did give the counsel of defendant such notice, they must find that defendant had no such notice; *second*, that under the facts of this case, the jury can not find for plaintiff, unless they are satisfied from the evidence that defendant, or his attorney, at the time of the execution of the mortgage, had actual notice of plaintiff's mortgage, and the burden of showing that defendant had notice is on plaintiff. The effect of the first charge is to call on the court to say there is no evidence that defendant had information or notice of any facts sufficient to put him on inquiry, as supposed in the foregoing charge given at the instance of the plaintiff, and no evidence of actual or constructive notice, other than that of the mortgagor, that he gave information of the prior mortgage to the attorney of defendant; and thus to narrow the inquiry to this question of fact, as to which the evidence was conflicting. The proposition of the second charge is, that, there being a want of evidence of constructive or implied notice, actual notice to defendant, or to his attorney, is essential to plaintiff's recovery. Whether or not the qualifying instructions should have been given, depends on the state of the proof, as shown by the record, and the tendencies of the evidence.

It is contended by appellee, in the first place, that there was constructive notice by the registration of the mortgage. All the mules, except three, were, at the date of the conveyance under which plaintiff claims, in the county of Bullock. The three excepted were at that·time in Montgomery county, but, about the first of 1886, were removed to Bullock county, where all the mules remained and were at the time of the execution of defendant's mortgage. The mortgage to J. & T. Davidson was recorded only in Montgomery county. By the statutes, conveyances of personal property to secure debts must be recorded, both in the county in which the grantor resides, and in the county where the property is at the date of the conveyance; and if removed to another county, it must be recorded, within six months from such removal, in the county to which the property is removed. As against creditors and purchasers without notice, such conveyances take effect from the date of registration; and when the property is removed to a different county from that in which the grantor resides, they cease to have effect

[Pollak v. Davidson.]

thereafter, unless recorded in such county within six months from the removal. The fact that the mules, originally in Bullock county, were sometimes brought during the day to work on a plantation in Montgomery county, and carried back at night, where they were kept all the time, did not operate to change the *situs* of the property as it was at the date of the conveyance. In order that registration may operate as constructive notice, it must be made in substantial conformity to the statutory requirements. The omission to have the mortgage recorded in Bullock county destroys the effect of its registration in Montgomery county, as constructive notice.—Code, 1886, §§1806, 1814; *Sanders v. Knox*, 57 Ala. 80; *Hardaway v. Semmes*, 38 Ala. 657.

The only witness examined in reference to actual notice is the mortgagor, introduced by plaintiff, who testified, that he had no recollection of ever having told defendant at any time about plaintiff's mortgage, and that his transactions touching the execution of defendant's mortgage were with his attorney. It will not be seriously contended, that any inference of actual notice to defendant *himself* can be drawn from this evidence. This was the entire evidence relating to this matter, except the evidence of the mortgagor, that on the day on which the mortgage was signed, and before it was signed, he informed the attorney, who represented the defendant, that "the Davidsons" had a mortgage on the property. This was denied by the attorney, who further testified that he had no knowledge of it until the commencement of legal proceedings by defendant against the mortgagor for the recovery of the property. By the qualifying charges, this disputed question of fact was properly referred to the jury. The only fact of which there is evidence tending to show that defendant was informed, is the indebtedness of the mortgagor to J. & T. Davidson. Upon this information, and the additional fact that they were merchants advancing to farmers, and doing business about one hundred and fifty yards from defendant's place of business, plaintiff claims that implied notice may be inferred. It can not be insisted that the proximity of their places of business is a fact sufficient to put defendant on inquiry as to the prior mortgage. The insufficiency, for this purpose, of knowledge of the indebtedness of the mortgagor, was expressly decided in *Bell v. Tyson*, 74 Ala. 353, where it is said: "We are aware of no rule of law which makes notice of the existence of a debt to be constructive notice of a secret lien created by an unrecorded mortgage by which such debt is secured."

Whether or not there be evidence is a question for the court; its sufficiency is a question for the jury. When there is a want of evidence to prove a fact material to plaintiff's recovery, the court should, on request of defendant, instruct the jury there is no evidence of such fact.—*Tyree v. Lyon*, 67 Ala. 1. On the uncontradicted evidence, the court would have been authorized, in the absence of evidence of notice to the counsel, to instruct the jury to find the issue as to notice in favor of the defendant. As the record fails to disclose any evidence tending to show information of facts sufficient to put defendant on inquiry, or constructive or actual notice, other than through his counsel, the court should have instructed the jury that defendant was a *bona fide* purchaser without notice, unless they were satisfied the mortgagor informed his counsel of the prior mortgage. The qualifying charges requested by defendant should have been given. Such charges are the only means by which a party may protect himself against the misleading tendencies and prejudicial effects of a charge unsupported by any evidence.

The second charge asked by plaintiff is to the following effect: If defendant had no notice of the prior mortgage, and his want of notice was the result of that want of diligence which the law required for its ascertainment; then he is chargeable with notice, and can claim no protection against the prior mortgage. The charges requested by defendant, which we have above considered, were also intended to qualify this instruction, and the foregoing observations apply. It may be further remarked, that the charge is obnoxious to the objection, that it refers to the jury a question of law—what diligence in making inquiry the law requires of a purchaser.—*Drake v. State*, 60 Ala. 62; *Riley v. Riley*, 36 Ala. 496; *Thomason v. Odum*, 31 Ala. 108.

It appears that the mules in controversy were seized under a writ of detinue, brought by the defendant against the mortgagor. They were taken possession of by the agent of defendant, and kept on the plantation upon which they were when seized, until shortly before the commencement of this suit, when they were removed to another plantation in a different county. On a settlement of the litigation, the mortgagor, after the commencement of this suit, purchased from the defendant six of the mules, which he has in possession. On these facts, defendant asked the court to charge the jury, that he was not liable for the mules returned to the mortgagor. If defendant had committed a previous conversion, on which this action is founded, his sale and return of the mules, after the commencement of suit, does not relieve the conversion of its tortiousness.

In the argument of the cause before the jury, counsel for plaintiff contended that they had the right to infer, from the failure of the defendant to testify, that if examined he would testify that he had notice of the prior mortgage. To meet this, defendant requested the court to instruct the jury, that the fact that defendant had not been examined as a witness, is no evidence that he had any notice of the prior mortgage. The rule in such case is thus stated by Mr. Wharton: "The refusal of the party, under any circumstances, to testify as to any facts with which he is familiar, must lead to the presumption which ordinarily holds against a party who withholds explanatory evidence in his favor."—1 Whart. Ev. § 486. To bring a party within the operation of such an unfavorable presumption, he must occupy a position analogous to that of a party who withholds clearer and more satisfactory evidence of the matter in dispute, which is in his power to produce, than that which is offered. The facts, to which the witnesses on the part of the adverse party have testified, must be apparently, or presumably, within his knowledge. When the evidence is conflicting, or circumstantial, and it appears to be in the power of a party to contradict or explain, a presumption can and should be indulged against him, if he should fail to testify without satisfactory reason. In *McGar v. Adams*, 65 Ala. 106, after declining to decide whether an unfavorable presumption should be indulged under the circumstances last stated, the court said: "But we do affirm that a presumption can not, and ought not, to be indulged against a party who does not introduce and examine himself as a witness, merely to support the uncontradicted evidence, favorable to him, which his adversary introduces." Neither should such presumption be indulged against defendant for not introducing himself to disprove facts essential to plaintiff's recovery, which he has failed to *prima facie* establish. He may remain silent, until plaintiff has shown a case which calls upon him to speak in denial or explanation.

At the time of the execution of the mortgage, the mortgagor and the counsel of defendant only were present. The defendant had no knowledge of what then and there occurred, and could neither contradict nor explain the testimony of the mortgagor. The utmost to which he could have testified would have been, that his counsel never communicated to him that he had been informed of the prior mortgage. The attorney having testified that he was not so informed, and had no knowledge of it, it is not presumable that he made such communication to defendant; and it may well be doubted whether such negative testimony would be admissible in mere corroboration of the attorney's testimony. Under the circumstances, no unfavorable presumption should have been indulged against the defendant, especially when it was shown that he had been, several days prior, and was at the time of the trial, in New York.—*Perkins v. Hitchcock*, 49 Me. 468.

We have examined all the assignments of error pressed in the argument. Several other charges were asked by defendant, as to which, without considering them specially, we remark, that they are either misleading, or suppose facts as a part of the hypothesis of which there is no evidence, or are argumentative, or invade the province of the jury.

For the errors mentioned, the judgment is reversed, and the cause remanded.

Chambers *v.* Seay.

Action by Agent against Principal, for Services rendered under Power of Attorney to sell Lands.

1. *Misjoinder of counts.*—Special counts in case, claiming damages for the breach of a duty imposed by a written contract, can not be joined with the common counts.
2. *Statute of limitations, in defense of action for value of services rendered.*—Under statutory provisions (Code, §§ 2615, 2618), three years is the bar to an action to recover the reasonable value of services rendered under a written contract.

APPEAL from the Circuit Court of Talladega.

Tried before the Hon. LEROY F. BOX.

This action was brought by George W. Chambers against John L. Seay, and was commenced on the 24th March, 1880. The plaintiff sought to recover, under the complaint as amended, the reasonable value of services rendered by him, as agent and attorney in fact for defendant, under a written contract by which defendant authorized him to sell a tract of land, his compensation to be "an undivided one-fourth interest in the proceeds of sale." The defendant revoked the agency in January, 1880, and soon afterwards himself sold the property for $20,000. The contract was dated February 28, 1878, and was signed by both parties. Its material stipulations are set out in the former report of the case (73 Ala. 372), and it is unnecessary to repeat them. Some of the counts in the complaint were in case, as decided by the court, and as shown by the former report; and these were struck out by amendment, after demurrer sustained. The court instructed the jury, in substance, that the action was barred by the statute of limitations of three years; and this charge is here assigned as error, with the ruling on the demurrer.

PARSONS & PARSONS, for appellant.

CECIL BROWNE, *contra.*

McCLELLAN, J.—The first three counts of the complaint are in *assumpsit,* claiming for money due by account, for money paid at the request of the defendant, and for work and labor done for the defendant, respectively. The original fourth count, and the fifth and sixth, respectively, claim damages for a breach of duty on the part of the defendant, the alleged duty being imposed by the written contract, which is set out, and each of these counts is essentially in case.—*Myers v. Gilbert,* 18 Ala. 467; *Whilden v. M. & P. Nat. Bank,* 64 Ala. 1. The sixth and seventh assignments of demurrer, taken to the misjoinder of counts, were, therefore, properly sustained.—*Chambers v. Seay,* 73 Ala. 379.

2. The complaint, having been amended, so as to conform to the ruling of the court on demurrer, the plaintiff claimed in the original counts, and on the amended fourth count, the sum of five thousand dollars as by account for money paid, and work and labor done at the request of the defendant, more than three years before suit brought. The general issue, and the statute of limitations of three years, were pleaded. The effort of plaintiff appears to have been to bring his cause of action within subdivision five of section 2615 of the Code of 1886; but the bill of exceptions, which purports to set out all the evidence, shows an utter failure in this effort. On the contrary, it is expressly stated, that "it was and is conceded by plaintiff, and agreed by and between

the parties," that the action was not upon the contract of
agency, "but was and is a suit to recover," not money loaned,
nor upon a stated liquidated account, but "the reasonable
value of services rendered under said contract," &c. It
clearly appears that these services were rendered, and
plaintiff's claim to be recompensed for them accrued, more
than three years before this suit was instituted. On this
state of pleadings and proof, the court, at the request in writing of the defendant, correctly charged the jury, that if they
believed "the evidence, they must find for the defendant on
account of the bar of the statute of limitations of three
years."—Code, § 2618.

Affirmed.

Sheppard *v.* Sheppard.

Statutory Proceedings for Allotment of Dower.

1. *Petition for allotment of dower; averment of husband's seizin.*—In a
petition for the allotment of dower, an averment that the husband "was
seized and possessed" of the lands described is, on demurrer, equivalent to an averment that he was seized in fee (Code, 1886, § 1892; 1876,
§ 2232); but it is the better course to follow the language of the statute.

2. *Right of dower, as affected by separate estate.*—In estimating the
widow's right of dower, or making an abatement from its value, on account of a separate estate held by her, "exclusive of the rents, income
and profits" (Code, 1886, §§ 2354-5; 1876, §§ 2715-16), lands allotted to
her as dower in the estate of a former husband must be computed, her
interest therein being an estate of freehold, and more than a mere right
to the rents, income, and profits.

3. *Assignment of dower in lands chargeable with trust.*—When it appears that the lands, in which an allotment of dower is sought, are
chargeable with a trust in favor of the husband's children by a former
marriage, on account of moneys belonging to their mother's statutory
estate, which were invested or used by him in the purchase of the lands,
an assignment by metes and bounds would be unjust (Code, 1886,
§ 1910; 1876, § 2248), and the court should decline jurisdiction, leaving
the parties to their remedies in equity; but the mere assertion of such
a claim by the heirs, without any evidence to support it, does not require the court to dismiss the petition.

APPEAL from the Probate Court of Cherokee.
Heard before the Hon. ROBERT R. SAVAGE.

WATTS & SON, and BURNETT & SMYER, for appellant.'

MATTHEWS & DANIEL, *contra.*

STONE, C. J.—The appellant, Martha Sheppard, filed her petition in the Probate Court praying the allotment of dower in lands, of which, as the petition alleges, her late husband, J. L. W. Sheppard, was "seized and possessed" at his death. The petition was contested by the administrator, and the heirs at law of the deceased husband. Contestants assigned numerous grounds of demurrer, and set up various objections in their answer to the petition, and many questions arose during the hearing as to the allowance or disallowance of testimony offered; but, with our view of the case, it will not be necessary to enter into a consideration of these various questions.

Section 2232 of the Code of 1876, under which this proceeding was begun, declares that the widow is dowable: 1st, of all lands of which the husband was seized in fee simple during the marriage; 2d, of all lands of which another was seized in fee to his use; 3d, of all lands to which, at the time of his death, he had a perfect equity, having paid all the purchase-money thereof.

The averments of the petition do not bring this case strictly within any one of these definitions; but, under the averments of seizin, evidence was admissible to show that such seizin was *in fee*. This court has held that such an averment of the character of ownership of the husband, in the petition for dower, was sufficient.—*Snodgrass v. Clark*, 44 Ala. 198. Still, we think that, in a statutory proceeding for the assignment of dower, it is the better course to adopt the language of the statutes.

One of the grounds of objection to the allowance of dower in this proceeding, set up in the answer of contestants, was, that the petitioner, at the time of the death of her husband, had a separate estate, which was equal to, or greater in value than her dower interest in the estate of her late husband. Section 2715 of Code of 1876 provides, that "if any woman, having a separate estate, survive her husband, and such separate estate, exclusive of the rents, income and profits, is equal to, or greater in value than her dower interest and distributive share in her husband's estate, . . . she shall not be entitled to dower in, or distribution of her husband's estate." It appears that petitioner had been a widow before her marriage to Sheppard, and dower had been assigned her in her former husband's estate. In the effort to show the value of petitioner's separate estate, much testimony was offered by contestants as to the value of the dower lands as-

36

signed petitioner as widow of her former husband. We need not pass absolutely on this question; but an estate in dower is a freehold, and, it would seem, must be classed as more than a right to the rents, income and profits. It is a marketable estate in the lands.

Another objection urged in the answer of contestants, to the allowance of the petition, was, that an undivided interest in the larger part of the lands in which dower was sought, belonged to the estate of Martha M. Sheppard, the former wife of J. L. W. Sheppard, and mother of the contesting heirs; and evidence was introduced, *prima facie* sufficient, to show that two thousand dollars of the statutory separate estate of said Martha M. Sheppard had been invested by the said J. L. W. Sheppard in the purchase of this land, in which dower was sought by the petitioner. Section 2248 of the Code of 1876 provides, that "when land out of which dower is demanded has been alienated by the husband, and from improvements made by the alienee, or from any other cause, an assignment by metes and bounds would be unjust, the judge of probate must decline jurisdiction, and application must be made to the court of chancery." In *Thrasher v. Pinckard*, 23 Ala. 621, this court said: "The Probate Court, being one of limited jurisdiction, can only allot dower in the mode pointed out by statute; and where the decree has to be moulded so as to meet the justice of the case, arising from the peculiar circumstances, a court of chancery alone has power to make the proper decree." If it be shown that any portion of the statutory separate estate of Martha M. Sheppard had been invested in the purchase of the lands, out of which the petitioner seeks to be endowed, there is a resulting or constructive trust in favor of the heirs of said Martha M. Sheppard, the contestants here, which the Probate Court has no jurisdiction to determine. Courts of equity entertain concurrent jurisdiction with the Probate Court in the assignment of dower, and only in a court of equity could the rights of all parties, in such a case, be adjudicated.— *Wood v. Morgan*, 56 Ala. 397.

We do not wish to be understood as holding that every suggestion of adverse claim or interest should devest the jurisdiction of the Probate Court in proceedings for the assignment of dower. What was said by this court in *Ballard v. Johns*, 84 Ala. 70, in a somewhat analogous proceeding in the Probate Court, we think applicable here. The adverse claim must be *bona fide*. If, on investigation, it is clear to the Probate Court that there is, in reality, no such adverse claim as is asserted, it may proceed to hear the application; but, if, during the pendency or trial of the petition, it is made known to the court that there is a substantial adverse claim asserted, or the court entertains serious doubts as to such adverse claim, the court should decline further jurisdiction of the matter. With the evidence in this case, we can not hold that the Probate Court erred in refusing to entertain jurisdiction of the appellant's petition.

Affirmed.

Manning *v.* Maroney.

Action on Bill of Exchange, by Indorsee against Drawer.

1. *Error without injury, in sustaining demurrer to special plea.*—The sustaining of a demurrer to a special plea, if erroneous, is error without injury, when the same defense was equally available under the general issue, which was also pleaded.

2. *When sworn plea is necessary.*—In an action on a bill of exchange by an indorsee against the drawer, the indorsement to plaintiff, or his ownership, not being denied by plea verified by affidavit (Code, §§ 2676, 2770), the validity of the transfer can not be questioned, and the bill is admissible as evidence.

3. *Admissibility of bill as evidence; preliminary proof of demand, protest, and notice; mutilation by identifying marks.*—In an action on a bill of exchange, the bill is admissible as evidence without preliminary proof of demand, protest, and notice of dishonor, or a waiver thereof, these facts being matter of defense; and it is not rendered inadmissible as evidence on the ground of mutilation, because of identifying marks as an exhibit to a deposition, written by the commissioner.

4. *Instructions to drawee not to pay; secondary evidence of letter beyond jurisdiction of the court.*—In an action by an indorsee against the drawer of a bill of exchange, who pleads the failure to give him due notice of dishonor, a letter written by him to the drawees, instructing them not to pay the bill, is admissible as evidence; and the letter being addressed to the drawees at their place of business in another State, and therefore presumptively beyond the jurisdiction of the court, secondary evidence of its contents may be adduced by the plaintiff, without accounting for its non-production.

5. *Demand and notice; averment and proof of.*—It has been long settled as a rule of pleading and evidence, that facts which excuse demand and notice are, in law, deemed proof of such demand and notice; consequently, an averment of demand and notice is proved by evidence of facts showing a waiver thereof.

6. *Waiver of protest and notice of dishonor.*—If the drawer of a bill instructs the drawee not to pay it, this dispenses with the necessity of protest and notice of dishonor.

7. *Set-off against commercial paper.*—By express statutory provision

(Code, § 2684), a bill of exchange, or other commercial paper, negotiated for value before maturity, is not subject to set-off.

8. *Set-off of partnership and individual demands.*—In an action by an
indorsee against the drawee of a bill of exchange, a demand due from
the payee to a partnership of which the defendant is a member, if available as a set-off in any case, is not so available without proof that the
other partners consented to such use of the claim, and that plaintiff had
knowledge of their consent; and consent given at the trial can not relate back.

APPEAL from the Circuit Court of Jackson.

Tried before the Hon. JOHN B. TALLY.

This action was brought by Frank M. Maroney, against
William Manning, and was commenced on the 17th January, 1877. The action was founded on a bill of exchange
for $90, drawn by the defendant on Hill, Fontaine & Co.,
Memphis, Tennessee, dated October 23d, 1886, and payable
to the order of LaFayette Maroney, by whom it was indorsed
to plaintiff. The complaint contained a special count on the
bill, alleging that it was not paid or accepted on presentation and demand, the defendant having notified the drawees
not to pay it; and the common counts were added. The
court overruled a demurrer to the special count, and sustained
a demurrer to the defendant's second plea, which averred
that "said bill was not in any manner presented to the drawees
for acceptance and payment by them, nor has said defendant,
the drawer of said bill, ever received any legal, proper, and
sufficient notice of the non-acceptance and non-payment
thereof;" and issue was joined on the pleas of *non assumpsit* and set-off.

On the trial; as the bill of exceptions shows, when the
plaintiff offered the bill in evidence, the defendant objected
to its admission, (1) because it did not appear on its face to
be the property of the plaintiff; (2) because it "has been de-
faced or mutilated," on account of words written on it by the
commissioner who took the deposition of one of the drawees,
identifying it as an exhibit; (3) because there was no proof
that it ever had been presented to the drawees for acceptance
or payment; (4) because there was no proof of notice to the
defendant of the dishonor of the bill. The court overruled
these several objections, and the defendant excepted. The
plaintiff offered in evidence the deposition of N. Fontaine,
one of the drawees of the bill, taken on interrogatories.
The third interrogatory asked the witness to examine the bill,
annexed as an exhibit, "and state whether or not said paper
was ever presented to Hill, Fontaine & Co. for payment or

[Manning v. Maroney.]

acceptance; and if it was, give the time, place, and by whom?" The witness answered, that the bill was sent to them in a letter by J. G. Winston, plaintiff's attorney, "for remittance, and was returned to him by us, by letter of November 18th, 1886, *as Hill, Fontaine & Co. had been instructed, by letter from William Manning, not to pay the same.*" The defendant objected to the italicized words, and moved to exclude them as evidence, "because they were not responsive to the interrogatory, and were in relation to the contents of a written instrument, the loss of which was not accounted for." The court overruled the objections, and the defendant excepted. The plaintiff introduced Thos. J. Cochran as a witness, who was a member of the firm of Jordan, Manning & Co., and who testified, that he wrote a letter to Hill, Fontaine & Co., at the instance of the defendant, instructing them not to pay said bill; but he did not recollect whether he signed the defendant's name to the letter, or whether the defendant himself signed it. The defendant himself, being called as a witness by plaintiff, admitted that he had instructed Cochran to write a letter to Hill, Fontaine & Co., telling them not to pay the bill; but he objected to the admission of this evidence, because the letter was not produced, nor its absence accounted for; and he excepted to the overruling of his objections.

The defendant offered in evidence, under the plea of set-off, an account for $13.84, in favor of Jordan, Manning & Co., against said LaFayette Maroney, the payee of the bill, due November 13th, 1886; and a note for $85.60, executed by said L. Maroney to said firm, dated December 28th, 1885, and due one day after date. The defendant proved that these claims were unpaid, and said T. J. Cochran testified in his behalf, that defendant was a member of said firm at that time, "and had the permission and consent of all the members of said firm to use said note and account as a set-off against this action." The plaintiff himself, while testifying, stated: "Before I bought said bill of exchange from my brother, I knew that he was indebted to said Jordan, Manning & Co., and had been to see them twice about his indebtedness." On this evidence, the court instructed the jury, "that unless the defendant held and owned said note and account prior to the indorsement of said bill of exchange to the plaintiff, and the plaintiff knew, at or before the transfer and indorsement of said bill to him, of said indebtedness by LaFayette Maroney to Jordan, Manning & Co., and that the defendant owned the same,—then the defendant was not entitled to claim the same as a set-off in this action." The defendant excepted to this charge, and he here assigns it as error, with the refusal of several charges asked by him, which it is unnecessary to set out, and the other rulings above stated.

LUSK & BELL, for appellant.

JNO. G. WINSTON, JR., and WATTS & SON, *contra.*

SOMERVILLE, J.—1. The defense set up in the second plea—viz., a failure to present the bill sued on, and to give due notice of dishonor—was equally available under the plea of the general issue, and the record shows that the defendant had the full benefit of it on the trial of the cause. Sustaining the plaintiff's demurrer to this plea is, for this reason, error without injury, if error at all.—*Phœnix Ins. Co. v. Moog*, 78 Ala. 284.

2. The objection interposed to the admission in evidence of the bill of exchange described in the complaint, was not well taken. The instrument was averred to be the property of the plaintiff, transferred to him by the indorsement of the payee; and there was no sworn plea, denying the fact of ownership. The validity of such transfer could not, therefore, be raised under the plea of the general issue.—Code, 1886, §§ 2676, 2770; Rule of Practice, No. 29, p. 810, Code (1886); *Agee v. Medlock*, 25 Ala. 281. The averment that the bill was indorsed to plaintiff by the payee is tantamount to an averment of the personal identity of the indorsee, *F. M.* Maroney, and the plaintiff *Frank* M. Maroney.

3. There was nothing in the objection, that the paper was mutilated, because of the memorandum indorsed on it by the commissioner for the purpose of identification, when it was attached as an exhibit to the deposition of the witness Fontaine; nor in the suggestion that preliminary evidence of demand, protest, and notice of dishonor, or waiver of them, should first have been offered, before offering the paper. This was mere matter of defense, not necessary to be negatived by anticipation on plaintiff's part before introducing the paper. The execution of the paper by the drawee, moreover, was sufficiently proved, and it was admissible under the other counts of the complaint.

4. The contents of the letter, written by order of the de-

fendant, Manning, to the drawees of the bill, Hill, Fontaine & Co., *instructing them not to pay the bill*, was properly admitted in evidence. We discover nothing in the record introduced on this point not entirely relevant. The drawees resided in Memphis, Tennessee, and the letter was received by them there. Presumptively, it continued to remain out of the jurisdiction of the court, and was in Tennessee at the time of the trial. If the contrary was true, it should have been proved by the defendant. Where a paper is beyond the jurisdiction, its contents can be proved by secondary evidence without proving its loss or destruction.—*Young v. East Ala. Railway Co.*, 80 Ala. 100; *Elliott v. Dyche, Ib.* 376; *Gordon v. Tweedy*, 74 Ala. 232.

5–6. It is objected that the statement as to the contents of the letter, which was disclosed by the witness Fontaine in his deposition, was not responsive to the third interrogatory, under which it was introduced. The inquiry made by this interrogatory was, whether the bill in suit had ever been "presented" to the drawees "for payment or acceptance." The answer shows both a presentation, and *excuse* for non-payment—viz., a specific instruction of the drawer *not to pay*. The rule is settled as one of pleading and evidence, and was long ago announced in this State, that facts which excuse demand and notice will, in law, be deemed *proof* of such demand and notice. Allegation of these facts may, therefore, be proved by any fact showing a waiver of them, demand and notice, and waiver of them, being in law equivalent of each other.—*Kennon v. McRea*, 7 Port. 175; *Shirley v. Fellows*, 9 Port. 300; *Spann v. Baltzell*, 46 Amer. Dec. 346; *Hibbard v. Russell*, 41 *Ib.* 733. The answer of the witness, in this view of the law, was responsive. and as such admissible, because the answer showed a good excuse for failure to give *notice of dishonor* to the defendant as drawer. "If the drawer of a bill or draft countermands payment, he thereby dispenses with presentment and notice of dishonor to himself. So, if he informs the payee that he has withdrawn the funds against which the bill is drawn." 3 Randolph on Com. Paper, § 1385; 2 Daniel Neg. Instr., §§ 1105, 1147; Byles on Bills, 286, 298; *Jacks v. Darwin*, 3 E. D. Smith, 558.

This instruction not to pay, by which the drawer brought dishonor on his own paper, was equally a good excuse for failure to *protest* the bill; the rule being that, generally, whatever will in law excuse, or amount to a waiver of notice of dishonor, will equally excuse protest.—3 Rand. Com. Paper, §§ 1148, 1161, In such cases, the drawer, being the real debtor, and having knowledge of the fact in advance that payment will be refused by the drawee, by reason of his countermand, can suffer no injury from the alleged negligence of the holder.—*Campbell v. Webster*, 2 C. B. 258.

7-8.   The instructions of the court as to the set-off were correct.   The bill was commercial paper, and being negotiated for value before maturity, was not subject to set-off or recoupment, by the express provisions of the statute. Code, 1886, § 2684; *Bank v. Poelnitz*, 61 Ala. 147.   In any event, unless the defendant, Manning, was the owner of the cross demands, prior to the indorsement of the bill of exchange to the plaintiff, and this fact was known to the plaintiff before he acquired title to the bill, the set-off would not be available in an action on the bill, as in the present suit. The note and account claimed by the defendant as a set-off, were the property of Jordan, Manning & Co., a partnership of which defendant was a member.   They were due by La-Fayette Maroney, the payee and indorser of the bill, not by the defendant.   As against such payee, they were not a legal set-off at the time of the indorsement, for want of mutuality.—*Cannon v. Lindsey*, 85 Ala. 198, and cases there cited.   And admitting that a partnership demand against the plaintiff in an action may, by consent of all the partners, be set off against a demand by the plaintiff against an individual partner, that principle can have no application here, because it does not appear that there was any consent of the partners to such use of their claim before the assignment of it to defendant, and that the plaintiff knew of such consent, even if that would avail.   The consent given at the trial can not relate back to the date of the assignment, so as to make the set-off good against the assignor; and unless it was good against him, it can not be so against the defendant, not being his debt, and the paper sued on being governed by the commercial law.—*Jones v. Blair*, 57 Ala. 457; Code, §§ 2684, 1765; *McKenzie v. Hunt*, 32 Ala. 494.

The charge given by the court recognized these principles, while the instructions refused, on request of the defendant, either ignored, or were in direct conflict with them.

The rulings of the court are free from error, and the judgment is affirmed.

Swann & Billups *v.* Gaston.

Ejectment by Trustees for Railroad Lands.

1. *Deed of railroad corporation. executed by agent.*—A conveyance of lands which belonged to the Alabama & Chattanooga Railroad Company, executed by J. C. Stanton as general superintendent and attorney in fact, without written authority from the board of directors, or other governing body of that corporation, passed no legal title or estate, as against the corporation, or the trustees who succeeded to its rights; but it would constitute color of title, under which a title might be acquired by possession held long enough to effect a statutory bar.

2. *Congressional grant of lands in aid of railroads; title of State, and statute of limitations against.*—Under the acts of Congress granting lands to the State of Alabama in aid of certain railroads (11 U. S. Stat. at large, p. 17; 16 *Ib.* 45), as heretofore construed, the legal title to the lands granted at once vested in the State, for the use and benefit of the designated railroad companies; and it continued in the State, except as to the lands sold during the construction of the road in continuous sections of twenty miles, until the construction of the road was completed; and while the title thus continued in the State, the statute of limitations did not begin to run in favor of an adverse possessor under color of title.

3. *Same; lands allotted to Alabama & Chattanooga Railroad Company; statute of limitations against trustees.*—The lands allotted to the two railroad companies which were consolidated into the Alabama & Chattanooga Railroad Company having been conveyed by it to the State, before the completion of the road, by mortgage dated March 2d, 1870, the legal title remained in the State, notwithstanding the completion of the road in May, 1871, until the lands were conveyed by it to Swann and Billups, as trustees for the railroad company, by deed dated February 8th 1877; and the statute of limitations did not begin to run against said trustees until that time.

4. *Conveyance (or mortgage) of lands; title afterwards acquired.*—A railroad company may convey by mortgage property to be afterwards acquired; and if it conveys lands to which it has only an equitable title, but to which it afterwards acquires the legal title, that title at once enures to the grantee, or mortgagee, both by the express words of the instrument, and by the statutory words of warranty, *grant, bargain, sell and convey.*

5. *Statute of limitations against State.*—On general principles, a statute of limitations does not apply to the State, unless it is expressly named or included, nor can possession be adverse to it; and by express statutory provision (Code, § 2613,), twenty years is the limitation of an action against the State.

APPEAL from the Circuit Court of Etowah.

Tried before the Hon. JOHN B. TALLY.

This action was brought by John Swann and John A. Billups, against James L. Gaston, to recover the possession of a tract of land, described as the south-west quarter of the north-west quarter of section 17, township 11, range 7 east, containing forty acres; and was commenced on the 13th July, 1885. The land sued for was embraced in the grant of lands to the State of Alabama, by act of Congress approved June 3d, 1856, in aid of certain railroads therein mentioned; and it was included in the lands afterwards set apart and allotted by the State to the two railroad companies which were consolidated into the Alabama & Chattanooga Railroad Company. The plaintiffs claimed the land under the deed executed to them, as trustees, by Governor Houston, in the name of the State, dated February 8th, 1877; while the defendant claimed under a conveyance executed to him, in the name of said railroad company, "by J. C. Stanton, general superintendent and attorney in fact," which was dated November 1st, 1870, and recited the payment of $100 as its consideration; and he pleaded adverse possession and the statute of limitations. The several acts of Congress, and the acts of the General Assembly relating to these lands, with the conveyances under which each party claimed, were in evidence; but it is not necessary to set them out, nor to state their contents, as the material facts are stated in the opinion of the court. On all the evidence adduced, the court charged the jury, on request, that they must find for the defendant, if they believed the evidence. The plaintiffs excepted to this charge, and they here assign it as error.

S. F. RICE, for appellants, cited *Ware v. Swann & Billups*, 79 Ala. 330; *Wright v. Roseberry*, 121 U. S. 488; *Jackson v. Vail*, 7 Wend. 125; *Wilson v. Hudson*, 8 Yerg. 398; *Thomas v. Hatch*, 3 Sumner, 170; 4 How. U. S. 169; *Kennedy v. Townsley*, 16 Ala. 246; *Hartley v. Hartley*, 3 Metc. Ky. 56; *Farley v. Smith*, 39 Ala. 38; 58 Iowa, 621; 13 Wall. 92; 75 Mo. 272; 61 Mo. 329; 20 W. Va. 485; 97 U. S. 497.

R. A. D. DUNLAP, *contra*, cited *Swann & Billups v. Lindsey*, 70 Ala. 507; *Ware v. Swann & Billups*, 79 Ala. 330; *Barclay v. Smith*, 66 Ala. 230.

CLOPTON, J.—Appellants' title to the land, to recover which they bring the action of ejectment, had its origin in the act of Congress of June 3, 1856, by which there was granted to the State of Alabama, for the purpose of aiding in the construction of certain railroads, "every alternate
VOL. LXXXVII.

[Swann & Billups v. Gaston.]

section of land designated by odd numbers, for six sections
in width on each side of each of said roads," with a reservation of any sections, or parts of sections, which had been sold
by the United States, or to which the right of pre-emption
had attached.   If the roads were not completed within ten
years, the lands unsold reverted to the United States.—11 U.
S. Stat. at Large, 17.   Under authority conferred by the
act, the legislature, by joint resolutions, assigned the lands,
granted for the purpose of constructing a railroad from the
North-East to the South-Western portion of the State, to
the North-East and South-West Alabama, and the Wills
Valley Railroads, respectively.—Acts 1857–8, p. 430.   These
roads were not completed within the time prescribed.   By
an act of the General Assembly, they were consolidated and
incorporated by the name of the "Alabama and Chattanooga
Railroad Company;" and all the franchises, rights and immunities granted or pertaining, and property belonging to either
of the companies, were vested in the consolidated company.
Acts, 1868, 207.   By an act of Congress, approved April
10, 1869, the grant made by the act of June 3, 1856, was
revived and renewed, subject to all the conditions and restrictions contained in the latter act, except that three years
from the passage of the act were allowed, within which to
complete the roads.—16 U. S. Stat. at Large, 45.   The Alabama & Chattanooga Railroad was completed May 17, 1871,
and became entitled to the lands.

The defendant entered into possession of the land sued
for, about November 1, 1870, under a deed executed in the
name of the Alabama & Chattanooga Railroad Company, by
J. C. Stanton, general superintendent and attorney in fact,
and has been in possession ever since, claiming in his own
right.   There being no evidence of any written authority
from the governing body of the company, for which Stanton
purported to act as agent, to execute the deed, it conveyed
no legal title or estate to defendant.—*Standifer v. Swan*,
78 Ala. 88.   This was admitted on the trial, and the deed
was relied on only as color of title, to show the character and
extent of defendant's possession.   His contention is, that his
continuous adverse possession matured into a title by operation of the statute of limitations of ten years.   The suit was
commenced July 13, 1885.   The material question is,. at
what time did the statute begin to run against plaintiffs'
cause of action.

Further statement of the provisions of the congressional

acts, and re-discussion of their construction, is unnecessary. The material provisions will be found stated in *Swann v. Lindsey*, 70 Ala. 507, where the acts were fully considered and construed. The construction was, that under the provisions of the act of June 3, 1856, the State had absolute power to sell one hundred and twenty sections included within a continuous length of twenty miles of the road; and when the Governor certified to the Secretary of the Interior that any twenty continuous miles of the road was completed, to sell another one hundred and twenty sections included in a continuous length of twenty miles; and so, from time to time, until the road was completed; that sales made in pursuance of these provisions vested in the purchaser all title of both the Federal and State Governments, whether or not the road was completed; and on the completion of the road within the prescribed time, the indefeasible ownership of the unsold lands vested in the State, or its appointee. This construction was followed and re-affirmed in the subsequent cases of *Standifer v. Swann*, 78 Ala. 88, and *Ware v. Swann*, 79 Ala. 330. The conclusion reached in each of these cases was, that the act of Congress operated a grant *in præsenti* to the State, until the completion of the road. Until then, the State alone could maintain an action for the possession; and until then, the running of the statute of limitations of ten years could not commence.

This construction is not controverted; but it insisted, that the statute began to operate from May 17, 1871, the date of the completion of the road; and as more than ten years elapsed after that time, before the commencement of the suit, that the statute is a full defense. It may be conceded, that if nothing intervened to prevent it, the statute commenced to run on the completion of the road, as the trust would have been executed, and the object of a suit brought thereafter, though in the name of the State, would be to enforce the rights of the company—a litigation in which the State had no real interest. This brings for consideration the legal effect and operation of certain conveyances made by the railroad company to the State, and by the State to the plaintiffs. On March 2, 1870, the Alabama & Chattanooga Railroad Company executed to the State a mortgage of the lands granted by the act of Congress, except such as had been previously sold; and on February 8, 1877, the State, by its Governor, conveyed the land to plaintiffs as trustees. The mortgage and deed were duly recorded. The mortgage

was made to secure the bonds of the company given in exchange for the bonds of the State, loaned to the company in
pursuance and by authority of an act of the General Assembly, entitled "An act to loan the credit of the State of Alabama to the Alabama & Chattanooga Railroad Company, for
the purpose of expediting the construction of the railroad of
said company within the State of Alabama."—Acts, 1869–70,
89. It conveyed "all the lands granted by the United States,
to and for the benefit of this company, and all the right, title,
interest and estate which said company now has, or may
hereafter lawfully acquire, in and to said lands;" reserving
the privilege and right to sell any part thereof in accordance
with the act of Congress, on condition that the proceeds shall
be applied to the payment of the bonds of the company
secured by the mortgage. Had defendant shown a sale
under this reserved right, by an authorized agent of the
company, his title would have been unimpeachable; but, in
the absence of such evidence, a purchase from purported
agents can avail nothing. The deed by the State to the
plaintiffs was made in consideration of the surrender of the
bonds loaned to the company, and the release and discharge
of the State from liability thereon, under authority of an act
of the legislature commonly known as the "Debt Settlement
Act."—Acts, 1875–6, 130.

At the time of the execution of the mortgage, the railroad
company had only a beneficial interest in the land; the road
not having been completed, the legal title was in the State.
The mortgage expressly conveys any title and estate which
the company might thereafter acquire. There can be no
question, that the company could include in the mortgage
property to be thereafter acquired. The only title and estate
which the company could thereafter acquire, was the legal
title and estate—the indefeasible ownership. The company
having the equitable interest, and an existing right to the
legal estate on complying with the prescribed condition, and
the mortgage including both the equitable and the subsequently acquired legal estate, the completion of the road did
not divest the State of the legal title, which it had at the date
of the mortgage. Though the company may have become
entitled to it, the mortgage operated, by its terms, to continue
it in the State.

Another view: The mortgage contains the words, *grant,
bargain, sell and convey.* These words, the statute declares,
must be construed, unless it otherwise clearly appears from

the conveyance, an express covenant that the grantor was
seized of an indefeasible estate in fee simple, and for quiet
enjoyment. The settled doctrine in this State is, that if a
person, having at the time no title, conveys land by warranty, and afterwards acquires title, such title will enure and
pass *eo instanti* to his grantee; and that the doctrine applies,
when the warranty is such as the law implies from the employment of the statutory words.—*Chapman v. Abraham*,
61 Ala. 108. If, therefore, the legal estate was acquired by
the completion of the road, it passed instantaneously in and
out of the company; so that there was no instant of time at
which the statute of limitations could have been put into
operation. The decisions above referred to, holding the title
of plaintiffs derived from the conveyance by the State sufficient to maintain ejectment, can be sustained only on the
ground, that the legal title was in the State at the date of
the conveyance, which was many years after the completion
of the road.

The ten years limitation does not apply to the State, not
only on the cardinal and elementary rule, that statutes of
limitation do not apply to the State unless it is expressly
named, or it was clearly intended to be included, but because
of exclusion by express provision, prescribing the limitation
of twenty years to "actions at the suit of the State against a
citizen thereof, for the recovery of real or personal property."—Code, 1886, § 2613. It is also well settled, that the
possession of the defendant during the time the title remained
in the State, though adverse, can not be taken into the computation under the plea of the limitation of ten years.
Kennedy v. Townsley, 16 Ala. 239; *Iverson v. Dubose*,
27 Ala. 418; *Farley v. Smith*, 39 Ala. 38; *Cary v. Whitney*,
48 Me. 516.

The suit was commenced less than twenty years from the
time defendant entered into possession, and less than ten
years after plaintiffs became the grantees of the State. It
follows from the foregoing principles, that the statute of
limitations is no defense to the action. The court erred in
giving the affirmative charge in favor of the defendant.

Reversed and remanded.

Paden & Co. *v.* Bellenger & Ralls.

|87
|107

1

Action on the Case by Mortgagee, for Conversion of Cotton.

1. *Mortgage on future crops.*—A mortgage executed in November, 1886, conveying the mortgagor's "entire crop to be grown in the year 1887, on my own or any other land in said county," does not convey the crop raised on a tract of land which did not then belong to the mortgagor, and in which he had no interest, though he afterwards bought it.

2. *General charge, when evidence is conflicting.*—When there is a conflict in the evidence as to a material fact, it is the right of the jury, if they can not reconcile the evidence, to accept either aspect as true; and a general charge in favor of either party is an invasion of this right.

3. *Liability of partnership for act of partner.*—A recovery can not be had against a partnership, for the conversion of cotton on which plaintiff claims an equitable lien, merely on proof that one of the partners bought it, not showing that he bought it on partnership account, or that the partnership had anything to do with it.

APPEAL from the Circuit Court of Etowah.

Tried before the Hon. JOHN B. TALLY.

A. E. GOODHUE, for appellant, cited *Burns v. Campbell*, 71 Ala. 288; *Varnum v. State*, 78 Ala. 28; *Mayer & Co. v. Taylor & Co.*, 69 Ala. 405; *Purcell v. Mather*, 35 Ala. 572; *Grantham v. Hawley*, Hob. 132; *Low v. Pew*, 108 Mass. 347; *Otis v. Sill*, 8 Barb. 112; Herm. Ch. Mortgages, § 46; *Pennock v. Coe*, 23 How. 117; *Hussey v. Peebles*, 53 Ala. 435; *Lomax v. LeGrand*, 60 Ala. 542; *Hurst & McWhorter v. Bell*, 72 Ala. 337.

R. A. D. DUNLAP, *contra*, cited *Booker v. Jones*, 55 Ala. 271; *Abraham v. Carter*, 53 Ala. 8; *Floyd v. Morrow*, 26 Ala. 353; *Smith v. Field*, 79 Ala. 335; *Leslie v. Hinson*, 83 Ala. 266; Jones Ch. Mortgages, 174.

McCLELLAN, J.—This is an action on the case, for the wrongful conversion by John S. Paden & Co. of certain cotton, on which the appellees, plaintiffs below, claim to have an equitable mortgage. According to the unbroken current of our decisions, as well as by the weight of authority in other States, it is essential to the creation of such an incumbrance, that its subject-matter should have a potential exist-

ence, as distinguishable from a mere possibility, or expectancy
on the part of the contracting parties, that it will come into
being.   While the thing itself need not have identity, or
separate entity, yet it must at least be the product, or growth,
or increase of property, which has at the time a corporal
existence, and in which the mortgagor has a present interest,
not a mere belief, hope or expectation, that he will in future
acquire such an interest.—*Varnum v. State*, 78 Ala. 30;
Mayer v. Taylor, 69 Ala. 403; *Grant v. Steiner*, 65 Ala.
499; *Burns v. Campbell*, 71 Ala. 288; *Low v. Pew*, 108 Mass.
347; *Otis v. Sill*, 8 Barb. 112; *Pennock v. Coe*, 23 How.
117; Herman Chattel Mortg., § 46.

The mortgage involved here was executed November 15,
1886.   It in terms conveys the "entire crop" of the mortgagor; "to be grown in the year 1887, on my own land, or
any other land in Etowah county."   The cotton alleged to
have been converted was grown on land which did not belong to the mortgagor when the instrument was executed.
Whether it was the product of land in which the mortgagor
had an interest at that time, the evidence is conflicting. The
testimony of the mortgagor tended to show that he had no
interest whatever in the land until after November 15, 1886.
The testimony of other witnesses tended to establish the fact
of such interest at that time.   It was the province of the
jury to reconcile this conflict, if they could, and failing in
that, they had a right to accept as true either aspect of the
evidence.   The affirmative charge given at plaintiffs' request
took away this right.   This was error, which must work a
reversal of the case.—*Carter v. Shorter*, 57 Ala. 253; *Belisle
v. Clark*, 49 Ala. 98.

The action is against a partnership, composed of John S.
Paden and another.   The evidence shows that the cotton
was sold to Paden, and that he was a member of this partnership; but there appears to have been no evidence that
he bought the cotton as a member of the partnership, or on
joint or partnership account.   In the absence of some proof
of this character, the general instruction, that a verdict
against the defendants be brought in, should not have been
given.

It may be, too, that the failure or absence of proof that
the cotton had in fact been converted by the defendants—
sold or disposed of in such sort that plaintiffs could not enforce their lien against it—the general charge should not
have been given.—*Thompson v. Powell*, 77 Ala. 392.   We,

[Berney National Bank v. Pinckard, DeBardelaben & Co.]

however, rest the decision of the case on the first point stated above.

Reversed and remanded.

Berney National Bank *v.* Pinckard, DeBardelaben & Co.

Bill in Equity by Transferree of Stock Certificates, to enjoin Sale under Attachment or Execution.

1. *Certificates of stock in private corporation; transfer on books; liability to attachment or execution.*—Under statutory provisions (Code, 1876, §§ 2043-4; 1886, §§ 1670-71), stocks in private corporations are placed on the same footing as other personal chattels, as to their liability to levy under execution or attachment; a transfer thereof, not recorded on the books of the corporation within fifteen days afterwards, is void as to *bona fide* creditors, or subsequent purchasers without notice; and a judgment creditor having a lien, and an attaching creditor who perfects his lien by the recovery of judgment, are equally *bona fide* creditors from the inception of the lien.

2. *Fi. fa. or vend. ex. on judgment in attachment case.*—The lien of an attachment is perfected by the recovery of judgment, and is not waived or forfeited by suing out a *fi. fa.* instead of a *vend. ex.* to enforce it, but the latter may still be sued out if necessary.

APPEAL from the City Court of Birmingham, in equity.

Heard before the Hon. H. A. SHARPE.

The bill in this case was filed on the 29th December, 1887, by Pinckard, DeBardelaben & Co., suing as partners, against the Berney National Bank, and the Bessemer Land and Improvement Company; and sought to enjoin a sale, under execution in favor of the bank, of certain shares of stock in said company, which had been issued to one W. W. Davin, and to compel the company to enter and record on its books a transfer of said certificate and shares to complainants. The certificate was for twenty shares of stock, and was issued to said Davin 15th April, 1887. On the 8th June, 1887, Davin had borrowed $2,000 from the Berney National Bank, giving his promissory note at sixty days, and pledging other stocks as collateral security. On the 8th August, 1887, the bank sued out an attachment on this debt against Davin, and it was levied by the sheriff on said twenty shares of stock, the secretary of the company having furnished him, on demand, a written statement that they were standing in Davin's

37

[Berney National Bank v. Pinckard, DeBardelaben & Co.]

name on the books of the company. The attachment suit
was prosecuted to judgment by default, November 15th,
1887, for $1,729.80, "amount of plaintiff's debt and dam-
ages, as ascertained by the court, on proof produced by
plaintiff, besides costs; for which execution may issue." An
execution was issued on this judgment, and under it the
sheriff had advertised said stock for sale, when the bill in
this case was filed to enjoin it. Davin had indorsed the certificate in blank, by signing his name to the printed transfer
and power of attorney on the back of it, placed it on the
market, and sold it; and the complainants alleged that they
purchased it in the regular course of business, for valuable
consideration, "at least thirty days prior to the levy of said
attachment." The answer of the bank to this averment was:
"This defendant has no knowledge that, at least thirty days
prior to the levy of said attachment, or at any other time before the levy of said attachment, in due course of trade or
otherwise, complainants purchased said shares of stock as
alleged in their bill; and because defendant has no knowledge in reference to said matters, it can not admit the same
to be true." The complainants took the deposition of said
W. P. Pinckard, who testified that they "bought said twenty
shares of stock, in open market, in due course of trade, prior
to the 8th day of August, 1887;" and this was the only evidence in reference to the time of their purchase.

The court overruled a demurrer to the bill, and, on final
hearing, rendered a decree for the complainants, granting
relief as prayed; and this decree is now assigned as error by
the bank.

WEBB & TILLMAN, for appellant, contended that attaching
creditors, whose lien was perfected by judgment, were within
the protection of the statute, equally with creditors who had
a judgment and execution; and that the protection accrued,
in each case, from the inception of the lien. They cited and
discussed the following cases: *Fisher, Parker & Co. v. Jones,*
82 Ala. 117; *Daniel v. Sorrells,* 9 Ala. 436; *Jordan v. Mead,*
12 Ala. 247; *Governor v. Davis,* 20 Ala. 366; *De Vendell v.
Hamilton,* 27 Ala. 156; *Preston v. McMillan,* 58 Ala. 94;
Hardaway v. Semmes, 38 Ala. 657; *Wood v. Lake,* 62 Ala.
493; *Tutwiler v. Montgomery,* 73 Ala. 267; *Bank v. Watson,* 105 U. S. 22; *Morehead v. Railroad Co.,* 2 S. E. Rep.
247; 63 Amer. Dec. 120, note; 60 Amer. Dec. 789; 51 Wisc.
519; 1 Wade on Attachments, 204; 9 Cent. L. J. 249.

[Berney National Bank v. Pinckard, DeBardelaben & Co.]

McIntosh & Altman, *contra.*—(1.) The bank was not a *bona fide* creditor when it received notice of complainants' ownership of the stock, and when application was made to have the transfer entered on the books. The bank then had no judgment, and the judgment afterwards rendered can not relate back to the levy of the attachment, so as to cut off the intervening equities of complainants. *Jones v. Latham,* 70 Ala. 164, is decisive of this point. See, also, 76 Ala. 377; 70 Ala. 403. It must be remembered, too, that the attachment was sued out against Davin before the debt was due, the note being entitled to days of grace as commercial paper. (2.) The attachment was waived, or abandoned; no judgment of condemnation was rendered, nor *vend. ex.* ordered or issued; but only a judgment in ordinary form, as on personal service, and an award of execution.

STONE, C. J.—We have many decisions in this State interpreting registration statutes. *Daniel v. Sorrells,* 9 Ala. 436, is a leading authority on the question it discusses. That case arose under the act "concerning the registration of deeds and patents," approved January 15, 1828.—Sess. Acts, 44-5; Clay's Dig. 256, § 8. It provided, that "all deeds, recorded within six months from the date of their execution, shall have force, and be valid and operative between the parties thereto, and subsequent purchasers and creditors." The question considered and determined in *Daniel v. Sorrells* was, who were creditors within the statute, who could take advantage of the failure to record deeds within six months after their execution? The decision was, that only *judgment creditors having a lien* could assert priority over such deed.

The principle settled in *Daniel v. Sorrells* was re-affirmed in *Jordan v. Mead,* 12 Ala. 247; *DeVendell v. Doe, ex dem. Hamilton,* 27 Ala. 156, and *Tutwiler v. Montgomery,* 73 Ala. 263.

The same construction of the word creditors was given in the following cases, in which the question arose on statutes not relating to registration: *Thomason v. Scales,* 12 Ala. 309; *Preston v. McMillan,* 58 Ala. 85; *Walker v. Elledge,* 65 Ala. 51; and *Dickerson v. Carroll,* 76 Ala. 377. These last two decisions, however, were rested on the peculiar language of our statute, which declares that "no trusts, whether implied by law, or created or declared by the parties, can defeat the title of creditors, or purchasers for a valuable consideration, without notice."—Code of 1886, § 1846. Without the statute, the rights of creditors, even with a lien, could not prevail over trusts implied by law.—*Preston v. McMillan, supra.*

Cases have been before us, in which controversies have arisen between parties claiming to be transferrees of stock in corporations, and creditors of the transferrors. The following are some of the cases: *Nabring v. Bank of Mobile,* 58 Ala. 204, in which the transfer had been made on the books of the company; no question arose in that case, which is material to the present one. *Jones v. Latham,* 70 Ala. 164, was the case of a creditor having an execution, followed by a levy on the stock; we held that the bill was imperfect for the want of necessary averments. In that case we interpreted section 2043 of the Code of 1876— § 1670, Code of 1886—and ruled that the word *creditors* in that section meant judgment creditors having a lien. No question of attachment lien arose in that case, for none had been issued. A judgment had been recovered against Rushing, in whose name the stock had been issued, and still stood on the books of the corporation, execution on the judgment, levy, sale and purchase by Jones. The bill in that case, like the present one, was filed by the alleged purchaser of the stock from Rushing, and sought to compel a transfer of the stock to him, Latham. We interpreted the one section, 2043 of the Code of 1876, and held that the word *creditor* in that section meant a judgment creditor having a lien. As we have said, we did not, and could not, consider the effect of an attachment levy, for the record presented nothing of the kind.

Fisher v. Jones, 82 Ala. 117, was the case of an attachment levied on the stock, and the question whether the attachment lien would prevail over a prior sale of the stock, which had not been transferred on the books of the corporation, was approached, but not decided. We held that there had been a transfer of the stocks on the books of the corporation, before the attachment was levied, and this rendered a decision of the other question unnecessary. Which of the rights will prevail over the other is an open question in this court, so far as any direct and necessary decision of the question is concerned.

The following are the facts of this case: Davin was indebted to the Berney National Bank, and on the 8th day of August, 1887, the bank sued out an attachment against him, which, on the same day, was levied by the sheriff on twenty shares of the capital stock of the Bessemer Land & Improvement Company, a private corporation under the laws of Alabama. The secretary of the B. L. & I. Co. had, on the demand of the sheriff, furnished him a written statement, that on that day twenty shares of the capital stock stood on the books of the company in the name of Davin, defendant in attachment. When the attachment was levied on the stock, the sheriff immediately gave notice to the secretary of the company, and so indorsed in his return. The sheriff also stated in his return, that "written notice of the above levy was this day given by me, in which notice the said W. W. Davin, defendant, was required to appear and plead, or demur to the complaint filed in this cause, within thirty days from this date." In the suit by the bank, judgment was recovered against Davin, November 15, 1887; and under process issued for its collection, the sheriff was about to sell the stock as the property of Davin.

Under our statute, the levy of an attachment creates a lien in favor of the plaintiff, on the property or effects attached.—Code of 1876, § 3280; Code of 1886, § 2957, and authorities cited. The lien, however, is inchoate, and does not become complete and enforceable, unless and until a judgment is recovered in the suit.—1 Brick. Dig. 162, §§ 105, 108, 109, 113.

The case made by the bill, and sustained by the proof, is as follows: Davin, having possession of a certificate of twenty shares of the capital stock of the Bessemer Land & Improvement Company, indorsed the same in blank, and the same was sold for a valuable consideration to Pinckard, DeBardelaben & Co. This was some time prior to the levy of the bank's attachment. Neither the secretary of the B. L. & I. Co., the bank, nor any of its officers, had any notice of this sale, until after the attachment was levied. After the levy, but before the judgment was recovered against Davin, Pinckard, DeBardelaben & Co. presented the certificate to the secretary of the B. L. & I. Co., and demanded that it be transferred to them on the books of the company. A by-law of the company had made a provision for such transfer. The secretary refused to make such transfer, and the present bill was filed to compel him to do so, and to enjoin the sale of the stock under the bank's process. The City Court, sitting in equity, granted the relief prayed.

The levy of the attachment in this case being prior to the date when the Code of 1886 went into effect—December 25, 1887—the question of error *vel non* must be determined by the statutes as found in the Code of 1876.

In *Jones v. Latham*, 70 Ala. 164, in which the creditor
claimed no attachment levy, but only a judgment, we said,
speaking of section 2043 of the Code, "We have uniformly
interpreted the words '*bona fide* creditors,' in statutes like
this, to mean judgment creditors having a lien." As we have
said, that was not a question in that case. Possibly, the proposition was stated too broadly, and was liable to mislead.
But is not the Berney National Bank a judgment creditor
having a lien? True, the judgment did not ante-date the
notice of transfer of the stock, but the attachment levy did.
And when the lien became complete by the recovery of the
judgment, may it not be said, that by force of our statute it
related back to the levy of the attachment, and fixed the lien
as of that date? But we need not decide this.

We think section 2043 of the Code of 1876—§ 1670, Code
of 1886—must be construed in connection with other sections in the same chapter. Section 2021 provides, that "the
shares or interest of any person in any incorporated company are personal property, and transferrable on the books of
company, in such manner as is or may be prescribed by the
charter, or articles of association, or by-laws and regulations
of the company; and such shares or interest may be levied
on by attachment or execution, and sold as goods and chattels; and the purchaser shall be the owner of the shares, or
interest bought by him, and the officer making the sale shall
transfer the same to the purchaser in writing, which shall be
registered on the books of the company." See Code of
1886, § 1673.

Section 2044 of the Code of 1876 provides, that "persons
holding stocks not so transferred or registered,   .   .   .
must have the transfer   .   .   .   made or registered on the
books of the company; or, upon failing to do so within fifteen days, all such transfers   .   .   .   shall be void as to
bona fide creditors, or subsequent purchasers without notice."
Code of 1886, § 1671.

We feel constrained to construe the foregoing provisions,
first, as placing stocks in private corporations on the same
footing as other personal chattels, as to their amenability to
levy either under execution or attachment; second, that if a
transfer of such stock is not recorded within fifteen days
after the transfer, then such transfer is void as to *bona fide*
creditors, or subsequent purchaser without notice; and, third,
that a judgment creditor having a lien, or an attaching creditor who perfects his lien by the recovery of judgment, is

each a *bona fide* creditor from the inception of the lien.   The
question as to priority of lien was settled as we have declared
it, in *Hardaway v. Semmes*, 38 Ala. 667.   See, also, *Jordan
v. Mead*, 12 Ala. 247; *Application of Thomas Murphy*,
51 Wisc. 519: *Weston v. B. R. & A. Mining Co.*, 5 Cal.
186; s. c., 63 Amer. Dec. 117; *Fisher v. Jones*, 82 Ala. 117.

We place our ruling above on the language of the statute,
which, as we interpret it, accords equal efficacy to attachment
levy, as it does to levy under execution.   But, a plaintiff in
attachment levied, does not thereby become a purchaser
(*Wollner v. Lehman*, 35 Ala. 274), and can assert no claim
as such.

We have ruled above that, under our statutes, Pinckard,
DeBardelaben & Co. were allowed fifteen days after their
purchase of the stock, within which to have it transferred on
the corporation books, and that failing to do so within that
time, the stock became liable to levy under execution or attachment, at the suit of any creditor of Davin, in whose
name the stock stood on the books.   The question of the
length of time elapsing between the purchase by Pinckard,
DeBardelaben & Co. and the levy of attachment, does not
appear to have been mooted or considered in the court below.   From any thing shown in the record, or in the argument, we infer it was deemed immaterial.   The bill raises no
such question, but states a time which was more than fifteen
days before the attachment.   The demurrer fails to object to
the bill on this account; and the testimony only shows that
the purchase antedated the attachment.   Under these circumstances, if we were to render a final decree on a question that was neither considered nor raised in the court
below, we might do an injustice.

It is contended for appellees, that if appellant acquired a
prior lien by the levy of its attachment, followed by a judgment on the claim, it forfeited or waived it by suing out an
execution, instead of a *venditioni exponas*.   There is nothing
in this.   The levy and judgment give the perfect lien, not
the final process for its enforcement.   If necessary, a *venditioni exponas* may yet be sued out.

The decree of the chancellor is reversed, and the cause
remanded, with instructions to dismiss the bill, unless there
is amendment both in the averments and the proof, so as to
show complainants are entitled to recover under the principles of this opinion.

Reversed and remanded.

Woodstock Iron Co. *v.* Fullenwider.

Statutory Action in nature of Ejectment.

1. *Adverse possession as between widow and heirs; estoppel against heirs; presumptions from lapse of time.*—The widow's possession of lands allotted to her as dower is not adverse to the heirs, and if she purchases the reversionary interest, at a sale made by the administrator, they can not assail her title, at law, during her life, even though the sale was void; and if the purchase-money was paid, and was applied by the administrator to the payment of debts, they would be estopped from denying the validity of the sale, without offering to do equity by refunding the purchase-money; and, having the equitable right to set aside the sale as a cloud on their title, on offering to do equity, if they allow the widow and those claiming under her to remain in undisturbed possession for more than twenty years, though less than ten years after her death has elapsed, the presumption will be indulged against them, that she acquired the legal title by voluntary conveyance from them, or by compulsory proceedings in equity.

APPEAL from the Circuit Court of Calhoun.

Tried before the Hon. JOHN B. TALLY.

This action was brought by Fannie Fullenwider and others, as heirs at law of Samuel Hudson, deceased, against the Woodstock Iron Company and the Anniston City Land Company, to recover the possession of a tract of land, which belonged to said Samuel Hudson at the time of his death; and was commenced on the 28th June, 1887. By consent of parties entered of record, a trial by jury was waived, and the case was submitted to the decision of the court, with a request for a special finding of the facts. On the facts found by the court, which are set out in the bill of exceptions, the court rendered judgment for the plaintiffs; and this judgment, to which the defendants excepted, is now assigned as error.

KNOX & BOWIE, CALDWELL & JOHNSTON, CASSADY & BLACKWELL, and BROTHERS, WILLETT & WILLETT, for appellants.

KELLY & SMITH, *contra.* (No briefs on file.)

SOMERVILLE, J.—The suit is one of ejectment under the statute, brought by the appellees as the heirs at law of

[Woodstock Iron Co. v. Fullenwider.]

Samuel Hudson, deceased, and was commenced on June 28th, 1887.

It is shown that the widow of Hudson owned a life-estate in the lands, based on her allotted right of dower; and that she purchased the reversionary estate at a sale of the lands made by the administrator of Hudson for the payment of the decedent's debts on March 20th, 1886—or more than twenty years before the commencement of this action. She received a deed from the administrator, paid the purchase-money to him, and he used the money in the payment of the debts of the estate. The defendants claim title through the widow, who did not die until June 25th, 1879—or less than ten years before suit brought. The possession of the defendants, and those under whom they claim, has been continuous, exclusive, open and under claim of ownership, since the date of the administrator's sale, or for more than twenty years.

The whole case of the plaintiffs is based upon the contention, that the proceedings in the Probate Court for the sale of the reversionary interest in the lands, owned by the decedent's estate, were void, and conveyed no title to the purchaser. The reasons assigned for this conclusion are because minors were interested in the estate, and no depositions are shown to have been taken as in chancery cases, proving the necessity of the sale; and because there was no order of the Probate Court authorizing the administrator to make a deed to the purchaser, besides some other grounds, which need not be named.—*Bland v. Bowie*, 53 Ala. 158; *Satcher v. Satcher*, 41 Ala. 26; *Doe v. Hardy*, 52 Ala. 291.

It is contended further by the plaintiffs (or appellees) that, under the authority of *Pickett v. Pope*, 74 Ala. 122, and other decisions of this court, neither the possession of the life-tenant, nor of the defendants as purchasers holding under her, could be *adverse* to the heirs as reversioners, until the death of the life-tenant, which occurred about eight years before the commencement of the action. For this reason, it is said, there was no right residing in the plaintiffs to sue at law; and hence there was no *laches*, or neglect on their part, which could be the foundation of any presumptions hostile to their title.

The defendants, who are appellants in this court, contend, on the contrary, that all irregularities of sale and defects of title, under the admitted facts of the case, are cured by the presumptions arising from the lapse of twenty years, under the broad doctrine of prescription, now so thoroughly established in this State.

The plaintiffs certainly had no right to sue in ejectment for these lands before the death of the widow, who was tenant for life; her possession, so far at least as concerns the legal title in the reversion, not being adverse or hostile to the heirs, during the continuance of such particular estate. *Pickett v. Pope*, 74 Ala. 122; *McCorry v. King's Heirs*, 39 Amer. Dec. 165; Tiedeman on Real Prop. § 715. The question is, whether any presumption will arise from the lapse of twenty years, sufficient to perfect the title of defendants, in view of the incapacity of plaintiffs to sue at law. In considering this question, we shall regard the contention of the appellees as well taken, so far as to assume that the sale of the administrator conferred no *legal* title to the reversion on the widow as purchaser under the probate proceedings in March, 1866.

Regarding the proceedings in the Probate Court as void at law for the reasons stated, what, we may inquire, were the equitable rights, if any, acquired under it by the purchaser? This question has been fully settled by our past decisions. Where land of a decedent is sold by the Probate Court for the payment of debts, or for distribution, and the proceeding is void for want of jurisdiction, or otherwise, and the purchase-money, being paid to the administrator, is applied by him to the payment of the debts of the decedent's estate, or is distributed to the heirs; while the sale is so far void as to convey no title at law, the purchaser nevertheless acquires an equitable title to the lands, which will be recognized in a court of equity. And he may resort to a court of equity, to compel the heirs or devisee to elect a ratification or rescission of the contract of purchase. It is deemed unconscionable that the heirs or devisees should reap the fruits of the purchaser's payment of money, appropriated to the discharge of debts, which were a charge on the lands, and at the same time recover the lands. They are estopped to deny the validity of the sale, and at the same time enjoy the benefits derived from the appropriation of the purchase-money. And this principle applies to minors, as well as adults.—*Bland v. Bowie*, 53 Ala. 152; *Bell v. Craig*, 52 Ala. 215; *Robertson v. Bradford*, 73 Ala. 116. See, also, *Ganey v. Sikes*, 76 Ala. 421.

All of our decisions, it is true, recognizing the doctrine of presumption by prescription based on the lapse of twenty

years of time, are founded upon the principle of some *laches*
on the part of one who, having the right and capacity to sue
either at law or in equity, neglects or omits to do so for such
period of twenty years. For the repose of society, it is presumed that the right, if it existed, has in some manner been
lost by reason of such act of acquiescence, based on some
omission or neglect.—*Long v. Parmer*, 81 Ala. 384, and
cases cited on p. 388; *Bozeman v. Bozeman*, 82 Ala. 389;
McCorry v. King's Heirs, 39 Amer. Dec. 165. In the
following cases, cited on the brief of appellants' counsel,
where life-tenants had purchased the reversion, under sales
which conferred no legal title to such reversionary interest,
important presumptions were allowed to prevail under the
operation of twenty years lapse of time, accompanied by possession and claim of ownership, involving the payment of
the purchase-money, the execution of conveyances, and the
presumed regularity in the execution of powers: *Matthews
v. McDade*, 72 Ala. 377; *Gosson v. Ladd*, 77 Ala. 223;
Kelly v. Hancock, 75 Ala. 229.

The plaintiffs in the present case, as reversioners, had
no right, as we have said, to sue at law. But they had a
right to go into a court of equity, to remove the cloud from
their title created by the probate court proceedings. This
cloud consisted of the administrator's deed, and other record
evidence of a sale, under the operation of which the purchaser had acquired an equitable title. Under an adverse
possession, such a title would become perfect in ten years
after the death of the life-tenant, and extrinsic evidence
would be necessary to show whether the holder of such particular estate was living or dead. The deed and other proceedings, therefore, were of a character to be used to
injuriously affect the complainants' title, and operated,
moreover, to impair the market value of the reversion, and
to prevent its sale by the owners in the event they desired
to dispose of it. And while one having the legal title to
land, with the right of possession, would be compelled first
to recover possession by ejectment, before invoking this
jurisdiction of equity to quiet it; yet the rule is different
where the complainants' title is equitable, or where, like a
reversioner or remainder-man, he is not entitled to possession
by reason of the existence of a life, or particular estate. In
the latter class of cases, the complainant may at once resort to
equity, to have the objectionable proceedings vacated as a
cloud on his title, especially when it is necessary to do some

act of equity as a condition precedent to its exercise. That act, in this case, would be to tender to the purchaser the amount bid at the sale,—whether with or without interest, we need not decide. That a reversioner or remainderman may file such a bill, on the same principle upon which he is permitted to redeem from a mortgage sale, we consider to be clear, both on principle and authority, his remedy at law being entirely inadequate. As observed in a recent case, holding this view: "A remainder [or reversion] is a present right, though the enjoyment is future, and the owner may desire to dispose of it, or in some way to make it available to his needs; and he is entitled to have it relieved from a cloud impairing its value, and perhaps rendering it wholly un-available."—*Aiken v. Suttle*, 4 Lea (Tenn.), 105; and cases cited on p. 110; 3 Pom. Eq. Jur. §§ 1220, 1398–1399, *note* 4; 1 High on Injunc. (2d Ed.), § 330; 3 Wait's Act. & Def. 190–191.

Here, then, was the capacity to sue in a court of equity, so as to sweep away a cloud on the title of the plaintiffs, and, by an offer to do equity, to have the equitable title of the defendants, acquired at the void sale, divested out of them by decree of a court of chancery. A failure to exercise this right for over twenty years is such *laches* as authorizes the inference that the right to do so is barred in any one of the modes in which that result may be effected. If the only existing right of action on the plaintiffs' part were at law—if his only *laches*, or slumbering on his rights, consisted in his failure to sue at law—then, as we have often said, "the only fact open to inquiry, in such cases, would be the char-acter of defendants' possession, either in its original acquisi-tion, or in its continued use, as being, on the one hand, per-missive and in subordination, or, on the other, hostile and adverse."—*Long v. Parmer*, 81 Ala. 384; and cases cited on p. 388. But the *laches* here imputed to the plaintiffs is the fact of having allowed the probate court proceedings to re-main unassailed for over twenty years—proceedings under which, though void at law, a good equitable title to the re-version had been acquired, accompanied with possession and claim of ownership, on the part of the purchaser and her sub-vendees, during the whole of this long period.

The fair legal presumption arising from this state of facts, in our opinion, is, that the purchaser, or those claiming title under her, have filed a bill in equity compelling the heirs of Hudson to convey to them the legal title; or else that a voluntary conveyance of such title has been made by such heirs, thereby converting the equitable into a legal title. *Bland v. Bowie*, 53 Ala. 152; *Bell v. Craig*, 52 Ala. 215.

The special finding of the Circuit Court on the facts was made under the provisions of the statute.—Code, 1886, §§ 2744-45. This statute makes it our duty to examine and determine whether the facts are sufficient to support the judgment, which was for the plaintiffs. It follows from the views above expressed that they are not. The court erred in rendering judgment on the facts for the plaintiffs. That judgment will be reversed, and a judgment will be rendered in this court for the defendants.

Reversed and rendered.

Cox *v.* Holcomb.

Bill in Equity for Reformation of Defective Conveyance of Homestead, or Specific Performance as Executory Agreement to Convey, and for Injunction against Judgment.

1. *Reformation or specific performance of conveyance of homestead.* A conveyance of the homestead by husband and wife, to which the certificate of acknowledgment is substantially defective (Code, § 2508), will not be reformed in equity, on the ground that the examination and acknowledgment of the wife were in fact properly made, but were not shown by the officer's certificate from ignorance or mistake on his part; nor will it be specifically enforced, as an executory agreement to convey.

APPEAL from the Chancery Court of Pickens.

Heard before the Hon. THOS. W. COLEMAN.

The bill in this case was filed by Mrs. Martha Cox, against D. G. Holcomb as the administrator of the estate of Robert Bridges, deceased, and Mrs. Frances Bridges, who was the widow of said Robert Bridges and the mother of the complainant; and sought relief against a defective conveyance of a tract of land, executed by said Bridges and wife to the complainant, on the facts stated in the opinion of the court. The chancellor sustained a demurrer to the bill for want of equity, and his decree is here assigned as error.

E. D. WILLETT, and J. C. JOHNSTON, for appellant, cited *Garth v. Fort*, 15 Lea, Tenn. 683; *Lowry v. Adamson*,

[Cox v. Holcomb.]

48 Texas, 621; *Johnson v. Taylor*, 60 Texas, 360; *Montgomery v. Simpson*, 25 Ark. 365; *Dalton v. Rust*, 22 Texas, 133; *Hutchinson v. Ainsworth*, 63 Cal. 286; *Brinkley v. Tomeny*, 9 Baxter, Tenn. 275.

D. C. HODO, *contra*, cited *Balkum v. Wood*, 58 Ala. 642; *Jenkins v. Harrison*, 66 Ala. 345; *Blythe v. Dargin*, 68 Ala. 370; *Van Cleave v. Wilson*, 73 Ala. 387; *Shelton v. Aultman & Taylor Co.*, 82 Ala. 315; *Scott v. Simons*, 70 Ala. 353; *Gardner & Gates v. Moore*, 75 Ala. 395; *Townsley v. Chapin*, 12 Allen, Mass. 478; *Donahue v. Mills*, 41 Ark. 421; *Downing v. Blair*, 75 Ala. 216.

CLOPTON, J.—On October 22, 1878, Robert Bridges and his wife, Frances Bridges, joined in a conveyance of real estate to appellant, upon a recited valuable consideration. The land conveyed included the homestead of the grantor. The officer's certificate of the wife's acknowledgment does not show a substantial compliance with the form prescribed by the statute in such cases—it omits to affirm a privy examination of the wife, and to exclude fear, constraint, or threats on the part of the husband. Appellant seeks by his bill to vacate and annul proceedings in the Probate Court, by which the homestead exemption was allotted to Frances Bridges, after the death of her husband, and to enjoin the enforcement of a judgment recovered by her against appellant, for the possession of the land exempted. The ground of relief is, that the officer before whom the wife's acknowledgment was made, omitted to certify her examination and acknowledgment in the manner required by the statute, from mistake or ignorance of the law, though, as the bill alleges, she was in fact examined separate and apart from her husband, and acknowledged that she signed the deed of her own free will and accord, and without fear, constraints, or threats on his part. The bill prays that complainant be allowed to prove that Frances Bridges was so examined, and made such acknowledgment, so as to constitute the deed a valid and legal conveyance; and failing in this, that the conveyance may be enforced as an executory contract.

In *Gardner v. Moore*, 75 Ala. 394, it was held, that where a mortgage of a homestead was executed by a married man and his wife, in strict conformity with the statute, a court of equity will assume jurisdiction to correct a misdescription in land conveyed and intended to be conveyed. It is not claimed

[Cox v. Holcomb.]

that there is any mistake in the description of the subject-matter, or terms of the conveyance. On the case made by the bill, the jurisdiction of the court is invoked to aid a defective certificate of acknowledgment, or to compel the specific performance of an agreement to convey by a married woman. While no case has been heretofore presented, in which the wife was in fact examined separate and apart from her husband touching her signature to an alienation of the homestead, and made the statutory acknowledgment of her voluntary signature and assent, and the officer before whom the acknowledgment was made omitted to certify in substantial compliance with the statute, the principles which underlie the case, and are decisive of the question involved, should be regarded as well settled. An alienation of the homestead by a married man, not executed by the wife in the manner prescribed by the statute, has been uniformly held to be a nullity,—inoperative to confer any rights. Such alienation does not possess the force and effect of an imperfectly executed conveyance. To give it operation, there must be a subsequent acknowledgment by the wife, properly certified, made voluntarily, and with intent to cure the defect.—*Balkum v. Wood*, 58 Ala. 642. The constitution and statute have reference to some mode of alienation by which the title passes *in præsenti*. They do not contemplate instruments which can be regarded only as agreements to convey. From the performance of an executory contract to alienate the homestead, which is a nullity because of the incapacity of the wife to make such agreement, she may withhold her signature and assent, and the court is powerless to compel performance. It is well settled by our decisions, that the conveyance of the homestead by the husband, though signed by the wife, if not executed in the manner essential to its validity, will not be enforced against her as a contract to convey. *Jenkins v. Harrison*, 66 Ala. 345; *Blythe v. Dargin*, 68 Ala. 370; *Gardner v. Moore, supra.*

By the statute, it is essential to a valid alienation of the homestead by a married man, that the voluntary signature and assent of the wife shall be shown by her privy examination before an officer authorized to take acknowledgments, and by the certificate of such officer, in the form prescribed by the statute, upon or attached to the deed.—Code, 1886, § 2508; *Scott v. Simons*, 70 Ala. 354. The power of the wife to consent to the alienation is derived from the statute. There can be no question, that if no sufficient examination and acknowledgment have been made, a court of equity will not compel the wife to correct the defective execution. When an order for re-execution is necessary, and the reformation only operates as a re-conveyance, the court will not undertake to reform it. The wife's signature and assent must be voluntary, under the constitution and statute. The omission of the statutory requirement, essential to a valid execution of the deed of a married woman, can not be supplied by the compulsory power of the court.—*Gebb v. Rose,* 40 Md. 387; *Russell v. Rumsey,* 35 Ill. 362.

We have been referred by counsel to decisions in other States, which uphold proceedings to correct defective official certificates in analogous cases. An examination shows that the decisions are rested on local statutes authorizing such proceedings; and some of the cases concede that, in the absence of statutory authority, the court would not assume to correct them.—*Johnson v. Taylor,* 40 Tex. 360; *Hutchinson v. Ainsworth,* 63 Cal. 286; *Koltenbroeck v. Cracraft,* 36 Ohio St. 584. As we have said, the officer's certificate of acknowledgment, in substantial compliance with the statutory form, is as essential to a valid alienation of the homestead, as the examination and acknowledgment of the wife required by the statute. A substantial compliance must affirmatively appear from the certificate itself, which is the sole and exclusive evidence of the voluntary signature and assent of the wife. Parol evidence is inadmissible to supply deficiencies.

It is manifest from the frame and prayer of the bill, that its purpose is to aid or supply the defective execution of the officer's certificate attached to the deed to complainant. The power of the officer to make such certificate is also statutory. Though a court of equity will relieve against the defective execution of a power created by a party, it is well settled that, with few exceptions, it can not relieve against the defective execution of a power created by statute, nor supply any of the formalities requisite to its due execution.—*McBryde v. Wilkinson,* 29 Ala. 662. The officer taking the acknowledgment may, during his continuance in office, voluntarily correct his certificate, or make a new one conforming to the statute, if the facts warrant; but a court of equity will not assume to correct or aid the defective execution of such statutory powers. It follows that the bill of complainant is wanting in equity.—*Wanall v. Kem,* 51 Mo. 150.

This conclusion, to which we are forced, may work hardship; but grantees can avoid such consequences, by taking care to see that their conveyances are properly executed.

Affirmed.

Prout & Robertson *v.* Webb.

Action by Warehouse-man against Banker, for Breach of Special Contract.

1. *Statute of frauds; contract not to be performed within one year; promise to answer for debt or default of another.*—A promise made by a private banker, advancing money to cotton-buyers, to a warehouse-man, to pay the warehouse charges on the cotton of persons dealing with him, if the warehouse-man would allow it to be shipped without prepayment of his charges, is not a contract "not to be performed within one year" (Code, §1732), although the parties acted under it for more than a year before a breach occurred; nor is it a promise to answer for the debt, default, or miscarriage of another person, within the terms of the statute; but it is an original promise or undertaking, founded on a two-fold consideration—benefit to the promisor, and detriment to the promisee.

APPEAL from the Circuit Court of Marengo.

Tried before the Hon. WM. E. CLARKE.

This action was brought by John C. Webb, against Prout & Robertson as partners, and was commenced on the 13th February, 1888. The original complaint contained two counts, the first being for the breach of a special contract, to which a demurrer was sustained because its averments were not sufficiently certain and definite; and the second was the common count for money had and received. On sustaining the demurrer to the first count, the plaintiff had leave to amend; and he then filed two additional counts, as follows:

(3.) "Plaintiff claims of defendants the sum of $500, and avers that he is engaged in the business of a warehouse-man and forwarding merchant, and, in his regular course of business as such, had in his possession 777 bales of cotton, upon which was due him the sum of $492.15 for his charges thereon; that he had a lien on said cotton for his said charges, of which defendants had notice; that defendants, being fully aware that plaintiff had a lien upon all cotton coming into his possession in the regular course of his business as warehouse-man and forwarding merchant, did prom-

38

ise and agree with the plaintiff, that if he would allow cotton under his control to be shipped from his warehouse by cotton-buyers who were dealing with defendants, without embarrassing such shipments by detaining cotton until his charges thereon were paid, they, said defendants, would pay such charges on all such cottons passing through their hands; that said 777 bales of cotton were shipped from plaintiff's warehouse by Th. Bernard & Co., cotton-buyers who dealt with defendants, and passed through defendants' hands; that plaintiff, relying upon defendants' said promise, suffered said cotton to go out of his possession, and to be shipped by said Th. Bernard & Co., without first collecting his charges; that the whole amount of said charges is still due and unpaid; that he has demanded of defendants the sum due him for said charges, and they have failed and refused to pay the same, or any part thereof," &c.

(4.) "Plaintiff claims of defendants the sum of $500, and avers that he is engaged in business as a factor, warehouse-man, and forwarding merchant, and, in his regular course of business as such, had in his possession 777 bales of cotton, upon which there was due to him the sum of $492.15 for charges and advances thereon, and on which he had a lien for said charges and advances, of which lien defendants had notice; that said defendants, being fully aware of plaintiff's lien upon cotton coming into his possession in the regular course of his business as above stated, did promise and agree with plaintiff, that if he would allow cotton under his control in his regular course of business to be shipped by cotton-buyers who were dealing with defendants, without embarrassing such shipments by detaining cotton until his charges thereon were paid, they, the said defendants, would pay said charges on all such cotton passing through their hands; that said 777 bales of cotton were shipped by Th. Bernard & Co., cotton-buyers who dealt as such with defendants, and passed through defendants' hands; that plaintiff, relying upon defendants' said promise, suffered said cotton to go out of his possession, and to be shipped by said Th. Bernard & Co., without first collecting his charges; that the whole amount of said charges is still due and unpaid; that he has demanded of defendants the sum due him for said charges, and they have failed and refused to pay the same," &c.

The defendants demurred to the complaint as amended, on the ground that there was a misjoinder of counts; and to the "1st, 3d and 4th counts severally, because it shows that plaintiff voluntarily abandoned the lien for whose destruction he sues, and voluntarily surrendered the possession of the cotton." The court overruled the demurrer, and the defendants then pleaded the general issue and the statute of frauds; on which pleas issue was joined.

On the trial, as the bill of exceptions shows, the plaintiff testified in his own behalf, that he had been carrying on the business of a warehouse-man, factor, forwarding and commission merchant in Demopolis, for twelve or fifteen years, while the defendants were carrying on business as bankers; "that defendants, in the course of their business, made advances to cotton-buyers, to enable them to buy cotton in that city; that when cotton was delivered to him, he gave the owner a receipt for the same, on which were shown all of his charges up to its date; that the receipt represented the stored cotton, and a purchaser of the cotton paid the value thereof less the charges shown by the receipt, and held the receipt as evidence of his title to the cotton, the ownership of the cotton always following the receipt; that the defendants, advancing money to cotton-buyers, took such receipts, and held the same as security for such advances; that up to November, 1885, or 1886, he had permitted buyers, who owned cotton in his warehouse, to ship the same before his charges were paid, relying on the shippers to pay the same, but about that time he became dissatisfied with this mode of business, and determined to quit it except as to one particular buyer; that he then informed defendants he would never ship any more cotton until his charges were paid, and they thereupon promised and agreed to guarantee his charges on all cottons, for which his receipts came into their hands, provided he would agree not to impede the shipment of such cottons by holding the same for the payment of his charges thereon, and he consented thereto." He testified, also, that the cotton season each year commenced on the 1st September, and ended on the 31st August following, though the buying of cotton generally ended early in May; that Th. Bernard & Co. followed the business of buying cotton in Demopolis during the season of 1887-8, their business being managed exclusively by said Th. Bernard; that the defendants introduced said Bernard to him in the early part of the season, saying that he would probably buy most of the cotton sold there that season; that said Bernard & Co. did buy a great deal of cotton during that season, and stored it in his warehouse,

taking his receipts for the same, and depositing them with
defendants as security for the money advanced to buy it; that
they paid all of his charges on such cotton prior to December 19th, 1887, invariably making payments by checks on
defendants, which showed on their face that they were given
for charges on cotton, and all of which were promptly hon-
ored by defendants up to that time; that between December
19th, 1887, and 7th January following, there accrued to him
charges amounting to $492.15 on 777 bales of cotton stored
with him by Bernard & Co., the account of which charges
was kept on his books against said Bernard & Co., and against
no other person; that Th. Bernard left the city early in January, 1888, leaving a clerk in charge of his office and business; that said account was made out and presented to said
clerk, who said that he could do nothing in Bernard's
absence; that payment was afterwards demanded of the defendants, who requested plaintiff to wait until Bernard returned, saying that they could do nothing in the matter without a check from him; that he repeatedly asked payment of
them, which they refused on the same ground; that on Bernard's return, he gave plaintiff a check on defendants for the
amount of the charges, but told him they would not pay it,
as he had no money to his credit with them; that Bernard
went with him to defendants' office when he presented said
check for payment, which was refused; that said account for
charges had never been paid, and he had no means of indemnity in his hands.

The defendants testified, as to the nature of their business
and that of the plaintiff, in substance as the plaintiff, but
said that they had never been engaged in the business of
buying or selling cotton in Demopolis; that they advanced
money to cotton-buyers on satisfactory security, their profits
accruing on account of interest and exchange; that they did,
on two separate occasions, guarantee plaintiff's storage account against two individual cotton-buyers, but this was done
by special agreement,—one five or six years ago, the other
in the Fall of 1885, or 1886; that they never made any
agreement in November, 1885, or at any other time, to be
responsible for plaintiff's charges on cotton; that at the beginning of the cotton season of 1887–8 they declined to advance money to any cotton-buyer, unless they were secured
against loss; that Th. Bernard came to Demopolis about that
time, representing Bernard & Co., secured them against loss,
and made arrangements to get money with which to engage

[Prout & Robertson v. Webb.]

in the cotton business; that they agreed to pay the checks of said Bernard & Co. when they came with the cotton receipts attached, and to advance to them such an amount of money as they thought they could safely advance on the security held; that they paid out a large amount of money on the checks of said Bernard & Co. during that season, but nothing at all on their account without checks; that Bernard & Co. bought said 777 bales of cotton as plaintiff had testified, taking plaintiff's warehouse receipts, checking on them to pay for the same, and depositing said receipts with them as security for the money advanced, which defendants paid out on their check; that when Bernard & Co. got ready to ship the cotton, defendants delivered the cotton receipts to them, taking their receipts for the same, and had nothing more to do with the cotton, or the receipts, until Bernard & Co. brought them a bill of lading for the cotton, with attached draft for the proceeds of sale when sold, and they thereupon placed said drafts, less exchange, to the credit of Bernard & Co. on their books, where they had been charged with the money advanced; that they then had no knowledge or information as to whether plaintiff had any charges, paid or unpaid, on the cotton, and did not know that his charges were unpaid until he informed them of the fact several days afterwards; that he did not then demand payment of them, nor claim that they were bound for his charges, but abused Bernard for not paying them, and said that the loss was owing to his own negligence; that plaintiff again came into their bank, on January 24th, 1888, in company with Bernard, and presented his check, which they refused to pay because they had in their hands no funds belonging to said Bernard, who was still indebted to them on account.

The bill of exceptions purports to set out "all the evidence in the case," the above being a summary of it. Thereupon, the court charged the jury, "that if they believed from the evidence that the defendants made the promise set out in the complaint, and testified to by plaintiff, the statute of frauds would not avail them as a defense." The defendants excepted to this charge as given, and also to the refusal of each of the following charges, which were asked by them in writing: (1.) "The jury can hold the defendants to no promise to answer for the debt, default, or miscarriage of Bernard & Co., unless the same was in writing." 2. "The plaintiff can not recover in this action upon any agreement that is not to be performed within one year from the making thereof, unless they believe from the evidence that the same was in writing." The court charged the jury, also, on request, that the plaintiff was not entitled to recover on the count for money had and received; and to this charge the plaintiff excepted.

The appeal is sued out by the defendants, who assign as error the rulings on the pleadings adverse to them, the charge given, and the refusal of the charges asked by them; and there is, by consent, a cross-assignment of error by the plaintiff, which requires no notice.

TAYLOE & JOHNSTON, and GEO. G. LYON, for appellants. (1.) The contract sued on was without consideration. Plaintiff's promise, as alleged and proved, was, "not to impede the shipments of cotton by holding the same for the payment of his charges." It was his legal duty not to impede the shipments, and he would have been liable to an action for damages if he had done so. (2.) The contract was void under the statute of frauds, because it was not to be performed within one year from the making thereof. It must be remembered that the contract was made late in the season, when the business of buying cotton was nearly over, as the court judicially knows; and the fact that the parties continued to act under it during the next season shows their intention as to its scope and extent—is a practical illustration of their understanding and intention; in fact, the alleged breach did not occur until the close of the next season.—12 Heisk. 655; *Doyle v. Dixon*, 93 Amer. Dec. 87; Smith on Contracts, 57–8. (3.) The contract was void under the statute of frauds, for the further reason, that it was a promise to answer for the debt, default, or miscarriage of other persons. The entire evidence shows that plaintiff regarded Bernard & Co. as his debtors, and made no claim of liability against defendants until after he had failed to make the money out of Bernard & Co. If any liability was incurred by Bernard & Co., or any credit was extended to them, defendant's promise was collateral, and within the terms of the statute.—Smith's Mer. Law, ch. 11; *Curtis v. Dennis*, 7 Metc. 510; 4 W. Va. 29; Brandt on Suretyship, § 56; 2 East, 325; Browne on Stat. Frauds, 228–30; *Clapp v. Webb*, 52 Wisc. 638; 55 Wisc. 645; 2 Story on Contracts, § 864; *Boykin v. Dohlande & Co.*, 37 Ala. 577; 22 Me. 395; 36 Me. 113; *Taylor v. Drake*, 53 Amer. Dec. 680; *Peabody v. Harvey*, 10 Amer. Dec. 103; *Puckett v. Bates*, 4 Ala. 390. (4.) The

[Prout & Robertson v. Webb.]

intention of the parties, under the facts in evidence, was a question for the jury, and it should have been submitted to them.—Brandt on Suretyship, § 63; 100 Amer. Dec. 66; 37 Ala. 583; 1 H. Bla. 10; 2 T. R. 80; *Scott v. Myatts & Moore*, 24 Ala. 489; Browne, Stat. Frauds, 226.

GEO. W. TAYLOR, *contra.*—(1.) The contract was supported by a two-fold consideration—benefit to one party, and detriment to another.—66 Ala. 490; 75 Ala. 452; 77 Ala. 217. (2.) The contract might have been fully performed within one year, and there was no provision for its longer continuance; nor can any presumption of further continuance be indulged in to defeat it.—*Brigham & Co. v. Carlisle*, 78 Ala. 243; *Derrick v. Brown*, 66 Ala. 165; *Heflin v. Milton*, 69 Ala. 356. (3.) The contract was executed, and nothing remained to be done but the payment of the money. *Westmoreland v. Porter*, 75 Ala. 452; Bishop, Contracts, §§ 672. (4.) The promise was an original and primary undertaking, supported by a sufficient consideration, and not collateral to the debt or liability of any other person.—*Bell v. Marx*, 48 Ala. 498; *Clark v. Jones*, 85 Ala. 127.

McCLELLAN, J.—The plaintiff below was a warehouseman and cotton-factor in the city of Demopolis. The defendants were private bankers in said city. The contract declared on was entered into, if at all, by and between them in these respective capacities, and in its very nature depended for its continued existence upon the continuation, on either hand, of the business engaged in at the time by Webb and Prout & Robertson, respectively. Either party might have continued to engage in the business, with respect to which the contract was made, for any number of years; and on the other hand, either party might have desisted from the business within a year from the date of the contract. A discontinuance by either party, within the year, would have determined the contract. The undertaking, therefore, belongs to that class of "agreements to continue to do something for an indefinite period, which may be determined by such a change in the circumstances of the parties as will make it unreasonable or unnecessary that they should be further bound, the contingency of such change in circumstances being implied in the nature of the contract," and which "are not within that provision of the statute of frauds which requires all contracts, which by their terms are not to be performed

within one year, to be in writing."—Browne on Stat. of
Frauds, 276a; 1 Reed, Stat. of Frauds, 199; Wood, Stat. of
Frauds, 485; *Talmadge v. R. & S. R. R. Co.*, 13 Barb. 493;
Adams v. Adams, 26 Ala. 279; *Brigham & Co. v. Carlisle*,
78 Ala. 244; *Heflin v. Milton*, 69 Ala. 356; *Derrick v. Brown*,
66 Ala. 165. And it is immaterial in such cases, so far as
the application of the statute of frauds is concerned, whether
the contract has or has not been performed within the year.
Browne on Stat. of Frauds, 279.

This contract was made in November, 1885, or 1886. It
was not restricted in its application to cotton bought by any
particular buyer or buyers, but was intended to embrace all
cotton stored in appellee's warehouse, which should be bought
by persons dealing with and through the appellants as to the
particular purchase. Bernard & Co. did not begin operations as cotton-buyers at Demopolis, until the fall of 1887.
It would, therefore, be a presumption too violent to be indulged, that the agreement of Prout & Robertson was made
in the interest of, or for the benefit of Bernard & Co., or
other cotton-buyer. On the contrary, the agreement was to
obtain with respect to all buyers who dealt with Prout & Robertson, and whose purchases passed through their hands.
From these dealings certain profits resulted to the appellants,
consisting of the interest on money which they advanced,
and of the exchange which they charged on the collection of
drafts for the proceeds of the cotton when sold. To facili-
tate Prout & Robertson in the dealings in which they were
thus interested, and out of which these profits were made,
Webb surrendered his lien on the cotton, in consideration of
their promise to secure him in the payment of his charges.
The "leading purpose" of Prout & Robertson, therefore, was
not to answer for the debt, default, or miscarriage of Bernard
& Co., but to subserve their own pecuniary or business interests. The contract by which this object was accomplished,
was supported by considerations moving directly between the
parties to it, and with which Bernard & Co. had no concern,
which were of benefit to the promisor, as well as of detriment to the promisee; and although it may be in form an
undertaking to answer for the debt of another, and although,
as a matter of fact, when performed, it may have that effect,
it is not within the third clause of the statute of frauds, and
need not have been in writing.—*Wilson v. Boynton*, 3 Met.
(Mass.) 396; *Emerson v. Slater*, 22 How. 28; *Castling v.
Aubert*, 2 East, 325; *Small v. Shœfer*, 24 Md. 161; *Leiber*

v. *Levy*, 3 Met. (Ky.) 292; *Westmoreland v. Porter*, 75 Ala. 459; Browne Stat. Frauds, 214b-249, and note; 1 Reed Stat. Frauds, 72.

The same conclusion would probably be reached upon other considerations presented by the evidence in this case; as, for instance, that appellants, through this arrangement, obtained possession and control of the property, through the bills of lading, which, in the course of these dealings, were deposited with them.—Authorities above cited; and *Williams v. Leper*, 3 Burr. 188; *McCrary v. Madden*, 1 McCord L. 486. But we are content to rest it on the position first taken.

The demurrers to the first count of the complaint were sustained, and leave granted plaintiff to amend. This was done by adding the third and fourth counts. Whereupon the defendants again demurred to the *first*, which was no longer in the complaint, and also to the third and fourth; and they now assign the overruling of their demurrer to that count as error. This is so palpably a mistake, that it need not be further considered.

The third and fourth counts are for the breach of the special contract, and seek to recover the amount of money which the defendants, it is alleged, agreed in that contract to pay to the plaintiff. They do not proceed on the theory, that a breach of duty imposed by the contract has been committed, whereby and in consequence of which plaintiff has been damaged in the sum claimed, but they seek to hold the defendants to the payment of the money that they obligated themselves to pay. The case made by these counts is, therefore, *ex contractu*, as upon an express agreement. The case made by the second count, for money had and received, is also *ex contractu*, as upon an implied promise; and these several counts are, therefore, properly joined.—*Whilden v. M. & P. Bank*, 64 Ala. 27.

The amended complaint on the special contract, and each count thereof, avers that the plaintiff was induced to forego his lien on the property, and to surrender his possession of it, by the agreement of the defendants to see that his charges were paid; and the demurrer to the third and fourth counts, on the assumption that they show a voluntary surrender of the property, or abandonment of the lien, under which plaintiff had possession of it, are not well taken. The rulings of the court below, so far as they were prejudicial to the defendants, were in accordance with the principles we have an-

nounced, and were free from error. Its rulings which went
to the prejudice of the plaintiff, and are, by agreement of
parties, brought to our attention by a cross-assignment of
error, need not be considered; since, in the view we have
taken of this case, they involve no injury to the appellee.

Affirmed.

Powell *v*. New England Mortgage & Security Co.

*Bill in Equity for Foreclosure of Mortgage, or Ratification
of Sale under Power.*

1. *Relieving married woman of disabilities of coverture, by decree in
chancery.*—In the exercise of the statutory jurisdiction formerly conferred on chancellors, to relieve married women of the disabilities of
coverture to the extent specified (Code, 1876, § 2731), relief can not be
granted by piecemeal, but the relief prayed and granted must be coextensive with the statute, neither more nor less; if the petition prays
only partial relief, or less than the statute authorizes, any decree rendered upon it is void; but, if the petition conforms to the statute, while
the decree goes beyond it, it is void only for the excess.

2. *Same; case at bar.*—Where the petition alleged that the petitioner
owned certain lands, "which are her statutory separate estate, and
which she desires to incumber or mortgage for the purpose of raising
money," and therefore prayed to be "relieved of all the disabilities of
coverture, to the end that she may sue and be sued as a *feme sole*, mortgage, convey, and otherwise dispose of her separate estate as fully and
freely as if a *feme sole*;" while the decree declared her "relieved of the
disabilities of coverture, with full power to convey, mortgage, buy, sell,
or otherwise dispose of her statutory and other separate estate, to sue
and be sued as a *feme sole*;" *held*, that the petition and decree, each,
was fatally defective, and conferred no power to mortgage her lands.

APPEAL from the Chancery Court of Montgomery.

Heard before the Hon. JOHN A. FOSTER.

The bill in this case was filed, on what day the record does
not show, by the New England Mortgage & Security Company, a corporation organized under the laws of Connecticut,
against Mrs. Virginia D. Powell and her husband, James W.
Powell; and sought the foreclosure of a mortgage on a tract
of land, executed by the defendants to the complainant, or a
ratification, at the election of the defendants, of an irregular
sale under a power in the mortgage, at which the complainant became the purchaser through an agent. The mortgage
was given to secure a debt for borrowed money, and was

dated November 17th, 1887; and was duly executed and acknowledged by said Powell and wife, and contained a power of sale on default. The bill alleged that Mrs. Powell, to whom the mortgaged lands belonged, had been relieved of the disabilities of coverture prior to its execution, "by proceedings in the Chancery Court of Montgomery," a transcript of which was made an exhibit to the bill. The transcript showed that, on the 21st December, 1878, a petition was filed in the name of Mrs. Powell, suing by her next friend, which alleged—"1st, that she is a resident citizen of Montgomery county, Alabama, over twenty-one years of age, and the wife of James W. Powell; 2d, that she is the owner of certain real estate and an interest in lands in Montgomery county, which are her separate statutory estate, and which she desires to incumber or mortgage for the purpose of raising money." The prayer of the petition was in these words: "Wherefore your petitioner prays, that your Honor will relieve her of all the disabilities of coverture, to the end that she may sue and be sued as a *feme sole*, mortgage, convey, and otherwise dispose of her separate estate, as fully and freely as if a *feme sole*." The consent of the husband was written at the bottom of the petition, and the case was submitted to the chancellor in vacation; and he rendered a decree in vacation, dated December 26th, 1878, as follows: "It is therefore ordered, adjudged and decreed, that Virginia D. Powell, wife of James W. Powell, of Montgomery county, be, and she is hereby, relieved of the disabilities of coverture, with full power to convey, mortgage, buy, sell, or otherwise dispose of her statutory and other separate estate, to sue and be sued as a *feme sole*."

The defendants demurred to the bill, assigning specially several causes of demurrer assailing the validity of the chancery proceedings. The chancellor overruled the demurrer, and his decree is here assigned as error.

WATTS & SON, for appellant.

THORINGTON & SMITH, *contra*.

STONE, C. J.—The question in this case is, whether certain proceedings had before the chancellor so far relieve Mrs. Powell of the disabilities of coverture, as to make the mortgage executed by her a binding lien on the land therein described. A transcript of those proceedings is made an ex-

[Powell v. New England Mortgage & Security Co.]

hibit to the bill. An attempt had been made, under section 2731 of the Code of 1876, to have Mrs. Powell relieved of her disabilities of coverture, as to her statutory and other separate estates, so far as to invest her with the right "to buy, sell, hold, convey, and mortgage real and personal property, and to sue and be sued as a *feme sole.*" The petition was addressed to the chancellor in vacation, and was acted upon by him in vacation.

This statute has been several times before us for interpretation. Our uniform ruling has been, that it is enabling, and that to obtain the benefits it offers, the whole, and not a part of the relief it tenders, must be set forth, and embodied in the prayer; in other words, that no fractional relief, less than the whole, can be obtained under this statute. The chancellor has no power to grant any relief, unless all the statute provides is asked for, and he can confer no greater or other powers than those enumerated in the statute. Asking to be relieved of only a part of the enumerated disabilities, falls short of putting the jurisdiction and powers of the chancellor into exercise; and any decree he may render on such petition is a nullity.—*Ashford v. Watkins,* 70 Ala. 156; *Cohen v. Wollner,* 72 Ala. 233; *Falk v. Hecht,* 75 Ala. 293. So, in *Meyer v. Sulzbacher,* 76 Ala. 120, 127, we said: "That the powers authorized by the statute to be conferred must all be conferred, or withheld together, as an entirety, and that this jurisdiction can not be exercised by piecemeal." If, however, the relief granted be greater than the statute allows, but yet both pleadings and decree cover the whole field of permissible relief, such decree will be void only for the excess.—*Meyer v. Sulzbacher, supra; Mohr v. Senior,* 85 Ala. 114.

The petition, under which Mrs. Powell obtained her relief, is fatally defective. It simply avers that she owns lands, her statutory separate estate, "which she desires to incumber, or mortgage, for the purpose of raising money." The prayer is, "that your Honor will relieve her of all the disabilities of coverture, to the end that she may sue and be sued as a *feme sole,* mortgage, convey, and otherwise dispose of her separate estate, as fully and freely as if she were a *feme sole.*" It will be seen that several of the provisions of the statute are ignored. The decree is fuller; but, to the extent it goes beyond the petition and its prayer, it is *coram non judice.* But, it is itself defective.

Reversed, and demurrer sustained. Remanded, with in-

[Carroll v. Richardson.]

structions to the chancellor to dismiss the bill, unless, perchance, the defects pointed out above can be cured by
amendment.

Reversed and remanded.

Carroll *v* Richardson.

Bills in Equity, between Legatees and Executor.

1. *When legatee may come into equity, against executor.*—A legatee to
whom the testator bequeathed his mercantile business, with stock of
goods, notes and outstanding accounts, directing that he "will assume
all the liabilities of the store, and continue the business as heretofore,"
and also devising to him the store-house in which the business was
carried on, can not maintain a bill in equity against the executor, to
recover the goods, notes and accounts, until after the expiration of
eighteen months from the grant of letters testamentary (Code, §§ 2134,
2192), unless the executor has reported the estate to be solvent, even
though he offers to give bond for the faithful administration of the
assets.

2. *Demurrer to cross-bill, when original bill is wanting in equity.*—On
appeal from an interlocutory order overruling a demurrer to a cross-bill
(Code, § 3612), the appellate court can not consider the sufficiency of
the original bill, to which a demurrer was interposed and overruled;
yet, if the original bill was wanting in equity, the overruling of a demurrer to the cross-bill is not a reversible error.

3. *When executor may come into equity.*—An executor may file a bill
in equity, asking the court to construe the will, to give him instructions
in the performance of his duties, and to remove the administration into
that court, when it appears that the provisions of the will are of doubtful construction, and that the legatees assert conflicting claims under it.

APPEALS from the Chancery Court of Butler.

Heard before the Hon. JOHN A FOSTER.

These two cases, involving controversies between J.Monroe
Carroll, a legatee and devisee under the last will and testament of John T. Perry, deceased, and J. C. Richardson, his
executor, were argued and submitted together in the court
below, on demurrers to each bill, and on motion to consoli-
date the two causes; and they were argued and submitted
together in this court.   Said J. T. Perry died on the 24th
June, 1887, and his last will and testament was duly admitted
to probate on the 28th July, 1887, on which day, also, letters
testamentary were granted to J. C. Richardson as sole executor; J. M. Carroll and E. Crenshaw, who were also named
as executors in the will, declining the trust.   The will was
dated February 10th, 1887, and contained the following

(with other) provisions: "*First*, my will is, that all my just debts and funeral expenses, including a monument over my grave, be paid out of my estate, as soon after my death as convenient. *Second*, after paying all my just debts and funeral expenses, as heretofore described, I give, devise and bequeath to my beloved sister, Mahala J. Rothenhoffer, all my personal property, except piano (which I give, devise and bequeath to my niece, Henrietta Dohrmeir), and my parlor set of furniture, including carpet and parlor fixtures of every kind, that is my parlor, to my niece, Bessie Dohrmeir. *Third*, I give, devise and bequeath $500 to each of my sisters, Mahala J. Rothenhoffer, Martha A. Fulmore, and Georgiana V. Carroll; which shall be paid over to them by my executors, within twelve months after my death, or sooner if practicable." Then follow devises of real estate, consisting of several store-houses and lots in Greenville, to his nephews and nieces; the first being to J. M. Carroll, of "two brick stores and lots on the corner of Commerce and Bolling streets," with these words added: "But, if he should die without issue, before the reversion or remainder shall come into his possession, then I give, devise and bequeath the same to my niece, Fanny Bell Dohrmeir, her heirs and assigns forever." The last clause of the will, after nominating the executors, added: "I hereby authorize them, or either of them, to do all things necessary to carry out the terms of this will, and to avoid, if possible, the necessity of going into any of the courts to settle up this will. It is my wish, in case of disagreement between any of the parties to this will, that the same shall be settled by arbitration, instead of going into chancery, or any other court with it."

This will, as propounded for probate, was attested by G. W. Bryan and J. M. Carroll as subscribing witnesses; and to it was annexed a certificate by A. B. Dulin as notary public, as to its acknowledgment before him by the testator, in the statutory form for the acknowledgment of a conveyance. Beneath the certificate these works were added: "*Codicil:* Additional to page 1 from second clause: Second, after paying all my just debts and funeral expenses, as heretofore described, I give, devise and bequeath to my beloved sister, Mahala J. Rothenhoffer, all my personal property, except my stock of merchandise, books, accounts, notes, mortgages, store fixtures, and everything belonging to said store now occupied by me, on corner of Commerce and Bolling streets, to my nephew, J. M. Carroll, who will assume

[Carroll v. Richardson]

all the liabilities of the store, and continue the business as
heretofore: and he would provide for the welfare of my
beloved sister, Elizabeth Kelley, and my sister-in-law,
Georgiana V. Carroll, as long as they live, and will accept."
This codicil was dated June 20th, 1887, and was attested by
G. W. Bryan and A. B. Dulin; and it was admitted to probate with the will.

According to the allegations of the bill afterwards filed by
Richardson as executor, the store-house of the testator remained closed from the day of his death, June 24th, to July
28th, when Richardson was appointed as executor; and the
keys of the building, and of the vault or safe in it, being
then delivered to him by Carroll, he took possession, and
found $1,825.86 in the vault. The goods being in a dam-
aged condition, the executor filed a petition asking an order
of sale from the Probate Court; and he proceeded to sell the
goods at private sale until October 29th, 1887, when Carroll
filed a bill against him, to enjoin any further sales, and to
require the executor to deliver the goods up to him; insisting that they were only charged with the debts of the business, until all the other property of the estate was exhausted,
and offering to give a bond of indemnity for the proper
application of the goods as assets. The executor had also
obtained from the Probate Court, on the 15th September,
an order for the sale of the other personal property, specifying and describing everything; and on the 16th October,
1887, the day appointed for the sale, a bill in equity was
filed against him and Carroll, by Mrs. Rothenhoffer and
other legatees, seeking to enjoin the sale of articles bequeathed to them, on the ground that Carroll had misappro-
priated money and other assets, which the executor should
recover and appropriate to the payment of the debts.

In the suit instituted by Carroll, the executor filed an
answer, which he asked might be taken as a cross-bill, and
he also demurred to Carroll's original bill. The chancellor
overruled the demurrer to the original bill, and also the demurrer to the cross-bill. Carroll appealed from the decree
overruling his demurrer to the cross-bill, and here assigned
it as error. In the suit instituted by Richardson, he asked
the court to construe the will, to instruct him in the discharge
of his duties as executor, and to remove the administration
of the estate into the Chancery Court. Carroll filed a demurrer to the bill, and he appealed from the decree overruling his demurrer, here assigning it as error.

TOMPKINS, LONDON & TROY, for appellant in each case, cited 3 Pomeroy's Equity, §§ 156–7; *Clay v. Gurley*, 62 Ala. 14; *McNeill v. McNeill*, 36 Ala. 109; *Taunton v. McInnish*, 46 Ala. 619; *Insurance Co. v. Webb*, 54 Ala. 688; *Shelton v. Carpenter*, 60 Ala. 201; *Grimball v. Patton*, 70 Ala. 626.

WATTS & SON, *contra*, cited *Trotter v. Blocker*, 6 Porter, 269; *Sellers v. Sellers*, 35 Ala. 235; *Cowles v. Pollard*, 51 Ala. 445; *Clay v. Gurley*, 62 Ala. 14; *Hollingsworth v. Hollingsworth*, 65 Ala. 321; *Wilson v. Crook*, 17 Ala. 59; *Stewart v. Stewart*, 31 Ala. 207; *Dudley v. Farris & McCurdy*, 79 Ala. 187; *Bozeman v. Gilbert*, 1 Ala. 90; 3 Porter, 231.

STONE, C. J.—These two suits refer to the estate of J. T. Perry, deceased. Mr. Perry left a will and codicil, each of which was proven and established as his last will and testament; and Richardson, one of the executors named in the will, qualified as such, and took upon himself the execution of the trust. The other two did not qualify.

The suit stated first above was instituted probably in less than six months after the probate of the will, J. M. Carroll being the complainant. The records fail to furnish the date when either bill was filed. Whether this be so or not, it is manifest that each of the bills was filed in much less than eighteen months after the probate of the will.

When a personal representative of a decedent's will or estate is appointed and qualifies, the result is, that the title to all personal effects of the estate, including *choses* in action, vests immediately in him, and that title relates back to, and takes effect from decedent's death.—1 Brick. Dig. 932, §§ 262, 264; 3 *Ib.* 463. § 130. It then becomes his duty to possess himself of all personal effects, that he may pay the debts, and perform the other functions of administration. Until the expiration of eighteen months after the appointment of a personal representative, the law does not impute to him a knowledge of the condition of the estate as to solvency or insolvency. Till then he can not be coerced to pay, or assent to a legacy.—Code of 1886, § 2192, and note. In the case of *Jackson v. Rowell*, at present term, we said: "Eighteen months are allowed after administration granted, for presenting or filing claims against decedents' estates; and a settlement can not be coerced until after the expiration of eighteen months (Code of 1886, §§ 2134,

[Carroll v. Richardson.]

2192), unless the executor or administrator becomes satisfied before that time that the estate is solvent, and so reports; in which event he may obtain an order of distribution as to the whole, or any part of the property."—Code of 1886, § 2191. See *Upchurch v. Norsworthy*, 12 Ala. 532.

There was a demurrer to Carroll's bill, which the chancellor overruled. There is no appeal from that ruling, and it neither is, nor can be assigned as error. Consequently, the sufficiency of that bill is not directly before us for review. Richardson answered Carroll's bill, and, under our statute, made his answer a cross-bill. To that cross-bill Carroll filed a demurrer, which the chancellor overruled. That ruling is assigned as error. A cross-bill is defensive in its nature and purpose; and if the original bill fails, the cross-bill, as a rule, has nothing to accomplish, and fails with it. We will not consider the sufficiency of the cross-bill, for, under the principles we have declared, Carroll's bill is without equity, and the demurrer to it ought to have been sustained. There is in this ruling no error of which appellant can complain.

There is not enough before us—indeed, facts are not sufficiently developed—to enable us to determine absolutely what course the executor ought to pursue in reference to the merchandise. It is clear that Carroll can not claim their delivery to him, either with or without security for his faithful administration of the trust. The executor should, as far as safety and the payment of the debts will permit, respect the wishes of the testator in the matter of the specific devises, bequests, and pecuniary legacies; for, next to the law of the land, the will is a law to him. The merchandise is probably perishable, and in any event would deteriorate in value, if kept on hands unreasonably. Much must be confided to the executor's discretion; while, if he acts recklessly, or in bad faith, and thereby injures the estate, he will render himself liable for the abuse. We know not how to be more definite on this subject.

Following pretty closely the foregoing suit, as we infer, came the bill of J. C. Richardson, as executor, stated second at the head of this opinion. That bill makes all the devisees and legatees under Perry's will parties defendant. The object and prayer of the bill, as amended, are two-fold: First, to obtain an interpretation of the will, and directions of the court in its administration; and, second, to have the administration removed into the Chancery Court. There was a demurrer to this bill by Carroll, which the chancellor overruled.

We hold that this bill, in each of its aspects, contains equity. The will itself, including the codicil, presents several questions of disputable solution, on which different legal minds might well differ. And it is shown that Mrs. Rothenhoffer and Carroll differ in the interpretation of the will, in the assertion of the interests they severally claim thereunder. And the question may arise, whether the codicil does not create a precatory trust, in favor of Mrs. Kelley and Mrs. Carroll; and on the other hand, whether the language is not too uncertain to authorize relief.—*Jones v. McPhillips*, 82 Ala. 102; 3 Pom. Eq. §§ 1156–7; *McRee v. McRee*, 34 Ala. 349; *Hollingsworth v. Hollingsworth*, 65 Ala. 321; *Cowles v. Pollard*, 51 Ala. 445. It is not our intention to express or intimate any opinion as to the proper interpretation of any clause of the will. The question of rightful interpretation, or rightful directions, is not before us. The chancellor has declared no interpretation, and has given no directions. He has simply decided that the bill makes a case calling for interpretation and direction, and from that decretal order the present appeal is prosecuted. There is no error in his rulings.

Affirmed.

Geo. Pacific Railway Co. *v.* Hughes.

Action for Damages on account of Personal Injuries.

1. *Contributory negligence between railroad companies at crossing.* In an action to recover damages for personal injuries sustained by plaintiff at a railroad crossing, the fact that the company on whose cars he was travelling was guilty of contributory negligence is no defense, though it may create a joint and several liability.

2. *Statutory liability of railroad companies, for injuries to persons or property; burden of proof.*—Under statutory provisions now of force (Code, §§ 1144–5, 1147, note), whether the action is for injuries to person or stock, the *onus* is on the railroad company to acquit itself of negligence, by showing (1) a compliance with the statutory requisitions as to blowing the whistle and ringing the bell, or (2) that such compliance could not have averted the injury; but this statutory rule does not extend to a case where the injuries are caused by a neglect of other duties at a crossing of two railroads, resulting in a collision whereby plaintiff, a passenger, was injured.

[Geo. Pacific Railway Co. v. Hughes.]

3. *Same; cases explained and limited.*—In the following cases, "presenting questions arising under section 1144 (Code of 1886), the decisions were correct on the points presented, but the principle was stated too broadly, and is liable to mislead : "*A. G. S. Railroad Co. v. McAlpine*, 75 Ala. 113; s. c , 80 Ala. 73; *L. & N. Ala. Railroad Co. v. Bees*, 82 Ala. 340; *M. & G. Railroad Co. v. Caldwell*, 83 Ala. 196; and in *L. & N. Railroad Co. v. Jones*, 83 Ala. 373, "the principle stated was scarcely called for, and is not correct when applied to the class of injuries there complained of."

APPEAL from the Circuit Court of Jefferson.

Tried before the Hon. LEROY F. BOX.

This action was brought by Thomas R. Hughes against the appellant corporation, to recover damages for personal injuries sustained by plaintiff from a collision of a street railway car, on which he was a passenger, and a train of cars belonging to the defendant. The collision occurred on the 16th March, 1888, at the intersection of two streets in the city of Birmingham, where the tracks of the two railroads crossed each other; and the action was brought on the 13th April, 1888. The court charged the jury, among other things, as follows: "When a person sues a railroad company for damages for injuries to his person, as in this case, he is required to show that he has been injured, and that the injury was inflicted by the defendant, or the defendant's employees or servants; and when he does that, the burden of proof is on the defendant to show that itself or its employees were not negligent at the time and place of the occurrence, and therefore, if the plaintiff was injured at all, he was not injured by reason of the defendant's negligence." This charge, to which the defendant excepted, is now assigned as error, with several other rulings, which require no notice.

JAMES WEATHERLY, for appellant.

SMITH & LOWE, *contra.*

STONE, C. J.—The East Lake Dummy Line of railway extends from the business part of the city of Birmingham, eastwardly to East Lake. It is a street railway, the cars of which are drawn by steam power, called a dummy engine. Within the corporate limits of Birmingham, at the intersection of First Avenue and Twenty-seventh Street, the East Lake railway track crosses two lateral tracks of the Georgia Pacific Railway Company, that were used in receiving and transferring cars from and to other railroads that center in

Birmingham.   The railroad crossings are in a public street,
or at the point of intersection of the two streets.   At this
crossing the injury was suffered, which gave rise to the present suit.   The injury was inflicted in March, 1888.

The plaintiff, Hughes, was a passenger on the dummy
line, going eastward.   While crossing the Georgia Pacific's
said tracks, a collision occurred between the coach in which
he was riding, and the front car of a train which the Georgia Pacific was pushing along its transfer track, with a view
of placing said cars, some ten in number, beyond the crossing.   The engine of the Georgia Pacific, which was moving
these cars, was at the other end of the train, about ten car
lengths distant—say three hundred feet—from the crossing.
Plaintiff, as the proof tends to show, was seriously hurt and
injured, and it is not claimed that he was himself guilty of
any negligence.   The testimony as to the cause, or proximate
cause of the collision, is in very marked conflict.   The one
line of proof, if true as presented, relieves the dummy line
of all omissions of duty—of all negligence—and places the
fault on the Georgia Pacific.   The other places the culpa-
bility on the dummy line.   Neither the court below, nor this
court, was or is charged with the ascertainment of the facts.
That was exclusively the province of the jury, under proper
instructions as to the law, to be given to them by the court.
We review the Circuit Court's rulings on the law, and nothing else.

A few questions were reserved on the admissibility of the
evidence.   They were not pressed in the argument, and we
think there is nothing in them.

The defense takes two positions.   *First:* That conceding
the Georgia Pacific was guilty of negligence, the dummy
line was also guilty of negligence, which contributed proximately to the collision; and plaintiff, being a passenger on
the dummy line, is under the same disability to sue and recover, as the dummy line would be if it were suing.   There
are some authorities which support this view, but we think
them unsound.   If each of the corporations was guilty of
negligence, which caused, or aided in causing the injury,
certainly it is a strange logic to contend, that because each
had an assistant in committing the tort, neither is liable to
the person injured by such compound tort.—*Western Railway of Ala. v. Sistrunk*, 85 Ala. 352; 2 Wood's Railway
Law, 1340, *et seq.*; *Chapman v. New Haven R. R. Co.*,
19 N. Y. 341; *Robinson v. N. Y. Cent. R. R. Co.*, 66 N. Y.

11; Shear. & Redf. Neg. § 46; Whart. Neg. § 395; *Wabash St. L. Co. v. Shacklet*, 12 Amer. & Eng. R. R. Cas. 166; Patterson, Accident Law, § 357. It may create a joint and several liability. It does not exonerate either.

The other defense relied on is, that the entire fault was that of the dummy line. If that be true, there should be no recovery against the Georgia Pacific. The only form in which this question comes before us is in the charges given and refused; notably, the charges relating to the burden of proof.

The act "to define the duties and liabilities of railroad companies in this State," was approved February 6, 1858. Sess. Acts 1857-8, p. 15. The 3d section of that act was amended January 31, 1861.—Sess. Acts, 37. As amended, the first and third sections were carried into the Code of 1867, as sections 1399, 1401. They were then carried, without change, into the Code of 1876, as sections 1699 and 1700. These sections remained without change, until February 28, 1887, when section 1700 was amended.—Sess. Acts, 146-7. Section 1699 of the Code of 1876 was carried, without any alteration which affects this case, into the Code of 1886, as section 1144. The act of February 28, 1887, which amended section 1700 of the Code of 1876, was not repealed, or affected in any manner, by the adoption of the Code of 1886. Such is the express language of the second section of the act "to adopt a Code of laws for the State of Alabama," approved February 28, 1887.—Sess. Acts, 47. It results, that the statutory law which governs this case is found in sections 1144 and 1145 of the Code of 1886, and in "the act to amend section 1700 of the Code," approved February 28, 1887.—Sess. Acts, 146.

Section 1144, Code of 1886, specifies many duties which "the engineer, or other person having control of the running of a locomotive on any railroad," must observe and perform. We will only mention those which seem to be applicable to this case: "He must also blow the whistle, or ring the bell, at short intervals, on entering into, or while moving within, or passing through any village, town or city. He must, also, on perceiving any obstruction on the track, use all the means within his power, known to skillful engineers, such as applying brakes and reversing engine, in order to stop the train." *Sec.* 1145. "When the tracks of two railroads cross each other, engineers and conductors must cause the trains of which they are in charge to come to a full stop, within one hundred feet of such crossing, and not to proceed until they know the way to be clear; the train on the railroad having the older right of way being entitled to cross first."

Before the amendment of section 1700, by the act of February 28, 1887, when suit was brought against railroad companies, for destruction or injury of stock or other property by their locomotives or cars, the burden of proof was declared to be on the railroad company, to show that the requirements of section 1699 of that Code were complied with, at the time and place when and where the injury was done. There was no such declaration or provision applicable to suits in which injury to the person was the ground of complaint. The requirements of section 1699, here referred to, are found in section 1144 of the Code of 1886, from which we have given extracts above. The amendment of section 1700 extended its provisions, so as to include cases in which a person was killed or injured; and, as the statutes stood when the plaintiff in this case was injured, and is still of force, the rule as to the burden of proof was and is still the same, whether the injury complained of is to person or property. The amended section is in the following language: "A railroad company is liable for all damages done to persons, stock or other property, resulting from a failure to comply with the requirements of the preceding section, or any negligence on the part of such company or its agents; and when any person or stock is killed or injured, or other property damaged or destroyed by the locomotive or cars of any railroad, the burden of proof in any suit brought therefor is on the railroad company, to show that the requirements of the preceding section [§ 1699 of the Code of 1876] were complied with, at the time and place when and where the injury was done."

Railroads are common carriers for hire, and as such, when they transport property, and it is injured in transit, or is not delivered, the burden is on the carrier to show that it bestowed all proper diligence on the service, and that the property was injured or destroyed without any negligence on its part.—*Steele v. Townsend*, 37 Ala. 247; *Leach v. Bush*, 57 Ala. 145; *Grey v. Mobile Trade Co.*, 55 Ala. 387. When the injury is to a person, or to property not being transported, then the statutes referred to above become important factors. We have had many cases before us which were more or less influenced by these statutes. Whenever an injury has been done to property, under circumstances which

[Geo. Pacific Railway Co. v. Hughes.]

call for the exercise of any of the cautionary signals or acts required by section 1144, Code of 1886, we have held that the burden is on the railroad company to prove that it complied with the requirements of that section. We have held, however, that a failure to comply, or, what is the same thing, to make proof that it did comply, while it creates a *prima facie* intendment that the railroad was in fault, is not conclusive of the plaintiff's right of recovery. It is only in cases where the injury complained of is reasonably traceable to the failure to comply with the requirements of the statute, that the failure, *per se*, gives a right of action. And we have held, further, that if, when the danger became visible, any appliances would have been powerless to avert the catastrophe, then it is not actionable negligence, if nothing be attempted. In each of these varying phases of defense, the burden is on the railroad company; that is, the burden is on it to prove that it complied with those requirements which were applicable to the case or crisis it had to deal with, or to show that none of those requirements could have availed to avert the injury. We have said the impossible need not be attempted. We subjoin a citation of most of our rulings, which, under the amended statute, are now alike applicable to each class of injury—that to person, as well as that to property: *M. & O. R. R. Co. v. Williams*, 53 Ala. 595; *Mobile & Montgomery R. R. Co. v. Blakeley*, 59 Ala. 471; *M. & C. R. R. Co. v. Copeland*, 61 Ala. 372; *S. &. N. R. R. Co. v. Thompson*, 62 Ala. 494; *Central R. R. & Bank. Co. v. Letcher*, 69 Ala. 106; *A. G. S. R. R. Co. v. McAlpine*, 71 Ala. 545; *E. T., V. & G. R. R. Co. v. Bayliss*, 74 Ala. 150; s. c., 77 Ala. 429; *Clements v. E. T., V. & G. R. R. Co.*, 77 Ala. 533; *E. T., V. & G. R. R. Co. v. Deaver*, 79 Ala. 216; *Same v. King*, 81 Ala. 177; *Ga. Pac. R. R. Co. v. Blanton*, 84 Ala. 154; *A. G. S. R. R. Co. v. Smith*, 85 Ala. 208; *Western Railway Co. v. Sistrunk*, *Ib.* 352; *N., C. & St. L. R. R. Co. v. Hembree*, *Ib.* 481; *L. & N. R. R. Co. v. Reese*, *Ib.* 497; *S. & N. R. R. Co. v. Williams*, 65 Ala. 74; 3 Brick. Dig. 726.

The following cases presented questions arising under section 1144 of the Code of 1886. The decisions were correct on the points presented, but the principle was stated too broadly, and is liable to mislead, if it has not aleady done so: *Ala. Gr. So. R. R. Co. v. McAlpine*, 75 Ala. 113; s. c., 80 Ala. 73; *S. & N. R. R. Co. v. Bees*, 82 Ala. 340; *M. & G. R. R. Co. v. Caldwell*, 83 Ala. 196. In *L. & N. R. R. Co.*

v. Jones, Ib. 373, the principle stated was scarcely called for, and is not correct when applied to the class of injury complained of in that case.

It is not our intention to modify the doctrine declared in *S. & N. R. R. Co. v. Shearer*, 58 Ala. 672; *S. & N. R. R. Co. v. Sullivan*, 59 Ala. 272; nor to weaken the authority of the principle declared in *Tanner's case*, 60 Ala. 621, further than that case may be qualified by *Womack's case*, 84 Ala. 149.

There is no case in our books which declares, clearly and specifically, to what extent, in cases like the present, the burden is on the railroad company to acquit itself of imputed negligence. The question has not heretofore been pressed upon our attention as it is in this case. Sections 1144 and 1145 each defines certain duties which railroad companies must observe. And we have declared it is their duty, when backing their trains within a city, town, or village, to maintain a lookout, which can survey and take in that portion of the track which their train is being pushed upon. This, for the safety of persons who might perchance be on the track. A disregard of any one or more of these duties would be negligence in the railroad company; and if injury to person or property resulted from it, and there was no concurring, proximate, contributory negligence on the part of the injured party, a suit can be maintained for damages resulting from such negligence. But, on whom, and to what extent, rests the burden of proof in such action?

We have seen that, under section 1700 of the Code of 1886, as amended, the burden is expressly placed on the railroad company, to show it complied with the requirements of section 1699, Code of 1876—§ 1144, Code of 1886. It fails to mention any other duty, or to cast the burden of proving it on the railroad company. It thus, by its silence, fails to place the burden of proof on the railroad company, in the matter of its compliance with section 1145, Code of 1886, and in the matter of maintaining a lookout, when it backs a train within the limits of a city, town or village. In fact, it is silent as to all matters of imputed negligence, save the disregard of the duties enjoined in section 1144 of the Code. This is significant. *Expressum facit cessare tacitum.* It is a rule of interpretation, that if a statute enumerates and commands certain duties, or specifies and declares certain exceptions, the implications are, that every thing not enumerated or specified is left without the influence of the

[Geo. Pacific Railway Co. v. Hughes.]

statute.—Sedg. Stat. Constr. (2d Ed.), 31, note. In 2 Amer. & Eng. Encyc. Law, it is said: "The burden of proof is, in general, upon the plaintiff, of showing, in a case of personal injury, negligence on the part of the carrier." This is the rule in the absence of the statute.

We feel constrained to hold, that the burden of proof was on the railroad company, only to the extent the statute places it—that is, as to all the matters enumerated in section 1144 of the Code; and if it seeks to excuse itself for a non-compliance with those requirements, then the burden is on it to show a state of facts which, under our rulings, will excuse it from making the attempt. As to all other matters raised by the issue, the burden is primarily on the plaintiff. But, the measure of proof required of him is graded by the issue it seeks to maintain. If it involves a negative—such as, that the train was not brought to a full stop within 100 feet of the crossing, or that it did not maintain a proper lookout to avert danger—then the rule of proof in such case is not so exacting. He must, however, in the first place, offer some testimony of the non-observance of the duty, before the defendant need offer any proof of its observance. When this primary proof is made by plaintiff, it then becomes a question of inquiry by the jury on the entire testimony before them. On the general subject of the burden of proof in suits like this, see 2 Wood's Railway Law, 1096, and note.

Under the principles we have declared, the first paragraph of the charge given by the court to the jury, to which exception was reserved, misplaced the burden of proof; and for that error, the judgment of the Circuit Court must be reversed.—*Thompson v. Duncan*, 76 Ala. 334.

We need not consider the other charges. What we have said will be a sufficient guide on another trial.

Reversed and remanded.

Lehman, Durr & Co. *v.* Glenn.

Action by Trustee under appointment of Foreign Chancery Court, against Subscriber for Stock in Private Corporation.

1. *Foreign chancery decree as evidence.*—A transcript, duly certified, of a decree rendered by the Chancery Court of Richmond, Virginia, under a bill filed by or on behalf of the creditors of a dissolved corporation, in which a trustee was appointed to act instead of the trustees named in a deed of assignment executed by the corporation, and authorized to collect unpaid subscriptions for stock, with other debts, is admissible as evidence against a stockholder in Alabama, in a suit brought against him by the trustee, if the court had jurisdiction of the subject-matter and the parties, and if the stockholders are to be regarded as parties; the decree being entitled, under constitutional provisions, to as full faith and credit here as in Virginia.

2. *Same; service on corporation*—The record in that case showing that process was served on the cashier and two directors of the corporation, two of whom appeared and answered, and that the court held this service sufficient to give jurisdiction over the corporation; the decree rendered is conclusive as to that fact, and it can not be here collaterally assailed.

3. *Same; conclusiveness on stockholders as parties.*—The corporation being properly brought in as a party to the foreign suit, the decree rendered is equally conclusive against it and the stockholders, so far as it affects the condition and *status* of the corporate assets, although the stockholders were not personally served with process; and the decree itself is conclusive as to this.

4. *Same; laches, and statute of limitations, as defenses to that suit; authority of court to make calls on stockholders; legal identity of corporations; right of trustee to sue.*—Said foreign chancery decree conclusively establishes, also, (1) that there was no *laches* on the part of said corporation, or its trustees, in the prosecution of that suit; (2) that the claims of creditors were not then barred by the statute of limitations; (3) that the court had authority to make calls or assessments on stockholders for their unpaid subscriptions, the directors having failed to make the necessary calls; (4) the legal identity of the two corporations under a change of name; and (5) the right of the trustee to maintain an action against a stockholder, on such unpaid call.

5. *Books of corporation, as evidence against stockholders.*—The books of a private corporation, showing subscriptions for stock, payments on calls, &c., are admissible as evidence against a stockholder, in an action to enforce his unpaid subscription as called for, especially when he does not by plea deny the genuineness of his subscription.

6. *Statute of limitations in favor of stockholders, as against corporation or creditors.*—When the terms of subscription bind the stockholders of a private corporation to pay the amounts subscribed by them respectively, "in such installments as may be called for by said company," in addition to a small sum in cash at the time of subscription; and the corporation, becoming embarrassed, executes a deed of assignment for the benefit of its creditors, not having called in all the stock subscribed;

the statute of limitations in favor of the stockholders, as to their unpaid subscriptions, against a trustee appointed and authorized by a court of equity to collect them, begins to run, not from the date of the assignment, but from the time when the court makes an assessment and call for them.

APPEAL from the Circuit Court of Montgomery.
Tried before the Hon. JOHN P. HUBBARD.

This action was brought by John Glenn, suing as trustee under appointment by the Chancery Court of the city of Richmond, Virginia, against the partners composing the firm of Lehman, Durr & Co.; was commenced on the 19th November, 1886, and sought to compel the payment of the defendants' unpaid subscription for stock in the National Express Company (or National Express and Transportation Company, its amended name), a corporation chartered under the laws of Virginia; said unpaid subscriptions, amounting to fifty per cent., having been assessed and called for by the decree of said Chancery Court in Virginia, in the suit in which the plaintiff was appointed trustee, and authorized to sue for and collect the unpaid subscriptions for stock. The original complaint contained three special counts, and the common counts were afterwards added by amendment, against the objection and exception of the defendants.

A corporation seems to have been chartered by the legislature of Virginia, in March, 1861, called the "Southern Express Company," but nothing was done under the charter; and the incorporation of another company was attempted in the Fall of 1865, under the name of the "National Express Company;" but, if this company was organized, the fact is not shown by the record, nor is the charter of either of these companies anywhere set out in the record. On the 12th December, 1865, an act was passed by the General Assembly of the State of Virginia, entited "An act to amend and re-enact an act to incorporate the Southern Express Company, passed March 22d, 1861, and to incorporate the National Express and Transportation Company," The defendants subscribed for ten shares, of $100 each, in the stock of the *National Express Company*, the subscription being entitled "Subscription list to the stock of the *National Express Company*: We, the undersigned, hereby subscribe the amount and the number of shares opposite to our names, to the *National Express Company*, and bind ourselves, our heirs, &c., to pay said amount in such installments as may be called for by said company, and to pay one per-cent. at the time of subscription." The plaintiff sued as trustee, under appointment by the Chancery Court of Richmond, Virginia, under a bill which sought to foreclose a deed of assignment executed by the *National Express and Transportation Company*; the decree of the court in that case having made an assessment on stockholders for their unpaid subscriptions, and authorized plaintiff, as trustee, to collect the amounts by suit or otherwise.

The deed of assignment executed by the corporation, which was dated September 20th, 1866, conveyed all of its property and assets by general words of description, "including office furniture, fixtures, and other effects and moneys payable to the company, whether on calls or assessments on stock of the company, or on notes, bill, accounts, or otherwise," to J. B. Hoge and two other persons as trustees, authorizing them to take possession of the property, to collect all the outstanding debts and demands without any unnecessary delay, to sell the property at private or public sale, and to make distribution of the proceeds among the creditors generally, after the payment of several preferred debts.

On the 28th November, 1871, W. W. Glenn, a judgment creditor of said corporation, filed a bill in equity in the Chancery Court of the city of Richmond, Virginia, on behalf of himself and all other creditors who might come in, against the corporation, its president and directors, and said trustees; asking the court to take jurisdiction of the assignment, to decide as to its validity, legal operation and effect, and to administer its trusts. The bill alleged that only twenty per-cent. of the subscriptions for stock had ever been paid in, or called for; that it was doubtful whether the trustees had power, under the deed of assignment, to enforce the collection of these unpaid subscriptions, and that it was necessary that they should be called in and appropriated as assets in payment of the debts of the corporation; and therefore prayed the appointment of a receiver, or trustee, with authority to collect, under the order of the court, these unpaid subscriptions. Process under this bill was served, November 25th, 1871, on J. R. Anderson, one of the directors of the corporation; and on the 4th December, 1871, on M. G. Harman, another director.

Nothing further appears to have been done in the case, until August 4th, 1879, when an amended and supplemental bill was filed in the name of John W. Wright, as administrator of said Glenn's estate; alleging his death, the appointment of said Wright as his administrator, the further wasting of the assets of the corporation, the cessation of all business by it, the death of one of the trustees, and other facts showing a necessity for the interposition and assistance of the court. The bill prayed relief as before; also, "that the claims of said W. W. Glenn and other creditors of said company may be established, and decreed to be paid; that said trustees, J. B. Hoge and J. J. Kelly, may be required to deliver up and surrender to this court all of the books of said company, of every kind and description, which came into their hands; that said trustees be removed from office, and, if necessary, another trustee, or other trustees, may be substituted in their place and stead, and the property and estate embraced in said deed of trust be conveyed to such substituted trustees, or to such receiver or receivers as may be appointed by the court," &c. Process on this bill was served, August 8th, 1879, on J. R. Anderson and Lorenzo Nowell, two of the directors, and M. B. Poiteaux, cashier; and the subpœna was returned by the sheriff with this indorsement as to the other defendants: "Executed in the city of Richmond, August 8th, 1879, as to the National Express and Transportation Company, by delivering to Jos. R. Anderson, a director, and M. B. Poiteaux, cashier of the said company, each a copy of the within *spa.* in chancery, each of whom is a resident of said city of Richmond; the president not being a resident of said city. The other defendants are not inhabitants." Publication was thereupon ordered against the non-resident defendants, and on the 6th November, 1879, decrees *pro confesso* were entered against all of the defendants except said Anderson and Poiteaux, each of whom had filed an answer. Anderson in his answer did not admit that he had ever acted as a director, but stated that he had resigned soon after his election, and that he had never attended a meeting of the board of directors. Poiteaux admitted that he had acted as cashier for several months, but was not indebted to the corporation, and did not have possession of any of its money, books, or papers; and he stated that he had never been a stockholder. At the same time, the court also entered an interlocutory decree, ordering an account to be stated by one of the commissioners of the court, of both its debts and its assets.

A decree was rendered in the cause on the 14th December, 1880, accompanied by an opinion, in and by which (1) the report of the commissioner was confirmed; (2) the deed

of assignment was held to be valid, and its legal effect was
to vest in the trustees all the property and assets of the corporation, "including the credits allowed by statute and by
the said company to its stockholders for the unpaid and un-
called for part of their several subscriptions to its capital
stock, and the right to receive and collect the same, according to the terms of the contract of subscription, for the purpose of said trust;" (3) the surviving trustees were removed,
on their declaration of inability to execute the trust, and
their wish to renounce it; (4) John Glenn was appointed
and substituted as trustee in their stead, was "clothed with
all the rights and powers, and charged with all the duties
of executing said trust, to the same effect as were the original trustees;" and (5) a call of thirty per-cent. was made on
stockholders, which the trustee was authorized to receive
and collect, by suit or otherwise. The latter part of the decree recites that the money realized from former calls on the
stockholders, amounting to twenty per-cent., have been exhausted, and the company has no property or assets available for the payment of the claims of creditors except the
subscriptions for stock remaining unpaid, which constitute a
trust fund for the payment of debts; that on account of death,
removal, insolvency, and other causes, much of said unpaid
subscriptions has been lost, and great difficulties encountered in realizing what remains good; that the company has
long since ceased and abandoned its business, and there has
not been for about fourteen years any meeting of either the
stockholders or the board of directors; and that at least
thirty per-cent. of said subscriptions is necessary to pay the
debts of the company and the costs and expenses of collecting and administering the fund.

On the 11th April, 1884, a petition was filed in the cause
by Thomas J. Jennings and others, stockholders and citizens
of Georgia, asking to have the decree set aside, and the
cause re-heard; alleging and insisting that they were not
made parties to the cause, that the corporation was not properly brought before the court, that the claims of creditors
were allowed without proof, and that all of them (except
Glenn's) were barred by the statute of limitations. On the
27th June, 1884, the cause was transferred to the Circuit
Court of Henrico county; and a decree was rendered by that
court, on the 4th March, 1885, dismissing the petition, and
overruling the several defenses set up in it. In the opinion
accompanying this decree, and made part of the decree

itself by reference, the court held—1st, that process was properly perfected on the corporation; 2d, that the stockholders were not necessary parties to the suit; 3d, that the decree rendered was conclusive on them, "when sued upon in other courts, of this State or any other;" and, 4th, that the claims of creditors were not then barred. Afterwards, on the 26th March, 1886, on the petition of Glenn as trustee, and on the report of the commissioner showing that the debts of the company exceeded the assets, including the thirty per-cent. of subscriptions already called in, nearly $400,000, the court made another decretal order calling in the remaining fifty per-cent. of subscriptions for stock; and this action was brought to recover of the defendants the amount due on their subscription under this last call.

The defendants pleaded the general issue, and several special pleas, which set up *laches*, lapse of time, the statute of limitations, and prescription of twenty years. The second plea alleged that the corporation became insolvent, and ceased to do business in October, 1866, and executed a general assignment of all its property and assets; that plaintiff's cause of action, if any, accrued more than six years before the commencement of this suit; that defendants have never acknowledged or admitted any liability or indebtedness, "wherefore plaintiff's cause of action is barred by *laches* and the statute of limitations of six years." The third plea alleged, in substance, that after said insolvency, cessation of business, and assignment by said corporation, "no call or demand was made on these defendants within a reasonable time, for or on account of any alleged subscription for said stock, for more than six years thereafter before the bringing of this suit," and therefore said demand is barred by *laches* and lapse of time. The fourth alleged that, after the insolvency of the company, and the execution of said assignment, "plaintiff and said company failed to make any demand within a reasonable time, and that no call or demand, for or on account of said alleged subscription, was made upon them for more than six years thereafter, nor did these defendants make any promise to pay said alleged subscription within six years before the bringing of this action; wherefore said demand is barred by *laches*, delay, and the statute of limitations of six years." The sixth plea alleged that said creditors' bill was filed in the Chancery Court at Richmond, Virginia, on the 28th November, 1871, "for the purpose of having said court to make a call for unpaid subscriptions to the

stock of said corporation," but no order of court was made
calling for unpaid subscriptions "until the Fall of 1880;"
wherefore said demand is barred by lapse of time, and by
laches on the part of plaintiff.   The seventh plea alleged unreasonable delay on the part of plaintiffs in the prosecution
of the suit in Virginia, whereby no call was made on stockholders until after the lapse of nine years after the commencement of that suit.   The eighth plea alleged that said subscription was made by defendants, if at all, more than twenty
years before the bringing of this suit; that they have not,
within twenty years before the bringing of this suit, recognized or acknowledged themselves or acted as stockholders,
or subscribers to stock in said corporation; wherefore
the defendants rely upon and claim the benefit of the
prescription of twenty years.   Issue was joined on the
second special plea, and a demurrer was sustained as to each
of the others.

On the trial, as the bill of exceptions shows, the plaintiff
offered in evidence the subscription list, above set out, with
certain books, records and papers of the said National Express and Transportation Company; and the court admitted
each of them, against the objection and exceptions of the
defendants.   The objections to each part of this evidence
were general, no particular ground of objection being specified.   The plaintiff also offered in evidence a transcript,
"duly authenticated under the act of Congress," of the record
and proceedings in the cause decided in said court in Virginia, the material portions of which are above stated.   The
defendants objected to the admission of the record as evidence, "because it appeared on the face of said record that
said court had never acquired jurisdiction of said corporation;
that no process had ever been served on said corporation, as
required by law, nor had said company ever appeared in
court; that no decree *pro confesso* had ever been entered
against said company; and that said record is not evidence
against these defendants."   The court overruled these objections, and admitted the transcript as evidence; and the defendants excepted.   Certain statutes of Virginia were also
read in evidence without objection, a printed copy of which
was made an exhibit to the bill of exceptions.   These statutes
relate to private corporations, the service of process on them,
the jurisdiction of the Chancery Court of Richmond, &c.

One of the plaintiff's counsel testified that, after said call
for thirty per cent. was made by the court in Virginia, "he

called on defendants to collect it, and was referred by them
to their counsel, to whom he submitted a copy of the record
of said cause, as shown by said certified transcript; that said
counsel informed him that he would advise defendants to
pay; and that they then paid him said thirty per-cent. call.
Defendants then asked said witness, if he showed their said
counsel the original subscription list, before he gave his
opinion; and the witness answered, that he could not say he
did.   The defendants thereupon moved the court to exclude
from the jury the declarations of the counsel," and excepted
to the overruling of their motion.

This being "substantially all the evidence," the court
charged the jury, on request of the plaintiff, that they must
find for him, if they believed the evidence.   The defendants
excepted to this charge, and they here assign it as error,
together with the allowance of the amendment to the complaint, and the several rulings on the pleadings and evidence above stated.

TROY, TOMPKINS & LONDON, for appellants.

WM. S. THORINGTON, *contra.**

SOMERVILLE, J.—This case is analogous, in its leading
facts, to *Glenn v. Semple*, 80 Ala. 159; s. c., 60 Amer Rep.
92.   Its merits may be disposed of by a few propositions
abundantly supported by authorities precisely in point.

1.   The decree of the Chancery Court of the City of Richmond, rendered on the fourteenth day of December, 1880,
on a creditors' bill previously filed in December, 1871, against
the National Express and Transportation Company and the
trustees of that corporation, is not only admissible as evidence
in this case against the defendants, as stockholders in said
company, but is entitled to as full faith and credit in the
courts of this State, as it would be in the courts of Virginia,
where the corporation was located and had its principal
office, and where the decree was rendered.   If the court had
jurisdiction of the subject-matter and of the parties, and the
stockholders are to be regarded as parties to that suit for
any purpose, this is the necessary legal effect of the decree
under the Constitution and laws of the United States.

---

* The counsel of both parties in this case referred to their respective
briefs in the case of *Semple v. Glenn*, which was submitted at the same
time, but is yet under advisement on application for rehearing.

Christmas v. Russell, 5 Wall. 291; *Maxwell v. Stewart,* 22 *Ib.* 77.

2. The record in that case, which is made a part of the record before us, shows sufficiently that the court acquired jurisdiction of the corporation itself, by service of process on the proper officers. This service was on two of the directors, one of whom appeared and answered; and also on the cashier of the company, who also appeared and answered. The Virginia court decided, that this service was sufficient to give jurisdiction; and that decision is binding on us. It can not be collaterally attacked. If erroneous, it should have been corrected on direct appeal. The precise point was so decided in *Glenn v. Springs* (U. S. Cir. Ct.), 26 Fed. Rep. 494; and again in *Glenn v. Williams,* 60 Md. 93.

3. The same cases also hold, that the decree rendered against the corporation in that case, was conclusive against the stockholders, so far as it affects the condition and *status* of the corporate property, although they were not personally made parties to the proceeding by service of process on them. The rule in cases of this nature is, that the interest of the stockholder is represented by the presence of the corporation, for all the purposes of that suit. It was said in *Glenn v. Williams, supra:* "When the court obtained jurisdiction of the corporation, every stockholder, in his corporate capacity, was a party to the cause, and was supposed to be represented by the president and the directors, who were intrusted with the management of the corporate interest of all the stockholders." It was observed, further, that the stockholders being distributed among the several States, many of them being non-residents of Virginia, ordinary process of the courts of that State could not reach them; and if the court were required to make them parties personally, the creditors of the corporation would be without adequate remedy. The unpaid subscriptions of stock are assets of the corporation, being a trust fund for the payment of its debts; and "as against a creditor, with an established debt against the corporation, by judgment or decree, the stockholder has no right to withhold the funds of the company, upon the ground that he was not individually a party to the proceedings in which the recovery was obtained."—*Glenn v. Williams,* 60 Md. 116; *Hawkins v. Glenn,* 131 U. S. 319; *Sanger v. Upton,* 91 U. S. 56; *Great Western Tel. Co. v. Gray,* 122 Ill. 630; s. c., Amer. Law Reg., vol. 27, p. 160, and *note* 168; *Vanderwerker v. Glenn* (Sup. Ct. Va.), S. E. Rep. 806.

[Lehman, Durr & Co. v. Glenn.]

4. The decree of the Richmond court also[1] conclusively determined the following points: *First*, that there was no *laches* on the part of the corporation, or its trustees, in the prosecution of that suit, or in obtaining the decree, which, as we have stated, was rendered on December 14th, 1880; *Secondly*, that the statute of limitations did not bar the claims of creditors up to that time; *Thirdly*, the authority of the court to make the call or assessment upon all who were stock-holders in the company; *Fourthly*, the legal identity of the National Express Company, to which the subscriptions were originally made payable, and of the National Express & Transportation Company, to which its corporate name was changed; *Fifthly*, the right of the trustee, Glenn, to bring this suit.—*Glenn v. Springs*, 26 Fed. Rep. 494; *Glenn v. Soule*, 22 Fed. Rep. 417; *Glenn v. Williams*, 60 Md. 93; *Sanger v. Upton*, 91 U. S. 56; *Hall v. U. S. Ins. Co.*, 5 Gill, 484; *Glenn v. Semple*, 80 Ala. 159; s. c., 60 Amer. Rep. 92; *German Passenger Railway Co. v. Fitler*, 60 Penn. St. 124; s. c., 100 Amer. Dec. 546; *note*, p. 552; *Hawkins v. Glenn*, 131 U. S. 319.

5. The books of the corporation were admissible, as *prima facie* evidence of the correctness of the subscriptions, as to all whose names there appear as owners of stock, especially in view of the fact that the defendants in this case interpose no plea denying the genuineness of their original subscription, and are shown to have paid one assessment made on their stock by decree of the court in 1880, which was an admission by them of their *status* as stockholders. There is no presumption that these names have been fraudulently inserted on the corporate books by an act of forgery. *Turnbull v. Payson*, 95 U. S. 418; *Glenn v. Orr*, 96 N. C. 413; *Glenn v. Springs*, *supra; Railroad v. Applegate*, 21 West Va. 172; *Vanderwerker v. Glenn* (Sup. Ct. Va., 1888), S. E. R. 106; Cook on Stockholders, § 73; 1 Morawetz Corp. (2d Ed.), § 75.

6. That the demand here sued for was not barred by the statute of limitations, is conclusively settled in *Glenn v. Semple*, 80 Ala. 159; s. c., 60 Amer. Rep. 92. See, also, Wait on Insolvent Corp., § 631. We there held, that the statute did not commence to run in favor of stockholders until December 14th, 1880, when the Richmond Chancery Court ordered the assessment of unpaid stock subscription sued for in that action. The assessment here sued for was made on March 26th, 1886; and the suit was brought in November 19th of the same year.

The questions here involved have a great many times come before the courts of this country for decision, and there has been a singular unanimity among them in the conclusions reached, all being in harmony with the views above announced. This is shown by the various cases above cited, in which the present appellee, Glenn, was party plaintiff.

The other assignments of error are not well taken, and the judgment of the Circuit Court is affirmed.

Morris *v.* Glenn.

Action by Trustee under appointment by Foreign Chancery Court, against Subscriber for Stock in Private Corporation.

1. *Liability of stockholders; by what law determined.*—The liability of stockholders in a private corporation, or subscribers for stock prior to the organization of the company, is governed by the law of the State by which the charter is granted, as if incorporated in the subscription as a part thereof.

2. *Transfer of stock; liability of transferror, under statutes of Virginia.* Under the statutes of Virginia, as proved in this case, a transferror or assignor of stock in a private corporation, which has not been fully paid for, is liable equally with the assignee for the unpaid part of the stock, at the instance of creditors, and may be proceeded against in the same manner.

APPEAL from the Circuit Court of Montgomery.

Tried before the Hon. JOHN P. HUBBARD.

This action, like the one preceding, was brought by John Glenn, as trustee under appointment of the Chancery Court of Richmond, Virginia, to recover of the defendant fifty per cent. of his subscription for the shares of stock in the Virginia corporation represented by the plaintiff, as assessed and called for by the decree of that court; and was commenced on the 19th November, 1886. The pleadings were, in substance, the same as in the other cases; and the evidence adduced on the trial was also the same, consisting of the original subscription list for stock in the National Express Company, on which the defendant's name appeared as a subscriber for ten shares of $100 each, the proceedings and decree in the chancery suit in Virginia, and several statutes of Virginia in force at the time the subscriptions were made. The "Stock Book" of the corporation, offered in evidence also

[Morris v. Glenn.]

by the plaintiff, showed that the certificate of stock issued to the defendant on the 12th March, 1866, "had been surrendered by him to the company, duly transferred and indorsed to W. C. Jackson, on the 12th March, 1866, and that a certificate for said ten shares was on that day issued to said Jackson;" and the plaintiff's evidence tended to show, also, that the defendant had paid the thirty per-cent. assessment called for by the decree of December 14th, 1880, but under protest and a denial of his liability. The defendant, testifying as a witness on his own behalf, admitted his subscription, his receipt of a certificate for his shares, its transfer to W. C. Jackson, as stated, and his payment of the thirty per-cent. assessment to plaintiff's attorney on demand; and he further testified, "that from the time of his transfer of said certificate to said Jackson, up to the demand made on him by plaintiff's said attorney, he had never heard of the stock; that he denied all liability on account of said stock, when approached by said attorney, but, being threatened with suit. agreed to pay said assessment to avoid the trouble and worry of a lawsuit;" that he finally accepted a receipt, which was in settlement of his liability on that assessment only; "and that he had never in any way, since said transfer in March, 1866, recognized or admitted any liability on account of said stock." The statutes of Virginia in force at the time of these subscriptions for stock, as offered in evidence, contained a provision in these words: "No stock shall be assigned on the books of the company, without the consent of the company, until all the money which has become payable thereon shall have been paid; and on any assignment the assignor and assignee shall each be liable for any installment which may have accrued, or which may thereafter accrue, and may be proceeded against in the manner before provided." This being "substantially all the evidence," the court charged the jury, on request of the plaintiff in writing, "that they should find a verdict for the plaintiff, if they believed all the evidence." The defendant excepted to this charge, and he here assigns it as error, with other rulings on the pleadings and evidence, which require no special notice.

TROY, TOMPKINS & LONDON, for appellant.—The prescription of twenty years was specially pleaded in this case, and was a complete defense to the action. The prescription is to be determined by the *lex fori*, and the statutes of Virginia do-not affect the question.—*Matthews v. McDade*, 72 Ala.

377. The partial payment made by the defendant, was simply a purchase of his peace, which does not affect his liability.—*Crawford v. McLeod*, 64 Ala. 240. The sufficiency and effect of the evidence as to this payment, if doubtful, should have been submitted to the jury.

W. S. THORINGTON, *contra*, cited the Virginia statutes set out in the record; also, *Canada Southern Railroad v. Gebhard*, S. C. Reporter, vol. 3, pt. 7, p. 363; *Glenn v. Busby*, Cent. Reporter, vol. 4, No. 10, p. 609; *McKim v. Glenn*, 66 Md. 479; *Glenn v. Scott*, 28 Fed. Rep. 804.

SOMERVILLE, J.—All the assignments of error in this case, except a single one, will be overruled, on the authority of *Lehman, Durr & Co. v. Glenn*, and *Semple v. Glenn*, decided at the present term.

One other question is raised, by reason of the fact that the appellant, Morris, is shown to have accepted and transferred his certificate of stock, prior to the time the assessment here sued for was made by order of the Chancery Court of Richmond, Virginia, on March 26th, 1886. This transfer did not discharge his liability to be further assessed, by reason of the provisions of the Virginia statute. The corporation being organized in that State, the subscriptions of stockholders must be held to have reference to the laws of Virginia, as fully as if these laws were a part of the subscription.—2 Morawetz Corp. (2d Ed.), § 874; *McDonnell v. Ala. Gold Life Ins. Co.*, 85 Ala. 401.

The Virginia statute provides, that "No stock will be assigned on the books without the consent of the company, until all the money which has become payable thereon shall have been paid; and in any assignment, the assignee and *assignor shall each be liable* for any installments which may have accrued, or *which may thereafter accrue*, and may be proceeded against in the manner before provided," by action or motion.—Code of Va. (1849; 1860; 1873), Ch. 57, § 26.

The precise point arose in *McKim v. Glenn*, 66 Md. 476, and again in *Glenn v. Scott*, 28 Fed. Rep, 804, decided by the United States Circuit Court of the Western District of Virginia, in September, 1886; and in each case, the statute was construed to continue in effect the liability of a transferror of stock, just as if no transfer had been made.

The judgment is affirmed.

Sayre *v.* Glenn.

Action by Trustee under appointment by Foreign Chancery Court, against Subscriber for Stock in Private Corporation.

1. *Subscription for stock, as debt against bankrupt's estate.*—An unpaid subscription for stock in a private corporation is not assets of the subscriber's bankrupt estate, which the assignee is bound to accept, nor is it a provable debt against the bankrupt's estate; consequently, a discharge in bankruptcy is no defense to the bankrupt against an assessment and call regularly made by a court having jurisdiction of the estate of the corporation, under a bill filed by its creditors.

APPEAL from the Circuit Court of Montgomery.

Tried before the Hon. JOHN P. HUBBARD.

This action, like the preceding, was brought by John Glenn, suing as trustee under appointment by the Chancery Court of Richmond, Virginia, against the defendant as a subscriber for stock in the National Express and Transportation Company; but it sought to collect the assessment of thirty per-cent. made by the decree of December 14th, 1880, and was commenced on the 1st November, 1884. The defendant pleaded the general issue, the statutes of limitation of six and ten years, and a special plea averring his discharge in bankruptcy on the 22d April, 1871, by the judgment and decree of the United States District Court at Montgomery, under a petition filed by him on the 1st June, 1870. The court sustained a demurrer to the plea of bankruptcy, and its judgment thereon is now assigned as error, with other matters.

R. M. WILLIAMSON, for appellant.

W. S. THORINGTON, *contra*, cited *Glenn v. Howard*, 65 Md. 40.

SOMERVILLE, J.—The questions arising in this case, except the sufficiency of the defense based on the plea of defendant's bankruptcy, are settled against the appellant in *Lehman, Durr & Co. v. Glenn*, and *Semple v. Glenn*, decided at the present term.

[Sayre v. Glenn.]

This plea sets up the fact, that the defendant, Sayre, on petition filed in the proper District Court of the United States, on the first of June, 1870, was duly adjudicated to be a bankrupt, and thereafter, to-wit, on April 22d, 1871, received his certificate of discharge, as provided for by the Bankrupt Law of March 2d, 1867.

To this plea a demurrer was sustained; and we think there was no error in this ruling. The ground of demurrer, which seems to us to be fatal to the sufficiency of the plea, is, that the demand in question was one not provable against the estate of the bankrupt, and was not therefore affected by the discharge.

The action is one for the assessment of thirty per-cent. upon an unpaid subscription to the capital stock of the National Express and Transportation Company. This assessment was ordered to be made by the Chancery Court of the city of Richmond, Virginia, by decree rendered December 14th, 1880. The subscription itself was for the sum of one thousand dollars, payable "in such installments as *may be called for* by said company, and to pay one per-cent. at the time of subscription.

The Bankrupt Law allowed proof to be made, not only of debts due from the bankrupt at the commencement of the proceedings in bankruptcy, but of "all debts then existing, but not payable until a future day," a rebate of interest being made.—U. S. Rev. Stat., § 5067. The law was also made to embrace "contingent debts and liabilities," the right of the creditor to share in dividends being made to depend upon the happening of the contingency before the order of the Bankrupt Court for a final dividend; or the ability of the court to ascertain and liquidate the "present value" of the debt or liability.—U. S. Rev. Stat., § 5068. The phrase "contingent debt" has been construed to mean, not a demand whose existence depended on a contingency, but an existing demand the cause of action upon which depends on a contingency.—*French v. Morse,* 68 Mass. 111; *Woodard v. Herbert,* 24 Me. 358.

It is our opinion, that a call of this nature made upon an unpaid subscription to corporate stock is not a provable debt within the meaning of the Bankrupt Law. The precise point was decided by the Court of Appeals of Maryland, in *Glenn v. Howard,* 65 Md. 40 (1885), where the question is fully discussed. It was suggested, that there was no right of action on the subscription until a call was made, either by the governing officers of the corporation, or by order of the Chancery Court having jurisdiction to make such an assessment. It might be that such call might never be made in any event; and if so, there would never exist any liability to pay anything on it. It was said not to be a debt *in præsenti*, payable *in futuro*. The demand, we may add, would thus be one whose existence would depend upon a contingency, rather than one that existed already, with a right of action on it depending on such contingency. It was accordingly held, that where a call was made on a subscription of stock identical with that here in controversy, after the discharge of the subscriber in bankruptcy, it would not be affected by the provisions of the Bankrupt Law, because the demand was one not provable under the law against the bankrupt's estate. A ruling of the same kind was made in *South Staffordshire R. Co. v. Burnside*, 5 Exch. 129, which has generally been since followed by the English courts. See, also, *Glenn v. Clabaugh*, 65 Md. 65; and *Riggins v. McGuire*, 15 Wall. 549; *Steele v. Graves*, 68 Ala. 21.

The assignee of the bankrupt was not bound to accept the stock in this corporation, as a portion of the bankrupt's assigned property, as it was of an onerous and unprofitable character; and it does not appear that he ever did so. The bankrupt proceedings do not, therefore, affect the question of the stockholder's liability.—*File Co. v. Garrett*, 110 U. U. 288; *Rugely v. Robinson*, 19 Ala. 404; *Glenn v. Howard*, *supra*.

The demurrer to the plea of bankruptcy was properly sustained.

The other assignments of error are without merit, and the judgment is affirmed.

Davis *v.* Memphis & Charleston Railroad Co.

Statutory Action in nature of Ejectment.

1. *Corporate existence of railroad company under provisions of charter.*—Where the corporate existence of a railroad company is, by its original charter, limited to fifty years, but, by an amendatory act, it is provided that, at the expiration of each subsequent term of ten years,

the State shall have the right, at its election, to take all the property of the company at the par value of its stock, and, if this election is not made within twelve months, then the charter of the company shall be continued for another term of ten years; the corporation has a capacity of perpetual existence, unless the election to purchase is exercised by the State.

2. *Conveyance to railroad company, for right of way.*—A conveyance of a strip of land to a railroad company, "for the term of fifty years, and so long thereafter as its charter shall continue," when the company has the capacity of perpetual existence, on default by the State to exercise a right of election to purchase its property, and also has power to condemn lands for a right of way under a writ of *ad quod damnum,* conveys the same interest and estate that would have been acquired by a judgment of condemnation under such writ.

3. *Condemnation of right of way by railroad company; nature of estate acquired; transfer to another corporation* —A judgment condemning lands for a right of way, under *ad quod damnum* proceedings at the suit of a railroad company, vests in the company an estate and interest commensurate with its corporate existence; and this estate passes to purchasers at a sale under a mortgage executed by the company, who are afterwards incorporated as a railroad company, or to another corporation, its assignee, so long as the contemplated use of the right of way is continued.

4. *Dissolution of corporation.*—When its corporate existence is not limited by charter, and there is no voluntary surrender of its franchises, a private corporation will not be deemed dissolved until its dissolution is judicially ascertained; neither its insolvency, nor a sale of all its property, nor cessation to do business, extinguishes its franchises; and while a voluntary surrender of its franchises from continuous non-user for a long time may be presumed, neither its dissolution, nor a forfeiture of its charter, can be declared in a collateral proceeding.

5. *Conveyance of base or qualified fee.*—A conveyance of a qualified, base or determinable fee in lands, leaves in the grantor only a possibility of reverter, which, though it may descend to his heirs, can not be granted or assigned so as to vest a title on which ejectment may be maintained.

6. *Presumption of title from lapse of time.*—After continuous *user* of a right of way by a railroad company for a period of fifty years, a grant in fee simple, or a judgment of condemnation under a writ of condemnation, will be presumed, though the land is part of a sixteenth section.

APPEAL from the Circuit Court of Morgan.

Tried before the Hon. HENRY C. SPEAKE.

This action was brought by Mrs. Ann Davis, a married woman, who was a daughter of James Fennell, deceased, against the Memphis & Charleston Railroad Company, to recover a strip of land one hundred feet wide, which was the defendant's road-bed and right of way, and was situated in sections sixteen (16) and twenty-one (21), township five (5), range five (5), west; and was commenced on the 14th October, 1887. The case was submitted to the court without a jury, on an agreed statement of facts; and the court rendered judgment for the defendant. Among the agreed facts were the following: "The north-west quarter of said

section twenty-one (21) was patented by the United States
to Joseph Sykes, and the south-west quarter of said section
sixteen (16) was granted by Congress to the State of Alabama, and by the State patented to individual purchasers in
1839. James Fennell acquired the legal title to said lands,
and went into possession thereof, except that portion now
sued for, under purchase from Joseph Sykes in 1843, and
held possession until his death; and in 1857, after his death,
on the division of his estate, said lands were allotted to the
plaintiff, his daughter, who has held such possession ever
since." The deed from said Sykes and wife to Fennell,
which was in evidence, expressly excepted "the railroad running through said lands, but any benefit or reversion therefrom which may accrue to go to the said Fennell." On the
7th February, 1834, Sykes had conveyed a right of way
through his lands, describing them as being "in sections
twenty-one (21) and (18)," to the president and directors of
the Tuscumbia, Courtland & Decatur Railroad Company,
"and their successors in office, for the term of fifty years,
and so long thereafter as their said charter shall continue;"
and the defendant claimed as the assignee and successor of
said railroad company, under conveyances and legislative
acts, the material portions of which are stated in the opinion of this court. The judgment of the court below, to
which the plaintiff excepted, is here assigned as error.

F. P. WARD, and L. W. DAY, for appellant.

R. C. BRICKELL, and MILTON HUMES, *contra.*

CLOPTON, J.—Appellant brings the statutory real action
to recover possession of a strip of land one hundred feet in
width, situated in the south half of section 16, and north-
west quarter of section 21, in township 5, range 5 west,
which covers the road-bed and right of way of the Memphis
& Charleston Railroad Company. The parties deduce title,
respectively, in this wise: The Tuscumbia, Courtland & Decatur Railroad Company was incorporated by an act of the
General Assembly, January 13, 1832. By the terms of the
act, the corporate existence was limited to a period of fifty
years.—Acts 1831-32, p. 67. On November 10, 1832, the
act of incorporation was amended. The fourth section of
the amendatory act provides: "That, at the expiration of
fifty years from the date of the said charter, and at each

subsequent term of ten years, the State shall be authorized to take all of said works, cars and estate of every description whatever, belonging to said company, at the par value of the stock of said company, if the State should elect so to do; but, if the State shall not, within one year after the expiration of any term of ten years, take said works, then the charter of said company shall be continued for a subsequent term of ten years."—Acts 1832-33, p. 7. The manifest operation of the amendatory act is, to remove the limitation of fifty years, as provided in the original act of incorporation, and to create a corporation endowed with capacity of perpetual existence, unless the State shall exercise its reserved right of purchase.

Joseph Sykes sold and conveyed, February 7, 1834, that part of the land in controversy, which is in the north-west quarter of section 21, to the Tuscumbia, Courtland & Decatur Railroad Company. The *habendum* clause of the conveyance reads: "*to have and to hold the said tract of one hundred feet of land above described, to the said president and directors of the said Tuscumbia, Courtland & Decatur Railroad Company, and their successors in office, for the term of fifty years, and so long thereafter as their charter shall continue.*" On April 29, 1843, Sykes sold and conveyed to James Fennell the half and quarter sections which include the land in suit. The deed contains the following exception: "*The railroad running through these lands excepted, but any benefit or reversion therefrom, which may accrue, to go to the said Fennell.*" The plaintiff claims by descent from her ancestor, James Fennell.

The conveyance from Sykes to the railroad company must be construed in connection with, and in reference to the amending act, providing for an indefinite continuation of the charter of the company, subject to the contingency of the State's exercise of the privilege to take the property at designated successive periods. By the fifth section of the original act of incorporation, the company was authorized to contract for, and receive conveyances of lands, stone or gravel, which might be required in the construction of the road; and if the owner and the company could not agree as to price, proceedings in condemnation were authorized. By this provision, *ad quod damnum* proceedings could be instituted only after an ineffectual effort to agree as to the price. The land was purchased from Sykes, and the conveyance received under this authority of the charter.

The estate or interest in land, acquired and taken for public use, is to be determined by the nature and extent of the use; the intendment being, that the estate or interest shall be commensurate with the purpose and duration of the use for which it is taken, when not otherwise provided. The operation of the amendment being to extend the duration of the corporate life, from a limited term of fifty years, to an existence uncertain and indefinite, but which might endure forever, had the land been taken and acquired under proceedings in condemnation, the company would have obtained an estate therein co-existent with the possible continuation of the corporate life. The acquisition of an estate in land for a public use, by the exercise of the right of eminent domain, is in the nature of a transfer by the State, to which the statute annexes the limitation or condition, that the estate acquired shall continue during the existence of the corporation, and so long as the land may be used for the purpose for which it is taken. The land having been contracted for, and the deed received from Sykes, by the same authority under which land may be condemned when the owner and the company can not agree as to price, and the deed having been made after the amendment of the charter, and containing the limitation—"for the term of fifty years, and so long thereafter as their said charter shall continue" substantially the same as that which is implied when land is condemned—his grant should be regarded as intended to have, and as having, the same legal effect and operation as condemnation under *ad quod damnum* proceedings. At common law, the general rule is, that real estate owned and possessed by a corporation at the time of its dissolution, reverts to the original owner. But this rule does not extend to real estate of which the corporation may have been divested by process of law during its existence. "It is the public use for which the land is taken, and so long as it is used for railroad purposes, it is immaterial what company or what individuals operate it."—2 Wood's Railway Law, § 242; *State v. Rives*, 2 Ired. 297; *Noll v. Dubuque B. & M. R. R. Co.*, 32 Iowa, 66; *Pollard v. Maddox*, 28 Ala. 321.

In the construction of the conveyance to the railroad company, as of all other written contracts, the intent of the parties becomes the primary inquiry; in ascertaining which, reference should be had, in connection with the terms employed, to the occasion, the relative position of the parties, and the objects designed to be accomplished. The Tuscumbia, Courtland & Decatur Railroad Company was among the earliest incorporated, and its railroad among the first built in this country. Its public necessity and utility were the moving considerations for its creation. These considerations, and its great convenience and benefit to the grantor, moved him to sell and convey the lands, which was evidently intended to form and constitute a part of the railroad track. By the contract between him and the company, the land was devoted to railroad uses—uses desired and contemplated to be permanent, whether or not the State exercised its reserved right of purchase. The estate conveyed, and its continuance, were designed to be commensurate with the uses to which the land was devoted. The term *charter* is not employed in the deed in its narrowest and most restricted sense, and should not be construed as referring only to the act of the legislature creating the corporation, which for convenience is denominated the charter, or to the mere corporate name. The signification is more comprehensive, and includes the rights, powers, privileges, immunities and franchises granted—the substance and not the shadow.

Under a decree made by the United States District Court, on a bill to foreclose a mortgage executed by the company, the railway, rolling-stock, shops, machinery and franchises of the Tuscumbia, Courtland & Decatur Railroad Company were sold by the marshal, September 22, 1847, and purchased by David Deshler. The sale was reported and confirmed by the court, and a conveyance executed to Deshler. On February 10, 1848, Deshler and his associates were incorporated by an act of the General Assembly, under the name of the Tennessee Valley Railroad Company. The preamble of the act recites the sale of the railroad, and all the property of the Tuscumbia, Courtland & Decatur Railroad Company, under a decree of the United States District Court, and that Deshler became the purchaser. The third section of the act provides, that upon payment of the purchase-money, all the right, title, interest and property in the latter company, including the right of way, and all rights, franchises and privileges, shall vest in the Tennessee Valley Railroad Company. In 1848, Deshler sold and conveyed to the latter company the railway, and all the property and franchises, purchased by him at the marshal's sale. The tenth section of the act made similar provisions for the continuance of the charter, subject to the State's exercise of the right to purchase at the expiration of fifty years, and at suc-

cessive periods of ten years, as contained in the charter of
the Tuscumbia, Courtland & Decatur Railroad Company.
Acts 1847-48, p. 79.

The Memphis & Charleston Railroad Company was incorporated January 7, 1850. By the seventh section it is provided: "It shall be lawful for the company, hereby incorporated, to acquire by purchase, gift, release or otherwise,
from any other company, all the rights, privileges and immunities of said company, and possess and enjoy the same
as fully as they were or could be possessed or enjoyed by
the company making the transfer."—Acts 1849-50, 183.
Under this legislative authority, the company acquired by
purchase and conveyance from the Tennessee Valley Railroad Company all their property, including the road-bed, and
all the franchises, privileges and immunities, which they had
used or enjoyed under or by virtue of their charter. It thus
appears that the Memphis & Charleston Railroad Company
has acquired by legislative authority all the property and
franchises of the Tuscumbia, Courtland & Decatur Railroad
Company, including their right to the lands in controversy,
and the franchise to use them permanently for railroad purposes, unless the State exercises its reserved right of purchase. · It is admitted that the Tuscumbia, Courtland &
Decatur Railroad Company entered upon, and took possession of the lands under the conveyance from Sykes, and remained in possession, using them as a part of their road-
bed, until the marshal's sale in 1847. It is further admitted, that Deshler entered into possession, and operated
the railway until he sold and conveyed to the Tennessee Valley Railroad Company, which had possession and operated
the railroad, until they sold and conveyed to the Memphis &
Charleston Railroad Company; and that the last named company had possession and operated the railway ever since.

There has been a continuous *non-user* of the franchise by
the Tuscumbia, Courtland & Decatur Railroad Company, for
more than forty years. When corporate existence is not
limited to a specified period, and there is no voluntary surrender of the franchises, a private corporation will not be
deemed dissolved until its dissolution is judicially ascertained. The franchises are not extinguished by insolvency,
or a sale of all the corporate property, or by a mere cessation to do business. It may be, that after a continuous *non-
user* for so long a time, a voluntary surrender of its franchises will be presumed; but neither its dissolution, nor its

charter can be declared forfeited in a collateral proceeding·
This can be done only by a direct proceeding by the State;
though, on its insolvency, or a sale of all the corporate
property, it will be deemed dissolved for the purpose of protecting and enforcing the rights of third persons.—*Duke v.
Cahaba Nav. Co.*, 16 Ala. 372; 2 Kent, 312; 2 Morawetz
Corp. §§ 1011-1015. There has been no voluntary surrender,pnor judicial forfeiture, of the charter of the Tuscumbia,
Courtland & Decatur Railroad Company. Their chartered
rights, immunities and franchises have been continued and
perpetuated by the legislative acts referred to, and now exist in the Memphis & Charleston Railroad Company, which
company possesses and enjoys them as fully as they were or
could have been enjoyed by the Tuscumbia, Courtland & Decatur Railroad Company. The latter corporation has ceased
to do business under its corporate name, but the rights and
franchises granted by the charter still exist, and are exercised by the defendant, though under a different corporate
name. The charter, as employed in the conveyance of
Sykes—representing and expressing the chartered rights—
continues.

Independent of this conclusion, plaintiff has not such title
to the lands in controversy as will maintain ejectment, or the
corresponding statutory real action. A fee is said to be qualified, base or determinable, when it is made to determine, or
liable to be defeated, on the happening of some contingent
event or act. Kent defines a qualified, base or determinable
fee, as "an interest which may continue forever, but the estate is liable to be determined without the aid of a conveyance, by some act or event circumscribing its continuance or
extent. Though the object on which it rests for perpetuity
may be transitory or perishable, yet such estates are deemed
fees, because, it is said, they have a possibility of enduring
forever."—4 Kent, 10; Tiedeman Real Prop. § 44. By the
original act of incorporation, the Tuscumbia, Courtland & Decatur Railroad Company had capacity "to purchase, receive
and hold, sell, convey and confirm real or personal estate, as
natural persons"—to acquire a fee simple. As we have
shown, the act amending the charter endowed the company
with the capacity of possible perpetual existence. The limitation in the conveyance of Sykes, that the estate granted
shall continue so long as the charter shall continue, constituted a defeasible or determinable quality, with a possibility
of the estate enduring forever. Purged of this quality, the

[Davis v. Memphis & Charleston Railroad Co.]

estate would have been a fee simple. But its existence in the grant constitutes it a base, qualified, or determinable fee. *State v. Brown*, 27 N. J. L. 13.

When a person grants only a portion of whatever estate he may have, the portion granted to determine on the happening of some event, in order that the residue may remain in the grantor as a reversion, the determinability of the estate carved out must depend on an event which, by the usual course of nature, must happen at some time. If it is defeasible or determinable on a contingency or event which, by possibility, may never occur, the interest remaining in the grantor is merely "a possibility of reverter." Conditions in a deed are reserved to the grantor, and only he, or his heirs, can take advantage of a breach. "Nothing which lies in action, entry or re-entry, can be granted over, in order to discourage maintenance." A possibility, or other thing not in possession, or vested in right, is not, by common law, the subject of an operative grant or assignment to strangers. "Where one grants a base or qualified fee, since what is left in him is only a right to defeat the estate so granted upon the happening of a contingency, there is no reversion in him; that is, he has no future vested estate in fee, but only what is called a naked possibility of *reverter*, which is incapable of alienation or devise, although it descends to his heirs." Tiedeman Real Prop. § 385; *Nichol v. N. Y. & E. R. R. Co.*, 2 Kernan, 121; s. c., 12 Barb. 460; *Ruck v. Rock Island*, 97 U. S. 693. It results, that no reversion remained in Sykes, which could be the subject of grant or assignment; and that Fennell, by his conveyance, acquired only a beneficial interest in the possibility of *reverter*, which is insufficient to maintain ejectment.

The record does not disclose in what manner the Tuscumbia, Courtland & Decatur Railroad Company acquired the portion of the land in controversy which is in section 16. But, after continuous adverse possession, under claim of right, by the company, and the derivative purchasers, including the defendant, for a period of forty years, we would presume, if necessary, a grant in fee simple, or that the land was taken by proceedings in condemnation.—*McArthur v. Carrie*, 32 Ala. 75; *Matthews v. McDade*, 72 Ala. 377; *Gosson v. Ladd*, 77 Ala. 223.

Affirmed.

41

Alexander Brothers *v.* King & Co.

Contest between Attaching Creditors, for Money in hands
of Sheriff.

1. *Action at law between partners.*—At common law, one partnership
could not maintain an action against another, when the two had a common partner; but, under statutory provisions making partnership demands joint and several, an action on a partnership demand may be
prosecuted against one of the partners individually (Code, § 2605); and
the fact that the partner not sued is also a partner in the plaintiff firm,
it seems, is no defense to the action.

2. *Contest between attaching creditors; what defects are available.*—A
junior attaching creditor, having first obtained judgment, can not claim
the proceeds of sale of the attached property, as against the prior attaching creditor, unless the prior attachment, or judgment thereon, is a
nullity; and the fact that the cause of action is a partnership demand,
the partner not sued being also a member of the plaintiff partnership,
does not render the proceedings or the judgment void.

APPEAL from the Circuit Court of Colbert.

Tried before the Hon. HENRY C. SPEAKE.

This was a contest between Alexander Brothers and F. R.
King & Co., attaching creditors of Paul C. Jones, involving
their respective rights to the proceeds of sale of the at-
tached property, in the hands of the sheriff. On motion of
F. R. King & Co., whose attachment was levied after that of
Alexander Brothers, the court awarded the money to them;
and this judgment, to which an exception was reserved by
Alexander Brothers, is here assigned as error.

KIRK & ALMON, for appellants, cited Code, § 2605; *Hall
v. Cook,* 69 Ala. 88; *Morris v. Hillery,* 7 How. Miss. 61;
Lindley on Partnership, 469-70; 2 Bates on Partnership,
§ 902; *Lacy v. LeBruce,* 6 Ala. 904.

J. B. MOORE, *contra,* cited *Tindal v. Bright,* Minor. 103;
Hazlehurst v. Pope, 2 Stew. & P. 259; *Smith v. Strader,*
9 Porter, 449; *Lacy v. LeBruce,* 6 Ala. 904; *Murdock v.
Caruthers,* 21 Ala. 785; 51 Ala. 305; 51 Mich. 480; 50 Vt.
668; 11 Oregon, 443; 14 La. 43.

CLOPTON, J.—On motion of appellees, the Circuit Court
made an order, that the proceeds of the sale of personal

property, levied on by the attachments sued out by appellants
and appellees, respectively, against Paul C. Jones, be applied
to the payment of the judgment which the latter recovered
March 20, 1889, in their attachment suit.   The attachment
of Alexander Bros. was first sued out and levied, and, so far
as the record discloses, is still pending.   It has the prior
lien, unless some valid reason is shown why it should be
displaced in favor of the lien of the attachment of F. R.
King & Co.   The reason assigned in the order directing the
application of the money is, that the attachment of Alexander
Bros. is founded on a debt contracted by the firm of Alexander & Jones, and Sydney J. Alexander is a member of both
firms, and that the Circuit Court has no jurisdiction to enforce the payment of the debt.

At common law, one partnership can maintain no action
against another, when one of the partners is a member of
both firms.   The reason is, that the common partner must
necessarily be the plaintiff and defendant, and that a judgment can not be rendered in favor of himself against himself.   But, by statute, "any one of the associates, or his
legal representative, may be sued for the obligation of all."
Code, 1886, § 2605.   This statute has been construed to
give a creditor the right to sue any one of the partners, for
a debt contracted by the firm, whether due by account or
otherwise; and that the effect of a suit so commenced is to
change, for the purposes of such suit, the obligation of the
partners from joint to joint and several.   The creditor may
declare on the debt, as the individual liability of the
partner sued.—*Duramus v. Harrison*, 26 Ala. 326; *Hall v.
Cook*, 69 Ala. 87.   Under a statute in Mississippi, declaring
the notes of partners joint and several, it was held, that
a member of a partnership may be co-plaintiff with the other
partners, in a suit on a promissory note against the members
of another firm, of which he is also a partner, provided he is
not joined as a defendant; and that the others can not set
up his liability as a defense.—*Morris v. Hillery*, 7 How. 61.
In *Lacy v. LeBruce*, 6 Ala. 904, it was held, that the death
of a common partner removed the impediment to a suit at
law to recover a demand due by one firm to the other, and
that the survivor of the one may sue the survivor of the
other.   The reason of the rule at common law having ceased
by operation of the statute, it would seem that the rule also
should cease.   But this we need not decide.

The order from which the appeal is taken can not be maintained, unless the attachment of Alexander Bros. is a nullity. It was sued out against Jones individually, and founded on his individual liability. It is manifest, that on the principles above stated, the attachment could not be quashed, dissolved or abated, and a complaint counting on the cause of action as therein set forth, would be held sufficient on demurrer. A judgment rendered in such proceedings would not be void. It is evident that the proceedings are not void on their face. On this motion, the court could not look to the extrinsic fact, that Sydney Alexander was a common partner of both firms, in order to determine that the court had no jurisdiction to render judgment against Jones on the attachment proceedings in favor of Alexander Bros., which is, in effect, to determine that the proceedings were not merely irregular, but invalid.—*Buchanan v. Thomason*, 70 Ala. 401. If it were conceded, that Alexander Bros. can not maintain the action, for the reason assigned by the judge in his order, this is matter which the defendant in attachment must set up by plea to the action. Strangers can not intervene, and set up collaterally the liability of the common partner, for the purpose of avoiding the prior lien created by its levy.

Reversed and remanded.

Sharpe *v.* National Bank of Birmingham.

Action on the Case for Conversion of Certificates of Stock.

1. *Count construed to be in case, and not in assumpsit.*—A count which claims damages of the defendant, for that whereas, plaintiff having procured a loan of money from defendant, and pledged certain shares of stock as collateral security, defendant undertook and promised, in consideration thereof, to hold said stock only as collateral security, and not to convert the same to his own use, nor to sell the same without notice to plaintiff; but, not regarding said promise and undertaking, and intending to injure and defraud plaintiff, defendant afterwards converted said stock to his own use, and sold the same without notice to plaintiff, whereby said shares of stock were lost to plaintiff, and he was damaged as aforesaid,—though informal, is a good count in *case*, and not in *assumpsit*.

2. *Error without injury in refusing to allow amendment.*—The refusal to allow an amendment of the complaint, by the addition of another count, if erroneous, is not a reversible error, when the record shows

that the plaintiff's case was tried on the original complaint precisely as it would have been if the amendment had been allowed.

3. *Pledge of stock as collateral security; remedies of pledgee.*—When shares of stock in a private corporation are pledged as collateral security for a debt, and default is made in the payment of the debt at maturity, the pledgee may file a bill in equity to foreclose the pledge by a sale under the order of the court, or he may exercise the implied power to sell without resorting to judicial proceedings; but, if he elects to pursue the latter remedy, the sale must be at public auction, in the absence of a special agreement, and reasonable notice must be given to the pledgor; and if he sells privately, without notice, becoming himself the purchaser, the relation between him and the pledgor is not thereby dissolved.

4. *Same; ratification of authorized sale.*—If the pledgor, when notified of the irregular or unauthorized sale, accepts its benefits, giving his note for the balance of his debt remaining unpaid, this is presumptively a ratification of the sale, and he can not afterwards impeach it; but, if he acted in ignorance of the fact that the pledgee himself was the purchaser, and did not intend to make an absolute and unconditional ratification without regard to the facts attending the sale, he may disaffirm it within a reasonable time after discovering that the pledgee was the purchaser.

5. *Pledge of stock by part-owner; estoppel between pledgor and pledgee.* If a part-owner of certificates of stock pledges them, with the consent of the other owner, as collateral security for his own debt, and they are converted by the pledgee, the pledgor is entitled to recover as if he were the sole owner, the pledgee being estopped from denying his absolute ownership.

APPEAL from the Circuit Court of Jefferson.

Tried before the Hon. LEROY F. BOX.

This action was brought by Thomas Sharpe, against the National Bank of Birmingham, and was commenced on the 29th October, 1883. The first count of the complaint claimed $15,000 damages, for that whereas, in the spring of the year 1878, the defendant loaned and advanced $1,200 to plaintiff, in consideration of plaintiff's promise and agreement to repay the same, as and when it became payable; and whereas plaintiff was the owner of twenty shares of the capital stock of the Newcastle Coal and Iron Company, a corporation organized under the laws of Alabama, of great value, which, at the special instance and request of the defendant, he then and there transferred and delivered to defendant, to be held by said defendant in pledge as collateral to secure the payment of said loans and advances; the defendant, in consideration of the premises, then and there undertook and promised to plaintiff that it, said defendant, would hold said shares of stock only in pledge to secure the payment of said loans and advances, and would not convert the same, or any part thereof, to its own use, and would not sell the same, or any part thereof, without first notifying plaintiff of its intention to sell the same, and affording him an opportunity to advise and aid in effecting such sale: "Now plaintiff avers that said defendant, not regarding its promise and undertaking aforesaid, but in violation thereof, and contriving and intending to injure, defraud and oppress plaintiff, did not nor would hold the said shares of stock only in pledge to secure the payment of said loans and advances, but afterwards, to-wit," &c., "converted said shares of stock to its own use, and sold the same, without first notifying plaintiff of its intention to sell the same, and affording him an opportunity to aid or advise in effecting said sale; whereby said shares of stock, being of the value aforesaid, became and were wholly lost to plaintiff, and he was damaged $15,000; wherefore he sues." Another special count, in the same form, claimed damages on account of the conversion by the defendant of the dividends on the stock alleged to have been received.

The court overruled a demurrer to the entire complaint, and to each count separately, but refused to allow the plaintiff to amend by adding a formal count in case; to which ruling the plaintiff excepted. After protracted pleadings, which it is not necessary to set out, the main defenses were, 1st, a general denial of liability; and, 2d, that plaintiff had ratified the sale of the stock, with knowledge of the facts. The facts of the case, and the rulings of the court in the charges given and refused, are stated in the opinion of the court. The plaintiff appeals, and assigns as error all the rulings of the court to which he reserved exceptions.

W. G. HUTCHESON, JAMES WEATHERLY, and WARD & HEAD, for appellant.—(1.) The plaintiff might have waived the tort, and sued for money had and received, but he did not: on the contrary, he declared in case for the wrongful sale or conversion of his stock, and was entitled to recover its highest value up to the time of the trial. The original complaint being in case, the amended count, which was strictly formal, ought to have been allowed.—*Life Insurance Co. v. Randall*, 74 Ala. 170; *Whilden & Sons v. M. & P. Nat. Bank*, 64 Ala. 1; 11 Amer. & Eng. R. R. Cases, 92. (2.) Whether the parties occupied towards each other the relation of mortgagor and mortgagee, or that of pledgor and pledgee, the sale of the stock by the defendant was equally unauthorized, and did not change their relative rights and duties. If a mortgagee becomes the purchaser at his own sale, it will be set aside on the timely application of the mortgagor, without regard to its fairness, or the fullness of the price paid.—*Cooper v. Hornsby*, 71 Ala. 62; *Garland v. Watson*, 74 Ala. 323; *McLean v. Pressley*, 56 Ala. 211; *Knox v. Armistead*, at present term, *ante*, p. 495. If the deposit of the stock constituted a pledge, the defendant had no right to sell without giving notice of his intention, in order that the plaintiff might have an opportunity to protect his own interests.—Jones on Pledges, §§ 602, 614, 721; Story on Bailments, §§ 308–10; 2 Kent's Com. 582; 4 *Ib.* 138–40; *Nabring v. Bank*, 58 Ala. 204; 2 N. Y. 443. (3.) The sale has never been ratified; for there can be no binding ratification without full knowledge of the facts, and while the plaintiff knew, of course, that the sale was made without notice to him, there is no pretense that he was informed of the purchase by the defendant.—*Andrews v. Hobson*, 23 Ala. 213; *Clark v. Taylor*, 68 Ala. 453; *Chapman v. Lee*, 47 Ala. 143; *Holt v. Agnew*, 67 Ala. 368; *Steinhart v. Bell*, 80 Ala. 208; Wharton on Agency, § 65; Story on Agency, § 529. (4.) The defendant was estopped from setting up the interest of Worl in the stock.

HEWITT, WALKER & PORTER, *contra.*—(1.) The original complaint was in *assumpsit*, while the proposed amendment was in *case*; and it was therefore properly disallowed.—*Insurance Co. v. Randall*, 74 Ala. 170; *Wilkinson v. Moseley*, 18 Ala. 288; *Bank v. Hudgins*, 3 Ala. 206; *Mardis v. Shackelford*, 4 Ala. 493; *Cook v. Bloodgood*, 7 Ala. 683; *Chambers v. Seay*, 73 Ala. 372; *Wilson v. Stewart*, 69 Ala. 302. (2.) In order to effect a valid sale of a pledge, the law does not require that the pledgee shall first demand of the pledgor to redeem, nor that the sale shall be at public auction. *Bryson v. Rayner*, 90 Amer. Dec. 69; *Fire Ins. Co. v. Dalyrymple*, 89 Amer. Dec. 779. (3.) The plaintiff received the benefit of the sale without objection, knowing how the proceeds were applied; and this, with his long acquiescence, estops him from now complaining of it.—*Gilmer v. Morris*, 80 Ala. 78; *Oil Co. v. Marbury*, 91 U. S. 587; 31 Penn. St. 161.

CLOPTON, J.—Before the trial was entered upon, plaintiff moved to amend the complaint by adding a count, formally and substantially, in case. The court refused to allow the amendment, evidently on the idea that the original complaint counts on a breach of the contract, and is in *assump-*

sit. In cases where the plaintiff has an election to sue in *assumpsit* for a breach of the contract, or to bring an action on the case, for a violation of duty growing out of the contract, it is often difficult to determine whether a count is in form *ex contractu* or *ex delicto.* The same facts have to be averred substantially in both instances, the difference being, that in one the complaint declares on the contract, and assigns breaches of the contractual stipulations; and in the other, the contract is stated as mere inducement, and the cause of action is founded on a breach of duty growing out of the contract, and imposed by law. In *Whilden v. Mer. & Plant. Nat. Bank*, 64 Ala. 1, the test is stated as follows: "It is from the facts stated in the body of the count the question must be determined; and when these indicate that the plaintiff is proceeding for a measure of recovery adapted only to the one form of action, it must be intended that the count belongs to that form of action, whether it is *ex delicto* or *ex contractu.*" Though the transaction may have had its origin in a contract, if the facts stated show that the cause of action is a violation or disregard of duties which the law implies from the contractual relations and conditions of the parties, the count will be regarded as in case.—*Mo. Life Ins. Co v. Randall*, 74 Ala. 170. The test of certain and easy application is, the measure of recovery to which the count is adapted

It may be conceded that the counts in the original complaint are not formally and technically in case. After stating the pledge contract, inapt words are used to aver the duties growing out of the contract, which the law devolved on defendant; such as, "the defendant, in consideration of the premises, then and there undertook and promised the plaintiff," followed by averments of violation and disregard of the legal duties which devolved on defendant as pledgee. But, considering all the averments, it seems that the contract is stated as inducement, and that the pleader did not intend by these words to allege that what follows them were express stipulations of the contract, but duties implied by law. The counts do not proceed for the recovery of the excess of the proceeds of the sale of the stock pledged, but for its value, as the measure of recovery. The amendment should have been allowed. Its refusal, however, would not operate a reversal, as it appears from the record that the whole case was tried as if the action was in form *ex delicto.* The plaintiff having had the same and as full benefit under the com-

[Sharpe v. Nat. Bank of Birmingham.]

plaint is it stood, as if the amendment had been allowed, we regard its rejection as error without injury.

The undisputed facts are: About February, 1878, the plaintiff placed with the National Bank of Birmingham twenty shares of the capital stock of the Newcastle Iron and Coal Company, as collateral security for debts due the bank, and its president individually. The debts were renewed or extended from time to time, the stock remaining in pledge. In October, 1879, the demands having matured, the president of the bank instructed the cashier to give the plaintiff par for his stock, credit him for the amount, and render him a statement of his account. The sale was private, and no notice thereof was given to the plaintiff, nor was there any demand of payment.

When the debt for which shares of stock are pledged matures, and is unpaid, the pledgee may file a bill in equity for a foreclosure of the pledge, and a sale under the order of the court, or he may exercise the implied power to sell without resorting to judicial proceedings. If he elects to pursue the latter remedy, the law requires, in the absence of an agreement, that the sale shall be made at public auction, and reasonable notice of the time and place given to the pledgor, that he may have opportunity to redeem the pledge. If there is a stipulated day for payment, demand of payment is not required; notice of the sale being considered as equivalent to a demand.—*Nabring v. Bank of Mobile*, 58 Ala. 204. The sale of the stock, having been made privately, and without notice, was inoperative to transmute the title, or to dissolve the relation of pledgor and pledgee, the bank being the purchaser; and retaining its possession. *Md. Fire Ins. Co. v. Dalrymple*, 25 Md. 242; *Middlesex Bank v. Minot*, 4 Met. 325; Cook on Stock, §§ 477-479.

These principles are not controverted; but defendant contends, that plaintiff, with knowledge that the sale was unauthorized and inoperative, ratified it. The ratification is claimed on the undisputed facts, that in December after the sale, plaintiff was informed that his stock had been sold at par, received a statement of his account, showing a credit of the proceeds of the sale, and a few days afterwards, without objection or further inquiry, settled with the bank by giving his note for the unsatisfied balance due by him. Unquestionably, plaintiff had the right, at his election, to ratify the sale, and receive the benefit of the credit of the proceeds, thereby relieving it of any imputation of tortiousness, or to treat it as futile, and be remitted to his rights, as they existed before the attempted sale. By giving his notes for the deficiency, after deducting the proceeds, without objection, and after being informed and receiving his account, was a ratification, if the other essential elements existed.—*Childs v. Hugg*, 41 Cal. 519.

Plaintiff, admitting that he knew his stock had been sold, and that notice of the sale was not given, seeks to avoid the ratification on the alleged ground, that it was made in ignorance of the fact that the bank was the purchaser, and that it was a private sale by the bank to itself. Defendant does not claim or pretend that this fact was communicated to plaintiff, or that he was otherwise informed of it at the time of the alleged ratification. As to this question, the court instructed the jury, that if, at the time the sale was reported to plaintiff, it was impeachable, and he knew it was impeachable, and elected not to impeach it, but to accept and enjoy its benefits, he can not now impeach the sale. When referred to the evidence, the charge imported to the jury, that if plaintiff had knowledge of the invalidity of the sale, on the ground only that the notice of the time and place had not been given, and elected to assent to and ratify it, he can not afterwards disaffirm it, though he was not informed that the pledgee became the purchaser at a private sale.

The salutary doctrine, that trustees and others, holding fiduciary relations, are incompetent to purchase the trust property at their own sales, applies with full force to pledges. Knowledge of all the material facts and circumstances is essential to an efficient and valid ratification of a sale made by a pledgee in disregard of the requirements of the law, and of the rights of the pledgor. It is readily supposable, that a pledgor might be willing to abide by a sale, though made without notice, and even a private sale, if made in open market, where there may be competition, and yet be unwilling to assent to a sale made by the pledgee to himself, without affording others an opportunity to buy. A confirmation, to be effectual and binding must be tantamount to a valid and binding agreement. Partial knowledge of the facts is insufficient; and knowledge of some of the grounds on which a sale may be avoided, there being others, is not the equivalent of information of all the material facts necessary to enable the party to form a correct judgment.

The ratification may be subject to objections and disabil-

[Sharpe v. Nat. Bank of Birmingham.]

ities, as well as the attempted sale; and is so subject, if made in ignorance of some of the material facts, unless it was done with the intent to ratify, irrespective of the character of the sale, and of who was the purchaser. When plaintiff received information of the material facts of which he was ignorant at the time he ratified the sale, he was entitled to disaffirm the ratification.—*Bannon v. Warfield*, 42 Md. 22; *Miller v. Board of Ed.*, 44 Cal. 166. If promptly disaffirmed, the disaffirmance would relate back, and operate to avoid the sale. On the case as presented by the record, the real matter of controversy between the parties arises at this point. The entire case would be simplified, and rendered easier of solution, if, assuming the uncontroverted facts, the investigation of the jury were directed to the inquiries, whether the ratification in December, 1879, was made with the intent to ratify without full knowledge of all the material facts; and if not, of ratification *vel non* after plaintiff received information of the character of the sale and the purchase by the bank. The evidence leaves in doubt the time when plaintiff obtained this information, and consequently it is an inference to be drawn by the jury. Having once ratified, it was especially incumbent on plaintiff, on obtaining information of these material facts, to act with promptness, and without unreasonable delay. Having assented to the sale, and having recognized it as valid and operative, by obtaining and retaining its benefits, he will not be permitted to continue to retain them, acting inconsistently with the repudiation of his former ratification, speculating upon the consequences of affirmance or disaffirmance, and inducing the defendant to regard it as in force, for an unreasonable time, and then repudiate it, when it may suit his convenience or advantage. Unreasonable and undue acquiescence, under circumstances, is tantamount to a ratification.

It is admitted that Linn, the president of the bank, died in August, 1882; and there is evidence tending to show that plaintiff was informed of the facts prior to his death. If the jury should so find, and further find that he retained the benefits of the sale, without objection brought home to defendant until shortly prior to the commencement of this suit, in October, 1883, his former ratification should be regarded as unimpeachable. But, if he did not receive the information until the spring or summer of 1883, the question of ratification should be submitted to the jury, to be determined by the conduct of the plaintiff, and on the entire evidence.

It appears that L. P. Worl owned a part interest in the stock, which was pledged by plaintiff, for his individual benefit, by Worl's authority and consent. The pledge, under such circumstances, did not create any relation of pledgor and pledgee between defendant and Worl, and devolved on defendant no duty to him. The relation existed alone between plaintiff and defendant, and estopped the latter from disputing the title of the former. If plaintiff is entitled to recover, his right of recovery extends to the entire stock pledged.

Reversed and remanded.

Hughes *v.* Hughes.

Bill in Equity by Legatees against Executor, to compel Final Settlement, set aside Sale of Land, and for Account of Profits on Re-sale.

1. *Purchase by executor or trustee at his own sale, and re-sale at profit.* A trustee is not permitted to traffic in the trust property for his own benefit, but holds the profits realized subject to be claimed by the beneficiaries on timely application; and this principle would probably apply to a sale of land by an executrix, where she was jointly interested with her sister as purchaser, and they afterwards effected a re-sale at a tenfold price; but such interest in the original purchase is not established, against the denials of the answer, merely by the deeds showing that the sister who was purchaser conveyed to the executrix, six years afterwards, a half interest in the land at the same price, and that they jointly effected the re-sale a few weeks afterwards.

2. *Correspondence of allegations and proof.*—There can be no relief on a controverted question without proof, and averments or admissions in pleadings are not open to disproof by the party making them.

APPEAL from the Chancery Court of Pickens.

Heard before the Hon. THOS. W. COLEMAN.

The bill in this case was filed on the 22d September, 1887, by Sallie B. Hughes and others, grandchildren of B. J. Hughes, deceased, and residuary legatees under his will, against Anna F. Hughes, the surviving executrix, who was a daughter of the testator, and against several other persons; and sought to compel a final settlement of the accounts and vouchers of the executrix, and more especially to set aside a sale of two city lots in Birmingham, or to hold the executrix liable for the price realized on a re-sale to Whitley & Trim-

ble, who were also joined as defendants to the bill. The
chancellor assumed jurisdiction of the estate, and made the
necessary orders for a statement of the accounts; but he refused to set aside the sale of the city lots, or to charge the
executrix with the profits realized on the re-sale. The complainants appeal from the decree, and here assign this part
of it as error.

E. D. WILLETT, and W. F. & J. C. JOHNSTON, for the
appellants.

M. L. STANSEL, contra.

STONE, C. J.—The question pressed upon our consideration is the sale of the Birmingham lots. The two lots were
sold by the exeutrixes in 1879, to the highest bidder for
cash, and brought seven hundred and sixty dollars. The
widow and a daughter of the testátor were the executrixes,
and another daughter became the purchaser, paid the purchase-money, and a deed was made to her in 1880. The
widow died soon afterwards, leaving Annie F. Hughes, the
daughter, sole surviving executrix, who proceeded to execute
the trusts conferred by the will. The bill was filed in September, 1887.

As we have said, the chief question pressed before us
grows out of the sale of the Birmingham lots to Mary
Hughes, daughter and sister of the executrixes. Complainants are grandchildren of testator, and are legatees under
the residuary clause of the will. The bill charges that there
was collusion bétween Annie F. Hughes, executrix, and Mary
Hughes, the purchaser, that the lots should be purchased in
the name of the latter, but that in fact the sisters were joint
purchasers—thus making Annie both buyer and seller; that
the title remained in Mary until 1886, and complainants did
not know until then that Annie was interested in the purchase. The bill further charges that, in 1886, Mary conveyed to Annie a half interest in the lots, on a recited consideration of three hundred and eighty dollars, one half of
the original purchase-price; and that about two months afterwards the two sisters, Annie and Mary, sold the lots to
Whitley & Trimble for eight thousand dollars. The bill
charges further, that when the first sale was made the price
of lots in Birmingham was rising, and there was no necessity for making the sale at that time. The will empowered

the executrixes to sell the real estate, and allowed them ten
years within which to exercise their discretion, and to make
sale. Testator died in 1878.

The answers deny that Annie, the executrix, was interested
in the purchase, and deny that there was any agreement that
she should have any interest in it. They set up that, after
Mary made the purchase, she became dissatisfied with it; and
that she, Annie, agreed to take a half interest with her, in
order to reconcile her to the investment she had made. The
answers further deny the averment that there was no necessity for making the sale, and set up that there was a necessity for the sale of that and other property, to provide for
two pecuniary legacies, aggregating four thousand dollars.
The record from the Probate Court, found in the transcript
before us, tends to prove the truth of this last averment. It
is not charged in the bill, that the market value of the lots,
when they were sold in 1879, exceeded seven hundred and
sixty dollars; nor is it averred whether any, or what improvements, were put on the lots between that time and the
sale to Whitley & Trimble.

The case was tried in the court below on bill and answers,
and the exhibits, without any testimony save that furnished
by the conveyances and the probate record. The chancellor
refused to charge the executrix with the profits made on the
Birmingham lots. The argument here pressed upon us is,
that the naked facts—sale to Mary, in 1879, for $760; con-
veyance in November, 1886, by her to her sister, the executrix, of a half interest for half the cost price; and sale by
the two sisters to Whitley & Trimble. for eight thousand
dollars—prove that Annie was interested in the original purchase. If this proposition be maintainable, it would probably follow that the beneficiaries can claim their share of the
profit realized on the re-sale. A trustee is not permitted to
traffic for his own benefit in property which he holds in trust;
and if he does so, the beneficiary, on timely application,
may claim the profit as his.—*James v. James*, 55 Ala. 525;
Pearce v. Gamble, 72 Ala. 341.

The facts stated are obnoxious to criticism, but they are,
of themselves, not enough to overcome the denials of the
answer, and make a case for relief.

It is contended in the second place, that the sale was invalid and void, because not made under the power in the will.
The contention is, that the probate record shows that the sale
was made under an order of court. There is nothing in this.

The bill not only fails to raise this question, but, properly interpreted, charges that the sale was made under the will. And if the bill had raised the inquiry, the proof fails to sustain it.   There can be no relief on a controverted question without proof, and averments or admissions in pleading are not open to disproof by the party making them.—*Lehman v. McQueen*, 65 Ala. 570; *McGehee v. Lehman, Ib.* 316; *Marshall v. Howell*, 46 Ala. 318.

All other questions presented are properly for consideration in taking the account and making settlement.   The settlement is yet to be had.

Affirmed.

Morrison Brothers & Co. *v.* Coleman.   [87 [105

Bill in Equity for Injunction against Obstruction of Navigable Stream.

1. *Navigable stream; allegations of bill for injunction against obstruction.*—When a bill is filed by a riparian proprietor on a running stream which is above tide-water, seeking an injunction against an obstruction of the stream more than two miles above his mill, whereby the floatage of the stream from above is impeded, he must show by specific averments how far up the stream is navigable, or, at least, that it is navigable up to the obstructions complained of, and how long; though it is not necessary to aver or show that it is navigable throughout the entire year.

2. *Receiver's certificate on homestead entry.*—A receipt given by the receiver of a land office of the United States, for money paid in full on a homestead entry (U. S. Rev. Statutes, §§ 2290-97), confers a title which, before the expiration of five years, enables the possessor to maintain or defend an action as owner.

APPEAL from the Chancery Court of Geneva.

Heard before the Hon. JOHN A. FOSTER.

The bill in this case was filed on the 4th March, 1889, by Morrison Brothers & Co., suing as partners, against John T. Coleman; and sought to enjoin and remove obstructions by the defendant in Spring Creek, a tributary of the Choctowhatchie River, more than two miles above the complainants' mill, whereby they were prevented from floating down logs from their lands above, and logs bought from other persons above.   After answer filed, the defendant submitted a motion to dissolve the injunction, both on the denials of the answer, and for want of equity in the bill. The chancellor sustained the motion, and dissolved the injunction; and this decretal order is here assigned as error.

C. H. LANEY, and WATTS & SON, for appellants, cited Angell on Water Courses, §§ 535–37; *Lewis v. Coffee County*, 77 Ala. 190; *Sullivan v. Spottswood*, 82 Ala. 163; *Gerrish v. Brown*, 51 Maine, 256; *Thompson v. Androscoggin Co.*, 54 N. H. 545; *Scott v. Wilson*, 3 N. H. 321; *Rhodes v. Otis*, 33 Ala. 578; 1 Green, Iowa, 348; 31 Maine, 9; 28 Maine, 534; 5 Pick. 199; 1 Pom. Equity, § 217; 1 High Inj. §§ 794-5, 805, 812, 814; *Nininger v. Norwood*, 72 Ala. 277; *Bryant v. Peters*, 3 Ala. 160; 44 Ala. 611; 17 Ala. 667; 56 Ala. 360; 52 Ala. 593; *Grady v. Robinson*, 28 Ala. 289.

STONE, C. J.—The present case raises the inquiry, whether Spring Creek, a tributary of Choctawhatchie River, above the ebb and flow of the tides, is a navigable stream. All the authorities agree that it is *prima facie* unnavigable. It was not meandered in the Government surveys; and being above tide-water, the burden is on him who asserts its navigability, to aver and prove it.

When such stream is, and when it is not navigable, is a question which has been many times before this court. If a navigable stream, then it is a public highway, and may not be obstructed. In *Rhodes v. Otis*, 33 Ala. 578, the question was very elaborately considered, Walker, C. J., delivering the opinion of the court. After collating many authorities, the summing up in that case contained the following language: "It does not appear that the public generally, or any large number of persons, will ever use the stream for such purpose. Indeed the short distance to which the stream can be used [six or seven miles], affords a strong argument that no large number of persons will probably ever use it for floating timber. The stream, even below the mouth of Tallahatta creek, can only be used for floatage in freshets from head water, or from back water from the Tombeckbee river. In case of freshets from head water, it can be used for floating rafts only for a very short time, because the creek, being a very short one, runs down very soon. . . . . The highest estimate of the aggregate of the brief periods when it might be used, for the short distance for floating rafts and logs on account of freshets and back water, is three months. The creek is not shown to have been excepted from the Government surveys. Upon such evidence it can not be said, that Bashi creek is a navigable stream."—*Peters v. N. O., M. & C. R. R. Co.*, 56 Ala. 528; *Walker v. Allen*, 72 Ala. 456; *Sullivan v. Spotswood*, 82 Ala. 163.

In the case of *The Daniel Ball*, 10 Wall. 557, speaking of streams above tide-water, the court said: "A different test must, therefore, be applied to determine the navigability of rivers, and that is found in their navigable capacity. Those rivers must be regarded as public navigable rivers in law, which are navigable in fact. And they are navigable in fact when they are used, or are susceptible of being used, in their ordinary condition, as highways for commerce, over which trade and travel are or may be conducted in the customary modes of trade and travel on water." In Angell on Water-Courses, § 535, is this language: "All rivers above the flow of tide-water are, by the common law, *prima facie*, private, but when they are naturally of sufficient depth for valuable floatage, the public have an easement therein for the purposes of transportation and commercial intercourse; and, in fact, they are *public highways* by water." This doctrine is amply supported by authority, and nowhere is it, perhaps, better or more clearly expressed than in *Morgan v. King*, 35 N. Y. 454. And we have declared substantially the same doctrine.—*Lewis v. Coffee County*, 77 Ala. 190; *Olive v. State*, 86 Ala. 88.

We declare, as the result of our own rulings and of the weight of authority, that a fresh-water stream above tidewater is navigable and a public highway, when, and only when it is susceptible of being used, in ordinary condition, for a highway of commerce, over which there may be trade, travel, transportation. or valuable floatage. We are not to be understood as affirming that, to be a navigable stream or public highway, it must be susceptible of the enumerated uses for the entire year. Most inland streams contain a greater volume of water in winter than in summer. Our precise meaning is, that for a season, or considerable part of the year, it must contain that depth of water, which fits it for such transportation. It excludes all those streams which have the requisite volume of water only occasionally, as the result of freshets, and for brief periods, as unnavigable, and private property.

The bill in the present case alleges that Spring Creek is a navigable stream and public highway. It alleges further, "that said stream has been used for the purpose above stated,

42

for, to-wit, the floating of saw-logs down said creek to the Choctawhatchie river, a navigable stream flowing across the State of Florida to the Gulf of Mexico, by the public generally, and by orators and their predecessors in title, for a long series of years, viz.: twenty years; and that said stream is navigable at all times, except in seasons of protracted drouth." The bill avers that Coleman, the defendant, had placed obstructions in Spring Creek two and a half miles above complainants' mill, and cut off their right and power to float logs from their lands above the obstruction, down to their mill.

Possibly we might indulge in a criticism of the language copied from the bill. We think, however, that on any construction, the averments of the bill are not sufficiently specific to justify the severe writ of injunction prayed for in this case. Complainants own a mill on Spring Creek near the point where it empties into Choctawhatchie River. The obstruction complained of is two and a half miles above, by the course of the stream. Still above that, complainants own timbered lands bordering on the stream. It is not averred how long Spring Creek is, how far up it is navigable, nor whether its navigability extends above the obstruction Coleman placed in it, or whether it could be, or ever had been used for floating logs above that point. On the most favorable construction for the complainants, the averment of their bill may be true in every part of it, and yet the navigability of Spring Creek may not extend above Coleman's obstruction. It is common knowledge that inland streams, even the largest, have a point above which they cease to be navigable. Pleadings, to be sufficient, must at least show a *prima facie* right of recovery.

The foot-note to the bill calls for an answer under oath, and the defendant so answered. We extract from it: "Respondent denies that Spring Creek is a navigable stream, and further denies that it is a public highway; denies that logs can be floated down said stream, only in cases of high water or freshets, and then only three or four days at a time; denies that said stream has ever been used as a navigable stream, or as a public highway." In another place, the answer says: "Respondent denies that said Spring Creek was ever used for transporting logs down to said mill, above where respondent has erected his mill on said creek, except by complainants, who have only used it for a few months." They had owned the property only seven months when the bill was filed.

[City of Demopolis v. Webb.]

We are not able to perceive that the answer does not answer categorically every averment that gives to the bill a semblance of equity. So, the injunction was rightly dissolved, for two reasons: want of equity in the bill, and the denials in the answer.

That defendant Coleman was so far the owner of the land he claimed as to be able to maintain or defend a suit concerning it, we have decided at the present term in *Case v. Edgeworth, ante,* p. 203; s. c., 5 So. Rep. 783.

Should complainants be advised to amend their bill, what we have said will be a sufficient guide for the purpose.

The decretal order of the chancellor, dissolving the injunction, is affirmed.

City of Demopolis *v.* Webb.

Bill in Equity by Municipal Corporation, for Injunction against Obstruction of Street and River Landing.

1. *Dedication of streets in city or town.*—If the owners of a tract of land have it surveyed and mapped out as a town, with streets dividing the blocks or squares, and each block sub-divided into lots, and sell off lots by their numbers and description on the map, this is a dedication of the several streets to the public, leaving the ultimate fee in the original proprietors.

2. *Acceptance of dedicated street.*—A legislative act incorporating a town as laid out by the proprietors of the land, declaring that "all the tract of land included in the plan of said town be and is hereby declared to be the limits of the same in conformity to said plan," is an adoption of the plan as a part of the charter; and an acceptance of the charter operates as an acceptance of the dedicated streets therein laid down, without further action on the part of the municipal authorities.

3. *Estoppel against denying dedication.*—A sub-purchaser of a lot in an incorporated city or town, described in his conveyance as fronting on a named street, according to the map and plat laid out by the original proprietors of the land, is estopped from denying the dedication of the street as a highway, and its acceptance as such by the proper authorities.

4. *Obstruction of street in city or town; legal and equitable remedies.*—The obstruction of a street in an incorporated city or town, although under claim of title to the soil, is an indictable nuisance, for which an action lies in favor of any person sustaining special damage; and a bill in equity may also be maintained by the city or town, to restrain its continuance, and abate it as a nuisance.

5. *Fee in streets of city or town.*—In the absence of statutory provisions to the contrary, a conveyance of a lot in an incorporated city or town, bounded by a public street, passes to the grantee the fee to the center of the street, subject to the public right of user; the fee to the other half remaining in the grantor, or original proprietor, and with it all riparian rights when the street is bounded by a navigable river.

6. *Right to collect wharfage.*—A right to collect wharfage may exist (1) as a franchise conferred by legislative grant, or (2) as an incident to the ownership of lands abutting on a navigable river, subject to reasonable legislative regulation; and where such proprietary rights existed prior to the adoption of the constitutional provision which has been of force since 1868 (Const. 1868, 1875, Art. I, § 26), and it has not been dedicated to the public, it can not be taken away by legislative enactment, without compensation to the owner.

7. *Injunction against collection of wharfage.*—An incorporated city or town can not maintain a bill in equity, to enjoin the collection of wharfage by a person who claims under the original proprietors of the land which was laid out into a town, without showing (1) that the user of the street abutting on the river is thereby obstructed, or (2) that the right to collect wharfage was dedicated to the public with the street, or (3) otherwise negativing its retention by the proprietors.

APPEAL from the Chancery Court of Marengo.

Heard before the Hon. THOS. W. COLEMAN.

The bill in this case was filed on the 11th June, 1888, by the "City of Demopolis," against John C. Webb and wife, and W. H. Creagh; and sought (1) to enjoin the continuance of a fence, which said Webb had erected across a part of Arch street near the river; and (2) to prevent the collection of wharfage by the defendants, at their landing on the river at or near the foot of said street. The chancellor held, on demurrer, that the bill contained equity, so far as it sought relief against the obstruction of the street by the fence, but not as to the collection of wharfage; and that there was a misjoinder of defendants, inasmuch as Webb alone was charged with the erection and continuance of the fence. Each party appeals from this decree, and assigns as error the rulings against them respectively.

GEO. G. LYON, and with him PETTUS & PETTUS, for complainants.—(1.) The bill clearly shows a dedication of Arch street to the public.—2 Smith's Lead. Cases, 6th Amer. ed., 224, mar. 209; *Godfrey v. Alton*, 12 Ill. 29; 52 Amer. Dec. 476; 18 Ohio, 18; 8 B. Mon. 237; 8 Wend. 85; 11 Wend. 486; 1 Hill, 190; 6 Hill, 407; 33 Amer. Dec. 267. The legislative charter shows a sufficient acceptance of the dedication.—2 Dill. Mun. Corp. 640, § 642 (505), note 1; *Desmoines v. Hall*, 24 Iowa, 234; *Requa v. Rochester*, 45 N. Y. 129; 22 Ala. 197. (2.) The defendants are estopped from denying the fact of dedication.—2 Dill. Mun. Corp., § 639 (494), note 3; 19 Ohio St. 238. (3.) The bill charges acts which constitute a public nuisance, and for which an action at law would lie in favor of any person sustaining special injury; but a court of equity will also inter-

[City of Demopolis v. Webb.]

fere by injunction, at the suit of the city.—2 Dill. Mun.
Corp., §§ 659 (520), 660; *State v. Mayor,* 5 Porter, 279;
Hoole v. Att'y Gen. 22 Ala. 195; 57 Ill. 283; 76 Ill. 231;
10 Bush, Ky. 288; 56 Ill. 451; 3 Paige, 210; 4 Paige, 510;
Eden on Injunctions, 259–65; 2 Story's Equity, §§ 923–4;
Mitf. Eq. Pl. 144–5; 3 Zabr. N. J. 712; 6 Paige, 133, 555;
3 Pom. Equity, § 1349; 6 John. Ch. 439; 3 Paige, 254;
10 Ala. 47. The jurisdiction of chancery is not taken away
by the provision of the charter giving the municipal authorities power to abate nuisances summarily.—*Hoole v. Att'y Gen.*
22 Ala. 195; *Watertown v. Cowen,* 4 Paige, 510; *Cincinnati
v. White,* 6 Peters, 431; 2 John. Ch. 371; 6 *Ib.* 439;
5 Vesey, 129. (4.) Arch street, as dedicated, extends to
low-water mark, and includes the lower landing; and this
gives the city all the rights of any other riparian owner.
Barney v. Keokuk, 94 U. S. 324; 10 Peters, 663. (5.)
The defendants are not riparian proprietors, though they
may own the fee to the center of the street in front of their
lots.—Gould on Waters, § 148; 2 Wall. 57; 67 N. Y. 512;
14 Allen, 145; 80 Penn. St. 119; 2 Minn. 114; 55 Ill. 486;
59 Ill. 196; 14 Iowa, 1; 18 Iowa, 179; 16 Wisc. 509;
18 Wisc. 118; 18 Wall. 57; 79 Amer. Dec. 288. (6.)
The bill is not multifarious, nor is there any misjoinder of
defendants.—*Lehman v. Mayer,* 67 Ala. 396; *Kennedy v.
Kennedy,* 2 Ala. 573; *Anderson v. Jones,* 68 Ala. 117;
1 Dan. Ch. Pl. 335; Story's Eq. Pl., §§ 284, 533; 23 Ala.
558; 47 Ala. 273; 79 Ala. 76.

GEO. W. Taylor, *contra.*—(1.) The remedy at law is
adequate and complete, (1) by ejectment, or (2) by statutory
proceedings in the nature of *quo warranto.*—2 Dill. Mun.
Corp., § 662; 79 Amer. Dec. 284; 9 *Ib.* 284; 69 *Ib.* 664;
64 N. Y. 75; Code, 1886, §§ 3170–71. (2.) It is only
streets in actual use, not speculative or projected streets, the
obstruction of which amounts to a nuisance.—2 Dill. M. C.
§ 680; 6 Mich. 176; 9 Mich. 111; 1 Amer. Dec. 647;
77 Amer. Dec. 491, note. (3.) To perfect a dedication of
land, acceptance is necessary, and use is essential.—*Gage &
Co. v. Railroad Co.,* 84 Ala. 224; 88 Mo. 155; 10 Amer.
Dec. 218; 91 *Ib.* 542, note; 1 *Ib.* 647. Dedication is a contract, and requires a grant by one party, or its equivalent,
and acceptance or user by the other.—88 Mo. 155. While
a reasonable time will be allowed for acceptance (48 Miss.
423; 31 Conn. 308), it will scarcely be presumed after the

lapse of sixty years, in the absence of user. The bill alleges
that the road leading to the landing was established in 1871,—
less than twenty years before the bill was filed; and user for
less than twenty years, without more, does not constitute a
highway.—68 Ala. 48; 84 Ala. 224. (4.) The bill should
have alleged that it was a free public wharf, since a wharf,
or landing, may be public in its use, and yet remain private
property.—1 Dill. 104; 1 Black, 1; 72 Amer. Dec. 365.
There can be no free public wharf, unless there is a public
road leading to it.—47 Amer. Dec. 548. (5.) The real
object of the bill is to get possession of the lands alleged to
be a street and landing, and the controversy is simply a dispute as to the legal title, Webb being in possession under
claim of title.—5 Porter, 279. 316; 64 Ala. 249; 66 Ala. 64;
3 Brick. Dig. 350, § 264. (6.) The right to charge and
collect wharfage is a riparian right, incident to ownership,
or a legislative franchise, and subject to legislative control.
11 Ala. 586; 1 Black, 1; 21 Amer. Dec. 89–95. A municipal
corporation has no right to regulate or control wharves,
except when authorized by its charter.—53 Ala. 561; 1 Dill.
103. Under the allegations of the bill, the complainant
never acquired any title to the wharf, or landing, but it remained in the original proprietors.—2 Dill. 629, 632, 648;
55 Ala. 413. Wharves, landings, &c., are not public
nuisances, unless they impede or obstruct navigation.—1 Dill.
M. C. 106; 21 Amer. Dec. 89–95; 95 Ib. 495, 644, 653;
Gould on Waters, § 140. (7.) Under the allegations of
the bill as to the collection of wharfage, the defendants were
guilty of usurping a franchise; of which only the State can
complain, and the remedy is by statutory proceedings in the
nature of *quo warranto*.—Code, §§ 3170–71; 45 Amer. Dec.
500. (8.) The bill is objectionable for multifariousness,
and for misjoinder of parties.—72 Ala. 302–07; 77 Ala.
278–81.

SOMERVILLE, J.—The bill is filed by the City of Demopolis, a municipal corporation, to restrain the continuance
of a fence erected by John C. Webb, one of the defendants,
across Arch street, a highway in said town, said obstruction
being alleged to be a public nuisance, and sought to be
abated as such. The bill further seeks to restrain the alleged
unlawful collection of wharfage by the said Webb and his
co-defendants, at a steam-boat landing on the margin of the
Tombigby river, which is averred to be an appropriation of

[City of Demopolis v. Webb.]

a part of said street, and an obstruction to the free use of
said landing by the public.   The highway in question—
called Arch street—is alleged to be on the east margin of
the river, running north and south, and extending from the
low-water mark to the lots on the west side of the street,
which are marked out and numbered on the map of the city.
Said street is also designated on this map, and is alleged to
have been duly dedicated to the public use.

There was a demurrer to the bill, some grounds of which
were sustained, and others overruled.   The case comes before us on cross-appeals by both the complainant and the
defendants.   We have been greatly enlightened in the investigation of this case by the able arguments of counsel, in
which great research is displayed.

It is objected, among other things, that the allegations of
the bill fail to show that Arch street was ever laid off, or
opened as a street, and in use as such prior to the alleged
obstruction.   In answer to this we may observe, that the bill
alleges with sufficient certainty a dedication of the street to
the public use, and the acceptance of such dedication by the
city authorities; and the defendants occupy an attitude
which estops them from denying the existence of this street
as a municipal highway.   The dedication itself was made by
the owners of the soil, in the clearest and most unmistakable
manner, by surveying and mapping out a town, under the
name of the town of Demopolis.   This town they laid off
into streets, blocks and lots, naming the streets, and number-
ing the lots, by marking them on this map or plat.   Among
these recognized highways was Arch street, the one here in
controversy.   The lots in said town were all described and
sold with reference to this plat, including certain lots occupied
by the defendant Webb, adjacent to, or fronting on Arch
street, upon which a ware-house has been constructed by the
proprietors, his co-defendants, from whom said Webb rents
the premises.   Improvements have been made, and a town
built up with reference to this plat, and upon the faith of an
implied covenant on the part of the dedicators that the highways and streets described shall always remain open for
public use.   "It may be stated as a general rule," as observed
in a recent leading case, "that where the owner of urban
property, who has laid it off into lots, with streets, avenues
and alleys intersecting the same, sells his lots with reference
to a plat in which the same is so laid off; or where, there
being a city map on which this land is so laid off, he adopts

such map by reference thereto, his acts will amount to a dedication of the designed streets, avenues and alleys to the public."—*M. E. Church v. Mayor of Hoboken*, 33 N. J. Law, 13; s. c., 97 Amer. Dec. 696. Under all the authorities, and upon every sound principle, this was a dedication of Arch street, as described on the map.—*City of Dubuque v. Maloney*, 9 Iowa ,451; s. c., 74 Amer. Dec. 358; *Cincinnati v. White*, 6 Pet. 431; *Godfrey v. City of Alton*, 12 Ill. 29; s. c., 152 Amer. Dec. 476; *Gardner v. Tisdale*, 60 Amer. Dec. 407; Angell on Highways, sec. 149.

The acceptance of the dedication by the public is sufficiently alleged. The act of the General Assembly of Alabama, approved December 15th, 1821, incorporating the town of Demopolis, provided, that "all the tract of land included in *the plan of said town* be, and is hereby, declared to be the limits of the same *in conformity to said plan*." Toulmin's Dig. p. 837. This was an adoption of the plan, or map, as part of the charter, with its streets there marked out and dedicated; and the acceptance of the charter operated, *ipso facto*, as an acceptance of such dedication, without further action on the part of the municipal authorities.—*Requa v. City of Rochester*, 45 N. Y. 129. The bill, moreover, alleges the actual use by the public, for over twenty years, of portions of Arch street near the two steamboat landings, in or adjacent to this street on the river margin.

But, as we have said, the defendants are in no situation to assert the non-existence of Arch street as a dedicated and accepted highway. They claim title to their lots by mesne conveyances running back to the original dedicators and proprietors—the same source through which the complainant derives its title to the street in controversy. In these conveyances, the lots on which the ware-house property is situated are described with reference to the original map or plat of the town, and stated to be bounded on the north by *Arch street* and Washington street. This estops the defendants from denying that Arch street is a public highway, having potential existence, whether actually opened or not. The case of *Providence Steam Engine Co. v. Providence Steamship Co.*, 12 R. I. 348; s. c., 34 Amer. Rep. 652, is an authority in support of this view. There, a riparian owner platted his land into streets, lots and squares, one of the streets being below high-water mark, and under tide-water at the time of dedication, having been subsequently reclaimed by filling out the uplands. It was closed by the owners of

[City of Demopolis v. Webb]

the adjoining lots, through the erection of a fence across the street. A bill was sustained to remove this obstruction as a nuisance. To the suggestion of the respondents that the street was never lawfully created, but existed only on paper, because the land over which it ran was overflowed by tide-water, the court answered: "Though it may be true that the way or street had no actual existence when the conveyance under which it is claimed was made, we think it had nevertheless what may be called a potential, or prospective existence, which would become actual whenever the place for it should be filled and incorporated with the upland; and though the conveyances, when executed, may have been ineffectual to create the way or street, because the site of it was flowed by tide-water, yet we think they were binding by way of estoppel on parties and privies, so that, in equity, at least, the said parties and privies could not refuse to allow the way or street as soon as the land designated for it became capable of supporting it. The ground of the estoppel," said the court, "is, that the easements and servitudes indicated by the plat constitute a part of the consideration for which all the conveyances referring to the plat were made; and therefore no person, while claiming under the conveyances, can be permitted to repudiate them, or to deny that they exist where they are capable of existing." We fully indorse this view of the law, as sustained both by reason and authority.—*City of Dubuque v. Maloney*, 74 Amer. Dec. 358; *Godfrey v. City of Alton*, 52 Amer. Dec. 476; *Van O'Linda v. Lothrop*, 21 Pick. 292; s. c., 32 Amer. Dec. 261.

It follows, we repeat, from this principle, that it is immaterial whether the street in question had been opened and used all its length through or not. The defendants purchased their lots in full recognition of its existence as a public street, or municipal highway, liable to be opened and used as such whenever the growing demands of an increased population and commerce might require it. They are estopped now to deny to it this character, upon the plainest principles of justice and right.

It is well settled, that a fence, or other like obstruction, erected across a street is a public nuisance; and it may be such although the obstruction is created under an accompanying claim of title to the soil. A right of action at law will lie for its maintenance, in favor of any one who may sustain from it a special or particular injury. For such nuisance an indictment will also lie, and any private person aggrieved by it may rightfully abate it by removal.—*Stetson v. Faxon*, 31 Amer. Dec. 123, and note p. 132; *Davis v. Mayor of New York*, 67 Amer. Dec. 186, note p. 203; *Harrower v. Ritson*, 37 Barb. (N. Y.) 303; *Milarky v. Foster*, 25 Amer. Rep. 531.

Chancery, however, will often assume jurisdiction to abate such a nuisance, by preventing its continuance through the aid of an injunction, where the fact of its existence is undoubted. This will be done, either on the ground of the irreparable nature of the injury, or to prevent a multiplicity of suits liable to be occasioned by its repetition or continuance, or other grounds which render the remedy at law inadequate. The disturbance of easements, existing or threatened, will especially be restrained with much favor.—3 Pom. Eq. Jur. §§ 1350–1351. Acting on these principles, this court in *State v. Mayor & Aldermen of Mobile*, 5 Port. 279; s. c., 30 Amer. Dec. 564, (1837) authorized an injunction to issue, restraining the erection of a market-house in one of the public streets of the city of Mobile, which was pronounced to be such an obstruction in the highway as to constitute a nuisance. A like jurisdiction exists to abate a nuisance already created, the remedy at law being inadequate, on the ground that one action, or even several, may not be sufficient to redress the plaintiff's grievances, by reason of the continuous nature of the injury. An appeal to the Chancery Court, moreover, is a more orderly method of settling such disputes, being less apt to lead to breaches of the peace, than the dangerous attempt to redress one's rights by taking the law in one's own hands.—*Town of Burlington v. Schwarzman*, 52 Amer. Rep. 571; *Hoole v. Attorney-General*, 22 Ala. 190; *Providence Steam Engine Co. v. Providence Steamship Co.*, 34 Amer. Rep. 652; *Dumesnil v. Dupont*, 68 Amer. Dec. 750.

That the city of Demopolis has the right to bring this suit is, in our judgment, clear, on both authority and principles of reason. Such jurisdiction was recognized and asserted long ago, by the English Court of Chancery, in *Mayor &c. London v. Bolt*, 5 Ves. 129, where an injunction was granted on the application of the corporate authorities of the city of London, to prevent a nuisance which threatened to be dangerous to the lives of the citizens.

In *Trustees of Village of Watertown v. Cowen*, 4 Paige Ch. 510; s. c., 27 Amer. Dec. 80, it was decided that the village of Watertown, in its corporate capacity, was so far the representative of the equitable rights of the inhabitants,

as to authorize the filing of a bill in its name to restrain the
erection of buildings on a public square, which were declared
to be a public nuisance, and liable to be abated as such,

So, it was held in *Town of Burlington v. Schwarzman*,
52 Conn. 181; s. c., 52 Amer. Rep. 571, that one who unlawfully erects a fence across a public street in a town, and
threatens to maintain it, could be restrained by injunction at
the suit of the town. The court, among other reasons,
thought that the liability of the town to pay damages, in
case of a person being injured by the obstruction, a sufficient
interest to enable it to appear as plaintiff in a complaint in
equity to prevent the threatened destruction. An equally
good reason is found in the power and duty to prevent and
remove nuisances, and to keep a general control of, and
supervision over all municipal highways, as incidental to
the right to repair and improve streets, to say nothing of
the express power in the city charter "to open all streets as
laid down on the maps of said city."—City Charter, Acts
1872–73, pp. 305, 310--311, § 19; *M. E. Church v. Mayor
of Hoboken*, 97 Amer. Dec. 698; note, 707; *Inhabitants of
Greenwich v. E. & A. R. R. Co.*, 24 N. J. Eq. 221. There
would be a great defect of justice, if the governing authorities
of a town or city, charged as trustees with the duty of protecting the public rights, were compelled to sit still with
hands tied, and witness the unlawful appropriation of the
municipal highways to private use, without any power to
prevent so monstrous an evil.

Mr. Pomeroy, discussing the subject of public nuisances,
observes: "A court of equity has jurisdiction to restrain existing or threatened public nuisances by injunction, at the
suit of the Attorney-General in England, and at the suit of
the State, or the people, or municipality, or some proper
officer representing the Commonwealth, in this country."
3 Pom. Eq. Jur. § 1349. See, also, 2 Dillon Mun. Corp.
(3d Ed.), § 659; 1 High on Inj. (2d Ed.), §§ 768, 769.

It is peculiarly appropriate, in our judgment, that this
jurisdiction should be asserted in this age and country at the
suit of towns and cities, as it harmonizes with the modern
American theory of remitting the governmental management
of local affairs, as far as convenient and practicable,
to the local authorities. For, as said by a learned judge,
"the law is made for the times, and will be made or modified by them."—*Lex. & Ohio R. R. Co. v. Applegate*, 8 Dana,
289; s. c., 33 Amer. Dec. 497.

It is needless to add, that the action of ejectment for a highway, by a municipality, even if the right be admitted to exist, as held by some authorities, is not a complete and adequate remedy in a case of this nature.

This suit, we hold, was properly brought in the corporate name of the City of Demopolis.

There is another feature of the bill, in addition to its purpose to abate the nuisance of obstructing Arch street by a fence erected across it. The further theory of the bill, if we correctly interpret it, is, that the collecting of wharfage at the lower river landing, by the defendant Webb, is an obstruction of the rights of the public in Arch street, which is alleged to run to the low-water mark on the river, and, therefore, to embrace the landing itself. It is argued, that the exercise of this right to collect wharfage is a franchise, and being without authority of law, it is an obstruction to the free use of Arch street, and as such is in the nature of a public nuisance.

Does the bill sufficiently negative the right of the defendants to collect wharfage, either in connection with their warehouse business, or by authority of the original proprietors of the soil, who dedicated Arch street to the public?

The defendants, as owners of the warehouse lots or property, to the south and east of Arch street, it may be admitted, can claim no right to collect wharfage as riparian owners. These lots are described as bounded by Arch street, and this street lies between these lots and the river, extending, as we have said, to the low-water mark. As owners of these attingent lots, therefore, in the absence of any statute to the contrary, the defendants by their deed became the grantees and owners of the ultimate fee only to the center of the street, not to the margin of the river, subject, of course, to the existing easement created by the dedication of the street.—*C. & W. Railway v. Witherow*, 82 Ala. 190, and cases cited on p. 195. Riparian rights can only attach to the ownership of .land which is bounded by a navigable stream, or, in other words, which abuts on the margin of the river.—*Yates v. Milwaukee*, 10 Wall. 497; Gould on Waters, sec. 148, p. 271. When, therefore, a street is bounded on one side by a navigable river, the ownership of lots on the other side running to the center, the fee of the half of the street bounded by the river presumptively remains in the original proprietor, subject to the public easement.—*Banks v. Ogden*, 2 Wall. 57; *Municipality, &c. v.*

[City of Demopolis v. Webb.]

Cotton Press, 36 Amer. Dec. 624. This is upon the principle, that a dedication, unaided by statute, does not pass the fee or legal title, but only an easement or right of way to the public, with such incidental privileges and powers of control as may be necessary to make it effective.—*Forney v. Calhoun County*, 84 Ala. 215; *Williams v. New York Cent. R. R. Co.*, 69 Amer. Dec. 651. As the owner of the fee or soil, he retains all property rights in it, incidental to ownership, which do not interfere with the use of the street for all reasonable purposes for which it may be needed by the public, and not incompatible with its improvement or development as required by the growth of the town or city of which it is the highway.—*Robert v. Sadler*, 104 N. Y. 229; s. c., 58 Amer. Rep. 498, 501, *note; Municipality, &c. v Cotton Press*, 36 Amer. Dec. 624; *Lorman v. Benson*, 8 Mich. 18; *Providence Steam-Engine Co. v. Providence Steamship Co.*, 12 R. I. 348; s. c., 34 Amer. Rep. 652, 661.

The right to collect wharfage may exist in either of two ways: (1) It may exist as a franchise conferred by legislative grant (*Lansing v. Smith*, 21 Amer. Dec. 89); or (2) it may exist as an incident to the ownership of land abutting on a navigable river, being a riparian right of the proprietor, and as such a right of property, subject, of course, to reasonable legislative regulation.—*Murphy v. City Council of Montgomery*, 11 Ala. 586; *Dutton v. Strong*, 1 Black (U. S.) 23; *Baltimore & Ohio R. R. Co. v. Chase*, 43 Md. 23; *Providence Steam Engine Co. v. Providence Steamship Co.*, 34 Amer. Rep. 652, 666; *Ball v. Slack*, 2 Whart. 508; s. c., 30 Amer. Dec. 279. It was declared in the Constitution of 1868 (Art. I, § 26), and is repeated in Article I, § 26, of our present State Constitution, "that all navigable waters shall remain forever public highways, free to the citizens of the State, and of the United States, without tax, impost, or toll imposed; and that no tax, toll, impost or wharfage shall be demanded or received from the owner of any merchandise or commodity, for the use of the shores, or any wharf erected on the shores, or in or over the waters of any navigable stream, unless the same is expressly authorized by the General Assembly."—Const. 1875, Art. I, § 26. We are called on to decide what effect this clause of the Constitution will exert on the rights of the parties defendant to this suit. It is not contended that the complainant, the city of Demopolis, is invested with any legal authority to conduct the business of wharfing on its own account; and without such authority conferred by charter, it can not be exercised.—*Mayor of Mobile v. Moog*, 53 Ala. 561. The contention is, that the dedication of Arch street was a dedication of that portion of it including the wharf, and that the exercise of the right of wharfage interferes with the easement of the public in the street, and being unlawful, because without express authority of law, the continuance of the business should be enjoined.

There may no doubt be a dedication of a public landing, or a wharf, as well as of a street, to the public use, if the intention of the proprietor to part with his property is made clear and unequivocal.—*Godfrey v. City of Alton*, 52 Amer. Dec. 476. Under our decisions, when a person owns land on a navigable river, his ownership is held to extend so far as to embrace the land between high and low-water marks. *Williams v. Glover*, 66 Ala. 189. But a landing, or wharf, may be private property, and the public be permitted to use it by license, or for a charge.—*O'Neill v. Annett*, 3 Dutch. 291; s. c., 72 Amer. Dec. 364. "The result of the authorities," says Mr. Gould in his treatise on Waters, "seems to be, that a dedication of land adjoining a river, for the purpose of public passage to and from the water, with, perhaps, the incidental right of temporary deposit, or a claim of prescriptive user, for the purpose of landing and embarkation, is valid; but that the right to incumber the land with lumber, merchandise, and the like, to a greater extent, or for a longer time, than would be permissible in a highway, is neither within the purpose of the dedication, nor valid as a custom."—Gould on Waters, § 105, p. 193.

In this aspect of the law, there are several defects in the bill fatal to its equity as a bill to enjoin the continuance of the wharfage business. (1.) There is no clear and unqualified averment in the bill, that the landing, or right of wharfage, was dedicated to the public, as well as the street. The very reverse is inferable from the statement, that the upper landing, as to which there is no controversy, was public and *free*. The lower landing, the only one in controversy, is alleged to have been *public*, which is not inconsistent with its permissive use by the proprietor as auxiliary to his own business, or for a charge of toll.—*Gage v. M. & O. R. R. Co.*, 84 Ala. 224. (2.) It is not alleged that the right of the public to an easement in Arch street—the right to pass and re-pass, to open and repair the street, or other privilege of improvement or user—is interfered with in any manner by

[City of Demopolis v. Webb.]

the wharfing business. (3.) The bill does not negative the fact, that the defendants are exercising, by privity of contract with the original proprietors, the right which may have existed in them to construct a wharf, and charge tolls at this landing. This, as we have said, was a property right incident to the ownership of the fee. If it existed prior to the enactment of the Constitution of 1868, and was not abandoned by dedication to the public so as to make it free, it could not be taken away by legislative enactment, without compensation to the owner.—*Municipality, &c. v. Cotton Press*, 36 Amer. Dec. 624. It is not made to appear, therefore, that the constitutional provision in question has abrogated the right of the original proprietor, or his assigns, to conduct the wharfing business, here sought to be enjoined. It may be observed, moreover, that the wharf itself is not shown to be constructed so as to injure the navigation of the river, or otherwise render it a public nuisance by preventing convenient access through the street.—*Lansing v. Smith*, 21 Amer. Dec. 89; 1 Dill. Mun. Corp., § 106; *Dutton v. Strong*, 1 Black, 23.

As to the question of parties. We think the chancellor correctly decided, that the only proper party defendant to the present suit was John C. Webb. The bill has equity only, in the present state of its averments, as one to abate the erection of a fence as a nuisance. This is charged to have been done by John C. Webb alone. The other defendants are not shown to have authorized, or participated in it, and are in nowise connected with it.

It follows from the above principles, that the rulings of the chancellor on the demurrer were correct, and his decree is in all respects affirmed. The costs of the two appeals will be equally divided between the appellant and the appellees.

Affirmed.

McCLELLAN, J.—While concurring in the conclusions reached in the foregoing opinion, I desire to add the following, as expressing my reasons for holding the demurrer well taken to those allegations of the bill which seeks to have the right of the public in respect to the river declared and enforced.

The bill alleges generally, that the whole of Arch street to the water's edge was dedicated to the public in 1819. Had the averments on this subject stopped here, they would, in my opinion, have been sufficient to show that the public

had the absolute right to the free and unobstructed use of
the street, not only in passing up and down it, and from
other streets on to it, and from it on other streets, but also
in passing from this street on to the river, and *vice versa*;
and this right of user pertained as well to the transportation
of property as the passage of persons.   The collection of
tolls or wharfage is wholly inconsistent with this right of user,
and incompatible with the dedication to the water line.   The
claim of the defendants of the right to construct, maintain
and charge for the use of a wharf at the lower landing, or
to collect fees for the passage of persons or property into or
off from the river at that point, can be sustained only by proof
of a reservation of these rights out of the original dedication, and their connection with them as successors of the
original proprietors.   As a matter of pleading, however, construing the allegations of the bill most strongly against the
complainant, subsequent paragraphs qualify the general averment of dedication to the water's edge, and state facts which,
either of themselves, or in their relation to the other facts,
admit of the conclusion that there was a reservation by the
original dedicators of the wharfing or landing privilege,
and the right to charge tolls, &c., and that the defendants
have succeeded to these rights.   The bill fails to negative, with
sufficient certainty, the existence of this right thus acquired
in the defendants; and the demurrer on this ground was
properly sustained.

STONE, C. J., dissenting.—I think the bill, considered in
its entirety, leaves no room for any inference that wharfage
privileges were retained in the dedicator.

Massie *v*. Byrd.

*Action on Promissory Note, by Payee against Maker's
Executrix.*

1. *Confederate money as consideration; past or executed consideration.*
In an action on a promissory note, given in April, 1866, for the amount
of Confederate treasury-notes collected by the maker, as agent for the
payee, during the late war, the measure of the plaintiff's recovery is
not the value of the Confederate notes in lawful currency, as it might

[Massie v. Byrd.]

be if the action was founded on the original indebtedness; and the rule as to a past or executed consideration do s not apply.

2. *When action accrues on note.*—When a promissory note, though made payable "one day after date," contains a further stipulation for the punctual payment of interest annually, and of the principal "on thirty days notice;" a right of action on it, for the principal, does not accrue until the expiration of thirty days after demand or notice, and the statute of limitations does not begin to run until that time.

3. *Same; presumption as to demand or notice.*—When a promissory note, payable thirty days after demand or notice, provides for the punctual payment of interest annually, and it is otherwise shown that a long credit was contemplated; partial payments being made until the death of the maker eight years afterwards, after which the note was filed as a claim against his estate, and an action brought against his personal representative more than ten years afterwards; *held*, that it would be presumed that a demand, putting the statute of limitations in operation, was made within the time prescribed as a bar by the statute of non-claim, and that this presumption was not overcome by proof of a demand in fact made after the expiration of that time.

APPEAL from the Circuit Court of Dallas.

Tried before the Hon. JOHN MOORE.

This action was brought by Mrs. Sarah Massie, against Mrs. Maria Byrd, as the executrix of the last will and testament of her deceased husband, Wm. M. Byrd; and was commenced on the 17th January, 1887. The action was founded on a promissory note for $4,500, which was signed by said Wm. M. Byrd, dated April 20th, 1886, and in these words: "One day after date, I promise to pay Sarah Massie forty-five hundred dollars, and will pay the interest annually, punctually, and the principal on thirty days notice.", The first count of the complaint alleged that the note was "payable on thirty days notice, which has been given;" and the second, after setting out the note, alleged that notice was given on the 8th December, 1886. Each count alleged that the note was subject to certain credits, or partial payments, indorsed on it; the payments aggregating $4,300, as specified in the second count, and extending from January, 1867, to December 22, 1885.

The defendant filed eight pleas, but the third and fourth were afterwards withdrawn. The first plea was the general issue; the second, want of consideration; the fifth, payment; and issue was joined on each of them. The sixth plea was the statute of limitations of six years. The seventh alleged, that the only consideration of the note was Confederate treasury-notes, of the face value of four thousand dollars, which said W. M. Byrd had collected, as the agent of the plaintiff, in 1863 and 1864, but the real value of which was not more than one thousand dollars; that said Byrd paid

43

[Massie v. Byrd.]

three hundred dollars, on account of the debt, at the time of the execution of said note, and afterwards made partial payments, specifying the dates and amounts, "which were more than the value of all of said Confederate treasury-notes so collected, with interest thereon; wherefore defendant says that said promissory note was paid by said Byrd before the commencement of this suit." The eighth plea was also a special plea of payment, in substance the same as the seventh, with the additional averment that the Confederate treasury-notes were collected by Byrd on account of the hire of slaves belonging to plaintiff, and for money loaned by her to one Kent; and with a difference in the amounts and dates of the partial payments.

The plaintiff joined issue on the sixth plea, and filed special replications thereto, numbered from 2 to 5 respectively, as follows: (2.) That said note, setting it out, was payable only on thirty days notice; that the said W. M. Byrd made partial payments on said note, each year, from the time it was given, until his death in the Fall of 1874, and promised in writing to pay it; that the defendant, as his executrix, made partial payments each year, through an agent, which were entered as credits on the note at the special instance and request of said agent, and that plaintiff relied on these as a constant acknowledgment of the debt. (3.) That the said W. M. Byrd made partial payments on said note up to the time of his death, specifying the dates and amounts; and that the defendant, as his executrix, made other partial payments up to December 22d, 1885. (4.) That the note required thirty days notice before it became payable, and the notice was not given until the 8th December, 1886, so that the statute of limitations did not begin to run until January 8th, 1887. (5.) That the statute of limitations did not begin to run, as to the principal of said note, until January 8th, 1887, notice having been given on the 8th December, 1886. The second replication was afterwards amended, by alleging that Byrd was the plaintiff's son-in-law for thirty years, and was a judge of the Supreme Court when said note was given, and was learned in the law; that intimate and confidential relations existed between him and plaintiff until his death, and continued between plaintiff and defendant, who was her daughter, up to the year 1885.

To these replications the defendant demurred and rejoined, as follows: "(1.) Defendant rejoins and takes issue on plaintiff's replication No. 3 to the sixth plea. (2.) And for special rejoinder to said replication defendant says, that this defendant did not make any payment on said note within six years next before the commencement of this suit. (3.) And defendant demurs to plaintiff's replication No. 2, and for ground of demurrer says, 1st, that said replication does not show that this defendant made any payment on said note within six years next before the commencement of this suit, or that any payment was made thereon, at any time within six years next before the commencement of this suit, by any other person thereunto authorized by this defendant." A demurrer was also interposed to the 4th and 5th replications, which was sustained by the court, but the demurrer to the 2d was overruled. The defendant then took issue on said 2d replication, and filed special rejoinders thereto, namely: (2.) That said W. M. Byrd died in September, 1874; that the defendant was, on the 26th October, 1874, duly appointed as his sole executrix, and has continued to be such ever since; and that on the 6th August, 1875, plaintiff presented said note to defendant for payment, by filing the same as a claim against the testator's estate in the Probate Court of Dallas county. (3.) That ever since the 26th October, 1874, the defendant has been, and is now, the sole executrix of the will of said Byrd; and that no payment was made on said note within six years next before the commencement of this suit, either by this defendant, or by any other person authorized by her. A demurrer was interposed by plaintiff to each of these special rejoinders, but was overruled; and a demurrer having also been overruled to the seventh and eighth pleas, the judgment-entry recites that the plaintiff "declined to plead further; and it is therefore considered by the court, that the defendant go hence discharged," &c.

The rulings on the pleadings adverse to the plaintiff, and the judgment of the court, are now assigned as error.

R. A. McCLELLAN, and WHITE & WHITE, for appellant. (1.) If a contract is founded on valuable consideration, there can be no inquiry, as between the parties, into its adequacy. In the absence of fraud or duress, parties *sui juris* are free to make their own contracts, and the courts can not inquire into the sufficiency of the consideration which induced them. *Bolling v. Munchus*, 65 Ala. 558; 19 Ala. 765; 77 Ala. 554; 71 Ala. 429; 66 Ala. 151, 160; 1 Chitty on Contracts, 28-32; 1 Parsons on Contracts, 463; 5 Pick. 380; 5 Bing. N. C. 577; 1 Metc. 93. (2.) The note having been given after the war, the word *dollars* means lawful money of the United States.—8 Wall. 1; 51 Ala. 224. Parol evidence could not be received to show that Confederate money was intended; and it is too late to set up that defense, after admitted payments far in excess of the alleged value of that currency. 103 U. S. 193. Moreover, the note is supported by a sufficient consideration, because it was given in settlement of past dealings and transactions between the parties.—59 Ala. 535; 81 Ala. 464; 77 Ala. 554, 562. (3.) By the terms of the note, the principal was payable "on thirty days' notice;" and notice was not given until Dec. 8th, 1886. Until that time an action on it would not lie, and the statute of limitations did not begin to run.—*Glenn v. Semple,* 80 Ala. 159; 1 Add. Contracts, 406, 407; Angell on Limitations, 113-15; 2 Parsons on Notes, 639-44; Wood on Limitations, 255-63; *Thorp v. Booth,* R. & M. 388; *Sutton v. Toomer,* 7 B. & C. 416; 4 B. & Ald. 594; *Clayton v. Gosling,* 5 B. & C. 360; 54 Md. 548; 2 Daniel on Bills, 1215; 3 Rand. 1608; 72 Mo. 640; 2 Taunt. 323; 8 Dow. & R. 347; 4 Harr. Del. 246; 7 Wait's A. & D. 252. No presumption of notice or demand can be indulged from the lapse of time, since the note shows on its face that long time was contemplated, and the maker might have paid at any time without demand.

PETTUS & PETTUS, *contra.*—(1.) The note was payable one day after date, and bore interest from that time. If the interest had not been paid, an action might have been at once maintained on it; and the plaintiff would have been entitled to recover the entire debt, principal and interest, the contract being one and indivisible.—*O'Neal v. Brown,* 21 Ala. 484; *Railroad Co. v. Henlein,* 56 Ala. 573; *Oliver v. Holt,* 11 Ala. 574. (2.) When a note is payable on demand, the statute of limitations begins to run from its date, and not from the time of the demand.—*McDonnell v. Br. Bank,* 20 Ala. 312; *Owen v. Henderson,* 7 Ala. 641; *Wright v. Paine,* 62 Ala. 344. (3.) If a demand was necessary to put the statute of limitations into operation, the filing of the note as a claim against Byrd's estate was a sufficient demand. *McDowell v. Jones,* 58 Ala. 35; *Allen v. Elliott,* 67 Ala. 436; *Pollard v. Scears,* 28 Ala. 487; *Jones v. Lightfoot,* 10 Ala. 24. (4.) If a demand was necessary, it was required to be made within a reasonable time; and reasonable time means the period allowed by the statute of limitations. *Wright v. Paine,* 62 Ala. 340; *Codman v. Rogers,* 10 Pick.

[Massie v. Byrd.]

119; *Railroad Co. v. Township*, 59 Amer. (36 Kans.) 578.
(5.) Confederate money, as a consideration, should be scaled
down to its purchasing power at the time it was collected.
Emerson v. Heard, 81 Ala. 443; *Dickie v. Dickie*, 80 Ala.
57; *Spence v. Railway Co.*, 79 Ala. 576; *Whitfield v. Riddle*, 52 Ala. 467; *Thorington v. Smith*, 8 Wall. 1. (6.)
Giving a note for a pre-existing debt does not amount to
payment, and does not change the legal obligation of the
debt.—*Day v. Thompson*, 65 Ala. 273; 3 Wall. 37-45;
12 Peters, 32; 1 Salk. 124. (7.) The consideration of a
note may be impeached by plea (Code, §§ 2667, 2769);
and when a partial want of consideration is shown, a recovery is defeated *pro tanto.—Holland v. Adams*, 21 Ala. 680;
Dickinson v. Lewis, 34 Ala. 638; *Kirkpatrick v. Henson*,
81 Ala. 470; Chitty on Contracts, 773; *Long v. Davis*,
18 Ala. 801; Chitty on Bills, 70-71, mar., and notes. (8.)
In making contracts, parties *sui juris* are allowed to exercise
their own judgment and discretion—to put their own estimate upon the value of the property, services, or other thing
in reference to which they are negotiating. But this principle applies only to contracts founded on a present or future
consideration. When the consideration is wholly past and
executed, and no new consideration is added, the law fixes its
value, and a recovery on a breach is limited to that value.
This distinction is recognized by text-writers, and illustrated
by numerous adjudged cases.—1 Parsons on Contracts,
472-3; Whart. Contracts, § 514; 2 Chitty on Contracts, 71,
11th Amer. ed.; 2 Amer. Lead. Cases, 125-6; *Roscorla v.
Thomas*, 3 Q. B. 234.

CLOPTON, J.—The suit, which is brought by appellant,
is founded on a promissory note made by the testator of appellee, of which the following is a copy:
"$4,500. One day after date I promise to pay Sarah
Massie forty-five hundred dollars, and will pay the interest
annually, punctually, and the principal on thirty days notice.
"April 20, 1866.   W. M. BYRD."
The seventh and eighth special pleas allege, that in 1863
and 1864 defendant's testator, as the agent of the plaintiff,
collected about forty-five hundred dollars, in Confederate
treasury-notes, and on April 20, 1866, paid her three hundred dollars, and executed the note sued on, for and in consideration of the Confederate treasury-notes so collected,
without any other consideration. The pleas further aver,

that the real value of the treasury-notes when collected was one thousand dollars, and that payments exceeding that amount were made on the note during the life-time of the testator. The defense thus set us is, want of consideration as to a part, and payment of the balance of the note.

In general, the consideration of a note is open to inquiry, and parol evidence of the actual consideration may be received for the purpose of determining its legality or sufficiency to support the contract. The note is evidence that it was made on sufficient consideration, but it may be impeached by plea.—Code, 1886, § 2769. When the consideration of a contract in writing is divisible—when two or more distinct things or matters enter into and constitute the consideration— inquiry may be made as to either one of such things or matters, for the purpose of determining its sufficiency, and a recovery may be had for the part of the contract supported by sufficient consideration, and defeated as to the balance. *Holland v. Adams*, 21 Ala. 680, and *Dickerson v. Lewis*, 34 Ala. 638, afford illustrations of this rule. Inadequacy of consideration is not, of itself, a ground of relief against a contract, unless it is so gross as to amount to fraud or undue advantage. Parties *sui juris* may determine, in making contracts, the adequacy of the consideration, and, if of real value, it need not be adequate in order to support a contract deliberately made with knowledge of the facts. In the absence of circumstances of fraud, imposition, or undue advantage or influence, there can be no inquiry into, and no adjustment of the value of the consideration, if valuable. When such circumstances are wanting, and the consideration is entire and indivisible, its extent and value are not subjects of inquiry in an action at law to enforce the contract, for the purpose of determining its partial sufficiency, and to defeat a proportional recovery.—*Bolling v. Munchus*, 65 Ala. 558; 1 Pars. Contr. 436.

But appellee invokes the rule as to a past or executed consideration. The general rule is, that an executed consideration will not support an express promise, unless induced at the instance or request of the party promising, or the past transaction is of such a nature that the law will imply a promise. When the promise is implied from the character of the executed transaction, a subsequent promise is supported, and will be enforced, only so far as co-extensive with the amount or value of the past consideration. If the prior promise, whether express or implied, is to pay a determinate

[Massie v. Byrd.]

sum, or value, for the definite ascertainment of which the contract or the law furnished the standard, a subsequent promise to pay a larger sum is unsupported by a sufficient consideration as to the excess. But, when the amount of a past unliquidated demand is ascertained and agreed on by the parties, a new promise to pay the amount so ascertained is supported by a sufficient consideration.

The pleas show that the consideration of the note is valuable, and entire and indivisible, consisting of a liablility or indebtedness on account of Confederate treasury-notes collected by the maker as agent of the plaintiff, which he had failed to pay over, or to account for, until the execution of the note. The duty and obligation of an agent, who collected Confederate treasury-notes during the war, was to pay them over to his principal. On his failure to do so, and their appropriation to his own use, the law did not. imply a promise to pay only their value in the currency of the United States. There was neither an express nor an implied promise to pay any determinate sum or value other than their face amount. The demand was unliquidated in respect to the amount that should be paid after the close of the war. It is true that, since then, the courts generally have enforced such contracts only to the extent of their just obligation, and that the measure of recovery is the value in lawful money of the United States, at the time of making the contract, of the Confederate dollars agreed to be paid.—*Whitfield v. Riddle*, 52 Ala. 467; *Wyatt v. Evans*, 52 Ala. 285; *Thorington v. Smith*, 8 Wall. 1. But, these and similar decisions rest, not on a partial want of consideration, but on an agreement or understanding of the parties, that the note was to be paid in Confederate dollars. If no such agreement or understanding was proved, the amount of the note was collectible.—*Cook v. Lillo*, 103 U. S. 792; *Confed. Note Case*, 19 Wall. 548. It may be, had the present action been founded on the original indebtedness of the defendant's testator, the plaintiff could have recovered only the value of the Confederate money collected. But when, after the restoration of peace, he deliberately, and with knowledge of the facts and his rights, executed the note sued on, payable in lawful money of the United States, he waived the right to limit plaintiff's recovery to the value of Confederate money in a suit on the note. This may often work a hardship, and probably the ends of justice would be better accomplished, if, on any sound principle, the recovery could be measured by

the value of the consideration.   But a different rule would
open the consideration of every contract in writing to investigation and adjustment in exact proportion to its real value.
Trustees of How. Coll. v. Turner, 71 Ala. 429.

The sixth plea of defendant sets up the statute of limitations, and raises the question, at what time did the statute
begin to run against the note.   The language of the statute
is: "Civil suits must be commenced after the cause of action
has accrued, within the period prescribed in this chapter, and
not afterwards."—Code, 1876, § 3223.   Under the statute,
the question is, when did the cause of action accrue on the
note?   Counsel for the appellee insist, that the note became
due and payable, by its terms, one day after date, and that
plaintiff could then have commenced an action, without any
demand being previously made.   In the construction of all
written contracts, the fundamental rule is the ascertainment
of the intention and mutual understanding of the parties.
Their condition, the terms and nature of the contract, and
the objects in view, all are to be regarded.   The substantial
purpose and purport, as collected from the entire instrument,
will control the separate parts, intended as the means of its
accomplishment.   The note consists of two promises—one
to pay one day after date; the other, to pay the interest annually, and the principal on thirty days notice.   It was given
about a year after the restoration of peace, in consideration
of an antecedent indebtedness, created by the collection of
Confederate notes, without claiming any reduction.   Considering the circumstances and the language of the note, it is
evident that the parties intended and contemplated delay,
probably long delay, in the payment of the principal, but
annual payment of the interest.   In construing the note,
some effect should be given to each word and phrase.   Looking to all the provisions of the note and the circumstances,
the words "one day after date," it seems, were intended and
used to fix the time from which interest should begin to run,
and after which the payee might, at any time, give notice to
pay the principal; and the other provisions were intended to
qualify the general operation of these words, and fix the
times when the interest and principal should be payable respectively.   It is not an unconditional and absolute promise
to pay the principal and interest one day after date.   This
construction accomplishes the evident purpose of the parties,
and gives effect to each part of the note.—*Jameson v. Jameson*, 72 Mo. 640.   As to the principal, the note has the same

effect and operation as a note payable thirty days after demand or notice.

The authorities all concur, that a note for the payment of money on demand becomes due *instanter*, and a cause of action accrues thereon at once, and that the statute of limitations begins to run from that date.—*Owen v. Henderson*, 7 Ala. 641; *Mobile Sav. Bank v. McDonald*, 83 Ala. 595. But they somewhat conflict as to the time when the limitation begins to run against a note payable a given number of days after demand. In *Palmer v. Palmer*, 36 Mich. 487, it was held, that a cause of action accrues, for the purpose of setting the statute of limitations in motion, as soon as the creditor, by his own act, and in spite of the debtor, can make the demand payable; and that a note, payable thirty days after demand, is barred in six years after the expiration of thirty days from its date. This case has been severely criticised, as abrogating the contract of the parties, and incorporating a provision in the statute not intended by the legislature. Without reviewing them, we may remark generally, that the great weight of authority supports the doctrine that on such note a cause of action does not accrue, and the statute of limitations does not begin to run, until demand is made. Wood on Lim. § 118; Angell on Lim. 95; *Rhind v. Hyndman*, 54 Md. 527, where the authorities are cited. In *McDonnell v. Br. Bank at Mont.*, 20 Ala. 313, the rule, that the statute begins to run against a note, payable so many days after demand, from the demand, is stated with seeming approval; the reason assigned being, that until that time the action does not accrue. We, therefore, hold, that by the contract of the parties, a cause of action did not accrue as to the principal of the note, until notice was given as provided therein.

Counsel for the appellee further insist, that if it be held that notice is essential to the accrual of a cause of action, it should have been given, and suit brought, within six years from the date of the note. In *McDonnell v. Br. Bank of Montgomery*, *supra*, the suit was against a clerk, for money collected on a judgment. It was held that, in the absence of a conversion, no action could be maintained until the clerk was in default by refusal to pay on demand, and that the statute dates its commencement from the demand; but it was also held that the demand must be made within a reasonable time after the collection of the money. In *Wright v. Paine*, 62 Ala. 340, which was a suit to recover money deposited, it was held that a demand was a condition precedent to the action; but it is said: "When a demand is essential, as a condition precedent to an action, it must be made in a reasonable time. . . . The demand was made, and nearly six years is permitted to elapse, the death of Winston intervening, before suit is brought, and no explanation of this delay is afforded. It would be a dangerous precedent; it would endanger the estates of the dead; it would render the rights of the living uncertain and insecure; it would open the door for the introduction of stale demands, which, it has been well said, have often more cruelty than justice in them; and it would be violative of the policy of the statute of limitations, and defeat the purposes it was intended to accomplish, if, without an explanation of the long delay in making demand, and the unwarrantable delay in bringing suit, after the fruitless demand, until Winston [the bailee] was dead, the statute was held not a bar."

From these cases, the following principles may be deduced: (1.) When a demand is a condition precedent to a cause of action, the statute of limitations does not begin to run until demand is made. (2.) But, in such case, the demand must be made in a reasonable time. (3.) Delay in making the demand, and bringing suit within such period, may be explained and excused. It will be observed that, in none of these cases, was a delay in making the demand contemplated or intended; and in *Palmer v. Palmer, supra*, where it was held that the limitation begins to run at the expiration of thirty days from the date of the note, it is said: "It may be otherwise, possibly, where delay is contemplated by the express terms of the contract, and where a speedy demand would manifestly violate its intent." In *Glenn v. Semple*, 80 Ala. 159, the rule was applied, that when money is to be paid, or a thing is to be done, on the happening of a contingency or uncertain event, no cause of action accrues, and the limitation does not run, until the contingency happens, or the event takes place. It was held, that when the terms of subscription to the capital stock of a corporation bind the subscribers to pay "in such installments as may be called for by said company," a cause of action does not accrue, and the statute does not commence to run, until a call is made by the company, or an assessment and call is made by the decree of a court having jurisdiction. Parties may make their own contracts, and may agree upon a long or short credit, or upon a given number of days or months after demand. The

[Massie v. Byrd.]

statute of limitations was not intended to abrogate these rights, or to prevent parties from agreeing upon a term of credit however long. The decisions of this court recognize an obvious distinction between cases where a demand is essential to a cause of action, and no delay in making the demand is contemplated, and where delay is contemplated and intended. In none of them is it held, that when a demand is a condition precedent to bringing an action, it must be made and suit brought within the period prescribed by the statute of limitations. Whether or not the action is barred, is made dependent on the particular circumstances of the case, without attempting to define or declare, inflexibly, what is a reasonable time, in which the demand must be made. In a court of law, this is a question for the jury.

Fully appreciating the beneficial policy of the statute of limitations, having for its purpose the discouragement of stale demands, the security of repose and quiet, and the protection of parties from unjust and oppressive litigation, when the circumstances of the transaction and the injustice of the claim can not be shown because of the lapse of time, we realize the importance and necessity of some rule, which will avail, even in cases where long delay may be contemplated or intended, to accomplish the purposes of the statute, and promote its policy, without infringing the contract of the parties, or extending the statute beyond its terms liberally construed. While the rule in equity, in respect to stale demands and the assertion of claims, which is applied in the cases cited, may not be strictly applicable in a court of law, which is governed alone by the provisions of the statute of limitations; "courts of law will presume a demand from the lapse of time, especially when the circumstances render it improbable that it should be neglected."—Wood on Lim. § 125. On this presumption a consistent rule may be predicated.

The note sued on was made in April, 1866, and it is averred in the replications to the plea of the statute of limitations, that notice was not given until December, 1886, after the lapse of more than twenty years. The maker died in 1874; but partial payments were made by him to 1873. The note was filed as a claim against the estate, within the time the statute requires claims against the estates of deceased persons to be presented. The purpose of this is to require and promote the speedy settlement of estates. The delay of giving notice, contemplated by the parties, evidently terminated with the death of the maker. The circumstances render it

[Massie v. Byrd.]

improbable that giving the notice would be thereafter neglected. Considering the long period the note was permitted to run, the termination of the contemplated delay by the intervening death of the maker, the policy of the statute of limitations, and the purpose of requiring the presentation of claims, and the actual presentation of the note as a claim against the estate of the deceased maker, we are of opinion, without attempting to establish an inflexible rule, applicable to all cases, that under the circumstances of this case, a court of law will presume that a demand was made within the statutory period for the presentation of claims against the estates of deceased persons. An analogous rule was held in *Keithler v. Foster*, 22 Ohio St. 27. It is said: "Since then it is settled in this State, that the statute begins to run in cases like this from the time of demand, it would be but reasonable to hold, in the absence of other special circumstances, where no demand is shown to have been made within the statutory period for bringing the action, that for the purpose of setting the statute in operation, a demand will be presumed at the expiration of that period from which the statute will begin to run." This seems to be a reasonable and logical rule, which meets the requirements of the law in both classes of cases, where delay is and is not contemplated or intended, and does no violence to the contract of the parties, nor unduly extends the statute of limitations. On this presumption, the application of the rule in equity, as made in *Wright v. Paine, supra*, may be rested, and all the cases harmonized, without disturbing the former rulings. The presumption may be overcome; but, in order to overcome its force, and arrest the running of the statute, circumstances must be shown sufficient to explain and excuse delay in the assertion of claims, that would otherwise be deemed stale. Mere proof that demand was made in fact at a time later than that at which the law presumes a demand, is of itself insufficient.

The second replication of plaintiff, as amended, alleges facts which are intended as an explanation or excuse for the delay in giving notice. The court overruled a demurrer to this replication, and hence its sufficiency is not a question for our consideration. There was no error in sustaining the demurrer to the fourth and fifth replications. Plaintiff's demurrer to defendant's second and third rejoinder to the second replication should have been sustained. The third replication alleges that partial payments were made on the

[Jackson v. Rowell.]

note by the defendant's testator to November, 1873, and by the defendant, as executrix, to December, 1885. The defendant joined issue on this replication, and for a special rejoinder averred that she did not make any payments on the note at any time within six years next before the commencement of the suit. As the replication alleges that such payments were made, and the rejoinder that they were not made, there was a sufficient joinder on an issue of fact. Under our system of pleading, as provided and regulated by the Code, and the forms of pleas established, a formal *similiter* in such case is unnecessary. These conclusions render unnecessary a decision of the other questions argued by counsel.

Reversed and remanded.

McCLELLAN, J., not sitting, having been of counsel.

Jackson *v.* Rowell.

Bill in Equity between Distributees, Widow and Administrator, for Distribution, Allotment of Dower, and Settlement.

1. *Decedent's estate; premature filing of bill for distribution.*—A bill filed by the distributees of a decedent's estate, within eight months after the grant of letters of administration, against the administrator and the widow, alleging that the decedent left no debts. and that the funeral expenses and other charges have been paid off by the parties interested in the estate, and praying a distribution and settlement, is prematurely filed.

2. *Homestead exemption to surviving widow; sufficiency of averments of bill.*—Where the bill, filed by distributees against the administrator and the widow, praying (among other things) a sale of lands for partition and distribution, alleges that the decedent's homestead was on a tract of land containing forty acres, of value more than $2,000; "that the dwelling-house and outhouses, with other improvements on said tract of land, are of such character, quality and value, as well as structure, that the dower of the said Eliza [widow] can not be carved out of said tract and the improvements thereon, and assigned by metes and bounds to her, and it is necessary to sell said property in order to assign the dower interest to her;" not stating the value of the dwelling with the grounds immediately connected with it, nor the value of the other portions of the tract, and neither negativing nor alleging the ownership of any other lands (except an adjoining tract containing about thirty acres),—the necessity for a sale is not shown, the right of homestead or substitutionary exemption of other lands (Code, § 2544) not being negatived.

3. *Homestead and substitutionary exemption.*—When the decedent's homestead, reduced to the lowest possible area, still exceeds $2,000 in value, the widow has a right to select other lands in lieu thereof (Code, § 2544), and she may select lands of less value than $2,000.

4. *Undue influence in procuring conveyance; averment of.*—Undue influence, such as will operate to set aside a conveyance, must be sufficient to overcome the grantor's will; and an allegation in a bill seeking to set aside the conveyance, that the grantor, "when he was very feeble both in mind and body, was persuaded and induced, through some undue and improper influence unknown to complainants, to execute said instrument," without more, is not sufficient to impeach it.

5. *Bill of sale as testamentary paper.*—A written instrument, in the form of a bill of sale of personal property, which recites a consideration of $500 in hand paid, but is never delivered, the words being added: "This bill of sale to be placed in the hands of W. A. P., to be delivered to the parties mentioned in the event of my death," is a testamentary paper, and can only take effect as a will.

APPEAL from the Chancery Court of Mobile.

Heard before the Hon. THOS. W. COLEMAN.

The bill in this case was filed on the 26th July, 1888, by Mrs. Emily R. Jackson and her three sisters, married women and daughters of Wm. H. Rowell, deceased, against their mother, Mrs. Eliza C. Rowell, their brother, Wm. H. Rowell, Jr., and Joseph Espalla as administrator of said decedent's estate: and sought principally the removal of the administration, and a settlement and distribution of the estate. The decedent died, intestate, on the 15th April, 1887, and letters of administration on his estate were granted, on the 17th December, 1887, to said Espalla; and the bill alleged that there were no debts against his estate, and that his funeral expenses had been paid "by those interested in the estate." At the time of his death, the decedent was seized and possessed of a tract of land containing forty acres, on which his dwelling-house was situated, and which, with an adjoining tract containing about thirty-three acres, constitute his homestead, and was cultivated by him as a truckgarden. The bill alleged that the smaller tract was worth about $10 per acre, but there was no averment as to the value of the larger tract, except that it largely exceeded $2,000. The original bill alleged that the larger tract was the homestead of the decedent at the time of his death, while an amendment alleged that the two tracts together constituted the homestead. The bill alleged, also, that the widow and son had gathered and sold the crops growing on the lands at the time of decedent's death; and it sought to hold them accountable for the proceeds thereof, as well as for the other rents and profits of the lands during their continued possession. The bill alleged that the widow's dower in the lands could not be assigned by metes and bounds, and prayed a sale for partition and distribution.

On the 6th April, 1887, the decedent and his wife joined in a conveyance of the smaller tract of land to their son, said Wm. H. Rowell, Jr., on the recited consideration of $2,600 in hand paid; and on the same day the son re-conveyed a half interest in the property to his mother for life. The conveyance to the son, made "Exhibit B," was acknowledged by the grantor and his wife, but there was no privy examination of the wife; and the bill sought to set it aside, on the grounds (1) that it was procured by undue influence; (2) that it was without consideration, and (3) that it was not valid as an alienation of a part of the homestead. On the same day, April 6th, 1887, another instrument was executed by the decedent, or in his name, in the form of a bill of sale to Wm. H. Rowell, Jr. and his wife, of all farming utensils, horses, mules, furniture, &c., on the recited consideration of $500 in hand paid. This instrument, made "Exhibit D" to the bill, was attested by two witnesses, and to it was appended the name of the decedent, "*per* Sam McOlliphant;" and at the foot these words were written: "This bill of sale to be placed in Wm. A. Pollard's hands, to be delivered to the parties mentioned in the event of my death." The bill insisted that this instrument, if effectual for any purpose, was testamentary, and had never been admitted to probate, and sought to hold the said defendant liable for the property, or, if it should be valid as a gift, then to charge him with its value as an advancement.

The chancellor sustained a demurrur to the bill, on several grounds, and his decree is now assigned as error.

W. E. RICHARDSON, and H. CHAMBERLAIN, for appellant.

D. C. & W. S. ANDERSON, *contra.*

STONE, C. J.—It is not our intention to declare that a bill will in no case lie, where its objects are substantially such as are set forth and prayed in the present bill. There are cases in which the varying rights and methods of relief so connect and complicate the subjects-matter, as that only courts of chancery can render adequate and complete relief. *Handley v. Heflin*, 84 Ala. 600; *Marshall v. Marshall*, 86 Ala. 383; s. c., 5 So. Rep. 475.

The bill in this case alleges that Rowell, the decedent,

died in April, 1887, and that Espalla was appointed administrator of the estate in December, 1887. This bill was filed in less than eight months after Espalla's appointment, and seeks, in effect, to take the administration out of his hands, and transfer it to the Chancery Court; and there, by a sale and division of the property, to have a settlement of the estate. It charges against the administrator that he has returned no inventory to the court, and that he has not taken possession of the personal property of decedent. These, under some circumstances, would be grounds for the removal of the administrator.

As an excuse, as we suppose, for filing the bill so early, the bill charges, "upon information and belief, that the said William H. Rowell, deceased, left no debts at all, and that there were no claims against the estate of said William H. Rowell, deceased, save his funeral expenses, and they have been paid off by those interested in the estate. Complainants show further, that no claims at all have been presented to said administrator against said estate of William H. Rowell, deceased." Eighteen months are allowed after administration is granted, for presenting or filing claims against decedents' estates; and a settlement can not be enforced until after the expiration of eighteen months (Code of 1886, §§ 2134, 2192), unless the executor or administrator becomes satisfied before that time that the estate is solvent, and so reports; in which event, he may "obtain an order of distribution as to the whole, or any part of the property."—Code of 1886, § 2191. The bill does not make a case for coercive distribution, and was prematurely filed.

The bill alleges that the decedent's homestead, at the time of his death, was on a forty-acre tract of land, and describes the tract by initial points, bearings and distances. There was and is a surviving widow. It charges "that said homestead . . exceeds by a large sum the sum of two thousand dollars in value. . . . The complainants charge that the dwelling-house and out-houses, and other improvements on the said tract of land, are of such a character, quality and value, as well as structure, that the dower of said Eliza C. Rowell (the widow) can not be carved out of said tract and the improvements thereon, and assigned by metes and bounds to said Eliza C. Rowell, and complainants charge that it is necessary to sell said property, . . . in order to assign the dower interest to said widow." The bill alleges that the decedent died seized of another detached

parcel of land of thirty-three acres, worth six hundred and
sixty dollars, without houses, which was cultivated in common with, and constituted a part of the homestead. There
is no averment that the decedent owned no other lands.

The frame of the bill, its averments and prayer, all tend
to show that the complainants denied the widow's right to
homestead exemption, on the alleged ground, that it could
not be so carved out as not to exceed two thousand dollars
in value. The averments, looking to this end, are mere conclusions, and are insufficient. They do not set forth facts
to support the conclusion averred. The value of the dwelling, with the grounds immediately connected, should have
been stated; for homestead can not be refused, if, when reduced to the lowest practicable area, it does not exceed two
thousand dollars in value.—Code of 1886, § 2543. And so,
the value of the lands not covered by the dwelling should
have been stated; so as to show whether exemption in lieu
of homestead can or can not be selected and allotted.—Code
of 1886, § 2544. And it would be no bar to this right of
substitutionary selection, that the other real estate selected
is worth less than two thousand dollars. The greater right
obviously includes the lesser. The averment, that the forty
acres, with its improvements, was worth more than two
thousand dollars, was and is not explicit enough to deny
to the widow her right of homestead.

Nor does the fact, if it be a fact, that the house was Mr.
Rowell's residence at the time of his death, together with
the ground it stands on, if it exceeded two thousand dollars
in value, preclude the widow from asserting claim in lieu of
homestead, under section 2544 of the Code. This, for the
obvious reason, that a homestead which exceeds two thousand
dollars in value, is not an exempt homestead; and it is only
when the homestead is exempt, that the widow is denied the
right of selecting other lands in lieu of it. A residence can
not, at one and the same time, be an exempt homestead, so
as to preclude the right of selection and claim of other lands
in lieu of it, and yet, by reason of excess in value, not be
exempt as a homestead, and thus preclude its selection as
such.

The averment that the dower can not be allotted by metes
and bounds is imperfect, because it does not negative decedent's ownership of other lands.

The bill, among other things, seeks to set aside an alleged
conveyance of the thirty-three tract of land, made April 6,

44

[Jackson v. Rowell.]

1887, by William H. Rowell, Sr., and wife, to William H. Rowell, Jr. That part of the bill which assails this conveyance, because it was insufficiently acknowledged and certified to convey the homestead, is inconsistent with the averment that the forty-acre tract was the actual residence, and was, itself, worth more than two thousand dollars. If its value equalled or exceeded two thousand dollars, the detached thirty-three acres could not be a part of what the law denominates the homestead, although it may have been a part of the plantation used in connection with the dwelling-house, in which the husband resided next before his death, and, therefore, subject to the widow's right of quarantine occupancy.—Code of 1886, § 1900.

The bill, however, contains the following averment: "Complainants show that, on the 6th day of April, 1887, and a short time ·before he died, and when the said William H. Rowell was very feeble both in mind and body, he was persuaded and induced, through some undue and improper influence unknown to complainants, to execute the instrument of which exhibit B [the deed] is a copy." This is the entire charge of undue influence. It is insufficient. Undue influence, to destroy the force of a deed, must be such as to overcome the freedom of the grantor's will. And pleadings, to be sufficient, must aver the facts in substance, which show the domination of the grantor's will.—*Shipman v. Furniss*, 69 Ala. 555; *Dunlap v. Robinson*, 28 Ala. 100; 2 Brick. Dig. 540, § 228.

Whether the deed from the elder to the younger Rowell was with or without consideration, is a question which complainants can not raise. In this connection, they can assert only such rights as the decedent could assert, if living.

Exhibit D, relating to the personal property, can not operate as a deed, or bill of sale. The only operation it can have will be as a will.

The widow, surviving her husband, and having no minor child, is entitled to the exemptions of personal property which the statute provides.—Code of 1886, §§ 2545-2546. The bill does not sufficiently aver to what extent, if any, the personal property exceeded the exemptions; and hence it must be adjudged insufficient on this question.

The decree of the chancellor is affirmed.

[Gilman, Son & Co. v. Jones.]

Gilman, Son & Co. *v.* Jones.

Trover for Conversion of Railroad Bonds.

1. *Validity of contract; by what law determined.*—The legality of an agreement made in New York, respecting railroad bonds involved in a pending suit in Alabama, and which is to be carried into effect here, "would probably be governed by the laws of Alabama," and it is so considered in this case.

2. *Champerty and maintenance.*—The whole doctrine of maintenance, as at common law, "has been so modified in recent times as to confine it to strangers who, having no valuable interest in a suit, pragmatically interfere in it for the improper purpose of stirring up litigation and strife;" and champerty, which is a species of maintenance, "does not exist in the absence of this characteristic."

3. *Same; contract for sale of bonds in suit, purchaser agreeing to pay costs and expenses.*—A contract for the sale of negotiable railroad bonds, issued by a corporation which has become insolvent, and whose assets are being administered under a creditors' bill in equity, claims of priority being asserted by different bondholders, is not champertous, although the purchaser, who is not a party to the suit, assumes the payment of the costs and expenses incurred in the future litigation respecting the bonds, when it further appears that he was largely interested in another intersecting railroad, and was endeavoring to effect for it a lease of a part of the road of the insolvent corporation, which could not be accomplished on account of the dissent of the selling bondholder. (STONE, C. J. dissenting.)

4. *Construction of contract for sale of railroad bonds, at price dependent on contingency.*—Under a contract for the sale of certain bonds issued by an insolvent railroad corporation, which are involved in a pending suit under a creditors' bill, where claims of priority are asserted by a judgment creditor and by different bondholders; the purchaser paying $6,000 in cash, and agreeing to pay the further sum of $14,000, "provided and whenever it is finally decided in said suit, or otherwise, that said bonds are finally decided in said suit, or otherwise, that said bonds are a superior lien to the other bonds of said railroad and to said judgment," but, "in case such priority of lien shall not be so finally established, then said $6,000 shall be deemed and taken as full payment;" it being finally decided that said bonds were entitled to a prior lien over the judgment and the other bonds which had been filed in the cause when the contract was made, but other bondholders, whose claims were afterwards filed, being allowed to share in this priority; *held*, that the seller was not entitled to recover the $14,000, the contingency on which it was payable not having happened.

5. *Error without injury in ruling on pleadings.*—In an action of trover, if a demurrer to a special count in case is erroneously sustained, the error is immaterial, when the record shows that the plaintiff had the full benefit of the same facts under the count in trover.

APPEAL from the City Court of Montgomery.

Tried before the Hon. THOS. M. ARRINGTON.

This action was brought by the surviving partners of the late firm of Gilman, Son & Co., against A. W. Jones and

D. S. Troy, to recover damages for the alleged conversion of fifty-eight railroad bonds; and was commenced on the 24th December, 1886. The bonds were issued by the New Orleans & Selma Railroad Company and Immigration Association, for $1,000 each, negotiable in form, as shown more particularly in the report of the case of *Morton & Bliss v. N. O. & Selma Railway Company*, 72 Ala. 566, and 79 Ala. 595. The said corporation became insolvent, and a judgment for $17,478.20 was recovered against it by R. M. Robertson, who then filed a bill in equity in the City Court of Selma, against the corporation, T. H. Du Puy, Gilman, Sons & Co., Morton & Bliss, and several other persons, bondholders and creditors; claiming priority over the bondholders and other creditors, and asking a sale and distribution of the assets of the corporation under the decree of the court. Answers were filed by Gilman, Son & Co., Morton & Bliss, and other creditors, asserting their respective claims, and other proceedings were had, as shown by the reports of the case above referred to. On the 16th August, 1879, while said suit was pending in the lower court, Gilman, Son & Co. sold their fifty-eight bonds to said A. W. Jones, and deposited them in the hands of said D. S. Troy, to be delivered to Jones on the happening of the contingency named in the written contract of sale; and on the 28th October, 1886, after the final decision of the suit, Troy delivered them to Jones, taking from him a bond of indemnity against any claim on the part of Gilman, Son & Co.

The contract for the sale of the bonds was made in New York, was reduced to writing, and signed by Gilman, Son & Co. as parties of the first part, and by said A. W. Jones as party of the second part. It contained the following provisions: (1.) "The parties of the first part sell, and the party of the second part purchases from them, fifty-eight bonds," describing them, "now in the possession of J. T. Holtzclaw and D. S. Troy, of Alabama, as custodians, for use in the prosecution of a suit for enforcement of, or involving the same, now pending in the City Court of Selma, Alabama." (2.) "The party of the second part purchases said bonds subject to all contingencies of the suit above referred to, except as herein specified. He pays $6,000 to the parties of the first part, upon the execution of this contract, the receipt of which is hereby acknowledged; and he agrees to pay the further sum of $14,300 to them, provided and whenever it is finally decided in said suit, or otherwise, that said bonds are a superior lien to the other bonds of said railroad of the same issue, and also to a claim against said corporation known as the Robertson judgment; such last mentioned payment to be made in cash, whenever such final decision is made by the proper authority, and upon delivery to him also, or to his assigns, of the said bonds. In case such priority of lien shall not be so finally established, then the $6,000 already paid shall be deemed and taken as full payment for said bonds, which shall then be delivered to him without any further payment, except settlement of all legal expenses hereby assumed by him." (3.) "It is understood·that an arrangement already exists with said attorneys, by which the said parties of the first part are to pay them a further sum of $250, and which they hereby also agree to pay; and by which said attorneys are to receive five per cent. commissions, in case they do not succeed in establishing such priority, or ten per cent. commissions in case they do succeed therein; and the party of the second part hereby agrees to settle with said attorneys, including all their fees and legal expenses incurred and to be incurred, except said sum of $250 to be paid by the parties of the first part." (4.) "The parties of the first part agree and consent that the suit or suits now pending may be carried on in their names until final termination; but said party of the second part is to arrange with said attorneys and counsel, so as to exonerate said parties of the first part from all further legal liability, except as aforesaid, by assuming their position with said attorneys in that respect; but the party of the second part is to have the control and direction of the said suit or suits, subject only to the right of the parties of the first part to employ additional counsel at their own expense, if they shall see fit to do so, in their own interest." (5.) "The parties of the first part, if requested by the party of the second part, will give instructions to the counsel employed, to apply for the appointment of the receiver of the property of said corporation, as the party of the second part may desire, or agree to a lease of the same on like request, and will also do, in and about said suit, on his request, and at his expense, all and whatsoever he may reasonably request them to do, in accordance with this agreement, for the purpose of making the sale [same?] more effectual, or more advantageous to said party of the second part." (6.) "A copy of this agreement shall be deposited with said D. S. Troy, in trust, with a request that he assent to its terms, and agree to hold

the said bonds in trust for the respective parties hereto, subject to the present agreement, and to be disposed of as
herein expressed.   In witness whereof," &c.

The original complaint contained only a count in trover
for the conversion of the bonds, but two special counts in
case were added by amendment, each of which set out the
written contract, and claimed damages because Troy delivered the bonds to Jones in violation of its terms, and without
payment to plaintiff of the $14,300, as stipulated therein.
The court sustained a demurrer to the first special count,
and this ruling is here assigned as error; but it is not necessary to set out that count in full, since this court does not
consider its legal sufficiency.   The defendants pleaded not
guilty, and a special plea alleging that the bonds were delivered to Jones, after the termination of the suit, in strict
compliance with the terms of the contract; and issue was
joined on these pleas.   On the trial, the plaintiffs offered in
evidence the written contract, and the final decree of the
City Court of Selma, in accordance with the last decision
of this court, as shown by the report in 79 Ala. 590.   By
the terms of this decree, as shown more fully by the report
of the case, it was held that Gilman, Son & Co. were entitled,
as *bona fide* holders for value, to a priority of lien over the
Robertson judgment, and over the claims of Morton & Bliss
and other bondholders; but it was further held that Seligman
& Co., of New York, as the holders of forty-seven bonds,
which they had taken as collateral security for a debt which,
with interest, amounted to about $30,000, and which they
had not filed in said court until after the rendition of the
first decree, were also *bona fide* holders for value to the
amount of their secured debt, and entitled to share in the
assets on terms of equality with Gilman, Son & Co.   The
correspondence between the parties, prior to the contract for
the sale of the bonds, was in evidence; and also several letters written by plaintiffs to Troy after the final decision of
the case by this court, claiming that the decision was in their
favor, and forbidding him to deliver the bonds to Jones
without payment of the $14,300.   Jones testified on behalf
of the defendants, as to the circumstances connected with
his purchase of the bonds, having gone to New York for
that purpose on the invitation of the plaintiffs; and stated
that he made the purchase in the interest of the owners of
the Selma & Greensboro railroad (he being one of them),
. which intersected the New Orleans & Selma road at Eliza-

[Gilman, Son & Co. v. Jones.]

beth Station, for the purpose of effecting a lease of the latter road between that point and Selma, thereby saving annually about $20,000 to their own road; the plaintiffs, as bondholders, having refused to sanction such lease pending the suit.

On all the evidence, of which the above is the substance, the court charged the jury, on request, that they must find for the defendants, if they believed the evidence. The plaintiffs excepted to this charge, and they here assign it as error.

BRICKELL, SEMPLE & GUNTER, for appellant.—(1.) The contract for the sale of the bonds is to be tested, not by the law of New York, where it was entered into, but by the law of Alabama, where the suit was pending, and where performance was to be had.—*Grell v. Levy*, 16 C. B. Rep. 73; *Richardson v. Rowland*, 40 Conn. 572; *Kentucky v. Bassford*, 6 Hill, N. Y. 526; Greenhood on Public Policy, 398; *U. S. Bank v. Daniels*, 12 Peters, 54; 1 How. U. S. 169. (2.) Under the laws of Alabama, as declared by repeated decisions of this court, the contract was void for champerty, because the purchaser was not a party to the suit, and because he assumed the payment of the costs.—*Holloway v. Low*, 7 Porter, 88; *Dexter v. Nelson*, 6 Ala. 68; *Elliott v. McClelland*, 17 Ala. 209; *Dumas v. Smith*, 17 Ala. 305; *Poe v. Davis*, 29 Ala. 676; *Ware v. Russell*, 70 Ala. 174; *Thompson v. Marshall*, 36 Ala. 512. These decisions recognize the doctrine of champerty, and show how far it has been relaxed by modern decisions, or affected by statutory provisions. See, also, *Prosser v. Edmunds*, 1 Y. & C. 484; 2 Story's Equity, § 1040, note *G*; 6 Hill, N. Y. 526; 2 My. & K. 140; White & Tudor's L. C. Eq., vol. 2, pp. 1632-39. (3.) Even if the contract be held free from the taint of champerty, Jones was not entitled to the possession of the bonds until he paid the $14,300, additional to the cash payment. By the terms of the decision, a superior lien for the whole amount of their bonds was declared in favor of Gilman, Son & Co., and no one was given a priority over them; and though Seligman & Co. were allowed to prove, for a part of their debt, on equal terms with them, it must be noted that they were not parties to the suit when this contract was made, and it is to be presumed that the parties contracted in reference to its *status* at that time. Suppose Jones had realized the full amount of these bonds out of the assets, could he have refused to pay the $14,300?

[Gilman, Son & Co. v. Jones.]

E. W. Pettus, and T. B. Roy, *contra.*—(1.) By the laws of New York, where this contract was made, both parties being there, and where it was executed (for the payment of the $6,000 was all the purchaser had to do), its validity can not be questioned.—*Sedgwick v. Stanton*, 4 Kernan, 301; *Peck v. Briggs*, 3 Denio, 107; *Mott v. Small*, 20 Wend. 212; *Coughlan v. Railroad Co.*, 71 N. Y. 443. The whole doctrine of champerty, as it existed at common law, has been greatly relaxed by modern judicial decisions, both in this country and in England, and modified by statutory provisions. Story' Equity, § 1050; § Benj. Sales, 705-6; *Williams v. Prothers*, 5 Bing. 309; 2 Ap. Cases, 186; *Fender v. Parker*, 11 Mees. & W. 675; *McPherson v. Cox*, 96 U. S. 404. The essence of champerty is the unlawful intention of fomenting litigation, and it does not exist where the purchaser has, or honestly thinks he has, an interest in the pending suit, whether in its conduct, its result, or its subject-matter. *Vaughan v. Marable*, 64 Ala. 61-7; *Johnston v. Smith*, 70 Ala. 108; *Thompson v. Marshall*, 36 Ala. 512; *McCall v. Capehart*, 20 Ala. 526; *Ware v. Russell*, 70 Ala. 179; *Price v. Carney*, 75 Ala. 546; *Broughton v. Mitchell*, 64 Ala. 210; *Insurance Co. v. Tunstall*, 72 Ala. 142. At common law, a *chose* in action was not assignable, and this was the chief foundation of the law against champerty; but, in Alabama, by statutory provisions long of force, any *chose* in action is assignable, and the assignor had a right to sue in the name of the assignor, on giving indemnity for costs, before he was allowed to sue in his own name.—*Brazier v. Tarver*, 4 Ala. 569; Code, §§ 1762, 2594, 2601. *Choses* in action on which suits are pending, are not excepted from the operation of the statute, and are clearly within its spirit and policy. Railroad bonds, such as these, are negotiable instruments, and are so made on principles of public policy. A pending suit does not destroy their negotiability.—*Winston v. Westfeldt*, 22 Ala. 760. The defendant's interest in the subject-matter of the suit is clearly shown by the evidence. (5.) The contract has been executed, and its validity can not now be assailed.—*Taylor v. Bowers*, 1 Q. B. D. 291; 103 U. S. 59; *Black v. Oliver*, 1 Ala. 450; 2 Benj. Sales, 680. (3.) Under the terms of the decision, the $14,300 never became payable.

SOMERVILLE, J.—The action is one of *trover* brought by the appellants against the appellees, for the alleged conversion of fifty-eight bonds, of one thousand dollars each, issued by the New Orleans & Selma Railroad Company. There are also two counts added by way of amendment, in *case*, based on the alleged unlawful use of the bonds, and of the decree of the Chancery Court in which they were merged.

The main point of controversy in the case is, whether the contract of August 16, 1879, between the plaintiffs, Gilman, Son & Co., on one side, and the defendants, A. W. Jones and D. S. Troy, as trustee, on the other, is void for *champerty*. Under this agreement, which was made in the State of New York, Jones purchased from the plaintiffs these bonds, for which a suit, by cross-bill, was then pending in the City Court of Selma, Alabama, sitting in equity.—*Morton v. N. O. & S. R. R. Co.*, 79 Ala. 590. They were to be held in trust by the defendant Troy, who then had custody of them as an attorney of the appellants, and were not to be delivered until the termination of the suit, and the payment of the agreed price. The litigation was to be continued in the name of the sellers, and the purchaser was to pay the attorney's fees, and "legal expenses incurred and to be incurred," except a retainer fee of two hundred and fifty dollars due by the present plaintiffs to their attorneys in that suit.

It is shown that in the State of New York, where this contract was entered into, there was no law of champerty which would render it illegal. The contract, consequently, was legal, when tested by the law of that State.—*Sedgwick v. Stanton*, 14 N. Y. 289; *Thallhimer v. Brinkerhoff*, 3 Cow. 623; s. c., 15 Amer. Dec. 308. But, as the agreement of the parties was to be carried into effect in the State of Alabama, where the suit was pending, the question of its legality would probably be governed by the laws of the latter State, according to the authorities, and we shall so consider it. 1 Addison, Contr. (Amer. Ed., Morgan), § 257, p. 391; *Grell v. Levy*, 16 C. B. (N. S.) 73; *Richard v. Rowland*, 40 Conn. 565.

Champerty is a species of maintenance, which at common law was an indictable offense. Maintenance was an officious intermeddling in a lawsuit by a mere stranger without profit. Champerty involved the element of compensation for such unlawful interference, by bargain for part of the matter in suit, or some profit growing out of it, or, according to some of the authors, as well also for the whole of the thing in dispute.—1 Hawk. P. C. 462-463; 3 Amer. & Eng. Encyc.

Law, 68–69; *Holloway v. Lowe*, 7 Port. 488; *Poe v. Davis*, 29 Ala. 683; *Ware v. Russell*, 70 Ala. 174. It would accomplish no good to quote at length the numberless definitions of these offenses given in the old books. Sir James Stephen, in his Digest of Criminal Law (note VIII), alludes to the vagueness with which these crimes are defined by the ancient common-law writers, and discusses the reasons why they have long since become obsolete. The ground of their origin is found in the familiar principle stated by Lord Coke: "Nothing," he says, "in action, entry or re-entry, can be granted over; for so, under color thereof, pretended titles might be granted to great men, whereby right might be trodden down, and the weak oppressed."—Co. Lit. 114a. It was a part of the law of maintenance, that no *chose in action*, which included all rights not reduced to possession, could be assigned or transferred. This was on the ground, as said by Mr. Chitty, that "such alienations tended to increase maintenance and litigation, and afforded means to powerful men to purchase rights of action, and thereby enable them to oppress indigent debtors, whose original creditors would not perhaps have sued them."—Chitty on Bills, *6-*7. It is common knowledge, however, that this rule, refusing to sanction, or give effect to the assignment of *choses* in action, was never adopted by courts of equity, either in England or in this country, and that courts of law, yielding to the growing exactions of commerce, finally allowed the assignees of such rights to maintain suits in the name of their assignors. 2 Story's Eq. Jur. § 1050. Such assignments are now expressly authorized by the statutes of this State.—Code, 1886, §§ 1762-63, 2594.

The peculiar state of society, out of which such a law grew, carried it to the most absurd extremes. Men were held indictable for aiding a litigant to find a lawyer; for giving friendly advice to a neighbor, as to his legal rights; for lending money to a friend, to vindicate his known legal rights; for offering voluntarily to testify in a pending suit, and other like offices of charity and friendship.—3 Amer. & Eng. Encyc. Law, 71. It is not surprising, therefore, that the law on this subject has gradually undergone a great change, which is recognized universally by jurists, judges and law-writers everywhere. This change has been called for by the new conditions of modern society, considered in its varied relations, commercial, political, and sociological. In many of its phases, it has been, both in America and

England, emphatically discarded, as "inapplicable to the present condition of society, and obsolete."—*Sedgwick v. Stanton*, 14 N. Y. 289, 296; *Masters v. Miller*, 4 Term R. 320; *Thallhimer v. Brinckerhoff*, 3 Cow. 623; s. c., 15 Amer. Dec. 308; *Richardson v. Rowland*, 40 Conn. 565; 2 Whart. Cr. L. (8th Ed.), § 1854, note. It is accordingly asserted, on high English authority, that no one has been punished criminally for the offense of maintenance or champerty within the memory of living man.—3 Stephen's Hist. Crim. Law, 234. Public opinion in England has advanced so far on this subject, that the Criminal Law Commissioners many years ago recommended very earnestly that the offenses of maintenance and champerty be abolished, observing of them, that they "are relics of an age when courts of justice were liable to intimidation by the rich and powerful and their dependents."—Stephen's Dig. Crim. Law, *note* VIII.

There is much reason, it thus seems, for the relaxation of the old doctrines pertaining to the subject, so that they may be adapted to the new order of things in the present highly progressive and commercial age. Necessity and justice have, accordingly, forced the establishment of recognized exceptions to the doctrine of these offenses. Among these may be enumerated the following instances: Relationship by blood or marriage will often now justify parties in giving each other assistance in law suits; and the relation of attorney and client; or the extension of charitable aid to the poor and oppressed litigant; and especially is an interference in a law suit excusable, when it is by one who has, or honestly believes he has, *a valuable interest* in its prosecution. It is especially with the last mentioned exception we are concerned in the present case, which, in our judgment, is controlled by it.

The principle is thus generally stated in 3 Amer. & Eng. Encyc. Law. p. 76: "It has been seen that the *gist* of the offense of maintenance is, that the interference is *officious;* where, therefore, a party either has, or honestly believes he has, *an interest*, either in the subject-matter of the litigation, or in the question to be determined, he may assist in the prosecution or defense of the suit, either by furnishing counsel, or contributing to the expenses, and may, in order to strengthen his position, purchase the interest of another party in addition to his own. The interest may be either small or great, certain or uncertain, vested or contingent; but it is essential that it be distinct from what he may acquire from the party maintained." In *Thompson v. Marshall*, 36 Ala. 504; s. c., 76 Amer. Dec. 328, this principle was applied to a case where one co-defendant, in a suit pending to rescind a conveyance for fraud, purchased the interest of his co-defendant in the property in litigation, and assumed a liability for his vendor's share of the costs and expenses of suit. The contract of purchase was held not to be champertous, because the interference was to protect a valuable interest, and was not, therefore, either an unlawful or officious intermeddling. So, in *McCall v. Capehart*, 20 Ala. 521, where certain persons, erroneously believing that they had an interest in a piece of land then in litigation, purchased the interest of the defendant, and indemnified him against the costs and damages of suit, the court held the transaction free from the taint of champerty, on the ground that the assistance was rendered by the defendants "under the honest belief that they were interested in the result of the suit, and not for the purpose of fomenting litigation."

The modern and better definitions of champerty incorporate this idea fully. Mr. Wharton says: "Maintenance is support given to a litigant in any legal proceeding in which the person giving the assistance *has no valuable interest*, or in which he assists for an improper motive."—2 Whart. Crim. Law. (9th Ed.), § 1854. In 2 Bouvier's Law Dict. (14th Ed.) 90, it is defined to be "a malicious, or at least officious interference, in a suit in which the offender *has no interest*, to assist one of the parties to it against the other with money or advice to prosecute or defend the action, without any authority of law." So, Mr. Addison involves in the definition the idea of agreeing to assist in the prosecution of a law suit, "in which the party making the agreement is *in no wise interested*, and with which he has no just or reasonable ground for interference."—1 Add. Contr. 256. Of course, it is necessarily true that, if the offense in question does not amount to maintenance, there can be no champerty in it, because, as we have said, champerty is but a species of maintenance.—2 Co. Inst. 207.

In *Thallhimer v. Brinckerhoff*, 3 Cow. 623; s. c., 15 Amer. Dec. 308, 314, a leading and learned case on the subject of champerty, it is said, "that any interest whatever in the subject of the suit is sufficient to exempt him who gives aid to the suitor from the charge of illegal assistance." And referring to such interferences, it is said: "Upon all such cases these laws were never intended to operate. They

[Gilman, Son & Co. v. Jones.]

were intended to prevent the interference of strangers having no pretense of right to the subject-matter of the suit, and standing in no relation of duty to the suitor. They were intended to prevent traffic in doubtful claims, and to operate upon buyers of pretended rights, who had no relation to the suitor, or the subject, than as purchaser of the profits of litigations." In *Ware v. Russell*, 70 Ala. 174; s. c., 45 Amer. Rep. 82, this court sustained an agreement between attorney and client, as free from champerty or maintenance, where the defendant in attachment, in consideration of professional services on the part of the assignee, assigned to his attorney the entire property in litigation, giving him the entire management and control of the suit, and stipulating for his own, the assignor's, active prosecution of it. It was said by BRICKELL, C. J.: "The corrupting element of the contract [of champerty] is its tendency to foment or protract litigation, its dependency for its value upon the termination of suits, and its introduction, to control and manage them, of parties *without other right or interest* than such as is derived from the contract." In *Call v. Calƒ*, 13 Met. 362, where two persons owned distinct rights to the exclusive use of a patent in two different places, near each other, it was held, that the interest which each had in maintaining the value and profit of his particular right would justify him in aiding the other to prosecute a suit for the infringement of the exclusive right of the latter. So it has been held, and is manifest, that any citizen may lawfully contribute to the lawful expenses of any public criminal prosecution, and the act will not subject him to the charge of maintenance. *Com. v. Dupuy*, Brightly (Pa.) 44. See, also, Story on Contr. § 579; Parsons Contr. *765-*766; 2 Story's Eq. Jur. § 1050.

We may safely say that the whole doctrine of maintenance has been modified in recent times, so as to confine it to strangers who, having no valuable interest in a suit, pragmatically interfere in it for the improper purpose of stirring up litigation and strife. And champerty, which is a species of maintenance attended with a bargain for a part or the whole of the thing in dispute, does not exist in the absence of this characteristic of maintenance. If the pecuniary interest of a person, even though he own no part of the immediate subject-matter of the suit, be so connected with it collaterally in any way as to be diminished or increased in value by the result of such suit, we can perceive no principle of public

[Gilman, Son & Co. v. Jones.]

policy that ought to forbid such person from taking proper care that such interest shall be properly protected in the courts. The forfeiture of the charter of a railroad, for example, on the line of which the owner of a factory or rolling-mill may have his plant, might result in his financial ruin; could it be said, in the light of modern views on this subject, that an agreement to aid in preventing the forfeiture would be champertous, and as such criminal, because the mill-owner held no stock in the railroad company, nor was otherwise immediately interested in the corporate charter or property? Interference in law suits, it has been said, to savor of maintenance, "must have some tendency to pervert the cause of justice" (*Stanley v. Jones*, 7 Bing. 369), or else, as said by Blackstone, "to pervert the remedial process of the law into an engine of oppression."—4 Bla. Com. 135. These elements of unlawfulness are entirely wanting in the supposed case.

Mr. Story asserts, that one "may purchase by assignment the whole interest of another in a contract or security, or other property, which is in litigation, provided there is nothing in the contract which savors of maintenance—that is, provided he does not undertake to pay any costs, or make any advance *beyond* the mere support of the exclusive interest which he has so acquired." And he puts his conclusion upon the ground, that a court of equity would, without special contract, *compel* the assignor to permit his name to be used in the suit, on the assignee's giving him indemnity for such costs. "Such indemnity, and such proceedings, under such circumstances," he adds, "are not deemed maintenance."—2 Story's Eq. Jur. § 1050. This seems to be the more correct and logical view, and better comports with the necessities of modern commerce, except as to transactions between client and attorney, which, by reason of their peculiar relations, ought perhaps to stand on a different basis from other contracts savoring of a maintenous character. *Ware v. Russell*, 70 Ala. 174; s. c., 45 Amer. Rep. 82; *Elliott v. McClelland*, 17 Ala. 206. Although, by the great weight of modern authority, contingent fees of a legitimate character charged for professional services, dependent on the amount of recovery, are not deemed within the rules against champerty and maintenance.—*Thallhimer v. Brinckerhoff*, 15 Amer. Dec. 321, *note*, and cases cited; *Stanton v. Embrey*, 93 U. S. 548; *Blaisdell v. Ahern*, 144 Mass. 393; s. c., 59 Amer. Rep. 99; *Walker v. Cuthbert*, 10 Ala. 213, 219.

VOL. LXXXVII.

But we prefer to place our decision in this case upon the broad ground, that the interest possessed by the defendant Jones in the pending suit, involving the fate of the Selma & New Orleans Railroad, was sufficient to rescue this transaction from the element of officious intermeddling, or pragmatical interference on his part. He and his associates owned another railroad, called the Selma & Greensboro Railroad, which was in operation between Akron and Marion Junction. The bed of the road extended from the latter point to Elizabeth Station, a point on the New Orleans & Selma road; and on this portion of the track, iron had formerly been laid, but was removed by the Confederate Government during the late war. The owners of the Selma & Greensboro road had no access to Selma, except over the track of the Alabama Central Railroad, and at a very heavy expense, by way of rental compensation. To avoid this expense, and thus appreciate the value and increase the profits of their road, they formed the plan of leasing or buying the Selma & New Orleans road, so as to connect with it at Elizabeth Station, and have an open route of their own to Selma. Negotiations were opened with the trustee of the litigant bond-holders, and the bond-holders themselves, all of whom except Gilman, Son & Co., the plaintiffs in this suit, gave their consent to have such lease to be legalized by approval of the Chancery Court in which the suit was pending. These particular bonds were purchased, and the agreement of August 16th, 1879, entered into, in order to consummate this enterprise. As stated by the record, the purpose of Jones was to enable him and his associates "to obtain the use of the New Orleans & Selma Railroad, to run their cars over from Elizabeth Station to Selma; and, soon after such purchase, the proposed lease was made with the approval of the court, and the Selma & Greensboro road was put in order and ironed afresh to Elizabeth Station, and used by it to run their cars to the latter point, and thence on the said New Orleans & Selma Railroad into Selma." It is argued by counsel, with much reason, that the interest which the purchasers had in the Selma & New Orleans road—the one in litigation—was emphasized by the existing right of the Selma & Greensboro road "to intersect, connect with, or cross" the former road at any point, and the duty of each road to receive and transport the cars of the other without delay or discrimination, as guaranteed by law.—Const. 1875, Art. XIV, § 21; *A. G. S. R. R. Co. v. S. & N. R. R. Co.*, 84 Ala.

570. We hold that these facts relieved the contract in question of all taint of champerty, irrespective of other considerations which we do not propose to discuss.

There are other grounds, which, in our opinion, would justify the conclusion reached by the City Court adverse to the plaintiffs, but we need not consider them.

The action of the court in sustaining the demurrer to the second count of the complaint becomes immaterial, in view of the fact that the plaintiff, in the trial of the cause, had the full benefit of the issues raised under that count, under the first count.

On the remaining point, we entertain no doubt. This involves the right of the plaintiffs to recover the further sum of $14,300.00, additional to the cash installment of $6,000, already paid. This sum was made payable by the terms of the contract only contingently, "whenever it is finally decided in said suit, or otherwise, that said bonds are a *superior* lien to the other bonds of said Railroad and Immigration Company of the same issue," and to what was known as the Robertson judgment, which was the basis of said chancery suit. "Superior" means higher in dignity, quality, or excellency.—Worcester's Dict. Here it manifestly means *prior*— superior lien meaning prior lien. This is made clearer, if possible, by a subsequent provision in the contract itself, that "in case such *priority* of lien shall not be finally established," then the six thousand dollars already paid shall be deemed full payment, without any further payment, except settlement of the legal expenses assumed by Jones. This, moreover, was the main question in controversy in the case to which the agreement had reference, the proceedings in which are made a part of the present record.—*Morton v. N. O. & S. Railway Co.*, 79 Ala. 590. The bonds of Gilman, Son & Co. were not decided to be a superior lien to all other bonds of the same issue. The record shows that an equal priority was accorded by the decree of this court to forty-seven other bonds held by Seligman & Co., as collateral security, for which they were allowed to prove on terms of perfect equality with Gilman, Son & Co., as *bona fide* holders without notice of any infirmity of title in them. This fact is fatal to the contention of appellants on this particular point.

We discover no error in the judgment of the City Court, either in sustaining the demurrer of appellees to the second count of the complaint, or in the charge given the jury, to find for the defendants if they believed the evidence.

Affirmed.

STONE, C. J., dissenting.—I do not think Jones shows such an interest in the litigation, or subject-matter of the suit, as relieves him of the imputation of maintenance. To have that effect, I hold that he must have had a pecuniary, or property interest. Mere benefit, or assistance to some other independent enterprise he was prosecuting, is not enough. Few, if any, contracts would be made, if the contracting parties did not each believe they were thereby securing to themselves some profit, benefit, or pleasure.

Cofer *v.* Moore.

Bill in Equity for Rescission of Contract, on ground of Fraud.

1. *Rescission of contract on ground of fraud.*—A court of equity will rescind a contract into which the party complaining was induced to enter by the misrepresentation of a material fact by the other party, on which he might properly rely, and by which he was injured; as here, where the complainant, a non-resident, was entitled to a half interest in the estate of his deceased grandmother, which estate was worth between $3,000 and $4,000, and was induced to sell his interest for $300 to a cousin, who was entitled to a part of the other half interest, and who was well acquainted with all the facts relating to the estate; and the contract being rescinded as against the party who procured it, a third person who was interested with him in the purchase, but who had no part in the fraudulent misrepresentations, can take no benefit under it.

APPEAL from the Chancery Court of Cullman.
Heard before the Hon. THOMAS COBBS.

W. T. L. COFER, and J. W. AUSTIN, for appellants.

PARKER & BROWN, *contra.*

CLOPTON, J.—Appellee seeks by the bill the cancellation of a conveyance of all his right, title and interest in and to the estate of Sarah Moore, to appellants, the ground of relief being that it was obtained by fraudulent misrepresentations. Sarah Moore, who was the grand-mother of complainant, and of the defendant, George G. Markland, died intestate in October, 1886, being at the time of her death a resident of the county of Cullman in this State. As heir and distributee, complainant is entitled to one half, and

45

Markland and his brothers and sisters, seven in number, to
the other half of the estate of decedent.   The charge of
fraud is, a misrepresentation as to the condition and value of
the estate, by which complainant was induced to sacrifice his
interest for an inadequate consideration.   The equity of the
bill rests on the general doctrine, that a party is entitled to
avoid a contract, into which he has been induced to enter, by
a misrepresentation by the other contracting party, of a fact
directly relating to the subject-matter, and material to the
transaction, upon which the party to whom it is addressed
may reasonably rely and act.   The bill alleges all the ele-.
ments essential to constitute a misrepresentation fraudulent.
There can be no question as to its equity.   Without specially reviewing the evidence, we remark, that it satisfactorily establishes the allegations of the bill.

The specific representations charged to have been made by
Markland are, that Sarah Moore had left a small estate,
which consisted of a house and lot in the town of Cullman,
and sixty or eighty acres of pine land, the entire estate being
worth about one thousand dollars; that there was no administration on the estate, but Charles Albes, their uncle, wanted
to be appointed administrator; that he, Markland, had applied for the appointment of himself, and if Albes was appointed, the heirs would not get anything; and also, that he
had bought the interest of some of the heirs for seventy-five
dollars each, and proposed to give complainant three hundred dollars for his interest, as he was entitled to one half.
This was an affirmative statement of existing facts, relating
to the subject-matter, and material to the transaction, in con-
tra-distinction to a mere expression of opinion, judgment, or
expectation.

Letters of administration had been previously issued to
Albes.   Markland had made application to the Probate
Court, to revoke these letters, and to grant the administration to him.   His application was refused, January 17,
1887.   A few days thereafter, he left Alabama, by agreement with his co-defendant, Cofer, to go to Arkansas, for the
purpose of purchasing, for the benefit of both, the share of
complainant in the estate.   On January 25, just eight days
afterwards, he arrived in Arkansas, where complainant resided, and had been residing for several years.   Immediately
after his arrival he had an interview with complainant, and
also with his mother and step-father, at which time he made
the representations charged.   On the following day the trade

was concluded, and the conveyance executed. The representations having been prior to the transaction, and being of such character that the natural and necessary consequence was to induce complainant to enter into the contract, the presumption arises, that they were made with the design to induce such action. But we need not depend on a presumption; the facts and circumstances clearly show that the purpose and design of Markland, in making the statement, was to induce complainant to sell his interest in the estate for a small price.

It is evident from the proof, that the estate consisted of two hundred acres of land, a house and lot in Cullman, and over twenty-eight hundred dollars of solvent notes, the aggregate value exceeding four thousand dollars. Markland, in his application to revoke the letters issued to Albes, which was verified by him, states that the property of the estate was worth about three thousand dollars. The falsity of the representations, of which Markland had actual and positive knowledge, is clearly shown. It is equally manifest that, under the circumstances, complainant was justified in relying upon the statements, and that they were the immediate cause of his entering into the contract of sale. He was ignorant of his grandmother's death, and also of the nature and value of her estate, until informed by Markland, who was his cousin, and had been in Alabama looking after the estate. Complainant had no opportunity to resort to any means, or make any examination, to ascertain the truth of the statements. They were concerning facts of which Markland had knowledge, and complainant was uninformed. Markland having made statements, of the untruth of which he had actual and positive knowledge, and also of complainant's ignorance, the intent to deceive necessarily results.—2 Pom. Jur. §§ 876-892.

The price at which Markland purchased complainant's interest was three hundred dollars, fifty dollars to be paid as soon as it could be sent by his co-defendant and co-purchaser, and the balance in thirty, sixty and ninety days, not exceeding one-fifth of the real value of his interest. While inadequacy of consideration, of itself, is not a ground of relief, unless so gross as to shock the conscience, when connected with suspicious circumstances or misrepresentations of material facts, it affords a vehement, if not conclusive evidence of fraud.

The defendant Cofer, in his testimony, denies that there

was any agreement or understanding between him and Markland, to resort to any means or misrepresentations to induce complainant to sell his interest. On his testimony, which is unimpeached, and uncontradicted, he must be acquitted of any fraudulent design or purpose. Notwithstanding, he can obtain no advantage or benefit from the fraud of Markland, who was his co-purchaser, and represented him in the transaction. The burden of fraud passes to him, though he may be innocent.

We concur in the rulings and conclusions of the chancellor.

Affirmed.

Louisville & Nashville Railroad Co. v. Hall.

Action by Brakeman against Railroad Company, for Damages on account of Personal Injuries.

1. *Railroad bridges across public road* —In the construction of a bridge across a public road, it is the duty of a railroad company to place the structure at such an elevation that trains can safely pass under it with their customary employes; yet it may be placed below the line of absolute safety, when inequality of surface, or other hindrance, occurring naturally, or in the proper construction or grade of the railroad track, renders such elevation impossible, or would greatly incommode the public in the use of the bridge, or unduly increase the expense to the railroad company; but in no case is it permissible to erect the bridge at an elevation so low that brakemen, while in the discharge of their duties on the top of a car, can not avoid danger by bending or stooping.

2. *Same; statutory regulations as to blowing whistle or ringing bell.* The statutory provision requiring the conductor or engineer of a moving locomotive or train of cars, on approaching a public road crossing, to blow the whistle or ring the bell (Code, § 1144), is intended for the protection of persons who are approaching or crossing the track of the road, and has no application to a case in which a brakeman sues for personal injuries, caused by his being struck by the bridge overhead while on top of one of the cars.

3. *Appliances and warning signals for protection of employes.*—In the use of appliances or instrumentalities for the protection of its employes, when approaching a public road crossing spanned by a bridge overhead, such as "whipping straps," a cautionary light on the bridge, &c., the duty and liability of a railroad company are determined by utility and the usage and custom of well-regulated railroads; if many railroads abstain from their use, the failure to use them is not negligence; and their use by a majority of railroads does not require all railroads to use them, nor impute negligence on account of the failure to use them.

[Louisville & Nashville R. R. Co. v. Hall.]

4. *Notice to brakeman of low bridge overhead; contributory negligence.* When a brakeman is employed on a railroad with which he is not familiar, and is required, in the performance of his duties, to pass under a low bridge spanning the track, which, though not high enough to allow him to pass in an erect position on top of a car, is yet high enough to meet legal requirements, it is the duty of the railroad company to give him reasonable notice of the danger; but, if, having been duly notified, he fails, from inattention, indifference, absent-mindedness or forgetfulness, to inform himself of the particular facts, or to take the necessary steps to avoid injury—in other words, if he fails to exercise the care, watchfulness and caution which men of ordinary prudence would exercise under the circumstances—he is guilty of contributory negligence.

5. *Sufficiency of complaint.*—Where the complaint claims damages on account of personal injuries sustained by a brakeman in the employment of a railroad company, by being struck by a bridge overhead across a public road, while on the top of a car in the discharge of his duties, the complaint must aver that the bridge was erected or maintained by the railroad company.

6. *Error without injury in ruling on pleadings.*—The sustaining of a demurrer to a special plea, if erroneous, is error without injury, when the record shows that the defendant had the full benefit of the same defense under another special plea.

7. *General notoriety as evidence.*—General notoriety is sometimes admissible evidence, as tending to prove notice of a fact, when notice thereof is material; but never to prove the existence of the fact itself.

8. *Expert testimony as to railroad appliances.*—The superintendent of a railroad, who has been employed on railroads for nearly twenty years, as fireman, brakeman, baggage-master, yard-master, and train-master, may give his opinion as an expert as to the value and usefulness of "whipping-straps," or ropes pendent from above, as cautionary signals to brakemen when the train is approaching a low bridge or tunnel overhead; but he can not give his opinion as to the prudent management of the defendant's railroad.

9. *Contributory negligence; burden of proof.*—Contributory negligence, when pleaded by itself, is an admission of negligence on the part of the defendant, but not when interposed with the plea of not guilty.

10. *Requisites of charge to jury.*—A charge to the jury should, if possible, be plain, simple, and easily understood, free from obscurity, involvement, ambiguity, metaphysical intricacy, or tendency to mislead; and if objectionable on any of these grounds, it should be refused, although, when closely analyzed, it may assert a correct legal proposition.

APPEAL from the City Court of Mobile.

Tried before the Hon. O. J. SEMMES.

This action was brought by William G. Hall, a minor suing by his next friend, against the Louisville & Nashville Railroad Company, to recover damages for personal injuries sustained by plaintiff while in defendant's employment as brakeman; and was commenced on the 28th Februray, 1888. The accident occurred on the night of October 26th, 1887, when plaintiff, being on the top of one of the cars in the discharge of his duties as brakeman on one of the defendant's freight trains, was struck by the timbers of a bridge overhead, which spanned a public road near Greenville in

Butler county, and was so badly injured that it became necessary to amputate one of his feet. The cause was tried on issue joined on the pleas of not guilty and contributory negligence, and resulted in a verdict and judgment for plaintiff for $20,000.

The complaint contained eleven counts, but a demurrer was sustained to the 10th and 11th counts. The 1st count alleged that, at and before the time of the injury, the defendant corporation was, as a common carrier, operating a railroad between Montgomery and Mobile, which passed through the corporate limits of the town of Greenville, and crossed a public street or road a short distance south of its depot in the town; that the defendant's charter provided that the company, "in the construction of said road, shall not in any manner obstruct any public road now established, but shall provide convenient passage for travel over said road;" that the railroad "crossed said public road south of Greenville, and the passage provided for travel over said road is by a bridge that crosses above said railroad track;" that the defendant's freight trains "are so arranged that they are stopped by means of brakes, which can only be managed by persons on the top of the cars," and for this purpose brakemen are employed by it, whose duty it is to stand and walk on the top of said trains, and to apply the brakes when signalled to do so; that said bridge across the public road "was, with gross negligence and reckless disregard of the lives of defendant's employes, improperly and dangerously constructed and maintained, in this: that it was constructed and maintained at such a height above the railroad track that there was danger of the brakemen on freight trains being struck by said bridge, and injured or killed;" that the plaintiff, while in the discharge of his duties as brakeman on the top of a freight train, on said October 26, 1887, was struck by the bridge overhead, knocked to the ground, and seriously injured as above stated; that he was at the time ignorant of the dangerous construction and condition of the bridge; and that said dangerous construction and condition of the bridge, at the time of said injuries, "either had not been discovered by the defendant, or else had not been remedied owing to the negligence of the defendant, or of some person in the defendant's service intrusted by it with the duty of seeing that the ways, works, machinery or plant of said road was in proper condition."

The 2d count alleged, in the same words as the 1st, that

the defendant was engaged as a common carrier in operating a railroad between Montgomery and Mobile, "which passes through the corporate limits of the town of Greenville, and crosses a public street or road a short distance south of defendant's depot there, by passing under the same; that the passage provided for travel over said road is by a bridge that crosses above said railroad track;" the dangerous construction of the bridge, the plaintiff's ignorance of its dangerous construction, &c., in substance the same as the first count, except in omitting any averment as to the provision in the defendant's charter. The 3d count was the same in substance, in its averments as to the construction and condition of the bridge, and the injuries suffered by the plaintiff while in the discharge of his duties as brakeman; but it did not allege his ignorance of its dangerous construction, nor that the defect had not been discovered or remedied on account of negligence on the part of the defendant, or of some person in its employment charged with that duty. The 4th count was substantially the same, but with less particularity in its statement of details. The 5th count alleged that, when the train approached the bridge, the engineer, or other person having control of the running of the engine and train, did not blow the whistle, nor ring the bell, one-fourth of a mile before reaching the public road crossing; and that the plaintiff had no notice, and did not know that the train was approaching said crossing. The 6th count alleged that the defendant's railroad "passes through the corporate limits of Greenville, and crosses a public street or road, a short distance south of Greenville, under a bridge that crosses above said railroad track;" that the bridge was of such a height as to be dangerous to any person standing or walking on the top of a train, as brakemen were required to do; that this fact was unknown to the plaintiff, who, in the discharge of his duties as brakeman, had got down to examine a "hot box," and when he climbed up again, the train having suddenly started, he was struck by the bridge overhead as he was walking to his position. The 7th count alleged that the defendant, on the 26th October, 1887, was operating a railroad between Montgomery and Mobile; that the ways, works, machinery or plant, connected with, or used in connection with said road, "was defective in this: that a bridge over said railroad, a short distance below defendant's depot in Greenville, was negligently constructed, so as to be dangerous to persons employed by defendant as brakemen on freight cars;" that plaintiff was employed as a brakeman on a freight train, and while in the discharge of his duties, on that day, was injured "by reason of said defective condition of said ways," &c. The 8th count alleged that, on the 26th October, 1887, the defendant was operating a railroad between Mobile and Montgomery, "and with one of its cars negligently run over and injured plaintiff." The 9th count alleged that, on said 26th October, 1887, plaintiff was a brakeman on a freight train on defendant's railroad, and was, "by the negligence of the defendant, violently brought into contact with a low bridge, which cut his head, knocked him senseless from the train," &c. Demurrers were sustained to the 10th and 11th counts, and they require no special notice.

The defendant demurred to each count of the complaint, assigning special causes of demurrer numbered consecutively from 1 to 31. The grounds specially assigned to the 1st count were: (1) that said count fails to show that plaintiff exercised reasonable and proper care in the performance of his duties on the train "at the time of the accident alleged to have resulted in his *death;*" (2) that it fails to show a violation of any duty legally owing by defendant to plaintiff in the premises; (3) that it fails to show any negligence on the part of the defendant; (4) that it fails to show that plaintiff had no such knowledge of the existence of said low bridge as would have enabled him, by due diligence on his part, to have avoided the alleged injury and damage;" (5) that it "shows that said alleged danger, due to the construction of said bridge, was a risk incident to plaintiff's employment, for which, when resulting in injury, no action lies;" (6) that it shows "that the alleged injury and *death* was caused by contact of plaintiff with said bridge while in the performance of his duties as brakeman, and fails to show that he was in the exercise of due care and diligence to avoid said accident, or that it could not have been avoided by due care and diligence on his part;" (7) that it fails to show any duty on the part of the defendant with reference to said bridge, whereby it became defendant's duty to maintain said bridge at any particular elevation; (8) that it shows said bridge was a public road bridge, and not a bridge constituting part of defendant's track or road. The same grounds of demurrer were assigned to the 2d count, and also, (10) that it does not show how or why it became necessary for plaintiff to stand or walk on the top of the train while it was passing under said bridge. The same grounds of demurrer were assigned to the 3d count as to the 1st and 2d, and also to the 4th count, with the additional assignment, (13) that said 4th count does not allege that said bridge was constructed or maintained by defendant. To the 5th count the same grounds of demurrer were assigned as to the preceding counts, and also, (15) that it fails to show how or why it became defendant's duty to notify plaintiff of the approach to said bridge; (16) that it shows that said alleged neglect was the neglect of a fellow-servant of plaintiff, for whose acts in the premises defendant is not liable to plaintiff; (17) that it fails to show any duty on the part of the defendant, requiring the engineer or conductor to blow the whistle or ring the bell on approaching the bridge. To the 6th count the same grounds of demurrer were assigned as to the 1st, 2d, and 4th, and also (19) that said count shows that plaintiff himself was guilty of proximate contributory negligence. To the 7th count the same grounds of demurrer were assigned as to the 1st, 2d, and 4th, and also to the 8th count, with the additional assignments, (21) that it does not show with sufficient particularity the nature of the neglect, or the circumstances under which plaintiff was injured as alleged; and (22) that it fails to allege or show the particular duty which the defendant owed the plaintiff in the premises. To the 9th count the same grounds of demurrer were assigned as to the 1st, 2d, 4th, and 8th, with the additional assignment, (23) that it does not show what right plaintiff had to be on top of the train at the time he was injured. The 24th, 25th and 26th assignments were addressed to the 10th and 11th counts, and require no notice; and the other assignments, addressed to each of the counts except the 8th," were: (27) because it does not show the nature of the defect in the bridge, "or how the defect proximately contributed to the injury and *death* of said plaintiff;" (28) because it is not alleged or shown that said bridge was constructed and maintained by the defendant, or that the defendant was in any way responsible for it; (29) because it is not alleged that defendant knew of said alleged defect in said bridge a reasonable length of time before the alleged injury, in which said defect might have been remedied; (30) because it is not shown that the defect in the bridge exposed plaintiff to unusual or unnecessary danger while in the performance of his duties; (31) because no legal duty on the defendant's part is shown, to construct and maintain the bridge at an elevation sufficient to enable a brakeman, while standing erect on the top of a car, to pass under it with safety.

The demurrers being overruled, except as to the 10th and 11th counts, issue was joined on the pleas of not guilty and contributory negligence. On the trial, the evidence showed that the railroad bridge crossed the public road on the side of a hill, and was about seventeen feet above the railroad track, the upper end being a few inches higher; and that the average height of freight trains was from eleven and a half to twelve feet. The plaintiff, testifying as a witness for himself, stated that he was in the 19th year of his age, and was making his fourth round trip, as brakeman, on the defendant's railroad between Montgomery and Mobile, when he was injured; that he did not know the road, and did not know where he was at the time he was injured, but afterwards ascertained that it was at the bridge south of Greenville; that he was not acquainted well enough with the landmarks of the road to know at what place he was; that if he knew there was a bridge at Greenville, he would not recognize it unless some one pointed it out to him at the time; that if it had ever been pointed out to him, he did not remember the fact, and that he had never noticed the bridge before. "Witness was then asked by his counsel, if there were any lights on the bridge, or any 'whipping straps,' to give warning of the approach to the bridge;" and answered, "that there were no 'whipping straps,' and he thought there were not any lights." To each part of this question the defendant objected and excepted. The plaintiff further testified, on cross-examination, "that he thought he was told about some low bridges, but did not know exactly where they were, and would not have known them when he got there unless he was told; that he knew there were low bridges on the road, which it would not be safe for a man to pass under while standing on the top of a car, but he would not have known the locality unless it was pointed out to him; that he might have been told there was a low bridge at Greenville, but he did not know when he got to Greenville." J. R. Gollithan, the conductor of the freight train, and two of the brakemen on the train, each testified on the part of the defendant, that they had warned the plaintiff against the danger of the low bridges on the road, and had specially mentioned the bridge at Greenville.

J. R. Porterfield, the town marshal of Greenville, was examined as a witness for the plaintiff, and testified as to the construction of the bridge by the defendant, its height, the steepness of the ascent to it when coming up the public road, &c.; and he was then asked, "Was it generally reported at Greenville, prior to the injury to plaintiff, that any person in the employment of the railroad company had been killed or wounded by said bridge while in the performance of his duty? What was the general reputation in the community on that subject?" The defendant objected to this question, "(1) because the evidence is irrelevant; (2) because it is incompetent to prove the fact of killing; (3) because it is incompetent to prove knowledge on the part of the defendant of the fact of killing; (4) because it is incompetent to prove the dangerous condition of the bridge; and (5) because a proper predicate has not been laid for the question." The court overruled the objections, and the defendant excepted. The witness answered: "I hardly know how to answer that question. It was thought that the bridge was probably too low." (Being reminded by the court that the question was whether some other person had been previously killed or injured.) "Yes, sir; but I wont be positive that this bridge killed him. They built a new bridge there in 1879, 1880, or 1881; and my recollection is, that this man was killed before it was built. I wont be positive whether this bridge did it or the other one; but my recollection is that a bridge knocked him off, and I saw him after he was dead. Railroad hands were with him, attended to him, and took care of him."

B. C. Epperson, the superintendent of that division of the defendant's road which lies between Montgomery and Mobile, was examined as a witness for the defendant, and testified that he had been employed on railroads for nineteen or twenty years, had served as fireman, brakeman, baggage-master, yard-master, train-master, and law agent, and had been on the Mobile and Montgomery division of the defendant's road about three years; that he had frequently heard of "whipping straps," and similar devices, for the purpose of giving notice of the approach to low bridges; that none of them were now used on his division of the defendant's road, and he did not know whether or not any were now used on the other divisions of the road; that their use is not increasing on the road, but, on the contrary, fewer are now used than formerly; that all train-men, and a majority of the officials with whom he had conversed, "ridiculed the idea of putting up straps, and said they were useless;" that the ob-

[Louisville & Nashville R. R. Co. v. Hall.]

jection to them was, that the men depended on the straps for
warning, and were not as careful as they otherwise would
have been; "that was his personal objection, and it is
what the majority seemed to think." During his examination the witness was asked these questions: "Whether these
straps, or ropes hung up in that way, tended to protect the
employes of the railroad from accidents at low bridges and
tunnels? "Whether the existence of these pendent ropes
and straps, as far as his observation or experience went,
tended to increase or diminish the number of accidents at
bridges and low tunnels?" "Whether he regarded the
L. & N. Railroad system as a prudently managed road?"
"Whether other railroads which he had seen, and which did
not use these appliances, were generally regarded in railroad
circles as prudently managed?" The court sustained objections to each of these questions, and the defendant excepted to its rulings.

The court gave an elaborate charge in writing to the jury,
ex mero motu, to which the defendant excepted as a whole,
and also reserved twenty-one (21) special exceptions to different parts of it. The opinion of this court states the objectionable parts of this charge, and it is unnecessary to set
it out in full. The court gave, also, ten charges in writing
asked by the plaintiff, among which were the following:
(3.) "A plea of contributory negligence confesses that the
defendant was guilty of the culpable negligence charged in
the counts of the complaint to which it is pleaded, except in
so far as the plea traverses or denies the negligence charged
in those counts, or sets up facts in qualification or avoidance
of such negligence; but this kind of confession of negligence only applies to the issue made by such plea under the
counts to which it is pleaded." (8.) "If the jury believe
from the evidence that the plaintiff, while in the employment of the defendant as brakeman on a freight train, received personal injuries by reason of a defect in the construction of a bridge over the defendant's track, and that
such defect arose from, or had not been discovered or remedied owing to the negligence of the defendant; then the
plaintiff is entitled to recover for the injuries so sustained,
although he may have known that such defect existed, provided he was guilty of no negligence which proximately
contributed to the injury; and provided, further, that he
knew the defendant, or some person superior to himself in

the service of the defendant, knew of said defect." To each of these charges the defendant excepted.

The defendant requested numerous charges in writing, duly excepting to the refusal of each, and among them the following: (13.) "Unless the jury believe from the evidence that the injury to the plaintiff resulted from gross negligence and reckless disregard for the safety and lives of its employes in general, as distinguished from simple negligence towards the plaintiff, the judgment must be for the defendant." (23.) "It was not a duty which the railroad company owed to the plaintiff while in its employment as a brakeman on a freight train, and while walking on the top of a train, approaching or passing under said bridge, that the engineer, or other person in charge of the running of the locomotive, should blow the whistle, or ring the bell, a quarter of a mile before reaching said public road crossing, and continue to do so, at short intervals, until the train had passed said crossing; and no negligence can be imputed to the defendant from the failure of the engineer to ring the bell or blow the whistle." (38.) "There is no legal testimony to show that whip-straps, or pendent cords, were a suitable or proper device to be employed by the defendant at the bridge in question, at or prior to the time of the accident, as a warning to employes of the approach to said bridge; and negligence can not be imputed to the defendant, because of the failure to provide such devices." (44.) "No exemplary, punitive or vindictive damages can be recovered in this case, even should the jury find that plaintiff is entitled to compensation for actual damages sustained by him.

The several rulings of the court on the pleadings and evidence, the charges given, and the refusal of the charges asked, are now assigned as error.

GAYLORD B. CLARK & F. B. CLARK, JR., for appellants.

R. INGE SMITH, and GREG. L. & H. T. SMITH, contra.

STONE, C. J.—We lay down the following legal propositions: When, in crossing a public highway, it becomes necessary for a railroad company to span it with a bridge, it is its duty, if reasonably practicable, to place the structure at such an elevation as that trains, with their customary employes, can pass under it unharmed.—Smoot v. M. & M. Railway Co., 67 Ala. 17; L. & N. R. R. Co. v. Allen, 78 Ala.

501; *Propst v. Ga. Pac. R. R.*, 83 Ala. 501; *H. & T. Railway Co. v. Oram*, 49 Tex. 341; *Wilson v. L. & N. R. R. Co.*, 85 Ala. 269. This is not an absolute, unbending requirement, but it will yield to a reasonable extent to circumstances, as many other natural and social rights must yield to other rights and interests, which duty requires to be conserved. If inequality of surface, or other hindrance, occurring naturally, or in the proper construction or grade of the railroad track, render such elevation impossible, or greatly incommode the public in the use of the bridge, or greatly or unduly increase the expense to the railroad company, then one inconvenience must yield somewhat to the other. In such case, the bridge may be so constructed as to extend below the line of absolute safety. A bridge, constructed and maintained with proper regard to these conditions, would not, without more, be negligence.—Patterson Railway Ac. Law, § 285; 2 Rorer Railroads, 1217; *Wells v. B., C. R. & N. R. R. Co.*, 2 Amer. & Eng. Railway Cas. 243; *Rains v. St. L., I. M. & S. Railway Co.*, 5 *Ib.* 610; *Clark v. Richmond & D. R. R. Co.*, 18 *Ib.* 78; *Baylor v. Del., L. & W. R. R. Co.*, 40 N. J. Law, 23; *Illick v. F. & P. M. R. R. Co.*, 35 N. W. Rep. 708. In no case, however, would it be permissible to so place the bridge, that brakemen on top of the train, in discharge of their duties, could not avoid danger by bending or stooping. A bridge, such as here last supposed, would be gross negligence, and *per se* a nuisance.—*Ill. Cen. R. R. Co. v. Welch*, 52 Ill. 183; *C. B. & Q. R. R. Co. v. Gregory*, 58 Ill. 272; *C. & I. R. R. Co. v. Russell*, 91 Ill. 298. If such bridge is so constructed as to extend below the line of absolute safety, then other duties rest on the railroad company.

The bridge in question was part and parcel of the public highway. The record affords evidence that, on the trial below, the question was considered, whether it was the duty of the defendant corporation "to blow the whistle, or ring the bell, at least one-fourth of a mile before reaching [a] public road crossing, . . . and continue to blow the whistle or ring the bell, at short intervals, until the train passed the crossing".—Code of 1886, § 1144. That statute has nothing to do with this case. Its design was to warn and protect persons who, at a public crossing, pass across and directly on the track, and who would be in danger of being struck and run over by an approaching train.—*Ala.*

Gr. So. R. R. Co. v. Hawk, 72 Ala. 112; *N., C. & St. L. R. R. Co. v. Hembree,* 85 Ala. 481.

Other questions were raised in the trial court, touching the duty of railroad companies to provide or furnish warning signals. Among these may be mentioned "whipping straps," and placing a cautionary light on the bridge. Considered abstractly, these are scarcely legal questions. Utility, and the usage and custom of well-regulated railroads, must determine the question of duty in this regard. If useless or hurtful, it can not be negligence to reject them. So, at most, if many well-regulated railroads abstain from their use, this absolves from all duty to resort to them. By the word *many,* we intend to be understood as meaning not a mere excess above the adjective *few.* *Many* denotes multitude; and while it is not the synonym of the word *majority,* our meaning is, that if a relatively large number, as compared with the whole number, abstain from their use, then to omit them is not, of itself, negligence. As to appliances —particularly new inventions, or changes claimed to be improvements—all railroads are not required to conform to one standard. Allowance is, and must be made, for diversity of opinion; and their use by a majority of roads does not necessarily require all railroads to adopt them.—*L. & N. R. R. Co. v. Allen,* 78 Ala. 494; *Ga. Pac. R. R. Co. v. Propst,* 83 Ala. 518; *Wilson v. L. & N. R. R. Co.,* 85 Ala. 269; *Baldwin v. C., R. I. & P. B. R. R. Co.,* 50 Iowa, 580.

When a brakeman is placed on a freight train, running on a road with which he is not familiar, and such train has to pass under a low bridge or bridges, the law, which simply voices the sentiment of humanity, requires that notice be given him of the danger he is to encounter. This notice must be reasonable; that is, he must be reasonably instructed, so as to put him on the look-out, and on inquiry and observation, that he may inform himself of the locality of the places of danger. The whole duty is not on the railroad company. The employe must give heed to the notice and instructions given him, and must employ his senses, his reasoning faculties and his attention, alike for his own safety and the welfare of the road. If he has not been sufficiently warned or notified to enable him by proper attention and diligence to learn where the points of danger are, then this would be negligence, for which the railroad company would be liable. On the other hand, if he has been sufficiently warned or notified, and from inattention, indifference, absent-mindedness, or forgetfulness, he fails to inform himself, or fails to take the necessary steps to avoid the injury, this is negligence, and he should not recover.—*Sullivan v. Man. Co.*, 113 Mass. 396; *B. & O. R. R. Co. v. Stricker*, 51 Md. 47; *Dorsey v. P. & C. Con. Co.*, 42 Wis. 583; *L., N. A. & C. R. Co.*, 16 N. E. Rep. 145; s. c., 17 *Ib.* 584; *St. L., Ft. S. & N. R. R. Co.*, 16 Pac. Rep. 146; *Wilson v. L. & N. R. R. Co.*, 85 Ala. 269.

It is not denied, in this case, that the space between the taller freight cars used on defendant's road, and the timbers of the bridge, would not permit a man of ordinary height, standing erect on the top of the cars, to pass under the bridge without being struck by it. The two principal, leading inquiries, then, are—*First:* Was the railroad company, under the rules above declared, justified in maintaining its bridge at the elevation shown in the testimony? If it was, plaintiff was not, merely on that ground, entitled to recover, for he had no cause of action. If the railroad company, under said rules, has failed to establish its right to maintain the bridge at the elevation proved, then negligence is shown, and, unrebutted, authorized a recovery by plaintiff. That *prima facie* right would be rebutted, if plaintiff was guilty of proximate, contributory negligence. *Second:* If, under the rules we have stated, the plaintiff was sufficiently notified or warned, and from inattention, indifference, absent-mindedness, or forgetfulness, he failed to inform himself, or failed to take the necessary steps to avoid the injury, this was proximate, contributory negligence, and is also a complete answer to the action. He must avail himself of the instructions given him, or furnished for his use; and taking into the account the surroundings and perils attendant upon the nature of the service he enters upon, he must bestow such care, watchfulness and caution as ordinarily prudent men would usually exercise in reference to their own safety, under like circumstances. There are perils in the very nature of such service, against which prudence can not always guard. Of these the employe takes the risk. He is guilty of contributory negligence, if, in his care, diligence, and watchfulness, he falls below the standard stated above. 3 Wood's Railway Law, 1481: *Wabash Railway Co. v. Elliott*, 98 Ill. 481; 4 Amer. & Eng. Railway Cas. 651; *Clark v. St. P. & S. City R. R. Co.*, 2 Amer. & Eng. Railway Cases, 240; *Wells v. B., C. R. & N. R. R. Co.*, *Ib.* 243; *P. & C. R. R. Co. v. Sentmeyer*, 92 Penn. St. 276, s. c.,

5 Amer. & Eng. Railway Cas. 508; *St. L., I. M. & So. Railway Co. v. Rains*, 71 Mo. 164; s. c., 5 Amer. & Eng. Railway Cas. 610; *Clark v. Richmond & Danville R. R. Co.*, 18 Amer. & Eng. Railway Cas. 78; *Gibson v. Erie Railway Co.*, 63 N. Y. 449; *Laflin v. B. & S. W. R. R. Co.*, 106 N. Y. 136; *Devitt v. Pac. R. R. Co.*, 50 Mo. 302; s. c., 3 Amer. Railway Cas. 533; *Owen v. N. Y. Cen. R. R. Co.*, 1 Lans. 108; *A. & W. P. R. R. Co. v. Webb*, 61 Ga. Rep. 586; *Same v. Johnson*, 66 *Ib.* 259; *I., B. & W. R. R. Co. v. Flanigan*, 77 Ill. 265; *T., W. & West. R. R. Co.*, 88 Ill. 112; *Gould v. C. B. & Q. R. R. Co.* 66 Iowa, 590. And evidence that the appliance has been long used with safety, is competent on the inquiry of contributory negligence. *Allen v. B., C. R. & N. Railway Co.*, 5 Amer. & Eng. Railway Cas. 620; *A. G. S. R. R. Co. v. Arnold*, 84 Ala. 159; *Laflin v. B. & S. W. R. R. Co.*, 106 N. Y. 136; *Loftus v. Union Ferry Co.*, 84 N. Y. 455; *Burke v. Witherbee*, 98 N. Y. 562.

The complaint contains eleven counts, and there were demurrers to each of them. We think the demurrers ought to have been sustained to those numbered eight and nine. Count No. 8 is meagre and defective in many particulars. Count No. 9 fails to aver that plaintiff was in the performance of any duty pertinent to his services as brakeman, when he was injured. Count 11 is defective, in that there is no duty resting on the engineer, as matter of law, to signal the approach to a low, or dangerous overhead structure. Possibly it would be well, if the law was so framed as to require notice to be given of such approach, by a signal which exposed employes would understand. The grounds of demurrer, in reference to the counts we have declared defective, which should have been sustained, are: in reference to count 8, assignments 21 and 22; to count 9, assignment No. 23. The trial court sustained the demurrers to counts 10 and 11, and we need not consider them.

A railroad corporation is "authorized to use, or to cross, or to change public roads, when necessary, in the building, construction, or maintenance of its roadway or track, but must place the road used, or crossed, or changed, in a condition satisfactory to the authorities," &c.—Code of 1886, § 1581 (1841). It is manifest that this statute approved March 8, 1876—Sess. Acts, 257—has reference to public roads in use as such at the time the road was constructed; or, at least, in case of a bridge, that it should have been

46

[Louisvillle & Nashville R. R. Co. v. Hall.]

erected or maintained by the railroad company. Each of the counts in the complaint is defective, in not averring that the bridge in question was erected or maintained by the railroad company. The 28th ground of demurrer ought to have been sustained. With this exception, each of the first six counts of the complaint is sufficient.—*S. & N. R. R. Co. v. Thompson*, 62 Ala. 494; *E. T., Va. & Ga. R. R. Co. v. Carloss*, 77 Ala. 443; *Hall v. Posey*, 79 Ala. 84; *M. & O. R. R. Co. v. Thomas*, 42 Ala. 672.

We will not consider the rulings on the demurrer to the third plea. The defendant could, and did have, under his second plea, the benefit of all defenses he could have made under the third.—3 Brick. Dig. 405, § 20.

Proof of general notoriety is generally admissible, as tending to prove notice of a fact, when such notice is a material inquiry; but it is never competent to prove the fact itself. That must be shown by other testimony. Applied to the present case, it was not competent testimony, on the inquiry whether the bridge in question had ever before been the means of killing a person. Seeing the dead body, was no proof that the person had been killed by the bridge, nor from the top of the train. Nor was there proof tending to show that the killing took place since the erection of the bridge which struck plaintiff. The trial court erred in receiving testimony of general notoriety.

The witness Epperson showed himself to be an expert. He should have been allowed to give his opinion, and his reason for it, as to the merits or demerits of the "whipping straps" as cautionary signals, and whether or not they were generally in use on roads regarded as well regulated. It was rightly ruled, that he could not give his opinion as to the prudent management of the Louisville & Nashville railroad, or any of its constituent sections.

The general charge given in this case, as we think the trial court intended it to be understood, is, in the main, free from error. We will first premise, however, that this case was tried, as to all the counts, on the double defense of not guilty, and proximate contributory negligence on the part of plaintiff. The effect of this double defense was, and is, that defendant denied all negligence on its part, and threw the burden of proof on plaintiff. As a further defense the defendant set up, that if found to have been guilty of negligence, then plaintiff was himself guilty of negligence, which contributed proximately to the injury he suffered. The burden was on the defendant to make good this phase of its defense.   Both lines of defense being interposed to the whole action, the defense of contributory negligence was not in whole, nor to any extent, an admission that the defendant had been guilty of negligence.

Some expressions in the general charge are subject to criticism.   We will quote certain passages, which possibly may have misled the jury, and. with them, will suggest such verbal alterations as will free them from all grounds of objection.   The alterations are placed in brackets.   They will be found to be, sometimes, merely explanatory, additional words, or phrases, while at other times, the words or phrases will be seen to be substituted for those found in the transcript. I begin with the first sentence in the first paragraph: "Which injuries [it is claimed] resulted from the negligence of the defendant, and [that] he would not have suffered [them] but for such negligence.   .   .   The defendant, on the contrary, [seeks to excuse itself for the low bridge, and alleges] first [that] it was necessary to build the bridge at the height at which it was built.   .   .   It being the law of this State, that a person entering the employment of a railroad [has a right to expect the railroad will furnish] safe appliances, &c.

.   .   In order to recover exemplary damages, it is not necessary that the defendant should have intended to commit the wrong, [if there was gross, reckless, or wanton negligence]—so gross as to evince an entire want of care," &c.

Charges to juries should, if possible, be plain, simple, and easily understood.   They should be free from obscurity, involvement, ambiguity, metaphysical intricacy, and tendency to mislead.   A charge obnoxious to any of these objections, should always be refused, even though, on dissection, it may assert a correct legal proposition.   The office and purpose of charges are to enlighten the jury, and to aid them in arriving at a correct verdict, as plain, common-sense men.   In other words, they should be made up of plain propositions of law, applicable to the tendency, or varying tendencies of the evidence, and they should go no farther.   Charges thus given greatly aid juries in their deliberations.

We do not know that we comprehend the meaning and import of charges 3 and 8 of the series styled "plaintiff's charges."   Charge No. 3 asserts, that when contributory negligence is pleaded, this is a confession "that the defendant was guilty of the culpable negligence which is charged in the counts of the complaint to which it is pleaded, except so far as the plea traverses or denies the negligence of defendant charged in those counts, or sets up facts in qualification or avoidance of such negligence." This is an assertion, that the plea of contributory negligence admits the negligence charged, unless the plea itself—not another plea —negatives, or avoids such negligence. We have shown above that this is not the true rule. A denial of the negligence charged, or plea of not guilty, although pleaded separately, repels all presumption of confession, which arises from the plea of contributory negligence when pleaded alone. And the last sentence of the charge does not heal the error, for each of the pleas, not guilty and contributory negligence, was pleaded to the entire complaint. Freedom from negligence is not one of the essentials of the defense of contributory negligence. There must be negligence in the defendant, before the plaintiff can contribute to its injurious results.—*M. & C. R. R. Co. v. Copeland*, 61 Ala. 376. Charge 3 is not only erroneous as a legal proposition, but the pleading furnishes no field for its operation.

Charge 8 hypothesizes, that there was a defect in the construction of the bridge, and that such "defect arose from, or had not been discovered or remedied, owing to the negligence of defendant;" and asserts that the plaintiff is entitled to recover for the injuries received, "although he may have known that such defect existed, provided he was guilty of no negligence which proximately contributed to the injury; and provided, further, that he knew that the defendant, or some person superior to himself in the service of the defendant, knew of said defect."

How the last proviso in this charge can become material on the inquiry of plaintiff's contributory negligence, is not perceived. It is undisputed that, by stooping, plaintiff could have passed the bridge in safety. The two phrases, "although he may have known that such defect existed," and "provided that plaintiff was guilty of no negligence which contributed to the injury," are incompatible with each other, when viewed in the light of the uncontroverted testimony. Having knowledge of the low bridge, and failing to stoop in passing it, would be proximate contributory negligence, even though every employe of the railroad had knowledge of the defect. Charges 3 and 8 should not have been given.

Charge 13, asked by defendant, was rightly refused. *L. & N. R. R. Co. v. Coulton*, 86 Ala. 129; s. c., 5 So. Rep. 448. Charges 23 and 38 of defendant's series ought to have been given, and charge 44, in the state of the testimony, should not have.been refused.　There is no testimony tending to prove gross, wanton, or reckless negligence.—*S. & N. R. R. Co. v. Huffman*, 76 Ala. 492; *Ala. G. S. R. R. Co. v. Arnold*, 80 Ala. 600; s. c., 84 Ala. 159.

Under the rules of law declared above, and in the state of the proof found in the record, each of the main questions of fact—negligence of defendant, and contributory negligence by plaintiff—was one of fact for decision by the jury.

Reversed and remanded.

Williams *v.* Evans.

Action on Special Contract for Price of Stock in Corporation.

1. *Fictitious stock in private corporation, under constitutional provisions.*—A subscription to stock in a private corporation, with the understanding that the corporation shall issue "five dollars of stock for one of subscription," is in violation of the constitutional provision which declares void the fictitious issue or increase of stock by private corporations (Art. XIV, § 6); and a contract for the sale of a part of the stock so subscribed, before it has been issued, accompanied with an order to the company to issue it to the purchaser, and to transfer it to him on the books, is equally illegal and void.

APPEAL from the Circuit Court of Elmore.

Tried before the Hon. JAS. R. DOWDELL.

This action was brought by H. G. Evans against E. M. Williams, to recover the price agreed to be paid for fifty shares of stock in the Decatur Land and Improvement Company; and was commenced on the 23d January, 1888.　The original complaint contained a special count on the written instrument, in the form of a bill of exchange, which was given for the agreed price, alleging its non-payment on presentment to the drawee, and the common counts; and a third count was added by amendment, which set out the terms of the contract.　The court overruled a demurrer to the third count, and, on the evidence adduced, instructed the jury to find for the plaintiff, if they believed the evidence.　The defendant excepted to this charge, and he here assigns it as error.

[Williams v. Evans.]

THORINGTON & SMITH, for appellants, cited Const. Ala., Art. XIV, § 6; *Fitzpatrick v. Dispatch Publishing Co.*, 83 Ala. 604; *Carrington v. Caller*, 2 Stew. 175; Greenhood on Public Policy, 585; *Barnes v. Brown*, 80 N. Y. 527; 1 Biss. 246, 255.

WATTS & SON, *contra*.

SOMERVILLE, J.—Upon first consideration, we were of opinion that the contract sued on in this case was not illegal, or invalid, as in violation of public policy. But, after further deliberation, we have come to the opposite conclusion.

It is too plain for argument that, under the evidence, if the plaintiff can recover at all, it must be under the third count, which claims the price agreed to be paid for the sale of fifty shares of stock in the Decatur Land Company. The bill of exceptions sets out all the evidence, and this evidence, in our opinion, shows a contract in violation of section 6, Article XIV, of the Constitution (1875), which provides, that "No corporation shall issue *stock*, or bonds, except for money, labor done, or money or property actually received; and *all fictitious increase of stock* or indebtedness *shall be void.*"

The plaintiff's own testimony shows that he had subscribed originally for $2,500 of stock in said company—say twenty-five shares—with the understanding, that the company was to issue to him "five dollars of stock for one dollar of sub-scription," which would be $12,500—a fictitious increase of five to one. The plaintiff sold $1000 (or ten shares) of the original stock, and "gave the defendant *an order* on the Decatur Land Company, *to issue to defendant fifty shares* of said land company stock, which was the amount called for by the $1000 of the original subscription, and to transfer the same to defendant on the books of the company." This stock was not then issued, but was to be issued on the day of the transaction.

The contract necessarily implied by this transaction is one which seems to us to be in violation of the section of the Constitution above quoted; and this is the consideration of the defendant's promise. It is a sale, not so much of the stock itself, as a transfer of a *subscription* to ten shares of the stock, based on an illegal agreement of the land company to issue fifty shares of such stock (a fictitious increase of forty shares), with an order on the company instructing it

[Young & Co. v. Cureton.]

to carry out the illegal transaction with the purchaser. A contract which contemplates the violation of a statute, or a constitution, as a mode of executing such contract, is illegal and void. It is based on an unlawful consideration, and, if executory, can not be enforced.

One of the purposes of this clause of the Constitution was to protect the public, as well as stockholders, against spurious and worthless stock by the process of *watering*—in other words, from fraudulently issuing and putting on the market fictitious corporate stock, which is based on nothing valuable as a consideration for its issue.—*Fitzpatrick v. Dispatch Pub. Co.*, 83 Ala. 604; *Memphis & Little Rock R. R. Co. v. Dow*, 120 U. S. 287; *Peoria & Springfield R. R. Co. v. Thompson*, 103 Ill. 187. It is greatly to the interest of the public that the policy of this provision should be enforced. We repeat that the present contract is in violation of this provision of the Constitution, and is void.

The court erred in the charges given.

Other questions need not be considered, as the defendant is entitled to the general affirmative charge in his favor, if requested.

Reversed and remanded.

Young & Co. *v.* Cureton.

Action for Price of Goods Sold and Delivered.

87
98
87
104
87
108
87
113 4

1. *Testimony of witness as to damages.*—A party, testifying as a witness, can not state "what damages" he sustained by the breach of contract of which he complains.

2. *Profits as damages.*—For the breach of an executory contract to deliver goods, the measure of damages is the difference between the agreed price and the market price at the place of delivery; and the profits which might have been realized on selling the goods by retail during the Christmas holidays, for which purpose they were intended, "are conjectural, merely speculative, and dependent on too many contingencies to constitute an element of recoverable damages."

APPEAL from the Circuit Court of Etowah.
Tried before the Hon. JOHN B. TALLY.

L. L. DEAN, for appellants, cited *Bell v. Reynolds & Lee*, 75 Ala. 511; *Martin v. Hill*, 42 Ala. 275; *Gray v. Waterman*,

40 Ill. 522; *Robertson v. Davenport & Patterson*, 27 Ala. 574; *Tucker v. Woods*, 12 John. 190; 11 John. 525; 1 Peters, 465; *Laroque v. Russell*, 7 Ala. 798; *Cuthbert v. Newell*, 7 Ala. 457; 40 N. Y. 422; 9 Wend. 325; 17 C. B. 21.

A. E. GOODHUE, *contra*, cited *Haas v. Hudmon*, 83 Ala. 176; *Brigham v. Carlisle*, 78 Ala. 247; *Pollock v. Gantt*, 69 Ala. 376; *Refining Co. v. Barton*, 77 Ala. 156; *Culver v. Hill*, 68 Ala. 66; *Parsons v. Sutton*, 66 Ala. 92; 2 Benj. Sales, 1120–22.

CLOPTON, J.—In this action, which was brought by appellee to recover the price of three barrels of whiskey, the defendants seek by special plea to recoup damages suffered by the alleged breach of an executory contract. The plea avers, that in November, 1887, plaintiff and defendants entered into a contract, by which the former agreed to deliver to the latter ten barrels of corn whiskey, at an agreed price, by the 25th day of December thereafter, and that the barrels in controversy were delivered in pursuance of such agreement, but that plaintiff failed to deliver the other seven barrels. All the assignments of error go to the rulings of the court on plaintiff's objections to certain questions propounded on behalf of defendants to each of themselves, while being examined as witnesses. It does not seem to admit of doubt, under the uniform decisions of this court, that the objections were properly sustained.

As witnesses, the defendants were asked, "what damages they sustained by the failure" of plaintiff to perform the contract? With some exceptions, witnesses will not be allowed to state their opinion, though it may be founded on facts, or the inferences or conclusions which they may have drawn from them. This case does not fall within any of the exceptions to the general rule. We assume, that no respectable authority can be found, which maintains the admissibility of the opinion of a witness as to the *quantum* of damages caused by the breach of an executory contract to deliver goods. This would be to put the witness in the place of the jury, whose province it is to draw the inferences and conclusions from the facts and circumstances in evidence.—*Montg. & W. P. R. R. Co. v. Varner*, 19 Ala. 185; *Chandler v. Bush*, 84 Ala. 102,

The other questions objected to were directed to the loss of profits. The general rule is, that the measure of damages, in cases like the present, is the difference between the price agreed to be paid, and the market value of the goods at the place of delivery. If goods are purchased for the purpose of fulfilling an existing contract of re-sale, and this is known to the seller, the profits that would have been realized from the re-sale would be recoverable, such damages being within the contemplation of the parties as a natural consequence of a breach of the contract to deliver. In such case, it becomes the duty of the purchaser to procure goods of the same kind from other sources, if reasonably obtainable. It appears from the evidence that the defendant, on the morning before Christmas, telegraphed to another party for whiskey, which was received by express; of what kind, or whether at the same or greater price and expense, is not shown. The defendants were engaged in the business of retailing, for which purpose the whiskey was purchased. There are no *data* from which to compute, with any degree of certainty, the amount of profits which would accrue in carrying on such business from sales at retail of any particular kind of liquor. They are conjectural, merely speculative, and dependent on too many contingencies to constitute an element of recoverable damages. The fact that the whiskey was purchased for the Christmas trade, is not such specific object, or special circumstance, as will take the case without the operation of the general rule as to the recoverability of profits. We need only to refer to the following cases: *Brigham v. Carlisle*, 78 Ala. 243; *Union Refining Co. v. Barton*, 77 Ala. 148; *Pollock v. Gantt*, 69 Ala. 373; *Beck v. West, ante*, p. 213. The evidence does not bring the case within the influence of the decisions in *Bell v. Reynolds*, 78 Ala. 511, and *Culver v. Hill*, 68 Ala. 66.

Affirmed.

Beard *v.* Johnson.

87
107

Statutory Action in nature of Ejectment.

1. *Homestead exemption in lands of husband and wife.*—Where the family homestead is on the lands of the wife, less in quantity than is allowed by law'Code, 1876, § 2820), the husband can not assert a claim of homestead in an adjoining tract belonging to himself, part of which he cultivates, the two tracts together containing more than 160 acres.

[Beard v. Johnson.]

᾽APPEAL from the Circuit Court of Coffee.

Tried before the Hon. JESSE M. CARMICHAEL.

This action was brought by John M. Beard, against Needham G. Johnson, to recover the possession of a tract of land containing 120 acres; and was commenced on the 31st August, 1887. The plaintiff claimed the land as purchaser at a sale under a power in a mortgage executed by the defendant and his wife to J. C. Henderson; and he offered in evidence the mortgage, with its several assignments, and the deed to himself as the purchaser at the sale. The mortgage was dated October 28th, 1884; and the bill of exceptions states that it "was not acknowledged by the defendant's wife, separate and apart from him, and had no certificate to that effect upon it." The defendant then testified, in his own behalf, "that he was a married man at the time said mortgage was executed, and the land conveyed by it was all the land he then owned; that he used and cultivated said land in making a support for himself and family; that he had rented out the cleared land, except about eight acres, which he himself was cultivating, and the same was then in possession of his renter; that said land adjoined a sixty-acre tract belonging to his wife, upon which he and his family resided; that he lived on the forty acres of her land which adjoined the land here sued for, and the other twenty acres belonging to her adjoined said forty; that at the time said mortgage was executed his renter was in possession of the land sued for, except the eight acres mentioned above; that he rented the lands sued for the year before the mortgage was executed, and the year afterwards, but took possession of it once each year. This being all the evidence, the court charged the jury, on request, that they must find for the defendant, if they believed the evidence." The plaintiff excepted to this charge, and he here assigns it as error.

H. L. MARTIN, for appellant, cited *DeGraffenreid v. Clark*, 75 Ala. 425; 71 Ala. 140.

W. D. ROBERTS, *contra.*

STONE, C. J.—Our statute, unlike former legislation in this State, and unlike the statutes in many other States, does not confine the exemption of the homestead to the head of the family. Section 2507 of the Code of 1886, following the provision of our constitution, secures this right "to every resident of this State." The plaintiff in this action, Beard, claims the land in controversy, as purchaser at mortgage sale, the mortgage executed by Johnson and wife in 1884. That mortgage was executed, acknowledged and certified, in sufficient form to convey lands not a homestead, but not sufficient to convey the homestead. The sole question in this case is, whether the claim of homestead exemption, set up by Johnson in the court below, was a bar to the action. The trial court held that it was.

The Code of 1886 went into effect December 25, 1887. Section 2507 of that Code stands in the place of section 2820 of the Code of 1876. The language of the later compilation differs from the former one, and from the provision of the constitution. Under the former, the phrase "owned and occupied by any resident of this State," is expressed as one of the conditions of exemption. These words are omitted from section 2507 of the Code of 1886. Whether this omission requires us to give to the language a different interpretation as to occupancy, or whether the word "homestead," and other words found in that section and in sections 2539 and 2544, Code of 1886, are tantamount to the adjective "occupied," we need not inquire in this case. It is possible, if not probable, that the phrase was omitted, because it was considered superfluous. Homestead, *ex vi termini*, means the family seat or mansion. The source of Beard's title being anterior to the adoption of the Code of 1886, the issue in this case must be determined by the terms of the Code of 1876, § 2820.

As we have said, the headship of a family, under our statute, is not made a condition of the right of homestead exemption. Hence, in *Bender v. Meyer*, 55 Ala. 576, we decided that, in a proceeding under our former statute, to subject the statutory separate estate of the wife to the payment of a debt for articles of comfort and support of the household, she could successfully claim her homestead exemption. In this case, the homestead was on lands of her statutory separate estate.— *Weiner v. Sterling*, 61 Ala. 98.

It is manifest that ownership, entire or partial, in fee or for a term, is one of the essentials of rightful claim of homestead exemption. If there is no ownership, there is no liability to execution, and no occasion, or field of operation, for the claim of exemption. And there can not, at one and the same time, "be two separate valid homestead claims, the one by the husband, and the other by the wife."—Smyth's

[Beard v. Johnson.]

Law of Homesteads, § 157. The debt being against one, and not against the other, it is clear that only the property of the one whose debt is sought to be enforced, can be the subject of the claim of exemption, and only the one owing the debt can assert the claim. To come within the statute, the debt sought to be enforced must be one to which the property, in the absence of the exemption, would be subject. And husband and wife can not unite in the claim of exemption, unless, possibly, the execution is for the collection of a joint debt of the two. On this proposition we decide nothing.

In the case before us, the homestead, or family residence, was on the lands of the wife. The husband owned adjoining lands, cultivated a portion of them in connection with his wife's tract, and put the residue to rent, by annual lettings. The two tracts combined were twenty acres in excess of the greatest quantity allowed as an exempt homestead—one hundred and sixty acres. The wife's land was the homestead, and, if claimed, was clearly exempt from any debt due by her. She owned it, and, together with the family, occupied it. We think it is manifestly against both the letter and spirit of the law, that the two holdings, being not in common, but by different persons, should be tacked, the one to the other, and thus become an individual homestead, claimable by either. She, owning, and, together with the family, occupying the homestead proper—the land on which they resided—was, without doubt, entitled to claim its exemption from debts. This disabled him, so long as that ownership and occupancy lasted, to assert homestead in other lands, on which the family did not reside.

This ruling must not be understood as at all conflicting with the decisions in *Tyler v. Jewett*, 82 Ala. 93, and *Dicus v. Hall*, 83 Ala. 159. In each of those cases, the ownership relied on was in one and the same person. In the first named of the cases, one part of the realty claimed was freehold, and the other leasehold; a mere difference in the quantity of the estate the occupant owned. In the other, the only question was, whether the detached parcels of land, collectively not in excess of the limit, could be set apart as exempt, when they were shown to have been owned and occupied by the same person, as one and the same homestead and direct source of family support.

If the sale under the mortgage was regular, and a conveyance made to the purchaser (these are not questioned in the present appeal), the plaintiff was entitled to recover.

Reversed and remanded.

Thompson *v.* Tower Manufacturing Company.

Creditors' Bill in Equity to set aside Fraudulent Conveyance.

1. *Receiver; appointment without notice.*—On the filing of a bill by simple-contract creditors, seeking to set aside, on the ground of fraud, a transfer by their insolvent debtor of his entire stock of goods to his mother, a receiver should not be appointed without notice, on the *ex parte* affidavits of the complainants' solicitors, stating their belief that the appointment *instanter* is necessary for the protection of complainants—that if notice of the application was given to defendants, "they would sell or dispose of said property before a receiver could be appointed, and thus leave complainants remediless;" and that the grantee, whose insolvency is not averred, "is already trying, and has tried, to dispose in whole of said property conveyed to her."

APPEAL from the City Court of Anniston, in equity.
Heard before the Hon. W. F. JOHNSTON.

The bill in this case was filed on the 19th April, 1889, by the Tower Manufacturing Company, and other New York creditors of V. L. Thompson, against him and his mother, Mrs. C. A. Thompson; and sought to set aside, on the ground of fraud, a conveyance of his entire stock of goods by said V. L. Thompson to his mother, and the appointment of a receiver to take charge of the goods. The bill alleged that V. L. Thompson was "legally insolvent," having no property which could be reached by the ordinary process of law, though he had moneys in his possession, the proceeds of recent sales of goods for cash, which he fraudulently withheld from his creditors; but there was no allegation of the insolvency of Mrs. Thompson. On the filing of the bill, before the service of process, the complainants submitted an application for the appointment of a receiver, supported by the joint affidavit of their several solicitors, to this effect: "that they believe it is absolutely necessary for the protection of complainants that a receiver be appointed *instanter* as prayed in said bill, and without notice to defendants; that they believe, if notice of said application was given to said defendants, they would sell or dispose of said property before a receiver could be appointed, and thus leave complainants remediless; and that said C. A. Thompson is already trying, and has tried, to dispose in whole of said property conveyed to her." A receiver was appointed on the filing of these affidavits, and the order appointing him is now assigned as error.

KNOX & BOWIE, for appellant.

BROTHERS, WILLETT & WILLETT, *contra*.

STONE, C. J.—In the absence of an averment that Mrs. C. A. Thompson was and is unable to respond to the recovery complainants allege they are entitled to, the order appointing the receiver in this case must be reversed, on the authority of *Moritz & Weil v. Miller, Schram & Co.*, at the present term, *ante*, p. 336. This order is made without prejudice to the right of the complainants to renew the application, on proper notice and proofs, as they may be advised. It should be a strong case of emergency and peril, well fortified by affidavits. to authorize the appointment of a receiver without notice to the other party.—*Hughes v. Hatchett*, 55 Ala. 631; *Brierfield Iron Works v. Foster*, 54 Ala. 622. In *Weiss v. Goetter*, 72 Ala. 259, notice of the application had been given, and affidavits were produced on both sides.

If it had been shown that Mrs. Thompson was insolvent, we will not say what would have been our ruling; for the bill avers that she is endeavoring to dispose of the goods. The averments of the bill, if made good, show a flagitious case of fraud.—*Tryon v. Flournoy*, 80 Ala. 321.

Decretal order appointing receiver reversed, and cause remanded.

Oates *v.* Clendenard.

Action on Stated Account; Plea of Misnomer.

1. *Bill of particulars, as waiver of plea in abatement.*—The right to file a plea in abatement is not waived by a previous demand for a bill of particulars.—Code, § 2670.
2. *Misnomer.*—The variance between the names *Clendenard* and *Clendinen* is sufficient to support a plea in abatement on the ground of misnomer.

APPEAL from the Circuit Court of Henry.

Tried before the Hon. JESSE M. CARMICHAEL.

[Oates v. Clendenard.]

J. G. COWAN, for appellant.—The demand for a bill of particulars was a waiver of the misnomer.—Bac. Abr., *Misnomer* (*E*); 1 Saund. Pl. & Ev., mar. 47–8; *Price v. Harwood*, 3 Camp. 108; *Bass v. Clive*, 4 M. & S. 13; *Halcy v. State*, 63 Ala. 89; *Miller v. State*, 54 Ala. 155.

STONE, C. J.—The complaint and summons in this case each describes the defendant as J. A. *Clendenard*, and the suit is against that name. The defendant pleaded in abatement, that his name is *Clendinen*, and by that name he has always been known and called, and that he has never been known or called by the name of *Clendenard*. There is no other plea shown in the record. It is not directly shown whether the plaintiff demurred to this plea, took issue on its averments of fact, or in what manner the issue was raised upon it. The plea of misnomer, it is shown, was filed in time. The judgment-entry is as follows; "Came the parties by their attorneys, and upon consideration it is adjudged, that the plea in abatement be, and the same is hereby sustained." There was then judgment that defendant go hence. The implications from this language are, that this judgment was pronounced on an issue of law; and such issue is ordinarily raised by demurrer.

There is, however, a bill of exceptions in the record, which contains the following statement: "On the consideration of the plea in abatement filed in this cause, it was shown to the court that a bill of particulars, under section 2670 of the Code, was demanded of plaintiff by J. A. Clendinen, on whom process was served, and being the party filing the said plea in abatement; and said demand was in the time allowed for pleading, and before filing said plea." This recital shows that testimony was adduced, and is inconsistent with the idea that the sufficiency of the plea was tested on demurrer. If there was anything in the objection, it is probable it should have been raised on motion to strike the plea in abatement from the file.—*Haley v. State*, 63 Ala. 89. We will treat this question as if it were properly raised in that form.

We do not think the demand of a bill of particulars should be held a waiver of the defense of misnomer. That notice was not a plea, nor in any sense a defense on the merits. It was, at most, a step, preparatory to defense, should the same become necessary under the rulings of the court on the plea in abatement. Counsel could not know what would be the fate of his plea; and if there was a meri-

torious defense, it would certainly be the dictate of prudence
to be prepared to make it. The notice in this case is not
like a demurrer, plea to the merits, or other step taken, or
ruling of the court invoked, which would be an admission
that the defendant was rightly in court. A notice to produce, or to furnish a bill of particulars, might become material on the trial of an issue formed on the plea of misnomer.

The variance in name, pleaded in this case, is certainly
substantial, and justified the ruling of the Circuit Court.
Munkers v. State, *ante*, p. 94, and authorities cited.

Affirmed.

Mobile Savings Bank *v.* McDonnell

*Bill in Equity by Creditor to set aside Mortgage, or Deed of
Trust, as Fraudulent.*

1. *Competency of party as witness.*—At common law, a party to the
record was not a competent witness in the cause, except in certain
cases, while, under statutory provisions (Code, § 2765), he is rendered
a competent witness generally, but is not allowed to testify as to any
transaction with a deceased person whose estate is interested in the
result of the suit, or who acted in that transaction in a fiduciary capacity; and the courts will not engraft the common-law exceptions on the
statutory provisions, where they are repugnant to the obvious policy of
the statute.

2. *Testimony of party as to transaction with deceased agent.*—In a suit
by a creditor seeking to set aside, as fraudulent, a mortgage or deed of
trust executed by his insolvent debtor to an incorporated bank, the
debtor himself being a party to the suit, he can not be allowed (Code,
§ 2765) to testify as a witness that the conveyance was withheld from
record, by agreement between him and the bank cashier, since deceased,
lest it might injure his credit; and the fact that a decree *pro confesso*
has been entered against him, does not remove his statutory incompetency.

3. *Unrecorded mortgage; validity as against creditors.*—An unrecorded
mortgage, which, after several renewals, is at last recorded within the
time allowed by the statute (Code, §§ 1810–11), is not void as against
simple-contract creditors, whose debts were incurred in the meantime,
unless it was withheld from record for the fraudulent purpose of upholding the credit of the debtor, or is otherwise impeached by proof of actual
or positive fraud on the part of the mortgagee; and under the facts of
this case (the *bona fides* of the secured debt being admitted, the mortgage conveying not more than one third of the debtor's property, the
law-day not being postponed for an unreasonable time, and it not being
shown that the mortgagee had notice of the debtor's insolvency), the
charge of fraud in fact is not sustained.

APPEAL from the Chancery Court of Mobile.

Heard before the Hon. THOS. W. COLEMAN.

The bill in this case was filed on the 17th October, 1887, by the executors of the last will and testament of James McDonnell, deceased, against the Mobile Savings Bank, W. J. Hearin as trustee, and Peter Burke and his wife; and sought to set aside on the ground of fraud, actual and constructive, a deed of trust executed by said Burke and wife to Hearin as trustee, to secure a debt of about $14,000 due to said bank. The deed of trust was executed on the 15th June, 1885, and was filed for record on the 27th July next afterwards; but the secured debt had been renewed several times, commencing in September, 1884, and a new mortgage executed on each renewal, and none of these mortgages were ever recorded. The bill alleged that Burke, at the time these transactions commenced, seemed to be doing a large and prosperous business, and was reputed to be a wealthy man, though he was in fact financially embarrassed, if not insolvent, and owed the bank nearly $100,000; that the bank, ascertaining his condition, determined to reduce his indebtedness, and not to extend further credit without security, but, knowing that publicity of the facts "would destroy his credit, render him unable to meet his liabilities, and thereby sacrifice said indebtedness to the bank, concealed said indebtedness from the public, and' thereby enabled him to obtain the indorsements of a number of his friends, upon paper which was afterwards, by pre-arrangement between him and said bank, given to it as security for part of said indebtedness; that said indorsements could not have been obtained, as said bank well knew, if the extent of Burke's indebtedness to it, and the evidence of said mortgages, or deeds of trust, after mentioned, had been known; . . that the purpose of allowing him to continue his business and to maintain his credit was to enable him to raise money and get security from other people, with which to reduce or secure the debt to said bank, and it was agreed and understood between him and said bank that said mortgage, or deed of trust, should not be recorded, but, for the purposes aforesaid, should be kept secret from the world;" that with a knowledge of the statutory provisions regulating the time within which mortgages were required to be recorded, "and for the purpose of protecting said property against judgment creditors and purchasers for value, and at the same time keeping the existence of said instrument a secret from the public, and there-

47

by maintaining the credit of said Burke, said Hearin, said bank and said Burke had an agreement and understanding between themselves, that said mortgage should not be recorded, but should be renewed every thirty or sixty days thereafter, or at some other frequent periods, until said Burke should pay off his said indebtedness, or until some complication in his affairs should necessitate the making public of said transaction;" and that said Burke executed a general assignment for the benifit of his creditors on Saturday, July 25th, 1885, two days before the last deed of trust was filed for record.

A joint answer was filed by the bank and Hearin, in which they stated the history of the various transactions between the bank and Burke, as shown by the books of the bank, whereby his indebtedness was reduced from $75,000 to $15,000; stated that these transactions were all conducted, on the part of the bank, by Thomas Henry, then president, and J. B. McMillan, cashier, both since deceased; denied that the bank had any notice of Burke's embarrassed condition; denied any fraud or concealment on the part of the bank, or any agreement or understanding that the deeds of trust should be withheld from record for the purpose of upholding Burke's credit, and insisted on the *bona fides* and validity of the deed of trust and the secured debt.

A decree *pro confesso* was entered against Burke, and his deposition was afterwards taken by the complainants. In reference to the first mortgage given to the bank, and its renewal from time to time, by agreement between himself and said McMillan, then cashier of the bank, Burke thus testified: "At first I objected to giving the mortgage, on the ground that it would affect my credit, and break up my business. He promised me most faithfully that no one would know anything about it, except himself and Major Hearin, who would be the trustee of the property, and that the same would not be put upon the record. I gave the mortgage on these conditions. It was agreed that the note and mortgage should be extended, from time to time as it fell due, for either thirty, sixty, or ninety days, as it should be convenient for me to pay the interest; except that I could not extend beyond ninety days at a time, because that was the limit for mortgages to be put upon record." The bank moved to suppress this part of the testimony of the witness, and other portions in which he referred to the agreement between himself and McMillan, because McMillan was dead, and had acted in the matter in a fiduciary capacity for the bank. The chancellor overruled the objections to the testimony of the witness, on the ground that he would be competent at common law, and that the statute was intended to enlarge rather than restrict the competency of witnesses; and on final hearing, on pleadings and proof, he rendered a decree for the complainants, holding the mortgage fraudulent and void. The defendants appeal, and assign this decree as error, with the overruling of their objections to the testimony of Burke.

T. A. HAMILTON, and OVERALL & BESTOR, for appellant.

GREG. L. & H. T. SMITH, *contra.*

SOMERVILLE, J.—The present bill is filed by the executors of James McDonnell, deceased, to set aside as fraudulent a deed of trust executed by Peter Burke on June 15th, 1885, to W. J. Hearin, as trustee for the Mobile Savings Bank, to secure a promissory note made by Burke and wife, of even date with the conveyance, for the sum of fourteen thousand dollars, and payable thirty days after date. This conveyance was a renewal of a series of prior mortgages on the same property, the first of which was executed on September 30th, 1884, to secure a debt of fifteen thousand dollars due by Burke to the Bank; and the others, four in number, being executed at various dates afterwards, extending to, and including the one in controversy. These conveyances were withheld from the record, none of them being registered except the last; and this was recorded on July 27th, 1887, on the day after Burke made a general assignment of his property to his creditors.

The question which we first consider is the admissibility of that portion of Burke's testimony which relates to the execution of the mortgage, and the alleged agreement between himself and the Bank that the instrument was to be withheld from the record, and its existence kept a secret, for the purpose of enabling Burke to maintain his credit with the public. Burke is a party defendant to the record in this case, and was introduced as a witness by the complainants, not by the Mobile Savings Bank, itself also a defendant to the suit. The transaction as to which he testified occurred between him and one McMillan, now deceased, who was then acting as cashier of the Bank, a relation of agency which was unquestionably of a fiduciary character.

We are clearly of opinion that Burke was not a competent witness as to this transaction, and that the chancellor erred in not excluding his testimony, so far as objected to by the appellant. He falls directly under the ban of the statute, both in letter and spirit, as declared in section 2765 of the present Code (1886). That section is to be construed in the light of the common-law rule, that all persons who were *parties* to the record, or had a pecuniary interest in the result of the suit, were incompetent to testify.—Stephen on Ev., Art. 107. The statute enlarges, to some extent, the former rule of competency, or, what is the same thing, narrows the old rule of exclusion; but it "preserves the common-law rule as to the class of excepted cases," at least where the proposed evidence does not violate the manifest policy of the statute.—*Dudley v. Steele*, 71 Ala. 423. It is substantially declared that, in civil suits, or proceedings, the common-law rule shall be abolished, which excluded a witness from testifying because he was a party to the record, or interested in the issue tried; and that hereafter, generally, both parties and interested persons shall be competent witnesses, except in certain cases. This exception provides, that "neither *party* shall be allowed to testify against the other, as to any transaction with, or statement by any deceased person, whose estate is interested in the result of the suit or proceeding, or ·when such *deceased person*, at the time of such transaction or statement, acted in any *representative or fiduciary relation* whatever to the party against whom such testimony is sought to be introduced, unless called to testify thereto by the opposite party."—Code, 1886, § 2765.

We repeat, by way of lending emphasis to the fact, that, as to the class of statutory exceptions, the common-law rule is preserved, and not abrogated, and that rule generally makes parties to the record incompetent. That this case falls among those excepted by the statute, scarcely admits of argument. The proposed witness, Burke, is a party to the record. Whether he is otherwise interested, makes no sort of difference.· McMillan, the agent of the bank, with whom the transaction occurred, is deceased, and was so at the time of the trial. We have often said, that the purpose and policy of the statutes are, to exclude the living from testifying against the dead, because the latter can not be heard in contradiction. A contrary rule would open broad the door to the entry of innumerable frauds. That a party to a suit is, under the statute, incompetent to testify as to a transaction with, or statement made by a deceased *agent* of another party to the record in the same suit, has several times been expressly decided by this court, and that is this precise case. *Warten v. Strane,* 82 Ala. 311; *Stanley v. Sheffield L. I. & C. Co.,* 83 Ala. 260. See, also, *Miller v. Cannon,* 84 Ala. 59.

The concluding clause of the statute—"unless called to testify thereto by the opposite party"—is only declaratory of the common-law rule, which permitted the immunity of incompetency to be waived by the opposite party,—by which is meant the party to the transaction whose rights would be affected by the testimony offered.—*Dudley v. Steele,* 71 Ala. 423.

In this view of the law, it is immaterial that the interest of Burke was equally balanced; his exclusion as a witness not resting on the ground of interest merely, but upon the independent fact of his being a party to the suit and record.

It next becomes our duty to consider this case disembarrassed of so much of Burke's testimony as may be construed to have reference to any transaction or conversation between himself and McMillan, pertinent to the mortgage in controversy, or any other collateral facts in issue. Burke being the only witness who testifies to any positive or express agreement between the parties to withhold the mortgage from registration, and to conceal its existence, we are left to make only such inferences on this subject as may be justified by the other evidence in the case.

The theory upon which the complainants' case must rest, then, is this: That Burke, at the time he executed the mortgage, was insolvent, and this fact was known to the Bank; that he was, however, reputed to be solvent and financially prosperous; and that the Bank fraudulently withheld the mortgage from the record, and permitted the mortgagor to remain in possession of the mortgaged property—a storehouse in which he was carrying on the mercantile business—for the specific purpose of giving him a fictitious credit; that the complainants' testator and others, being misled by the deceit, indorsed for, and loaned money to Burke, on the faith of the belief that no such mortgage existed, and thereby lost large sums of money, which they would not otherwise have lost.

It is manifest that the bill can be maintained only by proof of actual or positive fraud, either in the execution of the mortgage, or in the use made of it after its delivery to the Bank as grantee. Our statutes of registration go no further

than to protect subsequent purchasers for value, mortgagees
and judgment creditors without notice, against unrecorded
conveyances; and to neither of these classes do the complainants claim to belong, they being mere simple-contract creditors.—*Tutwiler v. Montgomery*, 73 Ala. 263; *Chadwick v.
Carson*, 78 Ala. 116; Code, 1886, §§ 1810-1811. The mere
failure to record the mortgage, without more, would not impair its validity as against a simple-contract creditor.

Nor is it pretended that the Bank, or any of its agents,
ever made any positive representations touching the solvency
or credit of Burke, which could have come to the ears of
McDonnell, so as to have influenced him in making loans to,
or indorsements for Burke. Even were this true, such a representation, even though false, would not constitute a basis of
an action for damages, unless it was either "in writing signed
by the party sought to be charged," or else made with the
intent to defraud, which would involve the false affirmation
of some alleged fact that the party making knows to be false,
or of the truth of which he has no knowledge, or well
grounded belief.—*Clark v. Dunham Lumber Co.*, 86 Ala.
220; 5 So. Rep. 560; Code, 1886, § 1734. Nothing can be
found in this principle which can lend plausibility to the contention of the appellees.

We can discover nothing in the facts of this case which
justified the conclusion, that there was any fraudulent intent
on the part of the Mobile Savings Bank in originally taking
the security. No question is raised as to the alleged *bona fides*
of the debt which it was given to secure; and the conveyance
embraced less than a third of the assessed value of the mortgagor's unincumbered property. If the instrument had been
recorded at once, there would scarcely have been any available pretext upon which its validity could have been successfully assailed. Especially is this apparent in view of the
fact, that the settlement between Burke and the Bank, on
September 30th, 1884, of which the first of the series of
mortgages constituted a part, operated to release McDonnell
from certain debts to the Bank, which he had incurred as indorser for Burke, of over fifteen thousand dollars—or a sum
greater than *that of the mortgage debt*. We can not suppose this release would have taken place, in this substitution
of securities, unless the mortgage had been given. It
enured, therefore, indirectly to McDonnell's benefit, as fully
as it would have done had he been the beneficiary in the instrument. Whoever may have ground to complain of being

damaged by its execution, he could not do so with any show
of truth or justice. Even fraud, without damage, gives no
ground of action in equity, or at law.

This leaves but one ground upon which to maintain the
bill, and that is the failure or refusal of the Bank to record
the mortgage, and the alleged fraudulent motive with which
this was done. There may, no doubt, be cases where a deed,
or mortgage, not at first fraudulent in its inception, may become so by being actively concealed, or not pursued, "by
which means creditors," as said in an old English case, "are
drawn in to lend their money."—*Hungerford v. Earle*,
2 Vern. 261; *Hildreth v. Sands*, 2 John Ch. (N. Y.) 35.
We are not dealing with the case of a deed, where the vendor is left in possession, contrary to the essential nature and
terms of the conveyance, but with a mortgage, where continued possession by the mortgagor, for a length of time not
unreasonably long, is consistent with the nature of the
security. In such a case, *a fortiori*, to make the withholding of the instrument from the record fraudulent, especially
as to debts afterwards created, it must have been done with
the purpose of upholding fictitiously the credit of the mortgagor, so as to enable him to obtain money or goods of
others, which he would not be likely to do if the instrument
were recorded. In other words, there must be an actual
intent to defraud, resulting in damage to some creditor of
the grantor.—*Tryon v. Flournoy*, 80 Ala. 321; *Danner
Land & Lumber Co. v. Stonewall Ins. Co.*, 77 Ala. 184;
Blennerhasset v. Sherman, 105 U. S. 100.

It is not certain that the Bank, through its officers, was
any better informed as to the solvency of Burke than Mc-
Donnell himself was. His credit seems at one time to have
been excellent with both of them. At the time of Burke's
suspension, he owed the Bank between seventy-five and
eighty thousand dollars, and he owed McDonnell, contingently, between fifty-five and sixty thousand dollars, which
soon afterwards actually accrued from this liability for previous lðans and indorsements, and was proved by McDonnell as a claim against the trustee under Burke's assignment.
Deducting the mortgage debt in question, this would leave
but a few thousand dollars of difference between the credits
thus extended by the two parties. In this estimate, we do
not, of course, consider Burke's debt which he at one time
owed the bank, and which was secured by pledge of Alabama
State bonds. It is made to appear that McDonnell and

Burke were personal friends, and very intimate in their social and business relations, being constantly in each other's
company, and often discussing business in which they were
both mutually interested. It is common knowledge, that
men in failing circumstances frequently conceal their financial condition, not so much for the fraudulent purpose of
retaining a fictitious credit, as with the hope that better
times may bring them financial relief by producing a favorable turn in the wheel of fortune. It may have been so with
Burke. He does not seem to have made a fair disclosure of
his financial *status* to his friend, who made an explicit demand on him for such an exhibit four or five months before
his failure by assignment, which, as we have said, was on
July 25th, 1885. The testimony of Boulet shows that this
exhibit of a balance-sheet of assets and liabilities made it
appear that he was worth two dollars for every one he owed.
It included the store-house embraced in the mortgage, but
made no disclosure of the mortgage incumbrance held on it
by the Bank. There is no intimation that the bank officers
ever knew of this statement, nor does it appear that McDonnell ever applied to them for any information as to the state
of Burke's indebtedness to that institution. If Burke, to
keep up his credit with McDonnell, made a statement which
showed him to be solvent, is it not just as probable that, with
a like object in view, he made one equally favorable to the
Bank? But it is said that the Bank refused to allow Burke
to continue to overdraw his account, and demanded the mortgage to secure a part of his indebtedness; and this showed
a knowledge of his insolvency, or reasonable ground to believe that he was insolvent. The first step argued only ordinary prudence, and the second may be interpreted into a
desire to be made safe by a common mode of security often
exacted of solvent debtors. But, supposing the bank officers
to have been in doubt as to the solvency of Burke, present or
future, it was a delicate matter with which to deal, and a
subject demnding at their hands great prudence. A suspicion, unjustly magnified, or a fact exaggerated, might have
brought even a solvent debtor to speedy embarrassment, or,
perhaps, to financial ruin. Financial credit, like female virtue, is often damned by being doubted. The fact, moreover,
that the mortgage originally taken in September, 1884, was
several times renewed, and was not recorded until Burke's
failure, lends credence to the view, that the mortgagee had no
well grounded belief that it was necessary to record it. Be-

[Mobile Savings Bank v. McDonnell.]

sides, it was recorded immediately, when demanded by the necessity of the mortgagor's failure. Discarding Burke's testimony, as we have done, we are at liberty to infer that the Bank was under no obligation created by an agreement not to record, and no one of the mortgages was withheld for a longer period of time than that authorized by the statute regulating the subject of the registration of such conveyances.

We fully recognize the doctrine of the well-considered case of *Blennerhassett v. Sherman*, 105 U. S. 100, where the authorities bearing on the subject of the fraudulent withholding of mortgages from registration are ably reviewed. There, an insolvent debtor had executed a mortgage upon his entire estate, for a very large sum of money. The secured creditor not only knew of the debtor's insolvency, but actively concealed the mortgage by purposely withholding it from the record, and in the meanwhile represented the mortgage debtor as having a large estate and unlimited credit— all this being done for the fraudulent purpose of giving him a fictitious credit—and by this means he was enabled to contract other debts which he could not pay. This fraudulent intent was properly held to vitiate the mortgage as a valid security, and to render it void. The case of *Hilliard v. Cagle*, 46 Miss. 309, seems to go to the extent of creating an estoppel in favor of creditors generally, without any actual fraud being imputed to the mortgagee in withholding his mortgage from registration. This view is contrary to the spirit of our registration statutes, and does not seem to us to be based on sound reasoning. It affords protection to those not intended to be protected by the statute—to other than subsequent purchasers for value, mortgagees and judgment creditors.

After a careful examination of all the legal testimony in this case, we do not feel authorized to find that the mortgage in controversy, covering less than a third of the assessed value of the debtor's property, and perhaps not more than a fourth of its real value, was either fraudulent in its execution, or was withheld from record for the fraudulent purpose imputed by the bill to the mortgagee.

The chancellor erred, in our judgment, in so deciding, and his decree must be reversed. A decree will be rendered in this court, adjudging the complainants not to be entitled to the relief prayed, and dismissing the bill.

Reversed and rendered.

[Mobile Savings Bank v. McDonnell.]

NOTE.—On application for rehearing, the case was held under advisement until November 7, 1889, when the following opinion was delivered:

SOMERVILLE, J.—We have given very careful attention to the application for rehearing in this case, and are constrained, after due consideration, to overrule it. This we have done after an attentive examination of all the authorities cited on the briefs of counsel, and many others besides.

The main point of contention is the admissibility of Burke's testimony. We held that, being a party defendant to the record—an indispensable party—he could not, therefore, testify to any transaction which occurred between him and McMillan, the deceased agent of his co-defendant, the Mobile Savings Bank, because he was prohibited from doing so by section 2765 of the Code (1886).

It is now urged that, inasmuch as a decree *pro confesso* was taken against Burke, this rendered him a competent witness to impeach for fraud the validity of the mortgage which he had executed to the Bank. The argument is, that this rendered him competent under the rules of the common law, and of equity practice, and, therefore, he is competent under the present statute, although he might be properly excluded if no decree *pro confesso* had been rendered. The point presented is one worthy of attentive examination, and has been argued by counsel on both sides with research, candor and ability.

We stated the rule of the common law to be, like that of the Roman law, that a party to the record was generally held incompetent to testify in a cause, by reason of the mere fact of his connection with the record, and irrespective of the question of his interest in the result of the suit. This rule, as Mr. Starkie observes, is not founded merely on the consideration of pecuniary interest, but, in part at least, "on principles of policy for the prevention of perjury." 3 Stark. Ev. *1061. Mr. Greenleaf adopts this as the better opinion, as the contrary principle would hold out to parties a strong temptation to perjury; and, therefore, he says, "the party is not admissible, without the consent of all the parties to the record, for the privilege is mutual, and not several."—1 Greenl. Ev. §§ 354, 329. The same view is supported by Mr. Stephen in his work on Evidence (Stephen's Dig. Ev., Art. 107); although the view of Mr. Best is, that

[Mobile Savings Bank v. McDonnell.]

a party, who is not interested, is a competent witness.—1 Best on Ev. § 168. The decisions, both in England and this country, are greatly conflicting on this subject, and, we may say, after much study of them, are environed by no little perplexity.

In this case, it is very important not only to ascertain the true rule in this respect, but the *reason* on which it is founded. The Supreme Court of the United States has many times had occasion to discuss the question, and is committed to the broad view, that (irrespective of statute) the party to a record, although divested of all interest, is disqualified to testify in the cause, if his testimony be objected to by any other party to the record. In *Stein v. Bowman*, 13 Pet. 209, an action at law, it was said the opposite rule "would hold out to parties a strong temptation to perjury, and we think it is not sustained either by principle or authority." "It would," said Mr. Justice McLean, "lead to perjuries, and the most injurious consequences in the administration of justice." "The exclusion," says Mr. Justice Nelson, in *Bridges v. Armour*, 5 How. 91, "is placed on the ground of public policy, which forbids a party from being a witness in his own cause," · · · the opposite rule "holding out to litigants temptations to perjury, and to the manufacturing of witnesses in the administration of justice." That court has thus alway adhered with great strictness to "the common-law rule, that a party to the record can not be a witness, either for himself or a co-suitor in the cause," until its abrogation by statute in the year 1864.—*United States v. Clark*, 96 U. S. 37, 44. There are many other courts that have taken the same view of this general rule of the common law, which is, of course, subject to many exceptions, based on necessity and convenience. It has, for example, been held that a party may testify to collateral facts in a suit; as, facts authorizing a continuance; the service of notice to produce papers; search for lost papers; and, perhaps, the fact of loss itself, with a view of introducing secondary evidence; or to the contents of a lost trunk or package, and other like cases.

It is especially insisted that another exception to the rule is, that a party defendant, against whom a judgment by default, or decree *pro confesso* has been rendered, is competent, on the ground that he ceases to be a party to the record. It is sought to sustain the admissibility of Burke's testimony on this ground—the record showing a decree *pro confesso* against him.

There are many cases on this question, and they are conflicting, both in England and the United States. In *Mant v. Mainwaring*, 8 Taunt. 139, a party to the record was held incompetent, although judgment by default had gone against him, and a release was executed by the plaintiff; while in *Worrall v. Jones*, 7 Bing. 395, a later case, it was held that a defendant, who had suffered judgment by default, and had no interest in the event of the suit, was, by his own consent, admissible as a witness for the plaintiff, the only objection urged being that he was a party to the record. The doctrine of the latter case prevailed in England, as to actions at law, until the year 1843, when an act of Parliament removed incompetency arising from crime or interest, but preserved the old common-law rule in actions at law as to parties "named in the record," who were still declared incompetent; and this continued to be the law until the act of 14 & 15 Vic. c. 99, § 1.—2 Taylor Ev. §§ 1347, 1349. And it was further deemed expedient, at the same time, to provide by special enactment that a defendant in a court of equity might be examined in behalf of the plaintiff, or of any co-defendant.—*Ib.*

The only ground on which the principle contended for can be logically sustained very clearly must be, that a judgment by default, or decree *pro confesso*, like a *nolle prosequi*, or separate verdict, terminates the suit as to such defaulting defendant, so that he ceases to be a party to the record; *or else*, that this ends his interest in the litigation, and that a party defendant, who has no interest, may testify against the protest of other parties who are prejudiced by his testimony.—1 Greenl. Ev. § 355.

There are several early cases in this State, prior to the Code of 1852, in which mere *nominal* parties to the record, without any interest in the event of the suit, were allowed to testify; and others where they were admitted to testify against their interest, when called by the opposite party. *Prewitt v. Marsh*, 1 S. & P. 17 (1831); *Duffee v. Pennington*, 1 Ala. 506 (1840); *Cunningham v. Carpenter*, 10 Ala. 109 (1846); *Burns v. Taylor*, 23 Ala. 255 (1853). So, in *Scott v. Jones*, 4 Ala. 695, a defendant in an action of assumpsit, against whom a judgment by default had been rendered, was held to be competent to prove the other defendants were his partners; and this ruling was followed in *Gooden v. Morrow*, 8 Ala. 486.

The rule in chancery cases, too, we admit, was, perhaps,

even more liberal in according to defendants the right to testify, where they were not interested. In *Colgin v. Redman*, 20 Ala. 650 (1852), a party defendant to a deed of assignment was allowed to testify as to matters in regard to which he had no interest, or which militated against his interest; it being said that "the mere fact that a witness was a party to a suit in chancery is no sufficient reason to exclude or suppress his deposition." In *Crawford v. Barkly*, 18 Ala. 270 (1850), a defendant in equity, against whom a decree *pro confesso* had been rendered, was allowed to testify, on the ground that he was not interested. And in *Royall v. McKenzie*, 25 Ala. 364 (1854), it was said, *arguendo*. that a defendant trustee might be a witness for his co-defendant in equity, if he had no interest in the suit; but the witness there was interested, and his exclusion was held proper on that ground. The case of *Montandon v. Deas*, 14 Ala. 33 (1848), contains a strong *dictum* in support of the view, that a party defendant, if his interest was precisely balanced, might testify against a co-defendant. But, in that case, it is shown clearly that no objection was interposed to the testimony, until the case reached the appellate court, and the case could have well been decided on this ground.

It is admitted that these decisions apparently go very far to sustain the contention of the appellant's counsel. Their force is weakened, however, as we shall seek to show, by the obvious fact, that they are opposed to the policy of our present statute, which seeks to avoid the strong temptations to perjury which might flow from allowing the living to testify against the dead. They ignore, moreover, that *reason* of the common-law rule, to which we have adverted, which was adverse to admitting *parties* to testify, on the ground, not of interest merely, but of that bias and prejudice begotten of forensic contention, which is often more potent than pecuniary interest. This policy was founded on man's inherent love of triumph, and his correlative aversion to defeat in all things, however profitless the result in pecuniary gain. This principle was well illustrated in the barbarous practice of wager by battle, which was once a common mode of settling lawsuits, criminal and civil, and was nothing more nor less than a duel to the death between ferocious litigants to settle a litigated lawsuit.

The policy of these decisions, we may further observe, was reprobated by the Code of 1852 (§ 2302), which removed all incompetency of witnesses based on crime (except perjury or subornation of perjury), or interest in the event of the suit (including liability for costs), "unless the judgment would be evidence for [or against] him in another suit," such objection going only to his credit. But it was declared that this section should "not be construed" so as to authorize *parties* to be witnesses, further than expressly authorized by other provisions of the Code.—Code, 1852, § 2302 This was a legislative declaration, in effect, that the common-law rule as to parties was sound in policy, and was to be maintained; and it tore up by the roots, so to speak, all previous decisions. From that time to the act of February, 1867, we find no case where a party to the record was held to be competent; and this act itself affirmed the same rule, inferentially, by removing the recognized incompetency of *parties as such*, irrespective of the question of interest, with certain *excepted cases.*—Rev. Code, 1867, § 2704. And so with all subsequent statutes.—Code, 1876, § 3057; Code, 1886, § 2765.

There is no occasion, in this view of the case, to declare these decisions overruled, although they are opposed by strong authority. For example, it is held in *Swanzy v. Parker,* 50 Penn. St. 441; 88 Amer. Dec. 549, where the cases are reviewed, that a defaulted defendant, although without interest in the suit, is incompetent to testify, because he is still a party to the record; and *Wolf v. Fink,* 1 Penn. St. 435, is an authority to the same point. So, in *DeWolf v. Johnson,* 10 Wheat. 368, a defendant against whom a decree *pro confesso* had been taken was held by the United States Supreme Court to be incompetent as a witness, and was excluded because he was still a party to the record. The latter is just this case.

It will be found generally true, that where contrary rulings have been made, and the reasons given, defaulted parties have been admitted on the alleged ground that they have ceased to have an *interest* in the suit. not on the ground that they had ceased to be *parties;* as in *Lupton v. Lupton,* 2 John. Ch. 614, a case in equity, and *Worrall v. Jones,* 7 Bing. 395, which was an action at law.

Under our present practice and existing statutes, unlike what they formerly were, shortly prior to the Code of 1852, it is very certain that a decree *pro confesso* does not now operate to discharge a defendant as a party to the record, or sever his connection with the cause. The most to be accomplished by it is as a conclusive admission of the facts alleged in the bill.—Code, 1886, § 3483. The defendant in default can still "appear and contest the decree on the merits of the bill, or may appear before the register on a reference." Code, § 3485. And he may also move to dismiss the bill for want of equity.—*Madden v. Floyd*, 69 Ala. 222. He is still invested with the authority to show himself an active and troublesome litigant, in this limited field of operation.

If we should even regard this question under discussion as a doubtful one under the old law—one on which the authorities everywhere have been at variance—the history and phraseology of our legislation show that the policy of our present statute, as embraced in section 2765 of the Code of 1886, was to prohibit parties from testifying as to certain transactions with deceased persons, within the specified exceptions, because of the injustice done the opposite party by reason of want of mutuality—his equal footing being destroyed by the death of his witness, with whom the alleged transaction or conversation occurred. It was observed in *Kumpe v. Coons*, 63 Ala. 448, that this statute "was intended as a revision of the whole subject of the competency of witnesses because of interest, or because of their relation to the suit or proceedings, and to substitute the rule prescribed by them, not only for the rules of the common law, but for the provisions of former statutes." In *Dudley v. Steele*, 71 Ala. 423, it was said that the statute, as now existing in section 2765 of the Code, enlarged the former common-law rule of competency, but "preserved the common-law rule as to the class of excepted cases." This clearly means those exceptional cases in which parties, or interested persons, were allowed to testify at common law, which do *not violate the policy, or contravene the plain purpose of the statute* as it now exists; as where one party to the record was called to testify in favor of the opposite party, against his own interest, which was the very case of *Dudley v. Steele, supra*. The case of *Dismukes v. Tolson*, 67 Ala. 386, is another illustration of our proposition. We there ruled, that original entries made by a defendant in his own shop-books, although admissible ordinarily in his own favor under certain restrictions, as an exception to the common-law rule excluding parties, could not be proved by himself, in a suit brought by the administrator of a deceased person, where such entries had reference to a transaction with the deceased in his lifetime. Such evidence was held to violate the policy of the statute, which was said to be, that "there should be no admissibility, unless there was mutuality; that when the lips of one party to a transaction are sealed by death, those of the other must in like manner be sealed by law."—*Miller v. Cannon*, 84 Ala. 59; *Welch v. Adams*, 56 Amer. Rep. 521; 3 Brick. Dig. 825-26, and cases cited.

To reiterate: parties to the record were incompetent witnesses at common law, except in certain cases. The statutes of this State now make parties competent to testify, except in a particular class of cases—*i. e.*, generically, where the transaction testified to was with a deceased person. We deduce the rule, that the common-law *exceptions*, whereby parties were held competent in certain cases, *will not now be engrafted on the present statute*, where such exceptions are *repugnant to the obvious policy of such statute*. Only such of these common-law exceptions as do not contravene the purposes of the present statute, will be recognized as now being in force. The present case, in our judgment, is not one of them.

Our conclusion is, that Burke remained a party to the record, notwithstanding the decree *pro confesso* against him; and being a necessary, and not a nominal party, he ought not to be allowed to testify, as to any transaction with a deceased agent of his co-defendant, the Savings Bank, unless called to testify thereto by such party, whose rights would be injuriously affected by his testimony.

The other objections to the opinion and judgment heretofore rendered in the cause will be overruled.

The application for rehearing is refused.

INDEX.

ACCOMPLICE. See CRIMINAL LAW. 1.

ACCORD AND SATISFACTION.

1. *Novation.*—If the mortgagor of personal property, having sold to a third person a part of the mortgaged property, afterwards executes another mortgage on other property, which is accepted by the mortgagee "in settlement of said matter for" the property so sold, or is so accepted by his agent, whose act is afterward ratified by him, this constitutes a valid substitutionary contract, healing the breach of the first, and is available to the purchaser as a defense to a subsequent action for the alleged conversion of the property sold to him. *Cobb v. Malone & Collins*, 514.

ACTION.

1. *Against agent of foreign corporation, for taxes.*—To sustain an action against the agent of a foreign corporation engaged in the business of lending money on mortgages, for taxes assessed on the gross receipts of its business, a valid assessment must be shown, as claimed, against that particular corporation. *State v. Sloss*, 119.

2. *When action lies for money paid.*—To maintain an action for money paid by plaintiffs to the holders of certain non-transferable "labor-tickets" issued by the defendant corporation to workmen in its employment, it must be shown that plaintiffs took the tickets at the instance or request of the corporation, acting through some agent lawfully authorized to bind it ; or, if the agreement was made by an agent not duly authorized, that it was afterwards ratified by the corporation. *Tabler, Crudup & Co. v. Sheffield Land, Iron & Coal Co.*, 305.

3. *When action lies for obstruction to navigable river.*—The obstruction of a navigable river is a public nuisance ; but an individual can not maintain an action on account of it, unless he shows some special injury to himself, independent of the general injury to the public. *Sipsey River Nav. Co. v. Geo. Pac. Railway Co.*, 154.

4. *Same; for pollution of running stream.*—An owner of land, through which a small stream runs, may maintain an action at law for damages, on account of injuries caused by the pollution of the stream and the deposit of sediment from a smelting furnace and washers for iron ore, by an upper proprietor. *Clifton Iron Co. v. Dye*, 468.

5. *Same; for obstruction of street.*—The obstruction of a street in an incorporated city or town, although under claim of title to the soil, is an indictable nuisance, for which an action lies in favor of any person sustaining special damage. *Demopolis v. Webb*, 659.

6. *Action by partnership.*—A suit may be maintained in the name of a late partnership, stating the names of the late partners, notwithstanding its dissolution. *Tompkins v. Levy & Bro.*, 264.

7. *Action against partner, for debt of partnership.*—In an action against a partner individually, the complaint containing the common counts only, a recovery may be had on proof of a debt against the partnership. *Clark v. Jones & Bro.*, 474.

48

ADVERSE POSSESSION—*Continued.*

3. *Adverse possession, under permissive possessor.*—A permissive possession does not become adverse, without an open and distinct disavowal of the title of the true owner, and the assertion of a hostile title brought to his notice; but, if the permissive possessor dies in possession, and the land is afterwards sold by his administrator for payment of debts, a deed executed to the purchaser purporting to convey the entire estate in the land, the purchase-money paid, and possession delivered, such possession is adverse to the true owner, and will ripen into a title if continued for the statutory period. *Woodstock Iron Co. v. Roberts,* 436.

4. *Continuity of possession, as affected by trespass.*—The intrusion of a mere trespasser on land, who enters without claim or title, does not interrupt the continuity of possession, unless continued so long that knowledge by him is presumed, and he fails to resort to legal remedies before adverse rights are acquired. *Ib.* 436.

5. *Actual and constructive possession.*—Possession under title, or color of title, is not limited to that part of the land which is actually occupied, but extends to the entire tract covered by the written instrument; while the possession of a trespasser, without color of title, extends only to the land actually occupied. *Ib.* 436.

See, also, LIMITATIONS, STATUTE OF.

AGENCY.

1. *Admission by agent, after termination of agency.*—The clerk of a steamboat, having authority to make purchases and to state accounts for the boat, can not bind the owners by his written admission of the correctness of an account after the termination of his agency, but must be examined as a witness to prove its correctness, if known by him. *Gunter v. Stuart,* 196.

2. *Cancellation of policy; authority of agent.*—An agency to procure insurance is ended when the policy is procured and delivered to the principal; and the agent has no power afterwards to consent to a cancellation, or to accept notice of an intended cancellation by the insurer. *Insurance Co's v. Raden,* 311.

3. *Same; dual agency.*—An express stipulation in the policy authorizing the company to terminate it at any time on giving notice to that effect to the assured, "or to the person who may have procured the insurance to be taken," can not be applied to a case where the same person acted as agent for both parties in procuring and issuing the policy, and notice of the intended cancellation was not given to the assured in person. *Ib.* 311.

4. *Ratification of cancellation.*—A ratification of the cancellation of a policy, which was procured for the insured by an agent of the insurance company, will not be presumed from his acceptance, after a loss, of a policy in another company, which was procured by the same agent, when it is not shown that the assured was fully informed of all the facts connected with the supposed cancellation and substitution, and of his legal rights as determined by those facts; nor will it be presumed from the institution of a suit on the substituted policy, which was induced by the misrepresentation of the agent to the attorneys of the assured. *Ib.* 311.

5. *Ratification of agent's unauthorized act or agreement.*—A payment by the defendant corporation, on presentation, of labor-tickets which the plaintiffs had taken from the holders to whom they were issued, on the faith of a promise by an agent of the corporation that they would be paid on presentation, is a ratification of the agent's promise, and authorizes plaintiffs to continue to purchase the tickets until notified that they would not be paid. *Tabler, Crudup & Co. v. Sheffield Land, Iron & Coal Co.,* 305.

ASSIGNMENT—*Continued.*

nishment at the suit of the client's creditors. *Sterrett v. Miles & Co.*, 472.

2. *Assignment of judgment or decree; suits by assignee.*—The statutory provisions relating to mesne or final process issued upon an as-signed judgment or decree (Code, §§ 2927-28), have no application to suits on such judgment or decree, whether at law or in equity. An action at law can not be prosecuted by the assignee in his own name, but he may maintain a bill in equity in his own name. *Moorer v. Moorer*, 545.

3. *General assignment for benefit of creditors; validity of.*—A general assignment for the benefit of creditors, which fixes no time for foreclosure, and reserves to the grantor the use of the property until foreclosure, is not on that account fraudulent as against creditors, since the assignee may at any time foreclose, and any creditor may compel him to do so. *Globe Iron Roofing & Corrugating Co. v. Thacher*, 458.

ATTACHMENT.

1. *What may be reached by attachment or garnishment.*—A written order from a client to his attorney, instructing him to pay to certain named creditors, when collected, money arising from claims placed in his hands for collection, does not operate an as-signment of the claims, or the money collected on them; and the ownership of the claims being thereby unchanged, the debtors are subject to attachment or garnishment at the suit of the client's creditors. *Sterrett v. Miles & Co.*, 472.

2. *Contest between attaching creditors; what defects are available.*—A junior attaching creditor, having first obtained judgment, can not claim the proceeds of sale of the attached property, as against the prior attaching creditor, unless the prior attachment, or judgment thereon, is a nullity; and the fact that the cause of action is a partnership demand, the partner not sued being also a member of the plaintiff partnership, does not render the proceedings or the judgment void. *Alexander Bros. v. King Co.*, 642.

3. *Practice in attachment suits, on interposition of claim by third person, and motion to dissolve attachment and dismiss levy.*—In an attachment suit, the defendant only appearing for the purpose of moving to dissolve the attachment and dismiss the levy, the attached property having been claimed by a third person as purchaser; although the court may correctly adjudge that the property is, on the facts proved, subject to the attachment, it should only render judgment overruling the defendant's motions, and delay final judgment, until the determination of the adverse claim to the property; and the defendant himself may assign as error the rendition of final judgment against him. *Abraham v. Nicrosi*, 173.

4. *Attachment on ground of fraudulent disposition of property.*—A proposal for a composition with his creditors by an embarrassed debtor, offering to surrender all of his property on condition of receiving a release in full, is good ground for suing out an attachment (Code, § 2630), when it appears that his scedule of assets includes claims which he had already transferred to one of his creditors as collateral security, and omitted property in which he had a valuable interest, and that the names of several small creditors were omitted, money being retained and laid aside to pay them. *Campbell v. Hopkins*, 179.

5. *Levy on stock in private corporation; transfer on books.*—Under statutory provisions (Code, 1876, §§ 2043-4; 1886, §§ 1670-71), stock in private corporations are placed on the same footing as othe personal chattels, as to their liability to levy under execution o

ATTACHMENT—*Continued.*

    attachment; a transfer thereof, not recorded on the books of the corporation within fifteen days afterwards, is void as to *bona fide* creditors, or subsequent purchasers without notice; and a judgment creditor having a lien, and an attaching creditor who perfects his lien by the recovery of judgment, are equally *bona fide* creditors from the inception of the lien. *Berney Nat. Bank v. Pinckard, DeBardelaben & Co.*, 577.

6. *Fi. ja. or vend. ex. on judgment in attachment case.*—The lien of an attachment is perfected by the recovery of judgment, and is not waived or forfeited by suing out a *fi. fa.* instead of a *vend. ex.* to enforce it, but the latter may still be sued out if necessary. *Ib.* 577.

7. *Replevy (or forthcoming) bond in attachment case, before justice of the peace.*—In an attachment case before a justice of the peace, a replevy bond conditioned to have the property forthcoming within *twenty* days after the rendition of judgment, is substantially defective as a statutory bond (Code, §§ 3334–41), and does not authorize a summary execution on a return of forfeiture; and the defect being one of substance, it is not cured by the statutory provision as to defects of form. (*Ib.* § 3357). *Cobb v. Thompson*, 381.

8. *Action on bond; lies when.*—Although an attachment may have been sued out vexatiously and maliciously, an action can not be maintained on the bond, unless it was also wrongfully sued out—that is, unless it was sued out without the existence of any one of the facts which authorize a resort to the process. *Calhoun v. Hannan & Michael*, 277.

9. *Burden of proof, as to ground for attachment.*—In an action on an attachment bond, the *onus* is on the plaintiff to prove the falsity of the affidavit on which the attachment was sued out. *Ib.* 277.

10. *Damages; error without injury.*—In an action on an attachment bond, a judgment on verdict for the defendants conclusively determines that the writ was not wrongfully sued out; and the rulings of the court on the pleadings and evidence, or in the matter of charges given or refused, relating only to the question of exemplary damages, if erroneous, could not have injured the plaintiff. *Ib.* 277.

11. *What may be reached by garnishment.*—On a sale of personal property, where the purchaser promises, as evidenced by the bill of sale, to pay the agreed price to several named creditors of the seller, ratably according to their respective debts, the assent of each creditor will be presumed, since the promise is apparently for his benefit; he may recover the money by action of debt, or *indebitatus assumpsit*, against the purchaser; and until he manifests his election, the money can not be reached by other creditors of the vendor. But, if he refuses to accept the money, the right to it revests in the vendor, and it is subject to garnishment at the suit of other creditors. *Leinkauff & Strauss v. Forcheimer & Co.*, 258.

ATTORNEY AT LAW.

1. *Priveleged communications between attorney and client.*—An officer, having the legal custody of a prisoner, should allow him every reasonable opportunity, consistent with his safe keeping, for private consultation with his attorney; yet he may testify to communications made in his presence, although they might be privileged as between the attorney and his client. *Cotton v. State*, 75.

2. *Argument of counsel to jury.*—Counsel should not be allowed, in argument to the jury, to state as fact that which is damaging to defendant, and of which there is no legal evidence. *Coleman v. State*, 14.

BILLS OF EXCHANGE, AND PROMISSORY NOTES—*Continued.*
lawful currency, as it might be if the action was founded on the original indebtedness; and the rule as to a past or executed consideration does not apply. *Massie v. Byrd*, 672.

BILL OF PARTICULARS.

1. *Bill of particulars, as waiver of plea in abatement.*—The right to file a plea in abatement is not waived by a previous demand for a bill of particulars.—Code, § 2670. *Oates v. Clendenard*, 734.

BONDS.

1. *Replevy (or forthcoming) bond in attachment case, before justice of the peace.*—In an attachment case before a justice of the peace, a replevy bond conditioned to have the property forthcoming within *twenty* days after the rendition of judgment, is substantially defective as a statutory bond (Code, §§ 3334–41), and does not authorize a summary execution on a return of forfeiture; and the defect being one of substance, it is not cured by the statutory provision as to defects of form (*Ib.* § 3357). *Cobb v. Thompson*, 381.

2. *Statutory claim bond; alteration adding name of another surety as co-obligor.*—After a statutory claim bond, having been signed by the principal obligor and two sureties, has been accepted and approved by the sheriff, it is his duty to return it at once to the court from which the process issued, and he has no authority, though retaining possession of the bond, to induce or accept the subsequent signature of a third person as surety; and such signature and acceptance being unauthorized, the liability of the original sureties is not thereby discharged or affected. *Anderson v. Bellenger & Ralls*, 334.

3. *Same; accepted on Sunday.*—A statutory claim bond, accepted by the sheriff on Sunday, is within the statute declaring void "all contracts made on Sunday" (Code, § 1749); and when the plaintiffs in the action bring suit on the bond, it is not necessary that a plea, alleging its invalidity because it was accepted on that day, should also allege the plaintiff's complicity in such acceptance. *Ib.* 334.

4. *Signature to bond procured by fraud and mistake.*—In an action on a statutory claim bond, it is a good plea by one of the sureties, that he was fraudulently induced by the sheriff to sign it after it had been accepted and approved with the signatures of the other two sureties only, and that he signed it under a mistake of fact induced by the misrepresentations of the sheriff. *Ib.* 334.

5. *Municipal bonds payable in gold coin.*—A grant of power to a municipal corporation to issue bonds, without limitation as to the kind of currency in which they shall be payable, confers the authority to make them payable "in gold coin of the United States of America, of the present standard weight and fineness." *Judson v. Bessemer*, 240.

BURGLARY. See CRIMINAL LAW, 4–6.

CERTIORARI. See JUSTICE OF THE PEACE.

CHAMPERTY. See CONTRACTS, 2.

CHANCERY.

JURISDICTION, AND GENERAL PRINCIPLES.

1. *Decedent's estate; removal of settlement into equity by administrator.* When an administrator seeks to remove the settlement of the estate into equity, it is immaterial whether or not proceedings for a settlement have been commenced in the Probate Court: in either case, he must aver and show some special ground for equitable intervention. *Cary v. Simmons*, 524.

CHANCERY—*Continued.*

2. *Same; advancements made by administrator for distributees.*—By statutory provision (Code, §§ 2150–60), an administrator may, on final settlement of his accounts in the Probate Court, be allowed a credit, as against the distributive shares of the several distributees, for moneys paid out and expended by him for their support and education during infancy; and this statute operating on the remedy only, it will be held to apply to and include such expenditures made before its passage, which would then have been allowed in equity; consequently such prior payments are now no ground for equitable interposition. *Ib.* 524.

3. *Same; removal of incumbrances on land.*—As to lands which never belonged to the intestate, but which accrued to the distributees, as tenants in common with the administrator, from some other source, the administrator may, by paying taxes, or removing incumbrances, acquire as against the distributees a claim for reimbursement; but such claim can not be enforced or allowed on settlement of his accounts, either at law or in equity—neither in the Probate Court, nor in the Chancery Court. *Ib.* 524.

4. *Same; partnership accounts; statute of limitations, as bar to suit for settlement.*—Where it appears that the administrator and his intestate had been partners in business, and the partnership was dissolved by consent, but no settlement of accounts was had; and the intestate then removed to Georgia, and there died after the lapse of several years; the administrator might have a settlement of the partnership accounts in equity, and a decree for any balance in his favor, which would bind any personal assets in his hands, notwithstanding the bar of the statute of limitations; but, when his bill shows that he had no personal assets, and that he seeks to charge the lands in the hands of the heirs, or the rents thereof, the statute of limitations is a bar to the suit. *Ib.* 524.

5. *Decedent's estate; premature filing of bill for distribution.*—A bill filed by the distributees of a decedent's estate, within eight months after the grant of letters of administration, against the administrator and the widow, alleging that the decedent left no debts, and that the funeral expenses and other charges have been paid off by the parties interested in the estate, and praying a distribution and settlement, is prematurely filed. *Jackson v. Rowell*, 685.

6. *When legatee may come into equity, against executor.*—A legatee to whom the testator bequeathed his mercantile business, with stock of goods, notes and outstanding accounts, directing that he "will assume all the liabilities of the store, and continue the business as heretofore," and also devising to him the store-house in which the business was carried on, can not maintain a bill in equity against the executor, to recover the goods, notes and accounts, until after the expiration of eighteen months from the grant of letters testamentary (Code, §§ 2134, 2192), unless the executor has reported the estate to be solvent, even though he offers to give bond for the faithful administration of the assets. *Carroll v. Richardson*, 605.

7. *When executor may come into equity.*—An executor may file a bill in equity, asking the court to construe the will, to give him instructions in the performance of his duties, and to remove the administration into that court, when it appears that the provisions of the will are of doubtful construction, and that the legatees assert conflicting claims under it. *Ib.* 605.

8. *Fraudulent conveyance, as cloud on title.*—A purchaser at sheriff's sale under execution, of lands which have been fraudulently conveyed by the judgment debtor, has a plain and adequate remedy at law, and can not, while out of possession, maintain a bill in

CHANCERY—*Continued.*

15. *Injunction against collection of wharfage.*—An incorporated city or town can not maintain a bill in equity, to enjoin the collection of wharfage by a person who claims under the original proprietors of the land which was laid out into a town, without showing (1) that the user of the street abutting on the river is thereby obstructed, or (2) that the right to collect wharfage was dedicated to the public with the street. or (3) otherwise negativing its retention by the proprietors. *Ib.* 659.

16. *Injunction against obstruction of navigable stream.*—When a bill is filed by a riparian proprietor on a running stream which is above tide-water, seeking an injunction against an obstruction of the stream more than two miles above his mill, whereby the floatage of the stream from above is impeded, he must show by specific averments how far up the stream is navigable, or, at least, that it is navigable up to the obstructions complained of, and how long; though it is not necessary to aver or show that it is navigable throughout the entire year. *Morrison Brothers v. Coleman,* 655.

17. *Injunction against pollution of running stream.*—The owner of land through which a small stream runs may maintain an action at law for damages, on account of injuries caused by the pollution of the stream and the deposit of sediment from a smelting furnace and washers for iron ore, by an upper proprietor; but a court of equity, balancing the probable injury to the respective parties, and considering the public interests involved in such industrial enterprises, will refuse to interfere by injunction, where it appears that the complainant has on his land another stream, amply sufficient for all the purposes to which he had ever applied the water of the polluted stream; that the upper proprietor owned a large tract of land chiefly valuable for its iron ore and other minerals, and had expended a large sum of money in the erection of a smelting furnace and other works necessary to convert the ore into pig metal; and further, that the stream was necessarily polluted by the sewerage of a neighboring town containing about fifteen hundred inhabitants. *Clifton Iron Co. v. Dye,* 468.

18. *Same; laches.*—In this case, an injunction should be refused on the additional ground of *laches,* it appearing that the defendant's first "washer" for the ore was erected more than three years before the bill was filed, the second one about one year afterwards, and that plaintiff did not object or complain until after the erection of the third. *Ib.* 468.

19. *Injunction against windows in party-wall.*—A court of equity will interfere by injunction, at the suit of one of the part owners of a party-wall, to prevent the other from making windows, or other openings in it. *Graves v. Smith,* 450.

20. *Injunction against statutory proceedings for condemnation of right of way between railroad companies.*—A court of equity will not interfere by injunction, at the suit of one railroad company, to prevent or restrain statutory proceedings by another for the condemnation of a part of its right of way, pending an appeal from the judgment of condemnation; since the appeal is an adequate remedy for the correction of errors and irregularities in the proceedings, if only irregular and erroneous, and the defendant is a trespasser if they are void; and the prosecution of the work by the defendant pending the appeal, having paid the assessed damages into court, does not add equity to the bill. *M. & G. Railroad Co. v. Midland Railway Co.,* 520.

21. *Relieving married woman of disabilities of coverture.*—In the exercise of the statutory jurisdiction formerly conferred on chancellors, to relieve married women of the disabilities of coverture to the extent specified (Code, 1876, § 2731), relief can not be granted

CHANCERY—*Continued.*

by piecemeal, but the relief prayed and granted must be coextensive with the statute, neither more nor less; if the petition prays only partial relief, or less than the statute authorizes, any decree rendered upon it is void; but, if the petition conforms to the statute, while the decree goes beyond it, it is void only for the excess. *Powell v. New England M. & S. Co.*, 602.

22. *Same; case at bar.*—Where the petition alleged that the petitioner owned certain lands, "which are her statutory separate estate, and which she desires to incumber or mortgage for the purpose of raising money," and therefore prayed to be "relieved of all the disabilities of coverture, to the end that she may sue and be sued as a *feme sole*, mortgage, convey, and otherwise dispose of her separate estate as fully and freely as if a *feme sole*;" while the decree declared her "relieved of the disabilities of coverture, with full power to convey, mortgage, buy, sell, or otherwise dispose of her statutory and other separate estate, to sue and be sued as a *feme sole*;" *held*, that the petition and decree, each, was fatally defective, and conferred no power to mortgage her lands. *Ib.* 602.

23. *Foreclosure of mortgage by trustee of tenant for life.*—As a general rule, when a person holds the legal title to property, charged with the duty of accounting for the rents and profits to a tenant for life, he is a trustee to that extent, and has no power to change the *status* of the property, except possibly in extreme cases, subject to the direction and approval of a court of equity; yet, where the widow and sole devisee of a deceased mortgagor, and grantor in a deed of trust in the nature of a mortgage, has conveyed all of her property to trustees, with a life interest in herself in the rents and profits after payment of taxes, repairs, &c., and a testamentary provision in their favor after her death, the trustees may maintain a bill to foreclose the mortgage, and the court may, if necessary to prevent danger from conversion of the trust fund, require proper security for the income during her life. *Kyle v. Perdue*, 423.

24. *Foreclosure of mortgage; extent of relief as to matters cognizable at law; interest.*—Under a bill to foreclose a mortgage on crops, a purchaser with notice being joined as a defendant, he may be held responsible, not only for the cotton then in his possession, but also for cotton received and sold by him before the bill was filed, although the mortgagee might maintain an action at law for its conversion; and he is chargeable with interest on the value of the cotton so sold, although, by agreement of the parties to the cause, he has been allowed to sell the cotton in possession, giving a bond to account for its value. *Comer v. Lehman, Durr & Co.*, 363.

25. *Accounts between partners.*—When one partner buys out his co-partner's interest in the partnership, giving his note for the balance of the purchase-money not paid in cash, with the understanding that it was subject to abatement on settlement of the partnership accounts, for any balance found in his favor; possibly this defense could not be made at law, against an action on the note, as it involved a settlement of the partnership accounts, and, therefore, the failure to make it does not bar equitable relief against the judgment.

26. *Receiver; appointment without notice.*—A receiver should not be appointed without notice, on the filing of a bill by a simple-contract creditor to set aside, on the ground of fraud, a transfer by an insolvent debtor of all his outstanding notes and accounts, when the bill merely alleges, on information and belief, that the transferees are rapidly collecting the notes and accounts, and placing them beyond the reach of creditors, but does not allege that they are insolvent, or unable to respond to any decree which might be

CHANCERY—*Continued.*

rendered against them; and the accompanying affidavit only states that, in the belief of the affiant, based on information, to give notice of the application would cause delay, which would probably defeat the receiver, and prevent him from taking possession and recovering the notes and accounts; it further appearing that all the defendants reside in the city in which the bill was filed. *Moritz & Weil v. Miller, Schram & Co.,* 331.

27. *Same.*—On the filing of a bill by simple-contract creditors, seeking to set aside, on the ground of fraud, a transfer by their insolvent debtor of his entire stock of goods to his mother, a receiver should not be appointed without notice, on the *ex parte* affidavits of the complainants' solicitors, stating their belief that the appointment *instanter* is necessary for the protection of complainants—that if notice of the application was given to defendants, "they would sell or dispose of said property before a receiver could be appointed, and thus leave complainants remediless;" and that the grantee, whose insolvency is not averred, "is already trying, and has tried, to dispose in whole of said property conveyed to her." *Thompson v. Tower Man. Co.,* 733.

28. *Receiver; appointment by register in vacation; how reviewed.*—Under statutory provisions regulating the appointment of receivers (Code, §§ 3515, 3614), an appeal lies to the chancellor, from an order of the register appointing a receiver in vacation, and an appeal to this court, from the chancellor's order confirming the appointment; but, if the defendant, not having taken an appeal from the appointment by the register, afterwards submits to the chancellor a motion to vacate the order, which motion is heard and overruled at the same time with a motion to dismiss the bill for want of equity, that ruling can not be revised on appeal from the refusal to dismiss the bill. *Miller v. Lehman, Durr & Co.,* 517.

29. *Reformation of conveyance and notes for purchase-money, on ground of mistake or fraud.*—A vendor of lands, having executed a conveyance to the purchaser, and taken his notes for the purchase-money, may maintain a bill in equity to reform and correct them, by inserting an express provision for the retention of a vendor's lien, on averment and proof that such provision was omitted by mistake or fraud, without fault on his part. *Kinney v. Ensminger,* 340.

30. *Same; signing or accepting writings without reading them.*—If the bill alleges that the complainant was not able to speak or understand the English language well, and that the contract was negotiated on his part by an agent, or an attorney in fact, who fraudulently colluded with the purchasers to omit from the writings the agreement for a retention of the vendor's lien, he relieves himself from the imputation of negligence, which generally attaches to a person who signs a writing without reading it, without inquiry, and without excuse for his neglect. *Ib.* 340.

31. *Reformation or specific performance of conveyance of homestead.* A conveyance of the homestead by husband and wife, to which the certificate of acknowledgment is substantially defective (Code, § 2508), will not be reformed in equity, on the ground that the examination and acknowledgment of the wife were in fact properly made, but were not shown by the officer's certificate from ignorance or mistake on his part; nor will it be specifically enforced, as an executory agreement to convey. *Cox v. Holcomb,* 589.

32. *Cancellation of instrument procured by undue influence.*—Undue influence, such as will operate to set aside a conveyance, must be sufficient to overcome the grantor's will; and an allegation in a bill seeking to set aside the conveyance, that the grantor, "when

CHANCERY—*Continued.*

he was very feeble both in mind and body, was persuaded and induced, through some undue and improper influence unknown to complainants, to execute said instrument," without more, is not sufficient to impeach it. *Jackson v. Rowell*, 685.

33. *Rescission of contract at suit of vendor.*—On a sale of town lots by a private corporation at auction, part of the purchase-money to be paid in cash, when a deed would be delivered, and notes and mortgages executed for the deferred payments; the general manager of the corporation having accepted from a purchaser his draft at thirty days instead of a payment in cash, and, by mistake, delivered the deed to the probate judge for registration, afterwards paying the fee, and retaining possession of the deed, the draft not having been paid; the right to a rescission in equity is barred by *laches* after the lapse of more than two years and a half, when it appears that the vendor still retained the notes and mortgage, and that the market value of the land had but recently increased. *Sheffield Land, Iron & Coal Co. v. Neill*, 158.

34. *Rescission of contract on ground of fraud.*—A court of equity will rescind a contract into which the party complaining was induced to enter by the misrepresentation of a material fact by the other party, on which he might properly rely, and by which he was injured; as here, where the complainant, a non-resident, was entitled to a half interest in the estate of his deceased grandmother, which estate was worth between $3,000 and $4,000, and was induced to sell his interest for $300 to a cousin, who was entitled to a part of the other half interest, and who was well acquainted with all the facts relating to the estate; and the contract being rescinded as against the party who procured it, a third person who was interested with him in the purchase, but who had no part in the fraudulent misrepresentations, can take no benefit under it. *Cofer v. Moore*, 705.

35. *Sale of lands under probate decree; setting aside in equity on ground of fraud.*—A sale of lands under a probate decree, on the petition of the administratrix of the deceased owner, will be set aside in equity at the instance of the heirs, on averment and proof that it was procured by fraudulent collusion between the purchaser and the administratrix, in payment of her individual debt to him. *Tillman v. Thomas*, 321.

36. *Same; sub-purchaser with notice.*—A sub-purchaser from the original fraudulent purchaser, having knowledge of facts sufficient to put him on inquiry, is chargeable with notice of the fraud, and can not claim protection against the equity of the heirs. *Ib.* 321.

37. *Specific performance of executory agreement to convey.*—A written instrument in the form of a deed, though defective as a conveyance for the want of attestation or acknowledgment, is a valid executory agreement to convey, the specific performance of which a court of equity will enforce, when it is shown that the consideration was paid, and that possession was given and taken under it. *Hall v. Caperton*, 285.

38. *Specific execution of defective instrument, as agreement to convey.* When a written instrument, purporting to convey land, is signed by the grantor, and has all the elements of a valid deed, except in the necessary attestation of subscribing witnesses, a court of equity will specifically enforce it, against the heirs of the deceased grantor, as an agreement to convey, unless some sufficient reason is shown why specific performance should not be decreed. *Sparks v. Woodstock Iron & Steel Co.*, 294.

39. *Same; case at bar.*—On the evidence shown by the record in this case, the court holds that the written instrument sought to be en-

CHANCERY—*Continued.*

46. *Purchase by executor or trustee at his own sale, and re-sale at profit.*
A trustee is not permitted to traffic in the trust property for his own benefit, but holds the profits realized subject to be claimed by the beneficiaries on timely application; and this principle would probably apply to a sale of land by an executrix, where she was jointly interested with her sister as purchaser, and they afterwards effected a re-sale at a tenfold price; but such interest in the original purchase is not established, against the denials of the answer, merely by the deeds showing that the sister who was purchaser conveyed to the executrix, six years afterwards, a half interest in the land at the same price, and that they jointly effected the re-sale a few weeks afterwards. *Hughes v. Hughes,* 652.

47. *Vendor's lien; priority as between sub-purchasers.*—As a general rule, in enforcing a lien or incumbrance on land, which has been sold and conveyed in parcels to different persons, a court of equity pursues the inverse order of alienation, first subjecting the unsold portions remaining in the hands of the incumbrancer; but the principle extends only to sub-purchasers with covenants of warranty, and is never allowed to work injustice, being subject to modification by particular facts and circumstances affecting the rights and equities of the several purchasers as between themselves. *Aderholt v. Henry,* 415.

48. *Same; case at bar.*—In this case, a bill was filed to enforce a vendor's lien on land, after the death of the purchaser, who had sold and conveyed some portions of it, with covenants of warranty, to different persons, charged some parcels with the payment of debts, and devised the residue to his children; and the executor having sold the parcels charged with the payment of debts, a purchaser of two lots or parcels paid the purchase-money for one, but failed to pay for the other, which was afterwards resold under a decree enforcing the vendor's lien of the executor, for less than the amount of the decree; and the purchaser at the resale having afterwards bought the decree in the original suit, and attempted to subject the other portions of the land to its satisfaction, *it was held*—1st, that the lot bought and paid for at the sale by the executor must be first subjected, because its owner was primarily liable for the unpaid purchase-money of the other lot; 2d, that the purchaser at the resale was not entitled to claim exemption from liability, but stood on an equality with the several devisees, and must each contribute ratably to the discharge of the common burden; and, 3d, that each portion should be estimated at its present value, including improvements erected by the owner. *Ib.* 415.

49. *Vendor's lien, when legal title is or is not retained; sale of real and personal property in gross.*—A vendor's lien, after he has conveyed the legal title, is a mere creation of equity, while it is a lien by contract so long as he retains the legal title; but, while the presumption is that he retains the legal title as security for the purchase-money, that presumption may be repelled by the terms and character of the contract, or by the circumstances; and when there is a sale of real and personal property for a sum in gross, no *data* being furnished by which the separate value of the land can be ascertained, it is immaterial whether a conveyance was or was not executed—a vendor's lien is not retained, and it does not arise by operation of law. *Sykes v. Betts,* 537.

50. *Same; contract for division of decedent's estate.*—Under a written agreement between two married sisters, their husbands uniting with them, for a "distribution and final settlement of the estate"

49

CHANCERY—*Continued.*

tory lien (Code, §§ 3018-48), to set aside subsequent conveyances of the property (with other property) as void, and to subject it to the satisfaction of his debt; or, in the alternative, as a simple-contract creditor without a lien, to set aside the conveyances as fraudulent   *Globe Iron Roofing & Corrugating Co. v. Thacher*, 458.

57. *Same.*—A bill filed in a double aspect, seeking to set aside a sale of lands under a probate decree, on the ground (1) that the proceedings are void on their face, or (2) that they are void for fraud in their procurement, is demurrable; but the objection must be taken by demurrer specially assigned. *Tillman v. Thomas*, 321.

58. *Demurrer; adequate legal remedy.*—A demurrer to a bill, on the ground that there is an adequate legal remedy, is properly overruled, when the legal remedy is adequate to only one of the two aspects in which the bill is filed. *Ib.* 321.

59. *Parties to bill.*—To a bill filed by the heirs at law of a deceased non-resident, against the surviving tenant in common, seeking a partition of lands and an account, and alleging that the decedent left no debts, and that no administration has been granted on his estate, a personal representative of his estate is not a necessary party. *Stevenson v. Anderson*, 228.

60. *Parties to bill.*—The personal representative of the deceased husband, though he might be a proper party, is not a necessary party to a bill filed by creditors, seeking to subject the proceeds of a policy of insurance on his life, as against the claims of his children, to the payment of their debts. *Tompkins v. Levy & Bro.*, 263.

61. *Parties to bill.*—When a bill is filed by the vendor of lands, seeking to correct his conveyance, and also the notes given for the purchase-money, by inserting an express provision for the retention of the vendor's lien, both of the makers of the notes are proper parties defendant, whether they were joint purchasers, or one was merely a surety for the other. *Kinney v. Ensminger*, 340.

62. *Parties to bill.*—The trustee in a mortgage, or deed of trust in the nature of a mortgage, where the mortgage debt has been bequeathed and devised by the defendant mortgagee to his widow, and she has conveyed all of her property to trustees, charged with the payment of taxes, repairs, &c , and the residue of the rents and profits payable to herself for life, with a testamentary provision in favor of the trustees after her death, may join with the said trustees in a bill to foreclose the mortgage, against the widow and the mortgagor. *Kyle v. Perdue*, 424.

63. *Intervention of third persons as parties by petition.*—By the general rule of practice in courts of equity, third persons can not be allowed to come in as parties to a pending suit on their own motion, or by petition, against the objection of the complainant; but are required to propound their interests by original bill in the nature of a cross-bill, or in the nature of a supplemental bill. *Ex parte Printup*, 148.

64. *Same.*—The only recognized exceptions to this general rule are—1st, that the beneficiaries of a trust are sometimes allowed to intervene by petition in a suit to which the trustee is a party; and, 2d, where a person has an interest in a fund which is in the custody, or under the control of the court, and he desires to secure its proper administration and distribution. *Ib.* 148.

65. *Same; waiver of objection.*—Although it is irregular, after an interpleader suit is regularly at issue, to allow a third person to intervene as a claimant of the fund, on his own petition; yet, if no objection to his intervention is made until after the lapse of more than seven years, when he has lost all other remedies by lapse of time, the objection comes too late. *Smith v. Alexander*, 387.

CHANCERY—*Continued.*

66. *Same; error without injury.*—If the party objecting was not, and could not have been injured, by allowing the petitioner to remain in the cause as a party, he can not complain of the ruling, even if it was erroneous; as when he disclaims all interest in that portion of the fund allotted to the petitioner. *Ib.* 387.

67. *Cross-bill*—The benefit of a set-off, in equity, can only be claimed by cross-bill. *Weaver v. Brown,* 533.

68. *Demurrer to cross-bill, when original bill is wanting in equity.*—On appeal from an interlocutory order overruling a demurrer to a cross-bill (Code, § 3612), the appellate court can not consider the sufficiency of the original bill, to which a demurrer was interposed and overruled; yet, if the original bill was wanting in equity, the overruling of a demurrer to the cross-bill is not a reversible error. *Carroll v. Richardson,* 605.

69. *Answer as evidence.*—When an answer is made on oath, as required by the foot-note to the bill, its denials can only be overcome by the testimony of two witnesses, or of one with proper corroboration. *Graham v. Gray,* 446.

70. *Correspondence of allegations and proof.*—There can be no relief on a controverted question without proof, and averments or admissions in pleadings are not open to disproof by the party making them. *Hughes v. Hughes,* 652.

71. *Same.*—When the bill seeks to establish a resulting trust in lands, a closer correspondence between the pleadings and the pooof is required than in other cases, except bills for the reformation or specific performance of contracts, which are strictly analogous. *Winston v. Mitchell,* 395.

72. *Dissolution of injunction on answer.*—An injunction should not be dissolved on the denials of the answer, unless they are full and positive, especially where irrenarable injury might result to the complainant from such dissolution. *Kinny v. Ensminger,* 340

73. *Same.*—On motion to dissolve an injunction, even when the answer contains a full and complete denial of the material allegations of the bill, the court is invested with a wide latitude of discretion, in the exercise of which it will consider and balance the probable resulting damages to the respective parties; and if it appears that irreparable mischief may result from a dissolution, or that greater injury may thereby result to the complainant than to the defendant from continuing the writ in force, a special injunction will be retained until final hearing. *Harrison v. Yerby,* 185.

CHANGE OF VENUE. See CRIMINAL LAW, 86-7.

CHARGE OF COURT TO JURY.

1. *Charge unsupported by evidence*—A charge to the jury which, though it asserts a correct legal proposition, is not supported by any evidence in the case, should not be given, because it tends to mislead the ury; but the giving of such a charge is not a reversible error, unless it is apparent that the jury were thereby misled, to the prejudice of the appellant, since he could protect himself by asking explanatory or qualifying charges. *Pollak v. Davidson,* 551.

2. *General charge, when evidence is conflicting.*—When there is a conflict in the evidence as to a material fact, it is the right of the jury, if they can not reconcile the evidence, to accept either aspect as true; and a general charge in favor of either party is an invasion of this right. *Paden & Co. v. Bellenger & Ralls,* 575.

3. *Charge not applicable to evidence.*—A charge asked which asserts a legal proposition not applicable to the facts of the case, though

CODE OF ALABAMA—*Continued.*

CODE OF ALABAMA—*Continued.*

COLLATERAL SECURITY. See PLEDGE.

CONFEDERATE STATES.

1. *Confederate money as consideration; past or executed consideration.* In an action on a promissory note, given in April, 1866, for the amount of Confederate treasury-notes collected by the maker, as agent for the payee, during the late war, the measure of the plaintiff's recovery is not the value of the Confederate notes in lawful currency, as it might be if the action was founded on the original indebtedness; and the rule as to a past or executed consideration does not apply. *Massie v. Byrd,* 672.

2. *Confederate money received by guardian.*—A guardian having been allowed a credit, on a partial settlement in 1870-71, for Confederate money received from a debtor during the late war, and left on his hands at the close of the war, the credit ought not to be disallowed on final settlement, on evidence showing merely that the money was collected on notes given for the purchase-money of land, which the guardian had received, in 1859-60, as his ward's distributive share on settlement of an estate; this evidence, without more, not being sufficient to overcome the presumption in favor of the allowance on annual settlement. *Bentley v. Daily,* 406.

CONFLICT OF LAWS.

1. *Liability of stockholders; by what law determined.*—The liability of stockholders in a private corporation, or subscribers for stock prior to the organization of the company, is governed by the law of the

CONFLICT OF LAWS—*Continued.*

State by which the charter is granted, as if incorporated in the subscription as a part thereof. *Morris v. Glenn,* 628.

2. *Validity of contract; by what law determined.*—The legality of an agreement made in New York, respecting railroad bonds involved in a pending suit in Alabama, and which is to be carried into effect here, "would probably be g verned by the laws of Alabama," and it is so considered in this case. *Gilman, Son & Co. v. Jones,* 691.

CONSTITUTIONAL LAW.

1. *Foreign corporations; constitutional and statutory restrictions on right to do business here; action by agent on contract violative of.*—An agent of a foreign corporation engaged in the business of lending money on mortgages, not having complied with the conditions imposed by constitutional and statutory provisions on the right to do business in this State (Const. Ala., Art. xiv, § 4; Sess. Acts 1886-7, pp. 102–04), can not maintain an action to recover compensation agreed to be paid him for procuring a loan from the corporation. *Dudley v. Collier & Pinckard,* 431.

2. *Private industrial corporation; declaration and certificate of incorporation; constitutional provisions as to title and subject-matter of laws, and as to amendatory laws.*—Under the statutory provisions which were of force in May, 1886, relating to the incorporation of private industrial enterprises (Sess. Acts 1882-3, pp. 5, 40; Code, 1876, §§ 1803-07), the board of corporators, on the completion of the organization of the company, the payment "in cash of at least twenty per cent of the capital subscribe l payable in money, and the payment of the remainder of the capital so subscribed, payable in money, being secured to be paid in such installments and at such times as may be provided in the written declaration required by section 1803 of the Code," and also the delivery of twenty per cent. of the property subscribed, "with security for the delivery of the remainder so subscribed, as may be promised [provided] by said written declaration required by section 1803," were authorized to certify these facts to the probate judge of the proper county, who thereupon issued to them a certificate of incorporation ; but these provisions did not require that the board of corporators should, in the written declaration required by said section 1803, specify when or how the unpaid portion of the subscribed capital was secured to be paid, nor make the failure to do so a defect fatal to the incorporation ; and to give them that construction would be to make them amendatory of said section 1803, in violation of constitutional provisions (Art. iv, § 2). *Bolling v. LeGrand,* 482.

3. *Constitutional provisions as to amending or extending laws by reference to title; estraying cattle on Bay Shell-Road in Mobile.*—The second section of the act "for the protection of life and property upon the Bay Shell-Road" in Mobile, approved February 17th, 1885 (Sess. Acts 1884-5, pp. 392-3), so far as it authorizes any officer or employe of the road company to take up any animal found running at large on its road, and to estray the same in the manner provided by the general law governing estrays, referring to said law only by the numbers of the article, chapter and title in the Code of Alabama, in which it is found, is violative of the constitutional provision (Art. iv, § 2), which provides, that no law "shall be revived, amended, or the provisions thereof *extended or conferred,* by reference to its title only, but so much thereof as is revived, amended, *extended or conferred,* shall be re-enacted and published at length." *Bay Shell-Road Co. v. O'Donnell,* 376.

CONSTITUTIONAL LAW—*Continued.*

4. *Charter of Bessemer, under constitutional provision as to title and subject-matter of laws; power to issue municipal bonds.*—The act approved December 12th, 1888, entitled "An act to amend the charter of the town of Bessemer, and to re-incorporate the same as the city of Bessemer, and to establish a charter therefor," is not violative of the constitutional provision which declares, "Each law shall contain but one subject, which shall be clearly expressed in its title" (Art. IV, § 2); the title and the body of the act, construed together, show a single purpose, and relate to a single subject; and the grant of power, in the 38th section, to issue negotiable bonds for specified municipal purposes, is germane to that subject as expressed in the title. *Judson v. Bessemer*, 240.

5. *Same; amendatory laws, and unconstitutional repealing laws.*—The subsequent statute amending the 38th section of said charter, "by striking out the word *fifty*, and inserting *thirty* in lieu thereof," is violative of the further constitutional provision, contained in the same article and section, that, in amendatory laws, so much of the former law as is amended "shall be re-enacted and published at length;" and said amendatory law being unconstitutional and void, the power of the corporation to issue bonds payable in fifty years, as at first provided, is unimpaired. *Ib.* 240.

6. *Constitutionality of statutes; rule of judicial construction.*—In adjudicating the constitutionality of a statute, it is the duty of the courts, in deference to the legislative department of the government, to so construe both the constitutional and the statutory provisions, if possible, that the statute may be upheld; but a constitutional provision, protective of the rights of persons and property, and remedial in its nature, is not to be construed so literally or strictly as to defeat the purposes for which it was intended; and a new provision, incorporated in a revised constitution, is to be construed in connection with the facts of public history, showing the causes in which it originated, and the mischief it was intended to remedy and prevent. *Garland v. Board of Revenue*, 223

7. *Bridge across Alabama river between Montgomery and Autauga counties, for railroad purposes, wagons, and persons on foot; constitutionality of law authorizing.*—The act of the General Assembly, approved February 27th, 1889, authorizing the Boards of Revenue of Montgomery and Autauga counties to erect a bridge across the Alabama river near the city of Montgomery, making it a "free foot and wagon bridge, or a railroad bridge, or both combined," to issue county bonds to pay for it, and to levy a special tax to pay the annual interest on the bonds (Sess. Acts 1889, p. 756), so far as it authorizes the counties to build a bridge for railroad purposes, or a foot and wagon and railroad bridge combined, is violative of the constitutional provision which declares that no county, city or municipality shall "lend its credit, or grant public money or thing of value, in aid of or to any individual, association, or corporation" (Art. XI, § 55); and is also violative of the constitutional limitation (Art. XI, § 5) imposed on the taxing power of the counties. *Ib.* 223.

8. *Title and subject-matter of laws, under constitutional provisions; act amending charter of Anniston.*—The act approved February 14th, 1887, entitled "An act to amend section 3 of an act entitled 'An act to incorporate the town of Anniston, Calhoun county,' approved February 4, 1879" (Sess. Acts 1886-87, pp. 307-32), is violative of the constitutional provision which declares, "Each law shall contain but one subject, which shall be clearly expressed in the title" (Art. IV, § 2), because it contains more than one sub-

CONSTITUTIONAL LAW—*Continued.*

ject, and because no one of its subjects is clearly expressed in its title. *Ex parte Reynolds,* 138.

9. *Prohibitory liquor laws in Butler county; amending and revising statutes.*—Beat No. 12 in Butler county was exempted from the operation of the general law regulating the granting of licenses to retail liquors, under the provisions of a special statute approved November 27th, 1886, which authorized a local election to determine whether or not the sale of liquors in that beat should be prohibited; another statute was approved February 19th, 1887, which prohibited the sale of liquors "within five miles of Goodwater Academy, Coosa county, and in the county of Butler except in Beat No. 12," while a general prohibitory law, applicable to the whole of Butler county, was approved on the 26th February, 1887, a subsequent day of the same session of the General Assembly; and each of these two acts went into effect on the 1st January, 1888. On the 20th February, 1889, during the next session of the General Assembly, the act of February 19th, 1887, was amended by excepting the town of Goodwater from its operation; but the amendatory law set out the title and the 1st section of the former act in full, including the exemption in favor of said Beat No. 12, and re-enacted it with the addition of a proviso excepting the town of Goodwater. *Held,* that the effect of this last statute was to revive the exemption in favor of said Beat No. 12, although it had been repealed by the general prohibitory law of February 26th, 1887. *Ex parte Pierce,* 110.

10. *Trial by jury, under constitutional provisions.*—A lawful jury, as the term is used in constitutional provisions, means a jury of twelve men, according to the principles of the common law; and a jury consisting of a less number, under statutory provisions, is not a lawful jury, unless an appeal is given to a higher court, where a jury of twelve men may be impanelled on demand. *Woodward Iron Co. v. Cabaniss,* 328.

11. *Jurisdiction of justice of the peace, under constitutional and statutory provisions.*—Under constitutional and general statutory provisions (Const. Ala., Art. vi, § 26; Code, § 839), the jurisdiction of a justice of the peace, in cases of tort, is limited to $50; and the special statute which gives him jurisdiction "of all actions for injury to, or destruction of stock, by the locomotive or cars of a railroad, if the sum in controversy does not exceed $100" (Code, § 1149), being a discrimination against corporations, is unconstitutional and void as to the excess of jurisdiction attempted to be conferred. *Brown v. Ala. Gr. So. Railroad Co.,* 370.

12. *Statutes relating to form of procedure.*—The statute requiring insanity, as a defense in criminal cases, to be pleaded specially, relates only to the mode of procedure, and applies to all cases tried since its passage, although the offense was committed before that date. *Perry v. State,* 30.

13. *Same.*—Statutes remedial in their character, or regulating the mode of proceeding in civil cases, apply to existing causes of action. *Brown v. Williams,* 353; *Cary v. Simmons,* 524.

14. *Fictitious stock in private corporation, under constitutional provisions.*—A subscription to stock in a private corporation, with the understanding that the corporation shall issue "five dollars of stock for one of subscription," is in violation of the constitutional provision which declares void the fictitious issue or increase of stock by private corporations (Art. xiv, § 6); and a contract for the sale of a part of the stock so subscribed, before it has been issued, accompanied with an order to the company to issue it to the purchaser, and to transfer it to him on the books, is equally illegal and void. *Williams v. Evans,* 725.

CONTINUANCE.

1. *Continuance on payment of costs; itemized bill of costs.*—When a continuance is granted to the defendant, "on the payment of all costs within ninety days, as a condition precedent, or judgment to go against him at next term," his consent to the terms is implied in his acceptance of the continuance; and the costs not being paid within the ninety days, the court may enter judgment by *nil dicit* against him on the first day of the next term, although he then offers to pay them; nor is it necessary that an itemized bill of costs should have been furnished to him by the clerk or sheriff. *Maund v. Loeb & Brother,* 374.

CONTRACTS.

1. *Validity of contract; by what law determined.*—The legality of an agreement made in New York, respecting railroad bonds involved in a pending suit in Alabama, and which is to be carried into effect here, "would probably be governed by the laws of Alabama," and it is so considered in this case. *Gilman, Son & Co. v. Jones,* 691.

2. *Champerty and maintenance.*—The whole doctrine of maintenance, as at common law, "has been so modified in recent times as to confine it to strangers who, having no valuable interest in a suit, pragmatically interfere in it for the improper purpose of stirring up litigation and strife;" and champerty, which is a species of maintenance, "does not exist in the absence of this characteristic." *Ib.* 691.

3. *Same; contract for sale of bonds in suit, purchaser agreeing to pay costs and expenses.*—A contract for the sale of negotiable railroad bonds, issued by a corporation which has become insolvent, and whose assets are being administered under a creditors' bill in equity, claims of priority being asserted by different bondholders, is not champertous, although the purchaser, who is not a party to the suit, assumes the payment of the costs and expenses incurred in the future litigation respecting the bonds, when it further appears that he was largely interested in another intersecting railroad, and was endeavoring to effect for it a lease of a part of the road of the insolvent corporation, which could not be accomplished on account of the dissent of the selling bondholder. *Ib.* 691.

4. *Contracts made on Sunday.*—A statutory claim bond, accepted by the sheriff on Sunday, is within the statute declaring void "all contracts made on Sunday" (Code, § 1749); and when the plaintiffs in the action bring suit on the bond, it is not necessary that a plea, alleging its invalidity because it was accepted on that day, should also allege the plaintiff's complicity in such acceptance. *Anderson v. Bellenger & Ralls,* 334.

5. *Contract in restraint of trade.*—A contract by which a partnership, engaged in the business of selling hardware, and selling out their stock of plow-blades and plow-stocks to a rival company, agree "not to handle any more plow-blades or plow-stocks," construed in connection with the attendant circumstances showing the extent of country over which the rivalry in business extended, is not an unreasonable restriction or restraint of trade. *M. & H. Hardware Co. v. Towers Hardware Co.,* 206.

6. *Contract for sale of railroad bonds, at price dependent on contingency.*—Under a contract for the sale of certain bonds issued by an insolvent railroad corporation, which are involved in a pending suit under a creditors' bill, where claims of priority are asserted by a judgment creditor and by different bondholders; the purchaser paying $6,000 in cash, and agreeing to pay the further sum of $14,000, "provided and whenever it is

CONTRACTS—*Continued.*

CONTRACTS—*Continued.*

so far that it can be ascertained with certainty that they would be completed, and the extent or amount thereof; but mere expectations, doubtful offers, or other vague or indefinite assurances of intention to purchase, without expression of quantity or value, are speculative merely, and not recoverable; opinions as to what sales he could, or probably would have made, are also speculative and contingent; nor can he prove or recover for the cost of his horse and buggy, the value of his services per month, or the damages to his credit by being thus thrown out of employment. *Beck v. West & Co.*, 213.

11. *Breach of contract, and waiver thereof; rescission.*—Under a contract by which plaintiff undertook to furnish materials and build a house for defendant at a specified price, to be paid as the work progressed on the certified estimate of the supervising architect, the defendant's failure to make partial payments on the certified estimates is a breach of the contract, but is waived by plaintiff's consent to wait for the money, and continuing to perform the work; and if the plaintiff himself violates the stipulations of the contract by furnishing materials and work of an inferior quality, and fails to correct the resulting defects, after repeated requests and promises to do so, the defendant may discharge him, and treat the contract as annulled and rescinded, notwithstanding the breaches on his part which had been thus waived. *Hewlett, Schwarz & Co. v. Alexander*, 193.

12. *Contract for construction of building; completion by owner, on default of contractor.*—On a contract for furnishing the materials and building a house, containing a stipulation that, on default by the contractor, and after notice to him, the owner might himself complete the building, deducting the expenses from the stipulated price, or the unpaid residue thereof, and accounting to the contractor only for the excess; if the expenses incurred in completing the house exceed the balance due to the contractor, no action lies in his favor. *Ib.* 193.

13. *Contract for sale of trees; damages for breach*—In an action for the breach of a contract, by which defendants sold to plaintiff all the standing trees on a tract of land suitable for saw-logs of specified size, at a named price per thousand feet, and afterwards sold all the timber on the land to a third person who entered and cut some of the trees to which plaintiff was entitled; the measure of damages is the market value of the trees so cut and carried away, *less* the price which plaintiff was to have paid for them, but which he had not paid. *Clements v. Beatty*, 2:8.

14. *Confederate money as consideration; past or executed consideration.* In an action on a promissory note, given in April, 1866, for the amount of Confederate treasury-notes collected by the maker, as agent for the payee, during the late war, the measure of the plaintiff's recovery is not the value of the Confederate notes in lawful currency, as it might be if the action was founded on the original indebtedness; and the rule as to a past or executed consideration does not apply. *Massie v. Byrd*, 672.

15. *Novation.*—If the mortgagor of personal property, having sold to a third person a part of the mortgaged property, afterwards executes another mortgage on other property, which is accepted by the mortgagee "in settlement of said matter for" the property so sold, or is so accepted by his agent, whose act is afterwards ratified by him, this constitutes a valid substitutionary contract, healing the breach of the first, and is available to the purchaser as a defense to a subsequent action for the alleged conversion of the property sold by him. *Cobb v Malone & Collins*, 514.

CONTRACTS—*Continued.*

16. *Promise to one person, for benefit of another.*—On a sale of personal property, where the purchaser promises, as evidenced by the bill of sale, to pay the agreed price to several named creditors of the seller, ratably according to their respective debts, the assent of each creditor will be presumed, since the promise is apparently for his benefit; he may recover the money by action of debt, or *indebitatus assumpsit*, against the purchaser; and until he manifests his election, the money can not be reached by other creditors of the vendor. But, if he refuses to accept the money, the right to it revests in the vendor, and it is subject to garnishment at the suit of other creditors. *Leinkauff & Strauss v Forcheimer & Co.*, 258.

CORPORATIONS.

1. *Foreign corporations; constitutional and statutory restrictions on right to do business here; action by agent on contract violative of.*—An agent of a foreign corporation engaged in the business of lending money on mortgages, not having complied with the conditions imposed by constitutional and statutory provisions on the right to do business in this State (Const. Ala., Art. XIV., § 4; Sess. Acts 1886-7, pp 102-04), can not maintain an action to recover compensation agreed to be paid him for procuring a loan from the corporation. *Dudley ". Collier & Pinckard*, 431.

2. *Action by corporation; proof of corporate character.*—In an action by a corporation, the plea of *nul tiel* corporation being interposed, the plaintiff is required to prove its corporate character, either by producing its charter, or by some admission on the part of the defendant, or to show facts constituting an estoppel. (But, by statute, a sworn plea is now required.—Sess, Acts 1888-9, p. 57.) *Schloss & Kahn v. Montgomery Trade Co.*, 411.

3. *Estoppel as between corporation and subscriber for stock.*—In an action by a corporation suing as such, against a subscriber to its capital stock before incorporation, the payment by the defendant of former installments as called for, and an averment that the installment sued on was "duly and regularly called in by plaintiff, and demand therefor made upon defendant," do not, without more, show an estoppel against him to deny that there ever was any corporation. *Ib.* 411.

4. *Organization of business corporation.*—By statutory provision (Code, 1886, § 1663; Code, 1876, § 1 06,) changing the rule of the common law, a business corporation may be organized before all of the capital stock has been subscribed for. *Ib.* 411

5. *Same*—Under statutory provisions relating to the formation of private corporations for business purposes (Code, 1876, § 1807), the judge of probate is required, "upon the completion of the organization of the company," as shown by the certified statement to him, to issue a certificate of the fact that the company is fully organized, and is authorized to commence business under its charter; but this certificate is not a condition precedent to the complete organization of the company, and the want of it does not establish the plea of *nul tiel* corporation, in an action brought by the company. *Sparks v. Woodward Iron & Steel Co.*, 294.

6. *Private industrial corporation; declaration and certificate of incorporation; constitutional provisions as to title and subject-matter of laws, and as to amendatory laws.*—Under the statutory provisions which were in force in May, 1886, relating to the incorporation of private industrial enterpris s (Sess. Acts 1882-3, pp. 5, 40; Code, 1876, §§ 1803-07), the board of corporators, on the completion of the organization of the company, the payment "in cash of at least twenty per cent. of the capital subscribed payable in money, and

CORPORATIONS—*Continued.*

the payment of the remainder of the capital so subscribed, payable in money, being secured to be paid in such installments and at such times as may be provided in the written declaration required by section 1803 of the Code," and also the delivery of twenty per cent. of the property subscribed, "with security for the delivery of the remainder so subscribed, as may be promised [provided] by said written declaration required by section 1803," were authorized to certify these facts to the probate judge of the proper county, who thereupon issued to them a certificate of incorporation; but these provisions did not require that the board of corporators should, in the written declaration required by said section 1803, specify when or how the unpaid portion of the subscribed capital was secured to be paid, nor make the failure to do so a defect fatal to the incorporation; and to give them that construction would be to make them amendatory of said section 1803, in violation of constitutional provisions (Art. IV, § 2). *Bolling & Son v. LeGrand,* 482.

7. *Acts or contracts of stockholders individually, before incorporation.* A corporation is a legal entity, and is not affected by the personal rights, obligations or transactions of its individual stockholders with third persons, whether before or after incorporation; although it may be charged with the engagements of its promoters in anticipation of incorporation, which it has ratified, or the benefits of which it has received, and although a court of equity will not allow partners or associates, by combining as a "paper corporation," thereby to evade responsibility for their individual obligations, but will hold the nominal corporation to a discharge thereof: yet this principle will not be applied, where an injunction is sought against a private corporation, to restrain its violation of a contract entered into, before incorporation, by its principal corporators and stockholders individually, when it is not averred or shown that the corporation was organized fraudulently, as a device to evade the personal obligation of the contractors. *M. & H. Hardware Co. v. Towers Hardware Co.,* 206.

8. *Private corporation; power to carry on mercantile business.*—A private corporation, authorized by its charter "to have, purchase, receive, possess and enjoy lands, rights, tenements, goods, chattels and effects, in any amount the body corporate may deem necessary to carry all the objects of said corporation into full force and effect; which objects are to mine lime rock and manufacture the same, to keep up and run such machinery as may be necessary to saw lumber and make barrels for the packing of said lime, and the same to sell, devise, grant, alien, and dispose of"— has no implied or incidental power to carry on a general mercantile business. *Chewacla Lime Works v. Dismukes, Frierson & Co.,* 344.

9. *Estoppel against corporation; contract ultra vires.*—Under the decisions of this court, a corporation which has received the benefits of a contract *ultra vires,* is not thereby estopped from setting up the invalidity of the contract, in defense of a suit to enforce it. *Ib.* 344.

10. *Variance in name of corporation; appeals from justice's court.*—In an action commenced in a justice's court, which, on appeal, is required to be tried *de novo,* according to equity and justice, without regard to any defect in the process or proceedings before the justice (Code, § 3405), the defendant corporation being sued by the name given by its amended charter, which also made it liable for all debts created by the corporation under its original name and charter; the cause of action, as indorsed on the justice's warrant, being an account for goods sold and delivered to it by its

CORPORATIONS—*Continued.*

amended name, while the proof shows that the goods were sold and delivered to the corporation before its change of name,—there is no material variance. *Ib.* 344.

11. *Name of corporation; variance.*---The *American Mortgage Company of Scotland,* and the *American Mortgage Company,* are, *prima facie,* different corporations; and an assessment of taxes against the latter, if regular on its face, will not support an action against an agent of the former. *State v. Sloss,* 119.

12. *Company, as corporation, or partnership.*---The name *Wetumpka Lumber Company* does not, *ex vi terminorum,* import that the company is a corporation, rather than an unincorporated association, or a partnership; nor does any presumption of incorporation arise from the fact that its business is transacted by and through a president and secretary; and where the plaintiffs declare against the defendant individually, but seek to charge him with the debt of the company as a partner, and adduce evidence *prima facie* establishing a partnership, the *onus* of proving incorporation is on the defendant. *Clark v. Jones & Brother,* 474.

13. *Liability of stockholders; by what law determined.*—The liability of stockholders in a private corporation, or subscribers for stock prior to the organization of the company, is governed by the law of the State by which the charter is granted, as if incorporated in the subscription as a part thereof. *Morris v. Glenn,* 628.

14. *Transfer of stock; liability of transferror, under statutes of Virginia.* Under the statutes of Virginia, as proved in this case, a transferror or assignor of stock in a private corporation, which has not been fully paid for, is liable equally with the assignee for the unpaid part of the stock, at the instance of creditors, and may be proceeded against in the same manner. *Ib.* 628.

15. *Certificates of stock in private corporation; transfer on books; liability to attachment or execution.*—Under statutory provisions (Code, 1876, §§ 2043-4; 1886, §§ 1670-71), stocks in private corporations are placed on the same footing as other personal chattels, as to their liability to levy under execution or attachment; a transfer thereof, not recorded on the books of the corporation within fifteen days afterwards, is void as to *bona fide* creditors, or subsequent purchasers without notice; and a judgment creditor having a lien, and an attaching creditor who perfects his lien by the recovery of judgment, are equally *bona fide* creditors from the inception of the lien. *Berney Nat. Bank v. Pinckard, DeBardelaben & Co.,* 577.

16. *Subscription for stock, as debt against bankrupt's estate.*—An unpaid subscription for stock in a private corporation is not assets of the subscriber's bankrupt estate, which the assignee is bound to accept, nor is it a provable debt against the bankrupt's estate; consequently, a discharge in bankruptcy is no defense to the bankrupt against an assessment and call regularly made by a court having jurisdiction of the estate of the corporation, under a bill filed by its creditors. *Sayre v. Glenn,* 631.

17. *Fictitious stock in private corporation, under constitutional provisions.*--A subscription to stock in a private corporation, with the understanding that the corporation shall issue "five dollars of stock for one of subscription," is in violation of the constitutional provision which declares void the fictitious issue or increase of stock by private corporations (Art. xiv, § 6); and a contract for the sale of a part of the stock so subscribed, before it has been issued, accompanied with an order to the company to issue it to the purchaser, and to transfer it to him on the books, is equally illegal and void. *Williams v. Evans,* 725.

50

CORPORATIONS—*Continued.*

18. *Corporate existence of railroad company under provisions of char-ter.*—Where the corporate existence of a railroad company is, by its original charter, limited to fifty years, but, by an amendatory act, it is provided that, at the expiration of each subsequent term of ten years, the State shall have the right, at its election, to take all·the property of the company at the par value of its stock, and, if this election is not made within twelve months, then the char-ter of the company shall be continued for another term of ten years; the corporation has a capacity of perpetual existence, unless the election to purchase is exercised by the State. *Davis v. M. & C. Railroad Co.*, 633.

19. *Conveyance to railroad company, for right of way.*—A conveyance of a strip of land to a railroad company, "for the term of fifty years, and so long thereafter as its charter shall continue," when the company has the capacity of perpetual existence, on default by the State to exercise a right of election to purchase its prop-erty, and also has power to condemn lands for a right of way under a writ of *ad quod damnum*, conveys the same interest and estate that would have been acquired by a judgment of condem-nation under such writ. *Ib.* 633.

20. *Dissolution of corporation.*—When its corporate existence is not limited by charter, and there is no voluntary surrender of its franchises, a private corporation will not be deemed dissolved until its dissolution is judicially ascertained; neither its insol-vency, nor a sale of all its property, nor cessation to do business, extinguishes its franchises; and while a voluntary surrender of its franchises from continuous non-user or a long time may be presumed, neither its dissolution, nor a forfeiture of its charter, can be declared in a collateral proceeding. *Ib.* 633.

21. *Deed of railroad corporation, executed by agent.*—A conveyance of lands which belonged to the Alabama & Chattanooga Railroad Company, executed by J. C. Stanton as general superintendent and attorney in fact, without written authority from the board of directors, or other governing body of that corporation, passed no legal title or estate, as against the corporation, or the trustees who succeeded to its rights; but it would constitute color of title, under which a title might be acquired by possession held long enough to effect a statutory bar. *Swann & Billups v. Gaston*, 569.

22. *Books of corporation, as evidence against stockholders.*—The books of a private corporation, showing subscriptions for stock, pay-ments on calls, &c., are admissible as evidence against a stock-holder, in an action to enforce his unpaid subscription as called for, especially when he does not by plea deny the genuiness of his subscription. *Lehman, Durr & Co. v. Glenn*, 618.

23. *Statute of limitations in favor of stockholders, as against corporation or creditors.*—When the terms of subscription bind the stock-holders of a private corporation to pay the amounts subscribed by them respectively, "in such installments as may be called for by said company," in addition to a small sum in cash at the time of subscription; and the corporation, becoming embarrassed, ex-ecutes a deed of assignment for the benefit of its creditors, not having called in all the stock subscribed; the statute of limita-tions in favor of the stockholders, as to their unpaid subscriptions, against a trustee appointed and authorized by a court of equity to collect them, begins to run, not from the date of the assign-ment, but from the time when the court makes an assessment and call for them. *Ib.* 618.

24. *Suit in equity against foreign corporation; certified transcript as evidence.*—A transcript duly certified, of a decree rendered by the Chancery Court of Richmond, Virginia, under a bill filed by or

CORPORATIONS—*Continued.*

30. *Dedication of streets.*—There can be no complete dedication of land to public uses, without an acceptance by the public, by use or otherwise; and where the owner of a tract of land adjoining the limits of an incorporated town or city, having had it mapped and subdivided into lots and blocks, separated by streets, afterwards sells a part of the tract extending to the middle of a street as laid down on the map, this narrows the street at that point to one half of its original width on the map. *Moore v. Johnston,* 220.

31. *Obstruction of street in city or town; legal and equitable remedies.* The obstruction of a street in an incorporated city or town, under claim of title to the soil, is an indictable nuisance, for which an action lies in favor of any person sustaining special damage; and a bill in equity may also be maintained by the city or town, to restrain its continuance, and abate it as a nuisance. *Demopolis v. Webb,* 659.

32. *Fee in streets of city or town.*—In the absence of statutory provisions to the contrary, a conveyance of a lot in an incorporated city or town, bounded by a public street, passes to the grantee the fee to the center of the street, subject to the public right of user; the fee to the other half remaining in the grantor, or original proprietor, and with it all riparian rights when the street is bounded by a navigable river. *Ib.* 659.

33. *Dedication of streets in city or town.*—If the owners of a tract of land have it surveyed and mapped out as a town, with streets dividing the blocks or squares, and each block sub-divided into lots, and sell off lots by their numbers and description on the map, this is a dedication of the several streets to the public, leaving the ultimate fee in the original proprietors. *Ib.* 659.

34. *Acceptance of dedicated street.*—A legislative act incorporating a town as laid out by the proprietors of the land, declaring that "all the tract of land included in the plan of said town be and is hereby declared to be the limits of the same in conformity to said plan," is an adoption of the plan as a part of the charter; and an acceptance of the charter operates as an acceptance of the dedicated streets therein laid down, without further action on the part of the municipal authorities. *Ib.* 659.

35. *Estoppel against denying dedication.*—A sub-purchaser of a lot in an incorporated city or town, described in his conveyance as fronting on a named street, according to the map and plat laid out by the original proprietors of the land, is estopped from denying the dedication of the street as a highway, and its acceptance as such by the proper authorities. *Ib.* 659.

36. *Injunction against collection of wharfage.*—An incorporated city or town can not maintain a bill in equity, to enjoin the collection of wharfage by a person who claims under the original proprietors of the land which was laid out into a town, without showing (1) that the user of the street abutting on the river is thereby obstructed, or (2) that the right to collect wharfage was dedicated to the public with the street, or (3) otherwise negativing its retention by the proprietors. *Ib.* 659.

37. *Act amending charter of Anniston.*—The act approved February 14th, 1887, entitled "An act to amend section 3 of an act entitled 'An act to incorporate the town of Anniston, Calhoun county,' approved February 4, 1879" (Sess. Acts 1886-87, pp. 307-32), is violative of the constitutional provision which declares "Each law shall contain but one subject, which shall be clearly expressed in the title" (Art. IV, § 2), because it contains more than one subject, and because no one of its subjects is clearly expressed in its title. *Ex parte Reynolds,* 138.

38. *Prohibiting sale of spirituous liquors in Anniston; local option;*

CORPORATIONS—*Continued.*

> *judicial notice of election.*—The provision contained in the charter of Anniston, giving the authority to "license, tax and regulate grocers, merchants, retailers," &c. (Sess. Acts 1888-9, p. 612, § 7, subd. 10), does not confer the power to prohibit the sale of spirituous liquors within the corporate limits; and if the power be conferred by the further provision empowering the municipal government to provide for the punishment of "any offense punishable by the laws of the State of Alabama" (subd. 22, § 7), it must be shown that the sale of liquor there is prohibited by law, since Calhoun county is governed by a "local option" law, and the court can not take judicial notice of the result of an election held under that law. *Ib.* 138.

39. *Sentence to hard labor, under municipal ordinance.*—A sentence to hard labor, imposed by a municipal court, which has power to punish only by fine or imprisonment, is illegal and void, and the defendant is entitled to be discharged on *habeas corpus.* *Ib.* 138.

40. *Charter of Bessemer, under constitutional provision as to title and subject-matter of laws; power to issue municipal bonds.*—The act approved December 12th, 1888, entitled "An act to amend the charter of the town of Bessemer, and to re-incorporate the same as the city of Bessemer, and to establish a charter therefor," is not violative of the constitutional provision which declares, "Each law shall contain but one subject, which shall be clearly expressed in its title" (Art. IV, § 2); the title and the body of the act, construed together, show a single purpose, and relate to a single subject, and the grant of power, in the 38th section, to issue negotiable bonds for specified municipal purposes, is germane to that subject as expressed in the title. *Judson v. Bessemer*, 240.

41. *Same; amendatory laws, and unconstitutional repealing laws.*—The subsequent statute amending the 38th section of said charter, "by striking out the word *fifty,* and inserting *thirty* in lieu thereof," is violative of the further constitutional provision, contained in the same article and section, that, in amendatory laws, so much of the former law as is amended "shall be re-enacted and published at length;" and said amendatory law being unconstitutional and void, the power of the corporation to issue bonds payable in fifty years, as first provided, is unimpaired. *Ib.* 240.

42. *Municipal bonds payable in gold coin.*—A grant of power to a municipal corporation to issue bonds, without limitation as to the kind of currency in which they shall be payable, confers the authority to make them payable "in gold coin of the United States of America, of the present standard weight and fineness." *Ib.* 240.

See, also, RAILROADS.

COSTS.

1. *Against guardian ad litem.*—The rule of this court has always been, not to tax a guardian *ad litem* with costs, though he be the unsuccessful appellant. *Brown v. Williams*, 353.
2. As to costs in criminal cases, see CRIMINAL LAW, 94-99.

CRIMINAL LAW.

ACCOMPLICES.

1. *Corroborating evidence.*—On a prosecution for receiving stolen money, a witness who, according to her own testimony, stole the money at the instigation of the defendant, and gave it to him, having further testified that, when he came back again, and gave

CRIMINAL LAW—*Continued.*

    her a message which purported to come from her mother, as had
been agreed upon between them, she replied, *"There aint no more
to get;"* *held,* that the testimony of another witness, who overheard this remark, but heard nothing else, would be corroborative evidence tending to connect the defendant with the commission of the offense (Code, § 4476), if the jury believed that it
referred to the money; but that this was an inference of fact
which only the jury could draw, and which the court could not
assume as matter of law in instructions to them. *Burney v.
State,* 80.

ARSON.

2. *Sufficiency of indictment; averment of ownership of building.*—An
indictment which charges the burning of a "cotton-house containing cotton of M. B." (Code, § 3781), is fatally defective, in not
alleging with sufficient clearness the ownership of the house.
Smoke v. State, 143.

ASSAULT.

3. *Mistake as to identity of person assaulted, and drunkenness, as defenses.*—Neither a mistake in the identity of the person assaulted,
nor the drunkenness of the defendant at the time, is a defense to
a prosecution for an assault. *Carter v. State,* 113.

BURGLARY.

4. *Sufficiency of indictment in averring ownership of house.*—An indictment for burglary, in breaking and entering the store-house
"of the Perry Mason Shoe Company," must either allege that
said company is a corporation, or, if it be a partnership, must
allege that fact, and state the names of the individual partners,
showing that the defendant is not one of them. *Emmonds v.
State,* 12.

5. *Possession of burglarious implements, as criminal offense.*—Under
statutory provisions, the possession of "any implement or instrument designed and intended to aid in the commission of burglary or larceny [in this State or elsewhere]," is declared to be a
misdemeanor (Code, § 3788); but, while the offense consists of the
possession, with the criminal intent to use the implements, the
bracketed words are no part of it, and the statute is to be read as
if they were omitted. *Davis v. State,* 10.

6. *Recent possession of stolen goods; flight.*—The possession of a part
of the stolen goods, recently after a larceny or burglary, imposes on the party the *onus* of explaining how he acquired
them; and being unexplained, in connection with proof of attempted flight when arrested for the offense, would authorize a
conviction for the offense. *Cooper v. State,* 135.

EMBEZZLEMENT.

7. *Embezzlement of public revenue; sentence to imprisonment in penitentiary.*—Under the provisions of the statute approved March
.6th, 1876, embezzlement of the public revenue was punishable by
fine and imprisonment in the penitentiary "not less than one
year," one or both, at the discretion of the court (Code, 1876,
§ 4275); but, by a statute approved the next day, regulating the
punishment of felonies (*Ib.* § 4450), when the sentence to imprisonment "is for twelve months or less," it must be in the county
jail, and not in the penitentiary; and this latter statute controls
a sentence to imprisonment under the former. *Herrington v.
State,* 1.

ENTICING AWAY LABORER.

8. *Constituents of offense; consent of employer.*—The consent of the
employer, expressed in writing, or given in the presence of a

CRIMINAL LAW—*Continued.*

credible person, is a defense to a prosecution for enticing away a laborer in service under a written contract (Code, § 3757); if the consent is conditional, as on payment of the amount due the employer, performance of the condition must be shown; and the person in whose presence the consent is given being presumed to be credible, in the absence of evidence to the contrary, the defendant is entitled to have the jury pass on the sufficiency of the evidence. *Prestwood v. State*, 147.

9. *Local jurisdiction.*—If the employer and the defendant resided near each other, but in adjacent counties, and the acts requisite to the consummation of the offense occurred in both counties, the jurisdiction is in either. (Code, § 3719.) *Ib*. 147.

EVIDENCE IN CRIMINAL CASES.

10. *Wife as witness for husband.*—In a criminal case, the wife is not a competent witness for her husband. *Hussey v. State*, 121.

11. *Testimony of physician as expert; hearsay.*—A practicing physician, who examined the deceased after he was wounded, and has given his own diagnosis of the case, can not be allowed to testify that other physicians concurred with him in opinion. *Ib.* 121.

12. *Dying declarations.*—The declarations of the deceased in this case, made to different persons, at intervals, during the three days he lived after receiving the fatal wound, always expressing the belief that he would die from the effects of the wound, were properly admitted as evidence, although some of his friends declared to him their belief that he was not seriously wounded, and one of his attending physicians had expressed to him the hope that he might recover. *Ib.* 121.

13. *Proof of character.*—A witness, testifying to the character of the defendant as a peaceable and quiet man, may be asked whether he "ever heard of his having any other difficulty than the one in question," and may testify that he had not. *Ib.* 121.

14. *Proof of character.*—Evidence of character, at least on direct examination, goes to general reputation only, and can not be extended to particular acts, or specified conduct; nor can a witness give his own opinion as to the person inquired about;—as, that he was a "model man," or "was a timid man, and would rather avoid than provoke a difficulty." *Ib.* 121.

15. *Same; cross-examination of witness; impeaching.*—Witnesses for the prosecution having testified to the good reputation of the deceased as a peaceable and quiet man, and having denied, on cross-examination, that they had ever heard of certain specified personal difficulties in which he was said to have been involved; the defendant can not prove the existence and general notoriety of those difficulties, for the purpose of discrediting their testimony. *Ib.* 121.

16. *Character of deceased; evidence as to.*—On a trial for murder, the prosecution may adduce evidence of the character of the deceased as a peaceable and quiet man, although the defense has only proved particular traits of his character, as a quick-tempered, violent man, easily provoked, and likely to provoke a difficulty. *Ib.* 121.

17. *Charge as to effect of evidence of good character.*—The court may properly instruct the jury in a criminal case, that proof of good character is not permitted to go to them for the purpose of shielding the defendant from the consequences of his conduct, but simply as a circumstance to be considered by them with the other evidence in the case; that if, from all the evidence, they believe the defendant guilty beyond a reasonable doubt, they should say so as firmly against a man of good character as bad; that good

CRIMINAL LAW—*Continued.*

character does not shield from the consequences of a criminal act, proved to the satisfaction of the jury beyond a reasonable doubt, though it may raise a reasonable doubt that the act was done with the criminal intent. *Ib.* 121.

18. *Testimony of defendant in his own behalf.*—In a criminal case, if the defendant fails or declines to testify in his own behalf, his failure does not create any presumption against him, and is not the subject of comment by counsel (Code, § 4473); but, if he elects to testify, and fails or refuses to explain or rebut any criminating fact, when he can reasonably do so, this is a circumstance in the nature of an implied admission, on which counsel may comment, and which the jury may consider in determining his guilt or innocence. *Cotton v. State*, 103; *Clarke v. State*, 71.

19. *Charge as to testimony of defendant.*—Where the defendant has testified in his own behalf, a charge instructing the jury that, in considering what weight they will give to his statements, "it is their duty to remember that he is the defendant, and interested in the result of the verdict: and they may, for this reason, if they think it sufficient, entirely disregard his statement, if it is in conflict with the other evidence," is erroneous, and ground of reversal. *Allen v. State*, 107.

20. *Same.*—When the defendant in a criminal case has testified in his own behalf, a charge instructing the jury that "the interest he has in the case may be considered by them in weighing his own evidence" is not erroneous. *Norris v. State*, 85.

21. *Charge as to testimony of defendant.*—A charge asked, instructing the jury that, "in considering the testimony of the defendant, while they may look to the fact that he is a party to the suit, yet that does not render him less creditable [credible?] than he would be if he were not a party," is properly refused. *Dick v. State*, 61.

22. *Admissibility of declarations, as part of res gestæ.*—This court can not revise the ruling of the trial court in refusing to admit the defendant's declarations as evidence, as a part of the *res gestæ*, when the declarations are not set out, and it is not shown that they related to the act charged, or threw light on it, or tended to elucidate it, or would have been beneficial to the defendant, or were in any way material. *Goley v. State*, 57.

23. *Same.*—The offer of the defendant to lift up the deceased, made two or three minutes after the shooting, is not admissible evidence as a part of the *res gestæ*, not being shown to have been made so immediately after the act as to authorize the presumption that it was part of the main fact, and not an afterthought intended to give a false coloring to it. *Ib.* 57.

24. *Charge as to weight or effect of evidence.*—It is the exclusive province of the jury to reconcile the testimony of the different witnesses, if possible, or, if irreconcilable, to determine whom they will believe, or what credit they will give to a witness who is contradicted or impeached; and a charge which institutes a comparison between the weight and force of the testimony of different witnesses, equally credible and having equal opportunities for knowing the facts, is properly refused, as tending to confuse and mislead the jury, and invading their peculiar province. *Norris v. State*, 85.

25. *Reasonable doubt; and "reason to believe."*—A charge asked, asserting the right to an acquittal if the jury "have reason to believe" certain facts hypothetically stated, is properly refused, since the expression is not the equivalent of *belief*, and does not correctly state the doctrine of reasonable doubt. *Munkers v. State*, 94.

26. *Charge as to circumstantial evidence.*—A charge asserting that, "to justify conviction, circumstantial evidence ought to exclude a

CRIMINAL LAW—*Continued.*

rational probability of innocence, and a conviction ought not to be had on circumstantial evidence, when direct and positive evidence is attainable," is properly refused, as tending to mislead and confuse the jury, when there is some direct and positive evidence, and the record does not show that any other was attainable. *Coleman v. State,* 14.

27. *Testimony as to defendant's arrest or surrender.*—The sheriff, by whom the defendant was arrested, or to whom he surrendered, having testified that, not being able to find the defendant, "he told his friends that he had a warrant for the arrest of the defendant, and sent him word to come in and give himself up—that the case against him amounted to nothing, and he would have no trouble to get out of it; that the defendant did come in and surrender a day or two afterwards, but he did not know the defendant got his message;" *held,* that this evidence was improperly admitted, against the objection of the defendant. *Ib.* 14.

28. *Charge as to sufficiency of evidence.*—A charge which instructs the jury, in a criminal case, that "the State is not required to prove the guilt of the defendant to a mathematical certainty," asserts a correct proposition. *Dick v. State,* 61.

29. *Conversations between third persons; admissibility as evidence.*—Conversations between third persons, tending to implicate the defendant, but not had in his presence, are not admissible as evidence against him; and if they did not relate to the particular offense with which he is charged, they would be inadmissible because irrelevant. *Tolbert v. State,* 27.

30. *Former testimony of absent witness.*—The testimony of a witness on a former trial of the defendant, or on his preliminary examination by a committing magistrate, is admissible as evidence against him on the trial, on proof that the witness is beyond the jurisdiction of the court, being either permanently or indefinitely absent. *Perry v. State,* 30.

31. *Charge as to reasonable doubt.*—A charge asked in a criminal case, asserting that "the probability of reasonably accounting for the death of the deceased by accident, or by any other cause than the unlawful act of the defendant, must be excluded by the circumstances proved; and it is only when no other hypothesis will explain all the conditions of the case, and account for all the facts, that it can be safely and justly concluded that it was caused by him,"—is properly refused. *Ib.* 30.

32. *Declarations, and conduct of conspirators, as evidence against each other.*—Under the rule laid down in the case of *McAnally v. State* (74 Ala. 9), when the evidence establishes, *prim f cie,* the existence of a conspiracy between the defendant and others, to commit the crime with which he is charged, the acts, declarations and conduct of the others, in promotion of the purpose or object of the conspiracy, or in relation to it, are competent and admissible as evidence against him; and such evidence was properly admitted in this case. *Johnson v. State,* 39.

33. *Declarations of defendant as evidence.*—Declarations made by the defendant himself, before or after the commission of the homicide with which he is charged, tending to connect him with it, are admissible as evidence against him, although a conspiracy between him and the other persons implicated may not be established. *Ib.* 39.

34. *Evidence of prior contradictory statements of defendant.*—The defendant testifying in his own behalf to an *alibi,* it is competent for the prosecution to prove his prior contradictory statements, by affidavit or otherwise, as to his whereabouts on the day named; but evidence of prior statements made, not inconsistent with his testimony on the trial, is not admissible. *Cotton v. State,* 75.

CRIMINAL LAW—*Continued.*

pair of steps running up on the outside, through a front hall with which it was connected by a door, is not a public house within the statute against gaming (Code, § 4052), because the front hall is public, and is used once or twice a week as a dancing hall. *Skinner v. State,* 105.

HABEAS CORPUS.

43. *When discharge ought to be granted.*—On petition for *habeas corpus,* the petitioner is entitled to be discharged, if he is confined under process or a judgment]which is void. *Ex parte State, in re Long,* 46; *Ex parte Reynolds,* 138. But not otherwise. *Ex parte Barker,* 4.

HOMICIDE; MURDER; MANSLAUGHTER.

44. *Charge as to self-defense; when properly refused.*—In a prosecution for murder, a charge requested, instructing the jury that the defendant is entitled to an acquittal, if the assault was unprovoked by him, and he appeared at the time to be so menaced as to create a reasonable apprehension of danger to his life, or of grievous bodily harm, and could not have retreated without danger to his life or person, is properly refused, when the evidence as to the assault is conflicting, and the defendant's own testimony shows that, when he fired the fatal shot, he was beyond the reach of the axe in the hands of the deceased. *Squire v. State,* 114.

45. *Self-defense; charge as to duty to retreat; explanatory charge.*—In a case of homicide, a charge instructing the jury that, "if the deceased was the assailant, the party assailed must retreat, unless retreat will endanger his safety, and must refrain from taking life, if there *is* any other reasonable mode of escape," states the rule in the ordinary language of the decisions; and if it be objectionable, as requiring the party assailed to act on the actual (and not an apparent) necessity, this qualifying principle should be invoked by an explanatory charge. (The 7th head-note to the case of *Tesney v. The State,* 77 Ala. 33, in stating that the charge therein set out "is erroneous," instead of "too narrow and restricted," is "not justified by the opinion of the court" in that case.) *Poe v. State,* 65.

46. *Same; charge ignoring duty to retreat.*—A charge requested, instructing the jury that, "if they believed the deceased was trying to draw a deadly weapon, or that he acted in such a manner as to convey to the defendant the impression that he was trying to draw a deadly weapon, for the purpose of attacking the defendant," who was armed with a shot-gun, "and thereby put defendant in fear of great bodily harm, he was justified in doing whatever was necessary to preserve his own life;" and a charge asserting that, if the deceased came towards the defendant, using angry and insulting language, "and placed his hand in his pocket in such a manner as to indicate to a reasonable mind that his purpose was to draw and fire, then the defendant was authorized to draw and fire first," each is erroneous, in excluding from the jury all consideration of the inquiry as to any duty to retreat. *Ib.* 65.

47. *Charge as to threats, with overt act, excusing retreat.*—No threats, or overt acts, which do not, actually or apparently, justify a reasonable apprehension of danger to life, or of great bodily harm, will justify the party assailed in killing his adversary, without resorting to retreat; and a charge requested which ignores the duty to retreat, without regard to the character of the threats, is properly refused. *Ib.* 65.

CRIMINAL LAW—*Continued.*

48. *To what witness may testify.*—On a prosecution for murder, a witness for the defense can not be allowed to testify that the defendant "was afraid" to work in the field alone, or to go out about his premises after dark, on account of threats made against him by the deceased; such testimony being merely the opinion of the witness, based on the conduct or declarations of the defendant himself, or unsupported by any fact at all. *Ib.* 65.

49. *Same.*—A witness who, as a member of the coroner's jury, had seen the dead body of the child alleged to have been murdered, may testify that its neck, which was broken, "looked like it had been struck with a hot iron, and looked scarred." *Perry v. State*, 30.

50. *Declarations of defendant as evidence.*—Declarations made by the defendant himself, before or after the commission of the homicide with which he is charged, tending to connect him with it, are admissible as evidence against him, although a conspiracy between him and the other persons implicated may not be established. *Johnson v. State*, 39.

51. *Same.*—The offer of the defendant to lift up the deceased, made two or three minutes after the shooting, is not admissible evidence as a part of the *res gestæ*, not being shown to have been made so immediately after the act as to authorize the presumption that it was part of the main fact, and not an afterthought intended to give a false coloring to it. *Goley v. State*, 57.

52. *Dying declarations.*—The declarations of the deceased in this case, made to different persons, at intervals, during the three days he lived after receiving the fatal wound, always expressing the belief that he would die from effects of the wound, were properly admitted as evidence, although some of his friends declared to him their belief that he was not seriously wounded, and one of his attending physicians had expressed to him the hope that he might recover. *Hussey v. State*, 121.

53. *Character of deceased; evidence as to.*—On a trial for murder, the prosecution may adduce evidence of the character of the deceased as a peaceable and quiet man, although the defense has only proved particular traits of his character, as a quick-tempered, violent man, easily provoked, and likely to provoke a difficulty. *Ib.* 121.

54. *Proof of character.*—A witness, testifying to the character of the defendant as a peaceable and quiet man, may be asked whether he "ever heard of his having any other difficulty than the one in question," and may testify that he had not. *Ib.* 121.

INDICTMENT.

55. *Arson; averment of ownership of building.*—An indictment which charges the burning of a "cotton-house containing cotton of M. B." (Code, § 3781), is fatally defective, in not alleging with sufficient clearness the ownership of the house. *Smoke v. State*, 143.

56. *Burglary; averring ownership of house.*—An indictment for burglary, in breaking and entering the store-house "of the Perry Mason Shoe Company," must either allege that said company is a corporation, or, if it be a partnership, must allege that fact, and state the names of the individual partners, showing that the defendant is not one of them. *Emmonds v. State*, 12.

57. *Forgery; averment of extrinsic facts.*—A written instrument which is on its face unintelligible, not purporting to create or discharge any pecuniary liability, nor otherwise showing that another person might be injured by it, will not support an indictment for forgery (Code, § 3852), unless extrinsic facts are averred supplying its deficiencies. *Fomby v. State*, 36.

CRIMINAL LAW—*Continued.*

58. *Gaming.*—An indictment which charges that the defendant "bet at a game played with cards, dice, or some device or substitute for either cards or dice, in a public house, highway, or other public place, or at an outhouse where people resort" (Code, §§ 4052, 4057), is fatally defective. unless it also alleges that a game *was played. Tolbert v. State,* 27.

59. *Receiving stolen goods.*—An indictment for receiving stolen money (Code, § 3794), must aver the number and denomination of the coins, or some of them, or must allege that the same was unknown to the grand jury; and an averment that it was "two hundred dollars in gold coin," without other descriptive words, is not sufficient. *Burney v. State,* 80.

JURORS AND JURY.

60. *Special venire in capital case.*—In a capital case, when the arraignment and the trial occur in the same week, the special *venire* should include, not "those summoned on the regular juries for the week" (Code, § 4320), but only those who have appeared, and who constitute the regular juries in fact; though the rule is different, when the trial is set for a subsequent week. *Dick v. State,* 61; *Cotton v. State.* 75.

61. *Same.*—In drawing a special *venire* for the trial of a capital case, under the provisions of the general jury law approved February 28th, 1887 (Sess. Acts 1886-7, pp. 151-8, § 10; Code, p. 134, note), the court has a discretionary power as to the number to be drawn, within the limits specified, and can not be required, on demand of the defendant, to draw fifty, the maximum number specified, which was the mimimum under the former law (Code, § 4320). *Clarke v. State.* 71.

62. *Peremptory challenges; when and how demanded.*—An exception reserved during the drawing of the special *venire*, in these words: "The defendant then made a motion that, as matter of law, he was entitled to twenty challenges. which motion the court overruled, and the defendant excepted," does not show a reversible error (Code. § 4330), when it does not appear that he in fact challenged or offered to challenge any juror who was drawn. *Ib.* 71.

LARCENY.

63. *Recent possession of stolen goods; flight.*—The possession of a part of the stolen goods, recently after a larceny, imposes on the party the *onus* of explaining how he acquired them; and being unexplained, in connection with proof of attempted flight when arrested for the offense, would authorize a conviction for the offense. *Cooper v. State,* 135.

64. *Assessed value of stolen property, as part of costs on conviction.*—On a conviction of larceny and sentence to hard labor for the county, the assessed value of the stolen property, or the part thereof which has not been restored to the owner, is an item of the costs, and payable as other items are (Code, § 3792); but the statute does not extend to convictions followed by a sentence to the penitentiary. *Skinner v. Dawson,* 348.

PEDDLING.

65. *Selling stoves by sample.*—Under an indictment which charges that the defendants engaged in the business of peddling in a two-horse wagon, without a license as required by law (Code, § 629, subd. 31, 40), a conviction can not be had on proof that they were the agents of a foreign company engaged in the manufacture of stoves; that one of them travelled about in a wagon, carrying a single stove with him, selling stoves by the sample,

CRIMINAL LAW—*Continued.*

and taking the purchaser's note payable on delivery within sixty days; and that the other afterwards carried the stoves around in a wagon, delivered them, and received payment of the notes, if the purchasers elected to pay cash at a reduced price. *Ballou v. State,* 144.

PLEAS AND DEFENSES.

66. *Insanity as defense; charges as to, when abstract.*—Charges as to the defense of insanity in criminal cases are properly refused, without regard to their correctness as abstract legal propositions, when there is no evidence in the case showing any form of mania, or mental incapacity, to a degree which confers irresponsibility for crime. *Perry v. State,* 30.

67. *Same; how pleaded; ex post facto laws.*—By statutory provision, insanity as a defense in criminal cases must be specially pleaded, and is not available under the plea of not guilty generally (Sess. Act 1888-9, pp. 742–6); and this statute, relating only to the mode of procedure, applies to all cases tried since its passage, although the offense was committed before that date. *Ib.* 30.

68. *Misnomer; pleadings as to*—The difference between the names *Munkers* and *Moncus* is sufficient to support a plea of misnomer, when a demurrer is interposed to it; if, by local usage, the names have the same pronunciation, issue should be taken on the plea, or a replication should be filed. *Munkers v. State,* 94.

69. *Mistake as to identity of person assaulted, and drunkenness, as defenses.*—Neither a mistake in the identity of the person assaulted, nor the drunkenness of the defendant at the time, is a defense to a prosecution for an assault. *Carter v. State,* 113.

RAPE.

70. *Assault with intent to ravish.*—Force is an essential ingredient of the crime of rape, and an intent to use force, if necessary, is essential to an assault with intent to ravish (Code, § 3751); yet, where it is shown that the defendant put his arms around the prosecutrix, forcibly held and pressed her, making indecent proposals, and only released her on her threats to call assistance, this is sufficient to support a conviction, although he may have had no intention to commit a battery on her. *Norris v. State,* 85.

71. *Evidence identifying defendants as perpetrators of offense.*—Where the defendants deny their guilt, though identified by the prosecutrix, and show that, before their arrest, she had given a description of the guilty parties which did not suit their appearance, it is competent for the prosecution to prove that, after their arrest, she identified and pointed them out among a large number of prisoners. *Cotton v. State,* 75.

72. *Complaint of prosecutrix; impeaching witness by proof of contradictory statements.*—On a prosecution for rape, the mother of the prosecutrix having testified that her daughter complained to her immediately after the commission of the offense, the defendant has a right to elicit the particulars of the complaint; and he may impeach the witness, a proper predicate having been laid, by proof of prior contradictory statements out of court. *Allen v. State,* 107.

73. *Consent implied from conduct.*—Although the prosecutrix may not have consented in fact, yet, if her conduct towards the defendant, at the time of the alleged rape, was such as to create in his mind an honest and reasonable belief that she had consented, or was willing for him to have connection with her, a conviction should not be had; and the court should so instruct the jury, on request. *Ib.* 107.

CRIMINAL LAW—*Continued.*

CRIMINAL LAW—*Continued.*

cation, does not render the seller criminally liable. *Carl v. State,* 17.

81. *Evidence as to intoxicating properties of article sold.*—In a criminal prosecution for the sale of intoxicating liquors in violation of a local prohibitory liquor law, the article sold being compounded by a druggist, and the bottles labeled *"Elixir Cinchona,"* or *"Cinchona Bitters;"* it is permissible for the prosecution to prove that it was bought and used by many persons as a beverage, the use to which it was applied being illustrative of its nature and properties; and a person who had swallowed it may state its exhilarating effect on himself, and, though not technically an expert, may testify that, "in his opinion, it would produce intoxication." *Ib.* 17.

82. *Prohibitory sale of spirituous liquors in Anniston; local option; judicial notice of election.*—The provision contained in the charter of Anniston, giving the authority to "license, tax and regulate grocers, merchants, retailers," &c. (Sess. Acts 1888-9, p. 612, § 7, subd. 10), does not confer the power to prohibit the sale of spirituous liquors within the corporate limits; and if the power be conferred by the further provision empowering the municipal government to provide for the punishment of "any offense punishable by the laws of the State of Alabama" (subd. 22, § 7), it must be shown that the sale of liquor there is prohibited by law, since Calhoun county is governed by a "local option" law, and the court can not take judicial notice of the result of an election held under that law. *Ex parte Reynolds,* 138.

SEDUCTION.

83. *Chastity of prosecutrix; charge on different aspects of evidence.*—The chastity of the prosecutrix, at the time of the alleged seduction, is an essential ingredient of the offense, and is to be presumed in the absence of evidence to the contrary; but a reasonable doubt of its existence entitles the defendant to an acquittal, and if the testimony of the parties is in irreconcilable conflict, as to the fact of prior illicit intercourse between them, he is entitled to have charges given based on the supposed truth of his own testimony. *Munkers v. State,* 94.

84. *Evidence corroborating prosecutrix.*—By statutory provision, a conviction of seduction can not be had on the uncorroborated testimony of the woman herself (Code, § 4015); the corroboration must be as to a material matter, must connect the defendant with that matter, and must be sufficient to satisfy the jury, beyond a reasonable doubt, of the truth of the woman's testimony; and the defendant's own admission to third persons of an engagement between him and the woman, and of his intention to marry her, are admissible as evidence against him, and sufficient to meet the statutory requirement, though they may not be sufficient to satisfy the jury beyond a reasonable doubt. *Ib.* 94.

TRESPASS AFTER WARNING.

85. *"Legal cause, or good excuse" for trespass.*—In a prosecution for trespass after warning (Code, § 3874), by driving a loaded wagon along a neighborhood road, which had been opened through the lands of the prosecutor, by his permission, to give convenient access to a cane-mill, and which was afterwards closed by him; it being shown that the defendant might have had access to the mill "by cutting out a new road, a short distance through open piney woods, perhaps 100 yards, and cause-waying a small boggy branch;" *held,* that a "legal cause or good excuse" for the trespass was not shown. *Wilson v. State,* 117.

CRIMINAL LAW—*Continued.*

TRIAL, AND ITS INCIDENTS.

86. *Change of venue.*—In a criminal case, a change of venue is a matter of right, if the application is made in due time, and is supported by sufficient evidence (Code, § 4485); but it is properly refused, when, on all the evidence adduced for and against the application, the court is not reasonably satisfied that an impartial trial and an unbiased verdict could not reasonably be expected in the county in which the indictment was found. *Hussey v. State*, 121.

87. *Same; counter affidavits.*—By the established practice in this and other States, on application for a change of venue, counter affidavits may be received against those offered in support of it; and this practice is not violative of the constitutional principle which gives to the accused the right to be "confronted by the witnesses against him." *Ib.* 121.

88. *When case is properly triable.*—The statutory provision requiring the criminal docket to be taken up on the second Monday of the term, when the term continues two weeks (Code, § 751), was intended to expedite speedy trials of criminal cases, and does not deny to the court the right to proceed with the trial of a criminal case before that time; and the further provision requiring the clerk of the court to set the trial of criminal cases for particular days, "except capital cases," and declaring that "no case so set shall be called for trial before such day" ¡*Ib.* § 4447), does not apply to a capital case improperly set for trial by the clerk. *Goley v. State*, 57.

89. *Severance of trial.*—Under the statute now of force (Code, § 4451), when two or more persons are jointly indicted, either one of them is entitled to a severance as matter of right, if he claims it in proper time. *Andy v. State*, 23.

90. *Trial on Good Friday.*—Although Good Friday has been declared a legal holiday (Sess. Acts 1888–9. p. 56), a trial may be lawfully had and judgment and sentence rendered on that day. *Bobbitt v. State*, 91.

91. *Trial by court, without jury; how considered on error or appeal.* When a criminal case is submitted to the decision of the court without a jury, as authorized by a special statute. the decision of the court on a question of fact, as to which the evidence is conflicting, or where inferences are to be drawn dependent on its sufficiency, will not be reversed, unless a verdict would be set aside on the same evidence; but, when the facts are undisputed, and only a legal conclusion is to be drawn from them, the decision is regarded as if given in charge to the jury, and its correctness is a question of law. *Skinner v. State*, 105.

92. *Same.*—A trial by jury not being demanded, in a criminal prosecution before the Criminal Court of Pike (Sess. Acts 1888-9, p. 631, § 7), this court can not review the conclusions of the judge on the evidence adduced. *Wynn v. State*, 137.

93. *New trial; refusal not revisable.*—By the settled practice of this court since its organization, a motion for a new trial is addressed to the discretion of the lower court. and its refusal is not revisable by this court on error or appeal. *Johnson v. State*, 39.

VERDICT; JUDGMENT; SENTENCE.

94. *Hard labor for county, on non-payment of fine and costs.*—On conviction of a misdemeanor punishable by fine only, or so punished in the particular case, followed by a sentence to hard labor for the county to enforce its payment, an additional term of hard labor may be imposed for the payment of the costs (Code, §§ 4502-04),

51

DAMAGES—*Continued.*

size, at a named price per thousand feet, and afterwards sold all the timber on the land to a third person, who entered and cut some of the trees to which plaintiff was entitled; the measure of damages is the market value of the trees so cut and carried away, *less* the price which plaintiff was to have paid for them, but which he had not paid. *Clements v. Beatty,* 238.

2. *Same.*—Under a contract by which defendants, tobacco merchants, employed plaintiff as a travelling salesman, agreeing to supply him with samples, to allow him as compensation one-half of the profits on sales effected by him, and to advance to him, by paying his drafts at the commencement of his work, $50 at the end of every two weeks, to be repaid out of his share of the profits, while he was to furnish his own outfit; on a breach by defendants, refusing to pay plaintiff's drafts, and instructing him to quit work before the expiration of the stipulated term, plaintiff is entitled to recover as damages, not only his share of the profits on sales perfected and consummated, but also on sales negotiated so far that it can be ascertained with certainty that they would be completed, and the extent or amount thereof; but mere expectations, doubtful offers, or other vague or indefinite assurances of intention to purchase, without expression of quantity or value, are speculative merely, and not recoverable; opinions as to what sales he could, or probably would have made, are also speculative and contingent; nor can he prove or recover for the cost of his horse and buggy, the value of his services per month, or the damages to his credit by being thus thrown out of employment. *Beck v. West & Co.,* 213.

3. *Profits as damages.*—For the breach of an executory contract to deliver goods, the measure of damages is the difference between the agreed price and the market price at the place of delivery; and the profits which might have been realized on selling the goods by retail during the Christmas holidays, for which purpose they were intended, "are conjectural, merely speculative, and dependent on too many contingencies to constitute an element of recoverable damages." *Young & Co. v. Cureton,* 727.

4. *Testimony of witness as to damages.*—A party, testifying as a witness, can not state "what damages" he sustained by the breach of contract of which he complains. *Ib.* 727.

5. *Damages for conversion by mortgagee, on return of property to mortgagor.*—In trover by the first, against a second mortgagee of personal property, the material question being whether the defendant was chargeable with notice, actual or constructive, of plaintiff's prior mortgage, the fact that the defendant, at the termination of a lawsuit with the mortgagor, sold and returned to him a part of the mortgaged property, does not relieve him of damages for its conversion, if otherwise he was guilty of a conversion. *Pollak v. Davidson,* 551.

6. *In action on attachment bond; error without injury.*—In an action on an attachment bond, a judgment on verdict for the defendants conclusively determines that the writ was not wrongfully sued out; and the rulings of the court on the pleadings and evidence, or in the matter of charges given or refused, relating only to the question of exemplary damages, if erroneous, could not have injured the plaintiff. *Calhoun v. Hannan & Michael,* 277.

7 *After judgment by nil dicit.*—After judgment by *nil dicit* in an action of trover, the only question to be referred to the jury, as to which evidence can be adduced, relates to the amount of damages. *Maund v. Loeb & Brother,* 374.

DEDICATION.

1. *Dedication of streets.*—There can be no complete dedication of land to public uses, without an acceptance by the public, by use or otherwise; and where the owner of a tract of land adjoining the limits of an incorporated town or city, having had it mapped and subdivided into lots and blocks, separated by streets, afterwards sells a part of the tract extending to the middle of a street as laid down on the map, this narrows the street at that point to one half of its original width on the map. *Moore v. Johnston,* 220.

2. *Same.*—If the owners of a tract of land have it surveyed and mapped out as a town, with streets dividing the blocks or squares, and each block sub-divided into lots, and sell off lots by their numbers and description on the map, this is a dedication of the several streets to the public, leaving the ultimate fee in the original proprietors. *Demopolis v. Webb,* 659.

3. *Acceptance of dedicated street.*—A legislative act incorporating a town as laid out by the proprietors of the land, declaring that "all the tract of land included in the plan of said town be and is hereby declared to be the limits of the same in conformity to said plan," is an adoption of the plan as a part of the charter; and an acceptance of the charter operates as an acceptance of the dedicated streets therein laid down, without further action on the part of the municipal authorities. *Ib.* 659.

4. *Estoppel against denying dedication.*—A sub-purchaser of a lot in an incorporated city or town, described in his conveyance as fronting on a named street, according to the map and plat laid out by the original proprietors of the land, is estopped from denying the dedication of the street as a highway, and its acceptance as such by the proper authorities. *Ib.* 659.

DEEDS.

1. *Registration as constructive delivery of deed.*—The intentional delivery of a deed by the grantor to the probate judge, for registration, may be a sufficient delivery to the grantee, though he never had actual possession, and was even ignorant of the existence of the deed; and a delivery for registration, by mistake of the grantor's clerk, may, by long acquiescence, operate as a valid and effectual delivery, on the presumption that the mistake has been waived. *Sheffield Land, Iron & Coal Co. v. Neill,* 158.

2. *Conveyance to railroad company, for right of way.*—A conveyance of a strip of land to a railroad company, "for the term of fifty years, and so long thereafter as its charter shall continue," when the company has the capacity of perpetual existence, on default by the State to exercise a right of election to purchase its property, and also has power to condemn lands for a right of way under a writ of *ad quod damnum,* conveys the same interest and estate that would have been acquired by a judgment of condemnation under such writ. *Davis v. M. & C. Railroad Co.,* 633.

3. *Conveyance of base or qualified fee.*—A conveyance of a qualified, base or determinable fee in lands, leaves in the grantor only a possibility of reverter, which, though it may descend to his heirs, can not be granted or assigned so as to vest a title on which ejectment may be maintained. *Ib.* 633.

4. *Deed of railroad corporation, executed by agent.*—A conveyance of lands which belonged to the Alabama & Chattanooga Railroad Company, executed by J. C. Stanton as general superintendent and attorney in fact, without written authority from the board of directors, or other governing body of that corporation, passed no legal title or estate, as against the corporation, or the trustees who succeeded to its rights; but it would constitute color of title,

DEEDS—*Continued.*

under which a title might be acquired by possession held long enough to effect a statutory bar. *Swann & Billups v. Gaston,* 569.

5. *Conveyance of lands; title afterwards acquired.*—A railroad company may convey by mortgage property to be afterwards acquired; and if it conveys lands to which it has only an equitable title, but to which it afterwards acquires the legal title, that title at once enures to the grantee, or mortgagee, both by the express words of the instrument, and by the statutory words of warranty, *grant, bargain, sell and convey. Ib.* 569.

6. *Covenant of seizin; breach of.*—A covenant of seizin is broken, if there is an outstanding estate in a third person, or a material deficiency in the quantity of land conveyed, or where the grantor has not substantially the same estate, both in quantity and quality, which he professes by his deed to convey; but the existence of a public easement, as a street or right of way, is not a breach of such covenant. *Moore v. Johnston,* 220.

7. *Conveyance of lot bounded by street.*—A conveyance of a lot bounded by a street, in an incorporated city or town, passes to the grantee the fee to the centre of the street, subject to the public easement; and the same rule applies to a conveyance of lots outside of the corporate limits, which have been laid off with a view to future extension of the corporate limits. *Ib.* 220.

8. *Same.*—In the absence of statutory provisions to the contrary, a conveyance of a lot in an incorporated city or town, bounded by a public street, passes to the grantee the fee to the center of the street, subject to the public right of user; the fee to the other half remaining in the grantor, or original proprietor, and with it all riparian rights when the street is bounded by a navigable river. *Demopolis v. Webb,* 659.

9. *Unrecorded deed; statutory protection to purchasers without notice.* As against subsequent purchasers and judgment creditors without notice, an unrecorded deed is inoperative and void (Code, §§ 1810-11); and possession, acquired or held under it, charges a purchaser or creditor with constructive notice *only* when there is an actual change of possession. *Troy v. Walter Bros.,* 233.

10. *Unrecorded mortgage; validity as against creditors.*—An unrecorded mortgage, which, after several renewals, is at last recorded within the time allowed by the statute (Code, §§ 1810-11), is not void as against simple-contract creditors, whose debts were incurred in the meantime, unless it was withheld from record for the fraudulent purpose of upholding the credit of the debtor, or is otherwise impeached by proof of actual or positive fraud on the part of the mortgagee; and under the facts of this case (the *bona fides* of the secured debt being admitted, the mortgage conveying not more than one third of the debtor's property, the law-day not being postponed for an unreasonable time, and it not being shown that the mortgagee had notice of the debtor's insolvency), the charge of fraud in fact is not sustained. *McDonnell v. Mobile Savings Bank,* 736.

11. *Registration of mortgage as constructive notice; removal of property to another county.*—A mortgage of personal property is required to be recorded, not only in the county in which the mortgagor resides, but also in the county in which the property then is; and on its removal to another county, the mortgage must be there recorded within six months afterwards (Code, §§ 1806-1814); and the fact that the mortgaged animals (mules) are carried over and worked in the former county by day, but carried back each night into the new county, does not dispense with the necessity for such new registration. *Pollak v. Davidson,* 551.

DEEDS—*Continued.*

12. *Constructive notice of mortgage, as implied from knowledge of indebtedness, character of business, &c.*—Knowledge of the existence of
a debt, is not constructive notice of an unrecorded mortgage given
to secure it; nor can notice of such unrecorded mortgage be implied from the additional facts, that the mortgagee was a merchant making advances to planters, and that his house of business was not more than one hundred and fifty yards distant from
that of the second mortgagee; nor are these facts sufficient to put
the second mortgagee on inquiry. *Ib.* 551.

13. *Sufficiency of consideration of deed.*—When a bill seeks to set aside
a conveyance of land as fraudulent against creditors, alleging that
the land was worth $1,000 or more, and the recited consideration
only $30; while the conveyance itself, made an exhibit to the bill,
shows that the grantor conveyed only whatever interest and title
he had by reason of his survivorship of his wife, to whom the
land belonged, no data being furnished from which the value of
his interest can be ascertained,—the deed can not be declared
fraudulent. *Moorer v. Moorer,* 545.

14. *Competency of party to testify to handwriting of subscribing witness
to deed.*—A party to the suit, who is the grantee in a deed which
he offers in evidence, may testify to the handwriting of the subscribing witness (Code, § 2765), on making satisfactory proof as
to his failure to produce the witness himself. *Calera Land Co. v.
Brinkerhoff,* 422.

15. *Written instrument operating partly as deed, and partly as will.*—A
written instrument in the form of a deed, signed by the grantor,
attested by two witnesses, and probated as a deed; by which the
grantor, reciting her physical incapacity to look after and care for
her property, her desire to have it cared for during her life, to
make provision for her comfort and welfare during her life, and
the further purpose of disposing of her property, and having the
utmost confidence in the grantees, and for the further consideration of one dollar in hand paid by them, bargains, sells and conveys to them, by present words, all her property of every kind
and description, to them and their assigns forever, "in trust nevertheless, and upon the uses and purposes hereinafter mentioned"
—namely, to take charge of said property, collect and receive the
rents and profits, keep the property in good repair, pay all taxes
and other charges or assessments against it, and pay the residue
to the grantor during life,—vests in the grantees a present right,
interest, and legal title to all the property, but charged with a
trust for the uses and purposes specified; although a subsequent
provision is added, which is testamentary in its character, and
can only take effect after the death of the grantor—namely, that
after her death the property "shall revert" to the grantees in fee
simple, in equal shares; and further, that in consideration of services rendered by them to her, and also one dollar in hand paid,
she sells and conveys to them all the property of which she may
die seized and possessed, "hereby revoking all other arrangements, either verbal or written, as to the disposition of my [her]
property." *Kyle v. Perdue,* 423.

DOWER.

1. *Petition for allotment of dower; averment of husband's seizin.*—In a
petition for the allotment of dower, an averment that the husband
"was seized and possessed" of the lands described is, on demurrer, equivalent to an averment that he was seized in fee (Code,
1886, § 1892; 1876, § 2232); but it is the better course to follow
the language of the statute. *Sheppard v. Sheppard,* 560.

DOWER—*Continued.*

2. *Right of dower, as affected by separate estate.*—In estimating the widow's right of dower, or making an abatement from its value, on account of a separate estate held by her, "exclusive of the rents, income and profits" (Code, 1886, §§ 2354-5; 1876, §§ 2715-16), lands allotted to her as dower in the estate of a former husband must be computed, her interest therein being an estate of freehold, and more than a mere right to the rents, income, and profits. *Ib.* 560.

3. *Assignment of dower in lands chargeable with trust.*—When it appears that the lands, in which an allotment of dower is sought, are chargeable with a trust in favor of the husband's children by a former marriage, on account of moneys belonging to their mother's statutory estate, which were invested or used by him in the purchase of the lands, an assignment by metes and bounds would be unjust (Code, 1886, § 1910; 1876, § 2248), and the court should decline jurisdiction, leaving the parties to their remedies in equity; but the mere assertion of such a claim by the heirs, without any evidence to support it, does not require the court to dismiss the petition. *Ib.* 560.

EJECTMENT.

1. *What title will support action; receiver's receipt on homestead entry.* As against a mere trespasser, a receipt given by the receiver of a land office of the United States, for money paid on a homestead entry (U. S. Rev. Statutes, §§ 2290-97), confers a title on which ejectment, or the statutory action in the nature thereof, may be maintained before the expiration of five years (Code, § 2782); and the defendant can not be heard to allege a breach of the conditions on which the entry may be perfected. *Case v. Edgeworth*, 203.

2. *Same.*—A receipt given by the receiver of a land office of the United States, for money paid in full on a homestead entry (U. S. Rev. Statutes, §§ 2290-97), confers a title which, before the expiration of five years, enables the possessor to maintain or defend an action as owner. *Morrison Bros. v. Coleman*, 655.

See, also, DEEDS, 3.

ERROR AND APPEAL.

1. *What is revisable; new trial.*—By the settled practice of this court since its organization, a motion for a new trial is addressed to the discretion of the lower court, and its refusal is not revisable by this court on error or appeal. *Johnson v. State*, 39.

2. *Bill of exceptions; matters of record.*—When matters which constitute a part of the record proper in the court below, are shown only by the bill of exceptions, the appellate court can not consider them for any purpose, but will disregard them *ex mero motu.* *Pendry v. Shows*, 339.

3. *Same.*—On appeal from a probate decree rendered on final settlement of an executor's accounts, this court can not consider an assignment of error based on an order setting aside a prior decree allowing a claim of exemptions filed by the widow, when such order and the decree setting it aside are shown only by the bill of exceptions; though the court may consider the transcript as showing the fact that the claim was filed, its date, and the property embraced in it. *Chandler v. Chandler*, 300.

4. *Same.*—Rulings on demurrer shown only by the bill of exceptions, are not revisable on error or appeal. *Beck v. West & Co.*, 213.

5. *Entries on docket, as part of record.*—Extracts from the docket of the court below, copied into the transcript by the clerk, but not made a part of the record by bill of exceptions or otherwise, are

ERROR AND APPEAL—*Continued.*

the mere unauthorized memoranda of the clerk, and can not be considered by this court for any purpose. *Baker v. Swift,* 530.

6. *Trial by court without jury; revision of finding on facts.*—A trial by jury not being demanded, in a criminal prosecution before the Criminal Court of Pike (Sess. Acts 1888-9, p. 631, § 7), this court can not review the conclusions of the judge on the evidence adduced. *Wynn v. State,* 137.

7. *Same.*—When a criminal case is submitted to the decision of the court without a jury, as authorized by a special statute, the decision of the court on a question of fact, as to which the evidence is conflicting, or where inferences are to be drawn dependent on its sufficiency, will not be reversed, unless a verdict would be set aside on the same evidence; but, when the facts are undisputed, and only a legal conclusion is to be drawn from them, the decision is regarded as if given in charge to the jury, and its correctness is a question of law. *Skinner v. State,* 105.

8. *Error without injury.*—When the plaintiff below recovered nominal damages only, but adduced no evidence which could serve as a basis for the computation or assessment of his damages, rulings adverse to him, even if erroneous, are no ground of reversal, and the court will not consider their correctness. *Sipsey River Nav. Co. v. Geo. Pac. Railway Co.,* 154.

9. *Same.*—In an action on an attachment bond, a judgment on verdict for the defendants conclusively determines that the writ was not wrongfully sued out; and the rulings of the court on the pleadings and evidence, or in the matter of charges given or refused, relating only to the question of exemplary damages, if erroneous, could not have injured the plaintiff. *Calhoun v. Hannan & Michael,* 277.

10. *Pleading over, after demurrer sustained; error without injury.* Where the record shows that, after demurrer sustained to a plea or replication, the party had the full benefit of the same matter under an amended pleading, the ruling on demurrer, if erroneous, could have worked no injury, and is not a reversible error. *Ib.* 277.

11. *Error without injury in ruling on pleadings.*—In an action of trover, if a demurrer to a special count in case is erroneously sustained, the error is immaterial, when the record shows that the plaintiff had the full benefit of the same facts under the count in trover. *Gilman & Sons v. Jones,* 691.

12. *Same.*—The sustaining of a demurrer to a special plea, if erroneous, is error without injury, when the record shows that the defendant had the full benefit of the same defense under another special plea. *L. & N. Railroad Co. v. Hall,* 708.

13. *Same.*—The sustaining of a demurrer to a special plea, if erroneous, is error without injury, when the same defense was equally available under the general issue, which was also pleaded. *Manning v. Maroney,* 563.

14. *Error without injury in refusing to allow amendment.*—The refusal to allow an amendment of the complaint, by the addition of another count, if erroneous, is not a reversible error, when the record shows that the plaintiff's case was tried on the original complaint precisely as it would have been if the amendment had been allowed. *Sharpe v. Nat. Bank of Birmingham,* 644.

15. *Error without injury in criminal case.*—As a general rule, the doctrine of error without injury does not obtain in criminal cases; yet, where evidence is erroneously excluded, but the record affirmatively shows that its admission could only have prejudiced the defense, the error will not work a reversal. *Marks v. State,* 99.

16. *Judgment reversed, as to erroneous punishment only.*—The defendant

ERROR AND APPEAL—*Continued.'*

and petitioner in this case having been convicted of a felony, and erroneously sentenced to the penitentiary for twelve months, instead of the county jail, this court, reversing the judgment, will not order his discharge, but will reverse the judgment back to the sentence; nor will it correct and render final judgment, though requested by counsel by agreement entered of record. *Herrington v. State,* 1.

17. *Costs, as against guardian ad litem.*—The rule of this court has always been, not to tax a guardian *ad litem* with costs, though he be the unsuccessful appellant. *Brown v. Williams,* 353.

ESTATES OF DECEDENTS. See EXECUTORS AND ADMINISTRATORS.

ESTOPPEL.

1. *Estoppel by words or conduct.*—In an action against a purchaser of goods at execution sale, by one claiming under a prior purchase from the defendant in execution, a charge asserting that, "if plaintiff used such words to and in the presence of defendant, at or near the time of the sale of the goods, as would cause a reasonably prudent man to act, and to alter his condition to his prejudice, on the faith of such statements, and defendant did alter his condition to his prejudice on the faith of such statements, then plaintiff was guilty of a fraud, and can not recover," is properly refused, because it submits to the jury the sufficiency of the statements to constitute an estoppel. *Knowles v. Street,* 357.

2. *Same.*—The breach of a mere executory agreement or promise does not constitute an estoppel *en pais;* as where plaintiff, in a conversation with defendant, relative to furnishing supplies to a third person to make a crop, said that he would not claim the crops in the fall if defendant would furnish the supplies, and defendant thereupon furnished supplies on the faith of a verbal mortgage only; these facts do not estop plaintiff from afterwards taking a mortgage on the crops for supplies subsequently furnished by him. *Weaver v. Bell,* 385.

3. *Estoppel against denying dedication.*—A sub-purchaser of a lot in an incorporated city or town, described in his conveyance as fronting on a named street, according to the map and plat laid out by the original proprietors of the land, is estopped from denying the dedication of the street as a highway, and its acceptance as such by the proper authorities. *Demopolis v. Webb,* 659.

4. *Estoppel against corporation; contract ultra vires.*—Under the decisions of this court, a corporation which has received the benefits of a contract *ultra vires,* is not thereby estopped from setting up the invalidity of the contract, in defense of a suit to enforce it. *Chewacla Lime Works v. Dismukes, Frierson & Co.,* 344.

5. *Estoppel as between corporation and subscriber for stock.*—In an action by a corporation suing as such, against a subscriber to its capital stock before incorporation, the payment by the defendant of former installments as called for, and an averment that the installment sued on was "duly and regularly called in by plaintiff, and demand therefor made upon defendant," do not, without more, show an estoppel against him to deny that there ever was any corporation. *Schloss & Kahn v. Montgomery Trade Co.,* 411.

6. *Estoppel by election between inconsistent rights.*—An embarrassed or insolvent debtor having sold certain bales of cotton, stating in the bill of sale that the purchaser promised and agreed to pay the purchase-money to several creditors, a specified sum to each; a creditor can not, while attacking the sale for fraud, claim his share of the money in the hands of the purchaser; and if he is unsuccessful in his suit attacking the sale, he can not afterwards assert a claim to the money, as against another creditor, who, having

ESTOPPEL—*Continued.*

accepted his share of the money, recovered a judgment for the balance of his debt, and sued out a garnishment against the purchaser; nor is the latter creditor estopped, by his acceptance of the money in the first instance, from afterwards maintaining such garnishment. *Lienkauff & Strauss v. Forcheimer & Co.*, 258.

7. *Estoppel between pledgor and pledgee.*—If a part-owner of certificates of stock pledges them, with the consent of the other owner, as collateral security for his own debt, and they are converted by the pledgee, the pledgor is entitled to recover as if he were the sole owner, the pledgee being estopped from denying his absolute ownership. *Sharpe v. Nat. Bank of Birmingham*, 644.

8. *Estoppel as between heirs and purchasers at administrator's sale; presumptions from lapse of time.*—The widow's possession of lands allotted to her as dower is not adverse to the heirs, and if she purchases the reversionary interest, at a sale made by the administrator, they can not assail her title, at law, during her life, even though the sale was void; and if the purchase-money was paid, and was applied by the administrator to the payment of debts, they would be estopped from denying the validity of the sale, without offering to do equity by refunding the purchase-money; and, having the equitable right to set aside the sale as a cloud on their title, on offering to do equity, if they allow the widow and those claiming under her to remain in undisturbed possession for more than twenty years, though less than ten years after her death has elapsed, the presumption will be indulged against them, that she acquired the legal title by voluntary conveyance from them, or by compulsory proceedings in equity. *Woodstock Iron Co. v. Fullenwider*, 584.

EVIDENCE.

Admissibility and Relevancy.

1. *Bill of exchange; preliminary proof of demand, protest, and notice; mutilation by identifying marks.*—In an action on a bill of exchange, the bill is admissible as evidence without preliminary proof of demand, protest, and notice of dishonor, or a waiver thereof, these facts being matter of defense; and it is not rendered inadmissible as evidence on the ground of mutilation, because of identifying marks as an exhibit to a deposition, written by the commissioner. *Manning v. Maroney*, 563.

2. *Evidence as to delivery and reception of invoice.*—Where the seller seeks to recover the goods from a sub-purchaser, the price being payable, on, delivery of an invoice, it is competent for the plaintiff to prove the sending and the reception of the invoice, as showing performance on his part, and that the purchase-money was due. *Harmon v. Goetter, Weil & Co.*, 325.

3. *Evidence as to value of goods.*—The goods sued for by the seller, the price never having been paid (as stipulated) on delivery of an invoice, being part of a stock of goods afterwards sold by the purchaser to the defendant, the validity of that sale is not involved in the issue; and evidence as to the value of the stock of goods, or offers to sell them, which might be admissible if the sale were attacked for fraud, is not relevant or competent. *Ib.* 325.

4. *Evidence as to intoxicating properties of article sold.*—In a criminal prosecution for the sale of intoxicating liquors in violation of a local prohibitory liquor law, the article sold being compounded by a druggist, and the bottles labeled *"Elixir Cinchona,"* or *"Cinchona Bitters;"* it is permissible for the prosecution to prove that it was bought and used by many persons as a beverage, the

EVIDENCE—*Continued.*

use to which it was applied being illustrative of its nature and properties. *Carl v. State,* 17.

5. *Evidence identifying defendants as perpetrators of offense.*—Where the defendants deny their guilt, though identified by the prosecutrix, and show that, before their arrest, she had given a description of the guilty parties which did not suit their appearance, it is competent for the prosecution to prove that, after their arrest, she identified and pointed them out among a large number of prisoners. *Cotton v. State,* 75.

6. *Testimony as to defendant's arrest, or surrender.*—The sheriff, by whom the defendant was arrested, or to whom he surrendered, having testified that, not being able to find the defendant, "he told his friends that he had a warrant for the arrest of the defendant, and sent him word to come in and give himself up—that the case against him amounted to nothing, and he would have no trouble to get out of it; that the defendant did come in and surrender a day or two afterwards, but he did not know the defendant got his message;" *held,* that this evidence wa~ improperly admitted, against the objection of the defendant. *Coleman v. State,* 14.

7. *Conversations between third persons; admissibility as evidence.*—Conversations between third persons, tending to implicate the defendant, but not had in his presence, are not admissible as evidence against him ; and if they did not relate to the particular offense with which he is charged, they would be inadmissible because irrelevant. *Tolbert v. State,* 27.

8. *Evidence as to character of house, or room.*—On a prosecution for playing cards in a public house, or for betting at a game played in a public house, evidence as to the character of the house, whether public or private, is relevant and admissible; the presumption being that the house is an entirety. *Ib.* 27.

9. *Proof of character.*—A witness, testifying to the character of the defendant as a peaceable and quiet man, may be asked whether he "ever heard of his having any other difficulty than the one in question," and may testify that he had not. *Hussey v. State,* 121.

10. *Same.*—Evidence of character, at least · on direct examination, goes to general reputation only, and can not be extended to particular acts, or specified conduct; nor can a witness give his own opinion as to the person inquired about;—as, that he was a "model man," or "was a timid man, and would rather avoid than provoke a difficulty." *Ib.* 121.

11. *Character of deceased; evidence as to.*—On a trial for murder, the prosecution may adduce evidence of the character of the deceased as a peaceable and quiet man, although the defense has only proved particular traits of his character, as a quick-tempered, violent man, easily provoked, and likely to provoke a difficulty. *Ib.* 121.

ADMISSIONS ; DECLARATIONS ; HEARSAY ; RES GESTÆ.

12. *Admission by agent, after termination of agency.*—The clerk of a steamboat, having authority to make purchases and to state accounts for the boat, can not bind the owners by his written admission of the correctness of an account after the termination of his agency, but must be examined as a witness to prove its correctness, if known by him. *Gunter v. Stuart,* 196.

13. *Husband's admissions, as evidence against wife.*—When the contract of sale is negotiated by the husband for the benefit of the wife, and the conveyance is executed to her, though his notes are given for the purchase-money, his subsequent admissions or declarations, when pressed for payment, that the vendor had retained a

EVIDENCE—*Continued.*

   lien on the land, are not competent or admissible as evidence against the wife. *Jackson v. Stanley*, 270.

14. *Evidence tending to prove possession; admission implied from silence.* Where the defendant in detinue denies his possession of the goods sued for, alleging that they were in the possession of the sheriff at the commencement of the suit, the plaintiff may prove, by a witness who was present, that the sheriff said, in the presence of the defendant, that he had not then made a levy under the other writs, and that the defendant said nothing. *Harmon v. Goetter, Weil & Co.*, 325.

15. *Failure of party to testify, as evidence against him.*—In an action by the first, against the second mortgagee, for a conversion of the mortgaged property, the failure of the defendant to testify in his own behalf, that he had no notice of the plaintiff's prior unrecorded mortgage, is not a circumstance from which an unfavorable presumption against him is to be indulged, when the record shows that he was absent from the State at the time of the trial, and that the plaintiff's evidence did not make out against him a *prima facie* showing of notice. *Pollak v. Davidson*, 551.

16. *Books of corporation, as evidence against stockholders.*—The books of a private corporation, showing subscriptions for stock, payments on calls, &c., are admissible as evidence against a stockholder, in an action to enforce his unpaid subscription as called for, especially when he does not by plea deny the genuineness of his subscription. *Lehman, Durr & Co. v. Glenn*, 618.

17. *General notoriety as evidence.*—General notoriety is sometimes admissible as evidence, as tending to prove notice of a fact, when notice thereof is material; but never to prove the existence of the fact itself. *L. & N. Railroad Co. v. Hall*, 708.

18. *Former testimony of absent witness.*—The testimony of a witness on a former trial of the defendant, or on his preliminary examination by a committing magistrate, is admissible as evidence against him on the trial, on proof that the witness is beyond the jurisdiction of the court, being either permanently or indefinitely absent. *Perry v. State*, 30.

19. *Dying declarations.*—The declarations of the deceased in this case, made to different persons, at intervals, during the three days he lived after receiving the fatal wound, always expressing the belief that he would die from effects of the wound, were properly admitted as evidence, although some of his friends declared to him their belief that he was not seriously wounded, and one of his attending physicians had expressed to him the hope that he might recover. *Hussey v. State*, 121.

20. *Affidavits on application for change of venue.*—By the established practice in this and other States, on application for a change of venue, counter affidavits may be received against those offered in support of it; and this practice is not violative of the constitutional principle which gives to the accused the right to be "confronted by the witnesses against him." *Ib.* 121.

21. *Admissibility of declarations, as part of res gestæ.*—This court can not revise the ruling of the trial court in refusing to admit the defendant's declarations as evidence, as a part of the *res gestæ*, when the declarations are not set out, and it is not shown that they related to the act charged, or threw light on it, or tended to elucidate it, or would have been beneficial to the defendant, or were in any way material. *Goley v. State*, 57.

22. *Same.*—The offer of the defendant to lift up the deceased, made two or three minutes after the shooting, is not admissible evidence as a part of the *res gestæ*, not being shown to have been made so immediately after the act as to authorize the presumption that it was

EVIDENCE—*Continued.*

part of the main fact, and not an afterthought intended to give a false coloring to it. *Ib.* 57.

23. *Declarations and conduct of conspirators, as evidence against each other.*—Under the rule laid down in the case of *McAnally v. State* (74 Ala. 9), when the evidence establishes, *prima facie*, the existence of a conspiracy between the defendant and others, to commit the crime with which he is charged, the acts, declarations and conduct of the others, in promotion of the purpose or object of the conspiracy, or in relation to it, are competent and admissible as evidence against him; and such evidence was properly admitted in this case. *Johnson v. State*, 39.

24. *Declarations of defendant as evidence.*—Declarations made by the defendant himself, before or after the commission of the homicide with which he is charged, tending to connect him with it, are admissible as evidence against him, although a conspiracy between him and the other persons implicated may not be established. *Ib.* 39.

25. *Evidence of prior contradictory statements of defendant.*—The defendant testifying in his own behalf to an *alibi*, it is competent for the prosecution to prove his prior contradictory statements, by affidavit or otherwise, as to his whereabouts on the day named; but evidence of prior statements made, not inconsistent with his testimony on the trial, is not admissible. *Cotton v. State*, 75.

26. *Privileged communications between attorney and client.*—An officer, having the legal custody of a prisoner, should allow him every reasonable opportunity, consistent with his safe keeping, for private consultation with his attorney; yet he may testify to communications made in his presence, although they might be privileged as between the attorney and his client. *Cotton v. State*, 75.

27. *Testimony of party as to transactions with decedent.*—In an action by a partnership against a private corporation, one of the plaintiffs can not testify as a witness in their behalf to a transaction or conversation between himself and the president or general manager, since deceased, of the corporation (Code, § 2765). *Tabler, Crudup & Co. v. Sheffield Land, Iron & Coal Co.*, 305.

28. *Testimony of party as to transaction with deceased agent.*—In a suit by a creditor seeking to set aside, as fraudulent, a mortgage or deed of trust executed by his insolvent debtor to an incorporated bank, the debtor himself being a party to the suit, he can not be allowed (Code, § 2765) to testify as a witness that the conveyance was withheld from record, by agreement between him and the bank cashier, since deceased, lest it might injure his credit; and the fact that a decree *pro confesso* has been entered against him, does not remove his statutory incompetency. *Mobile Savings Bank v. McDonnell*, 730.

29. *Nominal partner testifying as to transactions with decedent.*—In an action by a mortgagee against the widow of the deceased mortgagor, payment of the mortgage debt being suggested and pleaded (Code, §§ 1870, 2707), the plaintiff's son, who was in his employment as clerk when the mortgage was given, and held himself out to the public as a partner, though he had no interest in the business, may testify to transactions with the deceased mortgagor in reference to the mortgage debt, not being within the statutory disqualification (*Ib.* § 2765), either as a party, or as interested. *Huckaba v. Abbott*, 409.

30. *Testimony of defendant in his own behalf.*—In a criminal case, if the defendant fails or declines to testify in his own behalf, his failure does not create any presumption against him, and is not the subject of comment by counsel (Code, § 4473); but, if he elects to

EVIDENCE—*Continued.*

testify, and fails or refuses to explain or rebut any criminating fact, when he can reasonably do so, this is a circumstance in the nature of an implied admission, on which counsel may comment, and which the jury may consider in determining his guilt or innocence. *Colton v. State,* 103; *Clarke v. State,* 71.

BURDEN; WEIGHT; SUFFICIENCY.

31. *Contributory negligence; burden of proof.*—Contributory negligence, when pleaded by itself, is an admission of negligence on the part of the defendant, but not when interposed with the plea of not guilty. *L. & N. Railroad Co. v. Hall,* 709.

32. *Statutory liability of railroad companies, for injuries to persons or property; burden of proof.*—Under statutory provisions now of force (Code, §§ 1144-1147, note), whether the action is for injuries to persons or stock, the *onus* is on the railroad company to acquit itself of negligence, by showing (1) a compliance with the statutory requisitions as to blowing the whistle and ringing the bell, or (2) that such compliance could not have averted the injury; but this statutory rule does not extend to a case where the injuries are caused by a neglect of other duties at a crossing of two railroads, resulting in a collision whereby plaintiff, a passenger, was injured. *Geo. Pac. Railway Co. v. Hughes,* 610.

33. *Services of process, as shown by sheriff's return; evidence impeaching.* The return of a sheriff, showing service of process, imports verity, and casts on the party assailing it the burden of adducing evidence sufficient to overcome the presumption that the officer did his duty. *Paul v. Malone & Collins,* 544.

34. *Proof of payment.*—The *onus* of proving payment is on the party who asserts it; and if the evidence leaves the fact in doubt and uncertainty, he must fail. *Brown v. Scott,* 453.

35. *Action by corporation; proof of corporate character.*—In an action by a corporation, the plea of *nul tiel* corporation being interposed, the plaintiff is required to prove its corporate character, either by producing its charter, or by some admission on the part of the defendant, or to show facts constituting an estoppel. (But, by statute, a sworn plea is now required.—Sess. Acts 1888-9, p. 57.) *Schloss & Kahn v. Montgomery Trade Co.,* 411.

36. *Conclusiveness of annual settlement.*—On final settlement of a guardian's accounts, credits allowed him on an annual or partial settlement are presumptively correct (Code, § 2458), and the *onus* of disproving their correctness is on the ward. *Bentley v. Dailey,* 406.

37. *Burden of proof as to consideration and good faith of conveyance.* The fact that property has been conveyed by a debtor, on the recited consideration of an antecedent debt, raises a presumption of unfairness and bad faith, as between the debtor and his other creditors, and casts on him the *onus* of showing that the sale was fair, and made in good faith; and the proof must be fuller and clearer when the conveyance is made to a relative. *Calhoun v. Hannan & Michael,* 277.

38. *Burden of proof as to ground for attachment* —In an action on an attachment bond, the *onus* is on the plaintiff to prove the falsity of the affidavit on which the attachment was sued out. *Ib.* 277.

39. *Charge as to sufficiency of proof.*—When the burden of proof as to the truth or falsehood of an alleged fact is on the plaintiff, he must reasonably satisfy the jury in that regard; and the court may instruct the jury, on request, "that if the evidence leaves them confused and uncertain as to its truth or falsity, they must find for the defendant." *Ib* 277.

40. *Charge as to weight or effect of evidence.*—It is the exclusive province of the jury to reconcile the testimony of the different witnesses, if possible, or, if irreconcilable, to determine whom they

EVIDENCE—*Continued.*

will believe, or what credit they will give to a witness who is contradicted or impeached; and a charge which institutes a comparison between the weight and force of the testimony of different witnesses, equally credible and having equal opportunities for knowing the facts, is properly refused, as tending to confuse and mislead the jury, and invading their peculiar province. *Norris v. State,* 85.

41. *Charge as to sufficiency of evidence.*—A charge which instructs the jury, in a criminal case, that "the State is not required to prove the guilt of the defendant to a mathematical certainty," asserts a correct proposition. *Dick v. State,* 61.

42. *Charge as to circumstantial evidence.*—A charge asserting that, "to justify conviction, circumstantial evidence ought to exclude a rational probability of innocence, and a conviction ought not to be had on circumstantial evidence, when direct and positive evidence is attainable," is properly refused, as tending to mislead and confuse the jury, when there is some direct and positive evidence, and the record does not show that any other was attainable. *Coleman v. State,* 14.

EXPERTS; OPINION; LEGAL CONCLUSION.

43. *Testimony of physician as expert; hearsay.*—A practicing physician, who examined the deceased after he was wounded, and has given his own diagnosis of the case, can not be allowed to testify that other physicians concurred with him in opinion. *Hussey v. State,* 121.

44. *To what witness may testify.*—A witness may testify that a person went into the possession of lands, "and thereafter *controlled* them;" this being merely the statement of a collective fact. *Woodstock Iron Co. v. Roberts,* 436.

45. *Expert testimony as to railroad appliances.*—The superintendent of a railroad, who has been employed on railroads for nearly twenty years, as fireman, brakeman, baggage-master, yard-master, and train-master, may give his opinion as an expert as to the value and usefulness of "whipping-straps," or ropes pendent from above, as cautionary signals to brakemen when the train is approaching a low bridge or tunnel overhead; but he can not give his opinion as to the prudent management of the defendant's railroad. *L & N. Railroad Co. v. Hall,* 709.

46. *Testimony of witness as to damages.*—A party, testifying as a witness, can not state "what damages" he sustained by the breach of contract of which he complains. *Young v. Cureton,* 727.

47. *To what witness may testify* —On a prosecution for murder, a witness for the defense can not be allowed to testify that the defendant "was afraid" to work in the field alone, or to go out about his premises after dark, on account of threats made against him by the deceased; such testimony being merely the opinion of the witness, based on the conduct or declarations of the defendant himself, or unsupported by any fact at all. *Poe v. State,* 65.

48. *Same.*—A witness who, as a member of the coroner's jury, had seen the dead body of the child alleged to have been murdered, may testify that its neck, which was broken, "looked like it had been struck with a hot iron, and looked scarred." *Perry v. State,* 30.

49. *Same.*—A sheriff, or constable, testifying to a conversation had by them with the defendant, prior to his arrest, in which they asked him whether he had any of the money stolen from the prosecutor, not making any accusation against him, may testify "that he did not stand still, but kept turning around and kicking the ground, and would not look at them;" but not "that he was restless, nervous, and excited." *Coleman v. State,* 14.

EVIDENCE—*Continued.*

50. *Evidence as to intoxicating properties of article sold.*—In a criminal prosecution for the sale of intoxicating liquors in violation of a local prohibitory liquor law. the article sold being compounded by a druggist, and the bottles labeled *"Elixir Cinchona,"* or *"Cinchona Bitters;"* a person who had swallowed it may state its exhilarating effect on himself, and, though not technically an expert, may testify that, "in his opinion, it would produce intoxication. *Carl v. State,* 17.

MATTERS JUDICIALLY KNOWN.

51. *Local election.*—The court can not take judicial notice of the result of an election held under a "local option" law. *Ex parte Reynolds,* 139.

52. *Public facts.*—The courts will take judicial notice of the facts, that large sums of money have been invested in the recent development of the mineral resources of the State; that the utilization of these ores, which must be washed before using, necessarily requires the placing of sediment where it may flow into the streams which constitute the natural drainage of the surrounding country, and that this must cause a deposit of sediment on the lands below. *Clifton Iron Co. v. Dye,* 468.

OBJECTIONS.

53. *General objection.*—A general objection to the admission of a promissory note as evidence, not specifying any particular ground of objection, does not raise the objection that its execution has not been proved. *Calhoun v. Hannan & Michael,* 277.

54. *General objection to evidence partly admissible.*—A general objection to the admission of evidence, a part of which is admissible, may be overruled entirely. *Marks v. State,* 99; *Coleman v. State,* 19.

55. *Objection to party's own evidence.*—A party can not object or except to the admission of evidence which he has himself elicited. *Cotton v. State,* 75.

56. *Objections to question and answer.*—When an objection is made and sustained to a question propounded to a witness. but the record does not show what answer was expected, nor that the witness had any knowledge or information on the subject, this court can not consider the correctness of the ruling. *Tolbert v. State,* 27.

57. *Same.*—When a question is in proper form, and calls for evidence which is *prima facie* relevant and legal, the refusal to allow it is a reversible error, although the proposed or expected answer of the witness is not stated. *Hussey v. State,* 121.

PAROL EVIDENCE.

58. *As to consideration of mortgage.*—A mortgage given to secure payment for future advances by the mortgagee, is a valid security as between the parties; and when the recited consideration is an indebtedness by promissory note, oral evidence may be received to show that part of the actual consideration was supplies or advances to be afterwards furnished, and which were furnished. *Huckaba v. Abbott,* 409.

59. *As to terms of writing.*—A witness, testifying as to a written order drawn on an attorney by his client, directing him to pay certain creditors out of moneys. when collected, on claims placed in his hands for collection, which does not constitute an assignment in law, can not speak of it as an assignment. *Sterrett v. Miles,* 472.

PRESUMPTIONS.

60. *In favor of sheriff's return.*—The return of a sheriff, showing service of process, imports verity, and casts on the party assailing it the burden of adducing evidence sufficient to overcome the presumption that the officer did his duty; and on motion to set

EVIDENCE—*Continued.*

aside the return, the bill of exceptions reciting that "the defendant introduced himself as a witness, and his testimony *tended* to show that the summons and complaint were never served on him," &c., and that "this was all the evidence in the cause," these recitals are not sufficient to enable this court to say that the lower court erred in refusing to set aside the return. *Paul v. Malone & Collins,* 544.

61. *Identity of name, as showing identity of person.*—On application by an administrator for an order to sell lands for the payment of debts, when minors are interested in the estate (Code, §§ 2111, 2114), he is not a competent witness to prove the necessity for a sale; yet, if the order is granted, and application is made to set it aside at a subsequent term, the proceedings being regular on their face, it will not be presumed that one of the witnesses was the administrator merely because his name was the same. *Stevenson v. Murray,* 442.

62. *Presumption of title from lapse of time.*—After continuous *user* of a right of way by a railroad company for a period of fifty years, a grant in fee simple, or a judgment of condemnation under a writ of *ad quod damnum,* will be presumed, though the land is part of a sixteenth section. *Davis v. M. & C. Railroad Co.,* 633.

63. *Presumption from lapse of time, as against heirs.*—On a sale of lands by an administrator, the widow becoming the purchaser, if the purchase-money was paid, and was applied by the administrator to payment of debts, the heirs would be estopped from denying the validity of the sale, without offering to do equity by refunding the purchase-money; and, having the equitable right to set aside the sale as a cloud on their title, on offering to do equity, if they allow the widow and those claiming under her to remain in undisturbed possession for more than twenty years, though less than ten years after her death have elapsed, the presumption will be indulged against them, that she acquired the legal title by voluntary conveyance from them, or by compulsory proceedings in equity. *Woodstock Iron Co. v. Fullenwider,* 584.

64. *Presumption as to demand or notice.*—When a promissory note, payable thirty days after demand or notice, provides for the punctual payment of interest annually, and it is otherwise shown that a long credit was contemplated; partial payments being made until the death of the maker eight years afterwards, after which the note was filed as a claim against his estate, and an action brought against his personal representative more than ten years afterwards; *held,* that it would be presumed that a demand, putting the statute of limitations in operation, was made within the time prescribed as a bar by the statute of non-claim, and that this presumption was not overcome by proof of a demand in fact made after the expiration of that time. *Massie v. Byrd,* 672.

PRIMARY AND SECONDARY.

65. *Letter beyond jurisdiction of the court.*—In an action by an indorsee against the drawer of a bill of exchange, who pleads the failure to give him due notice of dishonor, a letter written by him to the drawees, instructing them not to pay the bill, being addressed to them at their place of business in another State, and therefore presumptively beyond the jurisdiction of the court, secondary evidence of its contents may be adduced by the plaintiff, without accounting for its non-production. *Manning v. Maroney,* 563.

66. *Certified copy of patent from land office.*—Under statutory provisions, a copy of a patent for lands issued by the United States may be certified by the "acting commissioner" of the General

52

EVIDENCE—*Continued.*

Land Office (Code, § 2787); and such certified copy is admissible as evidence without producing or accounting for the absence of the patent itself. (Overruling *Jones v. Walker*, 47 Ala. 175, as to the last point.) *Woodstock Iron Co. v. Roberts*, 436.

RECORDS AND JUDGMENTS.

67. *Annual settlements as evidence.*—On final settlement of a guardian's accounts, former annual or partial settlements made by him are a part of the record, and it is the right and duty of the court to look to them as evidence in the cause. *Bentley v. Dailey*, 406.

68. *Conclusiveness of annual settlements.*—On final settlement of a guardian's accounts, credits allowed him on an annual or partial settlement are presumptively correct (Code, § 2458), and the *onus* of disproving their correctness is on the ward. *Ib.* 406.

69. *Judgment as evidence.*—A judgment by default, rendered by a court of general jurisdiction, is admissible as evidence in a suit which seeks to enforce the demand as a lien on land, in the purchase of which the debt was created, although the record does not show the service of process, the presumption being indulged that the court had acquired jurisdiction of the person. *Weaver v. Brown*, 533.

70. *Foreign chancery decree as evidence.*—A transcript, duly certified, of a decree rendered by the Chancery Court of Richmond, Virginia, under a bill filed by or on behalf of the creditors of a dissolved corporation, in which a trustee was appointed to act instead of the trustees named in a deed of assignment executed by the corporation, and authorized to collect unpaid subscriptions for stock, with other debts, is admissible as evidence against a stockholder in Alabama, in a suit brought against him by the trustee, if the court had jurisdiction of the subject-matter and the parties, and if the stockholder are to be regarded as parties; the decree being entitled, under constitutional provisions, to as full faith and credit here as in Virginia. *Lehman, Durr & Co. v. Glenn*, 618.

VARIANCE.

71. *In name of corporation.*—The *American Mortgage Company of Scotland*, and the *American Mortgage Company*, are, *prima facie*, different corporations; and an assessment of taxes against the latter, if regular on its face, will not support an action against an agent of the former. *State v. Sloss*, 119.

72. *Same; appeals from justice's court.*—In an action commenced in a justice's court, which, on appeal, is required to be tried *de novo*, according to equity and justice, without regard to any defect in the process or proceedings before the justice (Code, § 3405); the defendant corporation being sued by the name given by its amended charter, which also made it liable for all debts created by the corporation under its original name and charter; the cause of action, as indorsed on the justice's warrant, being an account for goods sold and delivered to it by its amended name, while the proof shows that the goods were sold and delivered to the corporation before its change of name,—there is no material variance. *Chewacla Lime Works v. Dismukes*, 344.

EXECUTION.

1. *In attachment case.*—The lien of an attachment is perfected by the recovery of judgment, and is not waived or forfeited by suing out a *fi. fa.* instead of a *vend. ex.* to enforce it, but the latter may still be sued out if necessary. *Berney Nat.'Bank v. Pinckard, DeBardelaben & Co.*, 577.

2. *Setting aside sale.*—In ordinary cases, a court of equity will not take jurisdiction to set aside a sale of lands under execution by

EXECUTION—*Continued.*

the sheriff, even at the instance of a person who claims an equitable interest by purchase from the defendant, because he has an adequate remedy by motion to set aside the sale; but, when any distinct ground of equity intervenes, or when a motion to set aside the sale is not a complete and adequate remedy, he may invoke the jurisdiction of a court of equity. *Clark v. Allen,* 198.

EXECUTORS AND ADMINISTRATORS.

1. *Executor's power to sell property under will.*—A testamentary provision directing that all of the testator's property, real, personal and mixed, shall be collected together by the executor, and used in the settlement of debts, and that any residue, after the settlement of debts, shall be equally distributed among his children, does not confer any other or greater power of sale than is given by statutory provisions. *Chandler v. Chandler,* 300.

2. *Executor's authority to sell personally.*—Independent of testamentary provisions, an executor has the full legal title to all *choses* in action, and may dispose of them absolutely without an order of court; but he has not such power to dispose of the tangible personal property, and his sale without an order of court does not affect the right of exemption of the widow and children. *Ib.* 300.

3. *Payment of taxes by executor.*—An executor is entitled, on final settlement of his accounts, to a credit for taxes paid by him which were assessed during the year of the testator's death. *Ib.* 300.

4. *Allowance to executor, for costs paid.*—It being the duty of the executor to collect, by suit or otherwise, debts due the estate, he is entitled to a credit on final settlement, as against the widow and children, for costs paid in prosecuting a suit against a debtor. *Ib.* 300.

5. *Administrator and heirs as parties to bill.*—To a bill filed by the heirs at law of a deceased non-resident, against the surviving tenant in common, seeking a partition of lands and an account, and alleging that the decedent left no debts, and that no administration has been granted on his estate, a personal representative of his estate is not a necessary party. *Stevenson v. Anderson,* 228.

6. *When legatee may come into equity, against executor.*—A legatee to whom the testator bequeathed his mercantile business, with stock of goods, notes and outstanding accounts, directing that he "will assume all the liabilities of the store, and continue the business as heretofore," and also devising to him the store-house in which the business was carried on, can not maintain a bill in equity against the executor, to recover the goods, notes and accounts, until after the expiration of eighteen months from the grant of letters testamentary (Code, §§ 2134, 2192), unless the executor has reported the estate to be solvent, even though he offers to give bond for the faithful administration of the assets. *Carroll v. Richardson,* 605.

7. *Premature filing of bill for distribution.*—A bill filed by the distributees of a decedent's estate, within eight months after the grant of letters of administration, against the administrator and the widow, alleging that the decedent left no debts, and that the funeral expenses and other charges have been paid off by the parties interested in the estate, and praying a distribution and settlement, is prematurely filed. *Jackson v. Rowell,* 685.

8. *When executor may come into equity.*—An executor may file a bill in equity, asking the court to construe the will, to give him instructions in the performance of his duties, and to remove the administration into that court, when it appears that the provisions of the will are of doubtful construction, and that the legatees assert conflicting claims under it. *Carroll v. Richardson,* 605.

EXECUTORS AND ADMINISTRATORS—*Continued.*

9. *Removal of settlement into equity by administrator.*—When an administrator seeks to remove the settlement of the estate into equity, it is immaterial whether or not proceedings for a settlement have been commenced in the Probate Court; in either case, he must aver and show some special ground for equitable intervention. *Cary v. Simmons,* 524.

10. *Advancements made by administrator for distributees.*—By statutory provision (Code, §§ 2159-60), an administrator may, on final settlement of his accounts in the Probate Court, be allowed a credit, as against the distributive shares of the several distributees, for moneys paid out and expended by him for their support and education during infancy; and this statute operating on the remedy only, it will be held to apply to and include such expenditures made before its passage, which would then have been allowed in equity; consequently, such prior payments are now no ground for equitable interposition. *Ib.* 524.

11. *Removal of incumbrances on land.*—As to lands which never belonged to the intestate, but which accrued to the distributees, as tenants in common with the administrator, from some other source, the administrator may, by paying taxes, or removing incumbrances, acquire as against the distributees a claim for reimbursement; but such claim can not be enforced or allowed on settlement of his accounts, either at law or in equity—neither in the Probate Court, nor in the Chancery Court. *Ib.* 524.

12. *Partnership accounts; statute of limitations, as bar to suit for settlement.*—Where it appears that the administrater and his intestate had been partners in business, and the partnership was dissolved by consent, but no settlement of accounts was had; and the intestate then removed to Georgia, and there died after the lapse of several years; the administrator might have a settlement of the partnership accounts in equity, and a decree for any balance in his favor, which would bind any personal assets in his hands, notwithstanding the bar of the statute of limitations; but, when his bill shows that he had no personal assets, and that he seeks to charge the lands in the hands of the heirs, or the rents thereof, the statute of limitations is a bar to the suit. *Ib.* 524.

13. *Purchase by executor at his own sale, and re-sale at profit.* A trustee is not permitted to traffic in the trust property for his own benefit, but holds the profits realized subject to be claimed by the beneficiaries on timely application; and this principle would probably apply to a sale of land by an executrix, where she was jointly interested with her sister as purchaser, and they afterwards effected a re-sale at a tenfold price; but such interest in the original purchase is not established, against the denials of the answer, merely by the deeds showing that the sister who was purchaser conveyed to the executrix, six years afterwards, a half interest in the land at the same price, and that they jointly effected the re-sale a few weeks afterwards. *Hughes v. Hughes,* 652.

14. *Sale of decedent's lands for payment of debts; competency of administrator as witness; identity of name as showing identity of person.* On application by an administrator for an order to sell lands for the payment of debts, when minors are interested in the estate (Code, §§ 2111, 2114), he is not a competent witness to prove the necessity for a sale; yet, if the order is granted, and application is made to set it aside at a subsequent term, the proceedings being regular on their face, it will not be presumed that one of the witnesses was the administrator merely because his name was the same. *Stevenson v. Murray,* 442.

EXECUTORS AND ADMINISTRATORS—*Continued.*

15. *Correcting mistake in description of lands sold under probate decree.*
Under statutory provisions (Code, 1886, §§ 2129-30; 1876, § 2472;
1867, § 2128), when a mistake has been made in the description
of a decedent's lands sold under a probate decree, whether in the
petition, order, or other proceedings, the court ordering the sale
has the authority to correct it, on the application of the purchaser, or any one claiming under him; and the provisions regulating the practice in such cases, as now of force, being remedial
in their character, are applicable to sales made while the former
statutes were in force. *Brown v. Williams*, 353.

16. *Same; effect of decree correcting mistake; defenses against.*—A decree
correcting a mistake under these statutory provisions, only has
the effect of placing the parties in the same position they would
have occupied if no mistake had occurred, but it gives no validity
to the original order of sale; other defects in the order or in the
proceedings connected with it, assailing its validity, are no defense against the application; and the lapse of seventeen years
since the sale, no adverse possession being shown, is no bar to a
correction of the mistake. *Ib.* 353.

EXEMPTIONS.

1. *Homestead exemption in lands of husband and wife.*—Where the
family homestead is on the lands of the wife, less in quantity
than is allowed by law (Code, 1876, § 2820), the husband can not
assert a claim of homestead in an adjoining tract belonging to
himself, part of which he cultivates, the two tracts containing
more than 160 acres. *Beard v. Johnson*, 729.

2. *Exemptions of personalty in favor of widow and children.*—A liberal
construction has always been given to the statutory provisions
allowing exemptions to the widow and minor children of deceased
debtors; the right is not made to depend on a dissent from the
will, making a testamentary provision for their support; the
claim is allowed to attach to any kind of personal property, or
to the proceeds of any personal property which has been sold or
exchanged by the personal representative; and if the whole of
the personal property does not exceed $1,000 in value, and is in
the possession of the widow, her right of exemption does not require a selection, or formal claim to perfect it. But, when no
claim of exemptions has been interposed, a sale by the personal
representative, if made by authority, cuts off the right of exemption; though, if made without authority, the property may be
recovered by a succeeding administrator, and again become subject to a claim of exemption. *Chandler v. Chandler*, 300.

3 *Homestead exemption to surviving widow; sufficiency of averments
of bill.*—Where the bill, filed by distributees against the administrator and the widow, praying (among other things) a sale of
lands for partition and distribution, alleges that the decedent's
homestead was on a tract of land containing forty acres, of value
more than $2,000; "that the dwelling-house and outhouses, with
other improvements on said tract of land, are of such character,
quality and value, as well as structure, that the dower of the said
Eliza [widow] can not be carved out of said tract and the improvements thereon, and assigned by metes and bounds to her,
and it is necessary to sell said property in order to assign the
dower interest to her;" not stating the value of the dwelling
with the grounds immediately connected with it, nor the value
of the other portions of the tract, and neither negativing nor
alleging the ownership of any other lands (except an adjoining
tract containing about thirty acres),—the necessity for a sale is
not shown, the right of homestead or substitutionary exemption

EXEMPTIONS—*Continued.*

of other lands (Code, 2544) not being negatived. *Jackson v. Rowell*, 685.

4. *Homestead and substitutionary exemption.*—When the decedent's homestead, reduced to the lowest possible area, still exceeds $2,000 in value, the widow has a right to select other lands in lieu thereof (Code, § 2544), and she may select lands of less value than $2,000, *Ib.* 685.

5. *Homestead tract containing more than eighty acres; equitable rights of purchaser from debtor, as against purchaser at execution sale.* Where the owner of a homestead tract of land containing more than eighty acres, having made and filed a declaration and claim of exemption, which was valid though irregular, sold and conveyed the entire tract on the 6th March, 1880, putting the purchaser in possession; and the land was afterwards sold under an execution lien, which was existing at the time of this sale and conveyance, and the continuity of which was never broken; the plaintiff in execution becoming the purchaser with notice of the sale and conveyance by the debtor, and afterwards recovering a judgment at law for the land, against the grantee and his tenants, with damages for the rents; *held*, that the debtor's grantee acquired an equitable title to the homestead, not exceeding eighty acres of the entire tract, and was entitled to have it set apart in equity, and was also entitled to an [injunction against the judgment for damages (or rents), so far as the rents accrued or arose from the land allotted to him. *Clark v. Allen*, 198.

6. *Reformation, or specific performance, of conveyance of homestead.* A conveyance of the homestead by husband and wife, to which the certificate of acknowledgment is substantially defective (Code, § 2508), will not be reformed in equity, on the ground that the examination and acknowledgment of the wife were in fact properly made, but were not shown by the officer's certificate from ignorance or mistake on his part; nor will it be specifically enforced, as an executory agreement to convey. *Cox v. Holcomb*, 589.

FORGERY. See CRIMINAL LAW, 38.

FRAUD.

1. *Composition with creditors; fraudulent proposal.*—A proposal by an insolvent or embarrassed debtor to his creditors, offering to surrender all of his property to them on condition of receiving an absolute release from further liability, is fraudulent, and, if accepted, would avoid the discharge, when it appears that some of the assets included in his schedule had been previously transferred to one of his creditors as collateral security, and were in his hands only for the purpose of collection; that the names of several small creditors were omitted, because he had "laid aside the money to pay them, and regarded them as paid," although the payment was in fact not made for two or three days afterwards; and that he also omitted a power-press, on which he had paid one half of the purchase-money, the vendor retaining a lien until full payment was made. *Campbell v. Hopkins*, 179.

2. *Signature to bond procured through fraud or mistake.*—In an action on a statutory claim bond, it is a good plea by one of the sureties, that he was fraudulently induced by the sheriff to sign it after it had been accepted and approved with the signatures of the other two sureties only, and that he signed it under a mistake of fact induced by the misrepresentations of the sheriff. *Anderson v. Bellenger & Ralls*, 334.

3. *Fraudulent concealment, as avoiding statute of limitations, at law and in equity.*—The fraudulent concealment of facts on which a right

FRAUD—*Continued.*

of action depends, such as avoids the bar of the statute of limitations (Code, § 2630). is available at law, and will not uphold a suit in equity, in the absence of facts showing a necessity for special equitable relief. *Tillison v. Ewing*, 350.

4. As to equitable relief on ground of fraud. see CHANCERY.

FRAUDS, STATUTE OF.

1. *Promise to answer for debt, default, or miscarriage of another.*—When goods are sold to one person, or at his instance, for the use and benefit of another, and the sole credit is given to him, his promise to pay for them is an original and absolute undertaking, and not a promise to answer for the debt, default, or miscarriage of another (Code, § 1732); otherwise, if any credit whatever was given to the person for whom the goods were bought. *Clark v. Jones & Brother*, 474.

2. *Same; words of doubtful meaning.*—Where the plaintiffs testify that the defendant applied for the goods in the name of a company of which he was a member, but they refused to sell on the credit of the company, and proposed to let the company have the goods on his credit, to which he agreed; but further, on cross-examination, that they agreed to take, at the expiration of thirty days, the company's acceptance with the defendant's indorsement for the balance not paid for by the acceptance of a third person, which was received as cash; while the defendant denies that he ever offered, directly or indirectly, to become responsible for the goods: *Held*, that the words used might import (1) a collateral undertaking by defendant to indorse the company's acceptance, which would be within the statute of frauds, or (2) an original and independent promise to pay for the goods, with an understanding that plaintiffs would take, in lieu thereof, at the expiration of thirty days, the company's acceptance with the defendant's indorsement, which would be a novation of the original contract, and not within the statute of frauds; and the words being susceptible of these two meanings, it was a question for the jury to determine which was intended by the parties. *Ib.* 474.

3. *Same; charging goods on books to third person, and extending time of payment.*—The fact that the goods were charged on the plaintiffs' books to the company for which they were bought, with the words added, "*Vouched for by*" defendant, does not conclusively show that any credit was given to the company, especially when they were so charged at the instance and request of the defendant; and the fact that plaintiffs afterwards took the company's acceptance for the balance, and then their note with a further extension of time, though proper for the consideration of the jury in determining whether any credit was given to the company, does not conclusively establish, as matter of law, that credit was given, when it also appears that plaintiffs notified defendant, at the time, that they did not intend thereby to release him. *Ib.* 474.

4. *Same; contract not to be performed within one year; promise to answer for debt or default of another.*—A promise made by a private banker, advancing money to cotton-buyers, to a warehouse-man, to pay the warehouse charges on the cotton of persons dealing with him, if the warehouse-man would allow it to be shipped without prepayment of his charges, is not a contract "not to be performed within one year" (Code, § 1732), although the parties acted under it for more than a year before a breach occurred; nor is it a promise to answer for the debt, default, or miscarriage of another person, within the terms of the statute; but it is an original promise or undertaking, founded on a two-fold consideration—benefit to the promisor, and detriment to the promisee. *Prout v. Robertson & Webb*, 593.

FRAUDULENT CONVEYANCES.

1. *Sale of stock of goods by insolvent debtor to creditor; validity as against other creditors.*—A sale of his entire stock of goods by an embarrassed or insolvent debtor, in absolute payment of a *bona fide* existing debt, will be sustained as 'against other creditors, without regard to the question of fraudulent intent, when there is no material difference between the value of the property and the amount of the debt, and no use or benefit is reserved to the debtor himself. *Knowles v. Street,* 357.

2. *Conveyance by failing or insolvent debtor to creditor; validity as against other creditors.*—A failing or insolvent debtor may select one or more of his creditors, and pay them in full, even though he thereby disables himself to pay anything to the others; but, if the conveyance or arrangement, going beyond the limits of full payment or security, stipulates or provides, openly or secretly, 'for a benefit to the debtor himself beyond what the law allows or secures to him, it is fraudulent on his part; and if the grantee, or secured creditor, knows of the existence of other debts left unprovided for, or has knowledge of facts calculated to put him on inquiry as to them, he is charged with participation in the fraud. *McDowell v. Steele,* 493.

3. *Mortgage by embarrassed debtor to creditor, stipulating for long time; validity as against other creditors.*—A mortgage executed by an embarrassed (if not insolvent) debtor, conveying lands as security for a debt less than their value, which was to be paid in nine annual installments, the whole interest payable annually, and with power of sale on default in the payment of the third installment; followed on the next day by a second mortgage on the property, to the mortgagor's wife, who was the mother of the first mortgagee,—*held* fraudulent in law, both as securing a valuable benefit to the mortgagor, and as hindering and delaying another creditor, whose debt was reduced to judgment on the next day, of which debt the mortgagee had notice, actual or constructive, having knowledge of facts sufficient to put him on inquiry. *Ib.* 493.

4. *Fraudulent conveyance, as cloud on title.*—A purchaser at sheriff's sale under execution, of lands which have been fraudulently conveyed by the judgment debtor, has a plain and adequate remedy at law, and can not, while out of possession, maintain a bill in equity to cancel the conveyance as a cloud on his title. *Teague v. Martin,* 500.

5. *Sufficiency of consideration of deed.*—When a bill seeks to set aside a conveyance of land as fraudulent against creditors, alleging that the land was worth $1,000 or more, and the recited consideration only $30; while the conveyance itself, made an exhibit to the bill, shows that the grantor conveyed only whatever interest and title he had by reason of his survivorship of his wife, to whom the land belonged, no data being furnished from which the value of his interest can be ascertained,—the deed can not be declared fraudulent. *Moorer v. Moorer,* 545.

6. *Unrecorded mortgage; validity as against creditors.*—An unrecorded mortgage, which, after several renewals is at last recorded within the time allowed by the statute (Code, §§ 1810-11), is not void as against simple-contract creditors, whose debts were incurred in the meantime, unless it was withheld from record for the fraudulent purpose of upholding the credit of the debtor, or is otherwise impeached by proof of actual or positive fraud on the part of the mortgagee; and under the facts of this case (the *bona fides* of the secured debt being admitted, the mortgage conveying not more than one third of the debtor's property, the law-day not being postponed for an unreasonable time, and it not being shown that

FRAUDULENT CONVEYANCES—*Continued.*

the mortgagee had notice of the debtor's insolvency), the charge of fraud in fact is not sustained. *McDonnell v. Mobile Savings Bank,* 736.

7. *Validity of mortgage, as against creditors; allegations of fraud.* When a creditor files a bill to set aside, on the ground of fraud, a mortgage or deed of trust executed by an insolvent corporation, which purports to convey all of its property to secure the payment of certain interest-bearing bonds payable ten years after date, and which reserves to the corporation the right to use the property until foreclosure; alleging that it was really given to secure an antecedent debt to two banks, which had taken some of the bonds as collateral security, and was intended to hinder, delay and defraud other creditors; that these debts were partly simulated, and that they included usurious interest; these allegations, in connection with the provisions of the mortgage, are sufficient to impeach it, showing the reservation of a benefit to the debtor, a fraudulent intent, and participation by the beneficiaries. *Globe Iron Roofing & Corrugating Co. v. Thacher,* 458.

8. *Same.*—A mortgage executed by an insolvent debtor, though with a fraudulent intent on his part, for the benefit of certain *bona fide* creditors, who are not charged with knowledge or notice of such frudulent intent, or any participation therein, will not be declared fraudulent as against other creditors; and this p⁻inciple is not affected by the facts, that the debtor is an insolvent corporation, and that the preferred creditors, or some of them, are stockholders or officers. *Ib.* 458.

9. *General assignment for benefit of creditors; validity of.*—A general assignment for the benefit of creditors, which fixes no time for foreclosure, and reserves to the grantor the use of the property until foreclosure, is not on that account fraudulent as against creditors, since the assignee may at any time foreclose, and any creditor may compel him to do so. *Ib.* 458.

10. *Fraudulent sale of goods by insolvent debtor; right of purchaser, on payment of judgment, to claim as creditor under deed of assignment.*—A sale of goods by an insolvent debtor having been held fraudulent at the instance of attaching creditors, on the trial of a statutory claim suit instituted by the purchaser, the payment of their judgments by him, which were less than the assessed value of the property, does not subrogate him to their rights as creditors under a deed of assignment executed by the debtor after the sale of the goods, nor give him any other rights as a creditor to participate in the assets in the hands of the assignee, although a part of said assets consists of money paid by him in cash on the purchase of the goods. *Pritchett v. Jones,* 317.

11. *When creditor without lien may come into equity.*.—Under statutory provisions (Code, § 3544), a bill filed by a creditor without a lien, seeking to set aside a fraudulent conveyance by his debtor, alleging the existence, amount and consideration of his debt, the insolvency of his debtor, a conveyance by the debtor to his brothers, without valuable consideration, or on a simulated consideration, in secret trust for the debtor himself, and with the intent to hinder, delay and defraud his creditors, of which fraudulent intent it is alleged the grantees had knowledge, is not wanting in equity. *Miller v. Lehman, Durr & Co.,* 517.

12. *Insurance on life of husband, for benefit of wife;* validity as against creditors. *Tompkins v. Levy & Bro.,* 263. See INSURANCE.

FUGITIVES FROM JUSTICE. See CRIMINAL LAW, 4, 5.

GARNISHMENT. See ATTACHMENT.

GUARDIAN AND WARD.

1. *Annual settlement as evidence.*—On final settlement of a guardian's accounts, former annual or partial settlements made by him are a part of the record, and it is the right and duty of the court to look to them as evidence in the cause. *Bentley v. Bailey,* 406.

2. *Conclusiveness of annual settlements.*—On final settlement of a guardian's accounts, credits allowed him on an annual or partial settlement are presumptively correct (Code, § 2458), and the *onus* of disproving their correctness is on the ward. *Ib.* 406.

3. *Confederate money received by guardian.*—A guardian having been allowed a credit, on a partial settlement in 1870-71, for Confederate money received from a debtor during the late war, and left on his hands at the close of the war, the credit ought not to be disallowed on final settlement, on evidence showing merely that the money was collected on notes given for the purchase-money of land, which the guardian had received, in 1859-60, as his ward's distributive share on settlement of an estate; this evidence, without more, not being sufficient to overcome the presumption in favor of the allowance on annual settlement. *Ib.* 406.

4. *Allowance to guardian, for board of ward.*—An allowance to the guardian on an annual or partial settlement, for board paid to the ward's step-father on his account, is properly disallowed on final settlement, on the uncontradicted testimony of the ward that he owed nothing for board; the step-father, though living in the county, not being produced as a witness. *Ib.* 406.

5. *Costs, as against guardian ad litem.*—The rule of this court has always been, not to tax a guardian *ad litem* with costs, though he be the unsuccessful appellant. *Brown v. Williams,* 353.

HABEAS CORPUS. See CRIMINAL LAW, 43.

HOMESTEAD. See EXEMPTIONS.

HUSBAND AND WIFE.

1. *Wife as witness for husband.*—In a criminal case, the wife is not a competent witness for her husband. *Hussey v. State,* 121.

2. *Husband's admissions, as evidence against wife.*—When the contract of sale is negotiated by the husband for the benefit of the wife, and the conveyance is executed to her, though his notes are given for the purchase-money, his subsequent admissions or declarations, when pressed for payment, that the vendor had retained a lien on the land, are not competent or admissible as evidence against the wife. *Jackson v. Stanley,* 270.

3. *Transfer of promissory note by husband and wife.*—Under the statute regulating the separate estates of married women, which has been in force since February 28th, 1887 (Sess. Acts 1886-7, p. 81; Code, §§ 2346, 2348), a promissory note which is the separate property of the wife, having been made payable to her while sole and unmarried, may be transferred by her written assignment, to which the husband's consent is affixed in writing, as well as by a joint assignment. *Bullock v. Vann,* 372.

4. *Relieving married woman of disabilities of coverture, by decree in chancery*—In the exercise of the statutory jurisdiction formerly conferred on chancellors to relieve married women of the disabilities of coverture to the extent specified (Code, 1876, § 2731), relief can not be granted by piecemeal, but the relief prayed and granted must be coextensive with the statute, neither more.nor less; if the petition prays only partial relief, or less than the statute authorizes, any decree rendered upon it is void; but, if the petition conforms to the statute, while the decree goes beyond it, it is void only for the excess. *Powell v. N..E. Mortgage Security Co.,* 602.

HUSBAND AND WIFE—*Continued.*

5. *Same; case at bar.*—Where the petition alleged that the petitioner owned certain lands, "which are her statutory separate estate, and which she desires to incumber or mortgage for the purpose of raising money," and therefore prayed to be "relieved of all the disabilities of coverture, to the end that she may sue and be sued as a *feme sole*, mortgage, convey, and otherwise dispose of her separate estate as fully and freely as if a *feme sole*;" while the decree declared her "relieved of the disabilities of coverture, with full power to convey, mortgage, buy, sell, or otherwise dispose of her statutory and other separate estate, to sue and be sued as a *feme sole*;" *held*, that the petition and decree each was fatally defective, and conferred no power to mortgage her lands. *Ib* 602.

6. As to insurance on life of husband, for benefit of wife, see INSURANCE, 4-5.

INDICTMENT. See CRIMINAL LAW, 55-59.

INEBRIATES' ESTATES.

1. *Powers and duties of trustee; death of inebriate pending suit by trustee.*—The estate, powers and duties of the trustee of an inebriate's estate, under statutory provisions (Code, §§ 2502-06), like the committee of a lunatic in England, terminate with the death of the inebriate, though he still remains liable to account; and having filed a bill in equity to set aside a conveyance of land executed by the inebriate after his appointment, the suit abates by the death, and can not be continued or revived in the name of the heirs of the inebriate jointly with the trustee. *Ex parte Williams,* 547.

INFANCY.

1. *As exception to statute of limitations.*—By statute (Code, § 2624), an infant is allowed three years after attaining his majority, within which to bring suit, or make entry; but his disability is not allowed, in any case, to extend the period of limitations beyond the lapse of twenty years from the accrual of his right of action or entry; this being a statutory affirmation, as applicable to infants, of the doctrine of prescription. *Woodstock Iron Co. v. Roberts,* 436.

INJUNCTION. See CHANCERY, 12-20.

INSOLVENT ESTATES.

1. *Filing claim against; who may redeem as judgment creditor.*—A judgment rendered against a debtor while living, which is not presented as a claim against his insolvent estate within the time allowed by law (Code, § 2238), is forever barred as a debt against the estate; and the plaintiff therein, or his assignee, can not claim, as a judgment creditor (*Ib.* § 1883), the right to redeem lands sold under a mortgage executed by the debtor while living. *Walden v. Speigner,* 390.

INSURANCE.

1. *Cancellation of policy; authority of agent.*—An agency to procure insurance is ended when the policy is procured and delivered to the principal; and the agent has no power afterwards to consent to a cancellation, or to accept notice of an intended cancellation by the insurer. *Insurance Companies v. Raden,* 311.

2. *Same; dual agency.*—An express stipulation in the policy authorizing the company to terminate it at any time on giving notice to that effect to the assured, "or to the person who may have procured the insurance to be taken," can not be applied to a case where

INSURANCE—*Continued.*

the same person acted as agent for both parties in procuring and issuing the policy, and notice of the intended cancellation was not given to the assured in person. *Ib.* 311.

3. *Ratification of cancellation.*—A ratification of the cancellation of a policy, which was procured for the insured by an agent of the insurance company, will not be presumed from his acceptance, after a loss, of a policy in another company, which was procured by the same agent, when it is not shown that the assured was fully informed of all the facts connected with the supposed cancellation and substitution. and "of his legal rights as determined by those facts; nor will it be presumed from the institution of a suit on the substituted policy, which was induced by the misrepresentation of the agent to the attorneys of the assured. *Ib.* 311.

4. *Insurance on life of husband, for benefit of wife and children, or heirs; validity as against creditors.*—Under statutory provisions (Code, 1876, §§2733-4), since changed in phraseology (Code, 1886, §§ 2356), the husband might insure his own life in favor of his wife, paying annual premiums not more than $500, and might make the policy payable to her children, in the event of her death before his; and these statutory provisions operating in the nature of an exemption law, the proceeds of the policy could not be subjected by creditors to the payment of the husband's debts. But the interest of the wife terminated, on her death before her husband; and the policy being made payable to "her heirs, executors or assigns," her children acquired no interest which could prevail against the husband's creditors, on his subsequent death. *Tompkins v. Levy & Brother*, 263.

5. *Same.*—Where the husband takes out a policy of insurance on his own life, in favor of his wife, "her heirs, executors, or assigns," paying the premiums with his own funds, a provision to the effect that, after the expiration of fifteen years, on surrender of the policy, none of its provisions having been violated, the company would pay to him, his heirs, executors or assigns, the equitable value of the policy, "as an endowment in cash," is the reservation of a benefit to himself, and renders the policy fraudulent as against his creditors. *Ib* 263.

INTEREST.

1. *Against attorney, on money received from fund in court*—When a fund in court, in an interpleader suit, is paid to the attorney of one of the parties pending the litigation, on his own motion, he is properly charged with interest on it at the final hearing. *Smith v. Alexander*, 387.

JUDGMENTS AND DECREES.

1. *Assignment of judgment or decree; suits by assignee.*—The statutory provisions relating to mesne or final process issued upon an assigned judgment or decree (Code, §§ 2927-28), have no application to suits on such judgment or decree, whether at law or in equity. An action at law can not be prosecuted by the assignee in his own name, but he may maintain a bill in equity in his own name. *Moorer v. Moorer*, 545.

2. *Judgment by nil dicit; presumption in favor of.*—On judgment by *nil dicit* in regular form, the appellate court will presume, if necessary to sustain it, that it was so rendered because the defendant failed or declined to plead, and not because he failed to pay the costs as required by a former order granting him a continuance. *Maund v. Loeb & Bro.*, 374.

3 *Same; evidence as to damages.*—After judgment by *nil dicit* in an action of trover, the only question to be referred to the jury, as to

JURORS AND JURY—*Continued.*

    where a jury of twelve men may be impanelled on demand. *Woodward Iron Co. v. Cabaniss,* 328.

    See, also, CRIMINAL LAW, 60-61.

JUSTICE OF THE PEACE.

1. *Action for damages to stock; jurisdiction of justice of the peace.* Under constitutional and general statutory provisions (Const. Ala., Art. VI, § 26; Code, § 839), the jurisdiction of a justice of the peace, in cases of tort, is limited to $50; and the special statute which gives him jurisdiction "of all actions for injury to, or destruction of stock, by the locomotive or cars of a railroad, if the sum in controversy does not exceed $100" (Code § 1149), being a discrimination against corporations, is unconstitutional and void as to the excess of jurisdiction attempted to be conferred. *Brown v. Ala. Gr. So. Railroad Co.,* 370.

2. *Certiorari and supersedeas to justice of the peace; when proper remedy.*—When a forthcoming bond in an attachment case, before a justice of the peace, is illegally returned by the constable as forfeited, and a summary execution is thereupon wrongfully issued against the obligors, a petition for a *certiorari* and *supersedeas* from the Circuit Court is the proper remedy, since the defects would not be available on appeal from the justice's judgment. *Cobb v. Thompson,* 381.

3. *Replevy (or forthcoming) bond in attachment case.*—In an attachment case before a justice of the peace, a replevy bond conditioned to have the property forthcoming within *twenty* days after the rendition of judgment, is substantially defective as a statutory bond (Code, §§ 3334-41), and does not authorize a summary execution on a return of forfeiture; and the defect being one of substance, it is not cured by the statutory provision as to defects of form. (*Ib.* § 3357.) *Ib.* 381.

4. *Appeals; variance in name of corporation.*—In an action commenced in a justice's court, which, on appeal, is required to be tried *de novo,* according to equity and justice, without regard to any defect in the process or proceedings before the justice (Code, § 3405); the defendant corporation being sued by the name given by its amended charter, which also made it liable for all debts created by the corporation under its original name and charter; the cause of action, as indorsed on the justice's warrant, being an account for goods sold and delivered to it by its amended name, while the proof shows that the goods were sold and delivered to the corporation before its change of name,—there is no material variance. *Chewacla Lime Works v. Dismukes, Frierson & Co.,* 344.

LANLORD AND TENANT.

1. *Landlord's lien for rent, on goods in store-house.*—Under statutory provisions giving to landlords of store-houses, dwelling-houses and other buildings "a lien on the goods of their tenants for rent" (Code, § 3069-74), construed in the light of the rules of the common law governing the remedy by distress, the lien attaches, where the tenancy is continued, by express contract, or by implication, to goods brought on the premises after the expiration of the original term, and remaining there when the attachment is sued out to enforce it; and this lien must prevail against the claim of a third person in possession by purchase from the tenant. *Abraham v. Nicrosi,* 173.

LARCENY. See CRIMINAL LAW, 63, 64.

LIMITATIONS, STATUTE OF.

1. *Infancy as exception to statute.*—By statute (Code, § 2624), an infant is allowed three years after attaining his majority, within which to bring suit, or make entry; but his disability is not allowed, in any case, to extend the period of limitations beyond the lapse of twenty years from the accrual of his right of action or entry; this being a statutory affirmation, as applicable to infants, of the doctrine of prescription. *Woodstock Iron Co. v. Roberts,* 436.

2. *Adverse possession, under permissive possessor.*— A permissive possession does not become adverse, without an open and distinct disavowal of the title of the true owner, and the assertion of a hostile title brought to his notice; but, if the permissive possessor dies in possession, and the land is afterwards sold by his administrator for the payment of debts, a deed executed to the purchaser purporting to convey the entire estate in the land, the purchase-money paid, and possession delivered, such possession is adverse to the true owner, and will ripen into a title if continued for the statutory period. *Ib.* 436.

3. *Continuity of possession, as affected by trespass.*—The intrusion of a mere trespasser on land, who enters without claim or title, does not interrupt the continuity of possession, unless continued so long that knowledge by him is presumed, and he fails to resort to legal remedies before adverse rights are acquired. *Ib.* 436.

4. *Actual and constructive possession.*—Possession under title, or color of title, is not limited to that part of the land which is actually occupied, but extends to the entire tract covered by the written instrument; while the possession of a trespasser, without color of title, extends only to the land actually occupied. *Ib.* 436.

5. *Absence, or non-residence, as exception to statute of limitations.*—In computing the bar of the statute of limitations, the period of the defendant's absence from the State, and not of his non-residence, is to be deducted (Code, § 2622); yet, where the bill alleges that the defendant was a non-resident of Alabama, and resided in Tennessee, when the cause of action accrued, and ever since, this is sufficient, on demurrer, to avoid the bar. *Stevenson v. Anderson,* 228.

6. *Statute of limitations in favor of purchaser, as against tenant in common of vendor.*—The statute of limitations is not a bar, as against one tenant in common, in favor of a purchaser from the other, unless ten years have elapsed since his purchase, or unless he can claim the benefit of adverse possession by his vendor. *Ib.* 228.

7. *Adverse possession between tenants in common.*—Actual possession, such as the land reasonably admits of, is an essential element of adverse possession; an entry by two tenants in common, surveying and laying the land out in lots, without more, does not constitute such actual possession; and a sale and conveyance of one or more of the lots by one of them, after the lapse of ten years, does not, as against the other, establish an adverse possession of the other portions of the land. *Ib.* 228.

8. *Stale demands.*—As between tenants in common, a bill for partition is not a stale demand so long as a right of entry is not barred. *Ib.* 228.

9. *Statutory bar to action for value of services rendered.*—Under statutory provisions (Code, §§ 2615, 2618), three years is the bar to an action to recover the reasonable value of services rendered under a written contract. *Chambers v. Seay,* 558.

10. *Statutory bar to suit for settlement of partnership accounts.*—Where it appears that the administrator and his intestate had been partners in business, and the partnership was dissolved by con-

MORTGAGE—*Continued.*

purchaser with notice being joined as a defendant, he may be held responsible, not only for the cotton then in his possession, but also for cotton received and sold by him before the bill was filed, although the mortgagee might maintain an action at law for its conversion; and he is chargeable with interest on the value of cotton so sold, although, by agreement of the parties to the cause, he has been allowed to sell the cotton in possession, giving a bond to account for its value. *Ib.* 362.

4. *Verbal mortgage.*—By statutory provisions now of force (Code, § 1731), a mortgage of personal property is required to be in writing, and subscribed by the mortgagor, and a verbal mortgage has no validity. *Weaver v. Brown*, 385.

5. *Mortgage for future advances; parol evidence affecting consideration.* A mortgage given to secure payment for future advances by the mortgagee, is a valid security as between the parties; and when the recited consideration is an indebtedness by promissory note, oral evidence may be received to show that part of the actual consideration was supplies or advances to be afterwards furnished, and which were furnished. *Huckaba v. Abbott*, 409.

6. *Mortgage on future crops.*—A mortgage executed in November, 1886, conveying the mortgagor's "entire crop to be grown in the year 1887, on my own or any other land in said county," does not convey the crop raised on a tract of land which did not then belong to the mortgagor, and in which he had no interest, though he afterwards bought it. *Paden & Co. v. Bellenger & Ralls*, 575.

7. *Mortgage of lands afterwards acquired.*—A railroad company may convey by mortgage property to be afterwards acquired; and if it conveys lands to which it has only an equitable title, but to which it afterwards acquires the legal title, that title at once enures to the grantee, or mortgagee, both by the express words of the instrument, and by the statutory words of warranty, *grant, bargain, sell and convey. Swann & Billups v. Gaston*, 569.

8. *Registration of mortgage as constructive notice; removal of property to another county.*—A mortgage of personal property is required to be recorded, not only in the county in which the mortgagor resides, but also in the county in which the property then is; and on its removal to another county, the mortgage must be there recorded within six months afterwards (Code, §§ 1806-1814); and the fact that the mortgaged animals (mules) are carried over and worked in the former county by day, but carried back each night into the new county, does not dispense with the necessity for such new registration. *Pollak v. Davidson*, 551.

9. *Constructive notice of mortgage, as implied from knowledge of indebtedness, character of business, &c.*—Knowledge of the existence of a debt, is not constructive notice of an unrecorded mortgage given to secure it; nor can notice of such unrecorded mortgage be implied from the additional facts, that the mortgagee was a merchant making advances to planters, and that his house of business was not more than one hundred and fifty yards distant from that of the second mortgagee; nor are these facts sufficient to put the second mortgagee on inquiry. *Ib.* 551.

10. *Mortgage by embarrassed debtor to creditor, stipulating for long time; validity as against other creditors.*—A mortgage executed by an embarrassed (if not insolvent) debtor, conveying lands as security for a debt less than their value, which was to be paid in nine annual installments, the whole interest payable annually, and with power of sale on default in the payment of the third installment; followed on the next day by a second mortgage on the property, to the mortgagor's wife, who was the mother of the first mortga-

MORTGAGE—*Continued.*

gee,—*held* fraudulent in law, both as securing a valuable benefit to the mortgagor, and as hindering and delaying another creditor, whose debt was reduced to judgment on the next day, of which debt the mortgagee had notice, actual or constructive, having knowledge of facts sufficient to put him on inquiry. *McDowell v. Steele*, 493.

11. *Validity of mortgage, as against creditors; allegations of fraud.* When a creditor files a bill to set aside, on the ground of fraud, a mortgage or deed of trust executed by an insolvent corporation, which purports to convey all of its property to secure the payment of certain interest-bearing bonds payable ten years after date, and which reserves to the corporation the right to use the property until foreclosure; alleging that it was really given to secure an antecedent debt to two banks, which had taken some of the bonds as collateral security, and was intended to hinder, delay and defraud other creditors; that these debts were partly simulated, and that they included usurious interest; these allegations, in connection with the provisions of the mortgage, are sufficient to impeach it, showing the reservation of a benefit to the debtor, a fraudulent intent, and participation by the beneficiaries. *Globe Iron Roofing Co. v. Thacher*, 458.

12. *Same.*—A mortgage executed by an insolvent debtor, though with a fraudulent intent on his part, for the benefit of certain *bona fide* creditors, who are not charged with knowledge or notice of such fraudulent intent, or any participation therein, will not be declared fraudulent as against other creditors; and this principle is not affected by the facts, that the debtor is an insolvent corporation, and that the preferred creditors, or some of them, are stockholders or officers. *Ib*. 458.

13. *Unrecorded mortgage; validity as against creditors.*—An unrecorded mortgage, which, after several renewals, is at last recorded within the time allowed by the statute (Code, §§ 1810-11), is not void as against simple-contract creditors, whose debts were incurred in the meantime, unless it was withheld from record for the fraudulent purpose of upholding the credit of the debtor, or is otherwise impeached by proof of actual or positive fraud on the part of the mortgagee; and under the facts of this case (the *bona fides* of the secured debt being admitted, the mortgage conveying not more than one third of the debtor's property, the law-day not being postponed for an unreasonable time, and it not being shown that the mortgagee had notice of the debtor's insolvency), the charge of fraud in fact is not sustained. *Mobile Savings Bank v. McDonnell*, 736.

14. *Purchase by mortgagee, at sale under power.*—When a mortgage contains an express provision authorizing the mortgagee to purchase at a sale under the power, and he does become the purchaser, the mortgagor can not disaffirm the sale, and be allowed to redeem, except upon the allegation and proof of facts which would invalidate it if a third person had become the purchaser. *Knox v. Armistead*, 511,

15. *Injunction against sale under power in mortgage.*—When the bill prays an injunction against a sale under a mortgage, the complainant having purchased from the mortgagee, as agent of the mortgagor (to whom he had previously sold and conveyed), and alleging that the defendant fraudulently concealed from him the existence of the mortgage, which was then unrecorded; the injunction may properly be retained, notwithstanding the denials of fraud in the answer, when it appears that the mortgagor and vendor is a non-resident, and that he has transferred one of the

MORTGAGE—*Continued.*

complainant's notes for the purchase-money, to an assignee, who is asserting a prior lien on the land. *Harrison v. Yerby,* 185.

16. *Foreclosure of mortgage by trustee of tenant for life.*—As a general rule, when a person holds the legal title to property, charged with the duty of accounting for the rents and profits to a tenant for life, he is a trustee to that extent, and has no power to change the *status* of the property, except possibly in extreme cases, subject to the direction and approval of a court of equity; yet, where the widow and sole devisee of a deceased mortgagor, and grantor in a deed of trust in the nature of a mortgage, has conveyed all of her property to trustees, with a life interest in herself in the rents and profits after payment of taxes, repairs, &c., and a testamentary provision in their favor after her death, the trustees may maintain a bill to foreclose the mortgage, and the court may, if necessary to prevent danger from conversion of the trust fund, require proper security for the income during her life. *Kyle v. Perdue,* 423.

17. *Mortgage of property to be afterwards acquired; executory contract of pledge.*—A verbal agreement between private bankers and one of their customers who was engaged in the business of buying cotton, to the effect that they would advance money to be used by him in the purchase of cotton; that all cotton bought by him, and paid for by checks on them, should be their property, and they should have the right to take, hold and sell the same, until the money advanced for it had been repaid; and that on their failure to sell, the customer might ship and sell the cotton, but should give them a draft for the proceeds, with bill of lading attached,—does not create a legal mortgage, nor operate as a pledge of any particular cotton, until it has been delivered, or otherwise specifically appropriated. *Bank of Eutaw v. Ala. State Bank,* 163.

18. *Same.*—A subsequent agreement between the parties, after other transactions between them, to the effect that the bankers, on paying a note held by another bank, should take up and cancel a bill of lading for one hundred bales of cotton, held by that bank as security for the debt, and should hold all the customer's cotton then on hand, which he had bought with money advanced by them, until a specified future day, and, if not sold or shipped by the customer before that day, should have the right to take possession, ship and sell it, applying the proceeds of sale to the payment of the customer's indebtedness to them,—like the previous agreement, creates only an equitable lien, which, coupled with possession wrongfully taken, can not defeat an action by the owner of a superior equitable lien, who procured the legal title by an indorsement of the warehouse receipts after such wrongful possession taken. *Ib.* 163.

19. *Equitable lien with possession, as against prior lien with subsequent legal title.*—While possession of personal property wrongfully taken by a person who has an equitable lien on it, can not prevail against a prior or superior equitable lien, coupled with a legal title acquired after the wrongful taking; yet the title of the latter does not attach, as against the former, to property which was substituted by the owner, under whom each party claims, for a part of the property covered by the lien which he had disposed of. *Ib.* 163.

NEGLIGENCE.

1. *Negligence, as question of fact or law.*—The question of negligence, or contributory negligence, in any case, is properly left to the determination of the jury as a question of fact, unless the evi-

NEGLIGENCE—*Continued.*

dence is free from conflict, and the inferences to be drawn from it are clear and certain. *L. & N. Railroad Co. v. Perry*, 392.

2. *Contributory negligence between railroad companies at crossing.* In an action to recover damages for personal injuries sustained by plaintiff at a railroad crossing, the fact that the company on whose cars he was travelling was guilty of contributory negligence is no defense, though it may create a joint and several liability. *Geo. Pac. Railway Co. v. Hughes*, 610.

3. *Contributory negligence; burden of proof.*—Contributory negligence, when pleaded by itself, is an admission of negligence on the part of the defendant, but not when interposed with the plea of not guilty. *L. & N. Railroad Co. v. Hall*, 708.

4. *Notice to brakeman of low bridge overhead; contributory negligence.* When a brakeman is employed on a railroad with which he is not familiar, and is required, in the performance of his duties, to pass under a low bridge spanning the track, which, though not high enough to allow him to pass in an erect position on top of a car, is yet high enough to meet legal requirements, it is the duty of the railroad company to give him reasonable notice of the danger; but, if, having been duly notified, he fails, from inattention, indifference, absent-mindedness or forgetfulness, to inform himself of the particular facts, or to take the necessary steps to avoid injury—in other words, if he fails to exercise the care, watchfulness and caution which men of ordinary prudence would exercise under the circumstances—he is guilty of contributory negligence. *Ib.* 708.

NEW TRIAL.

1. *Refusal not revisable.*—By the settled practice of this court since its organization, a motion for a new trial is addressed to the discretion of the lower court, and its refusal is not revisable by this court on error or appeal. *Johnson v. State*, 39.

CASES OVERRULED.

1. *Ala. Gr. So. Railroad Co. v. McAlpine*, 75 Ala. 113; s. c., 80 Ala. 73, explained and limited by *Geo. Pac. Railway Co. v. Hughes*, 610.

2. *Jones v. Walker*, 47 Ala. 175, overruled by *Woodstock Iron Co. v. Roberts*, 436.

3. *L. & N. Railroad Co. v. Bees*, 82 Ala. 340, explained and limited by *Geo. Pac. Railway Co. v. Hughes*, 610.

4. *L. & N. Railroad Co. v. Jones*, 83 Ala. 373, explained and limited by *Geo. Pac. Railway Co. v. Hughes*, 610.

5. *M. & G. Railroad Co. v. Caldwell*, 83 Ala. 196, explained and limited by *Geo. Pac. Railway Co. v. Hughes*, 610.

6. *Tesney v. State*, 77 Ala. 33, 7th head-note held wrong in *Poe v. State*, 65.

PARTITION.

1. *Sale of lands for partition.*—To justify proceedings in the Probate Court for a partition of lands, or a sale for partition (Code, §§ 3237, 3253) each part owner must be interested in the entire lands sought to be sold or partitioned *Hall v. Caperton*, 285.

2. *Stale demands.*—As between tenants in common, a bill for partition is not a stale demand so long as a right of entry is not barred. *Stevenson v. Anderson*, 228.

PARTNERSHIP.

1. *Action by partnership.*—A suit may be maintained in the name of a late partnership, stating the names of the late partners, notwithstanding its dissolution. *Tompkins v. Levy & Bro.*, 264.

PARTY-WALL—*Continued.*

but each owns one half in severalty, with an easement in the other half; and each may increase the height, at least, of his half, if not of the entire wall, when it can be done without damage to the other proprietor; but, in the absence of statutory provisions, or express agreement between the parties, neither has the right to make windows or other openings in the wall; nor is such right conferred by an agreement giving either one the right "to use said party-wall free of expense in the erection of any building which he may wish to erect on said lot." *Graves v Smith,* 450.

2. *Injunction against windows.*—A court of equity will interfere by injunction, at the suit of one of the part owners of a party-wall, to prevent the other from making windows, or other openings in it. *Ib.* 450.

PAYMENT. See EVIDENCE, 34.

PEDDLING. See CRIMINAL LAW, 65.

PLEADING AND PRACTICE.

1. *Count construed to be in case, and not in assumpsit.*—A count which claims damages of the defendant, for that whereas, plaintiff having procured a loan of money from defendant, and pledged certain shares of stock as collateral security, defendant undertook and promised, in consideration thereof, to hold said stock only as collateral security, and not to convert the same to his own use, nor to sell the same without notice to plaintiff; but, not regarding said promise and undertaking, and intending to injure and defraud plaintiff, defendant afterwards converted said stock to his own use, and sold the same without notice to plaintiff, whereby said shares of stock were lost to plaintiff, and he was damaged as aforesaid,—though informal, is a good count in *case,* and not in *assumpsit. Sharpe v. Nat. Bank of Birmingham,* 644.

2. *Sufficiency of complaint.*—Where the complaint claims damages on account of personal injuries sustained by a brakeman in the employment of a railroad company, by being struck by a bridge overhead across a public road, while on the top of a car in the discharge of his duties, the complaint must aver that the bridge was erected or maintained by the railroad company. *L. & N. Railroad Co. v. Hall,* 708.

3. *Misjoinder of counts.*—Special counts in case, claiming damages for the breach of a duty imposed by a written contract, can not be joined with the common counts. *Chambers v. Seay,* 558.

4. *When sworn plea is necessary.*—In an action on a bill of exchange by an indorsee against the drawee, the indorsement to plaintiff, or his ownership, not being denied by plea verified by affidavit (Code, §§ 2676, 2770), the validity of the transfer can not be questioned, and the bill is admissible as evidence. *Manning v. Maroney,* 563.

5. *Bill of particulars, as waiver of plea in abatement.*—The right to file a plea in abatement is not waived by a previous demand for a bill of particulars.—Code, § 2670. *Oates v. Clendenard,* 734.

6. *Misnomer.*—The variance between the names *Clendenard* and *Clendinen* is sufficient to support a plea in abatement on the ground of misnomer. *Ib.* 734.

7. *Misnomer; pleadings as to*—The difference between the names *Munkers* and *Moncus* is sufficient to support a plea of misnomer, when a demurrer is interposed to it; if, by local usage, the names have the same pronunciation, issue should be taken on the plea, or a replication should be filed. *Munkers v. State,* 94.

8. *Pleading over, after demurrer sustained; error without injury.*—When the record shows that, after demurrer sustained to a plea or rep-

PLEADING AND PRACTICE—*Continued.*

lication, the party had the full benefit of the same matter under an amended pleading, the ruling on demurrer, if erroneous, could have worked no injury, and is not a reversible error. *Calhoun v. Hannan & Michael,* 277.

9. *Summons not signed by the clerk; waiver of defect.*—In a statutory action for the recovery of personal property *in specie,* the summons not being signed by the clerk, though the indorsement requiring the sheriff to take possession of the property was properly signed; the sheriff having taken the property from the possession of the defendant, and no objection to the defective summons being raised for four or five terms during which the suit was pending, before a judgment by default was taken; *held,* that the defect in the summons was waived. *Baker v. Swift & Son,* 530.

10. *Service of process as shown by sheriff's return; evidence impeaching.* The return of a sheriff, showing service of process, imports verity, and casts on the party assailing it the burden of adducing evidence sufficient to overcome the presumption that the officer did his duty; and on motion to set aside the return, the bill of exceptions reciting that "the defendant introduced himself as a witness, and his testimony *tended* to show that the summons and complaint were never served on him," &c., and that "this was all the evidence in the cause," these recitals are not sufficient to enable this court to say that the lower court erred in refusing to set aside the return. *Paul v. Malone & Collins,* 544.

11. *Error without injury, in sustaining demurrer to special plea.*—The sustaining of a demurrer to a special plea, if erroneous, is error without injury, when the same defense was equally available under the general issue, which was also pleaded. *Manning v. Maroney,* 563.

12. *Error without injury in ruling on pleadings.*—In an action of trover, if a demurrer to a special count in case is erroneously sustained, the error is immaterial, when the record shows that the plaintiff had the full benefit of the same facts under the count in trover. *Gilman, Son & Co. Jones,* 691.

13. *Same.*—The sustaining of a demurrer to a special plea, if erroneous, is error without injury, when the record shows that the defendant had the full benefit of the same defense under another special plea. *L. & N. Railroad Co. v. Hall,* 709.

14. *Error without injury in refusing to allow amendment.*—The refusal to allow an amendment of the complaint, by the addition of another count, if erroneous, is not a reversible error, when the record shows that the plaintiff's case was tried on the original complaint precisely as it would have been if the amendment had been allowed. *Sharpe v. Nat. Bank of Birmingham,* 644.

PLEDGE.

1. *Pledge of stock as collateral security; remedies of pledgee.*—When shares of stock in a private corporation are pledged as collateral security for a debt, and default is made in the payment of the debt at maturity, the pledgee may file a bill in equity to foreclose the pledge by a sale under the order of the court, or he may exercise the implied power to sell without resorting to judicial proceedings; but, if he elects to pursue the latter remedy, the sale must be at public auction, in the absence of a special agreement, and reasonable notice must be given to the pledgor; and if he sells privately, without notice, becoming himself the purchaser, the relation between him and the pledgor is not thereby dissolved. *Sharpe v. Nat. Bank of Birmingham,* 644.

2. *Same; ratification of unauthorized sale.*—If the pledgor, when notified of the irregular or unauthorized sale, accepts its benefits, giving

PRESCRIPTION. See Limitations, Statute of, 1.

PRESUMPTIONS. See Evidence, 60–64.

PROHIBITION.

1. *To Probate Court.*—Since an appeal lies from the Probate Court to the Circuit Court, in the matter of proceedings for the condemnation of a right of way at the suit of a railroad company, a writ of prohibition from the Circuit Court will not be awarded to prevent further proceedings. *Woodward Iron Co. v. Cabaniss*, 3¿8.

PUBLIC LANDS.

1. *Receiver's receipt on homestead entry.*—As against a mere trespasser, a receipt given by the receiver of a land office of the United States, for money paid on a homestead entry (U. S. Rev. Statutes, §§ 2290–97), confers a title on which ejectment, or the statutory action in the nature thereof, may be maintained before the expiration of five years (Code, § 2782); and the defendant can not be heard to allege a breach of the conditions on which the entry may be perfected. *Case v. Edgeworth*, 203.

2. *Same.*—A receipt given by the receiver of a land office of the United States, for money paid in full on a homestead entry (U. S. Rev. Statutes, §§ 2290–97), confers a title which, before the expiration of five years, enables the possessor to maintain or defend an action as owner. *Morison Bros. v. Coleman.* 655.

3. *Congressional grant of lands in aid of railroads; title of State, and statute of limitations against.*—Under the acts of Congress granting lands to the State of Alabama in aid of certain railroads (11 U. S. Stat. at large, p. l7 ; 16 *Ib.* 45), as heretofore construed, the legal title to the lands granted at once vested in the State, for the use and benefit of the designated railroad companies; and it continued in the State, except as to the lands sold during the construction of the road in continous sections of twenty miles, until the construction of the road was completed; and while the title thus continued in the State, the statute of limitations did not begin to run in favor of an adverse possessor under color of title. *Swann & Billups v. Gaston*, 569.

4. *Same; lands allotted to Alabama & Chattanooga Railroad Company; statute of limitations against trustees.*—The lands allotted to the two railroad companies which were consolidated into the Alabama & Chattanooga Railroad Company having been conveyed by it to the State, before the completion of the road, by mortgage dated March 2d, 1870, the legal title remained in the State, notwithstanding the completion of the road in May, 1871, until the lands were conveyed by it to Swann & Billups, as trustees for the railroad company, by deed dated February 8th, 1877 ; and the statute of limitations did not begin to run against said trustees until that time. *Ib.* 569.

RAILROADS.

1. *Corporate existence of railroad company under provisions of charter.*—Where the corporate existence of a railroad company is, by its original charter, limited to fifty years, but, by an amendatory act, it is provided that, at the expiration of each subsequent term of ten years, the State shall have the right, at its election, to take all the property of the company at the par value of its stock, and, if this election is not made within twelve months, then the charter of the company shall be continued for another term of ten years; the corporation has a capacity of perpetual existence, unless the election to purchase is exercised by the State. *Davis v. M. & C. Railroad Co.*, 633.

2. *Conveyance to railroad company, for right of way.*—A conveyance

RAILROADS—*Continued.*

of a strip of land to a railroad company, "for the term of fifty years, and so long thereafter as its charter shall continue," when the company has the capacity of perpetual existence, on default by the State to exercise a right of election to purchase its property, and also has power to condemn lands for a right of way under a writ of *ad quod damnum*, conveys the same interest and estate that would have been acquired by a judgment of condemnation under such writ. *Ib.* 633.

3. *Condemnation of right of way by railroad company; nature of estate acquired; transfer to another corporation* —A judgment condemning lands for a right of way, under *ad quod damnum* proceedings at the suit of a railroad company, vests in the company an estate and interest commensurate with its corporate existence; and this estate passes to purchasers at a sale under a mortgage executed by the company, who are afterwards incorporated as a railroad company, or to another corporation, its assignee, so long as the contemplated use of the right of way is continued. *Ib.* 633.

4. *Statutory proceedings for condemnation of right of way; appeal and trial by jury.*—Under statutory provisions authorizing the condemnation of a right of way by railroad corporations (Code, § 3210; Sess. Acts 1899, p. 112), the jury of appraisers may consist of only six men, and no appeal is given to a court of which a trial by jury is a constituent part; yet, under the general statute regulating appeals from the Probate Court (Code, § 3640), construed in connection with the constitutional provision which secures an appeal from "any preliminary assessment of damages," and gives a right of trial by jury, "as to the amount of damages, in all cases of appeal," an appeal lies from the Probate to the Circuit Court, and a jury of twelve men may be there impanelled to assess the damages. *Woodward Iron Co. v. Cabaniss,* 328.

5. *Condemnation of right of way of railroad corporation; interference with franchise of older corporation; jurisdiction of Probate Court.* Under statutory provisions authorizing and regulating proceedings for the condemnation of a right of way by railroad corporations (Code, §§ 1580-82, 3207-18), construed in connection with the constitutional provision pertaining to the exercise of the right of eminent domain (Art. I, § 24), a railroad corporation organized under the general statutes, without a special legislative charter, may institute such proceedings for the purpose of condemning a part of the right of way of an older corporation, and the Probate Court has jurisdiction to make an order of condemnation; but the right of condemnation in such case, and the jurisdiction of the court, are subject to the limitations hereinafter stated. *M. & G. Railroad Co. v. Ala. Midland Railroad Co.,* 501.

6. *Same; limitations on right of condemnation.*—Under such statutory proceedings, the right of condemnation does not authorize an unnecessary interference with the free exercise of the franchise of the older corporation, nor extend to that part of its right of way which is in actual use, and the use of which is reasonably necessary to the safe and proper management of its business—not merely used to prevent another corporation from condemning it; and a reasonably necessity must be shown for the condemnation of any other part. *Ib.* 501.

7. *Same; reasonable necessity as determined by practicability of another route, cost, etc.*—A necessity, such as authorizes one railroad corporation to condemn a part of the right of way of another, does not mean an absolute and unconditional necessity as determined by physical causes, but a reasonable necessity under the circum-

RAILROADS—*Continued.*

stances of the particular case, dependent upon the practicability of another route, considered in connection with the relative cost to one and probable injury to the other; and the right of condemnation is not made out, unless the petitioning company shows that the cost of acquiring and constructing its road on any other route clearly outweighs the consequent damage which may result to the older company, not including the question of competition for the business of a manufacturing (or other large) establishment on the line of the proposed route. *Ib.* 501.

8. *Statutory proceedings for condemnation of right of way between railroad companies; injunction against.*—A court of equity will not interfere by injunction, at the suit of one railroad company, to prevent or restrain statutory proceedings by another for the condemnation of a part of its right of way, pending an appeal from the judgment of condemnation; since the appeal is an adequate remedy for the correction of errors and irregularities in the proceedings, if only irregular and erroneous, and the defendant is a trespasser if they are void; and the prosecution of the work by the defendant pending the appeal, having paid the assessed damages into court, does not add equity to the bill. *M. & G. Railroad Co. v. Ala. Midland Railroad Co.,* 520.

9. *Same; payment of assessed damages into court.* — Under former statutory provisions, the petitioning railroad company, on paying into court the assessed damages, or condemnation money, was authorized to proceed with its work pending on appeal from the judgment of condemnation (Code, 1876, § 3593); but this statutory provision is not now of force, and the payment of money into court, pending the appeal, is not authorized, and has no effect on the rights of the parties. *Ib.* 520.

10. *Same; how far one railroad company may condemn part of another's right of way.*—Under statutory proceedings for the condemnation of a right of way by a railroad company (Code, §§ 3207-18), a part of the road-bed of another railroad can not be condemned, including a sufficient space on each side for the safe passage of trains; but the road-bed does not include all the space covered by necessary embankments and excavations. *Ib.* 520.

11. *Contributory negligence between railroad companies at crossing.*—In an action to recover damages for personal injuries sustained by plaintiff at a railroad crossing, the fact that the company on whose cars he was travelling was guilty of contributory negligence is no defense, though it may create a joint and several liability. *Geo. Pac. Railway Co. v. Hughes,* 610.

12. *Statutory liability of railroad companies, for injuries to persons or property; burden of proof.*—Under statutory provisions now of force (Code, §§ 1144-1147, note), whether the action is for injuries to person or stock, the *onus* is on the railroad company to acquit itself of negligence, by showing (1) a compliance with the statutory requisitions as to blowing the whistle and ringing the bell, or (2) that such compliance could not have averted the injury; but this statutory rule does not extend to a case where the injuries are caused by a neglect of other duties at a crossing of two railroads, resulting in a collision whereby plaintiff, a passenger, was injured. *Ib.* 610.

13. *Same; cases explained and limited.* — In the following cases, "presenting questions arising under section 1144 (Code of 1886), the decisions were correct on the points presented, but the principle was stated too broadly, and is liable to mislead:" *A. G. S. Railroad Co. v. McAlpine,* 75 Ala. 113; s. c., 80 Ala. 73; *L. & N. Ala. Railroad Co. v. Bees,* 82 Ala. 340; *M. & G. Railroad Co. v. Caldwell,* 83 Ala. 196; and in *L. & N. Railroad Co. v. Jones,*

RAILROADS—*Continued.*

83 Ala. 373, "the principle stated was scarcely called for, and is not correct when applied to the class of injuries there complained of." *Ib.* 610.

14. *Railroad bridges across public road* —In the construction of a bridge across a public road, it is the duty of a railroad company to place the structure at such an elevation that trains can safely pass under it with their customary employes; yet it may be placed below the line of absolute safety, when inequality of surface, or other hindrance, occurring naturally, or in the proper construction or grade of the railroad track, renders such elevation impossible, or would greatly incommode the public in the use of the bridge, or unduly increase the expense to the railroad company; but in no case is it permissible to erect the bridge at an elevation so low that brakemen, while in the discharge of their duties on the top of a car, can not avoid danger by bending or stooping. *L. & N. Railroad Co. v. Hall*, 708.

15. *Same; statutory regulations as to blowing whistle or ringing bell.* The statutory provision requiring the conductor or engineer of a moving locomotive or train of cars, on approaching a public road crossing, to blow the whistle or ring the bell (Code, § 1144), is intended for the protection of persons who are approaching or crossing the track of the road, and has no application to a case in which a brakeman sues for personal injuries, caused by his being struck by the bridge overhead while on top of one of the cars. *Ib.* 708.

16. *Appliances and warning signals for protection of employes.*—In the use of appliances or instrumentalities for the protection of its employes, when approaching a public road crossing spanned by a bridge overhead, such as "whipping straps," a cautionary light on the bridge, &c., the duty and liability of a railroad company are determined by utility and the usage and custom of well-regulated railroads; if many railroads abstain from their use, the failure to use them is not negligence; and their use by a majority of railroads does not require all railroads to use them, nor impute negligence on account of the failure to use them. *Ib.* 708.

17. *Notice to brakeman of low bridge overhead; contributory negligence.* When a brakeman is employed on a railroad with which he is not familiar, and is required, in the performance of his duties, to pass under a low bridge spanning the track, which, though not high enough to allow him to pass in an erect position on top of a car, is yet high enough to meet legal requirements, it is the duty of the railroad company to give him reasonable notice of the danger; but, if, having been duly notified, he fails, from inattention, indifference, absent-mindedness or forgetfulness, to inform himself of the particular facts. or to take the necessary steps to avoid injury—in other words, if he fails to exercise the care, watchfulness and caution which men of ordinary prudence would exercise under the circumstances—he is guilty of contributory negligence. *Ib.* 708.

18. *Expert testimony as to railroad appliances.*—The superintendent of a railroad, who has been employed on railroads for nearly twenty years, as fireman, brakeman, baggage-master, yard-master, and train-master, may give his opinion as an expert as to the value and usefulness of "whipping-straps," or ropes pendent from above, as cautionary signals to brakemen when the train is approaching a low bridge or tunnel overhead; but he can not give his opinion as to the prudent management of the defendant's railroad. *Ib.* 708.

19. *Sufficiency of complaint.*—Where the complaint claims damages on account of personal injuries sustained by a brakeman in the em-

RAILROADS—*Continued.*

ployment of a railroad company, by being struck by a bridge overhead across a public road, while on the top of a car in the discharge of his duties, the complaint must aver that the bridge was erected or maintained by the railroad company. *Ib.* 708.

20. *Congressional grant of lands in aid of railroads; title of State, and statute of limitations against.*—Under the acts of Congress granting lands to the State of Alabama in aid of certain railroads (11 U. S. Stat. at large, p. 17; 16 *Ib.* 45), as heretofore construed, the legal title to the lands granted at once vested in the State, for the use and benefit of the designated railroad companies; and it continued in the State, except as to the lands sold during the construction of the road in continuous sections of twenty miles, until the construction of the road was completed; and while the title thus continued in the State, the statute of limitations did not begin to run in favor of an adverse possessor under color of title. *Swann & Billups v. Gaston,* 569.

21. *Same; lands allotted to Alabama & Chattanooga Railroad Company; statute of limitations against trustees.*—The lands allotted to the two railroad companies which were consolidated into the Alabama & Chattanooga Railroad Company having been conveyed by it to the State, before the completion of the road, by mortgage dated March 2d, 1870, the legal title remained in the State, notwithstanding the completion of the road in May, 1871, until the lands were conveyed by it to Swann and Billups, as trustees for the railroad company, by deed dated February, 8th, 1877; and the statute of limitations did not begin to run against the trustees until that time. *Ib.* 569.

RAPE. See CRIMINAL LAW, 70–73.

RECEIVER. See CHANCERY, 26–28.

REDEMPTION OF REAL ESTATE.

1. *Who may redeem; widow of deceased mortgagor.*—Under statutory provisions giving and regulating the right to redeem lands sold under execution, or power of sale in a mortgage (Code, §§ 1879, 1888, 1891), the right is not conferred upon the widow of a deceased mortgagor, who joined with her husband in a mortgage of the homestead, under which the land was sold after his death; although his estate was insolvent at the time of his death, and was so declared after the foreclosure of the mortgage by sale under the power, and the premises were afterwards set apart to her as her homestead, subject to the mortgage incumbrance. *Walden v. Speigner,* 379.

2. *Who may redeem as judgment creditor.*—A judgment rendered against a debtor while living, which is not presented as a claim against his insolvent estate within the time allowed by law (Code, § 2238), is forever barred as a debt against the estate; and the plaintiff therein, or his assignee, can not claim, as a judgment creditor (*Ib.* § 1883), the right to redeem lands sold under a mortgage executed by the debtor while living. *Walden v. Speigner,* 390.

3. *Redemption by judgment debtor; surrender of possession on demand.* On bill to redeem by the judgment debtor (Code, §§ 1879-81), if it appears that he had rented out the land to a tenant, who quit the possession before the sale, and that the purchaser entered, within ten days, without demand, and without objection, this shows a substantial surrender of possession within ten days after the sale. *Aycock v. Adler,* 190.

4. *Same; outstanding title acquired by purchaser, or sub-purchaser.*—On bill to redeem by a judgment debtor, showing a substantial com-

REDEMPTION OF REAL ESTATE—*Continued.*

pliance with statutory requisitions, neither the purchaser, nor a sub-purchaser under him, can attack the validity of the debtor's original title, or set up, by cross-bill, a title subsequently acquired from a third person. *Ib.* 190.

SET–OFF.

1. *Set-off against commercial paper.*—By express statutory provision (Code, § 2684), a bill of exchange, or other commercial paper, negotiated for value before maturity, is not subject to set-off. *Manning v. Maroney,* 563.

2. *Set-off against note.*—A demand against an intermediate holder of a promissory note is not available as a set-off to the maker, either at law or in equity, unless founded on an agreement supported by a new consideration, in pursuance of which the intermediate holder procured it, or which was entered into by the parties while it was in his hands; and this rule applies to a non-commercial note transferred after maturity. *Brown v. Scott,* 453.

3. *Set-off in equity.*—When a note secured by mortgage is purchased by one of the heirs of the deceased mortgagor, and transferred as collateral security for his own debt, and the transferree files a bill to foreclose, he is only entitled to recover the amount of his debt, with attorney's fees and costs; and the transferror being indebted to the estate of the mortgagor, the other heirs may by cross-bill set off that indebtedness against the balance due on the mortgage debt. *Ib.* 453.

4. *Set-off against vendor's lien.*—In a suit to enforce a vendor' lien on land, the defendant may set off any legal demands existing in his favor, against the complainant, at the institution of the suit, on which he might maintain an action of debt or *indebitatus assumpsit* in his own name. *Weaver v. Brown,* 533.

5. *Same; conclusiveness of judgment.*—The complainant having obtained a judgment on the note for the unpaid purchase-money, before filing a bill to enforce his lien on the land, the defendant is not precluded from setting off a cross demand which would have been available as a set-off in the action at law, but which was not introduced in that suit. *Ib.* 533.

6. *Set-off of partnership and individual demands.*—In an action by an indorsee against the drawee of a bill of exchange, a demand due from the payee to a partnership of which the defendant is a member, if available as a set-off in any case, is not so available without proof that the other partners consented to such use of the claim, and that plaintiff had knowledge of their consent; and consent given at the trial can not relate back. *Huckaba v. Abbott,* 409.

SUSTITUTION OF LOST RECORDS.

1. *Amendment by striking out part of papers.*—On motion to substitute a judgment, the record of which has been lost or destroyed, an amendment may be allowed striking out the summons and complaint as a part of the papers to be substituted. *Peddy v. Street,* 299.

2. *Defense against substitution.*—On motion to substitute the record of a judgment which has been lost or destroyed, the copy proposed to be substituted reciting the service of process on the defendant, he may controvert the correctness of the copy in this particular, but not the recitals of the original judgment as to the service of process on him. *Ib.* 299.

SURETIES.

1. *Discharge of surety, by alteration of contract.*—A surety has the right to stand upon the very terms of his contract, and he is discharged by any alteration made without his consent, whether

SURETIES—*Continued.*

he is thereby injured or not, and even though it appears to be to his advantage, as by the addition of another as co-obligor; but alterations in the writing by a third person, who was not a party to it, can not change its legal operation and effect, and do not discharge the surety. *Anderson v. Bellenger & Ralls*, 334.

2. *Same; alteration of statutory claim bond, by adding name of another surety as co-obligor.*—After a statutory claim bond, having been signed by the principal obligor and two sureties, has been accepted and approved by the sheriff, it is his duty to return it at once to the court from which the process issued, and he has no authority, though retaining possession of the bond, to induce or accept the subsequent signature of a third person as surety; and such signature and acceptance being unauthorized, the liability of the original sureties is not thereby discharged or affected. *Ib.* 334.

3. *Signature to bond procured by fraud or mistake.*—In an action on a statutory claim bond, it is a good plea by one of the sureties, that he was fraudulently induced by the sheriff to sign it after it had been accepted and approved with the signatures of the other two sureties only, and that he signed it under a mistake of fact induced by the misrepresentations of the sheriff. *Ib.* 334.

TAXES.

1. *Action against agent of foreign corporation, for taxes.*—To sustain an action against the agent of a foreign corporation engaged in the business of lending money on mortgages, for taxes assessed on the gross receipts of its business, a valid assessment must be shown, as claimed, against that particular corporation. *State v. Sloss*, 119.

2. *Assessment of taxes against foreign corporation.*—An assessment of taxes against a foreign corporation, in these words: "Value of personal property, less exemptions, $15,200; State tax, $91.20; county tax $76.00; total tax, $167.20," does not show an assessment of two per cent. on the gross receipts of the corporation from the business in this State, and will not support an action against its agent to recover such assessment on receipts. *Ib.* 119.

TENANTS IN COMMON.

1. *Tenancy in common in crops, between owner of land and agricultural laborer.*—Under a contract between the owner of land and an agricultural laborer, by which the former agrees to furnish the lands and necessary teams, and the latter the labor, the crops to be divided equally between them, the parties are tenants in common of the crop until divided; though the statute (Code, § 3065) gives the laborer a lien, and process of attachment to enforce it. *Adams v. State*, 89.

2. *Adverse possession between.*—Actual possession, such as the land reasonably admits of, is an essential element of adverse possession; an entry by two tenants in common, surveying and laying the land out in lots, without more, does not constitute such actual possession; and a sale and conveyance of one or more of the lots by one of them, after the lapse of ten years, does not, as against the other, establish an adverse possession of the other portions of the land. *Stevenson v. Anderson*, 228.

3. *Statute of limitations in favor of purchaser, as against tenant in common of vendor.*—The statute of limitations is not a bar, as against one tenant in common, in favor of a purchaser from the other, unless ten years have elapsed since his purchase, or unless he can claim the benefit of adverse possession by his vendor. *Ib.* 228.

TRESPASS. See CRIMINAL LAW, 85.

54

WILLS.

1. *Written instrument operating partly as deed, and partly as will.*—A written instrument in the form of a deed, signed by the grantor, attested by two witnesses, and probated as a deed; by which the grantor, reciting her physical incapacity to look after and care for her property, her desire to have it cared for during her life, to make provision for her comfort and welfare during her life, and the further purpose of disposing of her property, and having the utmost confidence in the grantees, and for the further consideration of one dollar in hand paid by them, bargains, sells and conveys to them, by present words, all her property of every kind and description, to them and their assigns forever, "in trust nevertheless, and upon the uses and purposes hereinafter mentioned" —namely, to take charge of said property, collect and receive the rents and profits, keep the property in good repair, pay all taxes and other charges or assessments against it, and pay the residue to the grantor during life—vests in the grantees a present right, interest, and legal title to all the property, but charged with a trust for the uses and purposes specified; although a subsequent provision is added, which is testamentary in its character, and can only take effect after the death of the grantor—namely, that after her death the property "shall revert" to the grantees in fee simple, in equal shares; and further, that in consideration of services rendered by them to her, and also one dollar in hand paid, she sells and conveys to them all the property of which she may die seized and possessed, "hereby revoking all other arrangements, either verbal or written, as to the disposition of my [her] property." *Kyle v. Perdue,* 423.

2. *Bill of sale as testamentary paper.*—A written instrument, in the form of a bill of sale of personal property, which recites a consideration of $500 in hand paid, but is never delivered, the words being added: "This bill of sale to be placed in the hands of W. A. P., to be delivered to the parties mentioned in the event of my death," is a testamentary paper, and can only take effect as a will. *Jackson v. Rowell,* 685.

WITNESS.

1. *Competency of party as witness.*—At common law, a party to the record was not a competent witness in the cause, except in certain cases, while under statutory provisions (Code, § 2765) he is rendered a competent witness generally, but is not allowed to testify as to any transaction with a deceased person whose estate is interested in the result of the suit, or who acted in that transaction in a fiduciary capacity; and the courts will not engraft the common-law exceptions on the statutory provisions, where they are repugnant to the obvious policy of the statute. *Mobile Savings Bank v. McDonnell,* 736.

2. *Testimony of party as to transaction with deceased agent.*—In a suit by a creditor seeking to set aside, as fraudulent, a mortgage or deed of trust executed by his insolvent debtor to an incorporated bank, the debtor himself being a party to the suit, he can not be allowed (Code, § 2765) to testify as a witness that the conveyance was withheld from record, by agreement between him and the bank cashier, since deceased, lest it might injure his credit; and the fact that a decree *pro confesso* has been entered against him, does not remove his statutory incompetency. *Ib.* 736.

3. *Testimony of party as to transactions with decedent.*—In an action by a partnership against a private corporation, one of the plaintiffs can not testify as a witness in their behalf to a transaction or conversation between himself and the president or general

WITNESS—*Continued.*

tor, not making any accusation against him, may testify "that he did not stand still, but kept turning around and kicking the ground, and would not look at them;" but not "that he was restless, nervous, and excited." *Coleman v. State*, 14.

14. *Same.*—A witness who, as a member of the coroner's jury, had seen the dead body of the child alleged to have been murdered, may testify that its neck, which was broken, "looked like it had been struck with a hot iron, and looked scarred." *Perry v. State*, 30.

15. *Former testimony of absent witness.*—The testimony of a witness on a former trial of the defendant, or on his preliminary examination by a committing magistrate, is admissible as evidence against him on the trial, on proof that the witness is beyond the jurisdiction of the court, being either permanently or indefinitely absent. *Perry v. State*, 30.

16. *Contradicting or impeaching party's own witness.*—While a party can not, as a general rule, contradict or impeach his own witness, he may, when put at disadvantage by an unexpected answer, or for the purpose of refreshing the memory of the witness, ask him whether, at a certain time and place, he has not made other statements inconsistent with his testimony as just given. *White v. State*, 24.

17. *Same.*—The general rule which denies to a party the right to impeach his own witness, applies to a witness who is summoned and examined by and for each party; that is, the party who first introduces him, can not impeach him when introduced and examined by the other. *Ib.* 24.

18. *Evidence as to intoxicating properties of article sold.*—In a criminal prosecution for the sale of intoxicating liquors in violation of a local prohibitory liquor law, the article sold being compounded by a druggist, and the bottles labeled *"Elixir Cinchona,"* or *"Cinchona Bitters;"* a person who had swallowed it may state its exhilarating effect on himself, and, though not technically an expert, may testify that, "in his opinion, it would produce intoxication. *Carl v. State*, 17.

19. *Proof of character.*—A witness, testifying to the character of the defendant as a peaceable and quiet man, may be asked whether he "ever heard of his having any other difficulty than the one in question," and may testify that he had not. *Hussey v. State*, 121.

20. *Same.*—Evidence of character, at least on direct examination, goes to general reputation only, and can not be extended to particular acts, or specified conduct; nor can a witness give his own opinion as to the person inquired about;—as, that he was a "model man," or "was a timid man, and would rather avoid than provoke a difficulty." *Ib.* 121.

21. *Same; cross-examination of witness; impeaching.*—Witnesses for the prosecution having testified to the good reputation of the deceased as a peaceable and quiet man, and having denied, on cross-examination, that they had ever heard of certain specified personal difficulties in which he was said to have been involved; the defendant can not prove the existence and general notoriety of those difficulties, for the purpose of discrediting their testimony. *Ib.* 121.